Current Biography Yearbook 2019

H. W. Wilson

A Division of EBSCO Information Services, Inc.

Ipswich, Massachusetts

GREY HOUSE PUBLISHING

EIGHTIETH ANNUAL CUMULATION—2019

International Standard Serial No. 0084-9499

International Standard Book No. 978-1-68217-642-9

Library of Congress Catalog Card No. 40-27432

Current Biography Yearbook, 2019, published by Grey House Publishing, Inc., Amenia, NY, under exclusive license from EBSCO Information Services, Inc.

PRINTED IN CANADA

CONTENTS

LIST OF BIOGRAPHICAL SKETCHES

List of Biographical Sketches

List of Biographical Sketches

LIST OF OBITUARIES

List of Obituaries

List of Obituaries

Current Biography Yearbook 2019

Diane Abbott

Date of birth: September 27, 1953
Occupation: British politician

In 2017 Diane Abbott celebrated thirty years of service as a member of Parliament (MP) in Great Britain's Labour Party, which historically has been associated with the working class. She was among the first class of Black and Asian Britons to be elected MPs. As Abbott told *Ebony* (Mar. 1988), "We [second-generation Black Britons] have this compelling need to be involved in the political process and to challenge the racism that riddles English society." She would go on to do just that over the course of her lengthy political career.

Two decades later, in 2008, Abbott received the *Spectator* magazine's Parliamentarian of the Year Awarded for Speech of Year and the Law Society's Special Judge Award for opposing detaining terror suspects for forty-two days without trial.

Despite those accolades, Abbott remains a somewhat controversial figure, sometimes at odds with her own party and often spotlighting the ongoing problems of racism and sexism in British politics. She has also sought to empower ethnic minority Britons through philanthropic ventures as well as policy.

EARLY LIFE

Diane Julie Abbott was born in London, England, on September 27, 1953. During the early 1950s her parents each emigrated from the same village in Jamaica to England, where they met. Her father was a welder, her mother, a nurse; both had left formal schooling at age fourteen. Abbott has a younger brother. Their parents later divorced; her mother moved to Yorkshire when Abbott was an adolescent, leaving her with household chores in addition to her schoolwork.

In the early 1950s there were no rules to prevent discrimination in housing. Abbott told Stephen Bush for the *New Statesman America* (17 Jan. 2017), "My father was very aspirational, and so every weekend, he and my mother would drive round houses in Pinner, and every Monday they'd ring the estate agent, and the estate agent would say the house had gone. But, of course,

Photo by Chris McAndrew via Wikimedia Commons

the house wasn't gone." The Abbotts lived first in Notting Hill and later moved to Edgware.

EDUCATION

Abbott attended Harrow County Grammar School, where she was the only black girl in her class. She was active in theater and read avidly. She recalled to Bush, "I was an omnivorous reader, and in all these books, particularly these novels between the wars, if you went to university, you went to Oxford or Cambridge." During a visit to Cambridge University during her eleventh year, Abbott was taken with the architecture of the colleges.

Abbott's teachers discouraged her, despite her top grades, but she nevertheless gained admission there and attended Newnham College, Cambridge. She earned a master's degree in history in 1973. However, she felt like an outsider during her three years at Cambridge, both socially and economically. At the same time, she developed the sense that any obstacles in life existed to be overcome, an attitude that fueled her later political career.

CIVIL SERVICE AND MEDIA

Abbott began work as an administrative trainee in the UK's Home Office. About a year and a half later the National Council for Civil Liberties (NCCL) hired her as a race relations officer.

From 1980 until 1985, Abbott worked as a researcher for Thames Television and as a reporter for TV-am. She continued working as a press officer for local councils. Abbott also became a fixture on a BBC One political television show, *This Week*, with the Conservative pundit and politician Michael Portillo, with whom she had acted during high school. Abbott told Mary Riddell for the *Telegraph* (16 June 2010), "I don't watch the show, but so many people have told me that there's this on-screen chemistry that I'm bound to believe them. . . . We don't really socialise outside the show. My closest friends are women with similar backgrounds, and he has lots of grand Tory friends."

EARLY POLITICAL CAREER

In 1971, while at school, Abbott joined the Labour Party, which was founded in the early twentieth century and has been dedicated to better working conditions and wages. In 1982 she became a member of the Westminster City Council, one of Greater London's local governments. About a year later she ran unsuccessfully for Parliament. Then, in June 1987 she became the first black woman member of Parliament (MP), representing Hackney North and Stoke Newington, one of the poorest areas of London. Following her election, she visited the United States, meeting with black leaders such as Chicago mayor Harold Washington.

Much was made of her race at the time, but Abbott rejected the notion that she is somehow different from other blacks. She told *Ebony*, "I don't accept that I'm different from thousands of other Black people. There is enormous talent, energy and potential amongst Black people and it's about time society recognize that."

THATCHER CRITIC

Five years later Abbott was reelected, continuing to work for immigrants in her district from Greece, Turkey, and the Caribbean, as well as Hasidic Jews. Abbott was active in the Anti-Apartheid Movement (AAM) and in the Campaign for Nuclear Disarmament. She later served on the Foreign Affairs Select Committee.

Abbott did not hesitate to criticize Conservative prime minister Margaret Thatcher's policies, particularly against immigrants, which Abbott felt were unfair to racial minorities. She also opposed a poll tax, designed to replace a property tax, because it placed an outsized burden on the poor. Abbott also spoke for the religious rights of Hasidic Jews. As she wrote in *The House*, a publication of Parliament (3 May 2019), "Margaret Thatcher is mostly remembered for the poll tax, the miners' strike and the Falklands War. Her transformative effect on the British economy deserves to be equally well remembered. Remembered but not admired."

In 2000 she also began serving in the Mayor of London's Cabinet as the representative for equality and women's issues.

ALLIANCES AND PORTFOLIOS

Abbott became a close political ally of Jeremy Corbyn, a Labour Party leader. As she told Bush, "The thing that can be infuriating about Jeremy is that he likes to think the best of everyone. I'm always perfectly straight with him as to what I think, and even if he doesn't believe me at the time, he always does come round to my point of view."

In the early 2000s Abbott opposed centrist New Labour politicians like Tony Blair within the party ranks. Then, in 2010, she ran for leadership of the Labour Party, much to the amazement and dismay of some in the party. Abbott was criticized for attempting to become the face of Labour but maintained that the party leadership roster should include people other than white men in order to better reflect the country. She told Riddell, "I'm not thick-skinned at all, and of course I'm hurt by people attacking me as a person. On the Tube [subway], people shake my hand and say well done, but there's a very, very sour strand of thinking in Westminster, where insiders think it's outrageous I should run. But criticism goes with the territory."

Despite losing the leadership vote to Ed Miliband, Abbott became the shadow public health minister in October 2010. (In Great Britain, the official opposition party creates shadow cabinet positions that mirror those of the ruling party and challenge their counterparts on issues related to their specific portfolios.)

In May 2015 Labour candidates took only 30 percent of the vote, but Abbott kept her seat. That September she ran unsuccessfully for London mayoral candidate but became the party's shadow secretary of state for international development, a position she held for nearly a year. She then became shadow secretary of state for health in June 2016. That October Corbyn elevated her to shadow home secretary. In that role she has worked on police reform, anti-racism, and pro-immigration policies. Abbott temporarily stepped back from the role in 2017 because of difficulties with her diabetes, which was affecting her campaign performance.

After three decades of service, Abbott has remained highly popular. Known as a left-leaning politician, over the years Abbott has opposed the renewing of the Trident nuclear submarine system, tuition fees that keep many young people from top-tier schools, the war in Iraq, the sale of arms to Saudi Arabia that were used against Yemen, and construction of a third runway at

London Heathrow Airport. She has also supported abortion rights.

Abbott won reelection in June 2017 by a landslide, with 75 percent of the vote.

CONFLICTS
In a 2013 speech to the think tank Demos, Abbott charged that the economic anxiety among British men was leading to a toxic hypermasculine culture. As Harvey Morris quoted in the *New York Times'* blog *Rendezvous* (16 May 2013), Abbott said: "At its worst, it's a celebration of heartlessness; a lack of respect for women's autonomy; and the normalization of homophobia. I fear it's often crude individualism dressed up as modern manhood."

Reprisals were swift and vicious, although she urged people to read the entire speech rather than take remarks out of context. In fact, Dawn Butler cited Abbott's experience on the Labour Party's website (21 Nov. 2018) in an article about the status of female and minority MPs on the hundredth anniversary of women gaining the right to run for parliamentary office, saying: "My colleague Diane Abbott has been particularly affected by online abuse, receiving almost half of all the abusive tweets sent to female MPs in the run-up to the [2017] general election. We've been clear that when we are in Government this must end, and Labour will make the online intimidation of MPs a criminal offence." Abbott has also spoken out about the sexist and racist vitriol she has received online as a black female MP.

PHILANTHROPY
In addition to her policy work, Abbott has created nonprofit organizations dedicated to helping Black Britons. In 1993 she began Black Women Mean Business (BWMB) to support and promote black women in business. The organization grew out of conversations with her constituents and treasury select committee meetings during her first term in Parliament. From 1994 to 2002 BWMB hosted national conventions and seminars at which women received training, networked, and attended sessions for their professional development. It also shares research and produces reports and magazine issues relevant to Black women in business.

Abbott also founded the London Schools and the Black Child (LSBC) initiative in 1999 to raise achievement levels for Black British children. Its locus of attention was first Hackney North, later expanding to encompass all of London. Although LSBC targeted London specifically, the foundation's efforts reached throughout the country via semiannual conferences. Beginning in 2005, an annual LSBC awards ceremony at the House of Commons celebrated high-achieving students of African and African Caribbean origin. LSBC also works against the

reality that more white students from privileged backgrounds are accepted into top universities than are their black and Asian counterparts.

Both groups have been subsumed into the Diane Abbott Foundation, a charity devoted to research on racial disparities. Its aim is to narrow the gaps in achievement and representation between whites and persons of color.

PERSONAL LIFE
Abbott reportedly had a brief romantic liaison with Corbyn in 1979 when Corbyn was separated from his first wife. Abbott was later married to an architect from Ghana from 1991 until 1993. Their son, James Thompson (b. 1992), attended a secondary school in Ghana and then Cambridge.

One of Abbott's most politically controversial actions involved James. Frustrated with the quality of state schools, Abbott chose to send him to an independent school when he was ten, fully prepared to lose her seat as a result. Although that did not occur, she had to fend off charges of hypocrisy because of her past criticism of such actions by other politicians. She has cited the disadvantages of his inner-city peers and worries that he would be initiated into gang life as reasons for her choice. She has also suggested it was a culturally motivated decision for which other West Indian mothers applaud her.

As an adult, Abbott took piano lessons, an experience filmed for the BBC One program *Play It Again*. In addition, she enjoys watching television and visits family in Jamaica regularly.

SUGGESTED READING
Abbott, Diane. "Diane Abbott: 'You Can't Let Racism Hold You Back.'" Interview by Huma Qureshi. *The Guardian*, 20 Sept. 2012, www.theguardian.com/lifeandstyle/2012/sep/20/diane-abbott-racism-interview. Accessed 12 Aug. 2019.

Abbott, Diane. "Labour's Family Roots." *New Statesman*, 20 Sept. 2010, www.newstatesman.com/society/2010/09/labour-family-community. Accessed 12 Aug. 2019.

Bush, Stephen. "Having the Last Laugh." *New Statesman America*, 17 Jan. 2017, www.newstatesman.com/politics/uk/2017/01/having-last-laugh. Accessed 11 July 2019.

"Pioneers of Britain's Parliament." *Ebony*, Mar. 1988, pp. 76–84. *Google Books*, books.google.com/books?id=nMwDAAAAMBAJ&lpg=PA76. Accessed 11 July 2019.

Riddell, Mary. "Diane Abbott: It's Very Lonely Being a Single Mother." *The Telegraph*, 16 June 2010, www.telegraph.co.uk/news/politics/labour/7833158/Diane-Abbott-Its-very-lonely-being-a-single-mother.html. Accessed 29 July 2019.

Swift, Adam. "A Short Guide to Hypocrisy." *New Statesman America*, 3 Nov. 2003, www.newstatesman.com/node/158620. Accessed 11 July 2019.

—Judy Johnson

Zaradasht Ahmed

Date of birth: 1968
Occupation: Director

Filmmaker Zaradasht Ahmed had already spent years observing families in his native Iraq when, in 2010, he met Nori Sharif, a nurse working in the central Iraq town of Jalawla. Sharif was among a group of local medics that Ahmed trained to document life in conflicted areas of Iraq. Ahmed, a Kurdish Iraqi exile who has lived in Norway in the early 1990s, originally intended to use their footage for a documentary about the war in Iraq. However, after US troops unexpectedly withdrew from the country in 2011, he decided to shift his focus to a character-based film about Sharif, who, at his direction, proceeded to record post-occupation life in and around Jalawla, widely considered one of the most dangerous areas in the world.

The result was *Nowhere to Hide* (2016), a blistering, feature-length documentary that brought Ahmed a new level of international attention and critical acclaim. Largely comprised of raw footage shot by Sharif across five years of ever-worsening conditions in Iraq, the film was unanimously praised for its immersive and affecting look at the devastating effects of war, and it received several prestigious awards at international film festivals. Like Ahmed's other documentaries, which include *The Road to Diyarbekir* (2010) and *Fata Morgana* (2013), *Nowhere to Hide* highlights the theme of survival and perseverance, as Sharif, his family, and other Iraqi citizens maintain hope in the face of unspeakable horrors. In a self-penned account of the making of the film for *Al Jazeera* (14 Mar. 2018), Ahmed commented, "My ambition is to let the audience reflect on the human consequences of a brutal reality where all taboos are violated."

EARLY LIFE AND EDUCATION
Of Kurdish descent, Ahmed was born in 1968 in Sulaymaniyah, a city in northern Iraq located roughly three hours north of Jalawla. Although little has been reported on Ahmed's upbringing and family life, it is known that the filmmaker grew up amidst widespread violence and conflict. This instability was largely triggered by dictator Saddam Hussein, who, over the course of his twenty-three-year reign as Iraqi president

from 1979 to 2003, led various purges of political opponents and Iraqi ethnic groups, particularly Kurds. In an interview with Peter O'Dowd for the National Public Radio (NPR) program *Here & Now* (27 Aug. 2018), Ahmed described being part of Iraq's "war generation," a reference to the Iran-Iraq War and the Persian Gulf War, which dominated events in that country during the 1980s and early 1990s.

Upon finishing his formal education in Iraq in 1991, Ahmed, who had an early predilection for art, was conscripted into the national army. Rather than serve in the armed forces, however, he opted to flee to Europe. Though that decision carried grave consequences, namely the possibility of execution, Ahmed explained to Amelia Smith for the *Middle East Monitor* (10 Mar. 2017), "I didn't understand who to fight for so I defected; I left the army and I could not stay." He eventually settled in Norway and gained Norwegian citizenship.

In Norway, Ahmed studied visual art at the Rogaland School of Art, from which he graduated in 1997. He later earned a bachelor's degree in television and multimedia production from the University of Stavanger, graduating in 2006. Ahmed told O'Dowd that despite his exile status, he continued to hold a deep emotional connection to events in his home country. This undeniably shaped his worldview as a filmmaker.

ARTIST TO FILMMAKER
Ahmed's path to becoming a documentary filmmaker was influenced by two major world events: the September 11, 2001, terrorist attacks and the US–led invasion of Iraq in 2003. While Ahmed was living in Norway, he wanted to be identified simply as an artist and painter, and perhaps an Iraqi and a Kurd. However, after the September 11 attacks, people began defining him only by his Muslim faith, which introduced him to "a very ugly side [of Europeans] that I didn't see before," as he told Smith. The resultant 2003 invasion of Iraq was similarly pivotal. "It affected everything in my life and the way I am, my identity," he said to Smith.

At the time of the invasion, Ahmed was working as a visual artist, but he soon turned his attention to filmmaking, which would enable him to express himself on a wider scale. He got his start working as a freelance photographer and editor for Scandinavian television before graduating to the director's chair. Among Ahmed's first directorial efforts to receive attention was the film *The Road to Diyarbekir*. An award-winning, hour-long documentary about the legendary Kurdish singer Ciwan Haco, it first aired in Europe in 2010. In that film, Ahmed focuses on Haco's life as an exile in Gäyle, a small village in Sweden, and his decades-long efforts to return to Kurdistan after being blacklisted by the Turkish government. Those efforts crystallize when Haco is invited to perform a concert in Diyarbekir, the largest Kurdish city in Turkey, where he is greeted enthusiastically by over one million people.

Ahmed's next feature-length documentary, *Fata Morgana* (2013), similarly examined the themes of exile and identity. Screened to acclaim at festivals all over Norway, the film follows the travails of two young Moroccan vagrants, Mounir and Feisal, who attempt to flee their homeland in search of a better life in Europe. Ahmed first met Mounir and Feisal during a trip to Morocco in 2007; he tracked the men over a period of six years, during which the two took enormous risks to reach Spain from the Moroccan port city of Tangier. "I like long-term documentaries," he said to Dimitra Kouzi for *Kouzi Productions* (24 Nov. 2016). "I like to spend years on my films, on my subjects, on my characters because I believe that film is storytelling. It is also about some unique moments that we call the moments of truth."

ORIGINS OF *NOWHERE TO HIDE*

Ahmed adopted the same long-term approach for his documentary *Nowhere to Hide*, which he first began working on in 2008. He initially resolved to make a film about the ongoing military conflict in Afghanistan, one that aimed to capture the new, seemingly borderless war that had emerged there. He soon moved the concept to Iraq, however, after becoming intrigued and equally disheartened by the continued escalation of sectarian violence that had spread throughout that country since the US–led invasion in 2003.

As part of efforts to capture this "uncertain reality," as he put it to Smith, Ahmed recruited local medics and journalists to document activities in highly dangerous areas around central and northern Iraq that were inaccessible to the media, otherwise known as "no-go-zones." Over the course of a year, he taught them how to operate film cameras and how to conduct interviews. Among a group of twelve medics that Ahmed trained was Nori Sharif, a nurse. Sharif was then working at a hospital in Jalawla, in Iraq's Diyala province, an area that had come to be known as the "triangle of death" for its large number of insurgent attacks.

Despite having no prior knowledge about filmmaking, Sharif quickly distinguished himself as one of the most committed members of the group. Once the United States withdrew its troops from Iraq in December 2011 and the country transitioned to self-rule, Ahmed decided to focus his project exclusively on Sharif. This shift to a more personal character-based film offered Ahmed the opportunity to humanize the conflict in Iraq, which continued to worsen after the end of the US occupation. Ahmed, mostly directed Sharif from a distance (at a secure base set up in Sulaymaniyah), helping to give the footage a personal feel. As the filmmaker explained to Karzan Sulaivany for *Kurdistan 24* (28 Aug. 2018), "The film was meant to be emotional without borders, to make people attached to those who are involved in the film emotionally and not in a factual or news-based medium."

A DIFFERENT LOOK AT WAR

Filmed over a period of five years and assembled from approximately 300 to 400 hours of footage, *Nowhere to Hide* chronicles Sharif and his family's day-to-day struggles to survive in war-torn Iraq. This theme of desperate survival is established in the film's brief prologue, which opens with the image of a solitary, sweat-soaked, and white tunic-garbed Sharif stumbling through a bleak desert landscape. Sharif's family has been displaced from their home, and he is frantically searching for water for his children, who are sick.

After this opening sequence, the film flashes back three years to December 2011, when Ahmed first enlists Sharif to record and interview people in his community in the immediate aftermath of US occupation. Though initially optimistic about their future, the locals are soon filled with dread and terror as sectarian violence escalates. Sharif, meanwhile, is thrust from observer to subject as he finds himself amid near-daily attacks and suicide bombings. Sharif and his family remain in Jalawla until the city is seized by the Islamic State of Iraq and Syria (ISIS) terrorist group in late 2014, at which point they become nomadic refugees. The family then shuttles between various locations before finding safety at a refugee camp for displaced persons in Iraq's Baqubah province, which brings the film to its hopeful conclusion.

Featuring a spare guitar-based soundtrack by Norwegian composer Gaute Barlindhaug and singer Ciwan Haco, *Nowhere to Hide* earned widespread acclaim upon its debut in 2016. The many honors the film received included the coveted best feature-length documentary prize at that year's International Documentary Film Festival Amsterdam (IDFA), in Amsterdam, the Netherlands, the world's largest documentary film festival. It also took home the Amanda Award for best documentary at the 2017 Norwegian International Film Festival.

Nowhere to Hide was screened at film festivals all over the world, bringing Ahmed recognition as one of the first directors to shed light on what civilian life was like in post-occupation Iraq. Many critics praised Ahmed for his shrewd hands-off approach in making the film, allowing Sharif's raw, unfiltered footage to give viewers a rare glimpse into the experiences of innocent civilians forced to endure the horrors of war. Jeanette Catsoulis, in a review for the *New York*

Times (22 June 2017), wrote that the film "has a raw immediacy that's both appropriate and involving," and that despite its "rough" look, "the emotions [are] always hovering near the surface." In another review, for the *Washington Post* (6 July 2017), Ann Hornaday commented, "The great gift of Ahmed's film, and the way he has collaborated creatively with his subject, is that viewers can no longer read about faraway events in central Iraq as distant or abstract."

In 2018, *Nowhere to Hide* made its US broadcast premiere on the *POV* (initialism for Point of View) series on the Public Broadcast Service (PBS). Ahmed noted that he hoped his film would give people a different perspective on the Iraq war that will ultimately help to inspire change. "We are all human, we all feel the same things, we have to share and not close the door," he explained to Smith. "We have to lift the other people up. Help them, make the world a better place to live in."

SUGGESTED READING

Ahmed, Zaradasht. "Interview with Zaradasht Ahmed, Dir. Nowhere to Hide." By Dimitra Kouzi. *Kouzi Productions*, 24 Nov. 2016, kouziproductions.com/blog/2016/11/24/interview-with-zaradasht-ahmed-dir-nowhere-to-hide/. Accessed 15 Oct. 2018.

———. "*Nowhere to Hide*: Iraq Emergency Room–Filmmaker's View." *Al Jazeera*, 14 Mar. 2018, www.aljazeera.com/programmes/witness/2018/03/hide-iraq-emergency-room-180312071311633.html. Accessed 15 Oct. 2018.

———. "'Nowhere to Hide' Documents Family's Survival through 5 Years of Violence in Iraq." Interview by Peter O'Dowd. *Here & Now*, WAMU 88.5 American University Radio, NPR, 27 Aug. 2018, wamu.org/story/18/08/27/nowhere-to-hide-documents-familys-survival-through-5-years-of-violence-in-iraq/. Accessed 15 Oct. 2018.

Catsoulis, Jeanette. "Review: 'Nowhere to Hide' for an Iraqi Nurse Still Clinging to Hope." Review of *Nowhere to Hide*, by Zaradasht Ahmed. *The New York Times*, 22 June 2017, www.nytimes.com/2017/06/22/movies/nowhere-to-hide-review.html. Accessed 15 Oct. 2018.

Hornaday, Ann. "*Nowhere to Hide* Gives a Gift: Making Iraq under the Islamic State No Longer a Faraway Crisis." Review of *Nowhere to Hide*, by Zaradasht Ahmed. *The Washington Post*, 6 July 2017, www.washingtonpost.com/goingoutguide/movies/nowhere-to-hide-gives-a-gift-making-iraq-under-the-islamic-state-no-longer-a-faraway-crisis/2017/07/06/c9ea2714-5db0-11e7-9b7d-14576dc0f39d_story.html. Accessed 15 Oct. 2018.

Smith, Amelia. "'Tony Blair and George Bush Opened the Gate of Hell in Iraq.'" *Middle East Monitor*, 10 Mar. 2017, www.middleeastmonitor.com/20170310-tony-blair-and-george-bush-opened-the-gate-of-hell-in-iraq/. Accessed 15 Oct. 2018.

Sulaivany, Karzan. "*Nowhere to Hide*: Kurdish Filmmaker's Award-Winning Documentary Explores Human Suffering in War." *Kurdistan 24*, 28 Aug. 2018, www.kurdistan24.net/en/culture/61b39f48-ce2d-4df6-be15-ae-6351a3c960. Accessed 15 Oct. 2018.

SELECTED WORKS

The Road to Diyarbekir, 2010; *Fata Morgana*, 2013; *Nowhere to Hide*, 2016

—*Chris Cullen*

Njideka Akunyili Crosby

Date of birth: 1983
Occupation: Artist

Njideka Akunyili Crosby is an award-winning visual artist. Her mixed-media paintings combine paint, photography, and found materials, such as marble dust and fabric. Her work, "based on my autobiography," she told Jean-Philippe Dedieu for the *New Yorker* (5 Nov. 2015), combines references to her Nigerian upbringing and her adulthood in the United States in intimate domestic scenes. "I feel like my journey has created a character or person who doesn't fit in any box," she told Dedieu. Drawn from family photographs, magazine clippings, and staged photos with her husband, sculptor Justin Crosby, Akunyili Crosby's work often has a silk-screen effect that mimics the haze of dreams or memories. Her figurative style recalled for Dedieu a quote from the novel *Open City* (2011) by the Nigerian American author Teju Cole. "Nigeria was like that for me: mostly forgotten, except for those few things that I remembered with an outsize intensity," Cole wrote. "These were the things that had been solidified in my mind by reiteration, that recurred in dreams and daily thoughts: certain faces, certain conversations."

Akunyili Crosby has received a slew of awards for her work, including a MacArthur "genius" grant in 2017. Akunyili was stunned when she received the call; she had always dreamed of winning the grant in her fifties or sixties. She told Deborah Vankin for the *Los Angeles Times* (2 Nov. 2017) that she planned to spend some of her $625,000 prize on an extended trip to Nigeria. Other accolades include the Smithsonian American Art Museum's 2014 James Dicke Contemporary Artist Prize, the Studio Museum

Photo by Donato Sardella/Getty Images for Hammer Museum

of Harlem's 2015 Joyce Alexander Wein Prize, the 2015 New Museum's Next Generation Prize, and the 2016 Prix Canson for works on paper. She also appeared on *Foreign Policy*'s 2015 Leading Global Thinkers list.

EARLY LIFE AND EDUCATION
Akunyili Crosby was born in Enugu, a former coal-mining town in Nigeria, in 1983. Her father, J. C. Akunyili, was a physician. Her mother, Dora Akunyili, began her career as a pharmacology professor. In 2001, Nigerian president Olusegun Obasanjo appointed her director-general of the National Agency for Food and Drug Administration and Control (NAFDAC). At the time, Nigeria was vexed by a flood of deadly fake medicine. (Akunyili Crosby's maternal aunt, who had diabetes, was killed after receiving fake insulin.) Under Dora Akunyili's leadership, the fake drug market declined by 90 percent. She went on to become minister of information and communications. Though she died of cancer in 2014, Dora Akunyili remains a national hero.

Akunyili Crosby is the fourth of six children. Three of her siblings went on to become doctors, like their parents. As a child, Akunyili Crosby showed a natural affinity for the sciences and enjoyed poring over her father's book of diseases. After skipping a grade, she was accepted to boarding school at the prestigious Queens College in Lagos, the country's bustling capital, at the age of ten. It was a bit of culture shock for Akunyili Crosby, who was more familiar with life in grandmother's village, where she spent weekends and summers. The village was lit by kerosene lamps "so everybody goes to bed when the sun sets at seven, and there is *nothing*

to do. Get up at 5:30 and sweep the floor with palm fronds," she recalled to Sophie Heawood for the *Guardian* (3 Oct. 2016). Boarding school, she said, "was my first contact with a cosmopolitan life."

EARLY ART CAREER
When Akunyili Crosby was a teenager, her mother won a US green-card lottery for the family. In 1999, at the age of sixteen, Akunyili Crosby moved to Philadelphia with her sister. The girls spent a year taking classes at a community college and studying for the SATs. In addition to her rigorous course load of science classes, Akunyili Crosby decided to take a painting class, her first, for fun. Her teacher encouraged her to pursue painting, and she did, studying both fine art and biology at Swarthmore College, outside of Philadelphia.

She graduated in 2004 and returned to Lagos, where her family was then living. She broke difficult news to her parents: she wanted to pursue art, and she was seriously dating Crosby, a white American man. "That's why I feel like my art and Justin are so linked," she told Diane Solway for *W Magazine* (15 Aug. 2017). "Because it was all or nothing. You rebel or you don't." Her mother took the news in stride, but her father took longer to come around. One of her paintings, *I Still Face You* (2015), depicts a scene based on Crosby's first meeting with the family. In it, her father stands with his arms crossed. The tension in the room is palpable. Akunyili Crosby's trip home that year was emotionally fraught for other reasons, as well. Around Christmas, while the family was traveling to a reunion, her mother narrowly survived an assassination attempt.

GRADUATE WORK
Akunyili Crosby earned a post-baccalaureate certificate at the Pennsylvania Academy of the Fine Arts in Philadelphia in 2006. She went on to study at Yale University, where she became inspired by the paintings of legendary artist Kerry James Marshall. A 2009 portrait of a black woman particularly impressed her. "I don't think any work has had an effect on me like that," she recalled to Solway. "He was putting images in a space where you don't expect to see them. And I'm thinking, What am I looking at? It's this woman who is unapologetically black. Black, black, black. Not even a darkish brown aubergine." At Yale, Akunyili Crosby truly began to develop her artistic voice—though with little thanks to the institution itself. She graduated with an MFA in 2011 and won a coveted residency at the Studio Museum in Harlem the same year.

Later, Akunyili Crosby expressed distaste for Yale. "Yale was not a community," she told Heawood. "But I think of the Studio Museum as a family." At the Studio Museum, Akunyili

Crosby was introduced to the work of Kenyan-born artist Wangechi Mutu. She appreciated the way Mutu's work demonstrated, as Solway put it, "that an image could be composed of many others." Other influences include the nineteenth-century French painter Édouard Vuillard, contemporary American figurative artist Alex Katz, and contemporary British artist Chris Ofili.

DROWN AND OTHER WORK
One of the first of Akunyili Crosby's works to capture dealers' attention was *I Refuse to Be Invisible* (2010), a painting that depicts Akunyili Crosby dancing with her husband. She sold three paintings to the New York gallery Fredericks & Freiser while still at Yale. (A legal dispute arose later when the gallery refused to tell her who they sold the pieces to. She bought back one of the pieces—*Nyado: The Thing around Her Neck* from 2011—for $20,000, 150 percent more than its original price.) In 2016, Akunyili Crosby's painting *Drown* (2012), featuring a naked couple modeled after her and her husband, their bodies collaged with colonial images, sold at Sotheby's for $1 million, far more than its $200,000 estimate. In 2017, a portrait of her sister, similarly collaged with images of Nigerian women, called *The Beautyful Ones* (2014) and the first in the series of the same name, sold for more than $3 million.

The art market has a dangerous tendency to kill artists' careers by driving the prices of their work too high too soon. Unsurprisingly, Akunyili Crosby characterized her breakthrough as quite stressful. "People expect me to be happy [about the money], but it put a spotlight on me in a way I don't like at all," she told Solway. "I like operating quietly, on my own, in the background." (In 2018, she appeared in a documentary about the excesses of the market and the commodification of art called *The Price of Everything*.) Akunyili Crosby has since made an effort to sell her pieces to museums. In 2018, she donated her striking pseudo landscape painting *Bush Babies* (2017) to the Studio Museum of Harlem for a benefit auction. The piece sold for $3.4 million, a record for the artist.

Akunyili Crosby also enjoyed a solo show called "Front Room: Njideka Akunyili Crosby | Counterparts" at the Baltimore Museum of Art in 2017. The show appeared at the Modern Museum of Art in Fort Worth, Texas, in 2018. The same year, she created a mural called *Obodo (Country/City/Town/Ancestral Village)* for the Museum of Contemporary Art in Los Angeles. Her series "The Beautyful Ones," featuring portraits of Nigerian youth, went on display at the National Portrait Gallery in London in 2018.

ARTISTIC PROCESS AND STYLE
Akunyili Crosby is a painstaking artist, making only eight or nine works each year. She tacks the fruits of her meandering process—images sourced from the Internet and family photos, scraps of novels and books about postcolonial theory—on the wall of her Los Angeles studio.

Akunyili Crosby's work subtly positions commentary on racism and colonialism within intimate domestic scenes. *Ike ya* (2016), for instance, captures an intimate moment between Akunyili Crosby and her husband; in it, she sits on a living room couch, and he hugs her waist. A number of later works depict kitchens and other domestic spaces. The walls in her paintings are often covered with family photographs. "I wanted to put out pictures of these parts of Nigeria that I knew and experienced," Akunyili Crosby explained to Solway. "People forget that life exists in these places. There are serious things that are wrong in the country, but people exist and thrive. We hang out. We get married. We talk as a family. We lie in bed together. I can't make this point enough. It's hard to think people matter if you don't feel connected to them. And so it's about making that connection."

PERSONAL LIFE
Akunyili Crosby met her husband at Swarthmore. They were married—twice: once in a church and once in a Nigerian village wedding—in 2009. They have a son named Jideora and live in Los Angeles.

SUGGESTED READING
Dedieu, Jean-Philippe. "Njideka Akunyili Crosby's Intimate Universes." *The New Yorker*, 5 Nov. 2015, www.newyorker.com/culture/photo-booth/njideka-akunyili-crosbys-intimate-universes. Accessed 17 Feb. 2019.

Heawood, Sophie. "The Nigerian Artist Who Is Exploding the Myth of the 'Authentic African Experience.'" *The Guardian*, 3 Oct. 2016, www.theguardian.com/lifeandstyle/2016/oct/03/nigerian-artist-myth-authentic-african-experience-njideka-akunyili-crosby-harlem-studio-museum. Accessed 17 Feb. 2019.

Solway, Diane. "Nigerian Artist Njideka Akunyili Crosby Is Painting the Afropolitan Story in America." *W Magazine*, 15 Aug. 2017, www.wmagazine.com/story/njideka-akunyili-crosby-artist-painter. Accessed 17 Feb. 2019.

Vankin, Deborah. "Njideka Akunyili Crosby: The Painter in Her MacArthur Moment." *Los Angeles Times*, 2 Nov. 2017, www.latimes.com/entertainment/arts/la-ca-cm-njideka-akunyili-crosby-20171102-htmlstory.html. Accessed 18 Feb. 2019.

SELECTED WORKS
Drown, 2012; *The Beautyful Ones*, 2014; *Ike ya*, 2016; *Bush Babies*, 2017

—*Molly Hagan*

Lauren Alaina

Date of birth: November 8, 1994
Occupation: Singer and songwriter

Country singer Lauren Alaina first gained widespread public attention in 2011, when she came in second place on the television talent show *American Idol*, then in its tenth season. Although her debut album received average critical reviews, her 2017 sophomore album, *Road Less Traveled*, became the most-streamed country album by a female artist that year and landed on multiple "Best of 2017" lists, including those compiled by *Billboard* and *Rolling Stone*. In April 2018, at the Academy of Country Music (ACM) Awards, Lauren Alaina was named New Female Vocalist of the Year.

"It's been a crazy journey for sure, and it's crazy that it took six years to catch on and to get some traction," Alaina told Chuck Dauphin for *Billboard* (31 Jan. 2018). "I worked very hard on the music, writing on the *Road Less Traveled* for about four years." Alaina explained the differences between her first and second albums, telling Dauphin, "I didn't get to write the first album (2011's *Wildflower*) at all that much—just one song. . . . But I got to take my time on the [second] album, and got to write every song on it. They are my actual stories. I think that made a difference, and I think that made me believe in the music even more."

EARLY LIFE AND EDUCATION
The singer was born Lauren Alaina Kristine Suddeth on November 8, 1994, in Rossville, Georgia, not far from the Tennessee border. Her mother, Kristy, was a transcriptionist, while her father, J. J., worked in Chattanooga as a process technician for the chemical company BASF. She has one brother, Tyler.

Alaina started to sing by the age of three, performing at her family's holiday gatherings and in the choir of her church. (She is a devout Christian, who often professes her faith on social media and when speaking to journalists.) At age eight, she won a local talent contest, and the following year, she began appearing regularly at Chattanooga's popular annual Riverbend Festival. Other local victories followed, and when she was ten, she triumphed over a thousand other young competitors at a national talent search held in Orlando, Florida. She soon began singing

Photo by John Ramspott via Wikimedia Commons

with the Georgia Country Gospel Music Association's children's group. No matter how small or obscure the venue, however, Alaina took every opportunity she could to perform, frequently traveling to Nashville on the weekends to sing at clubs accompanied by her father on the guitar. In 2009 she won a talent show held at the Lake Winnepesaukah amusement park, a family-owned enterprise in Rossville.

Alaina attended Lakeview-Fort Oglethorpe High School in Fort Oglethorpe, Georgia, where she was a cheerleader. Although she hoped for a career in music, she also considered becoming a pediatrician or a special-needs teacher because of her love of children. When not in school she worked at the pizzeria chain Cicis, frequently singing as she stocked the salad bar or cleaned tables, much to the delight of patrons, as her manager later told reporters. She graduated from high school in 2013.

AMERICAN IDOL
In 2011 Alaina auditioned for the tenth season of *American Idol*, presided over by performers Steven Tyler, Jennifer Lopez, and Randy Jackson. Audiences got their first look at the bubbly teen during her initial audition in Nashville, where she sang Faith Hill's "Like We Never Loved at All" and then performed Aerosmith's "I Don't Want to Miss a Thing," with Tyler, the lead singer of Aerosmith.

During the segment of the show in which viewers are introduced to the contestants, Alaina tearfully cited her cousin Holly Witherow, who had been diagnosed with a brain tumor, as her inspiration for singing. Her hometown fans demonstrated their staunch support throughout the season. As *American Idol* paid for only one parent to accompany a contestant under eighteen, the family's neighbors raised money so that both of her parents could travel to Los Angeles to be with their daughter. Later in the season, Rossville dedicated May 14, 2011, as Lauren Alaina Day.

Throughout the competition, Alaina sang such tunes as "Hello, Goodbye" by the Beatles, "You Keep Me Hangin' On" by the Supremes, "(You Make Me Feel Like) A Natural Woman" by Aretha Franklin, and "Any Man of Mine" by Shania Twain. By the final round, which aired on May 25, 2011, the field of thirteen finalists had been whittled down to just her and Scotty McCreery, another young country singer. During the final show, Alaina sang a duet with former *Idol* winner Carrie Underwood, a personal hero of hers, before being named runner-up to McCreery. Following her second-place finish, she told Jennifer Still for *Digital Spy*, "I think everything happens for a reason and God has different plans for me. There are hundreds of thousands of people out there who would love to be second place in *American Idol* and I'm fortunate to get as far as I did."

WILDFLOWER

Following *American Idol*, Alaina was signed to a record deal with Mercury Nashville, 19 Recordings, and Interscope. She released her first single, "Like My Mother Does," in May 2011, which peaked at number thirty-six on the Billboard Hot Country Songs Chart. On October 11, 2011, she released her debut album, *Wildflower*, which garnered lukewarm reviews. "Lauren Alaina is at her best on *Wildflower* when she's selling teenage stories of love, loss and freedom," Billie Dukes wrote for *Taste of Country* on the day of its release. "At such a young age, it'd be unrealistic to expect her to deliver an instant classic. *Wildflower* is the musical equivalent of puppy love. It comes on strong but doesn't stand the wear and tear of time and repeated listens." Despite the criticism, Dukes conceded, "Alaina's debut project shows she has plenty of potential and will be capable of big things in the next few years." *Wildflower* peaked at number two on the Billboard Top Country Album Chart.

Such mixed feelings on the part of critics did not prevent Alaina from being invited to perform at the Grand Ole Opry, on such television programs as the *Ellen DeGeneres Show*, and in front of President Barack Obama at the White House for a 2011 PBS special. Additionally, she sang the national anthem at the 2011 Thanksgiving Day game between the Detroit Lions and Green Bay Packers, and she performed a song on the televised *American Country New Year's Eve Live* in 2011. Alaina remained in demand as an opening act throughout 2012, opening for Sugarland on their In the Hands of Fans Tour and appearing on the My Kinda Party Tour with Jason Aldean and Luke Bryan. She later opened for Underwood and Alan Jackson on their respective tours in 2016.

ROAD LESS TRAVELED

Alaina has acknowledged that she was bulimic throughout much of her teenage years and early career. "I was really sick. I don't know that person, I can't believe that was me," she told Jessie Van Amburg for *Time* (10 May 2016). "I just desperately wanted to be thin. . . . I was obsessed with it, which it was ridiculous because I had everything going for me. I was following my dream. Everything I wanted at the time, I was getting." She credits her mother's advice to look in the mirror each day and find positive things to focus on for her gradual recovery and healthier attitudes. In addition to her own eating disorder, Alaina was forced to contend with her father's alcoholism. Although he ultimately achieved sobriety, her parents divorced in 2013. Both remarried—her mother to Sam Ramker, who had been one of her father's good friends.

Alaina included these struggles when writing the songs for her second album, *Road Less Traveled*, which was released on January 27, 2017. Discussing all she had been through in the years before the album's release, Alaina told Taylor Weatherby for *Billboard* (8 Mar. 2017), "Those things gave me my story and made me who I am. I would go through those things a million times to feel the way I feel now and know the things I know now about myself. I really feel like I found myself, and when I found myself, I found the music along with it."

In a review of the album for *Taste of Country* (27 Jan. 2017), Cillea Houghton wrote, "Her vocals have matured vastly since her *Idol* days, exhibiting genuine emotion and pure control in her singing abilities." In particular, Alania was rewarded for her work on the album's title track and its subsequent music video, which won the CMT Music Award for Breakthrough Video of the Year in 2017. Houghton concluded: "*Road Less Traveled* stands out at the core with its lyrics, all about empowerment, positivity and loving yourself no matter what you're faced with in life—valuable lessons to learn from a young artist who's managed to overcome adversity and turn it into art that aims to empower us all." The song "Road Less Traveled" also inspired a television movie of the same name, which starred Alaina and premiered on CMT on November 10, 2017.

The same year Alaina was featured on the song "What Ifs" by childhood friend and fellow country singer Kane Brown. The song spent five weeks at number one on the Billboard Hot

Country Songs Chart, and the music video for the song won Alaina and Brown the 2018 CMT Music Award for Collaborative Video of the Year. Alaina was also awarded the 2018 ACM Award for New Female Vocalist of the Year.

PERSONAL LIFE

Known for her commitment to philanthropy, Alaina traveled to Pyeongchang, South Korea, for the Special Olympics World Games in 2013, as an ambassador for Project Unify. In 2017 she founded her own charitable organization, My Kinda People. Named after the title of one of her singles, the nonprofit supports special-needs children and other causes.

In July 2018 Alaina became engaged to model Alexander Hopkins, whom she began dating in 2012.

SUGGESTED READING

Alaina, Lauren. "*American Idol* Runner-Up Lauren Alaina: Q&A." Interview by Jennifer Still. *Digital Spy*, 26 May 2011, www.digitalspy.com/tv/ustv/a321723/american-idol-runner-up-lauren-alaina-qa. Accessed 16 Nov. 2018.

Alaina, Lauren. "Lauren Alaina Talks Overcoming Personal and Family Struggles through Honest New Album: 'I Was Freed with This Music.'" Interview by Taylor Weatherby. *Billboard*, 8 Mar. 2017, www.billboard.com/articles/columns/country/7717148/lauren-alaina-interview-road-less-traveled. Accessed 16 Nov. 2018.

Blumberg, Perri Ormont. "Rising Country Star Lauren Alaina Reflects on Her Biggest Year Yet: 'I'm Just Really Proud.'" *People*, 13 Apr. 2018, people.com/music/acms-2018-lauren-alaina-really-proud-biggest-year-yet. Accessed 16 Nov. 2018.

Dauphin, Chuck. "Lauren Alaina on Her Long Road to Becoming a Fresh Face in Country." *Billboard*, 31 Jan. 2018, www.billboard.com/articles/columns/country/8097285/lauren-alaina-interview. Accessed 16 Nov. 2018.

Dukes, Billie. Review of *Wildflower*, by Lauren Alaina. *Taste of Country*, 11 Oct. 2011, tasteofcountry.com/lauren-alaina-wildflower. Accessed 16 Nov. 2018.

Houghton, Cillea. "Album Spotlight: Lauren Alaina, 'Road Less Traveled.'" Review of *Road Less Traveled*, by Lauren Alaina. *Taste of Country*, 27 Jan. 2017, tasteofcountry.com/lauren-alaina-road-less-traveled-album. Accessed 16 Nov. 2018.

Van Amburg, Jessie. "*American Idol* Star Lauren Alaina Opens Up about Her Past Struggles with Body Image and Bulimia." *Time*, 10 May 2016, time.com/4324775/american-idol-lauren-alaina-bulimia. Accessed 16 Nov. 2018.

—*Mari Rich*

Jason Aldean

Date of birth: February 28, 1977
Occupation: Singer

Country music star Jason Aldean is known for a lengthy string of top-ten singles on the Billboard Hot Country Songs chart such as "Big Green Tractor," "Dirt Road Anthem," "Fly Over States," "Take a Little Ride," "Night Train," "Lights Come On," "A Little More Summertime," "Any Ol' Barstool," and "You Make It Easy." Aldean has taken home a slew of honors—including a Country Music Association (CMA) Award for Album of the Year for his 2010 hit record *My Kinda Party* and Academy of Country Music (ACM) Awards for Entertainer of the Year in 2016, 2017, and 2018.

Despite those accolades, some observers have pointed out that the innovations he has brought to the country genre are not universally beloved. "With his hard rock and hip-hop influenced brand of country music, the Macon, Georgia, native is, to his detractors, the embodiment of how far country has drifted from its roots," Joseph Hudak wrote for *Rolling Stone* (28 Nov. 2016). Still, Aldean has made an undeniable mark on his industry. "We did help to shape the sound of country music for a generation," he told Hudak about his own work as well as more progressive peers such as Luke Bryan. "There is somebody right now sitting in a room listening to our songs trying to figure out how to play them. They'll be the next wave of country superstars."

Long a fixture on the country music scene, Aldean came to widespread notice even beyond

Photo by Tim Mosenfelder/WireImage

the world of music because of a night he has described as the worst of his life. As a headliner at the Route 91 Harvest festival in Las Vegas on October 1, 2017, he was in the middle of performing his set onstage when a gunman opened fire, killing fifty-eight people and injuring hundreds more in what was considered the deadliest mass shooting in modern US history up to that point.

EARLY LIFE AND EDUCATION
The singer was born Jason Aldine Williams on February 28, 1977, in Macon, Georgia. (He later changed the spelling of his middle name to have a stage name he felt would stand out.) His mother, Debbie, and his father, Barry, were federal workers who divorced when he was three years old. He continued to live with his mother but spent his summers with his father, who had moved to Homestead, Florida. Of his parents' amicable divorce, Aldean told Hudak, "They've always gotten along. They knew that them not being able to stay married wasn't my fault and I shouldn't have to pay for it. I always had a ton of respect for them. . . . I have a great relationship with both of them."

Aldean attended Windsor Academy, a private preparatory school in Bibb County, Georgia. His father, who bought him a guitar, had made a habit of assigning him chords to practice each day during the summer, and he increasingly honed his skill. Although he particularly loved country acts like George Strait and Alabama, his tastes were wide-ranging. "I grew up listening to all kinds of music, everything from country to rock, pop, R&B and even rap, so for me, music is music and a great song is a great song," he explained to Lorie Hollabaugh for *The Boot* (29 June 2011).

Playing onstage for the first time at age fourteen, Aldean became hooked on performing, despite the crowd consisting of around five people at the Macon VFW hall. He then began appearing at local talent shows, and at about fifteen he had joined the house band at a Macon venue called Nashville South. At the time Aldean was also a longtime fan and player of baseball and initially thought that his future might be in the sport; he even attracted the notice of college baseball scouts. By the time Aldean graduated high school in 1995, however, he had a day job driving a Pepsi truck that allowed him to pursue his art by night. He would set about exploring the country music scene in both his hometown and surrounding areas, playing at popular venues such as Whiskey River, writing songs, and appearing at music festivals whenever he could get booked.

BREAKTHROUGH
In 1998 music producer Michael Knox heard Aldean performing at an Atlanta, Georgia, talent showcase. Knox had been looking for a country artist who could play arenas in a hard-hitting style, and he believed Aldean fit the bill. He signed the grateful performer to a contract as a songwriter with Warner/Chappell and helped him move to Nashville, Tennessee; however, Aldean's early years there were far from smooth.

Although Aldean at one point inked a recording deal with major label Capitol, it quickly fell through. "Capitol had tried to change my whole image," he explained to Hudak. "I wore the cowboy hat and boots, like now, but when I got there, it was during a time when boy bands were big. . . . They wanted me to not look like a cowboy. 'Don't wear a hat!' Every time I went onstage to play I was uncomfortable, it didn't feel natural, it didn't feel right to me." After being dropped by Capitol, more defeat followed. Label representatives would express interest but not follow through or would lose their position at the company before a deal could be made. "Things like that happened a lot. So it'd been seven years or so of frustration," he added to Hudak. And so, despite all his efforts, he still had no label-produced record. With no major recording label interested in him, Aldean started to seriously consider whether he would have to give up the dream and return to Georgia, even inquiring with connections back home about possible jobs.

Fortuitously, while performing at a showcase, he caught the ear of representatives at the independent label Broken Bow. Aldean, unsure at first about the amount of success he could have with an independent label, nevertheless signed with them and released his eponymous debut album in 2005. His album's first single, "Hicktown," made its way into the tenth position on the Billboard Hot Country Songs chart. "For the time, it was an anthem for a younger generation that maybe wasn't into a lot of the other, slicker stuff on radio," Aldean, who garnered the ACM Award for Top New Male Vocalist in 2006, recalled to Hudak. "And there was a changing of the guard of artists at the time. You had me, Miranda [Lambert], Eric Church, Luke [Bryan]— all of us hit at the same time. It was a different sound coming into the genre and I think we were at the forefront of that stuff."

MAKING HIS MARK AND HITS
After the release of his aptly named sophomore effort *Relentless* (2007), his next record, *Wide Open* (2009), spawned three singles that claimed the top spot on the Billboard Hot Country Songs chart—"She's Country," "The Truth," and "Big Green Tractor"—and firmly established his reputation as a force to be reckoned with on the country music scene.

That reputation was cemented by his 2010 album, *My Kinda Party*, which features the singles "Don't You Wanna Stay" (with Kelly Clarkson), "Dirt Road Anthem," and "Fly Over States," all of which peaked at number one on the Billboard Hot Country Songs chart. "Dirt Road Anthem," caused buzz because it includes several sections in which Aldean raps, albeit with a southern twang. Claiming the trophy for Album of the Year at the 2011 CMA Awards, *My Kinda Party* earned solid reviews from country music critics. Matt Bjorke, in a review for *RoughStock* (31 Oct. 2010), called *My Kinda Party* Aldean's "strongest album to date" and stated that the singer "may just be one of country music's best at making complete albums that are 'all killer, no filler.'"

Aldean followed that triumph with *Night Train* (2012), *Old Boots, New Dirt* (2014), and *They Don't Know* (2016), all of which topped the Billboard 200 chart. As he built his body of work, he continued to intrigue both new and loyal fans and anger traditionalists with his genre-bending style. "I know I'm not gonna please everybody when I make a record," he told Chrissie Dickinson for the *Chicago Tribune* (22 Oct. 2012). "I don't let that affect any of my decisions. . . . If we all did the same kind of music, it would be boring." In recognition of his success, he was presented with the ACM Award for Entertainer of the Year in 2016, 2017, and 2018.

MUSIC AFTER TRAGEDY

During a tour promoting *They Don't Know*, Aldean headlined the Route 91 Harvest country music festival taking place in Las Vegas, Nevada, in October 2017. Chaos ensued when, during a performance of his song "When She Says Baby," a gunman opened fire on the crowd from a hotel near the outdoor venue, killing fifty-eight. The weekend after the event, mainstream audiences had a chance to hear Aldean when he appeared on *Saturday Night Live* to perform a defiant version of the Tom Petty rock anthem "I Won't Back Down." He temporarily halted his tour out of respect for the victims and returned to Las Vegas to meet with some of those injured in the attack and recovering in a local hospital, while trying to cope with the tragedy himself. Still, he ultimately returned to the stage to resume the tour later that month. "For me, being able to talk to my guys, talk to people that I was close to, being able to talk about it to somebody who understood how I was feeling, that helped me tremendously. The other part of that was getting back on stage [and] mentally getting through some shows," he explained to Annie Reuter for *Billboard* (16 Feb. 2019).

Aldean's 2018 album, *Rearview Town*, debuted atop the Billboard 200 chart, becoming his fourth consecutive number-one album in the United States. At the ACM Awards in 2019, he was honored with the Dick Clark Artist of the Decade Award.

PERSONAL LIFE

Aldean and his first wife, Jessica Ussery, were high school sweethearts. They married in 2001 and had two daughters: Keeley, in 2003, and Kendyl, in 2007. The singer became the subject of a tabloid scandal in September 2012, when he was photographed getting inappropriately close to Brittany Kerr, a former *American Idol* contestant and pro basketball dancer, in a bar. Although he attributed the incident to drunkenness and a momentary lapse of judgment, he filed for divorce in April 2013 and married Kerr in 2015. Aldean and Kerr have two children together: a son, Memphis, born in 2017, and a daughter, Navy Rome, born in 2019.

SUGGESTED READING

Aldean, Jason. "Jason Aldean: The *Rolling Stone* Country Interview." Interview by Joseph Hudak. *Rolling Stone*, 28 Nov. 2016, www.rollingstone.com/music/music-country/jason-aldean-the-rolling-stone-country-interview-128109. Accessed 2 Mar. 2019.

Aldean, Jason. "Jason Aldean's Fans Follow Him down a 'Dirt Road.'" Interview by Lorie Hollabaugh. *The Boot*, Taste of Country Network, 29 June 2011, theboot.com/jason-aldean-interview-dirt-road-anthem. Accessed 2 Mar. 2019.

Bjorke, Matt. Review of *My Kinda Party*, by Jason Aldean. *RoughStock*, 31 Oct. 2010, roughstock.com/news/2010/10/19003-jason-aldean-my-kinda-party. Accessed 2 Mar. 2019.

Dickinson, Chrissie. "Jason Aldean Sticks to the Tried-and-True on 'Night Train.'" *Chicago Tribune*, 22 Oct. 2012, www.chicagotribune.com/entertainment/ct-xpm-2012-10-22-chi-jason-aldean-interview-20121022-story.html. Accessed 1 Apr. 2019.

Reuter, Annie. "Jason Aldean Reflects on Route 91 Harvest Festival Shooting: 'It Will Forever Be on My Mind.'" *Billboard*, 16 Feb. 2019, www.billboard.com/articles/columns/country/8498717/jason-aldean-reflects-route-91-harvest-festival-shooting. Accessed 1 Apr. 2019.

SELECTED WORKS

Jason Aldean, 2005; *Relentless*, 2007; *Wide Open*, 2009; *My Kinda Party*, 2010; *Night Train*, 2012; *Old Boots, New Dirt*, 2014; *They Don't Know*, 2016; *Rearview Town*, 2018

—*Mari Rich*

James P. Allison

Date of birth: August 7, 1948
Occupation: Immunologist

For immunologist James P. Allison, "science is a long and frustrating road," he noted in a press conference, as reported by Cindy George for the *Texas Medical Center* website (1 Oct. 2018). "There's no instant gratification," he added. Allison's career has aptly proven that point. A professor and researcher who earned his doctorate from the University of Texas at Austin in 1973, Allison spent several decades investigating the mechanisms controlling T cells—cells within the body that attack threats as part of the immune system's response—with the goal of developing a means of enabling those cells to fight cancer. His research led to the development of the antibody ipilimumab, which, after more than a decade of clinical trials, was approved for use in patients with metastatic melanoma in 2011.

In addition to that single drug, Allison's findings further invigorated the field of cancer immunotherapy and prompted researchers to seek additional ways of enabling the body to fight off cancer. "Since we're coming up with new tools all the time, I think it's just a really exciting period," he said in an interview for the website of the *Cancer Research Institute*. "The preclinical and clinical studies are just exploding with new ideas." In recognition of his critical contributions to the ongoing medical battle against cancer, Allison was awarded the 2018 Nobel Prize for Physiology or Medicine, which he shared with Japanese immunologist Tasuku Honjo.

EARLY LIFE AND EDUCATION

James Patrick Allison was born in Alice, Texas, on August 7, 1948. He was the youngest of three sons born to Albert and Constance Allison. His father was a doctor, and his mother was a homemaker. Allison's mother died of cancer when he was still a child, and the disease would later also kill his oldest brother and two uncles. Allison himself developed both prostate cancer and melanoma as an adult, both of which received successful early treatment. Although he did not begin his scientific career with the goal of developing cancer treatments, Allison later noted that his early experiences with cancer fueled his later passion for fighting cancerous cells.

Allison developed an interest in science at a young age and soon began designing his own experiments at home. He attended local public schools but by high school also began enrolling in summer science programs at the University of Texas at Austin. After graduating from high school in 1965, at the age of sixteen, he returned to the University of Texas as a full-time student. Although he initially considered following in his father's footsteps by pursuing a medical career,

Photo by Gerbil via Wikimedia Commons

he eventually decided to pursue a bachelor's degree in microbiology, which he completed in 1969. Allison remained at the University of Texas at Austin for his doctoral studies, earning his PhD in biological sciences in 1973.

While a graduate student, Allison first learned about the area of research that would shape his career. "I had a professor who told me there were these recently discovered cells called T cells, and he said he didn't even know if they existed or not, which gives you a sense of when my introduction to immunology occurred," he recalled in an interview with Jame Abraham for the *ASCO Post* (25 May 2018). "All we knew was that T cells went around the body looking for pathogens to attack, and they did it without hurting the healthy cells, which really intrigued me." Allison went on to devote much of his career to immunology, and particularly the study of T cells, which play a key role in the immune system's responses to threats such as viruses.

ACADEMIC CAREER

After completing his doctorate, Allison took a position as a postdoctoral fellow in the department of molecular immunology at the Scripps Clinic and Research Foundation near San Diego. After several years, he returned to Texas in 1977 to serve as an assistant biochemist and assistant professor at the University of Texas MD Anderson Cancer Center. He spent seven years at the center, during which time he was promoted to associate professor and served as an adjunct professor at the University of Texas at Austin. After a stint as a visiting scholar at the Stanford University School of Medicine, he joined the Department of Molecular and Cell

Biology at the University of California, Berkeley. He also served as an adjunct professor in the Department of Medicine at the University of California, San Francisco School of Medicine. Allison left California in 2004 and moved to Weill Cornell Medicine in New York, where he served as a professor until 2012.

Alongside his academic positions, Allison has been associated with a variety of research laboratories and institutions. He was an investigator at the Howard Hughes Medical Institute (HHMI) between 1997 and 2012, director of the Department of Cancer Research Laboratory at Berkeley between 1985 and 2004, and director of the Ludwig Center for Cancer Immunotherapy at the Memorial Sloan-Kettering Cancer Center (MSKCC) in New York from 2006 to 2012. While at Memorial Sloan-Kettering, he became more deeply involved in the world of drug development and immunology in humans. "[I] learned how to at least appreciate the complexity of clinical trials and appreciate the importance of understanding, again beyond just the clinical signal that they might give, how important it is to really understand what's going on," he told Brien Williams in a 2013 interview for the American Association of Immunologists Oral History Project. "The gratifying part of it, of course, was just seeing the people that were treated." He later returned to the MD Anderson Cancer Center in Texas, where he held several positions, including the roles of Vivian L. Smith Distinguished Chair in Immunology, chief scientific adviser, director of the center's Parker Institute for Cancer Immunotherapy, and chair of the Department of Immunology.

GROUNDBREAKING RESEARCH

Throughout his career as a researcher, Allison focused primarily on studying T cells to determine the mechanisms that control their response to foreign bodies. Research had revealed that while T cells attack threats such as viruses within the body as part of the immune system's response, they are ineffective against cancer cells. Allison found that the protein CTLA-4 is responsible for stopping T cells from attacking a particular threat, and he theorized that the protein acts as a safety mechanism to prevent the immune system from harming cells that should be within a person's body. Although often harmful to the human in question, cancer cells are not foreign threats; rather, they are human cells that keep dividing past the point when they should stop. As such, Allison noted, the immune system does not fully recognize cancer as a threat, and CTLA-4 prevents the body's T cells from attacking the cancer cells to the fullest extent possible.

In an attempt to slow or even stop the spread of cancer, Allison worked to develop a means of preventing CTLA-4 from halting the work of T cells so that the T cells could be allowed to defend the body by attacking the cancer cells. Doing so, Allison believed, would ultimately create a form of cancer treatment that would be much longer-lasting than its alternatives. "Once you've generated T cells that can recognize cancer, you've got them basically for the rest of your life," he explained in his interview for the Cancer Research Institute. "Whereas with every other drug, they kill a bunch of tumor cells and then the drugs go away." Allison partnered initially with NeXstar Pharmaceuticals and ultimately with the company Medarex to create an antibody that would block CTLA-4.

Medarex received approval to start clinical trials for the resulting antibody, ipilimumab, in 2000. The company was later purchased by the large pharmaceutical firm Bristol-Myers Squibb, and in 2011, the US Food and Drug Administration (FDA) approved the use of the drug, marketed as Yervoy, for some patients with melanoma. Other clinical drug development efforts based in part on Allison's research followed, drawing significant attention to an area of cancer research that had long been ignored. Although some scientists and members of the public objected to calling drugs such as ipilimumab cures for cancer, as they tended to extend the lives of patients without conclusively eliminating their cancer, Allison argued otherwise. "We have to redefine the word 'cure' a little bit," he told the Cancer Research Institute. "I think, for practical purposes, if you're alive and are having no trouble a decade after your treatment, then I think that's as good as a cure." Indeed, a significant portion of the patients with metastatic melanoma who participated in the original clinical trials lived for at least two years following the trials, with some remaining cancer free more than a decade later.

NOBEL PRIZE

In recognition of his research, Allison has received many awards and honors, including the American Association of Immunologists' Dana Foundation Award in Human Immunology Research, the Heath Memorial Award of the MD Anderson Cancer Center, and the American Cancer Society's Medal of Honor for Basic Research. In January 2018, the National Academy of Sciences (NAS) awarded him the Jessie Stevenson Kovalenko Medal. The most significant moment of recognition to date, however, came in October 2018, when the Nobel Prize Committee announced that Allison would be one of two recipients of that year's Nobel Prize in Physiology or Medicine, widely considered to be the highest honor in that field. Allison split the award—and the associated prize of nine million Swedish krona, or nearly US $1 million—evenly with Japanese researcher Tasuku Honjo of Kyoto University.

For Allison, who told Adam Smith for the *Nobel Prize* website (1 Oct. 2018) that winning the Nobel Prize was "the dream of a lifetime," the path that led him to receive such recognition was an unexpected one. "I'm a basic scientist. I did not get into these studies to try to cure cancer," he said, as reported by George. "I got into them because I wanted to know how T cells worked." Decades later, Allison had not only revealed further details about the functions of T cells but also determined how to help those cells fight one of the human body's deadliest foes.

Yet, despite the recognition he received and the promising results of his work, Allison remained focused on the need for additional research building upon his work and that of his colleagues. "The biggest challenge in immunotherapy now is figuring out why an immune drug works in some patients and not in others, or in some tumors and not in others," he told Abraham. "To do that we need to go back to basic science. That's how it's done; there's no easy answer, just hard basic science."

PERSONAL LIFE
Allison married Malinda Bell in 1969. They have one son, Robert. They divorced in 2012. He is now married to oncologist Padmanee Sharma. In his leisure time, he plays harmonica in the blues band The Checkpoints, which features other cancer and immunology researchers and has performed at events hosted by groups such as the Society for Immunotherapy of Cancer.

SUGGESTED READING
Allison, James P. "Allison Reflects on a Career in Immunology, Nobel Prize." Interview by Angelica Welch. *OncLive*, 4 Oct. 2018, www.onclive.com/web-exclusives/allison-reflects-on-a-career-in-immunology-nobel-prize. Accessed 9 Nov. 2018.

———. Interview by Brien Williams. *American Association of Immunologists Oral History Project*, 2013, www.aai.org/AAISite/media/About/History/OHP/Transcripts/Trans-Inv_023-Allison_James_P-2013_Final.pdf. Accessed 9 Nov. 2018.

———. "James P. Allison Interview." Interview by Adam Smith. *NobelPrize.org*, 1 Oct. 2018, www.nobelprize.org/prizes/medicine/2018/allison/interview. Accessed 9 Nov. 2018.

Devlin, Hannah. "James P. Allison and Tasuku Honjo Win Nobel Prize for Medicine." *The Guardian*, 1 Oct. 2018, www.theguardian.com/science/2018/oct/01/james-p-allison-and-tasuku-honjo-win-nobel-prize-for-medicine. Accessed 9 Nov. 2018.

George, Cindy. "MD Anderson Immunologist James P. Allison, Ph.D. Named Nobel Laureate." *TMC News*, Texas Medical Center, 1 Oct. 2018, www.tmc.edu/news/2018/10/md-anderson-immunologist-james-p-allison-ph-d-named-nobel-laureate. Accessed 9 Nov. 2018.

"James P. Allison, Ph.D." *Cancer Research Institute*, www.cancerresearch.org/immunotherapy/stories/scientists/james-p-allison-phd. Accessed 9 Nov. 2018.

Piana, Ronald. "For James Allison, PhD, Perseverance and Hard Science Are Paramount in Cancer Research." Interview by Jame Abraham. *The ASCO Post*, 25 May 2018, www.ascopost.com/issues/may-25-2018/james-allison-perseverance-and-hard-science-in-cancer-research. Accessed 9 Nov. 2018.

—*Joy Crelin*

Canelo Álvarez
Date of birth: July 18, 1990
Occupation: Boxer

"It's very important for me to give the fans the biggest fights and the most important fights, and I promise you I will always do that," Saúl "Canelo" Álvarez said, as reported by Dan Rafael for *ESPN* (17 Oct. 2018). Indeed, the professional boxer has kept that promise over the course of his professional career, which he launched in his native Mexico at the age of fifteen. A talented young athlete from a family of boxers, he quickly established himself as a champion and a celebrity in Mexico and caught the attention of retired boxer Oscar De La Hoya's Golden Boy Promotions, which set out to make Álvarez a star in the United States as well. Although he experienced some high-profile setbacks, including a painful loss to veteran boxer Floyd Mayweather Jr. in 2013 and a six-month suspension following failed drug tests in 2018, his career has had numerous highlights as well, among them many successful title fights and most notably his 2018 rematch against rival Gennady Golovkin.

Having signed a $365 million contract with the streaming service DAZN in late 2018, Álvarez appeared poised to usher in a new era of professional boxing. Álvarez, who prefers to speak Spanish and typically conducts interviews with English-language publications through an interpreter, called it "the second phase" of his career, as reported by Arash Markazi for *ESPN* (16 Dec. 2018). "The first phase has ended," he said. "I'm going to keep making history and moving forward."

EARLY LIFE AND CAREER
Santos Saúl Álvarez Barragán was born in Juanacatlán, Mexico, on July 18, 1990. He grew up in Juanacatlán, a small town outside of Guadalajara,

Photo by Presidencia de la República Mexicana

where his father sold ice pops known as *paletas*. Álvarez was the youngest of eight children born to Santos Álvarez and Ana Maria Barragán, and was one of seven brothers. All his older brothers would go on to become involved in boxing, and Álvarez's own entry into the sport was particularly inspired by his oldest brother, Rigoberto, who was already experiencing success in the sport during Álvarez's childhood. With Rigoberto's encouragement, Álvarez began boxing at a local gym and began training seriously by the age of eleven. During that period, he became known by the nickname Canelo—derived from *canela*, or cinnamon—due to his red hair. As a young teen, Álvarez distinguished himself in amateur competitions throughout Mexico, and he dropped out of school to focus on boxing.

Álvarez made his debut on the professional level in 2005, at the age of fifteen, and soon began to amass an impressive record, defeating nearly all the opponents he faced. His success in the ring earned him widespread attention within the Mexican media, turning the young athlete into a celebrity. "I turned around and all this happened suddenly," he told Pablo S. Torre for *ESPN* (3 Sept. 2013) of that period. "It was very weird. I didn't see it coming." Although primarily active in Mexico and not well known outside of that country, he also competed in the United States on occasion, including defending his World Boxing Association (WBA) Fedecentro welterweight title against Raúl Pinzón in Miami, Florida, in 2008.

SUCCESS IN THE UNITED STATES

With his impressive record and extensive Mexican media recognition, Álvarez eventually captured the attention of Golden Boy Promotions, a company founded by retired boxer Oscar De La Hoya. Álvarez signed with the company at the beginning of 2010, becoming the focus of efforts to establish him as a well-known and successful competitor in the United States. "We believe Saul is going to be a star," De La Hoya said, as reported by Roberto Andrade for *ESPN* (13 Dec. 2018). "He's already a big attraction . . . in Mexico and we're going to do everything we can to help him become a champion and a star in the United States." Álvarez made his debut at the MGM Grand casino in Las Vegas, a prestigious venue for boxing, in May 2010, defeating José Miguel Cotto in a technical knockout. Over the next years, he went on to claim several major boxing titles, including the World Boxing Council (WBC) Silver super welterweight title, the WBC World super welterweight title, and the WBA super welterweight world champion. (In boxing, super welterweight is also known as "junior middleweight" or "light middleweight.")

The highest-profile contest of Álvarez's career to that point came in September 2013, when he faced off against Floyd Mayweather Jr. at the MGM Grand. A veteran boxer about thirteen years Álvarez's senior, Mayweather had never been defeated in his professional career and represented a formidable opponent due to his wealth of experience in the sport. Álvarez trained extensively for the fight, including by analyzing footage of Mayweather's 2007 defeat of De La Hoya and by attempting to better understand Mayweather's own strategies and ways of moving. Although Álvarez avoided being defeated through a knockout or technical knockout during the match, the judges awarded the victory to Mayweather in a majority decision.

The loss to Mayweather marked Álvarez's first official defeat in his professional career, and he would later note in interviews that he had not been truly ready to take on such a daunting challenge. "At the time, I felt I was ready. Obviously, we were wrong," he recalled in an interview with the *New York Times* (17 Oct. 2018). "I didn't have the experience. It was the experience—or lack thereof—that defeated me." He noted, however, that his later experiences in the ring have aptly prepared him to take on Mayweather, who has retired and come out of retirement on several occasions, again in the future. "Now that I'm more mature, it would be a completely different fight," he said, as reported by the *Times*.

MAJOR BOUTS

Following his defeat by Mayweather, Álvarez returned to the MGM Grand for two successful fights in 2014, defeating Alfredo Angulo in

March and Erislandy Lara in July of that year. As he continued to train, he also increased his body weight, which enabled him to complete in different weight classes and face off against new opponents. Álvarez took the WBC world middleweight title in November 2015 after defeating Miguel "Junito" Cotto (brother of José Miguel Cotto) in a unanimous decision and the World Boxing Organization (WBO) light middleweight title after defeating Liam Smith in a knockout in September 2016. The year 2017 saw some of the most highly anticipated fights of Álvarez's career to that point, beginning with a competition against Julio César Chávez Jr., a fellow Mexican-born boxer and the son of famed champion Julio César Chávez Sr. Álvarez won the fight, held at Las Vegas's T-Mobile Arena in May 2017, in a unanimous decision.

In September 2017 Álvarez competed against Gennady "GGG" Golovkin, a Kazakhstani boxer who at that time held world middleweight titles in several different federations. Neither boxer managed to knock out the other during the fight's twelve rounds, although Golovkin succeeded in landing more punches on Álvarez than vice versa. At the end of the fight, the judges put forth a split decision that resulted in the fight being deemed a draw. Golovkin immediately began to call for a rematch, and Álvarez agreed, although he felt that he had been the true champion. "I felt I won the fight by 2 points," he told Miguel Maravilla for *Fightnews. com* (8 Mar. 2018). "He hit me with a lot of good shots but I hope that was his best punch." He looked forward to the rematch and told Maravilla, "I feel that there was a lot of openings that I didn't take advantage of."

SUSPENSION AND COMEBACK

In early 2018 Álvarez failed two drug tests when trace levels of clenbuterol, a substance considered to be a performance-enhancing drug, were found in his system. Although Álvarez stated that the positive result was due to his consumption of beef that had been contaminated with the substance, which is sometimes used in cattle feed in Mexico, he cooperated with the ensuing investigation. "I am an athlete who respects the sport and this surprises me and bothers me because it has never happened to me," he said in a statement released by Golden Boy Promotions, as quoted by Maravilla. "I will submit to all the tests that require me to clarify this embarrassing situation and I trust that at the end the truth will prevail." Álvarez was suspended from competition for six months, which resulted in the cancellation of a planned rematch against Golovkin in May 2018. Álvarez later commented in interviews that he had stopped eating meat while in Mexico to prevent any accidental consumption of clenbuterol in the future. While suspended,

Álvarez underwent surgery to remove a cyst from his knee.

Álvarez resumed competing in September 2018, returning to the T-Mobile Arena with Golovkin nearly a year after their previous matchup. The two fighters had a combative public relationship leading up to the fight, as Golovkin, still displeased with the result of their first fight, labeled Álvarez a cheater due to the positive drug tests and mocked him for his style of movement in the ring. Their rematch, however, resulted in a far less contentious decision on the part of judges than the 2017 draw, with the judges awarding the win to Álvarez in a majority decision. The victory earned Álvarez world middleweight titles and sparked rumors of an eventual third match between the two competitors. Although Álvarez was satisfied with his victory, he remained open to the idea of fighting Golovkin yet again. "If the fans want to see a third fight, then we'll do it," he told the *New York Times*.

NEW MILESTONES

In the fall of 2018, Álvarez signed a deal with the streaming sports broadcaster DAZN. The five-year deal, worth at least $365 million, specified that he would compete in eleven fights to be broadcast by the service. His contract was reported to be the most lucrative in sporting history, and the contract and his numerous sponsorships secured Álvarez fifteenth place on the Forbes list of the world's highest-paid athletes for 2018. For Álvarez, however, the DAZN deal was important not only because of the pay it guaranteed him but also because it would make his fights viewable with a low-cost monthly subscription rather than through the more expensive pay-per-view model. "The most important thing to me was being able to give the fans the opportunity to see me fight without having to pay the $70 or $80 for my fights on pay-per-view," he said, as reported by Rafael for *ESPN* (17 Oct. 2018). "That was the most important thing, more important than what I am making."

Álvarez made his debut with the service on December 15, 2018, in a fight against British fighter Michael "Rocky" Fielding at Madison Square Garden in New York City. Prior to the fight, Álvarez went up in weight again to compete in the WBA regular super middleweight class, which requires athletes to weigh between 160 and 168 pounds. As reported by Rafael for *ESPN* (16 Dec. 2018), Álvarez was comfortable with that change, noting that he felt "very good" and "very strong." He defeated Fielding in a technical knockout during the third round of the fight, winning a super middleweight title. Following the fight, Álvarez looked forward to his next match, scheduled for May 2019. "What I always want to do is to make the best fight, whether they're for world titles or not," he said, as reported by Rafael.

PERSONAL LIFE

Álvarez lives and trains in San Diego, California, and has also trained in the high-elevation Big Bear area of the state. He has noted in interviews that if he was not a professional boxer, he would like to compete in Formula One automobile racing.

Álvarez was once engaged to Marisol González, Miss Mexico Universe 2003 and sports reporter for Televisa. He has a daughter, Emily Cinnamon Álvarez.

SUGGESTED READING

Álvarez, Canelo. "Canelo Alvarez Is Back, and He'll Fight a Guy Named Rocky." Interview. *The New York Times*, 17 Oct. 2018, www.nytimes.com/2018/10/17/sports/canelo-alvarez-rocky-fielding-fight.amp.html. Accessed 16 Dec. 2018.

Andrade, Roberto. "The Evolution That Brought Canelo Alvarez to Madison Square Garden." *ESPN*, 13 Dec. 2018, www.espn.com/boxing/story/_/id/25526155/the-evolution-brought-canelo-alvarez-madison-square-garden. Accessed 16 Dec. 2018.

Maravilla, Miguel. "Interview: Canelo Alvarez." *Fightnews.com*, 8 Mar. 2018, fightnews.com/interview-canelo-alvarez/16213. Accessed 16 Dec. 2018.

Markazi, Arash. "Canelo Alvarez a Winner, and Not Only in the Ring." *ESPN*, 16 Dec. 2018, www.espn.com/boxing/story/_/id/25544184/canelo-alvarez-winner-not-only-ring. Accessed 16 Dec. 2018.

Rafael, Dan. "Canelo Alvarez Crushes Rocky Fielding, Now 3-Division Titlist." *ESPN*, 16 Dec. 2018, www.espn.com/boxing/story/_/id/25544321/canelo-alvarez-defeats-rocky-fielding-third-round-tko. Accessed 16 Dec. 2018.

Rafael, Dan. "Canelo Alvarez Signs 5-Year, 11-Fight Deal Worth Minimum $365 Million with DAZN." *ESPN*, 17 Oct. 2018, www.espn.com/boxing/story/_/id/25003974/canelo-alvarez-signs-5-year-11-fight-deal-worth-365-million-dazn. Accessed 16 Dec. 2018.

Torre, Pablo S. "The Last Best Contender." *ESPN*, 3 Sept. 2013, www.espn.com/boxing/story/_/id/9629500/can-canelo-alvarez-beat-legend-floyd-mayweather-espn-magazine. Accessed 16 Dec. 2018.

—*Joy Crelin*

Chris Anderson

Date of birth: January 14, 1957
Occupation: Entrepreneur

As a child, Chris Anderson was known for his curiosity. "I always wanted to know the *why* and the *how*," he told Vikas Shah for *ThoughtEconomics* (5 May 2018). "Some of my deepest memories are literally lying down at night when we were outdoors, looking up at the stars and being awestruck, wondering how all of this happened. . . . Wondering who we are, where we came from and what it all means." That sense of curiosity served Anderson well as an adult: in the 1980s, he built upon his fascination with the burgeoning field of personal computing to create Future Publishing, which would become one of the United Kingdom's most successful publishing companies of the following decade, beginning by publishing computer magazines for niche, yet devoted audiences. He went on to launch a new business, Imagine Media, in the United States and later merged his two ventures, creating the publishing powerhouse Future Network in the late 1990s.

A turning point for Anderson came in 2001, when he left Future Network—then struggling following the end of the dot-com boom—to focus on a newer acquisition, the nonprofit organization TED (Technology, Entertainment, and Design). Founded in 1984, TED then consisted of an annual, invitation-only conference dedicated to ideas and innovation. Under Anderson's leadership, TED expanded to encompass not only the annual conference but also global

Photo by James Duncan Davidson/TED via Wikimedia Commons

conferences, conferences dedicated to specific issues and demographics, and educational programs. The organization gained widespread attention beginning in 2006, when TED first began to make the short lectures known as TED Talks freely available online, and went on to become an influential cultural force as the talks delivered at TED-affiliated conferences and independent TEDx events spread across the Internet. For Anderson, expanding TED's reach was key to the goal of promoting ideas that are, in the organization's view, worth spreading. "I believe passionately that ideas are a force of unlimited power and it has never mattered more that we get behind the right ones," he told James Ashton for the *Evening Standard* (1 Mar. 2017).

EARLY LIFE AND EDUCATION

Christopher J. Anderson was born in rural Pakistan on January 14, 1957. At the time of his birth, his parents were both missionaries working to supply medical services to residents of the area. His father, John, was an eye surgeon whose dedication to improving the lives of others made a deep impression on the young Anderson. "He was passionate about sharing God's love in a way that he knew best, which was to try and bring eyesight to those who don't have it," he recalled to Mick Brown for the *Telegraph* (29 Apr. 2015) about his father. "I wouldn't recommend someone to become that kind of missionary nowadays, but the notion of a life of service, yes, that was inspiring for me." Alongside his two sisters, Anderson spent his childhood in Pakistan, Afghanistan, and India due to their parents' continuing work in those countries.

Throughout his early life, Anderson was an avid reader and a particularly curious child, traits he would later link in interviews to his adulthood approach to ideas and innovation. He initially attended Woodstock School, an American-run international school in India, before relocating to his parents' native England to attend the boarding school Monkton Combe. After completing his secondary education, Anderson enrolled in the University of Oxford, where he studied philosophy, politics, and economics. He earned his bachelor's degree from the university in 1978.

EARLY CAREER

Following university, Anderson began his career in journalism. In addition to working in print journalism as a reporter for the *South Wales Echo* newspaper, he worked as a radio producer for a time while living in Seychelles. Drawn to the developing field of computer technology, he became editor of a computer magazine in 1984. The following year, Anderson took the next major step in his career, launching the business Future Publishing as well as the company's debut publication, the computer magazine *Amstrad*

Action. Over the next years, the company's list of publications expanded significantly and came to encompass magazines focusing not only on technology-related topics but also on hobbies such as cycling. "A huge piece of luck was to discover after the event—we didn't know this at the time—that there was this giant trend away from generalist media to specialist magazines," Anderson explained to Ruth Nicolas for the *Independent* (11 July 1999). "Future just happened to be in one of those growth hotspots." After growing Future Publishing for nearly a decade, Anderson sold the company to the large publishing business Pearson in 1994 in order to finance new publishing ventures in the United States.

Upon moving to the United States and settling in San Francisco, California, Anderson launched a new, US–based publishing business, Imagine Media. In addition to publishing print magazines, among them *Business 2.0*, the company expanded into online publishing over the course of the 1990s and founded numerous websites, including several publications that later merged to form the entertainment website *IGN*. Four years into Anderson's tenure with Imagine Media, he and his business partners had the opportunity to buy Future Publishing back from Pearson and ultimately did so. They went on to merge Imagine Media and Future Publishing to form Future Network—later known simply as Future—and took the company public in 1999. Although Future Network's stock initially performed well, the later years were challenging ones for companies related to technology, publishing, and the Internet, as the end of the so-called dot-com bubble resulted in extensive layoffs, plummeting company valuations, and the closing of numerous businesses. Although Future Network survived, both the company and Anderson himself lost a substantial amount of money during the period, and Anderson stepped down from his position as director in late 2001.

TED

In 1996, during his time with Imagine Media, Anderson founded the nonprofit Sapling Foundation, an organization with the goal of using innovations from the media and business worlds to address key global issues. A key moment in Anderson's progression toward that role came two years later, when he attended his first TED conference in California. Launched in 1984 by the architect and designer Richard Saul Wurman, TED—Technology, Entertainment, and Design—began as a single conference that brought together a number of influential thinkers and enabled them to share ideas and innovations from their respective fields. Following Wurman's second TED conference, held in 1990, the event became an annual tradition that quickly gained traction among those seeking new ideas and solutions to global problems. While attending the 1998 conference, Anderson found himself instantly drawn to the concept. "I felt I'd come home," he told Brown. The Sapling Foundation later purchased TED in 2001 for $6 million.

Following Anderson's departure from Future Network, he focused his attention on TED, which represented a marked change from his previous work environment. "It was to some extent a deeply appealing landing ground on which to just kind of recover," he told Ashton. "I was shaken up. I'd gone from being a business rock star to a total loser in a year, and it really hurt." However, although Anderson had himself attended the conference in the past, he faced skepticism from longtime TED attendees. "What I discovered to my horror was that the majority of the TED community thought that because [Wurman] was leaving, TED was done," he told Melia Robinson for *Business Insider* (28 Aug. 2015). In response to such misconceptions, Anderson worked to win over the conference's community and succeeded in doing so in part through a talk he delivered at the 2002 conference, in which he opened up about the challenges he had faced during the previous years and the inspiration he drew from the multitude of ideas shared at TED.

IDEAS WORTH SPREADING

Over the next several years, Anderson focused both on curating the annual TED conference and on expanding the organization's reach. During its early years, the TED conference was open by invitation only, and the number of people who could hear and benefit from the short lectures delivered by guests was, therefore, limited. In 2006, however, the TED organization began to experiment with making videos of the lectures—known as TED Talks—available to view freely online. The earliest videos became tremendously popular, and the organization soon began to amass an extensive online archive of TED Talks that drew widespread attention to the conference. "Giving the talks away vastly multiplied the impact of TED," Anderson told David Hochman for the *New York Times* (7 Mar. 2014). "Suddenly, everyone was your marketing friend, and Facebook and Twitter became extensions of what we were doing." Deeply aware of the impact of TED's 2006 experiment, Anderson later delivered a TED Talk at TEDGlobal 2010 on the importance of online video in facilitating innovation. TED's vast online library of talks continued to expand over the following decade, and by 2016, TED Talks received more than three million views every day.

In his role as curator of the annual TED conference, which moved from California to Vancouver, Canada, in 2014, Anderson takes an optimistic approach that stems from the idea that the world's problems are not insurmountable. To that end the conference showcases not only ideas from within the fields of technology, entertainment, and design but also a variety of other scientific and philosophical topics, and TED speakers demonstrate significant enthusiasm for the topics they discuss. "So much of the attention wars that we all are immersed in are dominated by idiocy, triviality and shouting," Anderson told Hochman. "So, finding someone who can make a case and make it clearly in a way that's exciting and has a chance of being heard and being spread and acted upon, I mean that's a huge win."

In addition to the annual TED conference, the organization introduced several spinoff conferences, including TEDMED and TEDWomen, as well as the TEDGlobal series of conferences held throughout the world. TED likewise enabled independent events to operate under the TEDx brand for free in exchange for complying with certain policies. Other TED-sponsored initiatives included the TED-Ed educational programs, the TED Prize, and TED fellowships. Although some critics of the TED conference and its associated programs have accused the organization of elitism, censorship, and promoting the oversimplification of complex topics, Anderson disagrees with such assertions and prefers to focus on the organization's goals. "We have a shot at collaboratively building a better future, and we're only just started," he told Shah.

PERSONAL LIFE

Anderson was previously married to Lucy Evans, with whom he had three daughters. Their oldest daughter, Zoe, died of accidental carbon monoxide poisoning in 2010, and Anderson and his family went on to preserve a coral reef in her honor. Anderson met his wife, Jacqueline Novogratz, the founder of the nonprofit investment fund Acumen, when she delivered a TED talk. They married in 2008 and live primarily in the United States, where they own a home in New York City's West Village. Anderson is the author of the 2016 book *TED Talks: The Official TED Guide to Public Speaking*.

SUGGESTED READING

Anderson, Chris. "A Conversation with TED Curator and Owner, Chris Anderson." Interview by Vikas Shah. *ThoughtEconomics*, 5 May 2018, thoughteconomics.com/chris-anderson-ted/. Accessed 10 May 2019.

Ashton, James. "TED Talks Owner Chris Anderson on the Power of Public Speaking and Being the Ultimate Influencer." *Evening Standard*, 1 Mar. 2017, www.standard.co.uk/lifestyle/london-life/ted-talks-owner-chris-anderson-on-the-power-of-public-speaking-

and-being-the-ultimate-influencer-a3478766. html. Accessed 10 May 2019.

Brown, Mick. "'I Was Losing $1 Million a Day, Every Day for 18 Months': Meet Chris Anderson, the Man behind TED Talks." *The Telegraph*, 29 Apr. 2016, www.telegraph.co.uk/men/thinking-man/i-was-losing-1-million-a-day-every-day-for-18-months-meet-chris/. Accessed 10 May 2019.

"Chris Anderson." *TED*, 2019, www.ted.com/speakers/chris_anderson_ted. Accessed 10 May 2019.

Hochman, David. "No, His Name Is Not Ted." *The New York Times*, 7 Mar. 2014, www.nytimes.com/2014/03/09/fashion/Chris-Anderson-Curator-of-TED-Talks-Builds-his-Brand.html. Accessed 10 May 2019.

Nicholas, Ruth. "Profile: Chris Anderson: Media with Passion." *Independent*, 11 July 1999, www.independent.co.uk/news/business/profile-chris-anderson-media-with-passion-1105628.html. Accessed 10 May 2019.

Robinson, Melia. "The Head of TED Says This Talk Saved the Conference from the Brink of Extinction." *Business Insider*, 28 Aug. 2015, www.businessinsider.com/chris-anderson-ted-talks-2015-8. Accessed 10 May 2019.

—Joy Crelin

Kris Aquino

Date of birth: February 14, 1971
Occupation: Talk show host and actor

Kris Aquino is a Filipina talk show host and award-winning actor who has been dubbed the "Queen of all Media" in the Philippines. She came to the attention of the American public when she appeared in the hit movie *Crazy Rich Asians* (2018) as the austere Malay Princess Intan. It was a bit part—Aquino enjoys about five minutes of screen time—that belies Aquino's celebrity in the Philippines, where she has been omnipresent, as a television host and movie star, since the 1980s. Part of her appeal comes from her family name. Aquino is a member of a Filipino political family dynasty. Her late parents are two of the most revered figures in the country's history. Her politician father, Benigno "Ninoy" Aquino, was assassinated in 1983. Her mother, Corazon "Cory" Aquino, went on, after her husband's death, to become the president of the Philippines and is colloquially known as the "Mother of Asian Democracy." More recently, Aquino's brother, Benigno "Noynoy" Aquino III, served as the country's president from 2010 to 2016. In the Philippines, Aquino's celebrity is comparable to that of a reality television show

Photo by Emma McIntyre/Getty Images

star. (In American parlance, she is an amalgamation of a Kennedy, a Kardashian, and Oprah.) She is an actor and beloved talk show host, but her larger appeal lies in her willingness, to her family's distress, to share every detail of her rarified life. "If you say anything about me, you can say—the word is tactless," she once told Seth Mydans for the *New York Times* (3 May 2003). "When I open my mouth, people know that whatever comes out is true." Aquino might seem the family's obvious black sheep, but her knack for showmanship comes from her late father, a charismatic statesman. She displayed her talents at an early age, speaking at her father's rallies when she was just seven years old. "Through all these upheavals and historic events, Kris was a dynamic presence—articulate, forceful, convincing, at ease in the spotlight, unperturbed by all the attention," Doreen G. Yu wrote for the *Philippine Star* (12 Feb. 2012). "Fast forward to a quarter of a century later, and Kris is one of the hottest, most sought after celebrities in town."

GROWING UP IN A POLITICAL DYNASTY

Kristina Bernadette Cojuangco Aquino was born in Quezon City, northeast of Manila, on February 14, 1971. She is the youngest of five children; her siblings are Noynoy, Maria Elena "Ballsy" Aquino-Cruz, Aurora Corazon "Pinky" Aquino-Abellada, and Victoria Elisa "Viel" Aquino-Dee. A profile of her early life requires some understanding of her family's role in the larger political history of the Philippines. Both of her parents came from politically powerful oligarch families. Her father, Ninoy, was a rising political star who eventually became the chief rival of the country's dictator, Ferdinand Marcos. He was imprisoned for speaking out against Marcos in 1972. In 1978, Ninoy participated in a sham election from his prison cell. A seven-year-old Aquino made speeches at rallies on his behalf. According to Norma Japitana, writing for the *Philippine Star* (27 June 2011), Aquino "was the only one [of the children] who was thrust into the public eye" during this period. Japitana compared photographs of "young Kris straining to reach the microphone to give her father's message" to photographs of five-year-old John F. Kennedy Jr. saluting his father's casket in 1963. At the behest of Marcos's wife, Imelda, Ninoy was released to undergo heart surgery in the United States in 1980. For the next three years, the Aquino family lived in Newton, a suburb of Boston, while Ninoy taught at Harvard and the Massachusetts Institute of Technology (MIT). Multiple members of the family have cited this time as the happiest in the family's life.

Ninoy returned to the Philippines in 1983, whereupon he was assassinated by soldier escorts as soon as he disembarked the plane. His funeral—at which Aquino, then twelve years old, also spoke—became a defining moment in the popular democratic movement, while his widow, Cory, became a "national symbol" of dignity and hope, Mydans wrote. In 1986, she successfully campaigned for the presidency, buoyed by the People Power movement. Her election, Mydans wrote in her *Times* obituary (31 July 2009), "was a high point in modern Philippine history, and it offered a model for nonviolent uprisings that has been repeated often in other countries." Cory served as president for six years and faced down seven coup attempts. She was an imperfect leader, but when she left office in 1992, she had come to represent a democratic ideal that the people of the Philippines continue to strive for.

FILM CAREER

"My dad would always ask me, 'Do you want to be president some day? I'd say, 'I want to be a movie star,'" Aquino told Mydans in 2003. Aquino, along with her sisters, served as one of her mother's presidential assistants, though she also actively sought an acting agent. She made her first television appearance in 1986, but launched her film career—"much to her mother's consternation," as William Branigin put it for the *Washington Post* (14 Dec. 1994)—in 1990, when she starred in a romantic comedy called *Pido Dida: Sabay Tayo* (*Let's Do It Together*), as an orphan who marries a man that she had mistakenly thought was her brother. She was nineteen. The film received poor reviews, but broke box office records, outgrossing any foreign or domestic film ever shown in the Philippines. Aquino displayed her signature brand of flippancy and grace when

confronted with the critics who described her as a talentless socialite. "I think that everyone, regardless of who or what you are, should be given the chance to fulfill his or her own dream," Aquino told one interviewer, as quoted by a reporter for the *Deseret News* (3 Oct. 1990). "I want to be like [American actor] Michelle Pfeiffer, who can do both comedy and drama." She went on to star in a handful of other movies, including several true crime dramas such as *The Vizconde Massacre: God, Help Us!* (1993), *The Myrna Diones Story* (*Lord, Have Mercy!*) (1993), and the fictionalized *Humanda ka Mayor!: Bahala na ang Diyos* (*Get Ready Mayor!: It's God*) (1993)—earning her the nickname "the massacre queen," according to Branigin.

Aquino's early acting career, however, was defined by offscreen scandal. On the set of the 1994 film *Nandito Ako* (I'm here), twenty-four-year-old Aquino began an affair with her costar, forty-five-year-old Phillip Salvador. Salvador, a notorious womanizer, was married (divorce is banned in the Philippines), and Aquino was the daughter of the country's former president, a devout Roman Catholic who once described birth control as "intrinsically evil," Branigin wrote. Worse, Aquino was pregnant. She made the announcement on a celebrity talk show. For a brief period, Aquino and her mother were estranged. Aquino gave birth to a son, Joshua Salvador, in 1995. In 1994, Aquino was nominated for a prestigious Gawad Urian Award for her starring role in *The Fatima Buen Story* (1994). She later won a FAMAS Award, given by the Filipino Academy of Movie Arts and Sciences, for her supporting role in a family drama called *Mano Po* (2002); she was also nominated for a Gawad Urian Award for that performance. Aquino went on to appear in several of the film's five sequels. Her 2006 horror film *Sukob*, or "The Wedding Curse," was briefly the highest-grossing Filipino film of all time.

TELEVISION CAREER

Aquino is best known as a television host. She was appearing on television as early as 1986, the year her mother was elected. In 1995, she, along with cohosts Boy Abunda and Lolit Solis, launched a successful celebrity gossip show called *Startalk*. Though she left the show the next year, *Startalk* continued to air for many years. The same year, 1995, Aquino interviewed Bongbong Marcos, the son of the dictator responsible for her father's death, on the show *Actually, 'Yun Na!'* (Actually, that's it!), which she hosted from 1994 to 1996. In 1996, she became the host of an afternoon talk show called *Today with Kris Aquino*. She remained the host of that show until 2001. In 1999, she became a cohost on a Sunday talk show, similar to *Startalk*, called *The Buzz*. She left the show in 2010. In a tearful farewell, she told viewers that her departure was a "sacrifice" she was making on behalf of her brother, Noynoy, who had just been elected president. "I just don't want to be a burden," she said, as quoted by a reporter for the Manila *Business World* (20 May 2014). "I didn't want my stay here [at *The Buzz* to] have a negative effect on my brother. And I don't want that my personal life or my personal views should have an effect on him." She briefly returned to the show in 2014, leaving again the following year. The show went off the air shortly afterward.

Aquino's other popular shows include *Morning Girls*, which Aquino hosted with Korina Sanchez from 2002 to 2004. That year, she also hosted the short-lived *Good Morning, Kris*. From 2001 to 2007, Aquino hosted an evening quiz show called *Pilipinas, Game KNB?* (Are you game?). From 2010 to 2011, she served as a judge on *Pilipinas Got Talent*, the Philippines' entry in the international reality show franchise that spun off of *America's Got Talent* and *Britain's Got Talent*. She appeared in the 2013 comedy film *My Little Bossings* as a millionaire money manager who foists her son—played by Aquino's own younger son—off on an employee who is already caring for his own daughter and a street urchin whom he has taken in. The film was critically panned, but smashed box office records in its home country. In 2014, she starred in *Feng Shui 2*, the sequel to a 2004 horror film in which Aquino also appeared. *Feng Shui 2* became the highest-grossing Filipino horror film of all time. She took a brief leave from show business in 2016 for health reasons; when she returned, ABS-CBN, the network on which she had hosted talk shows for twenty-two years, was not interested in renegotiating her contract. In 2017, the travel special *Trip ni Kris* aired on rival network GMA, marking her return to television.

PERSONAL LIFE

In addition to Joshua, Aquino has a son, James Carlos "Bimby" Aquino-Yap, with Filipino basketball star James Yap. The couple were married from 2005 to 2012. (The marriage was annulled.) Six years later, their parting remains publicly acrimonious. Aquino shared a post criticizing Yap's absence as a father on her social media in 2018. She and her two sons live in Quezon City.

SUGGESTED READING

"Aquino Kin Seeks Stardom." *Deseret News*, 3 Oct. 1990, www.deseretnews.com/article/125156/AQUINO-KIN-SEEKS-STARDOM.html. Accessed 8 Nov. 2018.

Branigin, William. "An Ill-Conceived Scandal; Kris Aquino's Affair Rocks the Philippines." *The Washington Post*, 14 Dec. 1994, www.washingtonpost.com/archive/lifestyle/1994/12/14/an-ill-conceived-scandal-kris-aquinos-affair-rocks-the-philippines/a77b0cd3-2b0b-4ca9-afae-6e148c698f43/. Accessed 9 Nov. 2018.

Japitana, Norma. "A Beautiful Wedding for Ballsy Aquino." *Philippine Star*, 27 June 2011, www.philstar.com/entertainment/2011/06/27/699858/beautiful-wedding-ballsy-aquino. Accessed 8 Nov. 2018.

Mydans, Seth. "Corazon Aquino, Ex-Leader of the Philippines, Is Dead." *The New York Times*, 31 July 2009, www.nytimes.com/2009/08/01/world/asia/01aquino.html. Accessed 8 Nov. 2018.

———. "The Saturday Profile: A Famed Philippine Family's Bubbly Maverick." *The New York Times*, 3 May 2003, www.nytimes.com/2003/05/03/world/the-saturday-profile-a-famed-philippine-family-s-bubbly-maverick.html. Accessed 8 Nov. 2018.

Yu, Doreen G. "Oh, Kris!" *Philippine Star*, 12 Feb. 2012, www.philstar.com/other-sections/starweek-magazine/2012/02/12/776210/oh-kris. Accessed 10 Nov. 2018.

SELECTED WORKS

Pido Dida, 1990; *The Buzz*, 1999–2010 and 2014–15; *Pilipinas, Game KNB?*, 2001–7; *Mano Po*, 2002; *Crazy Rich Asians*, 2018

—*Molly Hagan*

Alejandro Aravena

Date of birth: June 22, 1967
Occupation: Architect

For Chilean architect Alejandro Aravena, the discipline of architecture should solve real-world problems—a point of view that has long put him at odds with much of the international architecture community, which he has characterized as overly focused on artistic expression and architectural theory. "Architects wanted to have a certain artistic freedom, and the price we paid as a discipline was irrelevance," he told Justin McGuirk for *ICON* (Jan. 2009). "You want to shock people to disguise the fact that you are irrelevant." In contrast, much of Aravena's award-winning body of work is deeply relevant to the populations his buildings serve, which include residents of multiple social housing projects.

Born and raised in Santiago, Aravena studied architecture in both Chile and Italy before beginning his career. A visiting professorship at Harvard University catalyzed the launch of his renowned firm Elemental. The so-called do tank focuses on socially conscious projects that meet the needs of vulnerable populations, including housing projects designed using Elemental's

Photo by Centro de Políticas Públicas UC via Wikimedia Commons

characteristic incremental housing approach. At the same time, however, Aravena seeks to look beyond basic needs to provide more beneficial living environments for his buildings' residents. "If architecture is about giving form to the places where we live, and life ranges from basic needs to artistic desires, the task of architecture and the difficulty of producing architecture is that it's not about choosing one or the other, but integrating the two of them," he told Rocky Casale in an interview for *Surface* magazine's Power 100 list (13 July 2016). "Not in one single project that we have done, not even social housing, did we forget that life cannot just be about mere satisfaction of physical needs."

EARLY LIFE AND EDUCATION

Alejandro Gastón Aravena Mori was born on June 22, 1967, in Santiago, Chile, to teachers Carmen and Gastón. He grew up in a middle-class family that valued education highly. At that time, private education was the primary path to university, and his family sacrificed financially so that he and his siblings, Cayo and Loreto, could pursue such educational opportunities. After completing secondary school, Aravena enrolled in the Pontificia Universidad Católica de Chile (PUC; Pontifical Catholic University of Chile) to study architecture.

During Aravena's years in university, the dictatorship of Augusto Pinochet limited Chileans' access to foreign publications, including architecture magazines. Such censorship might have limited the education of some aspiring architects, but Aravena found that those policies had the unintended effect of letting Chilean

architects develop their own pragmatic approach and avoid being overly influenced by the prevailing international trends. "We were saved from postmodernism," he explained to Michael Kimmelman for *T: The New York Times Style Magazine* (23 May 2016). "By default, we were left to find our own identity. Our professors were practitioners, not theorists, who taught how to get buildings built. It was, in retrospect, a very useful education." Aravena later credited his professor Fernando Pérez Oyarzun as a particularly strong influence and a major early supporter of his career.

After graduating in 1992, Aravena moved to Venice, Italy, to continue his education at the University of Venice's institute of architecture (IUAV) and the Accademia di Belle Arti di Venezia (Venice academy of fine arts). "I came to Italy to draw and measure architecture," he recalled to Laura Arrighi for *Elle Decor Italia* (16 Apr. 2018). "That period, for me, was an incredible time of learning and inspiration, especially if I think that not long before I was studying South American architecture. The exact opposite, it's physically fragile but culturally strong in a different sense. That contrast really fascinated me." Having expanded his architectural knowledge, Aravena returned to Chile to begin his professional career.

EARLY CAREER

Aravena established his first architectural firm, Alejandro Aravena Architects, in 1994. He worked primarily on businesses throughout his early career and soon grew dissatisfied with the limited projects available to him. Seeking a change, Aravena quit architecture for a time and supported himself by opening a bar. However, his longstanding interest in architecture remained. He returned to the field to design a mathematics building for PUC's San Joaquin campus, one of several campuses in Greater Santiago. The project was completed in 1999, and Aravena later designed two more buildings for the university and taught there as well.

As Aravena established himself further as an architect, he began to be regarded as an authority on architecture. He contributed to several books related to the field, including *Los hechos de la arquitectura* (Architectural facts, 1999), which he coauthored with Pérez and José Quintanilla. In 2000, he joined the faculty of the Harvard University Graduate School of Design as a visiting professor, an opportunity that shaped the trajectory of Aravena's later career.

Throughout his years as a working architect, Aravena had become disillusioned with the architectural community at large, believing many architects to be focused more on theoretical or artistic endeavors than on solving real-world problems. "I was kind of sceptical of architects trying to deal with problems that only interested other architects," he told Anna Winston for *Dezeen* (13 Jan. 2016). "The jargon, the way we talk about our issues, nobody except an architect understands. I guess that sense of irrelevance and isolation has always worried me."

At Harvard, Aravena met Andrés Iacobelli, an engineer then studying public policy. Iacobelli challenged Aravena to channel his ability to solve tangible problems into improving the design, functionality, and feasibility of social housing. Upon his return to Chile, Aravena focused heavily on that area of design, seeking to create forms of housing that would better serve Chile's low-income population.

ELEMENTAL

Since 2001, Aravena has led the Santiago architecture firm Elemental. In light of his commitment to creating meaningful solutions to problems that affect the public in Chile and beyond, he characterizes the firm as a "do tank," as opposed to a more theoretical "think tank." "The biggest challenge today is to try to engage non-architectural issues—meaning poverty, less segregation in cities, less violence—with our specific knowledge, which is to design and do projects," he told McGuirk of the firm's driving focus. Alongside partners Gonzalo Arteaga, Juan Cerda, Víctor Oddó, and Diego Torres, Aravena has worked on socially conscious projects that not only address the needs and wants of the specific populations benefiting from them, but also serve as reproduceable models. "Architects like to build things that are unique," Aravena explained to Kimmelman. "But if something is unique it can't be repeated, so in terms of it serving many people in many places, the value is close to zero."

Although Elemental worked on a wide range of projects over the years, the firm—and Aravena himself—became best known for its "incremental housing" approach to designing social housing. In its Elemental form, incremental housing entails the design and construction of a partial house that includes all the necessary and most costly structural elements—such as outer walls and roofing—and vital components such as a kitchen and a bathroom. With the essentials already in place, residents of such partially constructed houses can live comfortably within them and finish construction as they are able and to their own specifications. Elemental's first housing project based on that approach, Quinta Monroy, was built in Iquique, Chile, in 2004.

In addition to enabling social housing to be built for a significantly lower cost, incremental housing projects such as Elemental's enable residents to expand their living spaces as their families grow and to add value to their properties.

Aravena also noted in interviews that such homes, when completed, serve as valuable assets that can enable residents to take out loans, otherwise improve their financial standing, and break free from generational poverty. He further argued that such an approach will continue to be essential not only in Chile but also throughout the world. "There's [going to be] a billion people on the planet that will be needing housing," Aravena explained to Winston. "Unless we follow the incremental approach to tackle scarcity of means, we won't solve this problem. We have to operate with systems that can complete themselves, so families can arrive to their middle-class potential."

For his work on projects such as Quinta Monroy, Aravena and his partners at Elemental shared the Silver Lion—an award given to promising young architects—at the 2008 Venice Biennale of Architecture. The biennale is among the international architecture community's most prestigious events.

MAJOR PROJECTS

Aravena has worked on a variety of other major projects in Chile as well. Following February 2010, when an earthquake and tsunami devastated portions of Chile, Elemental was tasked with rebuilding portions of the city of Constitución, which had experienced widespread damage from flooding due to its location near the mouth of a river. Although the project was sponsored by the forestry company Arauco, which employed many residents of the city, Aravena remained committed to placing the needs and desires of the people first. "Residents in Constitución naturally suspected, because we were working for the forestry company, that all the benefits of reconstruction would go to the company, not them," he told Kimmelman. "That's why we knew from the start that the people had to participate in the reconstruction process. In effect, we needed to create the right client." Based on feedback from the people of Constitución, Aravena and his colleagues declined to build a seawall—one of the projects previously proposed for the city's waterfront area—and instead transformed the city's waterfront into open public space for use by residents and a natural barrier to frequent flooding. Elemental also designed the incremental housing project Villa Verde to provide new homes for some residents displaced by the earthquake and tsunami.

While Aravena has primarily worked in Chile throughout his career, he has also been responsible for several projects abroad. Among them was the design of a dormitory for St. Edward's University in Austin, Texas. In 2016, he served as director of the fifteenth International Architecture Exhibition at the Venice Biennale. As curator, Aravena sought to draw international attention to architectural responses to social and environmental issues through the exhibition's theme, Reporting the Front. The following year, Elemental won a competitive bid from among hundreds of firms to design a cultural center in Doha, Qatar.

In the 2000s and 2010s, Aravena gained widespread recognition for his work and has been the subject of several monographs. In 2010 he was named an international fellow of the Royal Institute of British Architects (RIBA). The same year as he headed the Biennale, in 2016, Aravena became the first architect from Chile to receive the prestigious Pritzker Architecture Prize, considered akin to the Nobel Prize for architecture.

PERSONAL LIFE

Aravena is married to fellow architect Giovana Franceschetto Fernandes, with whom he collaborated on the 2016 Venice Biennale. The couple have two children together, and Aravena also has a son from an earlier relationship.

SUGGESTED READING

Aravena, Alejandro. "Alejandro Aravena: How the Pritzker Prize–Winning Architect Is Changing the World with Beautiful, Practical Buildings." Interview by Rocky Casale. *Surface*, 13 July 2016, www.surfacemag.com/articles/alejandro-aravena-pritzker-prize. Accessed 12 Apr. 2019.

Aravena, Alejandro. "Alejandro Aravena: 'I'm Not Even Close to Being a Hero.'" *Strelka Mag*, 23 May 2016, strelkamag.com/en/article/interview-with-aravena. Accessed 12 Apr. 2019.

Aravena, Alejandro. "An Interview with Alejandro Aravena to Talk Design, Light, and the Biennale." Interview by Laura Arrighi. *Elle Decor Italia*, 16 Apr. 2018, www.elledecor.com/it/best-of/a20692736/alejandro-aravena-interview-milan-design-week-2018-artemide-eng. Accessed 12 Apr. 2019.

Chatel, Marie. "Spotlight: Alejandro Aravena." *ArchDaily*, 22 June 2018, www.archdaily.com/789618/spotlight-alejandro-aravena. Accessed 12 Apr. 2019.

Kimmelman, Michael. "Alejandro Aravena, the Architect Rebuilding a Country." *T: The New York Times Style Magazine*, 23 May 2016, www.nytimes.com/2016/05/23/t-magazine/pritzker-venice-biennale-chile-architect-alejandro-aravena.html. Accessed 12 Apr. 2019.

McGuirk, Justin. "Alejandro Aravena." *ICON*, Jan. 2009, www.iconeye.com/opinion/icon-of-the-month/item/3895-alejandro-aravena. Accessed 12 Apr. 2019.

Winston, Anna. "Architects 'Are Never Taught the Right Thing' Says 2016 Pritzker Laureate Alejandro Aravena." *Dezeen*, 13 Jan. 2016, www.dezeen.com/2016/01/13/alejandro-aravena-interview-pritzker-prize-laureate-2016-social-incremental-housing-chilean-architect. Accessed 12 Apr. 2019.

—*Joy Crelin*

Nolan Arenado

Date of birth: April 16, 1991
Occupation: Baseball player

After making his Major League Baseball (MLB) debut in 2013 with the Colorado Rockies, third baseman Nolan Arenado quickly emerged as one of the league's brightest stars. He distinguished himself with both his bat and his glove, winning multiple Silver Slugger and Gold Glove Awards (given annually to players voted the top hitters and fielders, respectively, at their position). His well-rounded play was also acknowledged with consistent All-Star nominations and even consideration in voting for the Most Valuable Player (MVP) Award. By 2019 Arenado was a beloved face of the Rockies franchise, which early that year rewarded him with an eight-year, $260 million contract extension. The deal made him one of the highest-paid MLB players by average annual salary.

Arenado's rapid rise to baseball superstardom was the result of both deep-rooted talent and persistent hard work. He excelled in high school baseball, leading the Rockies to select him in the second round of the 2009 MLB Draft despite his lack of college experience. As he progressed through the minor leagues his offensive

Photo by jenniferlinneaphotography on Flickr via Wikimedia Commons

skills were consistently strong, and with dedicated practice his defense improved to match. By the time Arenado was called up to the majors he was poised for the immediate impact that few prospects ever achieve. Yet despite his considerable personal successes—and occasional struggles—he remained motivated primarily by his love for the sport he began playing when he was only five years old. "It gets tough, but this is fun," he told Spencer Fordin for *MLB.com* (6 Aug. 2013). "We're playing a game that we love and we're trying to put on a good show."

EARLY LIFE AND EDUCATION

Nolan James Arenado was born on April 16, 1991, in Newport Beach, California. He was the second of three sons born to Millie and Fernando Arenado. His mother, a star softball player in high school, worked in insurance during his early life. His father, a Cuban immigrant, ran a family-owned travel agency. Arenado's younger brother, Jonah, went on to his own professional baseball career after being drafted in 2013. The boys grew up close to several cousins, one of whom also eventually pursued baseball full-time.

As the success of multiple Arenado children in professional baseball might suggest, the sport was an important one to the athletically inclined family. Arenado began playing at the age of five and soon demonstrated not only a talent for the game but also a competitive spirit that flourished within his home environment. "There was so much competitiveness going on in my household when I was growing up. I was always competing against my brothers and my cousins and my friends," he recalled to Patrick Saunders for the *Denver Post* (9 July 2016). "I always wanted to be the best in my group." A fan of the Los Angeles Dodgers as a child, Arenado also admired star players from a host of other major-league teams, including Derek Jeter and Albert Pujols.

Arenado played baseball for local travel baseball teams and at one point helped his Little League team win a championship. Upon entering El Toro High School in Lake Forest, California, he joined the El Toro Chargers and quickly distinguished himself as a rare talent. He impressed both local baseball fans and major-league scouts with his in-game performances and strong overall statistics, which included a batting average of .517 during his final season with the team. In light of his contributions to the El Toro baseball program, the program later retired his jersey number. Arenado graduated from high school in 2009.

MINOR LEAGUES

Following high school, Arenado initially planned to attend and play baseball for Arizona State University. In June 2009, however, the Colorado Rockies selected him fifty-ninth overall in the second round of the 2009 MLB Draft. The pick received little attention, and some scouts even suggested he did not have what it took to succeed in the majors. Still, having long hoped to play baseball professionally, Arenado decided to forgo college to join the Rockies organization, and signed with the team the next month.

He made his minor-league debut several days later, joining the Rockies' Wyoming-based rookie-level affiliate, the Casper Ghosts, for the 2009 season. Despite competing against mostly older players, Arenado continued to hit well. Over the next several years, he moved up through the Rockies organization, playing for the Class A Asheville Tourists in 2010 and the Class A Advanced Modesto Nuts in 2011. He also played for the Salt River Rafters during the 2011 fall league and put forward a strong performance, earning the title of league MVP.

By his 2012 season, which he spent with the double-A Tulsa Drillers, Arenado was one of the top prospects in all of baseball and anticipated that he might soon be called up to the major leagues. However, he struggled somewhat in 2012, and Rockies management publicly suggested he was not yet ready for promotion. Even after a strong spring training the following year he remained in the minors, joining the triple-A Colorado Springs Sky Sox for the beginning of the 2013 season. However, Arenado's stint with the Sky Sox was a short one, as in late April of that year he was finally added to the Rockies' major-league roster. Despite the challenge of waiting for the call-up and the high expectations that surrounded it, he worked to focus on the game itself rather than the significance of the moment. "I just try to do my job. That's the way I see it," he told Thomas Harding for *MLB.com* (28 Apr. 2013). "Hit the ball hard, make my plays and try to help this team win. This team is playing well right now. I want to be a part of it."

COLORADO ROCKIES

Arenado made his MLB debut with the Rockies on April 28, 2013. Over the course of the season, he was struck by increased intensity of the game at the major-league level. "I expected that coming in, and I definitely expected it with this team because we expect to win," he explained to Fordin. "But definitely the intensity and the support have been pretty cool. It definitely gets pretty crazy."

Arenado had mixed success at the plate in his rookie year, finishing with a batting average of .267, 10 home runs, and 52 runs batted in (RBIs) in 133 games played. However, he shone defensively, becoming only the second third baseman in MLB history to win the Gold Glove Award as a rookie and the first to achieve the feat in the National League (NL). It was the beginning of a streak that would see him set a record as the first infielder to earn the prestigious defensive award in each of his first six seasons. Yet despite Arenado's strong play, the Rockies finished last in the NL West division with a 74–88 record.

Arenado's next three seasons with the Rockies were marked by a variety of challenges and significant accomplishments. In May of 2014, he fractured his finger and was away from the team for more than a month as he spent time on the injured list and completed a rehabilitation assignment with the Sky Sox. In August, following his return to the majors, Arenado's performance earned him the title of NL Player of the Week for the first time. Despite playing fewer games than the previous year, he finished the 2014 season with eighteen home runs and sixty-one RBIs to go with a .287 average.

In 2015 Arenado broke out as a true star. That season he led the NL with 42 home runs and 130 RBIs, helping him earn his first Silver Slugger award. He was also selected as a member of that year's All-Star Game lineup. For Arenado, his success was the result of the experience he had gained as a player. "The experience factor has made a huge difference for me," he explained to Richard Bergstrom for *ESPN* (11 June 2015). "Knowing who I am as a ballplayer. When you first start off, you don't really know who you are or what you need to do, and once I found out what I needed to accomplish and what made me feel good, that's when things started changing for the better."

MLB STAR

Arenado further built on his experience in 2016. Playing in an NL-leading 160 regular-season games, he also led the league in home runs (41) and RBIs (133) for the second year in a row. His batting average climbed to .294, helping him win another Silver Slugger. He also continued his defensive excellence, achieving the second-best fielding percentage among NL third basemen and taking home several awards; his fourth Gold Glove across his first four seasons was an MLB first at third base. With such strong all-around play, he was again named an All-Star and finished fifth in NL MVP voting. However, the Rockies missed the postseason once again.

The 2017 season was another successful one for Arenado, who improved his average to .309 and led the NL with 43 doubles to go along with his 37 home runs and 130 RBIs. That year he started in the All-Star Game for the first time. His fifth straight Gold Glove to begin his career set an MLB record for infielders and trailed only outfielder Ichiro Suzuki's overall record of ten. In addition, he received the Platinum Glove Award as the best overall fielder in the NL, was named NL Player of the Month for July, and finished fourth in MVP voting. The Rockies also

improved, finishing with an 87–75 record to secure a spot in the NL Wild Card Game and giving Arenado his first play-off experience. The team faced the Arizona Diamondbacks and ultimately lost the single-elimination game, though Arenado hit a home run and scored twice.

In 2018 Arenado continued his run of excellence with another All-Star season. Offensively, he reclaimed the NL home run title with 38, tallied 110 RBIs, and finished with a .297 average for his fourth Silver Slugger win. On defense, he continued his Gold Glove streak and earned another Platinum Glove. His balanced performance saw him reach third in MVP voting. Yet in spite of his own strong performance, Arenado grew frustrated as the Rockies struggled once more, especially in the first half of the season. "I just get pissed because I don't want to lose anymore," he told Nick Groke for the *Athletic* (28 June 2018) at the time. "I've only been to the playoffs once and it was only one game. And I really want more than that." Arenado got his wish to a degree, as the Rockies managed to finish second in the NL West at 91–72 and defeated the Chicago Cubs in the Wild Card Game. However, they were promptly swept in their first NL Division Series appearance in nearly a decade by the Milwaukee Brewers.

RECORD-SETTING CONTRACT

Much speculation surrounded Arenado's future in the 2018–19 offseason, as he was set to enter free agency for the first time following the 2019 season. As a superstar playing on a team with little recent postseason success, he was seen as a candidate to eventually sign with a contending big-market team on a major deal. However, a slow market for free agents that offseason contributed to a wave of young players signing contract extensions with their current teams rather than waiting for the uncertainty of the open market. To the surprise of some analysts, Arenado was among them. In February 2019 he agreed to a $260 million contract that would keep him with the Rockies for eight years (though with the ability to opt out after three years). At the time it was announced, the deal made Arenado the highest-paid position player in baseball by average annual salary.

Arenado acknowledged that he could have left Colorado in search of an even bigger payday, but he remained devoted to the team with which he had spent his entire adult life. "It would be pretty cool to be one of those guys that stays with one organization their whole career," he said prior to the agreement, as quoted by Bob Nightengale for *USA Today* (26 Feb. 2019). "It just doesn't happen anymore. I'd like to change that." Once the deal was signed he continued that sentiment, telling Nightengale, "I grew up in this organization, so it feels like home in a way."

PERSONAL LIFE

Highly conscious of his diet and overall health since his high school days, Arenado focuses most of his free time on training. He has noted he was a big fan of the television show *The Office*, watching it every night before going to bed. Otherwise he has kept a low profile, even largely avoiding social media unlike many other sports stars. Arenado has also sought to be a role model for kids seeking his autograph. "I just want to be a good example and do the right things," he told the *Denver Post* (14 Apr. 2016).

SUGGESTED READING

Arenado, Nolan. "Rockies Q&A: Everything You Wanted to Know about Nolan Arenado." *The Denver Post*, 14 Apr. 2016, www.denverpost.com/2016/03/16/rockies-qa-everything-you-wanted-to-know-about-nolan-arenado. Accessed 10 May 2019.

Bergstrom, Richard. "Fans Should Get to Know New All-Star Nolan Arenado." *ESPN*, 11 July 2015, www.espn.com/blog/sweetspot/post/_/id/60227/fans-should-get-to-know-new-all-star-nolan-arenado. Accessed 10 May 2019.

Fordin, Spencer. "Arenado Takes His Turn in Chatting Cage." *MLB.com*, 6 Aug. 2013, www.mlb.com/news/rockies-rookie-nolan-arenado-takes-his-turn-in-chatting-cage/c-56073980 . Accessed 10 May 2019.

Groke, Nick. "'I'm Tired of Coming to the Ballpark and Losing': Nolan Arenado Feeling the Strain of Another Rockies Season Stuck in the Middle." *The Athletic*, 28 June 2018, theathletic.com/412562/2018/06/28/nolan-arenado-feeling-the-strain-of-another-rockies-season-stuck-in-the-middle-im-tired-of-coming-to-the-ballpark-and-losing/. Accessed 10 May 2019.

Harding, Thomas. "Prospect Arenado Ready to Face High Expectations." *MLB.com*, 28 Apr. 2013. www.mlb.com/news/rockies-nolan-arenado-ready-to-face-high-expectations/c-46052378 . Accessed 10 May 2019.

Nightengale, Bob. "Nolan Arenado Agrees to Eight-Year, $260 Million Contract to Stay with Rockies." *USA Today*, 26 Feb. 2019, www.usatoday.com/story/sports/mlb/columnist/bob-nightengale/2019/02/26/nolan-arenado-rockies-offer-record-extension-contract/2989636002/. Accessed 10 May 2019.

Saunders, Patrick. "Nolan Arenado's Star Power Born, Bred in Southern California Home." *The Denver Post*, 9 July 2016, www.denverpost.com/2016/07/09/nolan-arenados-star-power-born-bred-in-southern-california-home. Accessed 10 May 2019.

—*Joy Crelin*

Mike Babcock

Date of birth: April 29, 1963
Occupation: Hockey coach

"I'd like to be the best coach in my generation," professional ice hockey coach Mike Babcock told Brett Popplewell for *Sportsnet* (Feb. 2015). That goal is a challenging one, but that is perhaps to be expected from Babcock, whose perseverance in the sport of hockey has shaped his career since the mid-1980s, and even before then. A successful player at the junior and collegiate levels, Babcock hoped to play in the National Hockey League (NHL) in his early twenties but, after a single exhibition game with the Vancouver Canucks, knew that he would not be able to realistically achieve that dream. A year playing for the English team the Whitley Warriors, for which he also coached, reshaped his career trajectory, and he went on to coach at the junior, collegiate, and developmental levels before making his NHL coaching debut with the Mighty Ducks of Anaheim in 2002. A ten-year period with the Detroit Red Wings and two-Olympics stint with the Canadian men's ice hockey team followed, resulting in one Stanley Cup and two gold medals, respectively. In 2015, he took on a new challenge, joining the struggling Toronto Maple Leafs in an attempt to rebuild the franchise with a strategy incorporating "kitchen-table accountability," as he told Jonathon Gatehouse for *Maclean's* (2 Oct. 2015). "When you sit around your kitchen table with people you love, if you say something stupid, they call you on it right away—because they're honest with

Photo by Tom Gromak via Wikimedia Commons

you and they're making you better," he told Gatehouse. "That's what we're going to have here."

EARLY LIFE AND EDUCATION

Mike Babcock was born in 1963 in Manitouwadge, Ontario. The second of four children born to Mike and Gail Babcock, he has three sisters. Babcock's father worked in mining, and the family moved frequently due to his job, living in a variety of locales throughout Canada. The Babcocks spent a significant period in the Northwest Territories during Babcock's childhood, and he first learned to ice skate during that time. The young Babcock also enjoyed skiing and outdoor activities such as fishing, hunting, and camping. He was particularly influenced by his father's belief in hard work and his policy that one should not ask others to work hard if one is not willing to do so oneself, and he later noted in interviews that that influence significantly shaped his strategies for coaching hockey. "Everything I believe in comes from [my father's] philosophy," he said, as quoted by Tim Wharnsby for *CBC Sports* (21 May 2015). "I want to be successful. I always say to the guys, 'I want us to work hard and be able to be proud of that work ethic.' But if you ask for that, you better practise it."

After leaving the Northwest Territories, the Babcock family lived in Manitoba for a time before settling in Saskatoon, Saskatchewan. Having learned to play hockey in Manitoba, Babcock demonstrated a talent for the sport and began to compete on youth teams based in and around Saskatoon. He played for the junior-level Western Hockey League (WHL) team the Saskatoon Blades from 1980 to 1981 and later competed with the Kelowna Wings. "I never thought about being a coach, because I was thinking about being a player," he told Popplewell. "That was my dream." As a student at Holy Cross High School, Babcock played volleyball and ran track. Following his graduation, he enrolled at McGill University and joined the institution's hockey team, for which he played for four seasons. He also served as team captain for a time and, as part of a scholarship program, coached a hockey team made up of professors at the university. He earned his bachelor's degree in education with a specialization in physical education from McGill in 1986. He would later return to the school to take classes in sports psychology but did not receive an additional degree at that time.

EARLY CAREER

Although Babcock dreamed of playing hockey professionally and participated in a training camp with the NHL team the Vancouver Canucks, he had little luck in breaking into the league, playing in only a single exhibition game with the Vancouver team around 1985. "I didn't know I was feed, I didn't know I was just filling up the camp," he told Gatehouse about the experience. "I didn't know so many things, like details of the game that would have made me a better player. I just wasn't good enough." Although his career as an NHL player essentially ended as soon as it began, he was not quite ready to give up on a professional hockey career and instead traveled to England for the 1987–88 hockey season, which he spent with the Whitley Warriors. In addition to playing in thirty-six games with the team, he served as the Warriors' coach, beginning what would be more than three decades of work in that area.

Following his return to Canada, Babcock coached hockey for Red Deer College in Alberta and in 1991 began coaching the Moose Jaw Warriors of the WHL, with whom he spent two seasons. During the 1993–94 season, he coached for the University of Lethbridge and led the team to a Canadian Interuniversity Athletic Union (CIAU) national championship. He next moved on to the WHL's Spokane Chiefs, ultimately spending six seasons with that team. Meanwhile, the Canadian junior men's team coached by Babcock won the 1997 International Ice Hockey Federation (IIHF) World Junior Championship, marking the beginning of several stints in which he would serve as the coach for men's hockey teams representing Canada in international competitions. A new opportunity came in 2000, when he took a coaching position with the Ohio-based Cincinnati Mighty Ducks. A team within the professional American Hockey League (AHL), the Cincinnati Mighty Ducks was, at that time, the developmental team for the NHL's Mighty Ducks of Anaheim (later known as the Anaheim Ducks). Babcock spent two seasons with the team, both of which saw the Mighty Ducks compete in the AHL playoffs.

DEBUT AS NHL COACH

In May 2002, the Mighty Ducks of Anaheim announced that Babcock had been hired to replace former coach Bryan Murray as head coach for the team. Although some commentators expressed doubts about Babcock's ability and lack of NHL experience, Babcock himself was adamant that his years of experience at numerous levels of play made him a strong choice for the position and pointed out that despite the perceptions of some, he was hardly new to coaching. "You know those instant, overnight successes? Like the country musician who gets a hit after playing in Nashville bars for 15 years? That was me," he told Gatehouse about the experience.

Babcock began his tenure with the Mighty Ducks of Anaheim at the start of the 2002–03 season, which ended with the Mighty Ducks ranked second in their division. The team then advanced to the playoffs, where the Mighty Ducks became Western Conference Champions and went on to face the New Jersey Devils in the Stanley Cup Finals. Although the Mighty Ducks lost in the seventh game of the Finals, their success in the playoffs was a major milestone for the team, which had never been conference champion prior to that point. Babcock left the team after the following season, during which the Mighty Ducks did not qualify to compete in the playoffs. However, in 2004 his Canadian men's team won the adult-level IIHF World Championship.

DETROIT RED WINGS AND THE OLYMPICS

After leaving the Mighty Ducks, Babcock joined the Detroit Red Wings as coach beginning with the 2005–06 season. Over the course of his ten seasons with the team, the Red Wings appeared in the playoffs every single year. The 2007–08 postseason was a particularly meaningful one for the team, which progressed successfully through the playoffs before beating the Pittsburgh Penguins to claim the Stanley Cup, Babcock's first as coach. Although the Red Wings were strong contenders during the next several seasons, they were unable to duplicate the success of the 2008 playoffs and in 2009 lost in game seven of the Stanley Cup Finals. A firm believer in the strength of his team, Babcock later insisted in interviews that the Red Wings could have won on several occasions during his tenure as coach if not for factors such as injuries. "We could've won the Cup three years in a row. People on the outside who won the Cup may say no. I'm telling you, I've been there a number of times. We could have won the Cup all those years," he explained in an interview with Dante A. Ciampaglia for *Sports Illustrated Kids* (14 Jan. 2014). "That's how fine a line is. The fine line with injuries, the fine line with goaltending, the fine line with getting the right call at the right time, the post in versus the post out. It's hard to win."

Meanwhile, Babcock also experienced further success outside of the NHL season. The year 2010 saw him make his debut as coach of the Canadian men's hockey team for the Winter Olympic Games, held that year in Vancouver. "When you live in a country like Canada and the whole focus is on hockey and they ask you to coach their national team or Olympic team, obviously it's a moment of great pride," he later told Ciampaglia. "But it's also a moment of weight that you carry because in Canada you got to get it done." Babcock and the team ultimately represented their country well, claiming a gold medal by upsetting the United States. He again served as coach of the Canadian men's team at the 2014 Winter Olympics in Russia, overseeing the team's eventual claim of the gold medal upon its defeat of Sweden. The following year, he left the Red Wings.

TORONTO MAPLE LEAFS

Babcock reportedly signed an eight-year contract with the Toronto Maple Leafs prior to the 2015–16 season. At that time, the team had not won the Stanley Cup since 1967, and the franchise was struggling to compete and overcome its major rivals throughout the season. Babcock was determined to turn the team around and reestablish the Leafs as a contender within the NHL. "We're going to do everything we can to build a program. We're going to figure out the best players to play on this team, and we're going to go ahead," he told Gatehouse. "Our focus is very clear. We're going to regain the rightful place for this franchise." Despite his goals for the team, the Leafs fared poorly during his first season with the team, ending the season ranked last in the NHL.

Over the subsequent seasons, the Leafs made substantial improvements during the regular seasons and attained playoff spots for several seasons in a row. Following the 2016–17 season, the team won a wild card spot for the playoffs, where they were eliminated in the first round by the Washington Capitals. The Leafs earned their playoff spot through a higher finish in the NHL's Atlantic Division the following year but were again eliminated in the first round of the tournament, this time by the Boston Bruins. The team repeated that result in the 2019 playoffs, falling to the Bruins in a seven-game first-round series. "We're at the same point with the same result here today, so that part is disappointing," Babcock said following the loss, as quoted by Ailish Forfar for Yahoo! Sports (24 Apr. 2019). In response to fans and commentators unhappy with the team's performance and his work as coach, however, he argued, "We've improved our team drastically—you've witnessed it. This series we were a way better team than a year ago."

PERSONAL LIFE

Babcock and his wife, Maureen, have three grown children. The couple moved to Toronto not long after Babcock became the head coach for the Leafs in 2015. In recognition of his contributions to the sport of hockey, Babcock was named to the Order of Hockey in Canada in 2018.

SUGGESTED READING

Babcock, Mike. "Mike Babcock: 23 Men, 23 Ways to Coach." Interview by Jonathon Gatehouse. *Maclean's*, 2 Oct. 2015, www.macleans.ca/society/mike-babcock-23-men-23-ways-to-coach. Accessed 12 July 2019.

Babcock, Mike. "2014 Winter Olympics Interviews: Coach Mike Babcock, Team Canada Men's Hockey." Interview by Dante A. Ciampaglia. *Sports Illustrated Kids*, 14 Jan. 2014, www.sikids.com/

si-kids/2016/01/12/2014-winter-olympics-in-terviews-coach-mike-babcock-team-canada-mens-hockey. Accessed 12 July 2019.

Custance, Craig. "Why Mike Babcock Refers to Himself as a 'Thief.'" *ThePostGame*, 19 Dec. 2017, www.thepostgame.com/mike-babcock-coaching-leadership-craig-custance-hockey. Accessed 12 July 2019.

Forfar, Ailish. "Mike Babcock Offers Few Answers after Another Game 7 Loss." *Yahoo! Sports*, 24 Apr. 2019, sports.yahoo.com/babcock-provides-few-answers-after-another-game-7-loss-185926374.html. Accessed 12 July 2019.

Foster, Chris. "Ducks Enter Unknown Realm." *Los Angeles Times*, 23 May 2002, www.lat-imes.com/archives/la-xpm-2002-may-23-sp-dux23-story.html. Accessed 12 July 2019.

Popplewell, Brett. "The Perfectionist." *Sportsnet*, Feb. 2015, www.sportsnet.ca/hockey/nhl/mike-babcock-perfectionist/. Accessed 12 July 2019.

Wharnsby, Tim. "Mike Babcock: School of Hard Rocks." *CBC Sports*, 21 May 2015, www.cbc.ca/amp/1.3082494. Accessed 12 July 2019.

—*Joy Crelin*

Fredrik Backman

Date of birth: June 2, 1981
Occupation: Columnist and writer

American audiences were first introduced to Swedish author Fredrik Backman's oeuvre in 2014, when *A Man Called Ove* was published in English translation. The protagonist of the novel—a blockbuster in Sweden, where it was eventually adapted for both stage and screen—is a curmudgeonly senior who spends his days chastising neighbors for minor infractions like parking incorrectly and patrolling his housing complex to catch pet owners who fail to clean up after their animals. Six months after his wife dies, Ove plans to kill himself but reconsiders after a young Iranian family befriends him and begins counting on his help. The novel stayed on the *New York Times* Best Seller list for forty-two weeks. Describing Backman's immensely popular books, Mary Schmich asserted for the *Chicago Tribune* (7 June 2018): "They're sometimes called 'charming,' probably because they're witty and tender and include quirky characters, but that doesn't do justice to their depth."

American reviewers of *A Man Called Ove*, which initially sold modestly in the United States before gaining popularity by word of mouth, could not resist comparing it to another, very different, Swedish best seller by Stieg Larsson.

Photo by C. Fleetwood via Wikimedia Commons

"Step aside *Girl with the Dragon Tattoo*," Lynn Neary said on the National Public Radio (NPR) show *All Things Considered* (30 Sept. 2016), "a grumpy old man may soon be taking your place as America's favorite fictional Swede." Alexander Alter presented the same juxtaposition in the *New York Times* (28 Oct. 2016), deeming *A Man Called Ove* "one of Sweden's most popular literary exports since Stieg Larsson's thriller."

Peter Borland, the editor who originally acquired the US rights to *Ove* for Atria Publishing, told Alter that he was taken by how different the gentle, humorous book was to the graphically violent Nordic thrillers that had proven popular with readers in recent years. "It had a great voice, and it was different from everything else I was reading," he said. "It wasn't Scandinavian noir; it was Scandinavian . . . something else."

Translation rights to Backman's books have been sold in more than forty languages, including Arabic, Turkish, Latvian, Thai, and Korean, and collectively, some ten million copies have sold worldwide. Backman told Alter that it is sometimes difficult to adjust to that level of fame: "Everyone keeps telling you how great you are and what a great writer you are, and they want selfies, and that's not healthy, because you start liking that," he said. "You still have to write like you're writing for twenty people, or you're going to freak out."

EARLY LIFE AND EDUCATION

Fredrik Backman was born on June 2, 1981, in Brännkyrka, an area of South Stockholm, Sweden. He grew up in Helsingborg, a picturesque coastal city in the southern part of the country, across the Øresund Strait from Denmark. He grew up watching and playing a variety of sports, including soccer, tennis, ping pong, handball, basketball, and ice hockey (which is particularly popular in Sweden). In his youth, he had notions of becoming a journalist but opted to study comparative religion in college instead; he dropped out after three years.

Backman initially earned his living as a forklift operator in a food warehouse but dabbled in writing on the side, producing columns for a free local paper called *Xtra*, which launched in 2006. Later, he wrote pieces for *Moore Magazine*, a glossy men's publication, and *Café*, a monthly periodical comparable to *Esquire* or *GQ* in the United States. Still, he has told interviewers, at that point he viewed writing more as a hobby, rather than a serious career choice.

Backman maintained a blog for *Café*, and in it, he began touching upon a grumpy character he dubbed Ove—borrowing the name from an anecdote written by a colleague about an elderly man who got in a fight with a museum staffer over how to pronounce an artist's name. "The 'origins in the blog' story has turned into somewhat of an urban legend," he told Jen Forbus for the website *Shelf Awareness* (27 Apr. 2016). "I think publishers' PR departments love to keep telling it, but it's not really true. There were some elements of the character of Ove that I played around with in my blog and some things I wrote about my dad that the blog readers enjoyed, and that eventually found its way into the novel."

WRITING CAREER

Encouraged by the blog's popularity, Backman wrote the first draft of a novel, stringing together a series of comical vignettes about a character who is annoyed by almost everything he encounters. Advised by family members and friends that the stories, while amusing, did not constitute a coherent or compelling narrative, he began revising. "I went back and I started asking myself questions," he recalled to Forbus. "Who is this man? How was he raised? Who does he love? What makes him laugh? And it grew from there. I started to care about him."

He was not encouraged by the responses he received from publishers when he began submitting the finished manuscript. Most simply ignored him, while others sent polite but firm rejection letters. Finally, in 2012, the Swedish publisher Forum released *En man som heter Ove*. While fielding rejection letters, Backman had written a comedic but heartfelt collection of personal essays about parenting, *Saker min son behöver veta om världen* (*Things My Son Needs to Know about the World*), and as part of his deal,

Forum published that as well; the two books hit shelves in Sweden on the same day.

Ove became a surprise hit in Backman's home country, selling thousands of copies, and in early 2015 a stage play based upon it opened in Stockholm. At the end of that year, a movie of the same name reached the big screen, with actor Rolf Lassgård in the title role. (Lassgård has, somewhat ironically, made his name appearing in screen adaptations of popular Swedish crime thrillers by Maj Sjöwall, Per Wahlöö, and Henning Mankell—stalwarts of the Nordic noir genre.) The film won two statuettes at the Guldbagge Awards, which celebrate the Swedish film industry. It was also nominated in the categories of Best Foreign Language Film and Best Makeup and Hairstyling at the 2016 Academy Awards. Tom Hanks is slated to produce and star in an English-language version of the film.

American publishers were initially slow to lend their support, but in 2014 Atria cautiously printed 6,600 hardcover copies. Championed by independent booksellers, *A Man Called Ove* eventually shot to number one on the *New York Times* Best Seller list; it remained on the list for more than forty weeks.

MY GRANDMOTHER SAYS TO TELL YOU SHE'S SORRY

The following year Atria published *Min mormor hälsar och saäger förlåt* (*My Grandmother Says to Tell You She's Sorry*), a fanciful tale about an eight-year-old misfit whose deceased grandmother had crafted a tale of a fantastical world, complete with its own language, and charged her to navigate it. "Neither [the real nor the made-up] world is short on adventure, tragedy, or danger," wrote a reviewer for *Kirkus Reviews* (1 May 2015). "This is a more complex tale than Backman's debut, and it is intricately, if not impeccably, woven. . . . As in *A Man Called Ove*, there are clear themes here, nominally: the importance of stories; the honesty of children; and the obtuseness of most adults, putting him firmly in league with the likes of Roald Dahl and Neil Gaiman."

Britt-Marie, a minor character in *Grandmother*, is the protagonist of Backman's next translated volume, *Britt-Marie var här* (*Britt-Marie Was Here*). Published first in 2014 and translated in 2016, the novel follows a middle-aged woman who leaves her husband and ends up coaching youth soccer in a tiny backwater town. "I wanted to tell a very undramatic story that was extremely dramatic to *her* [Britt-Marie], if you understand what I mean," Backman explained to Forbus. "The novel really has all the same ingredients as *Star Wars* and *Lord of the Rings*: our hero goes on a quest, gets challenged, meets new friends, overcomes adversity, stands up to injustice, and eventually learns something about herself. My story didn't have all the laser swords and the space ships and the fire-breathing dragons, but it's still basically the same: the search for our destiny. The dream of changing the world and leaving our mark in it."

LATER WORKS

Backman's other novels are *Björnstad* (2016; *Beartown*, 2017) and *Vi mot er* (*Us against You*, 2018). Both take place in a small town in rural Sweden, whose fortune is inextricably linked to that of their local junior hockey team. "In general, I like to write about smaller communities, because in big cities people more often choose to surround themselves with people who are just like themselves," Backman told Sam Jenkins for the entertainment magazine *Watch!* (27 July 2018). "In a smaller community you don't get to be as picky about your company. That makes for funnier collisions of characters and therefore better stories."

Backman is also the author of the novella *Och varje morgon blir vägen hem längre och längre* (2015; *And Every Morning the Way Home Gets Longer and Longer*), which *People* magazine named one of the best new books of 2016. His short Christmas-themed work *The Deal of a Lifetime* was hailed as an instant holiday classic when it was translated in 2017, and *Things My Son Needs to Know about the World* is a 2019 translation of the parenting book Backman wrote early in his career.

PERSONAL LIFE

Backman often describes himself as socially awkward. He married Neda Shafti, a woman of Iranian descent, in 2009, and the couple live with their two children in Stockholm. Because he also serves as an at-home parent while his wife works outside the home full-time, he has trained himself to write anywhere and anytime. "I write on the back of envelopes, in my phone, and on my arm," he told Jenkins. "Most of all I always write in my head."

Backman has said that his father has advised him to treat his new-found financial security as a fluke of luck that will probably not last. "He's got a point," Backman told Forbus. "I think I'll eventually go back to having a real job, and I don't really think I'll be any less happy than I am now."

SUGGESTED READING

Alter, Alexander. "The Man behind *A Man Called Ove*, Sweden's Latest Hit Novel." *The New York Times*, 28 Oct. 2016, www.nytimes.com/2016/10/29/books/a-man-called-ove-fredrik-backman-sweden-success.html. Accessed 27 Apr. 2019.

Backman, Fredrik. Interview by Jen Forbus. *Shelf Awareness*, 27 Apr. 2016, www.shelf-awareness.com/max-issue.html?issue=196#m416. Accessed 27 Apr. 2019.

Backman, Fredrik. Interview by Sam Jenkins. *Watch!*, CBS.com, 27 July 2018, www.cbs.com/shows/watch_magazine/archive/1008683/author-profile-fredrik-backman/. Accessed 27 Apr. 2019.

Maher, John. "Atria Finds a Scandinavian Star." *Publishers Weekly*, 6 May 2016, www.publishersweekly.com/pw/by-topic/industry-news/publisher-news/article/70299-atria-finds-a-scandinavian-star.html. Accessed 27 Apr. 2019.

Masad, Ilana. "The Magic of Fredrik Backman." *Read It Forward*, 2016, www.readitforward.com/essay/magic-fredrik-backman. Accessed 27 Apr. 2019.

Neary, Lynn. "A Swedish Curmudgeon Wins Hearts, on the Page, and Now on Screen." *All Things Considered*, NPR, 30 Sept. 2016, www.npr.org/2016/09/30/495976398/a-swedish-curmudgeon-wins-hearts-on-the-page-and-now-on-screen. Accessed 27 Apr. 2019.

Schmich, Mary. "Meet *A Man Called Ove* Author Fredrik Backman and Many More at Printers Row Lit Fest." *Chicago Tribune*, 7 June 2018, www.chicagotribune.com/news/columnists/schmich/ct-met-schmich-printers-row-20180607-story.html. Accessed 27 Apr. 2019.

SELECTED WORKS

En man som heter Ove (*A Man Called Ove*), 2012; *Min mormor hälsar och saäger förlåt* (*My Grandmother Says to Tell You She's Sorry*), 2015; *Britt-Marie var här* (*Britt-Marie Was Here*), 2014; *Björnstad* (*Beartown*), 2016; *Vi mot er* (*Us against You*), 2018

—*Mari Rich*

Lucinda Backwell

Date of Birth: September 2, 1966
Occupation: Archaeologist

South African paleoanthropologist Lucinda Backwell has delved deep into the archaeological sites of her country and beyond to discover not only the physical artifacts left behind by early human cultures but also the links between those early humans and the people of her own time. A specialist in artifacts such as bone tools, which early cultures used for a variety of everyday purposes, Backwell is best known for her work on archaeological projects based in the Border Cave, located in eastern South Africa near Eswatini, where archaeologists have unearthed numerous tools and other material elements of early human culture. Backwell's work there drew attention in 2012 with the well-publicized discovery of artifacts such as early jewelry. To Backwell and her colleagues in paleoanthropology, such findings suggest that early human culture possessed a level of sophistication greater than earlier thought. "This find . . . shows the earliest evidence of modern human behavior as we know it," Backwell told Wilma den Hartigh for the website *Brand South Africa* (7 Aug. 2012). "What we found there shows that people made use of symbolism, they were innovative and had cognitive ability."

Backwell has been an important figure in South African archaeology since as early as 2001, when she and Francesco d'Errico published a paper suggesting that early humans in South Africa had used bone tools to extract termites from termite mounds for sustenance. Such papers, as well as Backwell's research into human hair found within fossilized hyena dung and her extensive writings on artifacts from the Border Cave, shed additional light on the daily lives of the early humans who once lived in South Africa but also aptly demonstrate some of the ways in which twenty-first-century humans remain deeply linked to their distant ancestors. "We are more [a]like than we think we are," Backwell told den Hartigh.

EARLY LIFE AND EDUCATION
Lucinda Ruth Backwell has an older sister named Patricia, who became a behavioral ecologist at the Australian National University (ANU). During her early life, Backwell did not plan to pursue a career in paleoanthropology but became intrigued about it through the influence of her sister. "She explained to me that we didn't always look like this, that when we first started walking upright our brains began to expand," Backwell recalled to Bianca Bothma for the website of the *Cradle of Humankind*, a World Heritage Site (31 Aug. 2011). "Having never heard the word evolution at school, the idea of change over time captured my imagination and has thrilled me ever since." Backwell has also credited her academic success to her mother, Maureen Eva Backwell, who provided emotional and financial support for her endeavors.

As an adult, Backwell enrolled in the University of the Witwatersrand, or Wits University, in Johannesburg, South Africa. There she studied paleoanthropology and completed a thesis titled "A Critical Assessment of Southern African 'Early Hominid Bone Tools,'" with which she earned her Master of Science degree from the university in 2000. Backwell's time at the University of the Witwatersrand enabled her to work alongside major figures in her chosen field, including the American paleoanthropologist Lee Berger and the Italian-born Francesco d'Errico, a visiting professor and researcher affiliated with the French national scientific research center;

d'Errico would also go on to work for a specialist commission at the University of Bordeaux in France. Backwell pursued doctoral studies jointly at Wits and Bordeaux, completing the dissertation "Early Hominid Bone Tool Industries" under Berger's supervision in December 2003. She earned her PhD in 2004, becoming the first South African woman to receive a PhD in paleoanthropology.

As a graduate student, Backwell received various awards in recognition of her research, including the S2A3 Medal for Original Research at the Masters Level from the Southern African Association for the Advancement of Science, as well as various merit scholarships.

EARLY ACADEMIC CAREER
After completing her doctorate, Backwell lectured at Wits University for more than a decade. She was recognized repeatedly for the quality of her teaching and in 2009 was named the best first-year lecturer by the university's Geological Student Society. Working for Wits's Evolutionary Studies Institute, Backwell held the title of researcher until 2011, when she rose to senior researcher. She was later named an honorary senior researcher. As a researcher, she is particularly fascinated by bones, fossilization, human behavior and culture, burial customs, and the Kalahari San people, past and present.

In addition to Wits, Backwell became affiliated with Argentina's national scientific and technical research council, Instituto Superior de Estudios Sociales–Consejo Nacional de Investigaciones Científicas y Técnicas (ISES-CONICET).

NOTABLE RESEARCH
As a paleoanthropologist, Backwell focuses on areas of archaeology dealing with ancient humans and their culture. She is particularly interested in tools made from bone, which early humans used in a variety of ways. Early in her career, Backwell received media attention for work with d'Errico dealing with bone fragments, believed to be tools, that had been found in two South African archaeological sites, Swartkrans and Sterkfontein, dating to the Lower Paleolithic period—generally defined as being between 2.5 million and 300,000 years ago. Although earlier researchers posited that primitive humans had used the tools to dig up tubers, which they would then eat, Backwell and d'Errico presented an alternative theory. In their paper "Evidence of Termite Foraging by Swartkrans Early Hominids," published in the *Proceedings of the National Academy of Sciences* (*PNAS*) in February 2001, the researchers suggested that the early human inhabitants of what is now South Africa may have instead used the tools to extract termites from termite mounds. Based largely on the

patterns of wear evident on the tools, Backwell and d'Errico concluded that the prevailing explanation for the tools was incorrect and indicated that early humans may have incorporated insects, such as nutrient-rich termites, into their diets. They noted that early human remains from that area showed the presence of a dietary carbon that indicates the consumption of an herbivore or plant-eating insects, such as termites.

Backwell again made headlines in 2009, when she and an international team of colleagues published a paper discussing what appeared to be early human hair extracted from a hyena coprolite, or piece of fossilized dung. The hair, aged at some 200,000 to 260,000 years old, set a record for the oldest human hair found to date. Study of that hair enabled the researchers to learn more about the appearance and physical characteristics of early humans, while later research revealed additional hair from a number of other large mammals that lived in the area at the time as well, including zebras and warthogs. "In the case of the human hairs in the coprolite, they told us a lot, because there were no bones," Backwell told Lorraine Boissoneault for *Mental Floss* (10 Apr. 2019). Although the fossilized nature of the coprolite made it impossible for researchers to extract DNA from the hairs, Backwell commented in interviews that genetic analysis of ancient human hair would be a significant step toward a greater understanding of early humans.

THE ORIGINS OF MODERN CULTURE
Much of Backwell's published work has been related to excavations at the Border Cave, located in KwaZulu-Natal province of South Africa. Occupied by ancient humans for a significant period, the cave has been excavated since the 1940s, and the cave itself and the artifacts located there have been analyzed using a variety of technologies.

Among the most notable items found were artifacts such as ancient bead jewelry, the discovery of which received significant media attention in the summer of 2012. Such artifacts suggested to Backwell and her colleagues that early humans who spent time in the area had a culture that was more advanced than previously thought. "They adorned themselves with ostrich egg and marine shell beads, and notched bones for notational purposes," Backwell explained to Erna van Wyk for a university press release published on the American Association for the Advancement of Science's website *EurekAlert!* (30 July 2012). "They fashioned fine bone points for use as awls and poisoned arrowheads. One point is decorated with a spiral groove filled with red ochre, which closely parallels similar marks that San make to identify their arrowheads when hunting." Simple counting devices

and beeswax glue were also discovered. The presence of what researchers consider signs of modern human culture raised possible connections beyond paleoanthropology, to linguistics and genetics, providing further clues about both the lives of early humans and their creative and cognitive capabilities.

Backwell and her colleagues' findings not only shed light on the early life of humans in the region but also illuminated connections between that early human culture and the present culture of the San people of southern Africa. "The dating and analysis of archaeological material discovered at Border Cave in South Africa has allowed us to demonstrate that many elements of material culture that characterise the lifestyle of San hunter-gatherers in southern Africa, were part of the culture and technology of the inhabitants of this site 44,000 years ago," she explained to van Wyk.

ADDITIONAL BORDER CAVE WORK
Although Backwell's work regarding the Border Cave received particular attention in 2012, she continued to research the cave and its contents over the next years, contributing to published work focusing on artifacts such as shell ornaments and poison production. An additional paper on excavations in the Border Cave, co-authored by Backwell and ten colleagues, was published in the *Journal of Field Archaeology* in September 2018. The projects examined ancient vegetation from the Border Cave's sedimentary record and attempted to sequence early humans' use of the site based on charcoal and grass bedding residues.

Although much work has already taken place, further questions about early humanity are constantly being raised, and the artifacts unearthed and studied by researchers such as Backwell and her colleagues enable scientists to tell a more detailed story of the development of human society and culture. "Innovations came, were used and were lost again. This shows that human evolution was not entirely gradual," Backwell told den Hartigh.

OTHER WORK
Throughout her career, Backwell has contributed to more than a half-dozen documentaries related to her areas of research, including programs produced for Discovery Channel Canada, the National Geographic Society, and France 5 Television. A prolific author, she has been widely published in *PNAS*, the *Journal of Archaeological Science*, and *Palaeogeography, Palaeoclimatology, Palaeoecology*, among other academic journals. Along with d'Errico, Backwell coedited the 2005 book *From Tools to Symbols: From Early Hominids to Modern Humans*, the proceedings of a conference held in honor of noted researcher

Phillip Tobias. In addition to the Border Cave, Backwell's coauthored papers and conference presentations have concerned finds from sites throughout South Africa as well as in other countries, such as Tanzania, Namibia, and China.

SUGGESTED READING

Boissoneault, Lorraine. "Unraveling the History of Human Hair." *Mental Floss*, 10 Apr. 2019, mentalfloss.com/article/576201/unraveling-how-hair-types-evolved. Accessed 13 Sept. 2019.

Bothma, Bianca. "Women Scientists Dig Success in South Africa." *Cradle of Humankind*, Maropeng and Sterkfontein Caves, 31 Aug. 2011, www.maropeng.co.za/news/entry/women_scientists_dig_success_in_south_africa. Accessed 13 Sept. 2019.

Den Hartigh, Wilma. "Solving Early Human Culture Riddle." *Brand South Africa*, 2012, www.brandsouthafrica.com/people-culture/arts-culture/early-san-culture. Accessed 13 Sept. 2019.

"Researchers: Modern Culture May Have Earlier Start." *Columbus Dispatch*, 30 July 2012, www.dispatch.com/article/20120730/NEWS/307309792. Accessed 13 Sept. 2019.

van Wyk, Erna. "Modern Culture 44,000 Years Ago." *EurekAlert!*, American Association for the Advancement of Science, 30 July 2012, www.eurekalert.org/pub_releases/2012-07/uotw-mc4072712.php. Accessed 13 Sept. 2019.

Wong, Kate. "Early Humans Ate Termites." *Scientific American*, 16 Jan. 2001, www.scientificamerican.com/article/early-humans-ate-termites. Accessed 13 Sept. 2019.

—*Joy Crelin*

Beauden Barrett

Date of birth: May 27, 1991
Occupation: Rugby union player

"Often when I'm playing well, there's a place I get to that I call 'light, bright and clear,'" New Zealand rugby union player Beauden Barrett told Ben Winstanley for *Square Mile* (17 Oct. 2018). "That's when I'm playing my best footie: when I'm running on instinct, my mind and my body are clear and I can just enjoy playing. That's where I aim to get each game." As Barrett's performance in both provincial and international rugby matches has made apparent, he has often succeeded in finding that light, bright, and clear mental zone, becoming a prolific scorer and a valuable contributor to his teams. The son of retired rugby player Kevin Barrett and the brother

Photo by André Richard Chalmers via Wikimedia Commons

of several fellow players, Barrett grew up playing New Zealand's national sport at home, for local youth teams, and later for the New Zealand Under Twenty national junior team. After beginning his professional career with the Taranaki provincial team, he joined the Hurricanes, part of the Super Rugby competitive league, and went on to be selected by New Zealand's national team, the All Blacks, in 2012. Although Barrett's years with the All Blacks saw the team win both the 2015 Rugby World Cup and several Rugby Championships and Barrett be named World Rugby Player of the Year two years in a row, he remained focused on excelling as an individual player and as a member of his team. "In New Zealand we're never satisfied," he told Tom English for *Rugby World* (25 Aug. 2018). "I want to become a better player, I want to take it to another level."

EARLY LIFE AND EDUCATION

Beauden John Barrett was born on May 27, 1991, in New Plymouth, New Zealand. One of eight children born to Kevin and Robyn Barrett, he grew up primarily in Pungarehu, in the Taranaki region of New Zealand, where his family operated a dairy farm. Throughout his early life in rural New Zealand, Barrett and his siblings spent a great deal of time outdoors, and his childhood was filled with a host of risky but exciting activities. "Climbing up trees that are I don't know how many storeys high," he recalled to English. "Driving motorbikes on the farm and going up these huge hills with the constant fear of falling off and really hurting yourself. Floating down stormy rivers in big rapids on a blown-up tractor tyre with my brothers and the fear of being flicked over onto a rock and going underwater." In 1999, the Barrett family traveled to Ireland, where Kevin Barrett's ancestors are from, and they lived for more than a year. Although they later returned to New Zealand, the experience was a meaningful one for Barrett, who has referred to Ireland as his second home in interviews.

While outdoor and athletic pursuits were popular in the Barrett household, no sport was more significant to the family than rugby. Barrett's father, Kevin, was a rugby union player who played for the provincial Taranaki Bulls team as well as the Hurricanes Super Rugby team throughout much of Barrett's early childhood, setting a powerful example for his children. "Growing up you see your parents playing sport and dad played rugby, so obviously that's all you know and that's what we loved as kids," Barrett told Tony Robson for *Stuff.co.nz* (29 Apr. 2011). Aspiring to follow in his father's footsteps, he learned to play rugby as a young child, training with his father as well as with his older brother Kane, who would go on to play for both Taranaki and the Blues Super Rugby teams. Barrett played for the Rahotu junior rugby club as a child and continued with the sport while completing his secondary schooling at Francis Douglas Memorial College.

EARLY CAREER

While still in his late teens, Barrett began to represent New Zealand in international junior-level competitions. He was called up to the New Zealand Rugby Sevens team in May 2010, joining the team to play in the final portions of the 2009–10 International Rugby Board (IRB) Sevens World Series. The team finished as runners up behind first-place winner Samoa. The following year, Barrett competed as a fullback on the New Zealand Under-20 national team in the IRB Junior World Championship, held that year in Italy. New Zealand put forth a strong performance in the championship, defeating England in the final match to claim the title.

As a child and teenager, Barrett was particularly set on one day playing for the Taranaki provincial team. "All I wanted to do was play for Taranaki because Dad played for Taranaki and I grew up watching so many of his games," he told English. "It was such a big moment for the province every time Taranaki played." A talented young player, Barrett first had the opportunity to play for the organization in 2008, when he joined Taranaki Under Eighteen. He joined the main Taranaki team in 2010 and the following year signed a contract with the organization that would keep him with Taranaki through 2013. However, he did not compete for Taranaki in 2013 or 2014, during which time he

focused primarily on competing internationally with the Hurricanes and the All Blacks. He rejoined the team for a game in 2015 but did not compete further with Taranaki during the next several years.

HURRICANES

During Barrett's first season with Taranaki, his strong performance during matches and significant potential as a player captured the attention of multiple of New Zealand's Super Rugby teams. A high-level of international competition, Super Rugby pits teams from several countries—including New Zealand, Australia, and South Africa—against each other in international competition. Having attracted attention from New Zealand teams within that league, including the Hurricanes and the Blues, Barrett ultimately joined the Hurricanes, another team for which his father had previously played. Barrett initially joined the Hurricanes as a member of the team's developmental squad. In mid-2011, however, Hurricanes leadership selected Barrett to accompany the team to competitions in South Africa, where he made his first appearance in a match against the team the Cheetahs. For Barrett, his sudden introduction to Super Rugby play was surprising. "I was happy just taking this development phases, not being rushed in. The focus this year was the under-20s. That, and a good season for Taranaki. Anything else, the preseason with the Hurricanes, has been a bonus," he told Robson. "I felt a bit of pressure at first, but was also really excited."

Although Barrett quickly proved himself as a strong addition to the Hurricanes, he remained conservative when it came to his career goals. "I just want to give Super Rugby a good crack, earn a starting place on the Canes and if I play well enough I may have a one in five chance of making it into the [All Blacks]," he told the *Taranaki Daily News* (26 Dec. 2011). Over the next several years, Barrett gave Super Rugby more than simply a "good crack," becoming a starter for the Hurricanes and helping the team amass numerous points during the seasons in which he played. In recognition of his strong performance in the 2016 season, he was named Super Rugby Player of the Year for 2016.

ALL BLACKS

Although pleased to be playing for Taranaki and the Hurricanes, Barrett harbored ambitions of playing for the senior-level New Zealand national rugby union team, known as the All Blacks because of their black uniforms. Having previously represented New Zealand internationally at the junior level, he had his first opportunity to play for the country as a senior-level player in 2012, when he joined the All Blacks roster. He played his first international test match against Ireland in June of 2012, helping the All Blacks achieve an impressive 60–0 victory. Although pleased with the victory, he was perhaps most excited simply to be playing for the team. "Every time you get the chance to wear that black jersey is a highlight in itself," he later told Hannah Fleming for the *Taranaki Daily News* (24 Dec. 2012). Barrett went on to play in four additional tests over the course of 2012, competing against teams from Argentina, Italy, Scotland, and Wales.

Barrett continued to compete with the All Blacks for the next several seasons, playing in eleven matches in 2013 and twelve in 2014. Throughout his early seasons with the team, he worked to avoid becoming complacent and sought to remember that every game was a new opportunity to prove himself. "I never thought, 'Right, I've made it now,'" he told English. "There were guys [on the team] who I had looked up to for years . . . so it took a lot of work on my self-belief to really accept that I could stay there and push on." The year 2015 was an especially important one for Barrett, who in September and October of that year accompanied the All Blacks to their first Rugby World Cup, held in the United Kingdom. After progressing through the pool stage, the All Blacks went on to defeat France in the quarterfinals and South Africa in the semifinals before facing Australia in the final match. The team beat Australia 34–17 to win the World Cup for the third time in the event's history.

Over the subsequent seasons, Barrett continued to compete with the All Blacks, contributing to the team's successes on the international stage. The All Blacks won the Rugby Championship—an annual tournament among the national teams of Argentina, Australia, New Zealand, and South Africa—in 2016, 2017, and 2018, and Barrett scored the most points of any player in the championship in 2016. In recognition of his strong performance on the international stage, Barrett was named World Rugby Player of the Year in 2016 and again the following year. He was shortlisted for World Rugby Player of the Year again in 2018, but the title ultimately went to Irish player Jonathan Sexton.

FURTHER ASPIRATIONS

Barrett's success as a player on the international stage prompted widespread speculation that he might one day choose to move abroad to play with an international rugby franchise, a potentially lucrative career move previously made by other New Zealand players. However, Barrett told interviewers that he planned to remain in his native country for the time being and hoped to progress further with the All Blacks. "If I get to an age, and a place, where I no longer have the drive or the desire to be an All Black and I feel it's time to leave because there are younger and better guys who need their chance to wear that jersey, then, yep, sure," he told English about the possibility of moving abroad. "But right at the moment, I'm fresh, I'm still young and I want to be around." Barrett particularly hopes to lead the All Blacks to another victory in the Rugby World Cup, the 2019 edition of which is set to begin in Japan in September of 2019.

PERSONAL LIFE

Barrett married accountant and social-media influencer Hannah Laity in January of 2019. When not playing rugby, he enjoys playing golf and practicing yoga. Along with his fellow members of the All Blacks, Barrett has been sponsored by the Swiss watch brand Tudor and has appeared in various advertisements for the company.

SUGGESTED READING

Cully, Paul. "All Blacks Star Beauden Barrett Set for Wedding, Rugby World Cup, and Then Japan." *Stuff.co.nz*, 13 Jan. 2019, www.stuff.co.nz/sport/rugby/all-blacks/109888454/all-blacks-star-beauden-barrett-set-for-wedding-rugby-world-cup-and-then-japan. Accessed 15 Feb. 2019.

English, Tom. "Beauden Barrett: 'I Want to Take It to Another Level.'" *Rugby World*, 25 Aug. 2018, www.rugbyworld.com/countries/new-zealand-countries/beauden-barrett-want-take-another-level-93538. Accessed 15 Feb. 2019.

Fleming, Hannah. "Barrett's Stellar Year—and It All Began Right Here." *Taranaki Daily News*, 24 Dec. 2012, www.stuff.co.nz/taranaki-daily-news/your-taranaki/8114610/Barretts-stellar-year-and-it-all-began-right-here. Accessed 15 Feb. 2019.

McLean, Glenn. "All Eyes on Young Taranaki Super Sub Barrett." *Stuff.co.nz*, 11 Oct. 2010, www.stuff.co.nz/sport/rugby/4217683/All-eyes-on-young-Taranaki-super-sub-Barrett. Accessed 15 Feb. 2019.

Robson, Rony. "Anything Dad Could Do—Beauden Has Followed." *Stuff.co.nz*, 29 Apr. 2011, www.stuff.co.nz/sport/rugby/super-rugby/squads/hurricanes/4939526/Anything-dad-could-do-Beauden-has-followed. Accessed 15 Feb. 2019.

Winstanley, Ben. "'Winning Is Not Enough for Us'—Beauden Barrett Is Coming for England (and the World)." *Square Mile*, 17 Oct. 2018, squaremile.com/sport/beauden-barrett-interview/. Accessed 15 Feb. 2019.

"Young Player Helped Bring Shield Home." *Taranaki Daily News*, 26 Dec. 2011, www.stuff.co.nz/taranaki-daily-news/editors-picks/6189310/Young-player-helped-bring-shield-home. Accessed 15 Feb. 2019.

—*Joy Crelin*

Regina Barzilay

Date of birth: 1970
Occupation: Computer scientist

Regina Barzilay is a computer scientist and the delta electronics professor of electrical engineering and computer science at the Massachusetts Institute of Technology (MIT). In 2017, she won the prestigious MacArthur Fellowship for her body of work, which includes research in computational linguistics (teaching machines how to read and analyze language) and using artificial intelligence (AI) to refine the detection and diagnosis of breast cancer. Her primary interest as a scientist is language. In 2010, Barzilay and a group of scientists created a program that automatically translates written Ugaritic, an ancient language last used in 1200 BC. The program demonstrates how computers can be powerful tools for translation, improving on existing programs like Google Translate. It took language specialists years to decipher Ugaritic after it was discovered in the late 1920s; the computer completed the same task within hours.

In 2014, Barzilay was diagnosed with breast cancer at the age of forty-three. "Going through it, I realized that today we have more sophisticated technology to select your shoes on Amazon than to adjust treatments for cancer patients," she told Meg Tirrell for CNBC (11 May 2017). "I really wanted to make sure that the expertise we have would be used for helping people." Barzilay was referring to the reams of data generated by mammograms, the imperfect, but only, screening test for the disease. With her research Barzilay hopes, among other things, that machines can learn to read mammograms more effectively than human doctors and generate more precise diagnoses and treatment plans.

In addition to the MacArthur Fellowship, Barzilay has also received the National Science Foundation Career Award and a Microsoft Faculty Fellowship.

EARLY LIFE AND EDUCATION

Barzilay was born in Moldavia in 1970. She grew up in a small Jewish community. When she was around nineteen, Barzilay and her family moved to Israel. She went to a kibbutz, or collective community, where she learned Hebrew (her first language was Russian), worked at an electrical factory, and harvested almonds on a farm. Soon after, she enrolled at Ben-Gurion University (BGU) of the Negev in Beersheba, Israel. She recalled her years as an impoverished student to Valerie Brown for *Bioengineering Today* (7 May 2018): "I didn't buy clothes for years. I remember going once on a date and the guy bought me chocolate milk in a package, and I thought he must be really rich, to buy chocolate milk in a

Photo by John D. & Catherine T. MacArthur Foundation via Wikimedia Commons

package." Barzilay graduated with a bachelor's degree in mathematics in 1993. After graduation, Barzilay taught secondary school math, but the job became tedious. She realized, she told Brown, that she would be "teaching from the same textbook" each year. Desiring a more intellectually rigorous career, she returned to BGU and earned a master's degree in computer programming in 1998. Barzilay then began pursuing her doctoral degree under the guidance of Kathleen McKeown at Columbia University in New York.

NATURAL LANGUAGE PROCESSING

Under McKeown, Barzilay focused on natural language processing, a subfield of computer science that explores how to teach machines natural (meaning human) language. In the 1970s and 1980s, natural language processing meant teaching machines the rules of language. The approach was not successful. While at Columbia, Barzilay chose to use frequency to accomplish the same goal. Instead of, as Brown put it, "handing the computer a complete guide" to language, Barzilay wanted the machine to teach itself by detecting patterns over time. "A lot of machine learning systems take as input the raw words, and you put the onus on the machine to be able to learn the structure on its own," Adam Fisch, one of Barzilay's doctoral students, explained to Brown. For her dissertation, Barzilay developed a program called Newsblaster. Newsblaster, the first program of its kind, was able to "recognize stories from different news services as being about the same basic subject, and then paraphrase elements from all of the stories to create a summary," a reporter for the *MIT Technology Review* (2005) explained.

Barzilay earned her PhD from Columbia in 2003. She then did a year of postdoctoral research at Cornell University, before joining the faculty at MIT as an assistant professor of electrical engineering and computer science. For her continuing work with Newsblaster and natural language generation, Barzilay won the National Science Foundation (NSF) Career Award in 2005. The following year, she earned the Microsoft Faculty Fellowship.

In 2010, Barzilay and a group of scientists at MIT created a program that translated an ancient language called Ugaritic by comparing it to the word patterns of Hebrew, its closest linguistic equivalent. "Using no more computing power than that of a high-end laptop," Tim Hornyak wrote for *National Geographic* (20 July 2010), the program translated the language in a few hours—a task that took scholars in the 1920s several years. "Traditionally, decipherment has been viewed as a sort of scholarly detective game, and computers weren't thought to be of much use," Barzilay told Hornyak. "Our aim is to bring to bear the full power of modern machine learning and statistics to this problem."

In 2011, Barzilay teamed up with her graduate student S. R. K. Branavan and David Silver, from University College London, to teach a machine to understand and play the complex computer game *Civilization*. Computers treat words like data—think of Google search terms—but the experiment sought to understand if computers could understand the meaning of words and use that understanding to complete a task. Game manuals, Barzilay told a writer for *MIT Electrical Engineering and Computer Science* (13 July 2011), have "very open text. They don't tell you how to win. They just give you very general advice and suggestions, and you have to figure out a lot of other things on your own." With no prior knowledge of the task or the language in which the game instructions were written, the machine learned to play by trial and error, and was eventually able to win about 80 percent of the games it played.

BREAST CANCER AND AI

While being treated for breast cancer, Barzilay learned that all treatment decisions were based on clinical trials, meaning that doctors everywhere were making decisions based on the experiences of 3 percent of patients. Barzilay believed that the medical records of all people with breast cancer and those that have been tested for it—data previously unused in research—might offer serious improvements to the way breast cancer is detected, diagnosed, and treated. "Looking back, there was clearly no tumor on the previous mammograms, but was there something in these very complex images that would hint at . . . a wrong development?" Barzilay told Tirrell of her own experience. "It clearly didn't just appear. Biological processes are in place to make a successful growth and it clearly impacts the tissue. So for a human who looks at it, it's very hard to quantify the change, but a machine may look at millions of these images. This should really help them to look at these signs." In other words, Barzilay was hoping that, if a machine could teach itself to play a computer game, perhaps it could also teach itself to diagnose cancer.

Working with scientists at Massachusetts General Hospital (MGH) and MIT's Computer Science and Artificial Intelligence Laboratory (CSAIL), Barzilay set out to find a more precise and noninvasive way to screen high-risk lesions for cancer. Using existing methods, doctors could only determine if a lesion was cancerous through surgery. According to Rowan Walrath for *Boston Magazine* (17 Oct. 2017), 90 percent of lesions are noncancerous, "making an invasive and expensive procedure totally unnecessary." Using patient information—including race, age, family history, biopsies, and pathology reports—from patients with high-risk lesions, the trial model was effectively able to identify cancerous legions, reducing the number of unnecessary surgeries by 30 percent. Still, using patient data in this way presents a potential conflict with the Health Insurance Portability and Accountability Act (HIPAA) and other privacy laws that restrict the use of a patient's personal information.

In 2018, Barzilay and her team developed "an automated model that assesses dense breast tissue in mammograms—which is an independent risk factor for breast cancer—as reliably as expert radiologists," Rob Matheson reported for *MIT News* (16 Oct. 2018). Matheson went on to report that it was the first time that a deep-learning model had successfully been used on real patients, in this case, patients at the breast imaging division at MGH. Instead of using a gaming manual, Barzilay gave the model tens of thousands of digital mammograms. It learned to distinguish among four types of breast tissue. "Breast density is an independent risk factor that drives how we communicate with women about their cancer risk," Adam Yala, a PhD student with CSAIL, told Matheson. "Our motivation was to create an accurate and consistent tool, that can be shared and used across health care systems." The model assesses images in less than a second and then sends that assessment to a radiologist for review. In over ten thousand mammograms at MGH, from January to May 2018, radiologists agreed with the model's assessment about 90 percent of the time.

For the sum of her work, in 2017, Barzilay won the MacArthur Fellowship, an Association for Computational Linguistics Fellowship, and an Association for the Advancement of Artificial Intelligence Fellowship.

In 2018, Barzilay became a faculty lead at MIT's new Abdul Latif Jameel Clinic for Machine Learning in Health, or J-Clinic, an organization dedicated to using machine-learning to advance health research.

PERSONAL LIFE

Barzilay's cancer is in remission. Her husband, Eli Barzilay, is also a computer scientist. The couple have a son named Tomer.

SUGGESTED READING

"Barzilay & Team Demonstrate Computer Learning from Language Understanding." *MIT Electrical Engineering and Computer Science*, 13 July 2011, www.eecs.mit.edu/news-events/media/barzilay-team-demonstrate-computer-learning-language-understanding. Accessed 5 Nov. 2018.

Brown, Valerie. "Regina Barzilay: Venturesome and Voracious for Data." *Bioengineering Today*, 7 May 2018, bioengineeringtoday.org/emerging-tech/regina-barzilay-venturesome-and-voracious-data. Accessed 5 Nov. 2018.

Hornyak, Tim. "'Lost' Languages to Be Resurrected by Computers?" *National Geographic*, 20 July 2010, news.nationalgeographic.com/news/2010/07/100719-science-technology-computers-lost-languages-translate-bible-hebrew/. Accessed 5 Nov. 2018.

"Innovators Under 35: Regina Barzilay, 34." *MIT Technology Review*, 2005, www2.technologyreview.com/tr35/profile.aspx?TRID=85. Accessed 5 Nov. 2018.

Matheson, Rob. "Automated System Identifies Dense Tissue, a Risk Factor for Breast Cancer, in Mammograms." *MIT News*, 16 Oct. 2018, news.mit.edu/2018/AI-identifies-dense-tissue-breast-cancer-mammograms-1016. Accessed 6 Nov. 2018.

Tirrell, Meg. "From Coding to Cancer: How AI Is Changing Medicine." *CNBC*, 11 May 2017, www.cnbc.com/2017/05/11/from-coding-to-cancer-how-ai-is-changing-medicine.html. Accessed 5 Nov. 2018.

Walrath, Rowan. "New Machine Learning Model Could Accurately Detect Breast Cancer." *Boston Magazine*, 17 Oct. 2017, www.bostonmagazine.com/health/2017/10/17/machine-learning-breast-cancer-mgh/. Accessed 6 Nov. 2018.

—*Molly Hagan*

Isabel Bayrakdarian

Date of birth: February 1, 1974
Occupation: Operatic soprano

When Isabel Bayrakdarian graduated from the University of Toronto in 1997, she faced a career-defining choice: pursue the career in engineering for which her studies had prepared her or take her chances in the highly competitive field of opera performance. A talented soprano who had sung in church choirs since childhood and had taken voice lessons as an adult, Bayrakdarian ultimately chose the latter option and quickly distinguished herself as a skilled performer through prestigious contests such as the 1997 Metropolitan Opera National Council Auditions and the 2000 Operalia. For Bayrakdarian, however, such achievements were far less important than the act of performing itself. "I just loved to sing, and to express and live the words that I was singing was pure oxygen to me," she told Wah Keung Chan for *myScena* (5 Apr. 2018). "I never compared myself to any other singer, which I think was the key to my success in competitions and beyond. I vowed to always give my best, but most importantly to enjoy the experience."

In addition to opera competitions, Bayrakdarian found success as a performer in operas such as *The Magic Flute* (including an American production in 2006 and a Canadian production in 2011) and *The Marriage of Figaro* (she turned in an early memorable performance in Los Angeles Opera's 2004 production). She was likewise successful in her career as a recording artist,

Photo by ArmenianEmbassy via Wikimedia Commons

which began in earnest in 2002 with the release of her debut album, *Joyous Light*. Particularly focused on performing and ensuring the preservation of traditional Armenian music, Bayrakdarian has combined that creative interest with a host of others to build a career that is varied and continually evolving. "It's not about competitiveness, and it's more than being challenged," she told Sarah Hampson for the *Globe and Mail* (7 Jan. 2006). "I think we have to be constantly improving. Otherwise, why did we come onto the planet?"

EARLY LIFE AND EDUCATION

Isabel Bayrakdarian was born in 1974 in Zahlé, Lebanon. She was the youngest of six children born to Ohannes and Lalig Bayrakdarian, members of Lebanon's Armenian community and children of survivors of the Armenian genocide of the early twentieth century. As a child, Bayrakdarian learned about her grandparents' experiences, which would inspire her later work to preserve and popularize traditional Armenian music through her recorded and live performances. "I don't consider myself political, but I am an artistic activist," she explained to David Ng for the *Los Angeles Times* (21 Oct. 2015). "I grew up hearing their stories. To this day, I feel their pain, because their pain wasn't resolved. . . . Keeping the songs alive gives voice to my grandparents and to all the Armenians who were silenced."

During Bayrakdarian's early childhood, her mother worked as a church choir director, and she began singing in church at a young age. She was also interested in sports and was particularly active in cycling during her time in Lebanon. When she was around fourteen, her family immigrated to Canada, settling in Toronto. Although her skill as a vocalist was already apparent, she did not initially plan to pursue a career in music, instead enrolling at the University of Toronto to study biomedical engineering. During that period, to indulge in her continued interest in and enjoyment of music (and, in part, "to be able to sing better in church," as she told Ng), she pursued formal vocal lessons through teacher Jean MacPhail at the Royal Conservatory of Music and entered singing competitions, winning her age division in the Canadian Music Competition around 1995.

EARLY CAREER

Although Bayrakdarian's university studies prepared her to enter the workforce as an engineer, she opted to pursue a career as an opera singer, a decision that was, in large part, bolstered by her successful performance at the 1997 Metropolitan Opera National Council Auditions. A competition with the goal of identifying talented young opera singers and assisting in their professional development, the National Council Auditions were particularly significant due to their connection to New York City's Metropolitan Opera, widely considered one of the world's prestigious opera houses. Bayrakdarian, however, who had not participated in a full-time vocal program at university, approached the competition and similar events from the perspective of an "outsider," which she told Chan was key to her success. "I was blissfully unaware of the pressures and the mind games that often sabotage a singer's performance in competitions," she recalled. Bayrakdarian was ultimately one of ten winners selected during that year's competition, and she also earned her degree from University of Toronto around this time.

Having turned down a lucrative contract for employment at a biotech company and having spent time performing with New York's Glimmerglass Opera immediately following graduation, in the hope of honing her vocal skills further, Bayrakdarian went on to study at the Music Academy of the West in 1998, a summer conservatory in California. Two years later, she entered the international opera competition Operalia, founded by acclaimed opera singer Plácido Domingo. She claimed first prize at the 2000 Operalia as well as one of the competition's Zarzuela Prizes, awarded to singers who performed works belonging to the Spanish zarzuela theatrical genre.

OPERA ROLES AND MAKING RECORDINGS

Over the following years, Bayrakdarian achieved several major career milestones, each demonstrating the versatility that would come to characterize her career. Having established herself as a talented opera performer, she made her debut with the prestigious Metropolitan Opera in 2002. That year, she also contributed vocals to the song "Evenstar" from the soundtrack to the film *The Lord of the Rings: The Two Towers*. For that recording, Bayrakdarian was tasked with singing in one of the Elvish languages created by the author of the *Lord of the Rings* novels, J. R. R. Tolkien. "It's hard," she told Ng about her experience singing in the language. "But you know what? You can get away with so much. After all, how many of you know Elvish?" The soundtrack for *The Lord of the Rings: The Two Towers* ultimately won a Grammy Award in 2004. The year 2002 also saw the release of Bayrakdarian's debut album, *Joyous Light*, which features an array of Armenian music.

Following the release of *Joyous Light*, Bayrakdarian went on to record numerous albums that further emphasize the breadth of her interests as a performer. The 2003 album *Azulão* features pieces by Spanish and South American composers, whereas 2004's *Cleopatra* collects performances of arias from several operas featuring the historical Cleopatra as a character. The year 2004 also saw her take on one of her best-recognized roles, one she would return to again in the future, once more as she appeared as Susanna in Los Angeles Opera's production of *The Marriage of Figaro*. Her 2005 recording, *Pauline Viardot-Garcia: Lieder, Chansons, Canzoni, Mazurkas*, along with her earlier albums, received widespread critical acclaim and won the Juno Award for classical vocal or choral album. During that period, she was also featured in the television documentary *A Long Journey Home*, which followed the performer during her first visit to Armenia. That 2004 visit also encompassed a performance with the Armenian Philharmonic Orchestra, portions of which were chronicled in the documentary.

AN ESTABLISHED CAREER

As Bayrakdarian's career continued to develop, she found that her increasing renown as a performer afforded her new opportunities to shape the artistic direction of her career. "At first, it's just about showing, auditioning, being known enough, impressing enough to get a break," she explained to Hampson. "Then, after five years, as of 2003 and 2004, it's more about proving. And now it's about choosing. And choosing means what repertoire to sing, where to sing, and with whom to sing." Her later albums reflected those choices, encompassing works by figures such as Austrian composer Wolfgang Amadeus Mozart; Armenian composer and music preservationist Gomidas (also known as Komitas); and Spanish composers Isaac Albéniz, Enrique Granados, and Manuel de Falla. The 2008 album *Gomidas Songs* earned her a Grammy nomination for Best Classical Vocal Performance.

Bayrakdarian's performances likewise continued to vary, from location to company, including a memorable portrayal of another one of her signature characters, Pamina, in the Metropolitan Opera's 2006 revival of *The Magic Flute*; singing as Blanche de la Force in Lyric Opera of Chicago's 2007 staging of *Dialogues des Carmélites*; continued performances as Zerlina in *Don Giovanni* (including as part of a 2009 Metropolitan Opera production); and a return to the role of Euridice for a 2011 Canadian Opera Company production of *Orfeo ed Euridice*. Throughout this time, she also continued to perform in numerous concerts, with both accompanists such as pianist and composer Serouj Kradjian (who is also her husband) as well as ensembles such as the Toronto Symphony Orchestra, the Manitoba Chamber Orchestra, and the Russian National Orchestra. "The atmosphere of music-making is very different depending on the medium of performance," she told Jenna Simeonov for *Schmopera* (19 Mar. 2018). "With full orchestral accompaniment, the control is—justifiably—in the hands of the conductor—so there's not much room for complete freedom. Voice/piano is very intimate, and an experience of complete freedom that I absolutely love. And right in between, there's the chamber group experience, which feels intimate enough that you don't need a conductor, but there's a constant sense of awareness of the need to be very sensitive to each instrument enveloping you (literally and figuratively) on stage."

TEACHING AND SINGING

After more than fifteen years, Bayrakdarian remained just as passionate about all phases of her career. She made adjustments as needed, which typically involved toning down her more demanding operatic performance schedule over time. She has noted in interviews that, for the most part, she has enjoyed the itinerant lifestyle of a performer, which she has credited with introducing her to new experiences and ideas. Her 2013 album, *Troubadour & the Nightingale*, highlights work by early Armenian troubadours and also features a piece by Kradjian.

In addition to performing and recording, Bayrakdarian became an associate professor in the voice program at the University of California, Santa Barbara, which recruited her after she had moved to California in 2012 to be closer to her mother. "It was truly a blessing, because it provided a meaningful musical outlet, while still being close to my mother," she told Chan. As a teacher, Bayrakdarian encourages students to put aside their need for validation from audiences or industry gatekeepers, which she notes can distract from the true purpose of performance. "The audience needs to be moved, and you move the heart, not the mind!" she told Chan. "I advise young singers first to learn and master the technique that will free up their instrument, then enjoy the process of learning about what their soul wants to express."

In 2016, she released a work of personal significance with *Mother of Light: Armenian Hymns & Chants in Praise of Mary*. The album originated in a religious pledge that the performer made following her mother's hospitalization for a stroke. "I said God, 'You take care of my mom, and I'll sing about your mom,'" she recalled in an interview for *CBC Radio* (9 Apr. 2018). *Mother of Light* also features vocal performances and percussion by several of Bayrakdarian's siblings. The album was nominated for the 2018 Juno Award for classical vocal or choral album of the year. Meanwhile, she reprised her role as Vixen Sharp-Ears for an Opera Santa Barbara production of *The Cunning Little Vixen* in 2017.

PERSONAL LIFE

Bayrakdarian and her husband, Kradjian, first met as teenagers and later began a relationship after reconnecting to work on a music project. They married in 2004. Bayrakdarian and Kradjian have collaborated on numerous projects, including albums and many live performances. They have a son and a daughter. Bayrakdarian lives in California when not traveling and performing elsewhere.

SUGGESTED READING

Bayrakdarian, Isabel. "Talking with Singers: Isabel Bayrakdarian." Interview by Jenna Simeonov. *Schmopera*, 19 Mar. 2018, www.schmopera.com/talking-with-singers-isabel-bayrakdarian/. Accessed 18 Jan. 2019.

Chan, Wah Keung. "Isabel Bayrakdarian on Competitions, Performing, Teaching and Life." *MyScena*, 5 Apr. 2018, myscena.org/wah-keung-chan/isabel-bayrakdarian-competitions-performing-teaching-life/. Accessed 18 Jan. 2019.

"Family Crisis Leads Opera Singer to Make Pact with God." *CBC Radio*, CBC Radio-Canada, 9 Apr. 2018, www.cbc.ca/radio/tapestry/family-crisis-leads-opera-singer-to-make-pact-with-god-1.4606793. Accessed 18 Jan. 2019.

Hampson, Sarah. "A Soprano on a Path to Greatness." *The Globe and Mail*, 7 Jan. 2006, www.theglobeandmail.com/arts/a-soprano-on-a-path-to-greatness/article700965/. Accessed 18 Jan. 2019.

Ng, David. "Soprano Isabel Bayrakdarian Hopes to Give Voice to Her Armenian Ancestors." *Los Angeles Times*, 21 Oct. 2015, www.latimes.com/entertainment/arts/la-et-cm-soprano-isabel-bayrakdarian-20151021-story.html. Accessed 18 Jan. 2019.

Ross, Jeremy. "An Interview with Soprano Isabel Bayrakdarian: Not Your Average Diva." *Living Out Loud*, 21 Oct. 2015, www.lol-la.com/an-interview-with-soprano-isabel-bayrakdarian-not-your-average-diva/. Accessed 18 Jan. 2019.

SELECTED WORKS

Joyous Light, 2002; *Azulão*, 2003; *Cleopatra*, 2004; *Pauline Viardot-Garcia: Lieder, Chansons, Canzoni, Mazurkas* (with Serouj Kradjian), 2005; *Mozart: Arie e Duetti* (with Russell Braun and Michael Schade), 2006; *Gomidas Songs*, 2008; *The Spanish Masters* (with Zuill Bailey), 2011; *Troubadour & the Nightingale*, 2013; *Mother of Light: Armenian Hymns & Chants in Praise of Mary*, 2016

—Joy Crelin

Nicole Beharie

Date of birth: January 3, 1985
Occupation: Actor

Nicole Beharie is an American actor and singer known for *Sleepy Hollow*.

EARLY LIFE AND EDUCATION

Nicole Beharie was born in 1985 in West Palm Beach, Florida. Her father served in the Foreign Service and his career required the family to relocate several times. Beharie spent parts of her youth in Panama, the United Kingdom, and Nigeria. She also spent several years in Washington, DC, and in Stone Mountain, Georgia, with her sister and grandmother.

While living in Nigeria, Beharie acted in her first play, a production of *Alice in Wonderland*. Beharie had developed an accent and was accustomed to using British turns of phrase in Nigeria. She had to lose the accent and learn not to use certain terms to avoid being bullied when she returned to the American South.

Her family moved to South Carolina for an extended period. Beharie attended Orangeburg Wilkinson High School in South Carolina and later transferred to the South Carolina Governor's School for the Arts and Humanities. She was the first student from the South Carolina Governor's School to earn acceptance to the Juilliard School in New York City.

In 2003 Beharie began her studies in the Juilliard School's prestigious drama program, pursuing a degree in acting and singing. She earned a Robin Williams Scholarship in 2006, enabling her to attend Juilliard tuition-free for two years. While attending Juilliard, she sang jazz in New York restaurants.

ACTOR AND SINGER

Beharie's professional acting career began before she had completed her studies at Juilliard. She accepted a role in *The Express* (2008), for which she missed her Juilliard graduation ceremony. That same year she appeared in her first starring film role as Dee Roberts, a single mother wrongfully convicted of drug dealing and her fight against the justice system, in *American Violet*. Beharie was widely praised for her performance.

She turned her attention to the stage and starred in an acclaimed 2010 Broadway production of *A Free Man of Color*. Beharie then appeared in the 2011 award-winning ensemble drama *Shame*, directed by Steve McQueen, about a man's struggles with sex addiction. Her next film was the romantic comedy *My Last Day without You* (2011), in which she portrays an aspiring singer. Beharie also performed several songs on the film's soundtrack. She had a two-episode guest spot on *The Good Wife* in 2011.

Beharie starred as the lead in *Apartment 4E* (2012), a mystery thriller in which Beharie's character shuts herself up in her apartment and her own world until she is interrupted by a knock at the door. In the same year, Beharie appeared in *The Last Fall*, a film about the personal trials of National Football League players, as well as *Woman Thou Art Loosed: On the 7th Day*, a suspense drama about a kidnapped child.

Next, she was cast in *42* (2013), a biopic of the first black Major League Baseball player, Jackie Robinson. In the film, Beharie portrayed Robinson's wife, Rachel. Though her performance was lauded, the film received mixed reviews.

Beharie's career breakthrough came later in 2013, when she began starring as Abbie Mills in the science-fiction drama series *Sleepy Hollow*. Her best-known role, Abbie Mills is a modern-day police officer working in Sleepy Hollow, New York, who works with the resurrected Ichabod Crane (the main character of Washington Irving's 1820 story) to solve a mystery that dates to the late eighteenth century. *Sleepy Hollow* quickly became a popular series and obtained a cult following known as "SleepyHeads." Beharie's character on the show was particularly popular with fans and critics.

Beharie decided to leave *Sleepy Hollow* in 2016, possibly due to the show hiring a new showrunner and declining in popularity and critical favor. In accordance with her intention to leave the show, Beharie's Abbie Mills character on *Sleepy Hollow* was killed in the season three finale, which aired in April 2016. The death of Abbie Mills generated immediate backlash from fans of the show, who widely expressed their anger on social media. *Sleepy Hollow*'s widely-panned decision to kill off Beharie's character also sparked controversy and discussion in the media about the role of minority actors in television series and the seeming frequency of their characters being killed.

Also in April 2016, Beharie announced that she would star, alongside Michael Ealy and Jesse Williams, in a remake of the 1990 cult hit *Jacob's Ladder*.

IMPACT

Beharie rose to widespread fame with *Sleepy Hollow*. Her performances on that series as well as in films such as *Shame* and *American Violet* have earned favorable reviews.

PERSONAL LIFE

Beharie's personal interests include science fiction, sustainable farming, and permaculture. She enjoys singing, as well. She dated her *Shame* costar, Michael Fassbender, in 2012 and 2013.

SUGGESTED READING

Butler, Bethonie. "After a Shocking Death on Sleepy Hollow, Fans Are Questioning How the Show Treats Characters of Color." *The Washington Post*. 12 Apr. 2016, www.washingtonpost.com/news/arts-and-entertainment/wp/2016/04/12/after-a-shocking-death-on-sleepy-hollow-fans-are-questioning-how-the-show-treats-characters-of-color/?noredirect=on&utm_term=.ba840014b2c6. Accessed 26 Apr. 2019.

Carson, Tom. "Tom Carson Reviews 42: Jackie Robinson Doesn't Get the Movie He Deserves." *GQ*. Condé Nast, 12 Apr. 2013, www.gq.com/story/tom-carson-reviews-42-jackie-robinson-doesnt-get-the-movie-he-deserves. Accessed 26 Apr. 2019.

Guiducci, Mark. "Here's to You, Mrs. Robinson: Ten Questions for 42's Nicole Beharie." *Vogue*. Condé Nast, 12 Apr. 2013, www.vogue.com/article/heres-to-you-mrs-robinson-ten-questions-for-42s-nicole-beharie. Accessed 26 Apr. 2019.

McNamara, Mary. "Yes, TV May Seem to Hold the Higher Ground on Diversity. Until You Notice Who's Doing All the Dying." *Los Angeles Times*. 21 Apr. 2016, www.latimes.com/entertainment/tv/showtracker/la-et-st-critics-notebook-death-meets-diversity-20160420-column.html. Accessed 26 Apr. 2018.

Perkins, Nichole, "Why *Sleepy Hollow* Just Lost Any Faith Fans Had Left in It." *Vulture*. New York Media, 9 Apr. 2016, www.vulture.com/2016/04/sleepy-hollow-just-lost-any-faith-fans-had-left-in-it.html. Accessed 26 Apr. 2019.

SELECTED WORKS

American Violet, 2008; *Shame*, 2011; *Apartment 4E*, 2012; *The Last Fall*, 2012; *42*, 2013; *Sleepy Hollow*, 2013–6

—*Richard Means*

Cody Bellinger

Date of birth: July 13, 1995
Occupation: Baseball player

Since joining the Los Angeles Dodgers in 2017, Cody Bellinger has proven to be key the team's success, both defensively as a first baseman and as an outfielder, but also offensively. Over his first three seasons, he made a name for himself as a clutch-moment power hitter with a low strikeout rate and a high slugging percentage. Although he faced a hitting slump during the 2018 season, he retooled his swing to return to

Photo by Ian D'Andrea via Wikimedia Commons

the power-hitting form baseball fans saw during his rookie season.

A two-time National League (NL) All-Star (2017 and 2019), Bellinger became the only player since the 2000s to have a .400 batting average going into the fiftieth game of the season (in an era when batting averages hover around .250). He is also only one of a handful who had hit more than 30 home runs by the 2019 All-Star break in midseason. In the *Washington Post* (16 July 2019), Neil Greenberg declared: "Based on their ratio of home runs to plate appearances in the first half of the season and the estimated plate appearances remaining in 2019, Bellinger and Yelich each have at least an 88-percent chance of hitting 50 or more home runs this year."

EARLY LIFE

Cody James Bellinger was born on July 13, 1995, in Scottsdale, Arizona, and grew up in Chandler, Arizona. His father, Clay Bellinger, was a Major League Baseball (MLB) player—for the New York Yankees from 1999 to 2001 and the Anaheim Angels in 2002—before becoming a firefighter. Growing up, young Bellinger was a Yankees fan and loved baseball, just as his father had. "I always told him at the very beginning, 'Dude, you can be a superstar on the field,'" Clay Bellinger said to Jorge Castillo for the *Los Angeles Times* (9 July 2019). "But you can be one off the field too, just being good to people."

Bellinger began playing baseball as a child. In 2007, he played in the Little League World Series with his team in Chandler, hitting five home runs in the first game of the series. He

then played first base for Hamilton High School, where he was known for his solid hitting. He had a .429 batting average as a senior but hit just a single home run during his whole high school career. When his offensive and defensive play earned the notice of scouts from the American and National leagues, Bellinger began to hope that he might go right to the majors instead of going to college. "I didn't want to go to college," Bellinger told Tom Verducci for *Sports Illustrated* (27 May 2019). "I went to Oregon two days to visit. And they were two sunny days. But me in college was not something I really wanted to do." While Bellinger was accepted to the University of Oregon with the intent to play baseball for the college, he also kept one eye on the 2013 MLB draft.

MINOR LEAGUE PLAY

Bellinger followed the 2013 draft closely, hoping an MLB team would pick him up in the early rounds. When round after round went by, however, he began to think that he would have to go to college after all. He was eventually picked up by the Dodgers farm system, as the eighteenth pick of the fourth round. One hundred and twenty-three players had been selected before him.

After receiving $700,000 at signing, he reported to the rookie level Arizona League Dodgers. Although he struggled during his first season in the minor leagues, striking out 46 times in 47 games, he was promoted in 2014 to the Ogden Raptors in the Pioneer League. In 2015, he moved up to the Rancho Cucamonga Quakes, where he made the All-Star teams in both the regular season and the postseason. His hitting power began to reassert itself in 2015, when a minor league instructor named Shawn Wooton suggested he change his swing to develop a higher launch angle. The change helped him lead the Quakes to a California League championship title with 3 home runs, 7 runs batted in (RBI), and a .324 batting average. He was also named that year's California League championship series most valuable player (MVP).

After an invite to work with the Los Angeles Dodgers during the team's 2016 spring training, Bellinger was moved up to the Double-A Tulsa Drillers. His hitting so impressed the Dodgers' scouts that he was again promoted later that season to the Triple-A Oklahoma City Dodgers. In Oklahoma City, he got 6 hits in 11 at bats and smashed 3 home runs in three games. He then joined the Glendale Desert Dogs during the Arizona Fall League, where he was selected to the All-Star Prospect Team and started in the Rising Stars Game.

2017 ROOKIE OF THE YEAR

In 2017, the Dodgers again invited him to spring training as a non-roster player. But this time, the team's management believed the first baseman had what it took to play full-time in the majors. The Dodgers placed him in left field for his debut on April 25. He hit his first MLB home run on April 29 and his first grand slam on May 6. His playing so impressed the baseball world that he was named the National League Rookie of the Month in May and June.

By season's end, Bellinger had wowed Dodger fans with his stellar defense, both in the outfield and at first base, and with his incredible hitting. He ended his rookie season with a .267 batting average, 39 home runs, and 97 runs batted in (RBIs), in 132 games. For his efforts, Bellinger was named to the NL All-Star team and was awarded the 2017 NL Rookie of the Year. After finishing first in the NL West, the Dodgers ended the postseason losing to the Houston Astros in the 2017 World Series four games to three in the best-of-seven series. Bellinger appeared in all 15 of the postseason games the Dodgers played, knocking in 3 homers and 9 RBIs.

SOPHOMORE SLUMP

Despite appearing in nearly every game the Dodgers played in during the 2018 regular season, Bellinger struggled at the plate. A major issue was that he could not consistently hit against left-handed pitchers, batting just .226 against them. Throughout the season he struck out 151 times. "I don't know what happened," Clay explained to Castillo. "He just couldn't get out of it. He was swinging at a lot of bad pitches, and when you're swinging at bad pitches in this game at this level, it's hard, man. It's hard when you're swinging at good pitches."

Defensively, Bellinger played well, putting in appearances at first base and across the outfield. By August, however, the Dodgers management decided to platoon—a method of sharing a position with another player to create tactical advantages—Bellinger with other players so that he would no longer face left-handed pitchers. Bellinger, who wanted to be an everyday player who played in every inning of every game, was disappointed with the situation. Despite the split playing time, he continued to work hard, garnering a .260 batting average, 25 home runs, and 76 RBIs for the season.

Bellinger did have some shining moments in the Dodgers' postseason, where he appeared in all 16 games in which the team competed. His most impressive contributions during the postseason were a walk-off single in game four of the 2018 National League Championship Series (NLCS), and a two-run homer in game seven to help the Dodgers defeat the Milwaukee Brewers and win the National League pennant. At the end of the series, Bellinger was named the NL NLCS MVP. The Dodgers then lost the World Series to the Boston Red Sox four games to one. Bellinger's struggles against lefty pitchers continued into the World Series, so much so that Dodgers manager Dave Roberts benched him during innings in which he would have faced left-handed pitchers.

COMEBACK AND DOMINANCE

During the off-season, Bellinger, determined to improve his hitting, worked with the Dodgers' hitting coaches, Brant Brown and Robert Van Scoyoc. They began by changing his stance, returning it to his 2017 form with his bat parallel to the ground and relaxed. Entering the 2019 regular season, the changes he made in the off-season proved to be dramatic. "Just the fact that he's been so consistent with his mechanics and his approach, he hasn't changed a lot of that, and that's been the most impressive thing," fellow Dodgers All-Star Max Muncy said to Castillo. "Guys go through a lot of changes over the course of the season, and he hasn't done any of that. He's been able to keep everything the exact same, and I feel that that's his biggest reason for success this year."

Halfway through the season, sportswriters began suggesting that it was possible for Bellinger to hit 60 home runs in 2019, which would be the first time any major league player has hit that many homers since 2001. Although the feat would not break records, it would place Bellinger in an exclusive hitter's club. Many observers believed Bellinger could do it, including Roberts. "Yes, it's sustainable, as long as he trusts the process," Roberts told Verducci. "It's sustainable as long as he just keeps taking good at-bats and is not thinking about numbers. It's sustainable as long as he keeps taking his walks. It's sustainable as long as he continues to use the whole field. It's sustainable as long as he sticks with his approach, because right now he can cover anything."

During the All-Star break in July, in which Bellinger started for the first time, he was one of just three players who hit 30 or more home runs. The others were Christian Yelich of the Milwaukee Brewers and Pete Alonso of the New York Mets. In early August, he hit his 100th home run in the major leagues. After 122 games, he was batting a staggering .320, with 42 home runs and 100 RBIs.

SUGGESTED READING

Castillo, Jorge. "Cody Bellinger's Transformation Driven by Desire to Be an Everyday Player." *Los Angeles Times*, 9 July 2019, www.latimes. com/sports/dodgers/la-sp-cody-bellinger-all-star-mvp-candidate-dodgers-hit-lefthandedpitching-20190708-story.html. Accessed 17 July 2019.

"Cody Bellinger." *ESPN*, 2019, www.espn.com/mlb/player/_/id/33912/cody-bellinger. Accessed 17 July 2019.

"Cody Bellinger #35." *MLB*, 2019, www.mlb.com/player/cody-bellinger-641355. Accessed 17 July 2019.

Greenberg, Neil. "We Could See the First 60 Home-Run Season Since 2001." *The Washington Post*, 16 July 2019, www.washingtonpost.com/sports/2019/07/16/we-could-see-first-home-run-season-since/. Accessed 17 July 2019.

Mukherjee, Rahul. "How Cody Bellinger Found His Zone." *Los Angeles Times*, 25 June 2019, www.latimes.com/projects/la-sp-cody-bellinger-comfort-zone/. Accessed 17 July 2019.

Verducci, Tom. "Cody Bellinger Is Making Batting Average Cool Again." *Sports Illustrated*, 27 May 2019, www.si.com/mlb/2019/05/27/cody-bellinger-video-la-dodgers. Accessed 17 July 2019.

—*Christopher Mari*

Photo by Saeima via Wikimedia Commons

John Bercow

Date of birth: January 19, 1963
Occupation: Politician

A Member of Parliament (MP) for Buckingham, John Bercow became the Speaker of the House of Commons, a nonpartisan role, in 2009. He is the 157th person to perform the role—and the first Jewish speaker in the chamber's three hundred–year history. As William Booth and Karla Adam put it in the *Washington Post* (27 Jan. 2019), he is "the most theatrical, sharp-tongued and proactive speaker in modern time." Bercow is an unusual figure in British politics. He embraced radical right-wing politics as a teenager. Notoriously arrogant and combative, he won a seat in the House of Commons in 1997. In the early 2000s, however, his ideology began to shift. He began embracing LGBTQ rights—long before other members of his party—and a host of other social issues drastically at odds with the conservative views he once held. His political ambiguity helped him win the speakership in 2009. Traditionally, the speaker serves as a kind of referee, keeping order in the infamously rowdy chamber and controlling the speaking clock, but Bercow interprets the role far more broadly and has introduced reforms aimed at making Parliament more efficient and accessible to everyday people. He also became known for his regular haranguing of members. He has described members as "incorrigible delinquents," and chided them for their "sedentary chuntering" and "finger-wagging." Fans of Bercow see him as a bracing anecdote to the incomprehensible fustiness of the House of Commons; detractors describe him as pompous and self-aggrandizing.

Bercow's activist interpretation of the speaker's role took on a new and extraordinary meaning after Brexit, the British decision to withdraw from the European Union (EU), in 2016. In the political and governmental chaos following the vote, Bercow fought to protect the sovereignty of Parliament through the difficult process of withdrawal.

EARLY LIFE AND EDUCATION

John Bercow was born on January 19, 1963, in Edgeware, Middlesex, in England. He grew up in Finchley, in northwest London. His grandfather was a Romanian immigrant. His father was a cab driver who instilled in his son a love of language. Bercow was raised Jewish—his mother, Brenda, converted to Judaism—and attended Finchley Reform Synagogue. As a child, he was a rising tennis star, but asthma forced him to stop serious pursuit of the sport. Bercow also took an interest in politics at an early age. Growing up, he revered Margaret Thatcher, a former Finchley MP who served as Prime Minister in the 1980s, and Enoch Powell, a conservative MP. Powell was best known for his racist 1968 "Rivers of Blood" speech, in which he painted a lurid picture of a Britain besieged by nonwhite immigrants, and was an advocate of a policy known as repatriation, in which immigrants would voluntarily choose to return to their countries of origin.

Teenage Bercow was captivated by Powell's ideas and, at eighteen, joined the ultraright wing Conservative Monday Club. "Powell convinced me that it was right to fear large-scale immigration," Bercow recalled to Anne McElvoy for the *New Statesman* (13 Nov. 2000). "This was 1981, the year of the inner-city riots, and my fear was that we were in a politically explosive situation." He remained with the club for only a short time, explaining, "I stayed with the Monday Club on the immigration and repatriation committee for eighteen months, until it became clear that there were a lot of people at the meetings who were really unpleasant racists and so I left."

Bercow graduated from Finchley Manorhill comprehensive school and went on to earn a degree in government from the University of Essex in 1985. The same year, he was appointed national chair of the aggressive and confrontational Federation of Conservative Students (FCS). During Bercow's tenure, FCS made t-shirts bearing the slogan "Hang Nelson Mandela," a reference to the antiapartheid leader who later became president of South Africa. Bercow was the last chairman of the FCS; the group was disbanded by Tory chairman Norman Tebbit in 1986.

EARLY POLITICAL CAREER

In 1986, Bercow became a councillor in Lambeth in South London—a position he held until 1990—and soon became the youngest deputy leader of the Tory party on the council. He then ran unsuccessfully to represent both Motherwell South and Bristol South in Parliament, in 1987 and 1992, respectively. Meanwhile, throughout the late 1980s and early 1990s, Bercow also worked as a political lobbyist for Rowland Sallingbury Casey, a part of the ad agency Saatchi and Saatchi. Within five years, he became a board director. Already known as a skilled orator, Bercow ran speaking classes for Tory MPs beginning in the late 1980s. In 1992, he became a special advisor to Jonathan Aitken, the chief secretary to the Treasury. The same year, Aitken was forced to resign; he later served a jail sentence for perjury and perverting the course of justice. After Aitken's resignation, Bercow took a job with Virginia Bottomley, who was then the National Heritage Secretary. Bercow was elected to the House of Commons in Buckingham in 1997. He quickly made a name for himself as an "attack dog," Brian Wheeler wrote for *BBC News* (24 June 2009), and gained promotion to the Tory's front bench, effectively making him a more visible spokesperson for the party.

In 1999, Bercow's conservative views began to change. Bercow identified that the beginning of his ideological shift was caused by an issue regarding the age of consent for gay and lesbian people. Bercow initially voted that there should be a different age of consent for LGBTQ people, but after speaking with those who identify as LGBTQ, Bercow changed his mind. "I came to the conclusion that there was no reason for statutory discrimination and told the Commons I had changed my mind. I then started to reflect deeply on other issues," he recalled to the London *Independent* in 2004, as quoted by Wheeler. In 2001, Bercow supported the party's decision to sever ties with the racist Monday Club, of which Bercow was once a member. In 2002, Bercow resigned his position on the front bench after Tory MPs were ordered to vote to ban gay and unmarried couples from adopting children. Between 2003 and 2004, he served as shadow secretary of state for international development. In 2007, much to his party's consternation, Bercow accepted a role in Labour Prime Minister Gordon Brown's government, as an advisor to a government review of support for children with learning difficulties. Trying to sum up his shifting views in an interview with James Graham for *Prospect Magazine* (2 Mar. 2019), Bercow became emotional, saying: "What we've got is a lot of very affluent people doing very well but people at the bottom of the pile . . . they're desperately struggling, they're eking out an existence . . . and any serious party of government with an ounce of compassion should want to protect those people."

PARLIAMENTARY REFORMS

In 2005, Bercow joined an obscure committee called the Speaker's Panel, in which he chaired debates and committees. In 2009, Speaker of the House of Commons Michael Martin was forced to resign amidst the explosive parliamentary expenses scandal. The scandal revealed that a number of MPs were abusing their government expense accounts. The same year, Bercow won the election to replace Martin with the backing of many Labour MPs. His tenure, the longest of any speaker since World War II, has included many memorable feuds. He was openly critical of Prime Minister David Cameron, arguing that the privileged Cameron was out of touch with the concerns of ordinary people; and he effectively barred President Donald Trump from addressing Parliament in 2017, for reasons of "racism" and "sexism."

True to his vow to modernize the speaker's role, Bercow eschewed the traditional wig, knee breeches and silk stockings—describing the antiquarian uniform, as quoted by Ellen Barry for the *New York Times* (19 Jan. 2019), as a "barrier between Parliament and the public"—in favor of suits with colorful ties. In 2010, he survived a Tory attempt to oust him from his post. While speaker, Bercow won praise for a number of reforms aimed at making Parliament more accessible and more accountable to ordinary people.

He oversaw the development of a new educational center that allows for more people to visit Parliament and emphasizes outreach work. He is known to give backbencher MPs more speaking time than was previously custom and champions the urgent question system, which allows MPs to call specific ministers to the House of Commons to immediately address topical issues on behalf of the government. Between 2009 and 2014, Bercow granted 159 urgent questions; in the same span of time, his predecessor approved only 42. He won reelection in 2015 and 2017.

BREXIT

As Graham explained, the role of speaker "is to be the defender of Parliament, and preserve its sovereign role from attack—whether that be from the monarch, or the modern executive." In 2016, the United Kingdom voted to withdraw from the EU, engendering political and procedural upheaval in Britain. After three years of negotiations regarding just how to withdraw from the bloc, in January 2019, Bercow controversially selected an amendment forcing Prime Minister Theresa May to bring her Brexit deal—attempting to answer unresolved questions about trade relations and immigration among a myriad of other issues—before Parliament. His decision provoked visceral rage in the chamber. May's deal lost by a historic 230 votes, the largest margin of defeat in UK history. A second vote, in March, was also defeated but by a lesser margin. The week following that vote, Bercow invoked an obscure parliamentary rule from 1604 that bars the House of Commons from being asked to make a decision on the same question twice. In other words, Bercow refused to put the Brexit deal to a third vote unless the plan was different from the one that had already been rejected. The pro-Brexit faction accused him of political sabotage—in 2017, Bercow admitted to a group of students that he had voted to remain in the EU—but Bercow was firm in his position. "It's not the speaker's job to deliver Brexit or to seek to stop Brexit," he told Karla Adam for the *Washington Post* (29 May 2019). "It is the speaker's job to champion the rights of Parliament."

PERSONAL LIFE

Bercow married Sally (Illman) Bercow in 2002. She is a Labour activist and outspoken media personality who has appeared on reality television shows like *Celebrity Big Brother*. A spin-off show called *When Paddy Met Sally*, featuring Sally and fellow *Celebrity Big Brother* contestant and former bare-knuckle boxer Paddy Doherty, aired in 2012. Bercow and his wife have three children and a cat named Order. As is tradition, Bercow and his family live in an apartment at the Palace of Westminster.

SUGGESTED READING

Adam, Karla. "House Speaker John Bercow on Theresa May, Brexit and Why He Won't Leave—Yet." *The Washington Post*, 29 May 2019, www.washingtonpost.com/world/europe/british-speaker-john-bercow-on-theresa-may-brexit-and-why-hes-staying-on/2019/05/29/089fba8a-7e6d-11e9-b1f3-b233fe5811ef_story.html. Accessed 11 June 2019.

Barry, Ellen. "John Bercow, Shouting for 'Order' among Chaos, Is Brexit's Surprise Star and Villain." *The New York Times*, 19 Jan. 2019, www.nytimes.com/2019/01/19/world/europe/brexit-speaker-john-bercow.html. Accessed 15 June 2019.

Booth, William, and Karla Adam. "Order! Order! The Sharp-Tongued Speaker of the House of Commons Is Changing the Rules—and Maybe Brexit." *The Washington Post*, 27 Jan. 2019, www.washingtonpost.com/world/europe/order-order-the-sharp-tongued-speaker-of-the-house-of-commons-is-changing-the-rules--and-maybe-brexit/2019/01/27/ff0c18c4-1b61-11e9-b8e6-567190c2fd08_story.html. Accessed 11 June 2019.

Graham, James. "'I Shouldn't Really Be Saying This': John Bercow on Brexit, Backbenchers and Why Nobody Dreams of Being Speaker." *Prospect Magazine*, 2 Mar. 2019, www.prospectmagazine.co.uk/magazine/james-graham-john-bercow-brexit-backbenchers-speaker-profile. Accessed 15 June 2019.

McElvoy, Anne. "The *New Statesman* Interview—Tory Boy." *New Statesman*, 13 Nov. 2000, www.newstatesman.com/node/152347. Accessed 11 June 2019.

Wheeler, Brian. "The John Bercow Story." *BBC News*, 24 June 2009, news.bbc.co.uk/2/hi/uk_news/politics/8114399.stm. Accessed 15 June 2019.

—*Molly Hagan*

Daniel J. Bernstein

Date of birth: October 29, 1971
Occupation: Cryptologist and mathematician

In 1992, mathematics graduate student Daniel J. Bernstein encountered a roadblock he had not expected. A talented programmer deeply interested in cryptography and cryptology, Bernstein had developed an encryption algorithm that he named Snuffle, as well as a research paper on his program. Hoping to avoid any legal complications, he contacted the US State Department to confirm whether he would be legally able to post the source code to his work and the research

Photo by Alexander Klink via Wikimedia Commons

EARLY LIFE AND EDUCATION

Daniel Julius Bernstein was born on October 29, 1971, in East Patchogue, New York. He attended Bellport High School, a public school serving East Patchogue and other towns in Long Island's Suffolk County. Bernstein performed well academically in high school, graduating early in 1987. Following graduation, he attended New York University, graduating in 1991 with a bachelor's degree in mathematics. He went on to pursue graduate studies in the Department of Mathematics at the University of California, Berkeley. There, he completed research into computational number theory under Dutch mathematician Hendrik Lenstra, and finished his dissertation, titled "Detecting Perfect Powers in Essentially Linear Time, and Other Studies in Computational Number Theory," in 1995. While still a graduate student, he began his career as a consultant and also worked on his own programming projects, most notably the encryption algorithm Snuffle.

ACADEMIC CAREER

After completing his PhD, Bernstein accepted the position of research assistant professor at the University of Illinois at Chicago, joining the university's Department of Mathematics, Statistics, and Computer Science in the College of Liberal Arts and Sciences. He was promoted to assistant professor in 1998, associate professor in 2001, and full professor in 2005. In 2003, Bernstein also began teaching in the Department of Computer Science in the College of Engineering, moving there permanently in 2008 when he was made a research professor. Beginning in 2012, he held a part-time professorship at the Technische Universiteit Eindhoven in the Netherlands.

In addition to his primary academic positions, Bernstein served as a visiting scholar at the University of Sydney in 2004 and visiting professor at the Danmarks Tekniske Universitet (Technical University of Denmark) in 2006. The year 2006 also saw him serve as senior scientific researcher in the Thematic Program on Cryptography at Canada's Fields Institute. Alongside his teaching positions, Bernstein served as principal investigator for National Science Foundation (NSF) on projects dealing with topics such as number theory and cryptography, as well as projects funded by the Cisco University Research Program and the National Institute of Standards and Technology (NIST), among others. Between 2002 and 2006, he was a research fellow of the Alfred P. Sloan Foundation. Bernstein at times struggled with what he described as issues of mismanagement regarding the grant funding he received, many of which he documented on his personal website.

paper online. The government responded that under the International Traffic in Arms Regulations (ITAR), the code for encryption tools were considered munitions, and Bernstein would have to register as an arms dealer and obtain an export license to post his work on the internationally accessible Internet. After several years of further communications with the US government, Bernstein ultimately filed a lawsuit in 1995 with the goal of changing the federal policy on encryption programs. "Cryptography is a powerful crime-fighting tool," he explained to Peter Cassidy for *Wired* (1 June 1996). "This is not a case of needing more laws. This is a case of needing more technology." After a lengthy legal battle, the US Ninth Circuit Court of Appeals ruled the US government's regulation of encryption software unconstitutional, determining that work such as Bernstein's qualified as speech and was thus protected by the First Amendment to the US Constitution.

In addition to his court case, Bernstein became widely known as a major researcher and programmer in the field of cryptography. Having completed his doctorate in 1995, he went on to begin a long career with the University of Illinois at Chicago, where he became a full professor in 2005. He was also affiliated for a time with the Netherlands' Eindhoven University of Technology (Technische Universiteit Eindhoven), where he began a part-time professorship in 2012. The author of numerous research papers and an editor of the 2009 book *Post-Quantum Cryptography*, Bernstein is also known for creating qmail, djbdns, and a variety of other tools designed to improve internet security for their users.

BERNSTEIN V. US DEPARTMENT OF JUSTICE

While a graduate student at Berkeley, Bernstein wrote an encryption program that he called Snuffle, which made use of the mathematical concept known as hash functions. Seeking to publish the code for his program and a set of instructions online and receive feedback from other members of the cryptography community, he contacted the US State Department in 1992 to determine whether he would be allowed to do so. Based on regulations such as ITAR, however, the US government informed Bernstein that the code for his encryption program was considered a form of munition. To publish his work online, where it might be accessed by individuals living outside of the United States, he would need to register as an arms dealer and apply for an export license. The government also indicated that he would be unable to obtain a license due to the nature of his program.

For Bernstein, the US government's policy of treating source code as munitions seemed counterintuitive. "What gets me worked up here is plain old crime," he told Cassidy. "I still remember the first computer intruder I ran into. How disgusted I was at finding out that he had been rifling through my files; how much time I spent trying to figure out if he had destroyed anything. In the years since, I've spent a lot of time thinking about how to stop these criminals. By now, I feel I can really help people protect themselves, but the State Department says I can't share my advice. That's totally disgusting." Believing that the government's policy violated his First Amendment right to freedom of speech, Bernstein partnered with the Electronic Frontier Foundation to sue the US government over the issue in 1995. In the ensuing court case, *Bernstein v. US Department of Justice*, Judge Marilyn Hall Patel ruled that software source code could be considered speech and that the government's attempts to block Bernstein from sharing his work online were unconstitutional. The Ninth Circuit Court of Appeals upheld that ruling in 1999, and Bernstein continued to challenge the federal government's stance on encryption programs over the subsequent years.

QMAIL

A skilled programmer as well as a researcher and teacher, Bernstein became known for a number of key projects, the results of which he made freely available online. One of the most significant of those was qmail, a mail transfer agent (MTA) that he began to work on in the mid-1990s after identifying issues in the security of popular MTAs used by internet service providers (ISPs) during that period. An MTA is a type of software that transmits email from the sender's computer to the recipient's computer. Security holes in popular MTAs such as Sendmail particularly concerned Bernstein, as they made computers vulnerable to malicious attacks.

Bernstein's work on qmail began in earnest late in 1995. "I had just finished teaching a course on algebraic number theory and found myself with some spare time," he wrote in his paper "Some Thoughts on Security after Ten Years of qmail 1.0" (2007), which summarized the history of the project. "The final kick to get something done was a promise I had made to a colleague: namely, that I would run a large mailing list for him." Bernstein began a beta test for qmail in January of 1996 and released qmail 1.00 in February of the following year. The program's June 1998 release, qmail 1.03, remained the definitive version for the next decade. Bernstein's new MTA proved popular among users and multiple large companies during the years following its release, among them Yahoo! and the ISP NetZero. Confident in his creation's high level of security, Bernstein offered a $500 reward to the first person to find and document a security hole in his program. He increased the reward to $1,000 in 2007 after no security holes were found.

DJBDNS

Bernstein also received extensive attention for his work on djbdns, a group of software elements designed to be a more secure alternative to the prevailing Domain Name System (DNS) servers. As was the case with qmail, the software was created in response to security vulnerabilities within popular options available to internet users. Bernstein also reportedly objected to the manner in which DNS server software such as BIND was written. By 1999, he began writing his own alternative, djbdns, which he released in an alpha version late that year. Another incarnation of the software, djbdns 1.05, was released in early 2001. Bernstein later placed his software in the public domain to encourage the free use and distribution of his work.

As with qmail, Bernstein announced that he would pay a reward to the first person to find a vulnerability in his djbdns. In 2009, an information security professional named Matthew Dempsky successfully identified and patched the first known security hole in djbdns. In response to that discovery, Bernstein acknowledged the bug and agreed to pay the promised reward. "Even though this bug affects very few users, it is a violation of the expected security policy in a reasonable situation, so it is a security hole in djbdns," he wrote to the djbdns mailing list, as reported by Ryan Naraine for *ZDNet* (6 Mar. 2009). "Third-party DNS service is discouraged in the djbdns documentation but is nevertheless supported. Dempsky is hereby awarded $1000."

OTHER WORK

Over the course of his career, Bernstein established himself as an expert in internet security and a major figure in cryptography and related fields. In addition to qmail and djbdns, he created a variety of other security-related tools, including daemontools, programs used to manage services with the UNIX operating system, and the Salsa20 and ChaCha families of ciphers, used for encrypting data. For Bernstein, the need to continually innovate in security and encryption remains constant due to both the increasingly connected nature of the world and invasions of personal privacy by both governments and corporations. "My views of security have become increasingly ruthless over the years," he explained in "Some Thoughts on Security." "I see a huge amount of money and effort being invested in security, and I have become convinced that most of that money and effort is being wasted. Most 'security' efforts are designed to stop yesterday's attacks but fail completely to stop tomorrow's attacks and are of no use in building invulnerable software. These efforts are a distraction from work that *does* have long-term value."

Alongside his teaching and programming work, Bernstein is a prolific public speaker and delivered more than 450 lectures between 1987 and 2019. Although his interests are wide ranging, he focused particularly on post-quantum cryptography during the second decade of the twenty-first century. The term *post-quantum cryptography* refers to forms of cryptography designed to withstand attacks by a quantum computer, a proposed computer that many cryptography experts believe would be able to break some of the encryption algorithms in common use on the twenty-first-century Internet. In addition to delivering numerous talks on the subject, Bernstein edited the 2009 book *Post-Quantum Cryptography* with fellow cryptography experts Johannes Buchmann and Erik Dahmen. Bernstein has published widely in major journals, in the proceedings of numerous conferences, and on his own website. A proponent of making research papers available to a wide audience, including individuals without access to costly print journals and databases, Bernstein typically posts copies of his papers online and urges other researchers to avoid publishing with journals or publishers that prohibit researchers from doing so.

SUGGESTED READING

Bernstein, Daniel J. *D. J. Bernstein*, cr.yp.to/djb.html. Accessed 18 Jan. 2019.

Bernstein, Daniel J. "Some Thoughts on Security after Ten Years of Qmail 1.0." *cr.yp.to*, 2007, cr.yp.to/qmail/qmailsec-20071101.pdf. Accessed 18 Jan. 2019.

"Bernstein v. United States Department of Justice." *FindLaw*, 6 May 1999, caselaw.findlaw.com/us-9th-circuit/1317290.html. Accessed 18 Jan. 2019.

Cassidy, Peter. "Reluctant Hero." *Wired*, 1 June 1996, www.wired.com/1996/06/esbernstein. Accessed 18 Jan. 2019.

King, Brad. "Professor's Case: Unlock Crypto." *Wired*, 19 Oct. 2002, www.wired.com/2002/10/professors-case-unlock-crypto. Accessed 18 Jan. 2019.

Naraine, Ryan. "Dan Bernstein Confirms DJBDNS Security Hole, Pays $1,000." *ZDNet*, 6 Mar. 2009, www.zdnet.com/article/dan-bernstein-confirms-djbdns-security-hole-pays-1000. Accessed 18 Jan. 2019.

Wright, Cory. "djbdns: More Than Just a Mouthful of Consonants." *Linux Journal*, Sept. 2008, nnc3.com/mags/LJ_1994-2014/LJ/173/10112.html. Accessed 18 Jan. 2019.

—*Joy Crelin*

Alia Bhatt

Date of birth: March 15, 1993
Occupation: Actor and singer

In 2019, Alia Bhatt was one of the highest-paid actors in Bollywood. She has starred in hits such as the rap musical *Gully Boy* (2019), about a rapper from the Mumbai slums, and *Raazi* (2018), a thriller in which Bhatt plays an Indian spy tasked with marrying behind enemy lines during the Indo-Pakistan War. By that time, she had won three Filmfare Awards, the Bollywood equivalent of an Academy Award. Though Bhatt has been acting in Bollywood films for less than a decade, her familial history is deeply entwined with the history of Hindi cinema. Her filmmaker father, Mahesh Bhatt, rose to prominence in the 1980s with films such as *Arth* (1982; Meaning) and *Saaransh* (1984; The Gist), and her paternal grandfather, director and producer Nanabhai Bhatt, was a Bollywood pioneer with a career spanning four decades. But since her official film debut in the teen romantic comedy *Student of the Year* in 2012, Bhatt has established herself as an artist in her own right. In an interview with Serena Chaudhry for *Reuters* (7 July 2016), Bhatt said she admired Academy Award–winning American actor Jennifer Lawrence. "Jennifer Lawrence is somebody I really look up to because I really like the kind of choices she makes," Bhatt said, noting that Lawrence has appeared in everything from high-budget action blockbusters to independent romantic comedies. Bhatt has been notable for similar choices, showcasing her versatility as a comedian and a dramatic artist. In

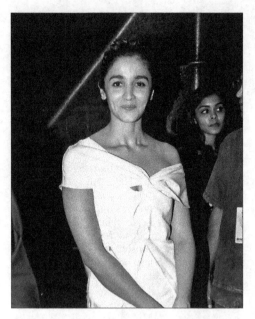

Photo by Bollywood Hungama via Wikimedia Commons

the same interview, Bhatt expressed an interest in working in Hollywood—but also Lollywood (Pakistan), Tollywood (Telugu-language Indian cinema), and Nollywood (Nigeria). Her decision to launch a YouTube channel, a charming chronicle of her daily life, in June 2019 might be a bid to find a larger international audience.

EARLY LIFE AND FAMOUS FAMILY

Alia Bhatt was born in Mumbai on March 15, 1993. Her father, Mahesh Bhatt, is a renowned filmmaker and producer of Hindi films. He is best known for classic films such as the semi-autobiographical *Arth*, about a film director who has an affair with a star performer; *Saaransh*, about a Bollywood starlet's disastrous relationship with the son of a local politician; and *Sadak* (1991; Road), in which a taxi driver attempts to rescue the prostitute he loves from her pimp, who forbids romantic attachments. Mahesh was better known for his womanizing and alcoholism, however, until he quit drinking in 1988. Her mother, Soni Razdan, is an English-born actor and film director. Bhatt has two half-siblings from her father's first marriage, Pooja and Rahul, and an older sister, Shaheen. Pooja became an actor and director, while Rahul became a fitness trainer and appeared in a season of the Hindi version of the reality show *Big Brother*. Shaheen, a screenwriter, published a memoir about growing up with famous parents and her struggles with depression, *I've Never Been (Un)happier*, in 2018. In an excerpt of the book published in the *Indian Express* (8 May 2019), Shaheen wrote of Alia, "She was disturbingly cute as a child, and even then she had an effortless knack of drawing people to her."

The sisters grew up in suburban Mumbai, where they enjoyed an upper-middle-class upbringing, Shaheen Bhatt wrote. "Contrary to what people believe, film directors in the '90s didn't exactly break the bank, and even if they did, my father—thanks to his own special brand of masochism—was supporting not one but two families, so while life was always comfortable, it was never lavish." The Bhatt sisters' relationship to their father developed over time. "For me, he was always like a celebrity who would walk in to the house," Alia Bhatt told *India Today* (19 Feb. 2019). "I didn't miss him as such because I did not really have him. But after a couple of years, he made sure he spent some time with us, played board games."

EARLY CAREER

Bhatt made her acting debut when she was just six years old, playing the younger version of actor Preity Zinta's character in the 1999 thriller *Sangharsh* (Struggle). The plot of the film is loosely based on the Academy Award–winning 1991 film *The Silence of the Lambs*, with Zinta playing the role of the rookie investigator. Bhatt graduated from the private Jamnabai Narsee School in Mumbai and planned to study drama in college. Instead, she was cast in a teen film called *Student of the Year* (2012) alongside Siddharth Malhotra and Varun Dhawan, the son of Bollywood director, David Dhawan. *Student of the Year* was a huge hit with audiences, despite its lack of known stars, and scored generally positive reviews from critics. Vinayak Chakravorty, in a review for *India Today* (19 Oct. 2012), described the trio as "a treat to watch" and the "primary reasons why you'll love this film." Bhatt made a cameo appearance in the film's 2019 sequel.

Student of the Year launched Bhatt's career, but her second film, a drama called *Highway* (2014), gave fans a taste of her range as an actor. In the film, written and directed by Imtiaz Ali, Bhatt plays a woman named Veera, who is engaged but feels stifled by the prospect of marriage. Before her wedding, she is kidnapped, and as the movie progresses, begins to fall in love with one of her captors, Mahabir (Randeep Hooda). Rachel Saltz, writing for the *New York Times* (20 Feb. 2014), was critical of the film—the tagline is "In bondage, she found freedom"—for its inability to balance its romantic ambitions and its dark subject matter. Still, she praised Bhatt's performance, writing: "Bhatt has an openness and emotional transparency that help make her character something more than a screenwriter's bad idea." Bhatt's performance earned her a special critic's award at the Filmfare Awards, Bollywood's equivalent to the Academy Awards.

UDTA PUNJAB AND DEAR ZINDAGI

Bhatt appeared in several more films in 2014, including a romantic comedy called *2 States*. In that film, Bhatt plays Ananya, a Tamil woman from southern India, who falls in love with Krish (Arjun Kapoor), a Punjabi man from northern India. Ananya and Krish must convince their parents to overcome their prejudice and support the union. The film, based on a 2009 novel of the same name by Chetan Bhagat, received mixed reviews. Saltz, for the *New York Times* (20 Apr. 2014), argued that the script gave the actors little room for characterization, while a reviewer for the *Times of India* wrote that the film would "charm and surprise" audiences looking for light fare.

The same year, Bhatt teamed up with *Student of the Year* costar Dhawan again in a romantic comedy called *Humpty Sharma Ki Dulhania*. In it, Bhatt's character meets Dhawan's character while shopping in Delhi for a wedding dress. Bhatt, who is also a singer—"Acting's my husband and singing is my boyfriend," she told Chaudhry—sings the song "Samjhawan" on the film's soundtrack. The film performed well with audiences; Bhatt and Dhawan starred in a sequel, involving different characters, called *Badrinath Ki Dulhania* in 2017. Saltz, in another *New York Times* review (12 Mar. 2017), was wary of that film's simplistic moral—men should respect women—but again praised Bhatt, writing that the actor gives the movie its "pop." Bhatt, she wrote, never falls into "the clichés of spunky Bollywood heroine."

Bhatt next starred in *Shaandaar*, a romantic comedy and an unexpected box office bomb, in 2015. In 2016, she appeared in the family drama *Kapoor & Sons* and the critically acclaimed crime drama *Udta Punjab*, for which she won another Filmfare Award. The film explores flourishing drug abuse in the Punjab region of India. In her review of *Udta Punjab* for the *Hindu* (17 June 2016), Namrata Joshi described Bhatt's performance in the role of Pinky, an abused migrant worker, as "utterly real, raw and vulnerable." The same year, Bhatt starred in another critically acclaimed film, *Dear Zindagi*. Written and directed by up-and-coming female director Gauri Shinde, *Dear Zindagi* features Bhatt as a cinematographer named Kaira who embarks on a journey of self-discovery with a psychologist named Jug (Jehangir Khan). Andy Webster, for the *New York Times* (25 Nov. 2016), named the film a critic's pick, describing it as a "resounding victory." Bhatt, he wrote, "benefits from Shinde's guidance, transcending her starlet status in a bitter tirade against Kaira's parents and a tearful confession to Jug." Bhatt was nominated for a Filmfare Award for Best Actress for the film, but beat herself, winning for *Udta Punjab* instead.

RAAZI AND GULLY BOY

In 2018, Bhatt earned her third Filmfare Award for her role in the historical thriller *Raazi*, set during the Indo-Pakistani War of 1971. Bhatt plays Sehmat, an Indian spy who marries a Pakistani man (Vicky Kaushal). The film is based on the 2008 novel *Calling Sehmat*, which was inspired by a true story. Rohit Vats, for the *Hindustan Times* (12 May 2018), praised the subtlety of the film as well as Bhatt's performance. "*Raazi* marks another step in the right direction for Alia. It required her to be restrained and mature, and she simply grabbed the opportunity with both hands." Other critics noted the film, and the nuance it required of its lead, as a turning point in Bhatt's career. *Raazi* was one of the top-grossing films in India in 2018. In 2019, Bhatt starred alongside Ranveer Singh in a rap musical about a rapper from Mumbai, *Gully Boy*. Singh plays Murad, a college student living in the Mumbai slums. (Gully means "street," and "Gully Boy" becomes his rap name.) Bhatt plays Murad's witty, higher-caste girlfriend, a medical student who must hide their relationship from her conservative family. The story is based on the true tales of Mumbai rappers Divine and Naezy. Jay Weissberg, for *Variety* (10 Feb. 2019), praised the film, though he was critical of a few plotting choices. "One of the joys of 'Gully Boy' is reveling in the chemistry between Singh and Bhatt, perfectly paired: Her ironic smile meets his open-faced grin and the screen lights up," he wrote.

Also in 2019, Bhatt starred in *Kalank*, a melodrama set in 1945, just before the partition of India.

SUGGESTED READING

"Alia Reveals Mahesh Bhatt Was Absent During Her Childhood: Friendship Started When I Entered Films." *India Today*, 19 Feb. 2019, www.indiatoday.in/movies/celebrities/story/alia-reveals-mahesh-bhatt-was-absent-during-her-childhood-friendship-started-when-i-entered-films-1459517-2019-02-19. Accessed 14 July 2019.

Bhatt, Shaheen. "Shaheen Bhatt: 'I Thrived on Being the Centre of Attention, Till Alia Was Born.'" *Indian Express*, 8 May 2019, indianexpress.com/article/parenting/health-fitness/shaheen-bhatt-i-thrived-on-being-the-centre-of-attention-till-alia-bhatt-was-born-5714817/. Accessed 14 July 2019.

Chakravorty, Vinayak. Review of *Student of the Year*, directed by Karan Johar. *India Today*, 19 Oct. 2012, www.indiatoday.in/movies/reviews/story/student-of-the-year-movie-review-119151-2012-10-19. Accessed 14 July 2019.

Chaudhry, Serena. "Bollywood Actress Alia Bhatt Sets Her Sights on Hollywood." *Reuters*,

1 July 2016, www.reuters.com/article/us-in-dia-bollywood-alia-bhatt/bollywood-actress-alia-bhatt-sets-her-sights-on-hollywood-idUSKCN0ZN1UW. Accessed 14 July 2019.

Joshi, Namrata. "Choppy, but a Wholly Worth-while Flight." Review of *Udta Punjab*, direct-ed by Abhishek Chaubey. *The Hindu*, 17 June 2016, www.thehindu.com/news/national/telangana/Choppy-but-a-wholly-worthwhile-flight/article14428736.ece. Accessed 14 July 2019.

Saltz, Rachel. "Celebrating Bondage over Bonds of Marriage." Review of *Highway*, directed by Imtiaz Ali. *The New York Times*, 20 Feb. 2014, www.nytimes.com/2014/02/21/movies/in-highway-a-bride-falls-for-her-kidnapper.html. Accessed 14 July 2019.

Vats, Rohit. "Raazi Movie Review: Alia Bhatt's Vulnerable Indian Spy Is Spotless and Super-lative." Review of *Raazi*, directed by Meghna Gulzar. *Hindustan Times*, 12 May 2018, www.hindustantimes.com/movie-reviews/raazi-movie-review-alia-bhatt-s-vulnerable-indian-spy-is-spotless-and-superlative/story-MVc-n1wyCuXb14FBwwdUn5K.html. Accessed 14 July 2019.

SELECTED WORKS

Student of the Year, 2012; Udta Punjab, 2016; Dear Zindagi, 2016; Raazi, 2018; Gully Boy, 2019

—Molly Hagan

Tyler "Ninja" Blevins

Date of birth: June 5, 1991
Occupation: Online personality

Tyler Blevins, known as Ninja to his fans, is a professional gamer. Blevins reached mainstream celebrity in March 2018 after rap superstar Drake joined him for a round of *Fortnite* on the Amazon streaming platform, Twitch. The stream had a record-breaking audience of 628,000 con-current viewers. It was a huge breakthrough for Blevins's career, but also a good illustration of his unique skill set. He is a formidable gamer, but more importantly, after years of streaming, he knows how to draw an audience. Blevins also exhibited unusual foresight about the popularity of *Fortnite*. He began his Esports career play-ing *Halo*, an extraordinarily popular first-person shooter game. (His gaming name, Ninja, comes from a move in *Halo*.) He moved on to other games, including *H1Z1* and *PlayerUnknown's Battlegrounds* (*PUBG*), but decided to go all-in on *Fortnite* in December 2017. *Fortnite*, a third-person shooter game, was released in September 2017. Its most rudimentary version is available

Photo by Robert Reiners/Getty Images

for free, and its battle royale concept is simple: one hundred avatars are dropped onto an is-land, and the last one standing wins. *Fortnite* is more cartoonish than the gory *Halo*, and avatars, called "skins" and assigned randomly in the free version, are various races and genders. Nick Paumgarten, writing for the *New Yorker* (21 May 2018), speculated that the game's "relative lack of wickedness . . . makes it more palatable to a broader audience." Regardless whether this is the case, within six months, *Fortnite* became the most popular video game in the world. It could be argued that Blevins, who tirelessly promoted his streams of the game through the winter of 2017–18, was instrumental to its rise.

Justin Charity summed up Blevins cultural significance, writing in the *Ringer* (10 Dec. 2018), "The games-streaming culture isn't new, but Ninja's prominence marks a new tier of professionalization." He is, for instance, the first professional gamer to appear on the cover of *ESPN* magazine. Recognizable for his ever-changing, candy-colored hair, Blevins streams ten to fourteen hours each day. He punctuates his play with silly banter, movie quotes, and celebrity impressions. But he has also stirred controversy. In March 2018, just weeks after his stream with Drake, Blevins caused an out-cry when he substituted a racial slur for a lyric while rapping along to "44 More" by Logic dur-ing another stream. Blevins apologized for what he characterized as a misunderstanding and the accidental use of the n-word while ad-libbing.

EARLY LIFE AND EDUCATION

Richard Tyler Blevins was born in Taylor, Michi-gan, near Detroit, on June 5, 1991. His family, including his two older brothers, Jonathan and Chris, moved to Illinois when Blevins was one. His father, Chuck, was an avid Sega player, whereas his mother, Cynthia, was skeptical of video games. She told her sons that they had to spend an hour outside for every hour they spent gaming. Blevins's early favorites included *Earthworm Jim* and *Ratchet & Clank*. He played midfield on the soccer team at Grayslake Central High School and continued to display an uncanny talent for video games. "He would drop his controller, then he'd still win," Jonathan recalled to Elaine Teng for *ESPN* magazine (18 Sept. 2018). He convinced his parents to let him go to his first gaming tournament in Columbus, Ohio, when he was seventeen.

Blevins graduated from high school in 2009 and enrolled at Silver Lake College, a Catholic liberal arts school in Wisconsin. He transferred to a community college after his first year and began working at the fast-food restaurant Noodles & Company.

EARLY CAREER

Blevins continued to play in *Halo* 3 tournaments and, according to the gaming news site *Dexerto*, began to make a name for himself in the larger gaming world in early 2010. Later that year, after the release of *Halo: Reach*, Blevins began to hit his stride. "Throughout the entirety of the *Reach* era Ninja never placed outside the top 16 at a major event," Mike Stubbs wrote for *Dexerto* (2 Apr. 2018). He teamed with professional gamers such as Michael "StrongSide" Cavanaugh and Dave "Walshy" Walsh.

In 2011, Blevins began streaming his play on Twitch, the year the platform was released. He created a new *YouTube* channel the same year, after managing to delete his earlier one. Blevins's early streams garnered few viewers, mostly family and friends, but over time, he learned how to draw a crowd. "Anything competitive is always going to get you more viewers," he told John Keilman for the *Chicago Tribune* (2 Aug. 2018). "When there's something on the line, it's just more exciting to watch. [One-on-one matches] in *Halo: Reach* were kind of my bread and butter." Once he began to earn a comfortable income from streaming, he quit both his studies and his job at Noodles & Company.

With the introduction of *Halo* 4 in 2012, Blevins was poised to become one of the most successful *Halo* players ever. Stubbs wrote that Blevins finished within the top four at every major event during the game's competitive era. But within a year, support for the game diminished. Blevins tried his hand at other games like *Call of Duty* but decided to focus on streaming, at the expense of tournament play.

In 2014, Blevins underwent surgery to fix a detached retina in his right eye and missed out on about a month of streaming during his recovery. The time lost was a tough blow to Blevins, who earns money for every hour spent streaming. Lost hours meant lost subscribers and lost revenue. By the time he returned, the release of *Halo: The Master Chief Collection*, had, in Stubbs's words, "breathed some life into the pro *Halo* scene." Blevins joined a top-level team, and the audience for his streams grew.

By 2015, Blevins had begun dabbling in an apocalyptic battle royale game called *H1Z1*. He took first place in the game in a 2015 invitational at TwitchCon, earning $20,000. For the next two years, he continued to divide his time between streaming *H1Z1* and playing pro *Halo*.

FORTNITE

In 2017, Blevins began playing the newly launched *PUBG*. In July, he retired from pro *Halo* to focus on streaming full-time. Still, later that year, he played at the Gamescom PUBG Invitational, taking first place in the squad's competition. Despite his success, his streaming numbers did not meet those of other pro *PUBG* players.

In December, Blevins decided to take a calculated risk on a new game called *Fortnite*. "I saw all the top streamers, every single one of them, which was at the time Doc, Summit, Shroud, JoshOG, all these guys, kinda like ripping into it a little bit," Blevins said on *Dexerto Talk Show*, as quoted by Stubbs. "Cartoony, not for me, I'm not gonna play it. Then I'm like this is it. I play the game for two days, and I was like this is fun, this is incredible, I can do crazy sh——t in this game and it can bring out the best of my personality. I stuck with it, I think I lost like 1,500 subscribers in like three weeks from switching from *PUBG* to *Fortnite*." Of his thinking at the time, he added, "I'm going to jump on it. I was late to *H1Z1* a little bit, I was super late to *PUBG*, I was like this ain't happening man, I was like I have an audience, I can do this." By the end of the year, Blevins was among both the top *Fortnite* players and the top streamers on Twitch.

"Ninja dominates *Fortnite* with a superstar athlete's strength and reflexes," Charity wrote. "He's quick, deliberate, and lethal; he's very good, and it can be gratifying to watch Ninja dominate a *Fortnite* match." Blevins also has a penchant for showy moves. Smart moves might reward you as a player, he told Kevin Draper and Jonah Engel Bromwich for the *New York Times* (18 Dec. 2018), but Blevins has other things to worry about. It might be strategically advantageous to book it for a safe zone, he said, but "as a flashy player, a streamer, I'm going to go for the kill every time."

By March 2018, Blevins had amassed a large enough following to attract rapper Drake into his orbit. Drake tweeted out a link to their live stream, breaking a Twitch record for concurrent viewers on the platform. Though Blevins was already popular among gamers, the spontaneous collaboration made him a mainstream celebrity. Blevins has since played with a host of other celebrities including football star JuJu Smith-Schuster and rapper Travis Scott. He was invited to the 2018 ESPY Awards, where he played *Fortnite* with NBA players Kevin Knox and Mario Hezonja and tennis player Taylor Fritz. At the year's end, Blevins, with sponsor Red Bull, hosted a twelve-hour *Fortnite* live-stream from Times Square on New Year's Eve.

BRANCHING OUT

Blevins's wife, Jessica "Jess" Blevins, a streamer who goes by the name JGhosty, is also his manager. Early on, she doggedly contacted companies pitching partnerships with Blevins. "Now it has really done a 180, because it's endless amounts of companies reaching out to *us* to work with Tyler," she told Dave Smith for *Business Insider* (16 Aug. 2018). In December 2018, Blevins released an album of electronic dance music that he curated, called *Ninjawerks Vol. 1*. In fall 2019, the Wicked Cool Toys company is set to release a series of Ninja-inspired toys. "We want him known in Hollywood. We want him known in the world of sports," Jess told Smith. "We want him as a household name, so we're trying to move him from just gaming to everywhere."

Blevins, in 2018, made an estimated $500,000-plus per month from his portion of Twitch subscription fees alone. (Watching Blevins is free, but viewers can subscribe to Blevins's channel, for extra perks, for $5 a month.) That figure does not include Blevins's income from his 20-million-subscriber-strong *YouTube* channel; sponsorships, including Red Bull, Uber Eats, and Samsung; or the money he receives from running ads on his channel.

PERSONAL LIFE

Blevins first met Jess at a *Halo* tournament in 2010. She messaged him on *Twitter* three years later, kick-starting their romance. They were married in August 2017, and their week-long honeymoon was Blevins's first vacation in eight years. The couple lives with their two Yorkshire terriers in a gated community outside of Chicago.

SUGGESTED READING

Charity, Justin. "From His Iron Gaming Chair, Ninja Rules the 'Fortnite' Generation." *The Ringer*, 10 Dec. 2018, www.theringer.com/2018/12/10/18133493/ninja-fortnite-gaming-2018-streaming. Accessed 16 Feb. 2019.

Draper, Kevin, and Jonah Engel Bromwich. "Ninja Would Like to Get Some More Sleep." *The New York Times*, 18 Dec. 2018, www.nytimes.com/2018/12/18/sports. Accessed 16 Feb. 2019.

Keilman, John. "He's Got Celebrity Pals, Millions of Fans and (Probably) Millions of Dollars: Meet Ninja, Chicago's *Fortnite* Superstar." *Chicago Tribune*, 2 Aug. 2018, www.chicagotribune.com/news/ct-met-ninja-fortnite-video-games-20180801-story.html. Accessed 16 Feb. 2019.

Paumgarten, Nick. "How Fortnite Captured Teens' Hearts and Minds." *The New Yorker*, 21 May 2018, www.newyorker.com/magazine/2018/05/21/how-fortnite-captured-teens-hearts-and-minds. Accessed 16 Feb. 2019.

Smith, Dave. "Meet Jessica Blevins, the 26-Year-Old Wife and Manager of the Most Popular Video-Game Player in the World Right Now." *Business Insider*, 16 Aug. 2018, www.businessinsider.com/jessica-blevins-tyler-ninja-interview-2018-8. Accessed 16 Feb. 2019.

Stubbs, Mike. "How Ninja Went from *Halo* Pro to the World's Biggest Twitch Streamer Playing *Fortnite*." *Dexerto*, 2 Apr. 2018, www.dexerto.com/news/ninjas-incredible-rise-from-halo-pro-to-the-biggest-twitch-streamer-in-the-world/47364. Accessed 16 Feb. 2019.

Teng, Elaine. "Living the Stream." *ESPN*, 18 Sept. 2018, www.espn.com/espn/feature/story/_/id/24710688/fortnite-legend-ninja-living-stream. Accessed 16 Feb. 2019.

—*Molly Hagan*

Christian Borle

Date of birth: October 1, 1973
Occupation: Theater actor

Widely regarded as one of the most talented stage performers of his generation, Christian Borle captivated audiences, critics, and peers alike with his effortless range and versatility, which allowed him to transition seamlessly from one role to another in a multitude of theatrical genres. Known for his extravagant acting style, Borle appeared in Broadway and Off-Broadway productions and won admiration for his onstage inventiveness and unflinching dedication to his craft. As Alexis Soloski wrote for the *New York Times* (5 Oct. 2016), "There's discipline in his work, but also something less predictable, an impetuous electrical current that powers his performances."

Photo by Montclair Film Festival via Wikimedia Commons

A graduate of the renowned Carnegie Mellon University (CMU) School of Drama, Borle launched his professional stage career in the mid-1990s. After well-received parts in musical comedies such as *Thoroughly Modern Millie* and *Monty Python's Spamalot*, in 2007 he earned his first Tony Award nomination for originating the role of Emmett Forrest in the Broadway musical *Legally Blonde*. Borle went on to win Tonys for his performances as the villainous Black Stache in *Peter and the Starcatcher* and as a caddish William Shakespeare in *Something Rotten!*, which opened on Broadway in 2012 and 2015, respectively. He had further starring roles in the musical *Falsettos* (2016–17) and as eccentric chocolatier Willy Wonka in the 2017–18 Broadway adaptation of Roald Dahl's children's novel *Charlie and the Chocolate Factory* (1964). Borle also branched out into television and film, most notably starring in NBC's short-lived musical drama series *Smash* from 2012 to 2013. He made his directorial debut in 2018, when he helmed an Off-Broadway production of James Hindman's two-character farce *Popcorn Falls*.

EARLY LIFE AND EDUCATION

Christian Dominique Borle was born on October 1, 1973, in Pittsburgh, Pennsylvania. He grew up in the Pittsburgh suburb of Fox Chapel. His father, Andre, was a doctor who served as a professor of physiology at the University of Pittsburgh; his mother, Lee, was assistant to the university's dean of medicine. Despite coming from a scientifically-minded family, Borle aspired to a career in the performing arts at an early age. His parents were patrons of the arts, and they encouraged him to pursue his passions.

Borle's parents took him to his first professional show, a production of William Shakespeare's *A Midsummer Night's Dream* at the Pittsburgh Public Theater, when he was in elementary school. Borle acted in school productions throughout his youth, but it was not until he started attending the local Shady Side Academy (SSA) that he first came out of his shell. During his sophomore year there, after delivering an impromptu singing performance at a school dance, he caught the attention of SSA's choir director, who invited him to try out for musicals. Borle soon landed the lead role of cowboy Will Parker in a production of the musical *Oklahoma!*, after which his passion for acting blossomed. Also an avid comic book reader, he considered trying to become a professional artist but decided to focus on drama.

After high school Borle entered the esteemed drama program at CMU, located in his hometown of Pittsburgh. There, he honed his acting and singing skills under the guidance of musical theater professor Gary Kline. "[Borle] was like Gumby, bendable and movable," Kline recalled to Cristina Rouvalis for *Shady Side Academy Magazine* (Winter 2011–12). "He wanted to learn everything. He has so much drive and spirit." Borle particularly showcased these qualities as a senior when, after not landing the lead role in a production of the musical *Cabaret*, he agreed to act in a variety of smaller parts.

EARLY CAREER

Upon graduating from CMU in 1995, Borle moved to New York City to launch his professional acting career. His first job was humbling, if brief: he worked as an elf at the Macy's department store Santaland but quit in the midst of the holiday season to accept an acting job in the rock opera *The Who's Tommy* in Germany. In 1998, he made his Broadway debut as a replacement for the role of Willard Hewitt in an adaptation of the film *Footloose* (1984). Meanwhile, he worked as a bartender to make ends meet.

Over the next several years, Borle cut his teeth performing in other Broadway roles, both as a supporting player and understudy. He had a stint as a disciple in a 2000 revival of Andrew Lloyd Webber's rock opera *Jesus Christ Superstar* and portrayed the dance captain in the short-lived 2002 musical *Amour*. He then won positive notices for his replacement turn as Jimmy Smith in an adaptation of the musical film *Thoroughly Modern Millie*, which ran on Broadway from 2002 to 2004 and won six Tony Awards. Around this time Borle earned mild fame for his appearance in a popular commercial for the online auction site eBay, in which he played a store clerk who parodies the famous Dean Martin song "That's Amore."

Borle received his big break in 2005, when he originated five different parts in *Monty Python's Spamalot*, Mike Nichols's Broadway adaptation of the 1975 cult film *Monty Python and the Holy Grail*. Borle's versatile performance, in which he portrayed everything from an effeminate prince to a not-yet-dead peasant, was well-received by critics and earned him a 2005 Drama Desk Award nomination for outstanding featured actor in a musical. *Spamalot*, meanwhile, received fourteen Tony nominations and ran for a total of 1,575 performances. "The opportunity to play a bunch of different parts in one show is just as thrilling to be given the opportunity to play one person in one season," the actor explained to Ruthie Fierberg for *Playbill* (24 Apr. 2017).

TONY AWARD WINNER

Borle quickly built on his success. In 2007 he originated the role of unlikely love interest Emmett Forrest in the musical *Legally Blonde*, which is based on the same-named 2001 film starring Reese Witherspoon. Though the show received mixed reviews, Borle landed his first Tony Award nomination for best featured actor in a musical and a second Drama Desk Award nomination in the same category for his performance. *Legally Blonde* ran on Broadway for 595 performances before closing in October 2008.

The following year, Borle played the iconic role of Bert in the Broadway adaptation of *Mary Poppins*, the 1964 musical fantasy film starring Julie Andrews. Replacing Adam Fiorentino in the whimsical role, which was made famous by actor Dick Van Dyke in the film version, Borle resolved to make the character his own. As he noted to Rouvalis, "I wanted to make him an actual person as opposed to a caricature, but parts of it had to be larger than life. It was a balancing act."

Borle left the cast of *Mary Poppins* in June 2010 to accept the role of anguished AIDS patient Prior Walter in an Off-Broadway revival of Tony Kushner's Pulitzer Prize–winning play *Angels in America*. Borle won excellent reviews for his take on the challenging role—a stark departure from his previous work—and earned a 2011 Drama League Award nomination. That same year he originated the supporting role of refined villain Black Stache in the Off-Broadway production of *Peter and the Starcatcher*, a prequel based on the tale of Peter Pan.

Borle reprised that role for the high-flying 2012 Broadway production of *Starcatcher*, which was adapted for the stage by his longtime friend, Rick Elice, from Dave Barry and Ridley Pearson's 2004 young-adult novel, *Peter and the Starcatchers*. In his review of the play for the *New York Times* (15 Apr. 2012), theater critic

Ben Brantley described Borle's performance as a "shameless star turn" and wrote that he was "as hammy, plummy and delicious as a Christmas dinner from Charles Dickens." For his over-the-top portrayal, Borle won his first Tony Award as best featured actor in a play and received his third Drama Desk Award acting nomination.

A "SCIENTIST OF COMEDY"

Between the Off-Broadway and Broadway debuts of *Starcatcher*, Borle also made the jump to television, starring in the Steven Spielberg–produced NBC musical drama series *Smash*. On the series, which ran for two seasons from 2012 to 2013, he played composer Tom Levitt, who collaborates with lyricist Julia Houston (portrayed by Debra Messing) in the staging of a musical based on the life of film icon Marilyn Monroe. The series enjoyed mild critical success, but it struggled to maintain a steady viewership, ultimately resulting in its premature cancellation.

After landing recurring parts on other television series like Showtime's *Masters of Sex* and CBS's *The Good Wife*, Borle made his return to Broadway in 2015, when he delivered an outrageous supporting turn as William Shakespeare in Karey and Wayne Kirkpatrick's original musical comedy *Something Rotten!* The boisterous comedy follows the misadventures of a playwriting duo who struggle to attain success in the shadow of a dastardly and flamboyant Shakespeare. In his *New York Times* review of the show (22 Apr. 2015), Brantley commented that Borle "brings his well-polished panoply of comic tics, winks and flourishes to his portrayal of Shakespeare as a glam rock star," calling him "a master of stylized excess." For his portrayal, Borle received his second Tony Award and his first Drama Desk Award for best performance by a featured actor in a musical.

Borle remained a featured player in *Something Rotten!* until July 2016. He left for a lead role as Marvin in a Broadway revival of William Finn and James Lapine's sung-through musical *Falsettos*, which opened at the Walter Kerr Theatre that September. Borle's fresh take on Marvin, a Jewish man from Manhattan's Upper West Side who ditches his wife and pubescent son to be with his male lover, was well-received by critics, garnering him his fourth Tony Award nomination. Commenting on Borle's inventive acting, Elice told Soloski: "He's a scientist of comedy, and he wants to know what the formula is."

Borle further tested out that "formula" in his next character portrayal: Willy Wonka in the high-ticket Broadway production of Roald Dahl's *Charlie and the Chocolate Factory*, which premiered at the Lunt-Fontanne Theatre in April 2017. Contrary to Gene Wilder's cheekily sinister turn as Wonka in the 1971 film adaptation of Dahl's book, Borle approached the role with the intention of highlighting the character's "humanity and sweetness," as he told Soloski. He acted in the role during the entirety of the tepidly reviewed musical's nine-month, 305-performance run.

2018 AND BEYOND

After his run in *Charlie and the Chocolate Factory*, Borle starred alongside his *Mary Poppins* costar Laura Michelle Kelly in an *Encores!* production of *Me and My Girl*, which had a limited run of seven performances at New York City Center in May 2018. That year he also made a series of small-screen appearances, including on the legal drama web series *The Good Fight* and the modern-day Sherlock Holmes reboot *Elementary*. Later that summer, he made his debut as a theater director, staging James Hindman's two-character farce *Popcorn Falls* at the Riverbank Theatre in Marine City, Michigan. In November 2018, he helmed a brief Off-Broadway production of that play at Manhattan's Davenport Theatre.

In addition to his theater and television work, Borle appeared in several Hollywood feature films, including small roles in the Jennifer Aniston vehicle *The Bounty Hunter* (2010) and in the Michael Mann crime thriller *Blackhat* (2015). In 2019 he took the role of Captain Walker in a fiftieth anniversary limited-run staging of *The Who's Tommy* at the John F. Kennedy Center for the Performing Arts in Washington, DC. He was also cast in a regular role on an ABC romantic drama series called *Until the Wedding*, which was written by *Smash* writer Becky Mode.

PERSONAL LIFE

Soloski described Borle as being "dryly funny and unnervingly charming" and as having "a distinctive face, with a nose that sallies forth, a chin that hangs back and a daredevil grin in between." Borle was married to his college sweetheart, the Tony Award–winning actor Sutton Foster, whom he acted alongside in *Thoroughly Modern Millie*, from 2006 to 2010.

SUGGESTED READING

Borle, Christian. "Christian Borle on the Thrill of Jumping from *Smash* to *Peter and the Starcatcher*." Interview by Kathy Henderson. *Broadway Buzz*, 9 Apr. 2012, www.broadway.com/buzz/161101/christian-borle-on-the-thrill-of-jumping-from-smash-to-peter-and-the-starcatcher/. Accessed 2 Mar. 2019.

Brantley, Ben. "Effortless Flights of Fancy." Review of *Peter and the Starcatcher*, directed by Roger Rees and Alex Timbers. *The New York Times*, 15 Apr. 2012, www.nytimes.com/2012/04/16/theater/reviews/peter-and-the-starcatcher-with-christian-borle.html. Accessed 2 Mar. 2019.

Brantley, Ben. "Review: 'Something Rotten!,' an Over-The-Top Take on Shakespeare." Review of *Something Rotten!*, directed by Casey Nicholaw. *The New York Times*, 22 Apr. 2015, www.nytimes.com/2015/04/23/theater/review-something-rotten-an-over-the-top-take-on-shakespeare.html. Accessed 2 Mar. 2018.

Fierberg, Ruthie. "How Two-Time Tony Winner Christian Borle Discovered His Own Versatility." *Playbill*, 24 Apr. 2017, www.playbill.com/article/how-two-time-tony-winner-christian-borle-discovered-his-own-versatility. Accessed 2 Mar. 2019.

Lee, Luaine. "With NBC's 'Smash,' Christian Borle Has Arrived." *SFGate*, 22 Feb. 2012, www.sfgate.com/news/article/With-NBC-s-Smash-Christian-Borle-has-arrived-3347834.php. Accessed 2 Mar. 2019.

Rouvalis, Cristina. "Alumni Profile: Christian Borle '91: Broadway Star Makes Leap to Network TV." *Shady Side Academy Magazine*, Winter 2011–12, www.shadysideacademy.org/alumni/featured-alumni/alumni-profile/~post/christian-borle-91. Accessed 2 Mar. 2019.

Soloski, Alexis. "First Christian Borle Gets Serious. Then He'll Be Wonka." *The New York Times*, 5 Oct. 2016, www.nytimes.com/2016/10/09/theater/christian-borle-falsettos-broadway.html. Accessed 2 Mar. 2019.

SELECTED WORKS

Thoroughly Modern Millie, 2003–4; *Spamalot*, 2005; *Legally Blonde*, 2007–8; *Mary Poppins*, 2009–10; *Peter and the Starcatcher*, 2012; *Smash*, 2012–13; *Something Rotten!*, 2015–16; *Falsettos*, 2016–17; *Charlie and the Chocolate Factory*, 2017–18

—Chris Cullen

Rutger Bregman

Date of birth: April 26, 1988
Occupation: Historian and author

Rutger Bregman is a Dutch historian and author who made an unexpected impression at the World Economic Forum in Davos, Switzerland, in 2019. The forum, an annual conference of world and business leaders, involves panels and discussions about how the world's elite might work together to make the world a better place. Bregman was invited to discuss aspects of his book *Utopia for Realists: How We Can Build the Ideal World*, published in the Netherlands in 2014, and published in the United States in 2017. Ostensibly there to talk about a universal basic income (UBI), an idea with growing

Photo by Victor van Werkhooven via Wikimedia Commons

popularity among the tech industry in Silicon Valley, Bregman later told Dylan Matthews for *Vox* (30 Jan. 2019), that the gathering made him "uncomfortable." Instead of speaking on just UBI, Bregman gave a speech about how the most productive thing the wealthy could do to help others would be to prevent tax evasion and focus on raising taxes. Videos from the conference and other interviews soon became popular online, giving both Bregman and his ideas popularity among the public.

Bregman, who is a writer for the Dutch outlet the *Correspondent*, is one of a burgeoning number of historians, thinkers, activists, and politicians advocating for radical solutions to serious global problems like income inequality and climate change. These ideas—including the Green New Deal proposed by Congresswoman Alexandria Ocasio-Cortez or presidential candidate Andrew Yang's support for UBI—are beginning to gain mainstream popularity. "I am part of a broad social movement," Bregman told Larry Elliott for the *Guardian* (1 Feb. 2019). "Ten years ago, it would have been unimaginable for some random Dutch historian to go viral when talking about taxes. Yet here we are."

EDUCATION AND EARLY CAREER
Bregman was born in 1988 and grew up in Zoetermeer, Holland. His mother was a teacher and his father served as a Protestant minister at the church just across the street from the family's home. He studied history at Utrecht University, earning his bachelor's degree in 2009 and his master's degree in 2012. During his master's program, he also taught history at the school. After

graduating, Bregman briefly considered earning a PhD, however, because he did not like the cloistered environment of academia, he instead decided to start his career. In the wake of the global financial crisis in 2008, Bregman told Elliot, "I thought that we needed historians to take the stage and explain what's going on. When I watched the crisis on TV, the only people being interviewed were economists, and these were the guys that didn't see it coming. I thought that we needed some historians there, so I left academia."

Around the same time, Bregman began publishing books describing his views on history and the economy. By 2015, he had published three books, including *De geschiedenis van de vooruitgang* (2013, The History of Progress) for which he won the Belgian Liberales Prize for Best Nonfiction Book of 2013.

THE CORRESPONDENT
Bregman spent a year working for a leftist Dutch newspaper before taking a job with the Dutch journalism outlet the *Correspondent* when it launched in 2013. Journalist Rob Wijnberg crowdsourced money to fund the site, which promised ad-free reporting of stories that were not driven by "breaking news." When the site launched, Wijnberg told Loes Witschge for *Nieman Lab* (5 Apr. 2013) that he hoped the site's purpose would evolve according to the interests of its contributors. "I want the correspondents to make their choices explicit—what do they think is important, and why should readers care about it? You do that by making clear that you're not following an objective news agenda, but a subjective journey through the world," Wijnberg explained. Bregman became "a kind of in-house historian," for the *Correspondent*, as Patrick Kingsley put it for the *New York Times* (1 Mar. 2019). He focused on subjects that were of interest to him and published an article about once a month. For his journalism with the *Correspondent*, Bregman was nominated for the prestigious European Press Prize twice. His articles for the website also inspired his fourth book.

UTOPIA FOR REALISTS
Utopia for Realists: How We Can Build the Ideal World was first published by the *Correspondent* in Dutch in 2014. A self-published English translation followed in 2017, and it has been translated into thirty-two languages, with different subtitles, including *And How We Can Get There* and *The Case for a Universal Basic Income, Open Borders and a 15-Hour Workweek. Utopia for Realists* was not an immediate success and Bregman worked to promote it. "I was my own PR employee at that point. I was emailing everyone—no interviews, no reviews. Nothing," he recalled to Tim Harford for the

Financial Times (9 Mar. 2018). The book later won endorsements from people like Harvard psychologist and author Steven Pinker, and it soon built a large enough following to become an international bestseller.

In *Utopia for Realists*, Bregman advocates for a UBI and a fifteen-hour workweek. He explains that throughout the twentieth century, with the rise of automation, plenty of thinkers predicted that people would have to work less in the future. In 1930, economist John Maynard Keynes predicted a fifteen-hour workweek by 2030. Instead, since the 1980s, people have been spending more time at work, not less. Bregman attributes this to the rise of what he believes are unnecessary jobs. Since the 1980s, there has been a rise in the number of jobs that are more difficult to quantify in terms of their benefit to the common good. Bregman described these often high-paying jobs for *Wired* (2 Mar. 2017), as "the growing armies of consultants, bankers, tax advisors, managers, and others who earn their money in strategic trans-sector peer-to-peer meetings to brainstorm the value-add on co-creation in the network society. Or something to that effect."

Bregman encouraged the radical reexamination of the concept of work and motivation behind it. Along with a guaranteed income, a shorter working week would leave more time for people to pursue meaningful, unpaid work that endeavors to make the world more beautiful, like making art, or more humane, like caring for family members. The third proposal of Bregman's book involves national borders. Bregman argued that borders are the world's leading cause of wealth inequity, and described measures to stem immigration to Harford as "apartheid on a global scale."

INFLUENCING THE PUBLIC

In 2017, Bregman was invited to give a TED talk. Titled "Poverty Isn't a Lack of Character; It's a Lack of Cash," the talk argued for a UBI to eradicate poverty. Bregman said that both austerity measures and current antipoverty initiatives operate from the assumption that poverty is a character flaw. He explained, citing research from behavioral scientist Eldar Shafir, that poor people made what were perceived as poor decisions because they were operating from a "scarcity mentality," unable to focus on the future outside of their immediate needs. Bregman argues that addressing those immediate needs is radically simple: give people cash. Bregman advocates for a UBI, in which every adult person receives a guaranteed amount of money from the government, believing that a basic income would allow people the freedom to choose their jobs and bargain for better wages.

Well-known proponents of UBI have included the civil rights leader Dr. Martin Luther King Jr., the libertarian economist Milton Friedman, and former president Richard Nixon. Bregman was surprised by the enthusiastic response to his TED talk for reasons that align with his bafflement of the Davos crowd. "You're talking for an audience of 1,500 people, many of them involved in kinds of charities," he recalled to Harford. "I was saying we should hand over the salaries of all these paternalistic bureaucrats and give them to the poor, who are the real experts on their own lives. And they were all clapping and laughing, and I was thinking on stage, 'But I'm talking about you! It's you!'"

In 2019, Bregman was asked to speak about the ideas in *Utopia for Realists*, including universal base pay, at the World Economic Forum in Davos, Switzerland. The wealthy participants at Davos, Bregman discovered, were far more interested in talking about philanthropy, or the donation of large sums of money for the common good, than what Bregman described as the "elephant in the room." When it came time for Bregman's panel, instead of answering a question about UBI and inequality, he gave a prepared speech in which he said, "It feels like I'm at a firefighters' conference and no one is allowed to speak about water," adding: "We've got to be talking about taxes. Taxes, taxes, taxes." Although some philanthropic efforts can produce great good, Bregman argued that there are limits to philanthropy as a solution to the world's ills. "Philanthropy is not a substitute for democracy or proper taxation or a good welfare state," he explained to Matthews. "I don't want to live in a society where we are dependent on the charity of one guy and his wife for something like that," Bregman said, referencing Microsoft founder Bill Gates, the Bill and Melinda Gates Foundation, and their ongoing efforts to eradicate malaria. Worse, the practice of philanthropy can obscure fundamental problems with the ways in which billion-dollar companies treat their employees or ultimately, how they tenaciously avoid paying taxes.

Some audience members applauded Bregman's speech. Others, like Ken Goldman, the former chief financial officer of the search engine Yahoo!, were angered by it. Following the conference, a video of the event made waves on the Internet, introducing Bregman to an international audience and giving him a larger platform with which to share his ideas. Bregman has been accused of idealism, but he argues that the world is suffering from a "crisis of imagination," as he told George Eaton for the *New Statesman* (19 Feb. 2018). "I was born in 1988, one year before the fall of the Berlin Wall, and people of my generation were taught that utopian dreams are dangerous," he said. "It seemed that the age of big ideas was over. Politics had just become technocracy and politicians just managers." His specific use of the term *utopia* is meant to inspire bigger thinking. In his book, he quotes the writer Oscar Wilde: "Progress is the realization of utopias."

PERSONAL LIFE

Bregman and his wife, Maartje, a photographer, live in Utrecht.

SUGGESTED READING

Bregman, Rutger. "Meet the Folk Hero of Davos: The Writer Who Told the Rich to Stop Dodging Taxes." Interview by Dylan Mathews. *Vox*, 30 Jan. 2019, www.vox.com/future-perfect/2019/1/30/18203911/davos-rutger-bregman-historian-taxes-philanthropy. Accessed 12 May 2019.

Bregman, Rutger. "Want Utopia? Start with Universal Basic Income and a 15-Hour Work Week." *Wired*, 2 Mar. 2017, www.wired.co.uk/article/universal-basic-income-utopia. Accessed 13 May 2019.

Eaton, George. "'I Want the State to Think Like an Anarchist': Dutch Historian Rutger Bregman on Why the Left Must Reclaim Utopianism." *New Statesman*, 19 Feb. 2018, www.newstatesman.com/culture/observations/2018/02/i-want-state-think-an-archist-dutch-historian-rutger-bregman-why-left. Accessed 13 May 2019.

Elliott, Larry. "'This Is about Saving Capitalism': the Dutch Historian Who Savaged Davos Elite." *The Guardian*, 1 Feb. 2019, www.theguardian.com/business/2019/feb/01/rutger-bregman-world-economic-forum-davos-speech-tax-billionaires-capitalism?CMP=twt_gu. Accessed 12 May 2019.

Harford, Tim. "Rutger Bregman: 'Basic Income Is All about the Freedom to Say No.'" *Financial Times*, 9 Mar. 2018, www.ft.com/content/44adcf46-2197-11e8-a895-1ba1f-72c2c11. Accessed 13 May 2019.

Kingsley, Patrick. "He Took Down the Elite at Davos, Then He Came for Fox News." *The New York Times*, 1 Mar. 2019, www.nytimes.com/2019/03/01/world/europe/davos-fox-news-bregman-carlson.html. Accessed 13 May 2019.

Witschge, Loes. "A Dutch Crowdfunded News Site Has Raised $1.3 Million and Hopes for a Digital-Native Journalism." *Nieman Lab*, 5 Apr. 2013, www.niemanlab.org/2013/04/a-dutch-crowdfunded-news-site-has-raised-1-3-million-and-hopes-for-a-digital-native-journalism/. Accessed 13 May 2019.

—*Molly Hagan*

Cecily Brown

Date of birth: 1969
Occupation: Painter

Cecily Brown is one of the most lucrative artists painting today. In 2018, she set a record for her work with *Suddenly Last Summer* (1999), which went for $6,776,200 at Sotheby's New York. She also became the first artist to display work inside the main hall of New York's famed Metropolitan Opera since Marc Chagall installed his site-specific murals for its opening in 1966. Her two, nearly twenty-six-feet wide paintings, *Triumph of the Vanities I* and *Triumph of the Vanities II*, depict characters at a wild cocktail party scene. She has had more than one hundred exhibitions displaying her work in galleries, foundations, and public museums since the 1990s.

Originally from the United Kingdom, Brown emigrated to the United States in the early 1990s and became a central figure of the New York City art scene, impressing art enthusiasts and critics alike with her bold, huge paintings, often sexual in nature, which skirt the line between figurative painting and abstract painting. For all her success, however, Brown understands the difficulty of trying to produce something strikingly original from traditional materials. "The boundaries of painting excite me. You've got the same old materials—just oils and a canvas—and you're trying to do something that's been done for centuries. And yet, within those limits, you have to make something new or exciting for yourself as well as other people," she said in an interview with Perri Lewis for the *Guardian* (20 Sept. 2009). "I have

Photo by Dominik Bindl/Getty Images

always wanted to make paintings that are impossible to walk past, paintings that grab and hold your attention. The more you look at them, the more satisfying they become for the viewer. The more time you give to the painting, the more you get back."

EARLY LIFE AND EDUCATION

Cecily Brown was born in 1969 in London, England, and was raised in Surrey. She knew that she wanted to be an artist when she was just three years old. She was also interested in acting. In her teens, she became a fan of David Bowie. "I was madly in love with him and his beauty, the lyrics sound so great," she said to Jackie Wullschlager for the *Financial Times* (10 June 2016). As a painter, she would pay homage to him with *Lady Grinning Soul* (2015), titled after one of his songs. "Painting is closest to poetry of all the arts: not being able to explain something . . . . You can't put your finger on it, that's what my work is about."

Brown's parents, novelist Shena Mackay and Robin Brown, divorced when she was twelve. When she was twenty-one, Mackay told her that her biological father was David Sylvester, a family friend, curator, and art critic. Of the revelation, Brown said to Wullschlager, "I was very, very surprised, but at the same time it absolutely made sense: how could I not see it? It was like a TV drama. It goes on being complicated. David always said I was much nicer to him before I knew he was my dad."

Knowing of Brown's artistic interests and abilities, Sylvester took her around to galleries and introduced her to artists, including Francis Bacon, with whom he was acquainted. From 1985 to 1987, she earned a B-TEC diploma in art and design at the Epsom School of Art in Surrey. Then, for the next two years, she took drawing and printmaking classes at Morley College, in London. In 1989, she enrolled at the Slade School of Fine Art, in London, England. While an undergraduate, she earned first prize in Christie's national art-student competition in 1990. She also traveled to New York as an exchange student, studying at the New York Studio School in 1992 before graduating from Slade in 1993 with a BFA with first class honors.

During her time in London, Brown began to associate with the Young British Artists (YBAs), a movement of visual artists known for the shock value of their work, as well as their wild lifestyles. Brown, however, did not entirely feel comfortable with the group. She wanted to create paintings that were both figurative and abstract, a concept that did not seem to be in line with the London art scene. "What I hated about the YBAs was that it was a closed club, it made me feel I could never be part of this so I may as well f—— off halfway round the world," she

explained to Wullschlager. "I didn't fit in England when I left. You couldn't do what I wanted to do without being attacked."

MAKING IT IN NEW YORK

Brown decided to settle in New York permanently in 1994. To a young artist looking to make a name for herself, the city felt like a breath of fresh air compared to London. In an interview for *Apollo Magazine* (3 Nov. 2018), she recalled to Rachel Wetzler: "You could just wander into an opening and people would actually talk to you. SoHo was still very alive with galleries, and there was loads of good art, stuff that I hadn't seen before, like Koons, Richard Prince, and Mike Kelley. I couldn't believe how much art there was everywhere."

When Brown first returned to New York, she supported herself by waiting on tables. When she took a position at an animation studio, she experimented with animation in her spare time and made an animated short film, *Four Letter Heaven*. Produced by Jeff Scher, the short opened at the Telluride Film Festival that year. Brown created the rotoscope animation by tracing over print footage of an X-rated film with watercolor, ink, and colored pencil. According to Brown's biography on *Guggenheim.org*, the film's "humor, sexual imagery, and energetic brushwork," became common themes and techniques in Brown's later work.

Brown's painting—which danced between figurative painting and abstract painting—was often inspired by her close studies of master artists like Degas, Delacroix, Hogarth, and Rubens. Gallery owner Jeffrey Deitch became interested in her work and began showing it. Her first success came in 1997, when she had a solo show, *Spectacle*, at Deitch Projects in New York, which included "a series of luridly coloured paintings of rabbits engaged in absurd, graphic orgies," as Wetzler described it. A year later, her second solo show at Deitch Projects, *High Society*, helped to cement her reputation as an up-and-coming artist.

In 1999, Brown moved from Deitch to the Gagosian Gallery, a major player in the New York City art scene. She began receiving greater public attention beginning in 2000, when she was photographed for *Vanity Fair* and *Interview* in revealing, fashionable clothing. The attention brought her some negative press from critics, who felt her art was not quite worth all the fuss. Reviewing Brown's work for the *New York Times* (21 Jan. 2000), Roberta Smith declared, "the majority of these paintings are uninteresting from any distance and ultimately vacuous. They suffer by comparison with any number of artists—from John Wesley to Jeff Koons and Sue Williams—who have made painting about sex funnier, more explicit and more original."

That said, Brown's work continued to find its way into group exhibitions as well as her own featured solo showings. In the first decade of the twenty-first century alone, she had had solo exhibitions in New York, Berlin, London, Boston, Hamburg, Madrid, Rome, Beverly Hills, and Vienna, among other cities. In the 2010s, her solo exhibitions have had an even greater exposure, appearing in Kiev, Ukraine; The Hague, Netherlands; Paris, France; and Santa Barbara, California, as well as in New York and London. Most notably, Brown's work has been collected by premier art museums such as the Solomon R. Guggenheim Museum, New York; the Whitney Museum of American Art, New York; the Tate Britain, London; the Museum of Contemporary Art, Los Angeles; the Museum of Fine Arts, Boston; the Museum of Modern Art, New York; and the Hirshhorn Museum and Sculpture Garden, Washington, DC, among others. Brown's reputation has continued to grow as her career has developed. In *Apollo Magazine*, Rachel Wetzler wrote: "Simultaneously channeling the Old Masters and Abstract Expressionism, her paintings combine rigorous compositional structure with a sense of intuitive intensity." Brown left Gagosian in 2015 and is represented by Paula Cooper in New York and Thomas Dane in London.

HOW SHE PAINTS

Critics and art lovers alike continue to be drawn to Brown's large, vibrant, powerfully brushed paintings. Her figures never quite materialize, nor do they ever become full abstractions. Yet her process is somewhat unusual, in that she does not work on a single painting at a time but always has multiple ones in development. "If you do something you like early on, the constant fear is losing it, but if you've got two or three or four going at once, they can all go in different directions," she explained to Wetzler. "One of the advantages of working on so many things at once is that you're always in the mood to work on something."

Brown says she enjoys starting paintings the most. She told Perri Lewis for the *Guardian*: "I always start in quite a loose and free way. I often put down one ground colour to begin with and then play off that. For the first day or two, everything moves very quickly—sometimes almost too quickly—then there's often this very protracted middle period of moving things around, changing things, editing."

On occasion, she gets stuck while in the middle of working on a painting and must force herself to put it aside to ensure that she does not take the work in the wrong direction. Another artistic challenge is when she gets very close to finishing and knows that a single wrong brushstroke at that point could ruin it for her. According to one interview, she had more than fifty works at various points of completion as of late 2018. Many of her paintings take years to complete.

PERSONAL LIFE

Brown is married to Nicolai Ouroussoff, an architecture critic who has written for the *New York Times*. The couple have a daughter, Celeste.

SUGGESTED READING

Brown, Cecily. "Cecily Brown: I Take Things Too Far When Painting." Interview by Perri Lewis. *The Guardian*, 20 Sept. 2009, www.theguardian.com/artanddesign/2009/sep/20/guide-to-painting-cecily-brown. Accessed 6 June 2019.

Brown, Cecily. "'Now I Can Steal from Myself as Much as from Other Artists'—An Interview with Cecily Brown." By Rachel Wetzler. *Apollo*, 3 Nov. 2018, www.apollo-magazine.com/now-i-can-steal-from-myself-as-much-as-from-other-artists-an-interview-with-cecily-brown/. Accessed 6 June 2019.

Ollman, Leah. "Review: Cecily Brown's Paintings Do Not Disturb." *Los Angeles Times*, 26 Sept. 2013, www.latimes.com/entertainment/arts/la-xpm-2013-sep-26-la-et-cm-cecily-brown-review-20130923-story.html. Accessed 6 June 2019.

Sheets, Hilarie M. "Cecily Brown's Paintings Are at the (Other) Met." *The New York Times*, 20 Sept. 2018, www.nytimes.com/2018/09/20/arts/design/cecily-brown-bonfire-of-the-vanities-metropolitan-opera.html. Accessed 6 June 2019.

Smith, Roberta A. "Art in Review; Cecily Brown." *The New York Times*, 21 Jan. 2000, www.nytimes.com/2000/01/21/arts/art-in-review-cecily-brown.html. Accessed 6 June 2019.

Wullschlager, Jackie. "Painting and Sex Have Things in Common; Lunch with the FT: Cecily Brown." *Financial Times*, 10 June 2016, www.ft.com/content/0051bdc0-2c99-11e6-bf8d-26294ad519fc. Accessed 6 June 2019.

SELECTED WORKS

Suddenly Last Summer, 1999; *Untitled (The Beautiful and Damned)*, 2013; *Lady Grinning Soul*, 2015; *Triumph of the Vanities I*, 2018; *Triumph of the Vanities II*, 2018

—*Christopher Mari*

Joy Buolamwini

Date of birth: January 23, 1990
Occupation: Computer scientist

A self-described poet of code, computer scientist Joy Buolamwini is focused on finding solutions to one of the twenty-first-century world's lesser known but particularly concerning problems. "I don't like to say, 'Oh, here's a problem,' and mike drop," she told Maria Temming for *MIT Scope* (3 Dec. 2016). Rather, Buolamwini—a Fulbright Fellow and Rhodes Scholar who pursued doctoral studies at MIT—has dedicated her career both to raising awareness of and actively addressing bias within the algorithms used in artificial intelligence and facial recognition technology. Design based on the flawed assumption that white men represent the default human form, some such algorithms cannot detect or correctly interpret the faces of people of color. For example, Buolamwini found that one facial recognition program could not detect her face unless she wore a white mask.

Such flaws have disturbing implications, particularly given the increasingly common use of facial recognition technology in everyday life. "If we do not improve the systems and they continue to be used, what are the implications of having innocent people identified as criminal suspects?" Buolamwini wrote for the *MIT Media Lab* website (14 Dec. 2016). "Considering the advent of self-driving cars, can we afford to have pedestrian detection systems that fail to consistently detect a particular portion of the population?" In light of such concerns, Buolamwini founded the Algorithmic Justice League, an organization dedicated to combating algorithmic bias, and established herself as an authority well positioned to speak out against the dangers of poorly designed and dangerous technology.

EARLY LIFE

Joy Adowaa Buolamwini was born in Canada on January 23, 1990, to John and Patricia Buolamwini. Her father was pursuing a doctorate at the University of Alberta at the time and went on to become a professor in medicinal chemistry and pharmaceutical sciences. Her mother is an artist. One of Buolamwini's grandfathers also worked as a professor at a pharmacy school. She has credited her family's background with both stoking her interest in science and helping her identify the ways in which science and art are interconnected. During her childhood, the Buolamwinis moved from Canada to Ghana, then to Mississippi, and finally to Cordova, Tennessee, near Memphis.

Buolamwini attended Cordova High School, where she served as president of the Cordova High Junior Classic League and participated in

Photo by Niccolò Caranti via Wikimedia Commons

the school's track-and-field activities. She excelled as a pole vaulter and dreamed of competing in the Olympics.

Buolamwini also began coding during that period, working on personal projects and creating websites for extracurricular groups. In 2007, while still in high school, she founded the web design company Jovial Designs, through which she would continue to hone her skills over the next several years. She graduated from Cordova High School in 2008.

COMPUTER SCIENCE TRAINING

After high school, Buolamwini enrolled in the Georgia Institute of Technology (Georgia Tech), where she studied computer science. She worked as a research assistant in the school's everyday computing lab and computational perception lab and served as a mentor within the College of Computing.

During her junior year Buolamwini traveled to Ethiopia, where she worked on a system for collecting health data to combat tropical diseases. The experience was an influential one for Buolamwini, as it demonstrated both the ability of technology to tackle global issues and the importance of carefully considering the ramifications of such technology. "I used to spend all my time coding stuff, very little time talking to people," she recalled to Temming. "When I went to Ethiopia during my junior year, that's when I stopped asking things like, 'Should this be a resistive or capacitive touch screen?' and started asking, 'Should we be building this technology in the first place? Who's benefiting here? What are the long-term goals?'"

In 2011 Buolamwini completed a software engineering internship at Yahoo! and received the Google Anita Borg Memorial Scholarship. Other undergraduate honors included recognition as a Stamps President's Scholar; a two-year recipient of the Astronaut Scholarship, started by John Glenn and other members of National Aeronautics and Space Administration's (NASA) Mercury 7 crew; and a Carter Center distinguished volunteer. She graduated from Georgia Tech's Flashpoint Start-Up Accelerator and earned her bachelor's degree with highest honors, both in 2012.

FULBRIGHT FELLOW AND RHODES SCHOLAR

Before and after completing her undergraduate degree, Buolamwini worked with a number of technology startups, including Excelegrade and Techturized Inc. / Myavana. In 2012 she traveled to Lusaka, Zambia, as a 2012–13 Fulbright Fellow. There she established the computer science–focused educational initiative Zamrize, for which she drew heavily on her earlier experiences working in Ethiopia. "The idea was to empower Zambian youth to become creators of technology," she told the *Rhodes Project* (2015).

Beginning in 2013 she traveled to the United Kingdom to attend the University of Oxford as a Rhodes Scholar, pursuing a master's degree in education with a specialty in learning and technology. In addition, Buolamwini piloted a new potential initiative for Rhodes Scholars known as the service year, in which she was able to work on a service project of her choosing. "We were selected to be scholars but not scholars alone, right?" she told the Rhodes Project. "For me, the prospect of doing another master's 'because it was nice' wasn't good enough. I knew I had to at least try to see if there was a different way to use the scholarship." During her service year Buolamwini launched Code4Rights, a project using technology and technology education to address human rights issues. For example, the project worked to create an app designed to support individuals who had experienced sexual violence.

GRADUATE RESEARCH

Following her return to the United States, Buolamwini enrolled in the Massachusetts Institute of Technology (MIT) to further her graduate studies. Her research initially focused on algorithmic bias, specifically the ways in which biases affect facial recognition technology's ability to recognize and identify women and people of color. Through her research, much of which was documented in her thesis, Buolamwini found that the data sets that facial analysis technology was typically trained on were male and light skinned. Even after supplying more diverse data sets, she found that existing technologies could determine the gender of light-skinned men with a high degree of accuracy but were far less accurate when assessing anyone else. She particularly found that women with darker skin were disproportionately misgendered as compared to their lighter-skinned counterparts. Buolamwini's thesis, "Gender Shades: Intersectional Phenotypic and Demographic Evaluation of Face Datasets and Gender Classifiers," was published in 2018 in *Proceedings of Machine Learning Research*. It has been written about in more than 230 articles in dozens of countries around the world.

Buolamwini would later create the short work *AI, Ain't I a Woman?* based in part on her research. An art piece that went on to be screened as part of a variety of museum exhibitions, *AI, Ain't I a Woman?* pairs a spoken poem by Buolamwini with examples of artificial intelligence's failure to correctly identify the gender of several famous African American women. Among them is the nineteenth-century abolitionist Sojourner Truth, the originator of the famous speech "Ain't I a Woman?"

After earning her master's degree in 2017, Buolamwini went on to pursue a doctorate within the MIT Media Lab's Center for Civic Media.

BIAS IN ALGORITHMS

As a graduate student, Buolamwini has worked extensively on algorithmic bias and the effects of such biases on artificial intelligence and facial recognition technology. Specifically, she asserts that algorithms used for facial recognition and similar technologies are shaped by the implicit biases of those who make them, and light skin and typical Caucasian facial features are often treated as the default. As such, some facial recognition software based on such algorithms have displayed notable flaws such as interpreting people of East Asian descent as having their eyes closed and not recognizing the faces of people with darker skin at all.

In addition, the means of assessing the effectiveness of such algorithms are inadequate. "Within the facial recognition community you have benchmark data sets which are meant to show the performance of various algorithms so you can compare them. There is an assumption that if you do well on the benchmarks then you're doing well overall," Buolamwini explained to Ian Tucker for the *Observer* (28 May 2017). "But we haven't questioned the representativeness of the benchmarks, so if we do well on that benchmark we give ourselves a false notion of progress."

Buolamwini has also called attention to the ways in which the camera technology used to capture images of the faces to be detected likewise displays signs of bias. "The default settings for digital cameras are influenced by the history of color film which itself exposes an optimization for lighter skin," she wrote for *Hacker Noon* (29 May 2017). "We have to keep in mind that default settings are not neutral. They reflect the Coded Gaze, the preferences of those who have the opportunity to develop technology. Sometimes these preferences can be exclusionary."

Buolamwini herself has experienced the results of such exclusionary preferences. As an undergraduate, a robot designed to detect human faces and interact with the humans it detected did not consistently respond to her. She later found that facial recognition software she attempted to use as a graduate student did not recognize her face as a face unless she wore a white mask.

COMBATING BIAS

In addition to calling attention to the problem of bias within facial recognition technology and artificial intelligence, Buolamwini has actively worked to combat such bias and prevent flawed technology from causing harm. She is particularly concerned about the use of facial recognition technology by law enforcement, especially given its inaccuracy. "Because algorithms can have real world consequences, we must demand fairness," she wrote for the *MIT Media Lab* website (14 Dec. 2016).

To raise awareness of the issue, Buolamwini delivered a talk on the subject at the TEDxBeaconStreet event in 2016 and established the Algorithmic Justice League, an organization that seeks to identify, mitigate, and highlight algorithmic bias to effect change. She has also contributed to various other initiatives to combat bias in facial analysis algorithms, including an Institute of Electrical and Electronic Engineers (IEEE) working group dedicated to the issue, and made a short film, *The Coded Gaze: Unmasking Algorithmic Bias*, that was presented at the Museum of Fine Arts in Boston, Massachusetts. In 2018 the *Algorithmic Justice League* cofounded the Safe Face Pledge, which calls for organizations to pledge not to use artificial intelligence and facial analysis technology for applications that could endanger human lives. Buolamwini's videos and films can be found on the Algorithmic Justice League website.

Widely recognized for her research and advocacy, Buolamwini was one of two grand-prize winners of the Search for Hidden Figures contest. The award, funded by PepsiCo, 21st Century Fox, and the New York Academy of Sciences, was inspired by the 2016 film *Hidden Figures*, which told the story of three African American women who worked as NASA mathematicians. Chosen from among more than seven thousand submissions, Buolamwini was selected to receive a $50,000 grant as well as a trip and various educational resources. "I'm honored to receive this recognition, and I'll use the prize to continue my mission to show compassion through computation," Buolamwini told Margaret K. Evans for the *MIT Media Lab* (18 Jan. 2017) following the announcement.

Additionally, MIT *Technology Review* designated Buolamwini one of its annual 35 Innovators Under 35. *Forbes* magazine also placed her on three of its top tech lists: America's Top 50 Women in Tech 2018, The World's Top 50 Women in Tech 2018, and 30 Under 30—Enterprise Technology 2019.

PERSONAL LIFE

Buolamwini lives in Cambridge, Massachusetts. Though still focused on artificial intelligence and facial recognition technology, she has commented in interviews that she hopes to explore a wide range of subject areas and industries over the course of her career. "I hope I never stop dreaming," she told the *Rhodes Project*. "I hope I'll continue to be somebody who tries to explore boundaries and create opportunities for others to do that as well—I can see myself potentially spending time in business, academia, policy, maybe even sports. I've always wanted to pole vault for Ghana in the Olympics!"

SUGGESTED READING

Buolamwini, Joy. "The Algorithmic Justice League." *MIT Media Lab*, 14 Dec. 2016, medium.com/mit-media-lab/the-algorithmic-justice-league-3cc4131c5148. Accessed 14 June 2019.

Buolamwini, Joy. "Algorithms Aren't Racist. Your Skin Is Just Too Dark." *Hacker Noon*, 29 May 2017, hackernoon.com/algorithms-arent-racist-your-skin-is-just-too-dark-4ed31a7304b8. Accessed 14 June 2019.

Buolamwini, Joy. "'A White Mask Worked Better': Why Algorithms Are Not Colour Blind." Interview by Ian Tucker. *Observer*, 28 May 2017, www.theguardian.com/technology/2017/may/28/joy-buolamwini-when-algorithms-are-racist-facial-recognition-bias. Accessed 14 June 2019.

Evans, Margaret K. "Media Lab Student Wins National Award for Fighting Bias in Machine Learning." *MIT Media Lab*, 18 Jan. 2017, www.media.mit.edu/posts/media-lab-student-recognized-for-fighting-bias-in-machine-learning. Accessed 14 June 2019.

"Georgia Tech Alumna Named Rhodes Scholar." *Georgia Tech*, 17 Nov. 2012, www.news.gatech.edu/2012/11/17/georgia-tech-alumna-named-rhodes-scholar. Accessed 14 June 2019.

"Joy Buolamwini Profile." *Rhodes Project*, 2015, rhodesproject.com/joy-buolamwini-profile. Accessed 14 June 2019.

Temming, Maria. "Programming for the People." *MIT Scope*, 3 Dec. 2016, scopeweb.mit.edu/programming-for-the-people-aa282fc76f23. Accessed 14 June 2019.

—*Joy Crelin*

Nicole Byer

Date of birth: August 29, 1986
Occupation: Comedian

Photo by Bryan Bedder/Getty Images for Turner

"Comedy can do so much more than make you laugh, but for me, personally, I'm in it for the laughs and the chuckles," Nicole Byer told Kelsea Stahler for *Bustle* (24 July 2018). Indeed, since taking her first class in improvisational comedy with the Upright Citizens Brigade (UCB) in 2008, Byer has committed herself to eliciting laughs and chuckles from audiences in New York, Los Angeles, and throughout the United States through her live performances, roles in television series such as *Loosely Exactly Nicole*, and appearances as herself on comedic programs such as MTV's *Girl Code*. With her characteristically truthful style of comedy and engaging personality, Byer has also flourished as a host, helping drive the popularity of the Netflix series *Nailed It!* following its debut in early 2018. A competition show in which contestants who are very bad at baking attempt to replicate delicious and beautiful desserts, *Nailed It!* in many ways encapsulates the spirit of perseverance and risk taking that has shaped Byer's professional career. "What can cake teach you about life?" she said, when asked by Estelle Tang for *Elle* (17 July 2018). "That practice makes perfect, and if you try something once it probably won't be perfect, and you have to keep working on it if you want to be good at it."

EARLY LIFE AND EDUCATION

Byer was born on August 29, 1986, in New Jersey. She grew up in Lincroft, an unincorporated community within New Jersey's Middletown Township. As a child, Byer wanted to illustrate children's books but eventually moved away from that career goal as she realized that she lacked the requisite artistic skills. She later determined that she wanted to be an actor and participated in school theater programs while attending Middletown High School South. Her theatrical aspirations were encouraged by her mother, who died when Byer was a teenager.

Although her father wanted her to stay in New Jersey and attend Rutgers University after high school, Byer remained focused on acting and moved to New York to enroll in a two-year program at the American Musical Dramatic Academy (AMDA). "The week before I was supposed to go, I saw a play called 'Taboo' and this guy in the box office was like SCAMDAAAAAA," she recalled to Lauren Clark for *Her Agenda* (8 Apr. 2012). "I ended up going and it turned out it's not a scam, but it's a bunch of 18 year olds running around the city with no parents."

After completing her program at AMDA in 2006, Byer struggled to find her way in New York until 2008, when she began to take classes in improvisational comedy offered by the UCB, a well-regarded comedy organization that had produced many successful comedians and actors since the 1990s. The experience marked a turning point for Byer, who shifted her focus to comedy. "[I] truly was like, 'Oh, this is the only thing I'm good at. I'm only good at making people laugh," she told Monique Madrid for *Vulture* (1 Apr. 2016). "I can't work in an office. I don't know Excel. I can't learn those skills, it's too late for me. Gotta do comedy.'" While studying and later performing with UCB, Byer befriended several fellow comedians with whom she would collaborate in the future, including Sasheer Zamata and Alison Rich.

EARLY CAREER

While living in New York, Byer held a variety of day jobs, including stints as an administrative assistant, a nanny, and a restaurant server. "I was a waitress for a while and sometimes, when I made people laugh, they'd leave me like a $50 tip," she recalled to Allison P. Davis for the *Ringer* (6 Sept. 2016). "What people with money don't understand is like, sometimes $50 means you make your rent. 'You're just like, my rent is done. I can make money to live and play.'" Alongside her day jobs, Byer performed comedy at the Upright Citizens Brigade Theatre, among other venues, and in 2010 was selected to perform at UCB's Maude Nights, which showcase UCB's high-level performers, beginning the following year.

With Zamata and fellow UCB comedian Keisha Zollar, she founded the improv group Doppelganger. The group later spawned the web series *Pursuit of Sexiness*, which starred Byer and Zamata as fictionalized versions of themselves. The duo also cowrote the series, the first season of which debuted online in 2013. A second season debuted in 2015, by which time Zamata was serving as a cast member on *Saturday Night Live*. For Byer, the web series was one of many projects she undertook semi-independently, a practice that she noted in interviews is essential for many up-and-coming performers.

MOVE TO LOS ANGELES

Byer experienced some success in New York, playing small roles on television shows such as the sitcom *30 Rock* and performing frequently at UCB–related events. Nevertheless, she decided to move to Los Angeles, California, in 2012 and went on to participate in 2013's CBS Diversity Sketch Comedy Showcase. Although Byer has not addressed the experience in interviews, soon afterward she created and starred in a caustic UCB Comedy video titled "Be Blacker," about typecasting and racial stereotypes. In an interview with Allison Takeda for *Brit + Co* (7 Feb. 2018), she later advised up-and-coming minority and plus-size entertainers: "If you don't think you're getting the opportunities that you deserve, do it yourself. . . . Just get your s—— out there and let the general public consume it." She concluded, "Make your own opportunities." Byers has also stated in interviews that she prefers to focus on inclusivity rather than diversity in media and champions body positivity.

Over the subsequent years, Byer continued to perform comedy in the Los Angeles area and found a variety of work as an actor, appearing in television shows such as *Angie Tribeca*, *Lady Dynamite*, *Young & Hungry*, and *Transparent*. She also later lent her voice to animated characters in shows such as *Apple & Onion*, *Star vs. the Forces of Evil*, and *BoJack Horseman*. Though primarily active in television, Byer also appeared in small roles in several films, including *Other People* (2016), *Mike and Dave Need Wedding Dates* (2016), and *All About Nina* (2018).

COMEDY PERSONALITY

Among audiences outside of the sketch and improvisational-comedy community, Byer first became widely known for her appearances on several digital and television programs released by MTV. In 2013 and 2014, she costarred in *Fast Food Heights*, a scripted comedy series set in a fast food restaurant that MTV made available through a variety of apps and online services. She was even better known for her frequent appearances on *Girl Code* (2013–15), a comedy show in which comedians give opinions and advice on issues relevant to young women. The comedians on *Girl Code* appear as themselves—or their comedic personas—rather than as fictional characters, and the show enabled Byer to share her characteristically truthful and sometimes raunchy brand of comedy. In 2016 she was cast in the short-lived MTV show *Ladylike*, a hidden-camera prank show that featured several *Girl Code* comedians and had a similar comedic point of view. Comfortable with and skilled at contributing to talking-head, panel, and round-table comedy programs, Byer likewise appeared on a variety of shows in that vein over the course of her career, including *Mind of a Man*, *Chelsea Lately*, and *@midnight*.

Additionally, Byer gained further attention with the 2016 premiere of *Party over Here*, a late-night sketch show broadcast on FOX. The show also starred UCB alumni Jessica McKenna and Rich, who, along with Byer, were tasked with performing a variety of sketches written primarily by the show's staff of comedy writers. Although often performed before a live audience, the show was not broadcast live, which allowed the actors to film multiple takes of sketches as needed. That practice represented a "challenging" adjustment for Byer, as she told Madrid, due to her lengthy history with live comedy. "With live you don't get a second take, so it was really hard getting out of the mindset of 'This take is it. This take is perfect take,'" she explained. Although *Party over Here* featured talented comedians and entertaining sketches, the show was ultimately canceled following a single ten-episode season.

LOOSELY EXACTLY NICOLE

The year 2016 also saw the debut of Byer's next scripted series, *Loosely Exactly Nicole*. As the title of the show suggested, the series was based loosely on events from Byer's earlier years, exaggerated as needed for the sake of comedy. The show aired on MTV, viewers of which had come to know and enjoy Byer's distinctive personality and point of view. "When I was developing the show, [MTV] told me they wanted a *Louie* [the often-misanthropic series starring comedian Louis CK]. And I was like, 'You don't want *Louie* from me,'" Byer recalled to Davis. "I'm cheerful, I don't get down on anything, that's my life. What you want is my voice."

Although *Loosely Exactly Nicole* was generally well received following the airing of its first ten-episode season, MTV later canceled the show as part of a pivot away from scripted series. Byer initially came to terms with the cancellation of the series and was surprised when the online service Facebook Watch expressed interest in resurrecting the show on its platform. She eventually agreed, and season 2 of *Loosely Exactly Nicole* was released on Facebook Watch from December 2017 through February 2018.

NAILED IT! AND OTHER PROJECTS

Among the most significant moments in Byer's career to that point came in 2018, when she began to appear as host of the Netflix reality series *Nailed It!* Taking inspiration from the many competitive reality programs aired on channels such as the Food Network, *Nailed It!* takes the unique approach of tasking amateur bakers who possess little skill at baking with attempting to replicate fancy desserts. Byer, pastry chef Jacques Torres, and an array of guest judges then taste and judge the contestants' creations, a responsibility for which Byer was unqualified prior to joining the show. "I was not into cake fails before hosting *Nailed It!*" she admitted to Tang. "Here's the thing. I just eat food. I'm not looking for pictures of it unless it's, like, tasty food at a restaurant. I'm not heavily into baking." At times, however, the baked goods created on *Nailed It!* are far from tasty. "There's always someone sweating on cake and it's so gross," Byer told Tang. Following the release of the show's first season in March 2018, *Nailed It!* gained a large following, and Netflix released a seven-episode second season and a seven-episode, holiday-themed third season called *Nailed It! Holiday!* over the course of 2018.

Byer remains active in live comedy and performs both on tour and when in Los Angeles. She even performed at the 2017 South by Southwest Comedy Festival. She is also the host or cohost of several podcasts, including *Why Won't You Date Me?* Launched in November 2017, *Why Won't You Date Me?* documents Byer's dating foibles and presents a funny and honest look at her personal life. "When I do anything I try to be very truthful, and my truth is I am single and desperate and want a boyfriend, so that's what comes through," she explained to Stahler of her approach. Byer likewise cohosts the podcast *90 Day Bae*, about the reality television series *90 Day Fiancé*, with friend and fellow comedian Marcy Jarreau and *What the Tuck?*, devoted to the reality contest *RuPaul's Drag Race: All Stars*, with fellow comedian Joel Kim Booster.

PERSONAL LIFE

Byer was briefly married to an Indian-born man between March 2007 and March 2008 and later commented in interviews that the marriage had been contrived to help her then husband gain US citizenship and her to pay off her credit-card debt. The incident would later form the basis of an episode of *Loosely Exactly Nicole*. When not filming or touring elsewhere, Byer lives in Los Angeles.

SUGGESTED READING

Byer, Nicole. "A Peek Inside Her Agenda: Nicole Byer." Interview by Lauren Clark. *Her Agenda*, 8 Apr. 2012, heragenda.com/power-agenda/nicole-byer. Accessed 18 Dec. 2018.

Byer, Nicole. "Nicole Byer Doesn't Know that Much about Cake, Actually." Interview by Estelle Tang. *Elle*, 17 July 2018, www.elle.com/culture/movies-tv/a22232378/nicole-byer-nailed-it-interview. Accessed 18 Dec. 2018.

Byer, Nicole, et al. "Inside 'Party over Here' with Nicole Byer, Jessica McKenna, and Alison Rich." Interview by Monique Madrid. *Vulture*, 1 Apr. 2016, www.vulture.com/2016/04/inside-party-over-here-with-nicole-byer-jessica-mckenna-and-alison-rich.html. Accessed 18 Dec. 2018.

Davis, Allison P. "Not Your Next Woke Sitcom." *The Ringer*, 6 Sept. 2016, www.theringer.com/2016/9/6/16042442/nicole-byer-is-not-your-teacher-8d96af3e5fd8#.ajem8m90i. Accessed 18 Dec. 2018.

McVey, Ciara. "Nicole Byer on Her New Facebook Watch Show, and Why She's 'Tired of Trump' on 'SNL.'" *The Hollywood Reporter*, 1 Mar. 2018, www.hollywoodreporter.com/news/nicole-byer-her-new-facebook-show-why-shes-tired-trump-snl-1090025. Accessed 18 Dec. 2018.

Stahler, Kelsea. "Why 'Nailed It' Star Nicole Byer Is Always So Thirsty." *Bustle*, 24 July 2018, www.bustle.com/p/why-nailed-it-star-nicole-byer-is-always-so-thirsty-9637437. Accessed 18 Dec. 2018.

Takeda, Allison. "Nicole Byer Can Find Humor in Anything—and She Does, on 'Loosely Exactly Nicole.'" *Brit + Co*, 7 Feb. 2018, www.brit.co/nicole-byer-loosely-exactly-nicole-season-2-interview. Accessed 18 Dec. 2018.

SELECTED WORKS

Fast Food Heights, 2013–14; *Pursuit of Sexiness*, 2013–15; *Party over Here*, 2016; *Loosely Exactly Nicole*, 2016–18; *Nailed It!*, 2018–

—Joy Crelin

Cardi B

Date of birth: October 11, 1992
Occupation: Rapper

Rapper Cardi B became a breakout hip-hop superstar following her hit single "Bodak Yellow

Photo by Tim Mosenfelder/Getty Images

EARLY LIFE

Belcalis Almanzar was born in the Bronx borough in New York City on October 11, 1992. She grew up in the borough's Highbridge neighborhood. Both of her parents are immigrants, and she was raised bilingual. Her Dominican father, who speaks to her exclusively in Spanish, worked as a cab driver. Her Trinidadian mother worked as a cashier. Her younger sister, Hennessy Carolina, has become a social media personality. Growing up, Cardi also spent a good deal of time with her grandmother who lives in the Washington Heights neighborhood of Manhattan. Cardi has, and was sometimes hospitalized for, chronic asthma. Because her mother feared she would die of an asthma attack in her sleep, Cardi was not allowed to attend sleepovers or parties at night.

Cardi graduated from Renaissance High School for Musical Theater & Technology in the Bronx, though she often skipped class to attend daytime parties. She also fell in with the Brims, a subset of the Bloods gang. Cardi's music—not to mention the "B" in her name—is littered with references to the Brims, but she has stated that she is wary of touting her gang affiliation as an endorsement. "I don't talk about it much," she told Caity Weaver for *GQ* (9 Apr. 2018). "Because I wouldn't want a young person, a young girl, to think it's okay to join it. You could talk to somebody that is considered Big Homie and they will tell you: 'Don't join a gang.' The person that I'm under, she would tell you, 'Don't join a gang.'"

After high school, Cardi enrolled at the Borough of Manhattan Community College, where she took classes in history and French. She began working as a cashier at the grocery chain Amish Market. On the advice of her manager, who suggested that Cardi might make more money dancing at the strip club across the street, Cardi began working as a stripper. She hoped to make enough money to leave a bad relationship but ended up loving her job. "I get really happy when people see me perform and they're rapping my music, but it's a different feeling when you're dancing and the men throwing you money because you look good," she told Davis. "It's just like when the rice is getting thrown at the bride." Cardi worked at various clubs and built a following. On her nineteenth birthday, she received a pair of Christian Louboutin high-heels—the "red bottoms" she refers to on "Bodak Yellow"—from an admiring customer. Around the same time, she began getting cosmetic surgery, paying $800 to receive illegal injections in a basement in Queens.

LOVE & HIP HOP

In 2013, Cardi began recording Vine videos. The popular platform allowed users to upload

(Money Moves)" in 2017. The song, ubiquitous during the summer of 2017, made Cardi the first solo female rapper to have a number one song since Lauryn Hill, with "Doo Wop (That Thing)," in 1998. More accolades quickly followed. In 2018, Cardi became the first rapper to have her first three Billboard Hot 100 entries—"Bodak Yellow," "MotorSport" with Migos and Nicki Minaj, and "No Limit" with G-Eazy and A$AP Rocky—in the top ten simultaneously. In 2019, her debut album, *Invasion of Privacy*, won the Grammy Award for Best Rap Album. Cardi's allure lies in her brash confidence, disarming sense of humor, sharp lyrics, and idiosyncratic delivery. Allison P. Davis, in her profile of Cardi for the *Cut* (12 Nov. 2017), described the infectious hook of "Bodak Yellow"—"I don't dance now, I make money moves"—as "a bildungsroman in two lines."

After dancing in strip clubs in her early twenties, Cardi became a social media star on Vine and Instagram. She then landed a spot on the reality television show *Love & Hip Hop*. Signed to Atlantic Records on the strength of persona, Cardi learned to translate both her winning off-the-cuff barbs and moments of candid vulnerability into hip-hop gold. For Cardi, the desire to make music is inseparable from her fierce desire for independence, expressed through savvy "money moves." "I have a passion for music, I love music," Cardi told Rawiya Kameir for the *Fader* (22 June 2017). "But I also have a passion for money and paying my bills."

six-second videos. Her often goofy, stream-of-consciousness musings on life, money, and sex earned her thousands of followers. Her account became so successful that Cardi quit dancing and began hosting parties and events as a social media influencer. Her videos also brought her to the attention of producers for *Love & Hip Hop*, a VH1 reality television show about women in New York pursuing careers in hip-hop. Cardi was cast in the show's sixth season in 2015. Though Cardi had been interested in rapping since high school, she was positioned on the show as a social media star, not an aspiring rapper. Still, she became the season's breakout star and returned to the show for the following season. In one episode, Cardi described herself, as quoted by Davis, as a "regular, degular, shmegular girl from the Bronx;" the phrase became part of her lore. Another impromptu phrase, a fan favorite, inspired the hook of Cardi's first single, "Foreva." The line, as rendered by Davis: "If a girl gonna have beef with me, she gonna have beef with me—[pause, dramatic turn]—foreva."

Cardi released her first mixtape, *Gangsta B—— Music Vol. 1* in March 2016. In 2017, she released her second mixtape, *Gangsta B—— Music Vol. 2*, including the hit single "Lick," featuring Offset, of the rap group Migos. Offset was fresh off the Migos smash hit "Bad and Boujee," but his clout did not seem to help her song find a larger audience. "I'd go play parties in every state," Cardi recalled to Davis, "and I would wake my a—— up at six in the morning to go to a radio interview, meet radio programmers, and beg them, 'Please play my song.' They didn't play my sh——t."

INVASION OF PRIVACY

On the strength of her small-scale celebrity, Cardi signed with Atlantic Records in 2017. The first single from the album, "Bodak Yellow," was released in June 2017. The song is a riff on rapper Kodak Black's 2015 song "No Flockin'." It was not an immediate hit; however, it received an early boost from model Blac Chyna, who played it in an internet video taunting her ex-husband Rob Kardashian during a fight. Thanks to key endorsements from a host of hip-hop royalty, including Lil' Kim, Missy Elliott, Nicki Minaj, and Beyoncé, the song continued to spread. By late summer it had achieved, as Davis evocatively put it, "open-car-window ubiquity." In December, Cardi released her second single, "Bartier Cardi," featuring 21 Savage. In his review of the song for *Pitchfork* (22 Dec. 2017), Sheldon Pearce wrote that it "builds on the momentum and promise of its predecessor, full of the same controlled aggression and unflappable slick talk. Her words crack and wallop, imposing her will, as she settles comfortably into the lap of luxury. Every stride she takes is an emphatic one." She

was also featured with A$AP Rocky on the G-Eazy song "No Limit" and appeared alongside Nicki Minaj on the Migos song "MotorSport." With the success of those songs, Cardi became the first rapper to have her first three Billboard Hot 100 entries in the top ten simultaneously.

In interviews after the release of "Bodak Yellow," Cardi expressed anxiety about living up to the song's success. Plagued by lack of sleep and chronic migraines, Cardi wrote daily and recorded at night. Her debut album, *Invasion of Privacy*, was released in April 2018. Jon Caramanica of the *New York Times* (10 Apr. 2018), praised the album, awarding it a critic's pick. He described *Invasion of Privacy* as "exuberant and impressive." Cardi, he wrote, "is more versatile than most rappers or pop stars of any stripe." The album features verses from rappers like Migos on the song "Drip," Chance the Rapper on the song "Best Life," and Bad Bunny on the song "I Like It," as well as verses from R & B singers Kehlani on the song "Ring" and SZA on the song "I Do." With the album, Cardi "emerges as a first-rate song-maker," as Pearce wrote in his enthusiastic *Pitchfork* review (10 Apr. 2018). The online music magazine rated her album an impressive 8.7 out of 10. In addition to rave reviews, *Invasion of Privacy* earned five Grammy Award nominations; it won the award for best rap album.

Also in 2018, Cardi was featured on the Bruno Mars hit single "Finesse;" the two teamed up again on the song "Please Me" in 2019. She was also featured on the Maroon 5 song "Girls Like You," a number one hit. Cardi was named to the 2018 Time 100 Most Influential People in the World, before releasing the single "Money," which she performed with dramatic piano accompaniment at that year's Grammy Awards. She also appeared on the song "Twerk" from up-and-coming rap duo, City Girls. In 2019, Cardi rapped a verse on "Clout," a song on Offset's solo debut, and released the single "Press."

On social media, Cardi is unabashedly honest about her relationship to fame, her bodily functions, and her sex life—but also about her interest in history and politics. She often posts commentary on the news and, in 2019, she posted an impassioned speech about the government shutdown on Instagram. In the viral video, Cardi lambasted President Donald Trump for compelling federal workers to work without pay.

PERSONAL LIFE

After a year of dating, Offset proposed to Cardi onstage at a concert in Philadelphia in 2017. They married in a secret ceremony in September 2017. Their daughter, Kulture Kiari Cephus, was born in 2018.

SUGGESTED READING

Caramanica, Jon. "Cardi B Is a New Rap Celebrity Loyal to Rap's Old Rules on 'Invasion of Privacy.'" Review of *Invasion of Privacy*, by Cardi B. *The New York Times*, 10 Apr. 2018, www.nytimes.com/2018/04/10/arts/music/cardi-b-invasion-of-privacy-review.html. Accessed 15 July 2019.

Davis, Allison P. "Regular, Degular, Shmegular Girl from the Bronx." *The Cut*, 13 Nov. 2017, www.thecut.com/2017/11/cardi-b-was-made-to-be-this-famous.html. Accessed 15 July 2019.

Kameir, Rawiya. "Cardi B Did It Her Way." *The Fader*, 22 June 2017, www.thefader.com/2017/06/22/cardi-b-cover-story-interview. Accessed 15 July 2019.

Pearce, Sheldon. Review of "Bartier Cardi" featuring 21 Savage, by Cardi B. *Pitchfork*, 22 Dec. 2017, pitchfork.com/reviews/tracks/cardi-b-bartier-cardi-ft-21-savage/. Accessed 15 July 2019.

Pearce, Sheldon. Review of *Invasion of Privacy*, by Cardi B. *Pitchfork*, 10 Apr. 2018, pitchfork.com/reviews/albums/cardi-b-invasion-of-privacy/. Accessed 15 July 2019.

Weaver, Caity. "Cardi B's Money Moves." *GQ*, 9 Apr. 2018, www.gq.com/story/cardi-b-invasion-of-privacy-profile. Accessed 15 July 2019.

SELECTED WORKS

Gangsta B—— Music Vol. 1, 2016; *Gangsta B—— Music Vol. 2*, 2017; *Invasion of Privacy*, 2018

—Molly Hagan

Janene Carleton

Date of birth: April 14, 1978
Occupation: Stunt performer

Whether they involve building-length falls, edge-of-the-seat car chases, elaborate fight sequences, or mind-boggling fire gags, stunts have always been a significant part of the filmmaking process. The men and women responsible for bringing those stunts to life, however, often go unnoticed, anonymously working in service of the actors they are doubling for. Among these intrepid and selfless stunt performers is Janene Carleton, who is widely regarded as one of Hollywood's top stunt doubles. Since launching her career in the mid-2000s, she has quietly amassed dozens of feature-film and television credits while serving as a stunt double for such high-profile actors as Angelina Jolie (*Salt*, 2010), Paula Patton (*Mission: Impossible—Ghost Protocol*, 2011), Jessica Biel (*The Tall Man* and *Total Recall*, 2012), and Kate Winslet (*The Mountain between Us*, 2017).

A former competitive horseback rider, Carleton, like most of her peers, is a well-rounded performer who specializes in everything from racing cars to weapons handling. She also maintains a strict diet and fitness regimen to keep up with the physical demands of her job. As stunt people fight to gain more recognition for their dangerous, oftentimes life-risking efforts, Carleton nonetheless revels in her under-the-radar status. "You work on all these big movies with these big people, but you have your anonymity," she explained to Holly Mackenzie in an interview for *GQ* (4 Dec. 2018). "You can go to the grocery store and do what you want to do."

EARLY LIFE

Carleton was born in 1978 in Kelowna, a city in British Columbia, Canada. Raised in the heart of British Columbia's Okanagan Valley, she "was fortunate to come from a family that did a lot of fun, active things outdoors," as she noted to Adam Proskiw for *iNFOnews.ca* (13 July 2014). "My family taught me not to fear trying new things and that's definitely helped in my career and my life."

Growing up, Carleton, who was blessed with natural athletic ability, regularly went horseback riding, hiking, snowboarding, dune-buggy riding, and motorcycling, all of which "helped me become a well-rounded performer," as she told Proskiw. It was her talent in horseback riding, however, that helped usher her move into stunt work. She joined the competitive equestrian circuit at a young age, participating in events that include the main disciplines of dressage, cross-country, and show jumping.

HORSE RIDING TO HOLLYWOOD

Carleton's entrée into Hollywood came through her work and experience with animals. Taking advantage of her passion for horses, specifically, she began training the animals for feature films and giving actors riding lessons. It was this work that first introduced her to the world of stunt performing, one which she naturally gravitated to. Drawing on her extreme sports background, she quickly immersed herself in the stunt profession by training for and expanding upon her experience in a wide variety of disciplines, including not just mixed martial arts but also racing cars, rock climbing, and weapons handling. As she explained regarding the importance of versatility to Mackenzie, "If you want to get hired, you have to be hirable, so you train in everything."

Carleton first started doubling actors as a stunt rider, which served as a direct stepping stone to providing stunts for other types of roles. In 2006, she landed her first feature-film credits, doing stunt work for the comedy *Scary Movie 4* and doubling for actor Dania Ramirez in the superhero film *X-Men: The Last Stand*. That same year, she also performed stunts in the television series *Stargate SG-1* and in the miniseries *Merlin's Apprentice*, doubling for actors Claudia Black and Meghan Ory, respectively.

When working as a stunt double, Carleton acts "as a kind of personal trainer, getting the actress ready for all the moves that they're going to do," as she said in an interview with Bilge Ebiri for *Cosmopolitan* (8 July 2014). She typically works with a stunt coordinator and a stunt rigger to prepare for scenes, then teaches the actor how to properly perform them. Contrary to widely held assumptions, she explained to Ebiri that "nine times out of ten, when there's a stunt, both the actress and the stunt double do it, so there's enough footage to cut the scene together."

BEING PREPARED AND TAKING RISKS

As she gained increasingly more experience, Carleton settled into the profession, adjusting to the process as well as the preparation and fitness maintenance required. Besides putting in the necessary training to pull off a wide array of stunts, Carleton, like other stunt doubles, must also maintain a specific weight and body type to serve as a believable stand-in for actors. In her interview with Mackenzie, she said that she adheres to an all-natural diet consisting mostly of lean proteins, complex carbohydrates, fruits, and vegetables while avoiding processed and deep-fried foods. She also regularly uses supplements to help her body recover faster from her intense, multidisciplinary training regimen. At the same time, she makes it a point to train without adding too much muscle (which comes easily to her) so she can more closely resemble actors. She accomplishes this balance by doing a lot of low-impact but core-strengthening activities such as yoga and Pilates. In an interview with Stephanie Ayre for *POP-SUGAR* (19 Oct. 2013), she also touted the mental merits of such activities: "Yoga also keeps me in a Zen state of mind, which is useful when working long hours under pressure which is often the case in the film industry."

Over the next several years, Carleton built her reputation among peers in the stunt community for her willingness to perform high-risk stunts. This included being set on fire for the low-budget, military-themed action film *Afghan Knights* (2007), in which she was forced to wrap her hands around another stunt performer and set him on fire. The stunt required Carleton to wear a fire-retardant jumpsuit and to cover her entire face and body with a clear, fire-retardant gel that appears invisible on camera. Still, she lost all the eyelashes on her left eye after the gel came off them on the day of filming. "Even if I know something's dangerous it doesn't stop me from wanting to do it," she explained to Proskiw.

On the small screen, Carleton performed stunt work for such popular television shows as the CW network's *Supernatural* (2006–8) and *Smallville* (2007–10), the Sci-Fi channel's *Battlestar Galactica* (2008), and Fox's *Prison Break* (2008). In 2009, she doubled for actors Ashley Judd, Emmy Rossum, and Carla Gugino in the films *Helen*, *Dragonball: Evolution*, and *Watchmen*, respectively.

STUNT DOUBLE TO THE STARS

The biggest gig of Carleton's career up to that point came in 2010, when she was hired to serve as a stunt double for Angelina Jolie, then one of the most high-profile actors in the world, in the spy thriller *Salt*. As this proved to be a case where she needed to slim down more quickly, she "was hungry for three months," as she quipped to Ebiri. In that film, Jolie portrays a Central Intelligence Agency (CIA) officer, Evelyn Salt, who is forced to go on the run after facing accusations of being a Russian double agent. In one of the film's action set pieces, Salt eludes federal authorities by jumping off a highway overpass onto a moving tractor trailer before transferring to another box truck, which she rolls off of after it brakes to a sudden halt. Carleton performed the stunt while attached to wires and all the vehicles were going at full speed. This work was recognized by her peers as the Best Overall Stunt by a Stunt Woman at the 2011 Taurus World Stunt Awards.

Based on such work, as a professional who rarely finds herself starstruck, Carleton continued to be in demand in subsequent years, often applying her varied stunt talents in action-packed blockbusters. She doubled for Paula Patton on the Tom Cruise franchise vehicle *Mission: Impossible—Ghost Protocol* in 2011 and for Jessica Biel on the films *The Tall Man* and *Total Recall*, both of which were released in 2012. She also did background stunt work, sometimes uncredited, on numerous other films, including the Twilight series (*The Twilight Saga: Eclipse*, 2010; *The Twilight Saga: Breaking Dawn—Part 1*, 2011; and *The Twilight Saga: Breaking Dawn—Part 2*, 2012), *The Green Hornet* (2011), *Underworld Awakening* (2012), *Jack Reacher* (2012), *White House Down* (2013), and *Robocop* (2014).

TOUGH BUT REWARDING WORK

Carleton showcased her equestrian skills as a stunt performer in director Matt Reeves's critically acclaimed science-fiction sequel *Dawn of the Planet of the Apes* (2014), in which she was required to ride a horse in an ape-like position. "Hanging out with horses," she told Proskiw, "is my idea of a good day at the office." She would again get a chance to work with the animals in the next installment of that series, *War for the Planet of the Apes* (2017), which was also directed by Reeves. That film's stunt team received a 2018 Screen Actors Guild (SAG) Award nomination for Outstanding Action Performance by a Stunt Ensemble in a Motion Picture.

Some of Carleton's most notable work as a stunt driver, meanwhile, came on the Marvel superhero film *Deadpool* (2016; she additionally served as Morena Baccarin's stunt double) and its sequel, *Deadpool 2* (2018), which star Ryan Reynolds as a wisecracking mercenary. She also went behind the wheel for car chases in the Fifty Shades film series, driving the so-called "hot" car during the chase sequence in the third and final installment, *Fifty Shades Freed* (2018).

At the same time, Carleton added working as a stunt performer with other high-profile stars to her résumé. She doubled for Kate Winslet in the action-adventure drama *The Mountain between Us* (2017), in which Winslet plays a plane crash survivor who is forced to survive in the wilderness with a stranger (played by Idris Elba). In the franchise films *Pirates of the Caribbean: Dead Men Tell No Tales* (2017) and *Avengers: Infinity War* (2018), she was part of the stunt crew.

PERSONAL LIFE

Carleton spends a good portion of her year traveling around the world—which she thoroughly enjoys—for shoots but frequently visits her parents in Kelowna, where she has a large extended family. A self-proclaimed animal lover, she owns a number of horses. She also remains a strong proponent of extreme sports, helping to launch an adventure program for one of Australia's top cruise lines, P&O Cruises, in 2013.

SUGGESTED READING

Carleton, Janene. "Angelina Jolie's Stunt Double Shares Her Fitness Secrets." Interview by Stephanie Ayre. *POPSUGAR*, 19 Oct. 2013, www.popsugar.com.au/fitness/Angelina-Jolie-Stunt-Double-Fitness-Diet-32147293. Accessed 5 Dec. 2018.

Carleton, Janene. Interview. By Bilge Ebiri. *Cosmopolitan*, 8 July 2014, www.cosmopolitan.com/entertainment/movies/a28386/hollywood-stunt-doubles-angelina-jolie-jennifer-lawrence/. Accessed 28 Nov. 2018.

Carleton, Janene. "The Real-Life Diet of Janene Carleton, Hollywood Stuntwoman and Master of Hard Falls." Interview by Holly Mackenzie. *GQ*, 4 Dec. 2018, www.gq.com/story/janene-carleton-real-life-diet. Accessed 5 Dec. 2018.

Proskiw, Adam. "Angelina Jolie's Badass Stunt Double Is from Kelowna." *iNFOnews.ca*, 13 July 2014, infotel.ca/newsitem/angelina-jolie%E2%80%99s-badass-stunt-double-is-from-kelowna/it11475. Accessed 28 Nov. 2018.

SELECTED WORKS

Afghan Knights, 2007; *Salt*, 2010; *Mission: Impossible—Ghost Protocol*, 2011; *Total Recall*, 2012; *Deadpool*, 2016; *War for the Planet of the Apes*, 2017; *The Mountain between Us*, 2017; *Fifty Shades Freed*, 2018

—*Chris Cullen*

Brandi Carlile

Date of birth: June 1, 1981
Occupation: Singer-songwriter

Brandi Carlile was the most nominated female artist at the Grammy Awards in February 2019. She received six nods, and although she did not take home prizes in the top categories of album of the year, record of the year, or song of the year, she claimed the other three awards for which she was in the running: best American roots performance and best American roots song (both for the hit single "The Joke") as well as best Americana album. Collectively, the awards were in recognition of work done for her 2018 album *By the Way, I Forgive You*, which she has said is one of her most poignant, exposing records yet.

As an openly gay artist, the Grammy Awards and nominations proved significant for Carlile, personally and as a testament to moving in the right direction in terms of greater inclusivity in the music industry. Having released the first of her six studio albums in 2005 she had, up to that point, only received one Grammy nod for her 2015 effort *The Firewatcher's Daughter*. Although her critically acclaimed music often defies categorization, some observers have noted her success in a genre whose fans are generally thought to be politically and socially conservative. "Brandi Carlile bent and broke Americana and folk stereotypes as an openly gay woman with outspoken progressive politics," Mary Louise Kelly explained in an interview with Carlile for the National Public Radio (NPR) show *All Things Considered* (14 Feb. 2018).

Though Carlile remained humble about the amount of work she had put into her career leading up to her Grammy wins, she also acknowledged the meaning of the milestone and the increased mainstream attention it could bring: "No kid sits in their bedroom learning how to play guitar and says, 'I don't want to give anybody my autograph' or 'I don't care if I ever win a Grammy.' You care," she told Nancy Kruh for *People* (1 Feb. 2019).

Photo by Kirk Stauffer via Wikimedia Commons

EARLY LIFE

Brandi Carlile was born on June 1, 1981, and grew up in and around Ravensdale, Washington, a rural town several miles outside of Seattle, alongside her brother and sister. Without any close neighbors in the rather isolated area, she and her siblings spent a lot of time outside and roaming in the woods.

Carlile hails from a long line of musicians: her great-grandmother was a country singer, as were her grandfather and her mother, Teresa. "[Singing] feels genetic to me, a personality trait almost," she told Aaron Kayce for the now defunct music magazine *Harp* (June 2007). "As soon as I was old enough to do anything, talk, walk, throw a ball, whatever it was, I was already singing." Teresa, who was part of a band, regularly played at local venues and amassed a small, but loyal following. If Carlile, who honed her singing craft by pushing herself as she sang to songs by country artists like Patsy Cline, had finished her chores, she was often allowed to go along. One day, when she was around eight years old, she sang on stage for the first time. While Seattle's grunge music scene was developing not far away, she had discovered Elton John, becoming a huge fan and later trying to teach herself to play the piano. "My friends at school would write 'Kurt' on their ripped-up jeans, and everybody was into Mudhoney and Temple of the Dog. Pearl Jam's 'Ten' was everything," she recalled to Chris Willman for *Variety* (5 Feb. 2019).

When she was about fourteen or fifteen years old, Carlile came out as gay. She was comfortable with her decision, so it was a surprising and traumatic experience (that she would later come back to when working on *By the Way, I Forgive You*) when her pastor refused to baptize her—doing so right before the ceremony was scheduled to take place. "I had my swimsuit on under my clothes, they'd invited my family and friends—everyone," she recalled to Eve Barlow for the *Guardian* (8 Feb. 2019). "That's when they decided to make an example of me. I'd been on a lot of stages in my life, but that was an irreversibly damaging public humiliation."

PURSUING A MUSIC CAREER

A poor student, Carlile began cutting classes at Tahoma High School and spending her time performing around Seattle instead. Eventually, she dropped out altogether. At one point, she served as a backup singer for an Elvis Presley impersonator, donning a poodle skirt for his 1950s numbers and a Las Vegas–worthy sequined dress for the 1970s tunes. Further inspired by the Indigo Girls, she had taught herself to play the guitar, a much more versatile instrument than the piano for traveling around to perform. She had also begun booking her own gigs in coffeehouses, restaurants, and bars, playing for a few dollars and a meal. Hustling, she would interact with audience members and procure contact information to get them to come out to more established shows. "Pretty soon," she told Marissa R. Moss for *Rolling Stone* (7 Mar. 2019), "I started selling out regular venues. I always thought that I was right on the verge of making it."

When a favorite local band, the Fighting Machinists, broke up, Carlile convinced twin brothers Tim and Phil Hanseroth, who had played guitar in addition to singing with the group and who also held day jobs, to join forces; they quickly melded both professionally and personally. "There is no Brandi Carlile without the twins," she told Willman. The three began performing locally and recording demo tapes of their acoustic songs. Gradually, as they had officially formed a band, they started getting more high-profile work, and in 2004 they opened for the iconic folk musician James Taylor, who had been exceptionally popular in the 1970s and still had a major following. Executives from Columbia Records were in attendance and signed the musicians the next day.

MAKING AN IMPRESSION

In 2005, the eponymous album *Brandi Carlile* was released, earning largely favorable reviews and landing Carlile on the list of artists to watch compiled by *Rolling Stone*. Following the release, the band toured widely, sometimes opening for such acts as Chris Isaak and Tori Amos. They also honed the tracks that would appear on the breakthrough sophomore album *The Story*, which was produced by T Bone Burnett and released in 2007 to enthusiastic reviews.

"It wasn't until 2007's *The Story* . . . that we realized even half of what we'd been dealt," Rachael Maddux later wrote for *Paste* (6 Oct. 2009). "Nearly a minute into the second song (the title track and lead single), something about her shifted from promise to absolute certainty as Carlile let loose a hurricane of lung power." The title track was used for a music video premiered as part of a special highlights episode of the popular television drama *Grey's Anatomy* in 2007 (various other tracks from Carlile's oeuvre have also been part of the show's soundtrack, introducing her to a wider audience) and was featured prominently in General Motors commercials during the 2008 Summer Olympics. *The Story* remained on the Billboard 200 album chart for twenty-five weeks, peaking at number forty-one, and reached the number-ten spot on the Billboard Top Rock Albums chart. In reflecting on Carlile's sophomore album, Molly Savard wrote for the entertainment site *Shondaland* (16 Feb. 2018), "Even then it was clear that the singer-songwriter had an old soul and an ear for the timeless, with gorgeous songs that artfully captured the divine ache of love and loneliness, the pain of loss, and the faith it takes to keep going."

EARNING RECOGNITION

Carlile's next efforts included *Give Up the Ghost* (2009), which won her a nomination for the GLAAD (Gay & Lesbian Alliance Against Defamation) Media Award for Outstanding Music Artist; *Live at Benaroya Hall with the Seattle Symphony* (2011), recorded during two sold-out shows; and *Bear Creek* (2012), which reached the top ten of the Billboard 200. *The Firewatcher's Daughter*, released in 2015, peaked at number nine on the Billboard 200 and earned Carlile her first Grammy nod, in the category of best Americana album. Even after so many years in the industry, the idea of being nominated for a Grammy had remained so foreign to her that when she got a text from a record label executive congratulating her, she texted back asking if he had meant to contact Brittany Howard of the Alabama Shakes, who also recorded on her label. "I was totally unaware of the whole cycle of any of the awards shows," she explained to Kruh, "because I just didn't think that was a world I was ever going to be allowed into."

Carlile's album *By the Way, I Forgive You* was released in February 2018. Coproduced by Shooter Jennings and Dave Cobb, the album was widely acknowledged to be the most intense and profound of her career. It included the evocative single "The Joke," an anthem that critics felt was particularly suited to the increasingly divisive political era in America. "There are so many people feeling misrepresented [today]," she explained to Ann Powers for NPR (13 Nov. 2017). "The song is just for people that feel under-represented,

unloved or illegal." Therefore, she was particularly grateful to have such an especially revealing and powerful record receive more mainstream recognition when it earned six Grammy nominations. Not only did she take home three of the awards in 2019, but *By the Way, I Forgive You* reached the number-five position on the Billboard 200.

PERSONAL LIFE

Carlile married her wife, Catherine Shepherd, on September 15, 2012. The couple met while Shepherd was working as a charity coordinator for Paul McCartney. They have two daughters: Evangeline Ruth (born June 15, 2014) and Elijah (born March 18, 2018). The family live in a log cabin in Maple Valley, Washington.

In 2008, Carlile and the Hanseroths established the Looking Out Foundation, which funds causes important to them, including the United Nations Children's Fund (UNICEF), the Women's Funding Alliance, and Doctors without Borders. She donates a portion of all her concert ticket sales to the foundation, and in 2017 *Cover Stories*, a benefit album featuring songs from *The Story* sung by such artists as Dolly Parton, the Indigo Girls, and Adele, was released. Proceeds from the project benefitted War Child, a British organization dedicated to protecting children in conflict zones.

"I'm pretty happy on the trajectory that I'm on, which is that I've got a pretty equal delineation in my life of the things that are really important: my family . . . my activism and faith, which are unbreakable and one in the same, and my music," Carlile told Savard.

SUGGESTED READING

Barlow, Eve. "Brandi Carlile on Her Song to Subvert the Grammys: 'It's a Call to Action.'" *The Guardian*, 8 Feb. 2019, www.theguardian.com/music/2019/feb/08/brandi-carlile-grammys-country-gay-marriage-cancun. Accessed 7 Apr. 2019.

Carlile, Brandi. "Brandi Carlile on Gay Motherhood and the Politics of Music." Interview by Molly Savard. *Shondaland*. Hearst Digital Media, 16 Feb. 2018, www.shondaland.com/live/a18005318/brandi-carlile-interview-music-motherhood/. Accessed 7 Apr. 2019.

Carlile, Brandi. "Brandi Carlile on Practicing Forgiveness, Even When It's Hard." Interview by Mary Louise Kelly. *All Things Considered*, National Public Radio, 14 Feb. 2018, www.npr.org/2018/02/14/582454085/brandi-carlile-on-practicing-forgiveness-even-when-its-hard. Accessed 7 Apr. 2019.

Kayce, Aaron. "Brandi Carlile." *Harp*, June 2007. *Internet Archive: Wayback Machine*, harpmagazine.com/articles/detail.cfm?article_id=5741. Accessed 7 Apr. 2019.

Kruh, Nancy. "Brandi Carlile Basks in Her Record Six Grammy Nods: 'People Who Say They Don't Care Are Lying.'" *People*, people.com/music/grammys-2019-brandi-carlile-six-nominations/. Accessed 7 Apr. 2019.

Maddux, Rachael. Review of *Give Up the Ghost*, by Brandi Carlile. *Paste*, 6 Oct. 2009, www.pastemagazine.com/articles/2009/10/brandi-carlile-give-up-the-ghost.html. Accessed 7 Apr. 2019.

Willman, Chris. "Brandi Carlile Steps Out of the Shadows and into the Grammys Spotlight." *Variety*, 5 Feb. 2019, variety.com/2019/music/news/brandi-carlile-grammys-by-the-way-i-forgive-you-1203127994/. Accessed 7 Apr. 2019.

SELECTED WORKS

Brandi Carlile, 2005; *The Story*, 2007; *Give Up the Ghost*, 2009; *Bear Creek*, 2012; *The Firewatcher's Daughter*, 2015; *By the Way, I Forgive You*, 2018

—*Mari Rich*

Photo by Leon Bennett/Getty Images

Jekalyn Carr

Date of birth: April 22, 1997
Occupation: Gospel singer and speaker

Jekalyn Carr is a gospel singer, actress, author, and motivational speaker from Memphis, Arkansas. The artist's mission is to inspire others through her work. The daughter of a minister and a gospel singer, Carr began singing when she was five and recording when she was seven. She scored her first hit single, the inspirational "Greater Is Coming," in 2012, when she was fifteen. She followed that with several critically acclaimed studio albums, including the Grammy-nominated album *One Nation under God* (2018). Her other hits include "You're Bigger," which was also nominated for a Grammy Award, and "You Will Win." "I always knew I would be successful in my music career," she told Bob Marovich for the *Journal of Gospel Music* (21 Feb. 2018). "But when you go from a vision to a reality, it's like, 'wow, this is actually happening!'"

In 2018 she published the motivational book *You Will Win! Inspirational Strategies to Help You Overcome*, inspired by the stories of people she met on tour. "As I began to travel, people shared their situations with me and it seemed as though they were allowing their situation to defeat them when it's supposed to be the other way around," she told Darren Paltrowitz for the *Hype Magazine* (20 Feb. 2018). She launched an annual motivational conference centered on *You Will Win* the same year. As several journalists

pointed out, 2018 was certainly a winning year for Carr, who also earned two Grammy Award nominations and made her silver-screen debut when she appeared as herself, singing her 2016 hit "You're Bigger," in the film *Never Heard* (2018).

EARLY LIFE AND CAREER

Carr was born on April 22, 1997, and grew up in West Memphis, Arkansas. Her mother, Jennifer Selvy Carr, is a member of the Arkansas-based family gospel-singing group the Selvy Singers. Carr's father, Allen Carr, is a former minister who became Carr's manager and frequent songwriting partner. Carr has a sister, Allundria, and a brother, Allen Lindsay Jr., and was home-schooled starting at the fourth grade.

Carr knew she wanted to be a singer when she was five years old. Her family encouraged her. "Actually my mom and dad, they heard me singing around the house and were like, it's something that God has given her," Carr told Lisa Washington for *WMC Action News* in Memphis, Tennessee (29 June 2011). As a preschooler with an uncanny ear, she chastised her siblings for singing off-key before demonstrating for them the correct one. (She has never received any formal vocal training.) Carr sang at school, in church, and occasionally with the Selvy Singers, where she often stole the show. She began pursuing a solo gospel career at an early age. She recorded her first independently produced album, *Blessed*, when she was seven years old. When she was nine, the Selvy Singers were interviewed for a gospel music documentary called *Rejoice and Shout* (2010). Carr, who was on set with her mother, broke into an a cappella version of the hymn "Amazing Grace," providing, as viewers noted, one of the most memorable scenes in the film. She then recorded the extended play (EP) record *Promise* in 2010.

By that time Carr, who had also begun preaching, was beginning to garner attention in gospel circles. At age fourteen she had already sung with several well-known gospel singers, including Grammy Award winner Myron Butler, Micah Stampley, Shirley Caesar, and, one of her personal heroes, Kim Burrell. Carr never considered her young age. She told Washington: "I always said when I go out, I don't want the people to see Jekalyn Carr, I want the people to see the God that's in me."

GREATER IS COMING

In 2012 Carr released her first hit single, "Greater Is Coming," with her family's independent record label, Lunjeal Music Group. Her budding career, as Marovich put it, was a "family affair." Carr's father served as her manager, and her older sister, who is also a singer-songwriter, handled the company's administrative work and appears on some of Carr's albums as a vocalist. "All of our writing is done in house, all of our producing is done in house," Carr told Marovich.

In 2013 the label signed an exclusive distribution deal with Malaco Records, through which she released her breakthrough album, *Greater Is Coming* (2013), which included the single of the same name. In the song, Carr sings that after one endures hardship, one is ready to receive the glory that God has in store, much as olives are shaken, beaten, and pressed into oil. The album reached number three on the Billboard Top Gospel Albums chart, while the single "Greater Is Coming" peaked at number seven on the Billboard Hot Gospel Songs chart. The song earned Carr her first Stellar Award for Children's Project of the Year and marked the true beginning of her career. "People would say, 'Where did she come from?' It may have seemed like overnight but the process started at five [years old]," she told Marovich. She attributed the timing of her breakthrough to her burgeoning career as an inspirational speaker, which grew out of her preaching. "For a minute, I thought that singing was all I was going to do," she told Marovich, "but when I was singing, it was as if I was doing inspirational speaking through my music. So it was a smooth transition. But it wasn't until I started focusing on that gift, that purpose of speaking, when my music started to expand."

"YOU'RE BIGGER"

Carr released her second studio album, *It's Gonna Happen*, in 2014. It spawned a hit single of the same name that peaked at number fifteen on the Billboard Hot Gospel Song chart. Like "Greater Is Coming," "It's Gonna Happen" contains an encouraging, inspirational message; in it she asks listeners to trust in God. Following the release of the album, Carr was named to the 2014 Ebony Power 100 list of influential people.

Carr's 2016 live album, *The Life Project*, was her first number-one album on the Billboard Top Gospel Albums chart. Its lead single, the expansive power ballad "You're Bigger," peaked at number two on the Billboard Hot Gospel Song chart, her biggest hit by that metric. Carr wrote the song with her sister. "We understand that there's a lot of people out there experiencing pain," Carr told Greg Garrison for the *Birmingham News* (2 Aug. 2016). "At the end of the day, this song reminds you to look at your circumstances and think, 'God, you're bigger than the universe. You're bigger than my hurt." "You're Bigger" was nominated for a Grammy Award for Best Gospel Performance/Song, a Gospel Music Association (GMA) Dove Award for Best Gospel Recorded Song, and a Billboard Music Award for Top Gospel Song.

In 2017 Carr further expanded her repertoire when she made her acting debut on the television series *Greenleaf*, about a megachurch in Memphis. Playing a young recording artist, she sang "Hold Me Close," which was later released on the *Greenleaf Soundtrack: Volume 2* (2017). The following year she made her silver-screen debut in the family drama *Never Heard* (2018). In the film—which follows a falsely incarcerated man as he finds strength in his religious faith and reconnects with his troubled son—Carr appeared as herself, singing her hit song "You're Bigger."

YOU WILL WIN

Carr released the album *One Nation under God* in 2018. The album, which peaked at number one on the Billboard Top Gospel Album chart, was preceded by the hit single "You Will Win." The song spent six weeks at number one on Billboard's Gospel Airplay chart. "You Will Win" was nominated for a Grammy Award for Best Gospel Performance/Song, and *One Nation under God* was nominated for a Grammy for Best Gospel Album. The album also won Carr her first GMA Dove Award for Best Traditional Gospel Album. The second single from *One Nation under God*, "It's Yours," reached number one on the Billboard Gospel Airplay chart in February 2019.

Alongside the album, Carr released her first book, the motivational *You Will Win! Inspirational Strategies to Help You Overcome* (2018). The idea for the book, which Carr began writing three years prior, came well before the song of the same name. "I knew that at some point God would use me to write a book. I just didn't know that *You Will Win* was the first one," she told Janice Malone for the *Tennessee Tribune*

(7 June 2018). It was the first book published by the Trinity Broadcasting Network. Winning, Carr writes in the book, is not a competition, but rather an acknowledgement of God's plans for different aspects of one's life. The book allowed Carr to expand her audience. "There are people who don't listen to gospel music but they will read a book," she told Marovich. "I want to give people the message in ways that they can grasp it."

To that end, Carr also launched an annual conference based on *You Will Win*. Jessie Clarks for the *Christian Beat* (4 Mar. 2019) called it "a natural extension of Carr's ministry—existing to embolden and inspire the people of God to live their most abundant life."

SUGGESTED READING

Carr, Jekalyn. "5 Questions with Jekalyn Carr." Interview by Janice Malone. *The Tennessee Tribune*, 7 June 2018, tntribune.com/lifestyle/entertainment/5-questions-with/5-questions-with-jekalyn-carr. Accessed 5 Mar. 2019.

Carr, Jekalyn. "Jekalyn Carr on Her New Book, Her New Album & Where Her Positivity Comes From." Interview by Darren Paltrowitz. *The Hype Magazine*, 20 Feb. 2018, www.thehypemagazine.com/2018/02/jekalyn-carr-on-her-new-book-her-new-album-where-her-positivity-comes-from. Accessed 5 Mar. 2019.

Clarks, Jessie. "Jekalyn Carr Announces 2nd Annual 'You Will Win' Conference." *The Christian Beat*, 4 Mar. 2019, www.thechristianbeat.org/index.php/gospel/5781-jekalyn-carr-announces-2nd-annual-you-will-win-conference. Accessed 5 Mar. 2019.

Garrison, Greg. "Gospel Singer with Billboard Hit Song Releases National CD in Birmingham." *Birmingham News*, 2 Aug. 2016, www.al.com/living/2016/08/gospel_singer_with_billboard_h.html. Accessed 5 Mar. 2019.

Marovich, Bob. "At 20, Jekalyn Carr Is in Her Winning Season." *Journal of Gospel Music*, 21 Feb. 2018, journalofgospelmusic.com/interviews/at-20-jekalyn-carr-is-in-her-winning-season/. Accessed 5 Mar. 2019.

Washington, Lisa. "Jekalyn Carr: A Star on the Rise." *WMC Actions News*, 29 June 2011, www.wmcactionnews5.com/story/14998319/jekalyn-carr-a-star-on-the-rise. Accessed 5 Mar. 2019.

SELECTED WORKS

Greater Is Coming, 2013; *It's Gonna Happen*, 2014; *The Life Project*, 2016; *One Nation under God*, 2018

—*Molly Hagan*

Shane Carruth

Date of birth: January 1, 1972
Occupation: Director; writer; actor

Shane Carruth is a self-taught filmmaker, writer, director, and actor. He has made two films: *Primer* (2004) and *Upstream Color* (2014), which won awards at the Sundance Film Festival.

EARLY LIFE AND EDUCATION

Shane Carruth was born in 1972 in Myrtle Beach, South Carolina. The eldest of four children, his father was an engineer and Air Force staff sergeant; thus, the family moved often during Shane's early childhood. After living in South Korea, New York, Virginia, and South Dakota, among other locations, the family settled in Dallas, Texas, when Carruth was in his early teens. He attended Stephen F. Austin State University, graduating with a math degree. After college, Carruth worked as a software engineer at several companies, including Hughes Electronics.

FILMMAKING CAREER

Despite working as a software engineer, Carruth had career aspirations focused on the creative. He tried his hand at writing a novel in his spare time and realized he was instead writing a screenplay. He then tried writing a screenplay and was dissatisfied with it. Deeply interested in making movies, he briefly worked as a sound engineer for an independent filmmaker but found it did not satisfy his ambition.

Carruth continued to work as an engineer while exploring avenues for breaking into the film industry. Then, when he was twenty-nine, he was in a car accident and suffered a head injury. He spent his recuperation watching movies, including films such as *The Conversation* (1974) and *All the President's Men* (1976), in which the use of information plays a central role. Inspired to start writing again, he wrote the screenplay for *Primer*, his first movie.

Carruth taught himself everything he needed to know to make *Primer*. In addition to writing the screenplay, he was the director, producer, filmmaker, editor, and actor. The movie was shot in Dallas over five weeks using Super 16mm film. Carruth scouted locations, cast actors, and edited and scored the film. On a tight budget, he shot each scene only once. He and a fellow software employee, David Sullivan, costarred, and his mother served as the caterer. Carruth eventually quit his software engineering jobs to work full time on the film and edited the movie on his home computer. The entire process took about two years, and the movie cost $7,000 to produce. Carruth submitted *Primer* to the 2004 Sundance Film Festival, where it won the US

Grand Jury Prize for dramatic film and the Alfred P. Sloan Prize.

Primer is a science-fiction film about two engineers who fiddle around in a garage during their spare time and invent a time-travel contraption. Along the way, they develop issues of trust related to their invention. The movie is dense with subplots, technical information, and scientific jargon. Many moviegoers viewed the movie as a puzzle and viewed it multiple times in an effort to decipher and understand it more fully. *Primer* attracted a cult following, and fans filled online forums with their musings on the film and its meaning.

After making *Primer*, Carruth was courted by individuals in Hollywood and spent months traveling to California and meeting with movie executives. He wrote a new screenplay, *A Topiary*, but after pitching it in 2010 was unable to get financing or secure a contract that gave him the level of control he desired. Lacking the money to produce *A Topiary*, he shelved it and decided to work independently.

For several years, Carruth worked in secret on a new film, *Upstream Color*. Determined to have total control over the film, he again served as the director, writer, photographer, composer, editor, and actor. He also composed the music for the movie. He secured a few private investors and took out a loan to fund the rest. He also decided to market and distribute the film himself—two things he knew nothing about—but which would give him control over how the movie was promoted.

Upstream Color, like *Primer*, is packed with details and confused many moviegoers—while attracting many to view the movie multiple times. Rather than following a straightforward linear narrative, the plot is circular and highly fragmented. The movie consists of layers of scenes—some only seconds long and some with no dialogue—that follow each other in rapid succession. Like *Primer*, it deals with deep philosophical questions—about identity, the place of humans in nature, and life cycles—which are more important than the plot. Unlike *Primer*, it was filmed using a large budget, resulting in scenes that are saturated with color and imagery.

The plot of *Upstream Color* involves a man and woman who ingested mind-altering worms, a scientist who controlled their minds, and the couple's attempts to deal with the bizarre behavior that follows. Carruth played the role of the man, and his costar was Amy Seimetz. Carruth entered *Upstream Color* in the 2013 Sundance Film Festival, where it won the US Dramatic Special Jury Prize for sound design.

Since the release of *Upstream Color*, Carruth has been working on a new movie, *The Modern Ocean*. He also appeared in a short romantic film, *We'll Find Something* (2015), written and directed by Casey Gooden, among other projects.

IMPACT

As an independent filmmaker, Carruth has defied tradition to make movies the way that he wanted them made. The result to date is two movies that are more art than commercial ventures—and his entree into making a movie with a Hollywood-size budget and big-name cast. *The Modern Ocean* went into development in late 2015. Its cast has been announced and includes major Hollywood stars, including Keanu Reeves, Anne Hathaway, Jeff Goldblum, Daniel Radcliffe, and Asa Butterfield.

PERSONAL LIFE

In interviews, Carruth has cited how filmmaking has consumed his time, leaving no time for relationships or other interests.

SUGGESTED READING

Baron, Zach. "Shane Carruth Will Have Another." *Grantland*. 2 Apr. 2013, grantland.com/features/getting-drunk-upstream-color-director-shane-carruth/. Accessed 25 Feb. 2019.

Carruth, Shane. Interview by Paul Dallas. "How Shane Carruth Constructs." *Interview*. 3 Apr. 2013, www.interviewmagazine.com/film/shane-carruth-upstream-color. Accessed 25 Feb. 2019.

Carruth, Shane. "Interview with Primer Director Shane Carruth." *SFFWorld.com*. 3 Oct. 2004, www.sffworld.com/mul/128p0.html. Accessed 25 Feb. 2019.

Olsen, Mark. "'Primer's' Shane Carruth Is In Total Control with 'Upstream Color.'" *Washington Post*. 17 Jan. 2013, www.washingtonpost.com/lifestyle/style/primers-shane-carruth-is-in-total-control-with-upstream-color/2013/01/17/9045b46c-5f52-11e2-b05a-605528f6b712_story.html?utm_term=.35fc7fbc1962. Accessed 25 Feb. 2019.

Raftery, Brian. "Buckle Your Brainpan: The Primer Director Is Back with a New Film." *Wired*. 19 Mar. 2013, www.wired.com/2013/03/primer-shane-carruth/. Accessed 25 Feb. 2019.

"We Talked to Shane Carruth about the Human Drama behind 'The Modern Ocean.'" *Motherboard*. 12 Aug. 2015, motherboard.vice.com/en_us/article/4x399m/we-talked-to-shane-carruth-about-the-human-drama-behind-the-modern-ocean. Accessed 25 Feb. 2019.

—*Barb Lightner*

Fabiano Caruana

Date of birth: July 30, 1992
Occupation: Chess grandmaster

In November 2018, the US chess community watched intently as chess grandmaster Fabiano Caruana faced Norwegian chess player Magnus Carlsen in the World Chess Championship. The first US–affiliated player to compete in the championship since 1972, Caruana faced a daunting challenge due to both the strength of his opponent—Carlsen had held the championship title since 2013 and defeated two previous challengers—and the mentally and physically taxing nature of competitive chess itself. "It is like a boxing bout," he explained at a 2018 press conference, as reported by Sean Ingle for the *Guardian* (8 Nov. 2018). "There's unlikely to be a quick knockout, so the aim will be mainly to try and outlast my opponent." Although Caruana did not cede any of the tournament's first twelve matches to Carlsen, he fell to the defending champion in the tiebreaker round of the tournament. Although the World Chess Championship did not result in a US victory, Caruana found that the event succeeded in bringing further public attention to chess within the United States, which he considered to be essential to the game's future success. "I think that chess could be marketed better. It could be presented better to the public. It's not so easy, it's not the most attractive game for people to look at," he told Ben Tippett for *Deadspin* (30 Jan. 2018). "I hope that someday we're able to bring chess to the outside world, not just to chess fans, but to everyone."

EARLY LIFE AND CAREER

Fabiano Luigi Caruana was born in Miami, Florida, on July 30, 1992. The only child of Lou and Santina Caruana, he moved from Florida to New York with his parents at the age of four, settling in the Park Slope neighborhood of Brooklyn. Caruana began playing chess at the age of five after his parents enrolled him in an after-school chess program. "I was a decent student but had some disciplinary problems, and they thought that would help me out," he recalled to Christopher Bollen for *Interview* (27 July 2015). He quickly demonstrated a talent for the game, and his teachers encouraged him to continue developing his skills. Over the course of his early years as a player, Caruana played at a variety of New York chess venues, including the Polgar Chess Center (named for Grandmaster Susan Polgar) in Queens and the Marshall Chess Club in Greenwich Village. He also had the opportunity to train with a number of accomplished players, including the grandmasters Miron Sher, Pal Benko, and Gregory Kaidanov.

Photo by Andreas Kontokanis via Wikimedia Commons

Caruana initially attended public schools in Brooklyn but later was largely homeschooled to balance his education with his chess training. His schedule likewise soon came to include chess events overseen by the US Chess Federation, where he was able to showcase his skills in competitions. "I started playing tournaments, and my results kept improving," he told Tippett. "I enjoyed playing chess, so I kept on doing it." Over the years, Caruana performed well at events such as the Pan-American Youth Championships and increased his rating as a player, achieving the rank of FIDE (Fédération Internationale des Échecs, or World Chess Federation) master in 2002.

INTERNATIONAL CHESS

In 2004, Caruana and his parents left the United States for Europe, where they lived for a time in countries such as Spain. "My parents wanted to visit Europe and explore a few countries for a few years, and it ended up being pretty much a decade that we were in Europe," he told Tippett. In addition to Spain, where Caruana trained with International Master Boris Zlotnik, the family spent several years in Budapest, Hungary, where he pursued further training with Grandmaster Alex Chernin starting in 2007, and also spent time in Switzerland. Although Caruana had long competed for the US Chess Federation, he switched his affiliation to the Italian Chess Federation during his time in Europe. "My situation with regard to choice of federations is somewhat unique," he explained to Bill Harvey for *Chess.com* (31 Oct. 2007) several years after his family's move. "Due to my dual citizenship, I can play for Italy or the United States, and due to my residency, I can play for Hungary. It's nice to have choices." Caruana noted that in addition to his Italian citizenship and European residency, his decision to switch to the Italian federation was motivated, in part, by the belief that the field of chess was less developed in the United States than it was in Europe.

Throughout his decade in Europe, Caruana continued to rise through the ranks of chess players, demonstrating that he was competitive not only in New York City's chess clubs but also on the international stage. He achieved the rank of international master in 2006 and the following year attained the title of grandmaster, the highest official title bestowed by FIDE. Only fourteen years old at the time, Caruana became the youngest US–born and Italian grandmaster to date as well as the twelfth-youngest grandmaster of all time. In addition to Zlotnik and Chernin, Caruana trained with Grandmaster Vladimir Chuchelov, who would go on to accompany him to tournaments such as the 2014 Sinquefield Cup, which Caruana won, beating world champion Norwegian grandmaster Magnus Carlsen by three points. A strong competitor, Caruana proved victorious at many chess tournaments while in Europe, among them several Italian Chess Championships.

RETURN TO THE UNITED STATES

Although Caruana at times visited and competed in the United States during his years living in Europe, he did not return to his native country permanently until 2014, when he moved to St. Louis, Missouri. Home of the prestigious Chess Club and Scholastic Center of Saint Louis and the host city for the US Chess Championship since 2009, the city was popular among high-level chess players and a fitting home for Caruana. Pleased to be back in the United States, where many of his family members and friends still lived, Caruana further reestablished himself as a US player in 2015, when he applied to switch his affiliation back to the US Chess Federation. "When I changed federations in 2005, I was thirteen and the chess scene in the US was not as good as it was in Europe," he explained to Bollen of his decision. "Now it's improved so much. It seems like the right moment to go back."

In the years following his return to the United States, Caruana remained active in both international and domestic competition. Having qualified for the 2016 World Championship Candidates Tournament, he traveled to Russia in March of that year to compete in the tournament, the winner of which would go on to challenge reigning champion Carlsen in that year's World Chess Championship. Caruana performed well in the eight-player tournament but was defeated by Russian grandmaster

Sergey Karjakin in the final round. Karjakin went on to play in the World Chess Championship, where Carlsen successfully defended his title. Although Caruana was unable to vie for chess's highest competitive title in 2016, he had a successful year overall, winning the US Chess Championship and accompanying the US chess team to the Chess Olympiad in Azerbaijan. At the Olympiad, Caruana and fellow US grandmasters Hikaru Nakamura, Wesley So, Samuel Shankland, and Ray Robson managed to defeat the competing teams and claim the gold medal in the open event, becoming the first US team to do so at the Olympiad since 1976.

As Caruana's continuing success in international and domestic chess competitions demonstrated, his many years of experience had not only taught him the skills necessary to excel at the highest level of play but also gave him the ability to withstand the strenuous nature of high-level tournaments. "During a tournament it's just purely chess, from morning to night," he told Tippett. "Usually it's for a few hours before the game that I'll prepare, look at their openings, try to figure out what I want to do, what they might do, try to predict what they're doing. On the other hand, they're trying to do the same thing, so we're both trying to surprise each other. Then I play the game, which could last from four hours on average." Like many other professional chess players, Caruana has emphasized the importance of physical fitness and endurance among chess players, whose success often relies on more than simply their mental abilities.

CHALLENGING CARLSEN

Although Caruana's tournament performances in 2017 were less successful than in previous years, his high chess rating nevertheless secured him a spot in the 2018 Candidates Tournament, in which he once again sought to defeat all competitors with the goal of playing against Carlsen in the World Chess Championship. Although he lost the twelfth round of the fourteen-round tournament, his performance in the other rounds in which he played earned him first place and the right to challenge Carlsen, who had held the title of world champion since 2013. For Caruana, Carlsen represented a serious and compelling challenge. "Part of Carlsen's success is that he has a very stable psychological demeanour," he explained to Ingle. "He rarely gets rattled, and when he loses a game he brushes it aside. Of course, the fact this is his fourth world championships is also in his favour. I will have to learn on the fly, but I feel I am more than ready for the challenge." In addition to representing a significant milestone for Caruana, his presence in the World Chess Championship was especially meaningful to the US chess community, as the United States had not sent a player to the championship since 1972, when Bobby Fischer defeated Soviet player Boris Spassky to claim the title.

In November 2018, Caruana faced off against Carlsen at the World Chess Championship, held that year in the United Kingdom. The two players were well matched, and each of the twelve games played during the main portion of the tournament ended in a draw. To break the tie, the tournament then moved into a series of rapid games, which placed additional time limits on the periods between moves. Carlsen won all three of the rapid games played, once again defending his standing as world champion. Although the loss was disappointing for Caruana, he congratulated Carlsen on his victory through social media following the tournament, referring to his opponent as one of the most talented players of all time. Caruana also expressed his hope that he would later compete in another World Chess Championship, the next of which is scheduled to take place in 2020.

PERSONAL LIFE

Caruana lives in St. Louis. In addition to playing chess, he practices yoga and enjoys athletic activities such as swimming and running, which he has noted in interviews are beneficial to his chess career. "As physical fitness becomes more and more a part of chess, players are starting to realize that one of the strategies is to tire out your opponent," he explained to Bollen. "The trend is to keep pushing and try to make the most out of whatever slight edge you might have." Caruana is also a fan of competitive poker.

SUGGESTED READING

Caruana, Fabiano. "Fabiano Caruana Tells Us What the Life of a Chess Grandmaster Is Really Like." Interview by Ben Tippett. *Deadspin*, 30 Jan. 2018, deadspin.com/fabiano-caruana-tells-us-what-the-life-of-a-chess-grand-1822282197. Accessed 11 Mar. 2019.

Caruana, Fabiano. Interview by Christopher Bollen. *Interview*, 27 July 2015, www.interviewmagazine.com/culture/fabiano-caruana. Accessed 11 Mar. 2019.

Harvey, Bill. "Young Superstars: Fabiano Caruana." *Chess.com*, 31 Oct. 2007, www.chess.com/news/view/young-superstars-fabiano-caruana. Accessed 11 Mar. 2019.

Hernández, Daisy. "A Chess Player's Challenge: Opponents His Own Age." *The New York Times*, 17 May 2003, www.nytimes.com/2003/05/17/nyregion/a-chess-player-s-challenge-opponents-his-own-age.html. Accessed 11 Mar. 2019.

Ingle, Sean. "Long Battle Expected as World's Top Two Chess Players Meet in London." *The Guardian*, 8 Nov. 2018, www.theguardian.com/sport/2018/nov/08/long-battle-expected-as-worlds-top-two-chess-players-meet-in-london. Accessed 11 Mar. 2019.

Jamieson, Alastair. "Fabiano Caruana Could Be First American World Chess Champion Since 1972." *NBC News*, 20 Nov. 2018, www.nbcnews.com/news/world/fabiano-caruana-could-be-1st-american-world-chess-champion-1972-n937846. Accessed 11 Mar. 2019.

Ramirez, Alejandro. "Caruana Switching Back to USA." *Chessbase*, 12 May 2015, en.chessbase.com/post/caruana-switching-back-to-u-s-a. Accessed 11 Mar. 2019.

—*Joy Crelin*

Maurizio Cattelan

Date of birth: September 21, 1960
Occupation: Conceptual artist

Maurizio Cattelan is an Italian conceptual artist who uses humor to convey serious ideas. He is often referred to as a prankster, or as New York City's Guggenheim Museum put on its website, the "court jester of the art world." Cattelan, who has no formal training, has been showing work since the early 1990s. His body of work was simply and aptly described by Calvin Tomkins for the *New Yorker* (4 Oct. 2004) as "a succession of startling and unforgettable visual images." One of his works, called *America*, was installed at the Guggenheim in 2016. It was a fully functioning toilet, located in the restroom of the museum, cast in 18-karat gold. Other famous works include *La Nona Ora* (The Ninth Hour) (1999), an ultrarealistic, life-sized wax figure of Pope John Paul II, pinned to the floor by a giant meteor; and *Him* (2001), a life-sized statue that, from behind, appears to be a young boy kneeling in prayer. Viewed from the front, the wax figure has the face of the adult Adolf Hitler. In 2011, Cattelan was cajoled into allowing the Guggenheim to present a retrospective of his work, but he required that they display the collection, which included over 100 pieces, dangling on wire cables from the museum's ceiling. His most obvious artistic forebears include Marcel Duchamp, the father of conceptual art, who famously displayed a urinal that he titled *Fountain* (1917), and Andy Warhol. In an interview with Michele Robecchi, a writer and curator, for *Interview* magazine (22 May 2009), Cattelan described Warhol as being "revolutionary without being militant." "He knew that believing in art as a society-changing weapon can be detrimental," Cattelan said. "The worst possible thing is when ideological art becomes didactic."

Photo by Espyyyy via Wikimedia Commons

EARLY LIFE

Maurizio Cattelan was born in Padua, Italy, on September 21, 1960. His father was a truck driver and his mother worked as a cleaner. During the first year of his life, Cattelan lived with family friends and relatives because his mother was suffering from lymphatic cancer. He soon returned to her care. She went on to have two daughters and lived twenty more years. She was a devoted Catholic, and when Cattelan was twelve, he got his first job selling religious images at a local church. One day, he recalled to Tomkins, he got bored and drew mustaches on some statuettes of St. Anthony. He never admitted to the crime, though in Cattelan's memory, the priest singled him out. "I know it was you," he recalled the priest saying. Cattelan moved out of his family home at eighteen. He stayed in Padua and supported himself by working as a janitor and a mailman. He was first introduced to the art world through a book by the late art historian Giulio Carlo Argan. Cattelan was intrigued by the photographs of contemporary artwork it contained. In 1985, he decided to quit his job as an assistant at a morgue and move in with his girlfriend, who lived in Forlì, near Bologna. As Tomkins described it, the move was a pivotal moment in Cattelan's life. He decided he never wanted to work for another person again.

EARLY CAREER

In Forlì, Cattelan began making furniture from salvaged materials for his girlfriend's apartment. He soon began selling his designs and developed a relationship with a dealer in Milan named Lucio Zotti. (Zotti went on to become a lifelong collaborator.) Cattelan spent increasingly more time in Milan, and a gallery in Bologna began showing his designs. He fell in with a group of artists, and as Tomkins put it, the "functional element" of his work gradually fell away. Organically, Cattelan began creating art. In 1989, he showed his first work, a black-and-white self-portrait called *Family Syntax*. He moved to Milan in 1990. In 1991, unable to produce a piece for a group gallery showing, Cattelan went to the local police station and filled out a report for a "stolen invisible artwork." The report was framed and hung in the gallery the next day as *Untitled*.

Cattelan enjoyed his first solo exhibition at the Massimo De Carlo gallery in Milan in 1993. For it, he bricked over the gallery door. Viewers were forced to peek through an opening in the window to observe, in the dark, an electric toy bear zooming back and forth on a wire—*Untitled* (1993). The same year, he was invited to show at the prestigious Venice Biennale. Again, he claimed artist's block; he sold his space at the show to an advertising agency, which displayed an ad for Schiapparelli perfume. He called it *Working Is a Bad Job*.

Despite, or perhaps because of, his burgeoning success, Cattelan recalls his early career as a frightening time. "Here I was, in my late twenties, with no art education or anything like that, desperately trying to come up with something clever without making a complete fool of myself," he recalled to Robecchi. "I was so afraid of doing something wrong that I ended up spending a lot of time on my own." He moved to the East Village in New York City in 1993. In a show at the Emmanuel Perrotin gallery in Paris in 1995, Cattelan persuaded Perrotin, the young gallerist, to wear a giant penis costume with rabbit ears every day for six weeks. The piece—*Errotin, le vrai Lapin* (1995)—was a reference to Perrotin's playboy reputation. Other Cattelan works involve gallerists in this way, thus reversing the power dynamic between artist and dealer. For *Untitled* (1999), De Carlo, of the gallery in Milan, agreed to be duct-taped to the gallery wall during the exhibition's opening. Later in the night, he had to be rushed to the hospital after suffering a lack of oxygen.

For a group show at the De Appel Foundation in Amsterdam in 1996, Cattelan stole an entire exhibit from a local gallery and reinstalled it at the foundation. In 1997, at another solo show at the Perrotin gallery, he made exact replicas of the work being presented at the gallery next door. (Later, Cattelan would enjoy employing doppelgängers to attend events and lectures pretending to be him.) In 1998, for *Untitled (Picasso)* for the Museum of Modern Art (MoMA), Cattelan made a Pablo Picasso costume, complete with a giant papier-mâché head. He hired an actor to wear the costume and pose for pictures with visitors outside the museum. In a speech written upon receiving an honorary degree in sociology from the University of Trento in Italy in 2004, Cattelan summed up his anarchic, prankster philosophy. He wrote, as quoted by Tomkins, "I do not know exactly why, but it seems to me that images do not belong to anybody but are instead there, at the disposal of all."

GUGGENHEIM RETROSPECTIVE AND RETIREMENT

In 2004, Cattelan created a work called *Now* featuring a life-sized wax figure of President John F. Kennedy lying in a coffin. In 2008, he created a piece called *Daddy, Daddy* for a group exhibition at the Guggenheim. It featured a statue of the title character of Disney's *Pinocchio* (1940) lying face down in a fountain of water in the museum, suggesting that the puppet had plummeted to his death from above. In 2010, two years after the financial crisis, Cattelan created a towering marble sculpture called *L.O.V.E.* Displayed in the Piazza d'Affari outside of the Milan stock exchange, it depicts a giant hand raising a middle finger.

By 2011, Nancy Spector, the chief curator at the Guggenheim, was actively trying to convince Cattelan to allow the museum to present a retrospective of his work. The subject, he recalled to Randy Kennedy for the *New York Times* (29 Sept. 2011), "put me in so much despair, truly." Years earlier, he had told Tomkins, "I think the moment you think you are successful, failure will be there for you." Cattelan told Kennedy that he pitched the idea to hang his works partly as a way of putting her off—but Spector loved the idea. "It was a eureka moment," she told Kennedy. It seemed an unusually appropriate way to view a body of work that "refuses to be seen in a coherent narrative," she said. The Guggenheim, designed by Frank Lloyd Wright, is a cylindrical space. A winding walkway takes visitors past artwork hung along its outer wall. Cattelan proposed to show his work, not on the walls, but hanging from the iconic rotunda, "like so many fat salamis in a butcher's window," as Kennedy put it.

Among works like *Him* and *La Nona Ora*, the retrospective, titled *All*, featured Cattelan's well-known *Ballad of Trotsky* (1996), a taxidermied horse hung from the ceiling by rope and pulley, and *Bidibidobidiboo* (1996), featuring a small squirrel slumped over a kitchen table having just committed suicide. Pulitzer Prize–winning art critic Jerry Saltz reviewed the show for *New York Magazine* (3 Nov. 2011). He noted that critics of Cattelan dismissed the artist's work as "sight gags, one-liners, and kitsch." "He's considered an entertainer more than an artist, a poseur joker who mocks the system that makes him able to be a millionaire poseur joker," Saltz wrote.

Still, Saltz concluded, the show was "some kind of masterpiece." "Far from being a one-shot chaotic burst, the installation becomes, for viewers, a slow burn," he wrote. "New objects come into view; you see work from below, then circle around and see it straight on, then from above . . . altering ideas about what you've experienced." Cattelan announced his retirement before the retrospective and joked to Kennedy that the announcement freed him from worrying about failure. Saltz identified some truth in this, writing that *All* is "Cattelan butchering everything he's ever done, playing hide-and-seek, hoping his art can somehow escape the scarring effects of being so visible."

Despite his retirement, Cattelan continues to make art in various forms. From 2002 to 2005, Cattelan and curators Massimiliano Gioni and Ali Subotnick presented pop-up shows at their Wrong Gallery—a three-foot doorway in Manhattan's Chelsea neighborhood. In 2012, Cattelan and Gioni opened a slightly larger space called Family Business. In 2010, Cattelan and photographer Pierpaolo Ferrari launched a magazine called *Toiletpaper*. The magazine's website sells products emblazoned with the images featured in the magazine. This mass-marketing approach was meant as a rebuke to the exclusivity of the art world. In 2017, filmmaker Maura Axelrod made a documentary about Cattelan called *Maurizio Cattelan: Be Right Back*. The title references an early show Cattelan put on in Milan. Under the auspices of creative block, he locked the door to the gallery and hung a sign that read, "Be right back."

SUGGESTED READING

Cattelan, Maurizio. Interview by Michele Robecchi. *Interview*, 22 May 2009, www.interviewmagazine.com/art/maurizio-cattelan. Accessed 21 Jan. 2019.

Kennedy, Randy. "Hanging with Cattelan." *The New York Times*, 29 Sept. 2011, www.nytimes.com/2011/10/02/arts/design/maurizio-cattelan-retrospective-at-guggenheim.html. Accessed 21 Jan. 2019.

Saltz, Jerry. "The Redemption of Maurizio Cattelan." Review of *All*, by Maurizio Cattelan. *New York Magazine*, 3 Nov. 2011, nymag.com/arts/art/reviews/maurizio-cattelan-all-saltz-2011-11/. Accessed 21 Jan. 2019.

Tomkins, Calvin. "The Prankster." *The New Yorker*, 4 Oct. 2004, www.newyorker.com/magazine/2004/10/04/the-prankster. Accessed 21 Jan. 2019.

SELECTED WORKS

La Nona Ora, 1999; *Him*, 2001; *L.O.V.E.*, 2010; *America*, 2016

—Molly Hagan

Pierre Charpin

Date of birth: June 16, 1962
Occupation: Designer

"I don't like arrogant objects," French designer Pierre Charpin said, as reported by Barry Samaha for *Forbes* (30 Aug. 2018). "As a designer, I think it is important to try to propose something that is not, how you say, a lot. I use simple things to express emotions." Indeed, simple yet compelling shapes, lines, and colors characterize much of Charpin's body of work, which includes a vast array of furniture pieces and household items created over the course of three decades. The child of two artists and a graduate of the Bourges School of Fine Arts, Charpin brings a distinctive artistic sensibility to the field of industrial design, creating pieces—such as the modular Slice armchair and the sleek, yet highly maneuverable PC Task Lamp—that are both visually pleasing and functional. Long the recipient of critical praise within the design industry, Charpin went on to be named designer of the year for 2017 by the French interior design trade fair Maison et Objet, a prestigious honor that brought international attention to his work. For Charpin, such recognition was welcome but perhaps somewhat unexpected. "I always did what I thought I had to do and not what I thought needed to be done," he told Daniel Scheffler for the *South China Morning Post* (6 Feb. 2017). "Recognition is a non-negligible moment that must be confronted with humility. It is a moment of sharing, sharing of sensibility." Through further design projects such as window displays created for the brand Hermès, Charpin has continued to share his design sensibility both with fellow members of the design community and with the world.

EARLY LIFE AND EDUCATION

Charpin was born on June 16, 1962, in Saint-Mandé, a suburb of Paris, France. He was the son of two artists, and his father, Marc Charpin, received extensive recognition for his work as a sculptor. The artistic nature of Charpin's upbringing would prove to be highly influential on his later work, shaping the evolution of his career as a designer. "From my childhood I was surrounded by people who produced shapes, people who were very committed to what they were doing," he told Scheffler. "And the very fact of having chosen design instead of becoming an artist was also a sort of reaction—more or less unconscious—not to be exactly like my parents; a way to find my own autonomy." After completing his primary and secondary schooling, Charpin enrolled in the Bourges School of Fine Arts (École des Beaux-Arts de Bourges, today the École Nationale Supérieure d'Art de Bourges), where he studied visual arts. He graduated from the institution in 1984.

Although painting was experiencing a resurgence in popularity during Charpin's years at the Bourges School of Fine Arts, he found that the medium did not appeal to him, and he instead gravitated toward the field of design and the creation of physical objects used in everyday life. Although he did not pursue formal studies in industrial design, the field to which much of his professional work would later belong, he found his training in visual art to be beneficial from a creative perspective. "I don't need to wait for an assignment to work, whereas other designers often work according to specifications defined by a design house," he explained to Oscar Duboÿ for *DAMN°* magazine (Sept. 2015). At the same time, Charpin's shifting career path required him to learn much about the design world outside of the classroom. "I had to learn about production systems and their impact on design on my own. It took me some time," he told Duboÿ. "Today, students leave school already knowing the business. But have I really learned it? I'm not sure I know anything."

DESIGN CAREER

By the early 1990s, Charpin had begun to prove himself as a talented designer of furniture and decorative items. He gained further experience as a designer in 1993 and 1994, during which time he moved to Milan, Italy, to work under British designer George Sowden. Following his time in Milan, Charpin returned to France, where he would spend most of the later decades. The designer of numerous works throughout the 1990s, he gained particular attention for works such as the Slice armchair, designed in 1996 and first distributed two years later. Consisting of an armchair and three modular ottomans that fit together, the chair offers the owner the ability to change the length of the chair, from as short as a regular armchair to as long as a chaise. In 2016, twenty years after its original design, the furniture brand Ligne Roset introduced a new version of the Slice chair, updated by Charpin and featuring new colors.

Over the course of his career, Charpin has created designs intended to feature a wide range of materials, including plastic, metal, glass, and ceramics. Although best known for the multitude of physical objects based on his designs, he also enjoys drawing, which he described for the website of the retailer the *Wrong Shop* (Apr. 2016) as "an activity in which I was completely autonomous, the sole master of my decisions, without the need for external expertise." In addition to the many design sketches he has produced over the decades, some of which went on to be published alongside interviews with or profiles of Charpin, he has produced drawn works of art for sale as limited-edition prints, including a series of drawings of monkeys created during a 2012 residency in Japan. Alongside his design work and other artistic endeavors, Charpin has also taught design, beginning at the École Supérieure d'Art et de Design (ESAD) in Reims, France. After leaving ESAD in 2008, he continued to teach at times at the École Cantonale d'Art de Lausanne (ECAL), in Lausanne, Switzerland.

MAJOR PROJECTS

The creator of numerous innovative yet functional pieces, Charpin draws inspiration from a wide range of sources. "I am inspired by all the things and people that stimulate my curiosity and my spirit," he told Devanshi Shah for *Architectural Digest India* (14 June 2017). Charpin's designs have included a variety of furniture items—including rocking chairs, a tennis umpire's chair, a Carrara marble side table, and the tables and shelving units of the 2011 Ignotus Nomen collection—as well as household décor and houseware items, among them the CIRVA collection of blown-glass vases, a crystal water pitcher, and a collection of leather and wood trays designed to hold loose change. Among the design projects Charpin found most challenging was that of the PC Lamp, developed in collaboration with fellow designer Sebastian Wrong. "It required a long development. There is three years between the first sketches and the beginning of the lamp production," he recalled to Shah. "Despite the technical complexity of designing a task lamp I have always wanted to propose a simple object formally, an object that is not technically demonstrative." The resulting task lamps, available in multiple configurations, debuted in 2016 and were sold through the Danish furniture and housewares company Hay, which had partnered with Wrong on new lines of merchandise. Charpin's collaboration with Wrong to create a design for Hay represented just one of his many collaborations with influential brands, among them Hermès, Alessi, Japan Creative, and Venini.

In addition to individual objects or collections, Charpin has contributed to a variety of larger scale projects, including exhibitions of his own work and that of other professionals. He has a longstanding relationship with Galerie Kreo, which has exhibited and sold his work since 2005. In 2014, he was tasked with decorating Appartement N°50, an apartment within the Cité Radieuse, a midcentury building in the French city of Marseilles that had been designed by twentieth-century French architect Le Corbusier and was considered one of the major works of the modern movement in architecture. The apartment's owner, Jean-Marc Drut, had invited a series of designers to decorate the apartment over the previous years, and Charpin became the latest in that series. The opportunity to decorate the apartment was compelling but required careful planning on the part of Charpin, who sought to achieve a specific balance with his work. "For me, it was clear that I didn't want to propose just an exhibition of my own objects in a famous apartment. I wanted to do some kind of arrangement with my own objects in a way that respected the lives of the owners," he explained, as reported by Rujana Rebernjak for the *Blogazine* (22 July 2014). "The challenge was to be present but not invasive." Filling the apartment with a variety of furniture items and objects he designed, Charpin created an overall aesthetic featuring pops of color that publications such as the *Blogazine* noted evoked the bright colors peppered throughout the building's concrete exterior.

WIDESPREAD RECOGNITION

Over the course of his decades as a designer, Charpin has received extensive recognition within the design community for the quality of his work. A book devoted to his designs, titled simply *Pierre Charpin*, was published in 2014 by the art-focused Swiss publisher JRP|Ringier and features illustrations, essays on his work, and an interview with the designer. Perhaps the most prestigious honor of Charpin's career to date came in late 2016, when the interior design trade fair Maison et Objet announced that Charpin would be named designer of the year for 2017. Although examples of his work had been featured at the Paris-based fair in previous years, the January 2017 fair marked his first opportunity to display a variety of his pieces in a dedicated showcase of his own design. Charpin's selection as designer of the year likewise drew further international attention to his work, and profiles of and interviews with Charpin went on to be featured in design-focused publications from around the world.

Charpin's international profile grew further in 2018, during which he began a new collaboration with the luxury brand Hermès. Although he had previously designed a selection of objects for the brand, the 2018 collaboration was highly public, as Charpin became the latest in a series of designers and artists to be selected to design a window display for the brand's New York City store. His ultimate design was displayed in the store's windows between August and November of 2018 and featured an image named La Serpentine, which included a colorful ribbon shape. "The theme of the year is Let's Play, so we started with a drawing of a ribbon and reinterpreted it with a computer, changing the proportions and colors," he explained of his process, as reported by Samaha. The design also featured a partial image of a horse, which Charpin explained "arrived after" the ribbon image. In addition to the store window, Charpin designed a silk scarf bearing the La Serpentine image, which Hermès made available for purchase by the public.

PERSONAL LIFE

Charpin works out of the Paris suburb of Ivry-sur-Seine, where he has a studio that formerly belonged to his father.

SUGGESTED READING

Charpin, Pierre. "In Conversation with Pierre Charpin, Maison&Objet's Designer of the Year." Interview by Shah Devanshi. *Architectural Digest India*, 14 June 2017, www.architecturaldigest.in/content/conversation-pierre-charpin-maison-et-objets-designer-year/. Accessed 15 Feb. 2019.

Charpin, Pierre. "'It Never Leaves the White Sheet.' Pierre Charpin's Obsession with Form." Interview by Oscar Duboÿ. *DAMN°*, Sept. 2015, www.damnmagazine.net/2015/09/13/it-never-leaves-the-white-sheet/. Accessed 15 Feb. 2019.

Charpin, Pierre. "Pierre Charpin on Monkey Drawings." *The Wrong Shop*, Apr. 2016, www.thewrongshop.co.uk/blog/interviews-and-writing/pierre-charpin-monkey-drawings/. Accessed 15 Feb. 2019.

"Pierre Charpin." *Maison&Objet*, Jan. 2017, www.maison-objet.com/en/paris/program/awards/designers-of-the-year/pierre-charpin. Accessed 15 Feb. 2019.

Rebernjak, Rujana. "Pierre Charpin for Appartement N°50." *The Blogazine*, 22 July 2014, www.theblogazine.com/2014/07/pierre-charpin-for-appartement-n50/. Accessed 15 Feb. 2019.

Samaha, Barry. "Hermès Unveils Store Windows Designed by Artist Pierre Charpin." *Forbes*, 30 Aug. 2018, www.forbes.com/sites/barrysamaha/2018/08/30/hermes-store-windows-pierre-charpin-interview/. Accessed 15 Feb. 2019.

Scheffler, Daniel. "Pierre Charpin Named Designer of the Year by Maison et Objet." *South China Morning Post*, 6 Feb. 2017, www.scmp.com/magazines/style/tech-design/article/2065734/pierre-charpin-named-designer-year-maison-et-objet. Accessed 15 Feb. 2019.

—*Joy Crelin*

Eric Church

Date of birth: May 3, 1977
Occupation: Singer-songwriter

Country rock singer-songwriter Eric Church is not only known for his allegiance to traditional country tropes, but also his ability to push the

Photo by Townsquare Media via Wikimedia Commons

genre in new directions and his fan-centered approach to selling music. "Country is not about hay bales or a fiddle," he told Josh Eells for *Rolling Stone* (25 July 2018). "It's about emotion and the organic way we make it." In the tradition of country outlaws like Merle Haggard, Willie Nelson, and Waylon Jennings, Church is both tremendously popular and a contemporary country outsider. Church, who made his debut in 2006 with the album *Sinners Like Me*, had his real breakthrough with the release of his third album, *Chief*, in 2011. That album spawned Church's first number-one hits, "Drink in My Hand" and "Springsteen."

Church is serious about honoring his fans. In 2015 he maneuvered an impressive surprise release of his album *Mr. Misunderstood*, bypassing his own record label to put physical copies of the album in the hands of fans. The year 2017 was a particularly difficult one for the singer, not only because of a series of personal struggles but because Church headlined at the Route 91 Harvest Festival in Las Vegas, Nevada, where the worst mass shooting to date took place. His heartfelt album *Desperate Man* (2018) was released about a year afterward.

EARLY LIFE AND EDUCATION

Kenneth Eric Church was born on May 3, 1977. He grew up in Granite Falls, a small town in North Carolina. His mother, Rita, was a kindergarten teacher; his father, Ken, worked in a lumberyard and eventually became the president of a local furniture company. His maternal grandparents lived down the street, and his maternal grandfather was the chief of police for decades. He had two siblings, Kendra and Brandon.

Church bought his first guitar and began writing songs when he was thirteen. Several years later he began playing sets at a local bar. He loved old country music, but growing up in the 1980s, rock was an inescapable influence. Speaking with Eells, Church described the rock band AC/DC's 1980 album *Back in Black* as "the most important thing to happen to me as a young man."

Church attended South Caldwell High School in Hudson, where he played football, baseball, golf, and basketball. After graduation, he enrolled at Appalachian State University in Boone, North Carolina. Church formed the Mountain Boys band with Brandon and two roommates. They played local venues throughout college and even pressed and released an album called *The Mountain Boys Live at the Blues Room*. Things were going well enough that Church contemplated dropping out of school, but his father promised him that if Church graduated, he would fund six months of music-making in Nashville. Church graduated with a degree in marketing in 2000.

Church arrived in Nashville with a portfolio of songs, though his writing was still unpolished. He received some tried-and-true advice: "It's writing to the chorus, every line fits, every line leads you somewhere," he recalled to Kelefa Sanneh for the *New York Times* (17 July 2006). To make ends meet, Church answered phones for the Shop at Home Network at night but was fired for talking a drunk caller out of buying two hundred knives at 3 o'clock in the morning.

SINNERS LIKE ME

In 2002 Church landed a songwriting contract with Sony/ATV Tree. Capitol Nashville signed him as a singer around 2003. But his stardom was slow to grow. He wrote some songs that found homes with other singers—Church has said that he always preferred songwriting to performing—including "The World Needs a Drink." It was released by country singer Terri Clark in 2004. Ever the perfectionist, Church continued to rewrite the song "eight or nine times," he told Sanneh, after he had already given it away.

To make his debut album, *Sinners Like Me* (2006), Church collaborated with rock producer Jay Joyce, who would go on to work on the artist's later albums too. The album's lead single, "How 'Bout You," peaked at number fourteen on the Billboard Hot Country Songs chart. The album debuted in the top ten of the Top Country Albums. Sanneh offered praise in the *Times*, describing *Sinners Like Me* as an "extraordinarily well-written album." "The songs they made are highly quotable, packed with wry observations and well-turned punch lines, and the tunes are as elegant as the words," he wrote. Church's economy and wit is demonstrated on songs like the single "Two Pink Lines," about a teenage couple's pregnancy scare, and "Before She Does," in which Church sings, "I believe that Jesus is comin' back / Before she does." The song "Lightning," a ballad about a death-row inmate, is the oldest on the album. Church wrote it when he arrived in Nashville and reckons it won him his first contract.

CHIEF

The success of *Sinners Like Me* earned Church a spot opening for the popular country group Rascal Flatts. But Church was fired from the tour after repeatedly taking too long with his set and was replaced with rising country star Taylor Swift. Church began headlining on the club circuit instead, which turned out to be a blessing in disguise. "Church did things the old-fashioned way: He built real fans," Nate Deaton, general manager at the KRTY radio station in San Jose, observed to Deborah Evans Price for *Billboard* (29 Nov. 2013). "They feel like they are a part of something. They go to the shows and they scream for two hours."

Church released his second album, *Carolina*, in 2009. Its lead single, "Love Your Love the Most," became Church's first top-ten hit. *Carolina* also produced a Church staple called "Smoke a Little Smoke," about the singer's appreciation for marijuana. A reviewer for the blog *Country Music Central* (25 Mar. 2009) described it as "a very risky and shifty album," incorporating elements of heavy metal. They concluded: "This album was not made to please the masses, but to please Church and those who want to, and should, take the time to listen." Among those listening was the Academy of Country Music (ACM), which selected him as the New Solo Vocalist of the Year 2010.

Church had built a small, loyal fan base, but his real breakthrough came with his next album, *Chief* (2011), titled after Church's nickname, which was, coincidentally, also the nickname of his grandfather. The album's first single, "Homeboy," about a man's relationship to his hometown, remains one of Church's most popular. The second single, "Drink in My Hand," topped the Hot Country Songs and Country Airplay charts, becoming Church's first number-one hit. The third single, "Springsteen," about how songs can carry memories about a particular moment in time, became his second number-one hit. *Rolling Stone* ranked *Chief* nineteenth on their list of the fifty best albums of 2011. They wrote, "Church is a country singer a rock fan could love—saluting Jesus and Springsteen, mixing up backwoods twang with power chords and [Rolling] Stones riffs." *Chief* debuted atop both the Top Country Albums and the Billboard 200 and earned album of the year honors at both the 2012 ACM and Country Music Association (CMA) Awards.

MR. MISUNDERSTOOD
Church released the live album *Caught in the Act* in 2013 and his exploratory fourth studio album, *The Outsiders*, in 2014. On the ABC television special *For the Love of Music: Nashville*, Church asserted, "Genres are dead," as quoted by Alison Bonaguro for the *Country Music Television* (CMT) website (4 Nov. 2013). "There's good music. There's bad music. And I think the cool thing about Nashville is it is at the epicenter of that kind of thinking. I'm a country music artist in Nashville, but Nashville is way, way, way bigger than country music." *The Outsiders* defied genre boundaries beyond Church's earlier work, eliciting passionate responses from listeners. Nevertheless, it spawned another number-one hit for Church, "Give Me Back My Hometown," on the Country Airplay chart and climbed to the top of the Billboard 200 within two months.

In 2015 Church released a surprise album called *Mr. Misunderstood*. Its origins were as surprising to Church as they were to fans. Beginning work on a follow-up to *The Outsiders*, Church found himself in an enviable state of flow. He wrote and recorded the entire album in about a month. "Whatever happened during the record of *Mr. Misunderstood*, God, I'd love to have bottled it," he told Jewly Hight for *Vulture* (Mar. 2016). "It happened so fast and explosively that there was no time to wonder where the inspiration came from." Church admitted that he hit a dry spell afterward, though.

In the studio, Church and his team devised an unorthodox release strategy. Without telling his record label, they bought a manufacturing plant in Germany where copies of the album were pressed into vinyl and CDs. (Church was adamant that doing a digital drop had become passé.) Church had copies of the album sent directly to members of his fan club and told his label at the eleventh hour. It was a political decision as much as an artistic one. "The way the music industry works is all based on hype," he explained to Hight. "The label gets the music first, and then it's media or critics, and then it's radio. All these people are telling the fans to get the record, which is backwards to me. You're trying to get it in the hands of the fans, but you give it to everybody else before you go to the fans. I like flipping that." The ploy worked: the album was his fifth to go platinum.

Mr. Misunderstood also proved popular with critics and awards bodies. Critic Jon Caramanica described it for the *New York Times* (10 Nov. 2015) as "a love letter to his influences," ranging from the Allman Brothers to Elvis Costello to Bessie Smith. The album garnered Church his second CMA Award for album of the year in 2016.

DESPERATE MAN
Church's next major album, *Desperate Man*, came after a particularly difficult year in his life. Church nearly died from a blood clot and, in June 2017, underwent emergency chest surgery to remove it. Weeks later, his younger brother died of alcohol withdrawal–related seizures. Then, two nights after he performed at the Route 91 Harvest Festival in October, a shooter opened fire on the crowd of attendees, killing fifty-eight people and wounding hundreds more. The massacre inspired him to write "Why Not Me," about James "Sonny" Melton, a Church fan who had died saving his wife's life.

The album, released in October 2018, gives voice to feelings of existential despair as well as political frustration, though it does not directly address the hardships Church had just experienced. In "The Snake," Church describes the major political parties as different kinds of venomous snakes, and in his interview with Eells, he shared his strong distrust of big business and national politics. "Though Church isn't working through his grief in public, he's not stoic," Stephen Thomas Erlewine in his review for *Pitchfork* (13 Oct. 2018). He continued, "The deliberate decision not to indulge in a grand gesture . . . means this album seems smaller than every record he's made since 2011's *Chief*. That modesty is the key to its very appeal: This is an album designed not for the moment but the long haul." The album peaked atop the Top Country Albums chart within two weeks.

PERSONAL LIFE
Church married Katherine Blasingame, a music publisher, in January 2008. The couple have two sons, Boone McCoy (b. 2011) and Tennessee Hawkins (b. 2015). Church and his family live outside of Nashville on a two-thousand-acre property on the Cumberland River, though he has written most of his albums at his Banner Elk summer home in North Carolina's Blue Ridge Mountains. In his spare time, he enjoys fishing, hunting, and golf.

Church and his wife support nonprofits dedicated to children's welfare and to animal shelters. They also established the foundation Chief Cares in 2013.

SUGGESTED READING
Bonaguro, Alison. "Eric Church Says 'Genres Are Dead.'" *CMT*, Country Music Television, 4 Nov. 2013, www.cmt.com/news/1716778/eric-church-says-genres-are-dead. Accessed 17 May 2019.

Caramanica, Jon. "On 'Mr. Misunderstood,' Eric Church Pays Homage to His Influences." *The*

New York Times, 10 Nov. 2015, www.nytimes.com/2015/11/11/arts/music/on-mr-misunderstood-eric-church-pays-homage-to-his-influences.html. Accessed 17 May 2019.

Church, Eric. "Understanding Eric Church." Interview by Jewly Hight. *Vulture*, Mar. 2016, www.vulture.com/2016/03/eric-church-on-mr-misunderstood-aging-success.html. Accessed 17 May 2019.

Eells, Josh. "Eric Church: The Defiant One." *Rolling Stone*, 25 July 2018, www.rollingstone.com/music/music-features/eric-church-desperate-man-nashville-country-700750. Accessed 16 May 2019.

Erlewine, Stephen Thomas. "Eric Church, *Desperate Man*." Review of *Desperate Man*, by Eric Church. *Pitchfork*, 13 Oct. 2018, pitchfork.com/reviews/albums/eric-church-desperate-man. Accessed 17 May 2019.

Price, Deborah Evans. "Eric Church: The Billboard Cover Story." *Billboard*, 29 Nov. 2013, www.billboard.com/articles/columns/the-615/5800892/eric-church-the-billboard-cover-story. Accessed 17 May 2019.

Sanneh, Kelefa. "If You're Looking at Eric Church, You're Looking at New Country." *The New York Times*, 17 July 2006, www.nytimes.com/2006/07/17/arts/music/if-youre-looking-at-eric-church-youre-looking-at-new-country.html. Accessed 16 May 2019.

SELECTED WORKS

Sinners Like Me, 2006; *Chief*, 2011; *Mr. Misunderstood*, 2015; *Desperate Man*, 2018

—Molly Hagan

Olivia Colman

Date of birth: January 30, 1974
Occupation: Actor

"When I really love a script, it's visceral," actor Olivia Colman told Roslyn Sulcas for the *New York Times* (22 Nov. 2018). "I can't explain why, but I feel it; I want to say those words, be that person." Indeed, over the course of her career in television and film, Colman has succeeded in embodying a vast range of characters, from a sitcom love interest or an abused wife to a dedicated police detective or the queen of England. Her layered and compelling performances have earned her widespread critical praise and a host of award nominations, including multiple Emmy, Golden Globe, and British Academy of Film and Television Arts (BAFTA) Awards.

Colman received particular notice for her portrayal of Queen Anne in the 2018 historical film *The Favourite*, a critically acclaimed work

Photo by Ibsan73 via Wikimedia Commons

set in early eighteenth-century England. Her work in the role earned her the Academy Award for Best Actress in a Leading Role in 2019. Despite the substantial recognition she received for that and other performances, however, the notoriously humble Colman tended to downplay the importance of her own efforts. "It was kind of easy for me because it had been done for me, really, the work," she explained to Rüdiger Sturm for the *Talks* (6 Mar. 2019). "I'm just an actor—I turn up, I do the best I can with the script I'm given, I try and make the director not fire me, and I have a lovely time."

EARLY LIFE AND EDUCATION

Sarah Caroline Olivia Colman was born on January 30, 1974, in Norwich, England. Her father worked as a surveyor, and her mother was a nurse. In addition to those professions, her parents had a side business of buying and renovating houses. Consequently, the family moved often during her early years, which the young Colman enjoyed. She attended the Norwich High School for Girls and in 1990 moved to Gresham's School, where she completed her final two years of education, graduating in 1992.

Colman's first experience of acting came in school plays, and a formative performance as Jean Brodie in a production of *The Prime of Miss Jean Brodie* at the age of sixteen convinced her that she had found her calling. After leaving Gresham's, however, still unsure of pursuing acting as a profession, she did not initially choose to study drama. Instead, she decided to study teaching at Homerton College, an institution affiliated with the University of Cambridge.

During her time in Cambridge she auditioned for and joined the Footlights, a drama club run by Cambridge students and responsible for producing many major contributors to British film and television. Colman's period with the Footlights sparked the beginning of what would be a lengthy association with actors and comedians David Mitchell and Robert Webb, with whom she would later appear in several television series.

However, despite such friendships, Colman ultimately decided to leave Homerton College, which had proven not to be a good fit. "They were bloody clever, but I wasn't and I left after a year," she told Stuart Jeffries for the *Guardian* (7 July 2013). She went on to study drama at the Bristol Old Vic Theatre School, from which she graduated in 1999.

EARLY CAREER

Colman struggled to obtain acting work during the earliest years of her career and took on a variety of jobs to support herself while auditioning. In the first few years of the twenty-first century she found work primarily on television, appearing in multiple episodes of sketch-focused television shows such as *Bruiser* and *The Mitchell and Webb Situation* as well as individual episodes of comedy series such as *The Office*. Colman also worked in radio during her first decade as a professional actor, lending her voice to several comedy programs aired on BBC 4.

Perhaps the best-known role of Colman's early career was that of Sophie Chapman, a character who appeared regularly on the comedy series *Peep Show*—which starred Mitchell and Webb—between 2003 and 2010. Although her work schedule precluded further appearances in the series for the latter portion of its run, she returned to the series for an episode of the show's 2015 final season. In addition to her television comedy work, which also included a role in the series *Green Wing* between 2004 and 2006 and *Beautiful People* from 2008 to 2009, she also appeared in the 2007 comedy film *Hot Fuzz* as well as an episode of the long-running science-fiction series *Doctor Who* in 2010. "I think it's just been a long slow burn," she later told Sturm of her career trajectory. "I've worked fairly consistently, and I'm really grateful—even for the years of not getting so many acting jobs because that means I really appreciate being able to do what I love now."

A turning point in Colman's career came in 2011, when she appeared in the independent drama *Tyrannosaur*. Her performance as a woman in an abusive relationship showcased her range as an actor, demonstrating that although she was best known for her comedic work, she was equally capable of putting forth a strong dramatic performance. Well regarded by critics, *Tyrannosaur* won the BAFTA Film Award for Outstanding Debut by a British Writer, Director, or Producer, and Colman herself won recognition for her memorable performance, including the British Independent Film Award for Best Actress. Although she appreciated the positive response to her work in the film, Colman later noted in interviews that she had to avoid being typecast in the period following the release of *Tyrannosaur*. "After *Tyrannosaur* came out I got five or six scripts about women who were victims of domestic violence who take revenge on their husbands," she recalled to Jeffries. "I thought, 'people are going to know the ending of this.'" In spite of such attempts, she succeeded in diversifying her body of work, appearing in projects such as the 2011 biopic *The Iron Lady*, the comedy series *Twenty Twelve* (2011–2012), and the 2013 romantic comedy *I Give It a Year*.

BROADCHURCH

In 2013, Colman became the focus of further attention for her performance as Detective Sergeant Ellie Miller, one of a pair of police detectives investigating the murder of a child in the drama series *Broadchurch*. For Colman, the role was compelling and one to which she was able to connect on a personal level. "I liked Ellie," she explained in an interview for the *BBC America* website prior to the show's premiere on that network. "I find it hard to play a character if I can't feel any of me in them. Especially if you are going to be playing that person for eight episodes you need to feel that connection." Colman's strong performance in the role earned her the BAFTA Television Award for Best Leading Actress in 2014.

Although the first season of *Broadchurch* told a story that was largely self-contained, two additional seasons were produced, each of which expanded upon the narrative of the first. "I must say my initial instinct was to leave it well alone," Colman told Chloe Fox for the British edition of *Vogue* (Feb. 2015) about the first season of the series. "I thought it was perfect as it was, and that it would be a travesty to touch it." However, she went on to add that once the show's writer and creator explained his vision for the second series, she was on board. The second season of *Broadchurch* premiered in the United Kingdom in 2015, while the third followed in 2017.

Colman's work on *Broadchurch* further solidified her reputation as a talented dramatic actor, and she followed the role of Ellie with numerous additional major roles in television and film. She was particularly pleased with the quality of the roles she was selected to play, noting that they tended to be more complex than the roles available earlier in her career. "You get to say more, there are more interesting characters, and the characters get more interesting as you get older," she told Sturm. "So, playing someone in my mid-forties, they've done more than someone in their mid-twenties." Among her projects were the miniseries *Mr. Sloane* (2014) and the film *The Lobster* (2015). She won particular acclaim for her supporting roles in two works released in 2016: the miniseries *The Night Manager*, for which she won a Golden Globe Award, and the first season of the critically lauded series *Fleabag*, for which she received a nomination for a BAFTA Television Award.

PLAYING THE QUEEN
Colman received further international acclaim in 2018 for her lead performance in the historical film *The Favourite*, set in the royal court in England in the early eighteenth century. Appearing alongside actors Rachel Weisz and Emma Stone, Colman plays Queen Anne, a monarch who ruled for a dozen years during that period and whose relationships with her close confidants form the basis of the film. The film was an exciting opportunity for Colman, who was thrilled to play a character whose appearance and behavior often diverged from societal expectations. "I wasn't meant to look nice or be nice, and it was liberating and brilliant," she told Sulcas. "I find it more embarrassing to try to look good. I think I've been fortunate to be cast in these roles, because it's very difficult for young women or men who are seen in one way, and then they are not allowed to age." A hit among critics, *The Favourite* was nominated for a total of ten Academy Awards, including the award for best picture. Colman herself won the Academy Award for Best Actress in a Leading Role and also received several other awards, including a Golden Globe and a BAFTA Film Award, in recognition of her performance.

Another opportunity to play a British queen came in 2018, when filming began for the third season of the Netflix historical drama *The Crown*. Focusing on the British royal family, the series starred actor Claire Foy as the young Queen Elizabeth II for its first two seasons. In 2017, however, the showrunners announced that Colman had been cast to play an older version of the queen in the third and fourth seasons of the show. "I was such a massive fan of the show, and I thought Claire Foy was just breathtaking," Colman told Sulcas about *The Crown*. The news that she had been selected for the role excited Colman, who was intrigued by the possibility of further exploring the inner life of the United Kingdom's longtime ruler.

Meanwhile, Colman portrayed Madame Thénardier in a miniseries adaptation of *Les Misérables* that aired first in the United Kingdom from late 2018 to early 2019 before being broadcast in the United States in 2019 as well. *Fleabag* also returned for a second season in 2019,

allowing her to reprise her acclaimed role as Godmother. She was nominated for a Primetime Emmy for Outstanding Supporting Actress in a Comedy Series for the role.

PERSONAL LIFE
Colman met her husband, Ed Sinclair, while living in Cambridge. Both aspiring actors, the two appeared in a theater production together and later "skipped off together into this nice, not-at-all-sensible world, where you were allowed to play forever," as Colman told Fox. Sinclair attended the Bristol Old Vic Theatre School alongside Colman but ultimately pursued a career as a novelist. They married in 2001 and have three children.

SUGGESTED READING
Colman, Olivia. "Olivia Colman: 'It Will Always Be a Mystery.'" Interview by Rüdiger Sturm. *The Talks*, 6 Mar. 2019, the-talks.com/interview/olivia-colman/. Accessed 13 Sept. 2019.

Colman, Olivia. "Olivia Colman Opens Up about *Broadchurch.*" *BBC America*, www.bbcamerica.com/shows/broadchurch/extras/an-interview-with-olivia-colman. Accessed 13 Sept. 2019.

Colman, Olivia. "Olivia Colman: The *Vogue* Interview." Interview by Chloe Fox. *Vogue*, Feb. 2015, www.vogue.co.uk/article/olivia-colman-interview-vogue. Accessed 13 Sept. 2019.

Colman, Olivia. "How Playing a Pair of Queens Made Olivia Colman an Oscar *Favourite.*" Interview by Julie Miller. *Vanity Fair*, 27 Nov. 2018, www.vanityfair.com/hollywood/2018/11/olivia-colman-the-favourite-crown-interview. Accessed 13 Sept. 2019.

Jeffries, Stuart. "Olivia Colman: 'It's Slightly Scary, the Tall Poppy Syndrome. It Could All Go Wrong.'" *The Guardian*, 7 July 2013, the-guardian.com/tv-and-radio/2013/jul/07/olivia-colman-scary-could-go-wrong. Accessed 13 Sept. 2019.

Sulcas, Roslyn. "Olivia Colman: Uneasy Lies the Head That Wears the Crowns." *The New York Times*, 22 Nov. 2018, www.nytimes.com/2018/11/22/arts/olivia-colman-the-favourite-the-crown.html. Accessed 13 Sept. 2019.

SELECTED WORKS
Peep Show, 2003–15; *Beautiful People*, 2008–9; *Tyrannosaur*, 2011; *Twenty Twelve*, 2011–12; *Broadchurch*, 2013–17; *Mr. Sloane*, 2014; *The Lobster*, 2015; *The Night Manager*, 2016; *Fleabag*, 2016–19; *The Favourite*, 2018

—Joy Crelin

Cristeta Comerford

Date of birth: October 27, 1962
Occupation: White House executive chef

In 1995, Cristeta "Cris" Comerford left her established role as chef at a Washington, DC, hotel restaurant to take a challenging and prestigious position: assistant chef at the White House. Over a decade in that role, she cooked for two different administrations alongside the other members of the White House kitchen staff, led at that time by executive chef Walter Scheib III. When Scheib resigned from his role in 2005, First Lady Laura Bush chose Comerford to fill the vacancy, making her the first woman and first person of color to hold the position of White House executive chef, a post created in 1961.

Comerford's longstanding working relationship with the kitchen staff and skills attained throughout her career made her a strong choice for the position and enabled her to maintain the collaborative nature of the kitchen as a workplace. "I always welcome everybody's ideas—more of a coaching leader," she explained to Jane Porter for *Real Simple* (5 May 2015). "You're there to look at everyone's talents and make sure you get the best of each team member." In addition to working on events for important visitors to the White House, Comerford and her staff have also cooked favorite meals for presidents and their families, all the while maintaining their commitment to producing delicious, high-quality food. "Seasonal and fresh ingredients make the best dishes. If you start with good products, it will be quite difficult to mess it up," she told Juan Machado in an interview for the Asia Society's *Asia Blog* (18 May 2015). "And the learning never ends. You have to be open to all cuisines and taste as many types of food as possible. Different cuisines and food open the door of possibilities to new and exciting things."

EARLY LIFE AND EDUCATION

Comerford was born Cristeta Pasia on October 27, 1962, in Manila, the Philippines. She grew up in the city's Sampaloc neighborhood. Her father, Honesto, was a school principal, and her mother, Erlinda, ran a dressmaking business. The tenth of eleven children, Comerford grew up in a large family for whom food was a major part of everyday life. "The constant smell of food is a very vivid memory for me," she told Porter. "My parents came from a town on the outskirts of Manila. My grandparents had a rice paddy, a fishpond, and livestock. Everything was right in their backyard. If you wanted to have chicken for dinner, you had to catch your own chicken and give it to Grandma so she could pluck it for you." Comerford's greatest culinary influence during her early life was her mother, who taught

White House photo by Tina Hager via Wikimedia Commons

Comerford not only how to cook delicious food but also how to be efficient in the kitchen.

After graduating from Manila Science High School, Comerford enrolled in the University of the Philippines–Diliman in Quezon City to study food technology. While there, she gained a deeper knowledge of the ingredients available to her and learned more about creating compelling flavor combinations. Despite her commitment to furthering her food education, Comerford left the university before completing her degree to immigrate with several relatives to the United States, where her older brother Juanito had already made a home for himself. The family settled in Chicago, Illinois, when Comerford was in her early twenties.

EARLY CAREER

Following her arrival in Chicago, Comerford began to pursue a career in the food industry, first taking a position at a Sheraton hotel near O'Hare International Airport. Responsible for assembling salads for the hotel's diners, she gained the nickname Salad Girl among her family members. Comerford later moved to another area hotel, the Hyatt Regency, where she gained further experience in professional cooking. As her career progressed, Comerford moved to the Washington, DC, area, where she became a chef at Le Grand Bistro, a restaurant located within a Washington, DC, Westin hotel. She also spent six months abroad in Vienna, Austria, where she mastered French cuisine at the restaurant Le Ciel.

Comerford's second major role in Washington was that of chef at the Colonnade, a restaurant within the city's ANA Hotel. Although she enjoyed running her own restaurant, she chose to leave the position in 1995 when an unusual opportunity presented itself. "The sous chef at the White House was leaving to open a restaurant," Comerford recalled to Porter. "Walter Scheib, the [executive] chef at the time, said, 'Hey Cris, are you interested?'" Intrigued by the opportunity to join the White House kitchen staff, who were responsible for serving the president and the president's family in addition to supplying food for state dinners and other events, Comerford accepted the position of assistant White House chef.

Throughout the next decade, Comerford distinguished herself as both a talented chef and a valuable contributor within the White House kitchen's collaborative environment. "She's an all-around great chef, no question about it," Scheib told Jose Antonio Vargas for the *Washington Post* (22 Aug. 2005). "Let me put it to you this way: In the years that I've worked with her, there's been so many dishes she's made for me, and I cannot think of anything she did that wasn't good." Although hired during the administration of President Bill Clinton, Comerford remained with the White House staff following the inauguration of the next president, George W. Bush, in January 2001.

WHITE HOUSE CHEF
In early 2005, Scheib stepped down from the executive chef position, at the request of First Lady Laura Bush. Comerford and fellow assistant chef John Meillor served as interim heads of the kitchen immediately after Scheib's departure, overseeing its operations during the transition. After a 450-candidate, six-month search for a new executive chef, Bush herself selected Comerford to fill the position in large part because of the chef's years of experience preparing high-quality food for the Bush family and their guests. "Her passion for cooking can be tasted in every bite of her delicious creations," Bush said upon announcing the promotion, as quoted by Marian Burros for the *New York Times* (14 Aug. 2005). For Comerford herself, the experience was both an exciting step in her career and a humbling one. "Being chosen from a long list of experienced, talented, and qualified chefs, it gives me great humility and a great sense of responsibility to do my job the best way I can," she told Machado. Although Comerford left Washington, DC, for a previously scheduled vacation following the announcement, she assumed the new role upon her return.

As executive chef, Comerford has prided herself on running an organized kitchen that is equally capable of cooking favorite breakfasts for presidents and preparing food for visiting dignitaries and told interviewers that she is a devotee of checklists and calendars. She has also noted in interviews that it is particularly important for the kitchen staff to remain mindful of both personal and cultural dietary restrictions, thus enabling the food they create to serve an important diplomatic purpose. In addition to running the White House kitchen, Comerford belongs to Le Club des Chefs des Chefs, a group of chefs who work for heads of state around the world and who communicate with each other about their experiences.

Comerford was reappointed and served as executive chef throughout both of President Barack Obama's two terms as well. During that period, she and her staff began to use fresh ingredients grown in the White House garden planted at the direction of First Lady Michelle Obama. Comerford remains as executive chef following the 2017 inauguration of President Donald Trump, who has made known his love of fast-food fare.

PUBLIC FIGURE
Comerford had long been known within the Washington culinary community for her work first at local hotels and later as an assistant chef at the White House, but gained widespread attention far beyond that community after being appointed to the position of executive chef. Along with numerous requests for interviews, that attention took less-common forms at various points throughout Comerford's tenure. In January 2010, Comerford appeared in a special episode of the Food Network program *Iron Chef America*. The televised cooking competition typically pits a challenger chef against one of the show's Iron Chefs and instructs them to each create several dishes featuring a specified secret ingredient within an hour in the show's Kitchen Stadium. In a team competition, Comerford and Iron Chef Bobby Flay faced off against Iron Chef Mario Batali and celebrity chef Emeril Lagasse to create five dishes featuring ingredients from the White House garden within two hours. First Lady Michelle Obama also appeared in the special episode, which complemented her ongoing efforts to promote healthy, local diets. Although the experience of competing on *Iron Chef America* was new to Comerford, she was nevertheless highly prepared for the challenge. "Kitchen Stadium and the White House, they're both immensely intense in terms of pressure," she explained to Rene Lynch for the *Los Angeles Times* (1 Jan. 2010). However, as she noted to Lynch, there was one major difference between the two: "One thing that the Kitchen Stadium has is a fog machine." Comerford and Flay ultimately won the contest, impressing the judges with their dishes which included ingredients from the garden such as sweet potatoes and Japanese eggplant.

In addition to her work and television appearances, Comerford has contributed recipes to a variety of publications, including the 2018 cookbook *The New Filipino Kitchen*. Although her career has reached a point that many chefs only dream of, she remains focused on producing excellent dishes and looking forward to the future. "People always say, 'The White House is the pinnacle of your career.' But when you reach a pinnacle, everything goes downhill from there," she told Porter. "You don't want to call it your pinnacle. You want to call it a stepping-stone for the next great thing."

PERSONAL LIFE

Comerford married fellow chef John Comerford in 1988; the former executive chef later moved to a work-from-home position to support his wife's White House career. The Comerfords have a daughter, Danielle (b. 2001), to whom they have passed down a love of cooking. Speaking of her husband, Comerford told Porter, "He's a great support system. He makes sure our daughter is driven to practices and doctors' appointments, and he does the cooking Monday to Friday. He's such a great partner. I couldn't ask for more." The family lives in Columbia, Maryland.

SUGGESTED READING

Adkins, Lenore T. "Meet a History-Making White House Executive Chef." *ShareAmerica*, Bureau of International Information Programs, US Department of State, 21 Nov. 2018, share.america.gov/meet-history-making-white-house-executive-chef. Accessed 12 Apr. 2019.

Burros, Marian. "White House Cook-Off Ends: Woman Becomes First Chef." *The New York Times*, 14 Aug. 2005, www.nytimes.com/2005/08/14/politics/white-house-cookoff-ends-woman-becomes-first-chef.html. Accessed 12 Apr. 2019.

Comerford, Cristeta. "Interview: White House Executive Chef on 'Culinary Diplomacy' and Learning to Cook in the Philippines." Interview by Juan Machado. *Asia Blog*, Asia Society, 18 May 2015, asiasociety.org/blog/asia/interview-white-house-executive-chef-culinary-diplomacy-and-learning-cook-philippines. Accessed 12 Apr. 2019.

Comerford, Cristeta. "7 Servings of Work Wisdom from White House Chef Cristeta Comerford." Interview by Jane Porter. *Real Simple*, 5 May 2015, www.realsimple.com/work-life/life-strategies/job-career/work-wisdom-cristeta-comerford. Accessed 12 Apr. 2019.

Lynch, Rene. "A Presidential 'Iron Chef America.'" *Los Angeles Times*, 1 Jan. 2010, www.latimes.com/entertainment/la-xpm-2010-jan-01-la-et-iron-chef1-2010jan01-story.html. Accessed 12 Apr. 2019.

MacVean, Mary. "The White House's Commander in Chef." *Los Angeles Times*, 14 Jan. 2009, www.latimes.com/style/la-fo-inaugurationbox14-2009jan14-story.html. Accessed 12 Apr. 2019.

Vargas, Jose Antonio. "Hail to the Chef." *The Washington Post*, 22 Aug. 2005, www.washingtonpost.com/wp-dyn/content/article/2005/08/21/AR2005082101106.html. Accessed 12 Apr. 2019.

—Joy Crelin

Nina Compton

Date of birth: October 16, 1978
Occupation: Chef and television personality

In 2013, chef Nina Compton stepped out of the kitchen at the Miami restaurant Scarpetta and onto American television screens, becoming one of the cast members of the latest season of the competitive reality program *Top Chef*. Despite more than a decade of experience as a professional chef and cook, apprenticeships at prestigious restaurants, and training from the Culinary Institute of America, the challenge at hand was a difficult one. "It's one of those things where you have no idea what you're going into," she explained to Todd A. Price for the *Times-Picayune* (27 May 2015). "You have to build yourself up and say, I'm going to win. And then the first day you think, oh, maybe I'm not going to win." Indeed, Compton finished second in *Top Chef: New Orleans*, but her popularity as a contestant—she earned the title of fan favorite following the conclusion of the season—propelled Compton toward her goal of opening her own restaurant. By 2018, she had opened not one, but two, restaurants in New Orleans. In each venue, Compton seeks to blend Caribbean, New Orleans, and European cuisines and especially to promote the ingredients and dishes of her native Saint Lucia. "We have a very good cuisine," she told Laura Janelle Downey for *Forbes Travel Guide* (19 Sept. 2014). "It's very fresh, very local and very easy to get fish and vegetables we can pick off the tree. I want people to say, 'I want that.'"

EARLY LIFE AND EDUCATION

Compton was born on October 16, 1978, in Saint Lucia. She was the fourth of five children born to Sir John George Melvin Compton and Lady Janice Compton. Her father was a politician who had served as premier of Saint Lucia while the country was a British colony and, following the nation's independence, served as prime minister on three separate occasions.

Photo by Erika Goldring/Getty Images

Compton's father was prime minister throughout much of her childhood. Due to her parents' obligations, she spent a significant amount of time with and grew very close to her maternal grandmother, Phyllis Clark, an Englishwoman who married a native Saint Lucian.

Food played an important role in the Compton household, and Compton was heavily influenced by her parents' enjoyment of cooking. "My mom was a baker, and she loved baking. My dad loved making stews with vegetables and saltfish," she told Downey. Perhaps most influential, however, was the time she spent with Clark. In addition to sharing the British tradition of afternoon tea with her granddaughter, Clark displayed an approach to food that had been greatly shaped by her experiences as a nurse and with food rationing during World War II. "She had a great respect for product. She would wrap up an onion that we would normally take for granted and probably throw away. Every single ounce counted for her," Compton recalled to Downey. "Seeing that for the first time really made me respect cooking because you had to make everything stretch. It was very eye-opening at a very young age."

Compton moved to the United Kingdom to attend boarding school. After completing her secondary school education there, she returned to Saint Lucia in 1997. Although she initially considered attending college to pursue studies in agriculture, she grew dissatisfied with that plan and hoped to pursue other options. "I didn't want to be mucking around with cows," she told Alex Witchel for the Washington Post (24 July 2018). After preparing home-cooked meals for her family and observing how happy dining together made them, Compton decided to discard her earlier plan and instead pursue a career in cooking.

EARLY CAREER

Compton began her professional cooking career at a Sandals resort in Saint Lucia, where she served as one of the kitchen's many employees. Seeking to explore a new environment, she transferred to the Sandals location in Jamaica. "Cooking there opened my eyes," she told Witchel. "I thought to give a dish taste I had to add butter or pork." Sampling local fare, including a life-changing coconut porridge, dramatically altered her perspective. "I said, 'That looks terrible,'" she told Witchel. "But it was creamy and sweet with ginger, nutmeg, caramelized plantains. All vegan, and those flavors were so enticing." After her tenure at Sandals, Compton traveled to the United States in 2000 to attend the Culinary Institute of America. Over the course of her time at the Culinary Institute, which continued into 2001, Compton honed her cooking skills and learned a variety of classic techniques that would further shape her approach to constructing delicious dishes.

Following her departure from the Culinary Institute, Compton completed an apprenticeship at the acclaimed New York City restaurant Daniel, run by French chef and restaurateur Daniel Boulud. Although a valuable experience for Compton, the apprenticeship had its share of stressful moments, including an incident in which Boulud's wife, who was dining in the restaurant, sent back a menu item that Compton had prepared. "I remember everyone in the kitchen stopped what they were doing—separating eggs, weighing flour—and started cursing in French. I prayed the floor would open up so I could disappear," she told Kristin Braswell for Bon Appétit (7 June 2019). "It was a crazy moment of failure, but working in a kitchen of that caliber, it was perfection or nothing."

Although New York City was home to many of the United States' top restaurants, Compton eventually moved to Miami in search of warmer weather. There, she worked at the restaurant Norman's, run by chef Norman Van Aken; the Biltmore Hotel's Palme d'Or; and the Miami location of Scarpetta, the Italian restaurant founded in Manhattan by chef and television personality Scott Conant. In 2008 she became Scarpetta's chef de cuisine.

TOP CHEF

While working at Scarpetta, Compton, applied to be one of the contestants on an upcoming season of Top Chef, a long-running competitive reality series aired on the cable channel Bravo. Since 2006, the series had pitted experienced chefs against each other in a series of culinary challenges to determine which talented professional would earn the title of top chef. Having made guest appearances on the program in earlier seasons, Conant encouraged Compton to pursue the opportunity, which would take her away from Scarpetta for the duration of filming. The show's producers selected Compton to compete in the upcoming season, which was set largely in New Orleans.

Aired in late 2013 and early 2014, *Top Chef: New Orleans* brought Compton to the attention of a new audience as she worked to cook while adapting to unusual circumstances, including cooking in improvised outdoor kitchens and designing a restaurant menu within a substantially abbreviated timeframe. She excelled throughout the competition, and placed second after the winner, Philadelphia-based chef Nicholas Elmi. Although disappointed with the outcome, Compton acknowledged that it was always a possibility. "On *Top Chef*, it's said again and again that it doesn't matter if someone has been solid throughout the season. Everything is based on that current meal," she told Laine Doss for the *Miami New Times* (3 Mar. 2014). "It's a tough pill to swallow, but you're only as good as your last service." Popular among viewers of the show, Compton was named the official *Top Chef* fan favorite for the season. "I think I came across as a likable character, and people now come to the restaurant and they start screaming when they see me and say they feel like they know me," she explained to Doss. "And I have a rapport with these people even though they haven't met me yet." Although Compton returned to Scarpetta following her time on *Top Chef*, she commented in interviews that her long-term goals were to open her own restaurant and to return to Saint Lucia for a culinary project of some kind.

RESTAURANTS

While Miami had been Compton's home for many years prior to her time on *Top Chef*, her experiences filming the show in New Orleans introduced her to a new city with a vibrant restaurant industry that meshed well with her own interests. "New Orleans is a beautiful place. People are so open-minded here—they are so open to new cultures," she told Stephanie Carter for the website of the *James Beard Foundation* (11 Oct. 2018). Compton decided to relocate to New Orleans, where she opened her first restaurant, Compère Lapin, in 2015. Although she had the support of her husband and business partner, restaurateur Larry Miller, she found that relocating and striking out on her own in a new city was a particularly challenging process. "I had no team behind me," she told Witchel. "I thought, 'There are tons of restaurants, we'll be fine.'" She recruited sous chef Levi Raines

based on a friend's recommendation and was impressed by his talent. The pair worked together to establish Compère Lapin as an exciting culinary destination within New Orleans.

Drawing from Compton's diverse influences and years of experience, the menu at Compère Lapin blends Caribbean cuisine with elements of continental European cuisine and local New Orleans traditions. Dishes at the restaurant included curried goat, which became one of the most popular items on the menu, and Compère Lapin received overwhelmingly positive reviews from local diners and food critics. Following the success of the restaurant, Compton, Miller, and Raines opened Bywater American Bistro, in March 2018. Two months later, Compton was recognized with the 2018 James Beard Foundation Restaurant and Chef Award for Best Chef: South, a prestigious honor for chefs from Alabama, Arkansas, Florida, Louisiana, Mississippi, and Puerto Rico. Although such recognition was in many ways a celebration of Compton's years of work and culinary talents, she preferred to focus on cooking rather than on awards and reviews. "The recognition is truly an amazing feeling, but I just continue [to] do what I love, which is cooking and making people happy with my food," she told Jessica Keller for *American Express Essentials*. "There's no better feeling than doing what makes you happy—and as a result, making others happy."

PERSONAL LIFE

Compton met Miller while they were both working at a private club in Miami. They live in New Orleans, in the converted rice mill that also houses Bywater American Bistro. A music lover, Compton emphasizes the importance of taking time to relax and recharge, particularly in light of the often-hectic nature of the restaurant industry. "People get so bogged down with work and everything else, they don't have that happy balance of personal life and work life," she told Carter. "You know what? The restaurants are not going to burn down if I wake up and I have a cup of coffee."

SUGGESTED READING

Braswell, Kristin. "New Orleans Chef Nina Compton Isn't Afraid of the Dish Pit." *Bon Appétit*, 7 June 2019, www.bonappetit.com/story/nina-compton. Accessed 12 July 2019.

Carter, Stephanie. "This Award Winner Stays Grounded amidst Sky-High Success." *JBF*, 11 Oct. 2018, www.jamesbeard.org/blog/this-award-winner-stays-grounded-amidst-sky-high-success. Accessed 12 July 2019.

Compton, Nina. "Nina Compton on Life after *Top Chef*." Interview with Laine Doss. *Miami New Times*, 3 Mar. 2014, www.miaminewtimes.com/

restaurants/nina-compton-on-life-after-top-chef-6591377. Accessed 12 July 2019.

Compton, Nina. "'Top Chef' Runner-Up Nina Compton Dishes on Life in St. Lucia." Interview by Laura Janelle Downey. *Forbes Travel Guide*, 19 Sept. 2014, stories.forbestravel-guide.com/top-chef-runner-up-nina-compton-dishes-on-life-in-st-lucia. Accessed 12 July 2019.

Keller, Jessica. "5 Minutes with . . . Chef Nina Compton." *American Express Essentials*, www.amexessentials.com/interview-with-chef-nina-compton/. Accessed 12 July 2019.

Price, Todd A. "Nina Compton of 'Top Chef,' Surrounded by Family, Finds a New Home in New Orleans." *The Times-Picayune*, 27 May 2015, www.nola.com/entertainment_life/eat-drink/article_a4218a32-40e8-556b-b500-aabb36575557.html. Accessed 12 July 2019.

Witchel, Alex. "For This 'Top Chef' Star, One Tropical Fruit Represents Both Past and Present." *The Washington Post*, 24 July 2018, washingtonpost.com/lifestyle/food/for-this-top-chef-star-one-tropical-fruit-represents-both-past-and-present/2018/07/23/61b7699c-8b75-11e8-8aea-86e88ae760d8_story.html. Accessed 12 July 2019.

—*Joy Crelin*

Iona Craig

Date of birth: ca. 1976
Occupation: Journalist

Iona Craig is a British Irish journalist best known for her award-winning coverage of Yemen. Her 2017 story for the *Intercept* about the Trump administration's botched Navy SEAL raid in a Yemeni village won the prestigious George Polk Award for Foreign Reporting in 2018. Craig, who spent her early adulthood working as a horse trainer, lived in Yemen from 2010 to January 2015. Her firsthand reporting has chronicled the Arab Spring uprisings in Yemen, the Yemeni Revolution, the ouster of authoritarian president Ali Abdullah Saleh, the American drone war, and the civil war and humanitarian crisis that began in 2014. Exact numbers are elusive, but the Armed Conflict Location and Event Data Project (ACLED) estimates that 6,000 Yemenis were killed between January 2016 and December 2018, and the estimated overall death toll was over 57,000 as of December 2018. That number does not include people who have died of malnutrition or disease. Craig is an adviser and spokesperson for the Yemen Data Project, an initiative that seeks to collect data related to the war and foreign airstrikes. "We don't do advocacy—it's about transparency and the fact that data can be used to hold the parties of the conflict accountable, because there is no independent monitoring or data collection going on," Craig said at the Center for Investigative Journalism's (CIJ) Logan Symposium, as quoted by Giulia Dessi for the British website *Journalism. co.uk* (23 Oct. 2018).

In 2014, Craig received the Martha Gellhorn Prize for investigative reporting. The prize jury noted her eyewitness investigation of a 2013 US drone strike that hit a traveling wedding party in Rada'a, Yemen, killing twelve people. The attack, a part of the ongoing US war on terror, offered evidence against the Obama administration's assertion that strikes precisely targeted terrorists and not civilians. Craig has also been the recipient of the 2014 Frontline Club Award for print journalism, the 2016 Orwell Prize for journalism, and the 2016 Kurt Schork Memorial Award for international journalism. She has written for a number of publications and news websites, including the *Intercept*, the *Times* of London, *USA Today*, National Public Radio (NPR), the BBC, and the *Los Angeles Times*.

EARLY LIFE AS A HORSE TRAINER

Craig was born in London in 1976 and spent most of her childhood in Gloucestershire. She began riding ponies when she was about three years old. Living near two well-known steeplechase trainers, she soon became interested in racing herself. She attended boarding school at Cheltenham Ladies College, where she often snuck out of class to go to the races.

She began racing in her teens, and after graduation, to the horror of her parents, embarked on a career as a horse trainer. "My father went to Oxford University and would admit himself that he didn't know one end of a horse from the other," Craig recalled to Teresa Genaro for *Forbes* (25 Sept. 2013). "My mother grew up in the countryside and rode when she was younger, but she really wanted me to go to university. I quite stubbornly said, 'No! I've got myself a job in Lambourn' and off I went." Craig worked in Lambourn as an assistant to Nicky Henderson, a five-time jump racing Champion Trainer, for five years. She suffered a nasty fall during this time, breaking her foot, her ankle, and her lower leg, but remained undaunted. She moved to Australia to work with Australian Racing Hall of Fame trainer Gai Waterhouse for a year, then worked for trainers Jack and Lynda Ramsden in Yorkshire. The Ramsdens encouraged her to begin training on her own.

By her mid-twenties, Craig was working solo. "The racing press said I was Britain's youngest horse trainer," she told Genaro, "but I'm not sure that's true." In 2003, at the age of twenty-seven, Craig earned her first win with a horse called

Nellie Melba. But by 2005, the year her father died, Craig had grown restless in the industry. Without a major sponsor or her own farm, Craig decided, she did not want to continue "plugging away" as a trainer, she told Genaro. In 2007, after thirteen years of horse racing, Craig decided to enroll at the City University of London as a journalism student. She earned her degree in 2010.

EARLY CAREER IN YEMEN

While studying journalism, Craig interned for the BBC's *Newsnight* and Bloomberg News. Those experiences made her realize that she did not want to work in an office. She also studied Arabic in a class at Westminster University during that time. Inspired by her father, who had spent his career working in the Middle East, Craig decided to travel to Yemen as a freelance journalist. "It was the only country in the Middle East my father hadn't been to, and there was a low level of interest in it from editors in London—no one even had any stringers there," she explained to Genaro. At the time, British (and American) news outlets were interested in the impoverished country as a training ground for the terrorist group al-Qaeda. Craig began working for the independent, English-language *Yemen Times* and simultaneously served as the Yemen correspondent for the London *Times* on a freelance basis. She arrived in Sana'a, Yemen's capital, in October 2010, two weeks before two bombs, sent from Yemen and bound for the United States, were intercepted in London and Dubai and defused. The "parcel bombs" were the subject of Craig's first published piece for the London *Times*. It was her first print byline in the United Kingdom, and it was a front-page story. She left *Yemen Times* in spring 2011 to focus on her work for the London *Times*.

The timing of Craig's arrival also coincided with the Arab Spring and the Yemeni Revolution in early 2011. Uprisings forced authoritarian president Ali Abdullah Saleh to hand over power to his deputy Abdrabbuh Mansour Hadi in 2012, but Hadi struggled to address the country's structural problems. The Houthi militia, champions of Yemen's Shia Muslim minority, began a separatist movement and took control of important areas in the north. The division set the stage for the country's civil war, pitting the Houthi rebels, who, the Saudis believe, are backed by Iran, against Hadi, who is backed by Saudi Arabia with crucial support from the United States and Britain. Life in Yemen steadily worsened. In the fall of 2013, Craig said that six of her friends had been kidnapped in the preceding months. Foreign journalists were being pressured to leave. By that time, there were, according to Craig, only four English-speaking journalists (herself included) permanently covering Yemen.

In 2014, Houthi rebels took Sana'a, officially sparking Yemen's civil war. Craig left Yemen in January 2015. By that time, she wrote in a blog post for the nonprofit *Index on Censorship* (14 May 2014), she had "gone on the run from government agencies on four occasions." After living under constant threat from the state, Craig was somewhat relieved to move. Hadi fled abroad a few months later in March, around the same time the Houthis banned foreign journalists from Yemen.

THE WAR IN YEMEN AND THE US NAVY SEAL RAID

Craig was one of the first journalists to reenter the country after the war started, traveling by boat from Djibouti in East Africa in May 2015, by which time the Saudis had begun a sustained bombing campaign against the Houthis. Craig reported that the Saudis were indiscriminately bombing civilians and rescuers, a war crime. Craig spent three weeks in the besieged port city of Aden and was disturbed by what she found there. The city was filled with people displaced by the bombings. The Saudi blockade kept shipments of food and fuel from entering the city by sea while the Houthis blocked shipments from the road. Craig reported that she saw trucks of flour turned away, while nine-dollar sacks of potatoes—"if you could find one," Craig told Stephen Snyder for *Public Radio International* (11 June 2015)—were selling for eighty US dollars. In addition to food, the fighting brought poor sanitation and shortages of medical supplies and water. (In 2018, Amnesty International estimated that two-thirds of the Yemeni population was dependent on humanitarian aid to survive.) She returned in July, staying for four months, two of which, she told James Warren for *Poynter* (21 Mar. 2017), were not voluntary.

Craig told Warren that her gender has been an invaluable asset to her reporting. Of traveling with a British Yemeni journalist for the BBC, Craig said, "We can travel around the country more easily and safely as women dressed in Yemeni female garb of all-black burqa, including face veil." The attire was crucial to her reporting on the Navy SEAL raid in January 2017. Craig was traveling to Yemen—her fourth time doing so since leaving in 2015—to fulfill a commission for *Harper's Magazine* about suicide bombers from a district in southern Yemen. (She had to apply for a travel grant from the Pulitzer Center; the money from *Harper's* did not even cover the cost of her flights.) Three days before she left, US president Donald Trump ordered a Navy SEAL raid in a small Yemeni village called al Ghayil. (Though Trump gave the mission the green light, press secretary Sean Spicer stated that planning began under the Obama administration in November 2016.) The Pentagon deemed the raid successful, reporting that fourteen al-Qaeda members (and one Navy SEAL) had been killed. It took several harrowing days for Craig to reach the village. She traveled the last leg of her journey with her translator, who posed as her husband. When she finally arrived in al Ghayil, she got a very different story.

In fact, the raid had gone quite poorly, notable for its confusion, extensive destruction, and high casualty rate. Interviewing witnesses and survivors, Craig discovered that the raid had killed twenty-five civilians, including ten children under the age of thirteen and six women. (Another victim was a man who had survived the 2013 wedding party drone strike.) According to Craig's report—published in the *Intercept* as "Death in Al Ghayil: Women and Children in Yemeni Village Recall Horror of Trump's 'Highly Successful' SEAL Raid" on March 9, 2017—it was unclear whether or not the men killed in the raid had any serious ties to al-Qaeda. Journalist Peter Maass, also writing for the *Intercept* (24 Feb. 2018), praised Craig's article, describing it as "a demonstration of how independent journalists are able to uncover important truths missed by traditional reporters." Despite her success, working freelance has taken its toll on Craig. Without grants from organizations such as the Pulitzer Center, Craig told Warren that more often, she is "paying to work."

SUGGESTED READING

Craig, Iona. "How a Freelance Journalist Told the Real Story of the U.S. Yemen Raid." Interview by James Warren. *Poynter*, 21 Mar. 2017, www.poynter.org/news/how-freelance-journalist-told-real-story-us-yemen-raid. Accessed 3 Dec. 2018.

Craig, Iona. "Yemen: The Persecution of Journalists Continues Unabated." *Index on Censorship*, 14 May 2014, www.indexoncensorship.org/2014/05/yemen-journalist-western/. Accessed 3 Dec. 2018.

Dessi, Giulia. "'The Greatest Data Project You've Never Heard Of:' Inside the Yemen Data Project." *Journalism.co.uk*, 23 Oct. 2018, www.journalism.co.uk/news/-the-greatest-data-project-you-ve-never-heard-of--inside-the-yemen-data-project/s2/a729383/. Accessed 4 Dec. 2018.

Genaro, Teresa. "From Racetrack to Reporter: Yemen Freelancer Iona Craig." *Forbes*, 25 Sept. 2013, www.forbes.com/sites/teresagenaro/2013/09/25/from-racetrack-to-reporter-yemen-freelancer-iona-craig/. Accessed 1 Dec. 2018.

Maass, Peter. "Iona Craig Won a Polk Award for Her Investigation of a SEAL Team Raid that Killed Women and Children in Yemen. Here's How She Did It." *The Intercept*, 24 Feb. 2018, theintercept.com/2018/02/24/iona-craig-won-a-polk-award-for-her-investigation-of-a-seal-team-raid-that-killed-women-and-children-in-yemen-heres-how-she-did-it/. Accessed 4 Dec. 2018.

Snyder, Stephen. "A Western Reporter Sneaks into Aden and Finds a Humanitarian Crisis in Progress." *Public Radio International*, 11 June 2015, www.pri.org/stories/2015-06-11/western-reporter-sneaks-aden-and-finds-humanitarian-crisis-progress. Accessed 3 Dec. 2018.

—*Molly Hagan*

Dan Crenshaw

Date of birth: March 14, 1984
Occupation: Politician

Republican Dan Crenshaw was sworn in to represent the Second Congressional District of Texas on January 3, 2019. Despite espousing views typical of most members of his party, Crenshaw was portrayed in the media as something of a game-changer for the GOP, largely because of his youth and military background. As Dan Zak wrote for the *Washington Post* (11 Nov. 2018), "Crenshaw seems poised to stand out. His potent life story, his striking presence and his military and Ivy League credentials have set him up as a rising star for a Republican Party in bad need of one."

He also become known for his media savvy. "Our biggest weakness is messaging, I think," Crenshaw told Al Weaver for the *Washington Examiner* (18 Jan. 2019), asserting the need for "getting people excited, making conservatism cool again." He continued, "I love digging deep into policy, but then thinking a lot more strategically on how to message that to people my age, people who aren't generally voting Republican."

Crenshaw also earned a measure of fame when comedian Pete Davidson disparaged him on *Saturday Night Live* because of his use of an eye patch. Crenshaw, who lost the eye while on active duty in the military, later agreed to appear on the show in response to the mean-spirited comment. As Lisa Lerer described for the *New York Times* (21 Feb. 2019), Crenshaw "offered a sincere plea for civility, and a political star was born."

EARLY LIFE AND EDUCATION

Daniel Reed Crenshaw, a sixth-generation Texan, was born on March 14, 1984. Because his father's work in the oil and gas industry took the family all over the world, Crenshaw was born in Aberdeen, Scotland, but spent his youth in Katy, Texas. His mother died of cancer when he was about ten years old. Right before Crenshaw

Official House Photographer, Franmarie Metzler via Wikimedia
Commons

next deployment took him to Ramadi, a city in central Iraq, and his service there earned him a promotion to lieutenant, as well as a Bronze Star Medal, a Combat Action Ribbon, and multiple Campaign Medals.

In January 2012 Crenshaw was deployed to Kandahar, Afghanistan. The following June, during a mission in the Helmand province, he was hit by an improvised explosive device (IED) that went off a few feet from him. He refused to be carried on a stretcher lest it expose the medics to enemy fire and walked to the helicopter to be evacuated to a military hospital in Germany, where he was put into a medically induced coma. When he awoke, he could not see; doctors had removed a length of copper wire that had embedded into his left eye during the explosion and removed what little remained of his right eye.

Crenshaw endured several surgeries and weeks of recovery before regaining limited sight in his left eye. Awarded several honors, including a Purple Heart, he refused to leave active duty. In 2014 he deployed to Manama, Bahrain, in support of Joint Special Operations Task Force-Arabian Peninsula, and in 2016 he was sent to Seoul, South Korea, where he served as the Maritime Special Activities lead for the Special Operations Command Korea. He earned a promotion to lieutenant commander during his final tours, along with several additional medals and honors, but on September 1, 2016, his combat injuries finally forced him to accept a medical discharge from the military.

entered high school, the family moved to Bogotá, Colombia. There he attended Colegio Nueva Granada, became fluent in Spanish, and played on his school's varsity soccer team.

As a youth, Crenshaw was fascinated by the memoir *Rogue Warrior* (1993) by Richard Marcinko, a member of the elite Navy SEALs, a special operations force that is part of the Naval Special Warfare Command. Inspired by the book, he set his sights on becoming a SEAL himself. In 2002 he won a Naval Reserve Officers Training Corps (NROTC) scholarship and entered Tufts University in Boston. He graduated from Tufts with a bachelor's degree in international relations in May 2006 and immediately entered the US Navy.

MILITARY CAREER

Crenshaw was commissioned as a naval ensign on May 20, 2006. The following month he embarked on Basic Underwater Demolition/SEAL Training (BUD/S) at the US Naval Amphibious Base in Coronado, California. During the infamous training period known as Hell Week—designed to test physical endurance, mental fortitude, pain and cold tolerance, and ability to function without sleep—Crenshaw fractured his shinbone. Once healed, he returned undaunted to resume the program.

In May 2008 Crenshaw completed SEAL qualification training—a feat only about one in four ultimately accomplishes. Promoted to lieutenant junior grade, he was assigned to SEAL Team Three and deployed to Fallujah, Iraq, where he conducted combat ground operations in support of Operation Iraqi Freedom. His

EARLY CAREER IN POLITICS

Crenshaw soon entered the Harvard Kennedy School of Government, earning a master's degree in public administration in 2017. Crenshaw quickly found work as a military legislative assistant for Congressman Pete Sessions, a Republican from Texas, but in November 2017, he resigned to make his own run for office. Ted Poe had announced his retirement as the representative of the Second Congressional District of Texas the same month, and Crenshaw, eager to fill the vacancy, was confident that his years in the military would serve him in good stead. "You don't make it through SEAL training without the mental fortitude," he told Matt Register for *Texas Business Radio* (9 Mar. 2018). "It's 90 percent mental. It's 10 percent physical. Don't get me wrong. It's a big 10 percent but if you go into anything wondering if you'll succeed, you probably won't because there's an option. If you ever have the option to fail, you might take that option. I don't know what that mentality is like."

As part of his early campaigning, Crenshaw embarked on a multiday 100-mile run through the congressional district—which includes large portions of northern and western Houston—to raise money for Hurricane Harvey relief. Harvey had flooded the greater Houston area with more than fifty inches of rain in September 2017, and many neighborhoods were still devastated. That type of grassroots effort allowed Crenshaw to place second in the March 2018 primary, bested only by more seasoned local politician Kevin Roberts. Crenshaw had, much to the surprise of many insiders, beaten Kathaleen Wall, who had received major backing from Senator Ted Cruz and Governor Greg Abbott and had spent a reported $6 million on her campaign. Following the primary Roberts and Crenshaw faced each other in a runoff in May 2018. Despite disparaging statements made against Crenshaw by some of Roberts's supporters, Crenshaw won the runoff with 69.5 percent of the vote.

He advanced to the general election against Democrat Todd Litton in November. As the election neared, it emerged that Crenshaw and a handful of other congressional candidates had been affiliated with a far-right Facebook group responsible for spreading conspiracy theories and racist and anti-Muslim posts. He responded that he had been unaware of the group's content and had merely shared campaign videos with them. That explanation satisfied Texas voters, and on November 6, Crenshaw defeated Litton with 52.8 percent of the vote to become Texas's youngest congressional representative.

POLITICAL OUTLOOK

The weekend after the election, Crenshaw won over viewers from across the country with his appearance on *Saturday Night Live*. Prior to the election, comedian Pete Davidson had made derogatory remarks about Crenshaw's eyepatch; following the election, the show's longtime producer, Lorne Michaels, called him to apologize for Davidson's remarks and offered Crenshaw a chance to spread his message to a national audience. While on the show, Crenshaw told the comedian, as quoted by Zak, "There's a lot of lessons to learn here. Not just that the left and right can still agree on some things but also this: Americans can forgive one another. We can remember what brings us together as a country." Crenshaw remained in high demand as a speaker and talk-show guest following his successful *SNL* appearance.

Crenshaw holds mainstream conservative views. He believes in what he characterizes as strong border security, opposes abortion, wants the Affordable Care Act (or Obamacare) repealed, and strongly advocates for Second Amendment rights. While he supports most of President Donald Trump's policies, he has expressed discomfort with the president's modes of expressing himself. "His style is not my style," Crenshaw told Zak. "I'll just say that. It's never how I would conduct myself." He went on to add, "Conservatives can hold multiple ideas in their head at the same time. ... You can disapprove of what the president says every day, or that day, and still support his broader agenda."

Crenshaw was assigned to the House Committees on the Budget and on Homeland Security. Within the homeland security committee, he sits on the Subcommittee on Emergency Preparedness, Response, and Recovery, and is the ranking member on the Subcommittee on Oversight, Management, and Accountability.

PERSONAL LIFE

Crenshaw wears distinctive eye patches, including one with wood grain and a military insignia that he sported at the 2019 State of the Union address. He also uses a dark-blue glass eye with a gold trident (the symbol of the Navy SEALs) in the center instead of a painted-on pupil.

Crenshaw married Tara Blake, the daughter of a career military officer, in 2013.

SUGGESTED READING

Crenshaw, Dan. "On Politics with Lisa Lerer: A Chat with Dan Crenshaw." Interview by Lisa Lerer. *The New York Times*, 21 Feb. 2019, www.nytimes.com/2019/02/21/us/politics/on-politics-dan-crenshaw.html. Accessed 23 Feb. 2019.

Crenshaw, Dan. "Texas Politics: Spotlight on Issues." Interview by Matt Register. *Texas Business Radio*, 9 Mar. 2018, texasbusinessradio.com/blog/dan-crenshaw-republican-congressional-candidate. Accessed 23 Feb. 2019.

Grieder, Erica. "Republicans Can Learn from Crenshaw Voters in Houston's 2nd Congressional District." *Houston Chronicle*, 13 Nov. 2018, www.houstonchronicle.com/news/columnists/grieder/article/Republicans-can-learn-from-Crenshaw-voters-in-13389515.php. Accessed 23 Feb. 2019.

Wallace, Jeremy. "Crenshaw Wins 2nd Congressional District Runoff as Roberts Concedes." *Houston Chronicle*, 23 May 2018, www.chron.com/news/politics/texas/article/Dan-Crenshaw-jumps-out-to-commanding-lead-in-2nd-12935633.php. Accessed 23 Feb. 2019.

Weaver, Al. "SEAL Veteran Dan Crenshaw's Mission: Make the GOP 'Cool Again.'" *Washington Examiner*, 18 Jan. 2019, www.washingtonexaminer.com/news/congress/seal-veteran-dan-crenshaws-mission-make-the-gop-cool-again. Accessed 23 Feb. 2019.

Zak, Dan. "Dan Crenshaw Started the Week as a Punchline and Ended It as a Star. The Real Story Came before That." *The Washington Post*, 11 Nov. 2018, www.washingtonpost.com/lifestyle/style/dan-crenshaw-started-the-week-as-an-snl-joke-and-ended-it-as-a-gop-star-the-real-story-came-before-that/2018/11/11/

d68d5c5c-e46e-11e8-ab2c-b31dcd53ca6b_
story.html. Accessed 23 Feb. 2019.

—*Mari Rich*

Stacey Cunningham

Date of birth: ca. 1974
Occupation: Executive, President of NYSE

"When the New York Stock Exchange was founded under a tree in 1792, women in the U.S. couldn't vote, write wills or even have property in their own names. Now, 226 years later, a woman will oversee the NYSE—the largest stock exchange in the world—for the first time," Julia Glum wrote for *Money* magazine on May 22, 2018, after it was announced that longtime trader and NYSE Group chief operating officer Stacey Cunningham had been chosen to lead the iconic institution, which boasted a market capitalization of some $23 trillion in June 2018 and thousands of listed companies.

Cunningham has credited Wall Street legend Muriel Siebert, who in 1967 became the first woman to become a full member of the New York Stock Exchange (NYSE), for blazing a trail in what is still a predominantly male industry. "I was a woman trader on the floor, and I never thought about it—I never thought for a moment whether or not that could happen, and whether or not that was an opportunity available to me," Cunningham told Tracy Byrnes and Julie Iannuzzi for the finance industry publication *The Street* (16 Mar. 2018). "And it's because Muriel paved the way. I think it's just really important to recognize that any time a woman pushes the boundaries and redefines the boundaries, she's redefining them for everyone else that follows her."

Although she is unquestionably pushing boundaries, Cunningham often explains to interviewers that she did not specifically set out to do so. "It wasn't, for me, about breaking glass ceilings or breaking barriers; it was about accomplishing what I set out to accomplish," she told Emily Stewart for *Vox* (14 June 2018). And, although the media focused on her gender when she was first appointed, she has focused on her role as leader of the exchange. "It means more to me to be the president of this place than it means to me to be the first woman," she said to Lucy Feldman for *Time* (9 Aug. 2018).

Some industry observers have asserted that Cunningham ascended to her new post at an evolving—and thus difficult—time for the NYSE. She takes such warnings in stride. "The future of equity markets is increasingly global, technology-focused and data-driven," she told

Photo by Patrick T. Fallon/Bloomberg via Getty Images

Dominic Rushe for the *Guardian* (20 July 2018), explaining that the organization "is uniquely positioned" to take advantage of its unparalleled renown and vast footprint to stay relevant and remain an industry leader.

EARLY LIFE AND EDUCATION

Cunningham was born around 1974 and was raised in New Jersey. She has three brothers and two sisters. The fourth out of six children, she has quipped to interviewers that she was one of the well-adjusted middle children of the family. Her father was a stock trader—although for many years during her childhood she thought his job involved socks rather than stocks—and among his most prized possessions was a LeRoy Neiman painting of the NYSE trading floor, which hung in his den.

From an early age, Cunningham loved math and science; she could not understand why more girls were not enthusiastic about those topics, and it seemed to her a natural choice to pursue engineering as a profession. She enrolled at Lehigh University, a large, private institution in Bethlehem, Pennsylvania, whose undergraduate classes had become coeducational in the early 1970s. When one of her sisters asked her to assess whether there were any boys worthy of dating in her program, Cunningham was shocked to look around and realize that she was the only woman in a sea of male students.

One summer during college, Cunningham attempted to get a job waitressing to earn extra money, but she was rebuffed because of her lack of experience. Her father arranged for her to serve as an intern at his brokerage firm instead.

"It just took one day. One day to change my career path," she recalled to Julia Glum of that day in 1994 when she first saw the NYSE up close. "The moment I walked into that building and onto the floor, I just knew it was the place that I belonged at that time." Cunningham felt a comfortable sense of community on the trading floor and enjoyed the buzz and pace, which reminded her of her hard-charging family.

When Cunningham graduated from Lehigh with a Bachelor of Science degree in industrial engineering in 1996, she headed directly back to the trading floor—confident that the ability to troubleshoot complex problems that she had developed during her engineering studies would serve her well there.

EARLY CAREER

Cunningham began her career as a trading specialist at JJC, which later became a subsidiary of Bank of America. As a trading specialist, she matched investors with securities listed on the NYSE, which was then still a private organization. She traded shares in Hershey Foods, Ambac Financial, and other companies.

By 2005 Cunningham was growing impatient with the tradition-bound practices at the exchange. "The trading floor back then was still entirely manual but the market had moved past that, and we hadn't yet made that transition to combining technology with the floor. It felt wrong to me," she told Nicole Bullock for the *Financial Times* (17 June 2017). "If you don't give the people on the floor the tools they need to compete in a modern environment, they are not going to be successful."

Ready for a complete change, she enrolled in a nine-month training program at New York City's Institute of Culinary Education. She completed her required internship at Ouest, a now-defunct restaurant on Manhattan's Upper West Side, where she found the high-pressure work conditions familiar. "The environment was so much like the trading floor. Things that would not be OK in really any other place tend to be OK on the trading floor and in the restaurant kitchen," Cunningham recalled to Bullock. "The way you interact with your co-workers during stress—everyone knows not to take it personally, for the most part. On the floor you might in the heat of the moment be aggressively fighting over a trade, and at the end of the day go grab a beer together."

FINANCIAL INDUSTRY EXECUTIVE

In 2007, when she was ready to return to the financial industry following her culinary hiatus, she joined rival exchange Nasdaq (originally an acronym for the National Association of Securities Dealers Automated Quotations), which ranks second in market capitalization only to NYSE and is located not far from the larger company, in Manhattan. At Nasdaq, Cunningham served as director of capital markets before being promoted to head of sales.

In late 2012 she returned to NYSE Group, just days before Intercontinental Exchange (ICE) announced plans to acquire the exchange for $8.2 Billion. Once that deal had closed, she was named vice president of sales and relationship management. She was later promoted to head of sales and relationship in 2013 and president of NYSE governance services in 2014 before becoming the exchange's chief operating officer (COO) in 2015. As COO, she oversaw the exchange's equities, equities derivatives, and exchange-traded products.

On May 22, 2018, ICE announced that Cunningham would be the exchange's sixty-seventh president, replacing Thomas Farley, effective on May 25. Since then, she has led efforts to overhaul and update the exchange's trading operations, including the rollout of NYSE Pillar, a state-of-the-art trading platform that connects all the exchange's markets. She told Feldman that, as president, she is often called upon to host business and government leaders wanting to confer about the world's capital markets. "When there's a global event that occurs, the world looks to the New York Stock Exchange to see how the markets are going to react," she said. Among other leaders, she has hosted former UK prime minister Tony Blair and former US secretary of state Colin Powell.

Critics of the NYSE have pointed out that "going public" on an exchange used to be considered a badge of honor for a startup company, with great ceremony accorded to the initial public offering (IPO). Now, however, many companies, including the likes of SpaceX and Airbnb, are choosing to stay private, thus avoiding pressure from shareholders and an increasingly complex regulatory landscape. Such observations have not dampened Cunningham's enthusiasm for the exchange. "There still are a good number of reasons as to why companies get the benefit of the public markets," Cunningham said to Stewart for *Vox.* "I think what's important, and where I'm focused, is that we spend our energy with politicians and regulators to make sure that we have the right rule set, because if a company like an Uber or an Airbnb waits until they're really large to access the public markets, it means that all the Main Street investors missed out on that growth. . . . We want to make sure that we have a framework in place that allows all investors to invest in the success of dreamers that are building large businesses. That's what makes this country so unique and so special, and so we want to make sure that we're protecting that."

Critics have also called out the fact that most trading is now done electronically, relying on artificial intelligence, thus making an exchange floor populated by human traders an anachronism. Cunningham has called upon the events surrounding the 2016 Brexit vote, when investors were jittery and the market was volatile, to explain the importance of human judgment. "One analogy we often use to describe how people add to that equation is an airline pilot," she told Rushe. "So, a plane can take off and land without a pilot. You don't need to have a human being in the cockpit. But that human being adds value, especially during the most tumultuous times."

PERSONAL LIFE

Cunningham, who lives in New York City, regularly works twelve- to fourteen-hour days and says that she generally goes to sleep thinking about the markets and wakes up doing the same. Among her own prized possessions is her father's LeRoy Neiman stock exchange painting, which he gave to her as a congratulatory gift when she assumed her position as head of the NYSE Group.

SUGGESTED READING

Byrnes, Tracy, and Julie Iannuzzi. "NYSE's Female Leaders Are Changing the World One IPO at a Time." *The Street*, 16 Mar. 2018, www.thestreet.com/video/14523159/companies-going-public-good-for-society.html. Accessed 2 Aug. 2019.

Bullock, Nicole. "Stacey Cunningham: Feeling the Heat on the Trading Floor and in the Kitchen." *Financial Times*, 17 June 2017, www.ft.com/content/58a80dd4-5089-11e7-bfb8-997009366969. Accessed 2 Aug. 2019.

Cunningham, Stacey. "The First Woman President of the NYSE Would Really Rather Not Talk about Her Gender." Interview by Emily Stewart. *Vox*, 14 June 2018, www.vox.com/identities/2018/6/14/17449032/new-york-stock-exchange-stacey-cunningham. Accessed 2 Aug. 2019.

Feldman, Lucy. "Stacey Cunningham, Head of the New York Stock Exchange, Talks History as She Changes It." *Time*, 9 Aug. 2018, time.com/5362170/stacey-cunningham-nyse/. Accessed 2 Aug. 2019.

Glum, Julia. "Meet the Next President of the New York Stock Exchange, a 43-Year-Old Former Intern Who Briefly Left to Become a Chef." *Money*, 23 May 2018, money.com/money/5286940/new-york-stock-exchange-stacey-cunningham/. Accessed 2 Aug. 2019.

Rushe, Dominic. "'We Need a Call to Action': Stacey Cunningham, the NYSE's First Female President." *The Guardian*, 20 July 2018, www.theguardian.com/business/2018/jul/20/stacey-cunningham-new-york-stock-exchange-first-female-president. Accessed 2 Aug. 2019.

Vara, Vauhini. "The New York Stock Exchange Has Its First Woman President. Is She on a Glass Cliff?" *The Atlantic*, 23 May 2018, www.theatlantic.com/business/archive/2018/05/nyse-president/561047/. Accessed 2 Aug. 2019.

—*Mari Rich*

Ana de Armas

Date of birth: April 30, 1988
Occupation: Actor

Ana de Armas is a Cuban-born actor who first earned widespread attention for her role as Joi in *Blade Runner 2049* (2017), the blockbuster follow-up to the 1982 cult classic, *Blade Runner*. The original film, directed by Ridley Scott and loosely based on a Philip K. Dick novel, takes place in a dystopian Los Angeles in 2019. The sequel, directed by Denis Villeneuve, takes place in the year of the title and stars Ryan Gosling, Harrison Ford, and Jared Leto. De Armas plays a hologram that Peter Debruge for *Variety* (29 Sept. 2017) described as "the soul of the film," in a world that probes the line between replicants (androids) and humans in a future dystopia.

De Armas studied at the National Theater School of Cuba and was cast in her first Cuban film at sixteen. At eighteen, she moved to Spain. Within weeks, she had landed a role on the popular Spanish television thriller *El Internado* (*The Boarding School*; sometimes called *El Internado Laguna Negra* [*The Black Lagoon Boarding School*]) about a haunted boarding school. After eight years of celebrity in Spain, de Armas moved to Los Angeles in 2014 as a total unknown. She was adamant about playing a variety of roles and fearful of being typecast. "It's weird when people say, 'You're a Cuban actress' or 'You're a Spanish actress.' They put a thing in front of what you are, but I'm like, 'I'm an actress,'" she told Lauren McCarthy for *W Magazine* (4 Oct. 2017). "I'll see what I can do, but don't put me in a place that you don't know yet. Don't put a label on my work before you see it." She made her Hollywood debut torturing actor Keanu Reeves's character in the erotic thriller *Knock Knock* in 2015. She went on to appear in supporting roles in a number of action films, including *War Dogs* (2016) and *Overdrive* (2017), before her breakout in *Blade Runner 2049*.

EARLY LIFE AND EDUCATION

Ana Celia de Armas Caso was born in Santa Cruz del Norte, Cuba, on April 30, 1988. She

Photo by Gage Skidmore via Wikimedia Commons

was raised in Cuba's capital city of Havana, where both her father, Ramon, and her mother, Ana, were workers. Her brother, Javier, became a photographer. She would later describe her upbringing as modest and close-knit. De Armas loved acting from an early age. "There wasn't a specific day or actor or anything like that, but I do remember that I would watch a movie and if there was any scene that I liked, I would run from the couch to the mirror and repeat it over and over again. I would get very emotional," she recalled to McCarthy. "When I was twelve, I heard about the National Theater School and I told my parents, 'That's what I want to do.' And that was it."

At fourteen, de Armas enrolled as a student at the National Theater School of Cuba in Havana. Two years later, while de Armas was still a student, Spanish director Manuel Gutiérrez Aragón cast her in her first film, a 1950s crime drama called *Una rosa de Francia*, or *Virgin Rose*. It was released in 2006. De Armas played the film's ingénue. She also appeared in the Spanish sci-fi film *Madrigal*, directed by Cuban auteur Fernando Pérez, in 2007. A few months shy of her graduation, de Armas decided to leave Cuba to pursue an acting career in Spain; her maternal grandparents were Spanish, allowing her to claim Spanish as well as Cuban citizenship.

De Armas noted that she left Cuba simply to have more opportunities as an actor. "I didn't leave Cuba to make more money or to have more food or live a better life, I left Cuba to grow as an artist and become involved in more interesting projects," she told Gabriel Lerman in an interview for the website of the *Golden Globe Awards*

(31 Aug. 2016). "Unfortunately there are a lot of good Cuban actors who do what they can with what they have and with the limited access to things they need. I knew that the amount of movies made in Cuba weren't many and that I had a ceiling as an actress. That was the only reason why I left."

CAREER IN SPAIN

Two weeks after moving to Madrid, the eighteen-year-old de Armas was cast in the television series *El Internado* (*The Boarding School*). The timing was serendipitous—she had arrived with only 200 euros in her pocket. "Of course, I didn't know that 200 euros was nothing, because in Cuba, 200 was a lot, and the money I had been saving from my movies," she told McCarthy. The show, which aired through 2010, was a thrilling mystery series about a secluded boarding school where supernatural things happen. It was a huge hit and made de Armas a star.

For eight years, de Armas enjoyed a thriving career in Spain. She appeared in a number of Spanish films, including the teen comedy *Mentiras y gordas*, or *Sex, Party and Lies* in 2009. She also appeared on a television show called *Hispania, la leyenda*, or *Hispania, the Legend*, set in Spain during the time of the Romans, and starred in a horror film called *El callejón*, or *Blind Alley*, in 2011. In 2014, she starred in a romantic movie called *Por un puñado de besos* ("For a handful of kisses").

HOLLYWOOD DEBUT

Despite her success in Spain, de Armas began to feel restless. "It was really exciting, but I got to the point like I had in Cuba where I thought, 'I want more than this,'" she told McCarthy. "I wanted something challenging." She, therefore, decided to move to Los Angeles in 2014 to pursue a career in Hollywood. Yet while she was a celebrity in Spain, she was totally anonymous in LA. She did not know anyone and did not speak any English—although she became fluent quickly. "As the Cubans say, when your rice and beans depend on that, your brain goes into survival mode," she told Olivia Gargan for *Wonderland* magazine (9 Oct. 2017). Her first few months in the United States were spent in intensive language study. "It was good exercise for my ego," she told McCarthy.

De Armas made her Hollywood debut in the erotic thriller *Knock Knock*, starring Keanu Reeves, in 2015. Based on the 1977 film *Death Game*, it was directed by famed horror director Eli Roth. In the film, de Armas's character Bel and her girlfriend Genesis (Lorenza Izzo) seduce Reeves's character Evan and then torture him. *Knock Knock*, far less gory than Roth's earlier offerings, received mixed to positive reviews. Multiple critics praised the dual performances of de

Armas and Izzo. "The economical, satisfyingly nasty scenario would be nothing without Izzo and de Armas, who—in addition to having the staggering good looks the plot requires—play off each other with ace comic timing and palpable menace," Ben Kenigsberg wrote for *Variety* (24 Jan. 2015).

BLADE RUNNER 2049

De Armas starred in another film with Reeves— a crime drama called *Exposed*—in 2016, playing a woman plagued by supernatural visions. However, the film was criticized for its lack of a cohesive plot. The same year, de Armas appeared in *Hands of Stone*, a biopic about Panamanian boxer Roberto Durán (Édgar Ramírez), featuring Academy Award–winning actor Roberto De Niro as Durán's coach, Ray Arcel. De Armas plays Durán's wife, Felicidad. In preparation for the role, de Armas spent New Year's in Panama with Durán's family. "They told us intimate stories about their lives that may not be in the film but definitely helped as a source of inspiration," de Armas told Lerman. "I think it's important to understand what drove these people to make the life decisions they did." The film received reservedly positive reviews, though it was criticized for its by-the-book boxing movie plot.

Also in 2016, de Armas appeared in the action comedy *War Dogs*, starring Jonah Hill and Miles Teller. Based on a true story, the film follows two friends who improbably become weapons suppliers for the US military. De Armas played a small role—the romantic interest of Teller's character—but the film won positive reviews. In 2017, de Armas appeared in the action thriller *Overdrive*, about two car thieves. Though she was again relegated to a supporting role in a muscular action movie, Stephen Dalton, who positively reviewed the film for the *Hollywood Reporter* (14 Aug. 2017) noted that de Armas "radiates more kick-ass charisma than her thankless sidekick role might suggest."

De Armas also enjoyed her breakout role in 2017, as a shape-shifting hologram called Joi in the long-awaited *Blade Runner* sequel, *Blade Runner 2049*. Joi is programmed to be the sexy companion of lead character K (Ryan Gosling), but over the course of the film learns the depth of her own unique emotions. "Joi is actually one of the most challenging roles I've had as an actress thus far," de Armas told Isaac Von Hallberg for *Flaunt* magazine (2 Oct. 2017). "Her character is very complex. She's a very strong woman; she's also very emotional and very joyful, like her name." The film was shot in Budapest over the course of five months. De Armas later described the process as emotionally and physically draining though spiritually rewarding. Viewing the film for the first time, de Armas felt overcome. She recalled to McCarthy: "I had to take 25 minutes after it was over with a box of Kleenex, just taking it in." *Blade Runner 2049* won enthusiastic praise from many critics—several described it as a modern classic—and won Oscars for best cinematography and best visual effects.

LATER ROLES

With her profile raised considerably, de Armas was later cast in a variety of roles, including in several projects set for release in 2019. She filmed scenes for the romantic comedy *Yesterday*, directed by Danny Boyle, but ended up being cut entirely from the finished movie when the filmmakers felt her performance as the third element in a love triangle was so strong it distracted from the main plot. In *The Informer*, based on the 2009 Swedish novel *Three Seconds*, she played a woman whose husband becomes an FBI informant. She also appeared in two other crime films, the whodunnit black comedy *Knives Out* and the drama *The Night Clerk*. Meanwhile, she was chosen as the female lead alongside Daniel Craig in the twenty-fifth James Bond film, *No Time to Die*, scheduled for release in 2020.

PERSONAL LIFE

De Armas was married to Spanish actor Marc Clotet from 2011 to 2013. She continued to live in Los Angeles after breaking into Hollywood.

SUGGESTED READING

Dalton, Stephen. Review of *Overdrive*, directed by Antonio Negret. *Hollywood Reporter*, 14 Aug. 2017, www.hollywoodreporter.com/review/overdrive-review-1029281. Accessed 21 Aug. 2019.

Debruge, Peter. Review of *Blade Runner 2049*, directed by Denis Villeneuve. *Variety*, 29 Sept. 2017, variety.com/2017/film/reviews/blade-runner-2049-review-1202576220/. Accessed 21 Aug. 2019.

Gargan, Olivia. "Ana de Armas." *Wonderland*, 9 Oct. 2017, www.wonderlandmagazine.com/2017/10/09/ana-de-armas/. Accessed 21 Aug. 2019.

Kenigsberg, Ben. "Sundance Film Review: 'Knock Knock.'" Review of *Knock Knock*, directed by Eli Roth. *Variety*, 24 Jan. 2015, variety.com/2015/film/reviews/sundance-film-review-keanu-reeves-in-knock-knock-1201413768/. Accessed 21 Aug. 2019.

Lerman, Gabriel. "Ana de Armas: The Cuban Actress Who's Taking Hollywood by Storm." *Golden Globes*, Hollywood Foreign Press Association, 31 Aug. 2016, www.goldenglobes.com/articles/ana-de-armas-cuban-actress-whos-taking-hollywood-storm. Accessed 21 Aug. 2019.

McCarthy, Lauren. "How Ana de Armas Went from Acting in Cuba to Starring alongside Ryan Gosling in *Blade Runner 2049*." *W*

Magazine, 4 Oct. 2017, www.wmagazine.com/story/ana-de-armas-blade-runner-2049. Accessed 21 Aug. 2019.

Von Hallberg, Isaac. "*Blade Runner 2049* Actress Ana de Armas Is Finding the Answers to All the Eternal Questions." *Flaunt,* 2 Oct. 2017, www.flaunt.com/content/people/ana-de-armas-eternal-feature. Accessed 21 Aug. 2019.

SELECTED WORKS

Knock Knock, 2015; *Hands of Stone,* 2016; *Overdrive,* 2017; *Blade Runner 2049,* 2017

—Molly Hagan

Morgan DeBaun

Date of birth: February 8, 1990
Occupation: Entrepreneur

In 2018 Morgan DeBaun's digital media company Blavity, which is geared toward black millennials, received $6.5 million dollars in venture capital in its first official round of funding. The infusion of cash represented a vote of confidence for the team behind Blavity, which has developed and grown steadily since it first launched in 2014. "In a time where the most iconic platforms for black entertainment face evident declines in revenue and viewership, a void has opened for a millennial-driven media outlet to emerge that reflects the progressive voice of today's generation," Julian Mitchell wrote for *Forbes* (5 Nov. 2015) regarding Blavity's success. "Since the definitive shift into digital media, extensive studies have concluded that African American millennials consume more content than any other demographic, are the most mobile-obsessive, and further prove to be the most active users on social media platforms."

Blavity attracts over a million unique monthly visitors with serious news features and other relevant content created by both staff and users. Its articles often go viral, thanks to the digital savvy of its millennial audience. Meanwhile, DeBaun, as cofounder and chief executive officer, has gained such recognition as being included on *Forbes'* 2016 list of the thirty top entrepreneurs and innovators under age thirty as well as its list of the top fifty women in tech in America in 2018. She and her team have continued to expand the company to better serve a wide range of audiences. By June 2018 Blavity Inc. was launched to house Blavity and its separate brands and platforms under one corporate umbrella.

DeBaun bristles at comparisons to another socially conscious, black female media figure, asserting to Nick Fouriezos for *OZY* (13 May 2018), "I don't want to be Oprah, but I do want to embody this world where I'm just going to be Morgan. If that doesn't fit, that doesn't matter. I'll just make the space."

EARLY YEARS

Morgan DeBaun was born in February 1990. Her parents raised her and her brother in a predominately white, upper-middle-class neighborhood in the suburbs of St. Louis, Missouri, but inculcated a strong sense of black identity in them. DeBaun has recounted to interviewers that her home had photos of Muhammad Ali and Martin Luther King Jr. The family also attended a black church, and she often read books presenting positive black role models, particularly biographies of iconic figures like Sojourner Truth and Maya Angelou. "It wasn't until elementary school that I started experiencing the tension between what I assumed to be normal versus the mainstream world," DeBaun recalled to Keryce Chelsi Henry for *NYLON* (27 Feb. 2016). "It was tough being black and gifted in a mostly white space." When she entered middle school, her parents enrolled her in a magnet school in the city, and she reveled in the diversity there.

DeBaun also began exhibiting a strong entrepreneurial streak, and she sensed an opportunity in her school's lack of vending machines. She regularly loaded up on discounted snacks and sweets at Costco and sold them to fellow students for a profit. Later she hit upon the idea of combining cheap packets of powdered drink mix with sugar and selling it at school, even though it was against the rules.

Photo by Patrick T. Fallon/Bloomberg via Getty Images

By around age fourteen, DeBaun had been introduced by her father to the concept of investing. "It's always been a part of who I am," she said, as quoted by Mandi Woodruff for *Yahoo! Finance* (5 Feb. 2016), "trying to figure out how to turn $1 into $1.25." She was far from narrow in her focus, however, and she participated in Model United Nations, field hockey, and chess, among other extracurricular activities. DeBaun graduated from Rosati-Kain High School in St. Louis in 2008.

HIGHER EDUCATION AND EARLY CAREER
Initially interested in teaching as a means of making a difference, DeBaun studied political science and entrepreneurship at Washington University in St. Louis, where she was a John B. Ervin Scholar. In 2010 she was elected student body president, and in that capacity, she honed her leadership and advocacy skills. She also served as a Des Lee Fellow with the United Way of Greater St. Louis, which gave her the opportunity to delve into urban revitalization. In addition to those activities, she worked for two start-ups, Quad Connect and backpack.tv.

Despite that impressive list of activities and accomplishments, DeBaun counts a completely different experience as the most formative of her college years: lunchtime, when she and other black students consistently gravitated to a large round table in the center of the campus cafeteria. "We would sit down, then another person would sit down, and then another 2 or 3 people would sit down. Then, before we knew it, there would more than 20 of us sitting there for hours," she recalled to Mitchell. "We would skip class and talk about critical race theories, what the Alphas did at the party, or whatever it may be. That moment when everyone would come to the table from different classes, parts of the country, and ethnicities of the diaspora—that was Black Gravity, or Blavity."

Upon earning her degree in 2012, DeBaun secured a job as a product manager with Intuit, a financial software company based in Mountain View, California. Over the years, she had also come to realize that, as with teaching, there were limitations to her ability to effect change through politics. Therefore, she had decided to enter the tech industry with the hope of being able to take part in products that could serve underrepresented communities. At one point working out of the company's Washington, DC office, she also spent time working for a start-up acquired by Intuit, steadily making her mark and taking on various roles in business development and strategic planning.

FOUNDING BLAVITY
At the same time, DeBaun felt culture shock and displacement after never having lived outside of the St. Louis area. To find a sense of connection, she often turned to internet forums and kept in contact with her peers from university. She and her peers sensed a need for an online platform for people, as significant cultural influencers, to engage and connect with the black community and share experiences, much as they had on campus, no matter where users were located. "It became apparent like, OK, there is a disconnect for me and also an information [disconnect] that the black community has in this country because we have not made it a priority to build our own new-age digital media brand that can distribute accurate information and stories that will never get covered anywhere else," she told Kelsea Stahler for *Bustle* (16 Aug. 2018). Ultimately, progressing from an email newsletter format, she and her fellow alumni and cofounders Jeff Nelson, Jonathan Jackson, and Aaron Samuels launched and began tweaking the *Blavity* website in July 2014.

Though DeBaun initially kept her day job at Intuit, she found herself at a more distinct crossroads after early August of that year, when a black teenager named Michael Brown was shot and killed by a white policeman in Ferguson, Missouri, setting off massive protests throughout the region. "Yes, I could have marched in the streets. Yes, I could have flown back to St. Louis, but really my unique contribution and the contribution of our Blavity team was being able to be a platform for people to get the word out about what was happening," she explained to John Ketchum for *CNN* (20 Apr. 2017). She then decided to focus on developing Blavity full time and left her position with Intuit that fall.

GROWING A MEDIA COMPANY
When DeBaun started a blog as a means of content marketing to drive traffic to the Blavity site, then a platform for short videos, she soon realized that more people were visiting the blog than the site itself. She and her team switched the site and their focus to curating written pieces, both from staff and users. "The people who make the best content on Instagram and Twitter are usually black," she told Carl Brooks Jr. for *Wired* (15 Feb. 2017). "With Blavity we built a platform to showcase that creativity." The site quickly became known for its timeliness and thought leadership, as well as its cultural relevance. When black students at the University of Pennsylvania were added to groups sharing racial slurs and images on a messaging app after the 2016 presidential election, for example, Blavity commissioned a piece directly from the director of the university's Black Cultural Center that included immediate, firsthand details about the incident. In another sign of Blavity's evolution, operations moved into the company's first official office in Los Angeles in 2016.

By early 2019 the umbrella organization Blavity Inc. encompassed a number of brands (both acquired and created) and platforms aside from the original Blavity site, including 21Ninety, a women's lifestyle site; Travel Noire, whose content focuses on travel and adventure; and Shadow and Act, which covers entertainment. The company also organizes popular conferences, including one aimed at empowering women. Another conference, AfroTech (with its own dedicated site), draws black programmers, entrepreneurs, and others in high-tech fields— a mission DeBaun sees as exceptionally important. "One of the specific stories that I love that I hear, are people who went [to Afrotech] last year and now nine months pass since the last conference and they're like launching their company or they've got funding from somebody that they met at that conference," she told Stahler. "I think that we'll probably see the ripple effect [in the industry] with more activity in three years as the startups that are being launched start to really scale."

DeBaun, who also founded M. Roze Essentials, a natural skin-care line for black women, is often a speaker and panelist at events planned by other organizations.

PERSONAL LIFE

DeBaun has been open about the challenges and time constraints of running a successful start-up company. "I have a spot on my calendar reserved for 'rest,'" she told Dayna Evans for *The Cut* (8 Nov. 2016). "It's usually about three hours where I'm not connected—I watch Netflix or I can write or I work on financial projections. It's time away from being pinged every five seconds." She has also found time for exercise and painting.

SUGGESTED READING

Brooks, Carl, Jr. "Inside Blavity, the Startup on a Quest to Be *the* News Source for Black Millennials." *Wired*, 15 Feb. 2017, www.wired.com/2017/02/black-news-matters-blavity. Accessed 12 May 2019.

DeBaun, Morgan. "Blavity's CEO on Taking Risks and Building a Community for Black Millennials." Interview by John Ketchum. *CNN Business*, 20 Apr. 2017, money.cnn.com/2017/04/20/technology/morgan-debaun-blavity/index.html. Accessed 12 May 2019.

DeBaun, Morgan. "How I Get It Done: Morgan DeBaun, Co-Founder and CEO of Content Platform Blavity." Interview by Dayna Evans. *The Cut*, New York Media, 8 Nov. 2016, www.thecut.com/2016/11/how-the-co-founder-of-blavity-gets-things-done.html. Accessed 12 May 2019.

DeBaun, Morgan. "Meet Morgan DeBaun: The Blavity Founder Bridging the Gap between Content and Tech." Interview by Julian Mitchell. *Forbes*, 5 Nov. 2015, www.forbes.com/sites/julianmitchell/2015/11/05/meet-morgan-debaun-the-blavity-founder-bridging-the-gap-between-content-and-tech/#5c278739751a. Accessed 12 May 2019.

DeBaun, Morgan. "Morgan DeBaun Is Putting Black Millennials' Voices Center Stage." Interview by Keryce Chelsi Henry. *NYLON*, 27 Feb. 2016, nylon.com/articles/morgan-debaun-interview. Accessed 12 May 2019.

Fouriezos, Nick. "An Oprah for Black Media's Internet Age?" *OZY*, 13 May 2018, www.ozy.com/provocateurs/an-oprah-for-black-medias-internet-age/85446. Accessed 12 May 2019.

Stahler, Kelsea. "How 'Blavity' Co-Founder Morgan DeBaun Became One of the Most Important Women in Silicon Valley." *Bustle*, 16 Aug. 2018, www.bustle.com/p/how-blavity-co-founder-morgan-debaun-became-one-of-the-most-important-women-in-silicon-valley-10133055. Accessed 12 May 2019.

—*Mari Rich*

Bryson DeChambeau

Date of birth: September 16, 1993
Occupation: Professional golfer

In 2015 Bryson DeChambeau became the fifth golfer ever to win the individual prize at the NCAA Division I Men's Golf Championships and the U.S. Amateur Championship during the same year. Although that would be a significant achievement for any golfer, it was a particularly meaningful one due to DeChambeau's unusual approach to golf, which he had honed since first reading the 1969 book *The Golfing Machine* while in high school. "The way I've built my golf game I've tried to make the least amount of moving parts," he told Dave Shedloski for *Golfworld* (27 May 2019). "So literally no matter the time of day . . . if I wake up in middle of the night and go and swing a golf club, I want to be able to make the same motion, execute the same thing no matter the situation. No matter what state I'm in."

Since making his professional debut on the Professional Golfers' Association (PGA) Tour in 2016, DeChambeau has put his precise swing and carefully calibrated clubs to good use, winning five tour events over the course of 2017 and 2018 and putting in strong performances in numerous additional competitions. DeChambeau's success in competition not only represents the realization of his childhood dream of playing professional golf but has demonstrated the merits

Photo by Mike Ehrmann/Getty Images

of an approach to play that some commentators have criticized as overly scientific. "I feel like I've been able to bring an idea to the world stage and shine a light on a different way to play, an easier way," he told Jim Gorant for *Popular Mechanics* (23 Apr. 2019). "I want to change the game."

EARLY LIFE AND EDUCATION

Bryson James Aldrich DeChambeau was born on September 16, 1993, in Modesto, California. His father, Jon, worked in the golf industry and had played in PGA Tour events as an amateur prior to DeChambeau's birth, while his mother, Jan, worked in sales. DeChambeau and his older brother, Garrett, grew up in Clovis, California. As a child, DeChambeau demonstrated a talent for mathematics and science and enjoyed activities focused on making and building things. "I liked building a lot of Legos and built houses and did some fun stuff with that," he said, as quoted by Gorant. "Those toys, I guess you could say, were put in front of me at a young age, and I became intrigued with them." In addition to such activities, DeChambeau played baseball, basketball, and soccer but focused particularly on golf, which he hoped one day to play professionally.

As a teenager, DeChambeau attended Clovis East High School, where he played golf and volleyball. During that period, as the director of golf operations at a Madera, California, golf club, DeChambeau's father hired a friend, Mike Schy, as a golf instructor for the club. Schy taught DeChambeau and gave him the book *The Golfing Machine*, first published in 1969 by Homer Kelley. DeChambeau soon memorized the book, which analyzed golf swing techniques from a scientific perspective and began to work on incorporating Kelley's findings into his own style of play. Those early efforts proved beneficial for DeChambeau, who won the 2010 California state junior championship and claimed second place at 2011 Callaway Junior World Golf Championships. He graduated from Clovis East High School in 2012.

COLLEGIATE CAREER

DeChambeau went on to enroll in Southern Methodist University (SMU), where he majored in physics and joined the SMU Mustangs men's golf program. A successful competitor during that period, he won a medal at the 2014 American Athletic Conference Championships and also competed in the National Collegiate Athletic Association (NCAA) Division I men's golf tournament during his sophomore season. In the summer of 2014, he competed in the Palmer Cup, an event held in England that brings together college and university players primarily from the United States and Europe. DeChambeau distinguished himself further in 2015 when he won the NCAA tournament in the individual division, becoming the first player in SMU's history to do so. He received numerous honors in recognition of his performance during his collegiate career, including selection for several different All-American teams.

In September 2015, the NCAA banned SMU men's golfers from competing in the following season's tournament in response to a series of rules violations allegedly carried out by the organization's previous head coach. The NCAA's decision not only affected the men's golf program but also rendered DeChambeau unable to defend his NCAA title. As such, he opted instead to leave SMU prior to his senior season and instead focus on noncollegiate amateur golf, with the goal of qualifying to play on the professional level. Although the decision was a difficult one for DeChambeau, he later came to consider it "a blessing in disguise," as he told Karen Crouse for the *New York Times* (4 Apr. 2016).

AMATEUR CAREER

In addition to competing in collegiate events, DeChambeau participated in amateur-level golf events while still in college and ranked among the top twenty amateur players. During the summer of 2014, he was part of the winning USA team that competed in the 2014 World Amateur Team Championships in Japan and also played in events such as the US Amateur Public Links. The latter event took place under the oversight of the United States Golf Association (USGA), which oversees many of the amateur events in the United States. The following year DeChambeau qualified for the US Amateur Championship and beat golfer Derek Bard to claim the title. He went on to play in England's Walker Cup, in which US golfers compete against a team of golfers from the United Kingdom and Ireland.

Although many of the events in which he played during that period were geared toward amateurs, DeChambeau also competed in several professional tournaments as an amateur, including the 2015 US Open. He did not progress past the cut stage in the event, which is one of professional golf's four major championships, alongside the Masters Tournament, the PGA Championship, and the Open Championship (or, British Open). In April 2016 he competed in the Masters, where he tied for twenty-first place and won the title of Low Amateur as the amateur-level player with the best final score.

Although such high-profile events were challenging for DeChambeau, he sought to remain calm and focus on his game. "Why be nervous?" he explained to *Golf* magazine (21 Jan. 2016). "There's no expectations. I'm not worried about anything. If I hit a bad shot I've got an opportunity to show my grace and my character. In that situation, there's no downside to it." In addition to valuable playing experience, DeChambeau's participation in a wide range of golf events won him attention from sponsors, and he signed a sponsorship agreement with Cobra Golf in April 2016.

PROFESSIONAL DEBUT

Although DeChambeau told *Golf* magazine that he "never [tries] to set goals" and is "more of a journey man," he had long aspired to play professional golf, which in the United States is overseen primarily by the PGA. He made his professional debut in the RBC Heritage PGA Tour event in April 2016. Although he tied for fourth in the event, his winnings were too low for him to qualify to play on the PGA Tour on a regular basis. He, instead, focused on competing on the *Web.com* Tour, a series of events for professional golfers who had not yet reached PGA Tour levels. In September 2016 he won the DAP Championship on the *Web.com* Tour, earning the right to compete on the PGA Tour during the 2016–17 season. DeChambeau also competed in the 2016 U.S. Open, where he tied for fifteenth place.

During the 2016–17 golf season, DeChambeau achieved a major career milestone, earning his first PGA Tour win at the 2017 John Deere Classic. He also tied for second at the Puerto Rico Open that year. Despite such achievements, his performance in the majors was disappointing, as he missed the cut at the U.S. Open and British Open and tied for thirty-third place at the PGA Championship. For DeChambeau, such disappointments prompted him to fine-tune his approach to ensure future success.

"Right after I won the John Deere, I missed the cut badly at the British Open. I knew something had to change, because you can't go and win an event and then miss the cut by seven or whatever," he explained to Shedloski. "After that FedEx Cup season, I said to myself I have to create something that will allow me to go through this [thought] process every single time and give myself the best chance to get the best adjustment and yardage out there, so I can hit the shots I need to hit."

DeChambeau's efforts to improve his performance proved successful in the 2017–18 season, during which he won three events on the PGA Tour: the Dell Technologies Championship, the Northern Trust, and the Memorial Tournament. He also won second place at the Arnold Palmer Invitational and served as a member of the US team that competed in the 2018 Ryder Cup. In the 2017–18 FedEx Cup, the championship within the PGA Tour, DeChambeau claimed third place thanks to his tour wins as well as strong finishes in other tour events. He also competed in all four majors that season and tied for twenty-fifth place at the U.S. Open.

In November 2018, after the 2018–19 PGA Tour began, DeChambeau won the Shriners Hospitals for Children Open. He likewise won the 2019 Omega Dubai Desert Classic on the European Tour, placed seventh in the Sentry Tournament of Champions, and tied for twenty-ninth place in the Masters. In June 2019 he tied for thirty-fifth place in the US Open at Pebble Beach Golf Links.

GOLFING STYLE

Over the course of his collegiate, amateur, and early professional careers, DeChambeau worked to refine his golfing style further, based on both information gleaned from Kelley's book and his own testing. Among the most important factors for DeChambeau was ensuring that all of iron and wedge clubs had shafts of the same length—37.5 inches—and had specific weights, which would, in turn, enable him to swing the clubs in a consistent way every time. He likewise developed a mental checklist of factors to consider when making a shot, including air density, wind vector, and the angle of the local terrain.

Since DeChambeau's early days as a golfer, he has faced some criticism for his approach, which some argued viewed golf as more of a science than an art. Critics also took issue with the speed of his play, finding it too slow. "I don't really worry about it too much," he told Luke Kerr-Dineen for *USA Today* (12 Apr. 2016) about such criticism. "Scientists out there are artists. They go out there and are imagining things that people aren't ever even thinking of. Coming up with these equations, that's an art." As De-Chambeau's success as a player demonstrated the potential of his approach to golf, he received further attention for his unique strategies, and in May 2019 he delivered a lecture on his approach at the Muirfield Village Golf Club in Dublin, Ohio.

DeChambeau has also worked with Bridgestone and Microsoft to develop a variety of data-driven golf-related products. "There will be a monumental leap in sport because of technology," he told Taylor Soper for *GeekWire* (17 Feb. 2017) about such projects. "There will be a couple people who come out, just like Tiger Woods or Michael Jordan, and make a huge leap that people won't expect because of technology."

PERSONAL LIFE

DeChambeau lives in Dallas, Texas. In addition to golf, he enjoys fishing.

SUGGESTED READING

"Bryson DeChambeau, 'The Golf Scientist,' Tames Abu Dhabi Field." *Golf*, 21 Jan. 2016, www.golf.com/tour-and-news/bryson-de-chambeau-golf-scientist-tames-abu-dhabi-field. Accessed 14 June 2019.

Crouse, Karen. "For a Golf Tinkerer, a Strategy Just Crazy Enough to Work." *The New York Times*, 4 Apr. 2016, www.nytimes.com/2016/04/05/sports/golf/for-a-golf-tinker-er-a-strategy-just-crazy-enough-to-work.html. Accessed 14 June 2019.

Gorant, Jim. "Bryson DeChambeau, the Mad Scientist of Golf." *Popular Mechanics*, 23 Apr. 2019, www.popularmechanics.com/culture/a27229236/golfs-mad-scientist. Accessed 14 June 2019.

Sampson, Curt. "A Crazy Good Amateur." *Golf-Digest*, 1 Sept. 2015, www.golfdigest.com/story/golf-world-bryson-dechambeau-crazy-good-amateur-summer. Accessed 14 June 2019.

Shedloski, Dave. "We Spent an Afternoon Listening to Bryson DeChambeau Talk Golf . . . and It Was Something." *Golfworld*, 27 May 2019, www.golfdigest.com/story/we-spent-an-afternoon-listening-to-bryson-dechambeau-talk-golf-and-it-was-something. Accessed 14 June 2019.

Soper, Taylor. "Meet the PGA Tour's Geekiest Golfer: Bryson DeChambeau on His Passion for Tech, Physics, Data." *GeekWire*, 17 Feb. 2017, www.geekwire.com/2017/meet-pga-tours-geekiest-golfer-bryson-dechambeau-passion-tech-physics-data. Accessed 14 June 2019.

—*Joy Crelin*

Laura Deming

Date of birth: 1994
Occupation: Scientist and venture capitalist

Many scientifically inclined twelve-year-olds may dream of one day working in a research laboratory, but in 2006, Laura Deming actually had the chance to do so. Fascinated from an early age with the science of aging—and the potential of preventing its most devastating effects on the human body, she contacted molecular biologist Cynthia Kenyon, a prominent researcher in that field, and ultimately joined Kenyon's laboratory as a volunteer. Deming's years at the Kenyon Laboratory are only part of her unusual educational and career trajectory, but they are in many ways emblematic of the approach that has made her a highly influential figure in the field of longevity research. "The best way to get ahead is to find the smart people and learn everything that you can from them," she told Karen Kaplan for *Nature* (16 May 2013). "Apply those insights to what you're doing. You will avoid a lot of mistakes."

Raised in New Zealand, Deming moved to the United States with her family to work with Kenyon and later enrolled in the Massachusetts Institute of Technology (MIT) at the age of fourteen. Two years later, however, she dropped out of the prestigious institution after being awarded the Thiel Fellowship, which required its recipients to leave behind their formal schooling to pursue their dream entrepreneurial projects. She ultimately founded the Longevity Fund, a venture capital fund dedicated to investing in

Photo by Kimberly White/Getty Images for TechCrunch

companies pursuing innovative research in aging, longevity, and age-related diseases. Although she initially struggled to find investors, the fund went on to raise tens of millions of dollars and make substantial investments in developing companies. "Earlier, our biggest challenge was getting other investors on board and convincing them that aging has become a place to play. Now that's a non-issue, which is great," she told Connie Loizos for *TechCrunch* (22 Aug. 2017). "Our job is to help the companies get other investors on board, so it's wonderful to see excitement in the space begin to build." Through her work with the Longevity Fund and other projects, she seeks to extend the number of years in which human beings are able to live healthy lives rather than simply to extend the human lifespan.

EARLY LIFE

Laura Deming was born in 1994 to Tabitha and John Deming. She grew up in Remuera, a suburb of Auckland, New Zealand. Her father disliked traditional education, so she and her brother were homeschooled. In Deming's case, her schooling took the form of extensive self-directed reading, particularly about scientific topics. "One of the things that was a huge luck factor for me was as a kid Dad loved science, so I was lucky in that he would encourage us to study things a lot faster, with a lot more passion, than others would have," she recalled to James Borrowdale for *Vice* (21 Aug. 2018). In addition to science, she proved particularly skilled in mathematics and developed a deep appreciation for the beauty of numbers.

While Deming was still a child, her scientific curiosity focused specifically on the area of aging, particularly efforts to understand—and potentially limit or control—the mechanisms that cause aging and age-related diseases. The concept of preventing the physically detrimental effects of aging became especially intriguing for Deming as she began to recognize how such effects shaped the life of her grandmother during their visits with one another. "My grandma had this wonderful spirit and wit, but she couldn't run around and play," she explained to Kaplan. "I thought about all these people I know who have arthritic joints and disease, and whether there was anything that could be done to help them. If there was a way to make that happen, I wanted to work on it."

EDUCATION AND EARLY CAREER

Deming became fascinated with the work of researcher Cynthia Kenyon, a molecular biologist then at the University of California, San Francisco (UCSF), who was conducting research into how genes affect aging. After emailing Kenyon, she gained permission to visit the Kenyon Laboratory (which she managed to fit into a trip to California for a family wedding), and she was later granted permission to volunteer in the laboratory and assist Kenyon and her colleagues with their research. In 2006, following her family's move to California, then twelve-year-old Deming began to contribute to the researchers' efforts to determine how certain genetic factors influence the longevity of worms known as *Caenorhabditis elegans*. For Deming, her years working in the Kenyon Laboratory were formative ones that shaped her outlook and career trajectory in key ways. "Cynthia was my first mentor—she taught me how to think and be creative," she told Kaplan. "She thinks as if there are no rules. Watching her changed how I am as a scientist." In addition to working in Kenyon's laboratory, she pursued coursework at UCSF and continued her self-guided education through reading and listening to online lectures.

In 2009 Deming moved to Massachusetts with her family and enrolled in the Massachusetts Institute of Technology (MIT). Although she had long been interested primarily in biology, she majored in physics during her time at MIT. She also joined the Sigma Kappa sorority and the MIT taekwondo team. In addition to pursuing her bachelor's degree, she worked in several different research laboratories during her time at MIT, including the Guarente Laboratory, where she participated in research focused on the enzyme SIRT1 led by biologist Leonard Guarente, and the Weiss Laboratory, led by synthetic biology researcher Ron Weiss. During the summer of 2010, she participated in the International Genetically Engineered Machine Competition at MIT, working on a project that concerned programmable and self-constructing biomaterials. She spent the following summer at researcher Ron Firestein's laboratory at the biotechnology company Genentech, where she worked on a potential lung cancer therapy.

THIEL FELLOWSHIP

During Deming's second year at MIT, a graduate student told her about a new fellowship offered by the Thiel Foundation and available—at that time—only to students under the age of twenty. Funded by billionaire entrepreneur Peter Thiel, the Thiel Fellowship is a two-year program that awards $50,000 per year to entrepreneurial students who leave school to pursue their ideas. Thiel had long expressed interest in the science of longevity, and Deming's scientific and entrepreneurial focus proved to be an ideal fit for the program. In May 2011 Thiel announced that Deming had been selected as one of twenty-four Thiel Fellows for that year.

Following her selection as a fellow, Deming took a leave of absence from her studies, as stipulated by the rules of the fellowship. After leaving MIT, she moved back to California, where she initially shared a home with other Thiel Fellows. Despite her two productive years at MIT, she was unsure whether she would ultimately return to the institution. She later decided to pursue a full-time career in venture capital, as she felt that she would find more opportunities there than in academia. "The funny part is I think I'll miss studying for exams," she told Jessica Leber for the *MIT Technology Review* (3 Feb. 2012) of her decision. "It's the sort of thing that was very fun—like a sudoku puzzle or a crossword puzzle can be fun. But I thought that I could learn a lot more about the biotech industry and business by diving right into it."

THE LONGEVITY FUND

After winning a coveted Thiel Fellowship, Deming embarked on an initiative that combined her entrepreneurial drive with her longstanding interest in the science of aging and longevity, founding a venture capital fund dedicated to providing funding for companies seeking to treat diseases related to aging. Deming held the position of partner in the Northern California–based fund, which she named the Longevity Fund. She initially struggled to find investors for the fund, a difficulty she later linked to the novelty of the research in question. "Not long ago, if you talked with most [venture capitalists] about aging, they didn't think there was anything there," she recalled to Loizos. "I think aging is such a young science, they hadn't heard about it. Meanwhile, I care a lot about it." Despite such difficulties, she succeeded in raising $4 million for her first fund. At the same time, she became a prolific public speaker, contributing to events such as the 2013 TEDMED conference as well as to panel and roundtable discussions related to topics such as aging and venture capital.

Over the course of its existence, the Longevity Fund provided early funding to a variety of companies exploring new ideas in biotechnology, pharmaceuticals, and genetics with the goal of extending human longevity and improving human health. Among others, the fund invested in Unity Biotechnology, a company dedicated to eliminating the buildup of cells that have lost their ability to divide; Metacrine, devoted primarily to developing new treatments for liver and gastrointestinal diseases; Precision Biosciences, which seeks to address diseases such as cancer through genome-editing technologies; and Decibel Therapeutics, a company focused on hearing disorders. As Deming has often noted in interviews, despite its name, the Longevity Fund is focused less on simply increasing the human lifespan and more on increasing the "healthspan"—that is, the period of life in which humans are healthy and able to engage in everyday activities. "It's very clear to everyone that we should be focusing on increasing the healthy part of the life, not just maximum lifespan in an old, decrepit state," she explained in an interview for the Milken Institute. "Our focus should be on how to let people live a healthier life for longer." She went on to raise $22 million for her second fund in 2017.

A NEW LONGEVITY FUND INITIATIVE AND PIONEER

In 2018 the Longevity Fund launched a new initiative, the accelerator program Age 1. Unlike the main fund, which makes substantial investments in a range of established companies, Age 1 seeks to enable the creation of new companies within the field of longevity research by providing funding and support to multiple new companies over a four-month period. Among other purposes, the program was designed to help would-be founders with innovative ideas overcome financial roadblocks that prevent some individuals from starting such businesses.

Deming has also worked extensively to promote future research into aging and health as well as the involvement of young people in science. Beginning in 2018, she began to serve as an adviser for Pioneer, a company dedicated to finding talented individuals from around the world—commonly referred to as "lost Einsteins"—who might not otherwise have the opportunities or connections necessary to pursue their chosen projects. "There are folks who are brilliant but who are constrained by luck basically to not have opportunities that they would have otherwise," she explained to Borrowdale.

PERSONAL LIFE

Deming lives in California. An avid reader since childhood, she particularly enjoys reading about the history of science.

SUGGESTED READING

Borrowdale, James. "This Kiwi Prodigy Wants to Help Make Your World-Changing Idea Happen." *Vice*, 21 Aug. 2018, www.vice.com/en_nz/article/8xb3mg/this-kiwi-prodigy-wants-to-help-make-your-world-changing-idea-happen. Accessed 16 Dec. 2018.

Deming, Laura. "Healthspan, Not Lifespan." *Milken Institute*, www.milkeninstitute.org/longevity-innovators/view/1326. Accessed 16 Dec. 2018.

Deming, Laura. "This 23-Year-Old Just Closed Her Second Fund—Which Is Focused on Aging—with $22 Million." Interview by Connie Loizos. *TechCrunch*, 22 Aug. 2017, techcrunch.com/2017/08/22/this-23-year-old-just-closed-her-second-fund-which-is-focused-on-aging-with-22-million. Accessed 16 Dec. 2018.

Deming, Laura. "Turning Point: Laura Deming." Interview by Karen Kaplan. *Nature*, 16 May 2013, www.nature.com/nature/journal/v497/n7449/full/nj7449-399a.html. Accessed 16 Dec. 2018.

Kelly, Caitlin. "Forgoing College to Pursue Dreams." *The New York Times*, 15 Sept. 2012, www.nytimes.com/2012/09/16/business/the-thiel-fellows-forgoing-college-to-pursue-dreams.html. Accessed 16 Dec. 2018.

Leber, Jessica. "Too Young to Fail." *MIT Technology Review*, 3 Feb. 2012, www.technologyreview.com/s/426789/too-young-to-fail. Accessed 16 Dec. 2018.

—*Joy Crelin*

Natalie Diaz

Date of birth: September 4, 1978
Occupation: Poet and activist

Photo by Jamestroud via Wikimedia Commons

Poet Natalie Diaz, whose first poetry collection, *When My Brother Was an Aztec*, was published in 2012, was awarded a "genius" grant from the John D. and Catherine T. MacArthur Foundation in 2018. Also named the Maxine and Jonathan Marshall Chair in Modern and Contemporary Poetry at Arizona State University (ASU) in 2018, Diaz, who identifies as Mojave/Pima and Latinx and is an enrolled member of the Gila River Indian Tribe, has directed a Mojave language revitalization program on the Fort Mojave Indian Reservation, where she grew up. While her work is significantly informed by her relationship with and place in multiple cultures and communities, including the LGBTQ community as a queer woman, it is also rather uniquely shaped by her former life as a professional basketball player. "Writing for me is no different than playing basketball, it's my body moving among and pushing up against and being moved by other bodies of language and the energy of language," she told Brandon Stosuy for the website the *Creative Independent* (14 Apr. 2017). In recognition of her work, she has earned, among other honors, a Lannan Literary Fellowship for Poetry, a Bread Loaf scholarship, the Holmes National Poetry Prize, and a Hodder Fellowship at Princeton University.

EARLY LIFE

Diaz was born on September 4, 1978, to Bernadette and Richard Diaz. She grew up with four brothers (Richard Jr., John, Belarmino, and Valentin) and four sisters (Nicole, Desirae, Gabrielle, and Franki Danielle) in a two-bedroom house on the Fort Mojave Indian Reservation, which encompasses approximately forty-two thousand acres of land along the Colorado River in Arizona, California, and Nevada. "I've seen the problems with being on a reservation, and at the same time, I see how rewarding living on a reservation can be," she told Lorraine Berry for *Gball* (Apr. 2000), an online magazine. "I see the things like alcoholism, the teen pregnancies, the drugs and stuff. On the other hand, I see the people for what they really are. They're so incredibly talented and good-natured and giving and caring. It's definitely something that has influenced me." Her mother is Mojave and Pima while her father, who worked in construction, is of Spanish heritage.

Particularly close with her great-grandmother growing up, Diaz enjoyed listening to her stories. Able to read from a very young age, she developed an affinity for books, which she coveted in the chaos of living with a large family. As a teen, she became involved in political causes. She traveled with Greenpeace, speaking about nuclear waste facilities and their negative effects on rural desert communities; such a facility had controversially been proposed to be located in Ward Valley, near Fort Mojave. Through her activism, she met the late activist and tribal judge Grace Thorpe.

PLAYING BASKETBALL

Diaz's parents encouraged her interest in the arts, like painting and writing, but also in basketball. While basketball is a popular sport on many American Indian reservations, Diaz had a particular talent for the game and was drawn to the cultural bridge and connection to the world outside of the reservation that being involved in the sport provided as well as the opportunity playing gave her to be herself. After racking up points and rebounds as a member of the basketball team at River Valley High School and earning a full athletic scholarship, she went on to play point guard for the Lady Monarchs at Old Dominion University in Norfolk, Virginia. During her freshman year in 1997, the team reached the National Collegiate Athletic Association (NCAA) finals. Later, Diaz recalled one particularly exhilarating moment from the game when the team advanced to the Final Four. The opposing team had the last shot with seconds left to tie the game or win. "I think one of their post players shot the ball in the paint. Everyone was flying up for the rebound. I didn't have the height that those girls did, but I remember seeing the ball—it was cool timing—and I went up and grabbed it. I grabbed the board so they didn't have the opportunity to put it back up. And that sealed our win," she recalled to Berry.

Although she continued to prove to be a crucial member of the team as she bested her career records, her college career was not always so glamorous. In an essay published on the website for *PEN America* (18 Dec. 2015) titled "A Body of Athletics," Diaz recalled how players from inner cities or reservations were typically discouraged from returning home for semester and holiday breaks "to keep us out of trouble." One year, she missed her grandfather's funeral.

Captain of the team her senior year, she was Old Dominion Female Athlete of the Year and was chosen as the most valuable player (MVP) of the Colonial Athletic Association (CAA) Tournament in 1999 and 2000. After graduating with a major in English and a minor in women's studies in 2000, she attended the Women's National Basketball Association (WNBA) Pre-Draft Camp. She told Berry that she was "hopeful" about her chances of being drafted.

MOJAVE LANGUAGE PRESERVATION

Though Diaz was not drafted, she did play professional ball for several years in Europe and Asia, including in countries such as Spain and Turkey. Around 2004, she was training at Old Dominion, her alma mater, to return overseas to honor a contract when she tore her anterior cruciate ligament (ACL), medial collateral ligament (MCL), and her meniscus. The knee injury ended her professional career, but while she was recovering, she decided to take some writing classes with encouragement from former professors. "I loved them," she told Michelle Schmidt for *Inland360.com* (1 May 2014). "I loved reading and writing. I took it as a sign that I was supposed to do this new thing." She began studying for her graduate degree, but it was not until late in her tenure, she has said, that she learned how to read poetry—meaning that she learned the

rhythm and the careful attention to detail absent from the rush of reading a novel—and then how to write it. She earned her Master of Fine Arts (MFA) degree in poetry and fiction from Old Dominion in 2007 and returned to the Fort Mojave reservation.

With her newfound attention to and passion for language, Diaz was pained to realize that the language of her ancestors was fading away. Despite knowing only a few Mojave words herself, she began serious efforts to preserve the Mojave language, including getting the support of ASU's Center for Indian Education by 2009. "Our values and our identity are fed by our language," she told Judi Davis for the *Tribal College Journal of American Indian Higher Education* (6 May 2013). "We learn how to speak to each other, how to talk about the land and water, how to tease, how to argue, how to mourn, and how to dream, all through the language."

As the director of the language revitalization program at the Fort Mojave reservation, she began working with the elders who speak Mojave, learning the language herself and recording conversations, stories, and songs as well as helping to teach the language in a way that it would be passed down within the community, including at younger ages. In her 2012 interview for *PBS Newshour*, she said that dreams are a particularly important aspect of Mojave culture. "My elder teacher says I was dreamed to be here, to be learning from him," she told Davis. She has conceded that some of her preservation efforts, particularly methods for capturing bird songs, run counter to Mojave tradition. "We're fortunate to have a very forward-thinking group of elders," she told Pete Zrioka for ASU's internal news website *ASU Now* (26 Mar. 2012). "Recording is very uncomfortable for them, but they've put the needs of the community and the survival of the language over their own comforts. They have a much deeper understanding of what will be lost."

WHEN MY BROTHER WAS AN AZTEC

Diaz's first collection of poems, *When My Brother Was an Aztec*, was published by Copper Canyon Press in 2012 and was largely praised by critics. Ryan Teitman, writing for *The Rumpus* (23 Oct. 2013), described it as a "commanding debut." The first section of the volume explores reservation life through a large cast of characters. There is a young basketball star whose career is cut short by pregnancy, and Jimmy Eagle, who is chased by the FBI for stealing a pair of cowboy boots. In another poem, "Hand-Me-Down Halloween," the speaker wears a white neighbor's Tonto costume. "There's both anger and tenderness in these poems," Teitman wrote. "They don't turn away from the scraping and fighting that people need to do . . . just to survive."

The book's second section—its "most striking," a reviewer for *Publishers Weekly* (25 June 2012) wrote—focuses on one of Diaz's brothers, who struggles with an addiction to methamphetamines. In the poem "My Brother at 3 A.M.," which uses a poetic form called a pantoum, Diaz recalls a time when her brother had shown up at the family's door believing that he was being chased by an evil spirit. She imagines her brother's death in the wrenching "No More Cake Here." In other poems, her brother becomes the subject of myths. The third section, on the other hand, is composed of poems that take on a variety of topics, from love to war and politics. Diaz was awarded both a Lannan Literary Fellowship for Poetry and the Louis Untermeyer Scholarship in Poetry from Bread Loaf in 2012, and *When My Brother Was an Aztec* was honored with a 2013 American Book Award.

In 2013 Diaz began teaching creative writing at the low residency MFA program at the Institute of American Indian Arts in Santa Fe, New Mexico, in addition to writing and continuing her efforts toward Mojave language revitalization. Having also been awarded the Holmes National Poetry Prize in 2014, she began teaching in the Department of English at ASU in 2017. The following year, not long after she received a MacArthur "genius" grant, she was made the Maxine and Jonathan Marshall Chair in Modern and Contemporary Poetry.

SUGGESTED READING

Davis, Judi. "Both Beautiful and Brutal: Natalie Diaz and the Mojave Language Recovery Project." *Tribal College Journal of American Indian Higher Education*, 6 May 2013, tribalcollegejournal.org/both-beautiful-and-brutal-natalie-diaz-and-the-mojave-language-recovery-project/. Accessed 14 May 2019.

Diaz, Natalie. "From Pro-Basketball Player to Poet—Diaz Aims to Reveal Native Warrior Spirit." Interview by Michelle Schmidt. *Inland360.com*, 1 May 2014, inland360.com/books/2014/05/from-pro-basketball-player-to-poet-diaz-works-to-show-natives-their-warrior-spirt/. Accessed 13 May 2019.

Diaz, Natalie. "Natalie Diaz on the Physicality of Writing." Interview by Brandon Stosuy. *The Creative Independent*, 14 Apr. 2017, thecreativeindependent.com/people/natalie-diaz-on-the-physicality-of-writing/. Accessed 13 May 2019.

Diaz, Natalie. "One on One with Natalie Diaz, Old Dominion University." Interview by Lorraine Berry. *Gball*, 2000, www.gballmag.com/pp_diaz.html. Accessed 13 May 2019.

Diaz, Natalie. Review of *When My Brother Was an Aztec*, by Natalie Diaz. *Publishers Weekly*, 25 June 2012, www.publishersweekly.com/978-1-55659-383-3. Accessed 14 May 2019.

Teitman, Ryan. Review of *When My Brother Was an Aztec*, by Natalie Diaz. *The Rumpus*, 23 Oct. 2013, therumpus.net/2013/10/when-my-brother-was-an-aztec-by-natalie-diaz/. Accessed 14 May 2019.

Zrioka, Pete. "Cultural Conservation: Keeping Languages Alive." *ASU Now*, Arizona State University (ASU), 26 Mar. 2012, asunow.asu.edu/content/cultural-conservation-keeping-languages-alive. Accessed 14 May 2019.

—*Molly Hagan*

Peter Doig

Date of birth: April 17, 1959
Occupation: Painter

In 2007, a painting by Peter Doig sold for $11.3 million, setting what was then a record sale for a living European artist. The event generated a great deal of excitement, and Doig's popularity continued to rise. In 2015, after one of his works sold at auction for an astonishing $26 million, art critic Jonathan Jones wrote for the UK *Guardian* (16 May 2015) that the event was "the latest chapter in the most unlikely and heartwarming success story in 21st-century art" and asserted, "Doig is a jewel of genuine imagination, sincere work and humble creativity. . . . Doig's art will last because it embodies a unique, beguiling vision. His paintings take the mind to new places, far-off places, forgotten places."

As Jones predicted, collectors continue to highly prize Doig's art. In 2017, one of his pieces (a depiction of a house in the woods that he had painted in the early 1990s) sold at auction for $28.8 million, placing him amongst a small handful of living artists whose work had commanded more than $25 million.

A Turner Prize nominee and the winner of a prestigious John Moores Painting Prize, Doig charmed critics and interviewers with his humility and seeming disregard for art-world laurels and the trappings of fame. At the time of the record-setting 2007 sale, he was living quietly in Trinidad, far from the bustle and glitter of the contemporary art world. In an interview afterward, he told Tim Adams for the *Guardian* (27 Jan. 2008), "It made me feel sick, really. . . . That someone should have put their hand in their pocket and spent that much money on a painting of mine seemed so unconnected to anything that I ever did."

Photo by Honkadori via Wikimedia Commons

EARLY LIFE AND EDUCATION

Peter Doig was born on April 17, 1959, in Edinburgh, Scotland. He has three siblings: Andrew, Dominie, and Sophie. His mother was a drama teacher. His father, a talented amateur painter, worked as an accountant for a shipping company, and as a result the family moved frequently. In 1962, the family settled in Trinidad, before moving to Montreal, Canada, in 1966. While living in Canada, Doig learned to play ice hockey and gained a reputation as an adventurous, free-spirited child.

After a great-aunt died and left an inheritance earmarked for education, Doig, then about twelve years old, was sent to a boarding school in the north of Scotland. He hated the academic rigor there and was in frequent danger of being expelled, so his parents allowed him to return home to Canada after three years. Shortly after his return, they moved to Toronto, and although Doig was happy to once again be with his family, he continued to struggle academically.

At age seventeen, Doig dropped out of school and found work in a series of local restaurants. At one point he traveled to Western Canada to work on oil rigs. To help pass the time there he drew landscapes in a sketchbook. Although by his own admission he showed little natural aptitude, when he returned to Toronto, he took art classes at an alternative high school.

ARTISTIC TRAINING

In 1979, when he was twenty years old, Doig decided to pursue art more seriously. He moved to London and signed up for a year of foundation classes at the Wimbledon School of Art, with a goal of eventually designing album covers for a living or doing something related to set design. To his surprise, after he had completed his foundation year, Doig was accepted to the prestigious St. Martin's School of Art. Although still not skilled at drawing, Doig discovered a way to work around that limitation. "I don't know how I got the idea, but I started photographing pictures I'd seen in magazines, and then projecting them on a larger scale, and trying out different compositions," he recalled to Calvin Tomkins for the *New Yorker* (11 Dec. 2017). "It just felt so totally liberating."

Doig graduated from St. Martins in 1983. Turning down the opportunity to earn an advanced degree at the Chelsea School of Art, he supported himself as a dresser at the English National Opera. During the summers, he returned to his parents' house in Canada, and he eventually decided to remain in that country. He found steady work designing film sets but was still plagued by restlessness. He consoled himself by painting in a studio he had set up in a barn on his parents' property. "I was quite desperately searching, making things that seemed random," he told Tomkins.

PAINTING CAREER

One night in 1987, Doig joined his sister Sophie in watching the horror movie *Friday the 13th* on videotape. One scene, of a terrified young girl alone in a canoe on a forbidding looking lake struck him. That same night he returned to the studio and began a painting based on the scene. He had found something of a theme and subsequently made several more paintings featuring canoes. "The canoe, the fragile, lightweight vessel that opened up Canada's vast interior, had an iconic appeal to Canadians, and also to Doig," as Tomkins explained.

In 1989, Doig returned to England and—determined to become a more skilled painter—he enrolled at the Chelsea School of Art. "Chelsea is a real painter school, and I was nervous because the students were all much younger, and on a roll—painterly painters forging their own way," he admitted to Tomkins. He earned a master's degree the following year and entered what critics have called one of the most productive periods of his career. Doig was tapped for group shows at the Whitechapel Gallery and the Serpentine, and in 1991, he won the Whitechapel Artist Prize.

Some art watchers point to a September 1992 review in the art journal *Frieze* as a turning point in Doig's career. In it, the curator Gareth Jones, asserted that Doig's figurative paintings "court risk, walking a fine line between attraction and repulsion." Solo shows at such highly regarded venues as the Victoria Miro Gallery and Gavin Brown's Enterprise in New York

City followed. Doig won the 1993 John Moore Painting Prize and was short-listed for the 1994 Turner Prize for his painting "Blotter." Picturing an adolescent standing on a frozen lake surrounded by woods, Doig has stated that the painting was influenced by his experimentation with the drug LSD during his teenage years. He explained to Adams, "It was an important, sometimes terrifying drug to experiment with, though only people who have taken LSD would really understand how it might have affected my work. 'Blotter' tries to catch the idea of all this activity in the head, but the body being still. It is something like being absorbed into the landscape, I suppose."

In 1995, he was invited to become a trustee of Britain's Tate Museum, a position he held until 2000. In 1998, Doig made his first sale at auction, a work on paper that commanded just $3,622. That year, however, when the Tate purchased his oil painting "Echo Lake" for $38,500, it set off a minor scandal for buying art by a trustee without an independently conducted appraisal.

RETURN TO TRINIDAD

Two years later, Doig was offered a residency in Trinidad with Nigerian-born artist Chris Ofili, who had gained a measure of infamy for creating a portrait of the Virgin Mary embedded with pieces of animal dung. Flooded by memories of his time on the island nation as a child, Doig purchased land there, and he and Ofili returned several times for visits. In 2002, Doig moved to Trinidad for the long term. "It is tempting to think he moved to Trinidad to escape the venality of the London art world, but it was less complicated than that," Adams explained. Doig told him: "It was more to do with being excited by somewhere else . . . and giving my family some of the childhood I'd had. . . . It seemed like a good alternative to London, because, although I had left there when I was seven, it was so familiar to me."

GROWING POPULARITY

It was after Doig left London for a quieter life in the Caribbean that buzz surrounding him intensified and prices for his work skyrocketed. During the 2000s, British mega-collector Charles Saatchi became a fan and purchased several pieces of Doig's work. In 2007, Saatchi resold Doig's 1991 canoe painting "White Canoe" for more than $11 million, much to Doig's displeasure. "You get seen as a different kind of artist, one whose work is of interest only to the megarich," he complained to Tomkins. He has been careful to note to journalists that it was Saatchi who received the money from that sale, not him, as is the case for any sale at auction.

While art world insiders buzzed about the $26 million that "Swamped," another of his canoe paintings, brought at auction in 2015, prices would reach even higher in subsequent years: in 2017, "Rosedale," a snowy scene in which a house is visible through the trees, fetched $28.8 million. Attempting to explain why Doig's work could command such stratospheric prices, Sotheby's auction-house executive Francis Outred told Stuart Jeffries for the *Guardian* (5 Sept. 2012), "He has been the flag bearer for painting when it came back into fashion. His works are very commercial objects, very traditional, very romantic and also incredibly complex."

In 2017, Doig was awarded the Whitechapel Art Icon Award for his contributions to contemporary painting.

CONTROVERSY

In 2016, Doig found himself at the center of a lawsuit. A former corrections officer claimed Doig had been incarcerated as a teen and while in custody painted an acrylic canvas of a desert scene. The man claimed that he had purchased the piece to help the young artist get back on his feet and that he now intended to sell it for millions. When the case went to court, Doig was able to prove that he had never been incarcerated and had not created the painting. (It was later discovered that the artist had been an inmate with a similar name: Peter Edward Doige. He had died in 2012.)

PERSONAL LIFE

Doig, who taught for several years as a professor at the Düsseldorf State Academy of Art in Germany, divides his time between Trinidad and London.

Doig met his first wife, Bonnie Kennedy, while they were both attending the Wimbledon School of Art. They raised their five children—Celeste, Simone, Eva, Alice, and August—in Trinidad. That marriage ended in divorce in 2012. Doig also has a daughter, Echo, with his current partner, the curator Parinaz Mogadassi.

SUGGESTED READING

Adams, Tim. "Record Painter." *The Guardian*, 27 Jan. 2008, www.theguardian.com/artand-design/2008/jan/27/art. Accessed 8 Oct. 2018.

Cottam, F. G. "Peter Doig: A Perfectionist in Paradise." *Independent*, 31 Jan. 2008, www.independent.co.uk/arts-entertainment/art/features/peter-doig-a-perfectionist-in-para-dise-776053.html. Accessed 8 Oct. 2018.

Gleadell, Colin. "For Love or Money: The Ascent of Peter Doig." *The Telegraph*, 27 Feb. 2018, www.telegraph.co.uk/luxury/art/love-money-ascent-peter-doig. Accessed 8 Oct. 2018.

Jeffries, Stuart. "Peter Doig: The Outsider Comes Home." *The Guardian*, 5 Sept. 2012, www.theguardian.com/artanddesign/2012/sep/05/peter-doig-outsider-comes-home. Accessed 8 Oct. 2018.

Jones, Jonathan. "Stroke of Genius: Peter Doig's Eerie Art Whisks the Mind to Enchanted Places." *The Guardian*, 16 May 2015, www.theguardian.com/artanddesign/2015/may/16/peter-doig-painting-art-scotland. Accessed 8 Oct. 2018.

Solway, Diane. "Peter Doig." *W Magazine*, 1 Nov. 2008, www.wmagazine.com/story/peter-doig. Accessed 8 Oct. 2018.

Tomkins, Calvin. "The Mythical Stories in Peter Doig's Paintings." *The New Yorker*, 11 Dec. 2017, www.newyorker.com/magazine/2017/12/11/the-mythical-stories-in-peter-doigs-paintings. Accessed 8 Oct. 2018.

—*Mari Rich*

Michelle Dorrance

Date of birth: September 12, 1979
Occupation: Dancer and choreographer

Michelle Dorrance is a tap dancer, dance teacher, and choreographer. The artistic director and founder of Dorrance Dance/New York, she was a 2015 MacArthur Fellow recipient.

EARLY LIFE AND EDUCATION

Michelle Dorrance was born on September 12, 1979, in Chapel Hill, North Carolina, to Anson Dorrance, a soccer coach at the University of North Carolina, and M'Liss Gary Dorrance, a former professional ballet dancer.

Dorrance had a passion for music and tap dance from a young age. She started tap dancing when she was four. Her early instruction was at the Ballet School of Chapel Hill, which her mother cofounded. When she was eight, she joined Gene Medler's North Carolina Youth Tap Ensemble. She also played several musical instruments, including the guitar and ukulele, studied ballet, and played competitive soccer.

As part of the NC Youth Tap Ensemble, she was taught by many of the masters of tap dancing and was exposed to a wide range of styles. Medler encouraged expression and innovation, which inspired Dorrance to experiment with multiple dance styles and music genres and incorporate them into her own unique art form.

During the 1980s Dorrance toured the country and traveled abroad with the ensemble and performed at festivals where tap dancing was featured. While a part of the ensemble, she experimented with improvisation and created her first dance choreography. When she was sixteen, she performed with the Squirrel Nut Zippers at an album-release show.

In 1997 Dorrance moved to New York City. She attended the Gallatin School at New York University (NYU). There she created her own major based on democracy and race in America, and she received a bachelor's degree in 2001.

DANCE AND CHOREOGRAPHY

After graduating college, Dorrance choreographed several pieces for the NC Youth Tap Ensemble. In 2002 she became a dance teacher at the Broadway Dance Center. For several years she performed with tap companies, including Manhattan Tap, Jazz Tap Ensemble, and Savion Glover's TiDii. Notable performances included the opening ceremonies for the 2001 Cannes Film Festival, the 2002 Winter Olympics, the Nijinsky Awards, the Jerry Lewis Telethon, and the Apollo Theater's seventieth anniversary concert.

In 2005 Dorrance choreographed *Music Box*, which used music by songwriter Regina Spektor and was performed at the Joyce Theater in New York. She then joined the Off-Broadway show *STOMP* in 2007 and performed with it for four years. Dorrance's performances received high praise from critics and audiences; reviewers described her dancing as electric, eclectic, and energizing.

In 2010 David Parker, a guest curator of the Danspace Project, invited Dorrance to create a piece for the project. She took a month leave of absence from *STOMP* and choreographed several pieces, which were performed at St. Mark's Church in New York City. She won a 2011 Bessie Award for *Three to One* and *Remembering Jimmy*, a memoir to tap master Jimmy Slyde.

Dorrance founded her own dance company, Dorrance Dance/New York, in 2011 and focused on choreographing her own pieces as well as directing her ensemble of dancers. She continued to tour and perform around the world, as well as teach others. Her performances were met with high praise, with critics crediting her for rejuvenating the art form by combining tap dancing with the movements of modern dance. More awards soon followed. She was a Field Dance Fund recipient and Princess Grace Award winner in 2012; it was the first time the latter had been given to a tap choreographer.

In January 2013, Dorrance premiered *SOUNDspace* at St. Mark's Church. The venue did not allow metal-soled tap shoes, which might damage the venerable building's floors, so Dorrance hand-made wooden taps for her dancers, creating an unusual sound. The piece incorporated unique elements, including hip-hop moves, a double bass, and body percussions, and the performance received a resounding response. She received the 2013 Jacob's Pillow Dance Award for her choreography. In July 2013, she premiered *The Blues Project*, which told the history of the blues, at Jacob's Pillow in Massachusetts. The following year she received the Alpert Award. In 2015 she was named a MacArthur Fellow and was awarded $625,000 over five years.

Dorrance has described her passion for tap dancing as a desire to create music with dance. She has always been drawn to tap because of its musicality, its expressiveness and storytelling power, and its use in American culture as a way of overcoming racism and oppression.

IMPACT

Dorrance is considered one of the most promising and influential tap dancers and choreographers of the early twenty-first century. She received a 2015 MacArthur Fellowship for her tendency to push boundaries. After receiving the award, she stated that she planned to use the award money to continue to move tap dancing forward and to help her dance company grow.

PERSONAL LIFE

Dorrance's instrument of choice for creating music is wood and tap shoes; she also enjoys playing bass with her childhood friend, indie pop musician Darwin Deez, as the band deez and deez.

SUGGESTED READING

"Bio." *Michelle Dorrance*. Michelle Dorrance, n.d. , www.michelledorrance.com/bio.html. Accessed 26 Apr. 2019.

Campbell, Karen. "Show Filled with Wondrous Feats." *Boston Globe*. Boston Globe Media, 20 Aug. 2007, archive.boston.com/ae/theater_arts/articles/2007/08/20/show_filled_with_wondrous_feats/. Accessed 26 Apr. 2019.

Campbell, Karen. "Michelle Dorrance, Making Tap for the 21st Century." *Boston Globe*. Boston Globe Media, 18 May 2013, www2.bostonglobe.com/arts/theater-art/2013/05/18/michelle-dorrance-making-tap-for-century/2oQssOmv4mJOafgRE3ZEoL/story.html. Accessed 26 Apr. 2019.

Dorrance, Michelle. "Tap Dancer and Choreographer Michelle Dorrance." Interview by Marty Moss-Coane. *Radio Times*, WHYY, 1 Nov. 2015, whyy.org/episodes/tap-dancer-and-choreographer-michelle-dorrance-2/. Accessed 26 Apr. 2019.

Dorrance, Michelle. "Michelle Dorrance: 'I Just Knew I Would Never Stop Tap Dancing.'" Interview by Robert Siegel. *All Things Considered*. NPR, National Public Radio, 30 Sept. 2015, www.npr.org/2015/09/29/444437486/michelle-dorrance-i-just-knew-i-would-never-stop-tap-dancing. Accessed 26 Apr. 2019.

Dunkel, Ellen. "For Tapper Michelle Dorrance, Time for Some Attention." *Philadelphia Inquirer*. Philadelphia Media Network, 29 Nov. 2015, www.philly.com/philly/entertainment/arts/20151129_For_tapper_Michelle_Dorrance__time_for_some_attention.html. Accessed 26 Apr. 2019.

Seibert, Brian. "Sounding Off." *Dance Magazine*. DanceMedia, 1 June 2013, www.dancemagazine.com/sounding_off-2306911631.html. Accessed 26 Apr. 2019.

SELECTED WORKS

Three to One, 2011; *Remembering Jimmy*, 2011; *SOUNDspace*, 2013; *The Blues Project*, 2013

—Barb Lightner

Kyle Dubas

Date of birth: November 29, 1985
Occupation: Hockey executive

Kyle Dubas, who was named the general manager of the Toronto Maple Leafs in May 2018, is considered one of the brightest young minds in the National Hockey League (NHL). Described by Alex Prewitt for *Sports Illustrated* (5 Oct. 2018) as "an avatar for the new age of NHL decision making," Dubas has long been at the forefront of the league in using analytics to evaluate players and teams. Known as a "rink rat," as Brendan Shanahan, president of the Maple Leafs, put it to Bruce Arthur for the *Toronto Star* (11 May 2018), he got his first job in hockey at the age of eleven with the Sault Ste. Marie Greyhounds, an Ontario Hockey League (OHL) franchise. He has since enjoyed a meteoric rise through the ranks.

Dubas's distinctions include being one of the youngest general managers in OHL history, when he assumed that role with the Greyhounds at the age of twenty-five in 2011. He entered the NHL and joined the Maple Leafs organization in 2014, when he was named the team's assistant general manager. In 2018, after serving about four years in that role, he was appointed the seventeenth general manager in the history of the team.

EARLY LIFE

Born on November 29, 1985, Dubas was raised in Sault Ste. Marie, a city in Ontario, Canada, with his younger twin sisters, Megan and Courtney. His father, Mark, is a sergeant with the Sault Ste. Marie Police Service, and his mother, Paula, is an ambulance dispatcher. His parents divorced when he was eight; both have since remarried. (He also has a half-sister, Julia.)

"It just really didn't feel like it was work," he recalled to Mark J. Burns for *Forbes* (25 Sept. 2014). "I enjoyed all aspects of the hockey and business end."

RISE THROUGH THE RANKS

Dubas's experience working with the Greyhounds prompted him to study sports management at Brock University, located in St. Catharines, Ontario. While there, he remained affiliated with the team as a regional scout. Despite those added responsibilities, he poured himself into his studies and regularly made the dean's list. In the interview with Burns, he said that his time at Brock, from which he graduated in 2007, was "by far, the best time of my life in every aspect."

Though there were already some questions and concerns about his age, while still attending the university, Dubas landed a job as an agent for the Ontario-based firm Uptown Sports Management. "I was 20 years old trying to recruit players, and other agents were telling guys, 'You can't let him represent you. He's 20. He'll screw up the pivotal moments in your career,'" he explained to Darren Yourk for the *Globe and Mail* (13 Oct. 2011). While he became the youngest player agent certified by the NHL Players' Association, he had already developed a strong reputation in local hockey circles for his sports knowledge and business acumen, which had been enough for Uptown executive Todd Reynolds to hire him. "He's a natural," Reynolds said, as reported by the *Canadian Press* (24 July 2014). "He's likable, he's got a great personality. He's smart, he knows the game, he loves it. He just soaks it up 24/7." Dubas spent about five years working as an agent, during which he logged thousands of miles in his car as part of efforts to recruit and represent players. Some of the players he represented included center Andrew Desjardins and forward Kyle Clifford, both of whom went on to play in the NHL. Additionally, he helped Uptown open offices in Europe.

Dubas's career trajectory changed in 2011, when the Greyhounds, looking for someone with the types of ideas that would move them forward, hired him to serve as their general manager; the decision was reportedly unanimous, as executives were impressed by the level of his preparation and vision. At age twenty-five, he became one of the youngest to hold that role in OHL history. "I think I certainly bring a level of energy and passion that maybe somebody who's been through the wringer a little bit doesn't have anymore," he said, explaining one of the advantages of being a younger general manager to Cynthia Vukets for the *Toronto Star* (29 Apr. 2011). His appointment came with resistance, however, as some local pundits accused him of nepotism due to his grandfather's former association with the

Photo by TheAHL via Wikimedia Commons

Like many of his Canadian peers, Dubas developed a love of hockey early on, and he started playing the sport as a boy. He learned the intricacies of the game from his grandfather, Walter, a steel mill worker who coached the Sault Ste. Marie Greyhounds for several seasons in the 1960s, during which the team competed in the Northern Ontario Junior Hockey League; the team later became an OHL franchise in 1972. Dubas attended many games over the years with his grandfather, whom he cites as his biggest hockey influence. He also credits his grandfather with instilling in him a strong work ethic and sense of urgency.

Taking these values to heart, at age eleven, Dubas began working for the Greyhounds as a stick boy and locker room attendant. He prepared players' sticks and water bottles before practices and games, washed the team's laundry, and cleaned their dressing room. Free discussions with both players and coaches during this time helped broaden his knowledge about the game. Traveling to the Greyhounds' home rink each day after school, when he did not have practice or a game of his own, he would often stay there until late at night.

When Dubas was fourteen years old, he was promoted to hockey operations assistant with the Greyhounds, at which point he became a full-time member of the team's staff. It was also at that time that his own playing career ended after he suffered a series of sport-related concussions. Throughout high school, he learned the operational side of the business under the mentorship of Craig Hartsburg, who then served as the general manager and coach of the Greyhounds.

team. Undaunted, he promptly began reshaping the team.

DIFFERENT APPROACH TO THE GAME

As part of his reshaping efforts, Dubas embraced an analytics-driven approach to overcome the Greyhounds' limited operating budget and lower revenues, which made it hard for the team to compete with cash-heavier rivals. Assembling a small research and development staff, he began using advanced statistics and metrics to evaluate player performance and to create on-ice strategies, which quickly helped him earn a reputation as one of the OHL's most innovative executives. Although the Greyhounds missed the play-offs in his first season, the team made consecutive play-off appearances in his next two seasons, taking home a West Division title in the 2013–14 season.

During this time, Dubas also demonstrated himself to be a risk taker by hiring Sheldon Keefe, a former NHL and OHL player with a troubled past, as coach in his second season. "He's very progressive, has a lot of really good ideas that challenge conventional thinking," Keefe, who also played a significant role in the Greyhounds' turnaround, explained to Tal Pinchevsky for *NHL.com* (22 July 2014). "As a coach, to get an edge, I learned a great deal from him." In Dubas's three seasons as general manager, the Greyhounds' overall record brought him attention from NHL executives.

Among them was the president of the Toronto Maple Leafs, Brendan Shanahan, then in his first year, who invited Dubas to discuss hockey with him at the team's headquarters in the summer of 2014. Impressed not only by Dubas's progressive tactics but also by his respect for old-school philosophies, Shanahan, an NHL Hall of Famer, soon approached Dubas about serving as the Leafs' new assistant general manager. Dubas eventually accepted the position in July 2014, replacing Claude Loiselle, who was fired as part of an executive management shake-up.

In his new role, Dubas was charged with overseeing the Leafs' research and development department, which he immediately helped bolster by partnering with the leading analytics company SAS. The company began providing the Leafs with real-time analysis of an all-encompassing range of NHL statistics, which the team would use to make decisions. Dubas's new-age contributions, which included a strong emphasis on advanced statistics centered around the concept of puck possession, were quickly recognized around the NHL and beyond. In 2015, he was named to *Forbes* magazine's list of thirty people under thirty in the sports category.

MAPLES LEAFS' GENERAL MANAGER

As the Leafs' assistant general manager, Dubas also oversaw the Toronto Marlies, the team's affiliate in the American Hockey League (AHL), the top developmental league of the NHL. With Dubas as their general manager, the Marlies finished atop the AHL in regular-season standings in both the 2015–16 and 2017–18 seasons and won the 2018 Calder Cup, which is awarded annually to the AHL play-off champion. During this time, Dubas also helped develop eight players who ended up on the Leafs' roster, including right winger Connor Brown, forward Kasperi Kapanen, and defenseman Travis Dermott.

Dubas's success with the Marlies was among the reasons Shanahan decided to name him the successor to Lou Lamoriello as the Leafs' general manager in May 2018. Dubas beat out fellow assistant general manager Mark Hunter for the position, which is regarded as "one of the most prestigious, onerous, responsibility-freighted jobs in all of hockey," according to Arthur. With his appointment, Dubas became the seventeenth general manager in club history and, at age thirty-two, one of the youngest at his position in the NHL. (He is older than the Arizona Coyotes' general manager John Chayka, who similarly has a background in statistical analysis.)

Since becoming the Leafs' general manager, Dubas has continued to implement the same cerebral, data-driven approach he used with the Greyhounds and Marlies. In this role, he holds the responsibilities of overseeing player personnel, negotiating contracts, and managing the team's salary cap, among other duties. One of Dubas's first significant moves as general manager included signing top free-agent All-Star defenseman John Tavares during the 2018 off-season.

Though Dubas's arrival in Toronto was described by Arthur as a "collision between hockey's past and its future, and its twin poles of thought," the young executive has tried to play down his label as a stats guru. "The two polarizing portions of the fight have taken me and tried to pull and say, this is what he is, or this is what he is," he stated to Arthur. "And the reality is I grew up in hockey, working in hockey every day—scouting, player development."

PERSONAL LIFE

Dubas and his wife, Shannon, whom he married in 2014, have a son, Leo. Despite his penchant for advanced statistics, Dubas was described by Prewitt as being "surprisingly analog," preferring print books over e-readers and moleskin notebooks to phone apps. "I know it's not the most technological way of doing it," he explained, "but it works well for me."

SUGGESTED READING

Arthur, Bruce. "Handing Leafs GM Reins to Creative Dubas Risky Play." *The Toronto Star*, 11 May 2018, www.thestar.com/sports/leafs/opinion/2018/05/11/handing-leafs-gm-reins-to-creative-dubas-risky-play.html. Accessed 21 Oct. 2018.

Burns, Mark J. "Assistant GM Kyle Dubas Injects Youth, Smarts into Maple Leafs Front Office." *Forbes*, 25 Sept. 2014, www.forbes.com/sites/markjburns/2014/09/25/assistant-gm-kyle-dubas-injects-youth-smarts-into-maples-leafs-front-office/#1bf5d4b0188e. Accessed 21 Oct. 2018.

Dubas, Kyle. "The New Ice Age." Interview by Cynthia Vukets. *The Toronto Star*, 29 Apr. 2011, www.thestar.com/sports/hockey/2011/04/29/the_new_ice_age.html. Accessed 21 Oct. 2018.

Hicks, Jeff. "Leafs Hire Dubas 'Wise Beyond His Years.'" *Sportsnet*, 22 July 2014, www.sportsnet.ca/hockey/nhl/leafs-hire-dubas-wise-beyond-his-years. Accessed 21 Oct. 2018.

Pinchevsky, Tal. "Dubas, 28, Took Fast Track to Maple Leafs Front Office." *NHL.com*, 22 July 2014, www.nhl.com/news/dubas-28-took-fast-track-to-maple-leafs-front-office/c-726933. Accessed 21 Oct. 2018.

Prewitt, Alex. "Cutting-Edge Rookie Leafs GM Kyle Dubas Working to Bring a Cup to Title-Starved Toronto." *Sports Illustrated*, 5 Oct. 2018, www.si.com/nhl/2018/10/05/kyle-dubas-toronto-maple-leafs. Accessed 21 Oct. 2018.

—*Chris Cullen*

Alan Duffy

Date of birth: ca. 1983
Occupation: Astronomer and science communicator

UK–born astronomer Alan Duffy became the lead scientist of the Royal Institution of Australia, an organization dedicated to science advocacy and education, in 2017. It was a natural step for Duffy, who dedicated much of his career to promoting a better understanding of the sciences to general audiences, both in his adopted home country of Australia and abroad. A deft public speaker, he became known for his ability to keep audiences engaged whether working from a stage, a television studio, or in a podcast. He developed a considerable following in print, on television and radio, and on the Internet as an effective science communicator. Throughout, he retained the sense of wonder and excitement

Photo by Mal Vickers via Wikimedia Commons

that first drew him to astronomy. "I think this really is a bit of a golden age of space exploration and I am lucky that I get that chance to get overly enthusiastic on air," Duffy said to Sue Green for the *Sydney Morning Herald* (3 Apr. 2016). "I do sometimes worry that not everyone is as excited as I am about an asteroid at 7 a.m."

In addition to his public speaking and outreach, Duffy also conducts his own scientific research, focusing on dark matter, dark energy, galaxy formation, and cosmology. As an associate professor and research fellow at the Centre for Astrophysics and Supercomputing at Swinburne University of Technology he developed complex computer models to help humanity's understanding of how the first galaxies in the early universe formed as well as the makeup of nearby galaxies. He also served as a member of the international scientific consortium SABRE, which seeks to directly detect dark matter for the first time. As Duffy stated on his Centre for Astrophysics and Supercomputing web page, "My role can be best described as doing cutting-edge research, then trying to explain it to as many people of all backgrounds as I can."

EARLY LIFE AND EDUCATION

Alan R. Duffy was born in Peterborough, England, the son of Kevin and Renee Duffy. When Alan was four the entire family moved to Northern Ireland, first settling in Belfast, then later in Ballyclare. During his childhood and continuing on through his teen years at Ballyclare High School, he became intrigued by the natural world. "I was naturally curious about everything," Duffy said in an interview with Chris

Jones for the *Belfast Telegraph* (27 May 2015). "It wasn't just astronomy—I was fascinated by electricity and how things worked."

During this same period, he became intensely interested in science fiction, including television shows like *Star Trek* and the works of acclaimed writers such as Isaac Asimov and Arthur C. Clarke. He also came to love science writing from esteemed thinkers like the renowned physicist Stephen Hawking. Hawking's book *A Brief History of Time* (1988) was a revelation to the young Duffy around the age of thirteen. "That was a key moment, discovering that book. He was explaining why we were learning maths and having to rote learn," Duffy told Green. "There was this universe to discover and explore and these were the tools."

Duffy conducted his undergraduate studies at the University of Manchester, enrolling in 2001 with an Entrance Scholarship and a Major Science Award. Thanks to the EU Erasmus Exchange Program, he was able to study at the University of Amsterdam and work on supercomputers at the observatory at Leiden University from September 2003 to June 2004. He received his MPhys (1st) in physics in 2005, then earned his PhD at the University of Manchester's Jodrell Bank Centre for Astrophysics in 2009, winning several other grants along the way. His thesis work discussed an investigation into the universe's large-scale structure.

RESEARCH WORK

In the fall of 2009 Duffy moved to Australia to become a postdoctoral associate at the University of Western Australia (UWA). The decision was the result of a bit of serendipity as he finished his time at the University of Manchester. As he told Jones, "It turned out that in Australia they were just beginning to build what would ultimately be the largest telescope that's ever been conceived of, never mind built. I happened to have done a bit of work at the start of my PhD on figuring out how to see as many galaxies as possible with a telescope and they asked me if I wanted to come down." As a result, he worked on the Australian Square Kilometre Array Pathfinder (ASKAP), one of the most advanced radio telescopes in the world.

Duffy began to attract attention for his research very early in his career. In 2011, he led a project that won a Research Development Award, and in 2012, he earned UWA's Best Publication by Early Career Research award. In 2012, he advanced to a postdoctoral research fellow position with UWA's International Centre for Radio Astronomy Research (ICRAR). That same year he moved to Melbourne, where he took another postdoctoral position at the University of Melbourne. In 2013, he won the ASA

Louise Webster Prize and was a state finalist for the 2013 Fresh Science Award.

In 2014, Duffy became an associate professor at Swinburne University of Technology in Melbourne. There he continued what had become his primary concern: studying the makeup and development of early universes. On his official web page at the Centre for Astrophysics and Supercomputing at Swinburne University of Technology, he explained, "I use supercomputers to uncover the nature of dark matter (a new type of particle that binds galaxies together) and the key physical laws that govern the formation of galaxies. I focus on two extremes of distance, the very close and the very far from us in the Milky Way." Among his work was the computer modeling of early galaxies as part of the DRAGONS (Dark-ages, Reionization And Galaxy-formation Observables Numerical Simulation) project.

EARLY GALAXIES AND DARK MATTER

One of Duffy and his colleagues' key discoveries was that early galaxies technically underwent a period of recession in terms of star formation. The finding was reported in a paper published in the *Monthly Notices of the Royal Astronomical Society* in 2017, and Duffy also explained it in more general terms in an article he wrote for *The Conversation* (16 July 2017). "Pristine gas from the Big Bang doesn't just exist as molecular hydrogen, it also comes in a lone atomic state known as neutral hydrogen," he stated in that article. "While the galaxies were indeed growing quickly from molecular hydrogen, the rest of the gas in the neutral hydrogen form was pouring inward and pilling up. The galactic economy simply couldn't process this neutral atomic hydrogen into molecular hydrogen and ultimately into stars fast enough." Duffy noted that later galaxies, such as the Milky Way, operate in a different way, closer to equilibrium. Ultimately, Duffy's computer simulations suggest the importance of dark matter since the dawn of the universe.

In addition to his work with computer simulations, Duffy became involved in efforts to detect dark matter directly. (Although scientists believe dark matter accounts for approximately 85 percent of all matter in the universe and about 25 percent of its total energy density, it remains theoretical.) He became a member of an international research group dedicated to investigating the phenomenon, specifically through the construction of the Stawell Underground Physics Laboratory (STUPL) begun around 2015. The project included a prospective dark matter detector known as SABRE (Sodium Iodide with Active Background Rejection Experiment).

Meanwhile, Duffy also became a member of numerous other professional and academic organizations. These included the International Astronomical Union (IAU), Science and

Technology Australia (STA), the Australian National Institute for Theoretical Astrophysics (ANITA), the Astronomical Society of Australia (ASA), and the Australian Telescope National Facility (ATNF), among others.

COMMUNICATIONS AND OUTREACH WORK

In conjunction with his scientific research, Duffy developed a parallel career based on his skill in explaining complex scientific concepts to lay audiences. Indeed, it was his work as a science communicator that raised his profile not only in the science community but also among the general public. His passionate commitment to outreach and education spanned a variety of media. He regularly wrote pieces for *The Conversation* as well as for *Cosmos*, Australia's most popular science magazine. In 2012, Duffy launched the YouTube video series *Pint in the Sky*, cohosted with cosmologist Katie Mack. He began cohosting the podcast *Cosmic Vertigo* with astronomer Amanda Bauer in 2017.

Over the years Duffy gave many media interviews for outlets ranging from local to international, earning praise for his clear and enthusiastic style and building a strong following on social media. He also appeared regularly on Australian news programs such as ABC's *News Breakfast*, *ABC Radio Sydney*, and *ABC Radio Melbourne*, among others. "Can you imagine sitting on the couch at breakfast time, trying to explain black holes to people?" Duffy told Jones. "It's insane. But it sort of suits that temperament of being a morning person and wanting to chat about science."

Duffy also served as the lead speaker, host, or moderator at a wide variety of science-oriented events and often visited classrooms. He worked steadily to interest audiences in topics such as cosmology, galaxy formation, the solar system, the night sky, and physics. Some of his more notable appearances include presenting during a national tour of the BBC lecture program *The Science of Doctor Who*, speaking at the Australian Skeptics conventions in 2017 and 2018, and presenting at a TEDx conference in the Sydney Opera House. He was ambassador for the Sydney Science Festival in 2016, and that same year he was a finalist for the national Eureka Award for Promoting the Understanding of Australian Science Research. In 2017, the Royal Institution of Australia, a national nonprofit seeking to provide better understanding to the general public about the sciences, appointed him lead scientist. In that capacity he became the face of Australia's Science Channel, a key outlet for science education.

PERSONAL LIFE

Duffy became an Australian citizen in 2014. He was engaged to Sarah Clarke in 2015, and the two married the next year. The couple had a daughter in 2018.

SUGGESTED READING

"About Me." *Prof Alan R Duffy*, www.alanduffy. com/about. Accessed 15 Aug. 2019.
"Alan R. Duffy CV." *Squarespace. com*, static1.squarespace.com/ static/5260bc02e4b0e912afef2198/t/52dd fd15e4b0f48cdba8a5b5/1390279957362/ Academic+CV+l.pdf. Accessed 27 Aug. 2019.
"Associate Professor Alan Duffy." *Centre for Astrophysics and Supercomputing*, Swinburne University of Technology, astronomy.swin. edu.au/staff/aduffy.html. Accessed 15 Aug. 2019.
Duffy, Alan. "The Great Galactic Recession." *The Conversation*, 16 July 2017, theconversation.com/the-great-galactic-recession-81033. Accessed 15 Aug. 2019.
Green, Sue. "Stargazer Teaches Earthly Realities." *The Sydney Morning Herald*, 3 Apr. 2016, www.smh.com.au/business/workplace/stargazer-teaches-earthly-realities-20160402-gnwv9d.html. Accessed 15 Aug. 2019.
Jones, Chris. "Dr Alan Duffy: Why This Ballyclare Boffin Has Stars in His Eyes." *Belfast Telegraph*, 27 May 2015, www. belfasttelegraph.co.uk/life/features/dr-alan-duffy-why-this-ballyclare-boffin-has-stars-in-his-eyes-31256104.html. Accessed 15 Aug. 2019.

—*Christopher Mari*

Jourdan Dunn

Date of birth: August 3, 1990
Occupation: Model

One of the highest-paid models in the world in 2014 and 2015, and a major figure in the world of modeling overall, Jourdan Dunn is in many ways emblematic of the new wave of supermodels that has challenged earlier preconceptions of the role of models in the industry. A fixture on both Fashion Week runways and magazine covers and outspoken about a variety of issues—including diversity in fashion, awareness of sickle cell disease, and her own experiences as a parent—Dunn has aptly demonstrated that models are not simply walking mannequins. "Before, models were only to be seen and not heard, but now [thanks to social media] we have a platform, we have a voice," she told Rebecca Gonsalves for the *Independent* (21 Sept. 2014). "People want to get to know us, to get to know our interests.

Photo by Ed Kavishe, Fashion Wire Press via Wikimedia Commons

I feel that you have to use that to your advantage by becoming a brand." Indeed, in the years since being discovered by a modeling scout at a Primark store in 2006, Dunn has done just that, expanding her personal brand to encompass not only her numerous lucrative advertising campaigns but also multiple clothing lines and web series showcasing her interest in cooking.

EARLY LIFE AND EDUCATION

Jourdan Sherise Dunn was born on August 3, 1990, to Dee Dunn and Rodney Alveranga. Born in Brent, a borough of London, England, she grew up in the west London suburb of Greenford. Her parents separated when she was a toddler. Dunn spent her childhood and teen years living with her mother, who worked as a receptionist and administrative assistant, and her younger brothers, Antoine and Kain. Dunn was also close to her extended family and often spent time cooking with her mother, aunt, and grandmother.

As a teenager, Dunn dealt with bullying at school that focused on her body, particularly her height and build. "In the fashion industry it's celebrated, but when you're thirteen and your family's from the Caribbean, it's not," she explained to Hayley Campbell for the *Guardian* (7 Oct. 2017). She later commented in interviews that the bullying she faced caused her to leave school for a time and pursue homeschooling. In light of such treatment, Dunn initially had no plans to become a model, instead aspiring to pursue a career as a dancer or an actor.

EARLY CAREER

In 2006, Dunn and a friend were in a Primark store in west London when a scout with the London-based modeling agency Storm Model Management noticed Dunn and approached her about becoming a model. Already familiar with Storm, which was particularly well known for having discovered the supermodel Kate Moss, Dunn quickly signed with the agency. Dunn began to make appearances in runway shows in 2007, including shows for major brands such as Marc Jacobs and Salvatore Ferragamo. The following year, she appeared in runway shows for brands such as Alexander McQueen, Prada, Duro Olowu, Givenchy, Rodarte, Chanel, Vivienne Westwood, and Thakoon. Dunn was particularly prolific during the 2008 spring/summer fashion season, appearing in more than seventy runway shows during that period.

With her immediate success on the runway, Dunn drew the attention of numerous fashion-focused publications, and the UK edition of *Vogue* highlighted her as a new model to watch. In addition to making live appearances at fashion events, she found extensive work as a print model, appearing in magazines such as *i-D*, various international editions of *Vogue*, and *Teen Vogue*. Dunn also starred in a 2008 advertising campaign for the retailer Topshop, appearing alongside fellow models Karlie Kloss, Kori Richardson, and Amanda Laine. Having established herself as a popular and talented model over the course of her early career, Dunn was named Model of the Year at the 2008 British Fashion Awards in recognition of her work.

Dunn's career continued to progress through 2009. She appeared in several major magazines, as well as in a Jean Paul Gaultier runway show. In 2010, Dunn continued to prove herself as one of the United Kingdom's most popular working models, securing contracts with major brands such as Burberry in 2011 and making a high-profile appearance in the closing ceremony for the 2012 Olympic Games in London.

INTEREST IN COOKING

A longtime lover of cooking, Dunn used her success as a model to draw viewers to her cooking web series *Well Dunn with Jourdan Dunn* from 2012 to 2013. Appearing on Jay-Z's YouTube channel, the series featured appearances by fellow models as well as entertainers and members of Dunn's family. A later series, *How It's Dunn*, premiered in 2015 and documented her travels in Thailand. The series showed her experiences learning about Thai cuisine. For Dunn, her forays into cooking programs are an extension of her childhood love of cooking, which her family nurtured throughout her early years. "I was always in the kitchen as a child, watching my grandmother, my auntie, my mum," she recalled to Bella Blisset for the *Daily Mail* (8 Nov. 2014). "In the Caribbean, where my family is from originally, you always cook just in case unexpected guests come over. I used to love seeing how they mixed different spices together to create a great dish." Dunn likewise showcased her love and knowledge of food as a guest judge on the cooking competition show *Chopped Junior*.

TOP MODEL

In 2014, Dunn signed a contract to be the new face of the cosmetics brand Maybelline. "My first memories of make-up are of raiding my mum's cosmetic bag as a child and being intrigued by the green and pink tube of Maybelline Great Lash mascara," she told Blisset following the announcement. "Now things have come full circle. It's genuinely a dream come true to be a face for the brand." The years 2014 and 2015 proved to be lucrative for Dunn, who was named to *Forbes* magazine's list of the world's highest-paid models both years. She also claimed her second Model of the Year title at the British Fashion Awards in 2015.

Over the course of her career, Dunn appeared in numerous advertising campaigns, including campaigns for fashion brands and retailers such as H&M, Kate Spade, DKNY, Balmain, and Michael Kors, as well as for the technology company HTC and social causes such as the #ActuallySheCan movement. Although Dunn herself had no shortage of career opportunities, she is particularly concerned about the lack of racial and ethnic diversity within her field and is outspoken about the need for fashion designers and major brands to hire more models of color. "I don't understand it. It seems crazy to me that this is even an issue that we're facing," she told Blisset. "Yes, when it comes to shows, I'm seeing more ethnic girls on the catwalks. But when it comes to magazine covers, it's still rare. I guess you'd have to ask the casting directors, modelling agents and magazines why that is still the case." Comments on the fashion industry's lack of diversity made by Dunn and some of her colleagues fueled widespread conversations within the fashion media, which continued to grapple with issues of inclusion and representation over the subsequent years.

CLOTHING LINES

In addition to modeling, Dunn made further inroads into fashion through collaborations with retailer Marks & Spencer and clothing brand Missguided. Her Marks & Spencer line, Lil' LonDunn, which launched in 2016, was designed for children and inspired by her experiences searching for clothing for her son. Lil' LonDunn is a largely unisex line and features a variety of pants, shorts, shirts, and outerwear. With Missguided, Dunn created the athleisure collaboration LonDunn + Missguided, for which she served as creative director. "I want to have the final say, because it's my name and it's a representation of me," she told Leanne Bayley for *Glamour* (23 Feb. 2017) of the project. "I don't want to have my name on it if other people have done all the work." The line launched in March 2017, while a second installment, referred to as Season 2 of the collaboration, debuted in September of that year. Dunn also enjoys acting and has appeared in several music videos as well as in small roles in films such as *Zoolander 2* (2016) and *Terminal* (2018). Widely recognized for both her work as a model and her activism, Dunn was named to the Forbes 30 Under 30: Art and Style list in 2018.

PERSONAL LIFE

Dunn lives and works in both London and New York. Born in 2009, Dunn's son, Riley, has the inherited blood disorder sickle cell disease. Dunn's interviews and media appearances in the years following his birth often focused on her relationship with him and experiences as a mother, and she has been candid about the challenges she faced in becoming a parent. Dunn has noted in interviews that she had not truly enjoyed modeling during the first years of her career and found a new sense of purpose following Riley's birth. "I just did it because I liked the money and wanted to continue my shopping sprees. But my son has put it into perspective for me—I have to do this, I want to, to set him up for life," she explained to Gonsalves. "I took it for granted that I had a great career in front of me, but now I realise my opportunities—the fact that I can provide for my family and be an ambassador for sickle-cell disease and raise awareness." Riley appeared alongside Dunn in a 2018 campaign for designer Brandon Maxwell as well as in some promotional material for Lil' LonDunn. Dunn has become active in raising awareness about the genetic condition and has hosted a series of Cell for Gratitude events to benefit the Sickle Cell Disease Association of America (SCDAA).

SUGGESTED READING

Bayley, Leanne. "Meet Your New *Glamour* Cover Star: Jourdan Dunn." *Glamour*, 23 Feb. 2017, www.glamourmagazine.co.uk/gallery/jourdan-dunn-glamour-magazine-2017. Accessed 18 Jan. 2019.

Blisset, Bella. "Supermodel and Supermum: An Interview with Jourdan Dunn." *Daily Mail*, 8 Nov. 2014, www.dailymail.co.uk/home/you/article-2825082/Supermodel-supermum-interview-Jourdan-Dunn.html. Accessed 18 Jan. 2019.

Brumfitt, Stuart. "Jourdan Dunn, the Girl That Set the World on Fire!" *i-D*, 13 Nov. 2013, i-d.vice.com/amp/en_us/article/43vwep/

jourdan-dunn-the-girl-that-set-the-world-on-fire. Accessed 18 Jan. 2019.

Dunn, Jourdan. "Jourdan Dunn: 'I Got Picked on for the Way I Looked at School.'" Interview by Hayley Campbell. *The Guardian*, 7 Oct. 2017, www.theguardian.com/lifeandstyle/2017/oct/07/jourdan-dunn-i-got-picked-on-for-the-way-i-looked-at-school. Accessed 18 Jan. 2019.

Gonsalves, Rebecca. "Exclusive Interview with Jourdan Dunn: Mother, One of the World's Best-Paid Models and Ambassador for Sickle-Cell Disease." *Independent*, 21 Sept. 2014, www.independent.co.uk/life-style/fashion/features/jourdan-dunn-model-mother-9747286.html. Accessed 18 Jan. 2019.

Newbold, Alice. "Jourdan Dunn on Juggling Motherhood and Modelling." *Vogue British*, 22 Jan. 2018, www.vogue.co.uk/article/jourdan-dunn-brandon-maxwell-spring-summer-2018. Accessed 18 Jan. 2019.

Sowray, Bibby. "Jourdan Dunn Is Officially Britain's Top Model." *The Telegraph*, 23 Nov. 2015, www.telegraph.co.uk/fashion/british-fashion-awards/jourdan-dunn-wins-model-of-the-year-british-fashion-awards/. Accessed 18 Jan. 2019.

—*Joy Crelin*

Ross Edgley

Date of birth: October 13, 1985
Occupation: Author and adventurer

British fitness expert and adventurer Ross Edgley earned widespread attention in the extreme sports community for his outlandish stunts, many of which pushed the boundaries of human physical prowess. A former water polo player turned sports scientist, he used his own body to accomplish first-of-their-kind strength and endurance feats. In 2016 alone, these included running a marathon while pulling a car, climbing the equivalent height of Mount Everest up a rope, and completing an Olympic-distance triathlon while carrying a hundred-pound tree trunk. The next year he created the sport of strongman swimming, which requires one to swim long distances while carrying a tree. In 2018 Edgley broke several records en route to becoming the first person to swim around the entire coast of Great Britain. As Miranda Larbi declared for *Metro* (23 Mar. 2017), "He's basically a real-life Action Man—times ten."

Edgley used his high-profile escapades to raise money for charity and to draw attention to his views on fitness and nutrition, which emphasized an individualized approach often at odds with the mainstream fitness industry. A cofounder of the UK–based sports nutrition company The Protein Works, he also authored the best-selling *The World's Fittest Book* (2018).

EARLY LIFE AND EDUCATION

Ross Edgley was born on October 13, 1985, and was raised in Grantham, Lincolnshire, England. He grew up in an athletic family. His father was a tennis instructor and his mother was a former sprinter, and one of his grandfathers was an accomplished marathon runner. Naturally, Edgley took up sports at a young age. Among these were swimming, which he would later describe as his first love, and water polo.

As a child Edgley fostered dreams of one day making the Olympic Games as a competitive swimmer. However, by age thirteen, he was a told by his swimming coach that he would have to grow another foot to even consider making that dream a reality. The short and stocky Edgley later turned his attention to water polo and earned a place on Great Britain's junior national squad. The physical and aggressive nature of that sport led to his adoption of strength and conditioning training, which ultimately enabled him to hold his own against stronger and bigger competitors. As Edgley explained to Jessica Carpani for the *Telegraph* (30 May 2018), "That was when I started to learn how to be strong in the water, because you're essentially swimming but also having a fight."

Edgley's interest in physical fitness led him to study sports science at Loughborough University's School of Sport, Exercise and Health Sciences, an internationally renowned institution

Photo by Luke Walker/Getty Images for Red Bull

located in England's East Midlands region. He received first-class honors for his dissertation, which focused on various strength and power training methods.

THE PROTEIN WORKS AND EARLY EXPERIMENTS

Upon completing his studies, Edgley became a strength and conditioning coach and performance nutritionist. He nonetheless started working outside the traditional realm of his field in an effort to push the boundaries of fitness. In 2012, he co-founded The Protein Works, which became one of the UK's leading sports nutrition companies. At the company, he began developing various nutritional supplements, such as pre- and post-workout shakes and snacks, for his own unique sports-based challenges.

Edgley performed the first of these fitness "stunts" in 2013, when he lost twenty-four pounds in twenty-four hours to highlight the difference between body weight and body fat. To achieve the feat, he took Epsom salt baths, used saunas, ingested natural diuretics like caffeine and vitamin C to use the bathroom twenty times, and worked out several times wearing sweat suits. He also limited himself to a carbohydrate-free, greens-rich diet and only 100 milliliters of water. The experiment quickly trended on social media sites, with Edgley seeking to shed light on the overemphasis on weight within the fitness community and society in general by proving that scale readings are determined by many factors beyond body fat.

Edgley next put his unconventional fitness wisdom to the test on close friend Andy Bolton, a legendary British power lifter and strongman noted for being the first person to ever deadlift one thousand pounds. Bolton, a seven-time world champion, learned that he had developed severe kidney complications, which forced him to start undergoing dialysis treatment three times per week. To help Bolton lose the weight necessary to be considered for a kidney transplant, Edgley put him on a supervised but highly individualized diet—with no strict calorie limits—and overhauled his training regimen. Under his supervision, Bolton dropped approximately one hundred pounds over a period of six months, stopped undergoing dialysis, and safely returned to competition.

PUSHING THE LIMITS OF HUMAN FITNESS

Edgley's desire to explore the possibilities of human physical fitness and to raise money for charities important to him led to a series of extreme stunts in 2016. In January of that year, he created the idea of the World's Strongest Marathon by running 26.2 miles while pulling a 3,000-pound Mini Countryman automobile. He spent months preparing for the strength-endurance feat, which was performed at the Silverstone Race Circuit in England and took more than nineteen hours to complete. Challenging a conventionally held belief, Edgley, who used the event to raise money for charities including the Teenage Cancer Trust, sought to illustrate how strength and stamina could be improved simultaneously.

In April 2016, Edgley again raised money for the Teenage Cancer Trust through what was billed as the world's longest rope climb. The feat required him to climb up and down a twenty-meter rope continuously until he reached the height of Mount Everest (29,029 feet, or 8,848 meters). Using US marine-inspired rope-climbing techniques, Edgley took just under twenty hours to reach his desired height goal, during which he endured painful rope burns on his hands and shins.

Four months after his rope-climbing stunt, Edgley embarked on a thousand-mile trek across England to raise money and awareness for Chester Zoo conservation projects. He covered that distance over the course of a month while running barefoot and carrying a 110-pound weighted Marine backpack. The run offered insight into the science behind barefoot running, though Edgley noted it was one of the most difficult challenges he had faced. As he told Larbi, "It was one of the hardest and most painful lessons, but also one of the most valuable: the body will always find a way to adapt and succeed if you're stubborn."

Edgley finished out 2016 in signature extreme fashion by completing the first-ever "tree-athlon"—that is, an Olympic-distance triathlon while carrying a hundred-pound tree trunk. After participating in a twelve-week triathlon training program, during which he also worked with the UK's Royal Marines, he set out for the Caribbean island of Nevis. There, he completed the grueling event, which consisted of a 1.5-kilometer swim, 40-kilometer bike ride, and 10-kilometer run. Edgley's decision to carry a tree on his back during the race was aimed at highlighting Nevis' goal of becoming the first carbon-neutral island in the world.

STRONGMAN SWIMMING AND *THE WORLD'S FITTEST BOOK*

Taking inspiration from his tree-athlon, Edgley devised the sport of strongman swimming, in which one swims long distances with a hundred-pound tree trunk attached to a rope around their waist. His goals included further pushing the limits of physical and mental endurance, continuing to raise awareness and funds for various causes, and inspiring all kinds of people to try swimming and other sports. "I'm built like a hobbit so I don't have the body of a professional swimmer," he told Fran McElhone for *Devon Live* (16 Jan. 2018). "But what's nice about strongman swimming is that there are no pre-conceived ideas about what the right physique should be."

During the summer of 2017, Edgley performed his first strongman swimming test with a ten-kilometer swim. That November, after completing a series of other test swims in England, he headed back to the Caribbean to undertake a thirty-five-kilometer strongman swim from St. Lucia to Martinique. Battling debilitating bouts of motion sickness, five-foot waves, and unforgiving tides and currents, he completed the swim in just thirty-two hours. He ultimately swam more than a hundred kilometers due to the water conditions, helping him establish a new world record.

Edgley's open-water feat paved the way for the most ambitious stunt of his career: an ocean swim world record attempt swimming around Great Britain. In January 2018, as part of his preparation, he completed a nonstop forty-eight-hour hundred-kilometer swim at the Royal Marines Commando Training Centre in Devon, England. Over the next five months, Edgley trained with the Royal Marines and independently at David Lloyd Cheshire Oaks' pool in Cheshire, England, swimming more than 100 kilometers per week and consuming more than 8,000 calories a day. During that time, he reached out to Matt and Susanne Knight, a husband-and-wife duo from Cornwall who had been previously known for shuttling surfers to big-wave surf spots in their fifteen-meter-long catamaran. The duo agreed to serve as Edgley's support crew, with Matt serving as his navigator and Susanne as his nutritionist.

The month before his record-breaking swim attempt, Edgley published *The World's Fittest Book* (2018). His first book, it features teachings and concepts from Olympic champions, world renowned strongmen, extreme athletes, and elite military personnel and draws on information culled from more than a thousand sports science journals. The idiosyncratic work, which took Edgley ten years to complete, became a *Sunday Times* best seller and went on to be released in more than a hundred countries around the world.

GREAT BRITISH SWIM AND BEYOND

On June 1, 2018, Edgley set off from Margate, a town on the southeast coast of England, on what was named the Great British Swim. He would swim 1,791 miles over the next 157 days to become the first swimmer to circumnavigate Great Britain. Seventy-four days into the journey, he broke the record for the longest staged sea swim propelled only by muscle power (without the aid of flippers). In completing the feat—equivalent to swimming from London to Moscow—Edgley swam anywhere from thirty to fifty kilometers

per day, swimming for a total of twelve hours a day in six-hour cycles. He spent the other half of his days on the support craft, where he rested and consumed up to 15,000 calories per day before returning to the exact spot he left off.

Over the course of the swim, Edgley experienced a plethora of health issues, including "salt mouth," which resulted in pieces of his tongue flaking off due to excess saltwater exposure, and severe chafing around his neck caused by his wetsuit. He also endured thirty-seven jellyfish stings and countless storms while swimming alongside dolphins, basking sharks, and on one occasion, even a minke whale. Edgley's travails were chronicled in a weekly vlog produced by sponsor company Red Bull. On that platform he summed up his goal for the project, as quoted by Amanda Jackson for CNN (30 Nov. 2018): "It's my hope that people remember the Great British Swim as an example or experiment in both mental and physical fortitude."

Upon making his way back to Margate on November 4, 2018, Edgley was joined by hundreds of other swimmers who swam the last half mile with him. In the days afterward, he quipped that he needed to learn how to walk again before embarking on his next epic adventure. In early 2019, he launched the World's Fittest Live Show, a tour in which he combined the teachings of his best-selling book with lessons he learned during his twenty-three weeks at sea.

PERSONAL LIFE

Edgley noted his exploits often distracted him from the ordinary aspects of a personal life. In addition to his athletic and sports science endeavors, he has written for a number of publications, including *GQ, Men's Health, Askmen.com,* and *Men's Journal.*

SUGGESTED READING

Carpani, Jessica. "Around the Island in a Million Calories: Strongman Swimmer Ross Edgley on His Next Challenge—To Swim around Britain." *The Telegraph,* 30 May 2018, www.telegraph.co.uk/health-fitness/body/around-island-million-calories-strongman-swimmer-ross-edgley/. Accessed 9 Feb. 2019.

Dean, Sam. "Why I Ran a Triathlon with a Tree Strapped on My Back." *The Telegraph,* 24 Nov. 2016, www.telegraph.co.uk/health-fitness/body/ran-triathlon-tree-strapped-back/. Accessed 9 Feb. 2019.

Edgley, Ross. "The Real Aquaman's Accidental World Record." *GQ,* 29 Nov. 2017, www.gq-magazine.co.uk/article/the-real-aquamans-accidental-world-record. Accessed 9 Feb. 2019.

Edgley, Ross. "Meet Ross Edgley: The Real Life Action Man Who Runs with Trees Tied to His Back." Interview by Miranda Larbi. *Metro,* 23 Mar. 2017, metro.co.uk/2017/03/23/

meet-ross-edgley-the-real-life-action-man-who-runs-with-trees-tied-to-his-back-6516769/. Accessed 9 Feb. 2019.

Hunt, Elle. "'Chunks of My Tongue Came Off – You Could See the Tastebuds': Ross Edgley on Swimming around Great Britain." *The Guardian*, 5 Nov. 2018, www.theguardian.com/lifeandstyle/2018/nov/05/chunks-of-my-tongue-came-off-you-could-see-the-tastebuds-ross-edgley-on-swimming-around-great-britain. Accessed 9 Nov. 2018.

Jackson, Amanda. "After 5 Months at Sea, Ross Edgley Completes Swim around Great Britain." *CNN*, 30 Nov. 2018, edition.cnn.com/2018/11/04/europe/ross-edgley-swims-around-great-britain-trnd/index.html. Accessed 9 Feb. 2019.

Quine, Oscar. "Adventurer Becomes First Man to Swim around the British Isles as He Reveals Singing Got Him through the Challenge." *The Telegraph*, 4 Nov. 2018, www.telegraph.co.uk/news/2018/11/04/adventurer-becomes-first-man-swim-around-british-isles-reveals/. Accessed 9 Feb. 2019.

—*Chris Cullen*

Photo by Daniel Harasymchuk via Wikimedia Commons

Esi Edugyan

Date of birth: 1978
Occupation: Author

"I like finding historical footnotes, things nobody has written big books about," the Canadian author Esi Edugyan said to Mike Devlin for the Victoria, British Columbia, *Times Colonist* (8 Sept. 2018). Often described as a historical novelist, Edugyan, who is of Ghanaian descent, has particularly focused on "footnotes" related to marginalized black people, which she has segued into a successful literary career. A graduate of the University of Victoria, she first burst onto Canada's literary scene with the publication of her debut novel, *The Second Life of Samuel Tyne*, in 2004; the acclaimed novel focuses on a Ghanaian immigrant who settles in rural Alberta, Canada, during the late 1960s. Her follow-up novel, *Half-Blood Blues* (2011), about a group of jazz musicians, including an Afro-German trumpet player, in Europe toward the beginning of World War II, won the Scotiabank Giller Prize, one of Canada's top literary honors, and was short-listed for the United Kingdom's prestigious Man Booker Prize.

Edugyan's 2018 novel *Washington Black* chronicles the life of an eponymous black boy who has grown up a slave on a plantation in Barbados. It garnered Edugyan a second Giller Prize and was also short-listed for the Man Booker Prize, among other honors. In addition to her novels, Edugyan has published a nonfiction work, *Dreaming of Elsewhere: Observations on Home* (2014), which explores cross-cultural identities. She has also held writer residencies in countries all over the world.

EARLY LIFE AND EDUCATION

Esi Edugyan was born in 1978 in Calgary, a large city in the western Canadian province of Alberta. Her parents had emigrated from Ghana and met in California before moving to Canada; her father worked as an economic forecaster and her mother was a nurse. Growing up in Calgary in the 1980s and 1990s, in an area that was not very racially diverse at the time, Edugyan did face incidents of racism and developed a keen awareness as a child of what it was like to feel like an outsider, which would become a major element in her work. "There was the sense of being very much the lone figure," she recalled to Cary Darling for the *Houston Chronicle* (20 Sept. 2018). "It's difficult because you feel a little bit representative of a whole, and people are looking to you that way."

Finding it difficult to identify not just as Canadian but also as Ghanaian, Edugyan turned to reading and writing early on to channel her conflicted feelings and emotions. She started writing poems around the time she became a teenager, which, by her own estimation, were "terrible," as she put it to Donna Bailey Nurse for *Quill & Quire* (July 2011). Still, her writing talent was eventually recognized by teachers at her high school, who encouraged her to apply to the writing program at the University of Victoria. There, she learned from writers such as Bill Gaston and Jack Hodgins and gained insight from the peer review process, graduating with a writing degree in 1999. In 2001, she earned a master's degree in creative writing from Johns Hopkins University in Baltimore, Maryland.

THE SECOND LIFE OF SAMUEL TYNE

Edugyan soon embarked on her literary career, which got off to a promising start when, in 2004, after having put a manuscript together often in the early morning hours, her debut novel, *The Second Life of Samuel Tyne*, was published to overall widespread acclaim. The novel, set during the late 1960s, follows an eponymous, disgruntled Ghanaian civil servant who moves his wife and twin daughters from Calgary to Aster, a fictional rural Albertan town, after inheriting his uncle's estate. Despite arriving there with hopeful aspirations, Samuel and his family's sentiments toward seemingly tranquil, small-town prairie life change once they become victimized by sudden bouts of racism and violence.

Edugyan based Aster on Amber Valley, a settlement in northern Alberta that was founded by African American homesteaders largely from Oklahoma in the early twentieth century. She had become inspired to write about the African American settlement after shockingly discovering its existence. Reviewers praised Edugyan's poignant portrayal of rural Alberta, which a writer for *Kirkus Reviews* (15 June 2004) described as "somber and bleak," commenting that her "spare prose, visceral images, and unfussy dialogue create a suitably ominous atmosphere." *The Second Life of Samuel Tyne* was nominated for the Hurston-Wright Legacy Award.

Despite the positive attention garnered by her first book, Edugyan soon grew disappointed by and disillusioned with the publishing industry when the manuscript for her second completed novel, which she ultimately shelved, was not acquired by a publisher. "I thought I could have gone off and studied law," she noted to Nurse regarding her consideration to give up writing for another career, "or anything else with very tangible, forward-moving results." Nevertheless, she recommitted herself to her craft as she held a series of international writing residencies, taking her to countries such as France, Iceland, Scotland, and Germany.

It was while at a residency in Stuttgart, Germany, around 2006 that Edugyan became interested in the history of black people in Germany. During her studies and German classes, she learned about a group of black Germans born from unions between German women and colonial African troops brought in by the French to occupy the Rhineland following the end of World War I. Struck by harrowing accounts she read about such black Germans, who were persecuted by the Nazis, she conceptualized a novel about a jazz ensemble, one of whom is an Afro-German, living in Europe at the height of Nazism at the beginning of World War II. As she explained to Shazia Hafiz Ramji for *Quill & Quire* (Oct. 2018), "When I come across a reference in a text that I find appealing or haven't heard before, I feel compelled to express something about it."

HALF-BLOOD BLUES

Initial reception of Edugyan's second novel, *Half-Blood Blues*, was tepid, however. "It was rejected universally," the author admitted to Devlin. "I knew that if [Half-Blood Blues] was going to sit in a drawer, then I was done." Furthermore, even as Canadian house Key Porter Books was close to publishing her sophomore effort, she was informed that its future in terms of publication in Canada was in limbo as much of the publisher's staff was laid off, and the fate of the company was unclear. "It was excruciating," she expressed to Mark Medley for the *National Post* (8 Nov. 2011). "All this hard work, and suddenly . . . it's all fallen apart." Fortunately, she found a new Canadian publisher through Patrick Crean, who had read an advance copy. *Half-Blood Blues* was later published in Canada by Thomas Allen Publishers in 2011 (it was first published in the United Kingdom earlier that year).

Set during the early days of Nazi occupation in Paris, France, in 1939, the novel is narrated by Sidney "Sid" Griffiths, an American bassist for a jazz band called the Hot-Time Swingers. Sid bears witness to the arrest of the group's virtuosic trumpet player, an Afro-German named Hieronymus "Hiero" Falk, by the Nazis, who send him off to a concentration camp. The band consequently dissolves, but Sid resurfaces in Germany more than fifty years later, where he and another former bandmate attend a jazz festival in Berlin named after Hiero. There, the two learn the truth behind Hiero's disappearance.

Simultaneously a celebration of German arts and culture, and a condemnation of the country's racist, genocidal, and war-ravaged history, *Half-Blood Blues* received universal acclaim from critics, many of whom praised Edugyan's lyrical depiction of mixed-race outsiders and her atmospheric rendering of the smoky European jazz clubs they called home. Nurse asserted, "Edugyan possesses an original literary mind—it's hard to think of another contemporary novelist who could fuse jazz, Jews, blacks, and the Holocaust into a cogent, riveting story."

Half-Blood Blues received a number of literary honors, including the 2011 Scotiabank Giller Prize, the 2012 Ethel Wilson Fiction Prize, and the 2012 Anisfield-Wolf Book Award. It was also short-listed for the Man Booker Prize, the Governor General's Award for English language fiction, and the Rogers Writers' Trust Fiction Prize.

In 2014, Edugyan published her first nonfiction work, *Dreaming of Elsewhere: Observations on Home*, a long literary essay that examines the idea of one's literal and figurative "home." The book draws on her lifelong experiences with racism and otherness, while also delving into her cross-cultural roots as a Canadian of Ghanaian descent.

WASHINGTON BLACK

Edugyan spent much of the following four years writing her third novel, *Washington Black*, which was published in 2018. Like her first two novels, *Washington Black* is rooted in a historical period. It is partly inspired by England's real-life 1860s and 1870s Tichborne case, in which Andrew Bogle, a former slave from Jamaica who was a servant for the wealthy English Tichborne clan, became involved when a man in Australia claimed to be Roger Tichborne, the family's long-lost son who had been presumed dead. Edugyan found herself most captivated by Bogle and the sense of displacement he must have felt.

After ditching a draft that adhered closely to the original case, Edugyan approached the novel with the goal of creating a character that retained "the psychology of somebody like Bogle, but who wasn't actually Bogle himself, and didn't have anything to do with the trial," as she explained to David Chau for the *Georgia Straight* (10 Oct. 2018). The resultant novel is set in the 1830s and told from the perspective of George Washington Black, a slave around the age of eleven living on a sugar plantation in Barbados. Wash, as he is nicknamed, is selected to work as a manservant for Christopher "Titch" Wilde, an English scientist and abolitionist and the brother of the malevolent plantation owner. Wash, who possesses innate artistic talent, aids Titch in the development of his hot air balloon, called the "Cloud-cutter," which the two used to flee from the sugar plantation, embarking on a globe-trotting adventure. In the process, Wash tries to make sense of his place in the world as a runaway slave.

Described by Edugyan to Darling as "a *post-slavery* narrative," *Washington Black* received rave reviews from critics. Chau proclaimed the novel to be Edugyan's "finest work yet," pointing out her "skill at conveying the magnitude of a life." Meanwhile, Ramji wrote, "Like Edugyan's previous novels, *Washington Black* brings nuance and magnetism to relationships between colonizer and colonized." The novel earned Edugyan the 2018 Giller Prize, making her one of only three writers to win the award twice. It was also short-listed for that year's Man Booker Prize and the Rogers Writers' Trust Fiction Prize in addition to the 2019 Andrew Carnegie Medal for Excellence in Fiction.

PERSONAL LIFE

Edugyan is married to the Canadian poet and novelist Steven Price, whom she met while they were attending the University of Victoria. The couple live with their two young children in Colwood, just outside of Victoria, on Vancouver Island. Calling Price her go-to sounding board and editor, she explained to Darling, "We definitely are deep into each others' work. . . . I think the novels would be completely different novels without his input. He's been so instrumental in my editorial process."

SUGGESTED READING

Chau, David. "Esi Edugyan Gauges the Power of the Past in Acclaimed New Novel Washington Black." *The Georgia Straight*, 10 Oct. 2018, www.straight.com/arts/1148676/esi-edugyan-gauges-power-past-acclaimed-new-novel-washington-black. Accessed 8 Mar. 2019.

Darling, Cary. "Esi Edugyan Drawn to Write Stories Outside the Margins." *Houston Chronicle*, 20 Sept. 2018, www.houston-chronicle.com/entertainment/books/article/Esi-Edugyan-drawn-to-write-stories-outside-the-13242704.php. Accessed 8 Mar. 2019.

Devlin, Mike. "Colwood Author Esi Edugyan Back with New Novel." *Times Colonist*, 8 Sept. 2018, www.timescolonist.com/entertainment/colwood-author-esi-edugyan-back-with-new-novel-1.23425075. Accessed 8 Mar. 2019.

Nurse, Donna Bailey. "Esi Edugyan: Writing the Blues." *Quill & Quire*, July 2011, quilland-quire.com/authors/writing-the-blues/. Accessed 8 Mar. 2019.

Ramji, Shazia Hafiz. "Esi Edugyan Makes History with Washington Black." *Quill & Quire*, Oct. 2018, quillandquire.com/authors/esi-edugyan-makes-history-with-washington-black/. Accessed 8 Mar. 2019.

Review of *The Second Life of Samuel Tyne*, by Esi Edugyan. *Kirkus Reviews*, 15 June 2004. *Kirkus*, www.kirkusreviews.com/book-reviews/esi-edugyan/the-second-life-of-samuel-tyne/. Accessed 22 Mar. 2019.

SELECTED WORKS

The Second Life of Samuel Tyne, 2004; *Half-Blood Blues*, 2011; *Dreaming of Elsewhere*, 2014; *Washington Black*, 2018

—Chris Cullen

Álvaro Enrigue

Date of birth: August 6, 1969
Occupation: Novelist and essayist

To Mexican-born writer Álvaro Enrigue, the "hardcore literary novel is under tremendous pressure," he told Thomas Bunstead for the *White Review* (Feb. 2017). "It was a technology invented to synthesize things that are better told now by political scientists, journalists, film directors, or TV series writers. It should be gone by now." As a novelist himself, however, Enrigue has sought to take that literary form in new directions. "My take on the problem of making a living as a dinosaur tamer is, then, to occupy the liminal spaces that the historians, philosophers and media people can't occupy yet," he told Bunstead. In the decades since the publication of his celebrated debut novel, *La muerte de un instalador* (The death of an installation artist), in 1996, Enrigue has done just that, publishing works that blend genres, styles, and eras to create thought-provoking narratives that incorporate the author's myriad interests. His novel *Muerte súbita* (2013), published in English as *Sudden Death* in 2016, garnered acclaim for its unique and purposeful blending of fact and fiction. For the politically conscious Enrigue, who often links historical eras to the challenges of the twentieth and twenty-first centuries, creating such works is of great importance. "It lets me live with myself," he told Ari Shapiro for *NPR* (9 Feb. 2016). "At least I'm trying to do something. I think that books change reality. I really think so."

EARLY LIFE AND EDUCATION

Álvaro Enrigue Soler was born in Mexico on August 6, 1969. He was the youngest of four children—three boys and one girl—born to parents Jorge and Maísa. His parents were avid readers whose extensive personal libraries would become a significant influence on their children: Enrigue's older brother Jordi Soler also became a writer. When Enrigue was a young child, his family moved to Mexico City, where they lived in the neighborhood Colonia Nápoles and later in El Carmen. Enrigue later recalled in essays and interviews that his childhood shaped his later life in a variety of sometimes unexpected ways. "We were, for sure, the less trendy kids wherever we went, and we paid our quota of bullying because of that," he recalled in an essay for *ESPN* (15 June 2018). "We wore supermarket clothes. My dad's car was a disgrace, and the other children were dancing to Gloria Gaynor and Rigo Tovar while we were discovering the Beatles in a set of records that came for free with our yearly subscription to *Selecciones del Reader's Digest.*" Among the major features of Enrigue's early life

Photo by Andrew Lih via Wikimedia Commons

was his family's avid support for the Cafeteros de Córdoba baseball team, a franchise that was not from Mexico City but at times visited to play against the Mexico City Red Devils.

After completing his secondary education, Enrigue remained in Mexico City to attend the Universidad Iberoamericana (the Ibero-American University), where he studied journalism. He would later return to the university to teach literature. In 1998, Enrigue moved to College Park, Maryland, to complete a fellowship with the Latin American literature program at the University of Maryland. He earned a master's degree from the institution in 2000. Enrigue went on to pursue doctoral studies over the course of more than a decade and completed a doctorate in Latin American literature at the University of Maryland in 2012. His doctoral thesis was published by the Spanish publishing company Editorial Anagrama under the title *Valiente clase media: dinero, letras y cursilería* (The valiant middle class: money, literature, and pretensions) during the following year.

LITERARY CAREER

After earning his bachelor's degree, Enrigue held a variety of jobs during the early 1990s, including positions as a literary critic and a radio journalist. He went on to serve for a time as editor of the magazine *Letras Libres* (Free Letters) and published a variety of short pieces in that publication. The year 1996 saw the publication of Enrigue's debut novel, *La muerte de un instalador*. The work gained Enrigue widespread recognition within Mexico, including the Joaquín Mortiz Prize. He followed that work with *El amigo* del héroe (The friend of the hero), published in 1998, and *El cementerio de sillas* (The cemetery of chairs), published in 2002. As a novelist, Enrigue developed an approach to literature that focused on that field's ability to interpret aspects of the real world. "I don't believe in inspiration at all. We live in a world that demands explanation. And fiction has the capability to offer explanations for things," he explained to Stephen Heyman for the *New York Times* (27 Jan. 2016). Also a writer of short fiction, Enrigue published the collection *Virtudes capitales* (Capital virtues) in 1998.

Enrigue's next major work, the 2005 book *Hipotermia* (*Hypothermia*) was particularly significant due to both the work's status as his first book to be translated into English and its blurring of the boundaries between literary formats, the latter a fact that became apparent only through the process of translation. "In Spanish Hypothermia is undoubtedly a novel, and in English it is very clearly a short-story volume, though it's exactly the same book," Enrigue told Scott Esposito for *Bomb* (15 Mar. 2016). "I worked line by line with the translator and the editor to make sure it was. It's so mysterious that I cannot add anything else—as though if in one language you were a mammal and in the other one a fish." Translated into English by Brendan Riley, *Hypothermia* received critical acclaim following its publication in 2013. Enrigue remained busy as a writer during the period between the publications of *Hipotermia* and *Hypothermia*, publishing the books *Vidas perpendiculares* (Perpendicular lives; 2008) and *Decencia* (Decency; 2011). He made his English-language debut in 2009 with the short story "On the Death of the Author," published in the anthology *Best of Contemporary Mexican Fiction*.

SUDDEN DEATH

In 2011 and 2012, Enrigue held the position of Dorothy and Lewis B. Cullman Center Fellow at the New York Public Library. A prestigious fellowship previously held by numerous successful writers, the position included a monetary stipend as well as office space and access to library resources. During his time as a Cullman Center Fellow, Enrigue worked on the manuscript for his next novel, *Muerte súbita*, a work set in the late sixteenth century and focusing, in part, on a fictional tennis game between two real-world figures, the Italian painter Caravaggio and the Spanish poet Francisco de Quevedo. Although Enrigue has at times objected to the classification of his work as historical fiction, he enjoyed making use of unexpected historical details in the novel, which expands upon its initial focus to address issues such as the sixteenth-century relationship between Europe and what is now Mexico. "Most of the weirdest stuff is real," he

told Garth Risk Hallberg for the *Millions* (7 Nov. 2018). "It is real that Galileo and Caravaggio were roommates—it's absolutely real. It's absolutely real that Galileo was writing his theory of the parabola as he saw Caravaggio playing tennis in the plaza. . . . That is the wonder of the novel, you know? It is the great lesson of [Spanish writer Miguel de] Cervantes: that you can put in whatever you want, and as long as it somehow relates to the story, it works." Prior to its publication in 2013, *Muerte súbita* won the Premio Herralde, a Spanish literary award that recognizes excellence in Spanish-language novels, and the novel went on to receive extensive praise in Mexico, Spain, and beyond.

Considering the literary community's enthusiastic reception of *Muerte súbita*, the novel became the second of Enrigue's novels to be translated into English for publication in the United States. The novel was translated by Natasha Wimmer, a translator with whom Enrigue was already familiar due to her earlier work on a novel by the Chilean novelist Roberto Bolaño. Although pleased that Wimmer would be translating his novel from the start of the process, Enrigue found that the final work exceeded his expectations. "Man! I can tell you that in the final stages of the editing I had to stop a second and wonder if I was reading her or myself," he told Esposito. "The way she got the respiration of my Spanish, the very complex language games—Mexican Spanish is full of expressions with a double sense that are used in both senses at the same time—and the not-always-rational way in which I use adjectives." Published in 2016 under the title *Sudden Death*, the novel impressed critics from a variety of publications, who commented positively on both the central conceit of the work and the thought-provoking explorations Enrigue carries out over the course of the narrative. Enrigue followed *Sudden Death* with *Ahora me rindo y eso es todo* (Now I surrender to you and that is all), a novel published by Anagrama in late 2018.

TEACHING CAREER

In addition to writing novels, short stories, and essays, Enrigue has taught at several different institutions, including the Universidad Iberoamericana, the University of Maryland, New York University, and Hofstra University. During the 2012–13 academic year, he served as a Program in Latin American Studies Fellow at Princeton University, where he was lecturer and a senior research assistant while also researching a project on Latin American journalism. Although Enrigue has primarily taught courses in Latin American literature and the Spanish language, he has also delved into a variety of related topics through courses such as Soccer as a Fine Art, taught at Hofstra. While teaching at

Columbia University, Enrigue sought to teach a classics course in part because he was working on a Western that drew inspiration from classical Greek and Roman works. "My American editor didn't take it super well when I told her that, instead of cloistering myself to finish the novel, I was going to teach this incredibly demanding wonder that is Columbia University's Classics Core Course," he recalled to Bunstead. "I answered to her that to read again Homer and Virgil is to write, and she conceded." In addition to his formal teaching work, Enrigue has appeared at a variety of festivals, readings, and other public events.

PERSONAL LIFE
Enrigue has two sons and a daughter, all from earlier relationships. He was previously married to fellow Mexican writer Valeria Luiselli, the author of works such as the 2019 novel *Lost Children Archive*. Enrigue moved to New York City in 2011.

SUGGESTED READING
Enrigue, Álvaro. "Álvaro Enrigue: Using the Past to Explain the Present." Interview by Stephen Heyman. *The New York Times*, 27 Jan. 2016, www.nytimes.com/2016/01/28/arts/international/alvaro-enrigue-using-the-past-to-explain-the-present.html. Accessed 14 June 2019.

Enrigue, Álvaro. Interview by Scott Esposito. *Bomb*, 15 Mar. 2016, bombmagazine.org/articles/álvaro-enrigue/. Accessed 14 June 2019.

Enrigue, Álvaro. Interview by Thomas Bunstead. *The White Review*, Feb. 2017, www.thewhitereview.org/feature/interview-alvaro-enrigue/. Accessed 14 June 2019.

Enrigue, Álvaro. "No Mexico, No Europe: *The Millions* Interviews Álvaro Enrigue." Interview by Garth Risk Hallberg. *The Millions*, 7 Nov. 2018, themillions.com/2018/11/no-mexico-no-europe-the-millions-interviews-alvaro-enrigue.html. Accessed 14 June 2019.

Enrigue, Álvaro. "What Connects a Legendary Mexican Baseball Team to the Orioles? Love, Loyalty and Family." *ESPN*, 15 June 2018, www.espn.com/mlb/story/_/id/23794413/alvaro-enrigue-connection-baltimore-orioles-legendary-mexican-baseball-team. Accessed 14 June 2019.

Enrigue, Álvaro. "When Caravaggio Plays Quevedo in Tennis, the Court Becomes a Sonnet." Interview by Ari Shapiro. *NPR*, 9 Feb. 2016. www.npr.org/2016/02/09/466145038/when-caravaggio-plays-quevedo-in-tennis-the-court-becomes-a-sonnet. Accessed 14 June 2019.

Felsenthal, Julia. "Married Mexican Writers Álvaro Enrigue and Valeria Luiselli on Their Buzzy New Novels and New York Life." *Vogue*, 3 Mar. 2016, www.vogue.com/article/alvaro-enrigue-valeria-luiselli-profile. Accessed 14 June 2019.

SELECTED WORKS
La muerte de un instalador, 1996; *Virtudes capitales*, 1998; *El amigo del héroe*, 1998; *El cementerio de sillas (The cemetery of chairs)*, 2002; *Hipotermia (Hypothermia)*, 2006; *Vidas perpendiculares (Perpendicular lives)*, 2008; *Decencia (Decency)*, 2011; *Muerte súbita (Sudden Death)*, 2013; *Ahora me rindo y eso es todo (Now I surrender to you and that is all)*, 2018

—*Joy Crelin*

Mary Callahan Erdoes
Date of birth: August 13, 1967
Occupation: Financial executive

Mary Callahan Erdoes is the chief executive officer (CEO) of J. P. Morgan's Asset & Wealth Management division, a position in which she oversees some $2.8 trillion for her clients. "When someone gives you their money to manage—isn't that one of the greatest expressions of trust?" she asked rhetorically during an interview with Pranay Gupte for the *New York Sun* (9 Jan. 2006), explaining that she feels honored to be working in her field.

She realizes that the reputation of banking (and bankers) among members of the general public has suffered greatly since the financial crisis of 2008. Still, she told Susan Young for *Harvard Business School Alumni Stories* (2016): "I am proud to be a banker. . . . We assist millions of people every single day—to buy their first home, get their first credit card, or pay for college."

Erdoes, who is also a member of parent company JPMorgan Chase's Operating Committee, has become known for promoting ethnic and gender diversity in the workplace through a variety of initiatives, such as the Women on the Move initiative started by Erdoes and several other leaders in 2013, and for being a devoted mentor to many. "If I could be a mentor to all 22,000 employees, I would," she told Young. "I love helping others discover things about themselves so they can blossom and grow."

Often referred to as a "rainmaker," a term that in the business world connotes someone who generates significant income, Erdoes is frequently mentioned as one of the most powerful people in her field; she topped *American Banker* magazine's list of most powerful women in finance in both 2017 and 2018, and in 2017 the

Photo by World Economic Forum via Wikimedia

editors of *Forbes* counted her among the one hundred most powerful women in the world.

EARLY LIFE AND EDUCATION

The eldest of four children, Mary Callahan Erdoes was born on August 13, 1967, to Patricia and Patrick Callahan Jr. She was raised in Winnetka, Illinois, an affluent suburb of Chicago. Her father was a partner at the iconic investment firm Lazard Frères, and when she was a child, she sometimes accompanied him to the office on the weekends. Her mother was active in Chicago's various philanthropic and social circles. Her maternal and paternal grandmothers were major influences in her life. Her paternal grandmother, Kay, a secretary before her marriage, was considered one of the most proficient mathematicians in the family, and her maternal grandmother, Izzy, taught Erdoes to balance a checkbook and help pay bills when she was still in grade school. One of Izzy's proudest moments came when Erdoes won an eighth-grade math competition, beating out the boy who was widely considered the smartest in the class.

For high school, Erdoes, who was a serious equestrian while growing up, attended Woodlands Academy of the Sacred Heart, a Roman Catholic girls' school. She graduated in 1985 and entered Georgetown University, where she majored in mathematics. Izzy, who knew people at the well-known Chicago money-management firm Stein Roe & Farnham, helped Erdoes get her first job there while still a student. Although her duties were rudimentary—sorting papers in the computer room—Erdoes took every opportunity to ask questions of the

managers and learn from them. Erdoes suffered from severe doubts about her mathematical abilities throughout her undergraduate years but earned her BS in 1989.

EARLY CAREER AND MBA

That year Erdoes joined Bankers Trust as an analyst. Because the markets were notably volatile during that period, she has characterized the job as a "baptism by fire" when speaking to interviewers. In a column for the *New York Times* (24 July 2005), she wrote of staying up till 3 a.m. to work on a spreadsheet once, only to have a male colleague take the credit for it. Upset, she called home. "I can still hear the words of wisdom from my mom that morning, 'Don't take no bullying from nobody,'" she wrote. "They were what put me back on my feet."

Deciding to earn an MBA, Erdoes entered Harvard Business School (HBS), and in 1993 she successfully completed the challenging program. "If you can master the case method, you can do anything," she recalled to Young. "Organizational behavior, manufacturing . . . it all got fused in my brain. I carry with me what I learned at HBS every day." With her newly minted degree she began working as a portfolio manager at Meredith, Martin & Kaye, and in 1996 she was hired in a similar capacity at J. P. Morgan Global Investment Management.

In 2000 J. P. Morgan and Chase merged. Although some journalists still confuse the financial entities, parent company JPMorgan Chase oversees administration and corporate governance; J. P. Morgan deals with institutional and corporate clients through Corporate & Investment Bank, Asset & Wealth Management, and Commercial Banking divisions; and Chase supports individuals and small businesses with its Consumer & Community Banking group.

THE TRILLION-DOLLAR WOMAN

In 2005 Erdoes was put in charge of private banking at J. P. Morgan, becoming responsible for high-net-worth clients around the world and managing some $300 billion in assets. Individual clients were required to have a minimum of $25 million in their accounts. "Our responsibility is to keep them wealthy—not just for their own generation but also generations to come," she explained to Gupte. In 2009 she was named CEO of J. P. Morgan Asset Management—a move that caused headline writers to refer to her as the "trillion-dollar woman," since the division was then worth some $1.3 trillion. That number quickly rose, however. In her first year, profits rose 20 percent to $1.7 billion. Overseeing the world's fifth-largest asset management company (which included the number-two hedge fund), Erdoes gained a reputation for fierce loyalty to her staff, protectiveness towards her clients, and unparalleled work ethic.

In recent years, Erdoes has been credited with expanding business in China; in 2016 her unit became the first fully foreign-owned asset management operation in Shanghai's free trade zone. "The free trade zone in Shanghai, a four-year-old pilot project, gives the New York–based banking giant a rare chance to go it alone in mainland China," Kevin Wack wrote for *American Banker* (25 Sept. 2017), explaining that although US banks have long sought access to the rapidly evolving Chinese market, they have been thwarted, for the most part, by government restrictions on foreign ownership of financial firms. J. P. Morgan's presence in China both allows access to wealthy Chinese clients and provides the company with insights into the Chinese market that can be shared with investors in other countries.

Erdoes has also won plaudits for her efforts to modernize and digitize her operations, a move, as she explained to Suleman Din for *American Banker* (23 Sept. 2018) that enables "more comprehensive analysis of enormous data sets, faster and more optimal execution in portfolios, and seamless delivery of all that we do in both human and digital form."

PERSONAL LIFE

Erdoes has served on the United Nations International Children's Emergency Fund (UNICEF's) board of directors since 2005, and in 2016 she joined the board of the Robin Hood Foundation, a New York City–based nonprofit group that fights poverty. Additionally, she has been a member of the Federal Reserve Bank of New York's Investor Advisory Committee on Financial Markets since 2013 and is a major donor to the Republican Party.

Erdoes met her future husband, Philip, while both were students at HBS. A serial entrepreneur turned business investor, he is the founder and CEO of Bear Ventures LLC, a private equity and venture capital firm. Erdoes has praised his intelligence and humor when describing him to interviewers.

The couple live in New York City and have three daughters. Like her father, Erdoes sometimes takes her children to the office with her on the weekend. Her family life, as she told Young, is "a little exhausting, sometimes unnerving, but always sheer joy."

SUGGESTED READING

Din, Suleman. "JPMorgan Chase's Mary Callahan Erdoes: The Most Powerful Woman in Finance." *American Banker*, 23 Sept. 2018, www.americanbanker.com/news/jp-morgan-chases-mary-callahan-erdoes-the-most-pow-erful-woman-in-finance-for-2018. Accessed 4 Oct. 2018.

Elkins, Kathleen. "Top JPMorgan Exec Shares Her Single-Best Piece of Career Advice." *Make It*, CNBC, 30 Sept. 2016, www.cnbc.com/2016/09/30/jp-morgan-exec-mary-callahan-erdoes-best-career-advice.html. Accessed 4 Oct. 2018.

Erdoes, Mary Callahan. "She Does the Math." *The New York Times*, 24 July 2005, www.nytimes.com/2005/07/24/business/yourmoney/she-does-the-math.html. Accessed 4 Oct. 2018.

Gupte, Pranay. "The Difference between Rich and Wealthy." *The New York Sun*, 9 Jan. 2006, www.nysun.com/business/difference-between-rich-and-wealthy/25541/. Accessed 4 Oct. 2018.

Vardi, Nathan. "Mary Callahan Erdoes: Wall Street's $1 Trillion Woman." *Forbes*, 12 Sept. 2011, www.forbes.com/sites/nathanvardi/2011/08/24/the-1-trillion-woman/. Accessed 4 Oct. 2018.

Wack, Kevin. "JPMorgan Chase's Mary Callahan Erdoes: The Most Powerful Woman in Finance." *American Banker*, 25 Sept. 2017, www.americanbanker.com/news/jp-morgans-mary-callahan-erdoes-the-most-powerful-women-in-finance-2017. Accessed 4 Oct. 2018.

Young, Susan. "Mary Callahan Erdoes, MBA 1993." *Harvard Business School Alumni Stories*, Harvard University, 2016, www.alumni.hbs.edu/stories/Pages/story-bulletin.aspx?num=5597. Accessed 4 Oct. 2018.

—*Mari Rich*

Paul Falkowski

Date of birth: January 4, 1951
Occupation: Scientist

Paul Falkowski is one of the most highly regarded figures in biological oceanography, which focuses on marine life. During his long career, which began in the mid-1970s, he conducted groundbreaking research on phytoplankton (the self-feeding components of the plankton community) and primary production (the synthesis of organic compounds from carbon dioxide in the air or water). Both fields of study are central to humanity's understanding of complex ocean ecosystems, but they also have wider implications in diverse areas, including astrobiology, evolution, and paleoecology. Falkowski earned numerous honors for his pioneering work, including the 2018 Tyler Prize for Environmental Achievement, a prestigious award considered to be the Nobel Prize of environmental scientific research.

Falkowski serves as a professor at Rutgers University, a position that has provided many opportunities to further his active research. On his Rutgers faculty webpage, he explained his ultimate goals at the most basic level: "My research interests are focused on three areas—origins of life, how electron transfer reactions are mediated, and how organisms transformed the geochemistry of Earth. . . . I am most interested in understanding how these kinds of processes have transformed our planet and may evolve on planetary bodies in our solar system and on extra-solar planets. There are only two questions I address: Where did we come from? And are we alone?"

EARLY LIFE AND EDUCATION

Paul G. Falkowski was born on January 4, 1951, in New York City, and took to science early in life. Neither of his parents had scientific backgrounds, but he enjoyed visiting the American Museum of Natural History and reading science books. He earned a Bachelor of Science degree from City College of the City University of New York (CUNY) in 1972, then completed his master's at City College in 1973. By this time, he was beginning to direct his attention to oceanography. "Everyone loves to talk about the romantic lure of the sea—and to some extent, it is real," he said in an interview with *Current Biology* (2007). "But I only started to seriously think about the oceans in graduate school."

Falkowski moved to Canada during the Vietnam War and earned his doctorate in biology and oceanography at the University of British Columbia, where his adviser was F. J. R. Taylor. Upon earning his PhD in 1975, he faced a decision: to work at a medical school in Canada or to go to sea as an oceanographer. He jumped at the chance of doing oceanography and briefly worked as a postdoctoral research associate at the University of Rhode Island.

BROOKHAVEN NATIONAL LABORATORY

In 1976 Falkowski was hired by the Brookhaven National Laboratory to serve as a staff scientist in the then-new Oceanographic and Atmospheric Science Division. There an older colleague advised him that "whatever I did for my doctorate research was history—and I should move on to new areas. I took that to heart," he told *Current Biology*. Much of his early research focused on photosynthesis and how the oceans affect the earth's carbon cycle. Falkowski was particularly interested in the way microbial communities were affected by climate change, and his work at Brookhaven proved key in giving rise to environmental biophysics. He was one of the first scientists to study how climate affects the diversity

of life, including both plants and animals in the oceans and on land, over millions of years.

Falkowski earned his tenure at Brookhaven in 1984. He went on to hold numerous senior positions at the laboratory, notably serving as head of the oceanographic division from 1987 to 1991 and being named a senior scientist in 1993. He was also deputy chair for environmental research in the applied science department from 1994 to 1998, and head of the environmental biophysics and molecular biology program from 1995 to 1998. Meanwhile, he took on various roles as a visiting scientist, lecturer, or professor with other institutions as well.

By the 1990s Falkowski was beginning to earn numerous accolades and recognition for his work. He had received a Medical Research Council Fellowship in Biophysics in 1976 and a John Simon Guggenheim Fellowship in 1992. He was also presented with the Thomas Byrne Award from the University of British Columbia in 1997 and the Huntsman Medal in 1998.

RUTGERS UNIVERSITY

In 1998 Falkowski moved his research group to Rutgers University in New Jersey. There he became a distinguished professor in the school's Department of Geological Sciences and Institute of Marine and Coastal Science—and the only biologist in the department. Despite the adjustment, it was "extremely rewarding to work with geologists," he noted to *Current Biology*. "I learned much more from my geological colleagues about the evolution of biological processes in relation to earth systems than I ever would have learned had I been appointed in a biology program."

In 2005 Falkowski was named the Board of Governors Professor in Geological and Marine Science at Rutgers, and in 2006 he also took the role of director of the Rutgers Energy Institute. In 2012 he became the university's Bennett L. Smith Chair in Business and Natural Resources. In addition to these positions, he also taught at the National Institute for Basic Biology in Okazaki, Japan; the Imperial College of Science and Technology in London, England; the University of California, Los Angeles (UCLA); the State University of New York (SUNY) in Stony Brook; and the University of Hawaii.

HOT OCEANS AND ANIMAL LIFE

Falkowski's research continued to evolve and focused particularly on oceanography's insights into broader questions. Much of his work involved understanding how oceans changed over time—including periods of warming, as during both the age of dinosaurs millions of years ago and modern times. This has the potential to help humanity understand the origins of life, as well as how life will be affected as the climate changes. Falkowski explained to Richard Harris for NPR's *Morning Edition* (2 Aug. 2013) how hotter oceans with disrupted circulation can "lead to a major change in the cycling of many elements of the planet, such as nitrogen, sulfur, carbon, and so on." His research also stressed how oceanic conditions can even significantly affect non-marine species. For example, he studied one warming period 56 million years ago that brought about the extinction of much of the life in the deep ocean and led to a proliferation of terrestrial grasslands, contributing to the evolution of large grazing mammals.

Throughout Falkowski's career, a common theme was the major threat posed to marine ecosystems by climate change, particularly human-induced global warming. However, not all his findings were negative. He was involved in important studies of coral reefs, vast ecosystems that supply habitat for roughly 25 percent of all ocean life but are considered highly sensitive to climate change increasing ocean acidification. Using ultrahigh-resolution microscopic imaging and other techniques, Falkowski and his fellow scientists found evidence that coral appeared to be more resilient than environmentalists had previously assumed. "Coral is not just a rock," he told Steph Yin for the *New York Times* (1 June 2017) after the publication of the study. "And because of that, we're pretty confident that they'll be able to continuing [sic] making their skeletons even if the ocean becomes slightly more acidic." Still, he noted that the fossil fuel carbon emissions linked to the heating and acidification of the oceans remains a dire concern.

OCEANS TO EXOPLANETS

Falkowski's research often involved subjects with implications well outside of what might traditionally be considered oceanography or marine biology. For example, his research group at Rutgers discovered four core chemical structures that can be combined to build the proteins within every living organism. They did this by essentially reverse-engineering the evolution of almost ten thousand proteins, taking them apart to better understand their individual parts. The work was recognized for its potential real-life applications in biomedical engineering. "Understanding these parts and how they are connected to each other within the existing proteins could help us understand how to design new catalysts that could potentially split water, fix nitrogen or do other things that are really important for society," Falkowski told Todd B. Bates for *Rutgers Today* (20 Jan. 2018).

Falkowski's work on the evolution of proteins also drew attention for its implications for possible extraterrestrial life. In 2018 he and his colleagues received a $6 million grant from NASA's Astrobiology Institute to better understand how life evolved on our planet and if these same "protein nanomachines" might have evolved on other planets or moons in our solar system or elsewhere. Falkowski's team, known as ENIGMA (Evolution of Nanomachines in Geospheres and Microbial Ancestors), sought to expand humanity's understanding of astrobiology. "Every organism on Earth moves electrons to generate energy," Falkowski explained to Bates in an interview for *Rutgers Today* (4 June 2018). "ENIGMA . . . is trying to understand the earliest evolution of these processes."

TYLER PRIZE AND OTHER HONORS

Falkowski continued to receive many honors as his career progressed. In 2000 he earned both the Hutchinson Award and the Board of Trustees Award for Excellence in Research from Rutgers University. He received the Vernadsky Medal from the European Geosciences Union in 2005, was appointed to the National Academy of Sciences (NAS) in 2007, and in 2008 was presented with the Gerald W. Prescott Award. He won the Ecology Institute Prize in Marine Ecology in 2010 and earned fellowships from the Radcliffe Institute for Advanced Studies in 2011 and the Ecological Society of America in 2012. In 2017 he was awarded an academic writing residency at the Rockefeller Foundation's Bellagio Center.

A crowning honor came in 2018, when Falkowski received the Tyler Prize for Environmental Achievement alongside marine ecologist James J. McCarthy. The annual prize, which was established in 1973 by philanthropists John and Alice Tyler and is administered by the University of Southern California (USC), is given to scientists for major achievements in environmental science, environmental health, and energy. Laureates receive a $200,000 stipend and a medallion. In commemorating Falkowski's work to date, the Tyler Prize website hailed him as "one of the world's greatest pioneers in the field of biological oceanography."

In addition to these awards, Falkowski is a member of dozens of learned societies and organizations, including the American Geophysical Union (AGU), the American Society of Limnology and Oceanography (ASLO), the New York Academy of Sciences (NYAS), the American Society of Plant Physiologists (ASPP, renamed as the American Society of Plant Biologists (ASPB) in 2001, the American Phycological Society (APS), The Oceanography Society (TOS), and the Executive Committee of NASA's SeaWiFS Science Team. He wrote more than 250 peer-reviewed articles, coauthored the textbook *Aquatic Photosynthesis: Second Edition* (2007) with John A. Raven, and published *Life's Engines: How Microbes Made Earth Habitable* (2015) for general readers.

Falkowski remains committed to the goal of ongoing learning. "My best advice to people thinking of a career in biology is to enjoy the prospect of being a student for the rest of your life," he told *Current Biology*. "That means accepting that you should always learn something every day—and while we can collectively 'master' a topic, individually we really don't know very much."

PERSONAL LIFE
Falkowski is married and has two children.

SUGGESTED READING
Bates, Todd B. "Rutgers Scientists Discover 'Legos of Life.'" *Rutgers Today*, 4 June 2018, news.rutgers.edu/rutgers-scientists-discover-legos-life/20180117#.XIaDVa3My8U. Accessed 11 Mar. 2019.

Falkowski, Paul. "NASA Funds Rutgers Scientists' Pursuit of the Origins of Life." Interview by Todd B. Bates. *Rutgers Today*, 4 June 2018, news.rutgers.edu/nasa-funds-rutgers-scientists'-pursuit-origins-life/20180604#.XIaDK-63My8U. Accessed 11 Mar. 2019.

Falkowski, Paul. "Q & A: Paul Falkowski." *Current Biology*, vol. 17, no. 9, 2007, pp. R301–2, doi:10.1016/j.cub.2007.02.053. Accessed 13 Mar. 2019.

Harris, Richard. "Our Once and Future Oceans: Taking Lessons from Earth's Past." *Morning Edition*, NPR, 2 Aug. 2013, www.npr.org/2013/08/02/208032918/our-once-and-future-oceans-taking-lessons-from-earths-past. Accessed 11 Mar. 2019.

"Paul G. Falkowski." *Department of Marine and Coastal Sciences*, Rutgers School of Environmental and Biological Sciences, 2019, marine.rutgers.edu/main/paul-falkowski. Accessed 11 Mar. 2019.

"2018 Tyler Laureates." *Tyler Prize for Environmental Achievement*, 2018, tylerprize.org/laureates/past-laureates/2018-tyler-laureates. Accessed 11 Mar. 2019.

Yin, Step. "In Coral Skeletons, Microscopic Portraits of Resilience?" *The New York Times*, 1 June 2017, www.nytimes.com/2017/06/01/science/coral-skeletons-ocean-acidification.html. Accessed 11 Mar. 2019.

—*Christopher Mari*

Kevin Feige

Date of birth: June 2, 1973
Occupation: Film producer

Longtime Marvel Studios president Kevin Feige is far more than one of the most bankable

Photo by Gage Skidmore via Wikimedia Commons

producers working in Hollywood today. A true visionary, he believed, beginning with the first *Iron Man* film, which debuted in 2008, that it was possible to build an interconnected series of films about Marvel superheroes with a great deal of film-to-film continuity. Such a series would emulate the way the heroes interact in the pages of comic books: teaming up, crossing over into one another's stories, and fleshing out a world to make it feel fully inhabited and lived in. "That was always the pinnacle of cinematic storytelling to me, something that was so enjoyed that people wanted to learn more and weave the larger mythology," Feige told Todd Gilchrist for *Variety* (18 Jan. 2019). "Marvel Comics have been doing that for 80 years. I wanted to replicate the experience of reading a comic book for filmgoers, and I want to continue to expand the definition of what a quote-unquote Marvel movie can be."

Feige has done just that—made a deeply compelling mythological world on screen, the Marvel Cinematic Universe (MCU), in which superheroes are real and relatable, in addition to being highly interactive with one another. His ambition has paid off, with his MCU films attracting a wide range of audiences worldwide; *Black Panther* (2018) was even nominated for the Academy Award for Best Picture in 2019. In January 2019, Feige was also presented with the David O. Selznick Achievement Award by the Producers Guild of America.

"Simple," director and producer Joe Russo answered when asked by Joanna Robinson for *Vanity Fair* (27 Nov. 2017) why other studios have not succeeded to the same extent in similar efforts to create shared cinematic universes. "They don't have a Kevin."

EARLY LIFE AND EDUCATION

Kevin Feige was born on June 2, 1973, in Boston, Massachusetts, and moved to New Jersey at the age of three. Raised in Westfield, he has always been in love with movies and wanted to have a career working in them. This desire was partly inspired by his grandfather, Robert E. Short, who oversaw the production of television shows, including soap operas, through his work with Procter & Gamble Productions.

Although comic books were a part of Feige's childhood, they were not a central part. He claims to have spent almost every Friday at the movies, but only went occasionally to the comic-book shop, where Wednesdays were the days for new comic books. Much of what he knew of comics came primarily through cartoons and films like Richard Donner's *Superman* (1978), the first film to treat a comic-book character with a level of seriousness and affection. Later, he came to love Tim Burton's films, *Batman* and *Batman Returns*, which came out in 1989 and 1992, respectively. What he loved most of all, however, were the original Star Wars films (1977–83), the original Indiana Jones series (1981–89), and the Back to the Future trilogy (1985–90).

In the early 1990s, after graduating from Westfield High School, Feige moved to the West Coast to attend the University of Southern California (USC) to study film. Getting into the university's film school, however, was not easy. In an interview for *Vanity Fair* (6 Dec. 2017), he recalled to Joanna Robinson, "I was rejected from the film school many, many times. . . . I applied every semester, basically, until I got in. There was a point where I thought, 'Oh, I'm just not getting in, so I'll have to go figure out another major.' At no point did I go, 'I have to figure out another career.' I always wanted to keep heading towards movies."

EARLY CAREER

While completing his studies, Feige scored an internship at the company owned by director and producer Richard Donner and his wife, producer Lauren Shuler Donner, the latter of whom is well known, in part, for producing the X-Men franchise, beginning in 2000 with *X-Men*, for 20th Century Fox. (*The Uncanny X-Men* is a flagship title for Marvel Comics, about a superhero team of mutant outcasts born with powers they are often initially unable to control.) After graduating in 1995 and having already been hired as a production assistant, he decided to work closely with Shuler Donner, whom he has credited as a great mentor. He explained to Robinson, "I would go to school, and then go in there

and work and got paid. I very much liked the notion of having a job before I graduated. That job was walking dogs and getting lunches and washing cars, but it was a job in the film business. I ended up not walking in my graduation ceremony because I was working, which I thought was a good excuse not to go."

Some of Feige's early tasks as a production assistant on pictures such as the 1997 action-drama *Volcano* are comical in hindsight; for example, he helped actor Meg Ryan learn how to use email for *You've Got Mail* (1998). But his extensive knowledge of comic books and devotion to the source material, particularly honed in an effort to be more involved in the creative process of filming, helped secure his first production credit as an associate producer on *X-Men*. His work on this film brought him to the attention of Avi Arad, the head of Marvel Studios at the time, who invited him to join the company. Before long, he was working alongside director Sam Raimi on his acclaimed Spider-Man trilogy, which began in 2002 with *Spider-Man*, as well as on other Marvel comics properties such as *Daredevil* (2003), *The Punisher* (2004), and *Fantastic Four* (2005).

What all these early Marvel film adaptations have in common, however, is the fact that Marvel had licensed its characters to various studios, notably 20th Century Fox and Sony, and forfeited creative control. Therefore, they were adapted for the screen with varying degrees of accuracy and success that Feige observed and learned from firsthand.

MOLDING A CINEMATIC UNIVERSE

Meanwhile, a plan had been put into motion and financing was secured around 2005 to allow Marvel Studios to independently produce its own film adaptations of the numerous characters to which it still held or regained the film rights. Feige became president of production around 2007.

Initially, Feige's goal was to produce individual films of the highest quality, no matter how well known the featured character, strict in their fidelity to the comics but also updated for the screen. The first two on the docket were the critically and commercially well-received films *Iron Man* (2008), starring Robert Downey Jr. as the armored titular hero, and *The Incredible Hulk* (2008), starring Edward Norton as the scientist who turns into a rampaging green monster. (Mark Ruffalo would later replace Norton in that role.) However, even in these early films, hints, often including postcredit teaser scenes, existed that a larger, connected world of films was emerging: the Marvel Cinematic Universe (MCU), in which all these comic-book superheroes would interact with each other, just as they had been doing since their creation. Feige explained this concept to Robinson: "We set out to make a great *Iron Man* movie, a *Hulk* movie, a *Thor* movie . . . and then be able to do what, at the time, nobody else was doing: put them together. Bring that experience that hardcore comic readers have had for decades of Spider-Man swinging into the Fantastic Four headquarters, or for Hulk to suddenly come rampaging through the pages of an Iron Man comic. We thought it would be fun for filmgoers to get that same—on a much bigger canvas—rush."

A SUCCESSFUL MCU FOUNDATION ESTABLISHED

By 2011, after the acquisition of Marvel Entertainment by entertainment giant Disney for $4 billion in 2009 and the release of the *Iron Man 2* film in 2010, most of the seeds of the MCU and the core of the Avengers superhero team were in place: *Thor* (2011), a film about the Norse god who comes to Earth to aid humanity, and *Captain America: The First Avenger* (2011), about an American super soldier who fought in World War II and who awoke from suspended animation in modern times, had been released to critical and commercial success. Feige would bring these characters together in *The Avengers* (2012), a long-anticipated film about the formation of a team of superheroes fighting to protect Earth.

Part of Feige's enormous success was the fact that he kept the essences of these characters in the films while removing parts that might not work on the big screen. Therefore, Thor's winged helmet makes only a brief appearance, but he still lives in a realm accessed via a rainbow bridge. In the *New York Times* (24 July 2011), Brooks Barnes noted, "Mr. Feige has accomplished this by maintaining a careful balance of conservatism and risk. In an industry that loves to fiddle, he actually sticks close to the original material, recognizing that there is a reason Marvel characters like Iron Man attracted fans in the first place. But Mr. Feige also makes unusual bets on untested actors and hires directors who would give many studios serious pause."

CONTINUING TO REDEFINE SUPERHERO FILMS

By the end of 2018, Marvel Studios had made twenty interconnected films within the universe grossing billions of dollars worldwide, including further installments in the Captain America, Iron Man, and Thor franchises. In addition to bringing together the original Avengers in several films (the fourth Avengers film, titled *Endgame*, finished principal photography in 2018), the various characters have also appeared in one another's solo films, and additional characters, such as those who make up the Guardians of the Galaxy, have been introduced into the universe to provide further diversity to the superhero roster. Among the films featuring them are *Ant-Man* (2015), in which a former thief is able to alter his size with the help of a special suit; *Doctor Strange* (2016), about the master of the mystic arts who studied magic in the Far East; *Ant-Man and the Wasp* (2018), notable because the Wasp is the first female Marvel superhero to be featured as a title character in a film; and *Black Panther* (2018), the studio's first film to focus solely on a black superhero—the king of Wakanda, a fictional African country with super-advanced technology. *Black Panther* is also significant because it became the first Marvel film to be nominated for the Academy Award for Best Picture in 2019.

Despite such a large catalogue of films under his belt, Feige, who accepted the David O. Selznick Achievement Award in January 2019 in recognition of his work, also continued to diversify the MCU. These efforts included a plan to bring back flagship heroes, such as Spider-Man, whose rights had been sold off to other studios. Through a deal with Sony, the web-slinging hero first returned to the Marvel fold with an appearance in *Captain America: Civil War* (2016) before starring in *Spider-Man: Homecoming* (2017). Feige also dug deeper into the Marvel catalogue to introduce to the MCU the female hero Captain Marvel, whose solo film hit theaters in March 2019. In considering the achievements of the studio, especially against initial odds, over the years, Feige noted to Gilchrist that "the quote-unquote superhero fatigue that people have been asking me about since years before 'Iron Man'" has not occurred. "Our instincts have always guided us, and the successes have always just encouraged us to keep following those instincts."

SUGGESTED READING

Barnes, Brooks. "With A Fan at the Helm, Marvel Safely Steers Its Heroes to the Screen." *The New York Times*, 24 July 2011, www.nytimes.com/2011/07/25/business/media/marvel-with-a-fan-at-the-helm-steers-its-heroes-to-the-screen.html. Accessed 8 Mar. 2019.

Feige, Kevin. "An Extended Conversation with Kevin Feige." Interview by Joanna Robinson. *Vanity Fair*, 6 Dec. 2017, www.vanityfair.com/hollywood/2017/12/marvel-kevin-feige-interview Accessed 8 Mar. 2019.

Feige, Kevin. "Kevin Feige on the 'Avengers 4' Title, Marvel Reshoots, Comic-Con, 'Black Panther 2', and More." Interview by Steve "Frosty" Weintraub. *Collider*, 30 Apr. 2018, collider.com/kevin-feige-interview-avengers-4/. Accessed 8 Mar. 2019.

Gilchrist, Todd. "How Kevin Feige Defied Naysayers to Build a Lucrative Universe." *Variety*, 18 Jan. 2019, variety.com/2019/film/awards/marvel-man-kevin-feige-defied-naysayers-to-build-a-lucrative-universe-1203109428/. Accessed 8 Mar. 2019.

Robinson, Joanna. "Secrets of the Marvel Universe." *Vanity Fair*, 27 Nov. 2017, www.vanityfair.com/hollywood/2017/11/marvel-cover-story. Accessed 8 Mar. 2019.

SELECTED WORKS

Iron Man, 2008; *Thor*, 2011; *Captain America: The First Avenger*, 2011; *The Avengers*, 2012; *Guardians of the Galaxy*, 2014; *Ant-Man*, 2015; *Doctor Strange*, 2016; *Spider-Man: Homecoming*, 2017; *Black Panther*, 2018; *Captain Marvel*, 2019

—*Christopher Mari*

Photo by Gage Skidmore via Wikimedia Commons

Dave Fennoy

Date of birth: January 20, 1952
Occupation: Voice actor

Known for his relaxed, mellifluous voice, Dave Fennoy became one of the most prolific and versatile voice actors of his day. A former musician and morning radio disc jockey, Fennoy launched his voice-over career in 1990 and eventually amassed hundreds of credits across a multitude of entertainment platforms, including television promos, commercials, animation, and video games. However, like many voice actors he spent the bulk of his career in relative obscurity. This began to change in 2008, when he began recording for the then-nascent streaming video service Hulu. Fennoy's brief, but distinctive advertisement bumper that aired before every program on the service brought him a new level of recognition.

In addition to becoming known as the "Hulu Guy," Fennoy also earned a cult following in the gaming community for his work across several popular franchises. Most notably, he voiced the character of protagonist Lee Everett in the highly acclaimed episodic video game series *The Walking Dead*. First released in 2012, the game built on the universe established in the comic books and television series of the same name. Fennoy has also worked as a voice-over instructor, and he noted that success in his esoteric line of work required the same amount of discipline, dedication, persistence, and luck as a traditional actor must possess. In an interview with James Collins for the acting and production career website *Mandy* (4 Apr. 2019), he nonetheless offered a simple piece of advice to prospective voice actors: "Get training, relax, and enjoy the ride."

EARLY LIFE AND EDUCATION

David Henderson Fennoy was born on January 20, 1952, in Silver Spring, Maryland, and grew up in Cleveland, Ohio. As a child, he began training for his voice acting career "without knowing it," as he told an interviewer for the Irish video game website *Bone-Idle* (17 Oct. 2012). That training came in the form of playful mimicry: he would imitate the voices of characters of cartoons he watched. Drawn to the performing arts, Fennoy acted in productions put on by the prestigious Cleveland community-based arts center Karamu House (considered the oldest African American theater in the United States). There he also studied art, dance, and music.

Fennoy remained actively involved in the theater as a high schooler at the Hawken School, a private preparatory institution. During his senior year there, he served as president of the student-run theater group the Players' Society, for which he directed and acted in several plays. After graduating, he attended Macalester College, in St. Paul, Minnesota, where he majored in theater. By that time, however, he had also started to devote his attention to music, so much so that he left college after several years to perform as a singer and guitarist at small venues across the United States and Europe.

Following two years on the road, Fennoy resumed his studies at Howard University, a historically black institution in Washington, DC. There he majored in jazz studies and minored in guitar. After earning his degree he moved to Berkeley, California, where, thanks in large part to his strong, soothing voice, he embarked on a career in radio.

RADIO TO VOICE ACTING

During the 1980s, Fennoy worked as a morning disc jockey for several San Francisco Bay Area radio stations under the stage name of Billy David Ocean. Prior to becoming a disc jockey, he worked as a copywriter and continuity director for the Berkeley-based radio station KRE/KBLX. He wrote and voiced commercials for the station but did so without consciously thinking of it as voice-over work. It was not until a disc jockey friend at the station informed Fennoy of the lucrative potential of voice-over that he considered it as a possible career option. "A light went on and never went off," Fennoy told Collins, "though it took a couple years before I did anything about it."

Eventually, Fennoy produced a demo tape that featured a compilation of his retail radio commercials, or spots, which were all performed in different voices. He submitted it to Joan Spangler, the top voice-over agent in San Francisco but had to be persistent just to get noticed. "It was several weeks before she took my call and had me in to tell me I was talented, but not ready, and to come back with a better demo in six months," he told *Bone-Idle*. Fennoy later booked his first voice-over gigs on his own. These included promotions for a local TV channel and various hotline jobs, such as announcing lottery results and even voicing a seductive, sexy man for a fantasy hotline for women. Eventually Spangler's agency signed him, and he found more work as a union member.

Initially, voice-over served as a side endeavor to Fennoy's regular radio job as the morning host at leading Bay Area station KSOL. However, in early 1990 he and the rest of KSOL's on-air staff were abruptly fired. He began cultivating contacts in Los Angeles, including agent Leigh Gilbert, with whom he had previously taken a voiceover workshop. A friend also helped him send a demo to figures in the animated cartoon industry, securing him several auditions. Not long afterward, he relocated to Los Angeles full time.

After many fruitless auditions, Fennoy eventually began to land a steady stream of voice acting gigs. These included minor television promos and voicing the character Robocop for a telephone game. It was his work in cartoons, however, that proved more substantial. In 1990 he broke through with the role of Dick Scott in a short-lived animated series based on the musical group New Kids on the Block. Throughout the 1990s he provided voices for shows such as *ProStars* (1991), *Darkwing Duck* (1991), *Sonic the Hedgehog* (1994), *Teenage Mutant Ninja Turtles* (1996), and *The Real Adventures of Johnny Quest* (1996).

THE HULU GUY

Fennoy's profile in the highly specialized, yet largely anonymous voice-over industry continued to rise in the 2000s. While much of this success was due to hard work and persistence, he also engaged in creative self-promotion. After making a name for himself among producers, agents, and casting directors around Los Angeles, he began sending annual holiday gifts to them to keep his name fresh in their minds for future gigs. He was featured in promos for national television networks such as the Disney Channel, CBS, ABC, Showtime, and ESPN. He also voiced advertisements for notable brands such as McDonalds, KFC, Corona Beer, Toyota, Lexus, Chrysler, and AT&T. Other projects included narration for programs on National Geographic and the Discovery Channel and gigs as an in-show announcer for several award shows, most notably the NAACP (National Association for the Advance of Colored People) Image Awards.

Fennoy was among twenty-one voice actors featured in the book *Secrets of Voiceover Success* (2005), by the veteran voiceover specialist Joan Baker. In it, among other things, he discusses some of the career obstacles he had to face, including as an African American man. Ultimately, he commented on his lifetime goal: "I want my voice to be remembered as one that could comfort and excite, a voice you trusted, that was warm and made you feel like you wanted to know the man behind the voice."

Arguably the biggest break of Fennoy's career came in 2008, when he became the voice of Hulu, an internet-based television streaming service. Fennoy landed the gig by chance after meeting a man at a party who, after overhearing his voice, pitched him the idea of working for the service, which officially launched in the United States in March of that year. Upon joining Hulu, Fennoy recorded a twelve-word advertisement introduction, or bumper, that aired before every program: "The following program is brought to you with limited commercial interruption by." The bumper soon became a highly recognizable part of the Hulu experience, coinciding with the service's rapid rise to popularity. Indeed, the line was so ubiquitous that several outlets published profiles of Fennoy, who became known as the "Hulu Guy." In one such article for *BuzzFeed News* (28 Jan. 2013), John Herrman described the bumper as "the defining sounds of Fennoy's career."

Fennoy was a ubiquitous presence on Hulu for six years, during which the service grew from thousands to tens of millions of subscribers per month. Nevertheless, he was unceremoniously fired by the company in June 2014 without being given an explanation. In response, some of his fans launched Twitter campaigns urging Hulu to hire him back, though with no success. In the wake of his firing, Fennoy expressed frustration but also commitment to moving forward, telling Adam Epstein and Zachary M. Seward for *Quartz* (11 July 2014), "Life goes on. My voice will be heard again."

THE WALKING DEAD SERIES

Concurrently with his Hulu tenure, Fennoy became one of most prominent voice actors in the gaming world. He lent his voice to characters in such iconic game franchises as World of Warcraft, Tomb Raider, Metal Gear Solid, Mass Effect, and Starcraft. However, it was the lead role of Lee Everett in the zombie video game *The Walking Dead* that brought him the most attention. First released by Telltale Games in 2012, the episodic adventure series is based on the wildly popular eponymous comic books and live-action television series. It follows Everett, a former college professor who, after being sentenced to prison for killing his wife's lover, finds redemption when he watches over and protects an orphaned eight-year-old girl, Clementine, during a deadly zombie apocalypse.

The first season of *The Walking Dead*, which spanned five episodes, received widespread acclaim and won over ninety game of the year awards. Much of that acclaim was attributed to Fennoy, whose authentic, multifaceted portrayal helped make the game more compelling. He earned six awards nominations and two wins for best voice in a video game. The game spawned two more five-episode seasons, released in 2013 and 2016, respectively, and a final four-episode season in 2018; Fennoy reprised his Everett character for the second and final seasons. "Lee's voice is my voice," Fennoy told Marty Mulrooney for *Alternative Magazine Online* (14 May 2012). "I just talk and let the emotions flow."

Credited with revitalizing the adventure game genre, the *Walking Dead* series was particularly noted for its well-developed narratives and for incorporating the element of player choice, which allows players to pick from a wide variety of scenarios that can determine future story outcomes. Because of this complexity, it took almost a year for Fennoy to record his lines for the series' first season. He had to record roughly 1,200 lines per episode, which each took up to three eight-hour sessions to complete. "Like any other acting gig, you want to know as much about the character as possible," he told *Bone-Idle*. "Who is he, where is he from, how old, what does he love . . . the questions go on and on to answer for yourself."

OTHER VOICE WORK

In addition to the *Walking Dead* series, Fennoy has voiced characters in other episodic games designed by Telltale. These included Bluebeard

in *The Wolf Among Us* (2013), Finch and additional voices in *Tales from the Borderlands* (2014), Gabriel the Warrior in *Minecraft: Story Mode* (2015), and Lucius Fox in *Batman: The Telltale Series* (2016). Some of his other notable gaming work included playing five different roles in the multiplayer battle arena game *Dota 2* (2013); the roles of Max Loken and Malcolm Latimer in the acclaimed postapocalyptic role-playing game *Fallout 4* (2015); and multiple characters in the massively multiplayer online role-playing game *World of Warcraft: Battle for Azeroth* (2018).

Meanwhile, Fennoy has continued to be an in-demand voice actor for animated shows and films. He voiced three characters for the Marvel Comics-inspired animated television series *Guardians of the Galaxy* from 2015 to 2016. He also portrayed multiple characters for Cartoon Network's comedy animated series *OK K.O.! Let's Be Heroes* from 2017 to 2018. In 2018, he handled three characters in DC Universe's direct-to-video animated superhero film *Suicide Squad: Hell to Pay*.

As an established and widely respected professional, Fennoy has often conducted workshops as a voice-over instructor. Yet while he remains passionate about his work, he has often discussed the disparity in recognition—and pay—between voice actors and traditional actors. He notes that the process behind voice-over is not much different from that of a traditional actor, save for the fact that he does not have to wear costumes or makeup. "Good acting is good acting," as Fennoy put it to the *Bone-Idle* interviewer.

PERSONAL LIFE

Though primarily recognized by his voice, Fennoy is also known for his long white dreadlocks, which have often earned him comparisons to the King Ezekiel character from *The Walking Dead* franchise. Living in Southern California, he records much of his voiceover work at his home, where he has his own studio equipped with a whisper room and a large collection of microphones. He has a daughter from his first marriage, which ended in divorce.

SUGGESTED READING

Baker, Joan. *Secrets of Voice-Over Success: Top Voice Actors Reveal How They Did It*. 2nd ed., Sentient Publications, 2009 PRINT.

"Dave Fennoy." *IMDb*, 2019, www.imdb.com/name/nm0271965/#actor. Accessed 17 June 2019.

Epstein, Adam, and Zachary M. Seward. "The Voice of Hulu Has Been Fired." *Quartz*, 11 July 2014, qz.com/233077/the-voice-of-hulu-has-been-fired/. Accessed 17 June 2019.

Fennoy, Dave. "INTERVIEW – In Conversation with Dave Fennoy (Lee Everett, The

Walking Dead: The Game)." Interview by Marty Mulrooney. *Alternative Magazine Online*, 14 May 2012, alternativemagazineonline.co.uk/2012/05/14/interview-in-conversation-with-dave-fennoy-lee-everett-the-walking-dead-the-game/. Accessed 17 June 2019.

Fennoy, Dave. "An Interview with Dave Fennoy, Voice of Lee Everett in 'The Walking Dead' Game." Interview by James Collins. *Mandy*, 4 Apr. 2019, www.mandy.com/news/dave-fennoy-voice-actor-the-walking-dead. Accessed 17 June 2019.

Fennoy, Dave. "The Walking Dead Interviews: Dave Fennoy as Lee Everett." *Bone-Idle*, 17 Oct. 2012, bone-idle.ie/index.php/the-walking-dead-interviews-dave-fennoy-as-lee-everett/. Accessed 17 June 2019.

Herrman, John. "How It Feels to Be the Voice of Hulu." *BuzzFeed News*, 28 Jan. 2013, www.buzzfeednews.com/article/jwherrman/how-it-feels-to-be-the-voice-of-hulu. Accessed 17 June 2019.

SELECTED WORKS

New Kids on the Block, 1990; *The Curse of Monkey Island*, 1997; *World of Warcraft*, 2004; *Metal Gear Solid 4: Guns of the Patriots*, 2008; *StarCraft II: Wings of Liberty*, 2010; *The Walking Dead* (video game), 2012; *Dota 2*, 2013; *Fallout 4*, 2015; *World of Warcraft: Battle for Azeroth*, 2018

—*Chris Cullen*

John John Florence

Date of birth: October 18, 1992
Occupation: Surfer

According to surfer John John Florence, surfing at its best is simply "perfect," as he told Zach Baron for *GQ* (15 May 2017). "You're perfectly present. You're perfectly in the moment. You're perfectly not thinking about anything else in the world," he added. "You're just surfing. You're surfing away with your friends or your family, and that's it. You're just there." Indeed, "just surfing" has been a constant in Florence's life since early childhood. The oldest son of an avid surfer, he grew up on the North Shore of Oahu, Hawaii, a world-renowned hotbed for the sport thanks to the ideal conditions of the area known as the Banzai Pipeline. Having honed his skills on the Pipeline's characteristic waves, Florence established himself as a young surfer to watch by the time he was thirteen. He went on to excel in professional competition, winning the Triple Crown of Surfing in 2011, 2013, and 2016.

Photo by Dane Siestas via Wikimedia Commons

Although a celebrity, Florence remains deeply tied to his roots and especially his Hawaiian home. "My life has revolved around the ocean since the beginning, and it's like that with everyone in this community," he wrote for the *Players' Tribune* (1 Mar. 2018). "The North Shore kind of has a small town feeling to it. Everyone knows everyone, and it seems like everybody here has something to do with the ocean." That lifelong connection to the ocean supported his rise to the top of the surfing world: Florence won back-to-back World Surf League Championship Tour titles in 2016 and 2017, solidifying his reputation as one of the greatest surfers of his generation and even of all time.

EARLY LIFE AND EDUCATION

John Alexander "John John" Florence was born on October 18, 1992, in Honolulu, Hawaii. He was the first of three sons born to Alexandra and John Florence, who divorced when Florence was five. His father later remarried, and Florence has a halfbrother from that relationship. Following their parents' divorce, Florence and his younger brothers Nathan and Ivan lived in the area of Oahu known as the North Shore with their mother, an avid surfer who had moved to Hawaii from New Jersey as a teenager.

Florence's mother shared her love of surfing with her sons, teaching them the basics when they were young. The sport became a fixture of everyday life for the family. "I remember these times when I was super young, like eight or so, and the waves were pretty big . . . and I was a little bit scared to go out on my board," he wrote for the *Players' Tribune*. "My mom wouldn't make me go, or pressure me, or anything like that. She'd just look at me and kind of shrug her shoulders and say, 'O.K., well I'm going out. . . . So I'd follow her out into the ocean. And every single time I did that, I'd have so much fun. I never regretted it.'"

Alongside his mother, one of the most formative influences of Florence's early life was his family's proximity to the Banzai Pipeline. Also known simply as Pipeline or Pipe, the name refers to an area of the North Shore's coastline that attracts numerous surfers due to the large, often tube-shaped waves created by several reefs below the water. Florence grew up surfing the Pipeline, and the area remains his home base even after he began visiting other top surfing spots around the world. "When I'm here, I surf it every day," he told Sean Doherty for *Surfer* (10 Dec. 2011) of the Pipeline. "It's like anything else: you do it often enough, you're going to get it down." In addition to serving as an invaluable training ground for Florence, the Pipeline hosted surfing competitions such as the Pipe Masters, and Florence was able to watch experienced surfers compete near his home throughout his early life. While surfing filled much of the young Florence's free time, he balanced his athletic pursuits with his schooling, attending Kahuku High School.

EARLY SUCCESS

As Florence's talent and skill as a surfer became increasingly apparent, he began to appear in competitions for young surfers, including events held by the National Scholastic Surfing Association (NSSA). He won his first title at the NSSA National Championships in 2003. Florence entered his first non-age-group tournament at age thirteen and in late 2005 set a record as the youngest person ever to compete in the Vans Triple Crown of Surfing, which encompasses the Hawaiian Pro, World Cup of Surfing, and Pipeline Masters events. Although he struggled at times during those events, he impressed onlookers with his handling of difficult waves and received widespread attention as a surfing prodigy. His efforts also helped win him the attention of numerous major sponsors, including the surfwear brand O'Neill, the footwear brand Vans, and the beverage company SoBe.

Over the course of Florence's early career he competed throughout the world, often traveling in the company of his family. Although his love of surfing remained as strong as ever, he began to find that his approach to the sport, which focused more on his own enjoyment than on all-out competition, was not conducive to professional success. That challenge became particularly apparent as Florence sought to enter the World Surf League (WSL, then known as the Association of Surfing Professionals) circuit of high-level competition, which saw him lose numerous tournaments. Negatively affected by the stress of losing, he began to consider quitting the sport to pursue another path.

Another challenge came in 2011, when Florence broke his back while surfing the Pipeline. Although the injury was a major setback that forced him to undergo physical therapy, the incident gave him a valuable opportunity to reflect on his sport and his approach to competition. "After all that losing, and after I broke my back, I came to a realization that competitions are actually a really unique opportunity to get to know yourself better, because you have all of these ups and downs and you have to figure out how to deal with those emotions," he wrote for the *Players' Tribune*. "I started to see competitions as a chance to learn about myself. And that's when I really started improving."

After recovering from his back injury, Florence surfed in a variety of WSL competitions, including numerous events on the WSL Qualifying Series and several on the higher-level WSL Championship Tour. His results included a first-place finish at the World Cup of Surfing and fifth-place finishes at both the Pipeline Masters and the Hawaiian Pro. Florence's cumulative success in those three competitions won him his first Triple Crown of Surfing, considered one of the most prestigious honors in the sport. He was the youngest winner in the history of the event. The 2011 season also saw his first win at the Volcom Pipe Pro, held in the Pipeline.

WORLD SURF LEAGUE CHAMPION

In the years following 2011, Florence remained a staple in WSL competitions, amassing success on both the Qualifying Series and the Championship Tour. In 2012, he won the Telstra Drug Aware Pro on the Qualifying Series and the Billabong Rio Pro on the Championship Tour, in addition to his second Volcom Pipe Pro. The following season saw Florence win his second Triple Crown, having placed second at the Pipeline Masters, fifth at the World Cup and thirty-third at the Hawaiian Pro. He also won his third consecutive Volcom Pipe Pro in 2013.

Florence won the 2014 Quiksilver Pro France, an event on the Championship Tour. However, that year he ended his streak of Volcom Pipe Pro wins, placing only forty-ninth in the competition. Despite that setback, Florence regained the Volcom Pipe Pro title the following year, placing first to claim his fourth win. "It feels pretty amazing. I'm pretty stoked," he told Jeff Mull for *Surfer* (2 Feb. 2015) following the competition. "To win four, I can't even believe it yet, to be honest. It's crazy, I'm just stoked to take this trophy home . . . again."

During the 2016 WSL season, Florence again showcased his dominance in the Triple Crown events, placing first at the Hawaiian

Pro, seventeenth at the World Cup, and fifth at the Pipeline Masters to win his third Triple Crown title. The season proved to be a particularly successful one, as he also placed first in the MEO Rip Curl Pro Portugal and Oi Rio Pro and achieved top-five finishes in several other Championship Tour events. By the end of the season, Florence's strong overall performance earned him the title of WSL World Champion. It was an achievement many saw as destined since his early days as a surfing phenom.

Even more impressively, Florence went on to repeat that achievement the following season. He reached the top of the 2017 WSL leaderboard thanks to nine top-five Championship Tour finishes, including first place at the Drug Aware Margaret River Pro. The back-to-back championships cemented his status as one of the leading surfers of the era and a near legendary figure in the surfing community, especially in Hawaii. Still, he remained characteristically low-key about the accomplishment and focused on the future. "It really hasn't fully sunk in that I won my second world title. It all happened so fast," he wrote in his *Players' Tribune* piece. "You put a lot of hard work into it throughout the year, and you're so committed and so focused on each event that you kind of lose track of where you are."

INJURY AND RETURN

In addition to professional competition, Florence was featured in many surfing films and documentaries throughout his career. Among the professional productions he was featured in were *Pipe* (2011), *Distance Between Dreams* (2016), and *Paradigm Lost* (2017). He became particularly well known for the 2015 film *View from a Blue Moon*, which focuses specifically on Florence and his traveling companions. Shot in 4K resolution, the film impressed critics with its compelling visuals and became the highest-grossing surfing film ever produced.

Florence began the 2018 WSL season with strong performances in Championship Tour events, for example placing ninth at the Oi Rio Pro. However, his attempt at defending his world title collapsed partway into the season, when he injured his knee while surfing in Bali, Indonesia. Although the injury forced him to take a break from surfing for a time, he kept busy during that period, competing in sailing and paddling competitions. He performed particularly well in the latter, placing second in the team division in the Molokai 2 Oahu paddle race alongside teammate Kona Johnson. Although Florence initially planned to return to surfing in time to compete in the Pipeline Masters in late 2018, he ultimately chose to withdraw from the competition. "I think I'm close to 100%, but I'm not there yet," he later wrote on *Instagram*, as quoted by Michael Ciaramella for *Stab* (16 Feb. 2019). "I noticed this week that I still don't have full trust in my movements, which has always been my test for returning to competition."

Due to his injury, Florence limited his surfing during late 2018 and early 2019. In February 2019, however, he posted several surfing videos on *Instagram*, signaling a potential return to competition. Florence returned to WSL competition in April 2019 for the Quiksilver Pro Gold Cast, where he tied for third place.

PERSONAL LIFE

When not surfing elsewhere, Florence continues to live in his childhood hometown on the North Shore of Oahu. In addition to surfing, he has regularly engaged in other sports such as skateboarding, snowboarding, and sailing. His other hobbies include beekeeping, photography, flying airplanes, and studying native Hawaiian plants. "I really just want to learn as much as I can about all sorts of things," he wrote in the *Players' Tribune*. "I'm one of those people who find it hard to stop doing things. I'm not big on sitting still."

Known for his quiet demeanor and light social media presence compared to many star athletes, Florence enjoys spending his time surrounded by friends and family. "I'm fortunate enough to be in a position where I can have a big team," he told Baron. "I don't have to worry about anything but going surfing."

SUGGESTED READING

Baron, Zach. "Surfer John John Florence's Very Wavy World." *GQ*, 15 May 2017, www.gq.com/story/at-home-with-john-john-florence. Accessed 12 Apr. 2019.

Ciaramella, Michael. "John John Florence Is Knee Braced Up and Still Carving Better Than 97 Percent of Pro Surfers." *Stab*, 16 Feb. 2019, stabmag.com/news/john-john-florence-is-back-to-his-old-tricks/. Accessed 12 Apr. 2019.

Doherty, Sean. "Island of the Mind: A Profile of John Florence." *Surfer*, 20 Sept. 2018, www.surfer.com/features/king-island-john-florence-profile/. Accessed 12 Apr. 2019.

Doherty, Sean. "The Surfer Profile: John John Florence." *Surfer*, 10 Dec. 2011, www.surfer.com/features/the-surfer-profile-john-john-florence/. Accessed 12 Apr. 2019.

Florence, John John. "Four for Florence." Interview by Jeff Mull. *Surfer*, 2 Feb. 2015, www.surfer.com/features/john-john-florence-volcom-pipe-pro/#jFEt6sZrgE9fAGZH.97. Accessed 12 Apr. 2019.

Florence, John John. "The Ocean Is Everything." *The Players' Tribune*, 1 Mar. 2018, www.theplayerstribune.com/en-us/articles/john-john-florence-surfing-world-surf-league. Accessed 12 Apr. 2019.

Marcus, Ben. "Over His Head." *Outside*, 1 Mar. 2006, www.outsideonline.com/1824146/over-his-head. Accessed 12 Apr. 2019.

—*Joy Crelin*

Photo by fotopress/Redferns

Luis Fonsi

Date of birth: April 15, 1978
Occupation: Singer

Though singer Luis Fonsi began his successful career in the late 1990s and became a major Latin R&B star in the 2000s, he reached a new level of worldwide recognition with his 2017 mega-hit "Despacito" (Slowly), which features reggaeton star Daddy Yankee. The song's remix, with pop star Justin Bieber, occupied the top spot on the Billboard Hot 100 for sixteen weeks, tying the record for the longest-running number one hit in Billboard history up to that point. "Despacito" also broke seven Guinness World Records, including most-streamed track worldwide and first music video to break five billion views on the streaming platform YouTube. With over six billion views by mid-2019, the song's music video became the most viewed video on the Internet.

Fonsi, who was born in Puerto Rico and grew up in Orlando, Florida, followed his deep-rooted love of music and performance in his rise to international stardom. A singer since childhood, he earned performance experience during his high school years as a member of a locally successful amateur a cappella group in the boy band style. He then attended the music program at Florida State University (FSU), determined to make singing his career. Fonsi rose to attention in the Latin music world after the release of his debut album *Comenzaré* (*I will start*) in 1998, and his renown grew throughout the 2000s. He became known for romantic pop ballads like the 2008 hit "No me doy por vencido" (I don't give up) and the earlier "Nada es para siempre" (Nothing is forever). The danceable "Despacito"—and later singles such as "Échame la culpa" (Blame me) with Demi Lovato and "Calypso" featuring Stefflon Don—showcase his versatility as a singer.

EARLY LIFE AND EDUCATION

Luis Alfonso Rodríguez López-Cepero was born on April 15, 1978 in San Juan, Puerto Rico, to Alfonso Rodríguez and Delia López-Cepero. He had a younger sister named Tatiana Rodríguez, and two younger brothers, Jean Rodríguez (who also became a singer) and Ramon do Salotti. Fonsi grew up singing in the children's choir in San Juan. His family moved to Orlando, Florida, when he was ten years old. Fonsi, who spoke little English, would later describe the move as a difficult one. "I had to leave my friends, my school, my cousins behind. Looking back, I realize how hard it was," he recalled to Peter Robinson for the *South China Morning Post Magazine* (18 Aug. 2017). "I felt like I was the only Latino around. That first year was just depressing—people were making fun of my accent and the way I dressed."

Eventually, Fonsi. joined the school choir, giving him an outlet to socialize. "It helped me kind of break out of my shell," he told Monivette Cordeiro for *Orlando Weekly* (20 Sept. 2017). "Music was always the easiest way for me to . . . express myself." As a student at Dr. Phillips High School in Orlando, he formed an a cappella group called the Big Guys under the guidance of his music teacher, Keith Galasso. Among the group's members was Joey Fatone, who later became a member of the popular boy band *NSYNC. The group performed all around the city, including everywhere from Orlando Magic basketball games to busking on street corners, singing doo-wop versions of hit songs.

Fonsi graduated high school in 1995 and earned a full scholarship to the Florida State University School of Music. During his time in college, he sang with the London Symphony Orchestra in 1997. However, he skipped one of the last rehearsals for the performance to see Michael Jackson perform at Wembley Stadium. "I almost got kicked out of concert choir," he recalled to Jay Cridlin for the *Tampa Bay Times* (14 Sept. 2017). "It was worth it!"

BREAKING INTO THE MUSIC INDUSTRY

After graduation, Fonsi won a recording contract with Universal Music Latin, and released his debut album, *Comenzaré*, in 1998. "I was really influenced by Brian McKnight, Stevie Wonder, Boyz II Men and all these other amazing R&B singers. But I wanted to keep my Latin heritage always present," he told Suzy Exposito for *Rolling Stone* (14 Feb. 2019). "So I said, 'How can I use everything I've learned and do it in Spanish, for a Latin American audience?'" His second album, *Eterno* (*Eternal*; 2000), featuring the hit song "Imagíname sin ti," made him a star. The song—which translates to "Imagine Me without You"—topped the Billboard Latin charts. The same year, he recorded a duet called "Si no te hubiera conocido" (If I hadn't met you) with pop star Christina Aguilera. His third album, *Amor secreto* (*Secret love*), was released in 2002.

Fonsi released his first English-language album, *Fight the Feeling*, the same year. The album came on the heels of successful English-language debuts from other Latin artists like Ricky Martin, Marc Anthony, and Shakira. Fonsi promoted his album heavily, opening for pop superstar Britney Spears on her Dream within a Dream tour in 2002. Still, *Fight the Feeling* received lukewarm reviews.

Fonsi released his next album, *Abrazar la vida* (*Embrace life*), in 2003. A reviewer for *AllMusic* (2003) expressed relief at Fonsi's return to Spanish-language pop balladry, noting that the record "finds Fonsi not only returning to singing in Spanish, but to his familiar musical background—the ultra-catchy romantic pop that initially launched him into the public eye." The reviewer went on to praise Fonsi's "heartfelt, emotive vocals wholly confident in their ability to caress a lover's soul." The album's title track reached the top of the Billboard Latin charts in 2004.

PALABRAS DEL SILENCIO

Fonsi released an album called *Paso a paso* (*Step by step*) in 2005. It was the first record on which he had cowritten most of the songs. It also featured the song, "Nada es para siempre (Nothing is forever)," a top hit on the Billboard Latin charts. He wrote the mid-tempo ballad while caring for his partner, actor Adamari López, who was being treated for breast cancer. The song was Fonsi's first to break the Billboard Hot 100, peaking at 90.

Fonsi released *Palabras del silencio* (*Words of silence*) in 2008, featuring the Mexican ranchera-influenced hit song "No me doy por vencido (I do not give up)." That song also broke the Billboard Hot 100 and had a nineteen-week run at the top of the Billboard Latin charts—setting a record for the longest such streak. The album also garnered another massive hit, a follow-up to "No me doy por vencido," called "Aquí estoy yo"

(Here I am). The ballad, featuring Mexican singer-songwriter Aleks Syntek, Noel Schajris of the Mexican duo Sin Bandera, and Spanish singer-songwriter David Bisbal, exhibits the clear influence of R&B groups like Boyz II Men. The song earned Fonsi a Latin Grammy Award for Song of the Year in 2009, and *Palabras del silencio* was nominated for the Grammy Award for Best Latin Pop Album.

Fonsi released his next album, *Tierra firme* (*Mainland*), in 2011. A reviewer for *Billboard* magazine (24 June 2011) described Fonsi's *Palabras del silencio*, as his "breakthrough," but wrote that "*Tierra Firme* is a step beyond in every sense of the word." They went on to praise the singer's inclusion of more introspective material, deeming *Tierra firme* "ambitious pop performed by a soulful singer who can touch his listeners on many levels." The album's hit single, "Gritar (Shouts)," was nominated for a Latin Grammy for Record of the Year.

Fonsi's next album, 8, was released in 2014. He wrote the gentle guitar ballad, "Llegaste tú" (You arrived), featuring the Dominican musician Juan Luis Guerra, for his infant daughter. The song was also nominated for a Latin Grammy Award for Record of the Year.

"DESPACITO" AND VIDA

Fonsi has said that the word "despacito"—which means "slowly" in English—came to him along with the chorus of the song that would bear the same name upon waking one morning in 2015. Working with his cowriter, Panamanian singer Erika Ender, Fonsi completed the song, and brought in Puerto Rican rapper Daddy Yankee to add another element. The song was released in January 2017. It had already broken into the Billboard Hot 100 when Fonsi received a call from Bieber, who had heard the song while touring in Colombia. Fonsi recalled to Madison Vain for *Entertainment Weekly* (9 June 2017): "It was a great call that I got when they told me he wanted to be a part of it. I know how it is when you're out on tour and your head is 'What's the next city? What time do I have to wake up for sound check?' And here he is in Colombia, he hears the song and he loves it—he sees how people react—and says, 'I need to be a part of this movement.'" The song's remix, featuring Bieber singing in English and Spanish, was released that April. By May, just in time to become the ubiquitous song of the summer, "Despacito" hit number one on the Billboard charts.

As the song raced up the charts, Fonsi saw the song as a turning point for Latin music and Puerto Rican reggaeton. "It says a lot about where Latin music is nowadays and where our culture is. We're breaking barriers down," he said, as quoted by Wayne Marshall for *Vulture* (22 Aug. 2017). "I think that's the biggest win out of all of this." "Despacito" was nominated for three Grammy Awards—record of the year, song of the year and best pop duo/group performance—and won four Latin Grammy Awards, for song of the year, record of the year, best urban fusion/performance, and short form music video, respectively. As the song's popularity showed no signs of waning, Fonsi decided to postpone the release of his new album. A second single, "Échame la culpa (Blame me)" featuring pop singer Demi Lovato, peaked at number 47 on the Billboard Hot 100 chart in November 2017. In 2018, Fonsi released a single called "Calypso" featuring British rapper Stefflon Don. He released his tenth album, *Vida* (*Life*), in 2019.

PERSONAL LIFE

Fonsi and Spanish model Águeda López were married between 2006 and 2010. In 2011, Fonsi and López had their first child, Mikaela. The couple married in 2014, and had a second child, Rocco, in 2016.

SUGGESTED READING

Cordeiro, Monivette. "Luis Fonsi Talks about Going from Singing on Orlando's Corners to Creating a Worldwide Hit." *Orlando Weekly*, 20 Sept. 2017, www.orlandoweekly.com/orlando/luis-fonsi-talks-about-going-from-singing-on-orlandos-corners-to-creating-a-worldwide-hit/Content?oid=7030053. Accessed 23 Aug. 2019.

Cridlin, Jay. "Before Clearwater Concert, Luis Fonsi Talks Florida Roots, 'Despacito.'" *Tampa Bay Times*, 14 Sept. 2017, www.tampabay.com/things-to-do/music/before-clearwater-concert-luis-fonsi-talks-florida-roots-despacito/2337456. Accessed 23 Aug. 2019.

Fonsi, Luis. "'Despacito' Singer Luis Fonsi Talks His Spanish-Language Hit." Interview by Madison Vain. *Entertainment Weekly*, 9 June 2017, ew.com/music/2017/06/09/despacito-luis-fonsi-interview/. Accessed 23 Aug. 2019.

Fonsi, Luis. "Luis Fonsi: King of the Radio Romantics." Interview by Suzy Exposito. *Rolling Stone*, 14 Feb. 2019, www.rollingstone.com/music/music-latin/luis-fonsi-interview-despacito-vida-792281/. Accessed 23 Aug. 2019.

Marshall, Wayne. "Everything You Ever Wanted to Know about 'Despacito.'" *Vulture*, 22 Aug. 2017, www.vulture.com/2017/08/everything-you-ever-wanted-to-know-about-despacito.html. Accessed 23 Aug. 2019.

Robinson, Peter. "Despacito Writer Luis Fonsi's 19-Year Journey to Musical Immortality." *South China Morning Post: Post Magazine*, 18 Aug. 2017, /www.scmp.com/magazines/post-magazine/long-reads/article/2107034/despacito-writer-luis-fonsis-19-year-journey. Accessed 23 Aug. 2019.

SELECTED WORKS

Comenzaré, 1998; *Eterno*, 2000; *Amor secreto*, 2002; *Fight the Feeling*, 2002; *Abrazar la vida*, 2003; *Paso a paso*, 2005; *Palabras del silencio*, 2008; *Tierra firme*, 2011; 8, 2014; *Despacito*, 2015; *Vida*, 2019

—Molly Hagan

Chris Froome

Date of birth: May 20, 1985
Occupation: Cyclist

Kenyan-born British cyclist Chris Froome has won all of cycling's three Grand Tours: the Tour de France, the Vuelta a España, and the Giro d'Italia. In 2017, he won his fourth Tour de France tournament. The following year, he focused on training specifically to win the race for the fifth time, a feat that has only been accomplished by four other riders: Jacques Anquetil, Eddy Merckx, Bernard Hinault, and Miguel Induráin. Froome told *BBC News* (2 Jan. 2019): "I'm getting to the point in my career now where I'm starting to think about what kind of legacy I want to leave behind and if I am able to win the Tour de France for a fifth time and join that very elite group of bike riders—only four other people have ever done that—it would just be incredible."

EARLY LIFE AND EDUCATION

Chris Froome was born on May 20, 1985, in Nairobi, Kenya. His father, Clive, was a former England Under-19 hockey player who moved to Africa from the United Kingdom to set up a business; his mother, Jane, worked in the physiotherapy field. After Chris's parents separated, his father moved to South Africa and his mother raised him and his two older brothers, Jonathan and Jeremy. The family struggled financially, so while his older brothers were sent to rugby boarding school in Warwickshire, England, Chris remained in Kenya with his mother.

Froome first became interested in cycling around age twelve. After winning a small charity race, Froome's mother asked David Kinjah, who was then the captain of the Kenya cycling team, to train him. "He was unusual but wasn't a boy you'd think of as a future champion," Kinjah said to Ian Chadband for the *Telegraph*. "Nothing special—except in his head. I thought he'd be a loner because even now in the village you don't see many white people. It was a bit odd for us spending days with a young white boy who was a bit shy and quiet. Soon, though, it was like we had known each other forever."

When Froome turned fourteen, he was sent to boarding schools in South Africa, first in Bloemfontein, then in Johannesburg. He continued to work with Kinjah and race whenever he could. Froome then attended the University of Johannesburg where he studied economics. He soon realized, however, that he could not handle both school and cycling. Froome told Matt Westby for *Sky Sports* (12 Sept. 2013). "It was always hard for me trying to balance my studies and training. I thought, 'OK, let me put the studies on hold. I am going to go for the cycling, give it everything for one year and if I can make something of it, then great, but if not, hopefully I can come back to my studies and carry on.'" After two years, Froome dropped out of college to focus on his cycling career.

GOING PRO
In 2007, Froome signed with the South African Konica Minolta team and found himself competing in Europe at the 2007 Giro delle Regioni. During the race, he won stage five and impressed everyone with his climbing and time-trialing. "I came over to Europe for my first stage race, which was the Giro delle Regioni, and I ended up winning a mountain-top finish there and coming second on another mountain-top finish," Froome recalled to Westby.

After his impressive showing at the Giro delle Regioni, he was offered a position on the Great Britain–registered team Barloworld on the recommendation of fellow South African rider Robbie Hunter. With Barloworld he raced in a wide variety of contests, including the 2008 Giro del Capo, the 2008 Giro dell'Appennino, and the 2009 Giro del Capo, in which he placed first. In his first Tour de France in 2008, he finished eleventh overall in the best young rider classification. He also placed second in the 2010 British National Time Trial Championship. Froome competed for Barloworld until 2010, when he joined the British cycling team Sky (now Team INEOS).

GRAND TOUR PERFORMANCES
In 2011, Froome placed in his first Grand Tour race when he finished second behind Juan José Cobo in the Vuelta a España. He soon began to think he might have what it takes to be a Grand Tour rider. "Up until then I found it very difficult to keep my performances consistently high throughout a stage race. I would have good days and showings of what I was able to achieve, but I would never be able to back it up all the way through," Froome told Westby. "But that Vuelta a España in 2011 was the first time that I was able to do that, and that gave me a lot of confidence and belief in myself that, actually, I do belong in this group of riders at the front of the general classification."

Photo by Hoebele via Wikimedia Commons

Like the other Grand Tour races, the Giro d'Italia and the Tour de France, the Vuelta a España is made up of twenty-one daylong stages over twenty-three days. The Tour de France is considered by many cycling enthusiasts to be the premier men's multistage bicycle race. For a rider to compete effectively in the Tour de France, he must have not only incredible endurance but also the ability to endure serious pain. "As a professional cyclist, you get to know that pain very well," he told *Raphia*, as quoted by Maya Oppenheim for the *Independent* (5 Aug. 2016). "You go to that 'place' so often in training and racing that it just becomes a part of you. It's not something completely new or foreign, it's more . . . I feel the pain, I acknowledge it, but I have trained myself to push on. There's a methodical side to it, a familiarity. You adapt to the pain."

With Team Sky, Froome began to dominate multistage races. He came in second overall in the 2012 Tour de France, then placed first in the 2013 Critérium International, the 2013 Tour de Romandie, and the 2013 Critérium du Dauphiné. Also in 2013, Froome won his first Tour de France, which immediately made him an international cycling star. After crashing multiple times during the 2014 Tour de France and retiring from the race, he returned to form in 2015, winning his second Critérium du Dauphiné and his second Tour de France. He then went on to win a third and fourth Tour de France in 2016 and 2017.

CLEARED IN DOPING CASE
In December 2017, the World Anti-Doping Agency (WADA) announced that Froome had

failed a doping test during the Spanish Vuelta in September 2017, when it was discovered that he had twice the permitted level of salbutamol, an asthma drug, in his bloodstream. Because it helps to expand lung capacity, it can be used as an endurance-enhancing drug. Froome was seen using inhalers, both during the Vuelta and in other races, and was well documented as using the drug to correct his asthma. Froome admitted that his asthma grew worse during the Vuelta, but denied wrongdoing. "My asthma got worse at the Vuelta so I followed the team doctor's advice to increase my Salbutamol dosage," Froome said, as quoted by the Associated Press (AP) and published in *Sports Illustrated* (13 Dec. 2017). "As always, I took the greatest care to ensure that I did not use more than the permissible dose. I take my leadership position in my sport very seriously. The UCI is absolutely right to examine test results and, together with the team, I will provide whatever information it requires."

Froome was not suspended from competition during the WADA investigation because it was possible that intense effort, fatigue, and dehydration could affect the urine concentration of the drug in doping tests. During that time, he placed first in the 2018 Giro d'Italia, however, he could not be confirmed the winner until the investigation was over. In July 2018, Froome was cleared of doping charges by the International Cycling Union.

JOINING CYCLING'S EXCLUSIVE CLUB

After Froome's 2017 Vuelta a España and 2018 Giro d'Italia wins were restored, Froome became the first cyclist to hold the first place title in three Grand Tours at the same time since Bernard Hinault did so in 1983. "It hasn't quite sunk in yet," Froome said to Sean Ingle for the *Guardian* (27 May 2018). "I am sure it will over the next few days when I have time to reflect. It is a dream to have all three leaders' jerseys in the space of ten months. I am still pinching myself. I can't believe I am here."

He did not fare as well in the 2018 Tour de France, in which he was pulled from his bike by a police officer who thought he was a spectator who had jumped onto the course. He also had to deal with crashes, unruly fans, and other interruptions before finishing third.

After the race, however, he began training with a goal to be in top form for the race the following year. In early 2019, Froome announced that he would not defend his title in the upcoming Giro d'Italia in order to focus on winning a fifth Tour de France title. "I've got some amazing memories from last year, but I think, with the Tour de France as my main objective, it's probably better that I skip the Giro d'Italia in 2019," Froome told *BBC News* (2 Jan. 2019).

PERSONAL LIFE

Froome married sports photographer Michelle Cound in 2014. The couple has two children, a son named Kellan and a daughter named Katie. In 2009, Froome was diagnosed with the parasitic disease bilharzia, which can be treated with medication but leaves him feeling lifeless when it resurfaces. In 2014, Froome published the autobiography *The Climb*, describing the effort he made to reach the upper echelons of the cycling world. In 2016, Froome was made an Officer of the Order of the British Empire (OBE) for his services to cycling.

SUGGESTED READING

Associated Press. "Chris Froome Fails Doping Test, Found to Have Double the Legal Limit of Asthma Drug." *Sports Illustrated*, 13 Dec. 2017, www.si.com/cycling/2017/12/13/chris-froome-failed-doping-test. Accessed 17 Apr. 2019.

Associated Press. "Tour de France Champion Chris Froome Is Cleared in Doping Case." *The New York Times*, 2 July 2018, www.nytimes.com/2018/07/02/sports/chris-froome-doping-tour-de-france.html. Accessed 17 Apr. 2019.

Chadband, Ian. "Tour de France 2013: The Incredible Rise of Chris Froome—and How He Was Almost Killed by a Hippo." *The Telegraph*, 27 June 2013, www.telegraph.co.uk/sport/othersports/cycling/tour-de-france/10144509/Tour-de-France-2013-the-incredible-rise-of-Chris-Froome-and-how-he-was-almost-killed-by-a-hippo.html. Accessed 17 Apr. 2019.

"Chris Froome to Skip Giro d'Italia to Focus on Tour de France." *BBC Sport*, 2 Jan. 2019, www.bbc.com/sport/cycling/46728045. Accessed 17 Apr. 2019.

Ingle, Sean. "Chris Froome Wins Giro d'Italia in Rome to Join Cycling's Exclusive Club." *The Guardian*, 27 May 2018, www.theguardian.com/sport/2018/may/27/chris-froome-wins-giro-ditalia-rome-first-briton-british-winner-cycling. Accessed 17 Apr. 2019.

Oppenheim, Maya. "Chris Froome: Cyclist Who Overcame Rare Parasitic Disease before Winning Tour de France Three Times Now Going for Gold." *Independent*, 5 Aug. 2016, www.independent.co.uk/news/people/rio-2016-chris-froome-olympics-cycling-tour-de-france-gold-medal-a7170411.html. Accessed 17 Apr. 2019.

Westby, Matt. "Tour de France: Chris Froome's Journey up Cycling's Ranks Comes to Glorious End in Paris." *Sky Sports*, 12 Sept. 2013, www.skysports.com/cycling/news/22854/8834543/tour-de-france-chris-froomes-journey-up-cyclings-ranks-comes-to-glorious-end-in-paris. Accessed 17 Apr. 2019.

—*Christopher Mari*

Anne Fulenwider

Date of birth: March 30, 1972
Occupation: Editor-in-chief

As editor-in-chief of *Marie Claire*, Anne Fulenwider was named *Media Industry Newsletter*'s Editor of the Year in 2013. Two years later, she was *Folio Magazine* Editor of the Year Eddie Award winner. Of her work, she told Dayna Wilkinson for *Harvardwood* (June 2016), "I'm constantly amazed and inspired by the women we cover in *Marie Claire*, women who have founded companies and social movements, entered politics, been entrepreneurial in a host of settings. I have no idea what's next, but I really love *Marie Claire*. It means so much to me to be part of this global network of women at such a pivotal time in our culture." Fulenwider oversees Lifetime's *Project Runway*, about the world of fashion designers, with which the magazine partners, and has appeared as a guest judge on *Project Runway All-Stars*. She also is on the board of several organizations, including the United Nations Foundation's Girl Up advisory board. In 2017, New York governor Andrew Cuomo named her to New York State's Council on Women and Girls, which is designed to ensure that the policies and programs of the state consider the rights of women and girls.

EDUCATION AND EARLY CAREER
Fulenwider was born on March 30, 1972, to Constance and Michael Fulenwider. She spent her early life in New York, serving as the editor of her high school newspaper. She then interned at a magazine in Rhode Island when she was just sixteen, before entering Harvard. While in college, she worked on articles for *Harvard Advocate* and enjoyed classes in creative writing, especially creative nonfiction. In 1995, she graduated magna cum laude with a bachelor's degree in English and American literature.

Fulenwider began her career in publishing with an internship at the start-up publication *Swing*, before moving on to an internship at the *Paris Review*. There, she became a senior editor and research assistant for editor George Plimpton as he worked on a biography of Truman Capote. She told Christina Amoroso for *New York Post* (10 June 2013), "The Paris Review was just fascinating. [George] had been working on and off for 10 years on a book about Truman Capote, and I ended up having the time of my life helping him finish this book."

Once the Capote book was completed, Fulenwider was out of a job. She gave a copy of the book to a former colleague who had gone on to work at *Vanity Fair*, mentioning she needed a new position. Encouraged to interview with her

Photo by Internet Week New York via Wikimedia Commons

former colleague's editor, Fulenwider did so and was hired.

WORKING FROM COAST TO COAST
After working for *Vanity Fair* for a couple of years, Fulenwider moved to San Francisco in 1998, influenced by the tech boom in the region and a lingering desire to go west. There, she slept on a college roommate's couch and worked several freelance jobs. Less than a year later, *Vanity Fair* lured her back to New York to fill in during a maternity leave and to offer her the new Fanfare section.

In 2008, Fulenwider left *Vanity Fair* for a position as an executive editor for *Marie Claire*, a monthly Hearst magazine whose target audience is women in their twenties and thirties. As she told Wilkinson, "I was leading the features team and had a huge amount of ownership of projects for the whole magazine. It was pretty heady for me at the time. I was inspired by *Marie Claire*'s interest in empowering women. I already had a daughter at the time and felt a responsibility to create excellent content for women." She served as executive editor until moving to rival publisher Condé Nast three years later.

In 2011, Fulenwider received a call inviting her to talk about an editor-in-chief position Condé Nast had open for their magazine *Brides*. As she explained to Taylor Dunn for *ABC News* (25 July 2017), "When they finally let me know what it was, I thought, 'Huh. Well, that's not what I thought it was going to be, but this is certainly a subject matter that . . . I'm not intimidated by . . . and it might be a really great way to learn how to be an editor-in-chief.'" She, therefore, left

Hearst and moved to *Brides* magazine to become editor-in-chief.

MARIE CLAIRE ONCE MORE

Fulenwider had been editor-in-chief for *Brides* for nine months when she received an opportunity she could not turn down; *Marie Claire* offered her the position of editor-in-chief to succeed long-time editor Joanna Coles, who was moving to another Hearst publication, *Cosmopolitan*. Fulenwider refused the position at first, given that she had brought several new hires on board for a project and had made big modifications to *Brides*. However, after consulting with her advisers and trying to imagine how she would feel when the announcement of the new editor-in-chief of *Marie Claire* came, but it would not be her name, she accepted the job in 2012. As she told Wilkinson, "I was blown away—it was the best opportunity I'd ever heard of. The timing wasn't ideal, but I've learned that things rarely happen at the perfect time." Unfortunately for morale and smooth running of operations, Coles took three top editors, as well as her personal assistant, with her. Several other key people left of their own accord for other positions.

Despite the challenges, the print magazine had a circulation of about a million readers and was active on all platforms of social media. Fulenwider instituted new features, such as the Image Maker Awards, which focus on makeup artists, stylists, and others in behind-the-scenes positions within the fashion industry. She also inaugurated an annual cross-country Power Trip, as well as Fresh Faces, celebrating new and talented women. The trip culminated in an annual "Power Issue," profiling fifty women who are changing the world around them. In addition, fifty influential women are honored annually at the New Guard luncheon.

Fulenwider credits her success to overcoming her natural introversion and honing her networking skills. She told Jacquelyn Smith for *Business Insider* (24 Mar. 2016), that connecting with people went beyond meet-and-greet, saying, "It's about being present in a conversation and genuinely curious about the person you're hoping to make a connection with." Her advice is to discover who might be attending an event and find three people with whom to connect, based on shared interests and the possibility of aiding one another.

WORKING TOGETHER

In March 2018, *Marie Claire* and *Esquire* printed a ten-page feature story on multiple sexual harassment cases, particularly the sexual harassment allegations against Harvey Weinstein. The joint project, entitled "Sex, Lies, and Human Resources," began months earlier with a meeting of editors from both publications. Speaking with Jay Fielden, who approached Fulenwider about the possibility of a joint article, Fulenwider said in an article for both *Esquire* and *Marie Claire* (6 Feb. 2018), that she agreed to the idea because, "We had to cover this in a way that moved the conversation forward. Part of that realization was that women can't make progress alone. By working with you guys, we could have an intelligent, thoughtful discussion, as *Esquire* has always elevated the conversation on what it is to be a man." She noted that the conversation had to respect the realities of differing opinions, not only between men and women, but also among women. Fielden admitted that the impulse among many men he knew and worked with was to either listen without comment or fear speaking about the issue at all.

The magazine also took on the issue of sustainability in beauty products and fashion in 2018, hosting the first forum on the topic. The first issue of *Marie Claire* devoted to the topic had been published some eight months previously. Many of *Marie Claire*'s readers are part of the drive for sustainability; their concern for sources of beauty products and clothing, as well as fair labor standards, have helped bring the issue forward.

At the same time, Fulenwider has no patience for people who do not comprehend that women can be interested in both makeup and current events, as she had been from the time she was a high school student. She told Hilary Milnes for *Glossy* (9 Jan. 2017), "Women's issues have always been at the forefront in my mind, and I've never understood why people think there can't be such a thing as a smart women's magazine, talking about global issues while getting excited about a new chrome nail polish." Her satisfaction with her work comes from a love of storytelling, as she explained to Fawnia Soo Hoo for *Fashionista* (9 May 2016), "I've always been interested in not just storytelling, but in learning about women's stories, so it seems completely inevitable that I would end up here."

PERSONAL LIFE

Fulenwider and her husband, Bryan Blatstein, a branding/media specialist, married in Martha's Vineyard, Massachusetts. They live in Brooklyn, New York, and have two children, Evie and Sammy. Fulenwider often takes the subway to work, and her forty-minute commute allows her time to read and prepare for the day ahead.

SUGGESTED READING

Dunn, Taylor. "'I Actually Said No the First Time.' Why Marie Claire's Editor-in-Chief Almost Turned Down the Job." *ABC News*, 25 July 2017, abcnews.go.com/Business/time-marie-claires-editor-chief-turned-job/story?id=48825457. Accessed 4 Oct. 2018.

Fulenwider, Anne. "Mag, Mag World." Interview by Christina Amoroso. *New York Post*, 10 June 2013, nypost.com/2013/06/10/mag-mag-world/. Accessed 5 Oct. 2018.

———. "Marie Claire's Anne Fulenwider: 'Women's Issues Have Always Been at the Forefront.'" Interview by Hilary Milnes. *Glossy*, 9 Jan. 2017, www.glossy.co/hot-topics/marie-claires-anne-fulenwider-womens-issues-have-always-been-at-the-forefront. Accessed 4 Oct. 2018.

Jones, Tashara. "Marie Claire's Top Editor Recalls First Time She Felt Like a Boss." *Page Six*, 17 June 2017, pagesix.com/2017/06/17/marie-claires-top-editor-recalls-first-time-she-felt-like-a-boss/. Accessed 4 Oct. 2018.

Smith, Jacquelyn. "Marie Claire Editor-in-Chief Says This Is How She Landed Every Job She's Ever Had." *Business Insider*, 24 Mar. 2016, www.businessinsider.com/marie-claire-editor-anne-fulenwider-on-networking-2016-3. Accessed 4 Oct. 2018.

Soo Hoo, Fawnia. "How Anne Fulenwider Went from an English Lit Major to 'Marie Claire' Editor-in-Chief." *Fashionista*, 9 May 2016, fashionista.com/2016/05/anne-fulenwider-marie-claire. Accessed 4 Oct. 2018.

Wilkinson, Dayna. "Anne Fulenwider AB '95." *Harvardwood*, 1 June 2016, www.harvardwood.org/mp201606. Accessed 6 Oct. 2018.

—*Judy Johnson*

Maya Gabeira

Date of birth: April 10, 1987
Occupation: Big-wave surfer

For big-wave surfer Maya Gabeira, no challenge is more thrilling than surfing a dauntingly large wave. "The sensation of being able to overcome fears and surf waves that are literally unforgettable—these are unique moments," she told Kim Feldmann de Britto for *Surf Simply* (2018). Since setting out to explore the world's best surfing spots at the age of seventeen, Gabeira has experienced many such unique moments, from her first time surfing at Hawaii's Waimea Bay to her mastery of a forty-six-foot wave off the coast of South Africa in 2009. Like many athletes dedicated to her dangerous—and sometimes fatal—sport, however, Gabeira has also experienced some substantial setbacks. In 2013, while attempting to set a world record for the largest wave surfed by a woman, she was severely injured and nearly drowned after a series of waves forced her into the water near Nazaré, Portugal. Although such an incident might have kept some surfers out of the water for good, Gabeira worked to recover from her injuries and resumed training with the goal of returning to Nazaré to attain the record. She succeeded in doing so in January 2018, surfing a sixty-eight-foot wave and thus setting a record that was eventually recognized by both the World Surf League (WSL) and the Guinness World Records. "To set the world record has been a dream of mine for many years," Gabeira told *Surfline* (1 Oct. 2018) following her achievement, "But of course, after the accident in 2013, it felt like a very distant dream. It took a lot of work to have a season like last year, to be 100 percent again, and to complete it with a Guinness World Records title is quite special."

EARLY LIFE AND EDUCATION

Maya Reis Gabeira was born in Rio de Janeiro, Brazil, on April 10, 1987. She was the younger of two daughters born to Fernando Gabeira, a leftist politician and former revolutionary, and fashion designer Yamê Reis. She has an older sister named Tami. Her parents divorced in 1999, and although Gabeira initially remained with her mother, conflicts between the two led her to move in with her father. Gabeira spent her early teen years living largely unsupervised during the work weeks, as her father was often away.

Gabeira began surfing at age fourteen, when a boyfriend introduced her to the sport. She did not initially have the confidence in the water that would come to characterize her later career. "I was scared of one-foot waves," she told Susan Casey for *Women's Health* (3 Nov. 2008). "It was challenging just to be in the ocean." However, Gabeira's surfing abilities improved quickly, and she soon began to take lessons at Rio de Janeiro's

Photo by Mark Thompson/Getty Images

Arpoador Beach, a popular surfing spot in the city. As her skills increased, so, too, did her devotion to the sport, which became a driving force for Gabeira. "Instead of buying shampoo I'd use the money I had to buy wax for my board," she recalled to Giuliano Cedroni for *Huck* (15 June 2009). When Gabeira was fifteen, she moved to Australia to continue her education as an exchange student. Although her parents wanted her to come home, she refused and eventually set out on her own at the age of seventeen.

EARLY CAREER

After leaving Australia, Gabeira moved to Oahu, Hawaii, an area known for its surf. Her experiences surfing at spots such as Waimea Bay were formative ones for the young surfer, who loved her sport but was unsure of whether she could pursue it professionally. "I didn't know I could make it," she told Cedroni. "But when I saw Waimea breaking for the first time I was sure that's what I wanted to do with my life. I said to myself: 'If I can do that I'll definitely be happy.'"

Over the next several years, Gabeira began to distinguish herself as a talented surfer, particularly in big-wave surfing. Unlike standard professional surfing, which encompasses events such as those belonging to the WSL Tour, the specialty of big-wave surfing entails riding waves that are at least twenty—and sometimes as much as eighty—feet tall. Due to the challenging and highly dangerous nature of big-wave surfing, Gabeira sometimes faced questions about whether she would rather compete in more conventional forms of the sport, but she always declined. "My thing is big-wave surfing, that's where I'm happy," she told Cedroni.

BIG-WAVE SUCCESS

By 2007, Gabeira established herself as a big-wave surfer to watch thanks to her seemingly fearless approach to the large waves she sought out. She won her first Billabong XXL Global Big Wave Award for Best Female Performance that year. Following her win, she earned the attention of sponsors such as the beverage brand Red Bull, which provided funding for her travels and equipment. She also established a strong working partnership with fellow Brazilian surfer Carlos Burle, who began to serve as her tow partner. Tow-in surfing—where the surfer is towed out to the wave by a partner aboard a jet ski or similar craft—enabled Gabeira to reach waves that, due to their size or distance from the shore, would be prohibitively difficult to reach by paddling. Such methods helped Gabeira achieve a number of impressive feats during her early years as a professional surfer. In 2009, she successfully surfed a forty-six-foot wave in South Africa, her personal best until 2018. She also won the Billabong XXL Global Big Wave Award three more

times consecutively between 2008 and 2010, and again in 2012. "Every year I feel more confident," she told Casey. "I just want to find the craziest waves that I can, get experience, and hang out with my heroes. And I'll just try to learn all I can from them." In addition to traveling and surfing, Gabeira appeared in a number of surfing documentaries chronicling the exploits of prominent professional surfers.

THE WIPEOUT AT NAZARÉ

Although Gabeira had succeeded in conquering numerous large waves, she dreamed of setting a world record for the largest wave ever surfed by a woman—a record that was, at that time, not included among the Guinness World Records. To prepare for that feat, Gabeira trained extensively in Brazil before traveling to Portugal, where she trained and prepared to set the record near the fishing village of Nazaré. The area off the coast of the village was known for having very large waves due to the topography of the surrounding ocean floor and had been first popularized among big-wave surfers in 2011, when American surfer Garrett McNamara set a world record there. Gabeira planned to use the tow-in method to reach the large waves and hoped to succeed in surfing one of them to set an impressive new record.

On October 28, 2013, Gabeira and her companions, including tow partner Burle, entered the water at Praia do Norte in Nazaré. After being towed out, she attempted to surf an eighty-foot wave that ultimately forced her into the water. She resurfaced following that first wipeout, but several later waves pushed her back underwater and tore off her flotation device, making it even more difficult for Burle to locate and retrieve her. Although he eventually managed to tow her to land, Gabeira had been unconscious in the water for some time and required cardiopulmonary resuscitation (CPR) before she regained consciousness. She also had broken bones due to the force of the waves that hit her.

RETURN TO SURFING

Following the incident in Nazaré, some prominent big-wave surfers criticized Gabeira for her attempt, arguing that she was not skilled enough to handle waves of that size, while others highlighted her demonstrated success in the sport and argued that even the most experienced big-wave surfers can experience devastating wipeouts. Gabeira herself focused on her survival, which she attributed in large part to her extensive training regimen, and her later period of recovery. "I was very happy to be alive," she told Matt Skenazy for *Outside* (3 Sept. 2014). "Still shaken and fragile, but I was happy that we went on that wave." After a period of hospitalization in

Portugal, she returned to Brazil to undergo further treatment and physical therapy.

Gabeira began surfing again in early 2014, initially limiting herself to small waves during a two-year recovery period that she spent primarily in Hawaii. During the months following the wipeout, she told interviewers that she no longer aspired to conquer Nazaré's waves. By 2016, however, she had again focused on setting a new women's big-wave record and was determined to learn from her previous attempt. "The fact I put my body back together again to a high level of performance was the touch of confidence I needed to overcome the fear and ultimately face those really big days," she told Lou Boyd for the Red Bull publication *Red Bulletin* (31 Jan. 2019). "I got to the point where I was super fit and I trusted my mind, knowing I was now a thousand times more prepared than in 2013." Gabeira moved to Nazaré, Portugal, in 2016, where she began to train to master the area's waves once and for all. A short documentary chronicling her return to the area, *Maya Gabeira: Return to Nazaré* (2016), was produced for Red Bull TV.

WORLD RECORD WAVE

Following her relocation to Portugal, Gabeira spent more than a year preparing for her mission. "I moved to Nazaré to be closer to the wave. I dedicated most of my time to the spot and I had years to focus on improving, on safety and on being around the best people to get where I wanted to be," she told *Surfline*. "That time was priceless, it taught me a lot." On January 18, 2018, Gabeira again entered the water near Nazaré, where she was at last successful. An official observer found that the wave Gabeira surfed measured sixty-eight feet and was the largest recorded wave ever surfed by a woman. The experience was a triumphant one for Gabeira, who had come back from a potentially career-ending wipeout to achieve her longtime goal.

Despite her success, Gabeira had a difficult time getting her achievement entered into the Guinness World Records, as the WSL had to certify the achievement first. However, the organization did not do so in a timely manner. "I went to the [WSL] awards ceremony, and that's when I realized it was never going to happen," she told Boyd. "My wave wasn't even shown that day. I realized I had to do something about it. I had to expose [the WSL] and put it out there publicly that the wave wasn't being looked at. I needed everyone to ask why. I needed to show everyone that women don't have the same platform [as men] for their waves to be judged." To call attention to the issue, Gabeira launched an online petition asking the WSL to certify her wave. In addition to amassing more than eighteen thousand signatures, the petition gained the WSL's attention. Eventually the organization certified the wave and enabled her achievement to be listed as an official world record.

PERSONAL LIFE

When not traveling to surf in areas such as coastal Brazil and Hawaii, Gabeira lives in Portugal. In addition to practicing her sport, she engages in a wide range of other physical activities to improve her strength, stamina, and ability to survive underwater.

SUGGESTED READING

Boyd, Lou. "Maya Gabeira: I Just Thought, 'This Is It, I'm Going to Die.'" *Red Bulletin*, 31 Jan. 2019, www.redbull.com/gb-en/theredbulletin/Maya-Gabeira-interview-surfing. Accessed 10 May 2019.

Casey, Susan. "Maya Gabeira: The Girl Who Will Surf Anything." *Women's Health*, 3 Nov. 2008, www.womenshealthmag.com/fitness/a19925873/maya-gabeira-interview/. Accessed 10 May 2019.

Feldmann de Britto, Kim. "Resurfacing: Maya Gabeira's Journey to a Guinness World Record." *Surf Simply*, 2018, surfsimply.com/people/resurfacing-maya-gabeiras-journey-to-a-guinness-world-record/. Accessed 10 May 2019.

Gabeira, Maya. "Maya Gabeira: Comandante." Interview by Giuliano Cedroni. *Huck*, 15 June 2009, www.huckmag.com/outdoor/surf/maya-gabeira/. Accessed 10 May 2019.

Haro, Alexander. "Maya Gabeira Talks about the Wave that Nearly Killed Her." *The Inertia*, 3 Oct. 2014, www.theinertia.com/surf/maya-gabeira-talks-about-the-wave-that-nearly-killed-her/. Accessed 10 May 2019.

"Maya Gabeira Sets Guinness World Record, Wins XXL Award for Nazaré Bomb." *Surfline*, 1 Oct. 2018, www.surfline.com/surf-news/maya-gabeira-sets-guinness-world-record-wins-xxl-award-nazare-bomb/35528. Accessed 10 May 2019.

Skenazy, Matt. "Maya Gabeira Takes a Breath." *Outside*, 3 Sept. 2014, www.outsideonline.com/1925936/maya-gabeira-takes-breath. Accessed 10 May 2019.

—*Joy Crelin*

Kuki Gallmann

Date of birth: June 1, 1943
Occupation: Conservationist

"Whatever is man-made can be somewhat reproduced," conservationist Kuki Gallmann told Allyn Stewart for *Town and Country* (24 Apr.

Photo by Louise Gubb/Corbis via Getty Images

2017). "The monuments to protect are the herds of elephant, the rhino, the forests, the natural springs, the life of the oceans." For Gallmann, the conservation of animals and wildlife is not simply a responsibility but also a calling. Born and raised in Italy but drawn since childhood to the continent of Africa, Gallmann later moved to Kenya, where she and her husband purchased a large ranch where they planned to live and raise their children. The deaths of her husband and her son, however, changed her priorities and the trajectory of her life. Gallmann soon established the Gallmann Memorial Foundation, turned her ranch into a wildlife conservancy, and began a wide range of efforts to protect the local wildlife from poachers and environmental threats, educate both children and adults about conservation, and provide support to local communities. Her memoir *I Dreamed of Africa*, published in 1991, called further attention to her efforts as well as to the family tragedies that fueled her dedication to protecting some of Kenya's most vulnerable species. "Once they go, they go forever," she told Stewart. "It is our collective responsibility to care for what is not ours to destroy."

EARLY LIFE AND EDUCATION

Gallmann was born Maria Boccazzi on June 1, 1943, near Venice, Italy. She spent her early years living in a village where her mother took refuge with her grandparents to avoid bombings during World War II. Meanwhile, her father, Cino, fought for the Italian resistance movement. Despite being captured by fascists and held in one of Italy's most notorious prisons, Cino Boccazzi managed to escape and ultimately

returned home after the war. A surgeon, as well as an avid traveler and mountaineer, he later authored multiple books, including a biography of the British military officer T. E. Lawrence.

As a child, Gallmann read avidly, an activity encouraged by her father, with whom she often read and recited poetry. She later credited her interest in traveling to Africa in part to her father, who told her stories about his travels in North Africa. After completing her schooling, Gallmann enrolled in the University of Padua to study political science. She ultimately left the university to marry, without finishing her degree. She separated from her spouse after about two years, however, and Gallmann and her young son moved in with her mother. Gallmann's parents also separated, and her mother began teaching art history at the University of Padua.

In 1970, Gallmann traveled to Kenya for the first time with her future second husband. The couple decided to move to Kenya permanently, with his two daughters and her son, in 1972. The blended family eventually purchased Ol Ari Nyiro, then a large cattle ranch in Laikipia County.

CONSERVATION WORK

Gallmann had long been interested in the welfare of animals, and she and her family had sought to prevent poaching and ensure the conservation of plant life on the Ol Ari Nyiro property. She immersed herself deeply in conservation beginning in 1983, inspired by the sudden deaths of her husband in 1980 and her son, an aspiring herpetologist, in 1983. "I had to do something that I wouldn't have done if my son had lived," she told the *Irish Times* (28 Apr. 1999). Following those events, Gallmann established the Gallmann Memorial Foundation, an organization dedicated to protecting Kenya's native wildlife, to educating visitors, and to promoting cross-cultural understanding. The latter was particularly essential to Gallmann, who feared that policymakers might make decisions affecting the natural world without possessing adequate knowledge of it. "The only solution was education, offering the chance of experiencing at first hand the land and traditions of their forebears and proving that one can and should coexist with the wild in harmony," she wrote in *I Dreamed of Africa* of the foundation's origins. In addition to organizing educational programs, Gallmann converted her property into the Laikipia Nature Conservancy.

By 2015, Gallmann's property encompassed a hundred thousand acres of land and was home to vulnerable and endangered animals such as elephants, lions, and rhinoceroses. Gallmann and her staff strive to protect the animals from poachers and provide veterinary care as needed and worked to ensure that animals had the ability to migrate safely across areas of land owned by Gallmann as well as those of adjacent local landowners. "We invaded their space, interrupted their migratory routes, mutilated them for their tusks," she told Stewart. "And, yet, patient and enduring, they keep trodding, fewer and fewer, along ancient routes guided by an ancient instinct." Gallmann likewise worked to combat erosion by planting native trees on the property and to educate local adults and children about nature and environmental sustainability through projects such as the Laikipia Wilderness Education Centre.

In addition to conservation of wildlife, Gallmann, her daughter, and her other staff have worked to protect the history and culture of local peoples and to promote peace among ethnic groups living in the area. The foundation has overseen some archaeological work on the property, established a school and a clinic, offered scholarships, and recorded songs, stories, and rituals of the local Kikuyu, Pokot, Samburu, Turkana, and Tugen cultures. They also operated a small luxury retreat for travelers, although the buildings were later burned down during a raid.

For her work as a conservationist, Gallmann was recognized with the Order of the Golden Ark, given by the Dutch government, in 1989. She has received a number of other awards as well.

WRITING CAREER

Gallmann initially became widely known outside of conservationist circles in 1991, with the publication of her memoir *I Dreamed of Africa*. Documenting her life from early childhood through 1989, the memoir chronicles Gallmann's marriages, her move to Kenya, the tragic deaths of her second husband and son, and the establishment and early years of the Gallmann Memorial Foundation. The memoir became a best seller and soon attracted the attention of film producers, who sought to adapt it for the screen. Although Gallmann was hesitant about allowing the story of her life to become the basis for a film, she ultimately agreed in the hope of sharing the beauty of her home. "Kenya doesn't have diamonds or oil, like some other African states. It only has its powerful natural beauty," she told the *Irish Times*. "If this film helps to bring people over to Kenya, then it will have been worthwhile."

I Dreamed of Africa was adapted into the 2000 film of the same name, directed by Hugh Hudson and starring Kim Basinger as Gallmann and Vincent Perez as Paolo. Gallmann served as a consultant on the project. The film performed poorly both among critics and at the box office, and Gallmann expressed some disappointment in the film, telling Hadley Freeman for the *Guardian* (5 May 2000), "Kim Basinger has given her own interpretation of me, and it's definitely not me." Nevertheless, the memoir itself

remained popular and was reprinted in 2007 and 2012. In addition to *I Dreamed of Africa*, Gallmann authored the memoir *African Nights* (1994) and the story collection *Night of the Lions* (1999).

SHOOTING

In April 2017, Gallmann became the center of international media attention when she was shot twice in the abdomen while driving on her property. The assailants were thought to be local Pokot and Samburu herders, who had been engaged in a longstanding dispute with government troops and landowners regarding the grazing of cattle on privately owned land. The issue had become direr due to a drought then taking place in Kenya, which rendered adequate grazing land particularly valuable. Laikipia County was marked by violence during that period, including the murder of a local landowner and the burning of buildings on various properties, including Gallmann's. In interviews following the shooting, Gallmann attributed the increase in violence to politicians, whom she accused of inciting violence against landowners during the lead-up to Kenya's 2017 elections. "The people who attacked me, they were militia," she told Tristan McConnell for the *Guardian* (18 June 2017). "Prior to every election I've seen there has been a similar build-up of violence." Gallmann survived the shooting and was flown by helicopter first to Nanyuki and then to the capital, Nairobi, for treatment.

The shooting called international attention to the political and economic unrest occurring in Kenya and prompted a debate in some publications about the role Gallmann and other conservationists of European origin play in East Africa. In an article published in the journal *African Studies Review* a year after the shooting, Graham Fox linked the incident to ongoing tensions between white owners of large tracts of land and African tribal herders and argued that white conservationists exert undue influence through their control of land—the last vestiges of colonialism. Fox noted that such conservationists secure funding from wealthy outsiders, direct development work, conduct research beyond government accountability, and exclude those who live by subsistence.

Despite such criticisms, Gallmann has remained adamant that her conservation and educational work in Laikipia is necessary and pledged to continue. "My aim is to try to prove that people and environment can survive together, you have to have a balance," she told McConnell. "The people have increased, the cattle have increased and the weather has changed. But I am an optimist in the capacity of the environment, if given a chance, to rejuvenate itself, and restore itself." After returning to the property, Gallmann resumed overseeing many of her ongoing initiatives and events, including the tenth annual Laikipia Highlands Games, an event for local athletes that is designed to promote both sport and interethnic peace.

PERSONAL LIFE

Gallmann married Mario Pirri around 1962; they separated a couple years later and divorced once it became legal to do so. The couple had one child, Emanuele, who died from a snakebite in 1983.

Gallmann later met and befriended her second husband, Paolo Gallmann, near Venice. The two began a relationship following a car accident that seriously injured Paolo, put him in a coma, and killed his first wife. Together, the Gallmanns had a daughter, Sveva, who was born following Paolo's death in a car accident in 1980. Gallmann has also two grown stepdaughters, Livia and Valeria.

SUGGESTED READING

Fox, Graham R. "The 2017 Shooting of Kuki Gallmann and the Politics of Conservation in Northern Kenya." *African Studies Review*, vol. 61, no. 2, July 2018, pp. 210–36, doi:10.1017/asr.2017.130. Accessed 8 Dec. 2018..

Freeman, Hadley. "'I Was Never Scared of the Elephants in My Garden.'" *The Guardian*, 5 May 2000, www.theguardian.com/film/2000/may/05/fashion. Accessed 9 Nov. 2018.

Gallmann, Kuki. *I Dreamed of Africa*. 1991, Penguin Books, 2012.

Gettleman, Jeffrey. "Armed Herders Invade 'I Dreamed of Africa' Author's Land in Kenya." *The New York Times*, 30 Mar. 2017, www.nytimes.com/2017/03/30/world/africa/kenya-kuki-gallmann-i-dreamed-of-africa.html. Accessed 9 Nov. 2018.

"A Lion in Her Bed." *The Irish Times*, 28 Apr. 1999, www.irishtimes.com/culture/a-lion-in-her-bed-1.178741. Accessed 9 Nov. 2018.

McConnell, Tristan. "Who Shot Kuki Gallmann? The Story of a Kenyan Conservationist Heroine." *The Guardian*, 18 June 2017, www.theguardian.com/global/2017/jun/18/who-shot-kuki-gallmann-the-story-of-a-kenyan-conservationist-heroine. Accessed 9 Nov. 2018.

Stewart, Allyn. "How Kuki Gallmann Became One of Kenya's Great Protectors." May 2015, *Town and Country*, 24 Apr. 2017, www.townandcountrymag.com/society/tradition/a9550775/kuki-gallmann-interview. Accessed 9 Nov. 2018.

SELECTED WORKS

I Dreamed of Africa, 1991; *African Nights*, 1994; *Night of the Lions*, 1999

—*Joy Crelin*

Destra Garcia

Date of birth: November 10, 1977
Occupation: Singer-songwriter

Destra Garcia is an award-winning Trinidadian soca singer and songwriter. Deidre Dyer, a writer for *The Fader* (30 Aug. 2016), described soca music as "the faster [paced], sexually suggestive kid sister of calypso," It was born, thanks to the pioneering musician Lord Shorty (Garfield Blackman), in Trinidad in the 1970s. Soca, the ubiquitous sound of Caribbean carnival, is a blend of African Trinidadian calypso with South Asian lyrics, melodies, and instruments. Originally spelled *sokah*, the genre is sometimes described as a contraction of "soul calypso" to underscore its connections to African American rhythm and blues. Garcia is one of the genre's most prominent stars. She earned the nickname "Queen of Bacchanal" after the smash success of early 2000s hits like "Whe Yuh Want" and the classic "It's Carnival," with soca superstar Machel Montano.

Garcia has managed to remain consistent in a volatile industry, and has been reliably churning out euphoric, undeniable dance hits for nearly twenty years. Over the course of her career, she has accrued fans all over the world, including some American pop royalty. In 2010, Garcia and Montano opened for Beyoncé in the superstar's first-ever concert in Trinidad, and more recently rapper Cardi B has recorded herself singing along to Garcia's "Bonnie & Clyde" and "Lucy."

Photo by Lionell Charles via Wikimedia Commons

Soca music has found new popularity in the United States, thanks to Caribbean artists like Rihanna and Nicki Minaj, who was born in Trinidad. Several years earlier, in 2010, Minaj had wanted Garcia to appear in her carnival-inspired music video, "Pound the Alarm" (2012). "I was shocked when Nicki came to Trinidad and was like, 'I want Destra in my video,'" Garcia recalled to Dyer. "But I wasn't there, I tour so damn much." Although it kept her from appearing in Minaj's video, Garcia's grueling, year-round touring schedule is part of her larger plan to make soca international.

EARLY LIFE

The eldest of Lloyd and Debra Garcia's four children, Garcia was born and raised in Laventille, a suburb of Port of Spain, Trinidad and Tobago's capital. She had a musical pedigree: her grandfather, Frankie Garcia, was a well-known Trinidadian jazz musician, and her father is a guitarist. Her family was also very religious. "Growing up, my mom did not allow me to wine"—gyrate one's hips to the rhythm—"in the house," Garcia told Dyer. "After Ash Wednesday, no soca was played. Certain things you can and cannot do." Her semiautobiographical 2015 hit song "Lucy" describes a journey from a pious childhood to being "loose," which Garcia describes as meaning free, sassy, and sexually liberated, as well as having "the freedom to just be yourself." As a teenager, she told Dyer, "you get introduced to carnival when you get your own money and you can buy your own ticket to fête, and then you get loose. Not because you're reckless, but because the music moves you. That's the power of soca."

Garcia grew up singing calypso, gospel, and R&B as a student at St. Crispin Anglican, a primary school. "My teacher, Janice Roach, was the one that found I had a good voice, a good tone, and she found that I was brave," Garcia recalled to Nigel Campbell for *Caribbean Beat* (1 Apr. 2019). "She wrote my very first calypso, 'Common Entrance,' and entered me in the primary schools' competition. And I won. My first try, my first attempt at singing in public after she trained me to use the microphone."

Garcia was just ten years old when she won that first competition. As a teen, she went on to win several junior Calypso Monarch competitions. The national Calypso Monarch contest is one of the major competitions held annually during carnival in Trinidad. Each year also brings a Soca Monarch and a Road March song, or favorite carnival song. Surprisingly, Garcia has yet to claim any of these titles. "It doesn't matter to me now, but sometimes in the back of my mind I ask myself, when I die and the future is looking back in the history books and they see [people's] names . . . and they don't see mine for winning a title, will they remember who Destra is? Will

they forget me?" she wondered to a reporter for *XX The Magazine* (10 Feb. 2018). She added, "I have grown to learn that the music is much more than a title. It is all about touching people with my music."

"IT'S CARNIVAL"

Garcia set out to pursue a career as an R&B singer, but a setback regarding a plan to record tracks for an executive in the United States led her to "try soca," as she put it to Campbell, instead. In 1999, Garcia appeared on the Third Bass (Adrian Hackshaw) single, "Ah Have a Man Already." The popularity of the song drew the attention of Roy Cape, a Trinidadian saxophonist who was with the Roy Cape All Stars until his retirement in 2017. Cape invited her to join the All Stars as a lead vocalist. With the All Stars, Garcia released a hit song called "Tremble It" in 2001. In 2002, she joined a soca band called Atlantik, where she formed a brief but successful songwriting partnership with Kernal Roberts, a singer, composer, and producer, and the son of calypso legend Lord Kitchener (Aldwyn Roberts). The two wrote the hit song "Whe Yuh Want," which appeared on Garcia's debut album *Red, White, Black* in 2003. The album also included "It's Carnival" (sometimes referred to as "Carnival"), Garcia's duet with soca star Machel Montano. Written by Roberts, the song samples Cyndi Lauper's 1984 pop ballad "Time after Time" and remains a carnival staple. Keryce Chelsi Henry, writing for *NPR* (18 Oct. 2018), described it as the quintessential example of a soca song. She notes its "pulsing beat" and its allusions to celebration. "The hook of the song serves double duty, demonstrating the genre's characteristic repetitive exclamations and instructing listeners to perform the Holy Trinity of movements to soca music—jump, wave and 'wine,'" she wrote. That year, Garcia won the Road March Title at Brooklyn, New York's Labor Day carnival and was runner-up in Trinidad and Tobago's Soca Monarch and Road March competitions.

QUEEN OF BACCHANAL

In 2004, Garcia released "Bonnie & Clyde," which she penned with Roberts, as part of the pre-release for her second album, *Laventille* (2005). Henry praised "Bonnie & Clyde" for its "unpredictable" elements. In the song, a woman waits anxiously for carnival so she can find the man she met the previous year. "Destra implies the celebration's omnipresence in her country by positioning it as a life-altering event where one can find (or lose) love, instead of simply praising its parties," Henry wrote.

In 2006, Garcia became a spokesperson for the major telecommunications company, Digicel. That same year she released an album called *Independent Lady*, which featured the hits songs

"Max It Up" and "Jumpin'." Her 2008 album, *Soca or Die*, features "I Dare You," one of the songs "I can't do a show without singing," Garcia told Dyer. In it, she sings: "Boy bring di wine, don't waste my time / Come test my wine / I dare you, I dare you." Henry wrote that Garcia plays up the song in live performances, inviting men on stage for a critique of their wine.

Garcia released the album *HOTT* in 2009, and *Welcome Back* in 2011. *The Queen of Bacchanal* (2014), was followed by *Bakanation* in 2015. The latter album included the hit song "Lucy," named after Garcia's "loose" alter ego. In it, she encourages people to shake off their inhibitions. The song quickly became a soca classic. Garcia was surprised by the song's success. "I thought, *Here I am telling a story about myself*," she recalled to Dyer. "But I didn't realize that it would touch so many people, because it's everybody's story."

In 2016, Garcia took a calculated risk. She released a crossover album, exploring pop, reggae, and electronic dance music (EDM), called *Queen*. She expressed fears that her fans might not like the new, less "loose" Destra, but she told Dyer that she felt compelled to branch out. "I'm just saying, in the years that I've been singing, I haven't gotten the chance to really explore my real God-given gifts," she said.

Garcia returned to her soca roots with her 2018 album, *Destraction*. That same year, Garcia, who was recovering from an ankle injury she sustained in 2017 when she fell off a stage while performing in Bermuda, asked her younger sister Kalifa to star in the music video for the single "Somebody." The video for "Family," which samples Nina Simone's classic "Feeling Good," features photographs of Garcia and her family. Garcia, alongside her mother Debra and her daughter, appears in the music video for "Doh Study People," a song about the pressures of social media. In 2019, Garcia branched out again, collaborating with the "Queen of Dancehall," Jamaican singer Spice, on the hit song "Trouble."

HONORS AND PERSONAL LIFE
As of 2019, Garcia has earned a bevy of nominations and awards for her work as a musician, including more than fifteen soca awards, six consecutive Copyright Music Organisation of Trinidad & Tobago (COTT) Awards, the 2013 International Soca Awards (Caribbean) Song of the Year Award, and the Black Canadian Awards Best International Act (Caribbean) Award for 2014 and 2015. In January 2018, the Port of Spain City Corporation presented her with the Downtown Carnival Committee Award for her contributions to soca and for promoting the nation's soca music locally and around the world.

Garcia and her longtime partner and manager, Brian Morris, had a daughter, Xaiya, in 2010. Garcia announced her engagement to Morris in 2017 by releasing a song called "Marry This Wine." The couple wed the following year.

SUGGESTED READING
Campbell, Nigel. "Destra Garcia: Queen of Queens." *Caribbean Beat*, Caribbean Airlines, Mar./Apr. 2019, www.caribbean-beat.com/issue-156/destra-garcia-queen-of-queens. Accessed 17 Apr. 2019.

"Destra Garcia, The Blooming Soca Queen." *XX The Magazine*, 10 Feb. 2018, xxthemag.com/2018/02/10/destra-garcia-the-blooming-soca-queen/. Accessed 17 Apr. 2019.

Dudley, Shannon. "Soca." *Encyclopaedia Britannica*, 25 May 2016, www.britannica.com/art/soca-music. Accessed 17 Apr. 2019.

Dyer, Deidre. "Soca Queen Destra Garcia Is Ready to Shake Up Pop." *The Fader*, Fader Media, 30 Aug. 2016, www.thefader.com/2016/08/30/destra-garcia-interview. Accessed 17 Apr. 2019.

Henry, Keryce Chelsi. "Destra Is the 21st Century's Liberator of Revelry." *NPR*, National Public Radio, 18 Oct. 2018, www.npr.org/2018/10/18/655849141/destra-is-the-21st-centurys-liberator-of-revelry. Accessed 17 Apr. 2019.

SELECTED WORKS
Red, White, Black, 2003; *Soca or Die,* 2008; *Bakanation,* 2015; *Queen,* 2016; *Destraction,* 2018

—*Molly Hagan*

Germán Garmendia
Date of birth: April 25, 1990
Occupation: *YouTube* personality and writer

Germán Garmendia is the rapid-fire Spanish-speaking star of the extraordinarily popular *YouTube* channel *HolaSoyGerman* (Hi I'm Germán). As of late 2018, the Chilean-born Garmendia enjoyed more than 34.8 million subscribers on the platform, making his channel more popular than those for pop stars Katy Perry, Taylor Swift, and Rihanna. His second channel, *JuegaGerman* (Play Germán), had more than 30.3 million subscribers, almost 3 million more than singer Ariana Grande.

In September 2011, Garmendia began posting short, comic video sketches describing elements of his everyday life. In one popular video from 2013 called "Los Hermanos" (Brothers), Garmendia applies his signature style—quick cuts, exaggerated facial expressions, and mile-a-minute speech—to the subject of what it is like to have a brother. "He rarely leans on snappy punch lines and largely steers clear of cruel or crass jokes," Lexi Pandell wrote for *Wired* (8 June 2018). "He's basically the internet's class clown." Garmendia's second channel, *JuegaGerman*, is "more personal," he told a reporter for the *BBC* (3 Oct. 2017). It began as a gaming channel but has become a catch-all for Garmendia's less curated material. As of late 2018, that channel is his most active. Garmendia has not posted a video on *HolaSoyGerman* in nearly two years. Garmendia told Pandell that the channel has not ended, however; "If I want to upload, I will," he told her in summer 2018.

Garmendia moved to Los Angeles in 2017 in hopes of pursuing a career as an actor and screenwriter in Hollywood. He brought with him some impressive bona fides including a best-selling book called *#ChupaElPerro* (2016), a book of advice for teenagers. As Pandell explained, the title is a Chilean expression that literally translated means "suck the dog," equivalent to the English expression "go to hell." The same year, Garmendia voiced a character in the Spanish-language version of *Ice Age: Collision Course* and appeared on the *Forbes* list of top-earning YouTubers in 2016, having made $5.5 million. In 2014, he was named Ícono Digital del año (Digital Icon of the Year) at MTV Latin America's Millennial Awards.

EARLY LIFE AND EDUCATION

Germán Alejandro Garmendia Aranis was born in Copiapó, a city in northern Chile, on April 25, 1990. He and his older brother, Diego, were raised by their mother, after Garmendia's father, a construction worker, died in a car accident on Christmas when Garmendia was three years old. He remembers his father from photographs and videos, if not from experience, Garmendia told the BBC. "People ask me, like, what is it like not to have a father, and for me it's like, you cannot miss something you never had," he said. He described his mother as a "hero," telling the BBC that she "did it all so we had everything she didn't have."

As a kid, Garmendia and his family moved around a lot, though never, in his telling, staying in one bad neighborhood long enough to be trapped by it. Garmendia, who learned English watching the American sitcom *Friends*, described himself as a "nerdy kid" with few friends. He was targeted by bullies for being "different," he said, though he now notes that his unique qualities are the key ingredients to his success. Garmendia spent his adolescence in the coastal city of Los Vilos, where, at thirteen, he formed a band with his brother called Zudex (later renamed Feeling Every Sunset). An average

student with no particular interest in attending college, he graduated from Escuela Técnico Profesional (ETP) in 2004.

HOLASOYGERMAN

Inspired by a vlogger friend, Garmendia posted his first video, "Las Cosas Obvias De La Vida" (The obvious things of life) on September 9, 2011. He reckons that it took him nearly two whole days to edit it. Something like forty people watched the video, he recalled to the BBC—a substantial audience for the site at the time. A couple viewers left comments encouraging Garmendia to upload more videos; so, he did. *YouTube* sent him an email each time he won a new subscriber. "Every like, three hours I got one subscriber," he recalled to the *BBC*. "My thought process was like, I can't believe someone just saw my video, liked it and decided to subscribe to my channel. But obviously I was like, super motivated. Every subscriber I got I was like, oh my god, I need to think of a new idea." Early enthusiasm for *HolaSoyGerman* was fairly benign, but then some fans began showing up at Garmendia's house, posting notes on the door to let him know they had been there. More recently, Garmendia had a problem with hundreds of people banging on his windows trying to catch a glimpse of him. In 2017, he revealed that once, a group of teenagers found his door unlocked and settled in his living room. He made a video imploring his fans to stay away from his house. For the most part, he has said, they have respected his wish.

JUEGAGERMAN

By 2013 Garmendia had over ten million subscribers. (He has been accused of buying followers, a charge he denies.) That same year Garmendia started his second channel, *JuegaGerman*. His first video on that channel featured him playing and commenting on the horror video game *Slender: The Arrival*. The video was about fifteen minutes long—much longer than his scripted, five-minute sketches on *HolaSoyGerman*. Over time, Garmendia has perfected his exuberant style. Videos, including his very first, feature sketches in which Garmendia exchanges rapid-fire dialogue with himself using quick cuts. In one video, titled simply, "Canciones" (Songs), he sobs theatrically over an acoustic guitar. In another, about teachers, he vamps across the frame with a lollipop and fake breasts. In her article about him, Pandell attributes Garmendia's success to the enduring popularity of Spanish-language telenovelas. Those programs, like *HolaSoyGerman*, she wrote, "melodramatized everyday life....Garmendia, it seems, filled a particular need at the nexus of cultural heritage and new media," she wrote. "His videos flirted not only with the exaggerated telenovela style but also with classic [Latin American] comedies, like the frenetic variety show *Sábado Gigante* and the 1970s Mexican sitcom *El Chavo del Ocho*, a slapstick series about a group of kids in housing projects." But Garmendia's global popularity—he was delighted to discover that Russian teenagers were watching his videos to learn Spanish—can be attributed to his "aggressively" normal videos, as Pandell put it. His topics are universal: siblings, music, relationships, food.

#CHUPAELPERRO AND ACTING

In April 2016, after the release of his book, *#ChupaElPerro*, Garmendia appeared at the International Book Fair of Bogotá in Colombia. Thousands of his fans mobbed the culturally hallowed event, purchasing a lion's share of the available 50,000 tickets. The festival's highbrow crowd was scandalized, though the festival has hosted other celebrities in the past. Reportedly, Garmendia signed autographs for twelve hours. The scene was reminiscent of one particular *HolaSoyGerman* meet-and-greet in Mexico City in 2014. Thousands of fans appeared to catch a glimpse of Garmendia, some succumbing to heat exposure. His handlers canceled the event, Pandell wrote, "when a riot broke out." One Colombian reviewer offered *#ChupaElPerro* tempered praise, pointedly noting that it was aimed at teenagers, not the adult literati. The advice the book contains, she added, is earnest and sincere. Among other things, Garmendia cites the virtues of travel, kindness, and taking a break from one's digital devices.

Garmendia signed with William Morris Endeavors (WME) in 2015 and voiced a character in the Spanish-language version of *Ice Age: Collision Course* in 2016. Like other *YouTube* stars, Garmendia has expressed an interest in pursuing a career as an actor—he is particularly inspired by frenetic comedians like Jim Carrey and Adam Sandler—or a filmmaker. But such opportunities have proved elusive. Hollywood continues to invest in internet-sourced talent, though it has yet to perfect the translation from *YouTube* screen to film. For instance, *Smosh: The Movie* (2015), starring the popular *YouTube* comedy duo, fared poorly at the box office. As Pandell put it, "There's no guarantee that followers interested in your free five-minute skits will pay to watch you in a feature-length film." She even suggested that some fans view such a leap as "selling out." Garmendia's success as an author and, perhaps moving forward, as a musician may portend that there are other, more fruitful paths for the *YouTube* star.

YOUTUBE FAME, PUBLISHING, AND MUSIC

In early 2018, the *BBC* ranked *HolaSoyGerman* the second most popular *YouTube* account in the world, despite the fact that Garmendia had not uploaded any videos to the channel since November 2016. He also published a novel called *Di Hola* (Say hello), about love and grief. He continues to post videos on *JuegaGerman*, though the content is less tightly constructed. Most of the videos involve video games. Garmendia plays the popular online game *Fortnite* in one video and offers an entire series exploring various scenarios of the game *Sneak Thief*. He is also a prolific purveyor of reaction videos, cringing and laughing at internet videos and clips from television shows. He employs a drum and cymbal to fully convey his reaction to a particularly embarrassing marriage proposal. These videos bear a striking similarity to *YouTube*'s biggest star, PewDiePie, a Swedish gamer named Felix Arvid Ulf Kjellberg who engages with memes and other internet ephemera. Unlike PewDiePie, who sometimes traffics in racism, anti-Semitism, and cruelty, Garmendia's videos are merely foolish. Other videos on *JuegaGerman* are styled more like vlogs. In one, Garmendia offers a tour of his first Los Angeles apartment. In another video, he tests the orthopedic Egg Sitter cushion, whose advertising claims you can use it to sit on an egg without breaking it. Garmendia sits on the egg, and it does not break.

Garmendia and his brother have a pop-rock band called Ancud, after a city in Chile. The brothers released their first EP, *Así es normal* (*This is normal*), in April 2016. Their music can be found on Ancud's *YouTube* channel as well as on the streaming service Spotify. On September 26, 2018, Garmendia released his cover of Ansel Elgort's single "Supernova" (2018) on his own self-titled *YouTube* channel. Garmendia's cover had received more than 1.3 million views by late 2018.

PERSONAL LIFE

Garmendia is dating Lenay Chantelle Olsen, a singer-songwriter and former MTV television host. Olsen is a *YouTube* star in her own right with more than 5.8 million subscribers as of late 2018. In October 2018, the couple appeared together in Garmendia's "Aniversario en Hawaii," on *JuegaGerman*. They live in Los Angeles.

SUGGESTED READING

Garmendia, Germán. "From Bullied Teenager to YouTube Superstar." *BBC*, 3 Oct. 2017. www.bbc.co.uk/programmes/p05hyj29. Accessed 13 Nov. 2018.

Jarvey, Natalie. "How Studios Are Cashing in on YouTube Stars." *The Hollywood Reporter*, 18 Mar. 2016, www.hollywoodreporter.com/news/youtube-stars-invade-hollywood-how-874812. Accessed 13 Nov. 2018.

King, Cecilia. "The Real Reasons Why YouTube's 5 Biggest Stars Became Millionaires." *The Washington Post*, 23 July 2015,

www.washingtonpost.com/news/the-switch/
wp/2015/07/23/how-these-5-youtube-stars-
became-millionaires-and-why-you-wont-be-
joining-them-anytime-soon. Accessed 13 Nov.
2018.

Matheson, Rosie. "HolaSoyGerman – German
Garmendia." *YouTube Famous: Making It Big
on the Internet*. Arcturus Publishing, 2015.

Pandell, Lexi. "Meet Germán Garmendia, The
Aggressively Normal YouTube Superstar Who
Wants It All." *Wired*, 8 June 2018, www.
wired.com/story/meet-german-garmendia-
the-aggressively-normal-youtube-superstar-
who-wants-it-all. Accessed 13 Nov. 2018.

—*Molly Hagan*

Johnny Gaudreau

Date of birth: August 13, 1993
Occupation: Hockey player

Standing five feet, nine inches tall and weighing barely 160 pounds, Johnny Gaudreau, the left winger for the Calgary Flames, holds the dubious distinction of having the lightest frame in the National Hockey League (NHL). The New Jersey native has nonetheless defied a lifetime of odds and doubters to become one of the league's most electrifying players. Selected by the Flames in the fourth round of the 2011 NHL Draft, Gaudreau had a storied three-year career at Boston College before making his NHL debut in the final game of the 2013–14 season. He has since wowed players, coaches, and fans alike with his dazzling array of offensive skills, which has been likened to "magic conjured in a flash," as Alex Prewitt wrote for *Sports Illustrated* (16 Mar. 2016). He earned All-Star selections in each of his first four seasons in the league, topping the sixty-point mark and tallying more than forty assists in each of those seasons.

Equally known for his on-ice discipline, Gaudreau received the NHL's Lady Byng Memorial Trophy for sportsmanship at the end of the 2016–17 season. A fixture in Calgary, he has balanced out his hockey talent with a humble demeanor that has helped him win widespread popularity around the league. The Flames' former head coach Glen Gulutzan described Gaudreau, who is nicknamed "Johnny Hockey," as "one of those guys that brings people out of their seats a bit when he touches the puck," as quoted by Wes Gilbertson for the *Calgary Sun* (26 Jan. 2018). "There are only a handful of guys in the league that do that, and he's certainly one of them."

EARLY LIFE

The second of four children, John Michael "Johnny" Gaudreau was born on August 13, 1993, in Salem, New Jersey. He grew up in nearby Oldsman Township with his two sisters, Kristen and Katie, and his brother, Matthew, who is sixteen months younger. His father, Guy Gaudreau, was an accomplished multisport athlete who played Division III hockey at Norwich University, in Northfield, Vermont. After settling in New Jersey, Guy helped open the Hollydell Ice Arena in Sewell, located roughly half an hour away from Oldsman Township.

Thanks in large part to his father, Gaudreau started playing hockey at a young age. In a self-penned article for the *Players' Tribune* (2 Feb. 2016), he quipped that his father "was sharpening my first pair of skates while I was still in the womb." He first learned how to skate at the age of two; his father would throw Skittles candies on the ice so Gaudreau would chase after them. Developing a natural love for the game, Gaudreau spent most of his free time growing up at his father's ice rink, where he and a group of friends would spend countless hours playing games of "shinny," or pick-up hockey. "Whenever he had the chance to be on the ice, he was on the ice," his father told Julie Robenhymer for *ESPN* (5 Feb. 2016). "That's when John's the happiest. That's what he lives for."

Gaudreau's passion for hockey was matched by his skills, and throughout his youth, he always played a year up from his normal age group in organized leagues. Still, despite often being the best player in his age group, he was repeatedly doubted and overlooked because of his small

Photo by mark6mauno via Wikimedia Commons

size. While Gaudreau was growing up, his father, who himself is just five feet eight inches tall, would feed Gaudreau and his younger brother steak, omelets, and chocolate milkshakes every morning in an effort to help them gain weight, but to no avail.

At age eleven, Gaudreau was passed over for a place on a regional select team that participated in USA Hockey's annual development camp. He tried out unsuccessfully for that team on four more occasions before earning a place on its under-sixteen squad, where he immediately became a top scorer. As Gaudreau wrote in the *Players' Tribune* article, "I was going to force people to ignore my size because of my production."

ROAD TO THE NHL

Gaudreau spent his freshman through junior seasons playing hockey at Gloucester Catholic High School in Gloucester City, New Jersey, where he was coached by his father. He led Gloucester to a state finals appearance as a junior, and then further raised his national profile in the summer of 2010, when he scored a slew of goals during an under-seventeen tournament conducted by USA Hockey. To better prepare himself for Division I college hockey, Gaudreau moved to Dubuque, Iowa, prior to his senior season to play for the Dubuque Fighting Saints of the United States Hockey League (USHL), the top level of American junior hockey. In sixty games with the Fighting Saints, he led the team with seventy-two points and guided them to the USHL title. "Even back then, he did things other players couldn't do," the Calgary Flames' general manager Brad Treliving recalled to Gilbertson.

Still, Gaudreau's future in the NHL remained uncertain, as many teams continued to express concerns about his size and ability to play offensively against bigger and stronger competition. After graduating from Dubuque, Gaudreau, then only five feet six and 137 pounds, admits that he entered the 2011 NHL Draft with few expectations. "My focus was never squarely on making it to the NHL," he explained in the *Players' Tribune* article. "I always just tried to advance to the next level, one rung at a time." However, the Flames looked past his physical shortcomings and selected him in the fourth round of the draft.

Upon reporting to his first Flames summer camp, Gaudreau was mistaken for an autograph-seeking fan by team staff members. Nonetheless, he again let his on-ice play speak for itself, and in the fall of 2011, he enrolled at Division I hockey powerhouse Boston College to continue his development. During the 2011–12 season, he led all freshmen and finished second on the Eagles with forty-four points, helping to lead the team to their third NCAA Division I

championship in five years. In response to a crucial goal Gaudreau scored in the national title game, longtime *ESPN* hockey analyst Barry Melrose said, as quoted by Chris Pawling for *NJ.com* (26 Apr. 2012), "He's tiny. He looks about 12 years old. But he's got hands of silk and he's got hockey sense. He sees the ice awesome."

DIMINUTIVE DAZZLER

Gaudreau would go on to have standout sophomore and junior seasons at Boston College, during which he also represented Team USA in international competitions. Among them were the 2013 World Junior Ice Hockey Championships, held in Ufa, Russia, where he scored seven goals in seven games en route to leading the United States to the gold medal. In 2014, during his junior season with the Eagles, Gaudreau played alongside his brother Matthew, then a freshman, and won the Hobey Baker Award as collegiate hockey's best player after scoring eighty points in forty games. (Matthew Gaudreau now plays professionally for the Worcester Railers in the East Coast Hockey League.) He subsequently signed an entry-level contract with the Flames, for almost $1 million per year, to commence his NHL career.

Gaudreau wasted little time proving his worth as a professional when, in his NHL debut during the 2013–14 season-finale against the Vancouver Canucks, he scored a goal on his first-ever shot. He went on to have a stellar rookie season, notching twenty-four goals and forty assists at the left-wing position to immediately establish himself as one of the Flames' top playmakers. He was named to his first All-Star team as an injury replacement and helped the Flames advance to the playoffs for the first time since the 2008–9 season. He finished third overall in the voting for the Calder Memorial Trophy, awarded annually to the NHL's best rookie.

Building on his rookie campaign, Gaudreau reached the seventy-point barrier for the first time during his second season in 2015–16, scoring a career-high thirty goals and amassing forty-eight assists in seventy-nine games. He finished sixth in the NHL in total points (seventy-eight) and was named to his second consecutive All-Star team. Earning the nickname "Johnny Hockey," he received attention around the league for his elusiveness, uncanny puck control, and on-ice creativity, generating unlikely scoring opportunities in high-traffic areas. Meanwhile, he became one of Calgary's marquee sports figures; his popularity there was such that he was asked to autograph everything from babies' pacifiers to Canadian coins. "I think he's subconsciously aware that he's a trailblazer for younger kids," Treliving told Prewitt. "He's saying, 'Look at me, I've done it, and I've been told I can't.'"

2016–17 SEASON AND BEYOND

Despite Gaudreau's electrifying play, the Flames failed to build off their performance from the previous year, missing the playoffs for the fifth time in six seasons. The Flames' head coach, Bob Hartley, was fired and replaced by Gulutzan. Nevertheless, prior to the 2016–17 season, the team showed their faith in Gaudreau as a franchise cornerstone by signing him to a six-year, $40.5 million contract extension. Gaudreau had a drop-off in production that season due to a finger fracture suffered in a game against the Minnesota Wild, which forced him to miss ten games. He quickly returned to form, though, earning a third straight All-Star selection and finishing with eighteen goals and forty-three assists in seventy-two games. The Flames, meanwhile, enjoyed a ten-win improvement from the previous year, but were swept by the Anaheim Ducks in the first round of the 2017 Stanley Cup playoffs.

One of the least penalized players in the NHL, Gaudreau was awarded the Lady Byng Award as the NHL's most "gentlemanly" player for the 2016–17 season after logging just four total penalty minutes. He would further solidify his place as a franchise cornerstone in 2017–18, when he recorded career-highs in assists (sixty) and points (eighty-four) and made his fourth consecutive All-Star team. His assists total led the Flames and ranked seventh-best in the NHL. The Flames, however, missed the playoffs with a disappointing 37–35–10 record, which resulted in the firing of Gulutzan at the end of the regular season.

Under new head coach Bill Peters, Gaudreau entered the 2018–19 season hoping to lead the Flames back to the postseason. Through the first two months of that season, he ranked among the top ten NHL leaders in points and assists. In the *Calgary Sun* article, the Flames' defenseman and team captain Mark Giordano lauded Gaudreau for his offensive playmaking ability and told Gilbertson that he "sees the game at a different speed" than other players.

PERSONAL LIFE

Gaudreau spends a good portion of the off-season with his family in New Jersey, where he is involved in a number of charitable endeavors. These include hosting an annual golf tournament that raises scholarship money for students who attend Gloucester Catholic. In 2017, he was elected to the Salem County Sports Hall of Fame.

SUGGESTED READING

Gaudreau, Johnny. "Here's Johnny." *The Players' Tribune*, 2 Feb. 2016, legacy.theplayerstribune.com/johnny-gaudreau-hockey-calgary-flames/. Accessed 26 Nov. 2018.

Gilbertson, Wes. "'Who Is This Kid?!': Flames Scout Knew Right Away Gaudreau Had Star Potential." *Calgary Sun*, 26 Jan. 2018, calgary-sun.com/sports/hockey/nhl/calgary-flames/who-is-this-kid-flames-scout-knew-right-away-gaudreau-would-be-a-star. Accessed 26 Nov. 2018.

"Johnny Gaudreau." *Hockey-reference.com*, www.hockey-reference.com/players/g/gaud-rjo01.html. Accessed 26 Nov. 2018.

Pawling, Chris. "Former Gloucester Catholic High School Star John Gaudreau Helps Boston College to National Ice Hockey Title." *NJ.com*, 26 Apr. 2012, www.nj.com/gloucester-sports/index.ssf/2012/04/former_gloucester_catholic_hig.html. Accessed 26 Nov. 2018.

Prewitt, Alex. "The Big Short: Pint-Sized Johnny Gaudreau Delivers Thrills." *Sports Illustrated*, 16 Mar. 2016, www.si.com/nhl/2016/03/16/johnny-gaudreau-calgary-flames-si-feature-best-small-nhl-players. Accessed 26 Nov. 2018.

Robenhymer, Julie. "Johnny Gaudreau Continues to Prove Doubters Wrong." *ESPN.com*, 5 Feb. 2016, www.espn.com/nhl/story/_/id/14660903/nhl-big-heart-overcomes-small-stature-calgary-flames-johnny-gaudreau. Accessed 26 Nov. 2018.

—*Chris Cullen*

Claudia Goldin

Date of birth: May 14, 1946
Occupation: Economist

Claudia Goldin, a labor economist and economic historian, pioneered research into the shifting role of women in the American economy. She is best known for her groundbreaking 1990 book, *Understanding the Gender Gap: An Economic History of American Women*. Goldin frequently describes herself as a detective, comparing her work to that of the famous literary character Sherlock Holmes. "You can see his mind at work. He goes out into the really dirty part of the town and lives there and hangs out and gets to know the [vagrant children]," she told Michael Fitzgerald for the *University of Chicago Magazine* (Nov.–Dec. 2014). "He collects all this and then sits down and comes up with a theory to help him solve the problem. That's what I do."

As a graduate student researching slavery in Southern cities, Goldin hitchhiked across North Carolina, digging through archives and gathering clues. Her award-winning work continues to lead her across the country in search of the roots of economic inequality as it pertains to race,

Photo by Eric Unverzagt via Wikimedia Commons

gender, and education. Goldin has published seminal articles about the effect of birth control on women's career and marriage decisions, posited the pollution theory of sexual discrimination in the workplace, and written books on such varied topics as public corruption and the free press, government regulation, and technology.

EARLY LIFE AND EDUCATION
Claudia Goldin was born in New York City on May 14, 1946 and grew up in a lower-middle-class neighborhood in the Bronx. As a child, she aspired to be an archeologist, but as a teen, influenced by a 1926 book about vaccines titled *The Microbe Hunters*, Goldin set her sights on becoming a bacteriologist. She attended the Bronx High School of Science and graduated in 1963.

As a student at Cornell University in Ithaca, New York, Goldin set out to study microbiology but soon became beguiled by other subjects, including history and the humanities. "Knowledge was deeper and broader than I had been led to believe at Bronx Science," she wrote in her 1998 autobiographical essay, "The Economist as Detective." "So little time, so many truths." During her sophomore year, Goldin studied with the economist Alfred Kahn. Kahn is best remembered for deregulating the airline industry in the 1970s, but as a professor in the 1960s, his enthusiasm for economics captivated Goldin. Goldin went on to graduate magna cum laude from Cornell with a bachelor's degree in economics in 1967.

ENTERING LABOR ECONOMICS
After graduation, Goldin enrolled as a graduate student at the University of Chicago in Illinois. She was interested in industrial organization and, inspired by Kahn, in regulation, but her encounters with others at the school encouraged her to broaden her scope.

An early mentor was the labor economist Gary Becker. Becker, who later became a Nobel laureate in 1992, was interested in the sociological side of economics—or rather, why people make particular economic choices. Becker, Goldin told Fitzgerald, "truly blew my mind open. I had never thought of economics the way he did it." Goldin worked alongside Becker as a research assistant. Becker later praised Goldin to Sophie M. Alexander for the *Harvard Crimson* (26 Apr. 2007), saying, "She's very good at the qualitative, at digging out data, interpreting data in light of economic analysis—not just putting down numbers but giving it an interpretation."

Goldin met another mentor (and future Nobel laureate) in Chicago, Robert Fogel. Fogel is remembered for studying the economics of slavery, though he had not yet published his work on that subject when he encouraged Goldin to pursue a similar line of inquiry in her dissertation. Goldin's dissertation was inspired by her roommate, a historian, and a 1964 book by Richard Wade called *Slavery in the Cities*, which argued that urban settings and slavery were incompatible. Backed by her research, Goldin found the reverse of Wade's premise to be true—that it was unlikely that the highly flexible system of slavery as it was practiced would have died on its own, even in an urbanizing country.

Goldin received her Master of Arts degree in 1969 and her doctoral degree in 1972. She started her career in academia in 1971 as an assistant professor at the University of Wisconsin–Madison.

THE GENDER WAGE GAP
Goldin continued to research areas related to her dissertation: slavery, Emancipation, and the labor of married black women after Emancipation. Eventually, she turned to the economics of family. Throughout the 1970s, Goldin studied the family as a unit but had an epiphany in 1980. She wrote in her essay, "I realized that something was missing," she wrote in "The Economist as Detective." "I was slighting the family member who would undergo the most profound change over the long run—the wife and mother." Sources regarding a woman's economic role in a family were thin. "Women were in the data when young and single and often when widowed," Goldin went on to explain. "But their stories were faintly heard after they married."

Goldin undertook a series of studies examining women's participation in the American labor force and how it had evolved over two hundred years. She published the result of this research, *Understanding the Gender Gap: An Economic History of American Women*, in 1990. It won both the 1990 Richard A. Lester Award for the Outstanding Book in Industrial Relations and Labor Economics and the 1991 Allan Sharlin Memorial Book Award.

In the book, Goldin identifies three specific eras of economic advancement for women. She argues that story of women in the labor force has not been one of steady progress but one of "distinct spells when the [wage] gaps narrowed," as Peter J. Walker put it in his profile of Goldin for the International Monetary Fund (IMF) quarterly *Finance & Development* (Dec. 2018). Those "spells" occurred in the early nineteenth century, as mechanization grew; the early twentieth century, as clerical work expanded; and the 1980s, after significant gains in women's higher education.

To wit, Goldin had joined Princeton University as an assistant professor in 1973, only four years after the school began admitting women. Six years later, she moved to the University of Pennsylvania, where she taught as an associate professor until 1985 and a full professor from 1985 to 1990. In 1990, Goldin was the first woman granted tenure in the Harvard University economics department; she is the Henry Lee Professor of Economics.

EDUCATION AND TECHNOLOGY

In 2008, Goldin published *The Race between Education and Technology* with Lawrence F. Katz, a fellow Harvard economist and colleague at the National Bureau of Economic Research (NBER). The book provides a history of American education and argues that a lack of investment in public higher education in the late twentieth century led to income inequality. The book examines that period through the lens of supply and demand: what is the relationship between the country's supply of educated workers and its demand for workers with technical skills in a rapidly modernizing society? Stephen Kotkin wrote in his review of the book for the *New York Times* (4 Oct. 2008): "The authors skillfully demonstrate that for more than a century, and at a steady rate, technological breakthroughs—the mass production system, electricity, computers—have been increasing the demand for ever more educated workers. And, they show, America's school system met this demand, not with a national policy, but in grassroots fashion, as communities taxed themselves and built schools and colleges." In the 1970s, technology began to outpace education. Communities had once taken it upon themselves to support high schools; no similar provision was made for higher education. This lack of investment, Goldin and Katz argue, has contributed to the wealth gap in the country today. *The Race between Education and Technology* won the Association of American Publishers' 2008 R. R. Hawkins Award for Excellence in Social Sciences, as well as the 2009 Lester Award.

LATER PUBLICATIONS

Goldin has published dozens of academic papers over the course of her career. Two of the most notable appeared in 2002. Goldin and Katz's paper "The Power of the Pill: Oral Contraceptives and Women's Career and Marriage Decisions" examined the effect of the birth control pill on the decisions of women in the workforce. The same year, Goldin published an NBER working paper titled "A Pollution Theory of Discrimination: Male and Female Differences in Occupations and Earnings."

The latter article challenges a model by Becker that posits that discrimination amounts to distaste, defined as a "desire for distance." Given that a vast number of men do not wish to physically distance themselves from women, Goldin argues that sexual discrimination requires a more nuanced model. Investigating the root of the designations "women's work" and "men's work," Goldin further argues that men bar female entry to certain occupations "because they feel that the entry of women into their occupations would pollute their prestige or status in that occupation," Goldin explained to Douglas Clement in an interview for the *Federal Reserve Bank of Minneapolis* (1 Sept. 2004).

In 2018, Goldin and Katz jointly edited an NBER conference proceeding titled *Women Working Longer: Increased Employment at Older Ages*. The book investigates why women, from the 1980s onward, have decided to remain in the workforce into their sixties and seventies. It examines such factors as educational attainment, work satisfaction, marital status, and retirement savings.

ADDITIONAL ROLES AND PROFESSIONAL RECOGNITION

Over nearly three decades, from 1989 to 2017, Goldin led NBER's Development of the American Economy program. She was the president of the Economic History Association from 1999 to 2000 and the American Economic Association from 2013 to 2014. In addition, she has worked on committees for various organizations, including the Fulbright Commission and the Alfred P. Sloan Foundation, and even served as an adviser on Social Security and for the Congressional Budget Office.

For her career achievements, Goldin received the Mincer Prize in 2009, the John R. Commons Award in 2010, and the IZA Prize in Labor Economics in 2016. She was awarded honorary degrees by several institutions and was elected to the prestigious American Academy of Arts and Sciences and National Academy of Sciences (NAS), in 1992 and 2006, respectively.

PERSONAL LIFE

Goldin and Katz are married. The couple enjoy hiking and birding. Goldin also trained their golden retriever, Pika, to be a competitive scent dog and a therapy dog.

SUGGESTED READING

Alexander, Sophie M. "Goldin Demystifies Gender Economics: Professor's Research Analyzes Causes of the Gender Gap." *The Harvard Crimson*, 26 Apr. 2007, www.thecrimson.com/article/2007/4/26/goldin-demystifies-gender-economics-gender-will. Accessed 11 Sept. 2019.

Fitzgerald, Michael. "Delight in Discovery." *The University of Chicago Magazine*, Nov.–Dec. 2014, mag.uchicago.edu/economics-business/delight-discovery. Accessed 10 Sept. 2019.

Goldin, Claudia. "The Economist as Detective." *Passion and Craft: Economists at Work*, edited by Michael Szenberg, U of Michigan P, 1998, pp. 98–112.

Goldin, Claudia. Interview by Douglas Clement. *Federal Reserve Bank of Minneapolis*, 1 Sept. 2004, www.minneapolisfed.org/publications/the-region/interview-with-claudia-goldin. Accessed 11 Sept. 2019.

Kotkin, Stephen. "Minding the Inequality Gap." Review of *The Race between Education and Technology*, by Claudia Goldin and Lawrence F. Katz. *The New York Times*, 4 Oct. 2008, www.nytimes.com/2008/10/05/business/05shelf.html. Accessed 11 Sept. 2019.

Walker, Peter J. "Time Traveler." *Finance & Development*, vol. 55, no. 4, Dec. 2018, pp. 41–43, www.imf.org/external/pubs/ft/fandd/2018/12/pdf/fd1218.pdf. Accessed 11 Sept. 2019.

—Molly Hagan

Henry Golding

Date of birth: February 5, 1987
Occupation: Actor

Henry Golding exploded onto the Hollywood scene as an up-and-coming leading man with charm, good looks, and charisma. Golding's rise was particularly meteoric as he had only released two films by the end of 2018—*Crazy Rich Asians* (2018) and *A Simple Favor* (2018)—and only one of which was a blockbuster international

hit. But many in Hollywood, as well as Golding's growing legion of fans, believe he has what it takes to become an extremely bankable movie star.

Henry Golding has a biracial ancestry: a British father and a Malaysian mother. Golding himself does not want to be defined by his ethnicity; he wants to transcend it while at the same time showing other Asian actors that there is a place for them too in American films and television. "I don't want to be defined as the *Asian* leading man," Golding said to Samuel Hine for *GQ* (13 Sept. 2018). "I want to be the leading man." Golding, however, also emphasized the importance of embracing his heritage, continuing, "If it means helping inspire other Asians to be leading men, hell yeah, I'll take it. You don't know how proud I am to have that associated with my name. Sadly, we're so underrepresented that we have to start with these labels to be proud of it, to normalize it."

EARLY LIFE AND CAREER

Henry Ewan Golding was born on February 5, 1987, in Sarawak, Malaysia. His mother, Margaret Likan Golding, hails from the Iban people of Sarawak; his father, Clive Golding, is from England. Golding and his older brother and sister spent their formative years in Malaysia, where their father worked as a helicopter engineer and their mother was a homemaker. Henry spent his days exploring the beaches of Malaysia's east coast until he was about nine, when the family decided to move to Clive Golding's home country, settling in Surrey, South London. "Everything was new," Golding recalled of the family's

Photo by World Travel & Tourism Council

world-spanning move to Sam Parker for *Esquire* (5 Sept. 2018). "The smells. The sweets in the corner shop. I remember distinctly walking to school for my first day of primary school and seeing the playground field was dewy. I'd never seen dew before. . . . So I put my hand down on it to play. I was like: *oh my god this is the weirdest thing.* That always stands out to me."

Golding's time in London was not easy at first. Being one of the few children of color in his school, he often found himself getting picked on and called racial slurs. But he stood up for himself, occasionally getting into fistfights. Then his fellow students began to leave him alone. He also found a passion playing soccer, which helped him fit in.

School was never particularly appealing to him. He has admitted in interviews that he enjoyed learning things on his own instead of being taught. He also developed a passion for cutting hair after getting a job sweeping up a barbershop on Saturdays. Before long, he was a respected stylist at an upscale salon on Sloane Street in London. Yet even then, he found in himself a desire to branch out, which was in part inspired by things some of his clients were telling him. Golding told Parker: "There were some clients from Malaysia who used to come in and they say: you'd do really well on TV, they love Asians with a British accent out there. I thought: that's interesting. I [remember] going back there in the summer and watching MTV Asia and thinking, that looks fun, I'd like to do that one day."

In 2008, Golding decided to go back to Kuala Lumpur, the capital of Malaysia. While there, he managed to find work as a television travel host on channels like Discovery and National Geographic. In 2014, he became a host for *The Travel Show*, a BBC program that took him to exotic vacation destinations. One of his most notable hosting gigs was when he filmed his *bejalai*—the Iban rite of passage into manhood—in the wilderness of Borneo. Titled *Surviving Borneo*, the six-part series was filmed over two months and premiered on Discovery Channel Asia in 2017.

CRAZY RICH ASIANS

In 2017, Golding received a phone call from director Jon M. Chu, who was then in the middle of a global casting call for the film adaptation of Kevin Kwan's novel *Crazy Rich Asians* (2013). After Chu was shown videos of Golding's hosting efforts by his accountant, Lisa-Kim Ling Kuan, he thought Golding would make an excellent leading man for Chu's film. Initially, Golding refused to audition, stating that he was not an actor and did not have acting experience. He later gave in, however, and went to the auditions in Los Angeles. Golding got the part after a second round of auditions, during which Chu told him to not be so serious and just be himself.

Despite Chu believing he had found the character of Nick Young in Golding, Golding's casting led to some online criticisms because of his ethnic background. The character does not have a white father like Golding does. Many critics charged that Chu was whitewashing the character by having a biracial actor portray Nick. Nevertheless, Chu and the film's producers remained steadfast behind Golding, believing him to be perfect for the role. "I think it's fair to question motives of why they're choosing me instead of someone else," Golding told Robert Ito for the *New York Times* (8 Aug. 2018). "It ensures that the studio knows, that everyone creating the story knows, that people are watching. . . . I never felt I wasn't suitable for the role because I was half-white. I've always seen myself as Asian, so I never had any qualms about that. I was much more concerned if I could act."

In the film, a Chinese American professor named Rachel Chu (Constance Wu) travels to Singapore to meet the family of her boyfriend, Nick Young, a fellow professor. On the way she discovers that Nick's family is immensely wealthy and that he is the heir to a vast fortune. During her visit, Rachel clashes with Nick's mother, Eleanor Young (Michelle Yeoh), a steely woman who believes that Rachel is not suitable for her son.

Crazy Rich Asians was Hollywood's first film with an all-Asian cast since *The Joy Luck Club* debuted to critical acclaim in 1993. Although the film had appealing newcomers like Golding mixed in with esteemed actors like Yeoh, a source novel that had sold millions of copies, a great romantic comedy script, and a $30 million budget, the pre-release press hinted at a general fear that it could very well flop. By the end of 2018, however, *Crazy Rich Asians* grossed more than $235 million worldwide, proved to be popular across demographics, and was nominated for a Golden Globe Award. Golding explained the widespread appeal of the movie to NPR's David Greene (15 Aug. 2018): "It's a story about Asians, but for me, it's the universality of the story in general. You could be Latino, you could be black, you could be Caucasian, you can be from Africa and realize that, like, the story transcends that of race. It's about love."

OTHER PROJECTS

After his star-making debut role, Golding found himself an in-demand leading man in Hollywood. His next film role—as the mysterious husband of Blake Lively's character in *A Simple Favor* (2018)—was brought to him by the film's director, Paul Feig. "I looked him up and found all these travel videos that he used to host and he was so charismatic and funny and charming. He was the perfect guy. I was like, 'He's Sean. He's the Sean role!'" Feig recalled to Evan Real for the

Hollywood Reporter (11 Sept. 2018). "But then I called [*Crazy Rich Asians* director] Jon Chu and said, 'You just worked with him. Is he a good actor?' And he said, 'He's the best. He's worked so hard and he's so directable.' From then, I was just in with Henry." Because of Golding's popularity in *Crazy Rich Asians*, his image and name were added to *A Simple Favor*'s posters and advertising shortly before it was released in September 2018. The film, a domestic comedy/mystery about a small town vlogger who investigates the disappearance of her mysterious rich best friend, received mostly positive reviews.

Following *A Simple Favor*, Golding worked on the film *Monsoon*, in which he portrays a gay British-Vietnamese man who returns to Vietnam some three decades after the war. Golding found the role appealing to him because he felt it would help challenge himself as an actor. "[*Monsoon*] is a much more subtle role," he told Parker. "It really stretched what I want to be able to achieve as an actor. It's the project where I found my feet, and felt like I deserve to be where I am." In December 2018, he began filming two films: the romance film *Last Christmas* alongside actor Emilia Clark and *Toff Guys*, a crime film directed by Guy Richie.

PERSONAL LIFE

Golding married Liv Lo, an Italian Taiwanese TV presenter and yoga instructor, in August 2016.

SUGGESTED READING

Desta, Yohana. "Henry Golding's Next Movie Almost Sounds Too Good to Be True." *Vanity Fair*, 18 Sept. 2018, www.vanityfair.com/hollywood/2018/09/henry-golding-emilia-clarke-last-christmas. Accessed 5 Nov. 2018.

Greene, David, and Karen Grigsby Bates. "'Crazy Rich Asians': Love, Loyalty and Lots of Money." *Code Switch*, National Public Radio, 15 Aug. 2018, www.npr.org/templates/transcript/transcript.php?storyId=638775885. Accessed 6 Nov. 2018.

Hine, Samuel. "Henry Golding, Leading Man and Lover of Expensive Timepieces." *GQ*, 13 Sept. 2018, www.gq.com/story/henry-golding-crazy-rich-asians-profile. Accessed 5 Nov. 2018.

Ito, Robert. "'Crazy Rich Asians': Why Did It Take So Long to See a Cast Like This?" *The New York Times*, 8 Aug. 2018, www.nytimes.com/2018/08/08/movies/crazy-rich-asians-cast.html. Accessed 6 Nov. 2018.

Parker, Sam. "Henry Golding Is Coming for Hollywood." *Esquire*, 5 Sept. 2018, www.esquire.com/uk/culture/film/a22991231/crazy-rich-asians-henry-golding/. Accessed 6 Nov. 2018.

Real, Evan. "Why 'A Simple Favor' Was the 'Perfect Next Step' for Henry Golding." *The Hollywood Reporter*, 11 Sept. 2018, www.hollywoodreporter.com/news/henry-golding-a-simple-favor-career-crazy-rich-asians-1142056. Accessed 5 Nov. 2018.

Ruiz, Michelle. "So You've Fallen in Love with *Crazy Rich Asians* Star Henry Golding." *Vogue*, 21 Aug. 2018, www.vogue.com/article/henry-golding-crazy-rich-asians-everything-you-need-to-know. Accessed 5 Nov. 2018.

SELECTED WORKS

The Travel Show, 2014; *Surviving Borneo*, 2017; *Crazy Rich Asians*, 2018; *A Simple Favor*, 2018

—Christopher Mari

Duff Goldman

Date of birth: December 17, 1974
Occupation: Pastry chef and television personality

"I used to call myself a pastry chef and now I call myself a baker," the chef, television personality, and entrepreneur Duff Goldman told Noah Rothbaum for the *Daily Beast* (5 Apr. 2018). "I really feel like my whole life I've been a baker masquerading as a pastry chef." That hazy distinction notwithstanding, Goldman has undoubtedly earned a reputation among food connoisseurs as one of America's most audacious and innovative bakers. He is the owner of Charm City Cakes, a cake business specializing in custom-made creations based in Baltimore, Maryland. Since officially opening Charm City in 2002, he has been credited with pioneering inventive approaches to making cakes, which has resulted in elaborate, one-of-a-kind creations that have repeatedly pushed the boundaries of baking and pastry arts.

One of the most in-demand cake makers in the country, Goldman was propelled to national fame in 2006, when he began starring on his own Food Network television series *Ace of Cakes*, which chronicled the daily operations of Charm City. The hugely popular series aired for ten seasons and opened the door to other television opportunities for Goldman. He has appeared on and hosted a slew of other Food Network shows, most notably *Kids Baking Championship*, which debuted in 2015. He later created a mini baking empire that includes a second Charm City location in Baltimore, a third in Los Angeles, California, and a chain of do-it-yourself cake-decorating studios based in Los Angeles called Duff's Cakemix.

EARLY LIFE AND EDUCATION

Jeffrey Adam "Duff" Goldman was born on December 17, 1974, in Detroit, Michigan. According to Goldman, his older brother, Willie,

Photo by Paul Archuleta/Getty Images

inadvertently nicknamed him Duff after repeatedly mispronouncing his first name as a child. Goldman spent part of his childhood in Overland Park, Kansas, before his family settled in Virginia. His father, Morrie, is a health club owner with a PhD in economics, and his mother, Jackie, is a multimedia artist from a line of creatives. His parents divorced in the mid-1980s, and his mother later remarried.

Goldman developed a lifelong love of food and cooking through his mother, who was also a skilled home cook. For Goldman, home life "usually centered around the kitchen," as he recalled in the book *Ace of Cakes: Inside the World of Charm City Cakes* (2009), which he cowrote with his brother. "Much time and care was taken up with buying, cooking, and of course devouring and savoring food—discussing it all the while." Further nurturing Goldman's love of cooking were the culinary icons Julia Child and Friedman Paul Erhardt, the German-born cook known as Chef Tell, whom he grew up watching on television.

It was not cooking but art, however, that initially captured his interest. Always fond of doodling and drawing, he eventually "found heaven in a spray can," as he put it in *Ace of Cakes*, after taking up graffiti art in his teens. Throughout high school, he partook in the illicit public art form, clandestinely spray-painting murals in various public spaces. When he was fourteen, his mother enrolled him in courses at the prestigious Corcoran School of the Arts and Design in Washington, DC, to harness his creativity. Still, in the ensuing years, "I walked a fine line

between the law and the needs of my creatively fertile mind," as Goldman noted in *Ace of Cakes*.

Goldman attended Virginia's McLean High School through sophomore year. The summer before his junior year, he transferred to Sandwich High School, located in Cape Cod, Massachusetts. During high school, he was active in such sports as football and lacrosse and continued to hone his artistic skills through graffiti as well as other art disciplines like metalwork.

CALLING IN THE KITCHEN

While attending Sandwich High School, Goldman continued working at a series of fast-food and greasy spoon establishments (at one point he had worked at McDonald's), in part, to earn income for his costly art supplies. These experiences ultimately prompted him to consider pursuing a culinary career, a decision that his parents did not initially encourage. To appease them, he agreed to earn an undergraduate degree before going on to culinary school. Consequently, upon graduating in 1993, he enrolled at the University of Maryland, Baltimore County (UMBC), where he studied history and philosophy.

During his junior year at UMBC, Goldman landed a job at chef-restaurateur Cindy Wolf's acclaimed Baltimore restaurant Savannah. There he was first introduced to the intricacies of baking and pastry production. Though mainly relegated to making cornbread and biscuits, Goldman became drawn to the methodical and scientific methods of baking, and the experience led him to resolve to become a pastry chef. After graduating from UMBC in 1997, he attended the Culinary Institute of America (CIA) at Greystone in California's Napa Valley.

At CIA, Goldman discovered a knack for baking and decorating cakes and quickly stood out among his peers with his artistic talent, enthusiasm, and ambition. "He was always innovative and the wild one when it came to ideas," Robert Jorin, his instructor, said, as quoted by Robert Gluck in the *Jerusalem Post* (1 Dec. 2012). "He was not the quiet person in the class. In the kitchen he got things done without hesitation." That single-minded determination led to Goldman boldly asking for and receiving an unpaid apprenticeship at the French Laundry, a renowned Napa Valley restaurant run by celebrated chef Thomas Keller. There he worked under pastry chef Stephen Durfee.

Upon receiving his baking and pastry arts certificate from CIA in 1998, Goldman left California to become executive pastry chef at the Vail Cascade, a resort in Colorado. He worked there for a brief time before landing a job baking bread and pastries at the Washington, DC, location of celebrity chef Todd English's noted restaurant Olives. There he worked under executive chef Steve Mannino. "The important part that all these great chefs taught me is how to dig real far into yourself and how to do your absolute best," Goldman explained, as quoted by Gluck. "It's about striving for excellence, making things as perfect as possible."

CHARM CITY CAKES

In 2000, after getting burnt out from long days at Olives, Goldman moved back to Baltimore and found work as a personal chef. Hoping to fund and make room for his dream of touring in a rock band, he launched his own cake business, Charm City Cakes, out of his apartment. Specializing in quirky creations, Goldman made several cakes per month as a side endeavor, mainly to help get the word out about his business. By 2002 it was pulling in enough money for him to quit his personal chef job and focus on decorating cakes full time. Charm City officially opened that year.

Thanks to word of mouth, savvy online marketing, and positive media coverage, Goldman's client list grew considerably, which enabled him to move Charm City to a bigger Baltimore location. Situated in an old church that has been retrofitted into a modern bakery, Charm City offers custom, made-to-order cakes for a wide variety of special occasions.

As the owner and chief creative force behind Charm City, Goldman has been credited with revolutionizing the art of making and decorating cakes. Charm City has earned widespread attention in the culinary world for its innovative, one-of-a-kind cakes, which are offered in an assortment of unique flavors, such as bananas foster and amaretto cream. The often-structural cakes are made with unconventional tools like paintbrushes, blowtorches, drills, and bandsaws, among others.

Unlike most cake shops, Goldman's small staff is composed mostly of artists and designers with no formal culinary training. This outside-the-box approach to hiring has resulted in elaborate cakes that have repeatedly helped redefine what is possible in baking and pastry arts. Their creations have included renderings of cultural icons, life-sized animals and cars, and three-dimensional specialty cakes featuring motors, lights, smoke, and sound. As Goldman told Anne Valdespino for the *Orange County Register* (4 June 2014), such baking feats are "an extension of the pursuit of excellence" and represent a commitment to making "the most amazing thing in the universe that no one's ever seen before—that's why you do it."

BECOMING A TELEVISION PERSONALITY: *ACE OF CAKES*

By 2005 Goldman had begun competing in the television contest *Food Network Challenge*. Struck not only by his outrageous cakes but also by his unique and engaging personality, executives at the Food Network had also expressed interest in a pilot pitch and eventually decided to create a weekly docuseries centered around Goldman and his team at Charm City. The series, titled *Ace of Cakes*, debuted in 2006 and quickly became a hit on the network.

Ace of Cakes aired for ten seasons over approximately five years on the Food Network, during which time Goldman became one of the network's most popular on-air personalities. Each unscripted episode was drawn from hours of weekly footage and chronicled the daily triumphs and travails of Goldman and his team. Cameras followed them as they rushed to meet tight deadlines making their elaborate custom cakes for a plethora of clients, which included sports, film, and television entities; private citizens; charities; and public institutions and organizations. Some of the more notable cakes showcased on the series included an edible replica of Wrigley Field, the Chicago Cubs' iconic ballpark; the Hogwarts castle for the premiere of the fifth Harry Potter film, *Harry Potter and the Order of the Phoenix* (2007); a recreation of the infamous bedroom scene from the 1973 horror film *The Exorcist*; and a model of the Hubble Space Telescope for the National Aeronautics and Space Administration (NASA).

The success of the series enabled Goldman to expand his business to the West Coast in 2011, when he opened Charm City Cakes West in Los Angeles. At the same time, he was recognized for his role as host with a nomination for a 2011 James Beard Foundation Award. The following year he debuted a do-it-yourself Los Angeles bakery, Duff's Cakemix, which allows customers to decorate their own cakes under the guidance of a team of helpers. A second Charm City Baltimore location opened in 2017, and two more Cakemix shops opened in California in 2017 and 2018. Particularly proud of helping other people to create in this way through Cakemix, he told Rothbaum, "I want one in every city."

EXPANDING HIS BAKING AND TELEVISION CAREER

In addition to *Ace of Cakes*, Goldman has hosted or served as a judge on such Food Network series as *Sugar High* (2011), *Holiday Baking Championship* (2014–17), *Duff till Dawn* (2015), *Worst Bakers in America* (2016), and *Dessert Games* (2017). He began serving as a cohost and judge, along with actor Valerie Bertinelli, on the Food Network program *Kids Baking Championship* in 2015. The show, which features children and young teenagers competing in various culinary challenges, "has arguably made him an even bigger star and famous with a new generation of foodies," according to Rothbaum. Meanwhile,

Goldman admitted to Rothbaum, "I never wanted to be on TV. I never chased this career. It just happened." That same year he published a cookbook, *Duff Bakes: Think and Bake Like a Pro at Home*, which features 130 recipes.

Another show starring Goldman, *Buddy vs. Duff*, aired on the Food Network in 2019. On the show, Goldman squared off against fellow baking icon Buddy Valastro, star of TLC's hit program *Cake Boss*, in a series of baking battles. He was ultimately crowned the winner of the six-episode baking competition, which "was, far and away, the most difficult thing I've ever done," as he said to Tess Koman for *Delish* (8 Mar. 2019).

PERSONAL LIFE

In January 2019 Goldman married his longtime girlfriend, writer Johnna Colbry, in a ceremony held at the Natural History Museum in Los Angeles. For the wedding, the Charm City team made five cakes.

An avid music lover, Goldman has played with various bands over the years. Additionally, he has been actively involved in numerous charities, including working with the Make-A-Wish Foundation, No Kid Hungry, and the Save a Child's Heart organization, among others.

SUGGESTED READING

Gluck, Robert. "No Ordinary Baker." *The Jerusalem Post*, 1 Dec. 2012, www.jpost.com/Jewish-World/Jewish-Features/No-ordinary-baker. Accessed 30 Apr. 2019.

Goldman, Duff. "Duff Goldman's Life Is a Piece of Cake." Interview by Anne Valdespino. *The Orange County Register*, 4 June 2014, www.ocregister.com/2014/06/04/duff-goldmans-life-is-a-piece-of-cake. Accessed 30 Apr. 2019.

Goldman, Duff, and Buddy Valastro. "Both Buddy Valastro and Duff Goldman Agree: Filming Their New Show Was 'Grueling.'" Interview by Tess Koman. *Delish*, 8 Mar. 2019, www.delish.com/food-news/a26767586/duff-goldman-buddy-valastro-interview. Accessed 30 Apr. 2019.

Goldman, Duff, and Willie Goldman. *Ace of Cakes: Inside the World of Charm City Cakes*. William Morrow, 2009 PRINT.

Rothbaum, Noah. "Celebrity Baker Duff Goldman's Next Act." *The Daily Beast*, 5 Apr. 2018, www.thedailybeast.com/celebrity-baker-duff-goldmans-next-act. Accessed 30 Apr. 2019.

—*Chris Cullen*

Gita Gopinath

Date of birth: December 8, 1971
Occupation: Economist

In October 2018 Gita Gopinath was named the chief economist of the International Monetary Fund (IMF), an economic organization under the United Nations (UN) charged with promoting international monetary cooperation. Although she made history as the first woman to take on that influential role, many observers noted she was simply a natural fit for the job, especially because of the considerable global economic uncertainty of the time. "Gita is one of the world's outstanding economists, with impeccable academic credentials, a proven track record of intellectual leadership, and extensive international experience," noted Christine Lagarde, managing director of the IMF, as quoted by Charlotte Beale for the World Economic Forum (2 Oct. 2018). "All this makes her exceptionally well-placed to lead our research department at this important juncture."

Gopinath's path to leadership of the IMF was marked by hard work and dedication. Hailing from a middle-class Indian family, she was devoted to her studies and excelled academically. After earning a PhD from Princeton University she pursued both research and a career as an economic adviser, serving in both governmental and institutional capacities and also as an editor of economic journals. She began teaching at Harvard University in 2005 and was named the John Zwaanstra Professor of International Studies and Economics in 2015. She became

Photo by World Economic Forum via Wikimedia Commons

particularly well known for her work challenging the wisdom of flexible exchange rates, a policy long supported by the IMF. This willingness to seek unconventional solutions eventually appealed to the IMF as the organization adapted to a turbulent global economy, and after taking over as chief economist Gopinath stated her intent to tackle major issues. "The one that is absolutely clear and present is that we are seeing the first serious retreat from globalization," she told Aaron Goldman for the *Harvard Gazette* (30 Nov. 2018). "I believe we are looking at a period of sizable uncertainty and a period where the downside risks are significant."

EARLY LIFE AND EDUCATION

Gita Gopinath was born in Kolkata, India, then officially known as Calcutta, on December 8, 1971, during the brief but bloody war with Bangladesh. Her father, T. V. Gopinath, was a farmer and her mother, V. C. Vijayalakshmi, ran a playhouse. She had an older sister named Anita. The family moved to Mysuru, a city in southwestern India, in 1980, when Gopinath was nine. The move contributed to her early mastery of multiple languages; already fluent in Hindi and English, she learned Kannada, the predominant language in Mysuru and the larger state of Karnataka, in a few months.

Gopinath attended a school called Nirmala Convent. As a child she excelled at sports but suddenly gave up athletics to focus on her studies after reasoning she would be more likely to find success that way. She also abandoned pursuits such as taking part in a fashion show and learning to play guitar. The dedication to academics quickly showed results: "The girl who used to score 45 per cent till class seven, started scoring 90 per cent," Gopinath's father recalled to Prathima Nandakumar for the *Week* (15 Oct. 2018). After earning her Secondary School Leaving Certificate (SSLC), Gopinath studied science at the SBRR Mahajana Pre-University College in Mysuru. She considered further pursuing science or medicine; but after becoming interested in international finance, she decided to study economics in college.

Gopinath attended Lady Shri Ram College of the University of Delhi in New Delhi, India, from 1989 to 1992. She graduated atop her class with an honors BA in economics and went on to earn an MA at the Delhi School of Economics in 1994. She then earned a full scholarship for a five-year PhD program in economics at the University of Washington. There her professor, impressed by her work, soon encouraged her to transfer to a more prestigious program and successfully lobbied the school to confer Gopinath a master's degree in 1996, though she technically fell short of the requirements. Gopinath transferred to Princeton, where she studied with

economists Kenneth Rogoff, who would go on to serve as the chief economist at the IMF from 2001 to 2003, and Ben Bernanke, who would serve as chair of the US Federal Reserve from 2006 to 2014. Bernanke later described Gopinath to Douglas Clement for the Federal Reserve Bank of Minneapolis's publication the *Region* (20 Dec. 2016) as a "very independent thinker" and "one of the strongest and most promising students I ever worked with." Gopinath earned her PhD from Princeton in 2001.

EARLY CAREER AND RESEARCH

After leaving Princeton, Gopinath took a job as an assistant professor of economics at the University of Chicago Graduate School of Business. As her academic career progressed, she also branched out into other ventures. In 2004 she began serving as an associate editor of the *Journal of International Economics*. She would maintain that position until 2013, when she became a special editor of the publication for a year. Also in 2004 Gopinath first became affiliated with the US National Bureau of Economic Research (NBER), as a faculty research fellow.

Gopinath left the University of Chicago to begin teaching at Harvard University in 2005 as an assistant professor of economics. She became an associate professor in 2009 and received tenure the following year. Speaking of her experience at Harvard, she told Goldman that she particularly enjoyed the "phenomenal people," including her students, and the "critical thinking and energy of this place." Meanwhile, she earned numerous fellowships, grants, and awards and continued to take additional advisory and research positions, as well as editorial roles. In 2005 she became a faculty associate at the Weatherhead Center for International Affairs, in 2008 she joined the research program of the British-based International Growth Centre, and in 2009 she became a visiting scholar at the Federal Reserve Bank of Boston. From 2007 to 2010 she was an associate editor of the *Journal of Economic Perspectives*, and she served on the editorial boards of the *American Economic Review* (2009–12) and the *IMF Economic Review* (2009–13).

In 2011 Gopinath was promoted to research associate at the NBER. That same year she was named to the World Economic Forum's list of young global leaders, boosting her profile as a rising star in the economics community. In 2013 she was named foreign editor of the *Review of Economic Studies*, becoming a managing editor the following year. Also from 2013 to 2014 she served as an adviser to India's Ministry of Finance. With Rogoff and coeditor Elhanan Helpman, Gopinath released volume 5 of the *Handbook of International Economics* in 2014. That year the IMF named her one of the top twenty-five economists under the age of forty-five.

A LEADING ECONOMIST

Over the second half of the 2010s Gopinath was increasingly recognized as one of the most prominent and respected economists of the time, both in the United States and internationally. At Harvard she was elevated to her named professorship in 2015, and in 2016 she became a member of the economic advisory panel of the Federal Reserve Bank of New York. Also in 2016 she began serving as an adviser to the chief minister of India's Kerala State. That appointment did stir some controversy, as Kerala was governed by the Communist Party of India and some constituents criticized her as a supporter of neoliberal economic policies. However, Gopinath saw "herself as not beholden to any political ideology," according to Andrew Mayeda for *Bloomberg* (22 Jan. 2019).

In 2017 Gopinath took on the role of co-director of the NBER's International Finance and Macroeconomics Program. By that time she was regarded as a particular expert on currency regimes, and her data-driven work was known for challenging established modes of economic thinking. For example, her research questioned the efficacy of floating exchange rates, a concept had been widely accepted since the 1950s, when noted economist Milton Friedman argued that fluctuations in a country's currency could help boost growth. Mayeda explained the prevailing stance of the IMF and other global monetary organizations: "Allow the currency to fall, the theory goes, and exports become cheaper relative to imports, so the country can sell more goods abroad and boost growth." Yet Gopinath suggested that such a view was too simplistic, with factors such as the dominance of the US dollar in international trade making the real economic effect much more complex. Her theories sought to focus on the practical effects of monetary policy rather than ideological underpinnings.

INTERNATIONAL MONETARY FUND (IMF)

In October 2018, Gopinath was appointed the chief economist of the IMF, succeeding Maurice Obstfeld. "This is a very exciting job for me," Gopinath told Goldman. "There is really no other place in the world where I can work with such a large number of highly qualified international macroeconomists, and that is a great source of excitement for me." She further suggested in her interview with Goldman that she saw the job—for which she took leave from Harvard—as comprising two distinct roles: research director and economic counselor. In the first capacity she managed a team of approximately one hundred researchers on the cutting edge of economics; in the second she served as the most influential adviser to the IMF's managing director on issues ranging from overarching policy to direct financial aid decisions.

Many analysts and commentators noted that Gopinath's research interests, and her willingness to challenge established economic thought, were assets at a time of much economic and political turmoil. In particular, the IMF and other economic institutions faced a significant worldwide shift away from globalization. As she assumed her new leadership position, Gopinath acknowledged the implications of this trend—and the potential path forward. "There is in general growing uncertainty about trade policy," she told Goldman. "While trade has reduced global poverty and raised livelihoods, its consequences for inequality, and on whether the rules of engagement are fair, are real concerns that need to be addressed."

Early in her IMF tenure, Gopinath often explored pressing issues in public-facing ways. For example, she addressed wealth inequality at a roundtable discussion with her counterparts at the World Bank and the Organization for Economic Cooperation and Development (OECD) in May 2019 that was filmed and made available online. In that conversation she noted that although income inequality had decreased globally over the last several decades thanks to gains in developing economies, it had risen sharply at the national level. She also suggested that the problem could be addressed, in part, by focusing on the economic status of women, citing IMF research to that point.

Gopinath also coauthored an *IMF blog* post (23 May 2019) warning of the negative impacts of the brewing trade war between the United States and China. The piece, which concluded that consumers in both countries were most hurt by such a conflict, was considered unusual in its direct criticism of prevailing US policy (the United States is the chief funder of the IMF and thus holds the most sway over the organization). The previous month the IMF had reduced its annual forecast of global economic growth to the lowest level seen since the 2008 global financial crisis, in part, due to rising tariffs.

PERSONAL LIFE

In 1999 Gopinath married Iqbal Dhaliwal, a civil servant who later became the executive director of the Abdul Latif Jameel Poverty Action Lab (J-PAL) at the Massachusetts Institute of Technology (MIT). The couple, who had a son named Rohil, met at the Delhi School of Economics. Even while living in the United States and often traveling the world, Gopinath maintained close ties to her heritage. "She stays connected with our relatives and friends in India. She still prefers simple food," her father told Nandakumar.

SUGGESTED READING

Beale, Charlotte. "Gita Gopinath Will Be IMF's First Female Chief Economist." *World Economic Forum*, 2 Oct. 2018, www.weforum.org/agenda/2018/10/gita-gopinath-appointed-as-imf-chief-economist/. Accessed 11 June 2019.

Cerutti, Eugenio, Gita Gopinath, and Adil Mohommad. "The Impact of US-China Trade Tensions." *IMFBlog*, 23 May 2019, blogs.imf.org/2019/05/23/the-impact-of-us-china-trade-tensions/. Accessed 10 June 2019.

Gopinath, Gita. "From Harvard to the IMF." Interview by Aaron Goldman. *The Harvard Gazette*, 30 Nov. 2018, news.harvard.edu/gazette/story/2018/11/from-harvard-to-the-imf-gita-gopinath-reflects-on-the-challenges-ahead/. Accessed 10 June 2019.

Gopinath, Gita. "Interview with Gita Gopinath." Interview by Douglas Clement. *The Region*, Federal Reserve Bank of Minneapolis, 20 Dec. 2016, www.minneapolisfed.org/publications/the-region/interview-with-gita-gopinath. Accessed 10 June 2019.

Mayeda, Andrew. "No Idea Is Off Limits for IMF's First Woman Chief Economist." *Bloomberg*, 22 Jan. 2019, www.bloomberg.com/news/articles/2019-01-22/nothing-s-taboo-for-new-imf-chief-economist-first-woman-in-job. Accessed 10 June 2019.

Murray, Brendan. "IMF Says US Is Paying China Tariff Costs, Contrary to Trump's Claim." *Bloomberg*, 23 May 2019, www.bloomberg.com/news/articles/2019-05-23/imf-says-u-s-paying-china-tariff-costs-contrary-to-trump-view. Accessed 10 June 2019.

Nandakumar, Prathima. "Gita Gopinath: From a Middle-Class Indian Girl to IMF's Chief Economist." *The Week*, 15 Oct. 2018, www.theweek.in/theweek/specials/2018/10/12/gita-gopinath-from-a-middle-class-indian-girl-to-imf-chief-economist.html. Accessed 11 June 2019.

—*Molly Hagan*

Ludwig Göransson

Date of birth: September 1, 1984
Occupation: Composer

When Swedish composer Ludwig Göransson enrolled in the film and television scoring program at the University of Southern California (USC) in 2007, he had no idea that just over a decade later, he would compose the score for one of the highest-grossing films of the year. "It definitely feels like I'm living a dream," he told Mesfin Fekadu for *AP News* (21 Nov. 2018).

"But I try not to pinch myself because I don't want to wake up." Having begun his career as an assistant to established composer Theodore Shapiro, Göransson composed music for television shows such as *Community* and *New Girl* before launching a productive partnership with director and fellow USC alumnus Ryan Coogler, for whom he would compose scores for the films *Fruitvale Station* (2013), *Creed* (2015), and the blockbuster Marvel superhero film *Black Panther* (2018).

Alongside such successes, which have earned him award nominations and widespread acclaim in his field, Göransson has established a second career as a producer for recording artists such as Childish Gambino, also known as actor-comedian Donald Glover. With the success of albums such as Childish Gambino's *Awaken, My Love!* (2016), Göransson has demonstrated the rare ability to juggle multiple careers while excelling in each. "My life has been running at a crazy tempo since I came here," he told Martin Brusewitz for *Scandinavian Traveler* (18 Oct. 2018). He added, "I've never stood still, just kept moving."

EARLY LIFE AND EDUCATION

Göransson was born on August 31, 1984, and raised in Linköping, Sweden. His mother was a botanist, while his father taught guitar. Following his father's example, Göransson began to learn to play guitar at the age of seven but only pursued playing the instrument seriously a couple years later, when he discovered and drew inspiration from the heavy metal band Metallica. "I wanted to be the best guitar player in the world," he recalled to Fekadu. Göransson's focus shifted somewhat, however, after his father gave him a portable tape recorder that allowed him to record his own songs. Göransson began to write his own music, developing skills that shaped his career to come.

After completing his secondary schooling, Göransson enrolled in the Royal College of Music in Stockholm, Sweden, where he studied jazz. Following his graduation, he toured Europe as part of a jazz quintet before traveling to the United States to join the graduate program in scoring film and television at the USC Thornton School of Music. "It was the first time I'd been in the US," Göransson told Brusewitz. "The first two years were very difficult." While at USC, he met Ryan Coogler, a fellow student and aspiring filmmaker who would go on to become a critically acclaimed director of feature films. Göransson's early work as a composer of film scores included the score for Coogler's 2009 short film *Locks*. Göransson completed his training at USC in 2008.

EARLY CAREER

After completing the film and television scoring program at USC, Göransson began to assist Theodore Shapiro, a composer known for his work scoring comedy films, such as *Wet Hot American Summer* (2001), *Old School* (2003), *Idiocracy* (2006), and *Blades of Glory* (2007). His first project with Shapiro was *Tropic Thunder* (2008), for which he worked as a programmer. "My first day at work was basically just to sit and watch Teddy record the score with a 100-piece orchestra while he was getting input from Ben Stiller. It felt a bit surreal," Göransson told Diana Kelly for *SCENE* magazine (2014). Shapiro was impressed by Göransson's skills and unique point of view as a composer, and the two continued to work together for the next several years, collaborating on films such as *Marley & Me* (2008) and *Year One* (2009).

Following a recommendation from Shapiro, Göransson came to the attention of the creative team behind *Community*, a television situation comedy set to air on NBC. He was ultimately hired as the composer for the series, which became his first major television project. "I record everything myself," he told Ted Drozdowski for *BMI* (25 June 2012) of the process of writing music for the show. "I play bass, guitar and keyboard. Every now and then they do spoof episodes of something like *Star Wars* or *Lord of the Rings* or *Glee*, and the show's creators know how important it is to have a big orchestral score for those, so they pay for me to go up to use the SeattleMusic film scoring orchestra." Göransson worked on *Community* from 2009 through 2015, remaining with the series following its cancellation by NBC and move to Yahoo Screen for its sixth season.

Göransson's work on *Community* both represented the beginning of a productive career as a composer for comedy series and enabled him to develop one of the most significant creative partnerships of his early career. The series' ensemble cast included Donald Glover, an actor and standup comic who also raps under the name Childish Gambino and had released several mixtapes already. During and after their time working together on *Community*, from which Glover departed in 2014, Göransson and Glover collaborated extensively on musical projects that earned the pair widespread popularity and critical acclaim.

TELEVISION WORK

Göransson's work on *Community* demonstrated that he was a talented composer well suited to writing music appropriate for television, and he went on to contribute music to the series *Satisfaction* (2014–15). In 2011, while still working on *Community*, he began to compose scores for the television comedies *Happy Endings* and *New Girl*, ultimately working on three different shows at once. While balancing multiple projects may have proven difficult for some composers, Göransson did not struggle to manage his various responsibilities. "It's about being organized," he explained to Drozdowski. "I have my schedule built so I work on each show for two days a week. I guess I've got my schedule set up so it works pretty fine." Göransson worked on sixteen episodes of *Happy Endings* (2011–13) in 2011 and 2012, but he remained with *New Girl* until the show's conclusion in 2018.

Additionally, Göransson contributed music to shows such as *Playing House*, the *Red Band Society* pilot, and *Survivor's Remorse*. In 2016 he began to compose the score for *Angie Tribeca*, a detective comedy series airing on TBS. That year also saw the premiere of Glover's dramedy *Atlanta*, to which Göransson also contributed. In 2018 he began to provide music for the Netflix series *Patriot Act with Hasan Minhaj*, and was selected as the composer for *The Mandalorian*, the first ever life-action *Star Wars* television series.

FILM SCORES

As Göransson established himself as a sought-after television composer, he continued to collaborate with Shapiro, with whom he worked on the scores for films such as *We're the Millers* (2013) and *Central Intelligence* (2016). His experiences at USC likewise proved key to his continued career development, as Coogler enlisted Göransson to compose the score for his 2013 feature film, *Fruitvale Station*. The film earned widespread critical acclaim, making Coogler one of Hollywood's most talked-about young directors, and Göransson's score was nominated for the 2014 Black Reel Award for Outstanding Score. Coogler and Göransson continued to work together over the following years, collaborating again on the 2015 film *Creed*.

A sequel to the Rocky Balboa film franchise, *Creed* posed an intriguing challenge for Göransson, in part because of the iconic nature of the earlier Rocky films' scores. In composing music for *Creed*, he sought to balance throwbacks to those well-known earlier pieces with unique material that underscored the film's status as a new work. Göransson was also responsible for cowriting original songs for actor Tessa Thompson to perform in her role as singer Bianca, one of the film's major characters. "I wrote all that music with Tessa before we started shooting. She and I talked to Ryan, read the script," he told Sam Coffey for *Awards Circuit* (16 Dec. 2015). He added, "We only had 10 DAYS to write all these songs that were supposed to be worthy of a young, up-and-coming, buzz-worthy Philly artist. We had to create not only the music, but the artist Bianca, what her signature sound would be." Göransson himself appeared on screen in

Creed as a member of Bianca's band, and several of the songs he cowrote for the film went on to be considered or nominated for awards for best original song.

BLACK PANTHER

Following *Creed*, Göransson went on to score the films *Everything, Everything* (2017), *Death Wish* (2018), *Venom* (2018), and *Creed II* (2018), among others. His most significant project to date, however, was the score for 2018's *Black Panther*, an installment in the Marvel Cinematic Universe of superhero films. Because the head of Marvel Studios, Kevin Feige, was a fan of *Creed*, Coogler was brought on to direct the high-profile project. "Feige also loved the music, so it was no problem when Ryan asked to have me on board," Göransson explained to Brusewitz about the origins of his involvement. "Otherwise, it might have been difficult. I hadn't worked on such a large production before and in Hollywood, people are nervous about bringing in inexperienced people. Everyone's afraid of losing their jobs."

In preparation for scoring *Black Panther*, which is set in the hidden, futuristic African country of Wakanda, Göransson traveled to South Africa and Senegal to meet with musicians and study local styles of music. The process of scoring the film proved to be complex, as *Black Panther* was set to feature both a score and a soundtrack curated by hip-hop artist Kendrick Lamar. Göransson worked to ensure that the soundtrack songs featured in the film and the score blended well, capturing the energy and emotions of the film. His work on the score earned him significant praise following the film's release early in 2018, and the score was later nominated for the 2019 Grammy Award for Best Score Soundtrack for Visual Media and the Golden Globe Award for Best Original Score–Motion Picture.

PRODUCER

Alongside his work in film and television scoring, Göransson expanded his career in a direction taken by few, if any, other professionals in his field. "Something that no one else is doing is tackling both sides of music in terms of film scoring and producing artists," he told Kelly. "I'm spending half of the day by myself writing new film scores and the other half of the day producing music." Göransson has produced music for artists such as Haim, Chance the Rapper, and Vince Staples; however, most of Göransson's work as a producer has come from collaborations with Glover in his role as rapper Childish Gambino, including the mixtapes *Culdesac* (2010) and *STN MTN/Kauai* (2014), the extended-play (EP) release *EP* (2011), and the albums *Camp* (2011) and *Because the Internet* (2013). "What's really fun, working with Donald, is he's such a Renaissance man. You never know where he's going to go, what he's going to do," Göransson told Fekadu. "Every project is musically very different from each other, but I still feel like they're emotionally very connected." Göransson appeared as himself in Glover's 2013 short film *Clapping for the Wrong Reasons*, released in conjunction with *Because the Internet*, and Glover also referenced their creative partnership in a line in the Childish Gambino single "Bonfire": "I put in work, ask Ludwig."

The greatest critical recognition for Göransson and Glover came following the release of Childish Gambino's 2016 album, *Awaken, My Love!* Unlike the artist's earlier recordings, *Awaken, My Love!* was a funk album that drew inspiration from the groundbreaking artists of the 1970s. The album was nominated for the Grammy Award for Album of the Year 2017, while the single "Redbone" was nominated for the awards for Record of the Year 2017 and Best R & B Song. The pair also received Grammy nominations for the 2018 songs "This Is America," for Record of the Year and Song of the Year, and "Feels Like Summer," for Best R & B Song.

In addition to composing and producing music for others, Göransson has written and performed his own original music under the name Ludovin. He released a six-song EP, *How to Find a Party*, in 2013. He lives in Los Angeles, California.

SUGGESTED READING

Agard, Chancellor. "*Black Panther* to 'This Is America': Composer Ludwig Göransson Reflects on His Prolific 2018." *Entertainment Weekly*, 14 Dec. 2018, ew.com/music/2018/12/14/ludwig-goransson-this-is-america-2018-interview/amp. Accessed 16 Dec. 2018.

Brusewitz, Martin. "Hollywood's New Music Man—Meet: Ludwig Göransson." *Scandinavian Traveler*, 18 Oct. 2018, scandinaviantraveler.com/en/people/hollywoods-new-music-man-meet-ludwig-goransson. Accessed 16 Dec. 2018.

Fekadu, Mesfin. "Ludwig Goransson Is Having the Best Year Ever. Period." *AP News*, 21 Nov. 2018, www.apnews.com/897fe0ea169b45359dee320f62afc045. Accessed 16 Dec. 2018.

Göransson, Ludwig. "*Community*: Exclusive Interview with Composer Ludwig Göransson." By Oscar Harding. *WhatCulture*, 31 Jan. 2013, whatculture.com/amp/tv/community-exclusive-interview-with-composer-ludwig-goransson. Accessed 16 Dec. 2018.

Göransson, Ludwig. "Interview: 'Creed' Composer Ludwig Göransson Talks to Score." By Sam Coffey. *Awards Circuit*, 16 Dec. 2015, www.awardscircuit.com/2015/12/16/

interview-creed-composer-ludwig-goransson-talks-score. Accessed 16 Dec. 2018.

Göransson, Ludwig. "10 Questions: Ludwig Göransson." Interview by Ted Drozdowski. *BMI*, 25 June 2012, www.bmi.com/news/entry/10_questions_ludwig_goeransson. Accessed 16 Dec. 2018.

Kelly, Diana. "Ludwig Göransson." *SCENE*, 2014, dianakelly.com/wp-content/uploads/2014/07/ludwig.pdf. Accessed 16 Dec. 2018.

SELECTED WORKS

Community, 2009–15; *Happy Endings*, 2011–12; *New Girl*, 2011–18; *Fruitvale Station*, 2013; *Creed*, 2015; *Angie Tribeca*, 2016–; *Black Panther*, 2018; *Venom*, 2018; *Creed II*, 2018

—Joy Crelin

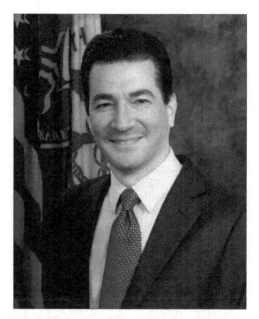

Photo by United States Government via Wikimedia Commons

Scott Gottlieb

Date of birth: June 11, 1972
Occupation: Physician and former government official

Dr. Scott Gottlieb served as commissioner of the US Food and Drug Administration (FDA) from May 2017 until his resignation in March 2019. The FDA regulates food, drugs, tobacco, medical devices, and cosmetics, among other things—accounting for 20 percent of American consumer spending each year. Powerful industries like the pharmaceutical and tobacco industries commonly complain that the agency takes too long to approve products, while consumer groups lobby for better quality control.

During his tenure as commissioner, Gottlieb surprised critics by proposing aggressive measures to address tobacco addiction, working to curb the opioid epidemic, and seeking to increase the availability of generic drugs. He had previously served as a deputy commissioner of the FDA during the George W. Bush administration at which time he was battling cancer. But most of his experience came from the business sector, working as a consultant for major pharmaceutical companies and investment banks and as a venture capitalist. The middle course he took at the FDA left a mixed record.

EARLY LIFE AND EDUCATION

Gottlieb was born on June 11, 1972 and grew up in East Brunswick, New Jersey. His father, Dr. Stanley Gottlieb, worked as a psychiatrist. His mother, Marsha, taught Hebrew at the East Brunswick Jewish Center.

Gottlieb attended Wesleyan University in Middletown, Connecticut. There, he was the editor in chief of the student newspaper, the *Wesleyan Argus*. He gained brief national attention after he was accused of leaving a threatening message on another student's answering machine. He later wrote several articles criticizing the school's justice system, contending that "he was needlessly subjected to a stressful and difficult process before being cleared," as Richard Perez-Pena put it for the *New York Times* (1 June 1994).

Gottlieb graduated with a bachelor's degree in economics in 1994 and took a job as a healthcare analyst for the investment bank Alex Brown & Sons in Baltimore. The following year he enrolled at the Icahn School of Medicine at Mount Sinai. He graduated with his MD in 1999 and completed his residency in internal medicine at Mount Sinai in 2002.

EARLY CAREER

Throughout the late 1990s and early 2000s, Gottlieb wrote for the *Journal of the American Medical Association* and, from 1998 to 2003, served as a medical staff writer for the *British Medical Journal*. From 2000 to 2002 Gottlieb wrote an investment newsletter called the *Gilder Biotech Report*, reporting on potential FDA decisions and developments in the drug and biotech industry. In a November 13, 2000, article for the American Medical Association (AMA) titled "Moving Your Career from Main Street to Wall Street," Gottlieb advised working physicians on how to put their medical knowledge to use as consultants for investment banks.

Later, Gottlieb expressed frustration with reports of doctors breaking confidentiality agreements to leak drug trial information to investors. He proposed an unusual solution, arguing that the FDA should make public such information as details of ongoing research on experimental drugs. "The FDA could and should release data contained in a company's (FDA) filings at each stage in the process. . . . Why shouldn't markets know what bureaucrats and insiders do?" he wrote for the *Gilder Biotech Report* in 2002, as quoted by Alicia Mundy in the *Seattle Times* (24 Aug. 2005).

In 2002 Gottlieb joined the American Enterprise Institute (AEI), a conservative think tank, as a resident fellow for a year. He would return to AEI in the same capacity in 2007 and serve as a contributor to *Forbes* magazine, authoring the *Forbes/Gottlieb Medical Technology Investor*, which advised readers on the intricacies involved in the purchase of heath-care related stock.. He also advocated speeding up the FDA's drug approval rate and complained that the FDA sent out too many public warnings about the potential side effects of a given drug, arguing that the FDA should alert only doctors first.

From 2003 to 2005 Gottlieb treated patients part time at Stamford Hospital in Stamford, Connecticut. Beginning in 2011 he also served as a clinical assistant professor and an internist in the NYU School of Medicine's Division of General Internal Medicine and Clinical Innovation.

EARLY GOVERNMENT APPOINTMENTS
In 2003 Gottlieb was named the director of medical policy development at the FDA and senior adviser to FDA commissioner Mark B. McClellan. Gottlieb followed McClellan to the Centers of Medicare and Medicaid Services in June 2004. He served as McClellan's senior adviser until that October.

Then, in 2005, Gottlieb was named the deputy commissioner for medical and scientific affairs, the number-two post, at the FDA. The appointment worried many in the medical community, who believed that Gottlieb's ties to Wall Street and major pharmaceutical companies presented a serious conflict of interest. Dr. Jerome Kassirer, the former editor of the *New England Journal of Medicine*, told Mundy, "Gottlieb has an orientation which belies the goal of the FDA," that is, to protect consumers.

Gottlieb served in that post for two years. During his tenure, he helped develop standards in HIV treatment and worked on biodefense countermeasures as a member of the White House Biodefense Interagency Working Group. Leaked emails revealed that Gottlieb pressed scientists after they rejected particular drugs or stopped particular trials—a highly unusual move for a deputy commissioner. In September 2005 *Time* magazine reported his questionable

behavior in an article about corruption in the Bush administration. Gottlieb also recused himself from decisions involving nine companies for a year.

HEALTH-CARE FINANCE AND MANAGEMENT
From 2007 to 2017 Gottlieb served as a venture partner for New Enterprise Associates Inc. (NEA), a venture capital firm focused on health-care and technology investments, in Chevy Chase, Maryland. NEA manages a multibillion-dollar portfolio.

Gottlieb also provided consulting services, through his consulting company Innovating Healthcare, to the pharmaceutical company Bristol-Myers Squibb. Gottlieb was also a managing director at the investment banking firm T. R. Winston & Company. By 2017 he was also the acting CEO of Cell BioTherapy, an animal biotech firm.

During that period, Gottlieb also sat on the boards of many pharmaceutical and biotech firms. In 2007 Gottlieb joined the board of directors at Molecular Insight Pharmaceuticals and MedAvante, which manages data for clinical trials. He went on to serve as an independent member of other boards. These included health-care insurer Bravo Health; drug researchers Aptiv Solutions (now ICON plc) and Tolero Pharmaceuticals; American Pathology Partners, a medical laboratory; Glytec, a digital therapeutics company; the biotechnology company Gradalis; and Daiichi Sankyo, then the second-largest pharmaceutical company in Japan. From 2010 to 2017 Gottlieb served as a member of the product investment board for GlaxoSmithKline, one of the world's largest pharmaceutical companies. His work for these companies provided a significant source of income: between 2013 and 2015 alone Gottlieb received more than $400,000 from pharmaceutical companies.

FDA APPOINTMENT
President Donald Trump nominated Gottlieb to head the FDA in March 2017. Gottlieb was viewed as a moderate choice compared to other candidates Trump could have selected. Industry executives praised Gottlieb's nomination; others expressed serious concern. "He is basically entangled in an unprecedented web of ties to big pharma," Dr. Michael Carome, health research director of Public Citizen, told Katie Thomas for the *New York Times* (10 Mar. 2017). "He is someone who has been an industry shill and has spent most of his career dedicated to promoting the financial interests of pharmaceutical corporations." Daniel Carpenter, a professor of government at Harvard University, expressed similar qualms. Were Gottlieb to be confirmed, Carpenter told Thomas, "he would be the most

interest-conflicted commissioner in American history, by far."

During his confirmation hearing, Gottlieb defended his support for a faster drug approval process, a desire shared by the pharmaceutical industry. Criticisms of this view, he told Congress (5 Apr. 2017), spring from "a false dichotomy that it all boils down to a choice between speed and safety." Gottlieb argued that the FDA could have both if it used the best practices and tools available.

The Senate voted 57–42 to confirm Gottlieb as commissioner on May 9, 2017. Upon confirmation, Gottlieb agreed to divest himself of his industry investments. He also recused himself for one year from decisions involving about twenty companies and ended outside affiliations.

COMMISSIONER

Gottlieb was sworn in on May 11, 2017. During his two-year tenure as FDA commissioner, he surprised critics by pushing for tougher restrictions on tobacco and nicotine. He advocated for lower nicotine levels, a ban on menthol cigarettes, and restricting flavors in electronic cigarettes to curb teen vaping. Had his proposal been adopted, the United States would have been the first country to limit the amount of nicotine in cigarettes. His stance on tobacco addiction won him praise from former critics. "He embraced science and embraced the goals of the agency," Peter Lurie, the president of the Center for Science in the Public Interest, told Julia Belluz for *Vox* (6 Mar. 2019). Some described him as the most aggressively antitobacco FDA chief in decades—a description that did not sit well with a coalition of Republican lawmakers that sought to block some of Gottlieb's proposals.

Gottlieb also helped pull the addictive opioid Opana ER from the market. However, he also oversaw approval for another potent opioid, Dsuvia, which many feared would be just as dangerous, if not more so. He also promoted harm-reducing opioid alternatives such as buprenorphine to help addicts in recovery. Under Gottlieb the FDA also cracked down on some herbal supplements, encouraged more generics to lower the costs of prescription drugs, and sped up drug approvals.

In March 2019 Gottlieb announced his resignation, citing a desire to spend more time with his family after having commuted weekly from Connecticut. The decision took many by surprise. "He was remarkably successful at keeping the agency moving forward at a difficult time and really focused on public health challenges, including the opioid epidemic and drug prices," Dr. Joshua M. Sharfstein, the former deputy commissioner of the FDA under President Barack Obama, told Sheila Kaplan and Jan Hoffman for the *New York Times* (5 Mar.

2019). "He surprised a lot of people in his willingness to take some risks for public health." Some observers feared his resignation jeopardized the initiatives he had begun, such as the e-cigarette proposals.

For his work as commissioner, Gottlieb was named among *Time*'s Health Care 50 list for 2018 and the AMA awarded him its Dr. Nathan Davis Award for Outstanding Government Service in 2019.

AFTER THE FDA

Gottlieb soon returned to NEA as a special partner on health-care investment and to AEI as a resident fellow. He also joined the board of directors at Pfizer, one of the world's largest pharmaceutical companies. This practice, known as the "revolving door" between the public and private sector, is common but ethically suspect. In July 2019 Senator Elizabeth Warren called on Gottlieb to leave Pfizer. She likened Gottlieb's decision to join the board to that of John Kelly, the former secretary of homeland security and White House chief of staff. Kelly helped craft the Trump administration's immigrant detention policies and, upon resignation, joined the board of Caliburn Inc., the parent company of an immigrant detention center in Florida.

PERSONAL LIFE

On June 13, 2004, Gottlieb married Allyson Brooke Nemeroff, then the national advertising director for the *New York Sun*, at the Women's National Republican Club in Manhattan. They have three daughters. The family lives in Westport, Connecticut.

Gottlieb was successfully treated for Hodgkin's lymphoma, a blood cancer, in 2006.

SUGGESTED READING

Belluz, Julia. "Scott Gottlieb Was the Most Aggressive Anti-tobacco FDA Leader in Years. Now He's Leaving." *Vox*, 6 Mar. 2019, www.vox.com/2019/3/6/18252176/scott-gottlieb-fda-vaping-tobacco. Accessed 8 Aug. 2019.

Healy, Melissa. "Four Things Americans Should Know about Dr. Scott Gottlieb, the New Head of the FDA." *Los Angeles Times*, 10 May 2017, www.latimes.com/science/sciencenow/la-sci-sn-scott-gottlieb-fda-20170510-html-story.html. Accessed 8 Aug. 2019.

Kaplan, Sheila, and Jan Hoffman. "F.D.A. Commissioner Scott Gottlieb, Who Fought Teenage Vaping, Resigns." *The New York Times*, 5 Mar. 2019, www.nytimes.com/2019/03/05/health/scott-gottlieb-resigns-fda.html. Accessed 9 Aug. 2019.

Mundy, Alicia. "Wall Street Biotech Insider Gets No. 2 Job at the FDA." *Seattle Times*, 24 Aug. 2005, www.seattletimes.com/nation-world/

wall-street-biotech-insider-gets-no-2-job-at-the-fda. Accessed 6 Aug. 2019.

Perez-Pena, Richard. "Private Colleges Are Criticized for Their Brand of Justice." *The New York Times*, 1 June 1994, www.nytimes.com/1994/06/01/us/private-colleges-are-criticized-for-their-brand-of-justice.html. Accessed 6 Aug. 2019.

Riggs, Mike. "Scott Gottlieb Is Not a Free Market Firebrand." *Reason*, vol. 50, no. 1, 2018, pp. 18–25. *EBSCOhost*, search.ebscohost.com/login.aspx?direct=true&db=a9h&AN=128534994&site=eds-live. Accessed 12 Aug. 2019.

Thomas, Katie. "F.D.A. Official under Bush Is Trump's Choice to Lead Agency." *The New York Times*, 10 Mar. 2017, www.nytimes.com/2017/03/10/health/fda-scott-gottlieb.html. Accessed 6 Aug. 2019.

—*Molly Hagan*

Kolinda Grabar-Kitarović

Date of birth: April 29, 1968
Occupation: President of Croatia

Kolinda Grabar-Kitarović is a diplomat and politician who became the president of Croatia in 2015 after running as the center-right Croatian Democratic Union candidate.

EARLY LIFE AND EDUCATION

Kolinda Grabar-Kitarović was born April 29, 1968, in Rijeka, Yugoslavia (now in Croatia). She grew up in Lubarska, a small town near Rijeka where her parents, Branko and Dubravka Grabar, worked in a butcher shop. She attended local primary schools and a secondary school in Rijeka. In high school, she participated in a foreign-exchange-student program, completing her last year of high school at Los Alamos High School in Los Alamos, New Mexico. After graduating in 1986, she returned to Croatia and earned a bachelor's degree in English and Spanish languages and literature from the University of Zagreb in 1993. During her college years, she served as a translator for foreign guests and translated academic works for a college professor.

In 1993, she joined the Croatian Democratic Union (HDZ) political party. She studied at the Diplomatic Academy in Vienna, Austria, during the 1994–95 school year, followed by further diplomacy studies at the Diplomatic Academy of the Ministry of Foreign Affairs in Croatia during the summer of 1995. She then completed a master's degree in international relations from the University of Zagreb in 2000.

Grabar-Kitarović later pursued additional studies, studying as a Fulbright scholar at George Washington University from 2002 to 2003, a Luksic Fellow at The John F. Kennedy School of Government at Harvard University in 2009, and as a visiting scholar at Johns Hopkins University.

POLITICAL CAREER

Grabar-Kitarović's work as a translator for a philosophy professor helped her gain entry to a diplomatic career when the professor became a minister of science and technology. He offered her a position as an assistant in the Department for International Cooperation in Croatia's Ministry of Science and Technology in 1992, and shortly afterward she was promoted to an adviser. From 1993 to 1997, she held several positions in the Ministry of Foreign Affairs, including special adviser to the deputy minister (1994–95) and director of the North America department (1995–97). She then became the diplomatic councillor for the Croatian Embassy in Canada (1997–1998), before becoming the embassy's minister councillor. In January 2001, Grabar-Kitarović returned to the Ministry of Foreign Affairs as the minister councillor.

Grabar-Kitarović began her political career in November 2003 when she was elected to parliament. One month later, she was appointed the Minister of European Integration, a post she held until February 2005. As the integration minister, Grabar-Kitarović was instrumental in initiating negotiations for Croatia's accession to the European Union (EU). In 2005, she was appointed the minister of Foreign Affairs. In this position, Grabar-Kitarović continued her negotiations for Croatia's entry into the EU and spearheaded negotiations for its entry into NATO. From 2008 to 2011, Grabar-Kitarović was Croatia's ambassador to the United States. In July 2011, she was appointed the assistant secretary general for public diplomacy for North Atlantic Treaty Organization (NATO).

Grabar-Kitarović ran for president of Croatia in the 2014 elections. She lost the first round to incumbent Ivo Josipović, but since he did not receive a majority of the votes, runoff elections were held in January 2015. Grabar-Kitarović won the second round, receiving 50.74 percent of the votes to Josipović's 49.26 percent. She campaigned on the need for national unity and consensus, as well as promises of economic recovery. At the time of her election, Croatia was in the midst of a six-year recession, with unemployment nearly 20 percent and high government debt. In a speech following her victory, Grabar-Kitarović stated her intent to transform Croatia into a prosperous, wealthy country and to resolve the issues dividing the country.

In February 2015, Grabar-Kitarović was sworn in as the president of Croatia. The position is primarily ceremonial, with the president representing Croatia abroad, influencing foreign policy, and heading the army. The president also is responsible for ensuring the government's stability and proper functioning. Citing the latter responsibility, Grabar-Kitarović announced her intent to be more than a figurehead. During her first year as head of state, she immersed herself in the European migration crisis, security issues, and diplomatic relations with other countries, including Iran, China, and Israel. She also kept one of her campaign promises when she had the bust of former Yugoslavian president Josip Broz Tito removed from the presidential palace.

IMPACT

Although Grabar-Kitarović resigned from the HDZ once she became president, her election helped her former party gain seats in the parliamentary elections of 2015, with a HDZ–led coalition gaining control of parliament. Coupled with a nonpartisan prime minister, Tihomir Orešković, who took office in 2016, the shift from a liberal, center-left government to a conservative, center-right government positioned Croatia to make reforms to reverse the country's longstanding economic decline.

PERSONAL LIFE

Grabar-Kitarović married Jakov Kitarović in 1996. They have two children. She is fluent in Croatian, English, Spanish, and Portuguese.

SUGGESTED READING

"Grabar-Kitarovic Elected Croatia's First Woman President." *BBC.* BBC, 12 Jan. 2015, www.bbc.com/news/world-europe-30765822. Accessed 29 Mar. 2019.

Kumar, Isabelle. "Croatian President Kolinda Grabar-Kitarovic from Peace, Recession to Feminism." *Euronews.* Euronews, 29 2015, www.euronews.com/2015/06/29/croatian-president-kolinda-grabar-kitarovic-from-peace-recession-to-feminism. Accessed 29 March 2019.

Veselica, Lajla. "Grabar-Kitarovic: Croatia's First Female President Sworn In." *Yahoo! News.* Yahoo, 11 Jan. 2015, news.yahoo.com/grabar-kitarovic-croatias-first-female-president-223833498.html. Accessed 29 Mar. 2019.

—*Barb Lightner*

Eliza Griswold

Date of birth: February 9, 1973
Occupation: Journalist and poet

Eliza Griswold earned international acclaim for her parallel careers in journalism and poetry, winning numerous awards for her diverse body of work. In 2019, she received both the Ridenhour Book Prize and the Pulitzer Prize for general nonfiction for *Amity and Prosperity: One Family and the Fracturing of America* (2018), an exploration of the effects of hydraulic fracturing (fracking) in Appalachia. She also served as a Nieman Fellow at Harvard University, a Guggenheim fellow, a senior fellow at the New America Foundation, and a distinguished writer in residence at New York University (NYU). Griswold's work has appeared in the *New Yorker*, the *Atlantic*, the *Nation*, and the *New York Times Magazine*, covering subjects including the environment, politics, and religion. She characterized her journalistic mission to Justine Isola for the *Atlantic* (Mar. 2008): "My job is to translate one side to another—conservative to liberal, religious to secular and back again. This is what all reporters do in different ways, whether they're writing about Google or God."

EARLY LIFE AND EDUCATION

Eliza Tracy Griswold was born on February 9, 1973, the only child of Phoebe Wetzel Griswold and Frank Griswold. Her father was the presiding bishop of the US Episcopal Church and US co-chair of the Anglican–Roman Catholic Dialogue theological organization; thus, religion was an important part of her formative years. "I grew up in a home where questions about faith and intellect were nightly dinner table conversation," she told the editors of the *New York Times Sunday Book Review* (5 Nov. 2010). "My parents' religious beliefs patterned their everyday lives."

Griswold graduated from Princeton University in 1995 with a degree in English. Her thesis was a compilation of poetry, and she would later credit that creative work with influencing her career path. She told Nina Bahadur for *Princeton Alumni Weekly* (1 May 2019), "I was able to imagine myself as a poet, as a writer, in a way that I wouldn't have been able to do otherwise."

Griswold went on to study creative writing at Johns Hopkins University, earning a master's degree in 1997. However, as she told Bahadur, "I never considered that I could actually support myself by being a writer. I didn't think that was a viable future." This changed when she began working in New York City at a literary agency and had the duty of sending royalty checks to writers. She began writing book reviews for *Vogue*, while also working on her poetry. Then she got a job as an assistant to the editor of *Paris Review*, George Plimpton, and was first exposed to participatory journalism.

REPORTER AND POET

During a brief stint at *Vanity Fair*, Griswold learned about honor killings in Jordan and was inspired to travel to the Middle East to report on the subject. "I really thought this story had to be told. I had never heard anything like it," she told Bahadur. "I was living in my parents' guest room, paying no rent, so I saved up my money and my vacation time and headed off." She ended up writing an article for the *New Republic*, which became the start of her freelance career. The piece was published in London's *Sunday Times Magazine*, which led her to take on further reporting assignments for that publication and eventually others.

Griswold's early years as a journalist were punctuated by the September 11, 2001, terrorist attacks against the United States. She traveled to Pakistan around the time of the attacks, reporting on the refugee camps there. She later visited many heavily Muslim parts of the globe, seeking to understand militant Islam. Many of her published pieces from this time sought to bring light to the complexity of the various sociopolitical conflicts seen to most Westerners as simply part of the so-called War on Terror. Along these lines, Griswold told Amy Crawford for *Smithsonian* (1 Dec. 2006), "We need to break down some of our monolithic language. Language should be as precise as possible in trying to assess exactly what's going on in a given situation."

In 2004, Griswold was honored with the first Robert I. Friedman Prize in Investigative Journalism. The award, given for journalistic work being done outside the United States, was specifically in recognition of an article published that year in the *New Yorker*, "In the Hiding Zone." The piece focused on the Islamic fighters in the Waziristan tribal region along the Afghanistan-Pakistan border.

Griswold's first collection of poetry, *Wideawake Field*, was published in 2007. The poems in the collection are based on her travels in Africa and Asia. Her poetic work won her the Rome Prize from the American Academy in Rome in 2010. She also completed a yearlong fellowship in Rome through the American Academy of Arts and Letters.

THE TENTH PARALLEL

In 2010, Griswold published her first nonfiction book, *The Tenth Parallel: Dispatches from the Fault Line between Christianity and Islam*. The book's title comes from a line of latitude 700 miles north of the equator, running through regions of North Africa, the Middle East, and South Asia known for their large, religiously diverse populations. In fact, Griswold notes how some evangelical Christians consider the area between the tenth and fortieth parallels (the "10/40 window") a battleground between Christianity and Islam. Approximately half of the world's total adherents of both religions live in that area, which is also known for its extensive poverty. Griswold spent much of seven years in six countries across Africa and Asia studying the frequent interactions between Christians and Muslims. The book was a result of her journeys. Key among Griswold's findings was that both faiths were growing exponentially in ways that the Western world failed to understand. "The current religious renewal in both Christianity and Islam today is a direct result of globalization," she told Isola. "As nations become increasingly irrelevant, religious identity becomes the next-greatest means by which people stake their claim as to who they are." Her book argues that recognizing the role of religion in global affairs is crucial to everything from combating terrorism to promoting economic development. Griswold also notes that her own background of religious experience provided the base of her investigation. She told Asma Hasan for *Publishers Weekly* (16 Aug. 2010), "I have always been interested in the overlap between human rights and religion, and the paradox of where religion doesn't protect human rights and where it does."

The Tenth Parallel was a critical and commercial success, landing on the *New York Times* Best Sellers list. In 2011, the book also received the J. Anthony Lukas Book Prize for exceptional nonfiction. The Lukas Prizes, a joint endeavor between the Columbia Graduate School of Journalism and the Nieman Foundation, were created to honor works that combine deep research, social concerns, and graceful prose.

I AM THE BEGGAR OF THE WORLD

While traveling in Afghanistan and Pakistan, Griswold discovered the Afghan folk poetry form known as *landay*. In their original language, Pashto, landays follow a two-line form that is many centuries old. The short works often deal with relationships between men and women, while grief, homeland, separation, and war are also common themes. These anonymous poems are generally composed by illiterate Pashtun women and passed down orally, adapted as needed in following generations. Yet poetry was typically forbidden to women in Afghanistan under the fundamentalist Islamic regime of the Taliban, making landays by nature an expression of protest.

Griswold and frequent collaborator Seamus Murphy, a photographer, sought to collect contemporary landays in an effort to document the unique tradition. As Griswold told Alex Zucker and Margaret Carson for *PEN America* (6 Aug. 2015), "We thought it would be a remarkable project to look at the impact that more than a decade of US occupation had had on the lives and songs of Afghans, especially women, through these two-line folk poems." Griswold was especially motivated by the death of a young Afghan woman whose brothers had beaten her for writing poetry and who later set herself on fire and died. She was also concerned that after US forces left the area, life would become even more precarious for the women.

As she did not speak Pashto, Griswold relied on collaborators to develop the translations that eventually were published as the collection *I Am the Beggar of the World: Landays from Contemporary Afghanistan* (2015). Two young Afghan women helped her collect examples of landays and get the literal sense of the poetry. She then worked with a variety of scholars and poets to interpret the central meaning of these sparse works and determine how to best translate that meaning into English. The resulting book was well received by critics, and won the PEN Poetry in Translation Award in 2015.

AMITY AND PROSPERITY

In 2019, Griswold rose to a new level of recognition when she won the Pulitzer Prize for general nonfiction for *Amity and Prosperity: One Family and the Fracturing of America*. The work examines fracking, a controversial process to increase yields of natural gas and oil from deep rock formations using pressurized liquid to fracture the rocks. Griswold spent seven years researching the book, which details the Haney family's experience with fracking in western Pennsylvania and their consequent health issues. After her children and animals grew sick, Stacey Haney faced denials from the mining companies operating near her house and eventually launched a legal case. Griswold was inspired to take the story in large part due to the decline of local media with the resources to investigate and draw attention to the issue.

Amity and Prosperity not only drew critical acclaim, it was influential in bringing the controversy over fracking into the public eye. "The response to the book has been heartening across the political spectrum," Griswold told Marylynne Pitz for *Pittsburgh Post-Gazette* (15 Apr. 2019). "It isn't just that activists have been excited about it. People who have been on the fence about fracking are grateful to have a careful account that is not politics." After the book's release, the main natural gas drilling company involved in the area, Range Resources, and co-defendants settled a three-million-dollar lawsuit that three families brought against them for falsifying lab results.

PERSONAL LIFE

Griswold often faced questions about being a woman while reporting from war zones and other dangerous areas. However, as she told Adam Pasick for *New York* (Mar. 2012), "Here's the secret: It's actually safer to be a woman doing this work. Most violence is random, and if you're a woman in a car and some nut comes up armed at a roadblock and sees you in the back of the car, chances are he'll hesitate. You get twenty seconds to get away, which is what you need. . . . You know, frankly, where I see the sexism? Editors who think twice about sending a woman where they send a man."

In 1996, Griswold married Christopher Allen, a banker, but the couple eventually divorced. She later married Steve Coll, a journalist and dean of the Columbia University Journalism School.

SUGGESTED READING

Bahadur, Nina. "Pulitzer Winner Eliza Griswold '95 Follows Stories That Need to Be Told." *Princeton Alumni Weekly*, 1 May 2019, paw.princeton.edu/article/pulitzer-winner-eliza-griswold-95-follows-stories-need-be-told. Accessed 5 Sept. 2019.

Griswold, Eliza. "An Interview with Eliza Griswold, Author of 'Waging Peace in the Philippines.'" Interview by Amy Crawford. *Smithsonian.com*, 1 Dec. 2006, www.smithsonianmag.com/travel/an-interview-with-eliza-griswold-author-of-waging-peace-in-the-philippines-140748663/. Accessed 5 Sept. 2019.

Griswold, Eliza. "One Nation, under Gods." Interview by Justine Isola. *The Atlantic*, March 2008, www.theatlantic.com/magazine/archive/2008/03/one-nation-under-gods/306689/. Accessed 5 Sept. 2019.

Griswold, Eliza. "2015 PEN Poetry in Translation Award: Four Questions for Winner Eliza Griswold." Interview by Alex Zucker and Margaret Carson. *PEN America*, 6 Aug. 2015, pen.org/2015-pen-poetry-in-translation-award-four-questions-for-winner-eliza-griswold/. Accessed 5 Sept. 2019.

Hasan, Asma, et al. "In Profile." *Publishers Weekly*, 16 Aug. 2010, www.publishersweekly.com/pw/by-topic/industry-news/religion/article/44177-in-profile.html . Accessed 5 Sept. 2019.

Pasick, Adam. "Duck, Cover: War Reporting While Female." *New York*, 5 Mar. 2012, p. 9. *Biography Reference Bank*, search.ebscohost.com/login.aspx?direct=true&db=brb&AN=72477929&site=eds-live. Accessed 5 Sept. 2019.

Pitz, Marylynne. "Eliza Griswold, Who Documented the Impact of Fracking in Washington County, Wins Pulitzer Prize." *Pittsburgh Post-Gazette*, 15 Apr. 2019, www.post-gazette.com/ae/books/2019/04/15/fracking-southwestern-Pennsylvania-Pulitzer-Prize-Nonfiction-Amity-Prosperity/stories/201904150111. Accessed 5 Sept. 2019.

"Up Front: Eliza Griswold." *The New York Times*, 5 Nov. 2010, www.nytimes.com/2010/11/07/books/review/Upfront-t.html. Accessed 5 Sept. 2019.

SELECTED WORKS
Wideawake Field, 2008; *The Tenth Parallel: Dispatches from the Fault Line between Christianity and Islam*, 2010; *I Am the Beggar of the World* (translation), 2015; *Amity and Prosperity: One Family and Fracturing of America*, 2018

—Judy Johnson

James Gunn

Date of birth: August 5, 1966
Occupation: Director and screenwriter

In 2012, James Gunn was a little-known screenwriter and director with offbeat and irreverent horror sensibilities when he was hired to develop the relatively obscure comic book series *Guardians of the Galaxy* for the big screen for Marvel Studios. Having spent a good amount of time reading Marvel comics growing up, Gunn was able to put his unique stamp on the first installment, which resulted in "the most personal franchise in the most successful cinematic universe in Hollywood history," as Adam B. Vary declared in a profile of the director for *BuzzFeed News* (3 May 2017). Following a flawed but relatable team of misfit cosmic superheroes, *Guardians of the Galaxy* became a major critical and commercial success upon its release in 2014, instantly catapulting writer-director Gunn from Hollywood outsider to the A-list. Gunn, who initially aspired to be a professional musician and began his career in the filmmaking industry in the mid-1990s with the legendary B-movie production company Troma Entertainment, went on to write and direct the sequel *Guardians of the Galaxy Vol. 2* (2017), which also became a global phenomenon.

Gunn's fast-rising career trajectory came to an abrupt halt in 2018 when Disney, Marvel's parent company, fired him for a series of offensive jokes he had made on social media around ten years earlier. The company, however, reversed its controversial decision and reinstated Gunn as the writer and director of the third installment of the Guardians franchise in 2019. As Gunn explained in an interview with Mike Fleming Jr. for *Deadline* (15 May 2019), "You hear in Hollywood that everybody's cutthroat . . . but there's also a lot of really good people. I'm always attracted to finding that goodness in places we don't expect, often in the characters in my movies."

EARLY LIFE AND EDUCATION

The oldest of six children, James Gunn was born on August 5, 1966, and raised in a tight-knit, yet dysfunctional Catholic family in Manchester,

Photo by Gage Skidmore via Wikimedia Commons

Missouri, a suburb of St. Louis. His father, James Sr., worked as an attorney. Gunn was often left to fend for himself due to his father's profession, which regularly required him to travel out of town; in his absence, Gunn's mother, Leota, would typically devote more attention to his younger siblings. In an article for *Newsday* (4 May 2017), Gunn admitted to Frank Lovece that his family "were all very large drinkers," but added that he and his siblings were raised in a deeply loving environment, which "gives you a measured, multifaceted view of family life."

Much of Gunn's family life revolved around laughter and the imagination. From an early age, he gravitated toward all things pop culture, developing a particular affinity for comic books and horror films. Influenced by low-budget horror classics like *Night of the Living Dead* (1968) and *Friday the 13th* (1980), he started making eight-millimeter comedic slasher films with his brothers around the age of twelve. As Gunn told Vary, "I was the kid in the neighborhood that was directing everyone else." Seemingly considering himself a "creative visionary," as his youngest brother, actor Sean Gunn, noted to Vary, Gunn taught himself how to make basic special effects—from gore to ray guns—by reading horror magazines like *Fangoria*.

As a teenager, Gunn's interests expanded to include punk and shock rock, as he became enamored with such music icons as Johnny Rotten and Alice Cooper. His various pop culture obsessions provided him solace while attending St. Louis University High School (SLUH), a Jesuit Catholic prep school for boys, where he had become increasingly alienated from many of his classmates. Upon graduating from SLUH in 1984, he attempted to pursue a music career. Around 1989, he formed a new-wave group called the Icons, which performed around St. Louis and the Midwest and released one album, titled *Mom, We Like It Here on Earth* (1994).

During his stint with the Icons (the band broke up in the mid-1990s), Gunn, who had come to realize that he was not a talented enough singer for a long-term career in the music world, attended Saint Louis University (SLU), where he discovered his passion for writing. He earned a degree in psychology from SLU in 1992, after which he moved to New York to study creative writing at Columbia University, eventually earning a Master of Fine Arts (MFA) degree.

FINDING HIS CALLING

Around that time, Gunn's path toward becoming a filmmaker began inadvertently at Troma Entertainment, an ultra-low budget, New York–based independent studio cofounded by Lloyd Kaufman in 1974. Gunn, who was then trying to become a novelist, interviewed at the studio with the intention of landing a side job making special effects. However, following his first meeting with Kaufman, he was commissioned to write the screenplay for *Tromeo and Juliet*, an adaptation characterized by sexuality and violence of the classic love story by William Shakespeare. Despite receiving just $150, the thought of having his name attached to a film proved to be a crystallizing moment for Gunn, who proceeded to write the script in about two weeks. In his interview with Vary, he explained that he felt "a weird sort of calling in filmmaking that I didn't feel with other things." He then added, "I feel like there are things in life you want to do, and then things you are called to do, and hopefully you can allow yourself to want to do whatever you're called to do."

Released in 1996, *Tromeo and Juliet*, notwithstanding its status as an exploitation film, was well received by critics and, thanks to its success, Gunn landed a full-time gig at Troma. Under the guidance of Kaufman, he learned the ins and outs of the industry, including everything from writing, producing, and distributing films to scouting locations and creating poster art. After helping Kaufman write the book *All I Need to Know about Filmmaking I Learned from the Toxic Avenger* (1998), about Kaufman and the history of Troma, he moved to Los Angeles, California, to launch his filmmaking career in earnest.

In 2000, Gunn published his first and only novel, *The Toy Collector*, which tells the story of a hospital orderly who pilfers pharmaceutical drugs to fund his toy addiction. That year he also wrote, coproduced, and acted in the low-budget indie comedy *The Specials*, which follows the daily adventures of a group of third-rate superheroes. Despite featuring an ensemble cast that included such actors as Rob Lowe and Thomas Haden Church, the relatively action-free film only earned just over $13,000 at the domestic box office. Nonetheless, it has since come to be heralded by such filmmakers as the Marvel Cinematic Universe director Joss Whedon, who has praised the film's unique human-driven approach.

In the meantime, Gunn "eked out a living in the gray area between movies, video games and cable projects," as Joe Williams wrote for the *St. Louis Post-Dispatch* (31 July 2014). Most notably, he wrote the screenplays for *Scooby-Doo* (2002), its sequel *Scooby-Doo 2: Monsters Unleashed* (2004), and the 2004 remake of George A. Romero's 1978 zombie classic *Dawn of the Dead*.

RISE TO HOLLYWOOD MAINSTREAM

Propelled by his success as a screenwriter, Gunn made his film directorial debut in 2006 with the horror-comedy *Slither*. The film, which stars Elizabeth Banks and Michael Rooker, portrays a small South Carolina town that is invaded by alien slugs. Seamlessly veering from horror to comedy, the film showcased Gunn's eccentric, offbeat style, and though it performed poorly at the box office, it received rave reviews from critics.

Gunn next created the comedy web short *Humanzee!* (2009), which follows a man (played by Gunn) who, after sending his sperm to a secret laboratory, receives a son in the mail who is a human-chimp hybrid. Around the same time, he had developed a short-form satirical web series for *Spike.com* consisting of sketch comedy–style pornography spoofs.

Gunn then wrote and directed the superhero dark comedy film *Super* (2010), which stars Rainn Wilson as Frank Darbo, an emotionally ravaged short-order cook who transforms himself into a crime fighter after his recovering addict wife (Liv Tyler) leaves him for a drug-dealing strip club owner (Kevin Bacon). Upon its release, the ultraviolent film received mixed reviews from critics and performed rather poorly at the box office. "*Super* was incredibly disorienting to people," Gunn told Vary. "I frankly felt misunderstood."

However, in 2012, Gunn unexpectedly found himself in the running to direct and revise the script (an initial conception of the story was developed by Nicole Perlman) for a film adaptation of *Guardians of the Galaxy*, one of Marvel's more obscure comic book titles. After meeting with Marvel executives, he delivered to them a seventeen-page document outlining his vision for the film. His treatment impressed Marvel

Studios president Kevin Feige enough to land him the job.

WORLDWIDE SUCCESS WITH *GUARDIANS OF THE GALAXY*

Modest expectations surrounded the release of *Guardians of the Galaxy* in 2014. The film follows a team of misfit superheroes from various planets who have joined forces to restore order in the cosmos. The team includes leader Peter Quill, or Star-Lord, a half-celestial, half-human rogue; Gamora, a green-skinned orphan-turned-assassin; Drax, a tattooed, muscular warrior with a deadpan sense of humor; Rocket, a genetically modified, wisecracking raccoon bounty hunter voiced by Bradley Cooper; and Groot, a tree-like alien voiced by Vin Diesel. Chris Pratt, then a relatively unknown television actor, was cast in the role of Quill while Zoe Saldana and Dave Bautista were cast in the roles of Gamora and Drax, respectively. Gunn's brother Sean was cast as Kraglin, first mate of the Yondu Ravager Clan.

Unlike with many of Marvel's previous slickly made, often corporate-driven blockbuster franchise films, Gunn infused *Guardians* with his own quirky personal stamp, resulting in a highly original take on the comic book genre; this included imbuing the film with humor, numerous pop culture references, self-referential flourishes, and a retro guitar-pop soundtrack. Audiences and critics enthusiastically responded to this approach, as *Guardians* raked in over $773 million at the worldwide box office and received widespread praise from critics. In a representative review for the *Hollywood Reporter* (24 July 2014), Justin Lowe called the film "an inventive space opera," commenting that Gunn and Perlman "have crafted a well-articulated universe with distinct settings and relatable, compelling characters devoted to a thrilling quest for redemption."

Gunn experienced similar worldwide success with *Guardians of the Galaxy Vol. 2*, which he again wrote and directed. That film picks up where the first left off, following Quill as he seeks to discover more about his biological father (played by Kurt Russell) while traveling through the cosmos with his fellow Guardians. It surpassed the original in worldwide box office receipts, grossing more than $863 million, and received generally positive reviews from critics. "I was able to do exactly what I wanted, and exactly be myself, and it worked," Gunn said of the two Guardians films to Vary.

FALLOUT AND REINSTATEMENT

In July 2018, Gunn was in the midst of completing the script for the third installment of the Guardians franchise when he was abruptly fired by parent company Disney. The move came in response to a series of resurfaced jokes considered provocatively tasteless that Gunn had made on the social media site Twitter around ten years earlier. Gunn immediately apologized for the tweets and accepted Disney's decision. At the same time, the company's move was widely criticized by many fans and various members of the entertainment industry, including several of his Guardians collaborators, and an online petition to rehire Gunn subsequently launched.

In March 2019, Gunn was reinstated by Disney as director of the third Guardians film following a series of productive meetings with company executives. "There's a lot of really positive stuff that's coming out of all of this, and one of those positives is I was able to learn," the director explained to Fleming Jr. of the experience. "People have to be able to learn from mistakes."

Besides shepherding the Guardians franchise, Gunn has played a behind-the-scenes role in the development of other Marvel franchise films. He served as an executive producer and consultant for the wildly successful *Avengers: Infinity War* (2018) and *Avengers: Endgame* (2019). In these films, the Guardians characters make an appearance to help the superhero team the Avengers fight against a common, formidable foe.

PERSONAL LIFE

Gunn began a relationship with actor Jennifer Holland in 2015. He was formerly married to actor Jenna Fischer, best known for her role as Pam Beesly on the NBC sitcom *The Office*. Wed in 2000, the couple separated in 2007 and divorced in 2008, but remain friends.

SUGGESTED READING

Gunn, James. "A Conversation with Director James Gunn." Interview by Jarrett Medlin. *St. Louis*, 26 May 2011, www.stlmag.com/A-Conversation-With-Director-James-Gunn/. Accessed 18 June 2019.

Gunn, James. "'Guardians of the Galaxy' Director James Gunn Breaks Silence on High-Profile Disney Firing, & What He Learned from the Career Crisis That Followed—Deadline Disruptors." Interview by Mike Fleming Jr. *Deadline*, 15 May 2019, deadline.com/2019/05/james-gunn-guardians-of-the-galaxy-suicide-squad-offensive-tweets-interview-news-1202610248/. Accessed 18 June 2019.

Lovece, Frank. "James Gunn Says 'Guardians of the Galaxy Vol. 2' a Family Affair." *Newsday*, 4 May 2017, www.newsday.com/entertainment/movies/james-gunn-says-guardians-of-the-galaxy-vol-2-a-family-affair-1.13566331. Accessed 18 June 2019.

Lowe, Justin. Review of *Guardians of the Galaxy*, directed by James Gunn. *The Hollywood Reporter*, 24 July 2014, www.

hollywoodreporter.com/review/guardians-galaxy-film-review-719882. Accessed 18 June 2019.

Vary, Adam B. "Marvel's Dark and Twisted Guardian." *BuzzFeed News*, 3 May 2017, www.buzzfeednews.com/article/adambvary/james-gunn-guardians-of-the-galaxy. Accessed 18 June 2019.

Williams, Joe. "St. Louis Director James Gunn Goes Galactic." *St. Louis Post-Dispatch*, 31 July 2014, www.stltoday.com/entertainment/movies/joe-williams/st-louis-director-james-gunn-goes-galactic/article_45cca4d9-6106-51bc-a665-26ea1e0ee660.html. Accessed 18 June 2019.

SELECTED WORKS

Tromeo and Juliet, 1996; *The Specials*, 2000; *Dawn of the Dead*, 2004; *Slither*, 2006; *Super*, 2010; *Guardians of the Galaxy*, 2014; *Guardians of the Galaxy Vol. 2*, 2017

—*Chris Cullen*

Sunetra Gupta

Date of birth: March 15, 1965
Occupation: Epidemiologist and novelist

A professor of theoretical epidemiology at the University of Oxford, Sunetra Gupta has been celebrated for her research on the evolution of pathogens as well as for her fiction novels. "A key challenge for me is to overcome the resistance towards accepting that I have two careers: scientists tend to regard my writing as a 'hobby' while writers often assume that science is a dreary day job," Gupta wrote in a post for the blog *Nature's Soapbox Science* (6 Apr. 2012). "The truth is that I am passionate about both." As a theoretical epidemiologist, Gupta focuses on using mathematical models to generate hypotheses about the processes that determine the population structure of pathogens. However, as Kimberly Nagy explained in an undated article for the *Wild River Review*, she "is equally playful and at home with the ambiguity (and thus possibilities) of language, whether describing her disdain for traditional punctuation . . . , exploring the consciousness of her characters, or comparing the languages of science and literature." As a writer, Gupta's successes include *A Sin of Colour* (1999), which won the Southern Arts Literature Prize and was long-listed for the prestigious Orange Prize, and *So Good in Black* (2009), which was long-listed for the DSC Prize for South Asian Literature.

EARLY LIFE AND EDUCATION

Sunetra Gupta was born on March 15, 1965, in Calcutta (now Kolkata), the capital of the Indian state of West Bengal. Her father, Dhruba, was a history professor, and her mother, Minati, taught math. Dhruba's academic career took the family to Ethiopia, Zambia, and England. The constant travel made life exciting for Gupta, but sometimes left the family financially unstable.

As a child, Gupta spoke Bengali to her parents and Amharic with her Ethiopian nanny. She easily picked up English after moving to Zambia when she was four. In 1976, the family returned to Calcutta. She has written evocatively and fondly of her native city, which later supplied the setting for some of her novels.

Once back in Calcutta, Gupta enrolled at La Martiniere, a missionary school for girls in which instruction was offered in English, allowing her to hone her language skills even further. She later transferred to Patha Bhavan, an experimental school founded by a group of intellectuals, many of them members of her father's social circle. There she immersed herself in Bengali literature and culture.

Outside of school, Gupta enjoyed listening to cricket matches on a cabinet radio in her cousin's living room, playing chess, and taking care of her pet rabbit. In school she particularly enjoyed math and science. She once kept a cockroach and an ant in a jar to observe their interactions. She toyed for a time with the idea of becoming a film director and wrote a succession of science fiction stories, a few of which she published in small Bengali magazines.

After secondary school, Gupta attended Princeton University in the United States. She first majored in physics, but she changed her major after thinking about how mathematics could be used to explain biology. During her senior year at Princeton, Gupta attended a creative writing workshop led by Joyce Carol Oates, which inspired her to begin writing in English instead of Bengali. She graduated from the school with her bachelor's degree in biology in 1987. In 1992, Gupta completed her PhD at Imperial College London.

SCIENTIFIC CAREER

After earning her PhD, Gupta won a three-year Training Fellowship from the Wellcome Trust, allowing her to undertake postdoctoral research in biomathematics. In 1995, she was awarded a Wellcome Senior Fellowship, which she used to study biodiversity at the University of Oxford.

Near the end of her fellowship, Gupta was nominated for a readership at Oxford (the equivalent of a tenure-track professorship at an American university). The head of the selection committee, however, argued strenuously that Gupta was not fit for a post at Oxford, claiming that she had engaged in a sexual relationship with a department chair. The accusations were quickly found to be baseless, and her accuser resigned in disgrace. Gupta was appointed to the readership in 1999, and in 2006, she was given the title of professor of theoretical epidemiology.

Talking about her work in an interview with Sarah-Jayne Blakemore for the *Scientific 23*, Gupta said, "I work on infectious diseases, but I'm not a doctor. I'm interested in the ecology and the evolution of infectious diseases, and how you can think about infectious disease as being the product of an interaction between two species—the host (us) and pathogen (the bug)." Gupta further explained, "Both hosts and pathogens evolve. . . . One way to investigate this is to construct theories about how it all works. That's where I come in. I use mathematical models to generate hypotheses about how pathogens and their hosts evolve, which I then go and test in the field or in the lab."

Over the course of her career, Gupta's research earned her the Zoological Society of London Scientific Medal in 2008; the Royal Society Rosalind Franklin Award in 2009; and the Royal Society Wolfson Research Merit Award in 2010. In the 2010s, Gupta's Evolutionary Ecology of Infectious Disease research group studied such conditions as malaria hemoglobin disorders and bacterial pathogens such as *Neisseria meningitides*, which can lead to meningitis and septicemia.

LITERARY CAREER

Buoyed by her father's firm conviction that one could pursue science and art concurrently, Gupta published her first novel the same year she earned her doctoral degree. *Memories of Rain* (1992) takes place during a single weekend in the life of Calcutta-born Moni, who dreams of returning to India with her young daughter after discovering her English-born husband's infidelity. In a review for the *Washington Post* (29 Mar. 1992) Shashi Tharoor called the book "the triumphant debut of a gifted and compelling voice" and opined: "In long rolling sentences that pile clause upon clause, emotion upon emotion, keenly observed detail upon poignantly imagined whimsy, Sunetra Gupta weaves a story as intricate and rich, yet as light and warm, as a . . . shawl." The novel was later awarded the Sahitya Akademi Award in 1996.

Gupta followed that debut with *The Glassblower's Breath* (1993), which led many reviewers to compare her to Virginia Woolf, given her female protagonist's similarities to Clarissa Dalloway. She next won attention with *Moonlight into Marzipan*, a 1995 book about a scientist who unwittingly discovers how to create life out of inanimate matter when he transforms copper from his wife's earrings into chlorophyll.

A Sin of Colour, her 1999 novel, garnered Gupta several literary honors. These included a Southern Arts Literature Prize; inclusion on the shortlist for the Crossword Book Award (an Indian award considered equivalent in stature to Britain's Booker Prize); and mention on the longlist for the Orange Prize (later known as the Women's Prize for Fiction), which is given to women from anywhere in the world writing noteworthy books in English. In an undated review for *Publishers Weekly*, a reviewer wrote, "In a novel of rare beauty, Gupta tells a mesmerizing tale of obsession, mystery and unrequited love spanning three generations. . . . These universal themes, couched in Gupta's elegant prose, allow the novel to transcend time and place."

Gupta's next novel, *So Good in Black*, was published in 2009 and eventually longlisted for the 2013 DSC Prize for South Asian Literature. The book unravels the evocative mystery of businessman Byron Mallick, who donated milk adulterated with chalk to a women's shelter and may have killed the shelter's founder to save his reputation. "Sunetra Gupta writes of ambiguities brilliantly," Claire Hopley wrote for the *Washington Times* (17 June 2011). "She is as much at ease describing the seashore and gardens of Bengal or the streets of Kolkata as she is describing Christmas in a country house in Ireland. . . . Long after the last page has been conned and the book set aside, readers will continue to reflect on this meditative and often fascinating work."

Gupta also translated the work of Nobel Prize–winning Bengali poet and musician Rabindranath Tagore, a great favorite of her father's. She even wove some of the translated verses into her novels.

PASSIONS COMBINED

In 2015, Gupta launched *Shooting Stars*, a website funded by her Rosalind Franklin Award. Cocreated with illustrator Ted Dewan, *Shooting Stars* features biographical profiles of women scientists through comic-like illustrations and dialog boxes. The website highlights such prominent figures as chemist and X-ray crystallographer Rosalind Franklin, astronomer Caroline Herschel, and mathematician Ada Lovelace.

PERSONAL LIFE

Gupta lives in Oxford with her husband, Adrian V.S. Hill, a renowned geneticist. The couple has two daughters, Olivia and Isolde. In 2015, Gupta was honored by the Royal Society in an art exhibition that featured portraits of influential women in science.

SUGGESTED READING

Gupta, Sunetra. "The Novelist and Biologist Discusses Metaphor and Science." Interview by Kimberly Nagy. *Wild River Review*, www.

wildriverreview.com/interviews/sunetra-gup-ta/. Accessed 21 July 2019.

Gupta, Sunetra. "On Craft: An Interview with Sunetra Gupta." Interview by Hilary Plum. *Kenyon Review*, Kenyon College, 10 Oct. 2011, www.kenyonreview.org/2011/10/on-craft-an-interview-with-sunetra-gupta/. Accessed 21 July 2019.

Gupta, Sunetra. "Professor Sunetra Gupta." Interview by Sarah-Jayne Blakemore. *The Scientific* 23, thescientific23.com/interview?id=9&name=Sunetra%20Gupta. Accessed 21 July 2019.

Gupta, Sunetra. "Transitions: From Scientist to Combining Science and Novel Writing." *Soapbox Science*, Nature, 6 Apr. 2012, blogs.nature.com/soapboxscience/2012/04/06/transitions-from-scientist-to-combining-science-and-novel-writing-professor-sunetra-gupta2. Accessed 21 July 2019.

Hopley, Claire. Review of *So Good in Black*, by Sunetra Gupta. *The Washington Times*, 17 June 2011, www.washingtontimes.com/news/2011/jun/17/book-review-so-good-in-black/. Accessed 21 July 2019.

"Sunetra Gupta." *Introductions Necessary*, 15 Mar. 2016, introductionsnecessary.com/2016/03/15/sunetra-gupta/. Accessed 12 Aug. 2019.

Tharoor, Shashi. "Out of India: A Thirst for the Past." Review of *Memories of Rain*, by Sunetra Gupta. *The Washington Post*, 29 Mar. 1992, www.washingtonpost.com/archive/entertainment/books/1992/03/29/out-of-india-a-thirst-for-the-past/c8cb2deb-4ff0-4ada-9166-96d754313058/. Accessed 21 July 2019.

SELECTED WORKS
Memories of Rainbows, 1992; *The Glassblower's Breath*, 1993; *Moonlight into Marzipan*, 1995; *A Sin of Colour*, 1999; *So Good in Black*, 2009

—*Mari Rich*

Tiffany Haddish

Date of birth: December 3, 1979
Occupation: Comedian and actor

Emmy Award–winning actor and comedian Tiffany Haddish is best known for her breakout role in the 2017 smash hit comedy *Girls Trip*, but her career has been a long time in the making. Haddish grew up in and out of the foster care system in South-Central Los Angeles. She discovered her love for comedy at the Laugh Factory, LA's famed comedy club, when she was fifteen and has been working toward a career in Hollywood

ever since. Haddish's 2017 memoir, *The Last Black Unicorn*, became a New York Times Best Seller, and the following year she became the first black female comedian to host *Saturday Night Live* in the show's forty-three-year history, earning an Emmy for her performance. In 2019, she filmed an hourlong follow-up to her hit Showtime comedy special, *Tiffany Haddish: She Ready! From the Hood to Hollywood* (2017).

Those accolades, in addition to her myriad successful film roles, illustrate Haddish's extraordinary ability to transform elements of her life into art. From the trauma of her childhood, to her recent exploits as an A-list celebrity, Haddish has built a lucrative career on her winning authenticity. It is not always easy, she admitted to Caity Weaver for *GQ* magazine (26 Mar. 2018). "Giving so much of yourself to so many different people—and then people love you. They want to hug, they want to talk to you, and sometimes you just feel like, man, *sleep*."

EARLY LIFE
Haddish was born on December 3, 1979, and raised in Colton and South-Central Los Angeles, California. Her father, Tsihaye Reda Haddish, an Eritrean Jewish immigrant, fled the authorities when Haddish was three and was later deported. (Haddish reconnected with him as an adult; he died in 2017.) Her mother, Leola, a successful businesswoman, remarried and had four more children. When Haddish was nearly nine, her stepfather allegedly cut the brakes of her mother's car, hoping to cash in on her life insurance. Her mother survived a terrible car accident but suffered serious brain damage as a result. Haddish

Photo by Staff Sgt. Eric Summers Jr. via Wikimedia Commons

and her siblings were supposed to be in the car with their mother, but Haddish had argued to babysit instead.

After the accident, Haddish's mother was unable to tie her shoes or pay the bills and also became physically abusive toward her. (Leola was later diagnosed with schizophrenia.) Haddish learned to crack jokes to deflect her mother's violent outbursts. "At that point it was not about being funny, it was a defense mechanism to avoid getting punched in the mouth," she recalled to Cara Buckley for the *New York Times* (17 Oct. 2018). Haddish, the oldest sibling, became the family caretaker until she was twelve. When Leola was arrested for assaulting a neighbor, Haddish and her siblings were split up and placed in foster care. "The state of California paid so much money to make sure I don't die 'cause they knew I was gonna be special," she jokes in her 2017 stand-up special, *She Ready!*. But Haddish's experience of the foster care system was bleak. She lived in group homes and with families where she was bullied and even molested. Haddish's grandmother gained custody of her when Haddish was fifteen. At about seventeen, she was raped by a man claiming to be a police cadet, and the following year, her foster care subsidy ran out, putting her out of her grandmother's house. She was a member of the class of 1998 at El Camino Real High School.

LAUGH FACTORY COMEDY CAMP

Haddish loved school, though through her various upheavals, she struggled to attend. She estimates that she was reading at a first- or second-grade level well into her teens. She was the class clown and often got in trouble for speaking out of turn. Performing became a refuge, and eventually Haddish won a drama competition in high school. "Whenever I would feel like I was about to cry I would crack a joke," she recalled to comedians Neal Brennan and Moshe Kasher for their now-defunct podcast, the *Champs* (8 Jan. 2015). Her social worker, tired of being called to the school for Haddish's transgressions, offered her what was in hindsight an unorthodox and serendipitous choice: attend therapy or attend comedy camp. Fifteen-year-old Haddish chose comedy camp.

The famed Laugh Factory in Los Angeles has run a camp for local teens from poor communities since 1984. Among Haddish's mentors were comedian Chris Spencer, who taught her how to write a joke, and comedy legend Richard Pryor. Haddish told Chris Barton for the *Los Angeles Times* (17 Aug. 2018) that the camp gave her a voice. "It was the first time I felt safe," she recalled. "It was the first time a man told me I was beautiful and I didn't think anything bad was going to happen. People were listening, and I learned communication skills, how to write a

joke. I learned a lot." She also got an important piece of advice from Pryor that sticks with her, as she recounts in her memoir: "People don't come to comedy shows because they want to hear about your problems, or about politics, or what's going on in the world, or celebrities. They don't care," she recalled him saying. "They come to comedy shows to have fun. So when you're onstage, you need to be having fun."

EARLY CAREER

After leaving her grandmother's house, Haddish became homeless three times, living out of her car. She often parked in Beverly Hills, she told Krista Smith for *Vanity Fair* (30 Jan. 2018), because if she was forced to be homeless, "I'm gonna be homeless in the best area." Haddish had various gigs, including a job as an energy producer, hyping attendees at bar mitzvahs and other parties, but she was haunted by traumatic memories of her rape. "I literally wanted to kill myself," she told Buckley. "I felt like everything in my life and everybody that came around was out to hurt me."

At her therapist's recommendation, Haddish started performing stand-up. She got her first big break appearing on the television competition *Bill Bellamy's Who's Got Jokes* in 2006. In her brief set, she won over the audience with her signature blend of candid asides and physical comedy. She landed bit parts in television shows like *That's So Raven*, *My Name Is Earl*, and *It's Always Sunny in Philadelphia*. In 2009, she appeared in a comedy film called *The Janky Promoters*, starring Ice Cube.

A few years later, in 2013, Haddish scored a role in the television parody series *Real Husbands of Hollywood*, starring Kevin Hart. She and Hart came up in the Los Angeles comedy scene together. Once, during one of her bouts of homelessness, Hart lent her three hundred dollars. At his urging, she got a hotel room, took a shower, and wrote out a list of career goals—among them, working with Jada Pinkett Smith and her idol Arsenio Hall. By 2018, she had accomplished most of them.

GIRLS TRIP

In 2014, Haddish landed a recurring role on the Tyler Perry series *If Loving You Is Wrong* and, in 2015, became a series regular on the NBC sitcom *The Carmichael Show*, starring stand-up comedian Jerrod Carmichael. She remained on the cast of the latter show until 2017. Then, in 2016, she appeared in the action comedy *Keanu*, starring Keegan-Michael Key and Jordan Peele, but in 2017, she received her big break: a role in *Girls Trip*, featuring Jada Pinkett-Smith, Regina Hall, and Queen Latifah. She heard about the film through crew members who had worked with her on the set of *Keanu*. "The transportation department, set [decoration], props. Who else sent me something? Sound. People was sending me the script like, 'Don't tell anybody I sent you the script. I read it and it's just like you,'" she recalled to Weaver. The film follows four college friends who have reunited to take a trip to New Orleans for the annual Essence Festival. She was encouraged to audition for the role of Dina, the wildest of the foursome. She auditioned a number of times, including via Skype, and eventually won the role, despite her status as a relative unknown. Producer Will Packer told Lacey Rose for the *Hollywood Reporter* (13 June 2018), "Tiffany *is* Dina."

Girls Trip became one of the biggest hits of 2017, garnering over $115 million at the domestic box office. To say that Haddish stole the show would be a vast understatement. "Her performance is so good it is jarring," Weaver wrote. Critic Peter Travers described her for *Rolling Stone* (21 July 2017) as a "Category 5 hurricane of laughs."

BEYOND *GIRLS TRIP*
Like *Bridesmaids* (2011) was for Melissa McCarthy and *The Hangover* (2009) for Zach Galifianakis, *Girls Trip* turbo-charged Haddish's career. She continued to win fans on the film's promotional tour. In an appearance on the late-night show *Jimmy Kimmel Live!* Haddish regaled the audience with a story about going on a swamp tour with Will Smith and Pinkett-Smith, the tickets for which she had purchased on the coupon website *Groupon*; her delightful anecdote went viral and spawned a partnership with that company. Haddish has made news for gossipy bits about other celebrities as well. Perhaps her most famous is about an actress who allegedly bit pop superstar Beyoncé.

Haddish's life and her comedy act have since become indistinguishable. When she hosted *Saturday Night Live*, Haddish wore the same white Alexander McQueen dress that she wore to the *Girls Trip* premiere. The dress was so expensive, she joked, that she planned to wear it again and again—and she has, at various red-carpet events, much to her fans' delight.

In 2018, Haddish appeared in *Uncle Drew*, a sports comedy starring NBA star Kyrie Irving; *Night School* with Kevin Hart; the political satire *The Oath*; and Tyler Perry's dramedy *Nobody's Fool*. She also began a starring role in the Tracy Morgan comedy series *The Last O.G.* on TBS. In 2019, Haddish is slated to appear in several films, including *The Lego Movie 2: The Second Part*, *The Kitchen*, and *The Secret Life of Pets 2*. "The goal is to get 80 movies by the time I'm 50," Haddish, who has seemingly accomplished everything she has ever set her mind to despite incredible odds, told Smith. "So, I got what? Twelve years? I got 12 years."

PERSONAL LIFE
Haddish was married to and divorced from William Stewart. She wrote in *The Last Black Unicorn* that he was physically abusive, a claim Stewart disputes, and in 2018 he sued her, her publisher, and her collaborator, Tucker Max, for defamation.

Much of Haddish's sizable income goes to providing care of her mother—whom she removed from a mental institution in 2018—and her elderly grandmother. She owns a home in South Los Angeles.

SUGGESTED READING
Barton, Chris. "Tiffany Haddish Helps Turn Darkness into Laughter at the Laugh Factory's Comedy Camp." *Los Angeles Times*, 17 Aug. 2018, www.latimes.com/entertainment/tv/la-et-st-comedy-camp-laugh-factory-20180817-story.html. Accessed 6 Mar. 2019.

Buckley, Cara. "Tiffany Haddish: 'My Career Is a Delicious Roast Chicken.'" *The New York Times*, 17 Oct. 2018, www.nytimes.com/2018/10/17/movies/tiffany-haddish.html. Accessed 6 Mar. 2019.

Jeffries, Michael. "The Remarkable Rise of Tiffany Haddish." *The Atlantic*, Sept. 2017, www.theatlantic.com/entertainment/archive/2017/09/the-remarkable-rise-of-tiffany-haddish/538872/. Accessed 15 Mar. 2019.

Rose, Lacey. "Tiffany Haddish, Hollywood's New Comedy Queen, Has One Crazy Story to Tell." *The Hollywood Reporter*, 13 June 2018, www.hollywoodreporter.com/features/tiffany-haddish-new-queen-comedy-has-a-crazy-story-you-1119446. Accessed 14 Mar. 2019.

Smith, Krista. "Why Tiffany Haddish Doesn't Consider *Girls Trip* Her Biggest Career Highlight." *Vanity Fair*, 30 Jan. 2018, www.vanityfair.com/hollywood/2018/01/tiffany-haddish-interview-in-the-spotlight. Accessed 12 Mar. 2019.

Travers, Peter. "'Girls Trip' Review: Comedy about Four Besties in NOLA Hits All the Right Notes." Review of *Girls Trip*, directed by Malcolm D. Lee. *Rolling Stone*, 21 July 2017, www.rollingstone.com/movies/movie-reviews/girls-trip-review-comedy-about-four-besties-in-nola-hits-all-the-right-notes-198843. Accessed 14 Mar. 2019.

Weaver, Caity. "There's Something Funny about Tiffany Haddish." *GQ*, 26 Mar. 2018, www.gq.com/story/tiffany-haddish-profile-2018. Accessed 11 Mar. 2019.

SELECTED WORKS
The Carmichael Show, 2015–17; *Keanu*, 2016; *Girls Trip*, 2017; *The Last O.G.*, 2018–

—*Molly Hagan*

Jonathan Haidt

Date of birth: October 19, 1963
Occupation: Social psychologist

Jonathan Haidt, an ethics professor at the New York University (NYU) Stern School of Business, takes in stride comments that it seems oxymoronic for a business school to employ a professor of ethics. The morality specialist accepted the post following a rash of newsworthy business scandals, including Bernie Madoff's $65 billion Ponzi scheme. Amid a widespread call for business schools to change their teaching models, Haidt designed an entirely new class. "I said, 'We're not going to teach MBA students, be ethical, be ethical, and then expect them to resist these incredible forces at work on them in real situations,'" he recalled to Brian Gallagher for *Nautilus* (7 Mar. 2019). "Rather, let's teach them ethical systems design. . . . [Let's] help leaders who want to create ethical organizations, help them to change the social forces, improve the culture."

Haidt also authored the best-seller *The Righteous Mind* (2012), which examines the bitter political polarization plaguing the United States, and coauthored *The Coddling of the American Mind* (2018), which asserts that it is vital for open, uncensored discussion of all points of view to be allowed on college campuses. Although often suspected of partisanship from both the Left and Right, he explained to Gallagher that he considers himself "someone who's not on either team." He added, "All social scientists should be committed to understanding society much more so than fighting for one side."

It takes a multidisciplinary approach, he believes, to address issues of societal importance effectively. "I am a social psychologist but I love all the social sciences, and I think to understand any complicated social problem, you need sociology, and psychology, and political science, and economics," he explained to Gallagher. "I see my role as someone who has spent his life studying morality from every possible angle. Historical, evolutionary, cultural, anthropological."

EARLY LIFE AND EDUCATION

Jonathan "Jon" Haidt was born into a Jewish family in New York City on October 19, 1963 and raised in the suburb of Scarsdale. Haidt's father, who had been raised during the Great Depression, wanted a practical, stable, economically secure career, so he chose chemical engineering and later entered patent law.

After graduating from Scarsdale High School in 1981, Haidt enrolled at Yale University. In 1985 he earned a bachelor's degree in philosophy with honors from Yale. In his senior thesis on free will and determinism, he posed the

Photo by Leigh Vogel/WireImage

following question: If the movement of every atom, electron, and neuron is determined by the state of the universe right before that movement, does that mean that we are predetermined to act in certain ways?

Haidt had learned computer programming in college, and he considered launching a computer consulting business. He toyed with doing so in Spain because he spoke Spanish and loved traveling in Europe. He quickly discarded that idea, however, on the grounds that there would be too many regulatory roadblocks and admittedly did not feel quite brave enough to make that drastic a leap. He also briefly considered earning a graduate degree in computer science but ultimately decided instead to pursue psychology. "I've always been the sort of person who is much more interested in ideas than in things or people," he told Gallagher.

Haidt entered the University of Pennsylvania, where he earned a master's degree in psychology in 1988. He continued his studies and completed a doctoral degree there in 1992, with the provocatively titled dissertation "Moral Judgment, Affect, and Culture, or, Is It Wrong to Eat Your Dog?" He spent three months studying in northeastern India on a Fulbright Scholarship; he later credited the experience with opening his eyes to a broader palette of moralities.

After graduating, he embarked on a two-year postdoctoral fellowship in cultural psychology at the University of Chicago. He then served for a year as a postdoctoral associate at the John D. and Catherine T. MacArthur Foundation's Program on Mental Health and Human Development.

EARLY CAREER

In 1995 Haidt was hired as an assistant professor of psychology at the University of Virginia, and he steadily climbed the academic ladder there, becoming an associate professor in 2001 and a full professor in 2009. He had a yearlong stint as a visiting professor at Princeton University in 2006–07 and spent the winter of 2008 as a visiting distinguished fellow at the University of California at Santa Barbara.

Haidt began his career, as the title of his dissertation suggests, by studying negative moral emotions, such as disgust and shame, but by about 1999 he had moved on to the still-fledgling field of positive psychology, examining the underpinnings of such feelings as admiration, awe, and optimism. To support that groundbreaking research, he was awarded the American Psychological Association's 2001 John Templeton Positive Psychology Prize.

His subsequent 2006 book, *The Happiness Hypothesis: Finding Modern Truth in Ancient Wisdom*, dissects ten established ideas (including "The whole universe is change and life itself is but what you deem it" from Marcus Aurelius and "What doesn't kill me makes me stronger" from Friedrich Nietzsche), questions them in light of modern scientific research, and extracts lessons still applicable to modern life. A November 2005 starred review in the respected industry periodical *Publishers Weekly* characterized Haidt as a "reductionist" but ultimately praised the book as "an erudite, fluently written, stimulating reassessment of age-old issues."

THE RIGHTEOUS MIND

Haidt next began investigating how moral psychology could be applied to the study of politics, with the aim of helping people understand the moral motives of people with whom they might disagree vehemently. In 2012 he published *The Righteous Mind: Why Good People Are Divided by Politics and Religion*, which he had begun conceiving after George W. Bush won the US presidency.

The product of a politically liberal family, Haidt originally believed that his research would make a strong case for liberalism. "Liberalism seemed so obviously ethical," he wrote in the book. Instead, he found himself agreeing at times with a range of conservative writers, from Edmund Burke to Thomas Sowell. "I realized, Wow, you actually need to expose yourself to critics, to people who start from a different position," he told Gallagher.

The book included suggestions for overcoming the effects of polarization, such as holding open primaries so that people outside each party's base can vote to nominate moderate candidates and requiring members of Congress to move their families to Washington, DC, to encourage friendship and cooperation across the aisle. "Many of Haidt's proposals are vague, insufficient or hard to implement. And that's O.K.," reviewer William Saletan wrote for the *New York Times* (23 Mar. 2012). "He just wants to start a conversation about integrating a better understanding of human nature—our sentiments, sociality and morality—into the ways we debate and govern ourselves. At this, he succeeds. It's a landmark contribution to humanity's understanding of itself." For his unique approach in the book, Haidt received the 2013 Media Book Prize from the Society for Personality and Social Psychology.

NYU AND NONPROFIT WORK

In the run-up to the book's publication, Haidt wanted to live in New York City, and during the 2011–12 academic year, he arranged a visiting professorship at NYU. In the fall of 2012 he accepted the post of Thomas Cooley Professor of Ethical Leadership there. At Stern he continued to develop his moral foundations theory, which proposes that a series of innate and universal psychological systems form the foundations of morality, with various cultures and factions placing special emphasis on some of them. These include adherence to authority, care for others, fairness, liberty, and sanctity or purity. His surveys suggest, for example, that political conservatives place great importance on loyalty, authority, and purity, whereas political liberals identify more with the concept of care for others, fairness, and liberty.

In 2013 Haidt launched the Ethical Systems collaborative through NYU. "I founded it by inviting lots of other professors, researchers who knew about accounting and finance and conflicts of interest, areas that I didn't know anything about—and together we summarized the research," he recalled to Gallagher. "We make it very easily available to business people all around the world for free." He explained that his organization approaches business as fundamentally good and valuable, though also potentially dangerous. "Business is incredibly powerful and when businesses go off the rails, when industries become predatory, a lot of people suffer," he acknowledged. "But when they're honest, when they make a good product, when they treat all their stakeholders well, the benefit to society is immense." Haidt continues to serve as its founding director.

Around the time Haidt moved to NYU, he noticed that there was little diversity in the viewpoints of his fellow social scientists. He found this alarming because it raises the probability of confirmation bias, distorting the science. In 2015 he and colleagues cofounded the Heterodox Academy to increase the quality of intellectual discourse and encourage productive disagreement in psychology, sociology, and law. He remains the chair of the board of directors.

THE NEED FOR CIVIL DISAGREEMENT

That same year Haidt and civil liberties lawyer Greg Lukianoff cowrote a controversial article that appeared in the September issue of the *Atlantic* magazine. "The Coddling of the American Mind"—as it was provocatively named by an editor in an echo of *The Closing of the American Mind*, a 1987 best-seller by Allan Bloom—criticized students and their universities for policing speech too zealously, heckling speakers with whom they disagreed, and shutting down intellectual inquiry. The article became one of the *Atlantic*'s five most-read pieces of all time and inspired a 2018 book, *The Coddling of the American Mind: How Good Intentions and Bad Ideas Are Setting Up a Generation for Failure*.

"Whether the subject is trigger warnings, 'victimhood culture,' or the supposed death of free speech, college students are an easy punching bag and target for generalizations," Jesse Singal wrote for *New York* magazine (26 Sept. 2018). "Because campus blowups have become more common in recent years, and far more visible thanks to social media, there's been a glut of half-baked perspectives about what they represent. I suspect that some left-of-center readers are going to be quick to shove *The Coddling of the American Mind* . . . into the hot-take pile—but that would be a mistake. It's a generally nuanced, carefully constructed book worth grappling with."

Haidt's TED talks on political polarization, religion, and how America could come together as a nation after the divisive 2016 election of President Donald Trump have proven very popular. The latter had been viewed nearly 2 million times by mid-2019.

Of the current state of the country, Haidt told George Eaton for *New Statesman America* (2 Jan. 2019), "I see nothing that gives me hope. However, I'm constantly reminded by my libertarian friends that people have often thought this way and they've always been wrong. . . . I'm not looking at property in New Zealand, I'm not planning to move my kids to another country, but I am expecting things to get worse in the next few years."

Haidt was named a Top 100 Global Thinker in 2012 by *Foreign Policy* magazine and a World Thinker in 2013 by *Prospect* magazine. His other honors include several teaching awards and the 2015 Beacon of Ethics Award from the Business Ethics Alliance.

PERSONAL LIFE

Haidt and his wife, photographer Jayne Riew, have a son (b. 2007) and a daughter (b. 2010). They are proponents of a movement known as "free-range parenting" and have allowed their children the freedom to play in a local park and run errands in their neighborhood from an early age. Haidt even became a founding member of the free-range parenting organization Let Grow.

In his mid-to-late teen years, Haidt became an atheist vehemently opposed to organized religion. His research as an adult led him to recognize the societal benefits of religion, despite remaining secular.

SUGGESTED READING

Eaton, George. "Jonathan Haidt Interview: 'I'm Jewish but I Want My Kids to Read *Mein Kampf*.'" *New Statesman America*, 2 Jan. 2019, www.newstatesman.com/culture/observations/2019/01/jonathan-haidt-interview-i-m-jewish-i-want-my-kids-read-mein-kampf. Accessed 3 July 2019.

Haidt, Jonathan. "Interview: Jonathan Haidt on What Underlies Polarization in America." Interview by Erich J. Price. *Merion West*, 30 Jan. 2019, merionwest.com/2019/01/30/interview-jonathan-haidt-talk-political-division. Accessed 3 July 2019.

Haidt, Jonathan. "The Psychology of Self-Righteousness." Interview by Krista Tippett. *On Being*, 19 Oct. 2017, onbeing.org/programs/jonathan-haidt-the-psychology-of-self-righteousness-oct2017/#transcript. Accessed 9 July 2019.

Haidt, Jonathan. "The Well-Meaning Bad Ideas Spoiling a Generation." Interview by Brian Gallagher. *Nautilus*, NautilusThink, 7 Mar. 2019, nautil.us/issue/70/variables/the-well_meaning-bad-ideas-spoiling-a-generation. Accessed 3 July 2019.

Jenkins, Holman W., Jr. "Jonathan Haidt: He Knows Why We Fight." *The Wall Street Journal*, 29 June 2012, www.wsj.com/articles/SB100014240527023038302045774465125225 82648. Accessed 3 July 2019.

Saletan, William. "Why Won't They Listen?" Review of *The Righteous Mind*, by Jonathan Haidt. *The New York Times*, 23 Mar. 2012, www.nytimes.com/2012/03/25/books/review/the-righteous-mind-by-jonathan-haidt.html. Accessed 3 July 2019.

Singal, Jesse. "How 'Coddled' Are American College Students, Anyway?" *New York*, 26 Sept. 2018, nymag.com/intelligencer/2018/09/the-coddling-of-the-american-mind-and-the-culture-wars.html. Accessed 3 July 2019.

SELECTED WORKS

The Happiness Hypothesis: Finding Modern Truth in Ancient Wisdom, 2006; *The Righteous Mind: Why Good People Are Divided by Politics and Religion*, 2012; *The Coddling of the American Mind: How Good Intentions and Bad Ideas Are Setting Up a Generation for Failure*, 2018

—*Mari Rich*

Matt Haimovitz

Date of birth: December 3, 1970
Occupation: Cellist

Matt Haimovitz is an award-winning, world-renowned cellist. Born in Israel and raised in the United States, Haimovitz was a musical prodigy. Famed violinist Itzhak Perlman took Haimovitz under his wing when Haimovitz was only eleven. After studying with Leonard Rose and Yo-Yo Ma, Haimovitz earned a recording contract at seventeen. Russell Platt, writing for the *New Yorker* (31 Mar. 2008) described Haimovitz as an "expressive maximalist" who "calls forth a dazzling spectrum of sounds from the depths of his instrument."

Over his decades-long career, Haimovitz has performed in vaunted concert halls and gritty punk clubs, playing a repertoire that ranges from Johann Sebastian Bach to Jimi Hendrix. Haimovitz plays a multimillion-dollar 1710 Matteo Goffriller cello, which he calls Matteo. "I'm just a steward with this instrument," he told Juan Rodriguez for the *Montreal Gazette* (12 Nov. 2015). "Think about Venice in 1710: one of the first composers to come to mind is Vivaldi, who taught at a girls' school. He very likely commissioned this cello for one of his girls. That's my connection to the history. This instrument was in Venice when Vivaldi was first writing his cello concerto." After thirty years of playing Matteo, Haimovitz dropped the instrument in 2017, breaking its neck. The accident revealed other problems within the cello, and it took five luthiers over a year to complete the extensive repairs.

Haimovitz, once on the verge of an illustrious career as a soloist in the traditional mold, is known for his eclectic taste in contemporary music and his imaginative renditions of classics, particularly Bach's suites for solo cello. He is, Jeremy Eichler wrote for the *New York Times* (26 Mar. 2006), the "classical musician who has strayed from the pack but taken his cello with him."

A MUSICAL PRODIGY

Haimovitz was born to Romanian Jewish parents in Bat Yam, Israel, near Tel Aviv, in 1970. His father is an engineer, and his mother is a classically trained pianist. Haimovitz displayed an early love for music. His mother recalls that when he was three, he attended concerts without complaint. The family moved to Palo Alto, California, when Haimovitz was four. At age seven, he begged his mother for cello lessons after hearing a recording of legendary cellist Mstislav Rostropovich. Irene Sharp, a well-known cellist, was Haimovitz's first teacher.

Photo by Hiroyuki Ito/Getty Images

In 1982, when Haimovitz was eleven years old, the violinist Itzhak Perlman invited him over for a spaghetti dinner to discuss music after hearing the prodigy in a master class. "He was interested in me cellistically," Haimovitz recalled to *People* (17 Aug. 1987). Perlman arranged for Haimovitz to study at the Juilliard School with master Leonard Rose that year, and Haimovitz's family moved to New York. Rose once described Haimovitz as "probably the greatest talent I have ever taught," as quoted by Eichler for the *New York Times* (2 May 2004). A thirteen-year-old Haimovitz once sat in for Rose at a chamber concert at Carnegie Hall with Rostropovich, Isaac Stern, Shlomo Mintz, and Pinchas Zukerman. When Rose became sick with leukemia, he asked his prized pupil, Yo-Yo Ma, to tutor Haimovitz. The young cellist occasionally met with Ma, who was constantly touring, on the road. "It was the two of us sitting on television sets and couches in hotel rooms," Haimovitz told Philip Kennicott for the *Washington Post* (2 Dec. 2011) of those early lessons, which included "more philosophical discussion" than technical instruction.

In 1984, Haimovitz made his debut as a soloist with conductor Zubin Mehta and the Israel Philharmonic Orchestra. That same year, for his New York debut alongside Ma, Marta Casals Istomin, widow of famed cellist Pablo Casals, loaned Haimovitz her late husband's Matteo Goffriller cello. After Rose died the same year, Haimovitz began studying with Ron Leonard, formerly of the Los Angeles Philharmonic. In 1986, he became the youngest musician to receive the Avery Fisher Career Grant.

EDUCATION AND EARLY CAREER

In 1987, Haimovitz, then seventeen, became the youngest artist ever signed to Deutsche Grammophon, a classical music label. The label signed Haimovitz to an exclusive ten-year deal under which he released six albums, starting with *Saint-Saëns, Lalo: Cello Concertos, Bruch Kol Nidrei* (1989), a 1987 recording with James Levine and the Chicago Symphony Orchestra. At the time, Haimovitz was touring with twenty to thirty orchestras each season and practiced three to four hours a day.

Haimovitz, who had graduated from the Collegiate School in Manhattan for high school in addition to Juilliard, enrolled at Princeton University, where he met composer and electric guitarist Steven Mackey. They improvised together, and for the first time, Haimovitz became interested in playing contemporary music. He continued to tour throughout his freshman year but eventually dropped out of school to focus on his music. Three years later, he returned to school, transferring to Harvard University, where he began working with contemporary and avant-garde composers like Luciano Berio, György Ligeti, Henri Dutilleux, and George Crumb, as well as composer and producer Luna Pearl Woolf, his future collaborator and spouse. He graduated magna cum laude in 1996.

BACH "LISTENING-ROOM" TOUR

Haimovitz began to tire of his hectic performance schedule and the repertoire he was being asked to play. "I started to realize it was really hard to play the [Dvořák] Concerto a thousand times and keep it fresh," he told Eichler. "I wasn't sure if that was really what I wanted to do." At nineteen, Haimovitz vetoed a recording of the concerto he made for Deutsche Grammophon with Levine and the Berlin Philharmonic. True to his wishes, the record was never released, but the label never asked him to record another concerto again. He finished out his Deutsche Grammophon contract with four contemporary classical records. Frustrated with his evolving taste, the company chose not to renew his contract.

Meanwhile, a restless Haimovitz moved to Europe, where he married Woolf and reconnected with Bach's suites for solo cello. The classic suites were once thought to be lost to time until Casals discovered them at a second-hand music shop in Barcelona in 1890 when he was thirteen years old. Haimovitz decided to make his own recording of the suites in an old church near his home in western Massachusetts. Haimovitz and Woolf released the album, *J. S. Bach: 6 Suites for Cello Solo* (2000) on their own record label, Oxingale.

Haimovitz chose to hold his album release concert at Iron Horse Music Hall, a 250-seat acoustical music club. It was an unusual choice for a venue, more suited to rock than classical music, but he played to a packed house. "It was the first time I felt like I had really reached a broad audience," he told Eichler. Inspired, he hired a singer-songwriter as a manager and set out on a club tour. Haimovitz came to call it the Bach "Listening-Room" Tour. As Eichler put it, "Haimovitz found that by stripping away any vestige of stuffy concert hall packaging, he could get the music to speak to listeners who knew nothing about its history or the prescribed etiquette for receiving its rewards. What's more, for the first time in his career, he began playing to audiences largely of his own generation." Playing Bach in these spaces, he later explained, imbued the music with the freshness that he yearned for while playing Dvořák in concert halls.

ANTHEM (2003) AND OTHER WORK

Haimovitz released an album called *Anthem* in 2003. The album is named for "Anthem," Haimovitz's rendering of Hendrix's version of "The Star-Spangled Banner." The album features the music of nine living American composers, including Woolf, Mackey, Tod Machover, Augusta Reed Thomas, and David Sanford, as well as Robert Stern, who died in August 2018. "While the listener may feel alienated by certain sonic spaces that Haimovitz discovers and shares with his audience, this disc remains a rich, fascinating, and truly multidimensional view of the cello's sonic potential," Zoran Minderovic wrote in a review for the website *AllMusic* (2003). Haimovitz went on a fifty-state tour, playing in pizza parlors, nightclubs, and the now-defunct punk mecca CBGB, where he was the first classical musician to play at the venue.

Between 2003 and 2013, Haimovitz released and appeared on a number of records through his Oxingale label. Among them are *Hyperstring Trilogy* (2003), an album featuring the music of composer and inventor Machover. For the album, Haimovitz played a hypercello, an instrument that translates cello notes into computer sounds. In 2005, Haimovitz released an album of Central European, folk-inspired contemporary music called *Goulash!* The album, which features works by Ligeti, Osvaldo Golijov, Adrian Pop, and Béla Bartók, is "shot through with an appealing sense of whimsy," Eichler wrote. It also features a four-cello version of the Led Zeppelin song "Kashmir."

In 2015, Haimovitz returned to the Bach suites with an album, released as part of the Pentatone Oxingale series, called *The Cello Suites according to Anna Magdalena*, inspired by the manuscript transcribed by Anna Magdalena Bach, the composer's second wife. In 2016, Haimovitz released another album in the series, called *Overtures to Bach*, for which he invited contemporary composers Woolf, Sanford, Vijay

Iyer, Roberto Sierra, Pulitzer Prize–winner Du Yun, and Philip Glass to each write a piece inspired by one of the six cello suites. The two albums were produced by David Frost, who won the 2016 Grammy Award for Best Classical Producer. In 2017, Haimovitz recorded *Philip Glass: Partitas for Solo Cello* for Glass's Orange Mountain Music label, which included the world premiere of Glass's Partita No. 2. That same year Haimovitz released his collaboration with pianist Christopher O'Reilly, *Troika* (Pentatone Oxingale series), featuring their arrangements of compositions by Sergei Rachmaninoff, Dmitri Shostakovich, Sergei Prokofiev, the Beatles, Viktor Tsoi, and Pussy Riot.

Haimovitz teaches cello as an associate professor at the Schulich School of Music of McGill University in Montreal, Canada, and previously headed the cello program at the University of Massachusetts, Amherst.

AWARDS AND PERSONAL LIFE
Haimovitz has won several awards and accolades over the course of his career. In addition to the Avery Fisher Career Grant, he has won the Grand Prix du Disque and the Diapason d'Or, both in 1991; the American Music Center's 2004 Trailblazer Award; and the 2006 ASCAP Concert Music Award for his advocacy of living composers. In 1999 he became the first cellist to win the Premio Internazionale "Accademia Musicale Chigiana."

Haimovitz and Woolf live in Montreal and have two daughters.

SUGGESTED READING
Eichler, Jeremy. "Music; The Pizza Parlor Prodigy." *The New York Times*, 2 May 2004, www.nytimes.com/2004/05/02/arts/music-the-pizza-parlor-prodigy.html. Accessed 15 Feb. 2019.

Kennicott, Philip. "Yo-Yo Ma, a Virtuoso at More Than the Cello." *The Washington Post*, 2 Dec. 2011, www.washingtonpost.com/lifestyle/style/yo-yo-ma-a-virtuoso-at-more-than-the-cello/2011/11/22/gIQAkvNnKO_story.html. Accessed 15 Feb. 2019.

Oestreich, James R. "Music: Classical Recordings; A Conversation between Composers, in Polish and Hungarian." *The New York Times*, 26 Mar. 2006, www.nytimes.com/2006/03/26/arts/music-classical-recordings-a-conversation-between-composers-in-polish-901059.html. Accessed 15 Feb. 2019.

Platt, Russell. "Cello Love." *The New Yorker*, 31 Mar. 2008, www.newyorker.com/magazine/2008/03/31/cello-love. Accessed 15 Feb. 2019.

Rodriguez, Juan. "Cellist Matt Haimovitz Draws from the Past, Plays in the Present." *Montreal Gazette*, 12 Nov. 2015, montrealgazette.com/entertainment/cellist-matt-haimovitz-draws-from-the-past-plays-in-the-present. Accessed 15 Feb. 2019.

Russell, Anna. "An Emotional Reunion between Cello and Cellist." *The New Yorker*, 17 Sept. 2018, www.newyorker.com/magazine/2018/09/17/an-emotional-reunion-between-cello-and-cellist. Accessed 15 Feb. 2019.

Steinberg, Martin. "A Broken-Hearted Matt Haimovitz Laments His Goffriller's Broken Neck." *Strings*, 14 Feb. 2017, stringsmagazine.com/a-broken-hearted-matt-haimovitz-laments-his-goffrillers-broken-neck/. Accessed 19 Feb. 2019.

SELECTED WORKS
Bach: 6 Suites for Cello Solo, 2000; *Anthem*, 2003; *Overtures to Bach*, 2016; *Troika* (with Christopher O'Reilly), 2017

—*Molly Hagan*

Andrew Haldane
Date of birth: August 18, 1967
Occupation: Economist

Andrew Haldane was appointed chief economist at the Bank of England, the central bank of the United Kingdom, in 2014. Working for the bank in a variety of positions since 1989, Haldane has taken the initiative of expanding the bank's research and data analytics functions. While previous chief economists have focused solely on monetary policy, Haldane has been praised for his multidisciplinary approach to his work, which draws upon complexity theory, world history, and political economy—a social science that examines the relationships between markets and the state as well as between individuals and society. In addition, he has been mentioned as a possible successor to Mark Carney, the institution's governor and highest ranking official.

"Central bankers aren't known as innovators or thought leaders, but Andrew Haldane . . . is an exception," John Cassidy wrote for *Time* (24 Apr. 2014) when the economist was named by that publication as one of the 100 Most Influential People in the World in 2014. Cassidy cited Haldane's assertion that government bailouts encourage financial institutions to take unwise risks, his acknowledgment that the Occupy Wall Street protesters made some good points, and his call for a "'reformation' in finance," and concluded: "In the City of London and on Wall Street, many people don't agree with what Haldane says. But they know they can't ignore him."

Photo by Niccolò Caranti via Wikimedia Commons

That sentiment is almost universally echoed by financial observers. Writing for the *Wall Street Journal* (31 Aug. 2012), Jason Zweig called Haldane "one of the world's smartest financial regulators," and Ralph Benko asserted in a profile for *Forbes* (22 Oct. 2012): "If Andy Haldane represents the new class of leading public servants—empirical, based in practical outcomes rather than on rather dubious theories—the world economy well may prove to be poised on the verge of a new golden age."

EARLY YEARS AND EDUCATION

Andrew Haldane, who is more often referred to as Andy, was born on August 18, 1967, in Guiseley, a town in Yorkshire, England. His father, George, earned a living as a professional trumpeter, playing at a succession of Britain's seaside resorts, and his mother, Maureen, was a homemaker. Haldane enjoyed watching from backstage as his father played, and as a child, he took up the trumpet; he abandoned lessons in his teens.

Haldane attended the Guiseley School in Leeds, West Yorkshire. He credits a teacher there, Peter Bates, for sparking his interest in economics. He was also heavily influenced by seeing the hardships that hit the United Kingdom during a period of mass unemployment in the 1980s—a period that convinced him that economics and effective public policy could combine to make people's lives better.

The first in his family to attend college, Haldane chose Sheffield University, in the northwest of England, reasoning that it was

both close to home (meaning that he could continue to play cricket with his local team on the weekends) and the alma mater of his respected teacher. Throughout his years at Sheffield he worked at a small fruit shop, earning less than £20 a week for what was sometimes physically demanding labor.

As an undergraduate, Haldane impressed Alec Chrystal, his professor of economics, who convinced him to continue his studies. He graduated from Sheffield with a bachelor's degree in economics and finance in 1988. Haldane then earned a master's degree in economics from Warwick University in 1989.

BANK OF ENGLAND

Shortly after obtaining his master's degree, Haldane—who has quipped to interviewers that he has only ever had one job interview in his life—joined the Bank of England in 1989. The Bank of England has a long and storied history. Established in 1694, it stands as one of the oldest such institutions in the world. Several other countries have modeled their own central banks on it. It was privately owned until 1946, when it was nationalized; in 1998, it became an independent public organization.

Upon being hired Haldane was assigned to the division dedicated to monetary analysis and made a member of the Monetary Policy Committee, an entity responsible for deciding what policy actions the bank should be taking—for example, raising or lowering interest rates—and explaining to the public the sometimes opaque reasons behind those decisions. Because it can take years for monetary policy to have a desired effect on the economy, monetary policy committee members need to consider such factors as probable inflation and growth—making setting policy an activity akin to a complex game of chess.

In 1993, Haldane was promoted to manager of the monetary policy division, a post he held until 1998, when he became head of international finance. He steadily moved on to head the divisions of market infrastructure, from 2003 to 2005, and systematic risk assessment, from 2005 to 2009. In 2009, he was made the executive director of financial stability, charged with making sure England's financial system is sound, identifying and monitoring risks in the financial system, and mitigating those risks when necessary. In those capacities, Haldane "had a knack for finding himself on the front lines of some of its biggest challenges," as Jennifer Ryan explained for *Bloomberg* (22 July 2015). She further explained that Haldane often found himself working in the departments that dealt with several economic changes as they were happening, including United Kingdom's departure from the European Exchange Rate Mechanism in 1992, Russia's financial crisis in 1998, and the 2008 collapse of the financial services firm Lehman Brothers.

PRO BONO ECONOMICS AND SPEECHES

In 2009, while still at the Bank of England, Haldane cofounded the nonprofit organization Pro Bono Economics, which encourages professional economists to donate their time and expertise to help charities function well financially. At the same time, he drew attention for a series of iconoclastic pronouncements and speeches. In a 2010 speech, titled "The $100 Billion Question," he calculated that the financial crisis of the previous year had cost the British economy more than £7 trillion and that the idea that some banks were "too big to fail" required a hidden public subsidy of at least £50 billion a year. Although more traditionally minded financial insiders were dismayed that he had so bluntly expressed those calculations, others applauded that he had helped bring about a much-needed political debate on banking reform. "Just as influential have been Haldane's radicalism and free-thinking in a central banking world where the key players are often a depressing blur of orthodoxy and conventional wisdom," Ben Chu wrote for the London-based *Independent* (1 Dec. 2013). "Haldane praised the Occupy movement, saying that the uninvited guests . . . were right to be hostile to the workings of the global financial system. . . . that same year, he delivered a dynamite speech which implied that regulators around the world were barking up the wrong tree by embracing complexity rather than simplicity in their banking reform principles."

During a 2012 speech made in Jackson Hole, Wyoming, Haldane made a striking analogy, as quoted by Benko. "Catching a frisbee is difficult. . . . Were a physicist to write down frisbee-catching as an optimal control problem, they would need to understand and apply Newton's Law of Gravity," Haldane explained. "Yet despite this complexity, catching a frisbee is remarkably common. . . . To ask today's regulators to save us from tomorrow's crisis using yesterday's toolbox is to ask a border collie to catch a Frisbee by first applying Newton's Law of Gravity." Haldane's made this assertion to explain that complex financial systems would be better managed by simple approaches than complex ones.

CHIEF ECONOMIST AND PUBLICATIONS

When Carney assumed the Bank of England's governorship in late 2013, he assigned Haldane to head a division dedicated to research and forecasting. There Haldane launched an advanced analytics unit and increased the focus on big data and financial technology. On June 1, 2014, Haldane was appointed the chief economist of the Bank of England, with a term scheduled to last until 2020. Following the appointment, there was much speculation that Haldane would one day succeed Carney as governor of the Bank of England; however, Haldane has declined to comment on the rumors.

In 2016, Haldane was confirmed as a Fellow of the Academy of Social Sciences (FAcSS). In 2017, he coauthored, with David Birch, the book *Before Babylon, Beyond Bitcoin: From Money That We Understand to Money That Understands Us*. In addition, he has served as the editor or coeditor of the books *Fixing Financial Crises in the 21st Century* (2004) and *The Future of Payment Systems* (2007) and has written a multitude of articles on various economic topics. In 2018, he was appointed to the chair of United Kingdom's newly created Industrial Strategy Council. The council works to monitor and advise the country's long-term strategy to improve productivity growth.

PERSONAL LIFE

Haldane lives near Walton-on-Thames, Surrey, and has a vacation cottage in Deal, on the coast of Kent. He and his wife, Emma Hardaker-Jones, a human-resources executive, have three children: Keir, Finn, and Autumn Grace. He purports to be averse to profligate spending thanks to his modest upbringing and never uses credit cards. Although his children do attend private schools, he considers their education to be a wise investment, rather than an extravagance.

Haldane is a trustee of the group National Numeracy, which helps adults and children across the United Kingdom to hone their math skills. He is also an ambassador for the volunteering network REACH.

SUGGESTED READING

Benko, Ralph. "Catching A Frisbee Is Difficult: The Bank of England Tells It Like It Is." *Forbes*, 22 Oct. 2012, www.forbes.com/sites/ralphbenko/2012/10/22/catching-a-frisbee-is-difficult-the-bank-of-england-tells-it-like-it-is/#2d5eff0323ac. Accessed 3 Feb. 2019.

Cassidy, John. "Andrew Haldane." *Time*, 24 Apr. 2014, time.com/70833/andy-haldane-2014-time-100/. Accessed 3 Feb. 2019.

Chu, Ben. "Andy Haldane: The Coming Man of British Banking." *Independent*, 1 Dec. 2013, www.independent.co.uk/news/people/profiles/andy-haldane-the-coming-man-of-british-banking-8975109.html. Accessed 3 Feb. 2019.

Evans, Steve. "Big Is Not Better When It Comes to Banks." *BBC News*, 18 Dec. 2009, news.bbc.co.uk/2/hi/business/8419658.stm. Accessed 3 Feb. 2019.

Mikhailova, Anna. "Feeling Poor as a Boy Scarred My Northern Soul." *The Times*, 28 Aug. 2016, www.thetimes.co.uk/article/

feeling-poor-as-a-boy-scarred-my-northern-soul-drlljp5tx. Accessed 3 Feb. 2019.

Ryan, Jennifer. "The U.K.'s Subversive Central Banker." *Bloomberg*, 22 July 2015, www.bloomberg.com/news/articles/2015-07-22/boe-s-haldane-plays-the-contrarian-to-carney-in-u-k-rate-debate. Accessed 3 Feb. 2019.

Zweig, Jason. "The Jackson Hole Speech People Should Long Remember." *The Wall Street Journal*, 31 Aug. 2012, blogs.wsj.com/total-return/2012/08/31/the-jackson-hole-speech-people-should-long-remember/. Accessed 3 Feb. 2019.

—*Mari Rich*

Photo by Richard Heathcote/Getty Images

Lydia Hall

Date of birth: December 14, 1987
Occupation: Professional golfer

Lydia Hall is a driven and accomplished Welsh professional golfer. Since joining the Ladies European Tour (LET) in 2007, she has played in over one hundred tournaments on a variety of courses all over the world and has distinguished herself with a handful of noteworthy performances. She was "over the moon," as she was quoted as saying in an article posted on the *LET* website (18 Aug. 2012), upon notching her first LET victory in 2012, when she won the ISPS Handa Ladies British Masters. Not long afterward, to gain more career opportunities and broaden her knowledge about other aspects of the golf industry, she enrolled in a renowned three-year program with the Professional Golfers' Association (PGA) of Great Britain and Ireland to earn a foundation degree; she began serving as a PGA teaching assistant with the Hensol Golf Academy, based in Wales, in 2015.

Never tiring of the challenge that each game of golf presents, Hall made history in 2016 when she became the first woman to win the Welsh National PGA Championship and the first woman to win a PGA national tournament. In addition to the LET, she has played in events on the LET Access Series, the developmental tour to the LET, and on the Symetra Tour, the feeder circuit for the Ladies Professional Golf Association (LPGA) Tour. In 2017, she proved victorious in the LET Access Series' WPGA International Challenge.

EARLY LIFE AND EDUCATION

Hall was born on December 14, 1987, in Bridgend, a town located in southern Wales. Her father, Wayne Hall, is a former rugby union player who represented Wales in one international match, against Western Samoa (present-day Samoa), in 1988; he played the "hooker" position, a specialist forward who has a key role in close-contact situations like scrums. Influenced by her father, Hall naturally gravitated toward sports as a young girl. She started playing golf at the age of eleven, in part after watching Tiger Woods, who was then taking the golf world by storm. Later, even after several years of professional play, she would continue to list her parents as her biggest influences and would express gratitude at being able to share some of her biggest career moments with them.

From the time she entered the sport, Hall practiced at the Southerndown Golf Club, in Bridgend, where she was coached by their head professional, John Peters. Under the guidance of Peters, she gradually progressed through the Welsh junior and amateur circuit beginning in the early 2000s. She earned a place on both the Welsh Under-21 and Welsh Ladies' teams in 2004. That same year, she was crowned the Glamorgan Ladies' and Girls' champion and captured a silver medal at the European Under-21 Team Championship.

From 1999 to 2007, Hall attended the Pencoed Comprehensive School. There, she earned A-levels in physical education and information technology. She then decided to pursue a professional golfing career. "The effort and determination that Lydia has shown since she was a kid has been absolutely fantastic," her father was quoted as saying in the article posted on the *LET* website.

TURNING PROFESSIONAL AND FIRST LET VICTORY

Hall officially turned professional in November 2007, earning her card to join the LET, Europe's top female golf tour, after placing second at the LET's Final Qualifying School at Italy's Le Fonti Golf Club. In an interview for *WalesOnline* (1 Nov. 2007), Peters said of her accomplishment, "It's fantastic to see it all come together and I am very proud of her. I knew she was talented and knew she could do it."

During her first four years on the tour, Hall did not achieve a single victory. Nevertheless, she strung together a series of confidence-boosting performances during that time. In 2010, she posted a top-ten finish as she tied for sixth position at the Lalla Meryem Cup in Morocco and played well at the Omega Dubai Ladies Masters in the United Arab Emirates. The following year, she tied twelfth at the latter event and recorded one of the best finishes of her career up to that point at the Tenerife Ladies Match Play in Spain's Canary Islands.

Hall's first LET win came at the 2012 ISPS Handa Ladies British Masters, which was held at the Buckinghamshire Golf Club in England. Over the course of the three-day event, which was renamed the European Masters in 2013, she shot rounds of sixty-six, seventy-one, and seventy-two, respectively, for a seven under par-fifty-four-hole total. Though she had trailed by two shots, she ultimately secured a one-shot victory over American Beth Allen. The win marked a culmination of her efforts to improve her game, which were helped immensely through comprehensive strength and conditioning work with Gareth Cooper, a former Wales rugby union player, at a gym in Bridgend.

SPONSORSHIP AND EXPANDING HER HORIZONS

Prior to her British Masters win, the amount of career earnings Hall had amassed often resulted in her skipping select LET tournaments solely due to the cost required to enter them. As she put it to Anthony Woolford for *WalesOnline* (24 Aug. 2012), "A tournament missed is £1,800 not spent." Though her victory granted her a two-and-a-half-year exemption on the LET, she still did not land significant financial backing from sponsors, who have historically placed a much higher emphasis on the men's game. "Everyone now says you must be doing well with sponsors but that's not really the case with the women's game," she explained in an interview for *National Club Golfer* (10 July 2013). "There are so many sports that take priority and they get all the exposure and it is difficult to compete with them." However, her persistence and dedication paid off when, in April 2013, it was announced that Lynx Golf UK, a company increasingly known for innovative equipment, had signed on to serve as her sponsor; that relationship continued over the subsequent seasons, and she still represented the brand as of early 2019.

Hall also made the decision to enter the PGA's qualifying training program, which is conducted in conjunction with University of Birmingham in England, to make herself more versatile as a golf professional. From 2014 to 2017, in between her time playing in tournaments, she took part in online instruction and fulfilled the additional requirements, including attending brief periods of residential classroom modules, learning about areas such as business management and sports science, to earn a PGA foundation degree in professional golf studies. In 2015, she joined the Hensol Golf Academy as a PGA teaching assistant. "It gives me an opportunity to teach and I really enjoy that," Hall, who has expressed an interest in coaching, said about her decision to pursue the degree, as quoted by Joe Urquhart in *National Club Golfer* (16 Aug. 2016). "It also gives me a balance in my life so I don't have to think all about playing all the time."

MAKING HISTORY

While in the PGA program, Hall continued to play in LET tournaments all over the world. In 2014, she finished tied at a place in the top ten at the Helsingborg Open in Sweden. Her progress was slowed the following season, however, when she missed about nine months due to a knee ligament injury. Undaunted, she returned in 2016 with a renewed enthusiasm and finished tied for second place at that year's Qatar Ladies Open, held at the Doha Golf Club in Qatar. That year, she also competed on the UK–based Women's Professional Golf Association (WPGA) circuit, playing four of the seven events in the WPGA One Day Series and later winning that year's WPGA Order of Merit.

In the middle of the WPGA series, Hall turned in a historic performance on the PGA circuit. In July 2016, she competed at the Welsh National PGA Championship, which was formed in 1904 and is one of the PGA's oldest tournaments. She won the thirty-six-hole tournament, which was held at the Tenby Golf Club, widely considered to be the birthplace of golf in Wales, by one stroke, after overcoming challenges by Matthew Tottey and Thomas Phillips. This triumph meant that she had become the first woman in golfing history to win the championship and the first to win a PGA national tournament.

Following her historic victory, Hall credited her success to her many years playing on the LET, which helped her "massively," as quoted by Urquhart. "I've been in this position—in the final group and leading. So I knew the kind of feeling I'd have, how to keep myself calm, to stay in the present and not think ahead." She went on to have the best year of her career in 2017, which was highlighted by a win at the LET Access Series' WPGA International Challenge, a fifty-four-hole tournament held in the English county of Suffolk. Also that year, she won all five of the WPGA One Day Series events she entered, earning the WPGA Order of Merit once more.

2018 AND BEYOND
In 2018, Hall finished second at the WPGA International Challenge. She also notched top-ten finishes at the Women's New South Wales Open in Australia and the Investec South African Women's Open, placing a tied fifth and ninth, respectively. Meanwhile, she competed on the US–based Symetra Tour, finishing sixth at the IOA Invitational in Milton, Georgia. She ended that season ranked twenty-eighth on the LET Order of Merit.

Among other goals, Hall has expressed an interest in gaining her LPGA Tour card and earning a place on the Solheim Cup team. The latter event is held every other year for professional female golfers representing teams from Europe and the United States. In 2017, in an interview with James Pontin for the BBC (3 Mar. 2017), she had said regarding the Solheim Cup, "I know deep down that my game is strong enough to be in that team." Additionally, as a professional golfer and instructor, she has said that she hopes to inspire and help young women wanting to break into the sport.

PERSONAL LIFE
When she is not competing, Hall, who stands five feet two inches tall, resides in Pencoed, Wales. In her spare time, she enjoys watching movies, listening to music, and socializing with friends and family.

SUGGESTED READING
Hall, Lydia. "Getting to Know Lydia Hall." *LET Access Series*, 7 Sept. 2018, letaccess.com/news_article.php?id=3954. Accessed 6 Feb. 2019.

Hall, Lydia. "Lady Golfer Interviews: Lydia Hall." *National Club Golfer*, 10 July 2013, www.nationalclubgolfer.com/news/lady-golfer-interviews-lydia-hall-2/. Accessed 6 Feb. 2019.

"Lydia Hall." *Ladies European Tour*, ladieseuropeantour.com/player/?player=130249. Accessed 6 Feb. 2019.

"Lydia Hall Earns Maiden Win at ISPS Handa Ladies British Masters." *Ladies European Tour*, 18 Aug. 2012, ladieseuropeantour.com/lydia-hall-earns-maiden-win-at-isps-handa-ladies-british-masters/. Accessed 6 Feb. 2019.

Urquhart, Joe. "Historic Lydia Hall Becomes PGA's First Lady." *National Club Golfer*, 16 Aug. 2016, www.nationalclubgolfer.com/news/lydia-hall-pga/. Accessed 6 Feb. 2019.

Woolford, Anthony. "Golf: Maiden Tour Win Timely Cash Boost for Wales Star Lydia Hall." *WalesOnline*, 24 Aug. 2012, www.walesonline.co.uk/sport/other-sport/golf/golf-maiden-tour-win-timely-2026283. Accessed 6 Feb. 2019.

—*Chris Cullen*

Rami Hamdallah
Date of birth: August 10, 1958
Occupation: Prime minister of the Palestinian National Authority

Rami Hamdallah is an academic who first became the prime minister of the Palestinian National Authority in 2013 and then, after briefly resigning, was reappointed to the position in 2014.

EARLY LIFE AND EDUCATION
Rami Hamdallah was born on August 10, 1958, in the town of Anabta in the northern West Bank, to a wealthy family who had large land holdings in the West Bank. He graduated from the University of Jordan in 1980 with a degree in English language. He then studied in the United Kingdom, earning a master's degree in linguistics from the University of Manchester in 1982 and a doctoral degree in applied linguistics from the University of Lancaster in 1988.

In 1982 Hamdallah joined the An-Najah National University in the West Bank as an English instructor. He later became the chair of the English department (1988–92), the dean of the Faculty of Arts (1992–95), and the vice president for academic affairs for the Colleges of Humanities (1995–98) at the university. In 1998 he became the president of the university.

As president, Hamdallah helped the university to expand by greatly increasing student enrollment and raising over $300 million to build a new campus in Nablus. He also added several new schools, including the schools of medicine, nursing, and engineering.

An active participant in the academic community, both within the West Bank and globally, Hamdallah has worked to advance learning and promote cooperation among institutes of higher education. He has served as a member of the boards of the Council for the Presidents of Palestinian Universities, the Palestinian European Academic Cooperation in Education (2000–2005), and the Commission for Universities and

Communities in the Euro-Med Region (joined 2009). He also has been a member of the steering committee for the Council of Arab Universities for Scientific Research and a vice president of the Palestinian Scientific Academy.

Hamdallah also has been a member of many nonacademic groups. In 2002 he became the secretary general of the Central Elections Commission. He served as the chairman of the board for the Palestinian Stock Exchange from 2003 to 2006 and from 2008 on. He has been a member of the board of the Yasser Arafat Foundation since 2011, was a trustee of the Palestinian Economic Policy Research Institute–MAS from 2008 to 2012, and is a member of the Palestinian Constitution Committee.

Hamdallah has published numerous academic papers and two books, mostly on language and higher education. Despite having several family members in politics (one was a mayor of Anabta; another was a member of the Jordanian Parliament prior to 1967), Hamdallah has been primarily interested in education, believing it is the key to the future for the people of Palestine.

POLITICAL CAREER
In 2013 President Mahmoud Abbas asked Hamdallah to be the prime minister of the Palestinian National Authority to replace Salam Fayyad. Despite being a widely respected academic, Hamdallah was not a member of a political party and was relatively unknown outside the academic community. Political analysts and the media reported that it was because he was an outsider and lacked political experience that Abbas chose him. His political neutrality was considered an asset, and his inexperience and lack of a power base indicated he would be unlikely to assert his own political agenda. Thus, it was perceived that Abbas chose Hamdallah because of his compliancy and willingness to go along with Abbas's goals. The Islamic fundamentalist group Hamas objected to Hamdallah's appointment primarily because it had not been consulted or involved in the decision-making process. Thus, the group refused at first to recognize Hamdallah as a legitimate prime minister.

In a written statement shortly after his appointment, Hamdallah pledged to work toward an independent Palestinian state and to support Abbas's political plans. He also stated his willingness to work with Hamas. Hamdallah was sworn in as prime minister on June 6, 2013. His appointment was a temporary one and he was intended to serve only through mid-August.

On June 20, 2013, Hamdallah submitted his resignation, tweeting that he was resigning due to "conflicts, confusion, and corruption" and that "Palestine needs a real political reform." Although Abbas accepted his resignation, Hamdallah agreed to stay on until his replacement could be found.

In May 2014, Abbas again appointed Hamdallah the prime minister and tasked him with forming a transitional coalition government. On June 2, 2014, a new cabinet was sworn in. In June 2015, Hamdallah formed a new national unity government with Hamas and the political party Fatah, once known as the Palestinian National Liberation Movement.

IMPACT
Despite predictions Hamdallah would be unable to effect significant change, he has created the first national unity government of the Palestinian National Authority since 2007. He also has overcome Hamas's objections to his appointment and has gained the group's acceptance as the head of the government. He has made inroads into the volatile Palestinian political environment and has remained committed to resolving the Palestinian conflict and creating an independent state. He has also appealed to the United Nations (UN) and the United States to protect Palestinians and to compel Israel to resume the peace process.

PERSONAL LIFE
Hamdallah met his wife while teaching at An-Najah National University. They became the parents of twin sons in 1989 and had another son in 1991. All three sons died in a car accident in 2000. Hamadallah and his wife later had a daughter.

SUGGESTED READING
Abu Toameh, Khaled. "Rami Hamdallah: A Yes Man for Fatah." *JPost.* 4 June 2014, www.jpost.com/Middle-East/Rami-Hamdallah-A-yes-man-who-poses-no-threat-to-Fatah-315359. Accessed 22 May 2019.

"BBC Reporting on the Hamdallah Resignation." *BBC Watch.* BBC, 23 June 2013, bbcwatch.org/2013/06/23/bbc-reporting-on-the-hamdallah-resignation/. Accessed 22 May 2019.

Beaumont, Peter. "Fatah and Hamas Agree on New Palestinian Prime Minister." *Guardian.* 29 May 2014, www.theguardian.com/world/2014/may/29/fatah-hamas-agree-new-palestinian-prime-minister. Accessed 22 May 2019.

Khoury, Jack, and Amos Harel. "Palestinian President Taps Academic as New PA Prime Minister." *Haaretz.* 3 June 2013, www.haaretz.com/abbas-taps-academic-as-new-palestinian-pm-1.5272501. Accessed 22 May 2019.

Makovsky, David. "New Palestinian Prime Minister Is a Victory for Fatah." *Washington Institute.* 4 June 2013, www.washingtoninstitute.org/policy-analysis/view/

new-palestinian-prime-minister-is-a-victory-for-fatah. Accessed 22 May 2019.

Rudoren, Jodi. "Palestinian Authority's New Premier Admired as 'Conscience.'" *The New York Times*. 3 June 2013, www.nytimes.com/2013/06/04/world/middleeast/hamdallah-palestinian-authoritys-premier-is-admired.html. Accessed 22 May 2019.

Weymouth, Lally. "A New Two-State Strategy for Peace." *The Washington Post*. 31 May 2015, www.washingtonpost.com/opinions/a-new-two-state-strategy-for-peace/2015/05/31/31330f4c-06da-11e5-bc72-f3e16bf50bb6_story.html?noredirect=on&utm_term=.9ddffdba6a96. Accessed 22 May 2019.

—*Barb Lightner*

Photo by Unknown, via Wikimedia Commons

Mona Hanna-Attisha

Date of birth: December 9, 1976
Occupation: Public health advocate

Dr. Mona Hanna-Attisha earned national attention beginning in 2015 for her role in exposing the water crisis in Flint, Michigan. The pediatrician and associate professor at Michigan State University (MSU), alerted to concerns over unsafe drinking water in Flint, conducted independent research on the issue. After finding elevated levels of lead—which can cause irreversible brain damage—in local children, she risked her career by immediately going public with the information and warning Flint residents to stop using tap water. Accused of conducting shoddy research and fomenting hysteria, Hanna-Attisha persevered and in late 2015 Michigan state officials finally admitted the drinking water in Flint was poisoned and began to take corrective action.

Hanna-Attisha used the recognition she earned to further pursue public health advocacy, including ongoing efforts to deal with Flint's water problems. She founded and served as director of the Pediatric Public Health Initiative, a program aimed at mitigating the impact of the crisis on Flint's children. She also became a vocal critic of the anti-immigration movement, noting how her own status as an immigrant showed how people coming to the United States can greatly contribute to the country. Above all, Hanna-Attisha dedicated herself to working for the social good of all people, including the disadvantaged. "I think it's my innate responsibility, it's my professional responsibility," she explained to Sumaia Masoom for the website *#MuslimGirl*. "I've always tried to fight for the underdog."

EARLY YEARS AND EDUCATION

The physician who would become widely known as Dr. Mona was born Mona Hanna in Sheffield, England, on December 9, 1976. Her parents had moved there from Iraq so her father could earn a doctorate, and when Saddam Hussein came to power in their home country, they decided not to return. After Hanna-Attisha was born, the family immigrated to the United States, settling in Michigan (first in the Upper Peninsula and later in Royal Oak) when she was four years old. This background would play a key role in shaping her outlook. "In 1980, my family arrived here full of hope, trading a future of war, fascism and oppression for one of peace, freedom and opportunity," she recounted in a *New York Times* opinion piece (11 Feb. 2017). "A future in Iraq might have included imprisonment or death at the hands of the government. It is through these everyday-grateful immigrant eyes that I first saw our country as a 4-year-old and still see it today."

Hanna-Attisha and her family endured hardship as they adjusted to American life, and even scraping up enough coins to buy a gallon of milk could be a challenge at times. However, her father eventually became an engineer at General Motors, and her mother found work teaching English to other immigrants. Her parents were a guiding influence in her life. "Together, they instilled in me and my brother an ethic of social justice and service-oriented work while providing us with a better life," Hanna-Attisha wrote. "The American dream was our reality." Living in a suburb of Detroit, Michigan, she enjoyed a middle-class upbringing and did well in school.

Hanna-Attisha would later credit her decision to enter medicine, in some part, to an experience that occurred when she was five. A car accident left her with a broken neck and fractured jaw, but she was greatly comforted by a young female doctor holding her hand and assuring her that everything would be alright. She determined that she would one day similarly comfort children.

Hanna-Attisha went on to receive her bachelor's degree and a master's degree in public health from the University of Michigan. She earned her medical degree from MSU, following which she completed her residency and chief residency at the Children's Hospital of Michigan, which was affiliated with Wayne State University.

FLINT WATER CRISIS RESEARCH
From the beginning of her medical career, Hanna-Attisha exhibited the humanistic approach to healthcare that had inspired her years before. In 2011, as a faculty member at Wayne State University, she was inducted into the Gold Humanism Honor Society in recognition of her compassion and empathy. She later became both a practicing pediatrician at Hurley Children's Hospital in Flint and an associate professor at MSU. It was while serving in those roles that she became involved in the issue that would bring her national fame.

The Flint water crisis began in the spring of 2014, when Flint officials (appointed by the Michigan state government to manage the city on an emergency basis) switched the city's water source from Detroit's system to the Flint River as a cost-cutting measure. The water from the Flint River, which was heavily polluted for decades, was not treated properly and, therefore, highly corrosive to old lead pipes. Soon after the switch, reports began to emerge of poor water quality. These included not only complaints of discolored, foul-tasting, and particle-filled tap water, but also concerns that lead and other harmful substances were leaching into the drinking supply. However, city officials insisted that the water was safe for human consumption, and many Flint residents, especially those who could not afford other sources, continued to use it for drinking and bathing. As a result, some people suffered hair loss, rashes, and even Legionnaires' disease.

In August 2015 Hanna-Attisha was visting with her high school friend Elin Betanzo, a certified water engineer. Betanzo brought up the rumors of high levels of lead Flint's water supply and the potential impact on the city's residents, especially young children. Childhood exposure to lead can result in serious brain damage and impact the entire course of a person's life; organizations such as the Centers for Disease Control and Prevention (CDC) and the American Academy of Pediatrics (AAP) suggest there is simply no safe level of lead exposure for young children. At the urging of her friend, Hanna-Attisha agreed to immediately research the issue. "I'd always seen my work through the lens of social justice," she wrote for the New York Times (9 June 2018). "To put it simply, health is justice, especially for the youngest among us."

However, Hanna-Attisha quickly ran into obstacles. Her attempts to obtain data on childhood lead levels from the state or country were rebuffed, so she turned instead to her hospital system's electronic data. Working rapidly, she and her research team concluded that the percentage of children with elevated blood levels of lead significantly increased after the water source changed. Throughout the city the numbers had more than doubled and, in some areas, had even tripled.

WHISTLEBLOWER
Armed with the results of her study, Hanna-Attisha contacted city leaders and state health officials, urging them to act to stop the tainted water. Yet her warnings were ignored. Frustrated, she decided to hold a press conference to get her findings out to the public. In her New York Times op-ed (9 June 2018) she noted, "It was an unusual thing for a local pediatrician to do. But that's what you do when nobody's listening. You get louder." Indeed, she risked her professional career by releasing research that had not been peer-reviewed or officially published.

Immediately after the September 24, 2015, press conference, Hanna-Attisha and her findings were summarily dismissed by government officials, who questioned the quality of her data and branded her as a troublemaker. However, she had the backing of numerous activists, religious leaders, and community members. In the face of mounting pressure from throughout the country, officials agreed to reexamine the data. In October, less than a month after the press conference, the city reconnected to the Detroit water system. The move represented a victory of sorts, but because damage had already been done to pipe infrastructure, experts advised Flint residents not to drink city water unless they were using lead-clearing filters, which the state agreed to supply.

Hanna-Attisha's whistleblowing research was formally published in the American Journal of Public Health in early 2016. She was also appointed to the Flint Water Interagency Coordinating Committee, the Michigan Child Lead Poisoning Elimination Board, and the Michigan Public Health Commission, all of which formed in response to the crisis. Thanks to her testimony before Congress, $100 million in federal funds (as well as some $250 million in state funding) were allocated to address Flint's water issues.

Among actions the state outlined were immediate water testing in all city schools, free testing of water for any resident requesting it, and rigorous anticorrosion treatment of the entire water system.

Although it was gratifying to be vindicated as a scientist—the governor of Michigan even issued a formal apology to her—Hanna-Attisha remained gravely worried about Flint's children. "These kids did nothing wrong," she told Masoom. "Just because they lived in a poor city that was bankrupt—and didn't treat its water properly, so we owe it to these kids now to really invest in them so that they have a bright future ahead of them." In 2016 she became the founding director of the Pediatric Public Health Initiative (PPHI), a venture of MSU and the Hurley Children's Hospital aimed at addressing the long-term effects of the lead exposure. Because the effects of lead poisoning may not become apparent for years in some cases, Hanna-Attisha stressed that it was important to use every resource possible to mitigate problems that may arise in the future. "We can't take away this exposure, but we are leaning on the incredible science of resilience and child development to limit the impact," she explained to Susan Davis for NPR's *Weekend Edition Sunday* (24 June 2018).

FURTHER ACTIVISM

Thanks to her work in drawing attention to the Flint water crisis, Hanna-Attisha was listed as one of the most influential people of 2016 by *Time* magazine. "I am honored and humbled," she remarked upon receiving the honor, as quoted by Geri Kelley for *MSU Today* (21 Apr. 2016). "However, the most influential people in my world are the people of Flint—the smart, strong and resilient people of Flint." Indeed, she leveraged her newly high-profile status mainly to continue to work on issues of public health and social justice. As she noted in the *New York Times* (9 June 2018), "My work couldn't stop with treating patients and training other pediatricians. I was becoming something new—an activist."

Hanna-Attisha won numerous awards for her advocacy efforts. These included the Ridenhour Prize for Truth-Telling, the PEN American Center James C. Goodale Freedom of Expression Award, the Rose Nader Award for Arab American Activism by the American-Arab Anti-Discrimination Committee, the Heinz Award for Public Policy, and the MIT Media Lab's inaugural Disobedience Award, among others. She was named Michiganian of the Year by the Detroit News in 2016 and a champion of science by the Union of Concerned Scientists. In 2018 she was inducted to the Michigan Women's Hall of Fame. That same year Hanna-Attisha published *What the*

Eyes Don't See, a personal account of the crisis in Flint; it was named one of the hundred most notable books of 2018 by the *New York Times*, among other honors. In 2019 Hanna-Attisha received the inaugural Vilcek-Gold Award for Humanism in Healthcare.

PERSONAL LIFE

Hanna-Attisha's family had Chaldean (Iraqi Christian) heritage, but she follows no particular religion. "I identify myself as just Iraqi American," she told Masoom. "I was very much raised Arab; I speak Arabic, we eat Arabic food, but we don't really practice anything." She has told interviewers that though she faced some ethnic discrimination growing up, mainly in high school during the Gulf War, her personality and her supportive community meant it had little negative effect on her.

Hanna-Attisha and her husband, fellow pediatrician Elliott Attisha, have two daughters, Nina and Layla. She noted that because of what she learned about the United States' crumbling water infrastructure, she is exceedingly careful about what she allows her children to drink.

SUGGESTED READING

"A Choiceless Choice: Mona Hanna-Attisha on Standing Up and Speaking Out." *Vilcek Foundation*, 28 May 2019, www.vilcek.org/news/current-news/mona-hanna-attisha-on-standing-up-and-speaking-out.html. Accessed 9 July 2019.

Hanna-Attisha, Mona. "How a Pediatrician Became a Detective." *The New York Times*, 9 June 2018, www.nytimes.com/2018/06/09/opinion/sunday/flint-water-pediatrician-detective.html. Accessed 9 July 2019.

Hanna-Attisha, Mona. "Meet the Whistleblower of the Flint Water Scandal." Interview by Sumaia Masoom. *#MuslimGirl*, 2016, muslimgirl.com/19283/interview-dr-hanna-attisha-whistleblower-flint-water-scandal. Accessed 9 July 2019.

Hanna-Attisha, Mona. "'What the Eyes Don't See' in Flint." Interview by Susan Davis. *Weekend Edition Sunday*, NPR, 24 June 2018, www.npr.org/2018/06/24/622959117/what-the-eyes-don-t-see-in-flint. Accessed 9 July 2019.

Hanna-Attisha, Mona. "Will We Lose the Doctor Who Would Stop the Next Flint?" *The New York Times*, 11 Feb. 2017, www.nytimes.com/2017/02/11/opinion/sunday/will-we-lose-the-doctor-who-would-stop-the-next-flint.html. Accessed 9 July 2019.

Kelley, Geri, et al. "Mona Hanna-Attisha Named One of *Time*'s Most Influential People." *MSU Today*, Michigan State University, 21 Apr. 2016, msutoday.msu.edu/news/2016/

mona-hanna-attisha-named-one-of-times-most-influential-people. Accessed 9 July 2019.

Riley, Rochelle. "Dr. Mona Hanna-Attisha Goes from Doctor to Global Hero." *Detroit Free Press*, 6 Feb. 2016, www.freep.com/story/news/columnists/rochelle-riley/2016/02/06/dr-mona-hanna-attisha-goes-doctor-global-hero/79772514. Accessed 9 July 2019.

—*Mari Rich*

Barbara Hannigan

Date of birth: May 8, 1971
Occupation: Soprano and conductor

For operatic soprano Barbara Hannigan, the key to a compelling musical performance does not lie in the interpretation of the musical composition, but rather, as she told Joseph So for *Ludwig Van* (5 Nov. 2017), "One has to become the music." Over the course of her distinguished career—during which she performed in major venues and with accomplished musical ensembles throughout North America and Europe—Hannigan has demonstrated talent for becoming one with the music itself as well as with the characters she portrays on stage. A repertoire-focused artist who often returns to her favorite works, she established a reputation for dramatic abilities that imbue the women she plays with degrees of emotion and nuance not always present in other productions. In recognition of her work, and her focus on contemporary music, Hannigan has received widespread critical acclaim and recognition both in her native Canada and around the world.

A singer since childhood and a graduate of the University of Toronto's well-regarded music program, Hannigan also turned her attention toward the field of conducting, making her debut in that role in 2011. She has received significant attention both for her work as a conductor and for the ways in which her experience as a singer shapes her approach. Ultimately, Hannigan considered both roles—between which she divided her time—to be natural offshoots of her musical self. "I am a musician, and whether I am leading an orchestra, singing a phrase, commissioning new works—I am always the same musician. Like a tree with branches reaching in different directions, I suppose," she explained to Leslie Barcza for *Barczablog* (21 Feb. 2015). Also devoted to developing the careers of the next generation of classical singers, Hannigan founded the mentorship program the Equilibrium Initiative in 2017 and taught master classes at a variety of institutions.

Photo by Lelli e Masotti via Wikimedia Commons

EARLY LIFE AND EDUCATION

Barbara Hannigan was born on May 8, 1971, in Waverley, Canada. She grew up in a rural area of the province of Nova Scotia, where she lived with her parents and three siblings in a household that valued hard work and creativity. Music was particularly popular among the children, who pursued lessons in various instruments. "We lived in the country and spent a lot of time in the car on the way to music lessons," she recalled to Barcza. "It must have been very difficult for my mother, with four kids, to manage us all, with our various activities, but we were most certainly supported in our musical endeavors." In addition to Hannigan herself, two of her siblings also pursued advanced studies in music.

By the time she was ten years old, Hannigan had decided that she seriously wanted to develop a career in music. Although she studied both singing and piano, she did not consider the possibility of becoming a conductor during that period. "Growing up in a small village on the east coast of Canada in the 70s and 80s, I thought women could only conduct choirs or, at best, school orchestras," she wrote for the *Guardian* (12 Mar. 2015). "I didn't know what sexism meant—that was just the way it was."

After completing her secondary education, Hannigan relocated to Toronto to study music at the University of Toronto, which was known for its music program and extensive music library. In addition to studying classical singing under operatic soprano Mary Morrison, Hannigan participated in a variety of musical ensembles during her time at the university. She earned her bachelor's degree from the school in 1993.

Hannigan then studied at the Banff Centre for the Arts, before spending 1995 to 1996 at the Royal Conservatory of the Hague. She earned a master's degree in music from the University of Toronto in 1998.

EARLY VOCAL CAREER

Beginning her career in music as a vocalist, Hannigan quickly gained a reputation as a talented and skilled singer whose soprano voice and dramatic abilities made her an excellent operatic performer. Her first major role as a soprano was as an understudy for the role of Anne Trulove in a production of the opera *The Rake's Progress*. She would later return to that role in various productions. In addition to her early stage appearances, Hannigan gained notice for her work in the 2001 contemporary opera *Toothpaste*, a short work that debuted on Canadian television in 2001.

Hannigan continued to build her reputation as a performer through engagements with a wide range of productions and ensembles, primarily in Europe but also in North America. For Hannigan, the location of the production was less important than the specific compositions being performed. "I'm repertoire driven. It's always been about what I want to sing, not where or even with whom," she explained to Wendalyn Bartley for the *Whole Note* (30 Jan. 2015). Among the numerous roles Hannigan played, one of her favorites became that of Lulu, the protagonist of the Alban Berg opera of the same name, who she first portrayed in 2012. She was particularly drawn to the multifaceted nature of the character, who can be interpreted in a range of ways. "For me, she is not a femme fatale, a sex kitten, or even the victim she's all too often played as. She's an endlessly fascinating, deliciously contradictory woman who might defy labels, but is always true to herself," Hannigan wrote for the *Guardian*. In 2014, she starred as Lulu in a filmed version of the play.

CONDUCTING DEBUT

Hannigan made her debut as a conductor in 2011 with a performance of the early twentieth-century work *Renard*, by composer Igor Stravinsky, at the Théâtre du Châtelet in Paris, France. "It wasn't that I was imagining making a career change," she recalled in an interview for the music festival *Klarafestival*'s website (2019). "I was basically doing one concert, that's it. But before the concert it felt like something special: a kind of responsibility I never experienced before." The reception to Hannigan's conducting debut was positive, and the experience fueled her increasing interest in pursuing that path. "I remember liking that feeling very, very much," she said in her Klarafestival interview. "I absolutely wanted to explore that further."

Over the next several years, Hannigan continued to develop her skills as a conductor through engagements with numerous major ensembles. These included both North American orchestras, such as the Toronto Symphony Orchestra and the Cleveland Orchestra, and European orchestras, such as the London Symphony Orchestra and the Munich Philharmonic Orchestra.

ORIGINAL ROLES

Although she at times performed older compositions, Hannigan was particularly interested in performing works from the twentieth and twenty-first centuries. Pursuing that interest in contemporary music, she starred in over eighty-five debut performances of new works. In 2012, she originated the role of Agnès in the opera *Written on Skin*, composed by George Benjamin. The following year, Hannigan starred in the premiere of the song cycle *let me tell you*, composed by Hans Abrahamsen and written by Paul Griffiths for the Berlin Philharmonic. Focusing on the character of Ophelia from William Shakespeare's tragedy *Hamlet*, *let me tell you* reinterprets the character through a new lens, a process that appealed to Hannigan. "When I perform the piece, my back story is about all the women who have found their voices over the last 400 years," she told Bartley. "Now we have a new Ophelia, and even though she retains the personality of the young Shakespearian Ophelia, she's now found her own words."

Hannigan also appeared in such roles as Marie in Bernd Alois Zimmermann's *Die Soldaten* (*The Soldiers*), for which she won Germany's Faust Award in 2015, and Elle in the 2015 production of *La Voix Humaine* at Opéra de national Paris. In 2016 and 2017, she appeared in productions of *Pelléas et Mélisande*, staged by Katie Mitchell and Krzysztof Warlikowski, respectively.

EQUILIBRIUM INITIATIVE

In 2017, Hannigan founded the Equilibrium Initiative, a mentorship program for classical singers still in the relatively early stages of their careers. "It's not an education program or a training program. Some of the musicians of Equilibrium are already singing with renowned ensembles and orchestras," she explained in her interview for the *Klarafestival* website. "What I'm trying to do is to help them with developing and maintaining their discipline, their focus, skills that are not just about singing and being a good musician but about being a good colleague and a healthy person serving not only to be successful but also to be truly satisfied with their career." In addition to benefiting from the mentorship program and its resources, singers affiliated with the Equilibrium Initiative had the opportunity to perform in major events such as the 2019 Ojai Music Festival, for which Hannigan served as music director. "It is a beautiful place with a generous spirit, and the audiences are open and curious!" Hannigan told Polina Lyapustina for *OperaWire* (1 June 2019) of the festival.

BALANCING SINGING AND CONDUCTING

In 2017, Hannigan released her first album, *Crazy Girl Crazy*, on which she both sang and conducted. The album incorporated a portion of the music from *Lulu* and featured her performances of work by composers Luciano Berio and George Gershwin. A collaboration with the orchestral collective LUDWIG, *Crazy Girl Crazy* received critical acclaim following its release and won the 2017 Grammy Award for Best Classical Solo Vocal Album.

In 2018, Hannigan conducted *The Rake's Progress*, her first full length opera, and sang the title role in Michael Jarrell's *Bérénice* at the Paris Opera. She released her next album, *Vienna: Fin de Siècle*, the same year, for which she received the 2019 JUNO Award for Classical Album of the Year: Vocal or Choral. In 2019, she took on the role of principal guest conductor with Sweden's Gothenburg Symphony. Although Hannigan worked to balance her singing and conducting careers, remaining active in both disciplines, she commented in interviews that conducting offered the ability to continue her career in music after the eventual end of her singing career, an event she considered inevitable due to the effects of aging on the voice.

PERSONAL LIFE

Hannigan was married to Gijs de Lange, a Dutch theater director, until 2015. Although based in Toronto during her early career, Hannigan spent much of her career in Europe. She briefly lived in the Netherlands before relocating to Paris, France, in 2017.

In recognition of her music successes, Hannigan was appointed to the Order of Canada in 2016. She was awarded an honorary doctorate by the University of Toronto, alongside mentor Morrison, in 2017.

SUGGESTED READING

Bartley, Wendalyn. "Barbara Hannigan—Being the Music." *The Whole Note*, 30 Jan. 2015, www.thewholenote.com/index.php/newsroom/feature-stories/25212-barbara-hannigan-being-the-music. Accessed 13 Sept. 2019.

Hannigan, Barbara. "Barbara Hannigan: No Jacket Required . . ." *The Guardian*, 12 Mar. 2015, theguardian.com/music/2015/mar/11/barbara-hannigan-conducting-britten-sinfonia. Accessed 13 Sept. 2019.

Hannigan, Barbara. "Barbara Hannigan on the Rake's Progress, Equilibrium and Brussels." *Klarafestival*, 2019, klarafestival.be/en/info/interview. Accessed 13 Sept. 2019.

Hannigan, Barbara. "Interview: Barbara Hannigan: Queen of the New." Interview by Joseph So. *Ludwig Van*, 5 Nov. 2017, www.ludwig-van.com/toronto/2017/11/05/interview-barbara-hannigan-queen-of-the-new/amp/. Accessed 13 Sept. 2019.

Hannigan, Barbara. "10 Questions for Barbara Hannigan." Interview by Leslie Barcza. *Barczablog*, 21 Feb. 2015, barczablog.com/2015/02/21/ten_barbara_hannigan/. Accessed 13 Sept. 2019.

Hannigan, Barbara. "Barbara Hannigan Interview: 'I Serve the Music, Not the Audience.'" Interview by Ben Lawrence. *The Telegraph*, 17 Sept. 2017, www.telegraph.co.uk/music/interviews/barbara-hannigan-interview-serve-music-not-audience/amp/. Accessed 13 Sept. 2019.

Lyapustina, Polina. "Creating Her Own Way—Soprano and Conductor Barbara Hannigan on Conducting, Equilibrium Project, and Ojai Festival." *OperaWire*, 1 June 2019, operawire.com/creating-her-own-way-soprano-and-conductor-barbara-hannigan-on-conducting-equilibrium-project-and-ojai-festival. Accessed 13 Sept. 2019.

—*Joy Crelin*

Yuval Noah Harari

Date of birth: February 24, 1976
Occupation: Historian and author

The Israeli historian and professor Yuval Noah Harari has earned considerable attention as a "big ideas" person, presenting broad ideas about the past and future of humanity. His work explores weighty and complex subjects such as human intelligence, consciousness, free will, and evolution. "The most important thing is the search for the truth," he told Carole Cadwalladr for the *Guardian* (5 July 2015). "I really want to understand reality, what's really happening here." Harari shot to fame with his first book for general audiences, *Sapiens: A Brief History of Humankind*, published in Hebrew in 2011 and in English in 2014. A discussion of the entire course of human history from the evolution of *Homo sapiens* to the twenty-first century, the book quickly became a best seller and brought the author a level of celebrity achieved by few academics. He followed up with two more popular successes: *Homo Deus: A Brief History of Tomorrow* (2016), which speculates on the future, and *21 Lessons*

Photo by Jonathan Nicholson/NurPhoto via Getty Images

for the 21st Century (2018), which seeks to supply insight on the present. Some of those ideas also formed the basis of several highly popular TED Talks, garnering millions of online views.

Harari's expansive ideas have proven popular not only with the general public, but also with many leaders around the world. He was praised by high-profile figures including former US president Barack Obama, Microsoft founder and philanthropist Bill Gates, and Facebook CEO Mark Zuckerberg. He consulted with many politicians and organizations, and in 2018 he addressed the World Economic Forum annual meeting about the future of humanity.

However, the same sweeping generalizations that make his writing accessible and influential also drew significant criticism from within the academic community. Some scholars have suggested Harari's ideas are simplistic and even questioned his command of facts and analysis.

EARLY LIFE AND EDUCATION
Yuval Noah Harari was born on February 24, 1976, and grew up in a secular Jewish home in a suburb of Haifa, Israel. As a young boy he had trouble understanding why the adults around him were fascinated by money, politics, and careers rather than deep philosophical ideas. He recalled to David Sexton of the *Evening Standard* (11 June 2018): "I made a promise to myself that when I was grown up, I would still care about the big questions."

Harari attended the Hebrew University of Jerusalem beginning in 1993, graduating with a bachelor's degree in history in 1996. He earned his master's degree in history from the same

institution in 1998. Later that same year he moved to the United Kingdom, where he studied history under Dr. Steven J. Gunn at the University of Oxford's Jesus College and earned a doctorate in 2002. During this time Harari went through a period of much self-doubt and confusion. This led him to discover Vipassana meditation, which he credited with changing his life. "I suddenly had a tool to scientifically observe directly my mind," he told Cadwalladr. "It gave me the ability to focus on what is really important."

ENTRY INTO ACADEMIA
From 2003 to 2005 Harari was a Yad Hanadiv Fellow, completing postdoctoral studies in history. He then became a lecturer in the history department at Hebrew University in 2005, specializing in military and medieval history.

Harari wrote numerous academic papers that were published in scholarly journals but received relatively little attention. He also penned a few books, including *Special Operations in the Age of Chivalry, 1100–1550* (2007) and *The Ultimate Experience: Battlefield Revelations and the Making of Modern War Culture, 1450–2000* (2008). He earned a number of accolades for his military history work, including the Polonsky Prize for Creativity and Originality in the Humanistic Disciplines, both in 2009 and 2012, and the Moncado Award from the Society for Military History in 2011.

SAPIENS: A BRIEF HISTORY OF HUMANKIND
Harari experienced a breakthrough when he changed his research focus to broad historical processes and their role in shaping humanity. His first book of popular history was *Sapiens: A Brief History of Humankind*, first published in Israel in 2011. It quickly became a best seller, leading to an adapted English version in the United Kingdom in 2014 and in the United States in 2015. That edition proved a major international hit, selling more than eleven million copies by 2018. It was eventually translated into more than fifty languages and was even optioned for film.

Harari found himself an instant celebrity, sought after for interviews and appearances as a public intellectual. "It's quite shocking to be now in a position that I write something and there is a potential of millions of people will read it," he told Andrew Anthony for the *Guardian* (5 Aug. 2018). "It's a privilege that I now have such an audience."

In *Sapiens*, Harari outlines the evolution of *Homo sapiens* about 150,000 years ago and the progression to modern-day human society. He breaks this history into four eras: the "cognitive revolution," in which humans developed imagination; the "agricultural revolution," which began about ten thousand years ago as crops began to be planted; the unification of humankind, during which political organizations began to form; and the scientific revolution, starting around the year 1500, in which objective scientific inquiry began to be prized. Throughout the book, Harari connects these revolutions to what he sees as successes and flaws in our progress. For example, he suggests that the agricultural revolution may have done more harm to humanity than benefit, because it exposed the species to a poorer diet, harder work, and greater risk of infectious disease.

Sapiens earned considerable critical acclaim that helped drive its enormous popularity. Many reviewers applauded Harari's writing style and stimulating ideas, and the book was notably praised by many influential public figures. However, it also drew significant negative criticism as well. For example, in a review for the *Guardian* (11 Sept. 2014), Galen Stawson wrote: "Much of *Sapiens* is extremely interesting, and it is often well expressed. As one reads on, however, the attractive features of the book are overwhelmed by carelessness, exaggeration and sensationalism." In the academic world, some critics suggested Harari often indulged in pop-science generalizations at the expense of facts and research.

HOMO DEUS: A BRIEF HISTORY OF TOMORROW
In 2016 Harari published his next book, *Homo Deus: A Brief History of Tomorrow*. It, too, went on to be an enormous international best seller, moving more than 5.5 million copies and receiving translations into more than fifty languages. While *Sapiens* examines where humanity has been, *Homo Deus* looks at the ways in which it might change as the twenty-first century progresses. Centrally, Harari contends that *Homo sapiens* will disappear over the next century as technology advances. He suggests that because human beings have largely overcome famine, many diseases, and traditional warfare, they will seek new challenges and become entirely new creatures. Biotechnology and big data will allow people to engineer themselves to develop godlike powers in pursuit of immortality and maximizing individual and collective happiness. But, he contends, this future might not be without cost, as superhumans with biological and technological advancements would help force the end of humanity as we know it.

As with Harari's earlier work, *Homo Deus* met with mixed reviews despite its great commercial success. The book was again widely seen as a well-written, engaging introduction to interesting concepts. However, some critics found that beneath the sharp prose, the broad themes were largely recycled ideas that had been examined in greater depth by other thinkers. In the *New York Times* (15 Feb. 2017), for instance, Jennifer Senior summed up the conflicted response to Harari's work, arguing that the author "has a

gift for synthesizing material from a wide range of disciplines in inspired, exhilarating ways. But an argument can look seamless and still contain lots of dropped stitches."

21 LESSONS FOR THE 21ST CENTURY
Harari followed up his two best sellers with *21 Lessons for the 21st Century* (2018), a collection mainly of earlier published essays. "In a way this was the easiest book to write because it was written in conversation with the public," Harari told Anthony. "Its contents were decided largely by the kinds of questions I was asked in interviews and public appearances." Building on many of the ideas presented in his earlier books, the essays touch on the variety of crises that humanity faces in the present. These include technological advances, threats to liberal democracy, economic and political instability, social changes, and existential issues.

Another commercial success, *21 Lessons* sold two million copies in the first few months after its release. However, reviewers were more sharply critical of the work, with many opining that it supplied few new ideas beyond *Sapiens* and *Homo Deus*. The academic community also stepped up its critiques, as various scholars accused Harari of obvious or vague pronouncements hidden behind philosophical posturing. He was also widely criticized for approving changes to a Russian translation that softened criticisms of Russia.

Some reviewers found real value in Harari's writing, however. "The title of Yuval Harari's latest best-seller is a misnomer: it asks many questions, but offers few answers, and hardly any lessons," Calum Chace wrote for *Forbes* (12 Nov. 2018). "But it is still worth reading. Harari delights in grandiloquent sweeping generalisations which irritate academics enormously, and part of the fun is precisely that you can so easily picture his colleagues seething with indignation that he is trampling on their turf. More important, some of his generalisations are acutely insightful."

For his part, Harari has expressed concern that audiences often either misunderstand him or assume too much about his efforts to explore complex ideas. "I don't have the answers, at least most of the answers," he said to Anthony. "So I hope that people will read the book not as an infallible guide to living in the 21st century but as a list of questions. You can't have answers before you have a debate. So we first need to start a debate."

PERSONAL LIFE
Harari met his future husband and personal manager, Itzik Yahav, in 2002 in Israel. They married in Canada in 2010 as Israel does not perform same-sex civil marriages but recognizes those conducted elsewhere.

Many of Harari's personal interests often turn up in his writings, including meditation, veganism, and opposition to factory farming.

SUGGESTED READING

Cadwalladr, Carol. "Yuval Noah Harari: The Age of the Cyborg Has Begun—and the Consequences Cannot Be Known." *The Guardian*, 5 July 2015, www.theguardian.com/culture/2015/jul/05/yuval-harari-sapiens-interview-age-of-cyborgs. Accessed 14 Aug. 2019.

Chace, Calum. "21st-Century Schizoid Man? A Review of '21 Lessons for the 21st Century' by Yuval Harari." *Forbes*, 12 Nov. 2018, www.forbes.com/sites/cognitiveworld/2018/11/12/21st-century-schizoid-man-a-review-of-21-lessons-for-the-21st-century-by-yuval-harari/#2d012db274a3. Accessed 13 Aug. 2019.

Gilad, Moshe. "Early Cracks in the Reputation of 'Know It All' Israel Philosopher Yuval Noah Harari." *Haaretz*, 1 Aug. 2019, www.haaretz.com/israel-news/.premium-early-cracks-in-the-reputation-of-yuval-noah-harari-1.7610839. Accessed 2 Aug. 2019.

Harari, Yuval Noah. "Yuval Noah Harari: 'The Idea of Free Information Is Extremely Dangerous.'" Interview by Andrew Anthony. *The Guardian*, 5 Aug. 2018, www.theguardian.com/culture/2018/aug/05/yuval-noah-harari-free-information-extremely-dangerous-interview-21-lessons. Accessed 14 Aug. 2019.

Senior, Jennifer. "Review: 'Homo Deus' Foresees a Godlike Future. (Ignore the Techno-Overlords.)" Review of *Homo Deus: A Brief History of Tomorrow*, by Yuval Noah Harari. *The New York Times*, 15 Feb. 2017, www.nytimes.com/2017/02/15/books/review-homo-deus-yuval-noah-harari.html. Accessed 12 Aug. 2019.

Sexton, David. "Sapiens Author Yuval Noah Harari on Rewriting the Rule Book after a Cult Best-Seller." *Evening Standard*, 11 June 2018, www.standard.co.uk/lifestyle/books/sapiens-author-on-rewriting-the-rule-book-after-a-cult-bestseller-a3860256.html. Accessed 12 Aug. 2019.

Strawson, Galen. Review of *Sapiens: A Brief History of Humankind*, by Yuval Noah Harari. *The Guardian*, 11 Sept. 2014, www.theguardian.com/books/2014/sep/11/sapiens-brief-history-humankind-yuval-noah-harari-review. Accessed 2 Aug. 2019.

SELECTED WORKS

Renaissance Military Memoirs: War, History and Identity, 2004; *Special Operations in the Age of Chivalry, 1100–1550*, 2007; *The Ultimate Experience: Battlefield Revelations and the Making of Modern War Culture, 1450–2000*, 2008; *Sapiens: A Brief History of Humankind*, 2011 (English trans., 2014); *Homo Deus: A Brief History of Tomorrow*, 2016; *21 Lessons for the 21st Century*, 2018

—*Christopher Mari*

Suzan Shown Harjo

Date of birth: June 2, 1945
Occupation: Activist

Long before NFL player Colin Kaepernick took a knee during the national anthem to protest racial injustice and oppression, the football field had supplied a backdrop for passionate activism. Suzan Shown Harjo, who has worked for decades on behalf of Native Americans, is a seminal figure in the fight against derogatory sports team names, stereotypic mascots, and offensive fan gestures, such as the so-called tomahawk chop.

Presented a Presidential Medal of Freedom, the United States' highest civilian honor, in 2014 by President Barack Obama, Harjo has held a variety of posts during her lengthy career, including coproducer of the nation's first regularly scheduled news and current affairs program devoted to Native American coverage, a congressional liaison for Indian affairs under President Jimmy Carter, executive director of the National Congress of American Indians (NCAI), and founding president of the Morning Star Institute, a nonprofit devoted to protecting tribal lands and advocating for effective cultural rights policies. In those roles, she has been instrumental in the passage of such important legislation as the American Indian Religious Freedom Act and the Native American Graves Protection and Repatriation Act, among other laws and policies.

In a profile for *Psychology Today* (5 Nov. 2014), Michael Friedman deemed her "one of the most revered human and civil rights leaders in the country," but Harjo has described her activism as almost axiomatic. "The people who raised me raised me to do what I'm doing," she told Tracy Fernandez Rysavy in an interview for *Green American Magazine* (Summer 2015).

EARLY YEARS AND EDUCATION

Suzan Shown Harjo was born on June 2, 1945 in El Reno, Oklahoma, to Freeland Edward Douglas, a Hodulgee Muscogee (Creek) tribal member, and Susie Rozetta Eades Douglas, a Cheyenne and Pawnee. She had two brothers, Dennis and Rickey. Her maternal great-great-grandfather, Bull Bear, was a Cheyenne peace chief.

Photo by Uyvsdi via Wikimedia Commons

Harjo spent her early years living on land her father had been allotted near the Oklahoma town of Beggs in a home without indoor plumbing or electrical power. Under the General Allotment Act of 1887, or Dawes Act, the federal government divided tribal lands into individual parcels, or allotments, in an effort to spur assimilation of European norms such as settled farming and end the tribes' collective use of land; unallotted lands were often sold to non-natives.

When Harjo was twelve years old, she moved with her family to Naples, Italy, where her father was stationed as a member of the US Army. A veteran of the Forty-Fifth Infantry Division called Thunderbird, he was assigned to the North Atlantic Treaty Organization (NATO) Allied Forces Southern Europe. A family trip to a series of World War II battle sites and burial grounds inspired her to write a poem that was published in an Italian magazine. When she returned to the US some years later, she settled in New York City.

EARLY ACTIVISM
Those trying to pinpoint the roots of Harjo's activism might turn to mid-1965, when she and her mother visited New York City's Museum of the American Indian (a precursor to the Smithsonian's national museum). Her mother recognized one of the garments on display as the burial clothing she had made for her own grandfather, and both were distressed to view a girl's buckskin dress with a bullet hole in the stomach. Harjo later contacted the NCAI and religious leaders from several tribes, and at a meeting in 1967, they brainstormed how to repatriate important

cultural artifacts, advocate for museum reform, and protect sacred, ancestral sites.

Meanwhile, Harjo began volunteering at the community radio station WBAI-FM, and in 1967 she and her husband were hired as producers. *Seeing Red*, as they called their Native American affairs show, broadcast from midnight to 4 a.m. and focused on contemporary Indian culture and social issues. The popular program was picked up by stations in a half dozen major cities throughout the country.

Harjo and her husband moved to Washington, DC, in 1974, so she could work as the news director of the American Indian Press Association. She also served for a time as a legislative liaison for NCAI, the National Indian Litigation Committee, and the Native American Rights Fund, a law firm representing Indian rights. In 1978 President Jimmy Carter appointed her to work with several subcommittees within Congress to put forth a Native American point of view on fishing rights, taxation, water and land management, and other such issues.

Thanks in large part to Harjo's efforts, in 1978, the American Indian Religious Freedom Act was passed. The National Museum of the American Indian Act followed in 1989, the Native American Graves Protection and Repatriation Act in 1990, and President Bill Clinton's executive order on Indian sacred sites in 1996. Because of her expertise, when the Smithsonian established the National Museum of the American Indian (NMAI), she served as a founding trustee from 1990 until 1996, overseeing the organization's exhibition and repatriation policies.

MORNING STAR INSTITUTE
In 1984 Harjo became the executive director of the NCAI, a post she held through 1989. The organization was founded in 1944 to battle detrimental federal policies and to protect tribes' treaty rights and status as sovereign nations. Also in 1984, she launched her own organization, the Morning Star Institute. Most prominent among the institute's various causes has been ending the use of American Indian mascots and names by sports teams and company logos. Harjo has recalled to interviewers that soon after moving to Washington, she and her husband had been invited to a professional football game, at which fans seated around them realized they were Native American and began pulling at their hair and prodding them. Disturbed, they left the stadium. Since then she has lobbied to persuade K–12 schools, colleges, and professional sports teams to drop names and mascots that reinforce derogatory stereotypes of Native Americans.

In 1992, under the auspices of the Morning Star Institute, she joined other plaintiffs in filing *Harjo et al. v. Pro Football, Inc.* with the US Patent and Trademark Office's Trademark Trial and

Appeal Board, to get the board to cancel the registration of the Washington Redskins. Although three judges ruled unanimously in favor of the plaintiffs, the team's owners appealed, and the ruling was subsequently overturned on the technicality that Harjo and her co-plaintiffs had waited too long to bring suit. As a result of the lawsuit, however, Harjo and her cause garnered a great deal of publicity, including appearances on televisions shows such as *Oprah*.

In 2006 she helped organize a similar suit, *Blackhorse v. Pro Football, Inc.*, which won a second favorable decision from trademark judges in 2014 and prevailed in a 2015 appeal, only for the 2017 Supreme Court decision in *Matal v. Tam* to vacate the lower court decision on the team trademarks and render the legal issue moot. In that case, the Supreme Court ruled that an Asian American band could call itself the Slants as a matter of free speech.

A MATTER OF MORALS
Despite those demoralizing losses, thanks to continued campaigns by Harjo and her allies, between 1970 and 2015, some two-thirds of teams with Native American mascots discontinued their use. The Washington team name represents a particularly egregious and tone-deaf example of inappropriate team names. Harjo explained to Rysavy that while working on repatriation of sacred objects and human remains, "the People, everywhere we went, talked about a history of fearing they would be skinned, people having a relative skinned, of coming upon trappers who had Indian skins." She continued, "This [bounty hunting] is the kind of history that comes to mind for Native peoples about the R-word name. This is the worst word that we can be called in the English language. This is the N-word for us."

Harjo told Friedman that there is a moral imperative to stand up to the owners of such teams. She excoriated the complicity of sports team fans who do not, saying, "That is more than a lack of integrity—that is saying, 'I recognize the problem, I recognize it's hurting you, I can't do anything about it because I'm only one person, so I'm going to keep on hurting you; I'm going to contribute to the greater hurt that's being caused for you and your people.'" She continued, "That's a person who helps in the demise of my grandchildren. And that is a dangerous person in society—someone who will go along with something even though they know it's a bad thing to do."

WRITING AND SCHOLARSHIP
Harjo, an accomplished poet, read her work during International Women's Day in the 1970s, sharing the stage with such figures as Alice Walker and Nikki Giovanni. Her work has been included in several anthologies and published in

such outlets as *New York Quarterly*, *Beltway Poetry Quarterly*, and the *Potomac Review*.

Having previously curated exhibits for the District of Columbia Arts Center, US Senate and House Rotundas, American Psychological Association (APA), and the Peabody Essex Museum, Harjo served as a guest curator and editor for the NMAI's exhibition *Nation to Nation: Treaties between the United States and American Indian Nations*, which went on display in 2014. She continues to act as a policy advocate, and her views can be read in the online publication *Indian Country Today*, for which she has addressed issues such as incidents of white officials targeting teenagers of color because of their hairstyles.

Harjo has also worked at a number of universities over the years. In the 1970s, she organized lectures at New York University. Later, in 1992, she became the first Native American woman to receive the Montgomery Fellowship at Dartmouth College and, in 1996, the first Native American person to be named a Stanford University visiting mentor. Additionally, she became the Eric and Barbara Dobkin Native American Artist Fellow, School of Advanced Research in 2004 and the inaugural Vine Deloria, Jr. Distinguished Indigenous Scholar at the University of Arizona in 2008. She also received an honorary doctorate from the Institute for American Indian Arts in 2011.

PERSONAL LIFE
Harjo met and married Frank Ray Harjo in the mid-1960s. Together, the couple had two children: a daughter, Adriane Shown, and a son, Duke Ray II. Frank Harjo died around 1982.

When Gayle Pollard Terry asked Harjo her opinion of Thanksgiving in a piece for *Los Angeles Times* (27 Nov. 1994), Harjo replied: "The spirit of Thanksgiving should be the spirit of all people, all the time. As a traditional Indian woman, one thing I'm obliged to do is greet the day and end the day with prayers of thanks for everything and every being of Mother Earth, not just for the people but for all the creatures and beings that live." She admitted, however, to feeling uncomfortable with some of the imagery surrounding the holiday, which she says reinforces the noble-savage and vanishing-people stereotypes and legitimizes the exploitation of Indigenous people.

SUGGESTED READING
Belson, Ken. "Redskins' Name Change Remains Activist's Unfinished Business." *The New York Times*, 9 Oct. 2013, www.nytimes.com/2013/10/10/sports/football/redskins-name-change-remains-her-unfinished-business.html. Accessed 12 Feb. 2019.

Friedman, Michael. "The Spirit of Suzan Shown Harjo." *Psychology Today*, 5 Nov. 2014, www.psychologytoday.com/us/blog/brick-brick/201411/the-spirit-suzan-shown-harjo. Accessed 12 Feb. 2019.

Harjo, Suzan Shown. "Grace of Water, Focus of Rock." *Talking Stick: Native Arts Quarterly*, vol. 12, no. 4, Oct.–Dec. 2009. *Amerinda*, www.amerinda.org/talkingstick/12-4/harjo.html. Accessed 12 Feb. 2019.

Harjo, Suzan Shown. "Something That Means Justice: An Interview with Suzan Shown Harjo." Interview by Tracy Fernandez Rysavy. *Green American Magazine*, Summer 2015, greenamerica.org/investing-can-change-world/something-means-justice-interview-suzan-shown-harjo. Accessed 12 Feb. 2019.

Murg, Wilhelm. "*OKG* Interview with Native American Activist Suzan Shown Harjo." *Oklahoma Gazette*, 6 Jan. 2016, www.okgazette.com/oklahoma/okg-interview-with-native-american-activist-suzan-shown-harjo/Content?oid=2948932. Accessed 12 Feb. 2019.

Terry, Gayle Pollard. "Los Angeles Times Interview: Suzan Shown Harjo: Fighting to Preserve the Legacy—and Future—of Native Americans." *Los Angeles Times*, 27 Nov. 1994, articles.latimes.com/1994-11-27/opinion/op-2126_1_suzan-shown-harjo. Accessed 12 Feb. 2019.

Weston, Jennifer. "Suzan Harjo." *Cultural Survival Quarterly Magazine*, Dec. 2010, www.culturalsurvival.org/publications/cultural-survival-quarterly/suzan-harjo. Accessed 12 Feb. 2019.

—Mari Rich

Rennie Harris

Date of birth: January 28, 1964
Occupation: Dancer and choreographer

For acclaimed dancer and choreographer Rennie Harris, dance has been a way of life virtually from birth. "I've always danced, there's no beginning or ending in that way for me," he told an interviewer for *Bomb* magazine (30 July 2009). "The first time I realized everybody didn't dance—'You don't dance? Really?'—it blew my mind! I thought everybody knew how to dance! I remember laughing, 'People go to class to learn how to dance?'" Having founded his first dance group at the age of twelve, the young Harris went on to distinguish himself as a talented performer within Philadelphia's hip-hop dance community during the early 1980s. A decade of work as a professional dancer followed, during which

Photo by Iris Schneider/Los Angeles Times via Getty Images

Harris toured with prominent hip-hop acts and showcased forms of dance originating primarily in African American communities throughout the United States.

In 1992 Harris took the next major step in his career, founding the dance company Rennie Harris Puremovement. Over the subsequent decades, Harris and the dancers in his company—as well as spin-off companies such as Rennie Harris Awe-Inspiring Works (RHAW) and the Rennie Harris Grass Roots Project—presented complex, moving, and exciting narratives through the medium of dance, particularly the styles of hip-hop and street dance that have long appealed to Harris. "Hip-hop adapts to its environment. It can be on the corner, [on stage], or if I'm in the cafeteria and we want to start jamming, we do it," he told Benjy Caplan for the *Miami New Times* (27 Feb. 2013). "I don't know ballet, modern dance, jazz. They're just movements, and they're my voice, because it's what I grew up in." Although Harris did not begin his career intending to become a choreographer, his ultimate career path has brought him substantial acclaim and honors, though such recognition has little to do with his creative process. "I get the urge to create something, and I go do it," he told Caplan.

EARLY LIFE AND CAREER

Lorenzo "Rennie" Harris was born in 1964 in Philadelphia, Pennsylvania. He grew up in North Philadelphia with his six younger siblings and his mother, Doris, a health-care professional and community activist. Harris was drawn to the world of dance as a young child and drew inspiration from depictions of dance in the media, including in the music- and dance-focused television program *Soul Train*. He was particularly inspired by the dance group the Campbell Lockers (later known simply as the Lockers), whose pioneering style of dance known as "locking" would significantly influence the evolution of hip-hop dance. Thanks to such influences, as well as the Philadelphia dance culture surrounding him, Harris spent his childhood developing his own skills as a dancer outside of the confines of formal lessons. "I trained at my mother's barbecues," he said of that period, as quoted by the *New Yorker* (2 June 2003). "I trained in the streets." Harris's intensive informal training led him to form his first dance group, Cobra III, at the age of twelve.

As Harris became increasingly involved in the Philadelphia dance scene, he turned particularly toward the form of African American dance known as "stepping." Also known as GQ after the men's magazine *Gentlemen's Quarterly*, stepping arose from and features movements like those in tap dance but does not use tap shoes. "Basically we mimed and mimicked the tap dancers, and although you couldn't hear our rhythms, we had rhythms that we used," he explained in an interview with Nicole Plett for the New Jersey news site *U.S.1 PrincetonInfo* (4 Feb. 2004). Alongside its movements, stepping drew sartorial inspiration from tap as well, requiring each dancer to wear a suit. "I went to Catholic school, so I had a suit," Harris told Plett. "If you didn't have a suit, you could go to a thrift shop for a three-piece suit or a double breasted suit and have a tailor take it in. Then we'd wear a derby or a velour hat. And we used to step against each other."

Although Harris later remarked in interviews that stepping became significantly less popular among Philadelphia dancers not long after he joined that community, he experienced success with the dance group the Step Masters, which specialized in that style. In addition to the Step Masters, Harris joined the hip-hop dance group the Scanner Boys as a teenager and performed with the group at a variety of events and Philadelphia venues during the early 1980s.

His talents for both stepping and hip-hop dance brought him to the attention of Smithsonian Institution representatives tasked with learning about hip-hop culture in Philadelphia. Harris's involvement with those efforts, which included lectures and performances, began what would become a decades-long career in preserving and championing early hip-hop dance styles that would incorporate both critically acclaimed performances and educational initiatives in Philadelphia and beyond.

RENNIE HARRIS PUREMOVEMENT

After graduating from the West Philadelphia Catholic High School for Boys in 1982, Harris initially found work as a dancer specializing in various styles of hip-hop dance. During the 1980s he performed as part of the first major hip-hop tour, the Fresh Festival, and as an opening act for a number of prominent hip-hop artists, including Salt-n-Pepa, Run-DMC, and Grandmaster Flash. That decade also saw Harris receive multiple citations from the city of Philadelphia in recognition of his work.

Although he continued to work as a hired dancer intermittently over the next two decades, working with artists such as Madonna, the Roots, and Will Smith, Harris shifted his focus primarily to choreography and stage performances during the early 1990s, a decision made in part due to the nature of his early career. "I spent my twenties touring, and I already felt kind of burned out at thirty. I'm running on extra fumes right now," he explained to Plett.

In 1992 Harris founded Rennie Harris Puremovement, a dance company focusing on hip-hop dance. Despite his extensive experience in that field, his effort was met with skepticism from some within the dance community. "People told me not to start a hip-hop company. They said there was no funding for any more companies," Harris later recalled to Debra Danese for *Phindie* (2 June 2019). "I was also told not to call myself a hip-hop theater company because no one would book me. But here I am, thirty years later, still going hard in the paint." Although Harris disbanded and re-formed Rennie Harris Puremovement on several occasions, the company became an enduring and important force in the American dance community, performing pieces choreographed by Harris and often blending a variety of styles of hip-hop, funk, and street dance. In addition to solo pieces performed by Harris himself, which included 1992's *Endangered Species* and 1995's *Lorenzo's Oil*, Rennie Harris Puremovement became well known for works such as *Students of the Asphalt Jungle* (1995), a longer production with multiple dancers.

In addition to Rennie Harris Puremovement, Harris founded the Illadelph Legends of Hip-Hop Festival in the late 1990s. The event later became a touring festival and came to feature performances, classes, lectures, and panel discussions related to hip-hop dance.

ACCLAIMED CHOREOGRAPHY

Despite receiving critical acclaim for his choreography throughout his career, he did not initially consider himself a choreographer at heart. "I never planned to do this," he told Caplan. "It wasn't until I was in my late 30s, actually, that I accepted I was a choreographer.

Before then, I got paid, so I danced. I got paid to choreograph, so I was a choreographer." Nevertheless, Harris's unique point of view and talents as both a choreographer and a dancer drew widespread attention to his work with both Rennie Harris Puremovement and other groups, in performances throughout the United States and internationally.

Though initially known for his short pieces, Harris won acclaim for a variety of longer works beginning around 2000, which saw the debut of his evening-length narrative work *Rome & Jewels*. Inspired by William Shakespeare's *Romeo and Juliet*, the piece told a full-length story through a mixture of dance, spoken-word, and deejay performances. Harris won the 2001 Bessie Award for choreography for *Rome & Jewels*, which would go on to tour throughout the United States. Another lengthy work, *Facing Mekka*, made its New York debut in 2003 and featured dancers from Rennie Harris Puremovement and a solo performance by Harris himself.

Given Harris's success in choreographing for the stage, some commentators in the media characterized his work as instrumental in bringing hip-hop dance and culture into US theaters. Harris, on the other hand, tended to disagree with that assertion. "Hip hop has always been in theater, mainstream culture only sees what it wants to see," he told Plett. "Of course it existed in both street and theater." However, Harris emphasized that unlike many other forms of dance, hip-hop originated outside the theater and then moved into the theater, rather than the other way around. "It can't go to the stage unless it existed in the community," he explained to Plett. "Everything we know as expression happens in the community and then it moves to the stage."

As his career progressed, Harris continued to explore the origins of hip-hop as well as the evolution of dance itself through works such as *Lazarus* (2018), created for the sixtieth anniversary of the founding of New York's Alvin Ailey American Dance Theater, and *Rennie Harris: Funkedified* (2018), which highlighted funk music and dance. The latter featured performances by both Rennie Harris Puremovement and the dance group the Hood Lockers.

RECOGNITION

Harris has not only received grants from bodies such as the Pew Charitable Trusts and the National Endowment for the Arts over the course of his career, but also the 2010 Guggenheim Fellowship, a prestigious honor awarded to mid-career individuals demonstrating excellence in the arts. A longtime teacher focusing on hip-hop dance and culture, he has delivered numerous lectures on those subjects at colleges and universities and held residencies at the University of Michigan, the University of the Arts in Philadelphia, the University of Colorado, Stanford University, the Ailey School, and the University of Texas. His time in Colorado led to the creation in 2014 of a new company, the Rennie Harris Grass Roots Project, which operated out of Boulder. Harris also received honorary doctorates from Bates College and Columbia College Chicago as well as the 2018 Dance Magazine Legend Award.

While Harris has earned acclaim throughout the United States, he is perhaps most proud of the recognition and performance opportunities he has received in his native Philadelphia. "Nothing beats seeing my company's picture and name on the billboard over Interstate 95," he told Danese. "To perform in my city, and to be supported by my city on such a level, is not only humbling, but leaves me speechless." In addition to carrying out performances by Rennie Harris Puremovement there, Harris serves as the director of RHAW (Rennie Harris Awe-Inspiring Works), a Philadelphia-based youth dance company founded in 2007. Among the group's noteworthy productions was the dance musical *Love American Style* (later performed under the title *LUV: American Style*), which RHAW began workshopping in 2013 and later performed in Florida, New York, and beyond.

PERSONAL LIFE

When not working elsewhere, Harris lives in the Philadelphia area. He has four children, the eldest of whom, Brandyn, has danced with both RHAW and Rennie Harris Puremovement. In addition to dance and choreography, Harris enjoys drawing and wants to write a children's book based on his artwork.

SUGGESTED READING

Caplan, Benjy. "Choreographer Rennie Harris Brings Love American Style to the Arsht." *Miami New Times*, 27 Feb. 2014, www.miaminewtimes.com/arts/choreographer-rennie-harris-brings-love-american-style-to-the-arsht-6394975. Accessed 16 Aug. 2019.

Harris, Rennie. "Rennie Harris Gets Funky: Interview with the Choreographer Ahead of FUNKEDIFIED." Interview by Debra Danese. *Phindie*, 2 June 2019, phindie.com/19578-rennie-harris-interview-funkified-merriam. Accessed 16 Aug. 2019.

Harris, Rennie. "Rennie Harris on Hip Hop and Dance." *Bomb*, 30 July 2009, bombmagazine.org/articles/rennie-harris-on-hip-hop-and-dance. Accessed 16 Aug. 2019.

Harris, Rennie. "Rennie Harris Talks Choreography, Street Dance and Taking Advice—with a Grain of Salt." Interview. *Dance ICONS*, International Consortium for Advancement in Choreography, 2017, www.danceicons.

org/pages/index.php?p=160330222542. Accessed 16 Aug. 2019.

"Off the Street." *The New Yorker*, 2 June 2003, www.newyorker.com/magazine/2003/06/02/off-the-street. Accessed 16 Aug. 2019.

Plett, Nicole. "Rennie Harris, Dazzling at 40." *U.S.1 PrincetonInfo*, 4 Feb. 2004. princeton-info.com/rennie-harris-dazzling-at-40. Accessed 16 Aug. 2019.

Ziv, Stav. "A Hip-Hop History: Rennie Harris Puremovement." *Stanford Daily*, 21 Jan. 2011, www.stanforddaily.com/2011/01/21/a-hip-hop-history-rennie-harris-puremovement. Accessed 16 Aug. 2019.

SELECTED WORKS

Endangered Species, 1992; *Lorenzo's Oil*, 1995; *Students of the Asphalt Jungle*, 1995; *Rome & Jewels*, 2000; *Facing Mekka*, 2003; *Love American Style*, 2013; *Lazarus*, 2018; *Rennie Harris: Funkedified*, 2018

—Joy Crelin

Photo by Mark Metcalfe/Getty Images

Lisa Harvey-Smith

Date of birth: 1979
Occupation: Astrophysicist

When British-born astrophysicist Lisa Harvey-Smith was twelve years old, a trip outdoors with her father changed the trajectory of her life and career. "That was kind of the moment I fell in love with the stars because that was the first time I really noticed them," she told Julie Hosking for the *West Australian* (8 Mar. 2018). "I just wanted to know more." From that moment on, astronomy became one of Harvey-Smith's greatest interests. Her effort to learn more about the field led her to complete a doctorate in astrophysics and work at some of Europe's most prestigious astronomical organizations before moving to Australia in 2007. There, she joined the Commonwealth Scientific and Industrial Research Organisation (CSIRO) as a researcher and went on to play a key role in the operations of the Australian Square Kilometre Array Pathfinder (ASKAP) radio telescope project as well as the proposed Square Kilometre Array (SKA), an international project that would be the most powerful radio telescope of all time.

Meanwhile, Harvey-Smith has established herself as a strong link between scientists and the public, working to communicate exciting scientific concepts in an accessible and appealing manner across a variety of media. "Science is absolutely for everyone. It's about solving problems for humanity," she told Julia Dean for *UN News* (6 Feb. 2019) about her motivation. "Even if it is about astronomy, it's about finding out where we came from, and what life is all about." In recognition of her work, Harvey-Smith was named Australia's first Women in STEM Ambassador in 2018.

EARLY LIFE

Harvey-Smith was born in Harlow, England. She and her two siblings grew up in Wethersfield, a village in Essex. Their mother, Liz, was the head teacher at a local primary school, and their father, Dave, cared for the children at home. Harvey-Smith's parents later separated.

Due to her parents' career paths and personal interests, education was valued highly in the young Harvey-Smith's household, but the family was skeptical of aspects of formal education such as standardized testing. Harvey-Smith's older brother had attended formal primary school but later completed his education at home, and Harvey-Smith followed his example after primary school, as she objected to the policies in place at the secondary school she was set to attend. "They had a uniform—they would have forced me to wear a skirt, and I wasn't going to do that," she recalled to Mark Dapin for the *Sydney Morning Herald* (12 May 2018). "The girls were forced to do netball and embroidery and things I hated, basically. And boys got to do woodwork and football and cricket. So I decided to stay at home and do whatever I wanted."

After leaving school, Harvey-Smith took charge of her own education. "I wasn't taught by anyone. I just absorbed hundreds of books," she told Dapin. She later returned to school to complete sixth form—the optional final years of secondary schooling in the United Kingdom—in the nearby town of Braintree.

ASTRONOMICAL EDUCATION

As a child and teenager, Harvey-Smith was active in sports such as soccer, judo, and javelin and also played several instruments. Her most consuming passion, however, developed when she was twelve years old, after her father showed her the planet Mars in the night sky. Immediately fascinated by the field of astronomy, she began pursuing studies in the topic and soon joined a local astronomical society, from which she was able to borrow a telescope. Harvey-Smith later had the opportunity to attend a Space School program at Brunel University in London, where the participants built rockets and learned about a variety of astronomical topics.

After completing her secondary education, Harvey-Smith began formal studies in astronomy and astrophysics at Newcastle University in 1998. However, she soon found the experience to be a disappointing one. "I thought, 'This is gonna be amazing,'" she told Dapin. "And it was really boring. There was hardly any astronomy in it. It just seemed like the professors didn't want to be there." Nevertheless, Harvey-Smith completed a master's degree at the institution in 2002.

Following her time at Newcastle University, Harvey-Smith went on to the University of Manchester, where she pursued doctoral studies in astrophysics with a specialization in radio astronomy. During that period, she worked at the Jodrell Bank Observatory, a radio telescope facility operated as part of the university's Jodrell Bank Centre for Astrophysics. "I sat right next to the telescope, and that was amazing," she told Dapin. "It felt like I was part of history, part of something big. Every day I felt really lucky to be there."

Despite the high-tech nature of the work she was doing, Harvey-Smith later noted in interviews that some of the technology she used during that period was almost quaint in comparison to the equipment to which she would later have access. "When I started my PhD we used 'Sun-brand' Unix computers, the type with no graphical user interface. Anything you did, you had to type in as text commands," she recalled in an interview for *MUP* (23 Aug. 2018). Having completed the thesis *Studies of OH and Methanol Masers in Regions of Massive Star Formation*, Harvey-Smith earned her doctorate from the University of Manchester in 2005.

EARLY CAREER

After completing her PhD, Harvey-Smith traveled to Germany and spent two months at the Max Planck Institute for Radio Astronomy. She went on to join the Joint Institute for Very Long Baseline Interferometry in Europe (JIVE) as a support scientist, working on additional radio astronomy research in the Netherlands between 2005 and 2007. During her early career, Harvey-Smith also applied to be an astronaut with the European Space Agency and was even selected for the agency's short list. Although she was not chosen to become an astronaut, she remained optimistic about going to space one day. "An astronaut isn't really a job that you go into, you have to be really good at other things, then you apply once you've had an established career," she told Hosking. "I just thought I'll try again next time!"

A key point in Harvey-Smith's career came in 2007, when she moved to Australia to complete a postdoctoral research fellowship at the University of Sydney. Although the fellowship lasted only two years, Harvey-Smith found that Australia was in many ways the ideal country in which to pursue astronomical research. "Australia is extremely good at astronomy—radio astronomy in particular," she explained to Marcus Strom for the *Sydney Morning Herald* (31 Aug. 2016). "It's great to be in a country where astronomy is a priority." After completing her fellowship, Harvey-Smith joined the Commonwealth Scientific and Industrial Research Organisation (CSIRO) as a project scientist in late 2009.

CSIRO

Much of Harvey-Smith's work with CSIRO involved the Australian Square Kilometre Array Pathfinder (ASKAP) radio telescope project. Located in Western Australia due to the low amount of radio interference in the area, ASKAP consisted of an array of radio-telescope technology used to observe and study areas of space and astronomical phenomena that cannot be viewed with traditional telescopes. Harvey-Smith became an ASKAP project scientist in 2012, served as acting head of science operations in part of 2017, and served as a research group leader within CSIRO in 2017 and 2018. She became a research astronomer with the group in New South Wales in 2018. Along with her research team, Harvey-Smith was a recipient of CSIRO's highest award, the Chairman's Medal, in 2015.

In addition to furthering astronomical research in its own right, ASKAP served as a preliminary step toward the development of the Square Kilometre Array (SKA), a proposed radio telescope project that would be located in both Australia and South Africa and would dramatically enhance the researcher's abilities to observe and collect data about astronomical phenomena such as black holes. Harvey-Smith was a key contributor to the international bid process that resulted in Australia becoming one of the countries to host the equipment that would make up the SKA, and she considered the project to be particularly important because of its international, collaborative nature. "It's not just one country," she told Hosking. "The whole international astronomy community is coming together to figure out what is the genuine next generation, next big step, in what our capabilities can be to study the universe."

COMMUNICATING SCIENCE
Even as Harvey-Smith established herself as a researcher and a major contributor to initiatives such as the ASKAP and SKA projects, she began increasingly focusing on the field of science communication. She found the work of making astronomy accessible to the public both professionally and personally fulfilling. "Working in research really made me uptight, and I didn't like who I was becoming," she explained to Dapin. "Working more with the media has relaxed me. And I like that side of me." She frequently spoke to the media about CSIRO's projects, and eventually branched out into speaking tours and television presenting, appearing on shows such as the Australian Broadcasting Corporation program *Stargazing Live*. Harvey-Smith was named one of the hundred most influential people of the year by the *Sydney Morning Herald* in 2012, and she was awarded the Eureka Prize for Promoting Understanding of Australian Science Research in 2016, largely in recognition of her work with CSIRO.

In 2018 Harvey-Smith published her first popular-science book, *When Galaxies Collide*, which discusses the idea that the Milky Way and Andromeda galaxies will collide and converge several billion years in the future. Harvey-Smith likewise delivered talks on that topic at events such as the 2018 TEDx Melbourne conference (the content of which was also made freely available online) and the Sydney Science Festival, for which she was the 2018 keynote presenter. "I'm really interested in speaking about science, trying to bring science and its real-world outcomes to people—to just make people excited about science and know what's going on around them," she told Hosking.

Long active in promoting issues relating to women and Lesbian, Gay, Bisexual, Transgender/Transsexual, Intersex and Queer/Questioning (LGBTIQ) individuals in the sciences, Harvey-Smith was able to take that work to a new level beginning in October of 2018, when the Australian government named her the country's first-ever Women in STEM Ambassador. "My immediate priority is to help develop and launch Australia's 10-year plan for Women in STEM [Science, Technology, Engineering, and Mathematics], which will provide a roadmap for developing and retaining the talent pipeline that we will need as a nation to embrace the new industries of the twenty-first century," she

said following the announcement, as quoted by Isabelle Dubach for the University of New South Wales (UNSW) Sydney Newsroom (15 Jan. 2019). Harvey-Smith worked out of UNSW Sydney in that role, having joined the university as an adjunct associate professor in 2017. She began serving as professor of practice in science communication at USNW Sydney in early 2019. She also became an adjunct professor at Western Sydney University in 2018.

PERSONAL LIFE
A dual British-Australian citizen, Harvey-Smith is a devoted supporter of the British soccer team Arsenal. An avid runner, she particularly enjoys completing ultramarathons. "It's a long, hard slog," she told Dapin, "but you get there and you feel amazing, and you feel amazing for months—or years—afterwards." Harvey-Smith also became an outspoken LGBTIQ activist, striving to act as an understanding adult for young people coming out after experiencing isolation in her own youth. She lives in Australia with her longtime partner.

SUGGESTED READING
Dapin, Mark. "Lisa Harvey-Smith: The Unorthodox Rise of a Top Australian Astronomer." *The Sydney Morning Herald*, 12 May 2018, www.smh.com.au/national/lisa-harvey-smith-the-unorthodox-rise-of-a-top-australian-astronomer-20180509-p4ze6w.html. Accessed 12 July 2019.

Dubach, Isabelle. "World-Renowned Astrophysicist and Champion of Women in STEM Joins UNSW." *UNSW Sydney Newsroom*, 15 Jan. 2019, newsroom.unsw.edu.au/news/science-tech/world-renowned-astrophysicist-and-champion-women-stem-joins-unsw. Accessed 12 July 2019.

Harvey-Smith, Lisa. "Q & A with Lisa Harvey-Smith–Author of When Galaxies Collide." *MUP*, 23 Aug. 2018, www.mup.com.au/blog/lisa-harvey-smith-author-interview-when-galaxies-collide. Accessed 12 July 2019.

Harvey-Smith, Lisa. "Women Can 'Punch through Glass Ceiling' and Take Their Place at the 'Top Table of Science.'" Interview by Julia Dean. *UN News*, 6 Feb. 2019, news.un.org/en/audio/2019/02/1032131. Accessed 12 July 2019.

Hosking, Julie. "Astronomer Lisa Harvey-Smith Hails Apollo Trailblazers." *The West Australian*, 8 Mar. 2018, thewest.com.au/lifestyle/astronomer-lisa-harvey-smith-hails-apollo-trailblazers-ng-b88733279z. Accessed 12 July 2019.

"Star-Gazing Professor Lisa Harvey-Smith Named the First Women in STEM Ambassador." *Western Sydney University*, 16 Oct. 2018, www.westernsydney.edu.au/newscentre/

news_centre/more_news_stories/star-gazing_
professor_lisa_harvey-smith_named_the_
first_women_in_stem_ambassador. Accessed
12 July 2019.
Strom, Marcus. "Eureka Prizes: Lisa Harvey-
Smith's Vision for Astronomy Lands Her
Award for Promoting Australian Research."
The Sydney Morning Herald, 31 Aug. 2016,
www.smh.com.au/technology/eureka-prizes-
lisa-harveysmiths-vision-for-astronomy-lands-
her-award-for-promoting-australian-research-
20160831-gr5cxx.html. Accessed 12 July
2019.

—*Joy Crelin*

Jayna Hefford

Date of birth: May 14, 1977
Occupation: Ice hockey player and executive

In 2018 Canadian ice hockey player Jayna Hefford became just the sixth woman to be inducted into the Hockey Hall of Fame. Hefford, whose legendary career spanned nearly two decades, retired from play in 2014 after winning four Olympic gold medals and one silver with Team Canada. Most famously, she scored the decisive goal in the gold-medal game against the United States at the 2002 Olympics. Hefford also played in twelve International Ice Hockey Federation (IIHF) Women's World Championships and won seven titles, becoming one of the most prolific scorers in the history of the tournament. "Heff"—as Hefford was often called— "was probably the best, big-game goal-scorer we ever had," her national team teammate Cassie Campbell-Pascall told Eric Duhatschek for the sports website the *Athletic* (6 Nov. 2018). "She was just one of the most underrated players in women's hockey, but for those of us who played the game, we considered her one of the best."

Hefford also played professional hockey, primarily with the Brampton Thunder. She led the two North American women's hockey leagues— the National Women's Hockey League (NWHL) and the Canadian Women's Hockey League (CWHL)—in scoring seven times, and at her retirement she was the NWHL's career leader in points, goals, and assists. In 2016 the CWHL named its Most Outstanding Player Award in her honor. In 2018, as the interim commissioner of the CWHL, she strove to improve players' pay and benefits. (Hefford herself never received a salary during her playing career.) However, less than a year later the league folded, highlighting the challenges women's hockey continues to face despite the emergence of stars such as Hefford.

Photo by hockeymedia via Flickr

EARLY LIFE

Hefford was born in Trenton, Ontario, on May 14, 1977. When she was a year old, her family moved to Kingston on Lake Ontario. Hockey was a major part of their family life. Her father, Larry, a longtime employee in the penitentiary system, played hockey growing up and remained an avid fan of the sport. Her mother, Sandra, a teacher, used to be a hockey coach. Her older brother, Mike, also played hockey.

Young Hefford expressed a desire to play as well, but as there were few options for girls hockey, her parents instead enrolled her in ringette, a similar game played on ice with a straight stick and a rubber ring, though it discourages body contact. Hefford was not impressed. "I remember playing one game and basically, after that game, I said, 'this is not hockey,'" she recalled to Duhatschek. She soon joined a local boys team before moving to a girls league by the time she was ten.

Because there were so few established girls teams, Hefford often played with others several years older than her. Her team traveled often and played whoever was available. Frequently this meant taking on boys teams one age level down, against whom Hefford held her own. She would later recall that she faced little of the obstruction and sexism that many other female hockey players report and long maintained her dream of playing in the male National Hockey League (NHL). "All the way growing up, I thought I'd play in the NHL," she told Duhatschek, "The most amazing thing about that was no one ever told me I couldn't. I never got the message as a young kid that I couldn't play in the NHL because I was a girl—or I shouldn't think that way because hockey is a boys sport."

MINOR AND COLLEGE HOCKEY

Hefford's youth coincided with the rise of professional women's hockey. She watched the first Women's World Championship in Ottawa in 1990, and women's hockey became an Olympic sport in 1992. "When I realized playing for Canada was an option that became a goal for me," Hefford told Wendy Graves for *Hockey Canada* (18 June 2019). She quickly progressed through the minor hockey system, playing for the Kingston Kodiaks from 1988 to 1996. She recorded over 1,400 points and set a goal record for any male or female player in Kingston history. In recognition of her impact, the city's hockey program retired her jersey number in 2012.

Meanwhile, Hefford also competed in the Ontario Women's Hockey Association. In the provincial championships she earned seven medals, winning gold in 1989, 1991, and 1993. In 1994 Hefford helped Team Ontario to its victory in the national women's under-18 championship tournament. In 1995 she captained Team Ontario and led the team to a gold medal at the Canada Winter Games.

Hefford attended the University of Toronto from 1996 to 1997 and played for its women's Varsity Blues hockey team (popularly known as the Lady Blues). At the end of her first season she led the collegiate league in points and was named Rookie of the Year. She eventually graduated with a bachelor's degree in physical education in 2004. During her college hockey career Hefford also played for the Mississauga Chiefs in the Central Ontario Women's Hockey League (COWHL) and made the All-Star team.

TEAM CANADA

Hefford's strong play earned her a place on the national women's hockey team in 1997. At nineteen she immediately helped Team Canada win the gold medal at that year's Women's World Hockey Championship by beating their chief rival, the United States. She remained with the national team for its first-ever Olympic competition, moving to Calgary, Alberta, to train.

The Canadians, who had never lost an international competition up to then, were heavily favored to win the gold medal at the Winter Games in Nagano, Japan, in 1998. However, Canada ultimately lost to the United States in the gold-medal game. Despite finishing with the silver medal, the loss profoundly disappointed Hefford and her teammates. "The pressure we had on us to win . . . was maybe unfair, but it was also something we put on ourselves," she recalled to Duhatschek. "I just remember feeling as if we'd let people down—that we'd let our country down and all the friends and family that had put so much into it.'"

Hefford bounced back by helping Team Canada win the Women's World Hockey Championship in 1999, 2000, and 2001. They defeated the US team in the gold-medal game each year. Hefford co-led all scorers at the tournament in 1999 and co-led her team in scoring in 2000.

Going into the 2002 Olympic Games in Salt Lake City, Utah, the Canadians were the underdogs, having lost all eight games to the US team that season. As usual, the two rivals faced off in the gold-medal game, and Canada struggled at times, drawing many penalties. However, near the end of the second period, Hefford broke away to score as the clock ran out, and her goal proved decisive as Canada won, 3–2. It was Canada's first Olympic gold medal in hockey in fifty years. Hefford would later consider her performance the top highlight of her career, as she told Graves: "If I had to narrow it down to one, winning our first Olympic gold medal in Salt Lake City is probably it. Just the idea of how that was done—being on a team that wasn't expected to win and having a bit of a Cinderella story."

OLYMPIC GOLD MEDAL STREAK

Hefford remained an integral part of Team Canada, leading the 2004 Women's World Championship in goals as the team won another gold medal. That year she won the IIHF's Directorate Award as the championships' top forward, an honor she repeated in 2005 when Canada came in second place. She would appear in six further Women's World Hockey Championships, winning gold in 2007 and 2012 and silver every other time.

Meanwhile, the Olympics remained a major goal for Hefford and her teammates, and they maintained Canada's dominance in women's hockey with a remarkable streak of victories. At the 2006 Olympic Games in Turin, Italy, Team Canada upset Team USA in the semifinals. They then beat Sweden, 4–1, to win gold.

At this point Hefford briefly considered retiring to accept a coaching job in Kingston. "When you're an Olympic athlete and you turn 30, everybody asks, 'when are you going to retire? What are you going to do next?' I wasn't ready to be done, but I also didn't know how long I was going to play," Hefford told Duhatschek. "If I was going to keep playing, I wanted to make sure I was an impact player. I didn't just want to coast along, just because I could."

Hefford, indeed, remained an impact player, helping Team Canada win another gold medal at the 2010 Olympic Games in Vancouver, British Columbia. Faced with defending their title on home turf, the team did not disappoint. In the first round Hefford tied an Olympic women's hockey record with six points in one game, and she finished second on the team in scoring overall. Canada defeated the United States, 2–0, in the final round, a game Hefford would recall as another one of the proudest moments of her career. "There was no better feeling than playing an Olympic Games in Canada," she told Chris Jurewicz for *Hockey Canada* (10 Sept. 2015). "Being able to share that moment of how proud our nation was at those games and the way they embraced the athletes was incredible."

Hefford made her final Olympic appearance at the 2014 Games in Sochi, Russia. Once again, Canada faced the United States in the gold medal game. Team USA led the game in the first two periods, but Team Canada rallied late to tie the game with less than a minute left. Canada ultimately won in overtime, 3–2, giving Hefford a record-sharing four Olympic gold medals in women's hockey. "I've never played in a game like that where the momentum had changed so quickly," Hefford recalled to Jurewicz. "Obviously to win an Olympic gold medal in overtime is something that's pretty special. Thinking back on that victory, the season we had and the challenges in that season, it still seems a little bit surreal."

RETIREMENT AND EXECUTIVE CAREER

Hefford announced her retirement from playing after the Sochi Olympics. She finished her international career ranked second all-time for Canada in points (291) and goals (157) and third in assists (134). She also held several NWHL/CWHL records through her career with the Brampton Thunder from 1998 to 2013. Hefford had become an assistant coach for her university hockey team, the Lady Blues, in 2012 and remained in that role until 2017.

In 2018 Hefford was named the interim commissioner of the CWHL. As commissioner she expressed her desire for a unified women's professional hockey league, preferably with the support of the NHL. "From a playing point of view, I know the players want to associate themselves with the league," she told Emily Kaplan and Greg Wyshynski for *ESPN* (6 Feb. 2019). She also continued to oversee the league's attempts to expand and improve revenue, with the goal of making professional hockey a viable career for women. Hefford often fielded questions about the financial challenges of playing full time; the CWHL only started paying players a stipend after her playing career ended.

In May 2019, the CWHL abruptly folded, unable to fund its next season. Top players for the NWHL announced a boycott, agitating for a unified league with better pay and working conditions. Yet Hefford remained upbeat: "These difficult times have created some really good conversations around not only women's hockey but women's sports," she told Graves. "The

uncertainty is there, but I'm really optimistic for the future of the sport."

PERSONAL LIFE

Hefford's partner, Kathleen Kauth, is a former US hockey player who played for the Brampton Thunder. The couple have three children together, daughters Isla and Arwen and son Lachlan.

SUGGESTED READING

Duhatschek, Eric. "From Ringette to the Olympics to the Hall of Fame: Jayna Hefford Reflects on a Prolific Hockey Journey." *The Athletic*, 6 Nov. 2018, theathletic.com/625674/2018/11/06/from-ringette-to-the-olympics-to-the-hall-of-fame-jayna-hefford-reflects-on-a-prolific-hockey-journey. Accessed 12 Aug. 2019.

Freeborn, Jeremy. "Jayna Hefford." *The Canadian Encyclopedia*, Historica Canada, 30 Jan. 2019, www.thecanadianencyclopedia.ca/en/article/jayna-hefford. Accessed 13 Aug. 2019.

Graves, Wendy. "For the Love of the Game." *Hockey Canada*, 18 June 2019, www.hockeycanada.ca/en-ca/news/2019-hcf-ohc-jayna-hefford. Accessed 12 Aug. 2019.

Hefford, Jayna. "Jayna Hefford on the CWHL, When There Will Be a Female GM or Coach in the NHL and More." Interview by Emily Kaplan and Greg Wyshynski. *ESPN*, 6 Feb. 2019, www.espn.com/nhl/story/_/id/25924293/jayna-hefford-cwhl-there-female-gm-coach-nhl-more. Accessed 12 Aug. 2019.

"Jayna Hefford." *Canada's Sports Hall of Fame*, 2019, www.sportshall.ca/events/jayna-hefford.html?lang=EN. Accessed 13 Aug. 2019.

"Jayna Hefford." *Hockey Hall of Fame*, 2019, www.hhof.com/htmlInduct/ind18Hefford.shtml. Accessed 13 Aug. 2019.

Jurewicz, Chris. "A Legend Says Goodbye." *Hockey Canada*, 10 Sept. 2015, www.hockeycanada.ca/en-ca/news/legend-says-goodbye-with-hefford-retirement. Accessed 12 Aug. 2019.

—*Molly Hagan*

Remy Hii

Date of birth: July 24, 1986
Occupation: Actor

When Remy Hii was a child, a career in acting "was never something that was on the radar," he told Rebekah Clark for *Icon* magazine (2019). "It never sort of revealed itself as something you can actually do." By the time Hii graduated from Australia's National Institute of Dramatic Art in

2011, however, acting was undoubtedly a viable career option. With several short films, television guest appearances, and stage plays already under his belt, Hii soon won the opportunity to showcase his talents in both the long-running soap opera *Neighbours* and the biopic miniseries *Better Man*. Having earned both attention and critical praise for his work, he went on to appear in a variety of roles in projects such as the Netflix original series *Marco Polo* and the Australian Broadcasting Corporation (ABC) crime drama *Harrow*.

It was in 2018 and 2019, however, that Hii's career reached a particularly significant turning point thanks to his roles in two films: *Crazy Rich Asians*, based on the best-selling novel of the same name, and *Spider-Man: Far from Home*, an installment in the Marvel Cinematic Universe of superhero films. In addition to expressing his excitement about both films, Hii emphasized the diversity of their casts and spoke out about the importance of seeing people of color—and especially actors of Asian descent—onscreen. "I just think of it as playing what is there," he told Laura Sirikul for the *Nerds of Color* (29 June 2019) in an interview about *Spider-Man: Far from Home*. "I think that the face of America—the face of an American—has always been there. Have we seen it on our screens? Not necessarily up until now. So I think that it's really cool in a film like this where you get to see a real high school and what that make up is."

EARLY LIFE AND EDUCATION

Remy Hii (who sometimes goes by Remi) was born in Malaysia to a Chinese Malaysian father and an English mother. He spent much of his early childhood in rural Papua New Guinea, where his father worked as a doctor with the World Health Organization (WHO). During that period, the young Hii had ample opportunities to exercise the creativity that would go on to shape his career as an actor. "We didn't have television and the power was on and off every other day so we sort of made do with storytelling and making things up and playing," he recalled to Clark, going on to explain that his childhood pastimes "didn't really translate into 'I'm going to be an actor.'" After his family moved to Australia when he was eight, Hii's burgeoning interest in storytelling and performance flourished, inspired, in part, by his experiences accompanying his mother to theatrical performances.

In Australia, Hii's family settled first in the city of Townsville, Queensland. They later moved to Brisbane. Due to the family's numerous moves, Hii attended six or seven schools during his childhood and teen years and at times struggled to fit in his new environments. However, he enjoyed studying drama while in school and later noted in interviews that he considered

Photo by Eva Rinaldi via Wikimedia commons

drama to be both a safe place and an escape. After graduating from Ferny Grove State High School in 2004, Hii studied human rights at the Queensland University of Technology.

EARLY CAREER

Hii began his acting career on the stage, initially performing with a cooperative theater company. He landed the lead male part in a 2007 production of the play *The Estimator* put on by the Queensland Theatre Company. He appeared in short films between 2009 and 2013 and played small roles in television shows such as the drama *East of Everything*. Seeking to develop his skills further, Hii moved to Sydney in 2009 to enroll in the National Institute of Dramatic Art (NIDA), a prestigious performing-arts school known for producing numerous successful actors. He graduated from NIDA in 2011.

Days after graduation Hii was cast in a major Hollywood film and traveled to Los Angeles, California, to prepare for the job. However, its production was abruptly cancelled before the start of filming, an event Hii later attributed to financial problems.

Following his return to Australia, Hii was cast in *Better Man*, a television miniseries based on true events. The miniseries focuses on the 2005 execution of an Australian named Van Tuong Nguyen following his arrest for drug trafficking in Singapore. To play the role of Nguyen, Hii researched the man extensively to gain an understanding of his life and motivations. "I was given a treasure trove of information by the producers with boxes of newspaper clippings. Pretty much anything that made it into print. No stone was unturned," he told David Knox for *TV Tonight* (23 July 2013). He also had the opportunity to interview some of Nguyen's friends and associates, including Nguyen's lawyer. The two-part show premiered in July 2013. Hii's performance won him the 2014 TV Week Logie Awards' Graham Kennedy Award for Most Outstanding New Talent, which came with a yearlong scholarship to the Stella Adler Academy of Acting and Theatre in Los Angeles.

SUCCESS IN TELEVISION
Shortly before the premiere of *Better Man*, Hii debuted on the long-running soap opera *Neighbours* as Hudson Walsh, a swimmer introduced as a love interest for the established character Chris Pappas (James Mason). For Hii, the experience of working on the show—an Australian institution since 1985—was key to his development as an actor. "It's a great family to be inducted into," he told Daniel Kilkelly for *Digital Spy* (20 June 2013). "And as a young actor just out of drama school, it's a fantastic place to really hone your skills. The opportunity to work with so many different directors is invaluable." Hii was a regular on *Neighbours* through late 2013 and continued to appear on the show into 2014, when his character's arc concluded.

Hii went on to find further success in television, including programs aired on Australian channels and available through online streaming services. Between 2014 and 2016 he appeared in the Netflix original series *Marco Polo*, a fictionalized depiction of the Italian explorer's time in the court of Kublai Khan. Hii plays the character Prince Jingim in the series, which necessitated a significant amount of training and fight choreography. "In a million years I never saw myself playing a prince in the Mongolian empire in a swords-and-sandals adventure shot in Hungary, Malaysia, Venice, Slovakia and Kazakhstan," he said of the experience to Don Groves for *IF* magazine (29 Jan. 2018). Hii returned to stage acting in 2016, appearing in a Sydney Theatre Company production of the play *The Golden Age* and, in 2017, appeared in a handful of episodes of the drama *Sisters*. That same year he played Benny in the thriller 2:22, which flopped.

Beginning in 2018 Hii took on another major television role in the ABC crime drama *Harrow*, portraying Simon Van Reyk, a forensic pathologist working under medical examiner Daniel Harrow (Ioan Gruffudd). "It was a heavy workload and lightning fast: that is Australian TV," he told Groves. "You prepare to the eyeballs and at the same time you are prepared to drop much of your homework to get it done. You never know what challenges will be thrown your way." The show was also distributed in the United Kingdom and United States. Hii returned for the series'

second season, which premiered on ABC1 in May 2019.

MAJOR FILMS
Although Hii had succeeded in establishing himself as a working actor in the years since graduating from NIDA, a key moment in his career came in 2018, when he was introduced to audiences worldwide via the romantic comedy film *Crazy Rich Asians*. Based on a best-selling novel by Kevin Kwan, the film featured a large ensemble cast that included Hii as the wealthy playboy Alistair Cheng. A critical success and box-office hit, *Crazy Rich Asians* drew significant attention to the lesser-known members of its cast, bringing Hii and his colleagues into the spotlight. "This film and the way audiences around the world have responded—in America, my God!—it is so incredible to be part of," Hii told Geoff Shearer for *U on Sunday* magazine (8 Sept. 2018). As Alistair plays a more substantial role in the two sequels to the novel *Crazy Rich Asians*, Hii expressed hopes of reprising his role in further film adaptations of the series.

Hii received even greater attention in 2019, when he played a supporting role in the Marvel superhero film *Spider-Man: Far from Home*. A sequel to *Spider-Man: Homecoming* (2017) and the follow-up to the blockbuster *Avengers: Endgame* (2019), *Spider-Man: Far from Home* was highly anticipated and marked a major milestone for Hii, who experienced a whirlwind casting process. "I sent this tape on a Monday and . . . on Tuesday they said, 'Look we really, really like you,'" he recalled to Clark. "On Friday they said, 'We need you to fly to London.' So in the space of a week from hitting that email, I had to have my bags packed for the next five months and I was on a plane. So the whiplash was extraordinary."

In the film, Hii plays Brad Davis, a classmate of protagonist Peter Parker (Tom Holland) and a would-be romantic interest of Peter's friend MJ (Zendaya). Following the film's premiere in July 2019, Hii became the focus of substantial media attention and used that opportunity to discuss his experiences making the film as well as to speak out about the continuing importance of diversity in film and television.

PERSONAL LIFE
A frequent traveler because of his work since 2014, Hii splits his time between shooting locations on multiple continents. Between gigs he returns to Sydney. By 2018, however, he longed to settle down in a more permanent home. "At first the bohemian lifestyle was really, really exciting and fun and then you start thinking, 'Well actually, I want to start growing some roots somewhere,'" he explained to Clark. "'I want to be able to return somewhere where I recognise the furniture.'"

Hii enjoys playing music and is also an avid photographer known for posting his work, including behind-the-scenes photographs from his film and television projects, on social media.

SUGGESTED READING

Clark, Rebekah. "Remy Hii: '[Film] Was Always Being Driven by a False Belief That If It's Not a White Character Then It Won't Sell.' *Icon*, 2019, icon.ink/articles/remy-hii-spider-man-far-from-home-film-interview. Accessed 16 Aug. 2019.

Groves, Don. "Actor Remy Hii Hails Progress towards On-Screen Diversity." *IF.com.au*, 29 Jan. 2018, www.if.com.au/actor-remy-hii-hails-progress-towards-on-screen-diversity. Accessed 16 Aug. 2019.

Hii, Remy. "Interview with Australian Actor Remy Hii (*Marco Polo, Betterman, Neighbours*)." By Joy Hopwood. *Joy House*, 15 July 2015, joyhouseproductions.wordpress.com/2015/07/15/interview-with-australian-actor-remy-hii-marco-polo-betterman-neighbours. Accessed 16 Aug. 2019.

Hii, Remy. "'Neighbours' Newcomer Remy Hii Talks Hudson Role, Chris Plot." Interview by Daniel Kilkelly. *Digital Spy*, 20 June 2013, www.digitalspy.com/soaps/neighbours/a491976/neighbours-newcomer-remy-hii-talks-hudson-role-chris-plot. Accessed 16 Aug. 2019.

Knox, David. "Raw Emotion the Key for Remy Hii." *TV Tonight*, 23 July 2013, tvtonight.com.au/2013/07/raw-emotion-the-key-for-remy-hii.html. Accessed 16 Aug. 2019.

Shearer, Geoff. "Crazy Rich Asians Star Remy Hii Calls His Suitcase Home." *U on Sunday*, 8 Sept. 2018, www.couriermail.com.au/lifestyle/uonsunday/crazy-rich-asians-star-remy-hii-calls-his-suitcase-home/news-story/fe77f4d289cdd0123a3063adf1c1f16d. Accessed 16 Aug. 2019.

Sirikul, Laura. "Remy Hii on His 'Spider-Man: Far from Home' Love Triangle with MJ and Peter." *The Nerds of Color*, 29 June 2019, thenerdsofcolor.org/2019/06/29/remy-hii-on-his-spider-man-far-from-homes-character-love-triangle-with-mj-and-peter-parker. Accessed 16 Aug. 2019.

SELECTED WORKS

Better Man, 2013; *Neighbours*, 2013–14; *Marco Polo*, 2014–16; *Sisters*, 2017; *Crazy Rich Asians*, 2018; *Harrow*, 2018–; *Spider-Man: Far from Home*, 2019

—Joy Crelin

Joe Hill

Date of birth: June 4, 1972
Occupation: Writer

Following the publication of his critically acclaimed and best-selling debut novel, *Heart-Shaped Box*, in 2007, writer Joe Hill continued to entertain, frighten, and impress readers and critics both within and outside of the horror genre with novels and short stories that display one of his core philosophies as a writer. "No matter where the stories began, the job is always the same," he told Blu Gilliand for *Cemetery Dance* (23 Oct. 2017). "You try and find some fresh, exciting, believable characters, and then you put them through hell. You go after them with your knives drawn." With novels such as *NOS4A2* (2013) and *The Fireman* (2016); collections such as *Strange Weather* (2017); and the Locke & Key comic book series, which launched in 2008, Hill has solidified his reputation as one of horror's particularly intriguing contributors.

The son of writers Stephen King and Tabitha King, Hill was raised in a writing-focused household and began working on his own novels as a young teen. Determined to forge his own path as a writer during the 1990s, he began submitting short stories and novels for publication under the pen name Joe Hill—the last name derived from his legal middle name, Hillstrom—to ensure that his parents' literary reputations did not influence publishers' responses to his work. His efforts ultimately proved successful, leading to a number of his stories appearing in a variety of publications as well as in the debut collection

Photo by Rick Friedman/Corbis via Getty Images

20th Century Ghosts (2005). Although his true identity was later revealed publicly, Hill succeeded in becoming a successful author in his own right, building a career that allowed him to explore a wide range of topics and genres. "It's hard to imagine things being much better than that," he told Guy Kelly for the *Telegraph* (23 June 2016).

EARLY LIFE AND EDUCATION

Joseph Hillstrom King, widely known by the pen name Joe Hill, was born in Maine on June 4, 1972, and raised in the city of Bangor. The second of three children born to writers Stephen and Tabitha King, he grew up in a household where the act of writing was a nearly constant presence. "I just thought that was what you were meant to do," he recalled to Kelly. "I thought you were meant to sit by yourself in a room and make up a bunch of stuff, then one day someone would pay you for it." Hill himself was particularly influenced by the genres in which his father—a prolific and popular author whose works inspired some of the best-known American horror films of the twentieth century—worked, among them horror, mystery, and fantasy. Hill's younger brother, Owen, was also influenced by their parents' professions and would go on to publish a variety of works under the name Owen King.

In addition to writing, the members of the King family were avid readers and enjoyed reading aloud to one another, an activity that Hill later recalled continued into his teen years. As a teenager, Hill began writing daily and completed several novel manuscripts during that period. He remained interested in writing throughout his time in high school and, following his graduation, enrolled at Vassar College to study English. He earned his bachelor's degree from Vassar in 1995.

EARLY CAREER

Following his years in college, Hill worked to launch his career as a published writer under the pen name Joe Hill, created by omitting his last name and shortening his middle name. He would later explain that he did so to conceal his relationship to his father, which he feared could affect his own work's reception within the publishing industry. "When I went into writing, I had to know that if someone bought one of my stories they'd bought it for the right reasons—that it is a good story—and not because of who my dad is," he explained to Kelly. The anonymity of this pen name ultimately allowed him to write in his preferred genre after he did not produce successful works outside of horror/fantasy in an attempt to avoid comparisons to his father's writing.

Hill worked on different projects during that period and devoted several years to a lengthy fantasy manuscript that ultimately did not find a publisher. Discouraged, he began to consider transitioning into screenwriting and worked on a variety of projects with his brother. "I sort of put aside my pride and started writing screenplays as Joseph King," he told Zach Dionne for *GQ* (6 Nov. 2017). "And my brother and I wrote screenplays together. And so I have this sordid former career where I wrote and everyone knew, everyone knew who my dad was, and Owen and I wrote stuff, and we got rejections too." The brothers did succeed in selling the screenplay for one of their collaborative projects, a feature film, but the project was never produced.

Although Hill struggled to prove himself as a writer for a time, he began to experience some success in the realm of short stories. Examples of his work were published in a variety of magazines and anthologies. A number of his stories went on to appear in his debut short-story collection, *20th Century Ghosts*, upon its publication in 2005. The book was received well by readers, calling attention to Hill and sparking speculation about his identity.

While some in the horror community were already aware of Hill's birth name and parentage by 2006, his identity became public knowledge that year following the publication of an article about him in the periodical *Variety*. Although that revelation drew further attention to his debut novel, *Heart-Shaped Box*, upon its publication in 2007, many horror enthusiasts emphasized the need to consider the novel, and Hill's future writing, on its own merits. A best-selling novel about an aging rock star's encounters with a vengeful ghost, *Heart-Shaped Box* received widespread critical acclaim. It earned special recognition within the horror community, receiving the 2007 Bram Stoker Award for Best First Novel from the Horror Writers Association.

COMICS WORK AND A SOPHOMORE NOVEL

In addition to his prose work, Hill became active in the comics industry early in his career and often noted in interviews that he felt particularly at home in that medium. "When I started writing comics, I felt almost instantly that I had discovered my element. It was the version of writing I liked best," he told Christian Holub for *Entertainment Weekly* (26 June 2019). "I felt, when I worked in comics, that my strengths were amplified, and the stuff I struggled with as a writer almost completely vanished." Hill is perhaps best known among comics readers for his Locke & Key series, created in collaboration with illustrator Gabriel Rodriguez. Begun in 2008, Locke & Key earned extensive praise over the following years, and Hill won the prestigious Eisner Award for Best Writer for his work in 2011. Although the series largely concluded its run in 2013 after more than thirty issues, some additional material was published during the later years.

Meanwhile, Hill had also gone on to collaborate with his father on the story "Throttle," first published in 2009 as part of *He Is Legend: An Anthology Celebrating Richard Matheson.* In 2010 he published his second novel, *Horns.* Well received and nominated for a Bram Stoker Award, *Horns* was later adapted into a film of the same name that premiered at the Toronto International Film Festival in 2013.

LATER PUBLICATIONS AND WORK
Over the course of the second decade of the twenty-first century, Hill published numerous critically acclaimed works, including both novels and story collections. His horror novel *NOS4A2* (2013) not only received recognition within its genre, including in the form of a Bram Stoker Award nomination, but also was included in *Time* magazine's list of the top-ten fiction books of 2013. "Whenever something like this falls in your lap, you mostly feel relief," Hill told Jeanné McCartin for *Seacoastonline.com* (7 Dec. 2013) following the announcement of the *Time* list. "It's a sign you haven't completely spent your creative spark, that there's still good work to come and it's not all behind you." A television series based on *NOS4A2* premiered on the television channel AMC in June 2019.

Having first established himself as a writer of short stories, Hill built upon the lessons he had learned in that medium when writing his novels. "Every bit, every scene, has to fiercely defend itself as a scene that stands, that's exciting and entertaining in its own right," he explained during an interview for the *Geek's Guide to the Galaxy* podcast, published in print in *Nightmare* magazine (July 2013). "Every scene should almost be like a miniature little short story that does something compelling and gets the reader pumped up and makes them want to keep turning the pages."

Hill remained active in comics projects as well, releasing the limited series *Wraith* (2013–14), a spinoff from *NOS4A2.* Returning to the novel format, he then followed *NOS4A2* with 2016's *The Fireman,* a postapocalyptic novel dealing with a frightening plague. In 2017 he released *A Little Silver Book of Sharp Shiny Slivers,* a collection of short writing that was released as a limited signed and numbered work by the specialty publisher Borderlands Press. The year 2017 also saw the publication of *Strange Weather,* a book collecting four separate novellas.

In addition to writing the Locke & Key comics, Hill became involved in an ongoing effort to bring the series' story to the screen in the form of either a television series or a film. Although the failure of a television pilot and a planned film adaptation called the likelihood of that plan into question, the streaming service Netflix eventually ordered an adaptation to series in 2018. In June 2019, DC Comics announced that Hill would be lending his name and vision to a new line of horror comics, Hill House Comics.

PERSONAL LIFE
Hill remains close with his parents and siblings, and his family at times functioned as a writing group of sorts. "We all share manuscripts and talk about what we're working on, so it's this big group where we can bounce ideas off each other and get concrete, page-by-page help," he told Kelly.

Hill had three children with his first wife; that marriage ended in divorce. In 2018, he married Gillian Redfearn, a publishing professional.

SUGGESTED READING
Dionne, Zach. "How Do You Write a Horror Novel When Your Dad Is Stephen King?" *GQ,* 6 Nov. 2017, www.gq.com/story/joe-hill-stephen-king-profile. Accessed 16 Aug. 2019.

Hill, Joe. "Interview: Joe Hill (Part 1)." *Nightmare,* July 2013, www.nightmare-magazine.com/nonfiction/interview-joe-hill-part-1/. Accessed 16 Aug. 2019.

Hill, Joe. "An Interview with Joe Hill." Interview by Blu Gilliand. *Cemetery Dance,* 23 Oct. 2017, www.cemeterydance.com/extras/an-interview-with-joe-hill/. Accessed 16 Aug. 2019.

Holub, Christian. "Exclusive: Joe Hill Is Writing and Overseeing a New Line of DC Horror Comics." *Entertainment Weekly,* 26 June 2019, ew.com/books/2019/06/26/joe-hill-dc-comics-hill-house/. Accessed 16 Aug. 2019.

Kelly, Guy. "Joe Hill: 'How I Escaped the Shadow of My Father, Stephen King.'" *The Telegraph,* 23 June 2016, www.telegraph.co.uk/men/the-filter/joe-hill-how-i-escaped-the-shadow-of-my-father-stephen-king/. Accessed 16 Aug. 2019.

McCartin, Jeanné. "Exeter Author Joe Hill Earns Top 10 Honor." *Seacoastonline.com,* 7 Dec. 2013, www.seacoastonline.com/article/20131207/NEWS/312070332. Accessed 16 Aug. 2019.

SELECTED WORKS
20th Century Ghosts, 2005; *Heart-Shaped Box,* 2007; *Horns,* 2010; *NOS4A2,* 2013; *The Fireman,* 2016; *Strange Weather,* 2017

—*Joy Crelin*

Tommy Hollenstein

Date of birth: ca. 1961
Occupation: Abstract impressionist painter

Tommy Hollenstein has not allowed being confined to a wheelchair to limit his artistic ambitions. He creates paintings by coating the tires on his power wheelchair with vibrantly colored paint or rolling through paint that has been spilled on the floor; he then repeatedly rolls over a piece of Masonite board that an assistant has primed with a base color, stopping regularly to clean off his wheels and let the layers of paint dry. "As each piece speaks to me, I keep on working the paint," he told Sam Maddox for *New Mobility* magazine (1 Apr. 2008), explaining that one of his pieces can have up to fifty layers of paint and take several weeks to complete. "It's like dancing as I spin back and forth and slide the tires."

The resulting artwork—which has been collected by celebrities such as guitarist Slash, actor Joaquin Phoenix, writer Dean Koontz, and drummer Ringo Starr—features abstract arrangements of lines, swirls, and splashes, and Hollenstein gives each an inspiring title, such as *Freedom*, *Soar*, and *Beyond*. "I want people to go get a positive feeling, to move beyond their expectations, their limitations, including people who are not disabled," he said to Maddox. "Go do something you dreamed about as a child. That's what I did."

Hollenstein hopes people focus on the art itself, rather than how it was created, or that it was created by a quadriplegic. He is gratified when he sells a piece to someone who knows little about him personally. "A lot of times people don't know about [my painting] process until it's discussed," he told Michelle Pelsue in an interview for the website of *Arts & Entertainment Ministries* (9 Oct. 2006). "When I use the bald tires and I go layer by layer, you don't see any tracks at all."

EARLY LIFE AND EDUCATION

Tommy Hollenstein was born around 1961. His father, Wally, managed a popular California restaurant called the Hungry Tiger before opening his own restaurant and catering business in 1972 at the Calabasas Inn. Hollenstein's mother, Jean, served in the US Marine Corps before marrying Wally. They raised Hollenstein and his four siblings (Sandy, twins Donna and Mark, and Tricia) in Canoga Park, a town located in the San Fernando Valley section of the Los Angeles Metropolitan Area.

Even as a child, Hollenstein was known for pushing limits. That sense of rebelliousness continued into his teens, and he loved any sport that involved speed or a sense of danger. He could

Photo by Valerie Macon/Getty Images

often be found in the so-called "Toilet Bowl," a massive drainage ditch not far from his house that was a popular place for young skateboarders to congregate and practice.

Later, as a student at Chaminade College Preparatory School, a private Catholic school in the San Ferdinando Valley, he took up surfing, regularly visiting Santa Barbara County, where one of his teachers owned property near the coast. Despite being a somewhat lackluster student, Hollenstein enrolled at Pepperdine University in Malibu, where he joined the surf team and began dealing drugs. He dropped out after three semesters. He later enrolled in the Nick Harris Detective Academy in Van Nuys, seeking to become a private investigator, and he began working to get his own drug use under control.

CATASTROPHIC CRASH

In March 1985, Hollenstein had been sober for just under a month and was one day away from completing his private detective's training. He went for a mountain bike ride through California's Bell Canyon, an area he knew well. At the bottom of a hill, however, was a newly dug construction trench. Hollenstein was traveling too fast to stop but too slow to leap over the chasm.

The resulting crash was catastrophic. When Hollenstein woke up in the hospital he was told that his neck had been broken between the fourth and fifth cervical vertebrae, and that at just twenty-four years old, he would never walk or ride a bike again. He spent the next six months in the hospital.

Still hoping he could pursue his desire to become a private eye, he returned to Nick Harris's school to take the final exam, which came in the form of a mock murder case staged in a local park. Despite being confined to a wheelchair, he was the only one taking the test to pass and was given a Future Private Eye of the Year Award.

With that honor under his belt, he was hopeful that he could find a job doing surveillance, planting bugs, and working with the high-tech gadgetry by then prevalent in the industry. He was, therefore, disappointed when all he could get was desk work. Disillusioned, he quit after nine months and worked instead selling medical supplies.

Mainly reliant on a small Social Security check, Hollenstein ultimately returned to drug dealing. One day, as he sat in his car outside a restaurant waiting for a customer, he was surrounded by more than a dozen FBI agents with guns drawn. In his car was two kilograms of cocaine. Rather than jail time, a lenient judge gave him a forty-year suspended sentence, six months of house arrest, five years of probation, and a $2 million suspended fine. Down but not out, Hollenstein had to figure out a new life path.

Since childhood, Hollenstein had been interested in art. He had always painted his bikes and surf boards in brilliant colors, and even once took a course in creating edible art. After his accident, his physical therapists tried teaching him to paint using a brush in his mouth—a popular approach for disabled artists—but it didn't appeal to him. "They tried to teach me in rehab, but it was just too confining," he recalled to Maddox. "I felt boxed in; it wasn't flowing. I basically didn't do anything for 12 more years."

ARTISTIC CAREER

Hollenstein finally reached a turning point thanks, in a roundabout way, to a group called Canine Companions for Independence, which was founded in 1975 in Santa Rosa, California, and had become the largest providers of assistance dogs for people with disabilities in the world. Two years after his biking accident, he had received a dog from the group, a yellow Labrador retriever he called Weaver. Weaver made it possible for him to get his own apartment and work in medical-supply sales. "The bond between the dog and I was just phenomenal, and as he started to get older, I really wanted to have something as a memory of him on my wall other than a photograph," Hollenstein recalled to Mark Groubert for *LA Weekly* (22 Apr. 2009). "So I kept thinking that someday I'm gonna roll through paint and have him walk through the same paint. It'll be like tire tracks and paw prints."

After Weaver suffered a stroke and his health began to deteriorate, Hollenstein realized that if he did not act soon, he might miss his chance. He poured puddles of paint on a canvas, and he rolled through them with Weaver walking next

to him. "The result was more than a keepsake," Maddox wrote. "It was epiphanous. Fireworks ignited in Tommy's imagination; he realized he had colors and shapes and feelings bubbling up."

It dawned on Hollenstein that this could be a source of artistic satisfaction—and maybe even some income—if he kept at it. He experimented with various types of paints and surfaces, eventually developing a style that some critics have compared to that of abstract expressionist Jackson Pollock, who is known for pouring and splashing paint onto canvases lying on the floor. Pollack's work is a prime example of what came to be known as "action painting," a term Hollenstein has also adopted for his own style.

In 2005, he mounted his first show at a local gallery and sold nine paintings. Two of those were purchased by actor Joaquin Phoenix, and he has since sold pieces to a variety of prominent figures, including businesswoman Lisette Ackerberg, whose collection includes work by such well-respected artists as Frank Stella, David Hockney, Pablo Picasso, and Willem de Kooning.

Hollenstein has shown his work at venues throughout California, as well as in Seattle, Boston, and other major cities. His exhibits often have inspirational titles, such as *Chasing Your Dreams into Reality*, *Wheels of Hope*, and *Helping Hands*. He sometimes gives live demonstrations of his techniques at the exhibitions.

He has licensed his designs to custom backpack company Boldface, which has featured them on a series of colorful backpacks. Among his most popular works is a piece he calls *Salvation*, a bright red cross plainly visible against a black background. "Some of my paintings I put things a certain way to tell a story," he told Pelsue. "Not many of them, but sometimes God will speak to me."

PERSONAL LIFE

Hollenstein devotes much of his time and effort to philanthropic causes. He gives ten percent of his income to Canine Companions for Independence and is a cocreator of the annual Land Meets Sea Sports Camp, which takes place in Long Beach, California, and is aimed at providing adaptive outdoor sporting activities to those living with disabilities.

A devout Christian, Hollenstein enjoys Christian music (as well as conventional rock music), which he listens to as he paints. "Sometimes the rhythms help me, but often it's the words I'm concentrating on," he explained to Pelsue. "Some of the songs kind of speak to me, remind me of certain things, [and] bring back memories. A lot of my paintings happen when I'm thinking of places I surfed, places I camped, places where God was showing me different things and I was missing it at that moment."

SUGGESTED READING

Burke, Barbara. "Malibu's Gallery Art Walk Offers Eclectic Sampling." *Malibu Surfside News*, 9 July 2019, www.malibusurfsidenews.com/p/life-arts-arts/malibus-gallery-art-walk-offers-eclectic-sampling. Accessed 4 Sept. 2019.

Groubert, Mark. "LA People 2009: Spin Artist—Tommy Hollenstein." *LA Weekly*, 22 Apr. 2009, www.laweekly.com/la-people-2009-spin-artist-tommy-hollenstein/. Accessed 4 Sept. 2019.

Hollenstein, Tommy. Interview by Michelle Pelsue. *Arts and Entertainment Ministries*, 9 Oct. 2006, a-e-m.org/interview-with-painter-tommy-hollenstein/. Accessed 4 Sept. 2019.

Maddox, Sam. "Tommy Hollenstein: Tracking Art." *New Mobility*, 1 Apr. 2008, www.newmobility.com/2008/04/tommy-hollenstein-tracking-art/. Accessed 4 Sept. 2019.

Morrison, Laurie. "Stories from the Art: Tommy Hollenstein." *Inland Empire Museum of Art*, 2013, iearts.org/exhibits_stories_from_the_art-tommy_hollenstein.htm. Accessed 4 Sept. 2019.

Thornton, John Paul. *Art and Courage: Stories to Inspire the Artist-Warrior Within*. Fire Opal Publishing, 2009.

"Tommy Hollenstein Shares the Healing Power of Artistic Expression." *Cure Medical*, 2017–2018, curemedical.com/tommy-hollenstein-art/. Accessed 4 Sept. 2019.

SELECTED WORKS

Wheels of Dreams, 2006; *Helping Hands*, 2008; *Wheels of Hope*, 2011; *Chasing Your Dreams into Reality*, 2019

—Mari Rich

Donald Hopkins

Date of birth: September 25, 1941
Occupation: Public health official

During the early 1980s public-health advocate Dr. Donald Hopkins took on a new mission: the eradication of a disease known as the Guinea worm disease (GWD) for its prevalence on West Africa's Guinea coast. GWD is transmitted when people drink water contaminated with small copepods that carry Guinea worm larvae. Once the larvae hatch, they grow into long thin worms that eventually emerge through the skin of their human hosts, a disturbing and excruciating process that has devastated the lives and livelihoods of entire communities in Africa and Asia.

As a Centers for Disease Control and Prevention (CDC) employee, Hopkins had been part of the successful global effort to eradicate smallpox. He became convinced that GWD could be prevented and eventually eliminated through water-treatment and educational efforts, but others were unsure. "People often said to us at the beginning of the Guinea worm program, 'This is not smallpox, you don't have a vaccine. You're going to have to change people's behavior—and you won't be able to do that,'" he recalled to Madeline Drexler for the *Harvard Public Health* magazine (Winter 2018). "Well, lo and behold, it turns out if we approach people the right way and give them the information that they need, people will change their behavior—because they don't want to have Guinea worm, either."

After joining The Carter Center, a nongovernmental organization that was founded by former President Jimmy Carter in 1987, Hopkins led a successful campaign to address the disease, reducing the number of cases per year from several million to fewer than thirty over three decades. Yet despite his success, Hopkins remains committed to eradicating the disease entirely, and the international effort to do so will not end until that takes place. "You must not think of this as entirely voluntary," he told Barry Yeoman for *Atlanta* magazine (23 Aug. 2017). "I've got the tiger by the tail and I can't let go."

EARLY LIFE AND EDUCATION

Donald Roswell Hopkins was born in segregated Miami, Florida, in 1941. He spent his early years in the Bahamian section of Miami's Coconut Grove neighborhood, where he lived with his parents, Joseph Leonard Hopkins and Iva Louise

Photo by Center for Neighborhood Technology via Wikimedia Commons

Hopkins, and nine siblings. Hopkins's mother worked as a seamstress and a house cleaner, while his father was a carpenter. Hopkins also had a large extended family, many of whom lived nearby in the same neighborhood.

Although Hopkins's parents had received limited education themselves, they stressed the importance of education to their children, and his mother was particularly adamant that the children learn as much as possible. "She had a passion for education for all of us. She was there for every recital, spelling bee, performance, and all of the graduations: high school, college, graduate school," Hopkins recalled to Drexler. "After she died, we found among her papers an essay that she had written when she was in school—and she had only gone to eighth grade, so she had to be very young when she wrote it. The title of the essay was, 'Why We Must Educate Our Children.'" Hopkins, who aspired to become a doctor from a young age, took his mother's lessons to heart and distinguished himself as a student, eventually gaining the opportunity to begin college at age fifteen, as a sophomore in high school. Having qualified for a scholarship, he promptly left high school to enroll in Morehouse College in Atlanta, Georgia.

As an undergraduate, Hopkins had several experiences that would shape the trajectory of his life and career. While reading a textbook, he first saw a photograph of a Guinea worm exiting an individual's body, and the disturbing image left a lasting impression on him. Later, Hopkins received a scholarship to study abroad at the Institute of European Studies (IES) at University of Vienna, Austria, during the 1960–61 academic year. While abroad, he and a group of classmates traveled to Egypt, where Hopkins saw people exhibiting signs of what he would later learn was the bacterial infection trachoma, which can cause permanent blindness. "As a fellow human being, I thought, 'I would really like to be able to help people like this,'" he recalled to Yeoman.

After returning to Morehouse and completing his bachelor's degree near the top of his class in 1962, Hopkins enrolled in the University of Chicago Medical School. He specialized in tropical medicine during that period, influenced in large part by the illnesses he had learned about over the previous years. Hopkins earned his MD in 1966.

ERADICATING SMALLPOX

In 1967 Hopkins joined an international public-health campaign led by epidemiologist William Foege. Staffed, in part, by employees of the World Health Organization (WHO) and the CDC, the campaign sought to eradicate the highly infectious and often deadly disease smallpox, which continued to devastate a number of countries around the world. Hopkins was sent to the West African nation of Sierra Leone, where he and his colleagues employed strategic vaccinations. Unlike some smallpox-prevention initiatives, which operated via mass vaccinations, the campaign of which Hopkins was a part focused instead on containing the disease by traveling to locations where outbreaks were taking place and vaccinating the individuals most likely to have been exposed. Through that targeted approach, the campaign succeeded in eliminating smallpox from Sierra Leone by 1969.

Hopkins, having gained valuable experience during his years in Sierra Leone, later briefly joined a group working to eradicate smallpox in India. The disease was officially considered eradicated in India in 1975, and the WHO declared smallpox eradicated worldwide in 1980. For Hopkins, the success of the smallpox-eradication campaign proved that tackling such public-health crises was difficult but certainly not impossible. "Here is a disease that people thought could not be eradicated," Hopkins recalled to Colleen Mastony for the *Chicago Tribune* (13 May 2007). "It was causing all this trouble around the world. I heard people saying early on that eradication would never happen." Yet, despite widespread doubts, it had.

CDC

Highly motivated to continue addressing global health issues, Hopkins continued his education at Harvard University, earning a Master of Public Health degree in 1970. He then joined the university's School of Public Health as a faculty member in 1974, taking an assistant professor position there. Having determined that he preferred working in the field over academia, however, he left the university in 1977. Hopkins went to India to work on the smallpox eradication campaign and then joined the CDC as the assistant director for international health. He remained in that role until 1984, when he was promoted to deputy director. Hopkins served as acting director in 1985 and subsequently returned to the deputy directorship until 1987.

During his years with the CDC, Hopkins continued work on a book he had begun writing while at Harvard. Titled *Princes and Peasants: Smallpox in History*, the work chronicled the history of smallpox from ancient times to the present and featured information on early attempts at cures, the development of a vaccine, and the eradication of the disease. In addition to his personal experience with the eradication effort, Hopkins drew from his time studying abroad in Austria, which had once been home to numerous major figures killed by smallpox. "It gave me the context that those archdukes and duchesses and Emperor Joseph I all died of smallpox," he told IES Abroad (formerly the Institute of

European Studies) in 2015. "I did research at the Austrian National Library, and I found out in a daily gazette that two weeks prior to his illness Emperor Joseph I had visited a hospital. That was a classic way that people contracted the disease." Published in 1983, *Princes and Peasants* received critical acclaim and was nominated for the Pulitzer Prize. A revised edition of the book, titled *The Greatest Killer: Smallpox in History*, was published in 2002.

GUINEA WORM DISEASE

In 1980, while still at the CDC, Hopkins began to develop a plan to eradicate GWD, or dracunculiasis, a nonfatal but nevertheless tremendously harmful and painful parasitic infection. Affected by drinking water having larvae of the parasitic nematode *Dracunculus medinensis* (meaning "fiery little serpent of Medina"), people with GWD host the worms for ten to fourteen months. When ready to emerge, the worms, which can grow to about three feet in length, exit the body through the person's skin. The emergent worms release larvae when someone with GWD submerges an affected body part in water.

As no treatment or vaccine for GWD existed, Hopkins proposed that the disease could instead be eradicated through prevention and public education. Over the next several years, Hopkins worked to convince health officials to carry out his plan. Although unsuccessful, he refused to be dissuaded. "When people said to me, 'You're not going to be able to eradicate Guinea worm disease,' I had heard all of that about smallpox. So I just brushed it off," he told Yeoman. A turning point came in 1986, when Hopkins delivered a presentation on GWD and his plan to address it for the Carter Center. He succeeded in convincing Carter himself of the need to address the disease and joined the Carter Center as a senior consultant and leader of the center's GWD–eradication program. Later that year, WHO formally resolved to eradicate Guinea worms.

Hopkins and his Carter Center colleagues began their campaign in Ghana in 1987 and additional initiatives in Pakistan in 1988 and Nigeria in 1989. As Guinea worm larvae spread through tainted water, the team initially focused on the costly process of digging new wells for affected areas. However, they soon determined that simple, inexpensive water filters could be used to remove the larvae and other contaminants from drinking water, which allowed them to expand their efforts significantly. Hopkins and his colleagues also sought to educate the public about the causes of GWD and ensure compliance with efforts to filter water and keep clean water sources free of larvae.

CONTINUING EFFORTS

The Carter Center's efforts to eradicate GWD continued into the early twenty-first century and proved highly successful. The number of GWD cases worldwide was estimated at more than 3 million in 1986; fewer than 25,000 individuals had the disease by 2007. Hopkins and his colleagues also succeeded in eradicating the disease within eleven countries between the start of the campaign and 2006. The campaign's work remained important in countries such as Ghana, which experienced a new outbreak in 2007 but was considered officially free of the worms by 2015. A challenge also arose in Chad, where domesticated dogs began to be infected, requiring further interventions. In 2018 the disease was present in humans in only two countries—Chad and South Sudan—and only twenty-eight human cases were reported that year. In the first two months of 2019, there were four human cases: one in Angola and three in Chad.

Over his tenure at the Carter Center, Hopkins took on an increasing array of responsibilities within the organization, becoming associate executive director for health programs and later the vice president and director of health programs. After a heart attack in 2015, Hopkins retired from his leadership positions but took on the title of special adviser for Guinea worm eradication. Despite reducing his active participation in the center's eradication efforts, he remained devoted to that mission and convinced of its eventual success. "We will have shown that you can eradicate something without a vaccine and without a curative treatment," he told Drexler. "Our main tool has been health education."

In recognition of his efforts to eradicate smallpox and GWD, Hopkins has received numerous honors and widespread acclaim. He was named a MacArthur Fellow in 1995 and later served on the MacArthur Foundation's board of directors from 2005 to 2016. He has also received Medal of Excellence from the CDC and the Distinguished Service Medal from the US Public Health Service and was inducted into the American Academy of Arts and Sciences in 1997. In addition, Hopkins has received recognition from the governments of several African nations, including Mali and Niger, and was named an honorary chief in Nigeria thanks to his work in the region.

PERSONAL LIFE

Hopkins met his wife, Ernestine Mathis Hopkins, when she was working as an electron microscopist at the University of Chicago Medical Center. The couple married in 1967. They live in Chicago's Lincoln Park neighborhood. Hopkins shares a home office with a preserved Guinea worm he named Henrietta, which serves as an ever-present reminder of his continuing commitment to eradicating GWD once and for all.

SUGGESTED READING

Basu, Moni. "Donald Hopkins Helped Kill Smallpox and Is Close to Slaying the Fiery Serpent." *CNN*, 6 May 2016, www.cnn.com/2016/05/06/health/man-who-kills-disease/index.html. Accessed 10 May 2019.

Drexler, Madeline. "Fierce Optimism: Donald Hopkins' Quest to Eradicate Guinea Worm Disease." *Harvard Public Health*, Winter 2018, www.hsph.harvard.edu/magazine/magazine_article/fierce-optimism. Accessed 10 May 2019.

Hopkins, Donald. "65 Faces of IES Abroad—Donald Hopkins." Interview. *IES Abroad*, Institute for the International Education of Students, 2015, www.iesabroad.org/study-abroad/alumni/profiles/donald-hopkins#sthash.PUbOpxpQ.7b4AJEdd.dpbs. Accessed 10 May 2019.

Mastony, Colleen. "Doctor Without Borders." *Chicago Tribune*, 13 May 2007, www.chicagotribune.com/news/ct-xpm-2007-05-13-0705112107-story,amp.html. Accessed 10 May 2019.

McNeil, Donald G., Jr. "Another Scourge in His Sights." *The New York Times*, 22 Apr. 2013, www.nytimes.com/2013/04/23/health/donald-r-hopkins-how-to-eradicate-guinea-worm-disease.html. Accessed 10 May 2019.

Whipple, Tom. "How to Eradicate a Disease." *1843: Stories of an Extraordinary World*, Nov.–Dec. 2014, www.1843magazine.com/content/features/tom-whipple/good-riddance. Accessed 10 May 2019.

Yeoman, Barry. "Dr. Donald Hopkins Helped Wipe Smallpox from the Planet. He Won't Rest Until He's Done the Same for Guinea Worm Disease." *Atlanta*, 23 Aug. 2017, www.atlantamagazine.com/health/dr-donald-hopkins-helped-wipe-smallpox-from-the-planet-now-hes-after-guinea-worm-disease. Accessed 10 May 2019.

—*Joy Crelin*

Niall Horan

Date of birth: September 13, 1993
Occupation: Singer-songwriter

Irish singer-songwriter Niall Horan released his chart-topping debut solo album, *Flicker*, in 2017. He got his start at age sixteen, on the UK reality singing competition show *The X Factor* in 2010. After he had auditioned individually and did not move through the competition, the decision was made to place him in a group with a handful of other teen hopefuls on the show: Harry Styles, Zayn Malik, Liam Payne, and Louis Tomlinson. Thus, the explosively popular boy band One Direction was born. The group ultimately inspired the kind of obsessive fandom that one historically associates with the Beatles.

However, in 2015, after Malik's departure from the group earlier in the year, it was announced just months prior to releasing their fifth record that the band would be taking a break. On the heels of Malik and Styles, Horan was the third member of the group to release a solo album, though his style proved distinct from those of his bandmates. A diehard fan of the 1970s soft rockers the Eagles Horan has fostered a sound that combines pop, classic rock, and folk. His mentor, Don Henley, an original member of the Eagles, praised Horan to Chris Martins for *Billboard* magazine (25 May 2017), telling him, "Niall is a solid guy whose focus is right where it ought to be: on songwriting. He's got the Irish charm and a healthy, self-effacing sense of humor, which is an essential survival tool in this business. I think that Niall will evolve into a resonant, thoughtful voice for his generation."

EARLY LIFE AND THE *X FACTOR*

Niall Horan was born on September 13, 1993, and raised in the town of Mullingar in County Westmeath, Ireland. His father, Bobby, worked as a butcher at the Tesco supermarket. After his parents divorced when he was around five, Horan and his older brother, Greg, eventually moved in with their father. He learned to be self-sufficient, cooking his meals, washing his

Photo by marcen27 via Wikimedia Commons

clothes, and waking himself up in the morning to walk to school. He attended St. Kenny National School for his primary education (where he had the title role in a production of the musical *Oliver!*) and later Coláiste Mhuire (St. Mary's College) in Mullingar, though he never graduated.

Horan grew up listening to classic rock artists like Crosby, Stills & Nash; Fleetwood Mac; and the Eagles, and he inherited his brother's neglected guitar when he was twelve. He was a natural singer, as well. As a teen, he appeared in a local talent show, performing a well-received rendition of the Jason Mraz song "I'm Yours." By that point, he had also been harboring ambitions of becoming a pop star himself, and in 2009, a contestant on the UK singing competition show *The X Factor* captured his attention. "I remember we were watching the X Factor and Olly Murs was on it; Niall was obsessed with him, he loved Olly Murs," a childhood friend told Liz O'Brien for the *Irish Examiner* (24 Aug. 2014). Murs, an English singer-songwriter, came in second in that 2009 season. "He was like, 'I'm going to be on X Factor,'" the friend recalled. "We were like, 'Yeah, yeah' and he said, 'No I am, I'm going to be on X Factor.'"

Horan was one of the first in line at the next local audition for the show. In 2010, at the age of sixteen, he first appeared before the judges singing Ne-Yo's "So Sick." Simon Cowell, an English music executive and notorious singing competition judge, told Horan that the R & B song was a poor choice and that he had been unprepared, but acknowledged that he had something special. Thanks to the concession of pop star and judge Katy Perry, he moved on to the next round. The subsequent formation of One Direction was part organic and part manufactured—and unique in that it played out on live television. Horan was one of a handful of talented teen boys competing that year. When none of them moved forward to the next level of competition individually, it was determined that Horan, Harry Styles, Zayn Malik, Liam Payne, and Louis Tomlinson would be combined into a group, allowing them to progress through the competition in a different category. One Direction had been born.

RISE OF ONE DIRECTION

Though One Direction did not win *The X Factor* competition that year—they came in third—the group signed a recording contract with Cowell's recording label, Syco. They released their first single, a huge hit called "What Makes You Beautiful," in September 2011 in the United Kingdom, before putting out their first album, *Up All Night*, there in November. As the album sold well almost immediately, they performed their first concert in England in December. In later interviews, Horan described the performance as the worst of his life. "We were just a

joke," he told Mark Savage for *BBC News* (15 Sept. 2017). "Anything we rehearsed just went out the window. It was our first ever gig and we just didn't know what the [expletive] was going on." Horan, who had been told on *The X Factor* that he needed time and practice to develop as an artist, would have to learn on the fly. The band's ascent was already in motion. When One Direction performed in the United States on the *Today Show* a few months later in March 2012, thousands of screaming fans turned out to see them. Upon releasing *Up All Night* in the United States that same month, according to *Billboard*, the band became the first UK group to have their first album debut at number one on the US Billboard 200 chart.

One Direction won the trophy for best new artist at the MTV Video Music Awards in 2012 and released their sophomore record, *Take Me Home*, which also entered the Billboard 200 chart at the top position, later that same year. In 2013, a documentary, directed by Morgan Spurlock and titled *One Direction: This Is Us*, premiered in theaters. The film chronicles the band's rise, combining concert footage and behind-the-scenes adventures from their 2013 world tour. The group's third studio album, *Midnight Memories*, which features the Billboard Hot 100 top-ten singles "Story of My Life" and "Best Song Ever," also appeared in 2013. The album itself became the band's third consecutive album to debut at number one on the Billboard 200 chart.

FOUR AND MADE IN THE A.M.

The following year, they released their fourth, largely critically acclaimed album, *Four*. As Andrew Unterberger, who reviewed the album for *Spin* (20 Nov. 2014), noted, the fact that the band remained relevant enough to make a successful fourth album was a feat in itself. By 2014, the band members were visibly maturing and beginning to move away from pure pop toward a classic rock sound. (Horan and Styles would further explore this influence in their solo work.) With a unifying theme, he described *Four* as "the most consistent-sounding Direction album yet." The record's debut at number one on the Billboard 200 chart marked it as the band's fourth consecutive album to achieve this feat and made Horan a member of the only group in the history of the chart to have their first four albums enter in the top position. Throughout this time, Horan and One Direction accepted awards recognizing their music in both the United Kingdom and the United States, including BRIT Awards in categories such as British Single (2012) and Global Success (2013) as well as the American Music Award for Artist of the Year in both 2014 and 2015.

However, just as the band began to find its groove, it began to break down. Malik left the group in early 2015. By August, it had been announced that the group, sans Malik, would be taking a break beginning in 2016. Horan and his remaining bandmates released a fifth album, titled *Made in the A.M.*, later in 2015. They played their last televised gig together at the Billboard Hollywood Party for *Dick Clark's New Year's Rockin' Eve with Ryan Seacrest* in December 2015.

FLICKER

In early 2016, Horan, along with two cousins, went backpacking throughout Southeast Asia. The trip was an opportunity to embrace his newfound freedom. "I didn't want the schedule anymore," he told Martins. During his time with One Direction, he recalled, "All me mates were backpacking, while I wasn't even allowed to go outside of the hotel." In September of that year, having signed with Capitol Records, he released his first solo single, titled "This Town." The gentle pop song features little more than Horan and an acoustic guitar—a stark departure from the broadening sounds of One Direction. The single suggested that Horan's tastes skewed closer to those of folk pop star Ed Sheeran—who wrote a handful of songs for One Direction, including the hit "Little Things"—than the more bombastic solo fare of bandmate Styles. Horan's second single, the hit "Slow Hands," peaked at number eleven on the Billboard Hot 100 chart following its release in early 2017. In writing the song, Horan said he was influenced by the funkier early solo work of Henley in the 1980s.

Horan's first solo album, *Flicker*, debuted at the top of the Billboard 2000 upon its release in October 2017. Craig Jenkins, who reviewed the album for *Vulture* (20 Oct. 2017), ably captured the project, writing, "*Flicker* is nice, clean folk-pop that keeps its sound pinned in the present while saluting the past." To paraphrase Jenkins, Horan's songs—"On the Loose" and "Since We're Alone"—borrow from the Fleetwood Mac hit "Dreams," but the product sounds more like the recent pop group Maroon 5. Jenkins gave the album a middling review, writing that it combined a few great songs—"Slow Hands" among them—with more forgettable filler. "Lacking the strength in numbers that One Direction provided, though, he's still learning how to carry a full album on his own," he wrote. Not all critics felt the same way, however. *Rolling Stone* named *Flicker* one of their top twenty pop albums of 2017.

PERSONAL LIFE

Horan is an avid golfer. In 2016, he helped launched Modest! Golf Management, a new division of the Modest! Management agency seeking to recruit golfers in the United Kingdom and Ireland. Still close with his parents, it was reported that he had paid off his mother's mortgage and offered to buy his father a new home after earning money through his music career.

SUGGESTED READING

Jenkins, Craig. "Niall Horan, the Heart of One Direction, Treads Water on *Flicker*." Review of *Flicker*, by Niall Horan. *Vulture*, 20 Oct. 2017, www.vulture.com/2017/10/review-niall-horans-album-flicker.html. Accessed 15 July 2019.

Martins, Chris. "Niall Horan Braces for Stardom Outside One Direction, with Advice from Justin Bieber & The Eagles." *Billboard*, 25 May 2017, www.billboard.com/articles/news/magazine-feature/7808513/niall-horan-interview-cover-story-one-direction-2017. Accessed 15 July 2019.

O'Brien, Liz. "Why There's No Place Like Niall Horan's Home." *Irish Examiner*, 24 Aug. 2014, www.irishexaminer.com/lifestyle/features/why-theres-no-place-like-niall-horans-home-283126.html. Accessed 15 July 2019.

Savage, Mark. "Niall Horan: 'One Direction's First Gig Was a Disaster.'" *BBC News*, 15 Sept. 2017, www.bbc.com/news/entertainment-arts-41246502. Accessed 15 July 2019.

Unterberger, Andrew. "Review: One Direction Hide in Plain Sight from Boy-Band History with 'Four.'" Review of *Four*, by One Direction. *Spin*, 20 Nov. 2014, www.spin.com/2014/11/one-direction-four/. Accessed 15 July 2019.

SELECTED WORKS

Up All Night (with One Direction), 2011; *Take Me Home* (with One Direction), 2012; *Midnight Memories* (with One Direction), 2013; *Four* (with One Direction), 2014; *Made in the A.M.* (with One Direction), 2015; *Flicker*, 2017

—*Molly Hagan*

Abby Huntsman

Date of birth: May 1, 1986
Occupation: Television personality

"There's no such thing today as someone being on TV with zero opinion," Abby Huntsman told Jeremy Barr for the *Hollywood Reporter* (17 Sept. 2018) shortly after becoming a host of ABC's popular daytime show *The View* in September 2018. "People don't want to watch someone that literally doesn't have a thought about anything." Throughout her career Huntsman repeatedly proved her willingness to express her opinion,

Photo by HuffPost Live via Wikimedia Commons

even when her views did not necessarily align with that of her audience. The daughter of Republican politician Jon Huntsman Jr., the US ambassador to Russia, she generally identified as Republican but began her career at more liberal-leaning outlets such as ABC, the Huffington Post, and MSNBC. She then raised her profile as a presenter for the conservative media channel Fox News, where she served as a more centrist voice from 2015 to 2018. Huntsman's move to *The View* drew controversy from both ends of the political spectrum, but she took the criticism in stride and maintained her independent outlook. "Many of my generation don't want to be labeled one thing or the other," she asserted to Erica Evans for the *Deseret News* (25 Sept. 2018). "With politics for example, we're at a time when both parties are at such an extreme. A lot of us are in that middle area, and that's where I sit."

EARLY YEARS

Abby Huntsman was born in Philadelphia, Pennsylvania on May 1, 1986, to Mary Kaye Huntsman and Jon Huntsman Jr. She was raised with her six siblings: Asha Bharati (who was adopted from India), Gracie Mei (adopted from China), William, Jon III, Elizabeth (known as Liddy), and Mary Anne. Her father was the scion of the wealthy family behind the major chemical manufacturer Huntsman Corporation, and his career as a diplomat and politician meant the family moved frequently. At various times she lived in Virginia, China, Taiwan, and Singapore, among other places. Huntsman spent many of her formative years in Salt Lake City, Utah, where her family was prominent in the Church of Jesus Christ of Latter-Day Saints, or Mormon Church.

Huntsman was a strong-willed child, later noting that she ran away from home multiple times when unhappy with some parental edict. She loved to sing and dance and often took it upon herself to perform for guests at her parents' parties. (Because of her father's position, some of those guests included high-level dignitaries and entertainment-world figures.) Her antics eventually convinced her parents to let her try out for theater productions, and at age seven she acted in her first play, beginning an enduring passion. Huntsman also became serious about playing tennis, twice winning the state championship during her high school years. A challenge, meanwhile, was learning to drive: she failed her driving test three times as a teen.

While still in high school, Huntsman worked as an intern at a local television station, washing the dishes after cooking segments and performing other low-level tasks. She later expressed pride in this humble introduction to working in television. "There is no question that I was given a lot of interesting and unique opportunities growing up," she told Mattie Kahn for *Elle* (19 Oct. 2015). "But I think people often misunderstand that I work as hard and want things just as badly as anybody else. . . . I thought, 'I'm going to do whatever it takes to get in those doors and prove myself and to learn and to work hard.' . . . I loved washing the dishes, because I was on set and I got to see what was going on firsthand."

POLITICAL BEGINNINGS AND EARLY CAREER

Huntsman entered her freshman year of college at the University of Utah and transferred to the University of Pennsylvania's Annenberg School for Communication as a sophomore. She later changed her major to political science and became immersed in the political life of the campus, joining a Young Republicans group and working on *Penn Red*, a conservative show that aired on the university's television station. That experience "was less about being a die-hard Republican than getting more people involved in politics," she recalled to Maria Yagoda for the *Pennsylvania Gazette* (27 Feb. 2014).

As a college student, Huntsman interned for noted television anchor and journalist Diane Sawyer, who served as an important mentor and role model. "She's probably the person I look up to most in this industry," Huntsman told Kahn. "I always think of her as someone that I hope I can try to be like, because she's represented herself in such a classy way and brought so many incredible stories into people's lives." With support from her family, Huntsman acclimated herself to the demanding newsroom environment.

After graduating from college in 2008, Huntsman worked briefly as a booker for the

ABC show *Good Morning America*. However, disliking the long hours and the machinations required to book in-demand guests, she soon joined the public-relations firm Burson-Marsteller instead. She even considered abandoning her goal of working in television news.

After her father announced in 2011 that he would run in the 2012 Republican presidential primary, Huntsman left her PR job to help manage his media appearances. She and her sisters Liddy and Mary Anne also contributed their own social media efforts to his campaign, launching a Twitter account dubbed @Jon2012girls and creating humorous videos. The account proved popular but drew some concern from her father's advisers for its unregulated content. In one typically irreverent tweet, the sisters jokingly attacked Republican frontrunner Mitt Romney— "How does Romney know anything about China? He's only been there once and that was for the Olympics. Panda Express doesn't count"— and they received particular attention for a video spoofing a campaign ad of primary opponent Herman Cain. "The campaign advisers were not happy about it, but my dad now admits we were the bright spot for him during a time that had many ups and downs," Huntsman told *Fox News Insider* (28 Aug. 2017).

Although Huntsman's father dropped out of the presidential race in early 2012, his candidacy supplied something of a launch pad for her. During and directly after the campaign she did political commentary, appearing on networks including CNN and MSNBC. During this period, she also became a contributing writer for the *Huffington Post* and worked on the HuffPost Live online video streaming network as a producer and host.

FROM *THE CYCLE* TO *FOX NEWS*

In 2013 Huntsman was named to the *Forbes* list of thirty influential media figures under thirty years old for her work at HuffPost Live. Her contributions also caught the eye of MSNBC executive Steven Friedman, who invited her to join the team at MSNBC's *The Cycle*, a roundtable show that covered politics and current events. There she was cast as the token conservative, often good-naturedly sparring against fellow panelists Krystal Ball, Touré, and Ari Melber. Huntsman remained with the show until it went off the air in July 2015.

Soon after *The Cycle* ended Huntsman joined Fox News—well known for its conservative leanings—as a general assignment reporter. However, she rejected simple political categorization. "I don't like to define myself as necessarily conservative," she told Evans. "For me, it just depends on what the issue is. I'm probably more fiscally a Republican. But socially, I'm just accepting of everything." Proving popular with viewers, in December 2016 she was made a co-host on the talk show *Fox & Friends Weekend*. However, she had her share of detractors as well, on both the left and the right. For example, many liberals criticized her interview of her father upon his appointment as US ambassador to Russia in 2017, noting that she avoided any mention of Russia's interference in American politics and generally posed unchallenging questions. On the other hand, some conservatives protested when she referred to President Donald Trump as a "dictator" on-air in 2018, prompting her to apologize and call the comment an accident.

Working in a highly partisan political climate, Huntsman often found herself defending her centrist views. In many cases this included both her criticisms and defenses of the highly controversial Trump and his administration. "I feel responsibility to speak from my heart and what I feel is true or not, or right or wrong," she told Evans. "I was probably far more critical of Trump than anyone else on our show, and the audience wasn't always thrilled about that. But I think it's important that as a country, we understand each other."

THE VIEW

In August 2018 it was reported that Huntsman would be leaving Fox News to become a cohost of the popular talk show *The View* on ABC. She welcomed the chance to return to the network where she had started her career, and the mainstream program fit her centrist outlook. She joined conservative Meghan McCain and more liberal hosts Whoopi Goldberg, Sunny Hostin, and Joy Behar on the show.

While her debut was relatively successful, Huntsman did receive backlash from both conservatives and liberals on social media for changing networks. She also found herself defending her former employer in her new role, especially amid reports of toxic culture and sexual harassment at Fox. "I would say it was a wonderful place to work," she asserted to Barr. "And there are so many great women there. . . . No one ever told the story about all the wonderful women that stayed, that were strong, and that kept it going, and kept it to where it is today. We always focus on the negatives and what the controversy is."

PERSONAL LIFE

Huntsman was raised as a Mormon but stopped being actively involved with the church because of her support for women's and LGBT rights. She married business analyst Jeffrey Livingston in 2010, and in November 2017 they had a daughter, Isabel Grace. The following year Huntsman published the children's book *Who Will I Be?*, which encourages young readers to be of service to their communities.

SUGGESTED READING

Barr, Jeremy. "Abby Huntsman on Why She Left Fox News for 'The View.'" *The Hollywood Reporter*, 17 Sept. 2018, www.hollywoodreporter.com/news/abby-huntsman-why-she-left-fox-news-view-1143488. Accessed 4 Dec. 2018.

Huntsman, Abby. "Abby Huntsman Thinks Fox News Is a Great Place to Be a Woman." Interview by Mattie Kahn. *Elle*, 19 Oct. 2015, www.elle.com/culture/career-politics/news/a31251/abby-huntsman-thinks-fox-news-is-a-great-place-to-be-a-woman/. Accessed 4 Nov. 2018.

Huntsman, Abby. "Q&A: Why Abby Huntsman Doesn't Like to Be Labelled 'Conservative.'" Interview by Erica Evans. *Deseret News*, 25 Sept. 2018, www.deseretnews.com/article/900033590/qanda-why-abby-huntsman-doesnt-like-to-be-labelled-conservative.html. Accessed 4 Dec. 2018.

Keegan, Kayla. "'The View' Cohost Abby Huntsman Has Quite an Interesting Background." *Good Housekeeping*, 28 Aug. 2018, www.goodhousekeeping.com/life/a22853341/abby-huntsman-husband-the-view/. Accessed 4 Dec. 2018.

Larson, Leslie. "Abby Huntsman joins NBC's Sorority of Political Daughters as She Makes Her Debut on the Cable Network's 'The Cycle.'" *New York Daily News*, 29 July 2013, www.nydailynews.com/news/politics/jon-huntsman-daughter-abby-joins-msnbc-cycle-article-1.1411439. Accessed 4 Dec. 2018.

Lizza, Ryan. "Those Huntsman Girls." *The New Yorker*, 14 Nov. 2011, www.newyorker.com/magazine/2011/11/14/those-huntsman-girls. Accessed 2 Jan. 2019.

Yagoda, Maria. "Hitting for the Cycle." *The Pennsylvania Gazette*, 27 Feb. 2014, thepenngazette.com/hitting-for-the-cycle/. Accessed 4 Dec. 2018.

—*Mari Rich*

Joel Thomas Hynes

Date of birth: 1976
Occupation: Writer, actor, and musician

Newfoundland native Joel Thomas Hynes has frequently been referred to as a quintessential multi-hyphenate artist. Beginning in the early 2000s, he carved out a successful career for himself as a novelist, playwright, screenwriter, actor, producer, director, and musician. He first burst onto the scene in 2004, when he published his debut novel, *Down to the Dirt*, a gritty exploration of Newfoundland life that received several literary honors. In the years following his debut Hynes continued to release other Newfoundland-set works known for their raw vernacular prose and self-destructive antiheroes, helping to hone his "international reputation as a bad boy of Canadian literature," as Sue Carter noted for the *Toronto Star* (1 Apr. 2017). He was awarded the coveted Governor General's Literary Award in English fiction for his fourth novel, *We'll All Be Burnt in Our Beds Some Night* (2017). In a review of that novel for *Quill & Quire* (Apr. 2017), Steven W. Beattie declared that Hynes had earned his status as "one of the most distinctive and recognizable voices in the Canadian literary canon."

As his literary career drew acclaim, Hynes also worked steadily in the Canadian film and television industry as an actor, screenwriter, and filmmaker. Among the many credits to his name, he earned attention as the creator, executive producer, and star of the hit CBC comedy series *Little Dog*, which debuted in 2018. That same year he also released his first full-length studio album as a musician, *Dead Man's Melody* (2018).

EARLY LIFE

Joel Thomas Hynes was born in 1976 in Calvert, a small coastal town in Newfoundland and Labrador, Canada. He was raised there in a rough-and-tumble environment, one that would later serve as a major inspiration for his writing. Growing up in the shadow of an older brother, Hynes identified with being an outcast from a young age. Consequently, he found solace in reading, which "came to me like magic," as he wrote in an

Photo by Canadian Film Centre via Wikimedia Commons

essay for CBC (1 Mar. 2018). "Reading gave me the foundation to become something better than I was told I was or could ever become."

Besides reading, Hynes gravitated toward music and other performing arts. One of his earliest influences was the Newfoundland-based sketch comedy troupe CODCO (an abbreviation of "Cod Company"). As a youth Hynes regularly watched the troupe's eponymous CBC television series with his family, who otherwise "weren't the type to do anything together," as he noted to an interviewer for CBC (17 Jan. 2019). The troupe, whose skits drew on Newfoundland's cultural idiosyncrasies, helped instill in him the power of humor and a lifelong pride for his native province.

Hynes's creative sensibilities were further shaped by his uncle, Ron Hynes, a noted folk singer-songwriter who was also something of a black sheep in the family. The musician would occasionally show up at Hynes's home with his latest albums and demos, which made real the possibility of pursuing a career in the arts. During his teens, Hynes, inspired by his uncle and authors like Jack Kerouac and John Steinbeck, started writing poetry and stories, many of which he transformed into songs. He wrote extensively throughout his time in high school, during which he also performed in various bands.

For Hynes, writing, as well as reading, often proved to be a saving grace from decadent and rebellious behavior. Like his uncle, who died of complications from cancer in 2015, Hynes struggled with drug and alcohol addiction. Throughout much of his teens and early adulthood he lived essentially as an outcast, all the while pursuing creativity no matter what the cost. "I've been struck by cars, woken up with my hair frozen to the ground, I've come home with black eyes and don't know where I got them," he told Daniel Miller for the Newfoundland and Labrador *Independent* (9 June 2011). "I've overdosed three or four times, I've almost bled to death a couple times."

MAKING HIS REPUTATION

Hynes drew heavily on his life experiences as he launched a cross-disciplinary career in the early 2000s. He began landing roles in Canadian television and film, making his acting debut in the television movie *Messiah from Montreal* (2001). From 2005 to 2006 he had a starring role on the sitcom *Hatching, Matching, & Dispatching*, alongside famed Canadian comedians Mary Walsh, a former CODCO member, and Mark McKinney, cofounder of the sketch comedy group Kids in the Hall. During the series' one-season run he also wrote three episodes.

Concurrently with his acting, Hynes produced works of fiction. His debut novel, *Down to the Dirt*, was published in 2004 to critical acclaim. It is told from the first-person perspective of Newfoundlander Keith Kavanagh, a booze-and-drug-addled ne'er do well who, along with his girlfriend Natasha and best friend Andy, desperately seeks to find his place in the world. Praised by critics for its rawness, dialogue, irreverent humor, and unflinchingly honest look at life on the margins, the novel won the Percy Janes First Novel Award and was nominated for several other honors.

In 2008, *Down to the Dirt* was adapted into a feature film, in which Hynes starred as Kavanagh. By then, Hynes had already published his follow-up novel *Right Away Monday* (2007), which revisits the same themes and milieu of his debut, focusing on a self-destructive protagonist, Clayton Reid, who is forced to face his demons after meeting an aspiring actress named Isadora. The novel received generally positive reviews, but it was not as commercially successful as *Down to the Dirt*. Comparing it to his debut, Hynes said to Miller, "It's darker; it's a lot more in-depth. It's a real reader's novel."

Hynes later published the chapbook *God Help Thee: A Manifesto* (2011), which had started out as a performance piece, and the prose-poetry collection *Straight Razor Days* (2012), which explores the subject of masculinity in Newfoundland in the twenty-first century. Meanwhile, he penned several well-received stage plays, including *The Devil You Don't Know* and *Say Nothing Saw Wood*. The latter is based on a real-life murder that occurred in Hynes's hometown in 1971, told from the perspective of the murderer.

In 2013, Hynes turned *Say Nothing Saw Wood* into a same-titled gothic novella. He then adapted it into a feature film the following year under the title *Cast No Shadow* (2014). He starred alongside his son, Percy Hynes White, in the film, which received numerous honors, including four Canadian Screen Award nominations.

GOVERNOR GENERAL AWARD WINNER

Hynes spent years scrapping and rewriting versions of his fourth novel, *We'll All Be Burnt in Our Beds Some Night*, before finally publishing it in 2017. Marking a departure from his earlier works in terms of setting, the novel centers around the character of Johnny Keough, who, like past Hynes protagonists, is tough, violent, and fond of chemical substances. Johnny is facing possible jail time for accidentally assaulting his girlfriend, but after she dies of a drug overdose he embarks on an epic road trip that takes him from Newfoundland to Vancouver, British Columbia, on a mission to scatter her ashes at her favorite beach.

We'll All Be Burnt in Our Beds Some Night garnered widespread plaudits from critics.

Beattie commented that Hynes has "an ear for colloquial rhythm and vernacular that is virtually unimpeachable," and wrote that the novel "offers the reader a kind of looseness and expansiveness that is absent from [his] earlier work." Meanwhile, Carter pointed out that the novel contains Hynes's characteristic "darkly comic situations," and, despite its second-half shift in setting, still features a colorful slice of Newfoundland "that is universal to hardscrabble small-town life."

The novel earned Hynes the 2017 Governor General's Award for English-language fiction, one of the most prestigious literary prizes in Canada. The book also won the 2017 Winterset Award and was longlisted for that year's Giller Prize. Yet Hynes frequently noted that he was not driven to please critics, to find commercial success, or by any other external motivations. "I run with my ideas first and I don't care if there's money on the other end of it, or if there's awards or anything like that on the other end of it," he explained to Terri Coles in another article for CBC (24 Feb. 2018). "I live for the kind of meditative qualities of creating."

LITTLE DOG AND MUSIC ENDEAVORS

During the 2010s Hynes also continued to remain active on the acting front, appearing in such television series as *Republic of Doyle*, *Rookie Blue*, *Orphan Black*, *Mary Kills People*, and *Frontier*. He also directed the award-winning short films *Clipper Gold* (2011) and *Little Man* (2013). This work ultimately paved the way for him to develop his first television series, *Little Dog*, which draws on his experiences as an amateur boxer. The CBC dark comedy series centers around Tommy "Little Dog" Ross, a former super welterweight contender from Newfoundland who is offered the chance to redeem himself after walking out on a bout five years earlier.

Upon premiering in March 2018, *Little Dog* received rave reviews from critics, many of whom made note of its strong writing and acting. Hynes starred in the title role and served as an executive producer on the series, which was renewed for a second season. He also wrote multiple episodes of the series. "I approach that role as a guy looking for love and approval, and looking to dredge up the inner strength to fight the big fight," he told the CBC interviewer (17 Jan. 2019). "I don't think of comedy, I don't think of drama."

Meanwhile, Hynes was also developing another facet of his career, as a musician. He had occasionally toured with bands for years, collaborated with Ron Hynes, and had tracks featured in various films and television shows. In 2015 he released an EP of four original songs, *JTH Live at the LSPU Hall*, and one was even a finalist in the CBC searchlight competition that year. Then, the same month that *Little Dog*

premiered, Hynes released his first full-length studio album, *Dead Man's Melody* (2018). The concept album, which was produced by Eamon McGrath, chronicles the dealings of a group of unsavory characters. It examines such Hynes-esque themes as doomed love, recklessness, violence, and death.

Hynes remained committed to his diverse career even as he acknowledged the difficulty of being involved in so many different fields. "I'm juggling a lot of creative endeavours and hoping for the best, and trying to work out a strategy that doesn't always pay off," he told Coles. "My approach hasn't always been the most conventional approach."

PERSONAL LIFE

Hynes entered rehab for alcoholism in 2010 and noted that getting sober improved both his personal and professional lives. He maintained deep roots in his native Newfoundland, even as his career led to long stints living in more commercial places such as Toronto and California. His son, actor Percy Hynes White, was the product of a relationship with Canadian actor, producer, and filmmaker Sherry White, who also served as the showrunner for *Little Dog* and collaborated with Hynes on many other projects.

SUGGESTED READING

Beattie, Steven W. Review of *We'll All Be Burnt in Our Beds Some Night*, by Joel Thomas Hynes. *Quill & Quire*, Apr. 2017, quillandquire.com/review/well-all-be-burnt-in-our-beds-some-night/. Accessed 2 Sept. 2019.

Carter, Sue. "Newfoundland and Joe Thomas Hynes: Writing about a Place He Loves." *The Star*, 1 Apr. 2017, www.thestar.com/entertainment/books/2017/04/01/newfoundland-and-joel-thomas-hynes-writing-about-a-place-he-loves.html. Accessed 2 Sept. 2019.

Coles, Terri. "From Newfoundland to California, 'Outcasts and Renegades' Keep Joel Thomas Hynes Busy." *CBC*, 24 Feb. 2018, www.cbc.ca/news/canada/newfoundland-labrador/joel-thomas-hynes-nlreads-1.4537404. Accessed 2 Sept. 2019.

Hynes, Joel Thomas. "Bottle Pit: An Interview with Joel Thomas Hynes." Interview by Michelle Butler Hallett. *Antigonish Review*, 22 Mar. 2009. *The Free Library*, www.thefreelibrary.com/Bottle+pit%3a+an+interview+with+Joel+Thomas+Hynes.-a0201371484. Accessed 2 Sept. 2019.

Hynes, Joel Thomas. "Joel Thomas Hynes: A Manifesto." Interview by Daniel Miller. *The Independent (Newfoundland and Labrador)*, 9 June 2011, theindependent.ca/2011/06/09/joel-hynes-a-manifesto/. Accessed 2 Sept. 2019.

Hynes, Joel Thomas. "Why Writer and Creator of the CBC Show Little Dog Joel Thomas Hynes Loves Reading." *CBC*, 1 Mar. 2018, www.cbc.ca/books/why-writer-and-creator-of-the-cbc-show-little-dog-joel-thomas-hynes-loves-reading-1.4557230. Accessed 2 Sept. 2019.

"Newfoundland's Joel Thomas Hynes Reflects on 'CODCO' and 'Little Dog.'" *CBC*, 17 Jan. 2019, www.cbc.ca/comedy/newfoundland-s-joel-thomas-hynes-reflects-on-codco-and-little-dog-1.4944663. Accessed 2 Sept. 2019.

SELECTED WORKS

Down to the Dirt, 2004; *Right Away Monday*, 2007; *Say Nothing Saw Wood*, 2013; *We'll All Be Burnt in Our Beds Some Night*, 2017

—*Chris Cullen*

Photo by Bryan Ledgard via Wikimedia Commons

Jason Isbell

Date of birth: February 1, 1979
Occupation: Singer-songwriter

Grammy Award–winning Americana singer-songwriter Jason Isbell "is on a roll," Jim Beviglia *American Songwriter* (10 July 2015) wrote in his review of the 2015 album *Something More Than Free*. "There's no better songwriter on the planet at this moment, no one operating with the same depth, eloquence, or feeling." Isbell has a talent for writing storytelling songs that feel strikingly real. He has been compared to Bruce Springsteen, the bard of New Jersey's working class, and Steve Earle. In addition to winning two Grammy Awards, including the award for best Americana album, in 2018, he also wrote a song for the critically acclaimed remake of *A Star Is Born* (2018). In the film, an alcoholic country star falls in love with a singer he mentors. Isbell was initially hesitant to work on the film—this is the story's fourth iteration—but was moved by an early version of the script. For the film's character Jackson Maine, played by Bradley Cooper, he wrote a song called "Maybe It's Time."

Elements of Isbell's own story are oddly parallel to the fictional Maine's. Only twenty-two when he joined the increasingly popular Southern rock band the Drive-By Truckers, he got an early taste of fame. He wrote a handful of classic songs, like "Outfit" and "Decoration Day," but left the band on poor terms in 2007. His early solo career was distorted by his struggles with alcoholism, but in 2012, supported by friends and family, he checked into rehab. His sobriety shaped his critically acclaimed "resurrection," as Dwight Garner put it in a profile of Isbell for the *New York Times* (31 May 2013), in the form of the 2013 album *Southeastern*. The Grammy Award–winning studio albums *Something More Than Free* and *The Nashville Sound* (2017) followed.

EARLY LIFE AND EDUCATION

Jason Isbell was born on February 1, 1979, to teenage parents. Raised in Green Hill, a small, rural Alabama community near the Tennessee border, he and his parents lived in a trailer in his grandparents' front yard in his early years. Eventually, they moved to a one-level house. His father, Mike, worked painting houses. Isbell showed an interest in music at a young age, crediting his grandfather, who often watched him while his parents were working, and his uncle with teaching him how to play mandolin and guitar. When he was around eight and was given his first electric guitar, the first song that he learned to play was Lynyrd Skynyrd's "Simple Man."

In his high school years, Isbell joined a band with a friend and was good enough to jam in local restaurants. The scene in and around tiny Green Hill was more serious than one might think, thanks to its proximity to Muscle Shoals, where artists like the Rolling Stones, Wilson Pickett, and Aretha Franklin once recorded. At first observing, he was eventually invited to play with the session musicians, such as David Hood, from Muscle Shoals who would regularly play at the restaurants. "Those older guys would record behind other people during the day and go out and play these intense R&B covers at night," he told Garner. "They took a real interest in me. They taught me a great deal."

After graduating from high school, where he played the trumpet and the French horn in a marching band, Isbell received an academic scholarship to the University of Memphis. In addition to continuing with the marching band, he studied creative writing, with an aim to improve his songwriting skills. For one gig at a Memphis, Tennessee, coffee shop, he wrote his own songs, and ended up making demos of the material, which he sent to FAME Studios in Muscle Shoals. Bored by a physical education class, he dropped out just a few credits short of graduation and headed back to the Muscle Shoals region in 2001.

DRIVE-BY TRUCKERS

Upon returning home, things were looking up for Isbell. FAME offered him a publishing deal in the form of a songwriting contract for $250 a week, based on the demos he had sent them. Around the same time, he was also playing casual gigs with Patterson Hood, one member of a band, formed in 1996, called the Drive-By Truckers. Isbell joined the band by accident. He jumped in when one of the guitarists did not show for an important gig late in 2001 and wound up going on tour. Shortly after becoming a Trucker, he wrote his two most famous Trucker songs, "Decoration Day" and "Outfit." "I knew we'd struck gold," Hood told Garner. "This chubby kid—he was 22 but looked like he was 15—was going to be one of the great songwriters of our time."

The Drive-By Truckers had been on tour to support their recently released, breakout third album *Southern Rock Opera* (2001). With Isbell, they released their highly anticipated follow-up, *Decoration Day*, in 2003. Stephen Haag, who reviewed the album for *Pitchfork* (28 Aug. 2003), favorably described it as an "emotional U-turn" from their earlier work. *Southern Rock Opera* is an epic—Haag even described it as the band's "magnum opus,"—while *Decoration Day* "casts a much smaller net, grappling with more personal struggles." Isbell's song "Outfit" is written from the perspective of his father. Haag described "Decoration Day," about a decades-long familial feud between two families, and a son who has no wish to continue it, as "the emotional core."

Isbell was still with the band when they released their next successful record, *The Dirty South*, in 2004. The album, like *Southern Rock Opera* before it, explores and breaks down mythologies of the South. But Isbell's contributed composition, the heavy and introspective "Goddamn Lonely Love," is more personal. Stephen M. Deusner, writing for *Pitchfork* (31 Aug. 2004), described it as a "starkly devastating closer" to the album, adding, of Isbell's formidable talent, "Although this is only his second album

as a Trucker, already he can hold his own with his seniors."

But all was not well in the band. Isbell had married bassist Shonna Tucker in 2002, and after the departure of the group's bassist Earl Hicks, she joined the band in 2003. By 2006, the year in which the group released the less impactful *A Blessing and a Curse*, Isbell and Tucker's marriage was falling apart, and the heavy-drinking band was constantly fighting. "We had gotten to the point where we just hated being around each other," Isbell told Garner. He was reportedly forced out of the band in 2007, and he and Tucker divorced.

EARLY SOLO CAREER

Isbell released a solo album titled *Sirens of the Ditch* that same year. Deusner, who also reviewed that album for *Pitchfork* (11 July 2007), described it, despite some missteps, as "a strong debut full of the kind of confident, charismatic songwriting that just can't be taught." However, as Hood served as a producer on the project and Tucker had bass credits, this debut solo work did not fully separate Isbell from his former group. With a new backing band, the 400 Unit, he followed it up with *Jason Isbell and the 400 Unit* in 2009. The album won praise for songs like "Streetlights," about a lonely, drunk musician making phone calls home as the bar closes, and "Soldiers Get Strange," about a returning veteran struggling to readjust to marital and civilian life.

Isbell released *Here We Rest*, also with the 400 Unit, in 2011. In his *Pitchfork* review (11 Apr. 2011), Deusner wrote that the album is plagued by the same problem as Isbell's earlier offering: a few songs on the record are standouts, but too many are just average. Deusner praised "Alabama Pines," which went on to win Song of the Year at the 2012 Americana Music Association's Americana Honors & Awards, and the more upbeat "Codeine," but described the album as "another spotty set." "It's a hard truth," Deusner concluded, "but so far Jason Isbell's solo career hasn't lived up to the promise he showed during his short tenure with the Drive-By Truckers." Despite such criticism, and even as Isbell struggled against continued alcoholism and finding his identity, he remained passionate about writing. He told Jonathan Bernstein for the *Village Voice* (19 June 2017) of the importance of songwriting, throughout his life, as a kind of therapy: "Even if this hadn't been my job, I would still have this thing that I could go to when things got too hard, which is explaining my own world to myself with songwriting. All the major difficulties in my life, all the really low points, I've been able to write my way out of those."

BREAKING OUT AS A SOLO ARTIST

With the encouragement of family, friends, and colleagues, particularly his girlfriend (later his wife), fellow singer-songwriter Amanda Shires, Isbell entered a Nashville treatment center in early 2012 to address his alcohol addiction. That summer, he began penning lyrics for his next album, *Southeastern* (2013), which, for many critics and fans, would represent a true breakout moment of his solo career. Garner described it as "prickly with loss, forgiveness, newfound sobriety and second chances." Deusner, in a review for *Pitchfork* (11 July 2013), stated, "*Southeastern* is easily Isbell's best solo album—his mostly richly conceived and generously written." The opening track, "Cover Me Up," a vulnerable song about love and sobriety, won song of the year while the record earned album of the year at the Americana Honors & Awards; Isbell won artist of the year.

Isbell released his next album, *Something More Than Free*, in 2015, which features such tracks as "Speed Trap Town" and "Children of Children," about the youth of his parents when he was born. The album won two awards at the Americana Honors & Awards, for album of the year and song of the year (for "24 Frames"). It also earned Isbell his first Grammy Awards, for best Americana album and best American roots song (again for "24 Frames").

THE NASHVILLE SOUND

Recorded with the 400 Unit, *The Nashville Sound*, Isbell's 2017 effort, is more bluntly political than his other work, inspired by the birth of his daughter in 2015, and the election of Donald Trump as president in 2016. In "White Man's World," a song about coming to terms with his own privilege, he sings, "There's no such thing as someone else's war." When asked why he chose to double down on his politics, he told Jon Freeman for *Rolling Stone* (17 Oct. 2018), "I'll never lose sleep over not selling more records, but I'll definitely lose sleep over keeping my mouth shut." In 2018 *The Nashville Sound* earned Isbell and the 400 Unit the Americana Honors & Awards honors for album of the year and duo/group of the year, and "If We Were Vampires" received the award for song of the year. The album also won Grammy Awards for best Americana album and best American roots song (also for "If We Were Vampires").

As for the future direction of his writing, Isbell has adapted as his life and the world around him have changed. "You have to look outward, and you have to really get better and better at empathizing with other people. I can't just keep writing about my own lonesome, drunken self, because I'm just not that person anymore," he explained to Bernstein. In addition to contributing a song to the critically and commercially successful film *A Star Is Born*, in 2018 he and the 400 Unit released *Live from the Ryman*.

PERSONAL LIFE

Isbell and Shires married in early 2013. They live with their daughter, Mercy, in Nashville. A devoted father, in 2018, during a discussion of his accomplishments, Isbell said to Hilary Hughes for *Billboard* (26 Dec. 2018), "My daughter read a couple of words, and that without question was the proudest that I was all year."

SUGGESTED READING

Bernstein, Jonathan. "Jason Isbell: 'I Thought I Understood What Everybody in America Was Like. I Was Wrong.'" *The Village Voice*, 19 June 2017, www.villagevoice.com/2017/06/19/jason-isbell-i-thought-i-understood-what-everybody-in-america-was-like-i-was-wrong/. Accessed 22 Jan. 2019.

Deusner, Stephen M. Review of *The Dirty South*, by Drive-By Truckers. *Pitchfork*, 31 Aug. 2004, pitchfork.com/reviews/albums/2509-the-dirty-south/. Accessed 22 Jan. 2019.

Deusner, Stephen M. Review of *Here We Rest*, by Jason Isbell and the 400 Unit. *Pitchfork*, 11 Apr. 2011, pitchfork.com/reviews/albums/15287-here-we-rest/. Accessed 22 Jan. 2019.

Deusner, Stephen M. Review of *Southeastern*, by Jason Isbell. *Pitchfork*, 11 July 2013, pitchfork.com/reviews/albums/18283-jason-isbell-southeastern/. Accessed 22 Jan. 2019.

Freeman, Jon. "Jason Isbell and Amanda Shires: The Rolling Stone Country Interview." *Rolling Stone*, 17 Oct. 2018, www.rollingstone.com/music/music-country/jason-isbell-amanda-shires-ryman-album-interview-738674/. Accessed 22 Jan. 2019.

Garner, Dwight. "Jason Isbell, Unloaded." *The New York Times*, 31 May 2013, www.nytimes.com/2013/06/02/magazine/jason-isbell-unloaded.html. Accessed 22 Jan. 2019.

Haag, Stephen. Review of *Decoration Day*, by Drive-By Truckers. *Pitchfork*, 28 Aug. 2003, pitchfork.com/reviews/albums/2508-decoration-day/. Accessed 22 Jan. 2019.

SELECTED WORKS

Decoration Day (with Drive-By Truckers), 2003; *Sirens of the Ditch*, 2007; *Southeastern*, 2013; *Something More Than Free*, 2015; *The Nashville Sound* (with the 400 Unit), 2017

—*Molly Hagan*

Jedidah Isler

Date of birth: 1982
Occupation: Astrophysicist

Many people develop an interest in the sky and space during childhood, but for some, that early interest develops into a full-blown career. Astrophysicist Jedidah Isler is one of those few. "The sky was mesmerizing and I couldn't get enough of it as a child," she told *Hive* (Dec. 2016). "I'd be thinking, 'This is the same sky that every person who has lived on Earth has seen throughout history.' It gave me a sense of connection to what has happened on the planet, but it also gave me a sense of wonder, mystery, and excitement. Once I realized there was a career that would allow me to feed that interest, I was off to the races." Having decided to become an astrophysicist at the age of twelve, Isler devoted the next decades of her life to following that dream, studying physics at Norfolk State University and Fisk University before earning her PhD in astronomy from Yale University in 2014. After holding several postdoctoral fellowships, Isler joined the faculty of Dartmouth College's Department of Physics and Astronomy as an assistant professor in 2018. Throughout that period, she continued to research her longstanding area of interest: blazars, a category of black holes at the centers of massive galaxies that are just beginning to be understood.

In addition to her groundbreaking research, Isler received significant attention for being the first African American woman to earn a PhD in astronomy from Yale University, a milestone that Isler has celebrated but also noted played little role in determining her educational trajectory. "I didn't start to be the first of anything. I started because I thought space was cool," she told Lucy Turnipseed for the Dartmouth College newspaper, the *Dartmouth* (31 Jan. 2019). "I think black holes are among the coolest things in the universe, so what I was doing was pursuing my dream and pursuing my interests as a scientist and researcher."

Dedicated to helping other people of color, and especially women of color, pursue their scientific interests as well, Isler has established herself as an advocate for inclusion in the sciences and has spoken out extensively about the need to combat both subtle and blatant forms of discrimination within academia. Isler has not only spoken and written widely on such topics, but also established the STEM en Route to Change (SeRCH) Foundation, which focuses on social justice in science, technology, engineering, and mathematics (STEM).

Photo by Jemal Countess/Getty Images for National Geographic Channel

EARLY LIFE AND EDUCATION

Jedidah Cherie Isler spent her early years in Virginia Beach, Virginia. Interested in space from the age of about eight, she grew up feeling a strong attachment to the sky above her. "I really just thought it was beautiful," she told Elizabeth Cook Jenkins for *Vanderbilt Magazine* (Spring 2016). "And I remember feeling a sense of calm whenever I looked up." Isler's family encouraged her celestial pursuits, and she received her first telescope, a birthday gift from her older sister, as a child.

At the age of twelve, Isler determined that she wanted to pursue a career in astrophysics, having learned about it from a book of careers that she had read. She remained dedicated to astrophysics from that point on, seeking out necessary courses and other opportunities to further her education in the right direction.

After Isler graduated from a small Christian high school, however, her father abandoned the family, plunging her into financial straits. Through financial aid, Isler was able to enroll in Norfolk State University (NSU), a historically black institution. There she studied within the Dozoretz National Institute for Mathematics and Applied Sciences. As NSU offered no astrophysics or astronomy major, Isler majored in physics. She graduated with a Bachelor of Science degree with honors in 2003.

GRADUATE WORK

After graduation, Isler took two years off from schooling for undisclosed personal reasons. She became motivated to pursue her dream again after seeing an American Physical Society (APS)

poster urging students of color to study physics. After contacting the APS about the poster, she was told of the Fisk-Vanderbilt Masters-to-PhD Bridge Program, which had just formed. Designed to promote diversity in science, the program was a partnership between Fisk University and Vanderbilt University, both located in Nashville, Tennessee. Isler became part of the first class of the program, which enabled her to take courses at both institutions. She earned a master's degree in physics from Fisk and received two research fellowships in 2007.

Although Isler chose to pursue doctoral studies elsewhere, she remained closely tied to the Fisk-Vanderbilt Masters-to-PhD Bridge Program and later worked on an alumni network for the program's graduates. "Alumni networks are extremely important for knowledge transfer and strategies," she explained to Jenkins. "Our bridge program is roughly 10 years old, which means we are just now getting a critical mass of students who have gone into enough different fields to compare notes."

After completing her master's degree, Isler moved north to study at Yale University in New Haven, Connecticut. There she earned a second master's degree in physics and went on to join the doctoral program in astronomy, at last getting to focus more significantly on the space-related subjects that interested her. "It was pretty amazing," she told Cyndi Moritz for *Syracuse University News* (25 Mar. 2014). "Getting to visit and even point large research telescopes was an incredible experience. By then I knew for sure that I had made the right decision in pursuing this field." Isler's dissertation, *In Like a Lamb, Out Like a Lion: Probing the Disk-Jet Connection in Fermi Gamma-ray Bright Blazars*, focused on blazars, a type of black hole that would become the focus of her later research. Isler earned her PhD in 2014, becoming the first African American woman within Yale's astronomy department to do so.

For her excellent and promising research, Isler was inducted into Yale's Edward Bouchet Graduate Honor Society and received the Ford Foundation Dissertation Fellowship, both in 2012. She also won a 2014 Rodger Doxsey Travel Prize from the American Astronomical Society (AAS). The Doxsey Prize enabled her to share the findings discussed in her dissertation at an AAS meeting that year.

EARLY CAREER

Isler began her career at New York's Syracuse University, where she was a Chancellor's Faculty Fellow from 2013 to 2015. During that period, she also belonged to the AAS Committee on the Status of Minorities in Astronomy and became a faculty advisory board member for the Women of Color in STEM Program at Syracuse. Beginning

in 2014, Isler also served as a Future Faculty Leaders postdoctoral fellow at the Harvard University-Smithsonian Astrophysical Observatory's Center for Astrophysics. She returned to Vanderbilt as a National Science Foundation (NSF) astronomy and astrophysics postdoctoral fellow in 2015. Isler was named a National Geographic Society Emerging Explorer for the year 2016.

In the fall of 2018, Isler joined the faculty of Dartmouth College in Hanover, New Hampshire, as an assistant professor of physics and astronomy. Thrilled to have attained her first professorship, Isler was also excited to have access to Dartmouth's astronomical equipment and resources. "I'm an observational astrophysicist, so it's really important that I be able to actually observe the sky, and Dartmouth has a really competitive suite of instruments with which to do that," she told Turnipseed. "The combination of having folks that are going to be sharp and ready to do the work and the raw resources to do that same work made it a really strong combination." Among other resources, Isler could incorporate data from the South African Large Telescope and the Arizona-based MDM Observatory, among other observatories, into her research.

BLAZARS

Since her time as a graduate student, Isler has dedicated her research to hyperactive, supermassive black holes, especially those known as blazars. Sometimes known as "blazing quasars," blazars are black holes in centers of galaxies. "As an astrophysicist, I have the awesome privilege of studying some of the most exotic objects in our universe," she explained in a 2015 TED Talk. She added, "What makes blazars so special is that they're some of the universe's most efficient particle accelerators, transporting incredible amounts of energy throughout a galaxy." What interests Isler most as a researcher are the streams of particles known as "jets" that come from them. "Think about a basketball spinning on your finger with the black lines pointed up and down—a loose analogy for the area surrounding the black hole," she explained to Moritz. "Then imagine a water hose shooting out from both the top and the bottom, where the black lines converge. Those are the jets and we want to know how they form and how they work."

In addition to her dissertation on blazars and their jets, Isler has authored or coauthored dozens of papers related to her research. Many were published in the *Astrophysical Journal* and the *Journal of Geophysical Research*. A prolific speaker, Isler has presented her research at several AAS meetings as well as at Syracuse, Brown University, Princeton University, Bryn Mawr College, and McGill University.

ADVOCACY

Alongside her research, Isler is equally passionate about advocating for people of color, and especially women of color, in astrophysics and other STEM fields. She is deeply aware of the importance of encouraging young women of color to pursue studies and careers in STEM but focuses especially on the changes and support needed to ensure that those who enter the field can stay in it.

Having faced both subtle and overt discrimination herself, Isler asserts that such discrimination and a host of related factors often limit the progress of women of color who are studying or working in science and at times force them out of those fields altogether. "I pushed through. I let my passion lead and I said, I'm going do astrophysics, no matter what," she explained for the *PBS NewsHour* videoblog *Brief but Spectacular*. "But I want to make sure that the next person doesn't have to make that same choice, that any person from any background, whether marginalized or not, can say, I love astrophysics and I want to do this thing."

To that end, Isler founded a nonprofit organization, the STEM en Route to Change (SeRCH) Foundation. The president and chair of the board hosts the nonprofit's monthly online panel Vanguard: Conversations with Women of Color in STEM (VanguardSTEM), which features panels on such issues as self-care, burnout, academic transitions, and bias. Isler is likewise active in mentorship initiatives and the alumni network for the Fisk-Vanderbilt Bridge Program.

PERSONAL LIFE

Isler is married and lives in Hanover, New Hampshire. In addition to teaching, conducting research, and furthering the cause of women of color in STEM, she has long harbored dreams of becoming an astronaut. "Space is amazing and the epitome of adventure," she told Jenkins. "I'm a Trekkie [a fan of the *Star Trek* franchise]. I love it. It's the final frontier."

SUGGESTED READING

Isler, Jedidah. "How I Fell in Love with Quasars, Blazars and Our Incredible Universe." *TED*, 2015, www.ted.com/talks/jedidah_isler_how_i_fell_in_love_with_quasars_blazars_and_our_incredible_universe/transcript?language=en. Accessed 12 Apr. 2019.

Isler, Jedidah. "Jedidah Isler." *Brief but Spectacular*, PBS NewsHour, www.pbs.org/newshour/brief/289083/jedidah-isler. Accessed 12 Apr. 2019.

Isler, Jedidah. "Q&A with Physics and Astronomy Professor Jedidah Isler." Interview by Lucy Turnipseed. *The Dartmouth*, 31 Jan. 2019, www.thedartmouth.com/article/2019/01/jedidah-isler-q-a. Accessed 12 Apr. 2019.

Isler, Jedidah, and Michio Kaku. "Saluting a New Guard of S.T.E.M. Stars, Part 4." *Hive*, Vanity Fair, Dec. 2016, www.vanityfair.com/news/2016/12/saluting-a-new-guard-of-stem-stars-part-4. Accessed 12 Apr. 2019.

Jenkins, Elizabeth Cook. "Rising Star: Jedidah Isler Is Forging New Paths in Astrophysics—and Diversity among Aspiring Scientists." *Vanderbilt Magazine*, Spring 2016, stories.vanderbilt.edu/rising-star. Accessed 12 Apr. 2019.

Mayol, Taylor. "The Astrophysicist at the Cutting Edge of Black Holes." *Ozy*, 9 Sept. 2016, www.ozy.com/rising-stars/the-astrophysicist-at-the-cutting-edge-of-black-holes/71552. Accessed 12 Apr. 2019.

Moritz, Cyndi. "Getting to Know: Astrophysicist Jedidah Isler." *Syracuse University News*, 25 Mar. 2014, news.syr.edu/blog/2014/03/25/getting-to-know-astrophysicist-jedidah-isler-74966. Accessed 12 Apr. 2019.

—Joy Crelin

Belinda Johnson

Date of birth: 1967
Occupation: Executive

When Belinda Johnson joined the home-sharing company Airbnb in 2011, the legal future of the service was precarious: by enabling users to rent out rooms or entire homes to guests for short periods of time, Airbnb was already in conflict or on the verge of conflict with a variety of local governments that were concerned about the practice's legality and tax implications. "The founders really recognized that part of what we were doing was not just changing the world, but requiring some law changes too," she told Tracey Lien for the *Los Angeles Times* (13 Dec. 2015). "So they really embraced the idea of finding a partner to help clear the path for the business."

As a lawyer with nearly two decades of experience managing and implementing the legal strategies of technology companies—among them the pioneering 1990s internet broadcaster *AudioNet*, later known as *Broadcast.com*—Johnson proved to be the perfect partner for Airbnb, bringing her extensive experience and characteristically communicative and proactive approach to the company. She went on to be promoted first to chief business affairs and legal officer, and in 2018 she was named chief operating officer (COO) of the company, becoming the first person to hold the position. In the latter role, Johnson continued to oversee the company's

Photo by Jerod Harris/Getty Images for Fortune

legal strategy, manage the operation of its various divisions and departments, and build productive relationships with governments and lawmakers. "Homesharing is about dialogue, not disruption," she explained at a gathering of Airbnb hosts, as reported by Jessi Hempel for *Wired* (13 June 2017). "Once your local officials meet you, they start to understand why homesharing is fundamentally good for cities and for society."

EARLY LIFE AND CAREER

Johnson was born Belinda Jean Sprung in 1967. Her father was a mortgage banker turned data storage entrepreneur, and her mother was a real estate professional. The family moved to Texas when Johnson was in elementary school and settled in Sugar Land, a city outside of Houston.

Growing up, Johnson participated in gymnastics. She attended John Foster Dulles High School in Sugar Land, from which she graduated in 1984. After high school, Johnson enrolled in the University of Texas at Austin, where she performed well academically and was inducted into the Phi Eta Sigma honor society during her first year. She earned her bachelor's degree in 1988 and went on to pursue legal studies at the University of Texas School of Law, where she completed her JD in 1991.

After being admitted to the Texas State Bar, Johnson began her career as a lawyer with several Texas-based firms. She joined the firm Johnson & Gibbs as an associate in 1991 and remained with the firm for four years before briefly joining Winstead, Sechrest, & Minick, PC—later known as Winstead PC—as a litigation associate. Johnson then moved to the Dallas–Fort

Worth, Texas, branch of the firm Littler Mendelson in the same role.

AUDIONET

A turning point in Johnson's career came in 1996, when she learned of the existence of the Texas-based technology company *AudioNet*. Then operating under the leadership of entrepreneur and investor Mark Cuban, the company broadcast streaming audio over the Internet and particularly specialized in content such as radio broadcasts of sporting events. Johnson was fascinated by the concept and approached *AudioNet* with the hope of being hired. "I reached out to those guys and said, 'Hey! You need a general counsel,'" she recalled to Hempel. "I didn't even understand exactly what they were doing, but I was excited by tech." *AudioNet* ultimately hired Johnson as its general counsel, a role she would hold for the next several years.

Throughout her time at *AudioNet* (later renamed *Broadcast.com*), Johnson successfully shaped the company's legal strategy and navigated a host of tricky legal and financial situations, including the company's initial public offering (IPO) of stock in 1998. Her approach earned acclaim from her colleagues at the company, including Cuban. "No one ever got rich betting against Belinda Johnson," he later told Leigh Gallagher for *Fortune* (2 Feb. 2018). "While most leaders might be looking at tomorrow, Belinda's already planned and built for next week." In 1999, the internet company *Yahoo* acquired *Broadcast.com* for $5.7 billion, incorporating the company's services into its own broadcast offerings.

Following the acquisition, Johnson decided to remain with the company, moving to California to work for *Yahoo*. She initially held the role of associate general counsel but was promoted several times over the course of more than a decade with the company, eventually becoming a senior vice president and deputy general counsel. During her time there, Johnson was responsible for managing the company's legal strategy regarding a variety of areas of concern, including copyright protection, piracy, and user privacy. Although her tenure with the company was a successful one, Johnson eventually began to consider leaving *Yahoo* in search of a new challenge. "I got to a point where I felt like I was no longer being challenged or growing professionally," she recalled to Leah Fessler for *Quartz at Work* (6 Feb. 2018). She added, "My entire career has been built by challenging myself despite uncertainties. That's when I decided to take some time to think about my next move." Johnson left in August 2011.

AIRBNB

Despite having spent more than a decade with a large company, Johnson retained the interest in small companies using technology in innovative ways that had first brought her to *AudioNet*, and the period following her departure from *Yahoo* represented a prime opportunity for Johnson to reenter that professional sphere. After learning about the company Airbnb, she became intrigued by its business model and engaged community of users and set her sights on joining the startup in a legal role. "I immediately understood the power of its community, and that this was an amazing company and an amazing opportunity," she told Lien. After making contact with Airbnb's leadership, Johnson joined the company as its general counsel in late 2011.

Founded in 2008 as *Airbedandbreakfast.com*, Airbnb offers a web-based platform through which hosts could initially rent out space in their homes—ranging from air mattresses placed on the floor to guest bedrooms—to visiting guests for short periods of time. As the service grew popular among users who preferred the personal touch, cost, and other benefits of Airbnb rentals to traditional hotel rooms, available lodgings expanded to include entire apartments or houses as well as less traditional forms of shelter, such as yurts, treehouses, houseboats, and even castles and islands. Over the years following its debut, Airbnb took in large investments from venture capitalists and expanded throughout the United States and, by 2018, into another 190 countries. However, the company's rapid expansion and popularity brought it into legal conflict with local governments in areas where its practices arguably broke laws related to the hospitality industry and short-term rentals, such as the collection of local accommodations taxes. As the company's general counsel and first executive hire, Johnson was tasked with handling such conflicts, which represented just the professional challenge she had been seeking. "I really love problem-solving, so I think the complexity of a business and being about to unwind that and make it simple, that's what I love to do, and that's what drew me to this opportunity," she explained to Lien.

RISING EXECUTIVE

After nearly four years with Airbnb, Johnson was promoted to chief business affairs and legal officer in mid-2015. In that position, as in her earlier role, she worked closely with Airbnb cofounder and CEO Brian Chesky to shape the company's legal and internal response to roadblocks and opportunities it faced, including fixing discriminatory behavior on the platform and expanding into new cities abroad. Johnson became particularly known for promoting more open dialogue with lawmakers and Airbnb hosts, favoring transparency and proactive communication over the relative secrecy preferred by other businesses within the sphere of industry-disrupting technology. In addition to her legal responsibilities, Johnson at

times took charge of unrelated projects when vacancies within the company made doing so necessary.

In February 2018, Airbnb announced changes to its leadership, including the departure of chief financial officer Laurence Tosi. At that time, Johnson was promoted to COO, a newly created role within Airbnb's executive structure. "I am very excited to take this on," she told Elise Taylor for *Vogue* (23 Feb. 2018) following the announcement. In that role, Johnson was tasked with ensuring that the four separate businesses operating under the Airbnb umbrella—Homes, Trips, Lux, and China—and all the company's departments functioned together to operate smoothly and to promote innovation. She also remained responsible for overseeing Airbnb's legal, policy, and communications strategies as well as its Customer Experience, Payments, and Trust Departments.

GAINING A PLATFORM

As Johnson's increasing prominence within Airbnb raised her profile within the business community, she has spoken out about the need for the institutional changes such as pay equity and mentorship opportunities that she believes must take place to facilitate women moving into business leadership positions in greater numbers. "When I think back to the early years of my career, I wish I would have been less tolerant of the norms of that time. Compared to today's generation, my generation didn't call attention to unfair practices like equal pay and promotion tracks as often," she told Fessler. "I look at the current generation of women in the workforce and am in awe of their courage to create change and take a stance on the issues that matter to them." In recognition of her growing influence, Johnson was included on *Forbes* magazine's list of the hundred most powerful women of 2018.

Johnson is also an advocate for travel as a means of cultural exchange. "Given the global nature of our organisation, I have to travel quite often for work. I am fortunate that I love what I do and enjoy the opportunity to experience new cultures and meet our hosts around the world," she explained to Shelly Anand for *India Today* (9 Dec. 2016). Johnson also often promotes the idea that travel can play an essential role in transforming individuals' points of view. "I wholeheartedly believe that travel leads to open minds and contributes to a better cultural understanding and acceptance of people from around the world," she told Anand.

PERSONAL LIFE

Johnson married William Brent Johnson, a writer and lawyer, in 1992. Her husband is the son of former National Football League (NFL) coach Jimmy Johnson. The couple have two children,

Lola and Roxy, and live in Redwood City, California. Johnson has noted in interviews that she sometimes hosts guests through Airbnb and uses the service herself while traveling for business.

SUGGESTED READING

Anand, Shelly. "Embrace Learning, Accept Change." *India Today*, 9 Dec. 2016, www.indiatoday.in/magazine/supplement/story/20161219-travel-embrace-learning-accept-change-belinda-johnson-airbnb-lifest-830030-2016-12-09. Accessed 15 Feb. 2019.

Fessler, Leah. "Airbnb's Belinda Johnson Is a Woman on the Rise: 'Envision What You Want, and Believe You Can Achieve It.'" *Quartz at Work*, 6 Feb. 2018, qz.com/work/1175702/airbnb-coo-belinda-johnson-thrives-by-saying-yes/amp. Accessed 15 Feb. 2019.

Gallagher, Leigh. "Inside the Shakeup at Airbnb: The Startup Loses a CFO, Gains a COO." *Fortune*, 2 Feb. 2018, fortune.com/2018/02/01/airbnb-cto-tosi-out. Accessed 15 Feb. 2019.

Hempel, Jessi. "'Airbnb's Sheryl Sandberg' Is the Valley's Quiet Superpower." *Wired*, 13 June 2017, www.wired.com/story/airbnbs-sheryl-sandberg-is-the-valleys-quiet-superpower. Accessed 15 Feb. 2019.

Lien, Tracey. "Belinda Johnson Steers Airbnb through Regulatory and Legal Turbulence." *Los Angeles Times*, 13 Dec. 2015, www.latimes.com/business/la-fi-himi-johnson-20151213-story.html. Accessed 15 Feb. 2019.

Sathian, Sanjena. "When Airbnb Goes to Court, They Call Her." *OZY*, 15 Feb. 2016, www.ozy.com/rising-stars/when-airbnb-goes-to-court-they-call-her/67214. Accessed 15 Feb. 2019.

Taylor, Elise. "Belinda Johnson, the New COO of Airbnb, Is Ready to Be the Next Great Female Leader in Silicon Valley." *Vogue*, 23 Feb. 2018, www.vogue.com/article/airbnb-belinda-johnson-coo-interview. Accessed 15 Feb. 2019.

—*Joy Crelin*

Gerlinde Kaltenbrunner

Date of birth: December 13, 1970
Occupation: Mountaineer

On August 23, 2011, mountaineer Gerlinde Kaltenbrunner accomplished a feat that only a select number of human beings had verifiably managed to that point: climbing to the summit of all fourteen "eight-thousanders," mountain peaks that are over 8,000 meters (26,246.72 feet) in height above sea level. Even more impressive, however, was the fact that she did so without the aid of porters or supplemental oxygen, a risky choice considering the hazards that mountains such as Everest and K2 pose to climbers, no matter how experienced. Indeed, Kaltenbrunner was no stranger to the dangers involved by the time she reached the summit of her final eight-thousander: in 2007, she narrowly escaped an avalanche that killed two of her fellow climbers, and in 2010, she was unable to help when climber Fredrik Ericsson fell to his death while just ahead of her on K2. Yet, neither incident, nor the countless similar ones that have taken place on the world's tallest mountains since the early twentieth century, dissuaded her from trying again. "When a mountain beckons, how can I not go?" she said at a speaking engagement in India, as quoted by Pooja Biraia Jaiswal in *The Week* (14 Jan. 2018). "Mountains are my world."

Raised among the Austrian Alps, Kaltenbrunner began hiking as a young child and completed her first climb at the age of thirteen. She began tackling the eight-thousander mountains in the mid-1990s, balancing her climbing expeditions with her career in nursing. After quitting to pursue climbing full time, she embarked on more than twenty expeditions to mountains around the world. Despite her extensive experience as a mountaineer, she remained deeply aware of the need to assess each mountain and each expedition on an individual basis. "It's important to reflect on the mountain over and over again. To ask yourself during an expedition whether this is still within the bounds of what you have taken as a risk," she told Patrick Mayer for *ISPO.com* (30 Jan. 2018). "Calmness,

Photo by Franz Johann Morgenbesser from Vienna, Austria via Wikimedia Commons

composure, humility—that comes automatically when you've been in the mountains for years."

EARLY LIFE AND EDUCATION
Kaltenbrunner was born in Austria on December 13, 1970. One of six children, she grew up in the municipality of Spital am Pyhrn, in the Austrian Alps. As a child, she loved sports and outdoor activities, particularly skiing. She developed an interest in mountain climbing through the influence of her church youth group leader, who led hikes and later took her on her first serious climbing trip, to the Austrian mountain Sturzhahn. Those early experiences proved formative for Kaltenbrunner, who later told Manuel Zierer for the website of sports products company *Keller Sports* (30 July 2018) that mountains have always "fill[ed her] with energy and a sense of power." Following her parents' divorce, she moved in with her older sister and began attending school in the town of Rottenmann. She later enrolled in the boarding school associated with the Rudolfstiftung Hospital in Vienna, where she studied nursing.

DEDICATION TO MOUNTAINEERING
As an adult, Kaltenbrunner worked to balance her career as a nurse, which she found rewarding, with her love of mountaineering. Although the Alps presented a degree of climbing opportunities, she was particularly interested in climbing the much taller mountains located elsewhere in the world. Expeditions to those mountains represented a significant financial investment, especially for little-known climbers without sponsorships. "I put all the money I earned as a nurse into different trekking and climbing expeditions to the Himalayas," Kaltenbrunner recalled, as quoted by Jaiswal. "You cannot expect sponsorships until you prove your worth in every way."

Kaltenbrunner is best known for her success in climbing eight-thousander mountains. Most of the mountains belonging to that category are in the Himalayan mountain range and are located primarily in Nepal and Tibet; they include Shishapangma, Annapurna I, Nanga Parbat, Manaslu, Dhaulagiri I, Cho Oyu, Makalu, Lhotse, Kangchenjunga, and Everest. The remaining four peaks—K2, Gasherbrum I, Gasherbrum II, and Broad Peak—belong to the Karakoram mountain range, which is located primarily in Pakistan, India, and China.

THE EIGHT-THOUSANDER MOUNTAINS
Kaltenbrunner completed her first eight-thousand-meter ascent at Broad Peak in 1994, which represented an exciting challenge for the mountaineer. "I was just concentrating really hard on doing everything right," she recalled to Zierer. "At such great heights, every single move is of great significance. I learnt early on that even the smallest mistake can have fatal consequences." Although she reached a peak that was more than eight thousand meters above sea level but lower than the mountain's true summit during that trip, she returned to Broad Peak more than a decade later and successfully climbed to the summit.

Though Kaltenbrunner had continued to work as a nurse, she left her job in 2003 to focus on climbing. While climbing was her passion, she has noted that her experience in nursing was valuable to her on multiple levels and proved useful during her mountaineering expeditions. "On the one hand, it means that I can help others," she told Zierer. "On the other, I feel that my experiences in the healthcare sector have helped me come to terms with the ephemeral nature of life." The latter point was particularly key for mountaineers seeking to climb the world's tallest peaks, which had seen the deaths of many climbers, newcomers, and veterans alike.

While climbing any of the eight-thousanders is a difficult and highly dangerous task due to factors such as elevation, weather conditions, and the constant risk of avalanches or falls, Kaltenbrunner's expeditions were particularly difficult due to her decision to make the climbs without the assistance of experienced porters—sometimes referred to as Sherpas due to the ethnic background of many of the local mountaineers employed as guides or porters in the Himalayas—or bottled oxygen. It is common to use supplementary oxygen when climbing extremely high peaks because of the low oxygen level in the air, which places climbers at risk of a variety of serious medical conditions. However, Kaltenbrunner was secure in her choice to climb the mountains without such assistance. "It was very important to me to climb these peaks with my own energy," she told *National Geographic* (9 Nov. 2011). "I wanted to feel good about how I climbed." She further shared her perspective on climbing in her 2009 memoir *Ganz bei Mir*, published in English as *Mountains in My Heart: A Passion for Climbing* in 2014.

WORLD'S HIGHEST PEAKS
Over the decades following her first expedition to Broad Peak, Kaltenbrunner embarked on expeditions to each of the other thirteen eight-thousander mountains. On several occasions, she had to make multiple attempts to climb to the summit of a particular mountain due to setbacks such as weather conditions, and at times, the setbacks she faced were far more tragic. In 2007, during her attempt to reach the summit of Dhaulagiri I, an avalanche hit one of the camps where she and several other climbers were staying, burying their tents in snow. Although she was able to dig her way out, two Spanish

climbers who were also at the camp died. Despite that near-death experience and the deaths of her fellow climbers, she remained intent upon ascending to the summit of Dhaulagiri I and succeeded in doing so the following year.

In 2010, five years after her first attempt to climb the mountain, Kaltenbrunner successfully reached the summit of Everest, the tallest peak in the world. The second-tallest mountain, K2, proved far more challenging, and she was forced to end multiple attempts before reaching the summit. In 2010, her party made it to about 400 meters (approximately 1,312 feet) below the summit when fellow climber Fredrik Ericsson fell to his death while climbing in an area known as the Bottleneck. "I shouted something, though I don't remember what it was," she recalled to Detlef Hacke and Gerhard Pfeil for *Spiegel Online* (24 Aug. 2010). "I stood there as if frozen and thought: 'Please! This can't be happening!' I held on tight to my ice tool. I didn't want to believe it." A veteran climber and skier, Ericsson had planned to ski down K2 after reaching the summit. Although Kaltenbrunner climbed down to search for Ericsson, she found only one of his skis. His remains were later located about 1,000 meters (around 3,281 feet) below the Bottleneck. Following Ericsson's death, Kaltenbrunner returned to base camp by herself.

ACHIEVING HER GOAL

The following year, Kaltenbrunner returned to K2, which she sought to summit by taking a more difficult route that would not take her through the Bottleneck again. She successfully completed the climb on August 23, 2011, becoming one of the small group of climbers confirmed to have reached the summit of all fourteen eight-thousander mountains. She was also the first woman to do so without using supplemental oxygen or being assisted by porters. After reaching that milestone, which earned her widespread recognition that included significant mainstream media notice, she told journalists that she did not plan to climb any more eight-thousanders in the future. "The subject is completed for me. I don't want to do any repetitions," she explained to Mayer. "I'm very happy that I've been able to return safe and sound each time. There are also very lovely five, six and seven-thousanders that I'd still like to pick up."

In recognition of her accomplishment, she was named *National Geographic*'s explorer of the year for 2012 and was later awarded the ISPO trophy at the international sporting goods trade fair in 2016. Although many journalists writing about Kaltenbrunner prior to her ascent of K2 attempted to present her as being in a competition to be the first woman to summit all fourteen eight-thousander peaks without supplemental oxygen or porters, she frequently rejected such narratives, noting in interviews that she did not consider herself to be competing with any other climbers. In addition to the eight-thousander mountains, she has climbed a variety of smaller mountains, including Muztagh Ata in China, Alpamayo in Peru, Nuptse in Nepal, and Denali (known at the time as Mount McKinley) in the United States.

PERSONAL LIFE

Kaltenbrunner was formerly married to German mountaineer Ralf Dujmovits, who accompanied her on many of her climbing expeditions. The two remained close friends following their divorce. In addition to mountain climbing, she enjoys sports such as skiing and mountain biking, and she trains intensively for her climbing expeditions. "I vary my workouts a lot and I focus on endurance and strength, but I don't have a training plan," she told Zierer. "For me, it's always been important to listen to my body and to feel what it needs and doesn't need at any given moment." She also practices meditation, which she has credited with helping her endure difficult situations on the mountains.

SUGGESTED READING

Brown, Chip. "K2." *National Geographic*, Apr. 2012, www.nationalgeographic.com/magazine/2012/04/k2-climb/. Accessed 9 Nov. 2018.

Jaiswal, Pooja Biraia. "Moved by the Mountains." *The Week*, 14 Jan. 2018, www.theweek.in/health/more/austrian-mountaineer-gerlinde-kaltenbrunner.html. Accessed 9 Nov. 2018.

Kaltenbrunner, Gerlinde. "Gerlinde Kaltenbrunner: Why I'll Never Climb Another Eight-Thousander." Interview by Patrick Mayer. *ISPO.com*, 30 Jan. 2018, www.ispo.com/en/people/mountain-legend-wont-let-gerlinde-kaltenbrunner-go. Accessed 9 Nov. 2018.

———. "'I Don't Think about Death.'" Interview by Detlef Hacke, and Gerhard Pfeil. *Spiegel Online*, 24 Aug. 2010, www.spiegel.de/international/zeitgeist/spiegel-interview-with-mountaineer-gerlinde-kaltenbrunner-i-don-t-think-about-death-a-713205.html. Accessed 9 Nov. 2018.

———. "10 Questions for Extreme Mountaineer Gerlinde Kaltenbrunner." Interview by Manuel Zierer. *Keller Sports*, 30 July 2018, www.keller-sports.com/guide/interview-gerlinde-kaltenbrunner/. Accessed 9 Nov. 2018.

"Mountaineer Gerlinde Kaltenbrunner." *National Geographic*, 9 Nov. 2011, www.nationalgeographic.com/adventure/features/adventurers-of-the-year/2012/gerlinde-kaltenbrunner/. Accessed 9 Nov. 2018.

—Joy Crelin

James Kaplan

Date of birth: September 10, 1951
Occupation: Author

James Kaplan is an American journalist, novelist, and biographer who is perhaps best known for authoring a two-volume biography of Frank Sinatra, the acclaimed twentieth-century singer, actor, and businessman who left his mark on generations of popular culture and who was as well known for his tempestuous private life as for his consummate artistry. Over the course of *Frank: The Voice* (2010) and *Sinatra: The Chairman* (2015), Kaplan delves into intimate detail about Sinatra's career as a chart-topping recording artist and actor; his complex relationships with his four wives, particularly Ava Gardner, whom Sinatra considered the love of his life; the strange attraction he had to power, whether from the mafia or politics; and his generosity and vindictive streaks. The books were widely acclaimed and are seen as some of the best Sinatra biographies yet published.

Kaplan—who has also been highly regarded as a writer of in-depth magazine profiles since the 1980s—is also the author of *Pearl's Progress* (1989) and *Two Guys from Verona* (1998); *The Airport* (1994), a nonfiction reflection on John F. Kennedy International Airport in New York City; and the coauthor of autobiographies by tennis star John McEnroe and entertainer Jerry Lewis, both of which became bestsellers.

EARLY LIFE AND EDUCATION

James Kaplan was born in 1951 in New York City, but grew up in rural Pennsylvania and northern New Jersey. One of his two brothers, Peter Kaplan, became a writer too, and later gained fame as editor of the New York *Observer* newspaper. James studied at New York University (NYU) and then transferred to Wesleyan University, from which he graduated with a degree in studio art in 1973. Shortly after his graduation, he enrolled in the New York Studio School in New York City's Greenwich Village neighborhood to continue to study painting. To support himself, he worked in the typing pool of the *New Yorker*, the prestigious literary and news magazine. At age twenty-three, he sold his first story to the *New Yorker*—a remarkable feat for someone so young, as even well-established writers often have difficulty selling to the magazine. Kaplan would continue to sell occasional stories to the *New Yorker* from the late 1970s to the early 1980s. One of his stories was selected for inclusion in *The Best American Short Stories 1978*.

During an extended period of travel, Kaplan visited Europe, Africa, Asia, and various parts of the United States. He also taught college in Mississippi. In the mid-1980s he spent several years as a Hollywood screenwriter. Beginning in the late 1980s, he began to develop a steady career as a writer of magazine profiles of notable creative figures, including musician Miles Davis, author John Updike, actor Jack Nicholson, comedian Jerry Lewis, and director Martin Scorsese. These profiles have appeared in major American magazines, including the *New Yorker*, the *New York Times Magazine*, *Vanity Fair*, *Esquire*, *Entertainment Weekly*, and *New York* magazine.

NOVELIST

Kaplan's first novel, *Pearl's Progress*, was published in 1989. It describes the misadventures of a young Jewish poet named Philip Pearl, who has moved from New York to teach English at a small university in Mississippi. Much of his time in Mississippi is spent lamenting the fact that he is not in New York City, and he has trouble relating to his fellow teachers and professors, whom he looks down on as bad poets and mediocre scholars. He also is frustrated by his students, whom he perceives as almost illiterate. He pines for the daughter of an Italian professor while sleeping with his old friend Jewel, who has a very jealous boyfriend. The comedic novel received mixed reviews upon its publication. A critic for *Publishers Weekly* (1 Feb. 1989) noted: "By turns hilarious and melancholy, this is the epitome of a first novel: its flaws are balanced by an appealing promise. . . . The book's plotting is somewhat confused; the story builds and then collapses without sufficient explanation. But then, little that Pearl encounters can be quite explained. Kaplan's writing is crisp, authentic and brimming with originality and wit."

Kaplan's second novel, *Two Guys from Verona*, was published in 1998, and describes the lives of two childhood friends living in suburbia: Will, a successful businessman who has inherited his father's box manufacturing company and who is married to a lawyer and has two terrific children; and Joel, who still works at the sub shop, lives with his mother and spends his time reliving his childhood memories, including a high school girlfriend who suffered from mental illness, a brother who died young, and his own mental breakdown. During the course of the novel, Will's life begins to fall apart, just as Joel's reconnecting with his old sweetheart has inspired him to reform his life and become an entrepreneur, opening a coffee bar. In *Publishers Weekly* (2 Feb. 1998), a reviewer noted: "At his best, Kaplan . . . sounds like a Jewish Updike, drawing a vivid set of characters from the sterile suburbs. The ending wraps up a bit predictably, but Kaplan's sense of the suburban mind (in all its variations) is right on." *Two Guys from Verona* was chosen by the *New York Times* as one of its Notable Books of the Year.

SWITCHING TO NONFICTION

Kaplan's turn toward book-length nonfiction began in 1994 with the publication of *The Airport: Terminal Nights and Runway Days at John F. Kennedy International*. The book describes in vignettes the working of New York's international airport, which has often been described as a frustrating experience (and worse) by those who have traveled through it. Among the people Kaplan describes working at the airport is Dr. Louis Abelson, who established the airport's onsite medical facility, and Sammy Chevalier, who directs the airport's bird patrol, which prevents flocks of birds from being sucked into jet engines. In a mixed review for *Publishers Weekly* (1 Aug. 1994), a critic declared: "Kaplan writes with style and wit, but his book seems even more a mosaic than JFK itself."

Kaplan's extensive experience writing celebrity profiles for magazines enabled him to co-author two celebrity autobiographies. The first, *You Cannot Be Serious* (2002), details the life of tennis star John McEnroe, who is considered among the best players of all time and was also famous for his volatile outbursts. The book received favorable reviews in *Sports Illustrated* and the *Washington Post Book World*, and went on to become an international best seller, topping the *New York Times* best seller list. Kaplan's other collaborative work was *Dean and Me* (2005), a memoir by comedian Jerry Lewis, who described his longtime comedic partnership with actor and singer Dean Martin. Martin and Lewis were once the most popular comedy duo in the United States and across the world but had a falling-out that prevented them from speaking for decades. *Dean and Me* earned acclaim from the *New York Times* and *Vanity Fair* and went on to be a *New York Times* best seller as well.

BIOGRAPHER OF FRANK SINATRA

If Kaplan is best known for any single piece of writing, it is his monumental two-volume biography of Frank Sinatra, considered one of the twentieth century's most significant entertainers, both as a singer and an actor. Sinatra dominated the pop charts from the 1940s to the 1960s, and continued to perform, despite fragile vocals and failing health, almost until his death in 1998. In the first volume, *Frank: The Voice*, which was published in 2010, Kaplan looks at Sinatra's life from his birth in Hoboken, New Jersey, through his years as a struggling singer in the 1930s, trying to emulate his idol Bing Crosby, through his success as a crooner for bobbysoxers in the 1940s, up through his decline as a performer in the late 1940s and into his remarkable comeback in the early 1950s, during which he signed with a new record label, Capitol, and won an Academy Award for best supporting actor for his performance in the film *From Here to Eternity*

(1953). The biography both details his gifts as an artist and his difficult personal life, in which he could be both remarkably generous and cruel—most notably in deserting his first wife, Nancy, the mother of his three children, for actor Ava Gardner. Noted *New York Times* book reviewer Michiko Kakutani named it one of her top ten books of 2010. In her review (31 Oct. 2010), she declared that Kaplan "produced a book that has all the emotional details and narrative momentum of a novel. . . . In recounting his subject's rise and fall and rise again—all before the age of forty—Mr. Kaplan gives us a wonderfully vivid feel for the worlds Sinatra traversed, from Hoboken and New York to Hollywood and Las Vegas, as well as the rapidly shifting tastes in music that shaped him and were later shaped by him." In a review for the *Los Angeles Times* (3 Nov. 2010), Tim Rutten called *Frank: The Voice* a "marvelously thoughtful, readable biography."

Kaplan's follow-up, *Sinatra: The Chairman*, was released in 2015 and met with similar, although more muted, praise. The second volume chronicles Sinatra's life as he reaches his zenith as a recording artist for Capitol Records and later Reprise Records (which he founded), as well as his later marriages, and his relationships with figures such as fellow entertainers Dean Martin and Sammy Davis Jr., mobster Sam Giancana, and President John F. Kennedy. It looks unflinchingly at his private generosity as well as his frequent public fights with reporters, fellow entertainers, and other figures. A critic for *Kirkus Reviews* (15 Sept. 2015) described it as "far more substantial than [the] initial volume." Another for *Publishers Weekly* (1 Sept. 2015) proclaimed: "The great singer-actor contains multitudes in this vast, engrossing biography. . . . Kaplan delves with gusto into Sinatra's seething contradictions."

PERSONAL LIFE

Kaplan lives in Hastings-on-Hudson, New York, with his wife, psychologist Karen Cumbus, with whom he has three sons.

SUGGESTED READING

Kakutani, Michiko. "And When I'm Gloomy, You Simply Gotta Listen to Me." Review of *Frank: The Voice*, by James Kaplan. *The New York Times*, 31 Oct. 2010, www.nytimes.com/2010/11/01/books/01book.html. Accessed 1 Apr. 2019.

Kaplan, James. Review of *The Airport: Terminal Nights and Runway Days at John F. Kennedy International*, by James Kaplan. *Publishers Weekly*, 1 Aug. 1994, www.publishersweekly.com/9780688092474. Accessed 3 Apr. 2019.

Kaplan, James. Review of *Pearl's Progress*, by James Kaplan. *Publishers Weekly*, www.

publishersweekly.com/978-0-394-50093-5. Accessed 3 Apr. 2019.

Kaplan, James. Review of *Sinatra: The Chairman*, by James Kaplan. *Kirkus Reviews*, 15 Sept. 2015, www.kirkusreviews.com/book-reviews/james-kaplan/sinatra/. Accessed 1 Apr. 2015.

Kaplan, James. Review of *Two Guys from Verona: A Novel of Suburbia*, by James Kaplan. *Publishers Weekly*, 2 Feb. 1998, www.publishersweekly.com/9780871137043. Accessed 3 Apr. 2019.

Rutten, Tim. Review of *Frank: The Voice*, by James Kaplan. *Los Angeles Times*, 3 Nov. 2010, www.latimes.com/archives/la-xpm-2010-nov-03-la-et-rutten-20101103-story.html. Accessed 1 Apr. 2019.

Waldie, D. J. Review of *Two Guys from Verona: A Novel of Suburbia*, by James Kaplan. *Los Angeles Times*, 8 Mar. 1998, www.latimes.com/archives/la-xpm-1998-mar-08-bk-26583-story.html. Accessed 1 Apr. 2019.

SELECTED WORKS

Pearl's Progress, 1989; *The Airport: Terminal Nights and Runway Days at John F. Kennedy International*, 1994; *Two Guys from Verona*, 1998; *You Cannot Be Serious* (with John McEnroe), 2002; *Dean and Me* (with Jerry Lewis), 2005; *Frank: The Voice*, 2010; *Sinatra: The Chairman*, 2015

—*Christopher Mari*

Isabelle Kelly

Date of birth: September 20, 1996
Occupation: Rugby player

In 2018, Australian Isabelle Kelly became the inaugural recipient of the women's Golden Boot award, given to the best female rugby league player in the world. The honor was all the more remarkable considering how early it came in her career. She began playing rugby league only in 2015 and in 2017 made her debut for Australia's national team, the Jillaroos, helping them win the World Cup that year. Kelly's rise to the pinnacle of success in rugby league also came in tandem with significant growth in popularity of the sport throughout Australia. By 2019, millions of women around the world were involved in rugby—which has two codes, rugby league and rugby union—and outreach efforts continued to increase interest. Kelly was among the star players credited with inspiring further generations of female players in the rugged, full-contact sport. "Girls are slowly starting to come into league," Kelly told Tony Webeck for Australia's *National Rugby League* (NRL) website (4 Feb. 2017). "They see myself or another girl representing Australia or New South Wales and they see that they can make it that far."

Although she grew up in a family of rugby league players, Kelly herself came to the sport late due to the lack of organization for women players. She excelled at other sports such as touch football but finally switched to rugby league once a women's team was founded in her area. Within months she was chosen for the New South Wales (NSW) team, and she became fully dedicated to the game. "I've loved every sport I've played but not as much as I love playing rugby league," she told Webeck. "It's a completely different feeling. . . . It's more aggressive, you can give it all you've got and it shows what your body is capable of."

EARLY LIFE

Isabelle Kelly was born in the city of Gosford in the Central Coast region of New South Wales on September 20, 1996. She grew up in a suburb called Chittaway Bay with her parents and four brothers. Her family was very involved in rugby league (which is also known simply as league, or in Oceania in particular, as football or footy). Her father, Ken, played the sport for the Manly-Warringah Sea Eagles club in the 1980s, and her brother Dylan also played professionally. "I think it's always been in my blood to play," Kelly told Webeck.

Despite this deep connection to rugby league, Kelly did not actually pursue the sport as a child or young adult, as there was simply no organized competition for female players. "When I

Photo by Mark Kolbe/Getty Images

was growing up there was no pathway so I had to play other codes," she told Alicia Newton for the *NRL* website (29 Nov. 2017). "I only really got to play when I started school because no female competitions were around." The other sports she played included touch football, in which she showed enough skill to eventually join the official NSW team. She also excelled at netball, a sport similar to basketball.

Kelly endured tragedy when her mother, Maree, died of a brain aneurysm in 2013. The next year Kelly graduated from high school at Tuggerah Lakes Secondary College (TLSC). It was around this time that she began to envision herself playing rugby league at an elite level. As she recalled to Newton, "I remember looking at the TV and the women's Test match [a competition between representative national teams] came on, and I said to my partner 'I want to be there one day.'"

TURNING TO RUGBY LEAGUE

Kelly got her chance to engage in higher-level rugby league competition when the Berkeley Vale Panthers club founded a women's team in the Sydney Metropolitan Women's Rugby League (SMWRL), becoming the first such organization in the Central Coast region. She made her debut as a player at the club level in 2015 and quickly proved formidable. Playing primarily the fullback position, she displayed a natural talent for scoring thanks to her speed and toughness. She also found herself more than up to the intense physicality of rugby league, becoming a strong tackler. "There are some big girls out there and you might not think you can get them down but then you can," Kelly told Webeck. She helped lead Berkeley Vale to considerable tournament success and earned several player-of-the-match honors.

Just a few months after her playing career began, Kelly joined the official NSW representative team, known as the Blues. Her debut with the team came in the highly competitive annual match against the Queensland Maroons in 2015. At the time the match was known as the Interstate Challenge but was later renamed to reflect the equivalent men's league's State of Origin series, one of the most popular sporting events in Australia. Kelly immediately established herself as a key member of the Blues, scoring the team's only try, similar to a touchdown in American football, as the match ended in a draw.

Kelly's made a point of watching Australia's national women's team, nicknamed the Jillaroos, to learn and improve her own game. Before long, her success in club and state-level play brought her to the attention to the national team, and in 2016 she was selected to join the squad. She made her official Jillaroos debut as an injury replacement at the 2017 Auckland Nines; nines are a type of competition in which each team fields nine players instead of the usual fifteen. Kelly switched between fullback and center for the national team, earning much respect from her teammates for her skills and dedication. "She's strong, she's fast, she knows a lot about the game," Jillaroos star Sam Bremner said of Kelly to Webeck. The team went on to sweep the New Zealand's Kiwi Ferns in the three-match series.

WORLD CUP CHAMPION AND 2018 STATE OF ORIGIN

Kelly continued to prove herself as a mainstay for the Jillaroos despite her relative lack of experience. Later in 2017 she made her Test debut with the team, again as a replacement for an injured teammate. National team coach Brad Donald was among those impressed by Kelly's all-around excellence. "She is only young and inexperienced around the game but she has got all the qualities of a Jillaroo," he told Brad Walter for the *NRL* website (9 Nov. 2018). "She just loves her footy and being around her mates."

Indeed, 2017 proved to be a breakout year for Kelly, particularly as the Women's Rugby League World Cup took place that November and December. Playing for the Jillaroos, she scored two tries in the pool stage in which Australia dominated England and the Cook Islands. However, she also stirred controversy when she was accused of biting an opponent in the match against England. She was cleared of the charge a day later. Kelly scored two more tries in the semi-final against Canada, which ended with another blowout victory for Australia. In the final the Jillaroos faced off against New Zealand, and Kelly again added two tries as Australia won a much tighter contest, 23–16. The championship was the second consecutive and overall title for the Jillaroos.

Fresh off the World Cup victory, Kelly continued to establish herself as one of rugby league's brightest stars. A highlight was the first official women's league State of Origin match between the NSW Blues and the Queensland Maroons in June 2018. Outside of Kelly's personal career, the match was a breakthrough moment for women's rugby in Australia. It was attended by nearly 7,000 spectators, setting a record for a women's rugby league crowd, and over 1 million more viewers watched on television. "Women's rugby league has come a long way," Brad Fittler, the coach of the NSW men's team, told Daniel Herborn for *CEO Magazine* (25 June 2018). "The quality with which they were playing was exceptional. I think there is a bright future for rugby league with women. . . . There were some big moments in the game, it was quite incredible."

Several of those big moments belonged to Kelly, who scored the first try for the Blues. The score was locked in a 10–10 tie for most of the match until Kelly, exhibiting her superior footwork, scored her second try, bringing home the win for the Blues. She was later awarded the Nellie Doherty Medal for player of the match, which she dedicated to her late mother. The team and fans were exuberant in what many called a victory for both NSW and the sport. However, the win also highlighted the challenges facing female rugby players, who often had to work second jobs to get by.

GOLDEN BOOT

Kelly continued to excel on the field through 2018. That year she joined the newly founded Sydney Roosters women's side for the inaugural season of the NRL Women's professional league. She also continued playing for the Jillaroos, and in October 2018 she scored the match-winning try against the Kiwi Ferns in the Women's International. A few weeks later, she was nominated for the first-ever women's edition of the Rugby League International Federation (RLIF) Golden Boot award for best rugby league player in the world. As she recalled to Josh Callinan for the *Newcastle Herald* (23 Mar. 2019), her initial reaction was confusion: "I was like what's the Golden Boot? It was the first one [for women] so I'd never heard of it."

Even after the reality of the nomination settled in, she never expected to win, especially as she was up against more established competition such as Jillaroo teammate Ali Brigginshaw and New Zealand superstar Honey Hireme. Yet in early November Kelly was announced as the recipient of the prestigious, groundbreaking award. "I honestly never thought I'd be where I am," she told Newton for the *NRL* website (8 Nov. 2018). "To be the actual winner, words can't explain."

Elevated to a new level of celebrity, Kelly approached her achievement as an opportunity to continue to advocate for women's rugby. She is a positive effect for young athletes, in general, from the Central Coast, or other areas with less exposure than major markets such as Sydney. "It just goes to show people can do what they want where they're from," she told Callinan.

In 2019 Kelly suffered an ankle injury, missing the National Women's Championship and raising questions about her health in the run-up to the 2019 State of Origin. However, she returned to play for the club CRL Newcastle in the NSW Women's Premiership and soon silenced her critics by finding her usual excellent form. The State of Origin match proved to be another tense competition. Although Kelly did not score, the Blues prevailed 14–4. The match also saw even greater turnout than the previous year, marking another step for the women's rugby league. Many commentators are thrilled at the fact that Kelly appears to have a long and illustrious career ahead of her and the potential to serve as a leading ambassador for her sport. "I can't think of anyone who has been more influential at representative level in the last year and she has potentially got ten to twelve more years ahead of her," Jillaroos coach Donald told Walter. "She has got the world at her feet."

PERSONAL LIFE

Kelly worked as a personal trainer to supplement her rugby career. She also served as a development officer for the NRL. In 2018 she was engaged to Jake Callister.

SUGGESTED READING

Boddan, Patrick. "Isabelle Kelly Wins Inaugural Women's Golden Boot Award for the Best Rugby League Player in the World." *The Daily Telegraph*, 11 Nov. 2018, www.dailytelegraph.com.au/newslocal/central-coast/sport/isabelle-kelly-wins-inaugural-womens-golden-boot-award-for-the-best-rugby-league-player-in-the-world/news-story/2120a5caa00a2d51909f2d8ccc1fa435. Accessed 24 June 2019.

Callinan, Josh. "Rugby League: Golden Boot Isabelle Kelly Set to Start 2019 with CRL Newcastle." *Newcastle Herald*, 23 Mar. 2019, www.theherald.com.au/story/5968923/rugby-league-golden-boot-isabelle-kelly-set-to-start-2019-with-crl-newcastle/. Accessed 20 June 2019.

Herborn, Daniel. "Inaugural Women's State of Origin Clash Draws One Million Viewers, Rave Reviews." *CEO Magazine*, 25 June 2018, news.theceomagazine.com/news/inaugural-womens-origin-game-success/. Accessed 20 June 2019.

Newton, Alicia. "Fast Rise to the Top for Jillaroo Kelly." *National Rugby League (NRL)*, 29 Nov. 2017, www.nrl.com/news/2017/11/29/fast-rise-to-the-top-for-jillaroo-kelly/. Accessed 20 June 2019.

Newton, Alicia. "Kelly Honoured to Create Golden Boot History." *National Rugby League (NRL)*, 8 Nov. 2018, www.nrl.com/news/2018/11/08/jillaroos-centre-isabelle-kelly-wins-womens-golden-boot-award/. Accessed 24 June 2019.

Walter, Brad. "Kelly Could Dominate for a Decade, Says Jillaroos Coach." *National Rugby League (NRL)*, 9 Nov. 2018, www.nrl.com/news/2018/11/09/isabelle-kelly-could-dominate-for-a-decade-says-jillaroos-coach/. Accessed 20 June 2019.

Webeck, Tony. "Jillaroos Rookie Set to Take Nines by Storm." *National Rugby League (NRL)*, 4 Feb. 2017, www.nrl.com/news/2017/02/04/jillaroos-rookie-set-to-take-nines-by-storm/. Accessed 19 June 2019.

—Molly Hagan

Sam Kerr

Date of birth: September 10, 1993
Occupation: Soccer player

When Sam Kerr was twelve years old, her goals as an athlete abruptly shifted. The child and sibling of Australian rules football players, she grew up playing the sport, which she described to Richard Parkin for the *Guardian* (5 June 2019) as "ingrained" in her. "You grow up with it, so I didn't know any different," she told Parkin. While she spent her childhood playing on boys teams, no teen girls or women's Australian rules football teams existed during that period, leaving the preteen Kerr no option but to switch to a different sport—in her case, soccer (also known simply as "football"). Although difficult for Kerr at the time, the switch proved to be a fortuitous one, as Kerr soon demonstrated a talent for the sport that would earn her a place on the Australian national team, known as the Matildas, at the age of fifteen. After several seasons playing with Australian W-League teams, Kerr began to showcase her skills in the United States as well, playing for professional teams such as Sky Blue FC and the Chicago Red Stars.

For Kerr, her success was attributable in large part to her particular manner of navigating the field and maneuvering around other players. "For me it's about getting in positions where the defender can't see you or doesn't think you'll be going. That's where my instincts kick in," she said, as quoted by Larry Buchanan et al. for the *New York Times* (9 June 2019). "I drift in and out of the game. Defenders switch off for a second and there I am." Kerr's strong performance on the field brought her numerous awards and major sponsorships, as well as significant attention at high-profile tournaments such as the 2019 FIFA Women's World Cup. Considered the face of Australian women's soccer, she became widely recognized as one of the best players in the world.

EARLY LIFE AND EDUCATION

Samantha May Kerr was born on September 10, 1993, in Western Australia. One of four children born to Roxanne and Roger Kerr and the only girl, she grew up in East Fremantle, Western Australia, a suburb of the city of Perth. Kerr displayed an interest in athletic activities from a young age and was active in several sports during her childhood, including cricket and track. Her preferred childhood sport, however, was Australian rules football, a distinctly Australian game that shares some similarities with American football, rugby, and soccer. Indeed, Australian rules football was a particular of the Kerr household; Roger Kerr had played in the West Australian Football League, and Kerr's older brother Daniel

Photo by Thewomensgame via Wikimedia Commons

played the sport for the West Coast Eagles. As no girls teams were available, Kerr played on boys' Australian rules football teams throughout her childhood and quickly distinguished herself as a talented player. "I was very good at it, I had good hand-eye co-ordination, my family was really embedded in the club, my brother played," she recalled to Parkin. "Everything was just easy for me."

Despite Kerr's skill as an Australian rules football player, her size and the lack of girls teams forced her to withdraw from organized competition. She soon shifted her attention to soccer but initially struggled to adjust to the change in sports. "It hurt going from one of the better players, one of the most popular players. I just went from being at the top of my game, as much as you can as a kid, to going to the bottom moving to football," she explained to Parkin. "I didn't know the rules, I didn't know offside, I didn't understand why no one would pass me the ball." She was also frustrated by the fact that her family knew little about soccer and so were not as enthusiastic about watching her play. Nevertheless, Kerr soon overcame those difficulties, becoming a valuable contributor to a variety of youth teams, eventually including the under-seventeen Australian national soccer team.

PROFESSIONAL SOCCER

Kerr began her professional soccer career while still a teenager, joining the team the Perth Glory in 2008 and playing her first games with the club during the following season. The Glory was one of the founding teams in the then recently formed W-League, the successor to the defunct Women's National Soccer League as the highest-level women's soccer league in Australia. Kerr's initial stint with the club lasted through 2011, during which time she began to emerge as a strong scorer. Meanwhile, she also played internationally with the senior-level Australian National Team, commonly known as the Matildas. Kerr made her debut with the Matildas at the age of fifteen, in a friendly match against the Italian national team. In 2011, she accompanied the team to that year's FIFA (International Federation of Association Football) Women's World Cup. The Matildas successfully progressed through the group stage of the competition but lost to Sweden in the quarterfinals.

Despite the high levels at which she played, Kerr did not always fully apply herself during her early years as a professional player. "I didn't take it seriously," she told Alyssa Roenigk for *ESPN* (18 June 2019). "I was just happy to be medium." This lack of passion was in part because women's soccer was not given much attention in Australia at the time. Kerr's attitude began to change, however, after she spent an extended period off the field while recovering from an injury. "You don't really know what you have until it's gone," she told Parkin. "It couldn't have become more real, because I had twelve months out of the game and all I wanted to do after that was get back out onto the field."

After several seasons in Perth, Kerr moved to Sydney to join Sydney FC in 2012. That season she led the team in goals and helped earn a W-League Championship. In 2013 Kerr won the award for Australian Female Footballer of the Year, a title she would go on to claim again in 2017 and 2018. That year she also joined the Western New York Flash of the US–based National Women's Soccer League (NWSL).

STAR STRIKER

Following a successful debut season in the NWSL, during which the Flash finished the regular season ranked first in the league before losing the championship match, Kerr remained with the team for the 2014 season. She also returned to the Glory in 2014, beginning what would become a regular schedule of splitting her year and playing time between Australia and the United States. Neither league was particularly lucrative, a recurring issue in women's soccer. Playing in the W-League was especially challenging for Kerr at times because few other players were able to devote themselves to professional soccer full-time. "Most of my teammates work 9 to 5, so the commitment level is different [in the W-League]," she explained to Roenigk. "Sometimes it's frustrating. You're giving up your life for the sport, and for a lot of players, it's just another part of theirs." Nevertheless, Kerr

remained committed to the Glory. Meanwhile, in the NWSL she was traded from the Flash to the New Jersey–based Sky Blue FC prior to the 2015 season.

Over the following years, Kerr solidified her reputation as a strong player on both the national and international levels. In addition to spending three seasons with Sky Blue and continuing her affiliation with the Glory, Kerr continued to play for the Australian national team. In 2015 she competed in her second World Cup, during which the Matildas lost to Japan, the eventual runner up, in the quarterfinals. She represented Australia at the Olympic Games in 2016 and the following year contributed to the Matildas' victory at the first Tournament of Nations. Kerr was named the 2017 Asian Football Confederation's (AFC) Women's Footballer of the Year in recognition of her work on the field. That year she also led the NWSL in goals, earning both the Golden Boot and most valuable player (MVP) league awards. Following the 2017 NWSL season, Kerr was traded to the Chicago Red Stars.

As Kerr continued to distinguish herself as one of women's soccer major players, she received significant attention from teams based in Europe, with several offering her contracts in early 2018. Although such teams could offer Kerr a higher salary and more prestige, she was averse to make such a move, as the demands of the European soccer season would prevent her from playing in Australia. "Playing in a nice stadium for a famous club and having more money wasn't going to make me a better player," she told Roenigk about her 2018 decision to turn down a European contract. "It took me a while to realize the best decision for me and my football was coming home." To influence her decision further, the Football Federation Australia (FFA) offered Kerr a sizable payment and the role of the W-League's marquee player, effectively making Kerr the face of Australian women's soccer. In 2018 she was also named Young Australian of the Year and voted fifth in the first-ever women's Ballon d'Or, a prestigious award for the best soccer player in the world.

2019 WORLD CUP

Kerr became the focus of widespread attention in 2019, when she served as team captain for the Matildas at that year's World Cup. Although she appreciated the support, the increased scrutiny represented a significant change for the women's national team. "Everyone's got behind us and loved the way we played but with that comes that pressure, the pressure to have to perform," she told Aimee Lewis for *CNN* (13 June 2019). "We like that, we like that we have high expectations, but it's new for everyone to have this type of pressure and to not disappoint people." The Matildas overcame an opening loss to

Italy to defeat Brazil and Jamaica and move out of the group stage. Kerr herself scored all four goals in the team's 4–1 victory against Jamaica. In the round of sixteen, however, Australia ultimately lost to Norway after a tied game ended in a shootout.

Despite the Matildas' mixed performance in World Cup tournaments in which she played, Kerr focused primarily on the team's successes. The Australian women's national soccer program improved significantly over her career, thanks in part to her transcendent scoring talents. Perhaps even more importantly, Kerr and the rest of the Matildas were credited with greatly increasing public interest in women's soccer. "In the US, I've seen 40,000 fans turn up to watch their women's team play. That's amazing. That's what we want in Australia," she wrote in an essay for the *Players Voice* (22 Nov. 2017). "All of us Matildas have a real competitive streak."

PERSONAL LIFE

Kerr met her longtime girlfriend, US soccer player Nikki Stanton, while they were both playing for Sky Blue FC. Stanton later went on to play alongside Kerr with the Chicago Red Stars and also competed for the Perth Glory.

SUGGESTED READING

Buchanan, Larry, et al. "Sam Kerr Can't Stop Scoring." *The New York Times*, 9 June 2019, www.nytimes.com/interactive/2019/06/11/sports/world-cup/sam-kerr-world-cup.html. Accessed 16 Aug. 2019.

Kerr, Sam. "Learning a New Life." *Players Voice*, 22 Nov. 2017, www.players-voice.com.au/sam-kerr-challenge-to-melbourne/#UWWEvdSakfJpjRez.97. Accessed 16 Aug. 2019.

Lewis, Aimee. "Sam Kerr: Australia's Million Dollar Player at the Women's World Cup." *CNN*, 13 June 2019, amp.cnn.com/cnn/2019/06/11/football/sam-kerr-matildas-australia-womens-world-cup-spt-int/index.html. Accessed 16 Aug. 2019.

Makkar, Sahil. "Soccer Superstar Sam Kerr Opens Up on Her Relationship with Fellow Athlete Girlfriend after Telling the Haters to 'Suck on That One.'" *Daily Mail*, 16 June 2019, www.msn.com/en-au/lifestyle/familyandrelationships/soccer-superstar-sam-kerr-opens-up-on-her-relationship-with-fellow-athlete-girlfriend-after-telling-the-haters-to-suck-on-that-one/ar-AACX7L0. Accessed 16 Aug. 2019.

Parkin, Richard. "Sam Kerr: 'I Was Total Crap in My First Season as a Footballer.'" *The Guardian*, 5 June 2019, amp.theguardian.com/football/2019/jun/06/sam-kerr-i-was-total-crap-in-my-first-season-as-a-footballer. Accessed 16 Aug. 2019.

Roenigk, Alyssa. "Which Aussie Rules Football? It's the Unstoppable Sam Kerr." *ESPN*, 18 June 2019, www.espn.com/soccer/fifa-womens-world-cup/story/3867377/which-aussie-rules-football-its-the-unstoppable-sam-kerr. Accessed 16 Aug. 2019.

"Sam Kerr Is Ready to Be in Chicago." *Chicago Red Stars*, chicagoredstars.com/sam-kerr-is-ready-to-be-in-chicago/. Accessed 16 Aug. 2019.

—*Joy Crelin*

Ro Khanna

Date of birth: September 13, 1976
Occupation: US Representative

For many aspiring politicians, a loss in a primary election would be a devastating setback, but for US representative Ro Khanna, his own losses—in 2004, to Tom Lantos, and in 2014, to Mike Honda—were crucial learning experiences that led him to the political stances that would later win him a congressional seat. "That loss was the best thing that ever happened to me," he told Ezra Klein for *Vox* (1 May 2019) about the 2014 primary election for California's Seventeenth District, which encompasses much of Silicon Valley. "It forced me to reflect. I had this optimism about technology and America, but who were the people I was leaving out?"

After winning his next election in November 2016 and joining the US House of Representatives the following January, Khanna worked to represent his district while also championing a host of progressive causes and encouraging the technology leaders among his constituents to spread economic opportunity throughout the country. Although not opposed to big business, Khanna believes that the technology industry has a responsibility to work toward the betterment of all Americans. "My concern is not with billionaires that are produced by innovation or entrepreneurship," he explained to Hamilton Nolan for *Splinter* (24 May 2019). "My concern is, how do we deal with wage stagnation in this country? How do we ensure that the bottom 40 to 50 percent gets a wage raise? . . . My concern is, how do we have upward mobility of people to participate in the American dream. That's my focus, and that's why I call myself a 'progressive capitalist.'"

EARLY LIFE AND EDUCATION

Rohit "Ro" Khanna was born in Philadelphia, Pennsylvania, on September 13, 1976. His father, Vijay, was a chemical engineer, while his

Photo by U.S. Congress/Eric Connolly via Wikimedia
Commons

mother, Jyotsna, worked as a substitute special education teacher. Khanna's maternal grandfather was Amarnath Vidyalankar, an Indian independence and human rights activist who had been imprisoned by India's British rulers for his activism and who later served as a member of the Indian parliament. Khanna was deeply inspired by his grandfather's experience; as he told Greta Brawner for *C-SPAN* (5 Jan. 2017), "It gave me a sense that one could make a difference and it mattered." Khanna and his younger brother, Vikas, spent their childhood in Pennsylvania's Bucks County, where Khanna played Little League baseball and attended local public schools. The family summered in India.

Khanna's own entry into political activism began as early as 1991, when the *Bucks County Courier-Times* newspaper published extracts from an essay the fourteen-year-old Khanna wrote in opposition to the United States' military conflict with Iraq. After graduating from Council Rock High School, he enrolled in the University of Chicago to study economics. As an undergraduate, Khanna canvassed for future US president Barack Obama, who, at that time, was running for the Illinois Senate. Khanna was inducted into the Phi Beta Kappa honor society and earned his Bachelor of Arts degree in 1998. He went on to attend Yale Law School, from which he received his law degree in 2001.

EARLY CAREER
Following his time at Yale, Khanna moved to California. He was admitted to the California state bar in 2003 and, the following year, began his career in law with the multinational firm O'Melveny & Myers. Over nearly five years, Khanna handled cases dealing with intellectual property, proprietary information, and antitrust issues for California's many technology companies. He also collaborated with the Mississippi Center for Justice on a pro bono basis, working for free to address cases of contractor fraud that were carried out after Hurricane Katrina devastated several coastal states in 2005.

Following the election of President Barack Obama in 2008, Khanna secured a job within the new administration. He left O'Melveny & Myers in July 2009 and, in August of that year, stepped into the role of deputy assistant secretary for the US Department of Commerce. During his two years there, Khanna worked to address the needs of domestic manufacturers seeking to export their goods to other countries. "We would work with some small- and medium-sized manufacturers and help them get access to foreign markets," he recalled to Kara Swisher for the podcast *Recode Decode* (14 May 2017). "We'd see what they needed to succeed in a global economy, how they could be more competitive, how they could sell more of their products abroad."

After leaving the Commerce Department in 2011, he joined the Palo Alto branch of Wilson Sonsini Goodrich & Rosati, a law firm with roots in Northern California's technology-focused Silicon Valley. During his tenure with the firm, Khanna also lectured in economics at Stanford University and legal subjects at Santa Clara University and San Francisco State University. In 2012 he published the book *Entrepreneurial Nation: Why Manufacturing Is Still Key to America's Future*. After leaving Wilson Sonsini in 2014, he went on to serve as vice president of strategic initiatives for Smart Utility Systems, a company specializing in energy efficiency technology, from February 2015 until November 2016.

POLITICAL CAMPAIGNS
Khanna's first political campaign took place not long after his move to California, when he began a primary challenge against Tom Lantos, the longtime US representative for California's Twelfth District. Although Lantos was a Democrat, he had supported both the Iraq War and the Patriot Act, a conflict and a policy with which Khanna strongly disagreed. In challenging Lantos, Khanna sought to express his dissent and to decrease support for the agenda of then president George W. Bush in Washington. "For the South Asian diaspora, that was a symbol," he explained to Klein. "It was about standing up for the 'other.'" Khanna captured only about 20 percent of the primary vote, and Lantos once again won reelection.

Nonetheless, Khanna's effort impressed Lantos, who brought him to the attention of House Democratic leader Nancy Pelosi, who in turn encouraged Khanna to try again in the future. "Pelosi saw that the only Indian face in politics at the time was [Republican representative and later governor] Bobby Jindal," Khanna recalled. "She saw there was a huge South Asian community. And so she told me, get involved, and after redistricting, there'll be an opening."

In 2014 Khanna challenged the incumbent Democratic representative from California's Seventeenth District, Mike Honda, in that year's primary election. At that time, the Seventeenth District encompassed portions of Alameda and Santa Clara Counties, which includes Cupertino, home of Apple's corporate headquarters, as well as tech-heavy cities like Sunnyvale and Santa Clara. A vote-splitting accusation was leveled against Khanna, but a judge in the lawsuit ruled down the middle, rejecting one of two opposition candidates Khanna had allegedly recruited while allowing the other to remain in the race. Nevertheless, Khanna enjoyed the support of technology industry leaders as well as many members of the public, and narrowly lost the election by fewer than five thousand votes.

Two years later, Khanna again challenged Honda, this time besting him by about two thousand votes. Due to the nature of California's top-two primary voting system, both Khanna and Honda went on to appear on the ballot during the general election. Khanna won the election with 61 percent of the vote and took office in January 2017 as a member of the 115th Congress.

US REPRESENTATIVE

Upon taking office, Khanna joined caucuses and task forces dealing with a variety of issues, including affordable drug pricing, reproductive choice, food waste, LGBT equality, NASA, and the Peace Corps. He served as vice chair of the Congressional Progressive Caucus as well as the chair of the No PAC Caucus, a small group of representatives who refuse to accept financial contributions from political action committees, or PACs. Khanna also cofounded the Congressional Antitrust Caucus, which focuses on issues relating to the consolidation of companies. Although his district is home to many of Silicon Valley's technology companies, and he is less focused on breaking up such large companies than some of his colleagues, Khanna objects to mergers and other corporate actions—such as Amazon's acquisition of the grocery chain Whole Foods—that he believes could decrease wages and inhibit innovation. "If you look across the economy, if you have multiple players in an industry, you have more customization, more innovation, greater choice for consumers," he told Alexis C. Madrigal for the *Atlantic* (19 June

2017). "The more you have consolidation, the less likely you are to invest in innovation. It becomes all about driving down cost and mass production. And that's not good for innovation in an industry."

Khanna ran for reelection in 2018 and easily retained his seat, defeating Republican challenger Ron Cohen with more than 75 percent of the vote. During his second term in Congress, Khanna was named to the House Committee on Oversight and Reform as well as the House Budget Committee and the Armed Services Committee.

Khanna has sponsored multiple pieces of progressive legislation, including the Grow American Incomes Now (GAIN) Act, the Corporate Responsibility and Taxpayer Protection Act (TPA), the Veterans Apprenticeship and Labor Opportunity Reform (VALOR) Act, the 21st Century Integrated Digital Experience Act (IDEA), and multiple resolutions to end US military involvement in Yemen. In keeping with his focus on technology, Khanna sponsored the Internet Bill of Rights and supported net neutrality, the principle (and longstanding practice) of equal access to web content of all types. He likewise supports major initiatives championed by the progressive wing of the Democratic Party, including Medicare for All (a universal, government-run healthcare system) and the Green New Deal climate resolution. He is also a proponent of term limits for members of Congress and Supreme Court justices.

PROGRESSIVE CAPITALISM

As the representative responsible for addressing the concerns of much of Silicon Valley, Khanna focuses extensively on how the technology companies based in his district can promote economic growth and spread employment opportunities and financial stability beyond that region. "Our country is going through a profound transition from an industrial age to a digital age," he told Swisher. "Silicon Valley needs to answer the call to service, needs to think not just about what's narrowly in our interest but how it can contribute to making this transition successful for everyone." In delineating his approach to economic issues, Khanna describes himself as a progressive capitalist. Although that description caused some commentators to question whether Khanna's viewpoint puts him at odds with political ally Senator Bernie Sanders, a self-described Democratic Socialist, the representative argued that their views were not contradictory and noted that he has historically "been willing to hold Silicon Valley accountable," as he told Nolan.

In 2019 Khanna joined Sanders's 2020 presidential campaign as a national cochair, a role he would fill alongside several other current and former politicians. Some speculated that

Khanna could go on to serve in a cabinet position should Sanders succeed in winning the Democratic nomination and the general election, but Khanna indicated otherwise. "I love representing Silicon Valley," he told Nolan. "I think it is a fabulous role, and an important role when we're going through a technology revolution, and I'd like to do this job for at least a decade."

PERSONAL LIFE
Khanna married Ritu Ahuja in August 2015. They have a son, Soren (b. 2017), and a daughter, Zara (b. 2018). When not working in Washington, DC, Khanna lives in Fremont, California, and enjoys college basketball, movies, and travel. He was one of three Hindus in the 115th and 116th Congresses.

SUGGESTED READING
Herhold, Scott. "Ro Khanna's Family Narrative Rivals That of Mike Honda." *East Bay Times*, 15 Aug. 2016, www.eastbaytimes.com/2015/06/17/ro-khannas-family-narrative-rivals-that-of-mike-honda. Accessed 14 June 2019.

Khanna, Ro. "Full Transcript: Silicon Valley Congressman Ro Khanna on Recode Decode." Interview by Kara Swisher and Tony Romm, hosted by Swisher. *Recode Decode*, Vox, 14 May 2017, www.vox.com/2017/5/14/15633280/transcript-silicon-valley-congressman-ro-khanna-jobs-technology-recode-decode. Accessed 14 June 2019.

Khanna, Ro. "Interview with Representative Ro Khanna." By Greta Brawner. *C-SPAN*, 5 Jan. 2017, www.c-span.org/video/?421129-6/interview-representative-ro-khanna. Accessed 14 June 2019.

Klein, Ezra. "Ro Khanna and the Tensions of Silicon Valley Liberalism." *Recode*, Vox, 1 May 2019, www.vox.com/recode/2019/5/1/18297169/ro-khanna-silicon-valley-bernie-sanders-tim-cook. Accessed 14 June 2019.

Madrigal, Alexis C. "A Silicon Valley Congressman Takes On Amazon." *The Atlantic*, 19 June 2017, www.theatlantic.com/technology/archive/2017/06/ro-khanna-amazon-wholefoods/530805. Accessed 14 June 2019.

Morgan, Richard. "Meet Ro Khanna, Silicon Valley's Man in the Middle." *Fortune*, 29 May 2018, fortune.com/2018/05/29/ro-khanna-reelection. Accessed 14 June 2019.

Nolan, Hamilton. "Ro Khanna, the Bernie Guy Who's Okay with Billionaires." *Splinter*, 24 May 2019, splinternews.com/ro-khanna-the-bernie-guy-whos-okay-with-billionaires-1834982445. Accessed 14 June 2019.

—*Joy Crelin*

Rachel Khoo

Date of birth: August 28, 1980
Occupation: Cook and television personality

"I've always felt the easiest way to get to know new culture is through its food even if you don't speak the language," Rachel Khoo told Anna Barnett for the London *Evening Standard* (24 Aug. 2018), describing food as a "universal language." Khoo, a native of England, is the author of such popular cookbooks as *The Little Paris Kitchen* (2012) and *The Little Swedish Kitchen* (2018). She has also introduced television audiences to her brand of creative but unpretentious cooking in several highly rated television series, including *The Little Paris Kitchen: Cooking with Rachel Khoo* (2012), *Rachel Khoo's Kitchen Notebook: London* (2014), and *Rachel Khoo's Kitchen Notebook: Melbourne* (2015).

Early in her career, Khoo established an appealing and relatable style. "Think of a cross between Amélie and an excitable Lizzy Bennet," Elizabeth Day wrote for the *Guardian* (14 July 2012). "In *The Little Paris Kitchen* . . . Khoo was shown whipping up classic French dishes in her tiny kitchen in the Belleville district. . . . The comparative modesty of her surroundings played into the romanticised notion of a winsome English girl living the Parisian dream in a picture-postcard artist's garret."

EARLY LIFE AND EDUCATION
Rachel Khoo was born on August 28, 1980, and spent her early years in Croydon, a borough in southern London. Her father hailed from a family of Chinese immigrants who had set down roots in Malaysia. He had left Malaysia around the age of sixteen and ultimately arrived in the United Kingdom, where he met Khoo's mother, a native of Austria. Food was an important part of Khoo's family life. "In Malaysia, they don't ask you how you are, they ask 'Have you eaten?'" she explained to Day. She added that family meals often included "schnitzel, stir fries, rendang curry and we always had a Sunday roast like beef with Yorkshire pudding, so it was a real melting pot."

Khoo, who has one younger brother, Michael, attended school in nearby Bromley until she was about twelve. Around that time, her father, who worked in the field of information technology, got an assignment in the German state of Bavaria, and the family lived in a rural area outside of Munich. While there, Khoo attended a local convent school, despite not speaking a word of German. "My first day I'm trying to find swimming so I'm miming swimming to the nuns. And then my second lesson I have a maths test and this Bavarian woman yells at me," she recalled to Stephen Armstrong for the *Evening Standard* (8

Photo by Arsineh Houspian/Fairfax Media via Getty Images

June 2012). "Education in Bavaria is tough. . . . But like my mum says, it's 'character building.' You learn to adapt." Khoo would later credit her ability to adjust readily to other environments and languages to that early period of her life.

After about four years in Germany, Khoo returned to England. Following her A levels, she entered Central Saint Martins, a renowned arts and design school. There, students had the ability to work in a range of media, and for one architectural assignment, she drew upon her love of food and used gingerbread in her construction. She also honed skills such as photography and graphic design that would prove crucial to the foundation of her future, largely self-made career.

FOLLOWING HER CULINARY DREAM

Upon earning an undergraduate degree in 2003, Khoo found a public relations job with the British clothing brand Thomas Pink, known for its men's shirts. After a few years in which she spent much of her time sending free shirts to celebrities in the hopes they would be photographed in them, Khoo became bored.

In 2006, with just a small amount of money and without knowing the language or any of the people, she moved to Paris. There she began taking French language classes and enrolled in Le Cordon Bleu, the venerable culinary school, for a pastry course. "My parents thought I was mad," she explained to Day. "It was: 'Why are you giving up a good job in London? You should pay off your student loan!' People at work were really jealous. They thought going to Paris to bake cakes sounded amazing."

Khoo supported herself by working as a nanny for a French family and supplemented that income with a job behind the perfume counter at the Printemps department store. Despite being on a tight budget, she ate well, subsisting on inexpensive but high-quality fare like fresh baguettes and cheese. "That kind of food is not really accessible to you in London," she told Day. "I really love that in Paris, there is no division [in food] by social class."

HER LITTLE FRENCH KITCHEN

After graduating from Le Cordon Bleu, Khoo found work at La Cocotte, a combination bookstore and café. There, she baked the café's pastries, ran workshops, and oversaw events for cookbook launches. A connection with cookbook author Marc Grossman led to her being introduced to his editor, who signed her on. She had two cookbooks published in French in 2010 by Marabout, the first containing recipes for cereal bars, muesli, and homemade granola and the second focusing on recipes for sweet and savory spreads. On the strength of that accomplishment and wanting to put together a more personal book based on her innovative, modern take on classic French recipes, she daringly emailed the major publishing house Penguin in London to make a pitch.

Following a warm response to her premise, Khoo needed to test the book's more than one hundred recipes. To do this conservatively and economically, she opened a pop-up restaurant in her tiny apartment in Paris. "I don't like wasting food," she explained to Armstrong. "And it's expensive as well, buying good-quality ingredients. So I was like, 'OK, if I have two people round for lunch, twice a week, I get to test recipes, I don't waste the food, and they can cover the cost of ingredients.'" She also enjoyed the opportunity to meet people, as working on the book left little time for social pursuits. Khoo's reputation quickly spread, and whenever she announced openings through social media, reservations filled in a short time. The book itself, titled *The Little Paris Kitchen* (her first English-language book) and published in 2012, proved to be very successful. It was later translated into Dutch, French, Italian, and German, among other languages.

Khoo also decided to pitch herself—a young Briton creating fabulous Parisian-inspired meals despite the constraints of both a tiny kitchen and a tiny budget—as the host of a cooking show. She made plain to the production company that she did not want to be sexualized and that there would be a focus on substance over style. (Despite that assertion, her fans found her personal style—which relied on prim but colorful 1950s-style dresses and crimson lipstick—vastly appealing.) Although her mother warned her that no one would ever want to watch a television show centered on a normal, ordinary woman cooking, when *The Little Paris Kitchen: Cooking with Rachel Khoo* aired on BBC Two in 2012, it was an immediate hit. The six-episode series was later shown in countries such as Australia, Germany, Brazil, Finland, and the United States.

FURTHER WRITING AND TELEVISION PROJECTS

Amid the whirlwind of activity surrounding the television show, Khoo found herself longing for something different and ultimately traveled in 2012 to Sweden. She worked briefly at famed chef Magnus Nilsson's Michelin-starred restaurant Fäviken, situated on a remote estate north of the Swedish capital, Stockholm. Even as she performed such mundane tasks as washing dishes, she became enamored of Swedish cuisine, with its simple, minimal ingredients and strong, fresh flavors. Eventually, she followed up the success of *The Little Paris Kitchen* with a book titled *My Little French Kitchen*, which was published in 2013. For this effort, she ventured away from Paris and toured the countryside, tasting foods and then crafting dishes and recipes inspired by them. Despite the occasional mishap, she reveled in the North African–inspired offerings she found in Marseille, the Spanish flavors of the Basque region, and the Germanic influences evident in Alsatian meals.

Khoo later enjoyed a string of successful television series and books based on her creative food passion. The program *Rachel Khoo's Kitchen Notebook: London*, which aired over the course of ten episodes worldwide in 2014, saw the chef return to the area in which she was raised to explore London's food scene. Another ten-episode series released that year, *Rachel Khoo's Kitchen Notebook: Cosmopolitan Cook* featured her traveling to discover culinary treasures in sites such as Istanbul, Turkey; Naples, Italy; and Barcelona, Spain. In 2015, in addition to publishing *Rachel Khoo's Kitchen Notebook*, she appeared in an episode of the series *A Cook Abroad* in which she ventured to Malaysia to experience firsthand her culinary heritage. The show *Rachel Khoo's Kitchen Notebook: Melbourne*, which chronicled her time discovering the multicultural food scene of one of Australia's most vibrant cities, was also broadcast that year.

In 2016, Khoo moved to Sweden and launched an online lifestyle platform and social media venture dubbed Khoollect, focused on food, travel, beauty, and fashion. That same year, she appeared as a guest judge on the Australian cooking competition *My Kitchen Rules* and co-hosted the first season of the baking competition *Zumbo's Just Desserts* on Australia's Channel 7 (and later available on the streaming service Netflix). Her book *The Little Swedish Kitchen* was published in 2018 and focuses on what she had learned about the balanced style of Swedish cooking. "The geographical location of Sweden and, therefore, short growing season meant that the range of produce is not as abundant," she told Barnett. "This influenced the cooking culture and forced cooks to be creative with a handful of ingredients. It's a very modern way of cooking."

PERSONAL LIFE

Khoo married Robert Wiktorin, a Swedish citizen, in 2015. She largely remains reserved about her personal life. However, in early 2017, she did announce on her personal blog that she had given birth to her first child.

SUGGESTED READING

Armstrong, Stephen. "Rachel Khoo: 'Some Chefs Have a Few Issues with My Image . . .'" *Evening Standard*, 8 June 2012, www.standard.co.uk/lifestyle/esmagazine/rachel-khoo-some-chefs-have-a-few-issues-with-my-image-7827530.html. Accessed 10 July 2019.

Day, Elizabeth. "Rachel Khoo: 'My Parents Thought I Was Mad to Go Off Baking Cakes in Paris.'" *The Guardian*, 14 July 2012, www.theguardian.com/lifeandstyle/2012/jul/15/rachel-khoo-paris-kitchen-interview. Accessed 10 July 2019.

Digby, Marie Claire. "Rachel Khoo: A Culinary Journey from France to Sweden." *The Irish Times*, 28 July 2018, www.irishtimes.com/life-and-style/food-and-drink/rachel-khoo-a-culinary-journey-from-france-to-sweden-1.3569268. Accessed 10 July 2019.

Khoo, Rachel. "A Conversation with Rachel Khoo, Author of The Little Swedish Kitchen." Interview by Anna Barnett. *Evening Standard*, 24 Aug. 2018, www.standard.co.uk/lifestyle/foodanddrink/rachel-khoo-interview-recipes-a3917641.html. Accessed 10 July 2019.

Khoo, Rachel. "Rachel Khoo: 'Chocolate I'm Not Fussed About, but Cheese: Wow.'" Interview by John Hind. *The Guardian*, 21 Oct. 2013, www.theguardian.com/lifeandstyle/2013/oct/21/rachel-khoo-life-on-plate-john-hind. Accessed 10 July 2013.

Yeap, Sue. "Khoo's Swede Treats." *The West Australian*, 31 July 2018, thewest.com.au/lifestyle/food/khoos-swede-treats-ng-b88897492z. Accessed 10 July 2019.

SELECTED WORKS

The Little Paris Kitchen: Cooking with Rachel Khoo, 2012; *Rachel Khoo's Kitchen Notebook: London*, 2014; *Rachel Khoo's Kitchen Notebook: Cosmopolitan Cook*, 2014; *Rachel Khoo's Kitchen Notebook: Melbourne*, 2015; *My Kitchen Rules*, 2016

—Mari Rich

Fadlo R. Khuri

Date of birth: September 13, 1963
Occupation: College president

Fadlo R. Khuri has been the president of the American University of Beirut (AUB) in Lebanon, one of the most prestigious universities in the Middle East, since 2015. He was elected to a second five-year term in 2019. Khuri was born in Boston, Massachusetts, but grew up in Beirut. Both of his parents taught at AUB, and his father, who also worked as a physician, briefly served as president after the school's president was assassinated during the Lebanese Civil War. During his tenure, Khuri has sought to instill students with intellectual courage at a time of global and regional unrest. He has presided over AUB's outreach to the country's large community of Syrian refugees, a population the Lebanese government has struggled to deal with. Khuri grew up during the Lebanese Civil War and sees education as the cornerstone of a free and humane government and citizenry. Khuri spent most of his career as an oncologist, with a focus on lung cancer. His specific areas of expertise include molecular oncology, the investigation of cancer on a molecular scale, and translational medicine, or the "translation" of research discoveries to clinical applications. He has published over 300 peer-reviewed articles, and serves as the editor-in-chief of the prestigious journal *Cancer*. In 2006, Khuri received the Nagi Sahyoun Award of the Middle East Medical Assembly for his lung, head, and neck cancer research and received the Richard and Hinda Rosenthal Memorial Award from the American Association for Cancer Research (AACR) in 2013. Before accepting his position at AUB, Khuri served as the deputy director of the Winship Cancer Institute of Emory University, where he held the Roberto C. Goizueta chair in translational cancer research at the university's medical school. Before that, he spent seven years at the University of Texas MD Anderson Cancer Center.

EARLY LIFE AND EDUCATION

Fadlo R. Khuri was born in Boston, Massachusetts, in 1963. His father, Raja N. Khuri, was a renal physiologist. His mother, Soumaya Makdisi Khuri, was a mathematician. Both had emigrated from Lebanon; the family, including Khuri's brother, Ramzi, now a physicist, and his sister, Jananne, now a psychologist, returned to that country in 1970. His mother taught mathematics at AUB, and his father became the school's dean of medicine in 1978. Several years later, from 1984 to 1985, Raja Khuri served as the acting president of the university after the president, Dr. Malcolm Kerr, was assassinated. Khuri grew up in Beirut during the Lebanese

Photo by Nidal Mawas via Wikipedia

Civil War, which lasted from 1975 to 1990. The conflict drew fuel from frictions among Lebanon's various ethnic populations, but Khuri grew up steeped in the cultural and intellectual melting pot of the university. He recalled to Peter Wortsman for *Columbia Medicine* magazine (Spring 2017), that when his parents were asked during the war which party they belonged to, they always replied: "We belong to the party of AUB." Of his own upbringing, Khuri said, "I was born a Lebanese, but raised intellectually by Koreans, Chinese, and Americans, by Christians, Moslems [sic], Jews, atheists, and communists alike." He quickly realized, he added, that "there really is no 'other' when you've figured out that you yourself are part of that 'other.'"

Khuri attended high school at the International College in Beirut and graduated in 1981. He enrolled as an undergraduate at AUB but left after his first year to attend Yale University in the United States. He graduated in 1985 and earned his medical degree from the College of Physicians and Surgeons at Columbia University in New York City in 1989.

EARLY CLINICAL CAREER

Khuri had planned to become a psychiatrist, but as a third-year medical student on his first day of surgery rotation, he cared for a beloved rabbinical scholar who was dying of pancreatic cancer. He recalled wondering, "How could such a good man have such a cruel and unkind death?" Ultimately, he told Wortsman, "My search for meaning in this painful event drove me into the field of cancer research." Among his mentors at Columbia were the late Bernard Weinstein, the director of the cancer center at Columbia and Presbyterian Hospital, and the late Leslie Baer, the director of the hypertension research program. Baer, he told Wortsman, "taught me how to write a thoughtful patient history, to include my reasoning, the rationale for a diagnosis, and plan of treatment."

On the recommendation of the late John Lindenbaum, then the vice chair of medicine at Columbia, Khuri began training at the now-defunct Boston City Hospital. His residency coincided with the early days of the AIDS epidemic. His work was grueling, but ultimately, he told Wortsman, rewarding. "It's easy to feel you're working for a job your first eight hours, but after that you need to know that it's more than a job, that it's a calling," he said. Khuri went on to complete a fellowship in hematology and medical oncology at New England Medical Center and Tufts University School of Medicine. He joined the Department of Medicine at the University of Texas MD Anderson Cancer Center in 1995. In 2000, Khuri contributed to important research involving viral therapy. In a study, Khuri and a team of colleagues administered a genetically altered adenovirus, a virus that causes the common cold, to treat head and neck cancer with some success. In 2013, he described progress in that area of research to Ann Hardie for the *Atlanta Journal-Constitution* (20 Apr. 2013). "We helped develop viruses that we injected into tumors that, when combined with chemotherapy, did a pretty good job controlling the growth of metastatic disease," he said. "Unfortunately, we couldn't get the viruses to all of the places where the cancer was. Now, we are developing newer viruses that can be given to patients intravenously."

In 2002, Khuri was recruited by Emory University, where he became a professor of hematology and oncology, and the director of the Discovery and Developmental Therapeutics program at the Winship Cancer Institute.

LUNG CANCER RESEARCH

Khuri, who was later named the Roberto C. Goizueta Distinguished Chair for Cancer Research at Emory, developed a specialization in lung cancer. A year after Khuri was born, in 1964, the US surgeon general released a groundbreaking report on the dangers of smoking cigarettes. The report concluded, among other things, that smoking causes lung cancer. The report had a profound effect on the young Khuri, who, upon his family's return to Lebanon, was disturbed by the prevalence of smoking, particularly the custom of serving cigarettes with Turkish coffee. Khuri and his brother Ramzi began snapping the cigarettes served at their family home. The tactic was effective, he wrote in an editorial for *Cancer* (30 May 2019). "Within three months,

the serving of cigarettes had ceased entirely in the Khuri households!" Khuri admits that, as an adult physician, he is not above similar tactics to convince his patients to quit smoking. In 2005, Khuri and fellow researcher Shi-Yong Sun produced a breakthrough in lung cancer research when they identified an important behavior of the mTOR (mammalian target of rapamycin) signaling pathway. The protein regulates cancer cell growth. The discovery essentially demonstrated why existing treatments were not as effective as they should have been. Khuri's research could lead to the development of new pathway-targeted treatments. When asked to sum up advances in the understanding of lung cancer, Khuri told Hardie of his work: "With cancer cells, genes and proteins behave differently than they do in normal tissue. That was our first really important discovery. Also, we have learned that while patients may seem similar, they can have dramatically different outcomes. Over the years, we have increasingly taken a personalized or precision-medicine approach to treatment."

PRESIDENT OF AUB

"The real challenge in life is about being able to reinvent and redefine yourself every 10 to 15 years," Khuri told Wortsman. Under this guiding principle, Khuri applied for the role of president of AUB in 2014. He was named the sixteenth president of the university in September 2015. He came to AUB—and continues to preside over it—at a difficult time in the region's history. Lebanon remains divided among religious and political factions, and a huge influx of Syrian refugees—nearly 2 million people entering a country of 4 million—has exacerbated tensions. High unemployment, economic instability and inflation, and a new government policy of forced deportation of refugees have rattled the country. Amid such unrest, Khuri hopes to cultivate the same intellectual and cultural diversity in which he was raised. "A full half of the population in many Arab countries is under the age of twenty-five," he told Wortsman. "Young people are not yet set in their ways. They're open to new ideas. The risk is that they can be turned toward ideological extremism, but they can also be influenced to do great good." Khuri has called for a renewed emphasis on the humanities at AUB, including the study of literature, Arabic, and philosophy. Too narrow a focus on applied studies, he argues, leaves out a critical part of the purpose of higher education. "I don't want to train fewer engineers; I just want those engineers to take more humanities courses, learn more about why we do things, as opposed to just how we do things," he told Wortsman.

As president, Khuri has made a point to reach out to Syrian refugees. In 2016, AUB's Center for Civic Engagement and Community

Service won the 2016 MacJannet Prize for global citizenship for its educational outreach to that community. Khuri has also proposed a national service and teaching model to address the high cost of college tuition. His proposal would offer debt-forgiveness, funded by the Lebanese government, for students who pledge to teach in rural areas after graduation. (Khuri himself spent time teaching in Palestinian refugee camps as a young man.) More recently, Khuri joined with *Annahar*, an Arabic-language Lebanese daily, to edit a special dispatch on the vital issues facing Lebanon, and how a focus on education can help bring positive change. "Lawmakers are essentially looking for short-term and band-aid solutions," Khuri told Georgi Azar for *Annahar* (26 Sept. 2018). "The purpose of the special issue with *Annahar* is to recognize the country's strengths and weaknesses and to propose viable long-term solutions, [and] we hope to build on these for years to come." In 2019, Khuri was re-elected to another five-year term as university president, set to begin in 2020.

PERSONAL LIFE

Khuri is married to Lamya Tannous Khuri. The couple met at Columbia, where Lamya graduated with a PhD in nutrition in 1993. They have three adult children: Layla, Raja, and Rayya.

SUGGESTED READING

"About the President." *American University of Beirut*, www.aub.edu.lb/President/Pages/about-the-president.aspx. Accessed 16 Sept. 2019.

Azar, Georgi. "When Journalism Meets Higher Education: AUB and *Annahar* Join Forces." *Annahar*, 26 Sept. 2018, en.annahar.com/article/868734-aub-and-annahar-join-forces-when-journalism-and-higher-education-collide. Accessed 16 Sept. 2019.

Hardie, Ann. "Sunday Conversation with . . . Dr. Fadlo R. Khuri, Clinical Researcher Dedicated to Eradicating Cancer." *Atlanta Journal-Constitution*, 20 Apr. 2013, www.ajc.com/news/local/sunday-conversation-with-fadlo-khuri-clinical-researcher-dedicated-eradicating-cancer/LSAhePK3DXIBB1MGx-6IMGO/. Accessed 16 Sept. 2019.

Khuri, Fadlo R. "A Very Personal War." *Cancer*, vol. 125, no. 16, 2019, pp. 2725–7, doi:10.1002/cncr.32191. Accessed 16 Sept. 2019.

Wortsman, Peter. "Alumni Profile: Fadlo R. Khuri '89." *Columbia Medicine*, Spring 2017, www.columbiamedicinemagazine.org/alumni-news-notes/spring-2017/alumni-profile-fadlo-r-khuri89. Accessed 14 Sept. 2019.

—*Molly Hagan*

Hayley Kiyoko

Date of birth: April 3, 1991
Occupation: Singer and actor

"I never felt like I had a community growing up," singer Hayley Kiyoko told Suzy Exposito for *Rolling Stone* (4 Mar. 2019). "We all just want to feel understood and loved. It sounds cheesy, but my listeners create that for me. My fans are my community." Indeed, a particularly devoted community of fans has surrounded Kiyoko—whom many of them often refer to as "Lesbian Jesus"—in the years since her debut as a solo artist in 2013, transforming her concerts into not only entertaining musical performances but also celebrations of connection, positivity, and pride.

A performer since early childhood, Kiyoko began her career as an actor in projects such as the television films *Scooby-Doo! The Mystery Begins* (2009) and *Lemonade Mouth* (2011) and as a member of the pop quintet the Stunners. Following the release of her debut extended-play record (EP), *A Belle to Remember*, in 2013, she established herself as a solo artist to watch, impressing critics and gaining dedicated listeners with the EPs *This Side of Paradise* (2015) and *Citrine* (2016) as well as her 2018 debut album, *Expectations*. She also remained active in film and television, appearing in series such as *CSI: Cyber* (2015–16) and *Five Points* (2018–). Although Kiyoko's success as both a singer and an actor is in many ways the fulfillment of a lifelong dream, she has focused in large part on the effects that her newfound visibility has had on her community of fans. "I think it's just important for people to lead by example," she told Steven J. Horowitz for *Billboard* (8 Mar. 2018). "My motto is to help people love themselves sooner. I can't teach them how to do that. They have to figure that out on their own—that's their journey."

EARLY LIFE AND EDUCATION

Hayley Kiyoko Alcroft was born in California on April 3, 1991. She was the second of three children born to Sarah Kawahara, a figure skater and award-winning skating choreographer, and Jamie Alcroft, a comedian and voice actor particularly known for his work in video games. Alongside siblings Alysse and Thatcher, she grew up in Westlake Village, a city within California's Los Angeles County. Due to her parents' occupations, she was introduced to the realities of careers in the performing arts early in life. "I grew up with one parent always gone," she recalled to Brittany Spanos for *Rolling Stone* (20 July 2018). "We grew up learning to adapt wherever we were. Work was always first."

In addition to learning to skate, Kiyoko was an avid dancer as well as a musician throughout her early years. She began playing the drums at

Photo by Ralph Arvesen via Wikimedia Commons

the age of five and went on to learn guitar and piano, and she later recalled in interviews that she began writing original songs while in elementary school. As her interest in storytelling and performance continued to develop, she determined that she wanted to pursue a career in that arena. "My dream was to be like 'NSync," she explained to Exposito. "My dream was to have screaming girls around and be successful and popular. . . . But I thought, 'I'm a girl, and I don't know if that'll ever happen.'"

While she was pinpointing her career goals in elementary school, Kiyoko also realized that she was romantically attracted to girls during the same period. Although she came out to her parents as gay while in sixth grade, she kept her orientation largely secret throughout much of middle and high school due to fears that she would be ostracized by friends and classmates. "I was a likable person and I didn't want to all of a sudden not be [likable]," she told Spanos. "I was scared." Such experiences would go on to influence her later work as a singer-songwriter, and a number of her popular songs would reflect the sense of longing and isolation she associated with that time in her life.

Having gotten herself an agent for pursuing commercial gigs while in middle school, Kiyoko was also active in the performing arts during her years at Agoura High School in Agoura Hills, California. She performed in school theatrical productions in addition to serving as president of her freshman class.

EARLY CAREER

While still in high school, Kiyoko appeared in two episodes of the youth-oriented television series *Unfabulous*. She likewise became increasingly active in music during that period, briefly performing as a member of the band Hede before joining the all-girl pop group the Stunners in 2007. Formed under the direction of the established recording artist Vitamin C, the group consisted of Kiyoko and four other young performers with both acting and singing backgrounds. In addition to Kiyoko, the group was particularly notable for its inclusion of the singer Tinashe, who would go on to find significant success as a solo artist.

Although Kiyoko spoke positively about the group in interviews from that time, she was later more critical of her time as a teen pop artist, which she viewed as a crucial learning experience. "I learned a lot of what to do and what not to do," she told Spanos. "I wanted to be in control of my art. I wanted to write my own music. I always wanted to be in control and call the shots." Although the Stunners had released a self-titled extended-play record (EP) in 2009 and toured as an opening act for pop star Justin Bieber the following year, the group did not release a full-length album before breaking up in 2011. Meanwhile, Kiyoko had graduated from high school in 2009; and although she was accepted into New York University (NYU), she deferred her acceptance for a year. She ended up declining to enroll in college, opting to focus on her developing career as an actor and musician.

Alongside her early music career, Kiyoko continued to act in increasingly major projects, including the 2009 live-action television film *Scooby-Doo! The Mystery Begins*. Originally aired on Cartoon Network, the film was based on the long-running Scooby-Doo cartoon franchise and featured Kiyoko as Velma Dinkley, one of the franchise's mystery-solving teenagers. After reprising the role of Velma in the 2010 sequel *Scooby-Doo! Curse of the Lake Monster*, she received further attention with the 2011 premiere of the Disney Channel television film *Lemonade Mouth*, in which a group of teenagers meet in detention and later form a band. *Lemonade Mouth* gave her the opportunity to display her musical talents further, and she was featured on the film's soundtrack alongside the other members of the main cast.

EPS

Although Kiyoko had found some success as a member of the Stunners, she hoped to explore genres of music that were more to her taste and create work that reflected her own experiences as a solo artist. After also gaining more experience and funds from her acting gigs, she released her first independent EP, *A Belle to Remember*, in 2013 and followed it two years later with the EP *This Side of Paradise*. While the latter work earned Kiyoko widespread attention as a solo artist, it was perhaps most meaningful for helping to establish her as one of the United States' few openly lesbian pop singers. "I was like, 'Holy s——, I don't have a choice. This is something that I have to do because no one else is doing it,'" she told Horowitz about the process of writing the EP. "It forced me to step into my own as an artist. And this is something I've always wanted to do—be loud and sing about sexy girls." Kiyoko received particular notice (including from major label Atlantic, which signed her that year) for her song "Girls Like Girls" and its corresponding music video, which she produced independently with the help of friends and made available for viewing online. Focusing on a love story between two teenage girls, the video earned praise from many publications as well as LGBTQ commentators, who credited Kiyoko with unambiguously increasing lesbian representation in the music industry and popular culture.

Although Kiyoko focused heavily on her music from 2013 on, continuing to direct her music videos and releasing her third EP, *Citrine*, in 2016, she still acted as well, appearing both on television and in films. For her role in the 2014 independent film *Hello, My Name Is Frank*, she won the award for best supporting actress at the Independent Filmmakers Showcase Film Festival. She appeared in several episodes of the television series *The Fosters* in 2014, played a major role on the short-lived crime series *CSI: Cyber* between 2015 and 2016, and in 2015 appeared in the film *Jem and the Holograms*. In 2017, she guest-starred in an episode of the award-winning HBO series *Insecure*, and the following year, she began to costar in the series *Five Points*, released through the online service Facebook Watch. In December 2018, Facebook announced that *Five Points* had been renewed for a second season.

EXPECTATIONS

The year 2018 also saw a major career milestone for Kiyoko, who released her debut full-length album in March. Titled *Expectations*, the album was inspired, in part, by her high expectations of herself and others and the "battle of balancing" such expectations that everyone goes through, as she told Erica Gonzales for *Harper's Bazaar* (2 Apr. 2018). *Expectations* likewise deeply reflected personal experiences during different periods in her life, including her teen years and young adulthood. "I tackled each track on its own. And I don't like when albums sound the same; like when literally every track sounds like the same song," she explained to Gonzales about the album's content. "So I really focused on dedicating each track to a different part of my life and times

that I had been going through." Her dedicated fan base responded positively to the album, and *Expectations* also drew critical attention thanks to singles such as "What I Need," which features fellow singer Kehlani, and additional tracks such as "Mercy/Gatekeeper," which focuses on her experiences with depression and post-concussion syndrome following a 2016 concussion.

Much as she had been for earlier songs such as "Girls Like Girls," Kiyoko was heavily involved in the creation of the music videos for *Expectations'* singles, directing or codirecting many of the projects. In addition to retaining creative control over her work, she has noted that her involvement in the music videos is especially key because it enables her to tell meaningful and important stories on her own terms. "I don't have as many resources as other artists. I'm working with lower budgets and having to be creative with utilizing what I've got to make my videos look more expensive than they are," she told Estelle Tang for *Elle* (14 Aug. 2017). "I'm very proud of every video, because it's a lot of hard work. I'm working to get these stories out, because it's important. They're not just music videos with glitter and fancy moves. There's meaning behind it."

In recognition of her work, Kiyoko was nominated for a variety of awards, including the MTV Video Music Award for Best New Artist. She claimed the title of Push Artist of the Year at the 2018 Video Music Awards and was named Rising Star at the 2018 Billboard Women in Music event. Although grateful for such recognition, she stays focused primarily on her connections with her fans and working toward increased LGBTQ visibility in both the music world and society. "We need more bravery in the industry," she told Exposito. "To know that being myself, and being proud of who I am, can help people love themselves more? Is an incredible feeling."

PERSONAL LIFE

Kiyoko is beginning to adjust to spending larger amounts of time on the road but has expressed in interviews that she has always enjoyed being able to take time to relax and recharge in nature, including going for walks.

SUGGESTED READING

Exposito, Suzy. "How Hayley Kiyoko Found Her People." *Rolling Stone*, 4 Mar. 2019, www.rollingstone.com/music/music-features/hayley-kiyoko-women-shaping-future-2019-802172/. Accessed 15 Mar. 2019.

Horowitz, Steven J. "Hayley Kiyoko on Her Debut Album 'Expectations' and Being a Queer Pop Star: 'It's Important for People to Lead by Example.'" *Billboard*, 8 Mar. 2018, www.billboard.com/articles/columns/pop/8235955/hayley-kiyoko-interview-expectations-sexuality. Accessed 15 Mar. 2019.

Kiyoko, Hayley. "Hayley Kiyoko: 'I Love Loving Girls, and I Love Myself.'" Interview by Erica Gonzales. *Harper's Bazaar*, 2 Apr. 2018, www.harpersbazaar.com/culture/art-books-music/a19646748/hayley-kiyoko-expectations-interview/. Accessed 15 Mar. 2019.

Kiyoko, Haley. "Hayley Kiyoko Talks about Her Insecure Guest Role." Interview by Estelle Tang. *Elle*, 14 Aug. 2017, www.elle.com/culture/movies-tv/news/a47373/hayley-kiyoko-insecure-guest-role/. Accessed 15 Mar. 2019.

Spanos, Brittany. "#20gayteen: The Year of Hayley Kiyoko." *Rolling Stone*, 20 July 2018, www.rollingstone.com/music/music-features/how-hayley-kiyoko-became-lesbian-jesus-695667/. Accessed 15 Mar. 2019.

Studarus, Laura. "Hayley Kiyoko Ushers in a New Era of Pop Honesty." *CR Fashion Book*, 4 Jan. 2019, www.crfashionbook.com/celebrity/a25737241/hayley-kiyoko-profile-interview-new-music/. Accessed 15 Mar. 2019.

SELECTED WORKS

A Belle to Remember, 2013; *This Side of Paradise*, 2015; *Citrine*, 2016; *Expectations*, 2018

—Joy Crelin

Karl Ove Knausgaard

Date of birth: December 6, 1968
Occupation: Author

Other than perhaps *Harry Potter* author J. K. Rowling, few writers in the twenty-first century have attained the sweeping success and celebrity as Karl Ove Knausgaard, whose six-volume, 3,600-page autobiographical novel *My Struggle* catapulted him to the top of the literary pantheon when its first installment was published in his native Norway in 2009. Minutely and unflinchingly reconstructing every aspect of the author's life, the genre-busting epic, which began appearing in English in 2012, has been widely regarded as a monumental literary achievement and has earned Knausgaard critical adulation around the world. The book's success has not come without controversy, though, thanks to its scandalous title—the book's original Norwegian title, of which the English is a literal translation, is *Min kamp*, bearing a deliberate resemblance to the infamous 1925 political manifesto by German dictator Adolf Hitler. In addition, Knausgaard's decision to include deeply private and shocking truths not only about himself but also about close friends and family members has been criticized.

Still, the books have been called "the most significant literary enterprise of our times," as the novelist Rachel Cusk declared in a review for the *Guardian* (12 Apr. 2013). Knausgaard, who built his reputation with the well-received literary novels *Ute av verden* (1998; Out of the world) and *En tid for alt* (2004; *A Time for Everything*, 2009), initially planned to quit his vocation after completing *My Struggle* but has since published a quartet of books based on the seasons, as well as several collections of essays. "I'm not looking for something to write about, ever," he explained to Liesl Schillinger for the *Wall Street Journal* (4 Nov. 2015). "If it is valuable, it will be inside of me, so I'll write about it one day."

EARLY LIFE AND EDUCATION

The younger of two brothers, Knausgaard—which is also spelled as Knausgård—was born on December 6, 1968, in Oslo, Norway. He grew up on Tromøya, the largest island in southern Norway. His parents worked in the nearby town of Arendal; his father was a schoolteacher and local politician and his mother was a nurse. As Evan Hughes noted in a profile of the author for the *New Republic* (7 Apr. 2014), Knausgaard spent much of his childhood "either in terror or in tears" caused by his father, a violent alcoholic who routinely mocked and occasionally beat him and his brother Yngve. He has said that his father, who left the family when he was a teenager, was a dominant figure in his life and that writing *My Struggle* was largely an attempt to purge the overpowering influence he held over him.

Precocious but introverted, Knausgaard turned to literature as a boy "to escape the world," as he put it in an interview with Ane Farsethas for the *Paris Review* (15 Dec. 2015).

Photo by Kjetil Ree via Wikimedia Commons

By his own estimation, he read through two bags of library books every week, devouring works by authors like Alexandre Dumas, Jules Verne, and Robert Louis Stevenson. One of the first books to leave a lasting impact on Knausgaard was Ursula K. Le Guin's classic children's fantasy novel *A Wizard of Earthsea* (1968), which his mother bought for him when he was ten.

When Knausgaard reached his teens, he started fostering aspirations of becoming a writer. As he recalled in a self-penned article for the *Telegraph* (12 Nov. 2016), his early writing efforts included short stories "about young men and freedom, in the style of [Jack] Kerouac and [Ernest] Hemingway." At sixteen, Knausgaard channeled one of his other passions, music, into a weekly newspaper column. After graduating from high school, he took a gap year to work as a schoolteacher in northern Norway. He was then admitted to the prestigious Writing Academy in Bergen, a city on Norway's southwestern coast.

Despite arriving at the academy with high writerly ambitions, Knausgaard was brought back down to earth when students and teachers harshly criticized his work. Their negative feedback caused the self-doubting Knausgaard to lose "all faith in my abilities," as he admitted in the *Telegraph* article, and forced him to reevaluate his future as a fiction writer. He consequently spent a year studying literature at the University of Bergen (UiB), during which he wrote criticism.

ROAD TO LITERARY STARDOM

Following his year of study at UiB, Knausgaard took a four-year hiatus, working various odd jobs while trying to make it as a writer. He worked at a campus radio station to fulfill his compulsory national service, worked as an orderly at a psychiatric hospital, and spent time on an oil rig in the North Sea, before returning to UiB to study art history. Throughout this period, he read widely, discovering groundbreaking literary works that would play a significant role in his artistic and intellectual development. Among the most notable of these was French novelist Marcel Proust's seven-volume pseudo-autobiographical novel *À la recherche du temps perdu* (1913–27; *Remembrance of Things Past*, 1922–31), to which *My Struggle* is frequently compared.

Still, Knausgaard's writing output during this time was minimal. Crippled by insecurities about his writing talent and jealous of his published friends, he acted out his frustrations by drinking heavily and committing petty crimes. Knausgaard's writing career began to take on a promising new trajectory in the mid-1990s, however, after a friend, the award-winning Norwegian writer Tore Renberg, offered him words of encouragement. Renberg showed a short story of Knausgaard's to his editor, Geir Gulliksen, who

put it in an anthology. Gulliksen then signed Knausgaard up for a novel. "I instantly quit studying to write something—anything—that could get me in print again," Knausgaard recalled in the *Telegraph* article. "That was all it took for me to start believing in myself again: one person telling me I was good enough."

Knausgaard, who by then had married his first wife, the journalist Tonje Aursland, spent sixteen months working on his debut novel *Ute av verden*, which was published by the Norwegian publishing house Tiden in 1998. Divided into three parts, the nearly 700-page novel is narrated by a twenty-six-year-old elementary school teacher, Henrik Vankel, who returns to the Norwegian town of his youth after having a sexual liaison with a female student. As he makes his way there, Henrik falls into long reveries about his past, exploring personal and family histories. Shifting genres and points of view, the novel was hailed for its innovative narrative technique and earned Knausgaard the Norwegian Critics Prize for Literature, making him the first debut novelist to win the award.

Knausgaard's second novel, *En tid for alt*, was similarly published to wide critical acclaim when it first appeared in 2004. The novel, which retells several stories from the Bible, delves into the mystery of angels through the perspective of a man who has decide to write a book about their history on earth. It won a number of awards, as Knausgaard garnered praise for his vivid descriptions of nature and penetrating psychological insight and became the first of his books to be published in English.

SUCCESS AND CONTROVERSY FOR *MY STRUGGLE*

Despite the success of his first two novels, Knausgaard remained dissatisfied with the quality of his writing. He started working on a novel about his father, but those efforts yielded only contrived and uninspiring results, leading him to fall into a long period of writer's block. Things began to change for the better in early 2008, however, when Knausgaard decided to take a new radical approach to his writing. Frustrated with contemporary fiction, Knausgaard resolved to write about his life in a completely unvarnished way, without concern for writerly flourishes and artful evasions. As he told Hughes, "I wanted to just *say* it, you know. As it is."

This approach immediately proved fruitful for Knausgaard, who proceeded to write what would become *My Struggle*. Writing at a frenzied pace that saw him produce upwards of twenty pages a day, he published the first volumes of the autobiographical opus in Norway in 2009 and released the others there in quick succession over the next two years. Totaling 3,600 pages, the volumes, which became an immediate sensation, cover Knausgaard's entire life, from early childhood to the present. Marked by a life-like intimacy and an extreme attention to detail, they feature a narrator named after the author who digresses into lengthy descriptions about everything from quotidian tasks to momentous and equally tragic life-changing events.

Among those events include the death of Knausgaard's father in 1998, which is the central focus of *My Struggle*'s Book One. In that volume, Knausgaard describes in shocking detail his and his brother's visit to their grandmother's house in scenic Kristiansand, Norway, where their father lived out his last days in drunken squalor. Finding not just heaps of empty bottles but also furniture and clothes sodden with urine and excrement, the brothers spend several painful days cleaning the house, during which they entertain their senile and seemingly alcoholic grandmother. It was this bravura section that prompted the most outrage from Knausgaard's family, particularly his father's younger brother Gunnar, who threatened legal action to stop the book's publication.

Throughout each of the books, Knausgaard, as part of his efforts to be wholly truthful, includes the real names and lives of numerous other close friends and family members, which caused further controversy. Notwithstanding this Faustian bargain, the books offer a full and unflinching self-portrait of the author. Book Two of *My Struggle* follows Knausgaard as he reaches middle age, honing in on his second marriage to the Swedish author Linda Boström; Book Three flashes back to his childhood and adolescence; Book Four focuses on his gap year as a school-teacher; Book Five chronicles the fourteen years he spent living in Bergen; and Book Six offers a look at the two years that spanned the publication of the *My Struggle* books in Norway, as well as a 400-plus-page meditation on Hitler's *Mein Kampf*, the book that inspired its title and provided another source of controversy.

REACHING A GLOBAL AUDIENCE

With *My Struggle*, Knausgaard quickly became a household name in Norway, which provided nonstop newspaper coverage of the volumes. Their popularity was such that they sold a half million copies in that country within the first years of their publication; it is estimated that one out of every ten Norwegians has read them. Many Norwegian companies, in fact, even began instituting "Knausgaard-free days" to temper discussion about *My Struggle* during work hours. Much of readers' obsession has been attributed to Knausgaard's fascinatingly minute descriptions and hyperrealistic evocations of the past, which earned him comparisons to Proust. "It was very shocking when I realized how people read it," Knausgaard explained to Liesl Schillinger. "I thought,

this is so private it's almost unreadable—but it worked the other way around."

Knausgaard first achieved global prominence in 2012, when the first volume of *My Struggle* appeared in English; it was published by Archipelago Books and translated by Don Bartlett. The other five volumes—also released by Archipelago and translated by Bartlett—were released in the United States yearly from 2014 through 2018. (The volumes have appeared with the respective subtitles: *A Death in the Family*, *A Man in Love*, *Boyhood Island*, *Dancing in the Dark*, *Some Rain Must Fall*, and *The End*.) Echoing the sentiment expressed by European-based reviewers like Rachel Cusk, American critics were effusive in their praise of the books. In his profile of Knausgaard, Hughes commented that reading *My Struggle* was "like opening someone else's diary and finding your own secrets." Meanwhile, in a review of Book Six for the *New York Times* (24 Sept. 2018), author Daniel Mendelsohn called Knausgaard's narration "weirdly addictive" and observed that the work blurs the boundaries between fiction and autobiography, with books that constitute "a kind of genre novel in which the author himself has become the genre."

Knausgaard also won admiration from many fellow writers, including the American novelist Jeffrey Eugenides, who credited him with breaking "the sound barrier of the autobiographical novel," as Hughes noted. *My Struggle* has since been translated into more than twenty languages and sold millions of copies, in addition to receiving many literary prizes. Commenting on the purpose of the complete work, Knausgaard explained to Schillinger, "The point of the book was not my life but what I made out of it in literature."

Although Knausgaard pledged to give up writing after completing *My Struggle*, he has remained active on the writing front, releasing, among others, four books named after the seasons. Labeled his Seasons Quartet series, the books are comprised of 240 essays on a wide range of topics, from objects like toilet seats and chewing gum to subjects like love and war; they were published in Norway from 2015 to 2016 and in the United States from 2017 to 2018. Knausgaard has additionally published several collections of essays.

PERSONAL LIFE

Knausgaard divides his time between London and Sweden. With Boström, whom he has since divorced, he has four children: Vanja, Heidi, John, and Anne. His three oldest children feature prominently in *My Struggle*, and Anne served as the inspiration behind his Seasons Quartet series.

Knausgaard is the cofounder of the Norwegian independent publishing house Pelikanen, which was established in 2010.

SUGGESTED READING

Cusk, Rachel. Review of *A Man in Love*, by Karl Ove Knausgaard. *The Guardian*, 12 Apr. 2013, www.theguardian.com/books/2013/apr/12/man-in-love-knausgaard-review. Accessed 18 Oct. 2018.

Hughes, Evan. "Karl Ove Knausgaard Became a Literary Sensation by Exposing His Every Secret." *New Republic*, 7 Apr. 2014, newrepublic.com/article/117245/karl-ove-knausgaard-interview-literary-star-struggles-regret. Accessed 18 Oct. 2018.

Knausgaard, Karl Ove. "After *My Struggle*: An Interview with Karl Ove Knausgaard." Interview by Ane Farsethas. *The Paris Review*, 15 Dec. 2015, www.theparisreview.org/blog/2015/12/15/after-my-struggle-an-interview-with-karl-ove-knausgaard/. Accessed 18 Oct. 2018.

———. "Karl Ove Knausgaard: All It Took Was One Person to Tell Me I Was Good Enough." *The Telegraph*, 12 Nov. 2016, www.telegraph.co.uk/books/authors/karl-ove-knausgaard-all-it-took-was-one-person-to-tell-me-i-was/. Accessed 18 Oct. 2018.

Mendelsohn, Daniel. "What's More Appealing: Eight Seasons of 'Suits' or Six Volumes of Karl Ove Knausgaard?" Review of *My Struggle: Book 6*, by Karl Ove Knausgaard. *The New York Times*, 24 Sept. 2018, www.nytimes.com/2018/09/24/books/review/karl-ove-knausgaard-my-struggle-book-six.html. Accessed 18 Oct. 2018.

Schillinger, Liesl. "Why Karl Ove Knausgaard Can't Stop Writing." *WSJ Magazine*, 4 Nov. 2015, www.wsj.com/articles/why-karl-ove-knausgaard-cant-stop-writing-1446688727?mod=e2tw. Accessed 18 Oct. 2018.

Wood, James. "Total Recall." *The New Yorker*, 13 Aug. 2012, www.newyorker.com/magazine/2012/08/13/total-recall. Accessed 18 Oct. 2018.

SELECTED WORKS

Ute av verden (*Out of the World*), 1998; *En tid for alt* (*A Time for Everything*), 2004; *Min kamp* (*My Struggle*), 2009–11; Seasons Quartet, 2015–16

—*Chris Cullen*

Virat Kohli

Date of birth: November 5, 1988
Occupation: Cricketer

Virat Kohli "always wanted to be a cricketer," he told Lokendra Pratap Sahi for the India *Telegraph* (7 Mar. 2011), adding, "I didn't have any back-up plans in case I couldn't become one." Luckily for Kohli—and for the teams on which he has played over the course of his career—no back-up plan was necessary. One of India's most accomplished and widely recognized batsmen, he has led domestic teams such as the Delhi first-class team and the Royal Challengers Bangalore of the Indian Premier League to numerous victories and contributed to India's success in international cricket competition. A member of India's winning 2011 Cricket World Cup squad, Kohli made his Test cricket debut with the national team in June of that year and went on to distinguish himself in Test play, becoming captain of the team in late 2014 and leading the team to extensive success in Test series abroad. In addition to his many accomplishments, Kohli—who was drawn to cricket as a child largely because of the Indian National Team and its fans—is particularly focused on the role he can play in promoting and ensuring the future success of his sport. "For me it's not about what I want to achieve as a cricketer, it's more to do with how I can inspire the next lot of players," he told Jo Harman for *Wisden* (24 Sept. 2018). "I feel that is more of a responsibility now, and not merely going on the park and hitting a ball."

Photo by NAPARAZZI via Wikimedia Commons

EARLY LIFE AND EDUCATION

Kohli was born on November 5, 1988, in Delhi, India. His father, Prem Nath, was a lawyer, and his mother, Saroj, was a homemaker. The youngest of three children, Kohli has an older brother and an older sister. Kohli began playing cricket at the age of five but did not initially display the talents that later made him one of India's best-known players; rather, he joked during a 2012 school visit that he "broke a lot of windows" during that period, as reported by Devadyuti Das for *Times of India* (25 Mar. 2012). By the time he was eight years old, however, he had become devoted to the sport as both a fan and a player and was particularly inspired by the Indian national cricket team and the team's passionate fans.

He began to pursue cricket more seriously with the encouragement of his parents. "My father was my biggest support," he recalled, as reported by Das. "He was the one who drove me to practice every day." During that period, Kohli trained under coach and former cricket player Rajkumar Sharma at the West Delhi Cricket Academy. Although Kohli enjoyed attending school as well and particularly enjoyed studying history and English, he began to attend school less often as his cricket career progressed, ultimately leaving to pursue professional play.

EARLY CAREER

In February 2006, Kohli made his debut in List A cricket, a short-format incarnation of the sport in which a game consists of only two innings. He went on to play his first first-class match, the highest level of domestic cricket competition, in November of that year. Competing for the Delhi cricket team throughout his domestic career, Kohli accompanied the team to the Ranji Trophy competition just a month after his debut and went on to help the team claim the trophy the following year. In April 2007, Kohli also began playing Twenty20 (T20) cricket, a relatively new form of the sport that resembles List A cricket in that each match consists of only two innings but differs from List A in the number of times the ball is allowed to be bowled.

The year 2008 was a particularly productive one for Kohli, who experienced international success as captain of India's national under-nineteen (U-19) team. The team competed in and won the U-19 World Cup in Malaysia. That year Kohli also joined the Royal Challengers Bangalore, a team that plays in the T20 Indian Premier League (IPL). A member of the team throughout the following decade, he became captain of the Royal Challengers in 2013. In addition to his domestic and U-19 international success in 2008, he made his one-day international (ODI) senior-level debut in August of that year. Kohli later achieved his first ODI century—a score of one hundred or more runs in an inning—in December 2009, in a game against Sri Lanka, and in June 2010 made his Twenty20 International (T20I) debut.

INDIAN NATIONAL TEAM

A frequent member of the Indian National Team's ODI squad since 2008, Kohli's strong performance as a batsman led him to be selected to compete for the national team's squad for the 2011 Cricket World Cup. Prior to that competition, India had not won the World Cup since 1983, and members of the national team's World Cup squad were set on claiming a victory for India. During the World Cup, India progressed through the early stages of competition before moving on to the knockout stage, where the team defeated Australia, Pakistan, and Sri Lanka to win the tournament. Although winning the World Cup was an important career milestone for Kohli, he noted that it was less meaningful for him than it was for others. "I didn't feel as emotional as other guys because it was my first World Cup. I saw the emotions in the eyes of the guys that hadn't won it for five World Cups," he said, as reported by Ankit Kumar Singh for the *Hindustan Times* (5 May 2018). "I didn't have any of those emotions. I pushed myself to like cry because everyone was crying." Kohli may have gained a greater understanding of such emotions in 2015, when he and the Indian National Team again competed in the World Cup but suffered a decisive loss to Australia in the semifinals.

Another major step in Kohli's career came later in 2011, when he made his Test cricket debut with the Indian National Team. Played only between national teams, Test cricket is both the longest and most prestigious cricket format and enables players to showcase their skills against the most talented representatives of rival countries. Kohli made his first appearance with the Test squad on June 20 of that year, playing in a three-day match against the West Indies team. Kohli scored nineteen runs during the match, which India ultimately won by sixty-three runs. He made his first Test century in January the following year, in a match against Australia.

CAPTAIN

As a member of the Indian National Team, Kohli particularly looked up to the team's captain, Mahendra Singh "MS" Dhoni. "He has allowed us to play our natural game, which has been encouraging," Kohli told Sahi of Dhoni's influence. "He has made us realize that even we have plenty of responsibility." In late 2014, however, Dhoni announced his retirement as Test captain, and Kohli, who had previously captained the national team's ODI squad at times, was selected to succeed his mentor in the position. Beginning in 2017, Kohli became T20I captain for the team as well, thus captaining for India in three formats of international cricket.

Over the years following Kohli's ascent to the position of Test captain, he remained a strong performer during matches in addition to fulfilling his leadership responsibilities, noting in interviews that he was not content to rest on his earlier accomplishments. "I walk out and I feel like I'm still a club cricketer playing my first match," he told Harman. "I still have to get that first run." With the national team, he competed in major events such as the 2016 International Cricket Council (ICC) World Twenty20, which was held in India for the first time in the competition's history. Although India was eliminated from the tournament during the semifinals, Kohli was named player of the tournament in recognition of his performance. The following year, he led the ODI squad to the ICC Champions Trophy tournament, in which India made it to the semifinals. In addition to playing Tests and ODI matches abroad throughout 2018 and early 2019, Kohli remained focused on the approaching 2019 Cricket World Cup, which represented an opportunity for India to become the world's cricket champion once again.

APPROACH TO CRICKET

Over the course of his professional cricket career, Kohli became known as an aggressive athlete whose style of play reflects that characteristic. Although he has admitted that his aggressive approach can be beneficial, he has noted that it is not something he has worked to cultivate. "Whatever I am, it's natural," he told Sahi. "I don't have to pretend to be aggressive, don't have to show the opposition that I am on the field. Being aggressive comes naturally to me, helps me perform." At times during the earlier years of his career, Kohli's attitude brought him into conflict with cricket leadership, including during a 2012 incident in which he made an obscene gesture toward heckling onlookers during a match in Australia. In the years after Kohli took on leadership positions with the Indian National Team, however, his public image mellowed somewhat, reflecting his increasing responsibilities and years of experience.

As Kohli developed further as a player, he also gained a greater understanding of the benefits of overall physical fitness and a strong routine on athletic performance. "I realized if you want to stay on top playing three formats in this day and age you need a routine," he told Michael Vaughan for the *Telegraph* (22 Nov. 2016). "You need a set pattern of your training, the way you eat, how healthy and fit you need to be. Being fitter made me mentally stronger. It was like a direct connection." He also told Vaughan that he wanted the national team under his leadership to be the "fittest Indian team that has played the game."

OTHER VENTURES

In addition to playing domestic and international cricket in multiple formats, Kohli is active in a variety of business ventures, including commercial sponsorships with companies such as the watch brand Tissot, the cellphone brand Jio, and the athletic wear company Adidas. While his cricket and business obligations have made his schedule a hectic one, he has noted that he enjoys his lifestyle. "It gives me a sense of working towards something all the time," he told Harman. "I don't feel the burden at all, to be honest. I love having the opportunity to be so busy in life." In addition to his existing business deals, Kohli had long expressed interest in entering the restaurant business and in 2017 became involved with the opening of a restaurant, Nueva, in New Delhi.

As one of India's most popular athletes, Kohli has become a celebrity both in India and abroad. In light of his widespread recognition, which includes a substantial social-media following, Kohli has sought to use his influence to promote the sport of cricket, particularly among children. "If I can inspire young boys in India to actually go out and play Test cricket and play for their country, that will make me very happy to know that I've done something for the society, I've done something for the sport, and I've made use of this time in my life," he told Eoin Connolly for *SportsPro* (27 May 2016).

PERSONAL LIFE

Kohli married actor and film producer Anushka Sharma in 2017. Although he acknowledges that his career and that of his wife necessitate a great deal of time in the public eye, he hopes to be able to keep his personal and professional lives separate. "I have a life. I have a family. I will have kids. They deserve all my time. That is something that is very, very clear and close to my heart," he told Wright Thompson for *ESPN* (22 May 2018). "I want no part of my career being flashed into my house. I want no part of my trophies, my achievements, nothing in my house when our kids are growing up." When not playing cricket elsewhere, Kohli lives in Delhi. He enjoys watching soccer and tennis in his free time and driving and traveling abroad with his wife.

SUGGESTED READING

Das, Devadyuti. "Superstar Virat Kohli Goes Back to School." *The Times of India*, 25 Mar. 2012, timesofindia.indiatimes.com/sports/ new-zealand-in-india-2016/top-stories/ Superstar-Virat-Kohli-goes-back-to-school/

articleshow/12397226.cms. Accessed 12 Mar. 2019.

Kohli, Virat. "Being Aggressive Comes Naturally: Virat Kohli—Young Turk Speaks about His Likes and Dislikes." Interview by Lokendra Pratap Sahi. *The Telegraph* [India], 7 Mar. 2011, www.telegraphindia.com/sport/being-aggressive-comes-naturally-virat-kohli-young-turk-speaks-about-his-likes-and-dislikes/cid/422139. Accessed 12 Mar. 2019.

Kohli, Virat. "Exclusive: Virat Kohli—'I Understand That Life Is Much Larger Than Any of This.'" Interview by Jo Harman. *Wisden*, 24 Sept. 2018, www.wisden.com/stories/interviews/virat-kohli-exclusive-interview. Accessed 12 Mar. 2019.

Kohli, Virat. "In the Middle—An Exclusive Interview with Virat Kohli." Interview by Eoin Connolly. *SportsPro*, 27 May 2016, www.sportspromedia.com/from-the-magazine/in_the_middle_an_exclusive_interview_with_virat_kohli. Accessed 12 Mar. 2019.

Singh, Ankit Kumar. "Virat Kohli Reveals His Lack of Emotion after 2011 World Cup Win—Watch Video." *Hindustan Times*, 5 May 2018, www.hindustantimes.com/cricket/virat-kohli-reveals-his-lack-of-emotion-after-2011-world-cup-win-watch-video/story-bqeZ-7KCvouPDkRb8EEdq5N.html. Accessed 12 Mar. 2019.

Thompson, Wright. "Keeping Up with Kohli." *ESPN*, 22 May 2018, www.espn.com/espn/feature/story/_/id/23531071/the-strange-life-india-cricket-god-virat-kohli. Accessed 12 Mar. 2019.

Vaughan, Michael. "Virat Kohli Interview: 'People Think I'm Superman'—Michael Vaughan Meets World Cricket's Biggest Star." *The Telegraph*, 22 Nov. 2016, www.telegraph.co.uk/cricket/2016/11/22/virat-kohli-interview-people-think-superman-michael-vaughan/. Accessed 12 Mar. 2019.

—*Joy Crelin*

Marie Kondo

Date of birth: October 9, 1984
Occupation: Consultant and author

So popular has Marie Kondo become since her first book, *The Life-Changing Magic of Tidying Up*, hit American bookstores in late 2014 that her name is being used as a verb: to Marie Kondo your home now means to engage in a massive project of cleaning and organizing, purging it of unneeded possessions and keeping only those things that "spark joy," in her parlance. The book, which Barry Yourgrau for the *New Yorker* (8 Dec.

2015) called "a tidy blend of confessional autobiography, life philosophy, decluttering strategies, and clothes-folding tips," has since sold more than 11 million copies in forty countries.

"Like any lifestyle guru, Kondo has rules," Molly Young wrote for *The Cut* (10 Feb. 2015). "T-shirts should be folded into taut packets, not floppy slabs. Kitchen sponges belong under the sink. Small change must not be left in piles throughout the house. (It is disrespectful.) The following items should be dumped without delay: credit-card statements, spare buttons, user manuals, makeup samples, mysterious cords." Despite the seeming severity of these guidelines, Kondo brings a tremendous amount of tenderness to the process, making it engaging and empowering rather than off-putting.

In a piece for the *Guardian* (30 Dec. 2018), Aaron Hicklin purported to understand the global appeal of the KonMari method, as it is officially known. (KonMari is a contraction of Kondo Mariko, as her name is rendered in Japan.) "Kondo has hitched tidying to the bandwagon of wellbeing," Hicklin wrote, "and is prone to saying things like: 'Putting your house in order is the magic that creates a vibrant and happy life.' And, 'To go throughout life without knowing how to fold is a huge loss.'" He added, "Making order from disorder feels like a balm for these turbulent times."

Kondo, who was named by *Time* magazine as one of the one hundred most influential people of 2015, now reaches an even wider audience through her hit Netflix show, *Tidying Up with Marie Kondo*, which debuted in early 2019. The series features Kondo descending on a different

family each episode to help them organize their possessions; as Christopher Harding wrote for the *New York Times* (18 Jan. 2019), however, she "is shown not just sprucing up people's homes but also reimagining them as sacred spaces." Kondo begins each session by quietly thanking the homes she enters for protecting their owners, and before discarding anything, she expresses gratitude for the item's service.

Kondo is adamant that her method is about much more than simply a clean physical space. "Basically, when you put your house in order, you put your affairs and your past in order, too," she wrote in *The Life-Changing Magic of Tidying Up*. "As a result, you can see quite clearly what you need in life and what you don't, and what you should and shouldn't do."

EARLY LIFE AND EDUCATION

Marie Kondo was born on October 9, 1984, in Tokyo, Japan. She has an older brother and a younger sister. Kondo has posited that her place in the middle of the birth order made her exceptionally eager to please her parents and to prove her independence to them. When she was in first grade, she began using an alarm clock to wake herself for school, where she surprised her teachers by staying inside to organize the classroom shelves, rather than going out to play at recess.

Happiest when engaged in solitary pursuits, she had begun paging through home and lifestyle magazines at the age of five, racing to the mailbox each month to get the family's copy of one such Japanese magazine, *ESSE*, and browsing food magazines at the local newsstand. Because her bedroom was small and lacked windows, she made a habit of clipping out nature photos that appealed to her and using them to decorate.

When she was about fifteen, Kondo came across a book called *The Art of Discarding*, by Nagisa Tatsumi. "I can still remember the shock of surprise I felt as I read it," she wrote in *The Life-Changing Magic of Tidying Up*. "I went straight to my room with a handful of garbage bags and stayed closeted for several hours. Although my room was small, by the time I finished I had eight bags full of stuff." After getting rid of clothes she never wore, old textbooks and toys, and a childhood collection of colorful erasers, she was astounded at how different the space looked. "My room seemed to have been transformed, and the air inside seemed so much fresher and brighter that even my mind felt clearer," she wrote. "Tidying, I realized, could have far more impact than I had ever imagined." At eighteen, Kondo got a part-time job at a Shinto shrine, where her duties included selling amulets to visitors and tidying up for the Shinto priest. She has acknowledged that the spiritual nature of her work is connected with her early job as a "shrine maiden," since those who practice Shintoism believe that inanimate objects contain a divine essence, or *kami*, in much the same way that people and animals are believed to.

Kondo attended Tokyo Woman's Christian University, where she ran a thriving sideline helping people tidy their homes. So immersed was she in the topic that her thesis was titled "How to Declutter Your Apartment—from a Sociological Perspective."

CONSULTANT AND AUTHOR

Within a short time after graduating, Kondo was running a tidying consultancy full time, with a six-month backlog of clients. Some of her wait-listed clients suggested she write a training guide so that they could begin the process on their own. When she came up with a book proposal, Tomohiro Takahashi, an editor at Sunmark, a Tokyo-based publisher of self-help and business books, was impressed. Over the course of eight months, he worked with her intensively on the book, which was published in Japan in 2010. Thanks, in part, to a savvy online marketing campaign, the volume sold well, and sales picked up even further after the devastating 2011 earthquake and tsunami in Japan, when many people were forced to redo their living spaces.

The Life-Changing Magic of Tidying Up became a best seller when it was published in the United States in 2014, and Kondo followed it up in 2015 with *Life-Changing Magic: A Journal—Spark Joy Every Day*, a journal that provided a space for users to reflect upon the meaning of the objects they owned, interspersed with quotes from her book. Her next book, *Spark Joy: An Illustrated Master Class on the Art of Organizing and Tidying Up*, was published in 2016 and had numerous illustrated instructions—including step-by-step guides to the KonMari method of folding clothing, an element of her work that has gained particular attention. Her most recent book is *The Life-Changing Manga of Tidying Up: A Magical Story*, published in 2017. This graphic novel tells the tale of Chiaki, a young woman in Tokyo who transforms her apartment and her life with Kondo's help. Collectively, according to the *KonMari* website, more than 10 million copies of the books have been sold around the globe.

The popularity of the books, perhaps unsurprisingly, sparked something of a backlash. "Since the English translation of *Tidying Up* hit shelves last fall, there has been no way to avoid the exuberant exhortations of Kondo acolytes at every brunch, happy hour, and dinner party; on Twitter, Instagram, and your college roommate's Facebook wall; at baby showers, bridal showers, and Mother's Day teas," Maureen O'Connor observed for *The Cut* (21 May 2015). "The 'KonMari method' for cleanliness is the new juice fast, the new Soul-Cycle, the new organic food. Which is to say: It is a method for self-improvement that inspires cultlike evangelism."

TIDYING UP WITH MARIE KONDO

Netflix premiered *Tidying Up with Marie Kondo* on January 1, 2019, cannily timing the debut for a day known for resolutions and self-improvement campaigns. The show has performed solidly with viewers, although critics are split between those who find it charming and addictive and those for whom it is too precious or unrealistic. Writing for the *Atlantic* (4 Jan. 2019), Sarah Archer was in the former camp: "Kondo's effect on people is transformative, and that's because her attitude is rooted in empathy rather than in judgment or in a prescriptive approach to outward appearances." She noted that *Tidying Up* is different from many other reality shows: "There's no sense of competition, and the ostensible makeover at the heart of every episode simply involves regular people becoming happier and more at ease in their own home. Kondo doesn't scold, shame, or criticize. Things spark joy or they don't, and it's fine either way." By contrast, in a review for the *Guardian* (4 Jan. 2019), Jack Seale opined, "Maybe Kondo should have laid out every scene in an editing suite and, after the necessary thank yous, carefully considered which ones sparked joy. The bulk of them would have gone in the bin."

PERSONAL LIFE

Kondo has been married to her husband, Takumi Kawahara, since 2012. When they met, he was working in sales and marketing; and when her brand took off, he left his corporate job to manage her career. He is now the CEO of Konmari Media, LLC. He also oversees her thriving social media accounts: she has over 3 million followers on Instagram.

Kondo and Kawahara have two young daughters, Satsuki and Miko, who already try to emulate her style of folding laundry. Kondo has admitted to journalists that it is hard to rigidly organize a playroom when your children are toddlers.

Yourgrau described Kondo as being "possessed of a winsomely deferential and yet authoritative air." On television, she most often wears white, because of the cleanliness it evokes, and she has also expressed fondness for light pink clothing with feminine detailing. Asked to name items that spark joy in her, she mentions an antique writing desk, a crystal she keeps in her bedroom, and an earthenware pot for cooking rice.

SUGGESTED READING

Archer, Sarah. "*Tidying Up with Marie Kondo* Isn't Really a Makeover Show." *The Atlantic*, 4 Jan. 2019, www.theatlantic.com/entertainment/archive/2019/01/tidying-up-with-marie-kondo-netflix-show-kon-mari-review/579400/. Accessed 22 May 2019.

Harding, Christopher. "Marie Kondo and the Life-Changing Magic of Japanese Soft Power." *The New York Times*, 18 Jan. 2019, www.nytimes.com/2019/01/18/opinion/marie-kondo-japan.html. Accessed 22 May 2019.

Hicklin, Aaron. "Don't Mess with Marie: Tidying Up with Author and Netflix Star Marie Kondo." *The Guardian*, 30 Dec. 2018, www.theguardian.com/global/2018/dec/30/dont-mess-with-marie-tidying-up-with-author-netflix-star-marie-kondo. Accessed 22 May 2019.

O'Connor, Maureen. "De-Cluttering Is the New Juice Cleanse (and Equally Annoying)."*The Cut*, 21 May 2015, www.thecut.com/2015/05/de-cluttering-is-the-new-juice-cleanse-annoying.html. Accessed 22 May 2019.

Seale, Jack. "*Tidying Up with Marie Kondo* Review—TV Destined for the Bin Bag of Shame." *The Guardian*, 4 Jan. 2019, www.theguardian.com/tv-and-radio/2019/jan/04/tidying-up-with-marie-kondo-review-tv-destined-for-the-bin-bag-of-shame. Accessed 22 May 2019.

Young, Molly. "Marie Kondo Will Change Your Life." *The Cut*, 10 Feb. 2015, www.thecut.com/2015/02/marie-kondo-room-purge.html. Accessed 22 May 2019.

Yourgrau, Barry. "The Origin Story of Marie Kondo's Decluttering Empire." *The New Yorker*, 8 Dec. 2015, www.newyorker.com/books/page-turner/the-origin-story-of-marie-kondos-decluttering-empire. Accessed 22 May 2019.

—*Mari Rich*

Jarrett J. Krosoczka

Date of birth: December 22, 1977
Occupation: Author and illustrator

Author and illustrator Jarrett J. Krosoczka has published more than thirty books since getting his start as a picture book author in 2001. His books have topped multiple New York Times Best-Sellers lists and have earned him a host of accolades from readers, librarians, and schools. His work enabled him to give two highly regarded TED Talks, which had together accrued more than two million online views by mid-2019. In addition to crafting delightful picture books such as *Punk Farm* (2005), he is also known for being the author and illustrator of the Lunch Lady

Photo by fourandsixty via Wikimedia Commons

and the Star Wars Jedi Academy graphic novel series and the Platypus Police Squad middle-grade novels.

In 2018 he penned and illustrated *Hey, Kiddo: How I Lost My Mother, Found My Father, and Dealt with Family Addiction*, a graphic memoir about his childhood experiences with a mother who was addicted to opioids. In interviews he has often described how humbled and grateful he is that he has had the opportunity to do such a wide variety of work in his career. Krosoczka told Sara Grochowski for *Publishers Weekly* (20 July 2018): "My favorite thing about all of this is that babies who read *Good Night, Monkey Boy* in 2001 were early elementary and preschool age when *Punk Farm* was published, and then they were around third grade when *Lunch Lady* was published. Now all those kids are in their middle to late teens. It's so cool. A lot of those families I still see at events."

EARLY LIFE AND EDUCATION

Jarrett J. Krosoczka was born on December 22, 1977, in Worcester, Massachusetts. He was raised by his maternal grandparents, Joseph and Shirley Krosoczka, because his mother had a substance abuse problem and was often in jail. Because of this, he saw his mother only occasionally but often exchanged letters and drawings with her. He did not meet his father until he was seventeen, at which point he also discovered he had two half siblings.

Krosoczka's drawing was inspired by his love of comic books and Saturday-morning cartoons. His grandfather encouraged his artistic talents, often by drawing alongside him. In sixth grade,

the funding for the art program in Krosoczka's school was cut. His grandparents responded by signing him up for classes at the Worcester Art Museum. This encouragement—along with a high school class on picture book art and story writing—inspired him to study illustration at the Rhode Island School of Design in Providence after high school.

While in college, Krosoczka spent his summers working as a camp counselor at the Hole in the Wall Gang Camp in Ashford, Connecticut, which serves children with disabilities and serious medical conditions. The experience changed the way he approached drawing. Prior to working at the camp his drawings had, as he explained to Steve Pfarrer for the *Daily Hampshire Gazette* (5 Feb. 2012), "mostly been violent monsters with knives and blood—typical teenage angst material. Seeing the things that these kids contended with changed my thinking."

Upon his college graduation in 1999, Krosoczka found a part-time job teaching at a community art center in Boston and began making submissions to publishing houses. He received a number of rejections before a fellow graduate suggested he submit his work to the editors directly.

PICTURE BOOKS AND GRAPHIC NOVELS

Krosoczka's first success came with an editor at Random House, who asked him to come to New York to show off his illustrations. The editor soon signed Krosoczka to a contract with the company's children's book imprint, Alfred A. Knopf Books for Young Readers. In 2001, when he was twenty-three, his first picture book, *Good Night, Monkey Boy*, was published. *Good Night, Monkey Boy* and Krosoczka's other early picture books—including *Baghead* (2002), *Bubble Bath Pirates!* (2003), *Punk Farm* (2005), *Giddy Up, Cowgirl* (2006), *My Buddy, Slug* (2006), and *Punk Farm on Tour* (2007)—were met with critical and commercial acclaim. *Punk Farm*, a picture book about rock band animals, won the 2005 Child Magazine Best Books of the Year Award and the 2007 Abilene ISD Mockingbird Award. The popularity of his picture books enabled him to visit schools and libraries to discuss his books with children.

During one such visit, to his former elementary school in 2001, Krosoczka was inspired by the school's longtime lunch lady, Jean Cargilia, to create his superhero graphic novel series. Cargilia told him all about her family and life outside of work. "I was like, 'Wait a minute, you leave the cafeteria? You have a life outside this?'" Krosoczka recalled to Pfarrer in 2012. "Even at twenty-three, I'd never thought of that. I had this sudden vision of her as this matriarch of a large family, instead of just this woman who'd been serving food in the school cafeteria when I was seven years old." Cargilia became the model for Lunch Lady, a school cafeteria worker who is secretly a crime-fighting hero. The series began in 2009 with *Lunch Lady and the Cyborg Substitute*, and by 2014, there were ten graphic novels in the series, including *Lunch Lady and the Author Visit Vendetta* (2009), *Lunch Lady and the Field Trip Fiasco* (2011), and *Lunch Lady and the Schoolwide Scuffle* (2014). The series has earned a number of recognitions, including the 2010 Children's Choice Book Award for Third Grade to Fourth Grade Book of the Year, a 2012 Charlotte Award nomination for *Lunch Lady and the Cyborg Substitute*, and the 2011 Children's Choice Book Award for *Lunch Lady and the Summer Camp Shakedown* (2010).

PLATYPUS POLICE AND JEDI ACADEMY

Krosoczka's next series was also conceived through a school visit. During a promotional tour for *Punk Farm*, he was inspired by a child's reaction to the book's illustrations to write a series about animals that are also police officers. Initially, he imagined the animals to be a Penguins Police Squad, but his editor soon nixed that idea as the market was already inundated with books about penguins. About his process to find another, less often used animal, Krosoczka told Steve Pfarrer for the *Daily Hampshire Gazette* (20 May 2015), "I basically went through the alphabet to find another animal that started with 'P.' And since platypuses are such strange animals, I thought kids would really like it, plus they'd also be fun to draw." The ensuing middle-grade chapter book series, the Platypus Police Squad series, followed a grizzled police veteran and his rookie partner. The first book in the series, *Platypus Police Squad: The Frog Who Croaked*, was published in 2013. He followed with three more illustrated chapter books—*Platypus Police Squad: The Ostrich Conspiracy* (2014), *Platypus Police Squad: Last Panda Standing* (2015), and *Platypus Police Squad: Never Say Narwhal* (2016)—all of which were met with considerable acclaim.

In 2016 Krosoczka took over the Star Wars: Jedi Academy series from its creator, Jeffrey Brown. Focusing on a new class of young students who are learning the ways of the force under Jedi master Yoda, Krosoczka wrote and illustrated four graphic novels for the series by 2019: *A New Class* (2016), *The Force Oversleeps* (2017), *The Principal Strikes Back* (2018), and *Revenge of the Sis* (2019).

As a critically acclaimed children's book author, Krosoczka has been honored numerous times throughout his career for his work. In 2003 he was named one of Print Magazine's Top Twenty New Visual Artists Under Thirty; he was a finalist for the 2010 Will Eisner Comic Industry Award; and a number of his books have made the recommended list in the Junior Library Guild Selection (2005, 2009, 2011–14).

CREATING HIS MEMOIR

Krosoczka published his graphic memoir, *Hey, Kiddo*, in 2018, after spending many years deliberating how to best write about his childhood experiences and, in particular, the difficult relationship he had with his mother because of her addictions. He had previously discussed her in his 2013 TED Talk "How a Boy Became an Artist"; however, he struggled with writing about her influence on his life. "Every time I sat down to write it, I hesitated, because I feared what people would think about what I was writing," Krosoczka told Grochowski. "I realized that I wasn't emotionally ready; if you're going to truly write a memoir, you can't cherry-pick memories and events to pacify those in your life. Everything was still very black-and-white to me then: there were heroes and villains of my life story."

Krosoczka forged a better relationship with his mother after his grandmother and grandfather died, in 2007 and 2010, respectively. The shift in their relationship as adults, and Krosoczka's own experiences as a parent, helped him eventually write about his childhood experiences. As he explained to Grochowski, "When you get older and become a parent, your perspective shifts; you start thinking about the people who came before you and what made them the way they are. Because time passed, I was able to write my mother's character in a much more nuanced and sympathetic way." Although she had been recovering from her addictions, Krosoczka's mother later relapsed and died in March 2017, while he was writing the script that would serve as the basis for *Hey, Kiddo*. The book provided an overview of his childhood with and without his mother, as well as the positive influences his grandparents had on his life.

During the writing process, Krosoczka had to decide what events to cover in the memoir, which was aimed at middle-grade readers. He decided to be as honest as he could be. "I didn't pull any punches because of one simple realization: There are difficult truths in our books because there are difficult truths in children's lives," Krosoczka wrote in an article for the *Washington Post* (26 Oct. 2018). "For me to write this harrowing tale of my upbringing, I needed to write openly and authentically so young people dealing with similar situations would feel less alone." *Hey, Kiddo* won the 2018 Cybils Award for Young Adult Graphic Novels and was a finalist for the 2018 National Book Award for Young People's Literature.

PERSONAL LIFE

Krosoczka and his wife, Gina, live in western Massachusetts with their three children and two pugs, Ralph and Frank.

In 2010, Krosoczka founded the Joseph and Shirley Krosoczka Memorial Youth Scholarships. Named after his grandparents, the scholarship funds art classes for underprivileged children in Worcester, where he grew up. He also helped establish School Lunch Hero Day, an annual celebration of the people who work in school lunchrooms across the country, and the Platypus Police Reading Squad, a program that asks police officers to read to children in libraries and schools.

SUGGESTED READING

"Biography." *StudioJJK*, www.studiojjk.com/biography2.html. Accessed 17 May 2019.

Grochowski, Sara. "A New Direction for Jarrett J. Krosoczka." *Publishers Weekly*, 20 July 2018, www.publishersweekly.com/pw/by-topic/childrens/childrens-authors/article/77565-a-new-direction-for-jarrett-j-krosoczka.html. Accessed 21 May 2019.

Krosoczka, Jarrett J. "What's Appropriate for Kids to Read? There's Value in Exposing Them to the Tough Stuff." *The Washington Post*, 26 Oct. 2018, www.washingtonpost.com/entertainment/books/whats-appropriate-for-kids-to-read-theres-value-in-exposing-them-to-the-tough-stuff/2018/10/25/148f0b80-d7b9-11e8-83a2-d1c3da28d6b6_story.html. Accessed 21 May 2019.

Pfarrer, Steve. "Mass. Children's Writer Flourishes after Setbacks." *Daily Hampshire Gazette*, 5 Feb. 2012. *Boston.com*, archive.boston.com/news/local/massachusetts/articles/2012/02/05/mass_childrens_writer_flourishes_after_setbacks. Accessed 21 May 2019.

Pfarrer, Steve. "Webbed Feet, Bills and Boomerangs Jarrett Krosoczka Unveils His Newest 'Platypus Police Squad' Book." *Daily Hampshire Gazette*, 20 May 2015, www.gazettenet.com/Archives/2015/05/Jarrett-hg-050715. Accessed 21 May 2019.

SELECTED WORKS

Good Night, Monkey Boy, 2001; *Punk Farm*, 2005; *Punk Farm on Tour*, 2007; Lunch Lady series, 2009–14; Platypus Police Squad series, 2013–16; Star Wars: Jedi Academy series, 2016– ; *Hey, Kiddo*, 2018

—Christopher Mari

KuroKy (Kuro Takhasomi)

Date of birth: October 28, 1992
Occupation: Professional esports player

Kuro Salehi Takhasomi, better known as KuroKy, became the highest-earning esports player in history in 2017 when his team won The International (TI), the largest and most prestigious annual tournament of the video game *Dota 2*. KuroKy specialized in *Dota 2*, a popular multiplayer online battle arena (MOBA) game, from its inception in 2011 and became one of only three players to appear in each of the first seven TIs. He competed with a variety of teams and found much success but was only able to capture the game's most coveted championship after personally forming Team Liquid in 2015. He served as the team's leader through various difficulties on the way to the record-setting TI7 victory. He also continued to set individual records, for example in 2018 becoming the first *Dota 2* player to reach one thousand professional wins and the first to play as each of the game's more than 115 playable characters, or heroes, in pro competition. Yet, as he explained in an essay for the *Players' Tribune* (8 Sept. 2018), "If there's one thing I've learned over the course of my *Dota 2* career, it's that there's nothing more important than good teamwork."

EARLY LIFE AND ESPORTS BEGINNINGS

KuroKy was born Kuro Salehi Takhasomi in Iran on October 28, 1992, but grew up in Berlin, Germany. His father worked as a cab driver. His mother did not work due to chronic illness. The family, which included a brother, did not have much money. When KuroKy later began earning money in esports, he gave much of his earnings to his parents. "I always wanted to give something back," he told Christian Baltes for the gaming website *joinDOTA* (18 Sept. 2013). "I can finally buy them some freedom."

As a child, KuroKy had a disability that made it difficult for him to walk. This led him to turn to video games, to which he soon became dedicated. His family got a computer when he was ten, further expanding his interest in gaming. Eventually he discovered the game *Warcraft III: Reign of Chaos* (2002) and then the related *Defense of the Ancients*, or *DotA*, a modification of *Warcraft*. Adopting the alias KuroKy, he quickly proved himself skilled in the complex gameplay of *DotA*, in which two teams of players compete to destroy the opponent's base.

Meanwhile the rising popularity of *DotA* and similar video games was giving rise to professional competition, a phenomenon that became known as electronic sports or esports. KuroKy was initially part of various German clubs that did not achieve true professional

Photo by Jeff Vinnick/Getty Images

status. He then joined the international team mousesports in 2008, when he was just sixteen. He made a splash right away, excelling in multiple roles in *DotA* including as a "carry," or a hero who carries the team to victory as the game draws to a close. He was named Carry of the Year at the GosuGamers Awards in 2008.

SUCCESS AND CONTROVERSY

As KuroKy established himself as a *DotA* star he formed close relationships with several fellow players. The most important of these was Estonian player Puppey, a.k.a. Clement Ivanov, whom he first met when Puppey played as a stand-in with mousesports in late 2008. Ray Ian Ampoloquio, writing for *Esports Ranks* (12 Feb. 2018), echoed a common refrain in describing Puppey as "the one player who arguably had the biggest impact on KuroKy and his career." The two clicked, and for the next two years played for several teams together, including Kingsurf.

However, in 2011 Puppey left to join the Ukrainian team Natus Vincere, more commonly known as Na'Vi. Frustrated with the state of esports, KuroKy considered quitting the game altogether. Ultimately he was convinced to remain as leader of his team, and he doubled down on his drive to be the best in the field. Also in 2011 *Dota* 2 was first released, giving KuroKy a new platform on which to compete. He participated in the first TI, held that same year, but his team was quickly eliminated.

For some time KuroKy struggled, moving between various teams and earning little. Then, in 2013, he joined Puppey on Na'Vi. The move signaled a professional milestone for KuroKy,

who changed roles to fit in on his new team and soon found considerable success. Na'Vi had already been considered the top *DotA* 2 team in the West, but with KuroKy they played even better and won many tournaments. They were significant favorites in TI3, but finished in second place.

After Na'Vi was disappointingly eliminated early in TI4, KuroKy left the team to found Team Secret with Puppey. The two recruited other top stars for what was supposed to be an organization owned by the players themselves. Team Secret compiled such a formidable roster, that many in the gaming world were "ready to give them the title of champions already before the start of TI5," as Ampoloquio wrote. The team won an unprecedented four straight LAN (Local Area Network) events leading up to TI5.

In his article for the *Players' Tribune*, KuroKy noted the intense pressure at TI matches, likening it to playing multiple Super Bowls. "The competition never lets up and you have thousands watching your every move in a packed arena and millions more streaming the action around the globe," he wrote. At TI5 the pressure seemed to catch up with him. Despite their star-studded roster, Team Secret ultimately and infamously "flamed out at the main event," as Stephen Chiu put it for *Slingshot Esports* (14 Aug. 2017). Just why the team lost was a source of controversy, with many fans blaming KuroKy. Observers noted that teammate Artour "Arteezy" Babaev appeared to be shouting at KuroKy as they played. Team Secret began to fracture following the TI5 loss, and the remainder of the season found Arteezy and KuroKy airing their grievances with one another online.

FORMING TEAM LIQUID

As Team Secret fell apart, KuroKy left to found his own team in 2015. He handpicked his teammates, most of them relative unknowns at the time, including key players Lasse "MATUMBAMAN" Urpalainen and Ivan Borislavov "MinD_ContRoL" Ivanov. The ultimate roster was built on a totally different philosophy than the veteran-oriented Team Secret. Chiu described KuroKy's plan: "Instead of picking established all stars to fill the roles and the swapping them whenever their form or the meta [currently-held wisdom about the best way to play the game] changed, he decided this would be his five-person squad for the entire year." Originally called 5jungz, the team was quickly signed by the esports organization Team Liquid. Joining the established brand brought coaches, a manager, a support staff and intensive boot camps to improve team chemistry.

Training ramped up in preparation for TI6, but Team Liquid made a poor showing and was eliminated early in the tournament. Following that disappointment, two members, Adrian "FATA" Trinks and Jesse "JerAx" Vainikka, left the team. They were replaced by Amer "Miracle-" al-Barkawi and Kanishka "BuLba" Sosale. The latter departed a few months later and his spot was filled by Maroun "GH" Merhej. As before, KuroKy prioritized team chemistry and fit when selecting his fellow players. "Because everyone at this level has tremendous skill, that's ultimately a relatively small part of the equation when it comes to success," he noted for the *Players' Tribune*. "What really separates the winners and losers isn't about how you handle yourself personally, but rather how you coexist with your teammates."

With its new lineup Team Liquid once again rose through the ranks of professional *Dota 2* competition. They made a strong showing in June 2017, defeating rival team Evil Geniuses to win the EPICENTER 2017 tournament. By TI7 in August, they were considered strong contenders for the title.

THE INTERNATIONAL 2017 AND BEYOND

According to KuroKy, he was confident entering TI7. Team Liquid entered the knockout round as favorites—but then promptly lost their first bracket game to Invictus Gaming. They still had a chance due to the tournament's double elimination structure, but the loss meant that the team was relegated to the loser's bracket. KuroKy and his teammates needed to win six matches in a row for a shot at winning the whole competition.

KuroKy detailed the events of the tournament in his *Players' Tribune* piece. "Our nerves got to us. The International is what we all play for. Every *Dota 2* player, no matter where they are in their career, dreams of winning this tournament," he wrote. "That fixation can sometimes be too much to bear when you finally get here." He noted that his teammates, especially the less experienced ones, seemed unfocused and nervous. Going against his usual taciturn nature, he gave a heated speech backstage to rally the team and loosen their spirits. As he wrote, "The one thing I kept saying was 'Don't think about winning! Just focus on performing well.' Because if you can do that, everything else will fall into place naturally."

Team Liquid then faced off against Team Secret. They lost the first game of the match, but after KuroKy delivered another energizing pep talk in the bathroom, they held on to win and move to the next round. From that point on, the team began to gel. They ultimately faced a Chinese team called Newbee in the Grand Finals. Team Liquid won three games to zero, marking the first time a TI tournament ended in a sweep. The winners earned $10 million of the total $24 million pool—the largest pool in esports history

to that point. KuroKy's cut was $2.1 million, which with his other earnings over the years made him the top-earning esports player ever.

With the TI7 victory KuroKy had achieved the longstanding goal of his career. However, the accomplishment was in some ways unsettling for the veteran gamer. "It was the greatest achievement of all of our careers," he wrote for the *Players' Tribune*. "But I guess that's also the reason I felt strange. Winning The International took away my one motivating factor." Ultimately, he vowed to win the tournament again.

That new goal quickly proved easier said than done. At TI8 Team Liquid was relegated to the loser's bracket once again before finishing in fourth place. KuroKy was open about the challenges facing the team as opponents became familiar with their style. "We are an 'old' team, that's the main problem," he said in a video interview with RuHub Media (7 May 2019). "Sometimes you either make a change and get some fresh blood, or you try to fix your problems. It's like being in a relationship and it takes time, it can take a long time. Right now we are in a stage where we want to play together, we like each other, and we just have to go through the struggles."

SUGGESTED READING

Ampoloquio, Ray Ian. "The First to a Thousand Wins: The Legend of KuroKy." *Esportsranks*, 12 Feb. 2018, esportsranks.com/first-thousand-wins-legend-kuroky/. Accessed 14 May 2019.

Carpenter, Nicole. "Dota 2 Pro KuroKy Has Played All 116 Heroes in Competitive Matches." *Dot Esports*, 30 Nov. 2018, dotesports.com/dota-2/news/dota-2-pro-kuroky-has-played-all-116-heroes-in-competitive-matches. Accessed 15 May 2019.

Chiu, Stephen. "Liquid's Arduous Journey to the Aegis Started at TI5." *Slingshot*, 14 Aug. 2017, slingshotesports.com/2017/08/14/team-liquid-arduous-journey-aegis-ti5/. Accessed 14 May 2019.

KuroKy. "KuroKy: 'Even My Dad Likes Mushi!'" Interview by Christian Baltes. *JoinDOTA*, 18 Sept. 2013, www.joindota.com/en/news/12215-kuroky-even-my-dad-likes-mushi. Accessed 14 May 2019.

KuroKy. "What We All Play For." *The Players' Tribune*, 8 Sept. 2017, www.theplayerstribune.com/en-us/articles/kuroky-dota2-the-international. Accessed 14 May 2019. Accessed 24 May 2019.

Liquid.KuroKy: 'I Want to Win 3 TIs' @ Interview with KuroKy." *YouTube*, uploaded by RuHub Media, 7 May 2019, www.youtube.com/watch?v=WmvkpXCe3Pk.

Van Allen, Eric. "Road to TI6: Team Liquid." *ESPN*, 3 Aug. 2016, www.espn.com/esports/

story/_/id/17210172/team-liquid.   Accessed 14 May 2019.

—*Molly Hagan*

Jocelyne Lamoureux-Davidson

Date of birth: July 3, 1989
Occupation: Hockey player

When Jocelyne Lamoureux-Davidson stepped onto the ice in the gold-medal women's ice hockey game at the 2018 Winter Olympics in PyeongChang, South Korea, she was deeply aware of the significance of the impending competition. The US women's team had not won a gold medal since the sport's Olympic debut in 1998; their opponent, Canada, had taken the gold four times in a row. The 2018 matchup, then, represented something that Lamoureux-Davidson and her teammates—who included her identical twin sister and perennial teammate, Monique Lamoureux-Morando—had long been hoping for: an opportunity to end Canada's dominance in their sport and demonstrate the skill and potential of women's ice hockey players in the United States. The team's motivation and preparation paid off, especially for Lamoureux-Davidson. After the game tied and went into overtime, she scored the decisive goal in the shootout, helping to lead Team USA to victory and earning her first Olympic gold medal.

A lifelong hockey player, Lamoureux-Davidson was raised in a family that was heavily immersed in the sport. Her skill on local and school teams led to her debut with the US national team as a teenager, and she made her first Olympic appearance in 2010. Along with her competitive play, Lamoureux-Davidson worked extensively to secure greater support for female hockey players and promote the sport, often in conjunction with Lamoureux-Morando. "What we strive [for] is to make USA Hockey a better place, to make the US national team and the program better," she told Mika Brzezinski in an interview for NBC News's *Know Your Value* (18 June 2018). "But outside of that, [it's] having a positive impact and using this platform that we're fortunate to have to impact so many more people beyond hockey."

EARLY LIFE AND EDUCATION

Jocelyne Lamoureux-Davidson was born Jocelyne Nicole Lamoureux on July 3, 1989, in Grand Forks, North Dakota. She and Lamoureux-Morando were the youngest children born to Jean-Pierre and Linda Lamoureux, who also had four sons. Jean-Pierre—typically referred to simply as Pierre—was a Canadian-born former hockey player for the University of North Dakota, while

Photo by Sara Melikian via Wikimedia Commons

Linda was a high school state champion swimmer who later became an avid marathon runner. Considering Pierre and Linda's backgrounds, athletic activities were a constant feature of life in the Lamoureux household, chief among them hockey.

Much like her siblings, Lamoureux-Davidson began to learn the fundamentals of the sport at a young age, learning to ice skate as a toddler and beginning to play hockey itself at the age of four. The family benefited from a nearby stream that had an area appropriate for skating on during the winters, which enabled the Lamoureux children to practice their skills more regularly than many other young players. In addition to hockey, Lamoureux-Davidson and Lamoureux-Morando played musical instruments, studied dance, and participated in sports such as gymnastics, track, soccer, swimming, and martial arts.

The Lamoureux sisters began playing organized hockey as children, joining boys' teams in Grand Forks. "We've always been together, always on the same team," she told Corey Seymour for *Vogue* (7 Mar. 2018). "We're super competitive with each other." The twins both earned high school scholarships to Shattuck-St. Mary's School, a private institution in Minnesota known for its hockey program. During her time at Shattuck-St. Mary's, Lamoureux-Davidson helped the school's women's hockey team win three national championships. She was named the school's best all-around athlete during her final year.

TEAM USA

Thanks to her exceptional hockey talents, Lamoureux-Davidson earned the attention of the US women's national team while still in high school. She and her sister first represented the United States in international competition as teenagers in 2006 at the Four Nations Cup, which brings together teams from the United States, Canada, Finland, and Sweden. The team came in second place that year, and Lamoureux-Davidson went on to several further appearances in the tournament, including first-place finishes in 2008, 2011, 2012, 2015, 2016, and 2017. She also played in the International Ice Hockey Federation (IIHF) Women's World Championships beginning in 2009. The US team claimed the gold medal in her championship debut, and Lamoureux-Davidson went on to contribute to the team's victories in 2011, 2013, 2015, 2016, and 2017 as well.

Beyond annual international competitions and championships, Lamoureux-Davidson was particularly focused on competing in the Winter Olympics, which she hoped to do alongside Lamoureux-Morando. "We train and do everything together. If one of us gets cut, it would be very tough." she explained to Mike Chambers for the *Denver Post* (12 Dec. 2009) during preparations for the 2010 Olympics. Both sisters did ultimately make the US Olympic team, and they traveled to Vancouver, British Columbia, for the high-profile competition. After moving through the early rounds, the team beat Sweden in the semifinal to set up the gold-medal game against Canada, the two-time defending Olympic champion. Despite their best efforts, the US women lost to Canada 2–0 and settled for silver medal.

The Lamoureux sisters returned for the 2014 Olympics, held in Sochi, Russia. Once again, the US team faced Canada in the final. The game initially appeared promising for the US team, which was winning by two goals until less than four minutes to play. However, Canada rallied to tie in the final seconds and ultimately won 3–2 in overtime. Despite earning the silver medal, the loss was painful for the US players, including Lamoureux-Davidson. "Inches from the gold medal, I guess," she told Wayne Drehs for *ESPNW* (20 Feb. 2014) after the game. "It only comes around once every four years. It just sucks."

COLLEGE HOCKEY

After graduating from high school in 2008, the Lamoureux sisters enrolled in the University of Minnesota, where they played for the university's Gophers women's hockey team. During her freshman season Lamoureux-Davidson amassed impressive statistics, ranking eleventh nationally in points per game, fifteenth in goals, and ninth in assists. She was nominated for the Patty Kazmaier Memorial Award, given to the United States' best female college ice hockey player, and was named to the All-WCHA (Western Collegiate Hockey Association) first team.

Following their freshman year of college, the Lamoureux sisters transferred to the University of North Dakota (UND). They did not play for the UND Fighting Sioux—renamed the Fighting Hawks in 2015—during their first year at the school, instead focusing on training for the 2010 Winter Olympics. Lamoureux-Davidson joined the college team for the 2010–11 season and remained through 2012–13, serving as a captain each year and setting team records in points, goals, and assists in a season. She was the recipient of numerous honors during her time at UND, including in 2012 when she became the first female UND hockey player to receive Academic All-America recognition, and finished as the WCHA's all-time points leader. Also successful in the classroom, she earned her bachelor's degree in physical education in 2013. She later began graduate studies in kinesiology.

In the years following her graduation, Lamoureux-Davidson found work as an athletic coach, including the women's hockey program at UND. In 2017, however, the university abruptly eliminated that program as part of an effort to cut expenses. The decision angered many of UND's current and former players, including Lamoureux-Davidson. "I understand that it's a business, and the NCAA is a business. But there was a way to make it work, and I don't think any solutions were tried," she told Seymour. "When you have one of the most prevalent men's college hockey programs in the country and a women's team of this caliber and literally the best facilities in the world . . . you should be offering a women's program as well."

FIGHTING GENDER INEQUITY IN HOCKEY

In addition to her work on the ice, Lamoureux-Davidson has been active in addressing issues of gender inequity in hockey, particularly regarding player pay and support. She and her teammates on the US women's hockey team organized in an attempt to reach an agreement with USA Hockey that would grant female hockey players the same benefits as their male counterparts, going so far as to threaten to boycott the 2017 world championships if their concerns were not addressed. The players' actions received widespread support, including from male hockey players, members of other professional sports leagues, and various politicians. The team ultimately came to an agreement with USA Hockey in early 2017. For Lamoureux-Davidson, the effort reinforced the importance of continually challenging inequality when it arises. "What our team went through taught us that doing what's right is not always easy, and the status quo is not always right," she told Seymour. "Our team firmly believes in giving young girls and women the same opportunities as boys."

In a related effort, Lamoureux-Davidson supported the movement to create one unified North American league for women's professional hockey, which was split between the National Women's Hockey League (NWHL) and the Canadian Women's Hockey League (CWHL). The field of professional women's hockey has also included independent teams such as the Minnesota Whitecaps, for which Lamoureux-Davidson played in 2016–17 (and which joined the NWHL in 2018). Supporters of the one league movement argued that consolidating women's pro teams into a single league would help the sport gain greater recognition and inspire new players. "You have to look at the growth and ask how you grow the fan base. Having the best players in the world play in two different leagues is not going to help that," Lamoureux-Davidson told Mike Murphy for *SportingNews* (29 Aug. 2018). "I think if you can create one league that gives young girls an opportunity to watch and give them role models, you're going to grow the sport and grow the fan base. It's really important for this sport to take the next step."

2018 OLYMPIC GAMES
Lamoureux-Davidson made her third attempt at winning an Olympic gold medal in 2018, when she returned to the US team for that year's Winter Olympics in PyeongChang, South Korea. After defeating Finland in the semifinals, the United States faced off against the Canadian team in yet another gold-medal match. By the start of the game's final period, Canada was ahead 2–1. However, Lamoureux-Morando scored another goal for the United States, tying the game. The game went into overtime, which proved scoreless, leading to a shootout round in which the teams take turns sending players to attempt to score in a one-on-one matchup against the opposing goalie.

When Lamoureux-Davidson's turn came in the shootout, she had a strategy in mind. "I'd been watching how she was reacting to earlier shots, and based on that I knew I was going to fake a shot—but after that it was just kind of reading her and her reaction," she explained to Seymour. "You go on instinct once you're there, but you go in with some idea of what you have planned to do." Her plan proved successful, as her deke fooled Canadian goalie Shannon Szabados and allowed her to slip the puck into the net. US goaltender Maddie Rooney then blocked Canada's final attempt, ending the game in a 3–2 victory for the United States. As the game-winning goal scorer, Lamoureux-Davidson earned much of the media attention for the US women's hockey team's first Olympic gold medal since 1998. Indeed, her fake-out move in the shootout was seen by many as an Olympic highlight.

PERSONAL LIFE
Lamoureux-Davidson married Brent Davidson, a former UND men's hockey player, in 2014. In the summer of 2018, she announced that she was expecting her first child, an announcement that came only two months after Lamoureux-Morando's pregnancy announcement. The sisters continued to work out and train while pregnant, which they documented on social media channels such as Instagram. "We want to be an example that you can continue to train through pregnancy and be healthy," Lamoureux-Davidson explained to Murphy. "We're still driven to play in a fourth Olympics. Being pregnant and having a family is just going to be a part of that journey. We're excited to share it. Hopefully that will inspire and motivate other moms and show what we can do."

SUGGESTED READING
Cassidy, Emily. "Peak Performance: US Olympians Jocelyne Lamoureux-Davidson and Monique Lamoureux-Morando Predict the Future [of Hockey] Is Female." Interview with Mika Brzezinksi. *Know Your Value*, NBC News, 18 June 2018, www.nbcnews.com/know-your-value/feature/peak-performance-u-s-olympians-jocelyne-lamoureux-davidson-monique-lamoureux-ncna883786. Accessed 18 Jan. 2019.

Chambers, Mike. "Lamoureux Twins Aim for Vancouver and Hope It's Together." *The Denver Post*, 12 Dec. 2009, www.denverpost.com/2009/12/12/lamoureux-twins-aim-for-vancouver-and-hope-its-together/. Accessed 18 Jan. 2019.

Drehs, Wayne. "Why It Wasn't the US Team's Night." *ESPNW*, 20 Feb. 2014, www.espn.com/espnw/news-commentary/olympics/article/10492375/espnw-was-supposed-olympic-moment-us-women-team-stunned-canada. Accessed 18 Jan. 2019.

"Jocelyne Lamoreaux-Davidson." *USA Hockey*, 2019, teamusa.usahockey.com/page/show/2874725-jocelyne-lamoureux-davidson. Accessed 22 Jan. 2019.

Murphy, Mike. "Catching Up with the Lamoureuxs: Olympic Heroes Talk Motherhood, 'One League,' Fight for Gender Equity." *SportingNews*, 29 Aug. 2018, www.sportingnews.com/ca/amp/nhl/news/jocelyne-monique-lamoureux-twins-sisters-olympics-goal-video-team-usa-whitecaps-nwhl-cwhl/18cgk99kn5x2213kskzxmv7d8q. Accessed 18 Jan. 2019.

Seymour, Corey. "Jocelyne Lamoureux, the Golden Goal Scorer of Team USA, Wants It

All." *Vogue*, 7 Mar. 2018, www.vogue.com/
article/jocelyne-lamoureux-team-usa-title-ix.
Accessed 18 Jan. 2019.

Smith, Gary. "House of Hockey." *Sports Illustrated*, 1 Feb. 2010, www.si.com/
vault/2010/02/01/105899244/house-of-hock-
ey. Accessed 18 Jan. 2019.

—*Joy Crelin*

Brie Larson

Date of birth: October 1, 1989
Occupation: Actor

Actor Brie Larson wants to tell "universal tales,"
as she said to Laurie Sandell for the *Hollywood
Reporter* (20 Jan. 2016). "I've struggled watching films where people dressed well and seemed
to have it together, where the worst thing that
happened was they fell in front of the guy they
liked at their office," she explained. "I don't relate to that." Indeed, while the characters Larson
plays often find themselves in unusual situations, their inner selves and relationships with
others reflect the emotional truths that she has
long sought to bring to the screen. A working actor since childhood, she found small roles in film
and television throughout the first decade of her
career but gained wider recognition beginning in
2009, when she debuted as teenager Kate Greg-
son in the Showtime series *United States of Tara*
(2009–11). Critically acclaimed roles in films
such as *Short Term 12* (2013) followed, and in
2016, she won the Academy Award for Best Actress in a Leading Role for her performance in
the 2015 independent drama *Room*.

Larson's career trajectory transformed further in 2019, when she made her debut as the
Marvel Comics hero Captain Marvel in the film
of the same name, the first installment in the
Marvel Cinematic Universe to focus solely on
a female hero. For Larson, the film represented not only an exciting new challenge but also
an opportunity to further the representation of
women in film. "The movie was the biggest and
best opportunity I could have ever asked for,"
she told Sana Amanat for *InStyle* (5 Feb. 2019).
"It was, like, my superpower. This could be my
form of activism: doing a film that can play all
over the world and be in more places than I can
be physically."

EARLY LIFE AND CAREER

Larson was born Brianne Sidonie Desaulniers on
October 1, 1989, in Sacramento, California. She
was the first of two daughters born to Heather
and Sylvain Desaulniers, both of whom worked
as chiropractors. Though shy, she developed an

Photo by Gage Skidmore via Wikimedia Commons

interest in acting by the age of six, and she soon
began to study at the prestigious American Conservatory Theater. In part to further help her career dream become reality, she moved with her
mother and sister to Los Angeles, where they
struggled financially during their early years in
the city; around this time, her parents also divorced. "We had a crappy one-room apartment
where the bed came out of the wall and we each
had three articles of clothing," she recalled to
Tim Lewis for the *Guardian* (19 Oct. 2013).
Due to her need for a flexible schedule while
pursuing acting work, she was homeschooled
for much of her childhood, and she eventually
completed her high school education around the
age of fifteen.

Throughout Larson's early years as an actor,
she primarily found work on television, beginning with a series of sketches on *The Tonight
Show with Jay Leno* (1998). She went on to appear in small roles in television series such as
To Have & to Hold (1998), *Touched by an Angel*
(1999), *Popular* (1999), and *Then Came You*
(2000). Beginning in 2001, she costarred in the
sitcom *Raising Dad*, which focused on the lives
of a widowed father and his two daughters. The
series aired on the WB for a single season but
was eventually canceled. She went on to costar
in Disney Channel's original movie *Right on
Track* (2003), about a pair of sisters who become
drag racing champions.

In addition to acting, Larson explored her
interest in singing during her early career, releasing the pop album *Finally Out of P. E.* in 2005.
The album was financially unsuccessful, and she
went on to focus exclusively on acting, although

she would later sing in some films. Although she continued to find acting work, including roles in the films *Hoot* (2006) and *Remember the Daze* (2007), she was disappointed with the state of her career after a decade as a professional actor. "My friends were going to college, and I was still auditioning. It became this real turning point," she told Krista Smith for *Vanity Fair* (25 Apr. 2017). "Am I supposed to do this? Is it worth how this makes me feel sometimes?" Although she considered quitting acting in favor of a new career path, she persevered, a decision she linked to her love of acting itself. "I realized then that story was too important to me," she told Smith.

BREAKTHROUGH ROLES
The year 2009 marked a turning point for Larson, who began to costar in the critically acclaimed television series *United States of Tara*. Although Larson was cast in the role of Kate, the teenage daughter of actor Toni Collette's titular Tara, the role was initially given to another actor. "I fainted, because I honestly believed this was it," Larson recalled to Idil Tabanca for *Bullett* (8 Nov. 2011) about learning that she had not gotten the part. "It was like being left at the altar." However, the team in charge of the series ultimately decided to replace the original actor who played Kate, and Larson was eventually offered the role. In addition to introducing Larson to a wider audience, *United States of Tara* provided her with further opportunities to work with and learn from actors such as Collette, whom she particularly admired. "All of a sudden I was there with bigger leagues, and I was thinking, *Oh my gosh, I hope I'm doing this right*," she told Tabanca. *United States of Tara* aired on the premium cable channel Showtime for three seasons between 2009 and 2011.

In the years following her debut on *United States of Tara*, Larson took on a series of increasingly prominent roles in films such as *Scott Pilgrim vs. the World* (2010), an adaptation of a graphic novel series (2004–10) by Bryan Lee O'Malley, and *21 Jump Street* (2012), a film reboot of the 1980s television show of the same name. In addition to acting, she had long aspired to direct and began to do so relatively early in her career, making her directorial debut in 2012 with the short film *The Arm*. The film won a special jury prize at the Sundance Film Festival, where it premiered. She later directed the short film *Weighting* (2013).

ROOM
Larson received particular attention for her performance in 2013's *Short Term 12*, an independent film set in a home for at-risk youth where Larson's character works. The film won awards from a variety of film festivals and critics groups following its release, and Larson received significant critical acclaim for her performance, which some critics suggested was worthy of a major honor such as an Academy Award. For Larson, the sudden influx of praise was disconcerting. "Suddenly there's this weird spotlight on you and it's a vomit of gold coins," she told Lewis. "It's wonderful, but it doesn't feel real." She went on to play supporting roles in films such as *Don Jon* (2013) and *Trainwreck* (2015) and returned to television with guest appearances in comedy series such as *Kroll Show* (2013) and *Community* (2013–14).

Another major milestone in Larson's career came in 2015 with the release of *Room*, an independent drama based on a 2010 book by Emma Donoghue. Larson plays one of the film's protagonists, a young woman who has been abducted and held captive in a one-room shed for several years along with her young son. The film received numerous accolades following its premiere at the Telluride Film Festival, and Larson's performance drew widespread praise. She went on to win the Academy Award for Best Actress in a Leading Role as well as the Golden Globe, British Academy of Film and Television Arts (BAFTA) Award, and Screen Actors Guild (SAG) Award in the equivalent categories, among many others.

Winning an Academy Award represented a life-changing shift in Larson's career. "Every single step of this last year has been a completely new experience and one that is totally outside of my comfort zone," she told Sandell in 2016. "I keep asking myself: How will my life be different? I have no idea. In this industry, where things change so quickly, I've found that having no expectations is the happiest way to go."

CAPTAIN MARVEL
In July 2016, Marvel Studios announced that Larson had been cast as the lead in *Captain Marvel*, an upcoming installment in the studio's series of superhero films. The first film in the Marvel Cinematic Universe to focus solely on a female hero, *Captain Marvel* features the character Carol Danvers, who gains an array of superpowers and takes on the title moniker. A character with decades of history in Marvel comics—much of it under the name Ms. Marvel—and a dedicated fan base known as the Carol Corps, Captain Marvel was among the most highly anticipated characters yet to be seen on screen, and the degree of international attention that would come with the role was somewhat daunting to Larson, who was initially conflicted about whether to take the part. "I had to sit with myself, think about my life and what I want out of it," she told Smith. "Ultimately, I couldn't deny the fact that this movie is everything I care about, everything that's progressive

and important and meaningful, and a symbol I wished I would've had growing up. I really, really feel like it's worth it if it can bring understanding and confidence to young women—I'll do it."

Having made Larson a household name, the success of *Room* also put her in the running for a host of other major roles, and she starred in films such as *Kong: Skull Island* (2017) and *The Glass Castle* (2017). At the same time, she tried her hand at directing feature-length films with *Unicorn Store*, a comedy in which she also stars. "I felt like, What better time for me to direct than now, when I don't have a stigma attached of this extra scrutiny, like, 'Oh, she's an actor—now she wants to be a director'?" she explained to Smith about the timing of her feature-length directorial debut. *Unicorn Store* premiered at the Toronto International Film Festival in 2017 and went on to be screened at the Edinburgh International Film Festival the following year.

Also featuring Samuel L. Jackson and Jude Law, among many other actors, *Captain Marvel* opened in the United States in March 2019, and Larson reprised the role of Captain Marvel for the filming of *Avengers: Endgame* (2019). Additionally, the streaming service Netflix announced that it had acquired *Unicorn Store*.

PERSONAL LIFE
Larson has numerous hobbies, including mushroom hunting and designing fonts, the latter of which she has found to be a productive means of decompressing while in the middle of shooting films. "I made three or four different fonts during *Short Term 12*—it was how I'd calm my mind between scenes," she explained to Lewis. "I have graph paper and gel pens and I would do the alphabet: just do 'a' over and over again until I got it perfect and then go to 'b' and then 'c.'"

SUGGESTED READING
Larson, Brie. "Brie Larson Talks 'Captain Marvel' and Her Goal to Make Art That Lasts." Interview by Perri Nemiroff. *Collider*, 4 Dec. 2018, collider.com/captain-marvel-brie-larson-interview/. Accessed 15 Feb. 2019.

Lewis, Tim. "Brie Larson Interview: 'I Just Wanted to Do Weird Stuff.'" *The Guardian*, 19 Oct. 2013, www.theguardian.com/film/2013/oct/20/brie-larson-short-term-12-interview. Accessed 15 Feb. 2019.

Sandell, Laurie. "Brie Larson's 20-Year Climb to Overnight Stardom: I'm 'Totally out of My Comfort Zone.'" *The Hollywood Reporter*, 20 Jan. 2016, www.hollywoodreporter.com/features/brie-larsons-20-year-climb-857011. Accessed 15 Feb. 2019.

Smith, Krista. "Cover Story: Brie Larson, Hollywood's Most Independent Young Star." *Vanity Fair*, 25 Apr. 2017, www.vanityfair.com/hollywood/2017/04/brie-larson-cover-story. Accessed 15 Feb. 2019.

Tabanca, Idil. "Actor Brie Larson Makes the Leap from 'Tara' to '21 Jump Street.'" *Bullett*, 8 Nov. 2011, bullettmedia.com/article/brie-larson-united-states-of-tara-21-jump-street/. Accessed 15 Feb. 2019.

Zinski, Dan. "*Captain Marvel*'s Brie Larson Set to Direct, Star in Films for Netflix." *Screen Rant*, 31 Jan. 2019, screenrant.com/captain-marvel-brie-larson-netflix-films/. Accessed 15 Feb. 2019.

SELECTED WORKS
Raising Dad, 2001–2; *United States of Tara*, 2009–11; *Scott Pilgrim vs. the World*, 2010; *21 Jump Street*, 2012; *Short Term 12*, 2013; *Room*, 2015; *Kong: Skull Island*, 2017; *The Glass Castle*, 2017; *Captain Marvel*, 2019

—Joy Crelin

January LaVoy
Date of birth: December 1975
Occupation: Actor and audiobook narrator

January LaVoy is an actor and an audiobook narrator who was named *Publishers Weekly*'s Audiobook Narrator of the Year in 2013. By then, LaVoy had been building her narrator profile for five years. She had recorded nearly 200 audiobooks as of 2019, winning several Audie Awards, which the Audio Publishing Association gives each year for the best audiobooks. She was one of the voices in the audiobook *Nimona*, an adaptation of a fantasy web comic, which was a finalist for the 2017 American Library Association Odyssey Award for Excellence in Audiobook Production. LaVoy told Alexis Gunderson for *Paste* (2 Feb. 2018), "If you had told me when I was 10 years old that I was going to get paid to read books out loud, I *definitely* would have thought you were making fun of me. I didn't know it was a job you could have. And if I had known that as a child, I would have actively pursued it, because [reading] is what I do all day anyway!"

EARLY LIFE AND EDUCATION
Born in Trumbull, Connecticut, to Kim Capristo and Alexander Merola, LaVoy knew from childhood that she wanted to act. Her maternal grandmother, Mary Lou Capristo, was involved in community theater at the Bridgeport Polka Dot Playhouse, serving as an administrator as well as an actor and director. LaVoy made her stage debut there at the age of three.

Photo by Walter McBride/Getty Images

LaVoy graduated from Connecticut's Fairfield University, a Jesuit school located about sixty miles from New York City, in 1997. She values the university's requirement that every theater major work in every aspect of a show. She told Joe Meyers for *CTPost* (16 Apr. 2017), "We had to make costumes, build sets. I can't tell you how many times I've been thanked by a crew member just because I've done those jobs, and I know that it's not magic that results in costumes being delivered and steamed every night."

Five years later, LaVoy received her master's degree in acting at the National Theater Conservatory in Denver. While trying to carve a career in theater in New York, she went on as many as 500 auditions annually, while waiting tables, cleaning apartments, and taking temporary jobs to pay the rent.

She was in graduate school when terrorists attacked New York City's World Trade Center on September 11, 2001. She had a rehearsal that night and was unhappy to be in the theater working on a production of *Cyrano de Bergerac*, which was due to open in three weeks. But as she told Meyers, the director said, "In three weeks, people will need a story about heroism and love. Trust me, they're going to need us." Because of his words, she told Meyers, "I realized theater is a gift, and that's why it isn't going away."

EARLY CAREER

In 2005 LaVoy performed the role of Kegan in John Fisher's play *Joy* at the Actor's Playhouse in New York City. She also appeared that year in a minor role in Steven Spielberg's film *War of the Worlds*. The following year LaVoy was cast in a revival of August Wilson's show *Two Trains Running*, in the role of the waitress Risa. The production won the Lucille Lortel Award for Outstanding Revival in 2007. She characterized the show as a great joy, telling T. J. Fitzgerald for *Broadway World* (16 Jan. 2008), "I still regularly see many of my castmates, whom I adore. I have never been more proud to be a part of a show." LaVoy played multiple roles in *Coraline*, a musical based on Neil Gaiman's 2002 novel of the same title, which opened in 2009.

In 2009 Fairfield University recruited LaVoy to play the role of Helen Keller in a work by Dr. John Orman, chair of the political science department and LaVoy's former teacher there. From Keller's letters and speeches, Orman created *Helen Keller Speaks*, a work that is part drama and part reading, to reveal the politically engaged woman he discovered. Like most people, Orman knew only of Keller's childhood and her relationship with Annie Sullivan, who taught the blind and deaf child. This part of Keller's life was immortalized in the 1959 play *The Miracle Worker* and its several film adaptations, shaping the public's perception of Keller. *Helen Keller Speaks,* however, explores Keller's adulthood, spanning the years from 1913 to 1919. During that time, Keller was involved in the struggle for women's suffrage and protested US involvement in World War I.

Orman cast LaVoy as Keller, though LaVoy, as an African American woman, was not an obvious choice to play a white historical figure. Of her role, LaVoy told Jan Ellen Spiegel for the *New York Times* (6 Mar. 2009), "As a woman of color, I am thrilled to be able to portray Helen Keller; it's a huge honor. If Helen Keller looked at me the way she did—through her hands—she would never know the color of me nor would she care." Proceeds from the production were sent to the American Foundation for the Blind (AFB).

ACTING CAREER

On the *ABC* daytime drama *One Life to Live*, LaVoy originated the role of Noelle Ortiz-Stubbs. The role was initially designed as a recurring character rather than a full contract role, which LaVoy told Fitzgerald "wasn't as intimidating as it might have been if I had known [it was a contract role] from the start." Initially hired in October 2008, LaVoy remained under contract until spring of the following year and returned as a guest in two episodes in 2011. Other acting credits include episodes of several of the shows in the Law and Order franchise. She has also appeared in other soap operas, such as *Guiding Light* and *All My Children*, as well as in the procedural drama *Blue Bloods* (2010–).

On Broadway, LaVoy was in the 2010 production of British playwright Lucy Prebble's *Enron*, which was based on the scandal surrounding the Houston-based energy company of the same name. Due to slow ticket sales, the show had a short run. In addition, she was featured in several Off-Broadway productions, including *Home* by Samm-Art Williams, in which three actors performed more than twenty-five roles. LaVoy is active in regional theater as well. She originated the role of Lena in Pearl Cleage's drama *What I Learned in Paris* at Atlanta's Alliance Theatre in fall 2012. She has also acted in theaters in Pittsburgh, Philadelphia, and Denver.

Known for her work on August Wilson's plays, in 2013 she was among nearly one hundred performers who gathered to record all ten of the plays that form Wilson's American Century Cycle, playing the role of Mattie Campbell in *Joe Turner's Come and Gone*. The same year, she played the role onstage in a production directed by Phylicia Rashad.

Commenting on LaVoy's performance in Adrienne Kennedy's play *Funnyhouse of a Negro*, critic Hilton Als wrote for *New Yorker* (6 and 13 June 2016), "LaVoy projects an emotional reality drawn not just from the script but from the nightmare of being. As she goes about her business, her star quality keeps us watching her for what she does now, and for what she will do in the future."

In 2017 LaVoy appeared in multiple roles in *Measure for Measure* at the Theatre for a New Audience (TFNA) in New York, which *New York Times* critic Charles Isherwood characterized as "the most sophisticated purveyor of revivals in the major Off-Broadway leagues." Founded in 1984, TFNA has produced twenty-eight of Shakespeare's plays as well as more than thirty other master works and contemporary plays.

AUDIOBOOK NARRATOR

LaVoy's work as a book narrator began in 2007, when she met representatives from the agency Innovative Artists while performing in a production of August Wilson's *Two Trains Running*. The show also featured two men Innovative Artists represented; the agents attended the show in support of their clients. LaVoy met them after the performance, and they invited her to a meeting. A year passed before LaVoy finally was allowed to audition for narration.

When she began recording in 2008, she did so using a pseudonym. The first book she recorded was a vampire novel with sex scenes; she feared recording the book would negatively affect her acting career. *One Life to Live*'s network was owned by Disney, so she felt she needed to be careful with her image.

A reluctant convert to audiobooks herself, LaVoy had a change of heart, as she told Michael Sangiacomo for *AudioFile Magazine* (Aug./Sept. 2015). "I used to think audiobooks were for commuters. Recently, a war photographer

presented me with three flags that flew over his camp in Afghanistan. He said audiobooks allowed them to shut out the war for several hours." She also learned that some prisons broadcast audiobooks to entire cell blocks. Because many imprisoned people are not literate, audiobooks may be the only way that they can experience literature.

To prepare for her work, LaVoy prefers to read the book once through in the way she normally would when reading for pleasure. She then goes back through the text, making notes about her emotions and any clues in the story as to the way a character sounds. For LaVoy, the emotional experience is primary. She often associates each character in a book she is recording with a different person she knows in real life, such as a relative or teacher, to make the voices distinct.

A major challenge came when she was to record the biography of Barack Obama's mother, *A Singular Woman*, by Janny Scott. As she told Shannon Maughan for *Publishers Weekly* (Feb. 2014), "Half the book takes place in Indonesia and involved some fascinating pronunciation. We were calling the embassy from the studio to make sure we got things right." She tries to accept all offers to record young adult (YA) fiction. As a child, she had few books with characters who looked like her. As a result, she is passionate about diversity in novels for young people. LaVoy has read books of many genres, but told Maughan, "My bread and butter are mysteries."

LaVoy has also done voiceovers for commercials. Her work in that area includes clients such as Toll House, United Health Care, The Home Depot, Revlon, and Obama for America.

PERSONAL LIFE

LaVoy was named for the main character in Jacqueline Susann's novel *Once Is Not Enough* (1973), which LaVoy's mother was reading while pregnant with LaVoy. LaVoy has said she would like to record the work.

In September 2011 LaVoy married Mat Hostetler, whom she met while they were earning their master's degrees at the National Theater Conservatory. They have two cats, named for theater personalities. She has completed several marathons and half-marathons, and volunteers with the 52nd Street Project in Hell's Kitchen, a program in which professional stage actors and playwrights mentor disadvantaged children from the neighborhood, helping them to create and put on plays.

Although LaVoy does read reviews of her performances, she does not let them dictate her choices, as she told Fitzgerald, saying, "I can honestly say that I've never let them affect my portrayals. I work very hard on all of my characters, and I stand by my choices." She also learned to keep lip balm in the recording studio as she reads, to prevent her lips from cracking and bleeding as they did after her first eight-hour marathon recording session.

SUGGESTED READING

Als, Hilton. "Two Stage Actresses to Watch." *The New Yorker*, 6–13 June 2016, www.newyorker.com/magazine/2016/06/06/cush-jumbo-and-january-lavoy-two-actresses-to-watch.   Accessed 22 Jan. 2018.

Gunderson, Alexis. "Diviners Narrator January LaVoy Talks Creating Audiobooks." *Paste*, 2 Feb. 2018, www.pastemagazine.com/articles/2018/02/diviners-narrator-january-lavoy-talks-creating-aud.html. Accessed 30 Jan. 2019.

LaVoy, January. "LaVoy Finds There Is One Life to Live." Interview by T. J. Fitzgerald. *Broadway World*, 16 Jan. 2008, www.broadwayworld.com/article/LaVoy-Finds-There-Is-One-Life-To-Live-20080116. Accessed 28 Jan. 2019.

LaVoy, January. "Talking Audio with January LaVoy." Interview by Shannon Maughan. *Publishers Weekly*, 7 Feb. 2014, www.publishersweekly.com/pw/by-topic/industry-news/audio-books/article/60964-talking-audio-with-january-lavoy.html. Accessed 18 Jan. 2019.

Meyers, Joe. "Trumbull Native January LaVoy Triumphs in New York Drama." *CTPost*, 16 Apr. 2017, www.ctpost.com/living/article/Trumbull-native-January-LaVoy-triumphs-in-New-11072154.php. Accessed 30 Jan. 2019.

Spiegel, Jan Ellen. "Giving Voice to Helen Keller." *The New York Times*, 6 Mar. 2009, www.nytimes.com/2009/03/08/nyregion/connecticut/08spotct.html. Accessed 24 Jan. 2019.

SELECTED WORKS

Two Trains Running, 2007; *One Life to Live*, 2008–9; *Coraline*, 2009; *Enron*, 2010; *Joe Turner's Come and Gone*, 2013

—*Judy Johnson*

Kai-Fu Lee

Date of birth: December 3, 1961
Occupation: Venture capitalist and artificial intelligence expert

Americans, especially those not immersed in the tech world, may not immediately recognize the name Kai-Fu Lee. Yet the computer scientist–turned–venture capitalist has fifty million followers on the Chinese social media site *Weibo* and a level of fame and respect that many rock stars would envy.

Lee has worked at such iconic companies as Apple and Microsoft, and he led Google's briefly successful foray into China, where he almost tripled market share—a noteworthy feat for an American company attempting to gain a foothold in a tech culture vastly different from that in the United States. Business analysts have asserted that Lee managed to perform as well as he did for Google because he is the rare tech executive with extensive experience in both countries and, therefore, has a deep understanding of the similarities and differences between them.

"Both the Silicon Valley system and the Chinese system are of intrinsic value, both will create tremendous wealth, and both will be wildly successful even a century from now, but I don't want to project who will surpass whom," Lee told an interviewer for 52 *Insights* (21 Sept. 2018). "It's not an arms race, they work in parallel universes." He has said that in some respects, China has a distinct advantage, however. He has noted that the enormous customer bases in Asia mean tech companies there have substantially more data to aid in machine learning, and thus their algorithms become "smarter" faster.

"Whether it is predicting what you are going to buy, publishing an ad that you might click on, or recognizing your face and speech, all those technologies work better with more data," he explained to Peter High for *Forbes* (15 Oct. 2018). "China simply has more users and more data per user . . . A Chinese company will have a better product than that of an American company with the same funding and products because China's product has AI [artificial intelligence] trained on more data."

Lee heads his own venture capital firm, Sinovation Ventures, a $2 billion fund, with fully one-third of that invested in AI–based enterprises. He has become known for his ability to spot so-called unicorns—start-ups valued at over $1 billion—and he has helped incubate dozens of those, including the bike-sharing enterprise Mobike and Meitu, a firm that makes photo and video apps.

EARLY LIFE

Kai-Fu Lee was born on December 3, 1961, in Taipei, Taiwan. His mother, Wang Ya-Ching, had left the area known in the West as Manchuria in 1931, when she was just twelve years old, unwilling to live and study under Japanese occupation forces. Traveling alone by train, she settled in Beijing, where she attended schools funded by the Chinese Nationalist government. When she was nineteen, by then trained as a physical education teacher, she attended a political rally and became captivated by one of the speakers, Lee Tien-Min, a widower with a young son and daughter. Tien-Min, who was then working as a counselor in a job-training facility, had lived

Photo by SheilaShang via Wikimedia Commons

an eventful life up until that point, joining the Chinese Nationalist army at age thirteen, earning a bachelor's degree in economics, editing a Nationalist newspaper for a time, and teaching at a military school in Chengdu.

The two married in 1939, settled in Sichuan Province, and had three daughters together within the next decade. When Tien-Min was forced to flee to Taiwan in 1949, following the civil war between the Nationalists and the Communists, Ya-Ching valiantly followed him with all five children in tow. They had one additional daughter before Lee was born; his birth was a surprise to everyone, since by then Ya-Ching was in her forties. Although he was unexpected, Lee was cherished by his father, who settled during the early 1960s into a career as a full-time legislator and part-time university professor; his mother; and his six older siblings.

EDUCATION

Always a precocious child, Lee begged to take the first-grade entrance exam a year early and passed easily. He often found himself in trouble at school, however. His mischievousness, he has said in his own defense, was simply the result of his boredom. (Once a teacher sealed his mouth shut with tape.)

Lee's brother Kai-Lin had settled in the United States to work as a research scientist at Oak Ridge National Laboratory in Tennessee, and he convinced Lee of the value of an American education. Thus, in 1973, accompanied by his mother, Lee arrived in Oak Ridge, where he attended a Catholic middle school and then a public high school.

In 1983 Lee graduated summa cum laude from Columbia University, earning a bachelor's degree in computer science. He next entered a PhD program in computer science at Carnegie Mellon University (CMU), where he focused on the still fledgling field of machine learning. Even before earning his doctoral degree in 1988, Lee was making waves in the AI world. He helped develop a Bayesian learning-based system for playing the board game Othello that became the first program of its kind to beat a human world champion, Brian Rose (who lost to the computer, 56–8). At CMU, he also did pioneering work in speech recognition—the process by which twenty-first-century platforms like Alexa and Siri hear and understand the human voice. He remains widely celebrated for his creation of Sphinx, the world's first large-vocabulary, speaker-independent, continuous speech recognition system, which he described in his dissertation.

Although Lee had multiple job offers, he elected to remain at CMU as a faculty member. There, funded by grants from the Department of Defense (DoD), he continued his work on speech recognition for another two years.

A SERIES OF IMPORTANT COMPANIES

In 1990 Lee, a big fan of Apple's Macintosh personal computer and ready for a change from academia, joined Apple, making the leap from pure research to product development. He became one of the company's youngest vice-presidents at age thirty-three and worked on interactive multimedia technologies. He left in 1996 to accept a post at Silicon Graphics, which dealt in the high-powered servers and design platforms used in Hollywood to make blockbusters like *Jurassic Park* and *Titanic*.

In 1998 Lee accepted an offer from Microsoft to move to Beijing, China, to help establish a Microsoft Research division there. He has admitted he faced an uphill battle: not only was it difficult to recruit top-notch researchers willing to uproot themselves from their comfortable lives in Silicon Valley, but the company was far from a trusted or respected name in Asia at that time. Despite those impediments, within a few years Microsoft Research China (now known as Microsoft Research Asia) was being widely acknowledged as one of the premier computer science research labs in the world.

In 2000 Lee left the research organization he had so painstakingly built and came back to the United States to head Microsoft's interactive services division. It was difficult returning to product development—particularly within a company so beleaguered by an ongoing antitrust investigation by the Department of Justice that executives were warned to carefully word each email they sent.

GOOGLE

In 2005 Lee left Microsoft for Google, the search-engine company having aggressively recruited him to oversee efforts in China and offered him a $2.5 million cash signing bonus. Microsoft, with a massive legal team at the ready because of its ongoing antitrust disputes, promptly sued, charging that Lee had violated his noncompete agreement. The case was scheduled to go to trial in January 2006, but the month before, the two tech behemoths announced they had reached a confidential settlement ending the dispute.

Lee, who had been barred from doing any technical development in the interim, was now free to make his mark on Google China. At the time the company's presence in the country amounted to little more than a simplified Chinese-language version of Google News. Lee quickly recruited a cadre of engineers and scientists and helped launch the China-based *Google.cn* search page. The search page was, however, merely an abridged version of what users in other countries saw, with a disclaimer running along the bottom that read: "Some results have been withheld because of the government restrictions."

Although the international tech community decried Google's acquiescence to government censorship, Lee and other executives argued that they were at least bringing as much information as possible to a repressed people. By 2009 Lee—who had been earning a reported $10 million a year—had helped win Google a third of the Chinese market and hundreds of millions of users in mainland China.

In September of that year, he announced his resignation, asserting that he was leaving an exceptionally strong leadership team in place and that he was ready to pursue other avenues. (In 2010, in the face of continued government interference, Google moved operations to the less restrictive environment of Hong Kong.)

VENTURE CAPITAL

That other avenue was a $115 million venture capital firm dedicated to early-stage tech start-ups. Known as Sinovation Ventures, as of 2019 the enterprise has assets of $2 billion under management and has helped more than three hundred companies incubate. "We primarily look for disrupting technologies or those that tend to grow in exponential phases, rather than those that take an existing pie and go to a zero-sum competition," Lee explained to High. "Moreover, we want to look for entrepreneurs who are exceptional leaders, detail oriented, and those that are good at execution. . . . We do not insist that the product they are building is perfect so long that it is a reasonable product going into a high growth space with promising entrepreneurs."

He enjoys working with Chinese entrepreneurs, as he told High, because "competitiveness, tenacity, work ethic, and desire to build uncopyable business models are specialties that give China a unique advantage." He is often called upon, however, to defend China against accusations that the country's tech sector has built its wealth solely upon intellectual piracy. He admits that there was an era when copying and then building upon American tech was common but has said that by around 2013, the Chinese internet had morphed into "an alternate internet universe, a space with its own raw materials, planetary systems, and laws of physics," as he wrote for the blogging site *Medium* (4 Oct. 2018). "It was a place where many users accessed the internet only through cheap smartphones, where smartphones played the role of credit cards, and where population-dense cities created a rich laboratory for blending the digital and physical worlds. [And because] the Chinese tech companies that ruled this world had no obvious corollaries in Silicon Valley, simple shorthand like 'the Amazon of China' or 'the Facebook of China' no longer made sense."

In some ways, Lee has said, innovation is easier in China because of strong government support. By way of example, he told Sissi Cao for the *Observer* (9 Oct. 2018): "Self-driving trucks need to be tested on highways before running on local roads, because highways are safer and more predictable. In the United States, the truckers' union lobbied Congress to block the testing of autonomous trucks over fears of job losses, whereas in China, the government actually built a highway specifically designed for testing self-driving vehicles (with sensors installed beneath the roads) to facilitate the project. So, you tell me which one is going to be ahead of the game?"

PERSONAL LIFE

Lee married his wife, Shen-Ling, on August 6, 1983. They have two daughters, Jennifer and Cynthia. Lee began to rethink his workaholic nature only after being diagnosed with stage IV lymphoma in 2013; it later went into remission. The greatest benefits of AI, he asserts, will be that it frees up humans for jobs in creative and care-giving fields—an epiphany he reached after his illness.

SUGGESTED READING

High, Peter. "Thoughts on the AI Superpowers from the Person Who Understands Them Best." *Forbes*, 16 Oct. 2018, www.forbes.com/sites/peterhigh/2018/10/15/thoughts-on-the-ai-superpowers-from-the-person-who-understands-them-best/#4b507df01d26. Accessed 27 Apr. 2019.

Lee, Kai-Fu. *My Journey into AI: The Story behind the Man Who Helped Launch 5 AI Companies Worth $25 Billion*. Cranberry, 2018.

Lee, Kai-Fu. "The Rising Tide: A Jobless Future Is Coming." Interview. 52 *Insights*, Ari Stein, 21 Sept. 2018, www.52-insights.com/interview-technology-automation-kai-fu-lee-the-rising-tide-a-jobless-future-is-coming. Accessed 27 Apr. 2019.

Lee, Kai-Fu. "What Motivates China's Entrepreneurs? An Interview with Kai-Fu Lee." Interview by Scott Malcomson. *New York*, 10 Oct. 2018, nymag.com/developing/2018/10/kai-fu-lee-scott-malcomson-chinese-entrepreneurship-global-tech.html. Accessed 27 Apr. 2019.

Lee, Kai-Fu. "Will China's Tech Boom Take Over Silicon Valley? A Conversation with Kai-Fu Lee." Interview by Sissi Cao. *Observer*, 9 Oct. 2018, observer.com/2018/10/kai-fu-lee-google-china-tech-advancements. Accessed 27 Apr. 2019.

Purtill, Corinne. "A Former Symbol of Silicon Valley's 'Crush It' Culture Now Regrets Working So Much." *Quartz*, 9 Dec. 2018, qz.com/work/1488217/a-former-symbol-of-silicon-valleys-crush-it-culture-now-regrets-working-so-much. Accessed 27 Apr. 2019.

Wickenden, Dorothy. "Kai-Fu Lee on China's Race to the Future." *The New Yorker*, 28 Jan. 2019, www.newyorker.com/podcast/political-scene/kai-fu-lee-on-chinas-race-to-the-future. Accessed 27 Apr. 2019.

—*Mari Rich*

Simone Leigh

Date of birth: 1967
Occupation: Artist

Artist Simone Leigh, who blends ceramic and video art, received the 2018 Hugo Boss Award, given for achievement in the field of contemporary art. Awarded biennially by the Solomon R. Guggenheim Museum, the honor carries a $100,000 stipend and an exhibit at the museum. The jury's award statement, as Robin Pogrebin quoted for the *New York Times* (18 Oct. 2018), stated, "We are particularly compelled by Leigh's longstanding and unwavering commitment to addressing black women as both the subject of and audience for her work." Regarding the award, Leigh told Pogrebin and Hilarie Sheets for the New York Times (18 Aug. 2018), "Because I was largely ignored, I had a long time to mature without any kind of glare, which worked out for me quite well. I'm more concerned with having the space and the time to be creative." Leigh's work

has explored her African heritage rooted in West and South Africa, as well as in the American South. As she told an interviewer for a profile featured on the *Earlham College* website, "Some critics have referred to my work as 'Afro-futurist,' but I think that comes from a confusion around visual culture. I am very interested in using ancient motifs from African art in my work, but African art was also very important in the development of modernism. So the works actually draws from varied histories, and seem out of time, which perhaps is why people think it looks like the future."

EDUCATION AND EARLY CAREER
Simone Leigh was born and raised in Chicago, Illinois. Her parents were missionaries of Jamaican descent, and her father was a minister for the evangelical Church of the Nazarene. Leigh has described in interviews how her strict Christian upbringing has influenced her work. "It's created my awareness of the possibility of transgression in almost any thought or act," she said, as quoted by Quinn Latimer for *Modern Painters* in 2008.

Leigh went to Earlham College, a liberal arts college established in Richmond, Indiana, by the Society of Friends. As a college student, Leigh interned at the Smithsonian National Museum of African Art and developed an interest in African ceramics as well as their collection and curation by European colonists during the nineteenth century. As Leigh told Latimer, "These objects |. . . arrive with a complete lack of authorship. Yet they're supposed to have this incredible importance for modernism. . . . African pots are often

Photo by Tiffany I. Smith via Wikimedia Commons

explained as primitive objects made by primitive people . . . but it took me a long time to acquire the skills to create what I wanted to make." Having a liberal arts degree helped in her efforts to learn how to make the pots themselves and also to understand the cultural and historical context in which they were produced and displayed. "It's an unusual pedigree for an artist—having a liberal arts degree and never seeking an MFA—but I know how to research and write, and that has been very beneficial for me," as she explained for a profile on *Earlham.edu*. She also credits art professor Michael Thiedeman with introducing her to "the tradition of American pottery." Leigh graduated with a bachelor's degree in art, with a minor in philosophy, in 1990.

In the 2000s, she received a number of grants and fellowships, including a residency at the Haystack Mount School of Crafts in 2000; a Kiln God Fellowship at the Watershed Center for the Ceramic Arts in 2001; a 2005 Herbert and Irene Wheeler Foundation Emergency Grant to Artists of Color; and a 2009 New York Foundation for the Arts Fellowship in Sculpture. In the mid-to-late 2000s, she was an artist in residence for Greenwich House Pottery, the Henry Street Settlement, and Hunter College, as well as a visiting artist for the School of Visual Arts in New York.

In 2009, Leigh took part in Artists in the Marketplace (AIM), a program of the Bronx Museum. Two years later, she was the artist in residence at Harlem's Studio Museum. In 2012, she facilitated art programs in Lagos, Nigeria, and Dakar, Senegal.

EXPLORING THE LEGACY OF SLAVERY

When Leigh began investigating the legacy of the transatlantic slave trade and African diaspora, she relied on familiar forms. Cowrie shells, which were used as currency in Africa, may have been accepted as payment when Africans sold other Africans into slavery. Watermelons, another shape she invokes, have a complicated history as a symbol, having stood for black freedom and economic self-sufficiency after the Civil War before becoming an antiblack racist stereotype during the Jim Crow era.

For one of her sculptures on exhibit at her 2014 solo show at the Atlanta Contemporary Arts Center, Leigh was inspired by Edward Weston's photograph, *Mammy's Cupboard, Natchez, Mississippi, 1941*. The pancake-house restaurant of that name was in the shape of a stereotypical "Mammy" figure; to enter the restaurant, one walked through the door in her hoop skirt, which Leigh viewed as a symbol of sexual violence toward black women. Using steel, Leigh created an eighteen-foot-tall hoop skirt, with the door in place, and decorated the interior with forty ceramic cowrie shells hanging at eye level.

For another of her show's sculptures, *Jug*, Leigh worked with Lizella clay found in Georgia. She used the traditional face jug shape but left it faceless. Instead, Leigh built up the form, using her fingers. For the sculpture *Tree*, Leigh referenced the African American tradition of hanging bottles from a tree as a talisman to catch and hold bad spirits. Her shapes are strung on wires hanging in a rectangular steel structure. In a review of the show, Rebecca Dimling Cochran wrote for *Sculpture* (Dec. 2014), "Never having visited the region, Leigh relied on research and mediated imagery, and her decision to focus on face jugs, bottle trees, Mammies, and Wedgwood china paints a picture that feels less about Leigh than about preconceived notions of the South. Fortunately, the individual works were thought-provoking enough to carry the show."

FREE PEOPLE'S MEDICAL CLINIC

In 2014, Leigh collaborated with Creative Time, the Atlanta Contemporary Art Center and The Kitchen to create *Free People's Medical Clinic*, a month-long exhibition and event at the Stuyvesant Mansion, the home of Dr. Josephine English, the first African American woman to be an obstetrician-gynecologist in New York State. Part of Creative Time and Weeksville Heritage Center's *Funk, God, Jazz, and Medicine: Black Radical Brooklyn* exhibition, Leigh's event was inspired by the free medical clinics offered by the Black Panthers during the 1960s as well as the work of medical pioneers such as Dr. English; Dr. Susan Smith McKinney Steward, the first African American woman doctor in New York State; and the United Order of Tents, a secret organization established by black nurses during the Civil War and the oldest continually existing society of African American women in the United States .

A BUSY YEAR

Leigh's summer 2016 exhibit, *The Waiting Room*, at New York's New Museum, built on the *Free People's Medical Clinic*. The exhibit's title alluded to a 2008 incident in which Esmin Elizabeth Green, a black woman, died of a pulmonary embolism after waiting for twenty-four hours in a Brooklyn emergency room waiting area without being seen by a doctor. The incident was a particularly egregious example of the medical establishment's racial disparity in their concern for and treatment of patients and their pain.

While *The Waiting Room* was on display, two African American men, Philando Castile and Alton Sterling were shot and killed by police officers, in Minnesota and Louisiana, respectively. In response to these and other acts of violence toward African Americans, Leigh gathered other artists to form Black Women Artists for Black Lives Matter (BWAforBLM). Inspired by the

United Order of Tents, more than one hundred members of the collective met throughout the summer, in secret and without museum staff, to plan a takeover of the New Museum on September 1, 2016, as an extension of *The Waiting Room*. For four hours, the group met on two different floors, in the façade, lobby, and theater for conversation, performances, and workshops. Leigh later curated a second BWAforBLM event at Project Row Houses in Houston's Third Ward. Of the events, Helen Molesworth wrote for *Artforum* (Mar. 2018), "Given the lack of any such systematic inclusion of black women in the fields of Western culture prior to this moment, this recalibration seems both deeply necessary and positively exhilarating."

Later that month, Leigh's work was on display at the University of California Los Angeles's Hammer Museum. The exhibit, *Hammer Projects: Simone Leigh*, was her first solo museum show in Los Angeles. It featured Leigh's ceramics, a site-specific installation, and a public program, and was organized by Institute of Contemporary Art, Los Angeles curator Jamillah James.

Leigh received the Herb Alpert Award in the Arts in 2016. The annual award recognizes five artists at mid-career working in the arenas of visual arts, theater, music, dance, and film or video, and includes a $75,000 prize. In a statement on the *Herb Alpert Award in the Arts* website, Leigh stated, "I am involved in social practice and performance art but I consider myself a sculptor—so much work can be done by an object."

BRICK HOUSE

In August 2018 Leigh became the inaugural winner of the High Line Plinth commission, a series of large-scale public works displayed in the High Line, a public park located on a historic elevated rail line above the West Side of Manhattan. Leigh's winning entry, *Brick House*, unveiled in April 2019, is a sixteen-feet high bronze sculpture of an African American woman, whose braids descend over her torso. The shape mimics the traditional bell-shaped form of dwellings in Cameroon. The work's title came from a song by the Commodores, as Leigh told Pogrebin and Sheets, "It was a celebration of black womanhood that we hadn't really heard. That was what was resonant about it—not necessarily a male gaze but that beauty was associated with mightiness and strength, as opposed to fragility. Being solid."

Brick House is Leigh's second public work; the first, *inHarlem*, was shown in 2016–17 in Manhattan's Marcus Garvey Park. The largest sculpture she has ever made, *Brick House* was built as high as the plinth that holds it over a spur of the elevated park would allow. As Cecilia Alemani, director and chief curator of High Line Art, told Pogrebin and Sheets, "It's an icon, it's a goddess—this very powerful feminine presence in a very masculine environment, because all around you, you have these towering skyscrapers and cranes. It's very rare that in the public sphere you see a black person commemorated as a hero or simply elevated on a pedestal." The sculpture will be on display through September 2020.

Instead of making a smaller model that would need to be expanded, Leigh was able to work at a foundry in Philadelphia to create the full-size sculpture in clay. Working at full scale allowed Leigh to make small changes. One change was in the tilt of the woman's chin. Leigh also altered the original design of the hair from rosebuds (one of her signature looks) to cornrows.

LUHRING AUGUSTINE EXHIBIT

As she worked on the High Line sculpture, Leigh also prepared for a September 2018 solo exhibit at the Luhring Augustine gallery in New York, which has represented her work since 2016. It included a twenty-five-minute video that the Berlin Biennial commissioned. Leigh directed the video, which included what she described as "inside jokes to black women." Some of the same women who had been in the 2014 *Free People's Medical Clinic* show reappeared in the video.

The exhibit also featured thirteen pieces, eleven of them ceramic, which Leigh fired using the labor-intensive salt-firing method. Another piece, *No Face*, was cast in bronze. Ten of the works displayed female busts and bodies, made to appear jug- or vase-like. Many are without faces or eyes; all clearly display features that 4Columns art critic Aruna D'Souza described as "unmistakably African" (21 Sept. 2018). "They will not see us, and will not allow us to see them in their completeness, these anonymous, sightless beings, but they still allow us to experience their intense, visceral beauty."

PERSONAL LIFE

Leigh's studio is based in the Crown Heights neighborhood of Brooklyn, where she lives with her daughter, Zenobia, and their Tibetan terrier, Kafka.

SUGGESTED READING

Cochran, Rebecca Dimling. "Simone Leigh." *Sculpture*, vol. 33, no. 10, 2014, pp. 74–5. *Art Full Text* (H.W. Wilson), search.ebscohost.com/login.aspx?direct=true&db=aft&AN=99221756&site=eds-live. Accessed 14 May 2019.

Davis, Samara. "Room for Care: Simeon Leigh's Free People's Medical Clinic." *TDR: The Drama Review*, vol. 59, no. 4, 2015, pp. 169–76. www.mitpressjournals.org/doi/10.1162/DRAM_a_00503. Accessed 23 May 2019.

Latimer, Quinn. "Introducing Simone Leigh." *Modern Painters*, vol. 20, no. 9, 2008, p. 56. *Art Full Text* (H.W. Wilson), search.ebscohost.com/login.aspx?direct=true&db=aft&AN=505351437&site=eds-live. Accessed 14 May 2019.

Molesworth, Helen. "Art Is Medicine." *Artforum*, Mar. 2018, www.artforum.com/print/201803/helen-molesworth-on-the-work-of-simone-leigh-74304. Accessed 14 May 2019.

Pogrebin, Robin, and Hilarie Sheets. "An Artist Ascendant: Simone Leigh Moves into the Mainstream." *The New York Times*, 18 Aug. 2018, www.nytimes.com/2018/08/29/arts/design/simone-leigh-sculpture-high-line.html. Accessed 14 May 2019.

—*Judy Johnson*

Ben Lerner

Date of birth: February 4, 1979
Occupation: Poet

Ben Lerner is an American poet, author, and educator best known for his award-winning poetry books and novels.

EARLY LIFE AND EDUCATION

Benjamin Lerner is an American writer of National Book Award–nominated poetry and fiction. He was born in Topeka, Kansas, in 1979. His parents, Steve and Harriet Lerner, are both clinical psychologists. His mother is also an author of nonfiction psychology literature.

Lerner began writing poetry while attending high school in Topeka. Upon graduating, he attended Brown University, where he earned a BA in political science and an MFA in creative writing in 2003. While at Brown, he cofounded, with Deb Klowden, the literary magazine *No: A Journal of the Arts*. Shortly after earning his MFA, he published a book of sonnets titled *The Lichtenberg Figures*, in 2004. Lerner earned a Fulbright scholarship, which took him to Madrid, Spain. While living in Madrid, he wrote the poems that would become his second published book of poetry, *Angle of Yaw* (2006).

Lerner later moved to New York City, where he expanded his writing to include works of fiction. Lerner is a professor of English at Brooklyn College at the City University of New York. He has also taught at the University of Pittsburgh and California College of the Arts.

WRITING CAREER

Lerner's published poetry received immediate acclaim and accelerated his career as a writer. His sonnet collection, *The Lichtenberg Figures*, won the Hayden Carruth Award for new and emerging poets. *The Lichtenberg Figures* also received recognition as a Lannan Literary Selection and a position on *Library Journal*'s list of 2004's best poetry books. Lerner has been praised for his experimentation with the form of poems, particularly with his sonnets, which often break the conventions of sonnet structure.

Published in 2006, *Angle of Yaw* was another critical success, earning a nomination for the National Book Award. In his first two books of poetry, Lerner established his voice as a writer. His poems are known for being complex and avant-garde in their composition, while also humorous. His poems often address social issues including violence and political turmoil but use playful or absurdist language to generate a humorous effect. Lerner published his third collection of poems, *Mean Free Path*, in 2010. A collection of love poems, *Mean Free Path* diverged thematically from his first two works.

Having published three books of poetry, Lerner began writing his first novel, *Leaving the Atocha Station*. He later acknowledged that the poetry community is skeptical of fiction, and he feared backlash from his peers for his decision to publish a novel. He published *Leaving the Atocha Station* in 2011. The novel is a satire of the poetry industry. Of the criticism he faced from fellow poets, Lerner has noted in interviews that, "Poets really haven't gotten the news that the novel is also dead."

His second novel, *10:04*, was published in 2014. The novel, which began as a long poem and later incorporated essays and short stories spotlights a series of encounters with people in Lerner's life, including his family and friends. The novel was praised by the *New York Times*, who called it "frequently brilliant" and identified it as belonging to "an emerging genre" of fiction.

In addition to teaching and writing, Lerner has worked as the poetry editor for *Critical Quarterly*. His poetry has also been anthologized in *12x12: Conversations in Poetry and Poetics* and *Best American Poetry, New Voices* (2008).

IMPACT

Lerner has earned several noteworthy literary awards, in addition to the Hayden Carruth Award and his nomination for the National Book Award for Poetry. He was once honored at the Lyrik Festival in Münster, Germany, at which he was designated to sign the book of the city in a special ceremony recognizing his poetry. For *Leaving the Atocha Station*, Lerner won the Believer Book Award in 2012. He won a Guggenheim Fellowship in 2013, a Terry Southern Fiction Prize in 2014, and a MacArthur Foundation Fellowship in 2015.

PERSONAL LIFE

Lerner is married to Ariana Mangual, a professor of education at Rutgers University. They live in Brooklyn, New York, with their daughter.

SUGGESTED READING

"Ben Lerner." *Poetry Foundation*, n.d., https://www.poetryfoundation.org/poets/ben-lerner. Accessed 31 July 2019.

Kim, Shijung. "Lerner Attempts to Reinvent Form in *Mean Free Path.*" *Harvard Crimson*, 9 Mar. 2010, www.thecrimson.com/article/2010/3/9/mean-free-path-lerner/. Accessed 31 July 2019.

Kunzru, Hari. "Impossible Mirrors." *New York Times*, 6 Sept. 2014, www.nytimes.com/2014/09/07/books/review/1004-by-ben-lerner.html. Accessed 31 July 2019.

Plunkett, Adam. "Hilarity and Form." *New Republic*, 30 July 2010, newrepublic.com/article/76657/hilarity-and-form. Accessed 31 July 2019.

Sehgal, Parul. "Drawing Words from the Well of Art." *The New York Times*, 22 Aug. 2014, www.nytimes.com/2014/08/23/books/ben-lerner-imagines-different-futures-in-his-novel-1004.html. Accessed 31 July 2019.

Witt, Emily. "Ben Lerner: 'People Say, "Oh, Here's Another Brooklyn Novel by a Guy with Glasses."'" *Guardian*, 3 Jan. 2015, www.theguardian.com/books/2015/jan/03/ben-lerner-1004-novel-books-interview. Accessed 31 July 2019.

SELECTED WORKS

The Lichtenberg Figures, 2004; *Angle of Yaw*, 2006; *Mean Free Path*, 2010; *Leaving the Atocha Station*, 2011; *10:04*, 2014; *The Topeka School*, 2019

—*Richard Means*

Jessica Lessin

Date of birth: May 11, 1983
Occupation: Journalist and executive

Since the advent of the Internet, news media organizations have increasingly relied on advertising to drive user traffic, page views, and revenue—often at the expense of delivering quality journalism. Jessica Lessin, the founder and editor-in-chief of the subscriber-based technology news site *The Information*, has tried to reverse this trend. A graduate of Harvard University, Lessin launched *The Information* in 2013 after spending the previous eight years as a reporter for the *Wall Street Journal*, where she became known for her hard-driving coverage of Silicon Valley and the technology industry. A self-described "reportrepreneur," she has focused her

site, which has no advertising, toward delivering in-depth and meaningful stories to an exclusive group of subscribers, namely business and technology professionals. The site has since experienced steady subscriber growth, expanded into new markets, and developed a reputation as one of the top news organizations covering technology. As Lessin explained to Lucia Moses for *Business Insider* (17 Apr. 2019), "Our mission is always to be the most trusted source for the business world. . . . We're just scratching the surface of people who are interested in all the news and data with tech eating every industry."

EARLY LIFE AND EDUCATION

Lessin was born Jessica Elizabeth Vascellaro in 1983, and grew up in affluent Fairfield County, Connecticut. She was raised by high-achieving parents, both of whom received their undergraduate degrees from Brown University in 1974. Her father, Jerome, is a partner and the chief operating officer of TPG, one of the world's largest private equity firms; her mother, Mary, is a former retail buying executive who serves as a board member of Generation Citizen, a New York–based nonprofit organization geared toward civics education.

Precocious and ambitious, Lessin began her journalism career while attending New Canaan Country School, a private, independent day school for students in kindergarten through ninth grade. She was in seventh grade when her English teacher recruited her to write for the student newspaper, *The Keys*. Developing a penchant for interviewing and for putting together a

Photo by Gabriela Bhaskar via Wikimedia Commons

publication, Lessin told Joe Pompeo for *Politico* (24 Oct. 2016), "I caught the bug early."

Lessin's "bug" for journalism carried over to Greenwich Academy, where she held writing and editing roles with the school newspaper. Upon graduating from there in 2001, she attended Harvard University, where she further dedicated herself to the craft of reporting. She joined the university's prestigious daily student newspaper, the *Harvard Crimson*, and landed summer internships at a series of news outlets, including the Associated Press and the *Boston Globe*. "I think what drew me to journalism was I didn't have to pick one career," Lessin explained in a conversation with *Matter* magazine director Corey Ford, as quoted by Rebecca Radnaev for *Medium.com* (13 Sept. 2016). "I could constantly learn across many, and that just seemed to be pretty awesome."

Lessin found such opportunities at the *Wall Street Journal*, which she joined less than a week after graduating from Harvard magna cum laude with a degree in history in 2005. She started out working as an intern in the economics bureau of the paper before landing a permanent position covering consumer technology for its personal journal section.

SILICON VALLEY INSIDER

Lessin worked at the *Journal* for eight years, during which she wrote nearly a thousand articles and established a reputation for her dogged reportage. After spending the first three of those years in the paper's New York bureau, she was transferred to San Francisco to cover Silicon Valley and the technology industry. She covered such future tech behemoths as Google, Yahoo, Facebook, and Twitter, and helped break a number of major news stories, including Microsoft's failed attempt to acquire Yahoo in 2008 and Google's withdrawal from China in 2010. "She's fiercely smart and an absolutely relentless journalist," Wendy Pollack, a former news editor at the *Journal*, noted to Nellie Bowles for the *San Francisco Chronicle* (13 Dec. 2013). "To be anything other than hard hitting would be unfathomable to her."

In 2011, Lessin was part of an investigative team that was a finalist for the Pulitzer Prize for a groundbreaking series on digital privacy. That year she became a senior technology reporter at the *Journal* and started covering Apple, Inc., "one of the most coveted tech beats in the world," as Radnaev wrote. It was while covering that high-profile beat, however, that Lessin grew increasingly frustrated with the ever-changing direction of the paper, which had begun moving away from high-impact investigative reporting in favor of shorter commodity news stories that were aimed at generating clicks and traffic. "The whole media industry became so obsessed with traffic, page views, comprehensiveness," she said to Ford. "Everyone had to have every story. My job as a reporter had really changed."

Unsure about what audience she was writing for and uninterested in covering the same stories as her peers, Lessin resolved to launch her own venture, one with the central aim of delivering quality news stories. To do so, Lessin opted not to follow the predominant, ad-driven business models used by other news organizations. Instead, she took a completely different approach: to build a reader base willing to pay for content. She ultimately quit her job at the *Journal* in 2013 to found *The Information*, a subscription-only digital news site geared toward technology and business professionals. "I got up in the morning to write stories other people weren't writing, to help business leaders make decisions," she explained to Peter Kafka on his *Recode Media* podcast, as quoted by Eric Johnson for *Vox* (18 May 2017).

BREAKING THE DIGITAL MOLD

Lessin used personal resources to launch *The Information*, which started with just five full-time and three part-time employees. Eschewing advertising, the site, which is run like a startup, relies solely on subscriber revenue. For $399 a year, or $39 a month, subscribers receive two stories a day—as opposed to the hundreds larger sites publish—and invitations to networking events around the world. To produce top-notch stories on the technology industry, Lessin has recruited first-rate journalists, including former *Journal* colleagues like Martin Peers, who edited her at the paper. "I knew she'd be successful and I wanted to be part of it," Peers, now the site's managing editor, told Pompeo.

Despite facing industry skepticism, Lessin proved her detractors wrong, as *The Information* became an immediate success. Thanks to its niche focus and high-quality journalism, the site quickly landed thousands of paying subscribers in tech and business, ranging from entrepreneurs to hedge fund managers. As its editor-in-chief, Lessin began overseeing, as well as writing, stories that influenced the way global business leaders made deals and decisions. Such stories, which have included behind-the-scenes scoops on company boardroom meetings and breaking CEO announcements, brought her to the attention of several notable publications: in 2014, *Business Insider* listed her as one of the 100 most influential women in technology on Twitter, and she was included on *Vanity Fair*'s annual New Establishment list.

Nevertheless, Lessin's role as a "reportrepreneur" has not come without difficulties. She has sometimes drawn criticism for being too close to the people she covers, which has led to questions about audience-pandering and objectivity.

Still, as Lessin explained to Melissa Marr for the *Columbia Journalism Review* (Fall/Winter 2016), "If you don't write the stories subscribers know to be true and tough, it's bad for business. You earn respect by being tough, not writing puff pieces."

COMPANY ON THE RISE

Lessin's mission to deliver tough and influential stories has not just earned her respect but has also enabled *The Information* to enjoy steady growth. By 2016, the site had more than doubled both its staff (to nineteen) and subscriber base (to an undisclosed number in the thousands). That year it published a slew of notable scoops, one of which included an exposé on Tony Fadell, the founder of the home automation company Nest Labs, which was acquired by Google in 2014. The story shed light on Fadell's tyrannical management style, which alienated employees and hampered Nest's ability to roll out new products; in its wake, Fadell resigned from his post as company head. "We know how to write really great articles," Lessin affirmed to Ford, "and that's not coming up with a clever aggregator."

Also in 2016, *The Information* opened an Asia bureau in Hong Kong as part of efforts to expand into new markets. Lessin hired the Pulitzer Prize–winning former *Wall Street Journal* reporter Shai Oster to run the bureau, which caters to many of the site's subscribers. Besides the United States, she has hosted networking events in China and other countries around the world to further connect with her readership. Such events have ranged from informal drink and dinner outings to fancy parties thrown at the homes of high-profile business and technology executives.

Over the past three years, *The Information* has added other subscriber options, including a premium, invitation-only subscription for professional investors that costs $10,000 a year and a student edition for only $234 a year. The site has also broadened its coverage to include the automotive and financial industries, policymaking, and legacy media. In 2019, it launched another new product, The Information Courses, which allows people to sample articles, data points, conference calls, and more materials on a specific topic.

Lessin has said that *The Information*, whose headquarters are in downtown San Francisco, may experiment with advertising in the future to add other revenue streams. However, it will continue to remain a subscription-focused site. *The Information* has grown to thirty-five staff members and tens of thousands of subscribers; around 300,000 people receive its weekly newsletter. Commenting on the site's long-term goals, Lessin boldly told Lucia Moses in the *Business Insider* article: "Our ambition isn't to build a subscription business—our goal is to build the most impactful news organization for the next century."

PERSONAL LIFE

Lessin lives with her husband, Sam Lessin, whom she met at Harvard and married in 2012. Sam is a tech entrepreneur and the former vice president of product management at Facebook who now writes a weekly column for *The Information*, in San Francisco. The Lessins count tech-industry heavyweights such as Facebook founder Mark Zuckerberg (who was one year behind them at Harvard) as close friends. The couple, whose wedding was described by *Business Insider* as the tech networking event of that year, have often been listed among the top power couples in the tech industry. They celebrated the birth of their first child in early 2017.

In addition to being featured in various print publications, Lessin has appeared on CNN, NPR, CNBC, and PBS. She often delivers speeches at conferences around the world.

SUGGESTED READING

Bowles, Nellie. "Tech Titans Fete News Start-up." *SFGate*, 13 Dec. 2013, www.sfgate.com/technology/article/Jessica-Lessin-s-startup-courts-broad-audience-5059958.php#photo-5587005. Accessed 26 Aug. 2019.

Johnson, Eric. "Jessica Lessin Built a Business to Prove Information Doesn't Have to Be Free." *Vox*, 18 May 2017, www.vox.com/2017/5/18/15654470/jessica-lessin-the-information-subscription-advertising-paywall-journalism-recode-podcast. Accessed 26 Aug. 2019.

Lessin, Jessica. "The Founder of The Information on What Media Companies Are Doing Wrong." Interview by Mathew Ingram. *Fortune*, 5 Aug. 2016, fortune.com/2016/08/05/jessica-lessin-the-information/. Accessed 26 Aug. 2019.

Marr, Melissa. "Inside (The) Information." *Columbia Journalism Review*, Fall/Winter 2016, www.cjr.org/the_profile/information_lessin_silicon_valley_digital.php. Accessed 26 Aug. 2019.

Moses, Lucia. "Jessica Lessin Thinks The Information Could Spend More on Journalism Than The New York Times or Wall Street Journal Some Day." *Business Insider*, 17 Apr. 2019, www.businessinsider.com/jessica-lessin-wants-the-information-to-be-the-most-impactful-news-outlet-2019-3. Accessed 26 Aug. 2019.

Pompeo, Joe. "The Morning Media Profile: Jessica Lessin's Rise from Reporter to Entrepreneur." *Politico*, 24 Oct. 2016, www.politico.com/media/story/2016/10/the-morning-media-profile-jessica-lessins-rise-from-reporter-to-entrepreneur-004826. Accessed 26 Aug. 2019.

Radnaev, Rebecca. "For Some Reason It's Kind of a 'Bad Thing' to Write Kick Ass Articles." *Medium.com*, 13 Sept. 2016, medium.com/matter-driven-narrative/for-some-reason-its-kind-of-a-bad-thing-to-just-write-kick-ass-articles-380e4d3492b4. Accessed 26 Aug. 2019.

—*Chris Cullen*

Lori Lightfoot

Date of birth: August 4, 1962
Occupation: Politician and lawyer

Photo by Daniel X. O'Neil via Wikimedia Commons

Democrat Lori Elaine Lightfoot, an outsider who had never held elective office, became Chicago's fifty-sixth mayor on May 20, 2019. She and her closest opponent, Toni Preckwinkle, made history: for the first time, the mayoral race was being contested by two African American women. Furthermore, as a lesbian, Lightfoot ran as a candidate closely connected to LGBTQ issues. With her election, Chicago became the largest city in the United States to elect an African American woman as mayor. In her inaugural address, Lightfoot said, "In Chicago, we will build together, we will celebrate our differences. We will embrace our uniqueness and we will make certain that all have every opportunity to succeed." Her inauguration included police officers in kilts playing bagpipes, as well as prayers by an imam, a pastor, a rabbi, and a priest.

EARLY LIFE AND EDUCATION

Lightfoot's parents, Elijah and Ann, each migrated from the South to Ohio, where they met at an Urban League dance. She was their fourth and youngest child. Before her birth, her father became seriously ill and fell into a coma; when he awoke, he was completely deaf. Despite that challenge, he continued to work multiple jobs as a handyman, janitor, and barber to support the family. Her mother also worked in low-wage jobs in nursing homes and mental hospitals before becoming a home health aide. Watching her parents' many struggles gave Lightfoot a lifelong commitment to fairness and social justice.

Her mother encouraged her daughter to excel academically. Lightfoot excelled in school and was elected class president three times while a student at Washington High School in Massillon, Ohio. She graduated in 1980; the school recognized her in 2013 as a Distinguished Citizen. Four years after graduating from high school and working her way through college, she graduated from the University of Michigan with a bachelor's degree in political science.

She then worked as a legislative aide in Washington, DC, for two years before receiving a full scholarship to the University of Chicago Law School. There she served as president of the Law Students Association and showed the kind of out-front advocacy on social issues that would characterize her rise in professional and political life: when a law firm interviewer made racist and sexist comments to another African American student, Lightfoot was instrumental in having the firm banned from on-campus interviewing for a year. In the wake of that decision, other national law schools also banned the firm from interviewing. Following her election as mayor of Chicago, Geoffrey R. Stone, dean of the Law School when Lightfoot attended, told Becky Beaupre Gillespie for *Chicago University Law School News* (3 Apr. 2019): "In her approach to this critical moment, Lori clearly demonstrated the leadership and judgment that have now taken her to this remarkable step in her career." Lightfoot also played quarterback for the intramural women's football team and for the law school newspaper, the *Phoenix*. She earned her JD in 1989. Lightfoot later served on the University of Chicago Law School Visiting Committee, an advisory body.

EARLY CAREER

Lightfoot chose to stay in Chicago after graduating from law school, joining the law firm of Mayer Brown. From 1996 until 2002, she was an assistant US attorney for the Northern District of Illinois. She followed that position with a two-year stint as the chief administrator of the Office of Professional Standards for the Chicago Police Department (CPD), investigating police misconduct.

Lightfoot then moved to the Chicago Office of Emergency Management and Communications from 2004 to 2005, when she became first deputy procurement officer of the Chicago Department of Procurement Services. During that time she went after corruption in city government, a daunting task at the time, and she left the job after only a few months.

Lightfoot then returned to Mayer Brown, rising to partner. In 2015 Mayor Rahm Emanuel appointed Lightfoot to chair the Chicago Police Board, which oversees the CPD; later that year she was appointed to chair the Police Accountability Task Force, created in the wake of the police shooting of African American teen Laquan McDonald.

The panel's report, with more than one hundred suggestions for improving relations, excoriated the CPD for systemic racism and conduct that destroyed the department's credibility with residents. The report raised Lightfoot's political profile. As Mitch Smith reported for the *New York Times* (3 Apr. 2019), when the report was released, Lightfoot said, "What we heard from people all across the city is they felt like they didn't even have a claim to the geography in front of their house, on their street, or in their neighborhoods."

The report and its aftermath put Lightfoot somewhat at odds with Emanuel, whom she publicly pressured to carry out its recommendations. In May 2018 Lightfoot resigned from the Chicago Police Board and announced she herself was running for mayor—initially against Emanuel, until he announced later that year he would not seek a third term.

RUNNING FOR MAYOR

Lightfoot left her position as a senior equity partner at Mayer Brown upon deciding to run for mayor. About her decision to enter the mayoral contest with no experience in elective office, Lightfoot told Tim Peacock for the *Windy City Times* (13 Feb. 2019), "I got into the race because I saw that there's a lot of great things that were going on in the city, but the prosperity certainly wasn't spread evenly around the city's neighborhoods. And I saw too many families that looked like the family that I grew up in and individuals who look like me, and under similar circumstances, really struggling."

Lightfoot ran on a platform of ending Chicago city government's notorious culture of corruption: her campaign slogan was "Bring in the Light," a play on her name and her promise to bring transparency to city government. She pledged to curb the power of the city's fifty aldermen, who almost completely controlled development in their respective wards through so-called aldermanic prerogative, creating opportunities for bribe and graft. Her campaign promises also included reforming policing, tackling the city's huge pension-fund shortfall, creating more affordable housing and better public schools, and addressing gun violence.

From a field of fourteen contenders in the first round of voting in February 2019, Lightfoot and Toni Preckwinkle, president of the Cook County Board of Supervisors, were the top two vote-getters, but neither topped 50 percent, triggering a runoff election on April 11. In the runoff, Lightfoot won a sweeping victory in all fifty wards, garnering nearly 74 percent of the vote. On election night, as Stephon Johnson reported for the *New Amsterdam News*, Lightfoot told her supporters: "Today, you did more than make history. You created a movement for change. They're watching us and they're seeing the beginning of something a little different." On the day of her inauguration, she signed an executive order banning aldermanic prerogative.

IMPROVING EDUCATION

In her inaugural address, Lightfoot suggested that the four stars in Chicago's city flag could represent the four guiding stars of her administration: public safety, education, stability (in finances, housing, and business), and integrity in city government.

When Lightfoot took office, Chicago Public Schools, the third largest school system in the country, had an enviable report card, with a nearly 80-percent high school graduation rate, which was an all-time high. Average test scores had zoomed, and students were learning at a rate faster than 96 percent of the nation's school districts.

However, conscious of the loud grievances from the Chicago Teachers Union about layoffs, school closures, and expanded charter schools under her predecessor, Lightfoot promised to freeze the number of charter schools in Chicago and to funnel money from magnet schools and into neighborhood schools. She intended to further expand early childhood education, building on the structure that offers free prekindergarten to all four-year-olds.

Another area of education Lightfoot highlighted in her inaugural address was the need for vocational education for those who were uninterested in getting a college degree. She said, "Every student should have the option to pursue vocational and technical training. We will work with businesses and unions to set up apprenticeships for those who want to learn a trade. We will then connect Chicago's employers with our job-ready students while they're in school, so they can get to work the day they graduate."

TACKLING PUBLIC SAFETY

Lightfoot also promised to address the city's high rate of gun violence, which spikes during the hot months of summer. As Mitch Smith, Julie Bosman, and Monica Davey reported for the *New York Times* (3 Apr. 2019), Lightfoot's website declared her contention that "no child should have to worry about the consequences of going to the park and no parent should have to keep their kids inside on a warm day for fear of violence."

In addition, Lightfoot faces a police department ridden with scandals, including excessive use of force and racism, as well as the city's high rate of homicide. Lightfoot pledged to attack the corruption in the CPD. As early as 2017 Lightfoot told Michel Martin for National Public Radio (7 Jan. 2017), "We need to have more federal gun prosecutions in Chicago. Our federal partners from the U.S. attorney's office, the ATF, the FBI need to be much more invested in this overall strategy. Chicago Police Department cannot tackle this issue by itself. This is not a problem that we're going to arrest our way out of."

She also commented on the need for improved police relations within the communities regarding the problem of reentry after serving prison terms, when offenders return to areas of the city that contributed to their crimes. After winning the election, Lightfoot asked that the grand jury investigation into the role of the three officers who had been acquitted (a fourth was convicted) in McDonald's death be reopened.

FIGHTING FOR LGBTQ RIGHTS

When Lightfoot was running her election campaign, she emphasized the need for progress in the city's treatment of members of the LGBTQ community. She cited the reality of only one LGBTQ liaison to the mayor's office for the whole city, as well as the issue of homelessness and violence, particularly against transgender people. In addition, she sought to address access to health care and the availability of drugs to prevent HIV/AIDS from spreading.

PERSONAL LIFE

As a young person, Lightfoot attended St. James AME Zion Church in Massillon, serving on boards and working with youth of the church. She was also a founding trustee of Christ the King Jesuit High School, created to serve African American students on Chicago's West Side.

Lightfoot married her longtime partner, Amy Eshleman, on June 1, 2014, the day same-sex marriages were first performed in Illinois. The couple live in the Logan Square neighborhood with their daughter, Vivian.

SUGGESTED READING

Camera, Lauren. "Learning on the Job: The Fight to Fix Chicago's Schools." *U.S. News & World Report*, 12 Apr. 2019, www.usnews.com/news/education-news/articles/2019-04-12/chicago-mayor-rahm-emanuel-leaves-a-legacy-of-improved-schools. Accessed 18 June 2019.

Guarino, Mark. "Lightfoot Promises 'Reform Is Here' as She Becomes Chicago's 56th Mayor." *The Washington Post*, 20 May 2019, www.washingtonpost.com/national/lori-lightfoot-promises-reform-is-here-as-she-becomes-chicagos-56th-mayor/2019/05/20/6f500a38-7b1a-11e9-a5b3-34f3edf1351e_story.html. Accessed 19 June 2019.

Johnson, Stephon. "CTU Says Election of Lightfoot Won't Stop Their Push for Education Reform." *New York Amsterdam News*, 11 Apr. 2019, amsterdamnews.com/news/2019/apr/11/ctu-says-election-lightfoot-wont-stop-their-push-e. Accessed 18 June 2019.

Lightfoot, Lori. "Full Speech: Mayor Lori Lightfoot's Inauguration." *YouTube*, uploaded by Chicago Sun-Times, 20 May 2019, www.youtube.com/watch?v=iyEH1reTOrU. Accessed 18 June 2019.

Morell, Claudia. "Former Federal Prosecutor Lori Lightfoot Sworn in as Chicago's Mayor." *NPR*, 20 May 2019, www.npr.org/2019/05/20/725139720/former-federal-prosecutor-lori-lightfoot-sworn-in-as-chicagos-mayor. Accessed 18 June 2019.

Peacock, Tim. "Elections 2019, Mayor: Lori Lightfoot Talks LGBTQ Policy, Police Accountability." *Windy City Times*, 13 Feb. 2019, www.windycitymediagroup.com/lgbt/ELECTIONS-2019-MAYOR-Lori-Lightfoot-talks-LGBTQ-policy-police-accountability/65496.html. Accessed 18 June 2019.

"Who Is Lori Lightfoot?" *Chicago Tribune*, 26 Jan. 2019, www.chicagotribune.com/politics/elections/ct-met-cb-lori-lightfoot-chicago-mayor-bio-20190124-story.html. Accessed 18 June 2019.

—*Judy Johnson*

Robert Lighthizer

Date of birth: October 11, 1947
Occupation: Attorney and government official

Robert Lighthizer has been the United States trade representative in the administration of President Donald Trump since May 2017. In that role, a cabinet-level position within the Executive Office of the President, he recommends trade policy to President Trump and represents the United States at the World Trade Organization (WTO). Lighthizer, a longtime international trade attorney, served as the deputy trade representative under Bill Brock during the administration of President Ronald Reagan in the 1980s. He also served as Senator Bob Dole's campaign treasurer and economic adviser during Dole's

Photo by Stephanie Chasez/White House Official Photo

unsuccessful bid for president in 1996. President Trump announced his selection of Lighthizer on January 2, 2017, and Lighthizer was approved by Congress in May.

Lighthizer's ascension to the post is emblematic of a dramatic shift in US trade policy. Lighthizer is usually seen, like Trump, as a protectionist, but Quinn Slobodian for *Foreign Policy* magazine (6 Aug. 2018) recently described what he called "Lighthizerism" as a more aggressive form of globalism. Lighthizer favors individual nations cutting bilateral trade deals and using an arsenal of political weapons to achieve the most advantageous outcome. As Slobodian put it, "Paradoxical as it may seem, Lighthizerism sees trade wars as the road to freer trade." He quoted Lighthizer telling Congress: "We're not talking about a level playing field. What we're saying to the country is, 'We'll give you better access than the rest of the world, and you give us approximately an equal amount of better access.'"

Lighthizer's personal negotiating style has some similarity to that of his boss. "His personal style is that, in meetings, he uses filthy humor and vulgar language to throw people off their stride," one trade lawyer told Matthew Korade, Adam Behsudi, and Louis Nelson for *Politico* (3 Jan. 2017).

EARLY LIFE AND EDUCATION
Robert "Bob" Emmett Lighthizer was born in Ashtabula, Ohio, on October 11, 1947, to Michaelene "Micki" and Dr. Orville James Lighthizer. His brother, Jim, grew up to become a Maryland state politician and expert on the US Civil War; he is president of the Civil War

Trust preservation society. One of Lighthizer's ancestors, the Bavarian-born George Lighthizer, crossed the Delaware River with George Washington's Continental Army during the Revolutionary War. "We've probably got some horse thieves in there," Jim Lighthizer joked to Shawn Donnan for *Bloomberg Businessweek* (20 Sept. 2018) of his family tree. "But there's no traitors."

Lighthizer grew up in Ashtabula, a former steel-manufacturing city on Lake Erie. Ashtabula was a blue-collar town, but Lighthizer grew up wealthy. Childhood friends recall him as opinionated and persuasive. One friend, David Lucas, told Dave DeLuca of the Ashtabula *Star Beacon* (9 Jan. 2017), that Lighthizer once convinced him to jump off a garage roof to retrieve a paper airplane. "I knew it was too far to jump, but he actually talked me into it," Lucas recalled. "I sprained my ankle, but they iced it and apologized, so I didn't care. He was known to be a good communicator even then."

Lighthizer attended Gilmour Academy, a preparatory school outside nearby Cleveland, and graduated in 1965. He went on to enroll at Georgetown University in Washington, DC. He earned his bachelor's degree in 1969 and his law degree, also from Georgetown, in 1973.

DEPUTY TRADE REPRESENTATIVE
After graduation, Lighthizer took a job with the Washington law firm Covington and Burling. In 1978 he was recruited to serve as the staff director of the Senate Finance Committee. (His recruiter was Elizabeth Dole, wife of Senator Bob Dole, the committee's senior Republican.) "I was probably the only conservative in the firm; that's why they recommended me," he joked to Karen Hosle for the *Baltimore Sun* (26 July 1996). Lighthizer worked closely with Dole, who was chairman of the Finance Committee from 1981 to 1983. Lighthizer remained close with the late senator for years and served on his unsuccessful presidential campaign in 1996. "Working for Dole is like being a priest," he told Hosle. "You can never leave. You've got the job for life." During his tenure on the Finance Committee, Lighthizer helped craft President Ronald Reagan's tax cuts in 1981 and the subsequent tax increase, to restore lost revenue from the cuts, in 1982.

In 1983 Lighthizer was named deputy trade representative under Bill Brock, overseeing industrial policy. The following year he led a series of international negotiations on steel imports. He was part of a team that sought to get countries to reduce their steel exports voluntarily—in the face of steep tariffs. "I try to be friendly in negotiations," he told Susan F. Rasky for the *New York Times* (30 Sept. 1984). "I'm not the theatrical type. The art of persuasion is knowing where the leverage is." Colleagues and opponents took a different view of Lighthizer's techniques. He earned the nickname Missile Man from the Japanese, after he folded up their proposal and flung it back to them as a paper airplane.

The agreements that resulted from the steel negotiations were later deemed violations of WTO trade rules, but as Korade, Behsudi, and Nelson wrote in 2017, "they are strikingly similar to the kind of deal-making Trump envisions as he seeks to fulfill his promise to get tough on China and other countries."

CAREER AS A TRADE LAWYER

In 1985 Lighthizer joined the Washington branch of the law firm Skadden, Arps, Slate, Meagher, and Flom as a trade lawyer. He became a familiar Beltway figure, known for his asceticism and discipline. One article reported that he did not drink coffee, another that he kept a strict diet and was devoted to rigorous exercise. In other areas of his life, Lighthizer was more flamboyant; he was known to enjoy his red Porsche 911 Targa. One of his most prominent clients was the US Steel Corporation, on behalf of whom he filed numerous lawsuits seeking to minimize foreign competition through US government protections. As a trade lawyer, Ana Swanson wrote for the New York Times (9 Mar. 2018), Lighthizer "embraced the view that countries like China, South Korea, and Mexico have bent or broken global trade agreements to take business from the United States, generating worrisome trade deficits and weakening American manufacturing." As economic adviser to Dole's 1996 presidential campaign, Lighthizer offered a reserved endorsement of the creation of the WTO, the international organization founded in 1995 that sets global rules for international trade. However, he reversed his position a few years later, deciding the organization impinged on US sovereignty without offering sufficient protection against other nations' bad behavior.

In 2008 Lighthizer published a March 6 opinion piece in the New York Times, "Grand Old Protectionists," criticizing then Republican presidential candidate John McCain for his embrace of free trade. Citing Reagan—and the aforementioned Japanese steel trade agreement that he negotiated—Lighthizer urged McCain to adopt an economic policy that split the difference between free trade and old-school protectionism. Of free traders like McCain, he wrote, "They embrace unbridled free trade, even as it helps China become a superpower. They see only bright lines, even when it means bowing to the whims of anti-American bureaucrats at the World Trade Organization." In 2010 he testified before Congress about China's brand of state-controlled capitalism. "They have a system, and their system is challenging our system," he said then, as quoted by Slobodian. Slobodian raised concerns about this particular outlook, and the tenor of Lighthizer's proposed solutions: "Lighthizerism, because it is structured around the idea of interstate competition, bends toward state capitalism. It reserves for government executives the sovereign right to decide when economic rules bind and when they do not. Democratic accountability is an impediment, from this perspective: an unfair disadvantage that the adversary does not share."

US TRADE REPRESENTATIVE

Lighthizer was an early fan of Trump. When Trump was debating running for president in 2012, Lighthizer wrote a May 9, 2011, opinion piece for the conservative Washington Times— "Donald Trump Is No Liberal on Trade"—praising Trump's tough talk about trade with China. Once president, Trump announced Lighthizer as his pick for trade representative in January 2017. Lighthizer was confirmed with bipartisan support, despite opposition from Senator McCain, in May.

Since assuming his post, Lighthizer has been a vitally important member of Trump's team. After a year of talks with representatives from Canada and Mexico, Lighthizer negotiated a new North American Free Trade Agreement called the US-Mexico-Canada Agreement (USMCA). The deal needs to be approved by Congress, though the Democratic lawmakers set to take over in the House of Representatives in 2019 remained skeptical. Many, including some inside Trump's own administration, find Trump's trade strategy—wielding tariffs as weapons—alarming. "Fundamentally, Trump seems to misunderstand how tariffs work, insisting that they act as a tax on foreign companies and translate into more American wealth," Annie Lowrey wrote for the Atlantic (6 Dec. 2018). "But the tariffs are acting, as one would expect them to act, as a tax on American consumers, raising domestic prices and slowing the domestic economy." Regardless, Lighthizer supports Trump's ongoing trade war with China and other countries, including Trump's decision to place hefty tariffs on imported steel and aluminum. In the spring of 2018 Trump imposed over $250 billion of tariffs on Chinese goods in retaliation for unfair trading practices; late that year Lighthizer was named chief negotiator in talks to resolve the trade war with China.

PERSONAL LIFE

Lighthizer is married with two grown children, Claire and Robert.

SUGGESTED READING

DeLuca, Dave. "Area Native Nominated as Trade Ambassador." Star Beacon, 9 Jan. 2017, www.starbeacon.com/news/local_news/area-native-nominated-as-trade-ambassador/

article_e05e0738-346e-5303-b438-ab3c-c92a2f6e.html. Accessed 4 Dec. 2018.

Donnan, Shawn. "The Tough Negotiator Turning Trump's Trade Bluster into Reality." *Bloomberg Businessweek*, 20 Sept. 2018, www.bloomberg.com/news/articles/2018-09-20/the-tough-negotiator-turning-trump-s-trade-bluster-into-reality. Accessed 4 Dec. 2018.

Hosle, Karen. "Casting a Reflection on Dole Advisor." *The Baltimore Sun*, 26 July 1996, articles.baltimoresun.com/1996-07-26/news/1996208007_1_bob-dole-lighthizer-policy. Accessed 5 Dec. 2018.

Korade, Matthew, Adam Behsudi, and Louis Nelson. "Trump Picks Lighthizer to Serve as U.S. Trade Representative." *Politico*, 3 Jan. 2017, www.politico.com/blogs/donald-trump-administration/2017/01/robert-lighthizer-us-trade-representative-trump-233116. Accessed 6 Dec. 2018.

Rasky, Susan F. "The Steel Trade Negotiations; the Experts Who Will Forge the New Quotas." *The New York Times*, 30 Sept. 1984, www.nytimes.com/1984/09/30/business/the-steel-trade-negotiations-the-experts-who-will-forge-the-new-quotas.html. Accessed 6 Dec. 2018.

Slobodian, Quinn. "You Live in Robert Lighthizer's World Now." *Foreign Policy*, 6 Aug. 2018, foreignpolicy.com/2018/08/06/you-live-in-robert-lighthizers-world-now-trump-trade. Accessed 5 Dec. 2018.

Swanson, Ana. "The Little-Known Trade Advisor Who Wields Enormous Power in Washington." *The New York Times*, 9 Mar. 2018, www.nytimes.com/2018/03/09/us/politics/robert-lighthizer-trade.html. Accessed 7 Dec. 2018.

—*Molly Hagan*

Evangeline Lilly

Date of birth: August 3, 1979
Occupation: Actor, author

Throughout her career as an actor, Evangeline Lilly has struggled with retiring from the profession. Her first rush of fame came during the six-season run of *Lost* (2004–10), the cult smash network series about a group of plane crash survivors on a deserted island in the Pacific. The international fame never sat well with her, though, and she left acting shortly after *Lost*'s end in 2010 to pursue a quieter life. However, she was lured back to acting with an intriguing role as a warrior elf in the 2013 second installment of Peter Jackson's three-film adaptation of J. R. R. Tolkien's novel *The Hobbit* (1937). Beginning in 2015, she has also been acclaimed for her

approach to the role of the Wasp in the Marvel Cinematic Universe series of superhero films.

Yet now that she has grown more comfortable with her life as an actor, Lilly has little interest in playing flat characters and remains very choosy about her roles. "I don't like the idea of playing a one-dimensional character who is just fearless, strong and killer and has instincts and just thrives in dangerous circumstances—that's really boring to me and I don't think it represents what most women feel inside," she remarked to Leigh Blickley for the *Huffington Post* (9 Dec. 2014). Upon reflection of her atypical and winding career path, Lilly has often expressed a sense of gratitude regarding the opportunities that she has been given. "I can only chalk it up to fate and destiny, to what I'm supposed to be doing," she told Jacob Stolworthy for *Independent* (1 Aug. 2018). "It's unprecedented and ridiculous—I don't know why I'm so lucky."

EARLY LIFE AND CAREER

Nicole Evangeline Lilly was born in Fort Saskatchewan, Alberta, Canada, on August 3, 1979, the second of three daughters, and later raised in British Columbia. Her father was a manager at a grocery store and her mother, who also worked for Estée Lauder, operated a day-care center from the family home. She was raised in the Baptist and Mennonite faiths, which played a large part in her outlook on life. She has also credited her upbringing, in which she and her family did not have much wealth, in shaping her feelings of self-worth. "My family didn't have a lot of money, and I'm grateful for that. Money is the longest route to happiness," she explained in

Photo by Gage Skidmore via Wikimedia Commons

an interview for *Women's Health* (9 May 2009). A Sunday school teacher for many years, she additionally harbored a passion for humanitarian work. At one point in her late teens, she worked as a missionary in the Philippines.

Lilly was also athletic and bookish, keeping a journal, writing stories, playing soccer, and serving on the student council. To help pay for her college tuition at the University of British Columbia, she worked several odd jobs, as a flight attendant, a waitress, and a grease monkey doing oil changes on big rigs. While an undergraduate, she was approached by representatives of a modeling agency who wanted her to sign with them. Initially, she had little interest in a modeling career, but signed anyway, hoping that any modeling jobs she received might help pay for her degree in international relations. Not really a fan of her original bookings in commercials, she eventually also found more enjoyable work as an extra, appearing on television in episodes of *Tru Calling* (2003) and *Smallville* (2002–4). She also appeared in films like *Stealing Sinatra* (2003), *Freddy vs. Jason* (2003), and *White Chicks* (2004).

LOST

Lilly had little acting experience and no formal training when she submitted her audition tape to producer and director J. J. Abrams, who was then developing, along with Jeffrey Lieber and Damon Lindelof, a new sci-fi-tinged show titled *Lost*. Abrams had been looking for some time for a lead actor to play the role of Kate Austen, one of the survivors of a plane crash on a mysterious island in the Pacific. He saw her tape and immediately knew he had found his Kate in Lilly, as she had just the right combination of qualities he had been looking for. Although still unsure about a life in acting, and having only seen part of the script, Lilly took the role and, in just enough time, secured a visa to film in the United States. She figured that if she were unhappy during the filming of the pilot, she would just go back to school. "I remember at the time thinking, I have *no* idea if I want to do this," she told Adam B. Vary for *BuzzFeed* (2 Dec. 2014). "I just know it's a one-in-a-million chance, and it happened. There's got to be some higher power at work that's opening this door for me . . . I'm just going to go for it."

ABC ultimately picked up the pilot. After *Lost* began airing in September 2004, it became a huge hit—a serialized television drama with enormous weekly ratings and a cult-like, devoted following of fans. Lilly, still unconfident in her acting ability and out of her element, remained wary at first. "I'm a pretty skeptical person and I'm a realistic person. In the early days, the buzz built around it, but I was still hesitant to wager on it," she said to Gayle MacDonald for the

Globe and Mail (11 Sept. 2005). During *Lost's* initial run, Gavin Edwards described fans' fascination with the show in *Rolling Stone* (6 Oct. 2005): "*Lost* is the strange, addictive, highly unlikely hit show that cross-pollinates *Survivor*, *Twin Peaks* and *Gilligan's Island*."

Despite Lilly's initial reservations, *Lost* maintained its popularity among loyal fans, running for six seasons before ending in 2010. In 2006, she and her castmates accepted the Screen Actors Guild (SAG) Award for Outstanding Performance by an Ensemble in a Drama Series. Many of the show's fans were frustrated when *Lost* did not connect every single dot in its mythology in its final episode. Years afterward, Lilly found herself still discussing and defending the series finale.

BECOMING AN ELF FOR THE HOBBIT FILMS

Lilly was never entirely comfortable with her fame, or even with being an actor, which, she said in her interview for *Women's Health*, she still did not consider her "ultimate dream." After making a sci-fi film, *Real Steel* (2011), she effectively retired from the world of acting, in part to pursue other options such as writing and humanitarian work, settling in Hawaii.

Director Peter Jackson, who had made the critically acclaimed *Lord of the Rings* film trilogy based on the novels of J. R. R. Tolkien, managed to get in contact with her through her partner after calling around Hollywood in search of her. Lilly recalled to Blickley, "In 2004 or 2005, I met him . . . and he said to me then, 'If I had met you before I made "Rings," I would have made you an elf.' And it broke my heart! I was like, 'But they're over! That means I'll never be an elf!' It was kind of crushing and also a massive compliment at the same time. Then, in the crazy twist of fate, 10 years later, he called me up and said, 'Would you like to play a warrior elf in "The Hobbit"?'"

The Hobbit, published in 1937, serves as a prequel to Tolkien's *Lord of the Rings* books. Jackson wanted to expand Tolkien's novel and make it a three-film series, the first of which was shown in theaters in 2012. Lilly's character, Tauriel, was a character Jackson created with her specifically in mind. The role was a dream come true for Lilly, whose favorite novel as a young girl had been *The Hobbit*. And the experience of playing the elf archer in two of the three Hobbit films—*The Hobbit: The Desolation of Smaug* (2013) and *The Hobbit: The Battle of the Five Armies* (2014)—proved to be immeasurably fulfilling for her. In an interview with Katie Kilkenny for the *Hollywood Reporter* (5 July 2018), she stated, "One of the highlights in my life was living in New Zealand for that year and being a part of that family. That helped open my eyes to the fact that, OK, this job can be a joy, it's just a matter of how you approach it, and what you do with it, how much I put myself out there, and to a certain degree, how much I work."

During that time, she also experienced success in her dream of writing, which she has often described as her real passion. Her first book, a work for children titled *The Squickerwonkers*, was published in 2014. Her aim is to develop an entire series around the characters in this initial cautionary tale, which she first conceptualized at the age of fourteen.

JOINING THE MARVEL UNIVERSE AS THE WASP

Around the time that she completed work on the Hobbit films, Lilly was contacted by representatives of Marvel Studios, which had produced a series of blockbuster films bringing Marvel Comics' enormous cast of superhero characters to life on the big screen. Marvel was casting for *Ant-Man*, a 2015 film about a superhero with the power to change his size at will. They wanted Lilly for the role of Hope van Dyne, the daughter of the original Wasp, who would later take on the shrinking superhero mantle herself and serve as Ant-Man's mentor and partner. Lilly readily agreed.

In *Ant-Man*, Hope helps the new Ant-Man, played by Paul Rudd, adjust to the powers and abilities created by her father, Hank Pym, the original Ant-Man, played by Michael Douglas. At the end of the first film, Pym shows Hope a prototype for a new Wasp costume that he has made for her, setting up the sequel film, *Ant-Man and the Wasp* (2018), which is the first Marvel movie with a female superhero as a titular character. Lilly described the differences between the two films to Ian Spelling for the *Columbus Dispatch* (28 June 2018): "I kind of felt guilty sometimes because I felt like, where 'Ant-Man' was very much about Ant-Man, the second film, in some ways, was very much about Wasp. I know Paul, and I know that he wouldn't begrudge that, that he would be thrilled about that, but everyone on the film really is excited about a female being titled in the Marvel Universe and being a leading superhero in the movie."

In the second film, Hope's character helps to rescue her mother, Janet van Dyne (played by Michelle Pfeiffer) from a microscopic reality known as the Quantum Realm. Both it—and Lilly's Wasp—are expected to play an important part in the Marvel Cinematic Universe in the future. With that in mind, Lilly wanted to make her Wasp a very distinct character. She said to Kilkenny, "In her fight scenes, as trivial as it might seem, I really pushed and fought for her to fight with elegance, grace and femininity. She moves differently than a man. I wanted her to have a signature style that little girls, like I was when I was a feminine, girly little girl, would be

able to fall in love with, emulate and relate to in their own movements."

PERSONAL LIFE

Lilly lives with her longtime partner, Norman Kali, in Hawaii. The couple have two children (born in 2011 and 2015). Still protective of her private life, she has continued her involvement with charitable work in Rwanda.

SUGGESTED READING

Edwards, Gavin. "Evangeline Lilly: Little Girl Lost." *Rolling Stone*, 6 Oct. 2005, www.rollingstone.com/tv/tv-news/evangeline-lilly-little-girl-lost-55094/. Accessed 3 Dec. 2018.

"Evangeline Lilly Uncensored." *Women's Health*, 9 May 2009, www.womenshealthmag.com/life/a19931784/celebrity-interview-evangeline-lilly/. Accessed 3 Dec. 2018.

Lilly, Evangeline. "Evangeline Lilly on How She 'Challenged' Herself to Speak Up on the *Ant-Man and the Wasp* Set." Interview by Katie Kilkenny. *The Hollywood Reporter*, 5 July 2018, www.hollywoodreporter.com/heat-vision/ant-man-wasp-evangeline-lilly-fought-speak-up-set-1124350. Accessed 3 Dec. 2018.

Lilly, Evangeline. "Evangeline Lilly Is 'Not Interested in Trying to Pretend to Be a Man.'" Interview by Leigh Blickley. *The Huffington Post*, 9 Dec. 2014, www.huffingtonpost.com/2014/12/09/evangeline-lilly-the-hobbit_n_6290220.html. Accessed 3 Dec. 2018.

Stolworthy, Jacob. "Evangeline Lilly Interview: After *Lost*, I Don't Trust I Can Be Safe Doing Nude Scenes." *Independent*, 1 Aug. 2018, www.independent.co.uk/arts-entertainment/films/features/evangeline-lilly-antman-2-the-wasp-lost-kate-austen-interview-nude-scenes-a8471791.html. Accessed 3 Dec. 2018.

Vary, Adam B. "Evangeline Lilly Tried to Quit Acting, but Acting Would Not Quit Her." *BuzzFeed*, 2 Dec. 2014, www.buzzfeed.com/adambvary/evangeline-lilly-ant-man-the-hobbit-squickerwonkers. Accessed 3 Dec. 2018.

SELECTED WORKS

Lost, 2004–10; *Real Steel*, 2011; *The Hobbit: The Desolation of Smaug*, 2013; *The Hobbit: The Battle of the Five Armies*, 2014; *Ant-Man*, 2015; *Ant-Man and the Wasp*, 2018

—Christopher Mari

Ada Limón

Date of birth: March 28, 1976
Occupation: Poet

Ada Limón is an American poet known for her 2015 book *Bright Dead Things*.

EARLY LIFE AND EDUCATION

Ada Limón was born in 1976 in Sonoma, California. Her mother is Stacia Brady, a visual artist who would later contribute to Limón's work as an illustrator for her book covers. Brady also managed a large horse ranch in California, so Limón grew up with horses, which would become a common motif in her poetry.

Limón attended the University of Washington for her undergraduate degree, studying theater at the School of Drama. In 2001 she earned an MFA from New York University.

After completing her MFA, Limón lived in New York for several years before relocating to Lexington, Kentucky. Limón splits her time between New York, Sonoma, and Lexington. She has worked as an educator and freelance writer in addition to her poetry work, serving as a faculty member at Queens University of Charlotte's low-residency MFA program and for the Provincetown Fine Arts Work Center's online education program.

Limón has also taught undergraduate and graduate courses at New York University and Columbia University, as well as the New Harmony Writer's Workshop at the University of Southern Indiana.

While living in New York, Limón worked at a travel magazine as a creative director, and as an events manager for entrepreneur and artist Martha Stewart. Limón was attending an event at Martha Stewart's home when she learned that her first poetry book would be published.

POET

As a poet, Limón writes with a personal, often autobiographical voice. She cites American poet Philip Levine, with whom she studied at New York University, as an influence on her work, in addition to Chilean poet Pablo Neruda, whom she says influenced her willingness to write love poems.

Limón's work has earned her several prominent grants and awards. She was selected as a fellow at the Provincetown Fine Arts Work Center in 2001. Additionally, she received grants from the New York Foundation for the Arts and won the Chicago Literary Award for Poetry.

Limón published her first poetry book, *Lucky Wreck*, in 2006. The collection won the 2005 Autumn House Poetry Prize. Nine months later, in 2007, she released her second collection, *This Big Fake World*.

In 2010 Limón published her third collection, *Sharks in the Rivers*. Much like her earlier works, the book's titular poem explores her personal fears. Limón joked in a 2011 interview that she always writes about the same topics, having published three books of poems centered on themes including love, fear, joy, and death.

Limón was selected to judge the National Book Award for Poetry in 2013. Two years later, her fourth and most successful book of poems, *Bright Dead Things*, was itself a finalist for the award, but lost to *Voyage of the Sable Venus* by Robin Coste Lewis.

Bright Dead Things collects a series of Limón's autobiographical poems that examine her emotional response to events in her life, including the loss of her stepmother, Cynthia, and her relationship with places she has lived, including New York and Kentucky. The book's poems are the result of Limón's efforts to be as honest and bare as possible, she said in a 2015 interview.

In addition to her poetry, Limón has written several unpublished works of fiction, including a young adult novel. As a freelance writer, Limón has contributed to publications including *Martha Stewart Living* and *GQ*.

IMPACT

Limón's poems have been featured in the *New York Times*, the *New Yorker*, and the *Harvard Review*. Her writing has received positive reviews from critics.

PERSONAL LIFE

Limón divides her time among New York, Kentucky, and California with her partner, a horse racing reporter. Limón has said that while she is of Mexican descent, she does not speak fluent Spanish and often feels strange at events where she represents Latina poets.

Limón has suffered from vertigo, a topic she has addressed on her personal blog. Limón said that while she often writes about her fears, her only true fear is running out of time to write.

SUGGESTED READING

"About Ada Limón." *Ada Limón*. Ada Limón, n.d. ,www.adalimon.com/about.html. Accessed 2 Jan. 2019

"Ada Limón." *Poets.org*. Academy of American Poets, n.d., /www.poets.org/poetsorg/poet/ada-lim%C3%B3n. Accessed 2 Jan. 2019.

"Bright Dead Things," by Ada Limón, 2015 National Book Award Finalist, Poetry." *National Book Award*, www.nationalbook.org/nba2015_p_limon.html. Accessed 2 Jan. 2019.

Limón, Ada. "In Spite of It All, We Are Still Here Living." Interview by Kaveh Akbar.

Divedapper, 18 May 2015, www.divedapper.com/interview/ada-limon/. Accessed 2 Jan. 2019.

Limón, Ada. "Poet Ada Limon Talks Art, Quiet, and Sharks." Interview. *Daily Fig*. Figment, 12 July 2011. Web. 27 Mar. 2016.

Limón, Ada. "The Rumpus Poetry Book Club Chat with Ada Limón." Interview by Brian Spears. *Rumpus*, 15 Sept. 2015, www.therumpus.net/2015/09/the-rumpus-poetry-book-club-chat-with-ada-limon/. Accessed 2 Jan. 2019.

Limón, Ada. "Starting with A: On Art & Anxiety." *Ada Limón*. Author, 3 Sept. 2015, www.adalimon.blogspot.com/2015/09/starting-with-on-art-anxiety.html. Accessed 2 Jan. 2019.

SELECTED WORKS
Lucky Wreck (2006); This Big Fake World (2007); Sharks in the Rivers (2010); Bright Dead Things (2015)

—*Richard Means*

Photo by Miguel Discart via Wikimedia Commons

Becky Lynch

Date of birth: January 30, 1987
Occupation: Professional wrestler

In 2002, Irish teenager Rebecca Quin's life changed dramatically when she walked through the door of a newly established school for aspiring professional wrestlers. Long a fan of professional wrestling, a form of sports entertainment that blends dramatic storylines with physically challenging stage combat, she soon began training for a career in wrestling herself and participated in her first match at the age of fifteen. After taking on the ring name Becky Lynch, her career reached a level her younger self could hardly have dreamed of, as she claimed two titles at 2019's WrestleMania 35—the first edition of that tournament headlined by women. "This girl that was failing P.E. at fifteen years old has somehow become the best sports entertainer in the world," Lynch mused in an interview with Tim Fiorvanti for *ESPN* (5 Apr. 2019). "So much so that they couldn't deny her the main event of WrestleMania."

As Lynch's statement suggests, however, her road to superstardom was hardly an easy one. After suffering a head injury while wrestling on the independent circuit at the age of nineteen, she took several years off from wrestling. She explored alternative careers but continued to feel drawn to the ring. After signing a contract with World Wrestling Entertainment (WWE) in 2013, she began the slow process of establishing herself in the industry. Refining her persona along the way, Lynch experienced a breakthrough in 2018 with a story line highlighting her increasing self-confidence and tied to the WWE's effort to promote gender equality. Fans responded positively to Lynch's new direction, giving her a surge in popularity that left even Lynch—known to fans as the Man—stunned. "I think one day, when I sit down and actually let it sink in, I feel like my head just might explode off my shoulders," she told Chuck Carroll for *CBS New York* (29 Mar. 2019).

EARLY LIFE AND EDUCATION
Becky Lynch was born Rebecca Quin on January 30, 1987, in Limerick, Ireland. She grew up on the outskirts of the Irish capital, Dublin. As a child, Lynch enjoyed watching professional wrestling programs with her older brother, and the two at times engaged in play matches of their own. Despite her early interest in wrestling, however, the idea of pursuing professional wrestling as a career did not occur to Lynch for much of her early life. "I never for a second even considered that I could be a wrestler. It was such an out-there dream. There was no wrestling school in Dublin, it didn't even register as a thing I could do," Lynch recalled to John Hyland for *Totally Dublin* (31 Mar. 2016). "Of course I looked at it and thought 'that's so cool, that'd be amazing,'" but I didn't think that I'd ever be doing it." With wrestling out of reach, she instead considered becoming a lawyer.

A turning point in Lynch's life and career trajectory came in 2002, when she and her brother learned about a new wrestling school that was opening in Bray, a town south of Dublin. The siblings decided to visit the school, led by a young wrestler named Fergal Devitt, who would later win international fame under the ring name Finn Bálor. "I show up to this little gymnasium in a school hall," Lynch told Fiorvanti of her first impressions. "Finn, at the time, was skinny as a rake, big smiley head on him. 'How are you, lads?' And I walked in. That was my introduction to wrestling."

Then fifteen years old but reportedly claiming to be sixteen to meet the school's age requirements, Lynch began the physical training necessary for a career in wrestling. She competed in her first match not long afterward, appearing alongside her brother. Her first one-on-one match came less than two years later, following a string of tag-team appearances. Lynch began to use the ring name Rebecca Knox during this period. Meanwhile, she also entered college, still thinking she would pursue a career in law.

EARLY CAREER

By the time she was eighteen years old, Lynch had decided she would dedicate herself to professional wrestling. Hoping to raise her profile and find more lucrative wrestling opportunities in North America, where women's wrestling was becoming more popular than it was in Ireland at the time, she dropped out of college and moved to Canada. Based in the Vancouver, British Columbia area, she also competed in the United States as well as in Japan. Lynch received some attention within the North American wrestling community in mid-2006, when she competed in two matches for the newly established wrestling company SHIMMER Women Athletes. She later returned to Europe, where she continued to wrestle professionally and also competed in bodybuilding.

Although professional wrestling storylines and the outcomes of matches are predetermined, competitors train extensively to execute physical maneuvers without seriously injuring one another. Legitimate injuries do occur and have the potential to derail a wrestler's career significantly. Such was the case for Lynch, who suffered a head injury during a match in 2006 and later stepped away from the ring to recover. Over the next several years, she supported herself by working a variety of jobs, including over two years as a flight attendant. Convinced her wrestling days were over, she enrolled in university to study acting. Yet despite her injury she remained drawn to combat sports and began studying martial arts.

After several years away from the world of professional wrestling, Lynch briefly returned to the field as a manager in 2011, managing the mother-daughter wrestlers Saraya Knight and Paige Knight in SHIMMER performances. Still seeking to become an actor, Lynch then worked as a stunt performer on the television show *Vikings* in 2012. Training for that role further excited her about the possibility of returning to the ring, and she went on to try out for a spot in the WWE. "I knew there was no way I wasn't getting it," she recalled to Fiorvanti. "I knew everything that happened, everything that had led me to that moment, all the jobs that I had done in between—the degree in acting, the stunt work, just everything—was going to bring me back to this. It was too meant to be." Lynch's tryout proved successful, and she signed a developmental contract with the WWE in 2013.

WWE

After signing with the WWE, Lynch returned to wrestling in live events held under the NXT brand. She made her debut on the television program *WWE NXT* in June of 2014. Over the course of her early years with the WWE, Lynch worked to develop the new ring persona of Becky Lynch, also known at times as the Lass Kicker. "It's been about stripping it back, and finding a certain element of my own personality then turning that up a bit," she told Hyland about the process of developing her persona. "She's a firecracker, you know? She just wants to get down to business, just wants to fight." She became known for her signature bright red-orange hair, and at first wore a distinctive steampunk-inspired costume. Lynch initially struggled somewhat to gain traction with NXT's fan base. However, she ultimately became part of a core group of female NXT wrestlers known as the Four Horsewomen, which also included wrestlers Charlotte Flair, Sasha Banks, and Bayley.

Having established herself as a member of the NXT roster, Lynch moved on to the WWE's RAW brand in 2015. She made her debut on the television show *Monday Night RAW* in July of that year. She went on to join the WWE's SmackDown brand in 2016 and became the first person to hold the SmackDown Women's Championship title, which she would claim for a second time in 2018. Although Lynch experienced some success and an increase in popularity during this period, she remained largely in the shadow of Flair, who was her friend both in real life and in the WWE story line. That dynamic fueled the next major shift in Lynch's in-ring character trajectory, as the league played up a sense of building resentment between the two wrestlers. The growing rivalry resonated with many fans. "I think everybody has that one friend, or that one person, who's just leeching, just taking everything they get, just leave you the scraps and expect you to be grateful," Lynch explained to Scarlett Harris for *Fanbyte* (3 Apr. 2019) about the in-story roots of the conflict.

The turning point in Lynch's story line came during the 2018 SummerSlam event, in which

Flair appeared to steal a victory out from under her. Although Lynch initially seemed to accept that action, she later attacked Flair, signaling that a shift to a more villainous persona had begun. Although the events of SummerSlam suggested that WWE leadership hoped for Lynch to be perceived as a heel—a villainous or antagonistic character in professional wrestling—the public response to her actions was largely positive. This ushered in a period in which Lynch's persona became more aggressive, confident, and successful in the ring, and her popularity skyrocketed. She began using the nickname the Man, which she explained in interviews reflected her newfound self-confidence. "This is about overcoming the odds," she told Justin Barrasso for *Sports Illustrated* (7 May 2019). "Believe in yourself, even when no one else does, that's what it means to be 'The Man.'" The persona also alluded to Lynch's feud with Flair, as Flair's father, Ric Flair, had used a similar nickname during his years as a professional wrestler.

THE MAN

Following the events of SummerSlam 2018, Lynch continued her rivalry with Flair as one of the best-received story lines in the WWE. She also began an in-story feud with Ronda Rousey, an established mixed martial artist who had launched a new career in professional wrestling. Although Lynch and Rousey planned to face each other in a match during the Survivor Series in late 2018, Lynch suffered a concussion due to an accident in the ring and was forced to cancel. She ultimately faced both Rousey and Flair in a three-wrestler match during WrestleMania 35, held in April 2019. During the match, the first WrestleMania main event ever to focus on female wrestlers, Lynch succeeded in defeating both rivals and claimed both the RAW Women's Championship title and the SmackDown Women's Championship title.

Lynch continued to compete widely after WrestleMania, appearing in both RAW and SmackDown events and facing numerous challengers who hoped to claim the titles she held. "Now's going to be the hardest part because not only do I have one target on my back, I have two targets on my back," she told Evelyn Lau for the *National* (12 Apr. 2019) after the event. "Everybody wants a piece of me, everybody's going to want to be knocking me down." Indeed, Lynch lost the SmackDown title in May 2019, though she retained her RAW title through the summer. Despite such setbacks, she continued to be a fan favorite and a key face of the WWE. Lynch remained focused on promoting professional wrestling, and especially women's wrestling, through her hard-earned time in the spotlight. "I refuse to take a second of this for granted," she told

Barrasso, noting her goal to "make WWE must-see TV."

PERSONAL LIFE

Lynch announced her engagement to fellow professional wrestler Seth Rollins, born Colby Lopez, in August 2019. The two had earlier appeared together in WWE programming on occasion, and Lynch acknowledged that their real-life relationship would cross over into the wrestling world. "I think seeing the potential to have two top stars fighting side by side as champions is something that we couldn't really ignore, so here we are," she told Joey Hayden for *The Dallas Morning News* (26 June 2019).

SUGGESTED READING

Fiorvanti, Tim. "How Becky Lynch Became the Man." *ESPN*, 5 Apr. 2019, www.espn.com/wwe/story/_/id/26431351/how-becky-lynch-became-man. Accessed 13 Sept. 2019.

Lynch, Becky. "Becky Lynch: 'I Refuse to Take a Second of This for Granted.'" Interview by Justin Barrasso. *Sports Illustrated*, 7 May 2019, si.com/wrestling/2019/05/07/wwe-becky-lynch-wrestlemania-mitb-interview. Accessed 13 Sept. 2019.

Lynch, Becky. "No Apologies: A Conversation with Becky Lynch." Interview by Scarlett Harris. *Fanbyte*, 3 Apr. 2019, www.fanbyte.com/features/becky-lynch-interview/. Accessed 13 Sept. 2019.

Lynch, Becky. "Queen of the Ring: Becky Lynch Interview." Interview by John Hyland. *Totally Dublin*, 31 Mar. 2016, www.totallydublin.ie/more/features-more/queen-of-the-ring-becky-lynch-interview/. Accessed 13 Sept. 2019.

Lynch, Becky. "Becky Lynch Interview: On WrestleMania, Ronda Rousey, NXT UK and Coming to Abu Dhabi." Interview by Evelyn Lau. *The National*, 12 Apr. 2019, thenational.ae/sport/other-sport/becky-lynch-interview-on-wrestlemania-ronda-rousey-nxt-uk-and-coming-to-abu-dhabi-1.848170. Accessed 13 Sept. 2019.

Lynch, Becky. "Becky Lynch Talks Seth Rollins, Returning to Dallas, and Her New Goal Now That She's Had Her Own WrestleMania Main Event." Interview by Joey Hayden. *The Dallas Morning News*, 26 June 2019, www.dallasnews.com/arts-entertainment/2019/06/26/becky-lynch-talks-seth-rollins-returning-to-dallas-and-her-new-goal-now-that-she-s-had-her-own-wrestlemania-main-event/. Accessed 13 Sept. 2019.

Lynch, Becky. "WWE Almost Fired Becky Lynch, Now She's Headlining WrestleMania 35." Interview by Chuck Carroll. *CBS New York*, 29 Mar. 2019, newyork.cbslocal.com/2019/03/29/

becky-lynch-headline-wwe-wrestlemania-
35-almost-fired-interview/amp/. Accessed 13
Sept. 2019.

—Joy Crelin

Ma Dong-seok

Date of birth: March 1, 1971
Occupation: Actor

Ma Dong-seok, also known as Don Lee, rose to
become one of South Korea's most popular actors. The former personal trainer is best known
for his roles in thrillers, and has been compared
to Dwayne "The Rock" Johnson, a fellow tough
guy with a soft side—or as Hong Kong's *Bastille
Global Post* (31 Aug. 2017) described Ma, "a
brawny man with a gentle heart." Although such
a description might make him sound like a typecast "good guy," Ma also used his size and force
to portray pure villains and proved himself versatile across genres.

Ma made his film-acting debut in the 2005
action comedy *Heaven's Soldiers* and went on
to appear in scores of Korean films, especially
crime-related works such as *The Neighbors*
(2012). He enjoyed breakout success with *Train
to Busan* (2016), an action-horror film with zombies, and followed with blockbusters such as
Along with the Gods: Two Worlds (2017) and *The
Outlaws* (2017), one of the highest-grossing Korean films ever. In 2019, it was announced that
he would make his Hollywood debut in *The Eternals*, a Marvel Studios superhero film based on a
Jack Kirby comic about near-immortal beings.
Ma signed on to portray the character known as
Gilgamesh, alongside stars Angelina Jolie, Selma
Hayek, and Kumail Nanjiani.

EARLY LIFE AND EDUCATION
Ma Dong-seok was born Lee Dong-seok in South
Korea in 1971. He and his family immigrated to
the United States when he was a teenager, and
Ma became an American citizen. He graduated
from Columbus State Community College in
Columbus, Ohio.

Growing up, Ma became interested in boxing in response to being picked on. As an adult,
he worked as a personal trainer for mixed-martial
artists such as Mark Coleman and Ultimate
Fighting Championship (UFC) heavyweight
champion Kevin Randleman. "When I was
young, my dream was always changing," Ma later
recalled during the press conference for his film
The Outlaws, as quoted by Kim Jae-heun for *Korea Times* (1 Oct. 2017). "At first, I wanted to become a baseball player, then a boxer and then a
police officer. My dreams to be a baseball player

and a boxer slowly faded away but I still want to
be a police officer and run after villains." Eventually, Ma returned to South Korea and began
living his dream as an actor.

EARLY CAREER
Ma made his acting debut with a bit part in the
2005 action comedy *Heaven's Soldiers*. In 2007,
he played a detective on the short-lived television police procedural *H.I.T.* In 2008, under the
name Don Lee, he appeared in the Manchurian
Western *The Good, The Bad, The Weird*. For
the next few years Ma appeared in bit parts in
a number of films, mostly in the thriller, crime,
and drama genres. Among them were the art ca-
per *Insadong Scandal* (2009), the hostage thriller
Midnight FM (2010), and the crime dramas *The
Unjust* (2010) and *Nameless Gangster: Rules of
the Time* (2012). Ma also occasionally appeared
in films beyond those genres—namely, the romantic drama *Pained* (2011), the true-life baseball drama *Perfect Game* (2011), and the romantic dramedy *Love 911* (2012).

Also in 2012, Ma received second bill-
ing in the thriller *The Neighbors*. Starring Yun-
jin Kim of the American television series *Lost*,
the film is based on a popular 2008 web comic
about a town plagued by a serial killer. Among
the film's ensemble cast, Ma's performance "as
a very tough ex-con you wouldn't want to cross
in the parking lot," Deborah Young wrote for
the *Hollywood Reporter* (8 Oct. 2012), was especially "noteworthy." Ma received a Best Supporting Actor Award at Paeksang Arts Awards for
his performance.

Photo by Hb1600 via Wikimedia Commons

Ma went on to play a former convict turned hospice resident in the 2013 comedy *Rockin' on Heaven's Door* and, also in 2013, a washed-up journalist in a fictionalized rendering of the tragic story of Korean actress Jang Ja-yeon, called *The Secret Scandal*. In the 2013 film *Rough Play* Ma played a gang boss, and he starred in *Murderer* (2014) as a serial killer. In 2014, he starred in the crime thriller *One on One*, about the murder of a high school student. The same year, Ma appeared in the period action film *Kundo: Age of the Rampant*. Critic Andy Webster described the Robin Hood–like tale for the *New York Times* (28 Aug. 2014) as a "martial arts spectacle" set in nineteenth-century Korea. Webster had few words of praise for the shallowly plotted epic but noted Ma's "barrel-chested, mace-wielding fighter . . . arrestingly occup[ies] the camera."

TRAIN TO BUSAN

Ma continued to find work on the silver screen but also branched into television around this time. On the show *Bad Guys*, which also premiered in 2014, Ma portrayed a convicted mob boss tasked with helping a detective catch violent criminals; the cast later reunited to film the spinoff movie *The Bad Guys: Reign of Chaos* in 2019. He landed a small role in the critically acclaimed period drama *The Royal Tailor* (2014), set during the Joseon dynasty, and he played another detective in *The Chronicles of Evil* in 2015. That same year he landed a bit part on an episode of the Netflix series *Sense8* and a supporting role in the crime thriller *Exchange*.

In 2016, Ma enjoyed breakout success with the zombie movie *Train to Busan*. The film takes place on a bullet train from Seoul to Busan in South Korea. A zombie on the train sets in motion the plot, an "allegory of class rebellion," as *Variety*'s Maggie Lee deemed it (13 May 2016). Jeannette Catsoulis praised the film's agile cinematography in her review for the *New York Times* (21 July 2016), writing, "As zombies chomp and multiply, an assortment of regular folks face them down while furthering an extended critique of corporate callousness. The politics are sweet, but it's the creatures that divert." Ma plays one of the film's heroic regular folks, a passenger with a pregnant wife. His performance earned him a best-supporting-actor award at the Korean Film Reporters Association (KOFRA) Film Awards in 2017.

The same year, in a departure from his action role in *Train to Busan*, Ma appeared in a dramedy about a self-centered movie star titled *Familyhood*. Ma plays a stylist fond of feminine clothing. The role helped earn him the nickname Mavely (combining Ma and the word "lovely").

THE OUTLAWS AND LATER FILMS

In 2016, Ma also joined the cast of the television series *38 Task Force* (also known as *Squad 38*), about a tax collector and a group of confidence artists who expose wealthy people who avoid paying taxes. The show lasted only one season, however. Ma portrayed a victim-turned-perpetrator in *Derailed* (2016), about teenage runaways whose plan to rob a man goes horribly awry.

In 2017, Ma starred in *The Outlaws*, after spending nearly four years developing the film with director Kang Yoon-sung. The film is based on the 2007 Heuksapa incident in Seoul's Chinatown. Ma plays a police detective determined to maintain control of a precarious peace between two rival gangs. In an interview upon the film's release, Ma reiterated his childhood dream of becoming a police officer. "I poured out many of my ideas into this film from doing research for the scenarios and meeting with close police officers to hear their actual combat experience with gangs," Ma told Kim Jae-heun in an interview for the English-language *Korea Times* (1 Oct. 2017). "I also showed my knowhow and combat skills that I learned as a fighter." The film was popular with both critics and audiences, becoming a top-grossing local film. Ma received a 2018 Golden Egg Award for Best Actor for his role.

Also in 2017, Ma starred in the family-dysfunction comedy *The Bros* and cameoed in the epic fantasy blockbuster *Along with the Gods: Two Worlds*. The latter film follows three guardians guiding a firefighter who died in the line of duty through the trials of the afterlife. He reprised his role as the lead in the film's hit sequel, *Along with the Gods: The Last 49 Days* (2018). The *Along with the Gods* franchise attracted over ten million viewers with each installment, setting box-office records in South Korea.

In 2018, Ma starred in *Champion*, about an American arm wrestler who competes on the Korean circuit. Noel Murray, who reviewed the sports drama for the *Los Angeles Times* (16 May 2018), found it to be unpalatably "lighthearted." However, Murray concluded: "Ma, though, is as sweet as he is imposing and brings depth to a shallow story. Whether he's crashing a wedding with the youngsters because he can't afford to buy them dinner, or he's enjoying the feeling of slamming an opponent's hand down to the table, his [character] Mark is a winning hero."

That same year Ma appeared in *The Soul-Mate*, a fantastical comedy about a patrol officer trying to reunite his soul with his body after an accident. He also headlined a pair of movies about abduction: in the small-budget thriller *The Villagers* Ma plays a high school gym teacher who sets out to solve the kidnapping of one of his students, and in *Unstoppable* he plays a retired gangster who tries to find his missing wife.

In 2019, Ma starred in *The Gangster, the Cop, the Devil* as a crime lord who joins a cop in catching a serial killer. In her largely positive review of the film, Haleigh Foutch considered Ma the main attraction, writing in *Collider* (16 July 2019) that he "is one of the best gentle giants in the biz, gifted at contrasting his hulking strength with the tender-hearted charm that makes him so loveable in [earlier] films." The movie earned a standing ovation at a noncompetitive screening at the Cannes Film Festival. Soon after its release, actor-director Sylvester Stallone bought the film with plans for an English-language remake, in which Ma was slated to star as well.

SUGGESTED READING

Catsoulis, Jeannette. "Review: All Aboard 'Train to Busan' for Zombie and Class Warfare." Review of *Train to Busan*, directed by Sang-ho Yeon. *The New York Times*, 21 July 2016, www.nytimes.com/2016/07/22/movies/train-to-busan-review.html. Accessed 17 Sept. 2019.

Foutch, Haleigh. "'The Gangster, the Cop and the Devil' Review: Ma Dong-seok Steals the Show (Again)." Review of *The Gangster, the Cop, the Devil*, directed by Lee Won-Tae. *Collider*, 16 July 2019, collider.com/the-gangster-the-cop-the-devil-review. Accessed 17 Sept. 2019.

Kim Jae-heun. "'The Outlaws' Actors Shine in Crime Action Film." *The Korea Times*, 1 Oct. 2017, www.koreatimes.co.kr/www/art/2017/10/689_237269.html. Accessed 17 Sept. 2019.

Lee, Maggie. Review of *Train to Busan*, directed by Sang-ho Yeon. *Variety*, 13 May 2016, variety.com/2016/film/reviews/train-to-busan-review-busan-haeng-1201772922. Accessed 17 Sept. 2019.

Ma Dong-seok. "Ma Dong-seok to Rise as New Hero in Crime Action Genre." Interview by Kim Jae-heun. *The Korea Times*, 1 Oct. 2017, www.koreatimes.co.kr/www/art/2017/10/689_237271.html. Accessed 17 Sept. 2019.

Murray, Noel. "Review: Star Power Distinguishes Lighthearted Korean Arm Wrestling Drama 'Champion.'" Review of *Champion*. *Los Angeles Times*, 16 May 2018, www.latimes.com/entertainment/movies/la-et-mn-mini-champion-review-20180516-story.html. Accessed 17 Sept. 2019.

Webster, Andy. "The Robin Hoods of Ancient Korea." Review of *Kundo: Age of the Rampant*, directed by Jong-bin Yoon. *The New York Times*, 28 Aug. 2014, www.nytimes.com/2014/08/29/movies/ha-jung-woo-stars-in-kundo-age-of-the-rampant.html. Accessed 17 Sept. 2019.

Young, Deborah. "The Neighbors: Busan Review." Review of *The Neighbors*, directed by Kim Hwi. *Hollywood Reporter*, 8 Oct. 2012, www.hollywoodreporter.com/review/the-neighbors-busan-review-377085. Accessed 17 Sept. 2019.

SELECTED WORKS
The Neighbors, 2012; *Train to Busan*, 2016; *The Outlaws*, 2017; *Along with the Gods: Two Worlds*, 2017; *Champion*, 2018; *Along with the Gods: The Last 49 Days*, 2018; *The Gangster, the Cop, the Devil*, 2019

—*Molly Hagan*

Paul MacAlindin
Date of birth: 1968
Occupation: Conductor

In 2008, conductor Paul MacAlindin opened a newspaper and read an unusual headline: "Iraqi Teen Seeks Maestro for Youth Orchestra." That chance discovery signaled a new chapter in MacAlindin's career, taking him from his home in Europe to Iraq's Kurdistan region, which became the home of the newly formed National Youth Orchestra of Iraq. Over the next several years, MacAlindin led an ensemble of talented young musicians, many of whom had originally learned to play by watching online tutorials. "Every day was a day of unpredictability, of trying lots of things out to see what worked," he told Daniel Magarry for the *Gay Times* (4 Nov. 2016). "A lot of what we tried failed completely, so we had a very strong need to make mistakes and learn from them." The orchestra was forced to shut down in 2014, after Iraq was invaded by the so-called Islamic State. Nevertheless, the experience would change MacAlindin's life—and those of his musicians—forever. "The lesson for me is to enter into as many challenges as possible in order to help others grow, because the most important resource I have for getting the best out of people isn't talent, but compassion," he told Eliahu Sussman for *School Band and Orchestra* (14 Dec. 2012).

In addition to documenting his time in Iraq in the 2016 memoir *Upbeat: The Story of the National Youth Orchestra of Iraq*, MacAlindin went on to bring his extensive experience to the district of Govan in Glasgow, Scotland, establishing a new orchestra there as well as a program for musicians living in the city as refugees.

EARLY LIFE AND EDUCATION
MacAlindin was born in Aberdeen, Scotland, in 1968. He was raised in Dunfermline, a large

town in southern Fife, just north of Edinburgh. MacAlindin's interest in music and performance first developed at the age of five, when he heard his first piece of classical music while riding in a car driven by his father. He quickly decided that he wanted to pursue a career in music one day and soon afterward began taking piano lessons. Also intrigued by dance, MacAlindin later began to study ballet. Although he enjoyed dance greatly, his artistic pursuits made him the target of bullying during his early life, but he later noted in interviews that the experience only pushed him farther into the more supportive world of the performing arts.

After completing his secondary education, MacAlindin enrolled in England's University of Surrey. Although he had long dreamed of a music-related career, his years of experience with and love of both musical performance and dance made it difficult for him to choose one specific area of study and career path. A turning point in his education came partway through his years as an undergraduate, during which he participated in a foreign-exchange program with Michigan State University. While studying in the United States, MacAlindin first had the opportunity to take courses in conducting, which he quickly found was a good fit for his particular approach to music. "To me, music is a very physical thing, and I have to move to think and express myself," he told the tech start-up Tezign in an interview posted on the platform *Medium* (9 Aug. 2017). "When I went to university to study music, I found myself too restricted by just playing an instrument. I wanted to physically move much more, and so I decided to combine music with ballet thus becoming a conductor."

After returning to Surrey, MacAlindin earned his bachelor's degree in music with honors in 1989. He went on to pursue graduate studies at the University of York, obtaining his master's degree in music performance in 1990, and later completed postgraduate certificates related to business and innovation through the Open University.

EARLY CAREER

During the 1990s, MacAlindin took on a variety of conducting jobs on a freelance basis, initially working with amateur orchestras in and around Glasgow, Scotland. Around 1993, he became an assistant to the conductor and composer Peter Maxwell Davies, who spent the mid-1990s working with high-profile orchestras such as the Royal Philharmonic Orchestra and the BBC Philharmonic Orchestra. Although that period was an influential one for MacAlindin, who learned a great deal about the workings of major musical ensembles, it was difficult at times due to his simultaneous romantic relationship with Davies. "I had to deal with the abuse from those

in the business who figured I was hanging onto his coat tails," he recalled to Brian Beacom for the *Herald* (3 Dec. 2017). "There was a lot of anger and resentment directed at Max because he was so successful but he had his back-up in the form of agents and PR people. What happened was the critics would come at his partners, the soft targets."

In addition to his work assisting Davies, MacAlindin distinguished himself as a conductor and music director in his own right, working with ensembles for the Cantiere Montepulciano, Düsseldorfer Symphoniker, and Psappha, among others. He moved to Germany when he was in his early thirties, seeking a new home base with a strong musical culture from which to continue his work as a freelance conductor. He went on to work with groups such as the New Zealand Symphony, the National Youth Orchestra of Scotland, and the Armenian Philharmonic Orchestra and in 2003 became the volunteer director of Musiker in Asyl (Musicians in Asylum). Based in the German city of Cologne, Musiker in Asyl offered asylum seekers living in the city opportunities to play music, perform publicly, and practice their German-language skills. MacAlindin continued the Musiker in Asyl program into 2007 and would revive it in Scotland more than a decade later in the form of Musicians in Exile.

NATIONAL YOUTH ORCHESTRA OF IRAQ

In 2008, MacAlindin was visiting his father in Scotland when he first became aware of the project that would shape the next stage of his life and career. "I was sitting in a pub in Edinburgh eating fish and chips and drinking a pint, flicking through a *Glasgow Herald* newspaper someone had left behind, and there was a headline reading 'Iraqi Teen Seeks Maestro for Youth Orchestra.' There was this seventeen-year-old girl from Baghdad who wanted to set up a youth orchestra," he recalled to Magarry. "I instantly knew it was something I had to do." Although well aware of the risks involved in traveling to Iraq—military conflicts and terrorism were ongoing there, and MacAlindin could face homophobia and violence—MacAlindin remained drawn to the project, particularly after discussing the youth orchestra with the Iraqi teenager, pianist Zuhal Sultan, who had developed the idea. After a significant period of back-and-forth discussions with the relevant music professionals, potential students, and government officials, MacAlindin traveled to Iraq to serve as musical director of the newly formed National Youth Orchestra of Iraq. The group initially took the form of an orchestra boot camp in the Kurdish city of Sulaymaniyah.

Over the course of his years with the youth orchestra, MacAlindin found that music could play a powerful role in bringing together young people from a variety of different cultural backgrounds, including those speaking different languages. "The first duty of every musician is to listen. If you can't do that, then everything else is a waste," he said to Caroline Sanderson for the *Bookseller* (10 Aug. 2016). "So it was about the very simple act of sitting people down next to one another, teaching them to listen; listening to them, feeding back positively, constructively, gently. We all had a sense that just by focusing on the art of listening and making music, we could do something that had never been done before." As the National Youth Orchestra of Iraq became more established, the group began to tour internationally, and both the orchestra and MacAlindin himself became the focus of international attention as symbols of the possibility of peace and intercultural cooperation. In addition to leading the orchestra, MacAlindin served as a board member of the European Federation of National Youth Orchestras during that period.

UPBEAT
In 2012, MacAlindin started writing a memoir about his time with the orchestra. "I felt I had to write it because the orchestra was such a huge chunk of my life; it's a very complex thing that I put myself through and I wanted to make sense of it all," he told Magarry. "I also wanted to write an honest and open account about my experience in Iraq and the people I met while working there. The book felt like the only way for me to bring closure to that part of my life." In 2014, during the National Youth Orchestra of Iraq's sixth year of existence, the group known as the Islamic State—also called the Islamic State of Iraq and Syria (ISIS), the Islamic State of Iraq and the Levant (ISIL), or Daesh—invaded Iraq. The invasion not only put an end to MacAlindin's efforts to plan a US tour for the orchestra, but forced the dissolution of the orchestra itself, as the ensuing violence made participating in such a venture too great of a risk. MacAlindin returned to the United Kingdom, where he began serious work on the memoir.

The resulting book, *Upbeat: The Story of the National Youth Orchestra of Iraq*, was published in the United Kingdom in 2016. Following the memoir's publication, MacAlindin and the youth orchestra became the focus of renewed media attention, portions of which focused on the fates of the young musicians MacAlindin had led. "The good news is that every player is physically still safe," he told Andrew Thomson for the *BBC* (13 Aug. 2016). "Some have managed to get out and claim asylum in Europe or America. But many are still back in Iraq. They are still making music but they are all far from safe for as long as ISIL exists."

WORK IN GOVAN
MacAlindin returned to Scotland in mid-2016 and settled in Glasgow, the city where he had lived and worked as a young conductor. Having gained valuable experience during the earlier decades, he set out to make a difference in his new home city as well, focusing particularly on the district of Govan. A former industrial center that had declined significantly during the late twentieth and early twenty-first centuries, Govan had developed a reputation as a dangerous district known for its poverty and crime. MacAlindin sought to combat that reputation, selecting Govan as his own home as well as the home base for a new orchestra, the Glasgow Barons, which he founded in June 2017. The Glasgow Barons have performed in the district and further support the local music scene by premiering new compositions by Scottish singer-songwriters.

For MacAlindin, his work in Govan is part of a long-term effort to support the musical community within the district. "I'm not parachuting in for a couple of days," he told Nan Spowart for the *National* (11 Dec. 2017). "You need to be constantly at it otherwise nothing will change and you also have to be ready to go two steps forward and one back." With the support of organizations such as Creative Scotland and the William Grant Foundation, MacAlindin has also introduced a number of additional programs in Govan, including a Musicians in Exile program for local refugees.

PERSONAL LIFE
MacAlindin lives in Glasgow. In addition to his music-related projects, he is a prolific public speaker and is also active in corporate training.

SUGGESTED READING
Beacom, Brian. "Scots Maestro's Mission to Save Music in Iraq." *The Herald*, 3 Dec. 2017, www.heraldscotland.com/arts_ents/15699531.scots-maestros-mission-to-save-music-in-iraq. Accessed 12 Apr. 2019.

MacAlindin, Paul. "Paul MacAlindin on Leading Iraq's National Youth Orchestra and Being LGBT in the Middle East." Interview by Daniel Magarry. *Gay Times*, 4 Nov. 2016, www.gaytimes.co.uk/community/52504/paul-macalindin-on-leading-iraqs-national-youth-orchestra-and-being-lgbt-in-the-middle-east. Accessed 12 Apr. 2019.

MacAlindin, Paul. "Paul MacAlindin: The Story of the National Youth Orchestra of Iraq." Interview by Tezign. *Medium*, 9 Aug. 2017, medium.com/@Tezign/paul-macalindin-the-story-of-the-national-youth-orchestra-of-iraq-d23b4d13dfaf. Accessed 12 Apr. 2019.

Sanderson, Caroline. "Paul McAlindin: 'The First Duty of Every Musician Is to Listen.'" *The Bookseller*, 10 Aug. 2016, www.thebookseller.

com/profile/paul-mcalindin-373556#.   Accessed 12 Apr. 2019.

Spowart, Nan. "Profile: Paul MacAlindin, the Conductor Bringing People Together from Iraq to Govan." *The National*, 11 Dec. 2017, www.thenational.scot/news/15713125.profile-paul-macalindin-the-conductor-bringing-people-together-from-iraq-to-govan. Accessed 12 Apr. 2019.

Sussman, Eliahu. "Paul MacAlindin & the National Youth Orchestra of Iraq." *School Band and Orchestra*, 14 Dec. 2012, sbomagazine.com/archive-articles/4329-23paul-macalindin-the-national-youth-orchestra-of-iraq.html. Accessed 12 Apr. 2019.

Thomson, Andrew. "Scots Conductor and the Orchestra That Crossed Iraq's Divides." *BBC Scotland*, 13 Aug. 2016, www.bbc.com/news/uk-scotland-highlands-islands-37057504. Accessed 12 Apr. 2019.

—*Joy Crelin*

Photo by Tohomohiro Ohsumi/Bloomberg via Getty Images

Yusaku Maezawa

Date of birth: November 22, 1975
Occupation: Entrepreneur

Ranked the eighteenth-wealthiest person in Japan in 2018 by *Forbes* magazine, billionaire entrepreneur Yusaku Maezawa is notable for his wealth but is perhaps better known for what he has chosen to do with it. The longtime, avid art collector made headlines in 2016 for spending $98 million on contemporary art over two days of high-profile auctions, and he went on to spend more than $110 million on a single piece, a painting by American artist Jean-Michel Basquiat, the following year. Although that price was one of the highest ever paid for a work by an American artist, financial considerations are less important to Maezawa than his own feelings about a particular piece of art. "I just follow my instinct," he said, as reported by Motoko Rich and Robin Pogrebin for the *New York Times* (26 May 2017). "When I think it's good, I buy it."

A former drummer in a punk rock band, Maezawa entered the business world in 1998, when he established the company Start Today as a mail-order CD retailer. The company's later expansion into the world of fashion with the clothing website *Zozotown* proved particularly successful, and *Zozotown* went on to become the premiere online fashion retailer in Japan within a matter of years. Renamed *ZOZO Inc.* in 2018, Maezawa's company has also sought to position itself as a manufacturer as well as a retailer of clothing, an effort still in its early stages by the start of 2019. "I think there's a chance

for us to become the No. 1 apparel company in the world," Maezawa predicted, as reported by Alex Martin for the *Japan Times* (1 Apr. 2018). In addition to reshaping how Japanese consumers purchase clothing, ZOZO Inc. has facilitated Maezawa's own personal projects, including his art collecting and his establishment of the Contemporary Art Foundation.

Maezawa attracted further attention in 2018 when he purchased every seat on the company SpaceX's proposed first tourist trip to the moon, scheduled for 2023. His goal, he said, was to travel into space alongside a selection of artists who would go on to create powerful works based on their experiences.

EARLY LIFE AND EDUCATION

Yusaku Maezawa was born in 1975 in Chiba Prefecture, a coastal region of central Japan that is considered part of Greater Tokyo. He was the older of two sons born to an accountant and a homemaker. Growing up in Chiba, Maezawa developed an interest in music at a young age and eventually began playing guitar. As a teenager, he took up the drums, as he believed that playing that instrument would give him more opportunities to play in bands. Maezawa attended Waseda Jitsugyo High School, a prestigious high school in Tokyo that is affiliated with Waseda University. He commuted more than an hour each way to school, an exhausting experience that later contributed to his decision to turn away from his planned university and career path.

While in high school, Maezawa and his friends formed a punk band, Switch Style, in which Maezawa played drums. The band proved relatively successful, and Switch Style eventually signed with a label and released the band's first extended-play (EP) record in 1993. The band later signed with the major label BMG Japan and released several records of varying lengths. In light of the success of the band, Maezawa opted not to attend university or pursue an office job. "I think what I hated was the feeling that I was running along tracks that had already been laid down," he told the *Times* of his decision, as quoted by Allyson Chiu for the *Washington Post* (18 Sept. 2018). "I could see the rails stretching in front of me—school, university, career. I could picture myself as one of those people jam-packed in a rush-hour train. I wanted to derail myself."

Maezawa also traveled to the United States after high school, spending six months in the country. During that time, he began collecting records and CDs of bands he enjoyed, particularly punk bands whose recordings were difficult to find elsewhere.

START TODAY

After returning to Japan, Maezawa identified a demand for a company selling records, CDs, and related merchandise such as T-shirts, particularly those created by punk bands and other rock groups with devoted fan followings. He launched his mail-order retailer, Start Today, in 1998 and, in 2000, began the company's online operation, which soon demonstrated to Maezawa the promise of online retail. The success of his company, however, came at the detriment of his music career. "I was president of my company while touring around the country with the band," he said, as reported by Martin. "When it became physically impossible to handle both, I chose my company—that was around when I was twenty-five or twenty-six." Maezawa officially quit Switch Style in 2001 to focus on his business full time.

Although Start Today had sold some clothing items since early in the company's history, the company opened a dedicated clothing subsidiary, Zozotown, in 2004. Also an online retailer, Zozotown initially specialized in selling clothing from a select group of Japanese fashion brands but eventually came to feature thousands of brands from both Japan and abroad. Start Today eventually separated the music and clothing divisions of the business, and Zozotown proved particularly successful over the subsequent years. Start Today was listed on the Tokyo Stock Exchange beginning in 2007 and moved to the exchange's First Section, the part of the exchange devoted to large companies, in 2012.

ZOZO

Renamed ZOZO *Inc.* in 2018, Start Today came to encompass several additional businesses in addition to Zozotown, among them the fashion app WEAR, the technology company ZOZO Technologies, and the secondhand clothing market ZOZOUSED. Maezawa served as chief executive officer of ZOZO *Inc.* and at times acted as the face of the company when announcing some of its new products and services. In 2017, Maezawa announced the launch of the clothing brand ZOZO, specializing in custom-fit clothing that would be created based on the buyers' measurements and delivered to the customer within a matter of weeks. To gather the necessary measurements, the company planned to use ZOZO-SUIT technology, which used a form-fitting suit covered in computer-identifiable markers and a companion app to create a digital avatar based on the customer's measurements. This would then allow the company to construct clothing made to fit that specific individual.

For Maezawa, there was a clear need for such a service, as he had himself struggled to find clothing that fit his specific body shape. "I think the desire for a perfect-fitting pair of denim [jeans] is universal," he said, as reported by Martin. "If we can provide denim to all the people in the world, for example, we will have seven billion customers." Despite the wave of publicity surrounding the ZOZOSUIT technology, however, the company announced that the technology would no longer be available after March 2019, as adequate data had been gathered to produce clothing for customers with varied body types.

ART COLLECTING

An avid collector since his teen years, when he focused on punk records and related merchandise, Maezawa remained interested in collecting a variety of items as an adult, a hobby facilitated by the extensive personal wealth the success of ZOZO *Inc.* had brought him. Among other items, he assembled collections of watches, cars, and antiques such as Buddhist statues and Japanese teacups. Maezawa became best known, however, as a collector of fine art, which he began collecting around 2007 with the purchase of a painting by pop artist Roy Lichtenstein. "It was a very big investment for me back then, about two million dollars," he recalled to Danielle Demetriou for the website of the auction house Christie's (14 Sept. 2017). "It was the first time I had bought a painting. I just loved the greens—Lichtenstein is very good at creating beautiful greens. I followed my intuition and I bought it." Particularly intrigued by the art of the twentieth century, Maezawa went on to purchase pieces by numerous other major figures from that era, including Spanish artist Pablo Picasso.

In May 2016, Maezawa drew significant international attention for spending $98 million on art over two days, purchasing pieces such as *Eat War* by Bruce Nauman, *Runaway Nurse* by

Richard Prince, and *Untitled* (1990) by Christopher Wool at contemporary art auctions at Christie's and Sotheby's. The following year, he became the center of even greater attention for his purchase of an untitled 1982 painting of a skull by American artist Jean-Michel Basquiat. Maezawa had previously paid more than $57 million for a different untitled Basquiat piece during his 2016 purchasing period and was interested in acquiring the skull painting as well. "I decided to go for it," he said, as reported by Rich and Pogrebin. Following a bidding war, Maezawa purchased the painting for $110.5 million, the most ever paid for a piece by Basquiat and one of the highest prices ever paid for a work by an American artist.

Following the 2017 auction, the Basquiat painting went on tour, temporarily featuring in displays at museums in the United States and in Europe. For Maezawa, that effort was in keeping with his overall approach to art, which he believes should be made accessible to the public. "I want to show beautiful things and share them with everyone," he said, as reported by Rich and Pogrebin. "It would be a waste just to keep it all to myself." Maezawa has commented in interviews that he hopes to open an art museum in Chiba Prefecture, where many of the pieces he has collected could be displayed. In addition, he has sought to encourage the continued creation of artistic works through the Contemporary Art Foundation. Established in 2012, the foundation holds art exhibitions and distributes grants to young artists and musicians, among other efforts.

#DEARMOON

In September 2018, Maezawa again made international headlines when he announced that he had purchased every seat on the space exploration company SpaceX's first scheduled tourist flight to the moon. "Ever since I was a kid, I have loved the moon," he explained in a press conference, as reported by Chiu. "Just staring at the moon filled my imagination. It's always there and has continued to inspire humanity. That is why I could not pass up this opportunity to see the moon up close." Although the flight was not scheduled to take place until 2023, Maezawa immediately announced plans for a project he called #dearMoon, in which a select group of artists would accompany him on the trip and make artwork inspired by the experience following their return to Earth.

PERSONAL LIFE

Maezawa primarily lives in Tokyo, although he has noted in interviews that he feels most comfortable in Chiba. "There's more fresh air and you can see the ocean," he explained, as reported by Martin. He has three children, to whom he hopes to pass down an appreciation for art. "Art is really good for kids," he told Demetriou. "Although they don't really understand yet what it is. They point at that plant over there and say, *is that art?*"

SUGGESTED READING

Chiu, Allyson. "Yusaku Maezawa Just Purchased Every Seat on the SpaceX Flight to the Moon. Who Is He?" *The Washington Post*, 18 Sept. 2018, www.washingtonpost.com/news/morning-mix/wp/2018/09/18/yusaku-maezawa-just-purchased-every-seat-on-the-spacex-flight-to-the-moon-who-is-he. Accessed 18 Jan. 2019.

Demetriou, Danielle. "The Art World's New Rock Star." *Christie's*, 14 Sept. 2017, www.christies.com/features/Yusaku-Maezawa-The-art-worlds-new-generation-rock-star-8530-1.aspx. Accessed 18 Jan. 2019.

Maezawa, Yusaku. "Exclusive: Japanese Billionaire to Take 'Message of Peace' to Space as First Moon Tourist." Interview by Julia Sieger. *France 24*, 11 Jan. 2019, www.france24.com/en/20190110-interview-yusaku-maezawa-first-tourist-moon-lunar-flyby-spacex-artists-zozotown. Accessed 18 Jan. 2019.

Martin, Alex. "Zozotown Founder Yusaku Maezawa Follows Eclectic Path." *The Japan Times*, 1 Apr. 2018, www.japantimes.co.jp/news/2018/04/01/business/corporate-business/zozotown-founder-yusaku-maezawa-follows-eclectic-path. Accessed 18 Jan. 2019.

Rich, Motoko, and Robin Pogrebin. "Why Spend $100 Million on a Basquiat? 'I Decided to Go for It,' Japanese Billionaire Explains." *The New York Times*, 26 May 2017, www.nytimes.com/2017/05/26/arts/design/110-million-basquiat-painting-yusaku-maezawa.html. Accessed 18 Jan. 2019.

Yamamoto, Mari, and Jake Adelstein. "Meet Yusaku Maezawa, the Billionaire Entrepreneur Rocking the Art World." *The Daily Beast*, 13 May 2016, www.thedailybeast.com/meet-yusaku-maezawa-the-billionaire-entrepreneur-rocking-the-art-world. Accessed 18 Jan. 2019.

—Joy Crelin

Post Malone

Date of birth: July 4, 1995
Occupation: Rapper and producer

Rapper Post Malone became an overnight sensation with the release of his breakout song "White Iverson" in 2015. Journalist Bijan Stephen for *GQ* magazine (25 Jan. 2018) wrote that Malone was among a "new wave of rappers blurring the borders of hip-hop." Malone's music "is a mélange of pop, R&B, rap, emo, punk, and indie rock, thrown together in unpredictable and

Photo by Glenn Francis via Wikimedia Commons

unpredictably compelling ways," Stephen wrote. Although Malone is sometimes seen as a divisive figure, fans agree that he is both extraordinarily talented and supremely juvenile. Some of his lyrics have been noted by critics as juvenile, and he commissioned a portrait of himself as a mythical centaur, holding an American flag, amidst a mound of crushed beer cans. Jayson Greene wrote, appreciatively, for *Pitchfork* (26 July 2018), "To avoid saying 'Post Malone is ridiculous' in a piece about Post Malone would be a journalistic failure."

Following his emergence in 2015, Malone released a slew of hits, and by 2018, he had broken a record previously held by the Beatles and rapper J. Cole with nine simultaneous top-twenty hits, including the megahits "Psycho," featuring singer Ty Dolla $ign, and "Rockstar," featuring rapper 21 Savage. Malone's hard-partying, quasi-nihilist attitude toward living can be seen as part of his allure. His loping bangers have a tinge of melancholy. Music critic Hua Hsu, for the *New Yorker* (14 May 2018), described "Rockstar" as a "menacing I.V. drip of a song," while Jon Caramanica, for the *New York Times* (9 May 2018), described Malone as "perpetually narcotized, endlessly plaintive, borderline disoriented."

EARLY LIFE AND EDUCATION

Austin Richard Post was born in Syracuse, New York, on July 4, 1995. He moved to Grapevine, a suburb of Dallas, Texas, when he was nine, after his father, Rich, got a job managing concessions for the Dallas Cowboys. Malone has a stepmother, Jodie, and a stepbrother named Mitchell. Thanks to his father, a former wedding

DJ, he loved music from an early age. He became interested in learning to play guitar after playing the video game *Guitar Hero II*. He won an eighth-grade talent show by singing a metalcore version of the Rihanna song "Umbrella." As a student at Grapevine High School, Malone was voted "Most Likely to Become Famous" for his eccentric brand of showmanship.

While in high school, Malone experimented with a variety of music genres. He played in both an indie band and a metal band, and he made a hip-hop mixtape called *Young and After Them Riches*. In addition, he traveled to open-mic nights, where he performed covers of the 1980s rock band Guns N' Roses as well as the hip-hop duo Outkast. He also uploaded music on the video website *YouTube*, including a popular cover of Bob Dylan's "Don't Think Twice, It's All Right." For an art project, Malone jokingly styled himself as a pop star called Leon DeChino. In a music video for a DeChino song called "Why Don't You Love Me," he danced in booty shorts and a leopard-print head scarf. Around the same time, he began using the stage name Post Malone, which he has stated was created using an internet rap-name generator. When not making music, Malone worked for the fast food chain Chicken Express.

After graduating high school, Malone enrolled at Tarrant County College in Fort Worth. He dropped out after only a few months, however, stating that he was not interested in school. Malone instead decided to move to Los Angeles, California, in 2014, with his friend Jason Probst. Probst had become an internet celebrity after posting a video of him and his friends joking around while playing the video game *Minecraft*. Probst and his crew hoped to capitalize from their internet fame, while Malone hoped to score a record deal. His early time in Los Angeles was difficult for Malone, who scrounged for spare change to buy cigarettes and slept in a closet. "I had to make it work," Malone recalled to Jonah Weiner for the *Rolling Stone* (17 Nov. 2017), "It was that or Chicken Express."

RAPID RISE AND *STONEY*

Within a year, Malone met rapper and producer FKi 1st. "Something stuck out about him," FKi 1st told Gail Mitchell for *Billboard* (25 Feb. 2016). "Then his dad showed me a video of Post singing and playing guitar. We both made the beat for 'White,' put it on *SoundCloud* and let people take over. The people always know." FKi 1st was referring to "White Iverson," a song in which Malone compares himself to basketball legend Allen Iverson. Malone uploaded the song to the music sharing website *SoundCloud* on February 4, 2015, where it became an overnight success. The next day, the song was endorsed by rappers Wiz Khalifa and Mac Miller on the social media site *Twitter*. Six months later, in August 2015, Malone signed with Republic Records. The same month, "White Iverson" was released as an official single and, in 2017, was certified five-times platinum. In 2016, he was featured alongside Ty Dolla $ign on rapper Kanye West's track "Fade," from West's album *The Life of Pablo*. He also opened for popstar Justin Bieber on his Purpose tour. The same year, Malone released his first album, *Stoney* (2016); the title of the album references his old nickname, Stoney Maloney. *Stoney*—which featured guest artists such as Bieber, singer Kehlani, and rapper Quavo from the hip-hop group Migos—went triple-platinum. In 2018, the album broke a record previously held by Michael Jackson's *Thriller*, having spent seventy-seven weeks in the top ten of the Billboard Top R&B/Hip-Hop Albums chart. The album's second single, "Congratulations" featuring Quavo, peaked at number eight on the Billboard Hot 1000 chart. Still, the album received poor reviews, with critics dismissing Malone as a one-hit wonder.

CONTROVERSY

In preparation for his second album, Malone tried to distance himself from the label of rapper in an effort to shirk uneasy questions about race and cultural appropriation. He expressed to Stephen his frustration with the concept of music genres, stating "It should just be music, you know?" Malone became successful, however, by creating rap and hip-hop music, genres traditionally created and produced by black artists. Though he is not the first white rapper to do so, his failure to honestly engage with the culture behind rap and hip-hop created controversy with some people. Hsu, who has written extensively about hip-hop, observed that for Malone, "hip-hop is an idiom, a stylistic flourish, a way to wear your hair, not a history or a tradition to which one pays homage, or at least lip service." As a response, Hsu quoted Malone as saying, "I'm just trying to keep living and make the music that I love." Stephen, a professed Malone fan who struggles with the rapper's comments about race, summed it up this way: "What's worse than appropriating a black sound without giving appropriate credit is doing that and not realizing why that might be wrong."

In 2015, Charlamagne tha God, cohost of the radio show *The Breakfast Club*, famously accused Malone of cultural appropriation. Two years later, in an interview with Weiner for *Rolling Stone* (17 Nov. 2017), the exchange came up again. "Like, maybe my music's not the best, but I know I'm not a bad person, so you're just being a hater," Malone said, further suggesting that the host did not like him because he was a white rapper. Charlamagne stuck to his original point, encouraging Malone to "give back to the black community in some form." Despite not commenting directly on accusations of cultural appropriation, Malone has remained adamant that music should be able to cross genres. Malone reiterated to Weiner, "Especially with the power of music, we can push past the world's flaws and make it a more beautiful place."

BEERBONGS & BENTLEYS

Malone released the song "Rockstar," featuring 21 Savage, as the lead single for his second album in 2017. It was Malone's first certified megahit, spending eight weeks at number one. The album, *Beerbongs & Bentleys* (stylized as *beerbongs & bentleys*), was released in April 2018. It set *Spotify* records for first-day and first-week streams, earning 431 million listens on the music-streaming website within the first week of its release. All eighteen songs on the album debuted on the Billboard Hot 100; nine of the songs debuted in the top twenty, breaking an earlier record set by the English rock band the Beatles and tied by rapper J. Cole. *Beerbongs* follow-up single, "Psycho" featuring Ty Dolla $ign, also peaked at number one. The album featured an impressive and eclectic roster of collaborators, including rappers Nicki Minaj and G-Eazy, singer Swae Lee, and Mötley Crüe drummer Tommy Lee, who cowrote the song, "Over Now."

Beerbongs is notable for its range, managing to combine elements of pop, hip-hop, and country. Still, critics were divided. Caramanica described it as so ambient as to inspire hypnosis. "It is a submerged—and submersive—listening experience," he wrote. "Strong, but rarely in a thrilling way." Evan Rytlewski, for *Pitchfork* (3 May 2018), wrote that it was "more assured and impressive than its predecessor, *Stoney*, but it's also more exhausting." He offered praise for "Rockstar" and "Psycho" specifically, but *Beerbongs* as a whole, he wrote, "overplays its hand, twisting potentially breezy songs into something false and performative." Greene, also for *Pitchfork*, was more enthusiastic. Malone, he wrote, has "grown in disorienting leaps as a recording artist." He praised the ballad "Stay," describing it as "sophisticated" with a "cat-like grace." He described "Better Now" as "one of the best and most affecting break-up songs of the year." Malone earned four nominations at the 2018 Grammy Awards: Record of the Year and Best Rap/Sung Performance for "Rockstar," Best Pop Solo Performance for "Better Now," and Album of the Year for *Beerbongs*.

In January 2019, Malone and Swae Lee's song "Sunflower," from the 2018 film *Spider-man: Into the Spider-Verse*, hit number one on the Billboard Top 100 chart.

SUGGESTED READING

Caramanica, Jon. "Post Malone and Rae Sremmurd, Hip-Hop Impressionists Shaping the Stream." *The New York Times*, 9 May 2018, www.nytimes.com/2018/05/09/arts/music/post-malone-beerbongs-bentleys-rae-sremmurd-sr3mm-review.html. Accessed 17 Feb. 2019.

Greene, Jayson. "Learning to Love Post Malone." *Pitchfork*, 26 July 2018, pitchfork.com/features/overtones/post-malone-is-ridiculous-but-thats-not-all-he-is/. Accessed 17 Feb. 2019.

Hsu, Hua. "Post Malone's White-Rapper Blues." *The New Yorker*, 14 May 2018, www.newyorker.com/magazine/2018/05/14/post-malones-white-rapper-blues. Accessed 17 Feb. 2019.

Mitchell, Gail. "Producer FKi 1st Talks Diplo, Post Malone and 'The First Time for Everything.'" *Billboard*, 25 Feb. 2016, www.billboard.com/articles/news/6889539/producer-fki-1st-talks-diplo-post-malone-and-the-first-time-for-everything. Accessed 17 Feb. 2019.

Rytlewski, Evan. Review of *Beerbongs & Bentleys*, by Post Malone. *Pitchfork*, 3 May 2018, pitchfork.com/reviews/albums/post-malone-beerbongs-and-bentleys/. Accessed 17 Feb. 2019.

Stephen, Bijan. "Don't Call Post Malone a Rapper." *GQ*, 25 Jan. 2018, www.gq.com/story/dont-call-post-malone-a-rapper. Accessed 17 Feb. 2019.

Weiner, Jonah. "Post Malone: Confessions of a Hip-Hop Rock Star." *Rolling Stone*, 17 Nov. 2017, www.rollingstone.com/music/music-features/post-malone-confessions-of-a-hip-hop-rock-star-116218/. Accessed 17 Feb. 2019.

—*Molly Hagan*

Maluma

Date of birth: January 28, 1994
Occupation: Singer

Maluma is a Latin Grammy Award–winning Colombian reggaetón star. He is part of a group of artists reimagining reggaetón in Colombia. "In Colombia, we have a lot of passion. We work a lot, and we have a lot of discipline because we are really tired that people know Colombia as a violent country," Maluma told the *Rolling Stone* (25 Nov. 2015). "We just want to change that face of the country, and the music that we're doing is the music that people want, that people love." The genre, influenced by hip-hop and Caribbean music, originated in Panama and Puerto Rico. It is one of the most popular genres of music in the world, thanks to 2010 hits such as Luis Fonsi and Daddy Yankee's "Despacito," and "Mi Gente," by J Balvin and Willy William. The songs held enormous crossover appeal, raising the popularity of the genre among listeners outside of Latin America. Remixes of the two songs featured American pop stars Justin Bieber and Beyoncé, respectively. Maluma released his first album *Magia* in 2012, after finding fame on the Internet as a teenager. He then collaborated with popular artists such as Shakira, Ricky Martin, French Montana, and Jason Derulo, before releasing his third album, *F.A.M.E.*, in 2018. Maluma also maintains a robust social media following with over 37 million followers on Instagram and millions more on *YouTube*. The music videos for his songs "Felices los 4" and "Corazón," garnered over one billion views each.

EARLY LIFE

Maluma was born Juan Luis Londoño Arias to Marlli Arias and Luis Londoño in Medellín, Colombia, on January 28, 1994. He has an older sister named Manuela. His stage name, Maluma, is a combination of the first letters of each of his family member's first names: Ma-Lu-Ma. He was fourteen when he got the name tattooed on his leg. He attended the Hontanares School in El Retiro.

Maluma took up soccer when he was eight, and soon began training with the elite team Atlético Nacional's youth academy. When he was fourteen, he started playing for another team called La Equidad, based in Bogotá, Colombia. He dreamed of becoming a soccer player, but

Photo by festivaldevinachile via Wikimedia Commons

he also harbored a fierce passion for singing and writing. In tenth grade, he won a singing contest with the song "Tengo Ganas" by Andrés Cepeda. He told Michelle Herrera Mulligan for *Billboard* (20 Apr. 2017) that, while in school, "I filled the margins of my schoolbooks with lyrics. My boys asked me to write beautiful letters for their ex-girls so they could get them back. I thought, 'I should be writing songs for myself.'" He wrote ballads and pop songs but was particularly drawn to reggaetón. "Where I lived, reggaetón was on fire," he told Mulligan. When he was fifteen, he and a friend wrote a song called "No quiero," and for his sixteenth birthday, Maluma's uncle arranged for him to record it in a studio. "From that very first day, I knew I wanted to do music and nothing else," he told Javier Delgado for *Miami Living Magazine* (2017). He began taking singing lessons, and as he became more absorbed with music, he passed up a slot on the starting line-up for the national soccer team. The decision "almost gave [my] father a heart attack," Maluma told Mulligan, but his heart was set on music.

SIGNED BY SONY MUSIC

Maluma soon began performing at local schools and built a following on social media. In 2011, he released the song "Farandulera," which gained significant traction on the Internet and local radio. The popularity of the song won him a deal with Sony Music Colombia in late 2011, and he released his first album, *Magia*, with the studio in 2012. At first, the album was released only in Colombia and Venezuela. It generated several hit songs, including "Obsesión," "Miss Independent," and "Pasarla Bien," and earned him a Latin Grammy nomination for Best New Artist. In 2013, he released the hit song "La Temperatura," featuring the Puerto Rican singer Eli Palacios. It reached number twenty-four on the Billboard Hot Latin Songs chart, the first of his songs to crack a US music chart. In 2014, Maluma teamed up with the American Puerto Rican singer Elvis Crespo on the song "Olé Brazil." The same year, he signed a recording contract with Sony Music Latin.

Maluma's next release was *PB.DB Mixtape* (2015). The mixtape included his single "La Temperatura," as well as the single "Carnaval," which incorporated pop and soca (a genre of Calypso music) and won Maluma comparisons to pop star Ricky Martin. In 2014 and 2015, Maluma served as a coach and mentor, respectively, on Telemundo's *La voz kids*—a junior, Spanish-language version of the American singing competition show *The Voice*.

PRETTY BOY, DIRTY BOY

PB.DB Mixtape set the stage for Maluma's second studio album, *Pretty Boy, Dirty Boy*, released by Sony Music Latin in 2015. *Pretty Boy, Dirty Boy* was more than three years in the making and served as Maluma's official international debut. The album reached the number one slot on the Billboard Top Latin Albums chart. Pier Dominguez, writing for *Track Record* (13 July 2016), described it as "an explicit bid for pop domination," mixing ballads and bachata—a popular style of Dominican dance music—with reggaetón. The album's first single, "El Tiki," was nominated for a Latin Grammy Award for Best Urban Fusion Performance. The second single, "Borró Cassette," a collaboration with the production duo the Rude Boyz, reached number one on the Billboard Latin Airplay, Latin Rhythm Airplay, and Tropical Songs charts. It also won Maluma the Kids' Choice Award Colombia for Favorite Song. The song was the first major hit for the Rude Boyz, and the production team also produced Maluma's next single, "El Perdador," about heartbreak. The song "Sin Contrato" was released as the albums fourth single in 2016. In the song, Maluma paints himself as a ladies' man, moving from woman to woman "without contract," as the song's title translates in English. A North American remix of the song featured the girl group Fifth Harmony. The album earned Maluma the 2017 Lo Nuestro Awards for Urban Album of the Year and Urban Artist of the Year.

In 2016, Maluma collaborated with Colombian superstar Shakira on the megahit song "Chantaje," produced by the Rudy Boyz. The song debuted at number one on the Billboard Hot Latin Songs chart and broke the Billboard Hot 100 chart. It was nominated for three Latin Grammy Awards: Song of the Year, Record of the Year, and Best Urban Fusion Performance. The music video was the fastest-ever Spanish-language video to garner one hundred million views online. Maluma also appeared on Shakira's ballad "Trap" on her 2017 album, *El Dorado*. The same year, he collaborated with Mexican singer-songwriter Thalía on the song "Desde Esa Noche," and with Ricky Martin on "Vente Pa' Ca." The video for "Vente Pa' Ca" was viewed nearly 1.5 billion times by 2018.

CRITICISMS AND F.A.M.E.

Maluma then released the hit song "Cuatro Babys," in 2016, featuring Trap Capos, Noriel, Bryant Myers, and Juhn. The song, about a man who is simultaneously sleeping with four different women, and its risqué music video were criticized as misogynistic, a charge often lobbied at Maluma, who sings about sexual conquests and posts pictures of himself surrounded by scantily clad women on his social media accounts. His music video for his 2018 hit single "Mala Mia," which features Maluma waking up under a pile of unclothed, passed-out women, faced similar critiques. Responding to the criticism, Maluma told Delgado, "As I said previously, there's nothing more beautiful and special than women. Then again, I'm a storyteller and for that I've been pointed at and called names, but those who know me well recognize what kind of person I am."

Maluma released "Felices los 4," the first single from his third studio album, *F.A.M.E.* (2018), in 2017. The song, the first of Maluma's own to appear on the Billboard Hot 100 chart, peaked at number forty-eight. In 2017, Maluma was nominated for a number of Latin Grammy Awards, including the awards for both Record of the Year and Song of the Year for "Felices los 4." He later performed "Felices los 4" at the 2018 MTV Video Music Awards. Following "Felices los 4," Maluma released three promotional singles that were not featured on the album, including "GPS," on which he collaborated with American rapper French Montana.

After its release in 2018, *F.A.M.E* peaked at number one on the Billboard Top Latin Albums chart. The second single from the album, "Corazón," featuring Brazilian singer Nego do Borel, was inspired by Maluma's tour in Brazil. In 2018, Maluma won his first Latin Grammy Award for Best Contemporary Pop Vocal Album for *F.A.M.E.* In his review of the album, Ben Beaumont-Thomas for the *Guardian* (18 May 2018) gave *F.A.M.E.* four out of five stars, stating that, "the chief strength of this well-written album is the sensuality in Maluma's delivery, all keening vowels that splinter into come-hither huskiness." The same year, Maluma appeared with American singer Jason Derulo on the bilingual version of "Colors," the official Coca-Cola anthem for the 2018 FIFA World Cup. The intro to the video features Maluma talking about his own past as a soccer player.

PERSONAL LIFE
Maluma began dating model Natalia Barulich in 2017. The couple met on the set of Maluma's "Felices los 4" video, in which she played his love interest.

SUGGESTED READING
Beaumont-Thomas, Ben. "Maluma: FAME Review—Sexy Reggaeton from Fit-But-You-Know-It Megastar." Review of *F.A.M.E.*, by Maluma. *The Guardian*, 18 May 2018, www.theguardian.com/music/2018/may/18/maluma-fame-review. Accessed 12 Dec. 2018.

Dominguez, Pier. "Maluma and the Evolution of the Latin Pop Star." *Track Record*, 13 July 2016, trackrecord.net/maluma-and-the-evolution-of-the-latin-pop-star-1819123818. Accessed 10 Dec. 2018.

Maluma. "Maluma: 'Music Is My Life.'" Interview by Javier Delgado. *Miami Living Magazine*, 2017, digital.miamilivingmagazine.com/i/786375-maluma/135. Accessed 10 Dec. 2018.

Mulligan Herrera, Michelle. "Reggaetón's Sexiest Star Maluma on Crossover Dreams (Hola Justin Timberlake!) and Struggling with Fame." *Billboard*, 20 Apr. 2017, www.billboard.com/articles/news/magazine-feature/7767639/maluma-reggaeton-sexiest-star-latin-feature. Accessed 10 Dec. 2018.

"Ten New Artists You Need to Know: November 2015." *Rolling Stone*, 25 Nov. 2015, www.rollingstone.com/music/music-lists/10-new-artists-you-need-to-know-november-2015-147133/. Accessed 10 Dec. 2018.

SELECTED WORKS
Magia, 2012; *PB.DB Mixtape*, 2015; *Pretty Boy, Dirty Boy*, 2015; *F.A.M.E.*, 2018

—Molly Hagan

Pippa Mann

Date of birth: August 11, 1983
Occupation: Race car driver

Pippa Mann is one of the top British race car drivers. A native of London, Mann began her motorsport career in karting before moving to European open-wheel racing, in which drivers race in single-seater cars whose wheels are outside of the car's main body. After a number of successes on Europe's premier Renault World Series circuit, Mann moved to the United States in 2009 for better career racing opportunities. She spent two years racing in the developmental Indy Lights series, and in 2011, made her debut on the NTT IndyCar Series, the top level of open-wheel racing in North America. That year she raced in the Indianapolis 500, the series' premier event and one of the most prestigious sports events in the world.

Since then, Mann, who overcame a devastating injury suffered towards the end of her debut 2011 IndyCar season, has made five more starts at the Indianapolis 500 (all as a member of Dale Coyne Racing), recording a career-best seventeenth-place finish in 2017. Along the way, she has added to her list of achievements, among which is being one of the few drivers to top the 230-mph barrier. Aside from racing, she is known for her many charitable efforts, particularly those aimed at raising breast cancer awareness. As Gregg Doyel wrote for *IndyStar* (16 May 2018), "In a sport where speed is everything . . . speed is just a side note to Pippa Mann."

Photo by Nave.notnilc via Wikimedia Commons

EARLY LIFE

Pippa Mann was born on August 11, 1983, in London, England, to Clive and Anna Mann. She grew up in Leiston, a town in England's eastern Suffolk region. Mann's interest in racing was sparked by her father, who was a motorsports enthusiast. As a young girl, she watched Formula One racing events on television with her father. Each year the two would travel to the Snetterton race track, in nearby Norfolk, to take in Touring Car competitions; they later made annual treks to England's famed Silverstone racing circuit to watch the British Grand Prix, the oldest race on the Formula One competition schedule.

Mann's own racing career did not begin until she was twelve years old, when she first raced a go-kart at a friend's birthday party. Instantly hooked, Mann joined a local kids' kart racing club, where an instructor quickly recognized her potential in the sport. "From the moment I started driving karts, I knew I didn't want to do anything else," she told Robin Scott-Elliott for the *Independent* (5 Jan. 2012).

When Mann was thirteen, her parents bought her a go-kart of her own, helping to accelerate her racing development. By age fifteen, she was competing in British national karting championships—much to the annoyance of her male competitors, who would assert their authority by trying to bump her off the track. As the only female driver in her age group, "I had to develop a thicker skin," Mann explained to Adam Luck for the *Daily Mail* (6 Oct. 2012). "It is not the size of the person in the fight that matters, but the size of the fight in the person."

ROAD TO INDYCAR

That "fight" crystallized when, at seventeen, Mann, who attended Saint Felix School in Suffolk, moved to Italy to pursue a career in professional karting. For three years, she competed in races on the Italian, European, and World Karting championship circuits. In 2003, Mann became the first British woman to win an international Formula A karting race.

During her time abroad, Mann worked as a waitress in a pizza restaurant to support herself financially. She also performed odd jobs for her team to help boost her profile. Those efforts were for naught, however, as Mann struggled for recognition in Europe's male-dominated world of motorsports. Consequently, Mann turned her attention to North America's IndyCar Series. She became intrigued by open-wheel racing after her father sent her an article about the American race car driver Sarah Fisher, who became the first woman to claim a pole position, the top qualifying spot for a race, in an open-wheel race in 2002.

Mann returned to England in 2003, after which she focused her attention on open-wheel racing. Over the next six years, she ascended the European ladder in that racing discipline, earning the chance to compete in the top-level World Series by Renault championship. During her World Series debut season in 2007, Mann became the first woman to notch points in that series, as well as the first one to start a race from a pole position.

To further advance her racing career, Mann moved to the United States in 2009 and signed with Panther Racing to drive in the Indy Lights series, the feeder circuit for IndyCar. After Panther Racing folded, she joined Sam Schmidt Motorsports for the 2010 Indy Lights season, which was marked by several notable achievements. She won a pole position at the world-famous Indianapolis Motor Speedway, as well as two other race tracks, and achieved a first-place finish for the first time in her career. She finished that season ranked fifth in the series' points standings, helping her progress to the IndyCar circuit, and was voted "most popular driver" by fans.

MAKING HISTORY AND OVERCOMING ADVERSITY

Mann made her IndyCar series debut in 2011 at that year's Indianapolis 500. She was the lone one-off newcomer that year to qualify for the race in their maiden attempt. Driving for the Indianapolis-based team Conquest Racing, Mann placed twentieth out of the traditional thirty-three-car starting field.

Following her impressive Indianapolis 500 debut, Mann signed a deal with the Rahal Letterman Racing Team, for whom she drove in three races over the remainder of the 2011

IndyCar season. In October 2011, less than two months after suffering minor injuries in a crash during a practice session for an IndyCar event in Loudon, New Hampshire, Mann competed at the Kentucky Indy 300, in Sparta, Kentucky, where she finished twenty-second. Just two weeks later, however, the dangers of her sport came into focus when she was involved in a devastating fifteen-car pileup at the IndyCar series season finale, held at the Las Vegas Motor Speedway in Nevada.

During the eleventh lap of the 200-lap, 300-mile race, Mann and fourteen other drivers collided with one another, and Mann's car, traveling at an estimated speed of 220 mph, went airborne and became engulfed in a fireball before landing upside down. Though Mann wore fireproof gloves, the fireball "had a blow-torch effect on one small area of my right hand," as she put it to Luck, causing severe burns to her pinkie finger. The injury required her to undergo three surgeries on her hand over the course of a single week. The collision also tragically claimed the life of one of her good friends, British racecar driver Dan Wheldon, who had won that year's Indianapolis 500.

Mann spent the next year recovering from her hand injury, during which she lost much of her funding. As a result, she involved herself in other racing-related endeavors to earn money, such as hosting racing tours and providing radio commentary for select races. All the while, Mann never once thought about walking away from the sport. "You couldn't do it if you were scared of crashing," she said to Scott-Elliott. "There are the bare facts, it's racing and you are going to come together with other cars and sometimes it's going to go wrong. It's a part of it."

RACING WITH A PURPOSE

Mann returned to the IndyCar series in time for the 2013 season, prior to which she was signed by Dale Coyne Racing. She qualified to start for the team at that year's Indianapolis 500, where she placed thirtieth. She then rounded out that season by making three large oval track starts with the team, finishing twenty-fourth, fifteenth, and twenty-fifth, respectively, at the Firestone 550 in Texas, the Pocono IndyCar 400 in Pennsylvania, and the MAVTV 500 IndyCar World Championships in California.

Mann would start at the Indianapolis 500 for Dale Coyne Racing during each of the next four seasons, finishing twenty-fourth in 2014, twenty-second in 2015, eighteenth in 2016, and a career-best seventeenth in 2017. During those years, she served almost exclusively as a one-off racer for the Indianapolis 500, competing in only a handful of other IndyCar events. In one of those events, the MAVTV 500 in 2015, Mann achieved the best placing of her IndyCar career, coming in thirteenth. During this time, she launched a "pink" racing campaign in conjunction with her team and the Susan G. Komen Foundation to help raise breast cancer awareness. Mann, whose grandmother and aunt died of breast cancer, became known for her signature pink racing attire and race car. Rather than having Susan G. Komen sponsor her number sixty-three car, however, Dale Coyne Racing made in-kind donations—in the form of space on Mann's racing car—to the foundation, which in turn auctioned off Mann's racewear to raise money. Mann has since raised more than $200,000 for the foundation.

Unlike most of her IndyCar counterparts, who race under the backing of lucrative sponsorship deals, Mann oversees all her own marketing, branding, and public relations. Accordingly, she is responsible for finding her own sponsors and for satisfying the agreements she makes with them. Such partnerships enable Mann to generate the kind of funding necessary to compete in IndyCar races. Much of Mann's funding comes from local Indiana businesses, companies, and individuals. Mann explained to Doyel, "I understand that I'm not a big-name driver. I understand that I'm going to have to work hard to be here, and I understand that barring miracles, quite frankly we are not competing to win the Indianapolis 500."

Notwithstanding this realization, Mann has distinguished herself with her racing ability. In 2017, she topped 230 mph during the Indianapolis 500's annual "Fast Friday" practice; during this practice, drivers push their limits with regard to speed, all aiming to reach more than 230 mph. She nonetheless did not qualify her Dale Coyne Racing entry for the 2018 Indianapolis 500. That year, however, she did race in the Lamborghini Super Trofeo North America, placing second in all four of her races and coming in fourth overall.

In February 2019, Mann was announced as the driver for Clauson-Marshall Racing's entry for that year's Indianapolis 500. She signed with the team after being approached by its owner, Tim Clauson, whose son, Bryan, was a former Dale Coyne teammate of hers. In 2016, Bryan Clauson died at age twenty-seven after sustaining fatal injuries in a midget racing accident. Afterward, the Driven2SaveLives campaign was established to honor Bryan's decision to be an organ donor. Speaking of her 2019 Indy 500 aspirations, Mann, who is a Driven2SaveLives ambassador, told Arni Sribhen for the *NTT IndyCar Series* website (18 Mar. 2019): "I am out for redemption. I want not only to be in the field, but I also want it to be my best run ever."

PERSONAL LIFE

In addition to her racing responsibilities, Mann serves as a performance driving instructor and coach. She helped found a program with the Indianapolis-based Lucas Oil School of Racing that works to create more racing opportunities for women. In 2016, she was selected by the Susan G. Komen Foundation to be on The List, which honors individuals for their impact in raising awareness about breast cancer. That year she was also recognized by the UK–based automobile magazine *Autocar* as one of the top 100 British women in the car industry.

Mann resides in Indianapolis with her husband, Robert Gue, an American race car engineer, whom she married in December 2012.

SUGGESTED READING

Davis, Flynn. "At Indy 500, Pippa Mann Represents Female Drivers in a Hot Pink Race Car." *Bustle*, 4 June 2014, www.bustle.com/articles/26778-at-indy-500-pippa-mann-represents-female-drivers-in-a-hot-pink-race-car. Accessed 3 Mar. 2019.

Doyel, Gregg. "Doyel: Why Pippa Mann Is the Most Important Driver in 2018 Indy 500." *IndyStar*, 16 May 2018, www.indystar.com/story/sports/columnists/gregg-doyel/2018/05/16/pippa-mann-race-2018-indy-500-organ-donation-cancer-awareness/614749002/. Accessed 26 Feb. 2019.

Fabrizio, Tony. "IndyCar Driver Pippa Mann's Breast Cancer Awareness Efforts Recognized in 'The List.'" *ESPNW.com*, 6 Oct. 2016, www.espn.com/espnw/culture/article/17708973/indycar-driver-pippa-mann-breast-cancer-awareness-efforts-recognized-susan-g-komen-list. Accessed 26 Feb. 2019.

Luck, Adam. "How I Survived the 200mph Fireball That Melted My Flesh and Killed My Best Friend, by Britain's Top Female Racing Driver." *Daily Mail*, 6 Oct. 2012, www.dailymail.co.uk/femail/article-2213923/How-I-survived-200mph-fireball-melted-flesh-killed-best-friend-Britains-female-racing-driver.html. Accessed 26 Feb. 2019.

Scott-Elliott, Robin. "Pippa Mann: 'The Big Thing in a Crash Is to Relax.'" *The Independent*, 5 Jan. 2012, www.independent.co.uk/news/people/profiles/pippa-mann-the-big-thing-in-a-crash-is-to-relax-6284929.html. Accessed 3 Mar. 2019.

Sribhen, Arni. "Mann's Return to Indy 500 Built on Disappointment of 2018." *NTT IndyCar Series*, 18 Mar. 2019, www.indycar.com/News/2019/03/03-18-Mann-Indy-500-new-chance. Accessed 18 Mar. 2019.

—*Chris Cullen*

Rose Marcario

Date of birth: ca. 1964
Occupation: Business executive

After becoming president and CEO of the California-based outdoor clothing company Patagonia in 2014, Rose Marcario led the company's efforts in sustainable business practices. Under her leadership, Patagonia doubled operations and tripled profits. Each year Patagonia contributes 1 percent of its net sales to environmental groups working at the grassroots level, a total of more than eighty million dollars by 2017. As she told Richard Feloni for *Business Insider* (16 Apr. 2019), "Companies are realizing that their customers and their employees expect them to take a stand. You can't live in the gray area anymore. There's too much at risk right now."

Marcario's leadership, particularly in establishing family-friendly policies, earned her designation as a Champion of Change under the Barack Obama administration. In 2015 *Fortune* also acknowledged her as one of the Most Powerful Women in Business. The following year *Fast Company* named her among the most creative, innovative chief executive officers of that year. In addition, *Business Insider* included her on its list of 100 People Transforming Business. Of her work, Marcario told Ryan Bradley for *Fortune* (14 Sept. 2015), "This is my last stop. It's my way to keep myself from becoming so completely disillusioned, you know?"

EDUCATION AND EARLY CAREER

Rose Marcario was born around 1964 and grew up in an Italian Catholic family on Staten Island in New York. Following her parents' divorce when she was ten, she moved to California. She later earned a Bachelor of Science degree from State University of New York at Albany and a master's degree in business administration at California State University Los Angeles.

Marcario began her career in private equity firms as well as in finance and technology. She later served as a senior vice president and chief financial officer (CFO) of General Magic, a spin-off from Apple Inc., before becoming the executive vice president of Capital Advisors.

After twenty-five years in jobs that required her to focus on quarterly profits above all else, Marcario began to reconsider her career. As she told Caroline Winter for *Bloomberg* (6 May 2013), "I went through what many people do at that age, in my 40s, the sort of crisis of conscience about whether my personal values aligned with my work, which is where I spend most of my waking life." Marcario quit in 2006. She spent the next few years meditating and studying Buddhism in India and Nepal, before returning to Los Angeles.

Photo by MANDEL NGAN/AFP/Getty Images

JOINING PATAGONIA

In 2008 Marcario joined Patagonia. Although she initially hesitated to take the CFO role, a conversation with founder Yvon Chouinard reassured her that Patagonia—a private, family-owned company founded in 1970—was a different kind of company. During her first few years, Marcario streamlined production and saved costs by identifying financial and environmental waste, devoted resources to improving e-commerce, and furthered Patagonia's philanthropic and environmental protection agendas. She was soon given the additional responsibility of chief operations officer (COO).

In 2009 Patagonia joined with Walmart to recruit major retailers, such as Adidas and Nike, to form the Sustainable Apparel Coalition. Patagonia became a B (benefit) Corp in 2011. The nonprofit group B Lab certifies companies that are determined to follow business practices that are environmentally and socially sound. As Marcario told Marie Leone for *CFO* (1 Oct. 2010), "I didn't think it was possible to blend a social and environmental mission with profit targets, but now I am a total convert."

When Patagonia restructured in 2013, Marcario became president and chief executive officer (CEO) of Patagonia's parent company, Patagonia Works. The same year she helped lead the company's launch of $20 Million and Change, an internal venture fund dedicated to assisting businesses in finding solutions to environment problems. It assists start-ups working to make the world a better place. As Marcario explained to Danielle Sacks for *Fast Company* (Feb. 2015), "We all have the same issues—transportation,

packaging, manufacturing, use of water, use of energy. These things are very basic. We can solve them. It's only by a failure of imagination that we don't." Also in 2013 the company developed Yulex, a plant-based rubber for wet suits using a desert shrub native to the American Southwest. Marcario and Patagonia did not hesitate to share the technology with the entire surf industry, choosing not to make the formula proprietary and instead believing that because it was better for the environment than rubber-based suits, it should be available to all companies.

In 2014 Marcario was named CEO of Patagonia Inc. In that position, she continued Patagonia's commitment of collaborations to promote the sustainable food industry, increase use of recycled material, and influence environmental change. Speaking of the need companies have to address climate change seriously, Marcario told Feloni, "I have a high level of optimism that these problems are solvable. I like to solve problems and I feel like we can get there. We have all the tools to get there. We have the technology to get there. We have the best innovative and entrepreneurial minds here in the United States to help do that." In addition to the usual measurements that businesses use to track profitability, Patagonia also tracks an in-store recycling program, as well as the amount of recycled material used in their fabrics.

CHALLENGING A PRESIDENT

In 2013 Marcario and Patagonia joined with local groups and tribal leaders to campaign for Bears Ears in Utah to become a national monument. The area—considered sacred by the Zunis, Hopis, Pueblos, and Utes—contains ancient petroglyphs carved in the rocks and the ruins of earlier cliff-dwelling civilizations. The company relies on public lands and national monuments for much of its business, and Patagonia employees had gone to the area for retreats and products testing. President Barack Obama officially designated the Bears Ears National Monument, which covers 1.35 million acres of land, in December 2016.

On December 4, 2017, however, President Donald Trump signed an executive order to cut the protected area of the Bears Ears National Monument by 85 percent and reduce the area of Grand Staircase-Escalante National Monument as well. The order came as a result of a request from Utah governor Gary Herbert, who had opposed the Bears Ears monument designation. Many feel the presence of uranium and mineral deposits there was at the root of the Trump decision. Following the decision, Patagonia, joining with American Indian tribes and several other companies, sued the federal government. In addition, Marcario led a successful boycott of the

Salt Lake City Outdoor Retailer Show, a biennial trade show that moved to Denver, Colorado.

Marcario argued that article 4, section 3, clause 2 of the Constitution gave the president authority to create protected land but not to undo a previous president's actions in protecting federal land. As Marcario wrote for *Time* (6 Dec. 2017), "We must also acknowledge that history shows when states control public-trust land, 70% is sold off—and then often used for oil drilling, mining and other industrial activities. This also means that hunters, fishers, outdoorsmen and families like yours can no longer enjoy them." She continued, "This is not about politics; it's about protecting the places we love and keeping the great promise of this country for our children and grandchildren." The lawsuit also advances that Patagonia will lose revenue if public lands in the nation shrink.

ENVIRONMENTAL ISSUES

Marcario and Patagonia raised awareness of and challenged a variety of environmental and social issues. The company contributed funding for the documentary *DamNation* (2014), about dam removal in light of China's efforts to build more dams. As Marcario told Sacks, "We felt that the environmental risk of not talking about the negative aspects of hydropower and how much methane gas it's emitting were too high. We were concerned about those issues not getting out." In 2015 the company used federal and state tax credits to help subsidize solar panels in Hawaii, where Patagonia has long worked. Solar power can require both a high entry cost and a high credit score, which many private individuals cannot afford or do not have. The thirteen million dollars Patagonia contributed went for private homes in the state. As Marcario told Sacks, "We had capital that we had to use, and we want to use every arrow in our quiver right now because we feel so urgent about what's going on."

Marcario also advocates repairing clothing and other items rather than replacing them. As she wrote for *Quartz* (25 Nov. 2015), "As individual consumers, the single best thing we can do for the planet is to keep our stuff in use longer. This simple act of extending the life of our garments through proper care and repair reduces the need to buy more over time—thereby avoiding the CO_2 emissions, waste output, and water usage required to build it." She went on to delineate the difference between product consumers, who rush to replace rather than repair, and owners, who care for their purchases. Employees at Patagonia's garment repair shop, the largest in the nation, repair about forty thousand items annually. The company also has more than forty how-to-fix-it repair guides for their products.

In 2018 Patagonia joined the clothing company Levi's to institute Time to Vote, a nonpartisan effort to allow employees time to vote in the midterm elections. Some four hundred companies gave their employees time off to cast their ballots. Patagonia closed all its stores that day to underscore the importance of voting. After the corporate tax cuts signed into law in 2018 resulted in a ten-million-dollar tax cut for Patagonia, the company decided that the money could best be spent in fighting climate change and donated the entire sum to nonprofit groups working on environmental issues, rather than putting the money back into the business.

PERSONAL LIFE

Marcario practices Shambhala Buddhism, following the leader Chögyam Trungpa Rinpoche, who funded Naropa University in Colorado. In 2013 she became a trustee of the university's board. She is also involved with such groups as Mojave Desert Land Trust and Joshua Tree National Park Association.

SUGGESTED READING

Bradley, Ryan. "The Woman Driving Patagonia to Be (Even More) Radical." *Fortune*, 14 Sept. 2015, fortune.com/2015/09/14/rose-marcario-patagonia. Accessed 29 June 2019.

Feloni, Richard. "Patagonia's CEO Says 'Capitalism Needs to Evolve' If We Want to Save the Planet." *Business Insider*, 16 Apr. 2019, www.businessinsider.com/patagonia-ceo-rose-marcario-says-capitalism-must-evolve-to-save-earth-2019-4. Accessed 1 July 2019.

Leone, Marie. "'I Hate CFOs Who Always Say No.'" *CFO*, 1 Oct. 2010, www.cfo.com/people/2010/10/i-hate-cfos-who-always-say-no-2. Accessed 20 June 2019.

Marcario, Rose. "The Most Eco-Friendly Clothes Are the Ones Already in Your Closet." *Quartz*, 25 Nov. 2015, qz.com/553614/the-most-eco-friendly-clothes-are-the-ones-already-in-your-closet. Accessed 1 July 2019.

Marcario, Rose. "Patagonia CEO Rose Marcario Fights the Fights Worth Fighting." Interview by Danielle Sacks. *Fast Company*, 6 Jan. 2015, www.fastcompany.com/3039739/patagonia-ceo-rose-marcario-fights-the-fights-worth-fighting. Accessed 28 June 2019.

Marcario, Rose. "Patagonia CEO: This Is Why We're Suing President Trump." *Time*, 6 Dec. 2017, time.com/5052617/patagonia-ceo-suing-donald-trump. Accessed 20 June 2019.

Winter, Caroline. "Patagonia's Latest Product: A Venture Fund." *Bloomberg*, 6 May 2013, www.bloomberg.com/news/articles/2013-05-06/patagonias-latest-product-a-venture-fund. Accessed 1 July 2019.

—*Judy Johnson*

James Martin

Date of birth: December 29, 1960
Occupation: Priest and writer

Father James Martin's religious order, the Society of Jesus (also known as the Jesuits), asks its members to "find God in all things." Martin's work after being ordained a Roman Catholic priest demonstrates that he took that mission to heart. He ministered to the poor and sick, worked with refugees, counseled first responders after the September 11, 2001, terrorist attacks, and discussed Christian ethics and spirituality in a wide variety of media appearances. But most notably, he authored a series of thought-provoking, critically acclaimed, and best-selling books about his experiences and views. His writings both promote his faith and challenge Catholic tradition, often drawing considerable controversy.

Perhaps the most controversial and high profile of Martin's books is *Building a Bridge: How the Catholic Church and the LGBT Community Can Enter into a Relationship of Respect, Compassion, and Sensitivity* (2017). Some conservative Catholics criticized the book for skirting around religious doctrine, while some progressive Catholics felt Martin did not go far enough in condemning the Church's official views of homosexuality and the LGBT community. In response, Martin pointed to the Jesuit mission of helping the most ostracized in society. "We are not afraid of going to the margins," he said to David Gonzalez for the *New York Times* (16 Sept. 2017). "That is what Pope Benedict and Pope Francis asked us to do. As Francis said to us, go to the peripheries where the Church has not been serving people or where people need it the most. There is no one more marginalized in the Church than LGBT Catholics. So, I'm right where I should be."

EARLY LIFE AND EDUCATION

James Martin was born on December 29, 1960, and grew up in Plymouth Meeting, Pennsylvania. He went on to study at the Wharton School of Business at the University of Pennsylvania, earning his bachelor's degree in economics in 1982. For about six years he worked at General Electric in the corporate finance department but grew disillusioned with the corporate world. At the same time, inspired by the life of Trappist monk Thomas Merton, he grew more interested in the Catholic Church.

In 1988, Martin entered the Society of Jesus, a Roman Catholic religious order founded in sixteenth-century Spain by Ignatius of Loyola. The Jesuits' mission is devoted to evangelization, ministry, education, and culture. Jesuit training is known for being rigorous. In addition to studying philosophy and theology, those training

Photo by Kerry Weber via Wikimedia Commons

in the order must also conduct full-time ministry before being ordained as priests. By the time Martin was ordained in 1999, he had earned a master's degree in divinity (1998) and another in theology (1999) from the Weston Jesuit School of Theology in Cambridge, Massachusetts, which later became part of Boston College.

During his training, Martin did ministry work in a variety of places. While in Massachusetts he served at a hospital, a homeless shelter, and a prison. He also worked in Jamaica with Mother Teresa's Missionaries of Charity, in Chicago with street gangs, and in Nairobi, Kenya, with the Jesuit Refugee Service aiding East African refugees.

PRIEST AND AUTHOR

Even as he officially became a priest, Martin began a parallel career as an author. His first book, *This Our Exile: A Spiritual Journey with the Refugees of East Africa* (1999), documented some of his ministry experiences while in training. His discussion of faith through the lens of his own experience would become a trademark of his writing, which proved accessible to readers and popular. Martin was living in New York City at the time of the September 11 terrorist attacks, and he ministered to the responders working at the site. He described the ordeal in his 2002 book *Searching for God at Ground Zero*.

During this time Martin also faced a different crisis, as the revelation of widespread sexual abuse by priests that the Catholic Church had tried to cover up became a major national scandal. Although most priests were not sexual predators, all were considered suspect in the public eye. "During the 2002 crisis I was spat upon in the subway on two occasions," Martin recalled in an op-ed for the *New York Times* (15 Aug. 2018). "At times [I] was embarrassed to wear my collar."

Despite these challenges, Martin was increasingly recognized as a skilled writer and an effective priest. His intellectual vigor, candor, and spiritual insights earned him widespread praise not only in Catholic circles, but in the mainstream secular media as well. His work in the pages of *America*, a national weekly Jesuit magazine, brought significant attention and eventually a place as editor-at-large for the publication. He also continued to publish books, including *My Life with the Saints* (2006), which was named a best book of the year by *Publishers Weekly*.

Although Martin's works usually focus on Christian spirituality, the prism of his own real-world experiences often conveys the subject in unusual ways. For example, his 2007 memoir *A Jesuit Off-Broadway: Center Stage with Jesus, Judas, and Life's Big Questions* is about his time working in 2005 as a theological adviser to the theatrical production *The Last Days of Judas Iscariot*. The book received a starred review from *Publishers Weekly* (9 July 2007), which declared that Martin's "ability to translate and dissect the gospel story of Judas for a troupe of thespians echoes through his writing, making this a book that is bound to draw applause from a diverse audience."

LIBERAL CATHOLIC COMMENTATOR

As Martin's public profile grew, he had pieces appear in national publications such as the *New York Times* and the *Wall Street Journal*. He also appeared as a guest commentator on radio and television programs including NPR's *Fresh Air*, PBS's *NewsHour*, and various news networks to supply a spiritual voice on many issues. The outlet that arguably brought him the most exposure, however, was Comedy Central's satirical show *The Colbert Report*, where he first appeared in 2007 and became a frequent guest. His role as a popular communicator for Catholicism made him well liked among many liberal Catholics and non-Catholics alike. However, many conservatives found themselves at odds with the progressive views he espoused.

Meanwhile, Martin continued writing books. Thanks to the quality of his writing and his newfound visibility, both *The Jesuit Guide to (Almost) Everything: A Spirituality for Real Life* (2010) and *Jesus: A Pilgrimage* (2014) became New York Times Best Sellers. This popularity was accompanied by largely positive reviews. And although his work in many ways reflected his liberal views, it remained firmly rooted in his faith and the basic tenets of Catholicism. As the reviewer for *Publishers Weekly* (24 Feb. 2014) wrote of *Jesus: A Pilgrimage*,

Martin "balances faith and reason in the classic Catholic tradition."

In 2016 Martin published his first novel, *The Abbey*. The book describes a spiritual crisis faced by Anne, a divorced mother coming to terms with the death of her young son, and how her life intersects with the lives of an abbot and a former architect and handyman. The novel was unlike any of Martin's earlier works, but he found the process of writing fiction liberating. In an interview with Jamie Arpin-Ricci for the *Huffington Post* (22 Oct. 2015), Martin recalled: "It was a freer process. But at the beginning I was pretty skittish about it. . . . I have no pretenses of being a great novelist, but then I figured, 'Well, I can certainly tell a story. I do that in most of my writing.' So I decided to simply tell the story in my own voice. That was extremely freeing."

BUILDING A BRIDGE AND FURTHER ADVOCACY

In April 2017, Pope Francis named Martin as a consultant to the Vatican's Secretariat for Communications. Yet with the publication of *Building a Bridge* that same year, Martin found himself facing more controversy from fellow Catholics than ever before. Many more conservative members of the Church argued that the viewpoints he expressed regarding outreach to the LGBT community were outside of Catholic teachings—even though the book was approved by his order's superiors and does not deviate from official doctrine. (For example, in the book Martin does not contend same-sex couples should be allowed to marry, which is against Catholic teaching.) He was attacked online and disinvited to a number of events in which he was to discuss his book.

Building a Bridge did find a welcome audience among many LGBT Catholics. Readers flocked to Martin's lectures by the hundreds to listen to his thoughts on the subject. In addition, many Church officials ordered his book to discuss it within their local communities and parishes. Still, some progressives also critiqued the book, arguing it did not go far enough to demand equal treatment of LGBT people by the Church. In an interview with Bill McCormick for the *Jesuit Post* (24 July 2017), Martin addressed the controversy head on: "What have I learned? That there can be common ground among people of reason and charity, but finding common ground with people with closed minds is harder."

Martin continued to prove he was not one to shy away from speaking his mind, even when doing so was sure to draw controversy. In 2018, for example, he publicly criticized Attorney General Jeff Sessions for trying to use passages from the Bible to justify the Trump administration's policy of separating migrant children from their parents. "To use Romans 13 to justify tearing kids away from their parents is insane," Martin said, as quoted by Peter Martinez for *CBS News* (20 June 2018). "It's really close to obscene."

Martin also suggested that Catholics were justifiably angered by the 2018 revelation of a systematic cover-up of child sex abuse by more than three hundred priests in Pennsylvania parishes going back decades—with some cases even occurring after the 2002 reforms implemented by the Catholic Church. "All this anger may seem like an un-Christian scourge, tearing the church apart," Martin wrote of the crisis in the *New York Times*. "In fact, it is good, healthy and clarifying."

SUGGESTED READING

Gonzalez, David. "Jesuit Priest Stands Up for Gay Catholics, Then Faces Backlash." *The New York Times*, 16 Sept. 2017, www.nytimes.com/2017/09/16/nyregion/james-martin-gay-catholics-criticism.html. Accessed 14 Nov. 2018.

Martin, James. "The Abbey: An Interview with Fr. James Martin, SJ." Interview by Jamie Arpin-Ricci. *Huffington Post*, 22 Nov. 2015, www.huffingtonpost.com/jamie-arpinricci/fr-james-martin-the-abbey_b_8341402.html. Accessed 15 Nov. 2018.

Martin, James. "Bridging Truth and Love: An Interview with James Martin, SJ." Interview by Bill McCormick. *The Jesuit Post*, 24 July 2017, thejesuitpost.org/2017/07/bridging-truth-and-love-an-interview-with-james-martin-sj/. Accessed 3 Dec. 2018.

Martin, James. "God & I: James Martin, SJ." Interview by Mario Conte. *Messenger of Saint Anthony*, 6 Oct. 2016, www.messengersaintanthony.com/content/god-i-james-martin-sj. Accessed 3 Dec. 2018.

Martin, James. "The Virtues of Catholic Anger." *The New York Times*, 15 Aug. 2018. www.nytimes.com/2018/08/15/opinion/the-virtues-of-catholic-anger.html. Accessed 14 Nov. 2018.

Martinez, Peter. "Father James Martin: Trump Administration's Biblical References 'Insane,' 'Close to Obscene.'" *CBS News*, 20 June 2018, www.cbsnews.com/news/father-james-martin-trump-administration-biblical-references-insane-close-to-obscene-cbsn-interview-2018-06-20/ Accessed 14 Nov. 2018.

McKinless, Ashley. "Father James Martin Appointed by Pope Francis to Vatican Department for Communications." *America*, 12 Apr. 2017, www.americamagazine.org/faith/2017/04/12/father-james-martin-appointed-pope-francis-vatican-department-communications. Accessed 14 Nov. 2018.

SELECTED WORKS

This Our Exile: A Spiritual Journey with the Refugees of East Africa, 1999; *Searching for God at Ground Zero*, 2002; *My Life with the Saints*, 2006; *A Jesuit Off-Broadway: Center Stage with Jesus, Judas, and Life's Big Questions*, 2007; *The Jesuit Guide to (Almost) Everything: A Spirituality for Real Life*, 2010; *Between Heaven and Mirth: Why Joy, Humor, and Laughter Are at the Heart of the Spiritual Life*, 2011; *Jesus: A Pilgrimage*, 2014; *The Abbey*, 2016; *Building a Bridge: How the Catholic Church and the LGBT Community Can Enter into a Relationship of Respect, Compassion, and Sensitivity*, 2017

—Christopher Mari

J. D. Martinez

Date of birth: August 21, 1987
Occupation: Baseball player

"My whole life, I've felt like I've always had to prove myself," outfielder J. D. Martinez told Scott Miller for *Bleacher Report* (17 July 2018). "It's never been easy, as easy as others who are in my position have had it. So I've always felt that drive." Indeed, Martinez's drive proved essential over the course of his early career, which saw the player deal with a host of injuries as well as his abrupt dismissal in 2014 from the Houston Astros, the team that had selected him in the twentieth round of the 2009 Major League Baseball (MLB) draft. Despite such setbacks, Martinez remained devoted to both his sport and his own improvement, logging increasingly successful seasons with the Detroit Tigers and Arizona Diamondbacks before joining the Boston Red Sox in 2018. In many ways, joining the Red Sox marked the start of a new era for Martinez. "When all my friends and family ask me what the difference is with this team, and stuff like that, I'm like, 'Honestly, there's no egos,'" he told *WEEI* radio hosts Dale and Keefe, as reported by Alex Reimer for the station's website (22 Aug. 2018). "Everybody is pushing for each other. . . . Everybody gets almost as excited when someone else hits a home run as they do when they hit a home run." The team's performance in the 2018 postseason reflected that synergy, earning the franchise its ninth World Series title—Martinez's first.

EARLY LIFE AND EDUCATION

Julio Daniel "J. D." Martinez was born on August 21, 1987, in Miami, Florida. His father, Julio, owned a roofing business, while his mother, Mayra, was a registered nurse. Martinez has five older half-sisters from his parents' previous marriages, several of whom lived in the household while he was growing up. As a child, Martinez developed an interest in baseball and benefited from the nearby presence of former professional baseball player Paul Casanova, who allowed local children to practice in his batting cage. "Growing

Photo by Keith Allison via Wikimedia Commons

up, it was almost like a drug, going into the cage and hitting," Martinez recalled to Ian Browne for *MLB* (4 Apr. 2018). "It was like a relaxation. I kind of fell in love with it back then." As a teenager, he played baseball for Charles Flanagan High School, contributing to the team's consecutive state baseball championships in 2005 and 2006. Despite such accomplishments, Martinez found his performance as a high school player to be lackluster. "I did well, but I didn't do really really well," he told Tony Capobianco for the *Miami Herald* (8 Sept. 2014). "I always hit fourth on the state championship team, but I never really stood out and made a big impression." He graduated from Flanagan High in 2006.

In June 2006, Martinez was selected by the Minnesota Twins in the thirty-sixth round of that year's MLB draft. While he did hope to continue playing baseball, he decided not to sign with the Twins, instead planning to play for a college or university. To help secure Martinez a spot on a college team, one of his high school coaches took him to visit a number of different institutions in the area, where Martinez demonstrated his baseball skills. Martinez ultimately enrolled at Florida's Nova Southeastern University (NSU). As a member of the NSU Sharks baseball team, Martinez developed his skills further and achieved impressive milestones, including a batting average of .428 during the 2009 season. Martinez was inducted into the NSU Hall of Fame in 2014.

MINOR LEAGUES

Martinez once again entered the MLB draft in 2009. The Houston Astros selected him in the twentieth round of the draft. He signed with the Astros in June and joined the team's minor-league organization the same month. Martinez played on two of the Astros' affiliate teams during his first season in the minors, beginning with the rookie-level Greeneville Astros before moving to the class-A short-season Tri-City Valley-Cats later in the season. Although he initially struggled to distinguish himself in the minor leagues, Martinez remained dedicated to improving his skills and contributing to the team however possible. "I showed up every day, I wouldn't play, but I'd take early work," he told Miller. "Ground balls, ground balls, ground balls. I'd come in with bruises, bloody lips . . . the bad hops, the ball would just wear off my face." He also worked to master hitting the high-velocity fastballs he encountered during games, hoping to improve his chances of becoming a regular player on the teams.

Martinez played in nineteen games for the Greeneville Astros and fifty-three games for the Tri-City ValleyCats over the course of his debut minor-league season. He moved up in the organization during the 2010 season, spending three months with the class-A Lexington Legends and two months with double-A Corpus Christi Hooks. That year, he was named the Astros Minor League Player of the Year. He remained with the Hooks for the start of the 2011 season, playing in eighty-eight games with the team between April and late July.

HOUSTON ASTROS

Martinez made his debut with the Astros on July 30, 2011, in a game against the Milwaukee Brewers. "My heart was racing 100 miles an hour," he told Capobianco of the experience. "Everything seemed so big." Although the Astros lost 2–6, Martinez succeeded in batting in a run while pinch hitting for pitcher Aneury Rodriguez. Following his debut with the team, he remained with the Astros for the rest of the season, playing in a total of fifty-three games. Martinez stayed with the Astros during the 2012 season, appearing in 113 games. He did, however, spend several weeks with the triple-A Oklahoma City RedHawks, playing twenty-three games with the minor-league team while working on his batting strategy.

Martinez incurred several injuries over the course of the 2013 season. He returned to the Corpus Christi Hooks while recovering from a sprained knee but spent the remainder of the season with the Astros, appearing in eighty-six games. Following the regular season, he played for the Leones de Caracas in the Venezuelan Winter League. In March 2014, Martinez joined the Astros organization for spring training preparation for the upcoming season, however, the Astros decided to release Martinez from the team. Although that decision was undoubtedly disappointing for Martinez, he later noted that the experience of being released was a key one for him. "I think it made me who I am," he told Browne. "I've always been hungry, but when people ask, 'What drives you? How do you stay so driven throughout this whole thing?' You just don't stop. It's every single day."

TIGERS AND DIAMONDBACKS

Following his departure from the Astros, Martinez quickly signed a deal with the Detroit Tigers. Although he was set to begin his time in the Tigers organization in the minor leagues, his contract stipulated that he would enter free agency—a status that allowed him to join any team that offered him a contract—once again if not called up to the main team by June 2014. He began the season with the triple-A Toledo Mud Hens, playing in eight games in the minors before moving up to the Tigers on April 21, 2014. At the end of Martinez's first season in Detroit, the Tigers qualified to compete in the American League Division Series (ALDS), Martinez's first time reaching the playoffs. Facing off against the Baltimore Orioles, the Tigers lost in three games.

The 2015 season brought several major milestones for Martinez, who was named to his first All-Star Game and received his first AL Silver Slugger Award, an honor given to the best batter in each fielding position. The subsequent seasons, however, presented new challenges, including a broken elbow in 2016 and an ankle injury early in the 2017 season. After stints with the Lakeland Flying Tigers and Toledo Mud Hens while his ankle recovered, Martinez was traded to the Arizona Diamondbacks in July 2017. He immediately joined the major-league team, putting forward a strong performance that earned him the title of National League (NL) Player of the Month in September of that year. Martinez ended the regular season with the highest slugging percentage (.690) and third-most home runs (45) in the ML. During the postseason, the Diamondbacks competed in the NL Wild Card Game, defeating the Colorado Rockies. The team proceeded to the NL Division Series (NLDS), where the Tigers were swept by the Los Angeles Dodgers.

RED SOX

In November 2017, Martinez entered free agency. He eventually accepted an offer from the Boston Red Sox in February 2018. While joining another new team—especially one with as lengthy a history as the Red Sox—might have been challenging for some players, Martinez remained undaunted. "I'm just going to go out there and play my game and do what I've been doing the last four or five years," he told Michael Silverman for the *Boston Herald* (17 Nov. 2018). Martinez quickly proved himself as a strong addition to the Red Sox and, in August, was named the American League (AL) Player of the Month.

Over the course of the season, he posted a batting average of .330, the second-highest in the AL and his major-league personal best. Martinez also ended the regular season second in the league in slugging percentage (.629) and number of home runs (43), and he led the AL in runs batted in (130). Martinez was named to the 2018 All-Star Game starting lineup, received the 2018 AL Hank Aaron Award, and became the first player ever to win two Silver Slugger Awards in a single season, for his positions as an outfielder and designated hitter.

The Red Sox finished first in the AL East at the end of the 2018 season, automatically entering the playoffs. After beating the New York Yankees in the ALDS, the team moved on to defeat the Astros in the American League Championship Series (ALCS). They then faced the Dodgers in the World Series, winning four games to one. Martinez himself played a significant role in the playoffs, scoring six runs, including three home runs, over the course of the competition. "It's definitely a dream come true," he told *CBS Boston* (2018) after the final World Series game. "It's one of these things where you feel like you're dreaming and you don't want to wake up."

PERSONAL LIFE

Martinez moved to Boston in 2018 after joining the Red Sox. He is reportedly dating former Miami Dolphins cheerleader Ariana Aubert, whom he met in high school.

SUGGESTED READING

Capobianco, Tony. "Former Flanagan High Player J. D. Martinez Regroups after Signing Minor-League Deal with Detroit Tigers." *Miami Herald*, 8 Sept. 2014, www.miami-herald.com/sports/high-school/prep-broward/article1962630.html. Accessed 18 Jan. 2019.

Kepner, Tyler. "In Home Run Era, Red Sox' J.D. Martinez Is More Than 'Just Dingers.'" *The New York Times*, 6 Oct. 2018, www.nytimes.com/2018/10/06/sports/red-sox-jd-martinez.html. Accessed 18 Jan. 2019.

Martinez, J. D. "J. D. Martinez: Winning World Series with Red Sox 'Like a Dream Come True.'" *CBS Boston*, 2018, boston.cbslocal.com/video/3962204-j-d-martinez-winning-world-series-with-red-sox-like-a-dream-come-true/. Accessed 18 Jan. 2019.

Martinez, J. D. "Let's Play 20 Questions with J.D. Martinez!" Interview by Ian Browne. *MLB*, 3 Apr. 2018, www.mlb.com/red-sox/news/red-soxs-jd-martinez-answers-20-questions/c-270788036. Accessed 18 Jan. 2019.

Miller, Scott. "How J. D. Martinez Rose from Division II Obscurity, MLB Reject to Elite Superstar." *Bleacher Report*, 17 July 2018, bleacherreport.com/articles/2781760-how-jd-martinez-rose-from-division-ii-obscurity-mlb-reject-to-elite-superstar. Accessed 18 Jan. 2019.

Reimer, Alex. "J. D. Martinez Tells D&K Chemistry Is Biggest Reason for Red Sox' Success." *WEEI*, 22 Aug. 2018, weei.radio.com/blogs/alex-reimer/jd-martinez-interview-slugger-says-chemistry-biggest-reason-boston-red-sox-success. Accessed 18 Jan. 2019.

Silverman, Michael. "Silverman: J.D. Martinez Undaunted by Challenge as He Makes Red Sox Debut." *Boston Herald*, 17 Nov. 2018, www.bostonherald.com/2018/03/08/silverman-jd-martinez-undaunted-by-challenge-as-he-makes-red-sox-debut/. Accessed 18 Jan. 2019.

—*Joy Crelin*

Queen Mathilde of Belgium

Date of birth: January 20, 1973
Occupation: Queen of Belgium

Queen Mathilde of Belgium is the seventh queen of Belgium and the first queen to have been born in Belgium.

EARLY LIFE AND EDUCATION
Queen Mathilde of Belgium was born Mathilde Marie Christiane Ghislaine d'Udekem d'Acoz on January 20, 1973, in Uccle, Belgium. She was born into nobility: her father, Patrick Paul François Marie Ghislain (who later became known as Count Patrick d'Udekem d'Acoz) was a judge who came from a line of nobles dating back to the thirteenth century, and her mother, Countess Anna Maria Komorowska (now Countess Anna Maria d'Udekem d'Acoz), was a Polish-born aristocrat. The eldest of five children, Mathilde grew up at Castle Losange in Villers-la-Bonne-Eau in Bastogne.

Mathilde attended elementary school in Bastogne and secondary school at the Roman Catholic Institut de la Vierge Fidèle in Brussels. She then studied speech therapy at the Institut Libre Marie Haps, also in Brussels, graduating in 1994. The following year, she opened a speech therapy practice and operated it until 1999.

As a young adult, Mathilde traveled extensively. She backpacked in Asia, the Middle East, and Asia with friends; spent three months in the United States; and worked abroad as an au pair. She also did volunteer work with a human services organization for persons with disabilities and in an impoverished community in Cairo, Egypt.

In 1996 she met Prince Philippe of Belgium, and they began a three-year courtship they kept private from the public and the media. Mathilde also enrolled in the Université Catholique de Louvain and studied psychology.

PRINCESS AND QUEEN
In September 1999, Mathilde and Philippe of Belgium announced their engagement. He was thirty-nine, and she was thirteen years his junior. The announcement took the kingdom by surprise, and the media in Belgium and beyond immediately drew parallels with the marriage of Lady Diana and Prince Charles in the United Kingdom. Prince Philippe, like Prince Charles, was older, considered somewhat stodgy and dull, and had been a bachelor long into his adulthood. Mathilde, like Diana, was beautiful, charming, and at ease with the public. She was also multilingual, speaking French, Dutch, English, and Italian.

In a country where the monarchy is a symbol of unity, the announcement came at a providential time. Belgium had been wracked with scandals, political feuds, and economic woes. The news cheered the country and filled it with hope for its future. Philippe and Mathilde embarked on a *joyeus entre*, or traditional tour of the country to introduce Mathilde to the people of Belgium. Belgians embraced their future queen. With roots in both the French-speaking Wallonia and the Dutch-speaking Flanders, she was acceptable to both communities and was considered a future queen for all Belgians. Equally welcome was that she had been born in Belgium, unlike the country's previous queens, all of whom were foreign-born.

Mathilde's youth, charm, and beauty also won over the public, and she became immensely popular, appearing on the covers of numerous magazines in the months leading up to her wedding.

Mathilde and Philippe of Belgium wed in a royal ceremony on December 4, 1999. The ceremony was held in French, Dutch, and German, the three official languages of Belgium. Upon her wedding, Mathilde was given the titles princess and duchess of Brabant.

Following her wedding, Mathilde gave up her speech therapy practice, but she continued her psychology studies. She earned a master's degree in psychology in 2002. She quickly immersed herself in royal duties and accompanied her husband on numerous trips abroad to promote Belgium and its commercial and economic interests. She also became active in several charities, especially those dealing with children and other vulnerable members of society. In 2000 the Princess Mathilde Fund was created from donations following the couple's wedding. The fund awards a 10,000-euro prize each year to an initiative supporting vulnerable people, particularly women and children.

Mathilde participated in humanitarian activities with several international organizations, including the World Economic Forum, the United Nations Children's Fund (UNICEF), and the Joint United Nations Programme on HIV and AIDS (UNAIDS). She was a delegate to the United Nations (UN) Conference on Children in 2002 and a UN ambassador for the International Year of Microcredit in 2005. In 2009 she was named the honorary president of UNICEF Belgium. She has also served as a special representative of the World Health Organization Europe (WHO/Europe), an honorary member of the board of Schwab Foundation for Social Entrepreneurship, and the honorary president of the Breast International Group.

In 2013 Philippe became the king of Belgium when his father, Albert II, abdicated the throne. Upon his ascension, Mathilde became the queen of Belgium.

IMPACT
Mathilde of Belgium's popularity has continued since she was first introduced to the public as the fiancée of Philippe of Belgium. She helped to restore both the public's confidence in the monarchy and its image. While political divisions continued to wrack the small kingdom, she proved to be a unifying force and strengthened the symbolism of the royal family in Belgium.

PERSONAL LIFE
Mathilde married Philippe of Belgium in 1999. They have four children: Princess Elisabeth (2001–), Prince Gabriel (2003–), Prince Emmanuel (2005–), and Princess Eléonore (2008–). In her spare time, Mathilde plays the piano and enjoys sports such as tennis and swimming.

SUGGESTED READING
Dahlberg, John-Thor. "Bridging Belgian Divide: Wedding Puts Language Gulf on Hold for a While." *Gazette* [Montreal] 4 Dec. 1999: A26. Print.

"Mathilde, Belgium's Perfectionist Popular New Queen." *GlobalPost*, 21 July 2013, www.expatica.com/be/mathilde-belgiums-perfectionist-popular-new-queen/. Accessed 26 June 2019.

"Queen Mathilde." *Belgian Monarchy.* Kingdom of Belgium, n.d. Web. 5 Jan. 2016.

Sutherland, Tracy. "Mathilde Waltzes into Hearts." *Australian*, 6 Dec. 1999: 11. Print.

Torfs, Michael. "Female Royals in the Spotlights." *FlandersNews.be.*, 5 July 2013, www.vrt.be/vrtnws/en/2013/07/05/female_royals_inthespotlights-1-1670442/. Accessed 26 June 2019.

—*Barb Lightner*

Meghan McCain
Date of birth: October 23, 1984
Occupation: Commentator and columnist

As a daughter of longtime Arizona senator John McCain, Meghan McCain had a bird's eye view of politics from childhood. Her mother, Cindy, told Greg Veis for *GQ* (18 Mar. 2008) that her husband and daughter were "very similar. They're both very intelligent and very direct in terms of—I mean this in a good way—their knowing what they want and knowing how to get there." Although she has no ambition to run for political office herself, McCain was involved in her father's campaigns, writing blog posts and articles about the needs of the Republican Party in particular. As Mahita Gajanan reported for *Time* (8 Oct. 2018) when McCain returned to her post cohosting ABC's *The View* following her father's death, she referenced his ideals, saying, "We can never surrender to what is happening in our country right now. I understand how divided and how scared a lot of people are, and it looks like the fabric of democracy is fraying. We do not surrender."

EDUCATION AND EARLY CAREER
The fourth of John McCain's children and oldest of his four children with his second wife, Cindy Hensley McCain, Meghan Marguerite McCain wanted to be an astronaut when she was a child and twice attended a space camp. She grew up and attended high school in Phoenix, Arizona. Despite growing up in a political family, McCain first became interested in politics while studying at Columbia University, as she told Larry King in an interview on *Larry King Live* for CNN (23 Mar. 2009): "It sort of happened in college. I was kind of rebelling in high school and not wanting to be a part of it. But it's in my nature, so it kind of grew on me."

In college she initially wanted to be a music journalist. She planned to intern at *Rolling Stone*, but after a call from her father to *Newsweek* editor Jon Meacham, she interned at the news magazine instead. She later told Helena Andrews-Dyer for the *Washington Post* (4 Nov. 2014), "The thing about having famous parents is that yeah, it will open some doors, but you have to like break the door down with your high heel and go into it and make it happen." She also interned at *Saturday Night Live*. McCain graduated from Columbia in 2007.

McCain's political independent streak began showing early in her adulthood: breaking with her father in the 2004 presidential race, she voted for Democratic nominee John Kerry over the Republican incumbent, George W. Bush, and she began describing herself publicly as socially liberal and economically conservative.

Photo by Jay Godwin via Wikimedia Commons

WRITING LIFE

However, McCain returned to the Republican fold in 2008, and for good reason: her father became the Republican presidential nominee that year. Hoping to harness the force of the Internet in support of her father, she began a blog about the campaign called *McCain-Blogette*, although it was poorly received, and the twenty-four-year-old was sidelined by her father's campaign manager.

In 2009 McCain began writing on politics and pop culture for the *Daily Beast*. In one of her columns, she criticized right-wing pundit Ann Coulter. In response, commentator Laura Ingraham went to Coulter's defense, knocking McCain as "plus-sized," and giving McCain an opportunity to criticize fat-shaming as shallow and damaging to women. As she told King, "I'm not going to be bullied around about my weight and what kind of standards I'm not fitting. . . . I just don't think weight should ever be brought into a topic when we're talking about politics or anything."

She wrote a children's book about her father in 2008 before turning to politics with her 2010 book, *Dirty Sexy Politics*, which discusses her experiences during the 2008 campaign. Writing for *New York Times* (10 Sept. 2010), Liesl Schillinger called it "a frank, dishy and often scathing chronicle of her experiences" and quotes McCain as saying it is also a "coming-of-age story." The book was also an attempt to interest people of her own generation in politics and a call for a more moderate, inclusive Republican Party.

POLITICAL STANDS

In the wake of her father's defeat at the hands of Democrat Barack Obama, conservative pundits unleashed a storm of attacks. Conservative talk-radio host Rush Limbaugh announced he hoped the Obama presidency would fail. When Larry King questioned McCain about her attitude toward Obama, citing Limbaugh's comment, she said, "I love my country. I'm an American. I love being an American and I don't want my country to fail and I don't want my president to fail."

Concerned by the growing polarization in American politics, McCain has staked out positions on both sides of the aisle: opposing abortion but favoring birth control, eventually favoring the Iraq War, taking the threat of climate change seriously, and being a notable supporter of LGBTQ rights. Summing up where she falls politically, McCain told King, "I consider myself a progressive Republican. I am liberal on social issues. And I think that the party is at a place where social issues shouldn't be the issues that define the party. . . . I actually take it as a compliment, that [she as] sort of this new young Republican can come forward and make progress and be successful in the ways that this party has currently failed."

BROADCAST MEDIA

McCain moved into broadcast media in the mid-2010s. In 2013 she hosted her own television show—part talk show, part reality show—called *Raising McCain* on the Pivot cable network, though it only lasted one season. She also hosted on that network's *TakePart Live* in 2013 and 2014. From 2015 to 2017 she cohosted Fox News Channel's *Outnumbered*, a program intended to mirror ABC's *The View*. The show focused on news, pop culture, and the relationships among the newsworthy. Around the same time, between 2015 and 2017, McCain also hosted a nationally syndicated radio program, *America Now*, on iHeartRadio's Premiere Network.

In October 2017, McCain became a permanent cohost of the ABC morning talk show *The View*, on which she had appeared many times before. McCain was added to represent the conservative point of view, which had been lacking since the 2013 departure of Elisabeth Hasselbeck. That perspective has created conflicts on the show, particularly between Joy Behar and McCain. Some of their different perspectives may be attributed not only to political but also generational differences; Behar is more than four decades McCain's senior.

Throughout her work with the media, McCain has not shied away from controversy. Both she and her mother have supported marriage equality for same-sex couples, supporting NOH8, the California organization that worked to defeat Proposition 8, a 2008 ballot measure intended to ban same-sex marriage in the state. She posed for a photo supporting NOH8 in 2010, with the accompanying statement on their website, "I am a proud member of the Republican Party and a proud supporter of marriage equality. . . . Marriage equality is not just a Democrat or Republican issue, it is a human one." This was one of a number of issues on which McCain disagreed with her father. In 2015 the Trevor Project, which works to end suicide among LGBTQ youth, presented McCain with the Ally Award for her support of LGBTQ rights.

MCCAIN AND TRUMP
The national political divisions that so concerned McCain have only grown since the 2016 presidential campaign ramped up, with businessman and reality television star Donald Trump gaining the Republican nomination and eventually the presidency on a platform of nativist populism. During the campaign, Trump helped to vilify and marginalize moderate Republicans such as John McCain, and the family did not forget it. Knowing that he was dying, John McCain prepared a guest list for his funeral, to which President Trump was not invited. He also persuaded a reluctant Meghan to deliver a eulogy at his funeral, giving her a national platform to, in part, articulate the McCain family response to the state of affairs in American politics.

The funeral service took place in Washington's National Cathedral on September 1, 2018. McCain took a swipe at Trump and his campaign slogan, Make America Great Again, in her eulogy, saying, "The America of John McCain is generous and welcoming and bold. She's resourceful, confident, secure. She meets her responsibilities. She speaks quietly because she's strong. America does not boast because she has no need to. The America of John McCain has no need to be made great again, because America was always great." Unusually for a funeral, this line was greeted with applause.

PERSONAL LIFE
McCain told Sandra Sobieraj Westfall for *People* (10 Dec. 2007), "I am my father's personality cloned in a woman's form." Of that personality, McCain also told Schillinger, "I'm a nonstop extrovert, a people person who loves mingling and gabbing and getting out in the world."

After a long engagement, McCain married Ben Domenech, publisher of the conservative website *The Federalist*, in 2017 at the McCain family's ranch in Cornville, Arizona.

SUGGESTED READING
Gajanan, Mahita. "Meghan McCain Says Her Father's Values Did Not Die with Him as She Returns to *The View*." *Time*, 8 Oct. 2018, time.com/5418602/meghan-mccain-the-view-john-mccain. Accessed 6 Feb. 2018.

King, Larry. "Interview with Meghan McCain; Stocks Soar: Economy Rebounding?" *Larry King Live*, CNN, 23 Mar. 2009, transcripts. cnn.com/TRANSCRIPTS/0903/23/lkl.01. html. Accessed 19 Feb. 2019.

McCain, Meghan. "He Was a Great Man." *Vital Speeches of the Day*, 1 Sept. 2018, www.vsotd. com/featured-speech/he-was-great-man. Accessed 6 Feb. 2019.

Schillinger, Liesl. "Daughter of John McCain Is a Rebel." *The New York Times*, 10 Sept. 2010, www.nytimes.com/2010/09/12/ fashion/12McCain.html. Accessed 28 Feb. 2019.

Segarra, Lisa Marie. "Meghan McCain Is Coming to *The View* as a New Co-Host." *Time*, 28 Sept. 2017, time.com/4960712/meghan-mccain-the-view-fox-news. Accessed 28 Feb. 2019.

Westfall, Sandra Sobieraj. "All in the Family." *People*, 10 Dec. 2007, people.com/archive/all-in-the-family-vol-68-no-24. Accessed 6 Feb. 2019.

SELECTED WORKS
My Dad, John McCain, 2008; *Dirty Sexy Politics*, 2010; *America, You Sexy B——h*, 2011 (with Michael Ian Black)

—*Judy Johnson*

Jelena McWilliams
Date of birth: July 29, 1973
Occupation: Chairperson of the FDIC

On June 5, 2018, Jelena McWilliams was sworn in as the twenty-first chairperson of the Federal Deposit Insurance Corporation (FDIC), an independent federal agency that insures deposits in banks and thrift institutions and oversees the safety and soundness of the US banking system. The FDIC, which was established in 1933 in response to the wave of bank failures that occurred in the 1920s and early 1930s, now insures trillions of dollars each year, and since its launch, no consumer has lost their deposited money due to a bank failure.

The agency, although independent, is not without some degree of partisanship; its regulations state that three members of its five-person board of directors are to be nominated by the president and may be of the same political party. McWilliams was nominated by President Donald Trump and confirmed by the Republican-led Senate to serve a six-year term, including five years as chair. She is nonetheless widely respected on both sides of the aisle, thanks in part to her earlier posts as an aide to Senator Olympia Snowe, a moderate Republican from Maine, and

Photo by Federal Deposit Insurance Corporation via
Wikimedia Commons

later as chief counsel, then deputy staff director, on the Senate Committee on Banking, Housing, and Urban Affairs, also known as the Senate Banking Committee. "She has been a quiet force for years in shaping Republican policy on the banking industry," Christina Rexrode and Ryan Tracy wrote for the *Wall Street Journal* (8 Dec. 2017). Former colleagues the journalists interviewed praised her vast knowledge of banking law (she was known to carry around a well-used copy of the 2010 Dodd-Frank Act) as well as her willingness to entertain opposing viewpoints. "She was someone you could disagree with, without her being disagreeable," Dwight Fettig, a former Democratic staff director on the Senate banking committee, told them.

McWilliams's conservative views are expected to have a great impact on the nation's financial landscape, especially given the Trump administration's push to revise the regulations of the Dodd-Frank Wall Street Reform and Consumer Protection Act. The Dodd-Frank Act was passed during the administration of President Barack Obama with the aim of more tightly regulating the business sectors responsible for the 2008 financial crisis, including banks, mortgage lenders, and credit rating agencies.

EARLY LIFE AND EDUCATION

Jelena McWilliams was born Jelena Obrenic on July 29, 1973, in Belgrade, Yugoslavia, (in what is now Serbia) to Branka and Obrad Obrenic. She has a brother, Nenad, who became a bookkeeper. During a 2019 speech at a National Diversity Coalition meeting quoted by James Freeman for the *Wall Street Journal* (15 Mar. 2019), McWilliams explained that she had been raised "on the

wrong side of the Iron Curtain" by "a family of great character and humble means." She related that her father had fought as a teenager during World War II, and that after the war men were needed to guard the borders, not study what were considered frivolous topics; schooling for girls, particularly poor ones, was not considered a priority. "Education was not even an option for my parents," she said in the speech. "Still, years later, these two uneducated, humble people instilled in their daughter a belief that education was the only path upwards."

McWilliams was a fan of American television shows like *Dynasty* and *Dallas*, and she became enamored with the idea of traveling to the United States, which looked, as she asserted in her speech, "like a brilliant jewel, a beacon of hope, a land of opportunity." Although her parents were concerned about allowing her to travel so far on her own, after much discussion they agreed.

McWilliams was eighteen when she landed in California as part of a high school exchange program. Her parents went into debt to scrape together the $500 she took with her. A month after she arrived, war broke out in her native country. Businesses and banks shut down, and her parents lost all that they owned. In her speech, McWilliams explained the importance of federally insured deposits by telling the story of her parents waiting all night in line at their bank during the conflict; by the time they got to the teller's window, the bank had run out of money. Her father was consequently forced, at the age of sixty-eight, to take a job as a day laborer, earning the equivalent of about $5 or $6 a day.

By the time McWilliams finished her senior year of high school, her $500 had dwindled to $50. She narrowed her college wish list down to the University of California at Berkeley (UC Berkeley) and Stanford, but because the Berkeley application cost $40 and the Stanford application cost $60, her final decision was an easy one. More difficult was making ends meet as a student. She could not afford to live near campus and instead drove eighty miles each way from the more affordable neighborhood where her host family lived. She took on odd jobs to pay for gas and food, such as selling knives door to door and working the night shift at a video rental store.

Despite those challenging circumstances, McWilliams excelled. Although she had originally planned to study astrophysics, she switched her major to political science and mass communications, thinking she might want to be an investigative journalist one day, perhaps covering the brutal, ongoing conflict in Yugoslavia. That gradually developed into a desire to shape political policy from within, and after she graduated from UC Berkeley with highest honors in 1999, she entered Berkeley School of Law, earning her degree in 2002.

PRIVATE LEGAL CAREER

McWilliams had worked as a summer associate in the Palo Alto office of the law firm Morrison & Foerster. When the firm offered her a full-time job in its corporate division, she eagerly jumped at the opportunity. In addition to being deeply interested in mergers and acquisitions, she had large student loans to pay.

She strove to be a model employee, taking on extra projects, working long hours, and becoming adept at participating in major corporate deals. One day, she was sent to a conference in Washington, DC. "I'd always had a political bug and I was in awe of D.C. and national politics," she recalled to Andy Cohen for *Berkeley Law* (8 Apr. 2019)."I walked to the Lincoln Memorial, looked out across the reflecting pool, saw the congressional dome in the distance, and said to myself, 'This is my town, I've got to be here.'" Although she had recently purchased a house in Silicon Valley and had sent for her parents to come live with her, she packed everything up and settled in Washington.

She found a job at Hogan & Hartson (now Hogan Lovells) and worked as tirelessly as she had at her former firm, often seeing the sun rise from her office after pulling an all-nighter.

A NEW PATH IN PUBLIC SERVICE

One day in 2007 McWilliams was somewhat idly perusing *USAJOBS.gov*, a government job board, and stumbled upon a legal post at the Federal Reserve, which functions as the central bank of the United States. She responded, but knew most applications submitted via *USAJOBS.gov* were simply ignored; she was, therefore, surprised to be called in for an interview within days. A few days after that, she was offered the job. Although it involved a 47-percent pay cut, she would be getting to work in an area important to her because of her family's own struggles: consumer protection, amid the subprime mortgage crisis that broke out that year.

"We would get calls from the consumers [saying] 'my husband lost his job and we are in the process of foreclosure' and something as dramatic as 'my husband, I am concerned he may take his life,'" she recalled to Rachel Witkowski in an undated interview for *American Banker*. "You sit there and you take in these calls and . . . you realize the impact of financial regulation on consumers and how dramatic it can be and it affects people's lives."

In 2010, McWilliams was assigned to a detail with Maine senator Olympia Snowe. McWilliams helped Snowe formulate amendments to the Dodd-Frank Act, and when the senator retired in 2012, McWilliams won a job as senior counsel for the Senate Banking Committee,

working under Senator Richard Shelby, a Republican from Alabama, and then Mike Crapo, a Republican from Idaho. In the five years she worked for the committee, she worked her way up to chief counsel and then deputy staff director.

In 2017 McWilliams was approached by Fifth Third Bancorp in Cincinnati, then the nation's twelfth largest bank. She was intrigued; despite her years of experience with banking policy and regulation, she had never actually worked at a bank. She accepted a post as the bank's chief legal officer, but soon after she settled in, she got a call from the White House. The Trump administration had gained a reputation as a difficult place to work, and many posts were going unfilled. James Clinger, previously the chief counsel for the House Committee on Financial Services, had turned down an offer to head the FDIC, and Trump wanted to nominate McWilliams instead. Excited at the prospect, she quickly agreed, although she had been at Fifth Third for only a short time.

Formally nominated in November 2017, McWilliams received rare bipartisan support and was approved by the Senate in May 2018. On her first day of work, she showed up with 256 brownies she had baked the night before. She also brought with her a keen focus on improving operations at the FDIC. "Sometimes it takes a person from the outside coming in and saying, 'Why should we do this a certain way or should we maybe change it?'" McWilliams told Witkowski. "It's kind of peeling the layers to understand how we function as an agency, both inside the agency and also compared to the other financial regulators."

One of her first initiatives was dubbed "Trust through Transparency," which made earlier unpublished internal metrics publicly available and was intended to make the FDIC more understandable and responsive to the average person. She is continuing to work on such issues as loosening Dodd-Frank regulations and making it easier for new financial institutions, particularly community-based banks, to launch.

PERSONAL LIFE

While in law school, McWilliams married John Neal McWilliams and had a daughter, Maya. The couple divorced during her original move to Washington, DC. She has two rescued Jack Russell terriers named Charlie and Laika.

During her National Diversity Coalition speech, she quipped that she can still get nostalgic at times "about superior European bread, Nutella, and great cafes," but she affirmed her love and gratitude for the United States. "I realize the US economy is not perfect. There is still much work to do to address the problems and hardships many Americans face," she said, "But for someone like me, the American dream is still alive and well, and I believe that it exists—and should exist—for others."

SUGGESTED READING

Ackerman, Andrew, and Gabriel T. Rubin. "Rewrite of Bank Rules Advances Slowly, Frustrating Republicans." *The Wall Street Journal*, 10 June 2019, www.wsj.com/articles/rewrite-of-bank-rules-bogs-down-11560159001. Accessed 3 Sept. 2019.

Cohen, Andrew. "Living the American Dream: Alumna and FDIC Chair Jelena McWilliams '02." *Berkeley Law*, Berkeley School of Law, 8 Apr. 2019, www.law.berkeley.edu/article/living-the-american-dream-alumna-and-fdic-chair-jelena-mcwilliams-02/. Accessed 3 Sept. 2019.

Freeman, James. "America's Most Inspiring Bureaucrats." *The Wall Street Journal*, 15 Mar. 2019, www.wsj.com/articles/americas-most-inspiring-bureaucrats-11552679489. Accessed 3 Sept. 2019.

Jopson, Barney. "New US Bank Regulator Is Mould-Breaking Conservative." *Financial Times*, 24 June 2018, www.ft.com/content/d728a13c-7414-11e8-aa31-31da4279a601. Accessed 3 Sept. 2019.

Maclay, Kathleen. "Trump Taps Alumna to Lead FDIC." *Berkeley News*, University of California, Berkeley, 14 Dec. 2017, news.berkeley.edu/story_jump/trump-taps-alumna-to-lead-fdic/. Accessed 3 Sept. 2019.

Rexrode, Christina, and Ryan Tracy. "From Belgrade to the Pinnacle of Washington's Banking World." *The Wall Street Journal*, 8 Dec. 2017, www.wsj.com/articles/from-belgrade-to-the-pinnacle-of-washingtons-banking-world-1512732600#_=_. Accessed 3 Sept. 2019.

Witkowski, Rachel. "Remaking the FDIC by Ripping Up the Rules." *American Banker*, SourceMedia, 2019, www.americanbanker.com/news/jelena-mcwilliams-rewriting-fdic-rules-as-challenges-loom. Accessed 3 Sept. 2019.

—*Mari Rich*

Meg Medina

Date of birth: June 11, 1963
Occupation: Writer

For writer Meg Medina, the process of overcoming challenges is one of the core elements of a compelling narrative. "I like characters that survive and persevere despite lots of obstacles," she told Sarah Lockwood for *RFM Online* (25 Aug. 2012). "That always ends up being a strong theme in anything that I'm writing. Mostly, it's

Photo by Rhododendrites via Wikimedia Commons

about strength." Surviving and persevering despite obstacles such as bullying, domestic abuse, and a host of others, the well-rounded and intriguing protagonists of Medina's works—always girls or young women, typically people of Latinx descent, and often specifically Cuban Americans—render her novels and picture books thought-provoking and entertaining reads that have won acclaim from major literary organizations and literary critics as well as teachers and young audiences. Since making her fiction debut in 2008 with the middle-grade novel *Milagros: Girl from Away*, Medina has published numerous well-received works, including the Newbery Medal–winning novel *Merci Suárez Changes Gears* (2018). In addition, she has dedicated her career to promoting diversity in children's literature, particularly as a means of counteracting harmful stereotypes and detrimental policies perpetuated by those with political power. "I worry for children right now, especially in Latino families, around the issue of immigration," Medina told Sue Corbett for *Publishers Weekly* (29 Jan. 2019). "These children are not deaf. They are hearing all of this political talk. We need books that sound and look the way we as Americans look, books that get into the corners of children's experiences."

EARLY LIFE AND EDUCATION

Medina was born on June 11, 1963, in Alexandria, Virginia. She grew up in the Flushing area of Queens, New York, where she lived with her mother and sister following her parents' separation. Numerous other relatives, including aunts and grandparents, lived with the family at various points while Medina's extended family immigrated to the United States from Cuba. As a child, Medina attended PS 22 in Queens and had a variety of hobbies and interests. "I loved reading—and writing, too, although I was also a child who had trouble sitting still, so I could be found playing tag or roller skating just as easily," she told Margot Abel for the website of the *Ezra Jack Keats Foundation* (2012). Despite her interest in writing, Medina did not seriously consider pursuing a career as a writer of fiction during that period. As a teenager, she worked for a time at a transistor factory in Queens, where her mother and members of her extended family were employed.

Following her graduation from high school, Medina enrolled in Queens College, a college within the City University of New York (CUNY), to study communications. While in school, she began to think more about becoming a writer thanks in part to the encouragement of one of her professors, Judith Summerfield. Medina earned her bachelor's degree from Queens College and later, after moving to Florida, pursued graduate studies in educational leadership at Nova Southeastern University. Upon entering the workforce, Medina worked a variety of writing-adjacent jobs in fields such as marketing and education. A turning point came in the late 1990s, when her family moved to Virginia. There, Medina began to connect with the local literary community, including the group James River Writers, with which she remained associated over the course of her writing career.

WRITING CAREER

Although Medina had incorporated writing into her career in various ways over the course of her career, she did not begin writing fiction seriously until the age of forty. "I think I was always a writer in one way or another. What I lacked was courage to do this kind of writing," she explained to Lockwood. "One day when I was forty, I was working at a school and with my typical forethought and planning I said, I quit! Today is the day that I'm leaving and beginning to write a novel." After departing from her job, Medina worked on her first novel every day for more than a year, spending several hours each day at her designated desk in her home's family room. The resulting work, *Milagros: Girl from Away*, was published in 2008. Geared toward middle-grade readers—typically defined as those between the ages of eight and twelve—the novel tells the story of the titular character's life on a fictional Caribbean island, encounters with pirates, and experiences off the coast of Maine. Medina's debut received positive reviews upon its publication and was nominated for the American Library Association's Best Books for Young Adults award in 2009. The book's success signaled that her decision to pursue a career in writing was the correct one.

Medina's second book, the 2011 picture book *Tía Isa Wants a Car*, was the first of several books by Medina to be published by Candlewick Press and marked the beginning of a strong working relationship with editor Kate Fletcher, whose work Medina has often praised in interviews. The book was based on events surrounding Medina's real-life aunt Isa, who was the first member of her extended family to buy a car. *Tía Isa Wants a Car* won an award from the Ezra Jack Keats Foundation, named for the twentieth-century children's book writer whose work *The Snowy Day* (1962) was among Medina's own favorites. She followed *Tía Isa Wants a Car* with *The Girl Who Could Silence the Wind*, her debut young-adult novel, in 2012.

CRITICALLY ACCLAIMED WRITER

As Medina established herself as a talented contributor to children's literature, she received widespread critical praise for her work, including both her young-adult novels and her picture books. Her 2013 novel *Yaqui Delgado Wants to Kick Your Ass* was widely praised by critics for its strong coming-of-age narrative, which deals with issues such as bullying and draws inspiration from Medina's early teen years. Although the novel was the center of some controversy due to its title, its critical reception largely outweighed such objections, and it won the prestigious Pura Belpré Medal from the Association for Library Service to Children and the National Association to Promote Library and Information Services to Latinos and the Spanish-Speaking. Medina went on to win a related award, the Pura Belpré Honor for narration, for the 2015 picture book *Mango, Abuela, and Me*. For Medina, such recognition was particularly important in calling attention to stories often overlooked by the dominant forces in children's literature. "I think all of those awards celebrate quality and authenticity, both of which are absolutely essential in works for young people," she told Sujei Lugo for the *Horn Book* (8 Feb. 2019). "They also represent voice. These are the stories told by the people who have lived the experiences. My dream is to continue to elevate these voices and to increase their exposure." The illustrator of *Mango, Abuela, and Me*, Angela Dominguez, likewise won a Pura Belpré Honor for her work on the book.

Medina received further critical recognition in 2016, surrounding the release of her young-adult novel *Burn Baby Burn*. A work of historical fiction set in New York City in the summer of 1977, the novel draws inspiration from Medina's childhood in New York as well as from the historical events of that period, which included a series of murders committed by the serial killer known as Son of Sam. "It was just an epic year in New York City's collective history," Medina told

Martha Schulman for *Publishers Weekly* (8 Mar. 2016). "It felt like everything was at the brink of disaster, and yet there was this energy, this scary yet thrilling chaotic energy. I remember the smell of urine, the graffiti, the sense that you could get mugged at any time." In addition to these events, the novel deals with subjects such as feminism and domestic abuse. Well received by critics, *Burn Baby Burn* was longlisted for the National Book Award.

CHANGING GEARS

In January 2018, Medina joined the master of fine arts in children's literature program at Hamline University as a guest author. She became an official member of the program's faculty in July of that year. The year 2018 also saw the publication of Medina's next book, the middle-grade novel *Merci Suárez Changes Gears*. Released in September of that year, the novel is a coming-of-age story that focuses on the titular sixth grader as she copes with changes at school and at home. Like many of Medina's works, the novel was shaped in part by her own life experiences, including her experience caring for elderly relatives. Medina also sought to continue her mission of writing about characters who are underrepresented in much children's literature, a mission that she considered particularly important at the time of the book's publication. "I always center Latinx families in my work, and that is certainly true of this book," she told Lugo. "It feels especially vital to me right now, when the national dialogue around immigrants has become so charged and so derogatory. It's important for all children—and Latinx children in particular—to have a counternarrative."

In addition to receiving overwhelmingly positive reviews, *Merci Suárez Changes Gears* was the recipient of the 2019 John Newbery Medal, a prestigious honor recognizing excellence in American children's literature and awarded by the Association for Library Service to Children. Although Medina's writing had received major awards in the past, receiving the Newbery Medal was particularly meaningful for her. "When [chair Ellen Riordan] said it was the Newbery committee and I had won the medal, all of the emotion I had been holding back, not only for this day, but over the entire course of my career as a writer, just came crashing forward and I sank to the floor of my bathroom and had a big messy cry," she recalled to Corbett. "Those poor people. I have no idea what I even said to them but I'm so grateful that they loved Merci and the Suárez family." *Merci Suárez Changes Gears* also received the Charlotte Huck Honor from the National Council of Teachers of English and was named one of the best children's books of 2018 by a number of publications, including *Publishers Weekly* and *School Library Journal*. Medina's next book, the picture book *Evelyn Del Rey Is Moving Away*, was scheduled for publication in 2020.

ADVOCACY

Alongside her work as a writer, Medina is active in the advocacy organization We Need Diverse Books, for which she has served on the executive and advisory boards, as well as in other movements related to diversity in children's and young-adult fiction. "I try to keep the issue alive and in the thinking of librarians, and teachers, and parents, and readers as they build their collections and make recommendations," she told Schulman. "And it's never an easy conversation when you're talking about change, when people have to notice blind spots. But we move forward if we have these conversations with grace and civility." In addition to writing and blogging, Medina makes frequent appearances at conferences and educational events, and her books are read widely in schools throughout the United States.

PERSONAL LIFE

Medina and her husband, Javier Menéndez, live in Richmond, Virginia. The couple met while growing up in Queens. Their mothers worked in the same factory, and Medina and Menéndez also worked there as teenagers. They lived in Florida, where their three children were born, before moving to Virginia in 1998.

SUGGESTED READING

Corbett, Sue. "Meg Medina on Winning the Newbery Medal." *Publishers Weekly*, 29 Jan. 2019, www.publishersweekly.com/pw/by-topic/childrens/childrens-industry-news/article/79135-meg-medina-on-her-newbery-win.html. Accessed 12 July 2019.

Lockwood, Sarah. "Meg Medina, Storyteller." *RFM Online*, 25 Aug. 2012, richmondfamilymagazine.com/article/an-rfm-chat-with-author-meg-medina/. Accessed 12 July 2019.

Medina, Meg. "Five Questions for Newbery Medalist Meg Medina." Interview by Sujei Lugo. *The Horn Book*, 8 Feb. 2019, www.hbook.com/?detailStory=five-questions-for-meg-medina. Accessed 12 July 2019.

Medina, Meg. "An Interview with 2019 Newbery Medal Winner Meg Medina, Author of Merci Suarez Changes Gears." Interview by Maria Burel. *BNKids Blog*, 5 Feb. 2019, www.barnesandnoble.com/blog/kids/an-interview-with-2019-newbery-award-winner-meg-medina-author-of-merci-suarez-changes-gears/. Accessed 12 July 2019.

Medina, Meg. "Q & A with Meg Medina." Interview by Martha Schulman. *Publishers Weekly*, 8 Mar. 2016, www.publishersweekly.com/pw/by-topic/childrens/childrens-authors/article/69601-q-a-with-meg-medina.html. Accessed 12 July 2019.

Medina, Meg, and Rebecca Sutton. "Meg Medina: Telling the Story of You." *NEA Arts Magazine*, 2014, www.arts.gov/NEARTS/2014v2-story-our-culture-arists-place-community/meg-medina. Accessed 12 July 2019.

SELECTED WORKS

Milagros: Girl from Away, 2008; *Tía Isa Wants a Car*, 2011; *The Girl Who Could Silence the Wind*, 2012; *Yaqui Delgado Wants to Kick Your Ass*, 2013; *Mango, Abuela, and Me*, 2015; *Burn Baby Burn*, 2016; *Merci Suárez Changes Gears*, 2018

—Joy Crelin

Hasan Minhaj

Date of birth: September 23, 1985
Occupation: Actor and comedian

Hasan Minhaj, known for his semiautobiographical, socially conscious brand of humor, has enjoyed a meteoric rise to the top of the comedy world. Minhaj spent a decade cutting his teeth on the national standup scene before receiving his big break in 2014, when he was hired to serve as a senior correspondent for *The Daily Show*, Comedy Central's groundbreaking late-night satirical news program. He held that role for roughly the next four years, during which he broadened his reach into film, television, and other entertainment endeavors.

Minhaj's profile rose in 2017, when he hosted the White House Correspondents' Dinner and debuted his first stand-up special, *Homecoming King*, on Netflix. The Peabody Award–winning special centers around Minhaj's personal life experiences and showcases his ability to generate laughs "via enthralling storytelling rather than punch lines," as Anna Menta wrote for *Newsweek* (26 Oct. 2018). In 2018, Minhaj began hosting his own weekly comedy show on Netflix called *Patriot Act*, making him the first Indian American to do so. Speaking of his comedic style, which incorporates technology, Indian terms, and American pop culture references into informed cultural commentary, he said to Jocelyn Anderson for *UC Davis Magazine* (30 Nov. 2016): "I'm not there to try to skewer people. I'm just trying to come at it with some human empathy. I consider myself to be an angry optimist."

EARLY LIFE AND EDUCATION

Hasan Minhaj was born on September 23, 1985, in Davis, a small city near Sacramento, California. His parents, Najme and Seema, immigrated there from Aligarh, India, shortly before his birth. Not long afterward, Minhaj's mother returned to India to complete medical school. He was subsequently raised by his father, a chemist, for the first eight years of his life. During this time, Minhaj's parents had a daughter, Ayesha, whom he did not meet nor learn about until after his mother returned to live with him and his father; Ayesha is three years younger.

As an Indian American growing up in Davis, Minhaj had a relatively normal suburban upbringing. Still, as one of the few students of color in his classes at Pioneer Elementary School and Holmes Junior High, he was bullied and "always felt like an outsider," as he told Anderson. Because of Minhaj's "outsider" status among his predominantly white peers, he was often subject to racist experiences, which he later used as fodder for his comedy routines. Among these was an incident in which a grade-school crush told him that his skin was "the color of poop."

Notwithstanding such humiliating episodes, Minhaj tried his best to assimilate into American culture, developing an affinity for basketball and hip-hop music. However, without cable television in the house, his exposure to standup comedy was limited to "the first 30 seconds of *Seinfeld*," as he quipped to Menta. Minhaj's first personal forays into comedy came as a member of the speech and debate team at Davis High School, where he learned that he could achieve higher scores from judges if he made them laugh. Driven in part by his fondness for crafting arguments around topical issues, he majored in political science at the University of California (UC), Davis, commuting the two miles from his family home.

Photo by CleftClips via Wikimedia Commons

COMEDY BEGINNINGS

It was at UC Davis where Minhaj's comedy career first took root. Watching a friend's recording of comedian Chris Rock's 2004 television special *Never Scared* during his first year proved eye opening and life changing. The special, in which Rock riffs on controversial subjects across the political and social spectrum, "just blew my mind," Minhaj recalled to Priya Arora for *India. com* (8 Nov. 2015). "It was one of the most innovative, creative things and forms of artistic expression I had ever seen."

Minhaj immediately started developing and performing his own stand-up material at comedy clubs in and around Davis and Sacramento. Meanwhile, he founded a stand-up/sketch comedy club at UC Davis called the Gridiron Gang, through which he got to open for bigger-name comedians who performed at the school, such as W. Kamau Bell, Moshe Kasher, and Ali Wong. Though his early routines were admittedly sophomoric, often poking fun at Indian American stereotypes, Minhaj has said that these initial experiences performing gave him the determination to pursue stand-up as a career. "It was something I really wanted to do," he told Anderson. "To me, I felt like I was a superhero. I would put on my costume and go out into the city."

After graduating from UC Davis in 2007, Minhaj moved to San Francisco, where he regularly performed at open mic nights held at such venues as the BrainWash Café, a laundromat-cum-comedy club located in the city's South of Market (SoMa) district. His profile on the city's stand-up scene increased the following year when he won a Best Comic Standing competition hosted by Sierra Mist. Minhaj's victory won him a coveted opening act gig at the leading Bay Area radio station WiLD 94.9's 2008 Comedy Jam, which featured comedians Gabriel Iglesias and Katt Williams, among others.

In 2009, Minhaj participated in NBC's Standup for Diversity and was a featured comedian on their National College Tour, in which he performed at thirty-seven schools across the country. That same year, he appeared in a successful Pizza Hut commercial and at the Aspen Comedy Festival and SF Sketchfest. Minhaj eventually moved to Los Angeles to break into Hollywood, but those attempts were unsuccessful, save for a handful of minor television roles. Frustrated with being tokenized, he, along with his friends Aristotle Athiras, Asif Ali, and Fahim Anwar, formed the sketch group Goatface, and in 2012, the quartet filmed a *YouTube* series called *The Truth*. The series showcased the group's culturally specific style of humor, which centers around race and identity.

THE DAILY SHOW AND HOMECOMING KING

Minhaj's status in the comedy world rose in late 2014, when he was hired by host Jon Stewart to serve as a senior correspondent for *The Daily Show*. He had been granted an opportunity to audition for the late-night news satire program after Michael Che moved on to coanchor the popular *Saturday Night Live* segment "Weekend Update." After passing a first round of auditions, Minhaj was asked to travel to the show's headquarters in New York City, where he did a screen test for Stewart; he performed an original sketch called "Batman vs. Bill Maher," which was inspired by an on-air spat between late-night host Bill Maher and actor Ben Affleck about Islam. Stewart told Dave Itzkoff for the *New York Times* (18 Oct. 2018) that Minhaj "was just undeniable. I can teach the false-news correspondent mechanics, but not the singularity of someone's talent." Stewart went on to call Minhaj a "great storyteller, introspective and humble."

Minhaj proved to be one of Stewart's last hires as the longtime host announced his departure from *The Daily Show* several months later. Still, the hiring came at a good time for Minhaj, who was on the verge of ditching his comedy career to attend law school. He would serve as a correspondent on the show until August 2018. During his tenure, he covered such major news stories as Pope Francis's first visit to the United States, the 2015 Iran nuclear deal, and the 2016 US presidential election. He also appeared in several recurring segments on the show, such as "Brown in Town," in which he reported on timely issues in places across the country.

Around the same time that he joined *The Daily Show*, Minhaj began performing his solo stage show, *Homecoming King*. The show, in which Minhaj riffs on everything from a high school prom date gone wrong to his relationship with his stern father, underwent various stages of development before officially debuting Off-Broadway in New York in October 2015. From 2016 to 2017, Minhaj took the show on tour with performances in forty cities all over the United States. A January 2017 performance in Minhaj's hometown of Davis was taped for the video-streaming giant Netflix, which released it as a one-hour stand-up comedy special in May of that year. The special received rave reviews from critics, many of whom praised Minhaj's comedic storytelling abilities, and earned him a 2017 Peabody Award. "Storytelling is the most powerful way to convey your narrative and to get empathy from other people," Minhaj explained to Arora.

PATRIOT ACT AND BEYOND

One month prior to the Netflix debut of *Homecoming King*, Minhaj hosted the 2017 White House Correspondents' Dinner. He landed the coveted honor after many other high-profile comedians passed on the event, which President Donald Trump, in a break from tradition, declined to attend. Given only nineteen days to prepare, Minhaj, along with his head writer, longtime friend Prashanth Venkataramanujam, won praise for his biting twenty-five-minute set, which offered a no-holds-barred roast of Trump, his administration, and the media. The full set went on to garner more than 2.2 million views on *YouTube*.

In the wake of his successful correspondents' set, Minhaj teamed up with Netflix again on the weekly comedy show *Patriot Act*, which premiered in October 2018 to critical acclaim. Created by Minhaj and Venkataramanujam, the show is filmed in front of an in-studio audience and reaches nearly two hundred countries. The first seven of its thirty-two planned episodes focused on such topics as affirmative action, hype culture, the dissemination of social media content, and Amazon's effect on the US economy. Minhaj's aim for the show is to use breaking news stories and hot-button issues as a vehicle for connecting with viewers on a more personal level. "My job is to be as funny as possible, and to the tell the truth," he explained to Joe Berkowitz for *Fast Company* (25 Sept. 2018). "If I can do those two things, hopefully I can reach people."

Minhaj's approach to reaching a wider audience has also meant a move away from the cookie-cutter format of other weekly comedy programs. Like *Homecoming King*, *Patriot Act* features a backdrop of wall-to-wall LED screens with ever-changing multimedia graphics, including news clips, statistics, and screenshots from social media, as well as inventive lighting effects to reflect changing mood and tone. Eschewing the conventional desk-and-chair setup, Minhaj hosts the show on a bare hexagonal-shaped platform, delivering his monologues while keeping in perpetual motion. Speaking to Itzkoff, Minhaj likened the show's look to "a woke TED Talk."

Minhaj has kept busy with other endeavors as well. In November 2018, he reunited with his sketch comedy group Goatface for a self-titled one-hour special that aired on Comedy Central. Meanwhile, he has appeared in several Hollywood comedy films, including *Rough Night* (2017) and *The Spy Who Dumped Me* (2018), which starred Scarlett Johansson and Mila Kunis, respectively.

PERSONAL LIFE

Minhaj loves hip-hop and basketball, collects sneakers, and has what Itzkoff described as an "occasional tendency to talk like an internet meme come to life." Minhaj married his college sweetheart, Beena Patel, a management consultant, in 2015. The couple had a daughter in March 2018 and live in New York City. Minhaj is a practicing Muslim and speaks Urdu; his wife is Hindu.

SUGGESTED READING

Arora, Priya. "Comedian Hasan Minhaj on 'Homecoming King' and the Power of Storytelling." *India.com*, 8 Nov. 2015, www.india.com/arts-and-culture/comedian-hasan-minhaj-on-homecoming-king-and-the-power-of-storytelling-683559. Accessed 7 Feb. 2019.

Berkowitz, Joe. "Hasan Minhaj and the Art of Persuasion." *Fast Company*, 25 Sept. 2018, www.fastcompany.com/90227535/hasan-minhaj-and-the-art-of-persuasion. Accessed 7 Feb. 2019.

Itzkoff, Dave. "Can Hasan Minhaj Make Topical Comedy Work on Netflix?" *The New York Times*, 18 Oct. 2018, www.nytimes.com/2018/10/18/arts/television/hasan-minhaj-netflix-patriot-act.html. Accessed 13 Feb. 2019.

Menta, Anna. "How Hasan Minhaj Went from Demeaning Auditions to Netflix's 'Patriot Act.'" *Newsweek*, 26 Oct. 2018, www.newsweek.com/hasan-minhaj-patriot-act-profile-1187920. Accessed 7 Feb. 2019.

Minhaj, Hasan. "Seriously Funny." Interview by Jocelyn Anderson. *UC Davis Magazine*, 30 Nov. 2016, magazine.ucdavis.edu/seriously-funny. Accessed 7 Feb. 2019.

Rao, Mallika. "Hasan Minhaj Invites You to Take Off Your Shoes." *The Atlantic*, 2 Dec. 2018, www.theatlantic.com/entertainment/archive/2018/12/netflixs-patriot-act-hasan-minhaj-makes-talk-show/577048/. Accessed 7 Feb. 2019.

SELECTED WORKS

The Truth, 2012 (with Goatface); *Homecoming King*, 2017; *Patriot Act*, 2018–; *Goatface*, 2018

—*Chris Cullen*

Bo Levi Mitchell

Date of birth: March 3, 1990
Occupation: Football quarterback

Bo Levi Mitchell, a dedicated quarterback who began playing in the Canadian Football League (CFL) in 2012, has been awarded multiple Most Valuable Player (MVP) and Most Outstanding Player honors for his record-breaking performances on the field. However, those personal accomplishments are less important to Mitchell than his ability to lead his team to the playoffs. "Championships first, then you can go to individual accolades," he explained to Chris O'Leary for the website of the Calgary Stampeders (13 Feb. 2019). "I want to continue to chase championships." After Mitchell joined the Calgary Stampeders in 2012, the team became a fixture in the CFL's postseason tournament and in the league's final and most prestigious annual match, the Grey Cup. The Stampeders claimed the Grey Cup in 2014 and 2018, both times thanks, in part, to substantial contributions by Mitchell himself.

A football player since childhood, Mitchell had a successful high school career in Katy, Texas, before going on to play two seasons each for Southern Methodist University and Eastern Washington University. More at home at the latter school, Mitchell impressed fans with his skills on the field but remained a risky pick for National Football League (NFL) organizations. After going undrafted during the 2012 NFL Draft, Mitchell shifted his attention to the CFL, signing a contract with the Stampeders in the spring of 2012. Following the end of his contract, he signed a new, four-year deal with the Stampeders in early 2019, reinforcing his commitment to propelling the team toward championship victories. "I think if you're doing that, if you're getting championships that often, the numbers, the passing records and all that stuff will come with it," he told O'Leary.

EARLY LIFE AND EDUCATION
Bo Levi Mitchell was born on March 3, 1990, in Katy, Texas. He grew up in Katy alongside two older brothers and a younger brother. His parents, Dwight Mitchell and Barbara Miller, divorced when he was seven. Athletic pursuits were popular in Mitchell's household, and he and his brothers began playing sports such as baseball and football early in life. His older brother Cory later played alongside Mitchell as a wide receiver for the Eastern Washington University football team. Although Mitchell was more confident in his skills as a baseball player, he was particularly devoted to football as a teenager, practicing extensively even when at home. "I never put the football down," he recalled to O'Leary for the Canadian Football League (CFL) website (22 Nov. 2018). "Every single day in the house I was throwing it, spinning it on my hand, just trying to get to know it."

As quarterback for the Katy High School football team, Mitchell distinguished himself as a strong player and had a particularly successful senior season, during which he passed for thirty-seven touchdowns and contributed to the team's undefeated record and victory at the state championships. Over the course of his high school career, Mitchell received significant attention from college scouts, primarily those affiliated with National Collegiate Athletic Association (NCAA) Division II teams. He also attracted the attention of the University of Hawaii's Division I program, and he committed to attend the university following his graduation from Katy High School in 2008. After Hawaii coach June Jones moved to Southern Methodist University (SMU), however, Mitchell changed his plans and opted to enroll in that Texas-based Division I school.

Photo by Derek Leung/Getty Images

Despite the prestige of SMU's football program, Mitchell was dissatisfied with his experience on the university's team. "Everyone at SMU was there for themselves and about getting to the NFL," he explained to O'Leary for the CFL's website. "It wasn't a team atmosphere." Mitchell started nineteen games over his two seasons with SMU and achieved a total of thirty-six touchdowns but struggled during his second season, because injuries limited the number of games in which he played. He also had a relatively high number of interceptions. Seeking a team that would be a better fit for him, Mitchell transferred to Eastern Washington University in January 2010. His mother and brothers later moved to Cheney, Washington—the home of Eastern Washington University—to be closer to him.

EASTERN WASHINGTON UNIVERSITY
Mitchell began playing for the Eastern Washington University Eagles football team during the 2010 season. Over the course of his first season with the Eagles, he served as starting quarterback for fourteen games and excelled on the team. Perhaps equally important, Mitchell felt far more comfortable with his new team than he had with its predecessor and appreciated the camaraderie among the players. "It felt like home," he told Dan Graziano for *ESPN* (23 June 2017). "It felt like high school football to me. Guys weren't there trying to be the big-name guys, out for the advancement of their careers. They were just there to play football together." Having performed well throughout the season, the Eagles competed in the NCAA's Division I Football Championship Subdivision (FCS) Football

Championship Game, in which they faced off against the University of Delaware and ultimately proved victorious, earning the team's first championship win. Mitchell played a key role in the game and was later named the team's Most Outstanding Player thanks to his performance.

During his second and final season with the Eagles, Mitchell experienced similar success as a quarterback, achieving thirty-three touchdowns and receiving the Walter Payton Award for his high-level performance within the FCS. In January 2012, he played in the National Football League Players Association (NFLPA) All-Star Game, which represented an opportunity to demonstrate his talents on the field and attempt to capture the attention of an NFL team. "I know I'm going to have a chance to showcase my skills, but my window will be small, which is something I will have to take advantage of because I won't get many opportunities," he told Jon O'Connor for *Bleacher Report* (2 Jan. 2012) during that period. "But that's all you can ask for as a player, get a chance, seize the moment, and shine when the lights are on." Although Mitchell entered the 2012 NFL Draft, he went undrafted due to his high number of interceptions while at SMU and his stature, which is smaller than that of the average professional quarterback. He instead shifted his focus to finding a position within the CFL.

CFL

In April 2012, Mitchell announced that he had signed with the CFL's Calgary Stampeders as a free agent, having earlier attended a camp run by that organization. He made his debut with the team in July of that year and immediately committed himself to becoming a leading member of the team's roster. "The first thing I told Dave (Dickenson) was, 'I want to be the best to ever play.' In order to make that happen, I have to become better every single year, every single week throughout the entire season," he told Troy Durrell for *Last Word on Sports* (2 Mar. 2016). "And also I need to make sure I'm always raising the elevation of the players around me. That's what you define as a great player, somebody who can raise the level of play of the guys around him, and that's something I always look to do." As a newcomer to the team, Mitchell's contributions were limited during his debut season, which saw the Stampeders compete in the Grey Cup—the CFL's championship game—in November 2012, but ultimately lose to the Toronto Argonauts.

After acclimating further to his career with the Stampeders during the 2013 season, Mitchell began to serve as starting quarterback on a regular basis in 2014, during which the team had a particularly successful season and postseason. After finishing the season ranked first in the CFL's West Division, the Stampeders beat the Edmonton Eskimos to win a spot in the Grey Cup. They then defeated the Hamilton Tiger-Cats to claim the championship. Mitchell was named MVP for his contributions during the Grey Cup, which included throwing for 334 yards. The later seasons were also successful for Mitchell, who was named the CFL's Most Outstanding Player in 2016, despite the Stampeders' loss to the Ottawa RedBlacks in the 2016 Grey Cup. The team again competed in the Grey Cup in 2017 but lost to the Argonauts.

STAMPEDERS CONTRACT RENEWAL

The 2018 season was a strong one for both Mitchell, who achieved thirty-five touchdown passes and 5,124 yards, and for the Stampeders, who finished the season ranked first in the West Division. During the playoffs, the Stampeders beat the Winnipeg Blue Bombers in the Western Final before facing the RedBlacks in the Grey Cup and earning a decisive victory. Again named the MVP of the Grey Cup, Mitchell also received his second Most Outstanding Player Award for his contributions during the 2018 season. As Mitchell's contract with the Stampeders was set to end after the season, the beginning of 2019 was a key period for the player, who had to decide whether to remain with the Stampeders or go elsewhere. In addition to speculation that he might move to a different team within the CFL, some in the sports media suggested that Mitchell might join the NFL, a possibility he never ruled out. "When my time comes, the NFL has been my dream since I was a kid. I'll take that shot," he told Graziano. For Mitchell, the process of making his decision was "stressful," as he told O'Leary for the *Stampeders* website. "You realize how many people your decision impacts but you're trying to make the best decision for you and your family, for your legacy, for winning and everything," he explained.

Although he received offers from multiple teams, Mitchell ultimately chose to remain with the Stampeders, signing a four-year contract with the team in February 2019. "It's great to have Bo back for four more years," team president and general manager John Hufnagel said in a press release, as reported by the *Cheney Free Press* (21 Feb. 2019). "He had lots of options out there and I'm pleased he's made this commitment to the Stampeders and that he's chosen to continue building on his already-impressive legacy in Calgary." Following the start of the 2019 season, Mitchell suffered a muscle tear that kept him off the field for the months of July and August. He returned to play in September of that year.

PERSONAL LIFE

Mitchell met his wife, Madison, after Eastern Washington University won the 2011 championship. The couple married in 2015. They have two daughters. Mitchell lives in Calgary, where he is active in community service and was twice awarded the Herm Harrison Memorial Award for Community Service.

SUGGESTED READING

Behrens, Tom. "Bo Levi Mitchell, CFL's Most Outstanding Player." *The Katy News*, 7 Sept. 2017, thekatynews.com/2017/09/07/bo-levi-mitchell-cfls-most-outstanding-player/. Accessed 13 Sept. 2019.

"Bo Levi Mitchell Signs Four-Year Deal with Calgary." *Cheney Free*, 21 Feb. 2019, www.cheneyfreepress.com/story/2019/02/21/sports/bo-levi-mitchell-signs-four-year-deal-with-calgary/24418.html. Accessed 13 Sept. 2019.

Graziano, Dan. "CFL Star QB Bo Levi Mitchell Not Ready to Give Up NFL Dreams." *ESPN*, 23 June 2017, www.espn.com/cfl/story/_/id/19705254/calgary-stampeders-quarterback-bo-levi-mitchell-not-ready-give-nfl-dreams-2017-cfl. Accessed 13 Sept. 2019.

Mitchell, Bo Levi. "Interview with Calgary Stampeders Quarterback Bo Levi Mitchell." Interview by Troy Durrell. *Last Word on Sports*, 2 Mar. 2016, lastwordonsports.com/2016/03/02/interview-calgary-stampeders-quarterback-bo-levi-mitchell/. Accessed 13 Sept. 2019.

Mitchell, Bo Levi. "O'Leary: A Candid Q&A with Bo Levi Mitchell." Interview by Chris O'Leary. *Stampeders*, 13 Feb. 2019, www.stampeders.com/2019/02/13/oleary-candid-qa-bo-levi-mitchell/. Accessed 13 Sept. 2019.

O'Connor, Jon. "NFLPA College All-Star Football Game: Enter Bo Levi Mitchell." *Bleacher Report*, 2 Jan. 2012, bleacherreport.com/articles/1005894-nflpa-college-all-star-football-game-enter-bo-levi-mitchell. Accessed 13 Sept. 2019.

O'Leary, Chris. "Long Read: Bo Finds His Balance in Unique Mop Season." *CFL*, 22 Nov. 2018, www.cfl.ca/2018/11/22/long-read-bo-finds-balance-unique-mop-season/. Accessed 13 Sept. 2019.

—Joy Crelin

Paul L. Modrich

Date of birth: June 13, 1946
Occupation: Biochemist

Paul L. Modrich is a leading biochemist who described the mechanism by which cells are detected and correct errors in mismatched base pairs in a strand of DNA. He shared the 2015 Nobel Prize in Chemistry for this work.

EARLY LIFE AND EDUCATION

Paul L. Modrich was born in 1946 in the small town of Raton, New Mexico. He has credited this area's rich biodiversity with sparking his interest in biology. Modrich's father, Larry, was a biology teacher and encouraged his son's interest. Modrich spent much of his childhood out of doors, exploring the nearby hills and playing basketball or baseball with friends.

During his junior year of high school in 1963, Modrich's father gave him advice that would shape his career: The previous year Harry Crick and James Watson were awarded the Nobel Prize in Physiology or Medicine for their discovery of the double-helix structure of deoxyribonucleic acid, DNA, and Larry Modrich suggested that his son learn about it.

After high school, Modrich traveled across the country to study biology at the Massachusetts Institute of Technology (MIT) where he got his first taste of lab work studying the genetics of bacteria-infecting viruses. He graduated from MIT in 1968 with a Bachelor of Science degree.

Following graduation, Modrich returned to the Southwest United States to pursue a PhD in biochemistry at Stanford University in California. There he studied the enzyme ligase, a protein which glues strands of DNA together during several essential genetic processes, including replication, repair, and recombination. He was able to demonstrate that ligase is essential for the survival of the *Escherichia coli* (*E. coli*) bacteria. He completed his PhD in 1973.

DESCRIBING MISMATCH REPAIR IN DNA

After getting his doctorate, Modrich moved back to the Northeast for postdoctoral work, joining Harvard University and studying enzymatic effect on DNA molecules. Afterward, he took his first teaching position at the University of California, Berkeley, but was frustrated by the lack of enthusiasm for his work on the part of graduate students. He then joined Duke University in South Carolina in 1976 as an assistant professor.

By the late 1970s, Modrich had begun working on the topic that would bring him fame as a biochemist: a system called mismatch repair (MMR). As an organism grows, supports itself, and reproduces, it must generate new cells. Each of these cells needs its own complete copy of the organism's genetic code, its DNA. Therefore, the DNA in living things is constantly being read and copied. These replications afford ample opportunity for errors to creep in, which can have disastrous consequences.

DNA is composed of four distinct units called bases: adenine (A), thymine (T), guanine (G), and cytosine (C). These bases pair up very specifically (A-T and G-C) to form the "rungs" in the ladder of the double helix formed by two complementary strands of DNA twisted. Very rarely, however, the enzyme that links up bases makes a mistake and matches the wrong two together.

In the early 1980s, Modrich developed a technique to analyze these mismatched pairs, which allowed him to identify and describe the process of mismatch repair in *E. coli*. Modrich was promoted to the position of James B. Duke professor of biochemistry at Duke in 1988.

In 1990, Modrich and his team demonstrated that humans, like the bacteria he had been studying, also have a mismatch repair system in their cells. Moreover, when this system is broken, it can lead to cancer. Specifically, the team was able to show that individuals with a common and heritable form of colon cancer also had mutations that inhibited their ability to produce the proteins needed in the human mismatch repair system. Modrich became an investigator with the Howard Hughes Medical Institute (HHMI) in 1994, while keeping his position at Duke.

IMPACT
Modrich was awarded the 2015 Nobel Prize in Chemistry along with two other biochemists, Aziz Sancar and Tomas Lindahl, for his contribution to understanding how DNA is able to maintain its integrity despite myriad error sources. The Royal Swedish Academy of Sciences, which awards the Nobel Prize, described the separate but related work of the three scientists as "a decisive contribution to the understanding of how the living cell functions, as well as providing knowledge about the molecular causes of several hereditary diseases and about mechanisms behind both cancer development and aging." Modrich's work on mismatch repair, in particular, has shed light on the root cause of several types of inheritable cancer and has opened new treatment avenues for this devastating illness.

PERSONAL LIFE
Modrich has an adult son and daughter from his first marriage. In 1980, he married fellow Duke biochemist Vickers Burdett. The two enjoy traveling and spending time in their New Hampshire cabin and another home in rural New Mexico, which they built together. Modrich's hobbies include trap shooting, amateur photography, and astronomy.

SUGGESTED READING
Akpan, Nsikan. "DNA Repair Research Wins 3 Scientist Nobel Prize in Chemistry." *NPR*. 7 Oct. 2015, www.npr.org/sections/thetwo-way/2015/10/07/446532519/dna-repair-research-nets-chemistry-nobel-for-3-scientists. Accessed 29 Mar. 2019.

Broad, William J. "Nobel Prize in Chemistry Awarded to Tomas Lindahl, Paul Modrich, and Aziz Sancar for DNA Studies." *The New York Times*. 7 Oct. 2015, www.nytimes. com/2015/10/08/science/tomas-lindahl-paul-modrich-aziz-sancarn-nobel-chemistry.html. Accessed 29 Mar. 2019.

Kresge, Nicole, et al. "Understanding DNA Mismatch Repair: The Work of Paul L. Modrich." *Jour. of Biological Chemistry* 282(3) 1916-24 (February 2007): e2, http://www.jbc.org/content/282/3/e2. Accessed 29 Mar. 2019.

"Our Scientists: Paul L. Modrich, PhD." *HHMI*. Howard Hughes Medical Institute, 2015, www.hhmi.org/scientists/paul-l-modrich. Accessed 29 Mar. 2019.

Quillin, Martha. "For Paul Modrich, Frenzy and Failures Yield Truths." *News & Observer*, 25 Dec. 2015, www.newsobserver.com/news/local/education/article51568805.html. Accessed 29 Mar. 2015.

"The 2015 Nobel Science Prizes: Wisdom, Ancient and Modern." *Economist*. Economist Newspaper, 10 Oct. 2015, www.economist.com/science-and-technology/2015/10/10/wisdom-ancient-and-modern. Accessed 29 Mar. 2019.

—*Kenrick Vezina*

Jason Momoa

Date of birth: August 1, 1979
Occupation: Actor

Since early in his career, actor Jason Momoa has gravitated to specific types of roles: men on the run, warriors, survivors, lone wolves, and similar characters who exist outside of, or in the spaces between, societies. "I identified with this outcast thing, and I really loved it," he told Emily Zemler for *Esquire* (19 Jan. 2017). "I don't think a lot of people are calling me to play doctors and lawyers, which is fine with me. I can put a suit on, but I don't really like to." Indeed, Momoa has worn few suits in his most memorable roles, which have included *Stargate: Atlantis*'s Ronon Dex, *Conan the Barbarian*'s titular hero, *Game of Thrones*' Khal Drogo, *Frontier*'s Declan Harp, and—perhaps most notably—the DC Comics hero Aquaman. Although long a fan favorite among viewers of his more niche projects, Momoa became widely acknowledged as a star in his own right thanks to the lattermost role, which he played in the films *Batman v Superman: Dawn of Justice* and *Justice League* before starring in the solo film *Aquaman* in 2018. While the film proved to be a massive financial success, grossing more than a billion dollars worldwide, Momoa was primarily concerned with ensuring that fans enjoyed his interpretation of the character. "I want to make Aquaman fans proud," he told James Hibberd for *Entertainment Weekly* (19 July 2018).

Photo by Gage Skidmore via Wikimedia Commons

EARLY LIFE AND EDUCATION

Joseph Jason Namakaeha Momoa was born in Honolulu, Hawaii, on August 1, 1979. His parents, Coni and Joseph, separated when he was a baby, and Momoa and his mother moved to her home state of Iowa. The family settled in Norwalk, a small city south of Des Moines. Momoa remained in Iowa during the school year for the remainder of his childhood but began spending his summers in Hawaii with his father at the age of twelve. During those visits, Momoa pursued outdoor activities, such as surfing and rock climbing, and developed a deep love of the ocean, which led him to consider pursuing a career in marine biology. "Even when I was a kid in Iowa I took marine biology courses so I could do that as a profession, that was my passion for the ocean," he told Christie Wilson for the *Honolulu Star Advertiser* (16 Dec. 2018). "I think that's just from being Hawaiian."

As a student at Norwalk High School, Momoa struggled to fit in. "I graduated with maybe 100 kids, all very much the same. I stood out," he told Hibberd. "I didn't kind of do the same stuff. I was a bit of a skateboarder, and I started rock climbing. I love Iowa, but I just didn't fit in. If you're a Hawaiian kid in Iowa, you're kind of a fish out of water. Then I went back to Hawaii and I got ostracized there too." Momoa would later link his difficulty fitting in with those around him to his later tendency to play characters who are outcasts or caught between two worlds, noting that his experiences gave him a greater understanding of such roles.

After graduating in 1997, Momoa moved to Colorado, where he spent time snowboarding and attended college. In keeping with his early dreams of becoming a marine biologist, he initially pursued studies in that field but later switched his focus to wildlife biology. Momoa soon left college, however, and moved to Hawaii, where he worked in a surf shop for a time.

EARLY CAREER

While living in Hawaii, Momoa met local fashion designers and pageant coaches Takeo Kobayashi and Eric Chandler, influential figures within the state's fashion industry. He began modeling for the designers and soon transitioned into acting. In 1999 he secured the role of lifeguard Jason Ioane on *Baywatch: Hawaii*, the final two seasons of the long-running syndicated series previously known simply as *Baywatch*. Following the series' end in 2001, Momoa reprised his role in the 2003 television film *Baywatch: Hawaiian Wedding*. Although Momoa's role in *Baywatch: Hawaii* launched his acting career, he had a difficult time finding work after his years on the series. "It [led] to getting no respect for about four years and I couldn't get an agent to save my life," he recalled to Pascale Day for *Metro* (24 Nov. 2017). "I just became a rock-climbing bum and I spent the little money I got from *Baywatch* and travelled the world."

Over the subsequent years, Momoa appeared in several films as well as the short-lived television series *North Shore* (2004–5), a soap opera set in a Hawaiian resort. A turning point in his career came in 2005, when he joined the cast of the Sci-Fi Channel (now known as Syfy) series *Stargate: Atlantis* (*SGA*). A spin-off from the series *Stargate SG-1* (1997–2007), which was in turn based on the 1994 film *Stargate*, *SGA* follows a group of humans from Earth and their allies as they explore and attempt to survive in the Pegasus Galaxy, where a vampiric species of aliens known as the Wraith have long subjugated the rest of the galaxy's population. Momoa's character, Ronon Dex, joined the series' main cast of characters during the show's second season and remained a primary character for the remainder of *SGA*'s five-season run.

For Momoa, his years on *SGA* offered an experience unlike any he had previously had as an actor. "You do a movie, you meet everyone, you go from place to place. It's like joining a circus," he explained to Ryan Lamble for *Den of Geek* (3 Apr. 2011). "Being on a show for four years, you know everyone. You know the grips. You feel safe and comfortable. You can play with your character a lot. It evolves over a long period of time." While the show received limited mainstream recognition during its run, *SGA* proved popular among fans of science-fiction television, and Momoa and his castmates amassed a dedicated fan base during that period.

BREAKTHROUGH ROLES

Following *SGA's* cancellation in 2009, Momoa appeared in several episodes of the television series *The Game*. He went on to star in 2011's *Conan the Barbarian*, an adventure film based on the character created by pulp writer Robert E. Howard and popularized further by a duo of 1980s films starring Arnold Schwarzenegger. Then the most significant film of Momoa's career, *Conan the Barbarian* also offered a new opportunity to introduce Momoa to a wider audience. "It was hard. I've never been the lead of anything," he told Lamble. "It was my first experience of being a lead, the weight of it on your shoulders, performing at that level." Although the film performed poorly at the box office and received largely negative reviews from critics, Momoa nevertheless received widespread attention beginning in April 2011, which saw the premiere of the long-awaited HBO fantasy series *Game of Thrones*, based on the *Song of Ice and Fire* novels by fantasy and science-fiction writer George R. R. Martin.

Appearing almost exclusively in the first season of *Game of Thrones*, Momoa plays the role of Khal Drogo, the leader of a tribe of nomadic Dothraki warriors and the new spouse of Daenerys Targaryen, one of the series' principal characters. Although already written to be an imposing figure, Khal Drogo became even more fully realized on screen thanks to a suggestion from Momoa. "I went up to [writer and creator] David Benioff, and said, 'I'm Conan. I've just done seventeen goddamn battles. You should probably have something that shows he's this amazing warlord. He should have a little bit of a fight,'" he told Lamble. The show's creators ultimately added a scene in which Khal Drogo rips out a rival's tongue, demonstrating the character's fighting prowess. In addition to showcasing his experience playing action-oriented characters, Momoa was tasked with learning to speak the Dothraki language, an experience he described to Lamble as "fantastic." Nearly all of Momoa's dialogue in *Game of Thrones* was delivered in the Dothraki language, which was based on Martin's novels but was constructed for the television series. As *Game of Thrones* became popular among viewers, Momoa's memorable performance earned him a larger following, and he went on to be nominated for the Screen Actors Guild (Award for outstanding performance by an ensemble in a drama series alongside the rest of the first season's cast.

OTHER ROLES

Much as he had in the years following his performance in *Baywatch: Hawaii*, Momoa initially struggled to find work after his appearance in *Game of Thrones*, in part because his performance in the series had caused some of the individuals involved in casting film and television projects to believe incorrectly that he did not speak English. Although he did find work in several projects, including the films *Bullet to the Head* (2012) and *Wolves* (2014), the period was difficult for Momoa professionally. "We were broke," he told Zemler. "I had to write and direct a piece with my friends to get money for my family." The resulting project was Momoa's feature-length directorial debut, the 2014 film *Road to Paloma*, which he cowrote with Robert Mollohan and Jonathan Hirschbein. The film stars Momoa as Wolf, a man who goes on the run from police after avenging his mother's murder.

Although *Road to Paloma* reached a limited audience, Momoa later credited the film with showing industry professionals more of his abilities and helping him to obtain more work, including a lead role in the SundanceTV series *The Red Road* (2014–15). In addition to *The Red Road*, a drama focusing on the conflicts between the American Indian and white residents of a small New Jersey town, Momoa went on to appear in a variety of projects, including the films *Sugar Mountain* (2016) and *Braven* (2018). Beginning in 2016, he starred in the Netflix series *Frontier*, a historical drama set in eighteenth-century Canada. A third season of the series premiered on Netflix in November 2018.

BECOMING AQUAMAN

Already a recognizable figure from earlier roles such as Khal Drogo, Momoa became a household name in 2017 and 2018 in a new role: that of the DC Comics superhero Aquaman. The role was perhaps an unlikely one for Momoa, who was offered the role by filmmaker Zack Snyder after unsuccessfully auditioning for the role of Batman in the 2016 film *Batman v Superman: Dawn of Justice*. "I was like, 'What?' Blonde? Tights? Orange and green shirt?" Momoa told Hibberd of his response to Snyder's suggestion that he play the character, also known as Arthur Curry. "I'm like, 'I don't know man, is this a joke?'" The offer was very much not a joke, and Momoa initially took on the role for a cameo appearance in *Batman v Superman*.

Following that brief appearance, Momoa again played Aquaman in the 2017 film *Justice League*, an installment in the DC Extended Universe (DCEU) that brings together characters from earlier and upcoming films. Although Aquaman plays a significant role in the film's events, *Justice League* does not delve deeply into the character, a fact that initially worried Momoa. "One of my concerns . . . when we did *Justice League* was that people were going to be like, 'Oh he's so grumpy,'" he told Hibberd. "But the whole idea Zack and I talked about was that [*Justice League*] is only like a half hour in his life, you know? So I had to stick to that character knowing in *Aquaman* we can explain why he is the way he is." Opening in US theaters in December 2018, *Aquaman* did just that, exploring the character's origin as well as his ascension to his rightful place as ruler of the underwater kingdom of Atlantis. In addition to grossing more than one billion dollars worldwide at the box office, *Aquaman* fared better with critics than most of the earlier DCEU films, thanks in large part to Momoa's engaging performance.

PERSONAL LIFE
Momoa has been in a relationship with fellow actor Lisa Bonet since 2005, when they met at a jazz club in Los Angeles. They married in 2017 and have two children together, Lola and Nakoa-Wolf. Momoa is also stepfather to Bonet's adult daughter, fellow actor Zoë Kravitz. Momoa and Bonet live in Topanga, California. The couple appeared together in both *Road to Paloma* and *The Red Road*. In addition to acting, Momoa enjoys a variety of outdoor activities as well as reading and playing guitar.

SUGGESTED READING
Day, Pascale. "Jason Momoa Admits *Baywatch* Almost Ruined His Career." *Metro*, 24 Nov. 2017, metro.co.uk/2017/11/24/jason-momoa-admits-baywatch-almost-ruined-his-career-7106907. Accessed 15 Mar. 2019.

Finn, Natalie. "The Secrets of Jason Momoa and Lisa Bonet's Epic Love Story." *E News*, 1 Aug. 2018, www.eonline.com/news/956097/the-secrets-of-jason-momoa-and-lisa-bonet-s-epic-love-story. Accessed 15 Mar. 2019.

Lamble, Ryan. "Jason Momoa Interview: *Game of Thrones*, Playing Conan and More." *Den of Geek*, 3 Apr. 2011, www.denofgeek.com/us/tv/20779/jason-momoa-interview-game-of-thrones-playing-conan-and-more. Accessed 15 Mar. 2019.

Leimkuehler, Matthew. "*Aquaman*: Iowan Jason Momoa Stars in the Season's Biggest Film. Here's What to Know before Seeing It." *Des Moines Register*, 20 Dec. 2018, www.desmoinesregister.com/story/entertainment/2018/12/20/aquaman-jason-momoa-iowa-need-know-box-office-dc-films-norwalk-childhood-james-wan/2375169002. Accessed 15 Mar. 2019.

Momoa, Jason. "Jason Momoa Ultimate *Aquaman* Interview." Interview by James Hibberd. *Entertainment Weekly*, 19 July 2018, ew.com/movies/2018/07/19/jason-momoa-aquaman-interview/amp. Accessed 15 Mar. 2019.

Wilson, Christie. "Hawaii-Born Actor Jason Momoa's 'Aquaman' Role Parallels Own Upbringing." *Honolulu Star Advertiser*, 16 Dec. 2018, www.staradvertiser.com/2018/12/16/hawaii-news/hawaii-born-actor-jason-momoas-role-in-aquaman-parallels-his-own-upbringing. Accessed 15 Mar. 2019.

Zemler, Emily. "Jason Momoa Is Happiest in the Mud and the Dirt." *Esquire*, 19 Jan. 2017, www.esquire.com/entertainment/movies/a52399/jason-momoa-interview-frontier-aquaman. Accessed 15 Mar. 2019.

SELECTED WORKS
Baywatch: Hawaii, 1999–2001; *North Shore*, 2004–5; *Stargate: Atlantis*, 2005–9; *Conan the Barbarian*, 2011; *Game of Thrones*, 2011–12; *Road to Paloma*, 2014; *The Red Road*, 2014–15; *Frontier*, 2016–18; *Justice League*, 2017; *Aquaman*, 2018

—Joy Crelin

Yuyi Morales
Date of birth: November 7, 1968
Occupation: Author and illustrator

The Pura Belpré Award, named after the first Latina librarian at the New York Public Library, honors writers and illustrators whose work "best portrays, affirms, and celebrates the Latino cultural experience in an outstanding work of literature for children and youth," as the prize website states. Since Yuyi Morales began writing and illustrating children's books, she has made numerous appearances on the list, garnering honorable mentions and winning gold medals an impressive six times, as of 2019, for her illustrations. Among them are *Just a Minute*, a colorful 2003 counting book featuring a skeleton wearing a hat; *Los Gatos Black on Halloween*, a 2006 picture book authored by Marisa Montes that is centered on the holiday and blends Spanish and English; and *Just in Case*, a 2008 follow-up to her counting book. In *Niño Wrestles the World* (2013), her pint-size protagonist imagines taking on a series of villains. *Viva Frida* is her 2014 biography of the painter Frida Kahlo, and *Dreamers*, her 2018 picture book, celebrates immigration based upon her own experience immigrating to the United States with her infant son.

In an interview with David Haldeman for the nonprofit *Humanities Washington* (30 Mar. 2015), Morales explained that, like most children's book authors, she hopes to instill a passion for reading in her audience: "I hope that what happens is the children see reading books, creating books, loving books, is a celebration," she said. "And that books can be a part of everything beautiful in life."

EARLY LIFE AND EDUCATION
Yuyi Morales was born in 1968 in the Mexican city of Xalapa, in the state of Veracruz, near the coast of the Gulf of Mexico. She has two younger sisters and one younger brother. Among the most

Photo by Larry D. Moore via Wikimedia Commons

notable aspects of her childhood was her mother's creativity. Her mother made all the family's clothing, such home furnishings as drapes and bedspreads, and a zoo's worth of colorful stuffed animals, which she sold in local marketplaces. She also encouraged Morales to make simple school assignments more creative.

Through her mother, Morales learned to sew, embroider, and crochet—she recalls crafting herself a vest when she was just five years old—but mainly she doodled and drew. She began by copying photos, and after hearing that Frida Kahlo made a practice of drawing her own face in the mirror, she started doing that as well. "Although I liked it a lot, it never occurred to me that it could be something that I would do for a living," she recalled to Roger Sutton for the *Horn Book* (20 Aug. 2018). "I had this belief, as a number of people do, that to be an artist is not possible, because artists should be these people who are almost destined to be something very, very special. Maybe you were born when the stars aligned, or you have signs in your body that tell you are an artist." Her father thought that she might make a good architect because of her drawing skill, but Morales, who loved sports, particularly competitive swimming, decided to study physical education and psychology at a local university and set her sights on a job as a swimming coach.

One field Morales would never even have been able to imagine was children's book publishing, as she was totally unaware of its existence. "Back in Mexico when I was growing up they didn't really have books for children. It wasn't part of my childhood at all," she recalled to Haldeman. She did, however, have access to the occasional Spanish-language translation of American comic books and graphic novels, and those cemented her love of visual narratives.

COMING TO AMERICA

After her studies, Morales worked for a time as a swim coach. A life-altering point came in 1994, however, when her partner, musician Tim O'Meara, received word that a family member back in San Francisco, California, was ill. They quickly traveled with their infant son, Kelly, to the United States. After marrying and understanding the terms of the visa that had enabled Morales to enter the country, they decided to remain in California. It was a difficult transition for Morales, who spoke only Spanish. "I lived a whole year in my mother-in-law's house and they spoke only English," she told Sue Corbett for *Publishers Weekly* (18 July 2014). "I became terrified of answering the telephone, worried I would not understand what the caller was asking."

Another integral moment in her life came when she discovered the local branch of the San Francisco Public Library. As libraries, particularly in their US form, were not available to her growing up in Mexico, she was immediately taken with the concept. Bringing her son frequently, she took particular delight in the children's section, especially the picture books aimed at four- to eight-year-olds, which featured simple enough language for her to decipher—and illustrations to help her figure out any words she did not know. In interviews, Morales has consistently expressed gratitude for the role that the library, and the librarians who steered her toward the books she came to love and taught her how best to make use of the library, played in her adaptation to life as an immigrant and her eventual career. "It became not just a library. It became a home. It became that place where I wanted to be more than in my own apartment. We could stay there for hours and hours," she explained to Sutton.

When she happened upon a section of instructional volumes on such topics as making homemade paper and bookbinding, an entirely new avenue opened for Morales. She purchased art supplies and began writing stories for the first time and crafting rudimentary books to give herself a voice again while preserving her culture. Ultimately, she enrolled in a continuing-education course offered by the University of California, Berkeley, on creating children's books and subsequently, through connections she made, became a longtime member of a critique group.

ESTABLISHING A CAREER

Morales's peers encouraged her to become affiliated with the Society of Children's Book Writers and Illustrators (SCBWI) and to try for a Don Freeman Grant, a prize meant to fund projects in progress. She sent in a dummy and paintings for a concept that became her book *Just a Minute* for consideration. Gaining further confidence after receiving the grant, she also had some of her work displayed at the organization's annual conference in 2000. There, it caught the eye of Jeannette Larson, an editor at Harcourt.

Larson, impressed by the color and energy of the pieces on display, invited Morales to illustrate a children's biography of the labor leader César Chávez, written by Kathleen Krull. "Illustrating that book opened every door for me and allowed me to start creating my own books," Morales explained to Corbett. Another publisher subsequently purchased the project she had completed with the SCBWI grant; *Just a Minute: A Trickster Tale and Counting Book* was published in 2003, the same year the Chávez book, *Harvesting Hope: The Story of Cesar Chavez*, hit bookstore shelves. In 2004, *Harvesting Hope* was named a Pura Belpré Honor Book for its illustrations, and *Just a Minute* won Morales the first of many Pura Belpré gold medals.

Despite initially working in a cramped apartment studio that could only fit a small drafting table and her chair, Morales went on to produce a steady stream of other books, including those that she both wrote and illustrated as well as those written by other authors to which she contributed her artistic talent. After providing illustrations for Amanda White's *Sand Sister* (2004), she earned her second Pura Belpré Award for illustrating Marisa Montes's *Los Gatos Black on Halloween* (2006), authored and illustrated *Little Night* (2007), and received a third Pura Belpré Award for *Just in Case* (2008). Between 2009 and 2012, the picture books in which her illustrations appeared included *My Abuelita* (2009), by Tony Johnston; *Ladder to the Moon* (2011), by Maya Soetoro-Ng; and *Georgia in Hawaii: When Georgia O'Keeffe Painted What She Pleased* (2012), by Amy Novesky.

GAINING FURTHER RECOGNITION

Among Morales's most beloved efforts have been 2013's *Niño Wrestles the World*, which earned her a fourth Pura Belpré Award and received praise from reviewers for its feisty hero and bold color palette, and 2014's *Viva Frida*. For that biography, she painstakingly handcrafted figurines and props, even laboriously embroidering intricate details onto the Kahlo figure's clothing; creatively staged various vignettes; and had O'Meara photograph them to illustrate the story. "She was very proud of her Mexican heritage, and she showed it in the way she dressed and all sorts of things," Morales told Haldeman, explaining that she had begun to learn more about Kahlo only after coming to the United States. "I didn't know how I felt about my identity as a Mexican woman, and it was her pride that had an impact on me and made me realize that I had

things to be proud of too." Not only did this book garner a fifth Pura Belpré Award for her, but it was also named a Caldecott Honor Book.

Morales has received increased attention, including a sixth Pura Belpré Award, since publishing her 2018 picture book *Dreamers*, which tells the tale of her own immigration to the United States from Mexico in the 1990s with her infant son. Many readers have viewed it as a repudiation of the hard-line anti-immigrant policies of US president Donald Trump, and Morales has affirmed that she wrote and illustrated the work after getting over the shock of the 2016 election. "The next morning, it felt like I'd experienced a bomb or earthquake . . . like my life had crumbled," she recalled in a conversation with book editor Neal Porter for *Publishers Weekly* (16 Aug. 2018). "In so many ways, [Trump] represented the opposite of everything I had worked for and grown into as a children's book author: how we treat others, how we communicate, how we fight against bullying, and how we build our perception of ourselves."

PERSONAL LIFE

Morales married Tim O'Meara. After their son, Kelly, graduated from high school and entered Sarah Lawrence College, Morales returned to Xalapa, where she constructed a work studio, and has since divided her time between Mexico and the United States. Although she has been happy about being back in Mexico, she finds that the libraries in her native country are still sadly lacking. "They don't have anything close to what there is in the United States," she lamented to Sutton. "If you want picture books, middle-grade books, any of those things, you have to go to the bookstore. The culture of libraries here is just starting to grow. It has a long way to go."

SUGGESTED READING

Corbett, Sue. "Yuyi Morales: *PW* Talks with the Award-Winning Illustrator." *Publishers Weekly*, 18 July 2014, www.publishersweekly.com/pw/by-topic/childrens/childrens-authors/article/63359-yuyi-morales.html. Accessed 25 Jan. 2019.

Morales, Yuyi. "Viva Yuyi: An Interview with Yuyi Morales." Interview by David Haldeman. *Humanities Washington*, 30 Mar. 2015, www.humanities.org/blog/viva-yuyi-an-interview-with-yuyi-morales. Accessed 25 Jan. 2019.

Morales, Yuyi. "Yuyi Morales Talks with Roger." Interview by Roger Sutton. *The Horn Book*, 20 Aug. 2018, www.hbook.com/2018/08/authors-illustrators/talks-with-roger/yuyi-morales-talks-roger. Accessed 25 Jan. 2019.

Morales, Yuyi, and Neal Porter. "In Conversation: Yuyi Morales and Neal Porter." *Publishers Weekly*, 16 Aug. 2018, www.publishersweekly.com/pw/by-topic/childrens/childrens-authors/article/77766-in-conversation-yuyi-morales-and-neal-porter.html. Accessed 25 Jan. 2019.

SELECTED WORKS
Harvesting Hope (written by Kathleen Krull), 2003; *Just a Minute*, 2003; *Los Gatos Black on Halloween* (written by Marisa Montes), 2006; *Just in Case*, 2008; *Niño Wrestles the World*, 2013; *Viva Frida*, 2014; *Dreamers*, 2018

—*Mari Rich*

Debbie Mucarsel-Powell

Date of birth: January 18, 1971
Occupation: Politician

The 116th Congress that convened in January 2019 had a record 131 women members across both houses. Among their number was Debbie Mucarsel-Powell, a Democrat who represents Florida's Twenty-Sixth Congressional District, which encompasses southern Miami-Dade County, as well as the Florida Keys, and which is nearly 70 percent Hispanic. She defeated incumbent Republican Carlos Curbelo in the historic midterm, flipping the seat from red to blue and becoming the first South American immigrant (and the first Ecuadorian American) ever to hold a seat in Congress.

"You know, only in a country like ours does an immigrant like myself get to a point where I can run for Congress in one of the most contested races and have a very strong possibility of winning," Mucarsel-Powell told Pamela Avila for the online lifestyle publication *Hello Giggles* (27 Aug. 2018) ahead of the vote. "And it's a testament to who we are as a nation. We can't lose that track and we can't lose our values as Americans."

"Her life story and the district she represents in South Florida—a community on the front lines of rising sea levels—give her a unique set of first-hand experiences with a set of issues the new House Democratic majority is on track to spotlight: gun violence, immigration, and climate change," Clare Foran wrote for *CNN* (4 Feb. 2019).

EARLY YEARS AND EDUCATION
Debbie Jessika Mucarsel-Powell was born on January 18, 1971, in Guayaquil, a large port city in Ecuador that is known as a point of embarkment for cruises to the Galápagos Islands. Her parents, Imelda Gil and Guido Mucarsel Yunes, divorced when she was young. When she was fourteen years old, she came to the United States with her mother and her three older sisters.

The four settled in a one-bedroom apartment in Southern California, and Imelda worked

Photo by United States Congress via Wikimedia Commons

double shifts as a home health aide most days while studying English at night. At age fifteen, Mucarsel-Powell began working at a local doughnut shop to help the family financially. Despite the hardships, they were confident that they had made the correct choice. "Even though at the beginning it was very difficult, we were welcomed in a way that I think we didn't expect," she recalled to Foran, "and we called this place our home quickly after that."

Back in Ecuador, Mucarsel-Powell had attended La Moderna, a primary school devoted to bilingual instruction, and once in California, she entered Pomona Catholic High School, an all-girl's institution. Upon graduating from high school in 1988, she gained admission to Pitzer College, in the Southern California town of Claremont. In 1992 she earned her bachelor's degree in political science and remained in the area to attend Claremont Graduate University.

While she was in graduate school, Mucarsel-Powell got a call from one of her sisters: their father, a businessman who had remained back in Ecuador, had been shot and killed outside his home in Urdesa Norte. "It was a very traumatic experience. It changed all of us," she told Foran. "You never forget. You learn to live with it, but you don't forget." Later, during a political ad she recorded in support of her congressional run, she said, "He never walked me down the aisle. My children never met their grandfather. My sisters and I never had the chance to say goodbye."

Mucarsel-Powell earned her master's degree in international political economy in 1996, having worked as an office manager for a shipping company to help pay her tuition.

EDUCATIONAL AND NONPROFIT MANAGEMENT CAREER

Mucarsel-Powell initially embarked on a career in the management of educational and nonprofit institutions. From 2000 to 2003, for example, she served as the associate director of development for corporate and individual giving at the Zoological Society of Florida (now called the Zoo Miami Foundation), and she subsequently joined the staff at Florida International University, a large research university in Miami. There she directed the development office until 2007, when she was tapped to become an associate dean at the university's Herbert Wertheim College of Medicine. During her tenure at the medical school, she helped fund an initiative called Neighborhood Help, which sent students into poor, underserved areas of the city in mobile clinics to provide primary care.

She became dismayed by seeing the many ways in which politicians set up roadblocks to make it harder to get a good education and reliable healthcare. "I've had my share of dealing with elected officials," she told Avila of that stage of her career. "What I continued to see was that elected officials in government positions were making it harder for these nonprofit organizations to do what they had to do."

POLITICAL CAREER

In 2016, frustrated, Mucarsel-Powell made a bid to represent District 39 in the Florida State Senate, running against a Republican incumbent who had advocated for severe budgets cuts to the state's education system. She had only three months to campaign because she filed late, however, and was ultimately unsuccessful. Still, she considered it to be an invaluable learning experience. "I didn't completely understand the politics of the different communities that are part of this district," she admitted to Avila. "Time is definitely always going to be helpful when you run because you need to establish close relationships with people that live in your community so that they understand who you are, what you stand for, and what you're going to do. Campaigning is not easy, and you really do need to earn people's trust, you need to earn their votes."

It was a lesson she drew upon when making her 2018 run to replace US Representative Carlos Curbelo, a Republican who had positioned himself as a moderate: willing to stand up to President Donald Trump on the issue of climate change and able to work with both political parties. His avowed moderation did not sway Mucarsel-Powell, who believed that Curbelo sided with the Trump administration on too many other issues. "When he voted to repeal the Affordable Care Act—in that moment, when I saw how arrogant he was to turn his back to his community, to take away all care for more than 100,000 people—that was the moment I knew I had to step in," she asserted to Avila. "That was the day I made the decision to run for Congress."

To those who considered her a political neophyte, she pointed out how much she had learned from her 2016 campaign and her many years of experience as a volunteer, working on the campaigns of several Democratic politicians, including John Kerry and Barack Obama. "People think I'm some random woman Democrat who decided to run in the 'Year of the Woman,'" Mucarsel-Powell told Lesley Clark for *McClatchy Washington Bureau* (5 Oct. 2018), referring to the record number of female candidates in the 2018 midterms. "But I've been doing this work for twenty years."

She easily defeated established politician Demetries Grimes in the Democratic Party primary, receiving 64 percent of the vote, and soon garnered strong testimonials from such high-profile figures as Obama and former vice president Joe Biden; she was also backed by EMILY's List, which endorses women candidates with progressive agendas.

Although political insiders considered Curbelo to be ahead for much of the race, with the help of a series of bilingual radio and television ads—which hammered home his vote to repeal Obamacare to its 90,000 recipients in the district—Mucarsel-Powell made headway, and on November 6, she defeated her opponent with 50.9 percent of the vote.

Upon taking her oath of office on January 3, 2019, Mucarsel-Powell got to work on the issues she had announced as important to her, including immigration. "This president [Trump] ran on criminalizing immigrants and instilling fear in Americans that immigrants are criminals, that we want to take people's jobs away, that we will commit heinous crimes," she told Avila. "And the reality is, it's just not true. Immigrants who come here are coming to the U.S. because they're fleeing violence in their own countries, and they're looking for an opportunity to just make it for their kids. My community relies heavily on immigrants. Half the people who live in Miami today were born in a different country. And they are our teachers, our nurses, our doctors." She vowed to bring attention to the underlying crises throughout Central and South America that were causing people to flee and has called for increased humanitarian aid to those places.

Given her father's death by gunfire—and spurred by the deadly mass shooting in Las Vegas that occurred soon after she launched her campaign—she has also made gun control a signature issue, and climate change ranks as yet another priority. Acknowledging that areas of her district like the Keys and the Everglades are at grave risk of flooding due to rising sea levels, Mucarsel-Powell explained to Foran: "We are ground zero for the effects of climate change in my district. We only have about ten to twelve years to change the direction that we're taking as it relates to climate change. We have to be bold. We have to be aggressive. There is no other way."

Mucarsel-Powell is a member of the House Judiciary Committee and its Subcommittee on Crime, Terrorism, and Homeland Security and Subcommittee on Immigration and Citizenship. Additionally, she sits on the Transportation and Infrastructure Committee and is a member of both the Water Resources and Environment Subcommittee and the Economic Development, Public Buildings, and Emergency Management Subcommittee. As for serving with the other women who are members of the 116th Congress, she told Foran, "There's definitely a sense of sisterhood. A lot of us are becoming good friends and helping each other and supporting each other—even when we disagree."

PERSONAL LIFE

Mucarsel-Powell and her husband, attorney Robert Powell, have three children: Willow, Jude, and Siena. During her campaign, opponents cited her husband's job, as general counsel for a ferro-alloys trading corporation affiliated with wealthy Ukrainian businessman Igor Kolomoisky, as evidence of nefarious ties, but the charge did not stick.

SUGGESTED READING

Avila, Pamela. "Debbie Mucarsel-Powell Lost Her Father to Gun Violence, and Now She's Fighting for a Better America." *Hello Giggles*, 27 Aug. 2018, hellogiggles.com/news/politics/shes-running-debbie-mucarsel-powell-florida/. Accessed 10 Feb. 2019.

Bradner, Eric. "This Congressional District Is Drowning. Will Voters Choose a Republican to Save It?" *CNN*, 15 Oct. 2018, www.cnn.com/2018/10/15/politics/florida-carlos-curbelo-house-district-climate-change/index.html. Accessed 10 Feb. 2019.

Clark, Lesley. "Citing Health Care, Debbie Mucarsel-Powell Wants to Be Part of Florida's Blue Wave." *McClatchy Washington Bureau*, 5 Oct. 2018, www.mcclatchydc.com/latest-news/article219016890.html. Accessed 10 Feb. 2019.

Daugherty, Alex, and Jimena Tavel. "Democrat Debbie Mucarsel-Powell Defeats Republican Carlos Curbelo." *Miami Herald*, 6 Nov. 2018, www.miamiherald.com/news/politics-government/article220860675.html. Accessed 10 Feb. 2019.

Foran, Clare. "Debbie Mucarsel-Powell Is an Immigrant Who Lost Her Father to Gun Violence. Now She's in Congress." *CNN*, 4 Feb. 2019, www.cnn.com/2019/02/04/politics/debbie-mucarsel-powell-barrier-breakers/index.html. Accessed 10 Feb. 2019.

Gloriosa, Alexandra. "Mucarsel-Powell Ousts Florida Republican Curbelo." *Politico*, 6 Nov. 2018, www.politico.com/states/florida/story/2018/11/06/mucarsel-powell-takes-cd26-for-democrats-685165. Accessed 10 Feb. 2019.

Herman, Elizabeth D., and Celeste Sloman. "Redefining Representation: The Women of the 116th Congress." *The New York Times*, 14 Jan. 2019, www.nytimes.com/interactive/2019/01/14/us/politics/women-of-the-116th-congress.html. Accessed 10 Feb. 2019.

—*Mari Rich*

Ryan Murphy

Date of birth: November 9, 1965
Occupation: Screenwriter and director

Ryan Murphy is a writer, producer, and director of feature films and television series. His television series are known for defying conventions and presenting controversial issues. His best-known television series are *Glee* and *American Horror Story*.

EARLY LIFE AND EDUCATION

Ryan Murphy was born in 1965 in Indianapolis, Indiana, to Jim Murphy, a newspaper circulation manager, and Jeannine "Andy" Murphy, a writer. He grew up in Indianapolis and attended Warren Central High School, where he joined the school choir and newspaper staff and performed in school plays and musicals. When he was fifteen, he came out to his parents and has been openly gay ever since.

After graduating from high school in 1983, he attended Indiana University in Bloomington. Again, he worked on the school newspaper and sang in the university's choir. During the summer following his freshman year, he interned at the *Knoxville News-Sentinel*, covering fashion. He graduated from Indiana University with a degree in journalism.

CAREER IN TELEVISION AND FILM

Murphy began his career as a journalist working for newspaper companies. He was an intern for the *Washington Post* and the *Miami Herald*, then he moved to Los Angeles, California, and worked for the *Los Angeles Times* and *Entertainment Weekly*. He also contributed articles to *Rolling Stone*.

In his free time, Murphy wrote screenplays. He sold his first script, *Why Can't I Be Audrey Hepburn*, in 1995. The script bounced between production companies, but it was never made into a film. In 1999 he created his first television series, *Popular*, a teen comedy that explored the tensions between different groups of students in a high school setting. He was the executive producer of the series and wrote most of the episodes. The series ran for two seasons before being canceled. In 2002, he wrote the screenplay for the television drama *St. Sass*.

Murphy's next television series was *Nip/Tuck* (2003), a drama that explored people's obsession with their appearance and the tensions between medical ethics and monetary pursuits experienced by two plastic surgeons. It dealt with many controversial issues and included blatant sexuality and graphic content, oftentimes pushing against—and beyond—the conventional boundaries of television. *Nip/Tuck* attracted an avid following, with many fans hooked by the over-the-top storylines and characters. Murphy was the executive producer and wrote and directed many of the episodes. He was nominated for an Emmy Award for his role as director in 2004. The series won the 2005 Golden Globe Award for best television drama series and the 2004 and 2005 American Film Institute (AFI) Awards for television program of the year. It ran for seven seasons, until 2010.

Murphy's feature film, *Running with Scissors*, an offbeat comedy drama based on a memoir by Augusten Burroughs, was released in 2006. He was both its director and screenwriter. The movie was generally panned by critics, but several of the film's actors were nominated for their performances, and Murphy won the 2006 Hollywood Breakthrough Award for his directing.

His next television series proved to be a huge hit with audiences, especially young viewers. *Glee*, which premiered in 2009, was a musical comedy about high school students. Inspired by many of Murphy's own experiences in high school, it included a cast of misfit students and an ambitious glee club director who was determined to create a stellar glee club. The show regularly explored issues facing lesbian, gay, bisexual, and transgender (LGBT) students and the need for acceptance. The series developed a cult following and ran for six seasons, ending in 2015. Murphy was the director and screenwriter. The series won the Gay and Lesbian Alliance Against Defamation (GLAAD) Media Award for outstanding comedy series in 2010 and the AFI award for TV program of the year in 2010 and 2011. Murphy received an Emmy Award for outstanding directing of a comedy series for *Glee* in 2010. The show, its cast, and crew were nominated and won a great number of awards.

Murphy's next film project was *Eat Pray Love* (2010), a drama starring Julia Roberts, Javier Bardem, and Richard Jenkins. He and Jennifer Salt cowrote the screenplay, based on a memoir by Elizabeth Gilbert. Murphy also directed the film. The movie was well received and grossed more than $200 million worldwide.

The comedy series, *The New Normal*, appeared in 2012 and was cocreated and written by Murphy. The series portrayed different types of families, including those with same-sex partners and a single parent. It was unsuccessful and canceled after one season.

Pioneering the anthology format, *American Horror Story* (2011) included an ever-changing cast of evil characters, including witches, ghosts, nymphomaniacs, and freaks, who commit depraved and ludicrous acts. Although only a handful of characters appeared in every episode, the rotating cast and guest stars included big-name celebrities such as Lady Gaga and Stevie Nicks. Murphy wrote most of the episodes and directed a small number of them. The series became immensely popular and garnered numerous award nominations. The show finished its fifth season in January 2016 and a sixth season is expected.

In 2014, Murphy directed *The Normal Heart*, a television movie about gay activist Ned Weeks's efforts to draw attention to the burgeoning HIV/AIDS epidemic in the early 1980s. It won the 2014 Emmy Award for outstanding television movie and the 2014 Critics' Choice Television Award for best movie.

The horror comedy *Scream Queens*, Murphy's second anthology series, appeared in 2015 with the true-crime anthology series *American Crime Story* following in 2016.

IMPACT

Ryan Murphy has produced creative works that expose viewers to ideas and content seldom covered in other television formats. Unafraid to push the envelope, he has shown a range of characters from despicable murderers to sensitive teenagers who just want acceptance. In 2013, the Gay and Lesbian Entertainment Critics Association honored Murphy by naming him the Wilde Artist of the Year in recognition of his work to break stereotypes about gay and lesbian individuals.

PERSONAL LIFE

Murphy married photographer David Miller in 2012. They have two young children, Logan and Ford.

SUGGESTED READING

Nusshaum, Emily. "Queer Eyes, Full Heart." *New Yorker*, 26 Nov. 2012, www.newyorker.com/magazine/2012/11/26/queer-eyes-full-heart. Accessed 27 Sept. 2019.

Rose, Lacey. "Ryan Murphy's Professional Highs and Personal Lows: 'I Don't Want to Be That Person Anymore.'" *Hollywood Reporter*, 14 Oct. 2015, www.hollywoodreporter.com/features/ryan-murphys-professional-highs-personal-831587. Accessed 27 Sept. 2019.

"Ryan Murphy." *Bio*. A&E Television Networks, www.biography.com/people/ryan-murphy-20874367.

—*Barb Lightner*

Saina Nehwal

Date of birth: March 17, 1990
Occupation: Badminton player

Saina Nehwal became the first Indian badminton player to win an Olympic medal when she won bronze at the 2012 Olympic Games in London. In 2015, she was the first Indian woman to be ranked number one in the world in the sport. Though she was knocked out of the 2016 Olympic Games in Rio de Janeiro early due to a knee injury, a spectacular finals victory against rival Indian player PV Sindhu at the Commonwealth Games in 2018 earned her the award for Comeback of the Year from the ESPN India Awards in 2019.

Badminton has increased in popularity in India, and since her teens, Nehwal has played a significant part as one of the sport's most prominent stars. Her parents were badminton players, and she decided to take up the sport herself after her family moved to Hyderabad when she was eight years old. Just around ten years after picking up a racket, she won a gold medal at the Commonwealth Youth Games and was named the most promising player of the year by the Badminton World Federation (BWF). From there, her star only continued to rise. Even as she has grown as a player and experienced numerous successes, she has mostly shied away from the limelight. "I am just a humble badminton player who wants to make India proud," she explained to Zaral Shah for the Indian lifestyle magazine *Verve* (5 June 2017).

EARLY LIFE AND EDUCATION

Nehwal was born in the northwestern Indian state of Haryana on March 17, 1990, and spent her early childhood in Hisar, India. Both her father, a scientist, and her mother were accomplished badminton players. When she was eight years old, her father accepted a new position and the family, which also included her older sister, moved to Hyderabad in southern India. Without her friends and unfamiliar with the regional language, Telugu, she was lonely, and she threw herself into sports. When karate became too intense, she tried badminton. Initially, she saw badminton as merely another activity. "At that

Photo by Bollywood Hungama via Wikimedia Commons

time, neither I nor my parents knew that I would end up playing badminton professionally. I used to see my parents playing it, I often held the racquet," she recalled to Shraddha Jahagirdar-Saxena for *Verve* (15 Aug. 2010). "When I started, my first stroke was a smash. I was very aggressive." After proving herself at a summer camp at the local Lal Bahadur Shastri Stadium, she earned the opportunity to receive further training.

With the encouragement of her mother, Nehwal began to take the sport more seriously and pushed through the challenges of the physically demanding training. "I would get up at 4 am and catch a bus at 4:30 am for the stadium 25 km away," she told Jahagirdar-Saxena. Meanwhile, she also attempted to juggle her studies. "I would skip the last two periods of school and practise till seven or eight. I often slept in the bus or even on the scooter," she added to Jahagirdar-Saxena. In 1999, she won her first under-ten tournament, which was at the district level, in Tirupati.

Badminton increasingly became Nehwal's priority, and her family eventually moved closer to the stadium. They accommodated her training in other ways, too, with her father borrowing money and even dipping into his retirement savings to finance her dream in the days before sponsorship. As she expressed to Nilima Pathak for *Friday* (28 Mar. 2013), her parents have been tireless supporters of her athletic career: "My family sacrificed a lot so I could pursue my passion."

EARLY CAREER

Nehwal, working her way through tournaments and events at a variety of levels from district to international, trained with well-known coach

Syed Mohammad Arif until he retired in 2004. She then began working with former Indian badminton superstar Pullela Gopichand. Meanwhile, despite having to miss a fair amount of class time, she also found support from teachers and managed to pass her class 10 exams. However, as balancing the rigors of competing with studying had become too difficult, she stopped attending school after class 11.

In 2005, Stan Rayan, writing for *The Hindu* (20 July 2005), described Nehwal as a "teen wonder" and speculated that one day her talent might surpass that of her famous mentor. In 2006, she took home a bronze medal in the badminton mixed team event at the 2006 Commonwealth Games. That same year, in addition to proving victorious at the Philippines Open, making her the first Indian woman to win a four-star badminton tournament, she became India's under-nineteen national champion and won her second Asian Satellite Badminton tournament. Off the court, she was made a brand ambassador for the "Save the Girl Child" campaign in India, which seeks to eradicate female infanticide and dangerous gender bias against girls.

At the 2008 Olympics in Beijing, she became the first Indian woman to make it to the quarterfinal in the singles event. However, she was disappointed. "I thought, for just a few seconds, that my god, I'm so close to winning this!" she recalled to Rudraneil Sengupta for the newspaper *Mint* (12 Apr. 2012). "And that's when it all went wrong. I got too tense and too excited, and I lost." Used to experiencing and learning from both wins and losses, later that year she won a gold medal in the women's singles event at the Commonwealth Youth Games. She also became the first Indian to win the BWF World Junior Badminton Championships, which took place in Pune, India. The BWF named her the most promising player of 2008.

2012 OLYMPIC GAMES

In 2009, Nehwal won the Indonesia Open, becoming the first Indian to win a BWF Super Series tournament. Ranked eighth in the world, she bested Chinese shuttler Wang Lin, ranked third, for the title in a match that lasted forty-nine minutes. The following year, she won the India Open Grand Prix Gold, the Singapore Open Super Series, and the Hong Kong Super Series in addition to defending her title at the Indonesia Open. She also claimed a bronze medal at the Badminton Asia Championships. By the beginning of July 2010, she was ranked third in the world. "This did not come easily," she told Amarnath K. Menon for *India Today* magazine (3 July 2010). "Along with my coach I have worked really hard to reach here. If I can be No. 3, I have it in me to be No.1." For her achievements, she was given the Rajiv Gandhi Khel Ratna award, the highest sporting honor in India. In October, she beat Malaysian player Wong Mew Choo to win gold in the women's singles event at the Commonwealth Games. After she won the Swiss Open Grand Prix Gold, she was runner-up at the Malaysia Open Grand Prix Gold and Indonesia Open in 2011. However, she struggled to achieve the heights she had reached during her previous season. In addition to winning the Indonesia Open for the third time in 2012, she came out on top at the Denmark Open Super Series Premier later in the year.

Still hoping to fulfill her dream of an Olympic medal, Nehwal competed in the 2012 Olympic Games in London. She was hoping to win the gold medal but lost the semifinal to China's Wang Yihan. She faced Wang Xin of China in a match for the bronze. Nehwal had defeated Wang Xin in the past, but this particular victory was a bit of an anticlimax. Wang Xin conceded the match after injuring her knee, and Nehwal, securing the bronze, earned even greater national acclaim by becoming the first Indian badminton player to win a medal at the Olympics. Shortly after, she published an autobiography titled *Playing to Win: My Life . . . On and Off Court* (2012).

INJURY AND COMEBACK

In 2014, Nehwal won the Australian Badminton Open Super Series, but she made the difficult decision to pull out of the Commonwealth Games in Glasgow, Scotland, and leave her title undefended due to multiple injuries that foreshadowed further physical trials to come. Meanwhile, rumors spread that the relationship between Nehwal and her longtime coach, Gopichand, had curdled. That same year, she moved to Bangalore to train at the Prakash Padukone Badminton Academy with former national champion Vimal Kumar. In early 2015, she became the first Indian woman to play in the finals of the All England Open, where she ultimately lost to Carolina Marin of Spain. Regardless, thanks to her accumulated accolades, she officially reached number one in the women's singles world ranking in early April. Though Marin defeated her once more at the 2015 BWF World Championships, she walked away with a silver medal.

Nehwal won the Australian Badminton Open Super Series in 2016, but otherwise, her season was defined by her injured knee. In a major upset, she was out of the running for a medal early at the Olympic Games in Rio de Janeiro. Later that month, she underwent knee surgery in Mumbai. After some recovery, in 2017 she logged a victory at the Malaysia Masters Grand Prix Gold and won a bronze medal at the BWF World Championships in Glasgow. In September of that year, she announced that she was returning to Hyderabad to train with her former coach, Gopichand.

In April 2018, Nehwal bested her rival, PV Sindhu, in the final of the Commonwealth Games in Australia. Sindhu was training with Nehwal's coach, Gopichand, and had become the second Indian woman, after Nehwal, to win an Olympic medal when she won silver in Rio in 2016. At the 2018 Asian Games, Nehwal made further history by becoming the first Indian woman to claim a medal—a bronze—at that tournament. Such impressive feats earned her ESPN India's award for Comeback of the Year in 2019. Kumar, her former coach, attributed her resurgence to her fighting spirit. "You have to appreciate her resolve to persist and get in some good results. She's a good example for the younger lot of how to deal with adversity," he told Susan Ninan for *ESPN* (6 Apr. 2019). "She tends to over-train but at the end of the day that's who she is and maybe that's what's gotten her so far."

PERSONAL LIFE
Nehwal married longtime boyfriend and fellow shuttler Parupalli Kashyap in Hyderabad in December 2018. The two met during training.

SUGGESTED READING
Jahagirdar-Saxena, Shraddha. "Super Saina." *Verve*, 15 Aug. 2010, www.vervemagazine.in/people/super-saina-nehwal. Accessed 8 Apr. 2019.

Menon, Amarnath K. "Smash Hit." *India Today*, 3 July 2010, www.indiatoday.in/magazine/cover-story/story/20100712-smash-hit-743381-2010-07-03. Accessed 9 Apr. 2019.

Nehwal, Saina. "Inspirational Icons: Saina Nehwal." Interview by Zaral Shah. *Verve*, 5 June 2017, www.vervemagazine.in/people/inspirational-icons-saina-nehwal-badminton-player. Accessed 8 Apr. 2019.

Ninan, Susan. "Saina Nehwal's Stellar 2018 Shows What She's Made Of." *ESPN*, 6 Apr. 2019, www.espn.com/badminton/story/_/id/26453545/espn-india-awards-2018-comeback-year-saina-nehwal. Accessed 8 Apr. 2019.

Rayan, Stan. "Saina Nehwal—Female Version of Gopi Chand." *The Hindu*, 20 July 2005, www.thehindu.com/2005/07/20/stories/2005072007131800.htm. Accessed 8 Apr. 2019.

Sengupta, Rudraneil. "'I See the Medal, and I Want It.'" *Mint*, 12 Apr. 2012, www.livemint.com/Leisure/rguu8xbDE6b8m0ZK9WON0H/I-see-the-medal-and-I-want-it.html. Accessed 8 Apr. 2019.

—*Molly Hagan*

Amanda Nguyen
Date of birth: 1991
Occupation: Activist

Rise CEO Amanda Nguyen founded the survivor-led civil rights organization dedicated to passing state and federal laws that protect survivors of sexual assault. The passionate activist was the driving force behind the Sexual Assault Survivors' Rights Act, passed by Congress and signed into law by President Barack Obama in 2016. Nguyen explained to Alanna Vagianos for *HuffPost* (20 July 2018), "Every time a survivor tells me his or her story it is like they are handing over a coal. It is a weight I carry but also it keeps my fire to fight alive."

For her efforts, Nguyen has been much commended. *Marie Claire* recognized her among their inaugural Young Women's Honors in 2016, and *Foreign Policy* also cited her as one of their 100 Leading Global Thinkers. In 2017 she was named in *Forbes* magazine's list of 30 Under 30 in the area of law and policy. She told Brooke Hauser for *Marie Claire* (2016), "The most important thing is just showing up. People don't realize how powerful their own voices can be. We asked people to call or tweet at their member of Congress. Elected officials see that, and it makes a difference." Her work has the potential to aid the millions of survivors of sexual assault in the United States.

EDUCATION AND EARLY CAREER
Nguyen was born in 1991 to parents who were refugees from Vietnam. From childhood, Nguyen wanted to become an astronaut. After graduation from high school in 2009, she went on to earn a Bachelor of Arts degree in astrophysics at Harvard University in 2013. While in college she also cofounded Wema Children, a Kenyan orphanage. Interested in the issue of sex trafficking, she created the first course in modern slavery written by a student.

Nguyen interned with the National Aeronautics and Space Administration (NASA) as part of their efforts to interest young people in space travel. For an article requesting advice for eighteen-year-olds, she told Sharon Attia for *New York Times* (26 Oct. 2018), "So often girls are told no. No, you can't do this or be this because society says you need to fulfill certain conditions. Well, to that I say, prove them wrong. If you work hard enough, you're just as good as anyone else."

TURNING POINT
When Nguyen was a senior at Harvard, another college student raped her. After leaving the hospital where she had gone to complete a rape kit (a collection of physical evidence gathered after a sexual assault allegation, including bodily

Photo by House Judiciary Committee Hearings via Wikimedia Commons

civil rights. As she told Neesha Arter for *Women in the World* (4 Feb. 2016), "This movement is grounded in the belief that the voices of ordinary citizens matter—no matter the background, no matter the age. That's why it is named Rise—to remind us that a small group of thoughtful, committed citizens can rise up and change the world." A petition Nguyen started on Change. org, urging Congress to support basic rights for rape survivors, garnered 140,000 signatures. Eventually, some of the money the group raised on crowdfunding sites like *GoFundMe* allowed twenty survivors to fly to Washington, DC, to share their stories with members of Congress.

WRITING SURVIVORS' RIGHTS INTO LAW

Nguyen solicited help from her friends and professors to draft the text of a bill to protect all survivors. Volunteers at Rise first studied existing state and federal laws and searched for best practices. They also created financial metrics to demonstrate that the proposed legislation would benefit districts financially. Within two months, in January 2015, the group had convinced members of the Massachusetts state legislature to introduce a bill for survivors' rights. Twenty-five legislators cosponsored the bill.

What followed was a hard slog. On one occasion in 2016, Nguyen, who had moved to Washington, DC, to work for the State Department, was set to fly back to Massachusetts because her bill was about to be voted on in the state house of representatives. At the last minute, her team told her the bill would probably not be brought up for a vote, because there were too many others ahead of it. She nearly canceled her flight, telling Alex Ronan for *Yahoo! News* (28 Oct. 2016), "I just thought to myself, 'Why should I even go? Why would I watch my own civil rights be slaughtered on the floor of the House?'"

Nguyen's Rise colleagues, however, encouraged her to make the trip. She and her team in Massachusetts spent fourteen hours that weekend talking to anyone at the state legislature who would listen. She told Ronan, "We walked in like, 'Hi, my name is blank, and I want to talk to you about this bill that really means a lot to me. It's about rape survivors, and I am a rape survivor.'" The bill was ultimately brought to a vote and passed in the House and later in the Senate. Nguyen observed, "There's nothing more powerful than hearing it straight from the people it has affected. We pushed the boundaries from a 0 percent chance to a 100 percent chance in 14 hours." Massachusetts governor Charlie Baker signed the bill into law on October 19, 2016. It ensures that forensic evidence from rape kits are preserved for the duration of the state's fifteen-year statute of limitations for rape cases, meaning Nguyen no longer has to file for an extension for her rape kit every six months.

fluids, hair, clothing fibers, and other items) and to obtain drugs to protect her from contracting HIV, Nguyen determined not to allow the event to keep her from graduating.

After her traumatic experience, Nguyen learned about other unpleasant legal realities for sexual assault survivors. Although the statute of limitations in Massachusetts for rape cases is fifteen years, a brochure Nguyen received leaving the hospital noted that her rape kit and its evidence could be destroyed in six months unless she filed an extension request, for which no instructions were given. In addition, when she contacted an advocacy center, Nguyen learned that if she identified her attacker and went to court, the judicial process could take up to two years. Rather than put her career on hold, Nguyen chose to postpone legal action, meaning she has had to file for an extension twice a year since then—not a simple process—to ensure her rape kit is preserved. "Twice a year, I'm reminded about my rape," she told Tracy Jan for the *Boston Globe* (7 Apr. 2016). "This six-month deadline reorients my life to the date of the rape."

Nguyen further discovered that standards for keeping rape kits varied from state to state. Some states keep the kits for only thirty days. Additional variations occur in the statute of limitations for pressing charges in rape cases. And in some states, it is difficult or impossible for survivors to gain access to their own medical information, such as the results of blood tests from their rape kit.

In response to all this, in November 2014 Nguyen founded the nonprofit organization Rise, a group of millennials devoting their time and energy to ensuring rape survivors have full

SURVIVORS' BILL OF RIGHTS ACT

Simultaneously, Nguyen and Rise pursued a bill of rights for sexual assault survivors at the federal level. She found support from a Democratic senator from New Hampshire, Jeanne Shaheen, who became the primary sponsor of the bill in the Senate. In the House of Representatives, Florida Democrat Debbie Wasserman Schultz championed the bill. It included only rights that existed in at least one state; no new legal steps needed to be written. It included nothing controversial, such as emergency contraception. Supporters included the Innocence Project, which advocates for those accused of sexual assault, because DNA evidence from rape kits can exonerate as well as convict someone.

As Nguyen told Vagianos, "We wrote this bill of rights not just to help survivors, but to help police officers, prosecutors, and the judicial system better do their jobs, and as a result, both survivors and our criminal justice system are able to seek the justice they deserve."

With high-profile support from celebrities like actor Terry Crews, the bill went on to achieve an extreme rarity in partisan Washington: unanimous passage in both the House and the Senate. President Barack Obama signed the Survivors' Bill of Rights Act into law on October 7, 2016, almost two weeks before the Massachusetts bill became law. With similar provisions about preserving rape kits and other victims' rights, the federal Survivors' Bill of Rights applies to federal cases, meaning those that take place across state lines, in the military, on federal land, or in other areas of federal jurisdiction. Nguyen and Rise have a goal of getting similar laws passed in all fifty states; by the end of 2018, nineteen states had done so.

FURTHER WORK

Nguyen has expanded her vision to focus on rape as a global issue. The latest Rise campaign is a push for the United Nations to adopt a Worldwide Survivors' Bill of Rights as a resolution. Their goal is to achieve a vote during the 2019 General Assembly session.

In 2018, two congressional representatives from California, Mimi Walters and Zoe Lofgren, nominated Nguyen for the 2018 Nobel Peace Prize, citing her "unprecedented efforts in bringing equal protection under the law and basic human rights to all survivors of sexual assault, regardless of geography." Responding to the nomination, Nguyen told Vagianos, "I was overwhelmed with shock, happiness, and pride. Because I knew that this nomination was not just for me, it was for the millions of survivors that have seen their civil rights penned into law." Ultimately, the prize went to two others working in sexual assault survivors' rights, Yazidi activist Nadia Murad and Congolese gynecologist Dr. Denis Mukwege.

Nguyen has also traveled to Florida to view six rocket launches into space. In her spare time, she builds model rockets and maintains a collection of meteorites. Her NASA goal is to become a mission specialist and to discover an exoplanet.

PERSONAL LIFE

Nguyen has experienced prejudice against her because of her Asian heritage. As she told Vagianos, "Asian American women are subject to hyper-sexualization which contributes to sexual violence. Yellow fever, the objectification of Asian female bodies and the stereotype that Asian women are submissive, is an example of this. The exotification of our bodies dehumanizes us and that dehumanization creates a greater chance for sexual violence."

In her Washington, DC, apartment, Nguyen has a large poster of Frida Kahlo, the famed Mexican artist who transformed the pain in her life into beauty.

SUGGESTED READING

Arter, Neesha. "Navigating the Broken System Was Worse Than the Rape Itself." *Women in the World*, 4 Feb. 2016, womenintheworld.com/2016/02/04/amanda-nguyen-is-taking-the-fight-for-sexual-violence-survivors-civil-rights-all-the-way-to-the-white-house. Accessed 9 Apr. 2019.

Hauser, Brooke. "The Unstoppables: Meet the Winners of Our First-Ever Young Women's Honors." *Marie Claire*, 12 Dec. 2016, www.marieclaire.com/culture/a24040/marie-claires-young-womens-honors/#amanda-nguyen. Accessed 9 Apr. 2019.

Huetteman, Emmarie. "Advocates Praise Senate Bill on Sexual Assault Victims' Rights." *The New York Times*, 24 May 2016, www.nytimes.com/2016/05/25/us/politics/advocates-praise-senate-bill-on-sexual-assault-victims-rights.html. Accessed 9 Apr. 2019.

Luhar, Monica. "'30 Under 30' Honoree Amanda Nguyen Is Fighting for Sexual Assault Survivors' Rights." *NBC News*, 2 Feb. 2017, www.nbcnews.com/news/asian-america/30-under-30-honoree-amanda-nguyen-fighting-sexual-assault-survivors-n715661. Accessed 9 Apr. 2019.

Nguyen, Amanda. "The Lenny Interview: Amanda Nguyen." Interview by Alex Ronan. *Yahoo! News*, 28 Oct. 2016, www.yahoo.com/news/lenny-interview-amanda-nguyen-160543674.html. Accessed 9 Apr. 2018.

Vagianos, Alanna. "The Rape Survivor Who Turned Her Activism into a Nobel Prize Nomination." *HuffPost*, 20 July 2018, www.huffpost.com/entry/rape-survivor-nobel-peace-prize-nomination_n_5b51e9a8e4b0fd5c73c49f7f. Accessed 9 Apr. 2018.

Williams, Rich. "In Pursuit of Justice." *State Legislatures*, vol. 43, no. 4, Apr. 2017, www.ncsl.

org/bookstore/state-legislatures-magazine/
state-lawmakers-work-with-sexual-assault-
survivors-to-fix-criminal-justice-system.aspx.
Accessed 9 Apr. 2018.

—*Judy Johnson*

Rachel Nichols

Date of birth: October 18, 1973
Occupation: Sports journalist

With her infectious enthusiasm for sports, reporter and television host Rachel Nichols became a popular figure among fans as well as
many of the athletes, coaches, and other figures
she covered. However, it was Nichols's unre-
lenting approach to her job and her fearless, no-
nonsense style of interviewing that helped her
earn a reputation as one of the most respected
professionals in the US sports media. Known
for asking tough but fair questions, Nichols has
gone toe-to-toe with some of the biggest names
in sports over the course of her career.

Initially a sports reporter for newspapers including the *Washington Post*, Nichols was hired
by the television channel ESPN in 2004. During the following nine years, she was a constant
presence on the network, providing coverage for
National Basketball Association (NBA) and National Football League (NFL) broadcasts. She
appeared regularly on such flagship programs as
SportsCenter and served as a sideline reporter on
Monday Night Football. In 2013 Nichols moved
to CNN, where she hosted her own acclaimed
show, *Unguarded with Rachel Nichols*, and
covered the NBA and Major League Baseball
(MLB) for sister networks TNT and TBS. She
returned to ESPN in 2016 to host *The Jump*, a
daily afternoon NBA talk show.

EARLY LIFE AND EDUCATION
Nichols was born Rachel Michele Alexander on
October 18, 1973, in Phoenix, Arizona. She grew
up in Potomac, Maryland, a suburb of Washington, DC. Her father, Ronald, was an attorney;
her mother, Jane, was an associate director
with the National Institute of Mental Health in
Bethesda, Maryland.

From an early age, Nichols developed a
strong passion for sports. As a child she played
soccer and was also involved in figure skating.
However, she was even more interested in following her hometown NBA, NFL, and National
Hockey League (NHL) teams. She was particularly drawn to the unpredictable nature of sports.
"I loved the storytelling of it," Nichols recalled in
a self-penned 2014 piece for the Shirley Povich
Center for Journalism. "For me it was like watching a movie, but it was happening live in front of

Photo by George Gojkovich/Getty Images

you, with heroes and villains, challenges to be
overcome and a beginning-middle-and-end."

It was this storytelling aspect that drew
Nichols to the idea of becoming a sports journalist. She became an avid reader of the *Washington
Post*'s sports section and idolized the trailblazing
sports reporter Christine Brennan, who in 1985
became the first woman to ever hold that paper's
NFL beat. Taking after Brennan (later the national sports columnist for *USA Today*) Nichols
wrote for the sports page for both her junior high
and high school newspapers. The summer after
she graduated from Winston Churchill High
School, in Potomac, in 1991, she interned with
the sports desk of *USA Today*.

From there, Nichols attended Northwestern
University's prestigious Medill School of Journalism in Evanston, Illinois. She later credited
the school with instilling in her the importance
of research and preparation when interviewing
subjects. While there, Nichols showed flashes
of her signature gumption when she successfully persuaded the dean to change the internship program's policy of barring journalism students from working in the sports sections of
local newspapers. She subsequently interned in
the sports section of several newspapers, including the *Washington Post*, before graduating from
Northwestern in 1995.

FIRST STINT AT ESPN
Right after college, Nichols landed her first journalism job at the Fort Lauderdale, Florida, *Sun-
Sentinel*, where she worked as a sports reporter.
Then, in 1996, she was hired in the same role
at the *Washington Post*, where she remained for
the next eight years. During that time, she was

mentored by Brennan and by columnists and future ESPN colleagues Tony Kornheiser and Michael Wilbon. She became one of the first women to cover the *Post*'s Washington Capitals NHL beat. That assignment, however, forced her to contend with frequent sexism, which she met with tireless professionalism. In the Shirley Povich Center piece, she noted, "Even those who had been most openly hostile toward me were acknowledging how hard I worked, how prepared I was and how much I knew."

As part of her responsibilities covering the Capitals, Nichols delivered pregame segments on a local cable network, which marked her entry into broadcast journalism. Attracted to "the immediacy of television," as she put it in an interview with Molly Knight for *Marie Claire* (5 June 2017), she eventually transitioned to that side of her field during the last years of her tenure with the *Post*. Nichols says that her experience as a print journalist, especially in interviewing, gave her the skills she needed to become a successful sports broadcaster. "When I sit down with someone for an interview, it's not just a random series of questions thrown at someone," she explained to Isaac Chotiner for *Slate.com* (17 Feb. 2017). "You are building a story and a narrative and it's a quest for information."

Nichols's verve for sports, coupled with her serious journalistic approach, eventually attracted the interest of the major sports television channel ESPN, which hired her as a reporter and correspondent in 2004. She became a mainstay on the network over the next eight years, during which she regularly appeared on *SportsCenter* to provide coverage of the NBA and NFL. She also contributed reports to *Sunday NFL Countdown*, covered topical sports issues for the investigative series *Outside the Lines* and *E:60*, and worked as a sideline reporter for *Monday Night Football*.

During her first tenure at ESPN, Nichols earned widespread attention for her fearless interviewing style. One of her more notable interviews came in 2011, when she interviewed basketball superstar LeBron James in the wake of "The Decision," an ESPN special in which James made his heavily scrutinized announcement that he would leave his hometown team, the Cleveland Cavaliers, to join the Miami Heat in free agency. Nichols met with James—whom she had first interviewed when he was a high school phenom—after he and the Heat lost the 2011 NBA Finals. She probed him with questions that addressed his vilification by fans and the media over his decision. "There were challenging questions, but it was a far-reaching interview," she noted to Ed Sherman for the Poynter Institute (25 Feb. 2016). "The feedback was, 'Hey, I understand him a lot better now.'"

CNN

In January 2013, Nichols brought her expertise to CNN. The cable network lured her away from ESPN as part of efforts to build its own sports broadcasting presence. There she hosted her own weekly show, *Unguarded with Rachel Nichols*, which featured half-hour episodes. On the program Nichols moderated provocative panel discussions and conducted candid interviews with major sports personalities.

During *Unguarded*'s run, Nichols particularly drew the attention of the sports world in September 2014, when she interviewed boxer Floyd Mayweather Jr. During the interview she repeatedly pressed the talented but controversial boxer about his history with domestic violence. She cited police reports in response to his denials of wrongdoing and asked him why fans should root for him given such facts. Though regarded as an unfair ambush by Mayweather's camp, the interview was lauded by many in the sports media and "marked a watershed moment for the national conversation around domestic violence," according to Knight. "I truly believe if you are asking a fair question, it shouldn't be scary to ask, and it shouldn't be scary to answer," Nichols told Sherman.

Less than a week after the Mayweather interview, Nichols grilled NFL commissioner Roger Goodell during a press conference held to discuss the league's new-at-the-time conduct policy on domestic violence. The conference had been largely prompted by the Ray Rice scandal, in which Rice, a Pro Bowl running back for the Baltimore Ravens, was shown on video brutally assaulting his fiancé in early 2014. Nichols's aggressive questioning of Goodell, which addressed the league's slow response to the scandal, earned her plaudits from peers, so much so that she trended on the social media site *Twitter*.

During her tenure at CNN, Nichols also reported for its sister networks TNT and TBS, covering the NBA and the *NCAA* Tournament for the former and MLB games for the latter. For *Unguarded*, she received a Gracie Award in the category of outstanding on-air talent for a sports program. However, despite receiving critical acclaim, the show was canceled in 2014 after just one season due to cost-cutting measures at CNN.

RETURN TO ESPN

In 2016, Nichols was recruited back to ESPN, where she debuted a daily NBA studio show on the network called *The Jump*. Erik Spanberg described the program for *Sports Business Journal* (18 Mar. 2019) as "a no-frills show not driven by highlights and one that puts [Nichols] on equal footing with a rotating cast of former players. . . . And one that doesn't spoon-feed the audience." With an ever-changing cast of analysts offering recaps of games and discussing stories and issues pertinent to the league and beyond, the show was tailored to Nichols's strengths. "Part of the concept for the show was I never wanted to be asking a question I already had the answer to," she told Spanberg. "I know the league."

Nichols continued her trademark hard-hitting journalism on *The Jump*. For example, in September 2018, she interviewed Dallas Mavericks owner Mark Cuban in response to an NBA investigation that revealed longstanding patterns of sexual harassment within his organization. The program also landed a number of other notable and timely interviews, earning it a reputation as a leading correspondent of the NBA and further boosting Nichols's profile among serious sports fans. To prepare the in-depth analysis *The Jump* delivered, she conducted regular interviews with players and coaches and watched several hours of basketball every day to seek out potential storylines. "What appealed to me about this job was the opportunity to lead the conversation," she said to Knight. "You get people to tune in by saying something different or more layered than they're getting somewhere else. The misconception, though, is that it has to be the loudest. It just has to be the most interesting."

PERSONAL LIFE
Nichols married film and music video director Max Nichols, the son of the film and stage director Mike Nichols, in 2001. The couple have twin daughters.

SUGGESTED READING

Deitsch, Richard. "The Case for . . . Rachel Nichols." *Sports Illustrated*, 13 Oct. 2014, www.si.com/vault/2014/10/13/106646996/the-case-for--rachel-nichols. Accessed 3 Apr. 2019.

Nichols, Rachel. "Rachel Nichols Doesn't Think Asking Tough Questions Is Scary at All." Interview by Alex Wong. *GQ*, 18 Feb. 2016, www.gq.com/story/rachel-nichols-espn-interview. Accessed 3 Apr. 2019.

Nichols, Rachel. "Rachel Nichols . . . in Her Own Words." *The Shirley Povich Center for Sports Journalism*, 2014, povichcenter.org/still-no-cheering-press-box/chapter/Rachel-Nichols/index.html. Accessed 3 Apr. 2019.

Nichols, Rachel. "Rachel Nichols Is One of the Sports World's Few Female Voices—But That's Not Why She's a Game-Changer." Interview by Molly Knight. *Marie Claire*, 5 June 2017, www.marieclaire.com/culture/interviews/a27458/rachel-nichols-espn-the-jump-show/. Accessed 3 Apr. 2019.

Nichols, Rachel. "Should the Worldwide Leader Stick to Sports?" Interview by Isaac Chotiner. *Slate*, 17 Feb. 2017, slate.com/culture/2017/02/espns-rachel-nichols-on-why-she-doesnt-stick-to-sports.html. Accessed 3 Apr. 2019.

Sherman, Ed. "Rachel Nichols Returns to ESPN, and She Isn't Pulling Punches." *Poynter*, 25 Feb. 2016, www.poynter.org/reporting-editing/2016/rachel-nichols-is-returning-to-espn-and-she-isnt-pulling-punches/. Accessed 3 Apr. 2019.

Spanberg, Erik. "No Fear: Rachel Nichols." *Street & Smith's Sports Business Journal*, 18 Mar. 2019, www.sportsbusinessdaily.com/Journal/Issues/2019/03/18/Media/Nichols.aspx. Accessed 3 Apr. 2019.

—*Chris Cullen*

Katie Nolan

Date of birth: January 28, 1987
Occupation: Sports personality

In 2014, a short video about the role and representation of women in the sports media industry captured widespread attention in the sports community and beyond. Released as part of the Fox Sports 1 web series *No Filter*, the video was the creation of the series' host, Katie Nolan, a longtime sports fan and then up-and-coming television personality. She was inspired to speak out by her insider observations of the male-dominated industry and especially the ongoing debate regarding the National Football League's (NFL) handling of domestic abuse. "I thought, as a woman in sports, I had to say something," she told Jack Dickey for *Sports Illustrated* (24 Nov. 2014). "I'm happy I got my point out there, that women should be represented more in sports media. They really should be."

After the publicity generated by the *No Filter* video, Nolan became increasingly popular for her unique take on the sports world. Her signature blend of opinion and comedy carried over to her work for Fox Sports television, including *Garbage Time with Katie Nolan*, which won a Sports Emmy Award. Nolan's move to the ESPN network in late 2017 provided further visibility, as she hosted both a podcast, *Sports? With Katie Nolan*, and a late-night series, *Always Late with Katie Nolan*, beginning in 2018.

EARLY LIFE AND EDUCATION
Katherine Beth Nolan was born in Boston, Massachusetts, on January 28, 1987. Her mother was a bartender who had formerly worked as a speech pathologist, while her father was an accountant. She has an older brother named Kevin. Nolan grew up in Framingham, a suburb of Boston, where she attended local schools and was active in dance as well as gymnastics. She competed in rhythmic gymnastics in the Junior Olympic Games during the late 1990s. In addition to athletic pursuits, Nolan loved to write

Photo by Andrew Toth/FilmMagic

and also enjoyed creating pretend radio shows, which she recorded onto cassette tapes. Meanwhile, she began following professional sports largely through the influence of her mother, who listened to sports radio to better converse with customers at the bar.

After graduating from Framingham High School in 2005, Nolan enrolled in Hofstra University, which she selected due to its strong programs in public relations, her prospective major, and dance, her preferred minor. As the university was located on Long Island, New York, Nolan spent her college career surrounded by fans of New York's sports teams such as the New York Yankees and the New York Giants—historical rivals of the Boston-area teams she supported, such as the Boston Red Sox and the New England Patriots. She noted that this became particularly interesting in 2007, when the Red Sox won Major League Baseball's World Series. "It's fun to be the contrarian when everyone hates you, as long as your team is winning," she told Neil Best for *Newsday* (5 Mar. 2015). "As a contrast, I was also at Hofstra when the Patriots lost to the Giants in the Super Bowl [in 2008] and that was awful."

Along with keeping up with sports, Nolan completed several public-relations internships during her time at Hofstra. She also had a part-time job as a bar mitzvah dancer. She earned her bachelor's degree from Hofstra University's Lawrence Herbert School of Communication in 2009.

EARLY CAREER

After graduating from college, Nolan moved to New York City without already having a job lined up, which she described to Best as "the stupidest thing you can possibly do." She spent a year in New York, during which she worked at a gym, but then returned to Boston, where she found work as a bartender. "I'm a really good bartender," she later told Dickey. "That's the only skill I can confidently say I have."

While working as a bartender in Boston, Nolan began writing a blog titled *Bitches Can't Hang*, which featured comedic posts about current events and popular culture. The blog captured the attention of *Guyism*, a male-interest website, which hired Nolan to write and star in videos that would be posted online. Nolan moved back to the New York area to work on *Guyism* projects, which included the video series *Guyism Speed Round*. Although Nolan appreciated her time with *Guyism* and the opportunities it brought her, she later acknowledged that the work that had first brought her to *Guyism's* attention had perpetuated damaging or otherwise unproductive stereotypes about women. "Now I'm like, you were just buying into this idea of what a woman is that [men] defined, and then you perpetuated it by being like, *I'm not like them*," she told Clay Skipper for *GQ* (29 Oct. 2018). "I chose the wrong side, and I still am like upset about that. And I'm most upset because it got me a job that I deserve either way, but I got by being mean about women."

CROWD GOES WILD

After working for *Guyism* for a time, Nolan drew attention from an unexpected source: representatives of the newly established sports television channel Fox Sports 1. "One of my bosses came to me and said Fox wanted me for their new 24-hour sports channel, and that if I went, the company that owned *Guyism* would get money," she recalled to Dickey. "It was like a dowry. Oh, you'll give us a cow, and we'll give you Katie." Although Nolan's initial audition for the channel went poorly—a result she later attributed in part to her inexperience with teleprompters—she fared far better in later auditions. The channel hired Nolan for the show *Crowd Goes Wild*, which premiered on Fox Sports 1 in August of 2013.

Starring veteran television host Regis Philbin and a panel of other sports television personalities, *Crowd Goes Wild* was intended to be a lively, sometimes comedic take on the latest events in sports. Nolan initially served as the social media correspondent for the show, tasked with sharing information from websites such as Twitter, and was set apart from the other members of the cast. As the show developed, however, she became an increasingly major contributor to the program and gained further opportunities to share her opinions and humor with the show's audience. Although Nolan was pleased with the opportunity and particularly enjoyed working with Philbin, she found that the show's atmosphere was "chaotic," as she told Dickey. "On Mondays it felt like we were doomed. Tuesdays we felt we were getting the hang of it. By Wednesday we thought we had a hit. On Thursday someone was threatening to quit. And by each Friday, I was like, I don't want to do this anymore," she explained. While sports television critics commented positively on Nolan's work and that of some of her castmates, *Crowd Goes Wild* received mediocre reviews overall and struggled to draw an audience. The network canceled the show in April of 2014.

A NEW VOICE IN SPORTS

During Nolan's time with *Crowd Goes Wild*, she began to write and star in *No Filter with Katie Nolan*, a video series for Fox Sports 1's online platform. She remained with Fox following *Crowd Goes Wild*'s cancellation and continued to work on *No Filter* into 2015. Although largely comedic, *No Filter* also enabled Nolan to speak out about some serious issues within the world of sports, including the role of women in sports media. In 2014, she linked that topic to the controversy surrounding professional football player Ray Rice, who had been physically abusive to his fiancée and whose abuse had been documented on video. Despite the severity of the incident, the National Football League (NFL) suspended Rice for only two games, which sparked widespread discussions of how the league should truly handle such incidents. However, as Nolan and others observed, the conversations about the issue within the sports media were male dominated, as women were largely relegated to supporting roles. "Women in sports television are allowed to read headlines, patrol sidelines, and generally facilitate conversation for their male colleagues," Nolan explained in a 2014 *No Filter* video, as quoted by Alyssa Bailey for *Elle* (11 Sept. 2014). "And, while the Stephen A. Smiths, Mike Cairns, Dan Patricks, and Keith Olbermanns of the world get to weigh in on the issues of the day, we just smile and throw to commercial."

Nolan argued that the role of women in sports television must evolve and that the NFL "will never respect women and their opinions as long as the media it answers to doesn't," as quoted by Bailey. Following its online release, Nolan's video was shared widely, reaching a broad audience. While some sports fans criticized Nolan for speaking out and claimed that she simply wanted her own show, Nolan herself later clarified in interviews that she was speaking about an industry-wide problem rather than her own specific career. In general, her message received widespread support.

Following the cancellation of *Crowd Goes Wild*, Fox Sports leadership sought a new place on television for Nolan but struggled with the logistics, as Nolan was based in New York and most Fox Sports 1 programming was produced in California. The network launched a new show helmed by Nolan, *Garbage Time with Katie Nolan*, in March 2015. A weekly half-hour show filmed in New York, *Garbage Time* differed from Nolan's previous work in format but continued to feature the blending of content that had become her signature. "We're trying to blend humor and sports, which is a very difficult blend. You have to sort of straddle the line," she explained to Best. "But the goal really is to make something that's fun to watch, that doesn't take itself too seriously, but that also if there is an issue in sports we feel we need to talk about, we can address it." In conjunction with the show, Nolan starred in a *Garbage Time* podcast that featured notable guests and discussions similar to those in the television show. Following its premiere, *Garbage Time with Katie Nolan* received significant critical praise. The show won a 2016 Sports Emmy Award for outstanding social TV experience and was also nominated for the award for outstanding studio show weekly.

MOVE TO ESPN

In early 2017, Fox Sports 1 revealed plans to move *Garbage Time* to Los Angeles, California, and alter the show's length while retaining Nolan as host. Although initially excited, Nolan became unhappy with the proposal, in large part because the network wanted her to sign a new deal before the details of the show had been finalized. "I just didn't trust that I would move my life to LA and they would protect it or listen to me about it. They wanted me to sign the deal before we developed the show," she told Skipper. Nolan opted not to agree to the deal, and *Garbage Time* aired its final episode in February of 2017.

Following the end of *Garbage Time*, Nolan spent much of 2017 not working, as she remained under contract with Fox for the better part of the year. In October 2017, however, the major sports network ESPN announced that it was hiring Nolan, although the channel's plans for her were uncertain. "When I was a little girl, I always dreamed that one day announcements regarding my specific assignments would be forthcoming," she joked upon the announcement, as quoted by Matt Bonesteel for the *Washington Post* (4 Oct. 2017). During the months following her hiring, she made a variety of guest appearances on ESPN programs, began to host a version of the program *SportsCenter* on the social-media app Snapchat, and launched an ESPN podcast, *Sports? With Katie Nolan*. In September 2018, nearly a year after she joined the network, Nolan returned to the screen with *Always Late with Katie Nolan*, a late-night series broadcast via the ESPN subscription service ESPN+.

Nolan was based in Hoboken, New Jersey, as her career got off the ground. She has often commented that she hopes to move back to Boston one day and possibly establish her own production company.

SUGGESTED READING

Bailey, Alyssa. "Fox Anchorwoman Accuses Sports Media of Sexism." *Elle*, 11 Sept. 2014, www.elle.com/culture/movies-tv/news/a24545/fox-sports-anchor-called-out-fox-for-sexism/. Accessed 12 July 2019.

Bonesteel, Matt. "To the Surprise of No One, ESPN Is Hiring Katie Nolan." *The Washington Post*, 4 Oct. 2017, www.washingtonpost.com/news/early-lead/wp/2017/10/04/to-the-surprise-of-no-one-espn-is-hiring-katie-nolan/. Accessed 12 July 2019.

Nolan, Katie. "Can Katie Nolan, Host of Garbage Time, Be Fox Sports' Breakout Star?" Interview by Richard Deitsch. *Sports Illustrated*, 8 Mar. 2015, www.si.com/more-sports/2015/03/08/katie-nolan-qa-interview-fox-sports-noise-report. Accessed 12 July 2019.

Nolan, Katie. "Katie Nolan Is Ready to Put it All Out There." Interview by Clay Skipper. *GQ*, 29 Oct. 2018, www.gq.com/story/katie-nolan-always-late-interview. Accessed 12 July 2019.

Nolan, Katie. "Katie Nolan on Bartending, Regis and 'Tweeter' and One-Upping Bumgarner." Interview by Jack Dickey. *Sports Illustrated*, 24 Nov. 2014, www.si.com/extra-mustard/2014/11/19/katie-nolan-interview. Accessed 12 July 2019.

Nolan, Katie. "Q&A with Katie Nolan, Host of Garbage Time on Fox Sports 1." Interview by Neil Best. *Newsday*, 5 Mar. 2015, www.newsday.com/sports/media/q-a-with-katie-nolan-host-of-garbage-time-on-fox-sports-1-1.10017208. Accessed 12 July 2019.

Nolan, Katie. "10 Questions with Katie Nolan, the Fiery Host of Garbage Time." Interview by Charlotte Wilder. *Boston.com*, 3 Dec. 2015, www.boston.com/news/untagged/2015/12/03/10-questions-with-katie-nolan-the-fiery-host-of-garbage-time. Accessed 12 July 2019.

SELECTED WORKS

Crowd Goes Wild, 2013–14; *No Filter with Katie Nolan*, 2013–15; *Garbage Time with Katie Nolan*, 2015–17; *Always Late with Katie Nolan*, 2018–

—Joy Crelin

Ryan North

Date of birth: October 20, 1980
Occupation: Author

In February 2003, Carleton University student Ryan North created a digital comic strip in which a large *Tyrannosaurus rex* delights in stomping on things while a *Utahraptor* seeks to dissuade him from doing so and a *Dromiceiomimus* looks on. The comic strip's layout and images would supply the template for North's long-running *Dinosaur Comics* webcomic, which became known for its humorous writing in addition to its largely static visuals. Although North went on to earn a master's degree in computational linguistics following the creation of *Dinosaur Comics*, he decided to focus on comics full time, initially dedicating himself solely to *Dinosaur Comics* but later writing for print comics series such as *Adventure Time*, *The Midas Flesh*, *The Unbeatable Squirrel Girl*, and *Jughead*. He established himself further as a writer with works such as *To Be or Not to Be* (2013), the first book in his Choose-Your-Own-Path Shakespeare series, and 2018's *How to Invent Everything: A Survival Guide for the Stranded Time Traveler*. Alongside such projects, North has continued to write and publish *Dinosaur Comics*, which aptly demonstrated that its visuals were secondary to the characteristic humor and offbeat ideas that are still featured in the work more than fifteen years after its first publication. "I used to worry that I had a finite supply of ideas, that I should hold on to each of them in case it was the last. But then I talked to other cartoonists and I realized, ideas are cheap, you can have a million ideas," North told Brian Wolly for *Smithsonian.com* (14 July 2011). "The tricky part is the follow-through: making good ones work, making the best out of the raw material!"

EARLY LIFE AND EDUCATION

North was born in Ottawa, Canada, on October 20, 1980. He was the first of two sons born to Anna and Randall North. Although he would later build a career in both online and print comics, he was not significantly exposed to comics until he was in his late teens. "I always liked comics, but they weren't something I could really read that often," he told Kyle Schoenfeld for *Nineteen Questions* (15 Feb. 2016). "We grew up in a small town, and there was no comic book store in that town, so all I got was Archie Comics at the supermarket and knowledge of Batman and Superman through cultural osmosis, basically." After getting a job, however, his newfound disposable income enabled him to begin buying comics, and he soon became deeply immersed in the medium. An avid reader, North was also a fan of the novelist Kurt Vonnegut, and particularly his 1969 novel *Slaughterhouse-Five*.

Photo by Okras via Wikimedia Commons

After graduating from high school, North enrolled in Carleton University in Ottawa, where he earned his bachelor's degree in computer science and minored in film studies. North went on to attend the University of Toronto as a graduate student, pursuing a master's degree in computational linguistics. He published several coauthored papers in that field between 2004 and 2007 and in 2005 completed a master's thesis titled "Computational Measures of the Acceptability of Light Verb Constructions."

While an undergraduate and graduate student, North began to engage with internet culture through the creation of websites that displayed his characteristically offbeat sense of humor. "I used to have a page that was called 'Ryan's Page of Fun and Robot Erotica,' and all that was on there was this one picture of these two robots holding hands," he told the *Geek's Guide to the Galaxy* podcast in an interview transcribed for *Lightspeed* magazine (Nov. 2013). "When I was an undergrad, we got free web space with the university, and I had no use for it, so I just put up my page of 'Fun and Robot Erotica,' and I updated that once every semester." North displayed a penchant for prank emails and other lighthearted online antics that would eventually develop into more complex humorous projects, including an effort to encourage any would-be vandalizers of the online encyclopedia Wikipedia to focus their efforts solely on the Wikipedia entry on chickens.

DINOSAUR COMICS

In 2003, while in his final year at Carleton University, North began what would become his longest-lasting and perhaps best-known online project, the webcomic *Dinosaur Comics*. Featuring clip-art illustrations of a *Tyrannosaurus rex*, a *Dromiceiomimus*, and a *Utahraptor* as well as a tiny cabin, car, and human figure, the first *Dinosaur Comics* strip became the visual model for all future strips in the comic, all of which share the same images and format but feature new dialogue and captions. For North, *Dinosaur Comics* represented an opportunity to create a humorous comic strip despite his lack of artistic abilities. "I'd wanted to do a comic for a while, but being wholly unable to draw kinda limited that ambition, until I came up with this workaround," he told Wolly. "I think the lesson here is that comics are awesome, and even those who really have no business doing them will love them enough to find a way!" In addition to the text displayed on the comic strips themselves, *Dinosaur Comics* became known for featuring bonus comedic text that appeared when hovering a computer's cursor over the comic, among other Easter eggs.

After completing his master's degree, North faced a choice between seeking out a job in his academic field or devoting himself to making a living from *Dinosaur Comics* and related projects. He decided to focus on comics full time and initially brought in an income by selling T-shirts. "When I first started, I remember thinking, like every day, 'I need three people to buy a shirt today so that I can pay rent and eat food.' And it would happen," he recalled during his appearance on the *Geek's Guide to the Galaxy* podcast. "I would try to imagine these three presumably topless people being like, 'Yes, today is the day I buy a shirt.'" In addition to T-shirts, North went on to sell physical collections of his comics as well as socks, plush dinosaurs, notepads, and other merchandise.

PRINT COMICS

While *Dinosaur Comics* offered limited visuals, North's strong writing and distinct humor and creative point of view made the comic widely popular and garnered North attention from mainstream comics professionals such as BOOM! Studios editor Shannon Watters. Having read and enjoyed *Dinosaur Comics*, Watters enlisted North to write comics based on *Adventure Time*, a popular animated series airing on Cartoon Network. Working in collaboration with illustrators Shelli Paroline and Braden Lamb, North wrote for the *Adventure Time* comics series between 2012 and 2014. His run on the series was popular among critics, and *Adventure Time* won the 2013 and 2014 Harvey Award for Best Original Graphic Publication for Younger Readers as well as the 2013 special Harvey Award for humor. The series likewise won the 2013 Eisner Award for Best Publication for Kids.

Although North left *Adventure Time* in 2014, he hoped to continue working with Paroline and Lamb, with whom he "got along like gangbusters, both personally and creatively," he told Schoenfeld. He had the opportunity again while working on the 2014 series *The Midas Flesh*, a science fiction series based in part on the myth of King Midas. "When I wrote *Midas Flesh*, I wanted to do it with Shelli and Braden again, and they made themselves available," he explained to Schoenfeld. "What great people! Everyone should hire them to do everything." First published in the form of individual comics issues, *The Midas Flesh* was later collected into two volumes.

THE UNBEATABLE SQUIRREL GIRL
A key point in North's career in print comics came when Wil Moss, an editor at Marvel Comics, approached North to request that he pitch a series based on the lesser-known Marvel character Squirrel Girl. Also known as Doreen Green, the character was introduced in the early 1990s but was little used compared to many other Marvel heroes, in part due to her odd array of squirrel-related powers. Although North knew little about Squirrel Girl, he gave himself a crash course in the character over the span of a weekend. "By Monday I knew two things: that I wanted there to be a Squirrel Girl comic and that I really wanted to be the person writing it," he told Marcy Cook for the *Mary Sue* (7 Jan. 2015). "What appealed to me was how she really was this silver-age character in the modern age: she's down with having super powers, she thinks they're awesome, and she's ready to fight crime with them! NO SWEAT." North's Squirrel Girl series, *The Unbeatable Squirrel Girl*, launched in 2015 and was relaunched later that year. Well regarded by critics and readers, *The Unbeatable Squirrel Girl* was nominated for the Eisner Award for Best New Series in 2016 and the following year won the Eisner Award for Best Publication for Teens.

In addition to *The Unbeatable Squirrel Girl*, North wrote fourteen issues of the comic *Jughead*—focused on the titular Archie Comics character—between 2016 and 2017. Derek Charm served as the illustrator for the series during North's tenure, and *Jughead* won the 2017 Eisner Award for Best Humor Publication. Alongside such long-term series, North has written numerous short comics stories that have been published in anthologies such as the Marvel Comics anthologies *Original Sins* (2015) and *A Year of Marvels* (2017) as well as the collections *Defend Comics!* (2017) and *Boom Box Mixtape* (2018), among others.

PROSE PUBLICATIONS
Although North is best known as a writer of comics, he has also written or otherwise contributed to a variety of prose works. Alongside Matthew Bennardo and David Malki, North edited *Machine of Death* (2010), an anthology of short stories based on the premise that a machine exists that can tell people in vague terms how they will die but not when or specifically how it will happen—a concept first proposed by the *T. rex* in a *Dinosaur Comics* strip. The trio followed *Machine of Death* with the 2013 anthology *This Is How You Die*, to which North contributed a story titled "Cancer." That year, North also published *To Be or Not to Be*, the first installment in his Choose-Your-Own-Path Shakespeare series. Funded through the crowdfunding website *Kickstarter*, *To Be or Not to Be* raised nearly $600,000 in contributions during its campaign. North later also published the similar works *Romeo and/or Juliet* (2016) and *William Shakespeare Punches a Friggin' Shark . . . and/or Other Stories* (2017).

North published his first picture book, *How to Be a T. Rex*, in 2018. That year also saw the publication of *How to Invent Everything: A Survival Guide for the Stranded Time Traveler*, which arose in part out of North's recurring musings about how poorly he would fare if he were ever to become stranded in the past. "I don't know anything. I'd show up being like, 'hey past, the future is great, we got computers' and they'd be like 'how do you get computers' and I'd say 'I don't know,'" he told Angela Chen for the *Verge* (12 Oct. 2018). "I wanted to be a competent time traveler." Blending facts and humor, *How to Invent Everything* explores how a time traveler stranded in the past could go about inventing critical processes and technologies, from farm crop rotation to hot air balloons.

PERSONAL LIFE
North lives in Toronto, with his spouse, Jennifer Klug, and their dog, Noam Chompsky. In addition to his work as a writer, he was the creator of the online advertising network Project Wonderful, which he ran until shutting down the service in 2018.

SUGGESTED READING
North, Ryan. "*Dinosaur Comics* Creator Ryan North Explains 'How to Invent Everything.'" Interview by Angela Chen. *The Verge*, 12 Oct. 2018, www.theverge.com/platform/amp/2018/10/12/17964238/ryan-north-how-to-invent-everything-science-history-technology. Accessed 16 Dec. 2018.

North, Ryan. "I Am Ryan North, Author and Cartoonist and I One Time I Messed Up Walking My Dog So Badly It Made the News. AMA!" *Reddit*, 7 June 2016, www.reddit.com/r/IAmA/comments/4mzern/i_am_ryan_

north_author_and_cartoonist_and_i_one/. Accessed 16 Dec. 2018.

North, Ryan. "Interview: Ryan North." *Lightspeed*, Nov. 2013, www.lightspeedmagazine.com/nonfiction/interview-ryan-north/. Accessed 16 Dec. 2018.

North, Ryan. "Interview with Ryan North, Creator of *Dinosaur Comics*." By Brian Wolly. *Smithsonian.com*, 14 June 2011, www.smithsonianmag.com/science-nature/interview-with-ryan-north-creator-of-dinosaur-comics-15523444/. Accessed 16 Dec. 2018.

North, Ryan. "Interview: Ryan North on 'Dinosaur Comics.'" By Rick Marshall. *Comicmix*, 31 July 2008, www.comicmix.com/2008/07/31/interview-ryan-north-on-dinosaur-comics/. Accessed 16 Dec. 2018.

North, Ryan. "Interview: *Unbeatable Squirrel Girl*'s Ryan North Talks Nuts, Fighting Galactus, & Hazelnut Lip-Smacking." By Marcy Cook. *The Mary Sue*, 7 Jan. 2015, www.themarysue.com/interview-squirrel-girl-ryan-north/amp/. Accessed 16 Dec. 2018.

North, Ryan. "Ryan North." Interview by Kyle Schoenfeld. *Nineteen Questions*, 15 Feb. 2016, nineteenquestions.com/2016/02/15/ryan-north/. Accessed 16 Dec. 2018.

SELECTED WORKS

Dinosaur Comics, 2003–; *Adventure Time*, 2012–14; Choose-Your-Own-Path Shakespeare series, 2013–; *The Midas Flesh*, 2014; *The Unbeatable Squirrel Girl*, 2015–; *Jughead*, 2016–17; *How to Be a T. Rex*, 2018; *How to Invent Everything*, 2018

—*Joy Crelin*

Rachel Notley

Date of birth: April 17, 1964
Occupation: Politician

Canadian politician Rachel Notley was elected the premier of Alberta in 2015, marking the first time the New Democratic Party (NDP) took control of the province and ending forty-four years of Progressive Conservative rule. The victory was in many ways the culmination of a long political legacy, as Notley's father had cofounded the Alberta NDP, and she was involved in activism from a young age. She entered politics after a successful legal career focused on labor issues, winning her first seat in 2008 and becoming the Alberta NDP leader in 2014.

Notley's liberal platform as premier called for increasing social services and combining economic growth with environmental protections. In a province heavily dependent on the fossil fuel industries, balancing those goals proved difficult. Indeed, economic challenges were widely seen as the key factor in the NDP's loss to the United Conservatives in Alberta's 2019 elections, which saw Notley unseated as premier. She later remained leader of her party, heading the official opposition. As Notley admitted to Clare Clancy for *Edmonton Journal* (15 Apr. 2019), "As a New Democrat in Alberta I will always feel that I have to work twice as hard as anybody else."

EARLY LIFE AND EDUCATION

Notley, the oldest of three children, was born on April 17, 1964, in Edmonton, Alberta, and raised in northwestern Alberta near Fairview. She grew up with horses and was always eager to ride after returning home from school. By age ten, she was attending protest rallies against cruise-missile testing with her mother, Sandy, a devout Anglican whose faith motivated her activism. A native of Massachusetts, Sandy had been involved in movements such as registering black voters in the southern United States and opposing South Africa's apartheid system. Notley's father, Grant, was a founder and leader of the Alberta branch of the NDP. He lost many elections throughout her childhood before securing the NDP's first seat in the provincial legislature in 1971; in 1982 he became the leader of the official opposition.

Following graduation from Fairview High School, Notley worked in Paris for a year as an *au pair* and learned French. She then attended Grand Prairie Regional College, where she earned a reputation for questioning authority. In one notable incident, she even confronted her

Photo by Connor Mah via Wikimedia Commons

father at a town hall–style event on student debt and poverty. Tim Harper quoted her for the *Star* (5 May 2015) as announcing, "I am a student, very poor. My parents make too much money for me to get a loan, yet my parents are so cheap and I am so hungry. What would you recommend for me to do?" Notley's audacity reportedly impressed and amused other NDP members, and though her father was not happy with the stunt, he did give her twenty dollars before he left.

Notley's youth was also marked by tragedy, however. In 1984 her father died when the small plane he was traveling in crashed in bad weather. The rest of the family supported each other emotionally and financially, living frugally and saving carefully. Ultimately Notley obtained her Bachelor of Arts degree in political science, graduating with honors from the University of Alberta in 1987. She then earned a law degree from Osgoode Hall Law School at York University, where she founded a student branch of the NDP.

LEGAL CAREER AND ENTRY INTO POLITICS

After graduating from law school in 1990, Notley worked in Edmonton for the Alberta Union of Provincial Employees. She helped clients find jobs and get workers' compensation benefits. She then took an occupational health and safety job with British Columbia's Health Sciences Association (HSA) in 1994. While living in Vancouver, BC, Notley spent one year as an assistant to BC attorney general Ujjal Dosanjh, focusing on pension benefits for same-sex partners and other legal issues in the LGBTQ community, domestic abuse law, and community safety. "She was very politically savvy. She was bright but not impulsive," Dosanjh told Gary Mason for the *Globe and Mail* (15 May 2018). "She had great political smarts. She was a wonderful sounding board. And just really, really likeable."

Back at the HSA, Notley was heavily involved in the major project of rewriting BC's health and safety law. She returned to Edmonton in 2002 and became involved with the National Union of Public and General Employees (NUPGE). She also occasionally worked as a tutor and a business law instructor before taking a part-time role with the United Nurses of Alberta.

After volunteering for the NDP over the years, Notley decided to enter politics in 2006. Two years later she won a seat as a member of the Legislative Assembly (MLA) for the Edmonton-Strathcona electoral district. One of only two NDP candidates to win, she took on many responsibilities in the shadow cabinet. She quickly proved a popular legislator, winning reelection in 2012, and also became known for her frugal spending.

NDP LEADERSHIP AND 2015 ELECTION

In 2014 Notley won election as leader of the Alberta NDP with 70 percent of the vote. In her acceptance speech, as Dean Bennett reported for the *Globe and Mail* (18 Oct. 2014), she proclaimed: "Politics should be about more than nervously promising to clean up the mess you've made. It should be about more than issue management. It should be about more than efforts to distract people from things that matter. Politics should be about hope. It should be about optimism. And it should be about the wherewithal to build something better."

As head of her party, Notley led the NDP into Alberta's 2015 provincial elections. However, the generally conservative-leaning province had been solidly in the control of the Progressive Conservative Party for over four decades, and few initially expected any change. But plunging global oil prices had hurt the fossil fuel–reliant Alberta economy significantly, stoking public desire for political change. Spurred by strong funding, Notley campaigned with the hope of winning rather than the aim of just becoming the official opposition. Her performance at a mid-campaign debate galvanized support, and polls showed the NDP leading the race. Still, although Notley reportedly began preparing for victory, few others believed such a major upset would really take place.

The upset proved very real on election day, as the NDP quadrupled its usual share of voters and captured fifty-four seats in the legislature, giving it a solid majority. Nearly half of the NDP caucus was female. It was by far the greatest success the party had ever had in Alberta. Notley was sworn in as premier on May 24, 2015, and made a point of ensuring that her cabinet was gender-balanced and inclusive. "Change has finally come to Alberta," she said in her victory speech, as quoted by Josh Dehaas for *CTV News* (16 Apr. 2019). "New people, new ideas, and a fresh start for our great province."

TERM AS PREMIER

Notley's administration was marked by efforts to boost the provincial economy while improving environmental regulations and introducing social justice initiatives. Among her policies were a ban on political donations from unions and corporations, an increase in corporate taxes, a minimum wage increase, a school fee reduction, and a child benefit program. The United Nations Declaration on the Rights of Indigenous Peoples was put into effect, and an inquiry was opened into abuse of Indigenous women. She also oversaw a revision of Alberta's employment and labor standards as well as an overhaul of the system for royalties from the energy industry.

The energy industry and related environmental issues proved a tricky area for Notley.

She sought to present a new, more ecofriendly Alberta that would aim to cut carbon emissions sharply; for example, she attended the United Nation's 2015 Paris climate talks. However, her province's heavy reliance on the oil and gas industries meant that her positions were often more conservative than those of NDP members elsewhere. Most notably, she strongly supported the development of pipelines like the stalled Keystone XL that would allow resources from Alberta's oil sands to reach ports and command higher prices. To offset some of the staunch opposition of environmentalists, mainly for climate-related reasons, Notley released the Climate Leadership Plan, which instituted taxes on fossil fuel consumption. The plan proved controversial but was credited with influencing Prime Minister Justin Trudeau's approval of the major Trans Mountain pipeline expansion project in 2016. "We could not have approved this project without the leadership of Premier Notley," Trudeau was widely quoted as saying. That project continued to face intense opposition and was delayed several times, but Notley maintained her support.

Meanwhile, Alberta and the Notley administration faced other challenges. In May 2016, a major forest fire broke out in Fort McMurray, forcing the entire city of more than eighty thousand to evacuate and destroying more than 2,400 buildings. It was considered the costliest disaster in terms of insurance ever to hit Canada. During and after the devastating event, Notley earned widespread admiration for her immediate and level-headed response.

Notley did earn criticism on other fronts, however, most importantly regarding fiscal issues. Although her policies were credited with helping Alberta's overall economy improve slowly, this was largely achieved with planned deficit spending. The government borrowed heavily to pay public sector employees (even with a two-year wage freeze for teachers and nurses) and to fund ongoing services and infrastructure projects. Alberta's debt swelled to over C$50 billion, and the unemployment rate remained high, fueling attacks by opposition figures.

2019 ELECTION
Alberta's economic struggles posed a steep challenge for Notley and the NDP entering provincial elections in early 2019. The chief threat came from the United Conservative Party (UCP), which had formed in 2017 with the express aim of rallying Progressive Conservatives and other conservative groups to unseat the NDP. Despite the UCP's consistent lead in polls, Notley was considered still popular among voters, and she held out hope that her government could maintain its majority. "Alberta elections have a way of surprising you," she said at a rally, as quoted by Clancy.

Nevertheless, the NDP was soundly defeated in the election, which saw the UCP win a majority. UCP leader Jason Kenney, who had been a federal cabinet member, succeeded her as Alberta premier. However, Notley kept her seat as MLA of her district and became leader of the opposition. Her concession speech emphasized her administration's achievements as well as hope for the future. "This may feel like a step back but remember we have made tremendous progress," she said, as quoted by Dehaas. "Tonight's vote is not the result we had hoped or worked so hard for. But no matter what our role is in legislature, we will not rest."

PERSONAL LIFE
Notley married Lou Arab, an NDP organizer and former communications officer with the Canadian Union of Public Employees. The couple have two children, Ethan and Sophie.

Notley is a self-identified dog lover. She also started running to help her quit smoking and regularly runs with a group of friends on Sundays despite her busy schedule. She has also often participated in half-marathons.

SUGGESTED READING
Bennett, Dean. "Rachel Notley Becomes New Leader of Alberta NDP." *The Globe and Mail*, 18 Oct. 2014, www.theglobeandmail.com/news/alberta/rachel-notley-becomes-new-leader-of-alberta-ndp/article21156348. Accessed 9 May 2019.

Clancy, Clare. "Notley Says Alberta's Elections Tend to Yield Surprise Results." *Edmonton Journal*, 15 Apr. 2019, edmontonjournal.com/news/politics/leader-profile-on-notley. Accessed 9 May 2019.

Cosh, Colby. "How Rachel Notley Became Canada's Most Surprising Political Star." *Maclean's*, 21 May 2015, www.macleans.ca/politics/how-rachel-notley-became-canadas-most-surprising-political-star. Accessed 9 May 2019.

Dehaas, Josh. "Why Rachel Notley Lost the Alberta Election." *CTV News*, 17 Apr. 2019, www.ctvnews.ca/politics/why-rachel-notley-lost-the-alberta-election-1.4383295. Accessed 9 May 2019.

Harper, Tim. "Alberta's Giant Killer Grew Up with NDP Titans." *The Star*, 5 May 2015, www.thestar.com/news/canada/2015/05/05/albertas-giant-killer-notley-grew-up-with-ndp-titans-tim-harper.html. Accessed 9 May 2019.

Mason, Gary. "Notley's Way: How the Alberta Premier Became Determined." *The Globe and Mail*, 15 May 2018, www.theglobeandmail.com/news/alberta/the-alberta-ndps-rachel-notley-she-is-a-child-of-the-party/article24338069/. Accessed 9 May 2019.

Thomson, Graham. "Rachel Notley." *The Canadian Encyclopedia*, Historica Canada, 22 Mar. 2019, www.thecanadianencyclopedia.ca/en/article/rachel-notley. Accessed 9 May 2019.

—*Judy Johnson*

Cassper Nyovest

Date of birth: December 16, 1990
Occupation: Rapper and producer

Cassper Nyovest is one of the most popular hip-hop artists in South Africa. In 2015, he became the first South African artist to sell out the Ticketpro Dome stadium in Johannesburg. There followed a campaign to fill larger and larger stadiums, including the First National Bank (FNB) Stadium, the largest stadium in Africa. Though falling just shy of his sell-out goal, Nyovest's #FillUpTheDome concert series garnered him thousands of fans across the continent. Nyovest, who was born and raised in Mafikeng, South Africa, dropped out of school as a teenager to pursue music. For nearly ten years, Nyovest struggled to break through and for a time had to return to live with his parents; his younger sister eventually lent him cab fare to Johannesburg so he could try his luck again. Nyovest's dogged persistence paid off. After appearing on rapper Hip Hop Pantsula (HHP)'s single "Wamo Tseba Mtho," Nyovest scored two hits of his own: "Gusheshe" and the ubiquitous "Doc Shebeleza," inspired by Nyovest's hero, the kwaito star of the same name. His 2014 debut album *Tsholofelo*, named for his sister, catapulted him to fame. Nyovest, known for his flashy displays of wealth and bravado, has gone on to exhibit a more mellow side, but his hunger and motivation remain. "I don't ever want to get to a place where nobody knows who I am, where I'm not celebrated and people don't love me as much as they do right now," he told *CNBC Africa* (23 Dec. 2016), "I don't ever wanna get to that place."

EARLY LIFE
Cassper Nyovest was born Refiloe Maele Phoolo on December 16, 1990, in Mafikeng, near South Africa's border with Botswana, where he also spent his childhood. His mother and father, Muzuki and Letsebela Phoolo, worked as teachers. "My father is a great man cuz he made a lot of great people," he told Gabriel Myers Hansen for *Music in Africa* (6 Apr. 2018). "[He] was never like a successful businessman, but he taught successful businessmen. There are so many people that came from him, from his teachings. I'm one of them." Nyovest has two sisters. His brother, Khotso Motebang Phoolo, was also a rapper;

he died in a car accident in 2003. Nyovest's parents separated soon after their son's death, when Nyovest was fifteen.

Nyovest was performing with his school's theater program by the age of six and knew early on that he wanted to pursue a career in music. He started rapping at twelve, and in 2004, he and his friends formed a group called Childhood Gangsters. After the group disbanded, he joined the eight-person group Slow Motion. He was also a talented dancer, and won the popular dance competition television show *Jika Majika* when he was a teenager.

Nyovest attended high school at Sol Plaatje Secondary School in Mafikeng, where he played soccer, cricket, and basketball, but academics did not hold his interest. After he failed his tenth-grade exams, his parents sent him to live with his grandmother in Potchefstroom. The move was not academically inspiring, and ultimately Nyovest dropped out of school at sixteen. "It was a very emotional part of my life, and [my parents'] as well because they are passionate about education," he recalled to *CNBC Africa*. "I sat them down and said look I'm not saying I wanna quit school and sit at the corners and smoke weed and drink my life away. I want to work, on my dream and my purpose." Nyovest moved to Johannesburg, South Africa's largest city and capital, in 2008.

EARLY CAREER
Nyovest was signed to the label Impact Sound, run by producer Thabiso Tsotetsi. Nyovest told *CNBC Africa* that Tsotetsi "didn't wanna be associated with a child who dropped out of school

Photo by Kevin Mazur/Getty Images for Global Citizen Festival: Mandela 100

so he watched from a distance." For two years, little happened with Nyovest's career. In 2010, he tried to launch his own record label, called Press Play Music, but the venture fared poorly. Nyovest was forced to return home to Mafikeng, where he slept on a mattress given to him by his grandmother. Soon, one of his sisters, Tsholofelo, lent him her last 100 rand (about eight US dollars) to take a cab back to Johannesburg.

The same year, 2010, Nyovest wrote a song called "Holla at a Pantsula" and released it on YouTube. (Pantsula is a South African subculture revolving around an energetic form of dance; the name is used for both the dance style and those who practice it.) The song, which samples the 1981 Grover Washington Jr. song "Just the Two of Us," garnered him significant attention within the music industry and among the general public. The rapper, HHP, was impressed with Nyovest's work and invited him to rap on a song called "Wamo Tseba Mtho." It marked the beginning of a turbulent friendship. Nyovest went on tour with the rapper in 2011, and HHP paid him for every show. Nyovest appeared on several more HHP songs, including "Papada" and "Past Time," before HHP's death in 2018. At the rapper's memorial, as quoted by Sabelo Mkhabela for *Okay Africa* (31 Oct. 2018), Nyovest recalled that his "biggest dream" when he was starting out was to sign with HHP's label. "And he told me I'm not an artist that should be signed, I could be a businessman, as big as [hip-hop mogul] Lil Wayne, he would always tell me that. And I was thinking this guy is crazy, I'm hungry, I'm just trying to release this album." In the end, however, Nyovest heeded HHP's advice.

TSHOLOFELO

In 2013, Nyovest released his first single, "Gusheshe," featuring rapper Okmalumkoolkat. The title refers to the South African term for the coveted BMW 325iS. The song was a major hit, earning Nyovest four awards at the South African Hip Hop Awards in 2013, including song of the year, best collaboration (with Okmalumkoolkat), best video, and best freshman. The popularity of "Gusheshe" paved the way for the successful debut of his first album, *Tsholofelo* (2014), named after the sister who had loaned him the money to return to Johannesburg. (Her name means "hope" in Tswana.) The same year, Nyovest launched his own record label, Family Tree. "Artists get only eight percent of their record sales, [it's the] industry standard, and 50 percent of their show money," he explained to *CNBC Africa*. "I didn't want that, I wanted 100 percent of everything."

Nyovest described *Tsholofelo* as "a collage of music" to Tshepang Tlhapane for *Live SA* (25 June 2014). "It has one story line though, the whole album is Ntwana ya ko kasi (kid from the

hood) trying to make it in the big city and make history." The album's second single was called "Doc Shebeleza," after a legend of kwaito music, or South African house music. A remix of the song features American rapper Talib Kweli. Andy Petersen, for the South African music magazine *Platform* (23 July 2014), called "Doc Shebeleza" "one of the most distinctive hip hop singles to come out of the country in the last few years." Nyovest's third single was a diss track called "Phumakim," on which Nyovest took shots at rival rapper AKA, engendering a well-known beef.

Petersen wrote that the album as a whole draws references from US hip-hop, but also from kwaito and South African artists such as HHP. He concluded of *Tsholofelo*: "This is an artist in motion—one unafraid to exhibit his growth. *Tsholofelo* is certainly not a perfect album, but it is a very good one. And it hints strongly of someone who is only going to get better."

FILL UP THE DOME

In 2015, Nyovest released the lead single for his sophomore album *Refiloe*, a trap song called "Mama I Made it." On one verse, he addresses his mother, rapping: "But you, you let me drop out of school / All of your friends used to call you a fool / Now when I go home I pull up in a coupe." He also announced his intention to "fill up the Dome," or sell out the 20,000-seat Ticketpro Dome stadium in Johannesburg. Nyovest put up millions of his own money to prove that local artists could draw the same crowds as international acts. In October 2015 he became the first South African artist to sell out the Dome. He released the self-titled *Refiloe* the day of the concert, handing out a copy to each attendee—a stunt that caused the album to go gold almost immediately. Tecla Ciolfi, for the South African music blog *Texx and the City* (13 Nov. 2015), described *Refiloe* as "an echoing, memorable album" that focuses on Nyovest's turbulent teenage years.

In 2016, Nyovest announced his intention to sell out the Orlando Stadium, also in Johannesburg. Nyovest did not entirely sell out the Orlando, but came close, filling up the stadium just short of its 40,000-seat capacity and nearly doubling his audience from the year before. In 2017, Nyovest aimed to fill the FNB stadium in Johannesburg, the largest stadium in Africa, by selling 75,000 tickets. (The stadium seats nearly 95,000.) He won international headlines when 68,000 people filled the venue, also known as Soccer City or the Calabash. Again, Nyovest put up his money to finance the spectacle, even selling his sports car collection. "At that moment, my dream meant more than having a car," he told Hansen. "Having a car doesn't mean anything when the stadium is empty. . . so, I would [rather] do without everything I didn't need to make sure that this dream comes true."

THUTO AND SWEET AND SHORT

In 2017, Nyovest released his third album, *Thuto* (2017), named for his older sister. (Her name means "learning" in Tswana.) The cover of the album features a contemplative Nyovest, striking a thinker's pose—though the rims of his glasses and his jewelry shine gold in the black-and-white photo. "This [picture] sets the mood for the music on *Thuto*: ruminations on the past and its travails, sometimes cheery predictions for the future, and a deep-seated appreciation for the present," Uzoma Ihejirika wrote for *This Is Africa* (3 July 2017). American singer-songwriter Goapele is featured on the songs "Confused" and "Destiny," belonging to the album's introspective and vulnerable first half. The song "Ng'yekeleni," of the second, "chest-thumping" half, as Ihejirika put it, features American rap legend Black Thought, also known as Tariq Trotter, of the Roots.

Nyovest's next album, *Sweet and Short* (2018), expresses his love for kwaito music. It was released on the eve of Nyovest's bid to "fill up" the Moses Mabhida Stadium in Durban, South Africa. Although he was successful at drawing a large audience to the venue, he lost millions on the concert because of a lack of sponsors. On *Sweet and Short*, Nyovest samples HHP and offers a rendition of the Doc Shebeleza hit "Gets Getsa." Carlos Ncube, for *Music in Africa* (6 Dec. 2018), expressed disappointment with the album as a whole, describing a "lack of synergy between the songs." "The offering would have made more sense if it were presented as throwback mixtape," he wrote.

SUGGESTED READING

Ciolfi, Tecla. Review of *Refiloe*, by Cassper Nyovest. *Texx and the City*, 13 Nov. 2015, texxandthecity.com/2015/11/cassper-nyovest/. Accessed 16 May 2019.

Hansen, Gabriel Myers. "Cassper Nyovest: I'm in Position to Lead African Hip-Hop." *Music in Africa*, 6 Apr. 2018, www.musicinafrica. net/magazine/cassper-nyovest-im-position-lead-african-hip-hop. Accessed 16 May 2019.

Ihejirika, Uzoma. Review of *Thuto*, by Cassper Nyovest. *This Is Africa*, 3 July 2017, thisisafrica.me/lifestyle/review-cassper-nyovests-thuto/. Accessed 16 May 2019.

Mkhabela, Sabelo. "Cassper Nyovest Shares the Story of How His First Collaboration with HHP Came About." *Okay Africa*, 31 Oct. 2018, www.okayafrica.com/cassper-nyovest-first-hhp-collaboration/. Accessed 16 May 2019.

Ncube, Carlos. "Cassper Nyovest Shares Love for Kwaito on *Sweet and Short*." Review of *Sweet and Short*, by Cassper Nyovest. *Music in Africa*, 6 Dec. 2018, www.musicinafrica. net/magazine/cassper-nyovest-shares-love-kwaito-sweet-and-short. Accessed 16 May 2019.

Petersen, Andy. Review of *Tsholofelo*, by Cassper Nyovest. *Platform*, 23 July 2014, pltfrm.co.za/album-review-cassper-nyovest-tsholofelo/. Accessed 16 May 2019.

"South African Rapper Cassper Nyovest Continues to Break Barriers." *CNBC Africa*, 23 Dec. 2016, www.cnbcafrica.com/news/southern-africa/2016/12/23/casper-nyovest-rapper-music/. Accessed 16 May 2019.

SELECTED WORKS

Tsholofelo, 2014; *Refiloe*, 2015; *Thuto*, 2017; *Sweet and Short*, 2018

—*Molly Hagan*

Alexandria Ocasio-Cortez

Date of birth: October 13, 1989
Occupation: Politician

On June 26, 2018, Alexandria Ocasio-Cortez, a native of the Bronx who had never run for public office, defeated ten-term US representative Joe Crowley in the Democratic primary in New York's Fourteenth Congressional District. Ocasio-Cortez, a self-proclaimed democratic socialist, garnered more than 57 percent of the vote, stunning those who had counted on Crowley's larger war chest and entrenched authority—as chair of the House Democratic Caucus, he held the fourth-highest ranking position in House Democratic leadership—to carry him to easy victory. (Crowley had not faced a primary challenger in almost a decade.) Political observers credited Ocasio-Cortez's win to a savvy grassroots campaign and progressive agenda that included strong gun control, Medicare and higher education for all, and the dissolution of the US Immigration and Customs Enforcement (ICE) agency.

After that upset—fueled in part by a compelling viral video in which Ocasio-Cortez, who is of Puerto Rican descent, declared, "Women like me aren't supposed to run for office"—few were surprised on November 6, 2018, not long after her twenty-ninth birthday, when she soundly defeated Republican candidate Anthony Pappas in her bid to represent the Fourteenth District, a Democratic stronghold that encompasses areas of the Bronx and Queens and in which half the residents are Hispanic and nearly half are foreign-born. That victory made her the youngest woman ever elected to Congress—and an

Photo by Mark Dillman via Wikimedia Commons

integral part of a new wave of young congress-women of color.

EARLY LIFE AND EDUCATION

Alexandria Ocasio-Cortez was born on October 13, 1989, to Sergio Ocasio-Roman, an architect who ran his own small business, and his wife, Blanca. Sergio had been born in the South Bronx and Blanca hailed from Puerto Rico.

The couple initially raised Ocasio-Cortez and her younger brother, Gabriel, in the Parkchester section of the Bronx, a community of some 170 mid-rise, brick apartment buildings that had been erected by the Metropolitan Life Insurance Company to provide middle-income housing. Originally segregated, the units were largely occupied by African American, Hispanic, and South Asian residents by the time of Ocasio-Cortez's birth.

When she was five years old, Ocasio-Cortez's father, worried about the quality of the schools in the Bronx, moved the family north to a small but comfortable home in the New York suburb of Yorktown in Westchester County, purchasing the two-bedroom dwelling for $150,000 with the help of relatives. Her political opponents would later seize upon this fact to prove that she was misrepresenting herself as "a girl from the Bronx," when in fact she grew up in the wealthier northern suburb.

However, Ocasio-Cortez, who often traveled the forty minutes back to the Bronx to visit extended family, maintains she has always felt a deep connection to the borough. "My aunt and my uncle were just talking last Christmas about how they literally heard Malcolm X evangelizing on street corners. That is the institutional memory of my family and multigenerational New York families," she recalled to Bridget Read for *Vogue* (25 June 2018), explaining that three generations of the Ocasio clan had by then counted the Bronx as home. "It's actually kind of a rarity, and the reason it's a rarity is because of the changes that the city has gone through. This city is becoming too inaccessible and too unaffordable for normal people to live in anymore."

Not all the family members who remained in the Bronx fared well. "Their stories are not really mine to tell," she told David Remnick during an interview for the *New Yorker* (23 July 2018), "but growing up they were wearing t-shirts with pictures of their friends who had died—and that's just scraping the surface."

Ocasio-Cortez was a highly motivated and accomplished student—despite insinuations from some of her teachers that she might not be ready for advanced work. As a teen she read the *New York Times* each day and became outspoken about her political and social views. (Her mother has quipped to journalists that it was difficult to get her to stop talking at the dinner table.) With an eye to becoming a physician, she threw herself into her science classes, and in 2007 she garnered a second-place prize in the highly competitive Intel Science and Engineering Fair, with a project that explored the anti-aging effect of antioxidants in roundworms. (As part of her prize, an asteroid, 23238 Ocasio-Cortez, was named in her honor.) Invited to give a presentation to the local Board of Education, she was so poised that one late-comer, missing her introduction, thought he was listening to a representative of a tech company, rather than a high school senior.

Ocasio-Cortez, who volunteered as a phone-bank caller for the Obama campaign in 2008, next entered Boston University, where she paid tuition with a cobbled-together package of loans and scholarships and majored in biochemistry.

Early in her sophomore year, her father died of cancer. Rather than becoming mired in grief, Ocasio-Cortez took just one week off from college and then tackled her studies with a new sense of purpose. "The last thing my father had told me in the hospital was 'Make me proud,'" she told Remnick. "I took it very literally." She switched her major to economics and international relations and began working part time in Senator Edward Kennedy's Boston office, where she worked to solve problems presented by constituents.

After earning her bachelor's degree in 2011, Ocasio-Cortez returned home to help her mother, who had been forced to take on work as a house cleaner and school bus driver to make ends meet after Sergio's death. For her part, Ocasio-Cortez founded a small publishing company, Brook Avenue Press, dedicated to producing children's books that contained positive depictions of life in the Bronx. (Her critics have pointed out that during her brief stint as a business owner, she came out in favor of tax deductions for startup costs, a position they characterize as hypocritical.)

That venture was less than successful, and Ocasio-Cortez turned to waiting tables and tending bar to earn money. In 2016, with the family house in danger of foreclosure, Blanca sold it and moved to Florida, where she found work as a secretary. Ocasio-Cortez, who spent some of her free time teaching courses in community leadership to high school students for the National Hispanic Institute, returned to Parkchester to live.

POLITICAL CAREER

Despite the demands of waiting on tables and tending bar, Ocasio-Cortez remained involved in political activism. In 2016 she volunteered on Bernie Sanders' presidential campaign, helping set up his Bronx headquarters in a former nail salon and knocking on doors to get out the vote. She also protested the Dakota Access Pipeline at the Standing Rock Sioux Reservation, took part in a 100-day vigil after Hurricane Maria, and explored the Black Lives Matter movement.

When it became apparent that Sanders was losing his bid, some of his staffers—reasoning that they had proven that grassroots, non-corporate campaigns could be viable—started the organization Brand New Congress (BNC), aimed at recruiting candidates similar in ideology to Sanders for the House and the Senate. One day, the group got a letter from Gabriel Ocasio-Cortez, who was writing on behalf of his politically minded sister. A BNC staffer subsequently called Ocasio-Cortez, who happened to be in Standing Rock at a protest. She was initially hesitant. "Where did I get off?" she asked Remnick rhetorically. "I mean, I'm going to tell people that I, as a waitress, should be their next congresswoman?"

Still, she was intrigued by the possibility of making a real difference in a major race. Working with the group, she learned about policy issues, debate tactics, the fine points of the Federal Election Commission (FEC), and how to use social media effectively. She particularly excelled when interacting with potential supporters personally, and over the course of a year, she and her campaign workers sent some 170,000 text messages, made about as many phone calls, and knocked on as many doors as possible in the Fourteenth District. (One of her most popular Twitter posts included a photo of her tattered walking shoes with the comment: "Respect the hustle.") She also forged ties with such local groups as the Bronx Progressives, the 7 Train Coalition, and Queens Neighborhoods United, winning over even those who had lost faith in electoral politics. It was a tactic diametrically opposed to that used by the powerful incumbent, Joe Crowley, who ran a more tradition-bound campaign with glossy mailings and much less field work.

Political observers have opined that one of her most effective moves was spending a modest $10,000 to make a two-minute-long campaign video that depicted her on a subway platform, in a neighborhood deli, buying cupcakes from a group of children, and in other workaday settings. In the voiceover, after her comment that "women like me aren't supposed to run for office," she declared: "It's time we acknowledged that not all Democrats are the same. That a Democrat who takes corporate money, profits off foreclosure, doesn't live here, doesn't send his kids to our schools, doesn't drink our water or breathe our air cannot possibly represent us. What the Bronx and Queens needs is Medicare for all, tuition-free public college, a federal jobs guarantee, and criminal-justice reform."

While Crowley was the son of a police officer and had attended a public college in Queens, Ocasio-Cortez managed to paint him as an out-of-touch elitist beholden to big-money donors. His cause was not helped by his complacency: by the time he realized Ocasio-Cortez posed a serious threat he had skipped two of three debates with her, earning the ire of the *New York Times* editorial board and setting himself up for charges that he was discounting her because she was a young minority woman. When she trounced him in a near-landslide on June 26; however, he conceded graciously.

While Ocasio-Cortez acknowledged that her youth, gender, and ethnicity had played a part in her victory, she told Remnick, "When you hear 'She won just for demographic reasons,' or low turnout, or that I won because of all the white 'Bernie bros' in Astoria—maybe that all helped. But I *smoked* this race. I didn't edge anybody out. I *dominated*. And I am going to own that."

Similarly, she dominated in the general election on November 6, winning some 78 percent of the vote and becoming the youngest woman ever elected to Congress. (Newly elected Iowa Democrat Abby Finkenauer is a close second: also twenty-nine, she is older than Ocasio-Cortez by some ten months.)

PERSONAL LIFE

Although she will now have to maintain a home in Washington, DC, Ocasio-Cortez continues to live in her eclectic neighborhood in the Bronx: journalists have commented on the nearby sari emporium, halal grocery stores, and corner pizza parlors. She is still paying student loans and until shortly before the election had no health insurance.

SUGGESTED READING

Langone, Alix. "Meet the 28-Year-Old Former Bartender Who Will Likely Become the Youngest Congresswoman Ever." *Time*, 27 June 2018, time.com/money/5323399/alexandria-ocasio-cortez-career/. Accessed 18 Oct. 2018.

Newman, Andy, Vivian Wang, and Luis Ferré-Sadurní. "Alexandria Ocasio-Cortez Emerges as a Political Star." *The New York Times*, 27 June 2018, www.nytimes.com/2018/06/27/nyregion/alexandria-ocasio-cortez-bio-profile.html. Accessed 18 Oct. 2018.

Ocasio-Cortez, Alexandria. "A No-Nonsense Conversation between Alexandria Ocasio-Cortez and Kerry Washington." Interview by Kerry Washington. *Interview Magazine*, 5 Sept. 2018, www.interviewmagazine.com/culture/a-no-nonsense-conversation-between-alexandria-ocasio-cortez-and-kerry-washington. Accessed 18 Oct. 2018.

Read, Bridget. "28-Year-Old Alexandria Ocasio-Cortez Might Just Be the Future of the Democratic Party." *Vogue*, 25 June 2018, www.vogue.com/article/alexandria-ocasio-cortez-interview-primary-election. Accessed 18 Oct. 2018.

Remnick, David. "Alexandria Ocasio-Cortez's Historic Win and the Future of the Democratic Party." *The New Yorker*, 23 July 2018, www.newyorker.com/magazine/2018/07/23/alexandria-ocasio-cortezs-historic-win-and-the-future-of-the-democratic-party. Accessed 18 Oct. 2018.

—*Mari Rich*

Katelyn Ohashi

Date of birth: April 12, 1997
Occupation: Gymnast

In January 2019 Katelyn Ohashi, a gymnast at the University of California, Los Angeles (UCLA), became an overnight sensation after a video of her perfect 10.0 floor routine went viral. The video, which had garnered over 117 million views online by July 2019, was notable for Ohashi's technical prowess—it was the sixth perfect score of her collegiate career—but also for her infectious enthusiasm and her shimmies and claps between dizzying flips and splits, all set to a medley of music by the Jackson 5, Earth, Wind & Fire, Tina Turner, and Michael Jackson.

"Performing is my favorite thing," Ohashi told Victor Mather for the *New York Times* (15 Jan. 2019) of her evident joy in the viral video. "What you see is how I feel."

Ohashi's joyful performance belied the anguish of her athletic journey, however. The Seattle native had begun practicing gymnastics at age three. By the time she was nine, she had moved halfway across the country to train in a more rigorous environment. Like most young, female elite gymnasts, who peak in their teens, Ohashi's sights were set on the Olympics. At sixteen, she bested future gold medalist Simone Biles to win the prestigious 2013 American Cup. It was her first senior meet at the international level, but unfortunately, it would also be her last. Sidelined by serious injuries and an eating disorder, Ohashi found refuge as a member of UCLA's gymnastics team, an organization that values healthy living and community over winning at any price.

EARLY LIFE AND TRAINING

Katelyn Michelle Ohashi was born to Richard and Diana Ohashi in Seattle, Washington, on April 12, 1997. She is the youngest of four, with three older brothers, Ryan, Kyle, and Kalen. She grew up outside of Seattle, in Newcastle, Washington. Her mother, a former high school gymnast, maintains that Ohashi was a gymnast before she even emerged from the womb. "My whole pregnancy I'm like, 'This kid's doing cartwheels,'" she recalled to Mike Vorel for the *Seattle Times* (10 Feb. 2019). As a toddler, Ohashi climbed tables and doorjambs. Her mother enrolled her in a gymnastics class when she was three. Ohashi's potential was evident, and she was encouraged to pursue elite training. In 2006, when Ohashi was nine years old, her family made the difficult decision to let her train at Great American Gymnastics Express (GAGE) near Kansas City, Missouri, with coach, Al Fong. Ohashi's mother and one of her brothers, Kalen, moved halfway across the country with her. In 2009, when Ohashi was twelve, she finished tenth at her first elite nationals meet. The same year, Ohashi, her mother and Kalen moved again. They settled in Plano, Texas, where Ohashi trained at the World Olympic Gymnastics Academy (WOGA) with her coach, Valeri Liukin, a former Olympic gold medalist for the Soviet Union and the father of 2008 American gold medalist Nastia Liukin. Ohashi attended Spring Creek Academy, a special school that allowed her to practice gymnastics for seven hours a day, six days a week. In an interview with Rich Myhre for the *Everett Herald* (16 Mar. 2012), a young Ohashi admitted that the arrangement, particularly the family separation, was difficult. "But I think it's worth it," she said. "And I'm hoping it'll pay off." In 2012, at the Pacific Rim Gymnastics championships, Ohashi placed

Photo by Timothy Nwachukwu/NCAA Photos via Getty Images

first in all-around, uneven bars, balance beam and floor exercise in the junior division. Her beam routine was harder than any other being performed in the world. "For Katelyn, the sky's the limit. Nothing less," her coach, Liukin, told *International Gymnast Magazine* at the time, as quoted by Myhre. "I'm not exaggerating one single bit. Under very careful coaching, there is nothing impossible for that kid."

2013 AMERICAN CUP
After her performance at the national championships, some speculated that Ohashi was good enough to make the five-woman United States team for the 2012 Olympic Games in London. But gymnasts must be sixteen years old to compete in the Olympic Games. Ohashi missed the cut-off by a little more than four months. She set her sights instead on the 2016 Olympic Games in Rio de Janeiro.

In 2013, Ohashi bested Simon Biles to win the American Cup. Some have criticized the elite, international competition as a showcase for American athletes, but it remains a good indicator of Olympic talent; Biles went on to become a four-time Olympic champion. Other recent American Cup winners include all-around Olympic gold medalists Nastia Liukin and Gabby Douglas. The competition was Ohashi's international senior debut. "It feels so great to be out here—it's a great way to start my senior career," she told *USA Gymnastics* (2 Mar. 2013) after the meet. "I want to keep upgrading my routines and focus on cleaning them up and being consistent." Little did Ohashi realize at the time that the American Cup would be the last meet of

her elite career. Shortly after the American Cup, Ohashi realized that she had been competing with a fractured back and two torn shoulders. She was also struggling with an eating disorder. Ohashi dropped out of elite competition to save her body and was surprised by the decision's initial effect on her. "It was a relief," she told Daniela Tijerina for *Rolling Stone* (2 Mar. 2019). "Then, once I figured out I didn't have anything else I knew how to do, it was devastating."

NCAA CAREER AND BLOG
Ohashi graduated from Plano Senior High School in 2015. After a yearlong break from gymnastics, she enrolled at UCLA in 2016. She joined the gymnastics team, helmed by longtime coach Valorie Kondos Field, known as Ms. Val. "It took me finding Ms. Val and UCLA and having a different goal and path to follow, to finally find joy and love within the sport again," Ohashi said in a video for the *Players Tribune* (8 Aug. 2018). "I haven't been able to feel this type of happiness in a long time. It's not the outcome. It's not me standing on the podium with medals. It's me being able to walk out with a smile on my face and truly being happy with myself."

In January 2017, Ohashi and her friend Maria Caire launched a blog called *Behind the Madness*. On it, she writes about her struggles with injuries and body image. In one post, titled "Dear Standards" (24 Aug. 2017), Ohashi shares excerpts of her teenage diary. In one entry from 2010, when Ohashi was thirteen, she writes that her coach attributes any mistakes in her performance to her weight. She writes about how each day she measures her thighs with her hands to gage weight gain. In another entry from 2011, Ohashi writes about how her mother hides the unhealthy food she buys for Ohashi's brother. "I understand that this might be for my own benefit but at times it feels as if everywhere I look someone is telling me or doing something to let me know that I am already too big," she writes. She confides that after finding and eating some of the hidden food, she forces herself to exercise until her "conscience is clean enough to fall asleep." In December of that year, she writes about being kicked out of practice for being too heavy. Ohashi shared similar stories in her video for the *Players Tribune*, saying that she was once described as "a bird that was too fat to lift itself off the ground." Ohashi is not the only gymnast to feel abused by the sport. Margzetta Frazier, one of Ohashi's UCLA teammates, captured Ohashi's divided spirit, torn between her love of gymnastics and anger at the suffering she endured in pursuit of her dream. "Elite gymnastics is messed up," Frazier told Carla Correa for the *New York Times* (18 Feb. 2019). Her choice of words suggested a culture of silence surrounding abuse in the sport. "I don't care how many people come at me for that. Because they know it's true. It's decades of evil. And I feel bad saying that, because I love gymnastics and I've had some great coaches."

Ohashi thrived in the tightknit world of UCLA gymnastics. In 2018, the UCLA team won its seventh national championship, Ohashi was the NCAA floor champion. A video of her floor routine, set to the music of Michael Jackson, garnered over 90 million views online. In 2019, her viral routine at the Collegiate Challenge at the Anaheim Convention Center Arena in January, inspired by the choreography for the video for Janet Jackson's 1989 hit "Rhythm Nation," earned her a perfect 10 score, international exposure, and an interview on *Good Morning America*. Ohashi graduated from UCLA in 2019 with a degree in gender studies and continues to speak out about her experiences.

At ESPN's Excellence in Sports Performance Yearly (ESPY) Awards in July 2019, Ohashi won two awards for her viral routine. She won the ESPY Award for Best Play, beating Kawhi Leonard's series-winning buzzer beater in game 7 of the National Basketball Association Eastern Conference Semifinals, and the ESPY Award for Best Viral Sports Moment.

SUGGESTED READING

Correa, Carla. "How a Ballet Dancer Brought Balance to U.C.L.A. Gymnastics." *The New York Times*, 18 Feb. 2019, www.nytimes.com/2019/02/18/sports/valorie-kondos-field-ucla-gymnastics.html. Accessed 15 July 2019.

Mather, Victor. "For Katelyn Ohashi, Viral Gymnastics Joy Was No Act." *The New York Times*, 15 Jan. 2019, www.nytimes.com/2019/01/15/sports/katelyn-ohashi-ucla-gymnastics.html. Accessed 15 July 2019.

Myhre, Rich. "Gymnast Katelyn Ohashi Made Big Sacrifices for a Big Goal." *Everett Herald*, 16 Mar. 2012, www.heraldnet.com/sports/gymnast-made-big-sacrifices-for-a-big-goal/. Accessed 15 July 2019.

Ohashi, Katelyn. "Dear Standards." *Behind the Madness*, 24 Aug. 2017, behindthemadnesssite.wordpress.com/2017/08/24/dear-standards/. Accessed 15 July 2019.

Ohashi, Katelyn. "I Was Broken." *The Players Tribune*, 8 Aug. 2018, www.theplayerstribune.com/en-us/videos/katelyn-ohashi-gymnastics-ucla. Accessed 15 July 2019.

Tijerina, Daniela. "Gymnast Katelyn Ohashi's Leap of Faith." *Rolling Stone*, 2 Mar. 2019, www.rollingstone.com/culture/culture-features/gymnast-katelyn-ohashi-ucla-interview-796878/. Accessed 15 July 2019.

Vorel, Mike. "Newcastle Native, UCLA Gymnastics Sensation Katelyn Ohashi Has Always Had Talent. Now, Her Joy Is Back." *The Seattle Times*, 10 Feb. 2019, www.seattletimes.com/sports/college/ucla-gymnast-newcastle-native-and-viral-sensation-katelyn-ohashi-finds-her-voice-and-joy/. Accessed 15 July 2019.

—*Molly Hagan*

Shohei Ohtani

Date of birth: July 5, 1994
Occupation: Baseball player

For Japanese baseball player Shohei Ohtani, joining the Los Angeles Angels represented a significant adjustment. "Everything was different—the baseball, the culture," he said in a press conference, as reported by the Associated Press (21 Nov. 2018). "I was aware right away of a higher level of power, technique and speed." Nevertheless, Ohtani—who typically gives interviews through interpreter Ippei Mizuhara—was well prepared for the major leagues, having distinguished himself as both a pitcher and a batter over five seasons with Japan's Hokkaido Nippon-Ham Fighters. Although he struggled somewhat during spring training, Ohtani put forth a strong performance during his debut season with the Angels and went on to win the title of American League (AL) Rookie of the Year.

An avid baseball player since early childhood, Ohtani participated in a rigorous baseball program while in high school and in 2013 joined the Fighters, a major-league team within Nippon Professional Baseball. In 2016 Ohtani accompanied the Fighters to the Japan Series (the Japanese equivalent of the World Series) and played a decisive role in the team's victory over the Hiroshima Toyo Carps. Although he had experienced significant success in Japan, moving to the United States represented a host of new possibilities for Ohtani to develop as a player and progress in his career, and his debut season with the Angels hinted at the potential of seasons to come. "I didn't really know what to expect here, so I didn't really set any expectations for myself," Ohtani said, as quoted by Kyle Glaser for *Baseball America* (4 Oct. 2018). "But once I got here, I feel like I got the level of competition early, even though there were some struggles."

EARLY LIFE AND EDUCATION

Shohei Ohtani was born on July 5, 1994, in Mizusawa (now Oshu), Japan, the youngest of three children. His father, Toru, worked at an automotive assembly plant and played for a corporate recreational baseball team, while his mother, Kayoko, had played competitive badminton. An energetic child, he was particularly adventurous during his early years and "would try anything,"

Photo by Keith Allison via Wikimedia Commons

his father told the newspaper *Mainichi* (11 Dec. 2017). "If you didn't take care to watch him, it was dangerous." Ohtani began playing baseball while in primary school and soon demonstrated a talent for the sport, which he went on to play for the Ichinoseki Little Senior team. His father served as a coach for Ohtani's team during that period.

In 2010 Ohtani began attending Hanamaki Higashi in Iwate, a high school particularly known for its strong baseball program. Players played the sport year-round and lived in dormitories, where they were responsible for a variety of chores. Pitchers—including Ohtani—were specifically responsible for cleaning the toilets, per baseball coach Hiroshi Sasaki's wishes. "The pitcher, especially in Shohei's case, is literally and figuratively at the highest point on the field," Sasaki told Tim Keown for *ESPN* (6 Apr. 2018). "Once they get up there, they are at the pinnacle, so for the rest of the day I tell them, 'You have to do the lowest job.' Shohei never complained." While in high school, Ohtani competed in a number of major high school–level events, including the National High School Baseball Invitational Tournament in 2012. He gained significant attention for his play, including from Japanese teams and scouts from US franchises.

NPB CAREER

Although Ohtani considered joining a US baseball franchise after high school, he was drafted by the Sapporo-based Hokkaido Nippon-Ham Fighters, a team within the Nippon Professional Baseball (NPB) Pacific League, which convinced him of the benefits of staying in Japan. After joining the team in 2013, at the age of eighteen, Ohtani played a variety of positions during his debut season, filling roles such as outfielder and pitcher. He played in seventy-seven games and pitched in thirteen over the course of the season, during which he achieved a batting average of .238 and an earned-run average (ERA) of 4.23. Over the next several seasons, Ohtani continued to develop as a player, impressing baseball fans with his dual ability to pitch and hit. He made the All-Star Games five years running, as a starting pitcher in 2014 and 2015 and a starting designated hitter in 2016 and 2017.

The year 2016 was a particularly strong one for Ohtani, who in July of that year won the NPB Home Run Derby. During the regular season he managed a batting average of .322 and a career-low ERA of 1.86, in addition to scoring a career high of twenty-two home runs. In October, the Fighters beat the Fukuoka SoftBank Hawks in the Pacific League Climax Series and won the right to compete in the Japan Series, the NPB championship. The Fighters ultimately faced the Hiroshima Toyo Carp in a six-game series and, with a record of four games to two, won the series for the first time since 2006. Ohtani was a valuable contributor to the Fighters' victory, serving as both a pitcher and a designated hitter at various points and batting in the final, game-winning run in game 3. He was named most valuable player (MVP) for his league. The 2017 season was also a strong one for Ohtani, who achieved a new career-high batting average of .332, despite struggling with leg injuries and missing half the games that season.

In November 2017 Ohtani announced that he planned to leave the Fighters and move to the United States, where he hoped to play for a Major League Baseball (MLB) team. After several weeks of speculation regarding his eventual destination, Ohtani signed with the Los Angeles Angels of the American League (AL) as a free agent in early December. In addition to signing a six-year contract with the team, Ohtani received the league-minimum salary of $545,000 and a signing bonus of more than $2.3 million. He joined the Angels for spring training in early 2018 and initially struggled to adjust to the necessary level of play, which prompted some sports commentators to argue that Ohtani was not yet ready to play in the US major leagues.

MLB DEBUT

Ohtani made his debut with the Angels on March 29, 2018, in the season opener against the Oakland Athletics. Although the Angels lost the game, Ohtani immediately proved his value to the team, hitting a single during his first time at bat. "I had some good at-bats, and some not so good at-bats," he said following the game, as reported by Paul Gutierrez for *ESPN* (30 Mar. 2018). "That (first) at-bat, I'm probably never going to forget the rest of my life. Now I have to have better at-bats to help the team." Following his major-league debut, Ohtani was named the AL Rookie of the Month for April and also earned the title of Player of the Week during that period. He was named Rookie of the Month again in September.

Over the course of the 2018 season, which the Angels finished ranked fourth out of five in the AL West, Ohtani played in 104 games with the Angels, had a batting average of .285, and hit fifty-nine runs and twenty-two home runs. He pitched in ten games (starting in all of them) and had an ERA of 3.31. In addition to distinguishing himself as a strong addition to the Angels, he notably became the first player in MLB history to hit fifteen home runs and complete fifty strikeouts in a single season, drawing comparisons to baseball legend Babe Ruth. Ohtani went on to be named the 2018 AL Rookie of the Year, a title that underscored the substantial contrast between his underperformance during spring training and his later achievements. "I have no satisfaction showing (people) up or anything like that because looking at my numbers during spring training, I can't really blame them for saying those type of things," he said, as quoted by Glaser. "Maybe I really was not major league-ready at that time. But that time was really important to me now that I look back at it. Without those struggles, maybe I wouldn't have had success this year. I tried to take positive stuff out of it."

Ohtani made regular game appearances throughout the 2018 season but did not play for much of June due to a torn ligament in his elbow. That preexisting injury was caused by years of high-speed pitching and had worsened during his early weeks with the Angels, and he decided to undergo surgery that October. "I'm glad I had the surgery," he said in a press conference, as reported by the Associated Press. "Of course, there was some reluctance over whether to have it, but considering the long term I decided it was necessary." Although Ohtani was able to return to play following the surgery, he and his team did not expect him to pitch in a game until 2020.

SOPHOMORE SEASON

The Angels began the 2019 season on March 28, with a game against the Oakland Athletics; however, Ohtani did not rejoin the team's roster until May 7, when he returned to the field as designated hitter in a game against the Detroit Tigers. He played regularly throughout May and early June, scoring twenty runs and nine home runs over his first thirty-five games. In keeping with expectations following his elbow surgery, he did not pitch during that period and instead filled the role of designated hitter. Nevertheless, Angels leadership remained focused on his recovery and planned to have him fill the roles of both a hitter and the starting pitcher once he could do so. "I want him out there doing both disciplines because that's what he's trained for," Billy Eppler, the general manager of the Angels, told Glaser. "I know that's a goal of his and I think now that people have seen it, I think it's a goal of everybody to continue to see him do that."

In addition to fulfilling his goals with the Angels, Ohtani expressed interest in playing baseball in the 2020 Summer Olympics in Tokyo, Japan, which were set to be the first Olympic Games since 2008 to feature the sport. "As baseball is back in the program, I'd love to take part, I think that's just natural," Ohtani said, as reported by the Associated Press.

PERSONAL LIFE

Ohtani lived in the Fighters' team dormitories but moved to the Los Angeles area after joining the Angels, whom he chose in part because of Mike Trout, a humble, baseball-minded superstar Ohtani admired. Despite the language barrier, Trout soon befriended the younger player.

Ohtani has at times commented on the challenges associated with adjusting to living and playing in the United States, telling Ryan Fagan for *SportingNews* (21 Mar. 2018), "When I came here I tried not to change anything, just tried to keep everything the same as my days in Japan. And if that doesn't work out, obviously there are going to be some adjustments I need to make here. I'm starting to learn those adjustments and trying to work on that right now."

SUGGESTED READING

Fagan, Ryan. "Shohei Ohtani on Mike Trout, Baseball Cards and Adjusting to MLB Spring Training." *SportingNews*, 21 Mar. 2018, www.sportingnews.com/us/mlb/news/mlb-shohei-ohtani-los-angeles-angels-japan-mike-trout-adjust-pitching-hitting-babe-ruth-autographs/16fc563u5osm41ja6c9w9f00mq. Accessed 14 June 2019.

"Father of Baseball Star Ohtani Coached Son with Life Tips in 'Very Ordinary' Upbringing." *Mainichi*, 11 Dec. 2017, mainichi.jp/english/articles/20171211/p2a/00m/0sp/014000c. Accessed 14 June 2019.

Glaser, Kyle. "2018 MLB Rookie of the Year: Shohei Ohtani." *Baseball America*, 4 Oct. 2018, www.baseballamerica.com/stories/2018-mlb-rookie-of-the-year-shohei-ohtani. Accessed 14 June 2019.

Gutierrez, Paul. "Angels' Ohtani: 'Never Going to Forget' First At-Bat, a Single." *ESPN*, 30 Mar. 2018, www.espn.com/mlb/story/_/id/22955841/

shohei-ohtani-los-angeles-angels-singles-first-major-league-bat. Accessed 14 June 2019.

Keown, Tim. "The One's Baseball's Been Waiting For." *ESPN*, 6 Apr. 2018, www.espn.com/espn/feature/story/_/id/23042516/los-angeles-angels-star-shohei-ohtani-trying-never-seen. Accessed 14 June 2019.

Lee, Joon. "Amid the Mania, Shohei Ohtani, Like Mike Trout, Tries to Limit the Distractions." *Bleacher Report*, 17 Apr. 2018, bleacherreport.com/articles/2770853-amid-the-mania-shohei-ohtani-like-mike-trout-tries-to-limit-the-distractions. Accessed 14 June 2019.

"Shohei Ohtani Says Right Elbow Surgery Was 'Necessary,' Reflects on Rookie Year." *ESPN*, 21 Nov. 2018, www.espn.com/mlb/story/_/id/25344717/shohei-ohtani-los-angeles-angels-reflects-first-mlb-season. Accessed 14 June 2019.

—*Joy Crelin*

Viktor Orbán

Date of birth: May 31, 1963
Occupation: Politician

Viktor Orbán is a Hungarian politician who has been elected prime minister three times beginning in 1998.

EARLY LIFE AND EDUCATION

Viktor Orbán is a Hungarian politician elected to three terms as prime minister of Hungary. He began his career as a champion of liberal democratic reformation in Hungary, advocating free market economics and western democratic ideals. In his later political career, he aligned with conservatives and generated global controversy by erecting a border wall in 2015 to bar the passage of foreign refugees into Hungary.

Orbán was born on May 31, 1963, in the Hungarian village of Alcsútdoboz. He has revealed that his childhood was working class and that his father was an often-violent authoritarian. He attended Eötvös Loránd University, where he earned a degree in law, and later spent a few months on scholarship at Pembroke College at Oxford University in the United Kingdom. He ended his studies at Oxford in 1989 after the start of the Velvet Revolution in Prague.

Although he entered politics at a young age, Orbán was at one time a professional soccer player for a Hungarian club team. As a politician, he has worked to boost the presence and popularity of the sport in Hungary. Orbán's early political career was characterized by his involvement in attempts to reestablish Hungary's image as a progressive democracy in the wake of the Soviet era. In 1987, at age twenty-four, Orbán was a founding member of Hungary's Federation of Young Democrats political party, also known as Fidesz. Orbán made his first major political appearance in 1989, when he gave a pro-Western democracy speech to a crowd attending a ceremony in Budapest for the reburial of Imre Nagy, a Hungarian premier and revolutionary who was executed by the Soviets. At that speech, he renounced communism, called for open elections, and demanded Soviet forces leave Hungary. Orbán's bold ideology won him attention and favor as a new political player for Hungary. He was soon elected as a member of parliament in 1990, in one of the country's first votes as a post-Soviet multiparty democracy.

PRIME MINISTER OF HUNGARY

Fidesz struggled to compete with the liberal Alliance of Free Democrats and lost the national election in 1994. Historians have observed this as the turning point in Orbán's political leanings. Seeing that there was not a dominant conservative party in Hungary at the time, Orbán adopted a new identity for Fidesz, rebranding it as a right-wing alternative to its former self.

Orbán's Fidesz party won three national elections, making him prime minister, first in 1998, later in 2010, and again in 2014. His early work as prime minister encouraged economic growth and saw Hungary join North Atlantic Treaty Organization (NATO) in March 1999. He lost reelection in 2002 amid corruption scandals within his party.

In the years between his first premiership and his 2010 election, Hungary's economy had collapsed, enabling Orbán to run again as a reform candidate, though this time more sharply conservative than the incumbent Socialist Party. In his later premierships, Orbán has dismissed many of his formerly touted views and has angered former political allies and heads of state.

In 2015 Orbán ordered the construction of a 109-mile fence along Hungary's border with Serbia, intended to block refugees from Syria, Iraq, Afghanistan, and North Africa from entering the European Union (EU) along the short border. The fence, constructed of barbed wire, created global controversy for Orbán, who is seen as unsympathetic to the plight of refugees from war-torn Middle Eastern states. Orbán's critics have pointed out that his construction of the fence is antithetical to his once-held views about post-Soviet Europe, during which he advocated greater freedoms and liberal social reforms. He has gained criticism from other members of the EU for his views on Muslim refugees, his expressed desire to return to Christian intellectualism, and to maintain a homogeneous population in Hungary. He has also raised questions among his peers for his Putinist sympathies.

With regard to his strong shift to the right, Orbán classified his early political work as that of a freedom fighter, whereas in his later years, he was obligated to become more pragmatic. "It would be irresponsible not to have changed my mind and behavior," he told *Politico*. "The meaning of liberalism has changed."

IMPACT

Orbán has been a major figure in Hungarian politics since his emergence in 1987 as the co-founder of Fidesz. Today, Fidesz is the leading nationalist-conservative party in Hungarian politics, despite its start as a liberal youth movement. At the time of his election in 1998, Orbán was the youngest Hungarian prime minister elected in the twentieth century.

PERSONAL LIFE

Orbán has said he relaxes by watching soccer and reading books. Orbán is married to Anikó Lévai, a lawyer. The couple has five children.

SUGGESTED READING

Higgins, Andrew. "Hungary's Migrant Stance, Once Denounced, Gains Some Acceptance." *The New York Times.* 20 Dec. 2015, /www.nytimes.com/2015/12/21/world/europe/hungary-viktor-orban-migrant-crisis.html. Accessed 2 Jan. 2019.

"Hungary PM Viktor Orban: Antagonising Europe since 2010." *BBC News*, 4 Sept. 2015, / www.bbc.com/news/world-europe-16390574. Accessed 2 Jan. 2019.

Mackey, Robert. "Hungarian Leader Rebuked for Saying Muslim Migrants Must Be Blocked 'to Keep Europe Christian.'" *New York Times*, 3 Sept. 2015, www.nytimes.com/2015/09/04/world/europe/hungarian-leader-rebuked-for-saying-muslim-migrants-must-be-blocked-to-keep-europe-christian.html. Accessed 2 Jan. 2019.

"Point Taken, Mr. Orban." *The Economist.* Economist Newspaper, 26 Sept. 2015, www.economist.com/europe/2015/09/24/point-taken-mr-orban. Accessed 2 Jan. 2019.

Puhl, Jan. "Fortress Hungary: Orbán Profits from the Refugees." *Spiegel Online.* Spiegel, 15 Sept. 2015, http://www.spiegel.de/international/europe/viktor-orban-wants-to-keep-muslim-immigrants-out-of-hungary-a-1052568.html. Accessed 2 Jan. 2019.

Rev, Istvan. "Hungary's Politics of Hate." *The New York Times*, 26 Sept. 2015, www.nytimes.com/2015/09/26/opinion/hungarys-politics-of-hate.html. Accessed 2 Jan. 2019.

Schleifer, Yigal. "How Hungary's Viktor Orban Is Slowly Destroying His Country's Democracy." *Slate*, 3 Oct. 2014, www.slate.com/news-and-politics/moment-magazine. Accessed 2 Jan. 2019.

Waller, Luke. "Viktor Orbán: The Conservative Subversive." *Politico*, 2 Dec. 2015, www.politico.eu/list/politico-28/viktor-orban/. Accessed 2 Jan. 2019.

—*Richard Means*

Maité Oronoz Rodríguez

Date of birth: ca. 1976
Occupation: Chief Justice of the Supreme Court of Puerto Rico

Maité Oronoz Rodríguez is the Chief Justice of the Supreme Court of Puerto Rico, and the first openly LGBT chief justice in the United States. Oronoz Rodríguez succeeded retiring Chief Justice Liana Fiol Matta in 2016. (In Puerto Rico, Supreme Court justices serve until they are seventy years old.) Alejandro García Padilla, who was then governor of Puerto Rico, announced Oronoz Rodríguez's nomination, saying, as quoted by Trudy Ring for the *Advocate* (13 Feb. 2016), "It is time for a generational change." Oronoz Rodríguez joined the court in 2014. At the time, she was the court's youngest associate judge, and when appointed chief justice she became the youngest justice to preside over it. Oronoz Rodríguez is part of a larger sea change in the Puerto Rican judiciary. Obed Betancourt reported for San Juan's *Caribbean Business* (26 July 2016) that, in 2016, "the judicial system comprised 59% female judges versus 41% male ones." The majority of law clerks, Betancourt reported, were also women.

Prior to her time on the bench, Oronoz Rodríguez, who was educated at Villanova University and Columbia University, served as chief legal counsel to the mayor of San Juan and deputy solicitor general for the Commonwealth of Puerto Rico. In 2019, the National Center for State Courts (NCSC) gave Oronoz Rodríguez the Distinguished Service Award for her leadership in the "restoration of court services" following hurricanes Irma and Maria.

EDUCATION AND EARLY CAREER

Oronoz Rodríguez was born around 1976 in the capital city of San Juan and lived there throughout her childhood. Her father, Mario Oronoz, was an attorney. Her mother, Dolores "Maggie" Rodríguez de Oronoz, served on Puerto Rico's Court of Appeals. She has two brothers, Mario and Fernando. Oronoz Rodríguez graduated from Villanova University in Pennsylvania with a bachelor's degree in history in 1998. During her time as an undergraduate, she spent a year studying at the University of Florence in Italy. She earned a master's degree in history from the University of Puerto Rico in Río Piedras in 1999. She attended law school at the university, where she served on the law review from 2000 to 2001 and earned her juris doctorate in 2002. She then went on to earn a master of law degree from Columbia University in 2005.

From 2002 to 2004, Oronoz Rodríguez clerked for Federico Hernández Denton, the chief justice of the Supreme Court of Puerto Rico. She served as the deputy solicitor general for the Commonwealth of Puerto Rico from 2005 to 2008. She briefly served as acting solicitor general in 2009 before taking a job in private practice with the San Juan firm Sepulvado & Maldonado.

SUPREME COURT OF PUERTO RICO

In 2013, San Juan mayor Carmen Yulín Cruz appointed Oronoz Rodríguez to direct the Office of Legal Affairs of the City of San Juan. A year later, in 2014, Governor Alejandro García Padilla nominated her to replace Liana Fiol Matta, who was assuming the role of chief justice, as an associate judge on the Supreme Court of Puerto Rico. "She represents enthusiasm, dedication to public service and an open and creative mind," García said of Oronoz Rodríguez in a statement quoted by Natalie Daher for NBC (15 July 2014). Oronoz Rodríguez's nomination was a milestone for the commonwealth, as she was the first openly gay person nominated to the Supreme Court of Puerto Rico. The senate confirmed her appointment in June 2014. In a press release, the civil rights organization Lambda Legal called it "a historical step towards achieving a judiciary that reflects Puerto Rico's full and rich diversity."

After her nomination was announced, it was reported that Oronoz Rodríguez was being investigated by the Office of Government Ethics following a complaint by Jorge Navarro of the conservative New Progressive Party (NPP). The investigation concerned Oronoz Rodríguez's decision to hire her former employer, the law firm Sepulvado & Maldonado, while she was acting as chief legal counsel to the city of San Juan. The office concluded that Oronoz Rodríguez's conduct did not violate Puerto Rico's code of ethics.

CONTROVERSIAL CONFIRMATION

In 2016, García nominated Oronoz Rodríguez to be the court's chief justice upon the retirement of Fiol Matta. "I accept this nomination with the energy and force of a new generation, with my love for Puerto Rico and my unwavering commitment to the judicial branch and justice," she said, as quoted by Ring. Three former chief justices, including José Andreu García, Hernández,

and Fiol released a joint statement in support of the nomination.

There were a number of people who were opposed to Oronoz Rodríguez's ascent to the highest seat on the court, however. Some, like the conservative, antigay group Puerto Rico for Families, felt that Oronoz Rodríguez should not have been nominated in the first place. Furthermore, the swift confirmation of Oronoz Rodríguez's nomination generated its own controversy. The senate majority, the Popular Democratic Party (PDP), a centrist party equivalent to the Democratic Party in the United States, voted to confirm Oronoz Rodríguez within days of her nomination. No public hearings were held, and the confirmation passed without a single vote from the minority parties in Puerto Rico's legislature. "The confirmation itself is not the issue, but the way it was carried out definitely is," NPP minority speaker Larry Seilhamer told Ángel Rodríguez for *Caribbean Business* (23 Feb. 2016). "The chief justice of the Supreme Court is in charge of one of the three major branches of government. To make a decision of this magnitude without senators and the people learning about her positions on various important issues related to the judicial branch and Puerto Rico in general is inconceivable." Members of the social democratic Puerto Rico Independence Party (PIP) voiced other concerns. Senator María de Lourdes Santiago told Rodríguez: "Apart from the way this confirmation has been carried out, my objections are mostly based on the poor performance that Justice Oronoz Rodríguez has shown regarding human and civil rights in Puerto Rico." Oronoz Rodríguez, García, and Senate President Eduardo Bhatia are all members of the PDP.

SUPREME COURT CHIEF JUSTICE

As chief justice, Oronoz Rodríguez has pushed to make legal services more accessible to the public. In 2017, the judicial branch began holding local events to educate people about such topics as the rights of the elderly, or drug court. To a similar end, Oronoz Rodríguez has led the charge for modernization, overseeing the creation of an accessible database for all civil cases in San Juan. Over time, Oronoz Rodríguez hopes to implement electronic filing and notifications, and digitization of judicial files across all regions.

In September 2017, the island of Puerto Rico was struck by two catastrophic hurricanes, Hurricane Irma and Hurricane Maria. Hurricane Maria alone killed over 3,000 people. In the aftermath, Oronoz Rodríguez met with groups of lawyers from the American Bar Association (ABA) to discuss allowing outside attorneys to represent Puerto Ricans in matters relating to these natural disasters. Over 1 million people affected by Maria—Puerto Rico has a population of just over 3 million—have applied for aid from the Federal Emergency Management Agency (FEMA). As of February 2019, a year and a half after the hurricanes, less than half of those applications had been approved. Lawyers in Puerto Rico and from the US mainland have scrambled to help victims file for aid, and appeal FEMA's decisions, but differences between the two legal systems have made efficient legal aid arduous. The legal system in Puerto Rico, a former Spanish colony, was modeled on the Spanish civil code.

PERSONAL LIFE

Oronoz Rodríguez is married to Gina Méndez Miró, a lawyer and former chief of staff for Senate President Eduardo Bhatia. Méndez currently serves as a judge on Puerto Rico's Court of Appeals and her appointment did not sit well with many Puerto Ricans, who saw it as a conflict of interest. Further complicating matters, one reporter pointed out that Oronoz Rodríguez's mother, a former appeals court judge herself, chairs the evaluation committee for judicial appointments. In 2018, Oronoz Rodríguez was forced by petition to announce that she would not intervene in cases decided by her wife.

Oronoz Rodríguez and Méndez have two children, twins born in 2018.

SUGGESTED READING

Betancourt, Obed. "Puerto Rico Judicial System Presided by Women." *Caribbean Business*, 26 July 2016, caribbeanbusiness.com/puerto-rico-judicial-system-presided-by-women/. Accessed 10 Apr. 2019.

Daher, Natalie. "First Openly Gay Justice Sworn onto Puerto Rico's Supreme Court." *NBC News*, 15 July 2014, www.nbcnews.com/news/latino/first-openly-gay-justice-sworn-puerto-ricos-supreme-court-n156591. Accessed 16 Apr. 2019.

Ring, Trudy. "Lesbian Nominated to Head Puerto Rico Supreme Court." *The Advocate*, 13 Feb. 2016, www.advocate.com/politics/2016/2/13/lesbian-nominated-head-puerto-rico-supreme-court. Accessed 10 Apr. 2019.

Rodríguez, Ángel. "Legislators Slam Quick Confirmation of Oronoz as Chief Justice." *Caribbean Business*, 23 Feb. 2016, caribbean-business.com/legislators-slam-quick-confirmation-of-oronoz-as-chief-justice/. Accessed 11 Apr. 2019.

—*Molly Hagan*

Naomi Osaka

Date of birth: October 16, 1997
Occupation: Tennis player

By the time tennis player Naomi Osaka was twenty years old, she had earned victories at some of her sport's most prestigious events. Although relatively unknown outside of the tennis community during her early years as a professional player, she propelled herself to the forefront in 2018, winning both her first Women's Tennis Association (WTA) title and her first Grand Slam title. The latter came at the US Open, where she notably defeated six-time champion Serena Williams and became the first Japanese woman and the first known player of Haitian descent to win a Grand Slam event. Although those victories were career-shaping ones for Osaka, her success was in many ways consistent with her earlier approach and history as a player. "Ever since I can remember, I played better against bigger players on bigger courts," she told Brook Larmer for the *New York Times* (23 Aug. 2018).

A tennis player from the age of three, Osaka began playing in International Tennis Federation (ITF) and WTA competitions as a young teen and quickly established herself as a talented player. With a powerful forehand shot that could exceed one hundred miles per hour, she became a formidable competitor despite her relatively young age. She reached a top-forty ranking in the WTA in the 2016 season, and her victories in 2018 confirmed her status as a premier up-and-coming star in the game. Already a celebrity in Japan, where she was born and for which she has competed, her international profile only continued to rise, and she kept her focus on the future. "Life is more than one tournament; it's not like I'm done playing tennis," she said in the fall of 2018, as quoted by Jon Wertheim for *Sports Illustrated* (26 Nov. 2018). "I don't expect myself to just win one Grand Slam. Not to be cocky or anything but I feel like the more confidence I put in myself, the more I play better, so I try to tell myself that if I believe in myself then there's a lot of good things that will happen."

EARLY LIFE AND EDUCATION

Naomi Osaka was born in Osaka, Japan, on October 16, 1997, to Japanese-born Tamaki Osaka and Haitian-born Léonard François. The family moved to the United States when Osaka was three years old, first moving to New York, where they lived with her paternal grandparents. They moved to Florida in 2006, settling in the Boca Raton area.

When Osaka and her older sister, Mari, were young, their father learned of the success of the American tennis-playing sisters Venus and Serena Williams and decided to encourage his own

Photo by si.robi via Wikimedia Commons

daughters to play the sport. Osaka began playing tennis at age three, and François initially served as her coach. Both girls demonstrated talent in the sport, and a degree of competitiveness developed between the two. "I don't remember liking to hit the ball," Osaka told Larmer of her early years as a tennis player. "The main thing was that I wanted to beat my sister." Following the family's move to Florida, the Osaka siblings were homeschooled so that they could focus extensively on their tennis training.

EARLY CAREER
Osaka began to compete in professional tennis events as a teenager, mostly skipping the junior competition circuit that players typically begin with. Although she had spent much of her life in the United States, she represented Japan in international competition, as her family believed that she would have more opportunities in that country's tennis organization. Osaka initially began to play in events on the International Tennis Federation (ITF) Women's Circuit, a professional women's tennis tour considered lower ranked than the high-level circuit run by the WTA. She made her debut on the ITF circuit in 2012, playing at events primarily in Florida and elsewhere in the southeastern United States. At one ITF event held in Amelia Island, Florida, Osaka notably progressed to the semifinals of the competition, where she lost to her sister, the eventual champion. She began to compete in WTA events in 2013, making early appearances at qualifiers in Quebec City, Canada, and Tokyo, Japan, but primarily appeared in ITF events over the course of that year.

For Osaka, adjusting to competitive play at times proved challenging. "Playing sports growing up, for me, it was always like a roller coaster. You would have one good result and then the next day have a bad result," she recalled to Vera Papisova for *Teen Vogue* (11 Sept. 2018). "I think you should think that it's not really the outcome, it's the process. You just gotta keep going and fighting for everything, and one day you'll get to where you want. But, the way people are, they're never satisfied, so, of course, you're going to want to get farther!"

The 2014 tennis season saw Osaka compete in both WTA and ITF events. She impressed onlookers in the 2014 Bank of the West Classic singles competition, during which she progressed to the second round before being eliminated. In 2015 she began to compete in the qualifying rounds at the Grand Slam events—the most prestigious events in professional tennis, consisting of the Australian Open, the French Open, Wimbledon, and the US Open—but did not secure a spot in the competitions themselves. Nevertheless, Osaka put forth several strong performances over the course of 2015, including a trip to the finals at an ITF event in Gifu, Japan, where she lost to Chinese player Saisai Zheng. She advanced to the finals at competition in Great Britain later that year and went on to compete in a WTA 125K series event in Hua Hin, Thailand, where she placed second, behind Kazakhstani player Yaroslava Shevdova.

DEVELOPING PLAYER
Osaka continued to progress as a professional player in 2016. She played in three of the four Grand Slam events that year, defeating numerous players to reach the third round of each. Although the prospect of facing off against a multitude of highly ranked competitors might daunt some players, Osaka sought to remain focused on the game itself rather than rankings or past successes. "I never feel pressure from playing someone that's supposed to be, like, better than me, sort of," she said, as quoted by Courtney Nguyen for the *WTA* website (2016). "I'm just going to go in there happy and hopefully try to pull off an upset."

Osaka's approach proved helpful as she continued to distinguish herself as an up-and-coming player to watch. Following her exit from the 2016 US Open—a difficult loss to US player Madison Keys after leading for much of the match—she began to be coached by notable tennis figure David Taylor. She had success at events such as the 2016 WTA Premier tournament in Tokyo, Japan, where she competed in the final round. Osaka finished 2016 ranked fortieth in the WTA and was selected as WTA Newcomer of the Year for her strong performance. By that time, she had achieved considerable celebrity in

Japan as one of the country's top players, and she strove to improve her Japanese-language skills to better communicate with the media.

In 2017 Osaka proved successful at the Grand Slam events, reaching the second round of the Australian Open, the first of the French Open, and the third of Wimbledon and the US Open. She also competed for the Japanese national tennis team in the 2017 Fed Cup. However, she failed to take a significant step forward from the previous year and ended the season ranked sixty-eighth in the WTA. Following the 2017 season, Osaka began training with German coach Sascha Bajin, who had previously worked with major players such as Serena Williams and Caroline Wozniacki.

BREAKTHROUGH YEAR

The 2018 season proved a turning point for Osaka. The year started off strong in January when she progressed to the fourth round of the Australian Open, beating highly ranked players before falling to the top-ranked Simona Halep. She made it to the third rounds of both the French Open and Wimbledon. She likewise achieved significant milestones at non–Grand Slam events such as the Miami Open, where she beat her hero Serena Williams in the first round before falling to Ukrainian player Elina Svitolina in the second. In March 2018, Osaka claimed her first WTA title at the WTA Premier Mandatory event in Indian Wells, California, defeating Russian player Daria Kasatkina to win the title and more than $1.3 million in prize money.

The most significant event of 2018 for Osaka, however, came in August and September at the US Open. She defeated Laura Siegemund, Julia Glushko, Aliaksandra Sasnovich, and Aryna Sabalenka in the early rounds of the women's singles competition to move on to the quarterfinals, where she faced off against and beat Ukrainian player Lesia Tsurenko. She defeated Keys in the semifinals before entering the final round, where she faced Serena Williams, a veteran of the Grand Slam tournaments who had previously won the US Open on six occasions and was seeking to tie a record with her twenty-fourth major singles victory. However, Osaka defeated Williams to claim her first Grand Slam title and $3.8 million in prize money.

Although the moment was theoretically a triumphant one for Osaka, the final match-up became the center of widespread controversy due to Williams's clashes with the referee during the game and the penalties he imposed on her, which Williams's supporters argued were biased and unnecessarily harsh. "I didn't really hear anything because I had my back turned, so I didn't really know there was anything going on at the moment," Osaka said of the incident during a press conference after the match, as reported by the *US Open* website (8 Sept. 2018). Because of those events and the negative reactions of many fans and media commentators, Osaka was left with mixed feelings about her victory. "I just feel like I had a lot of emotions, so I had to kind of categorize what was which emotion," she said at the press conference. She even apologized to fans for the way the match turned out, earning praise from many sports outlets for her tact.

Following the US Open, Osaka went on to compete in the finals at a WTA Premier event in Tokyo and the semifinals at a Premier Mandatory competition in Beijing, China. In October, she made her debut at the WTA Finals, where she was eliminated from competition by US player Sloane Stephens. However, her season ended later that month with a hamstring injury. Considering her strong performances during 2018, Osaka ended the year ranked fifth in the WTA and led the tour in total prize money earned. She continued to look forward, noting that she hoped to compete for Japan in the 2020 Olympics, set to be held in Tokyo.

PERSONAL LIFE

Alongside her strong performances on the court, Osaka became known for her characteristic sense of humor and her tendency to reference memes and pop culture when talking to reporters. "I feel like I'm a child of the Internet, and the Internet has raised me," she told Ben Rothenberg for the *New York Times* (21 Jan. 2016). She also considered herself very shy, which she noted occasionally combined with her deadpan humor to confuse the media, especially in Japan. In addition to playing tennis, Osaka enjoys video games such as Overwatch.

SUGGESTED READING

Farzan, Antonia Noori. "Japanese, Haitian, and Now a Grand Slam Winner: Naomi Osaka's Historical Journey to the US Open." *The Washington Post*, 10 Sept. 2018, www.washingtonpost.com/news/morning-mix/wp/2018/09/10/japanese-haitian-and-now-a-grand-slam-winner-naomi-osakas-historic-journey-to-the-u-s-open. Accessed 16 Dec. 2018.

Larmer, Brook. "Naomi Osaka's Breakthrough Game." *The New York Times Magazine*, 23 Aug. 2018, www.nytimes.com/2018/08/23/magazine/naomi-osakas-breakthrough-game.html. Accessed 16 Dec. 2018.

Nguyen, Courtney. "Osaka's Star on the Rise." *WTA Tennis*, 2016, www.wtatennis.com/news/osakas-star-rise. Accessed 16 Dec. 2018.

Osaka, Naomi. "Interview: Naomi Osaka, Final." *US Open*, 8 Sept. 2018, www.usopen.org/en_US/news/interviews/2018-09-08/2018-09-08_interview_

naomi_osaka_final.html. Accessed 16 Dec. 2018.

Osaka, Naomi. "Naomi Osaka on Mental Health and Training to Face Her Idol at the US Open." Interview by Vera Papisova. *Teen Vogue*, 11 Sept. 2018, www.teenvogue.com/ story/naomi-osaka-us-open-champion-mental-health-serena-williams?verso=true. Accessed 16 Dec. 2018.

Rothenberg, Ben. "Another Win for a Player Getting in Touch with Her Japanese Roots." *The New York Times*, 21 Jan. 2016, www.nytimes.com/2016/01/22/sports/tennis/naomi-osaka-australian-open-win-elina-svitolina-japan.html. Accessed 16 Dec. 2018.

Wertheim, Jon. "Naomi Osaka's Breakout 2018 Season Marked the Emergence of a Star." *Sports Illustrated*, 26 Nov. 2018, www.si.com/tennis/2018/11/26/naomi-osaka-us-open-title-serena-williams-2018-moments-sportsperson. Accessed 16 Dec. 2018.

—*Joy Crelin*

Natalie Panek

Date of birth: ca. 1983
Occupation: Aerospace engineer

An aspiring astronaut since childhood, aerospace engineer Natalie Panek has spent her entire career working toward facilitating the future of space exploration. As an employee of the Canadian aerospace company MacDonald, Dettwiler and Associates, she worked on advanced robotics technology such as the Next Generation Canadarm and the *Rosalind Franklin* Mars rover, which potentially represent significant steps forward for space programs worldwide. Although thrilled to be working on such projects, Panek recognizes that her work is much more than simply a fun career. "It's not just that I enjoy my job; it's that I love engineering change and using innovation and creativity to find solutions to complex and advanced problems," she told the website *Women You Should Know* (27 Aug. 2013). "I have witnessed firsthand the positive impact that transformative technology can have on society. How we can revolutionize the way we live and work using innovation and how rewarding this feels." Although Panek's dream of becoming an astronaut ended in 2017—when she was removed from the Canadian Space Agency's astronaut shortlist due to potential health concerns—she remained focused on the importance of striving to achieve one's goals. "It's awesome to set far-reaching goals and it's OK if you don't get there because there's so many opportunities to learn along the way," she explained at a 2017 seminar, as reported by Dave Waddell for the *Windsor Star* (2 Nov. 2017).

EARLY LIFE

Panek was born in Canada. She grew up in Calgary, Alberta, where her parents enjoyed spending time outdoors. They were dedicated hikers and campers, and Panek spent much of her early life exploring the Canadian Rocky Mountain region with her parents. Those childhood experiences fostered a love of exploration in Panek, and she would later link that interest in venturing into the unknown with her developing fascination with outer space. Hoping to become an astronaut one day, Panek pursued studies in science and engineering and soon learned the importance of mentors and role models in encouraging her to further her aspirations. "I was the only girl in my high school physics class, but I had this amazing female teacher who just pushed us all to challenge our limits," Panek told Joshua Ostroff for the *Huffington Post* (8 Mar. 2016). "Having her, having someone who will motivate you and push you, is a start. It's about having those role models." Panek further told Ostroff that she also drew inspiration from fictional role models, including the character Samantha Carter, an astrophysicist and US Air Force officer featured in the science-fiction television series *Stargate SG-1*.

EDUCATION AND INTERNSHIPS

After graduating from high school, Panek enrolled in the University of Calgary in 2002, where she studied mechanical engineering. While an undergraduate, Panek completed a

Photo by George Pimentel/WireImage

production engineering internship with Devon Energy, between 2005 and 2006. She also participated in the 2005 American Solar Challenge, in which teams of college students sought to create solar-powered vehicles that they would then race across North America, traveling from Texas to Calgary. As a member of the University of Calgary's team, Panek worked on developing the university's solar car and later became one of the four team members tasked with driving the vehicle, a process Panek found particularly interesting. "You're driving on the highway with everyday vehicles and transport trucks, and it's so neat to see the looks on people's faces when they see something they've never seen before," she recalled to Erin Carson for *Tech Republic* (17 July 2015). Panek graduated with her bachelor's degree in 2007.

She then pursued graduate studies at the University of Toronto, enrolling in the institution's aerospace, aeronautical, and astronautical/space engineering program. There, Panek conducted research related to combustion in microgravity and gained hands-on experience in operating scientific equipment and collecting data. At the same time, Panek was intent upon pursuing a career in space exploration, ideally as an astronaut. She was particularly interested in becoming an intern with the National Aeronautics and Space Administration (NASA) in the United States. Achieving that goal proved difficult, as NASA internships were available to a very limited number of Canadians, and Panek was rejected each time she applied. However, she was unwilling to allow the opportunity to slip away. "After my fourth rejection I just decided to call to ask why," she told Ostroff. "I didn't think I'd get anyone on the phone, but [the recruiter] gave me the intern position on the spot. I asked for feedback and he said, 'Look, you were in the top and if you really want to come, come.'" Panek spent the summer of 2008 as an intern at the NASA Goddard Space Flight Center, located outside of Washington, DC.

Panek earned her master's degree in 2009, after which she participated in a space studies program run by the International Space University, a nonprofit institution focused on space exploration. In addition to her studies and internships, Panek honed her skills as a science educator during her early career, including as a recreational programs assistant at the Ontario Science Centre. In that role, which she held from 2007 until 2010, she assisted with recreational education programs and special events related to space and engineering.

MACDONALD, DETTWILER AND ASSOCIATES

In 2010, Panek joined the Ontario-based company MacDonald, Dettwiler and Associates (MDA) as a junior member of the technical staff in the robotics division of the company, which focuses on space technology such as satellites, surveillance systems, and robotics systems for use by space programs. She was promoted to intermediate member of technical staff in 2012. During her early years at MDA, Panek worked on a variety of major robotics projects, including the Next Generation Canadarm program. The original Canadarm was a robotic arm used by NASA's Space Shuttle Program beginning in the 1980s. By the time Panek joined the company, MDA's robotics division sought to create prototypes of new, smaller robotic arms and related devices that could be used to repair satellites, assist in docking spacecraft, and perform other essential functions in space. In addition to such work, Panek contributed to efforts to overcome roadblocks to space research such as the accumulation of lunar dust on and in equipment.

Panek became a full member of the technical staff in mission systems in 2014, where she was a key member of the team responsible for working on the chassis and locomotion system for a new Mars rover. A collaboration between several manufacturers, the rover was set to travel to Mars in 2020 as part of the ExoMars mission, a joint project of the European Space Agency (ESA) and the Russian agency Roscosmos. In the mission's first stage, which launched in 2016, the agencies put the ExoMars Trace Gas Orbiter in orbit around Mars to study gases in the planet's atmosphere. The ExoMars rover, which in 2019 was named *Rosalind Franklin* after one of the scientists responsible for discovering the structure of the DNA molecule, would be tasked with the corresponding mission of collecting and analyzing samples of materials from the planet's surface to locate any potential signs of organic material on the planet. For Panek, working on robotic components of the *Rosalind Franklin* rover was both challenging and exciting. "The fun part is testing," Panek said of the process, as reported by Waddell. "We're just starting to get to play with the hardware and see if it'll hold up." In December of 2018, Panek was promoted to senior engineer in mission systems.

DREAMS OF SPACE

Although Panek enjoyed working on technology that would one day be used to explore another planet, she continued to hope to be able to travel into space herself. "It's . . . this really cool pursuit of the unknown, and trying to find out what's out there, and lifelong learning," she told Carson. Panek likewise hoped to increase the numbers of Canadian women who have traveled into space, as each of those demographics remained underrepresented within the ranks of astronauts. As of 2018, only ten Canadians had ever gone into space, only two of whom were women.

With her lifelong pursuit of a career in space exploration, academic background, and years of hands-on robotics and engineering experience, Panek proved to be a strong candidate upon entering the selection process for the Canadian Space Agency's astronaut program. Although she made the shortlist for the program, she was rejected in early 2017 because of the agency's concerns that the white streak in Panek's hair—which she has had from a young age—could be indicative of potential future health problems. The rejection was deeply disappointing for Panek, who had spent years working toward her dream. "In some sense, it feels like the biggest failure of my life," she said, as reported by Waddell. "But in some sense, it's a unique opportunity to share a story about perseverance."

WOMEN IN STEM

In addition to her work at MDA, Panek has established herself as an advocate for women in science, technology, engineering, and mathematics (STEM) fields and has worked to encourage girls and young women to pursue studies in the fields that most interest them. "Dive head-on into challenging careers. Do not be afraid of risk and take on leadership roles to revolutionize what women can accomplish in challenging fields that can influence the foundations of our generation and the next," she told *Women You Should Know* when asked what advice she would give to the next generation of women in STEM. "Develop strong teamwork skills, competence, toughness, discipline, responsibility, and confidence to help propel innovation and expand the realm of possibility."

Panek has spoken out about the underrepresentation of women in STEM and sought to address that issue by serving as a mentor for preteen and teenage girls interested in science and engineering through programs such as Cybermentor, run by the University of Calgary. A prolific public speaker, Panek has delivered talks on women in STEM as well as a variety of space-related topics. In 2015, she delivered a talk at the TEDxToronto conference on the importance of addressing the issue of space junk, miscellaneous debris from satellites and other human-made objects in orbit around Earth.

PERSONAL LIFE

Panek has received a number of awards as recognition for her work in aerospace engineering. In 2013, she received the University of Calgary's Graduates of the Last Decade Award and, in 2015, she was named one of Forbes 30 Under 30 in Manufacturing.

SUGGESTED READING

Carson, Erin. "Natalie Panek: Rocket Scientist. Women in STEM Advocate. Pilot. Aspiring Astronaut." *Tech Republic*, 17 July 2015, www.techrepublic.com/article/natalie-panek-rocket-scientist-women-in-stem-advocate-pilot-aspiring-astronaut/. Accessed 15 Feb. 2019.

Levine, Romi. "#UofTBTS16: U of T Alumni Share Their Wisdom with the Class of 2020." *University of Toronto*, 13 Sept. 2016, www.utoronto.ca/news/uoftbts16-u-t-alumni-share-their-wisdom. Accessed 15 Feb. 2019.

Ostroff, Joshua. "Rocket Scientist Natalie Panek Wants to Go to Space. And Take More Women with Her." *Huffington Post*, 8 Mar. 2016, www.huffingtonpost.ca/2016/03/08/natalie-panek-international-womens-day_n_9150768.html. Accessed 15 Feb. 2019.

Panek, Natalie. "Ever Wonder What a Rocket Scientist's Job Is Really Like?" Interview by Georgie Binks. *Flare*, 23 Nov. 2015, www.flare.com/tv-movies/what-its-really-like-to-be-a-rocket-scientist/. Accessed 15 Feb. 2019.

Panek, Natalie, Robert Thirsk, and Laura Lucier. "Making an Astronaut: When Dreams Lift Off into Reality." Interview by Mike MacKinnon. *University of Calgary*, explore.ucalgary.ca/making-astronaut-when-dreams-lift-reality. Accessed 21 Feb. 2019.

"STEM Rock Star Natalie Panek Is Revolutionizing How We Think about Women in Tech." *Women You Should Know*, 27 Aug. 2013, womenyoushouldknow.net/stem-rock-star-natalie-panek-is-revolutionizing-how-we-think-about-women-in-tech/. Accessed 15 Feb. 2019.

Waddell, Dave. "Rocket Scientist Encourages Young Women to Shoot for the Stars in Their Career Choices." *Windsor Star*, 2 Nov. 2017, windsorstar.com/news/local-news/rocket-scientist-encourages-young-women-to-shoot-for-the-stars-in-their-career-choices. Accessed 15 Feb. 2019.

—*Joy Crelin*

Katie Paterson

Date of birth: 1981
Occupation: Artist

Scottish artist Katie Paterson rose to critical acclaim with works that blur or even eliminate traditional boundaries between disciplines, forms of media, and the ostensibly divergent fields of art and science. "My art practice is multi-disciplinary, exploring ideas relating to the landscape, geology, space, time and the cosmos; using technology to bring together the commonplace and the cosmic," she told art writer Rajesh Punj in

Photo by Oliver Mark via Wikimedia Commons

a 2014 interview published on Punj's website. "The imagination always plays a key role." This approach was reflected in notable conceptual pieces including an installation allowing the public to listen to the real-time melting of an Icelandic glacier, a map locating every dead star known to astronomers, and a beaded necklace made of fossils that traces the evolution of life. In 2014 she began the ambitious *Future Library*, a collaborative undertaking meant to unfold over a hundred years as a forest grows and is eventually turned into never-before-seen books.

Paterson's work has earned praise for drawing on science to create new means of conceptualizing the natural world and humankind's place in it. By 2019 she was recognized with several major exhibitions, and many critics hailed her as one of the most significant artists of the day, worthy of consideration alongside past masters such as the British Romantic painter J. M. W. Turner. "I don't know if I'm sometimes the luckiest person ever," she told Patrick Barkham for the *Guardian* (28 Jan. 2019), but she also recognized the deep connections linking her to a long tradition of groundbreaking art: "Ultimately, we're all drawn to the unspeakable wonder of everything."

EARLY LIFE AND EDUCATION

Paterson was born in Glasgow, Scotland, in 1981. Growing up in Scotland, Paterson knew that she wanted to become an artist when she was still "very, very, young," as she told Alicia Reuter for *Freunde von Freunden* (12 Nov. 2014). "It was pretty clear that that was what I was going to do.

Or at least, there wasn't anything else that I was going to be able to do." After completing her primary and secondary schooling, Paterson enrolled in the Edinburgh College of Art (ECA), where she pursued studies in a variety of artforms. "I couldn't settle on a discipline," she recalled in an interview for the *Nothing in the Rulebook* blog (23 May 2018). "It makes sense now because I still don't really settle when it comes to any disciplines." Paterson earned her bachelor's degree from the ECA in 2004.

A formative moment in Paterson's budding career and artistic perspective came in the period immediately following her graduation from the ECA, during which she traveled to Iceland and worked for a time at a hotel. Paterson's time in Iceland kindled in her a new awareness and appreciation of the natural world, both on Earth and in the wider universe. "Being in Iceland adjusted my perceptions and senses about living on, and belonging to, a planet that revolves around a vast star, amongst billions of others," she explained to Punj. "It took being in Iceland's otherworldly nature to remind me of this. . . . I looked upwards and all around, and became interested in geology and time, the moon and the wider cosmos."

Greatly inspired by her time in Iceland, Paterson returned to the United Kingdom and enrolled in the Slade School of Fine Art, a school within the University College London (UCL). She earned her master's degree from the institution in 2007.

EARLY CAREER

Paterson began to receive attention for artistic work developed while she was still at the Slade School of Fine Art, most notably the project *Vatnajökull (The Sound Of)*. Active in 2007 and 2008, the piece consisted of a telephone number that connected to a microphone located within a glacial lagoon in Iceland. Upon calling the publicly accessible number, an individual would be able to hear the glacier melting as the sound picked up by the microphone. Proving quite popular, *Vatnajökull (The Sound Of)* received extensive praise for its inventiveness and exploration of themes including ecology, scale, and distance, even after the project's end. "I have been asked to re-create it a lot but I do not want to do it again," Paterson told Karen Wright for the *Independent* (31 July 2014). "I do not want to be an artist who re-creates. I want to be doing the next thing. I have so many ideas. I want to do them all. If not all of them, at least the next."

Over the subsequent years, Paterson continued to explore the intersections between art and the natural world, creating pieces with roots in scientific data. *Light Bulb to Simulate Moonlight* (2008) involved sets of lightbulbs designed to replicate a human lifetime's worth of moonlight, according to spectral analysis. The 2009 piece *All the Dead Stars* consisted of a map showing the locations of all dead stars identified by astronomers up to that point.

Due to the scientific information and resources crucial to the creation of much of Paterson's artwork, her projects often required collaborations with experts in the relevant disciplines. Indeed, that collaborative nature of her work became one of her characteristic features as an artist. "In the beginning, I had to be a bit brazen," she told Reuter of her early attempts to reach out to experts. "I'd send out e-mails and call people and say, 'Okay. This is really weird, but I've got a request.' But it's amazing. People are really generous. I think especially in the sciences. Scientists can be really happy that you're interested in what they're doing and they want to share it with you." Paterson delved more deeply into the world of scientific research during the 2010–11 academic year, during which she served as artist in residence within the UCL astrophysics department.

METEORITES AND FOSSILS

As her exploration of the intersection between art and science deepened, Paterson's steady flow of ideas translated into numerous completed works. Continuing a theme, many of those related to outer space and celestial bodies. For *100 Billion Suns* (2011), Paterson used confetti cannons to represent gamma ray bursts. Perhaps most notable, however, was *Campo del Cielo, Field of the Sky*, a project begun in 2012 in which she made a cast of a meteorite, melted the meteorite down, and then returned the metal to its earlier form using the cast. Paterson's goal was to return the remade meteorite to space, and this was successfully achieved with the aid of the European Space Agency, which transported the piece to the International Space Station in July 2014. The meteorite once again reentered Earth's atmosphere in February 2015. Later that year the project was short-listed for the International Prize for Contemporary Art by the Foundation Prince Pierre de Monaco.

Paterson continued to explore the possibilities of mimicking the natural movements of objects in space with *Second Moon*, carried out in 2013 and 2014. For this project, Paterson placed a piece of material from the moon in a box and shipped it around the world by air, creating an orbit of sorts that followed the moon's orbit. The package was tracked using an app that showed its real-time location along with the locations of the original moon and other solar system bodies.

In addition to her cosmic pieces, Paterson also sought to explore and contextualize the development of life on Earth through her work. That mission is particularly evident in her 2013 work *Fossil Necklace*, which documents the evolution of life through its very materials. All 170 of the necklace's beads were made from genuine fossils, which Paterson purchased from dealers and at times searched for herself on Scotland's coast. "The necklace shows the first creatures to have eyes, the first creatures to have wings, the first creatures to breathe, the very first cellular life ever to evolve on the planet," she told Reuter. "Then it traces around the whole of Earth's geological time and history. Eventually, it comes to us at the end. It even traces the migration of people across the planet."

FUTURE LIBRARY

Launched in 2014, the project *Future Library* was perhaps Paterson's most ambitious work to date, both in the timeframe involved and the required cooperation of numerous parties. Like most of Paterson's art, the project had roots in the natural world. "I was drawing tree rings, and as I was doing that I very quickly made a visual connection between tree rings and chapters in a book and paper and trees and time," she told *Nothing in the Rulebook*. "I had a vision of a forest that was growing a book, and that the book was made of chapters of tree rings—and it would evolve and grow over time." As Paterson expanded upon that vision, she developed a concept for an artistic work that had never been attempted: At the start of the *Future Library* project, a forest would be planted. One hundred years later, the trees would be harvested and processed into paper. During the hundred years in which the trees were growing, one writer per year would donate an unpublished manuscript to the project, to be stored away unread. After the forest was turned into paper in the year 2114, the paper would be used to publish the texts, at last revealing their content to the public.

Despite the many challenges such an initiative presented, Paterson succeeded in setting the *Future Library* project in motion in 2014. With support from the city of Oslo, Norway, she had one thousand Norwegian spruce trees planted in a forest nearby. "It's still part of the city, but not—it feels like you're miles away," she told Reuter of the location. "When you're in there you can't hear or feel the city." Professional foresters would be charged with maintaining the trees and eventually harvesting them. Oslo also dedicated a room in its public library to store the unread manuscripts. Canadian writer Margaret Atwood became the first author to join the project, contributing her manuscript *Scribbler Moon*. She was followed by writers David Mitchell, Sjón, Elif Shafak, and Han Kang.

The *Future Library* was designed to draw attention to the concepts of collaboration and the passage of time. The Future Library Trust was established to ensure the continuation of the project over its hundred-year span, and other organizations and individuals became involved. Paterson served as an original trustee, knowing that the work would have to be completed by another generation.

OTHER WORK
The *Future Library* project attracted significant media attention, helping to boost Paterson to a new level of recognition. She earned a steady stream of group and solo exhibitions at museums around the world and also produced commissioned works. Among other honors, she won the 2014 South Bank Sky Arts Award for visual arts. She continued to win acclaim for her unique examinations of humanity in the vast context of time and space on geological and cosmological scales. "It's the point of mind-boggling which interests me," she explained to the *Scotsman* (8 Jan. 2019) about the unifying feature of much of her work. "The point when your mind is stretching to go a little bit further, the point where words stop—I think that's where my interests often begin."

In 2019 Paterson debuted the conceptual work *First There Is a Mountain*, in which individuals use sand to create miniature representations of some prominent mountains, reflecting her ongoing interest in issues of scale and the environment. That year she also published the book *A Place That Exists Only in Moonlight*, a collection of short texts, reminiscent of poems, that describe imaginary art pieces. It also continued Paterson's cosmic focus, as the cover was printed with a special ink mixed with what she described as cosmic dust—moon dust, meteorite fragments, and similar substances that she ground into powder herself. "I breathed in some really crazy things from outer space and then I sent it off to the ink people," she told Barkham. A portion of Paterson's ideas for imaginary artworks were also displayed at the Turner Contemporary gallery in England as part of a major retrospective of her work.

PERSONAL LIFE
Paterson lived in Berlin, Germany, for several years and operated a studio in the Kreuzberg area of the city before moving back to Scotland. She maintains a relationship with fellow artist Martin John Callanan, with whom she has a son.

SUGGESTED READING
Barkham, Patrick. "'I've Breathed in Some Crazy Things from Outer Space'—Katie Paterson's Cosmic Art." *The Guardian*, 28 Jan. 2019, amp.theguardian.com/artanddesign/2019/jan/28/katie-paterson-interview-turner. Accessed 15 Mar. 2019.
"Ones to Watch in 2019: Katie Paterson, Artist." *The Scotsman*, 8 Jan. 2019, www.scotsman.com/lifestyle/culture/art/ones-to-watch-in-2019-katie-paterson-artist-1-4853334/amp. Accessed 15 Mar. 2019.
Paterson, Katie. "Behold the Future—Katie Paterson Interview." Interview by Rajesh Punj. *Rajesh Punj*, 2014, www.rajeshpunj.com/behold-the-future-katie-paterson-interview. Accessed 15 Mar. 2019.
Paterson, Katie. "Creatives in Profile—Interview with Katie Paterson." Interview by Professor Wu. *Nothing in the Rulebook*, 23 May 2018, nothingintherulebook.com/2018/05/23/creatives-in-profile-interview-with-katie-paterson/amp. Accessed 15 Mar. 2019.
Paterson, Katie. Interview by Alicia Reuter. *Freunde von Freunden*, 12 Nov. 2014, www.freundevonfreunden.com/interviews/katie-paterson. Accessed 15 Mar. 2019.
Paterson, Katie. Interview by Kate Murphy. *The New York Times*, 20 Sept. 2014, www.nytimes.com/2014/09/21/opinion/sunday/katie-paterson.html. Accessed 15 Mar. 2019.
Wright, Karen. "Katie Paterson, Artist: 'I Do Not Want to Re-Create. I Want to Be Doing the Next Thing." *Independent*, 31 July 2014, www.independent.co.uk/arts-entertainment/art/features/katie-paterson-artist-i-do-not-want-to-re-create-i-want-to-be-doing-the-next-thing-9640246.html. Accessed 15 Mar. 2019.

SELECTED WORKS
Vatnajökull (The Sound Of), 2007–8; *All the Dead Stars*, 2009; *100 Billion Suns*, 2011; *Campo del Cielo, Field of the Sky*, 2012–14; *Fossil Necklace*, 2013; *Second Moon*, 2013–14; *Future Library*, 2014–; *First There Is a Mountain*, 2019

—Joy Crelin

Otto Pérez Molina

Date of birth: December 1, 1950
Occupation: Former president of Guatemala

Otto Pérez Molina is a retired general, a cofounder of Guatemala's Patriotic Party, and the former president of Guatemala. He resigned from office in September 2015 after being accused of defrauding the state of millions of dollars.

EARLY LIFE AND EDUCATION
Otto Fernando Pérez Molina was born on December 1, 1950, in Guatemala City, the youngest child of Jaime Pérez Marroquín and Victoria Isabel Molina. Pérez Molina grew up with two older brothers, Jaime and Mynor. He began his military career at the age of sixteen as a "knight

cadet" at the Polytechnic School of the Americas. In interviews, Pérez Molina has stated that he was a distinguished student and was known by his teachers for his leadership skills, discipline, and honesty.

Most of Pérez Molina's military experience occurred during the bloody, thirty-six-year Guatemalan civil war—the conflict between the government and leftist rebel groups fighting for the land rights of rural poor and indigenous Mayans, which lasted from 1960 to 1996. Pérez Molina rose through the ranks of the Guatemalan army, and he gained national notoriety on March 23, 1982, when he led a group of young officers in a coup against Guatemalan president José Efraín Ríos Montt. In 1990 Pérez Molina graduated from the Senior Management Program at the prestigious Instituto Centroamericano Administración de Empresas (INCAE Business School). He also attended the Inter-American Defense College, a military academy located in Washington, DC, in 1991.

POLITICAL CAREER

Pérez Molina first became known in political circles in the early 1990s when he was appointed director of military intelligence and was instrumental in reversing President Jorge Serrano Elías's 1993 attempt to dissolve congress and replace the members of the Guatemalan supreme court. From 1993–95 Pérez Molina served as chief-of-staff to President Ramiro de León Carpio, during which he negotiated with Guatemala's insurgent forces to sign the peace accords that ended the nation's civil war. For the remainder of the decade, he served in a number of roles including as army inspector general and as the lead Guatemalan delegate on the Inter-American Defense Board. He retired from the military with honors in 2000.

Pérez Molina cofounded the right-wing Patriotic Party in February 2001. After a brief run for president in 2003, he joined a coalition that supported the candidacy of the conservative party's Oscar Berger. Pérez Molina was elected to congress that year and was commissioned by the Berger government to run the Defense and Security Committee. Pérez Molina ran for president again in 2007 but lost to the National Unity of Hope (UNE) candidate, Álvaro Colom. He conducted his third presidential campaign in 2011 with Roxana Baldetti as his running mate. Buoyed by the Patriotic Party motto of, "Firm hand, head, and heart" and a promise to crack down on crime, Pérez Molina was elected president on November 6, 2011, with 54 percent of the vote. Baldetti was the first woman to be elected vice president of Guatemala.

At the forefront of Pérez Molina's presidential agenda was the issue of poverty. In the wake of food shortages, a global recession, and a series of natural disasters, over half of Guatemala's population was experiencing food insecurity and were living in poverty. Pérez Molina's initiatives however, made minimal impact. Although Guatemala's gross domestic product (GDP) grew almost 4 percent during the first year of his presidency, this progress was negated by a 2.5 percent increase in birth rates and a 3.45 percent inflation rate. In September 2012, Pérez Molina claimed that his administration's "iron fist" approach had lowered the nation's murder rate by 13 percent and kidnappings by 25 percent. That same day, he made international headlines by proposing to the UN General Assembly the legalization of drugs, arguing that the less Guatemala spent fighting drug cartels, the more money it could direct toward the nation's social welfare issues.

Pérez Molina's presidency was marked by a number of scandals. In 2011 he was accused of having participated in war crimes, including mass murder and forced resettlements during the civil war. In April 2015, the Guatemalan Justice Department and the United Nations International Commission against Impunity in Guatemala (CICIG) accused Pérez Molina and other officials of taking bribes in exchange for lowering tariffs for companies importing products. The customs corruption ring, known in the media as "La Línea," was discovered through a series of wiretaps and is estimated to have defrauded the state of $35 million. Baldetti resigned her position in May 2015 amid the scandal. The Guatemalan congress elected former constitutional court judge Alejandro Maldonado as acting vice president. In September 2015, after months of citizen protests and revocation of his prosecutorial immunity, Pérez Molina also resigned. He was arrested the following day and Maldonado took office as temporary president. Jimmy Morales, a former television comedian, was elected to the presidency in October 2015 and took office in January 2016.

While still imprisoned in April 2016, a new corruption charge was filed against Pérez Molina relating to several money laundering schemes the government alleges he and Baldetti orchestrated while in office. Gustavo Martinez, Pérez Molina's son-in-law, who served as his secretary while Pérez Molina was president, was also implicated and was arrested on charges of influence trafficking.

IMPACT

Allegations of Otto Pérez Molina's corrupt actions have sent Guatemala into what many analysts believe is the country's worst political crisis since the end of its civil war. Pérez Molina denies the allegations that he allowed top officials to systematically abuse their power. Such corruption has hollowed out Guatemala's government and institutions and redirected millions of dollars away from citizens, thereby exacerbating the nation's poverty, violence, and lawlessness.

PERSONAL LIFE

Pérez Molina and his wife Rosa Maria Leal Flores de Pérez have two children, Lisette and Otto.

SUGGESTED READING

Ahmed, Azam, and Elisabeth Malkin. "Otto Pérez Molina of Guatemala Is Jailed Hours after Resigning Presidency." *The New York Times*. New York Times, 3 Sept. 2015, www.nytimes.com/2015/09/04/world/americas/otto-perez-molina-guatemalan-president-resigns-amid-scandal.html. Accessed 29 Jan. 2019.

Allison, Mike. "Guatemalan President Otto Pérez Molina's First Year in Office." *Al Jazeera*, 18 Jan. 2013, www.aljazeera.com/indepth/opinion/2013/01/20131141236279913806.html. Accessed 29 Jan. 2019.

Associated Press. "Guatemalan Ex-President Linked to New Scandal." *Wall Street Journal*, Dow Jones & Co., Inc., 15 Apr. 2016, www.wsj.com/articles/guatemalas-former-president-linked-to-new-scandal-1460770956. Accessed 29 Jan. 2019.

Goldman, Francisco. "From President to Prison: Otto Pérez Molina and a Day for Hope in Guatemala." *The New Yorker*. Condé Nast, 4 Sept. 2015, www.newyorker.com/news/news-desk/from-president-to-prison-otto-perez-molina-and-a-day-for-hope-in-guatemala. Accessed 29 Jan. 2019.

Llenas, Bryan. "Guatemalan President Argues Drug Legalization and Calls Out US Anti-Drug Effort." *Fox News Latino*. Fox Entertainment Group, 27 Sept. 2012, www.foxnews.com/politics/guatemalan-president-argues-drug-legalization-and-calls-out-us-anti-drug-effort. Accessed 29 Jan. 2019.

—*Emily Turner*

Sundar Pichai

Date of birth: July 12, 1972
Occupation: Internet executive

Engineer Sundar Pichai was named the chief executive of Google in 2015, the same year the company restructured its sprawling business and created a parent company called Alphabet. (Pichai joined Alphabet's board in 2017.) His shareholdings make him one of the highest-paid CEOs in the United States. Pichai, who began working for Google in 2004, had previously helped develop Chrome, the company's web browser, and Android, its smartphone brand. Google was founded as a search engine by Larry Page and Sergey Brin in 1998, and David Gelles for the *New York Times* (8 Nov. 2018) wrote that it has become "arguably the most influential company in the world."

Pichai was interested in bringing the Internet to those who do not have it through mobile devices. In 2014, he launched a campaign to reach 1 billion new smartphone users. Pichai, who was born in Chennai, India, began that campaign with a host of programs to bring smartphones to more people in India. Google is paying for free wifi at Indian railway stations and making cheaper phones that use a minimum of data. Pichai also launched a social program called Internet Saathi, which aims to bring rural Indian women online, employing women to ride bikes to remote villages to teach other women how to use smartphones and tablets. Because of these efforts, Pichai is enormously popular in India; when he visits, the soft-spoken CEO is treated like a rock star.

Excluding the experimental ventures overseen by Alphabet, there are several important products that fall under Google's—and thus Pichai's—purview: Google Search, Gmail, YouTube, Android, Chrome, Google Maps, and the Google Play Store. Pichai has visions of further expansion. In 2017, he shifted the company's focus from mobile to artificial intelligence (AI). He has said, as quoted by Catherine Clifford for *CNBC* (1 Feb. 2018), that AI could be as important to the development of humanity as "electricity or fire."

Pichai's idealism is countered by concern about Google's growing global power. His role as CEO places him in the top tier of tech executives, along with people like Mark Zuckerberg of Facebook or Jeff Bezos of Amazon, whom Matt Honan for *Buzzfeed News* (27 Mar. 2016) described as the "new American industrialists." The global reach of their companies, Honan wrote, makes the corporate titans of a century ago, such as US Steel and Standard Oil, "look like Piggly Wiggly by comparison." In the European Union (EU), Google was fined a staggering $5 billion for violating antitrust laws with its Android mobile operating system in 2018. Like Facebook, the company also must contend with accusations of censorship. In late 2018, Google came under fire for its Dragonfly project, a censored search engine for the Chinese market that could enable state surveillance of users' searches. More than 700 Google employees signed a petition condemning the project on November 27, 2018. "We object to technologies that aid the powerful in oppressing the vulnerable, wherever they may be," they wrote in part. Yet Pichai remained enthusiastic about Dragonfly, telling an

Photo by Maurizio Pesce via Wikimedia Commons

audience at the Wired 25 Summit, as quoted by Violet Blue for *Engadget* (30 Nov. 2018), that China presents a "wonderful, innovative market." He continued, "We wanted to learn what it would look like if we were in China, so that's what we built internally. . . . Given how important the market is and how many users there are, we feel obliged to think hard about this problem and take a longer-term view," he said.

EARLY LIFE IN INDIA

Pichai Sundararajan was born in Chennai (then known as Madras), the capital of the southeastern Indian state of Tamil Nadu, on July 12, 1972. His father, Regunatha, worked as an electrical engineer for the British company GEC, and his mother, Lakshmi, worked as a stenographer before the birth of Pichai and his brother, Srinivasan. The family lived in a two-room apartment; Pichai and his brother slept on the living room floor. They were a traditional, middle-class family though they lived for years without a telephone or a refrigerator. "We waited a long time to get a refrigerator, too, and I saw how my mom's life changed: she didn't need to cook every day, she could spend more time with us," Pichai recalled to Jemima Kiss for the *Guardian* (1 Dec. 2017). "So there is a side of me that has viscerally seen how technology can make a difference." He recalls experiencing a drought when he was growing up. It was such a fraught experience, Pichai told Gelles, that he cannot sleep without a water bottle next to his bed. As a child, Pichai was an avid reader; he enjoyed science and engineering and playing street cricket with neighborhood friends. Schoolmates from Jawahar Vidyalaya, a

secondary school in the Ashok Nagar neighborhood of Chennai, remember him as bright but also shy.

EDUCATION

Pichai attended the Indian Institute of Technology (IIT) at Kharagpur, an elite engineering college, where he studied metallurgical engineering. He encountered his first computer and struggled to keep up with his Hindi-speaking peers. (Pichai grew up speaking Tamil.) Repeating what he thought was a standard Hindi greeting, he once got in trouble for saying to a cafeteria staff worker, "Hey, stupid!" Pichai graduated in 1993 and won a scholarship to study materials science and semiconductor physics at Stanford University in California. His father withdrew nearly a year's salary from savings to pay for his son's plane ticket; it was the first time Pichai had ever flown in an airplane. Upon his arrival in California, Pichai was immediately taken with the state. "I always wanted to be in the Valley," he told Gelles, though he said he still struggled to understand computers. "I kind of knew that's where everything happened." Pichai planned to stay at Stanford and complete his PhD but dropped out after completing his master's degree to take a job as an engineer and product manager at the Silicon Valley semiconductor firm Applied Materials. Several years later, Pichai returned to school, earning an MBA from the University of Pennsylvania's Wharton School of Business in 2002. He briefly worked for the New York consulting firm McKinsey & Company before taking a job with Google in 2004. As the story goes, a friend was debating taking a job at Google. Pichai tried to convince them not to, but he ended up persuaded to interview at Google himself.

GOOGLE CHROME AND ANDROID

Pichai interviewed for a position at Google on April 1, 2004, the same day that the company released its email platform, Gmail. "I remember doing my interviews through the day, and people kept asking me, 'What do you think of Gmail?' but I hadn't had a chance to use it. I thought it was an April Fools' joke," Pichai recalled to a group of students at IIT Kharagpur in 2017, as quoted by Aatif Sulleyman for *Gizmodo* (5 Jan. 2017). He finally got to see the platform in his fourth interview, "and then [by] the fifth interview I was finally able to start answering," he said. After three more interviews, Pichai got the job. His first project was Google Toolbar, a web extension that allowed users to search Google from within Internet Explorer. The job convinced him that Google needed a browser of its own—"a puzzling mission . . . when it was completely unclear why the company would need one," Honan wrote. Pichai worked on the browser with ten engineers. Pleased with the prototype, he showed it to Brin and Page, but they were skeptical. Despite a tumultuous release on Labor Day 2008—they released it a day earlier than planned after reporters in Europe began publishing marketing materials—Chrome quickly grew in popularity. Ten years later, in 2018, Chrome is the most widely used browser in the world, accounting for nearly 60 percent of the worldwide market.

Pichai's success with Chrome effectively launched his rise within the company. He was promoted to vice president and later senior vice president. He took over Google apps, including Gmail, and began reporting directly to the famously mercurial former CEO, Page. Twitter tried to hire Pichai away in 2011, the same year Pichai created Chrome OS and the inexpensive Chromebook laptops. In 2013, at Page's behest, he took over Google's mobile brand, Android, from its cofounder Andy Rubin. Rubin brought Android to Google in 2004. As of 2017, Android software runs more than 80 percent of the smartphones sold around the world.

In 2014, Pichai was rumored to be under consideration for the top job at Microsoft. Ultimately, though, he stayed at Google and replaced Page as CEO in August 2015. Despite Pichai's impressive resume, he seemed an unusual choice. Pichai is the opposite of his predecessor: quiet, unassuming—Honan followed Pichai around a tech conference in 2016; without his nametag, no one recognized him—and crucially, diplomatic. Facing scrutiny for various infractions—from sexual harassment to pay discrimination to invasions of privacy—Google benefits from its new CEO's friendly and judicious demeanor. Inside the company, Pichai is popular with most employees, who describe him as collaborative and empathetic. Others seemed to have a mixed view of Pichai's ability to please. One former Google manager told Honan: "He gave the *best* meetings. He never aligned with [any of Google's often divisive executives]. He always shot right down the middle. How could you ever really know what someone like that is really thinking?"

PERSONAL LIFE

Pichai met his wife, Anjali Pichai, a chemical engineer, when they were both students at IIT. They have two children, Kavya and Kiran, and live in Los Altos, California.

SUGGESTED READING

Blue, Violet. "Google's China Search Engine Drama." *Engadget*, 30 Nov. 2018, www.engadget.com/2018/11/30/google-s-china-search-engine-drama/. Accessed 1 Dec. 2018.

Clifford, Catherine. "Google CEO: AI Is More Important Than Fire or Electricity." *CNBC*, 1 Feb. 2018, www.cnbc.com/2018/02/01/google-ceo-sundar-pichai-ai-is-more-important-than-fire-electricity.html. Accessed 1 Dec. 2018.

Gelles, David. "Sundar Pichai of Google: 'Technology Doesn't Solve Humanity's Problems.'" *The New York Times*, 8 Nov. 2018, www.nytimes.com/2018/11/08/business/sundar-pichai-google-corner-office.html. Accessed 29 Nov. 2018.

Honan, Matt. "Searching for Google CEO Sundar Pichai, the Most Powerful Tech Giant You've Never Heard Of." *Buzzfeed News*, 27 Mar. 2016, www.buzzfeednews.com/article/mathonan/searching-for-google-ceo-sundar-pichai-the-most-powerful-tec. Accessed 29 Nov. 2018.

Kiss, Jemima. "Google CEO Sundar Pichai: 'I Don't Know Whether Humans Want Change That Fast.'" *The Guardian*, 1 Dec. 2017, www.theguardian.com/technology/2017/oct/07/google-boss-sundar-pichai-tax-gender-equality-data-protection-jemima-kiss. Accessed 29 Nov. 2018.

Sulleyman, Aatif. "Gmail's April 1 Launch Almost Ruined Google CEO Sundar Pichai's Job Interview." *Gizmodo*, 5 Jan. 2017, www.gizmodo.co.uk/2017/01/gmails-april-1-launch-almost-ruined-google-ceo-sundar-pichais-job-interview/. Accessed 29 Nov. 2018.

—*Molly Hagan*

Lydia Polgreen

Date of birth: 1975
Occupation: Journalist

In December 2016, *New York Times* senior editor and rising star Lydia Polgreen accepted an offer to become the editor-in-chief of *HuffPost*, the online news and opinion outlet originally known as the *Huffington Post*. Many news industry insiders were surprised when Polgreen accepted the job: since 2002 she had enjoyed a thriving career at the venerable *Times*, serving in such high-profile capacities as deputy international editor, Johannesburg bureau chief, New Delhi correspondent, and chief of the West Africa bureau, and she had covered such important events as the ethnic cleansing in Darfur and the turmoil in the Democratic Republic of the Congo. Among the many laurels she had garnered along the way were the 2006 George Polk Award for foreign reporting, the 2008 Livingston Award for international reporting, and a 2008 Overseas Press Club Award; in 2007 the World Economic Forum designated her as one of its Young Global Leaders.

Polgreen understood why observers were surprised to hear she would be leaving the *New York Times*, wHere she had been universally respected and beloved. Polgreen asserted that, influenced in part by the results of the 2016 presidential election, she was attracted to *HuffPost*'s "explicitly progressive mandate and identity," as she described it to Sydney Ember for the *Times* (6 Dec. 2016). However, she was also motivated by the chance to reach out to the wide cross section of the public that feels politically disempowered, including those who voted for Donald Trump. "For me, it's less about who you voted for and more about where you stand in the overall political and economic power arrangements," she told Johana Bhuiyan for *Vox* (12 Feb. 2018). "We need to be focused on issues that affect people's lives and write about them in really relevant ways to people's experiences."

Although Polgreen told Susan Lehman of the *New York Times* (21 Dec. 2016) that leaving the paper was "the hardest decision" she had ever made, she was excited at the prospect of building "a news organization, in the tradition of the great working-class tabloids, that speaks for and to people who feel left out."

EARLY LIFE AND EDUCATION

Lydia Frances Polgreen was born in the United States in 1975 but her father's job as a development consultant took the family all over the world; they moved to Kenya when she was four years old, and much of her childhood was spent there and in Ghana. Of her diverse family background, she told Aaron Hicklin for *Out* magazine (31 Mar. 2017): "My mother is an African immigrant [from Ethiopia], my father is a disabled veteran, and my grandparents on my father's side were sort of WASPy Goldwater Republicans who had a Catholic son, a gay son, and a son who married an African." Her parents had met when her father, a Baha'i missionary, was traveling in Ethiopia; her mother was a lapsed Seventh-day Adventist.

In a personal essay for the *New York Times* (5 Dec. 2013), Polgreen wrote that being biracial posed no problems during her childhood. "In the swirl of expat life in Nairobi, there was nothing unusual about that," she asserted. "My elementary school classes were full of kids who were half Kenyan, half British; half Chinese, half Rwandan; half Indian, half Filipino." Growing up amid the regular unrest in Africa gave her an appetite for current events. For example, during the 1982 coup in Kenya, she told Andy Stiny for the *Santa Fe New Mexican* (18 May 2018), she was "simultaneously horrified and thrilled." Attending high school in Accra, Ghana, she was editor of the student newspaper, and she once scored an interview with reggae musician Ziggy Marley through sheer persistence—an event

that revealed to her how much she enjoyed persuading people to open up to her, as well as how good at it she was.

Polgreen returned to the United States for college, attending St. John's College, a liberal-arts school in Annapolis, Maryland, where she studied philosophy, graduating in 1997. Thinking she might want to eventually teach philosophy but needing to start working to pay back her student loans, she took a clerical job at an office in suburban Virginia, helping foreign workers apply for H-1B visas. "At some point I thought, 'This can't be how my life is going to go. This isn't for me,'" she recalled to Hicklin. "I'm not a person who should ever be looking at the clock, waiting for things to be over—that's not my destiny."

A friend was then interning at *Washington Monthly*, a political magazine in the capital, and suggested she apply for a position there as well. Although she was reluctant to accept an unpaid internship, Polgreen reasoned that she could wait on tables at night—anything that would enable her to leave her soul-crushing clerical job. Being at the magazine reminded her how much she had loved reporting in high school, and in 1999 she entered the prestigious Columbia School of Journalism, where she earned a master's degree in 2000.

JOURNALISM CAREER

Polgreen got her start in newspapers working as a city hall reporter for the *Albany Times Union* in upstate New York and covering local news for the *Orlando Sentinel* in Florida. She eventually caught the attention of editors at the *New*

Photo by Emma McIntyre/Getty Images for AOL

York Times, who recruited her for a training program aimed at writers "who didn't have the kind of background or résumé that you would typically have to get hired at the *Times*," as she told Hicklin.

In 2002 she was hired as a *Times* metro reporter, and one of her early stories, about how Starbucks locations were alleviating the city's shortage of public restrooms, made it onto the front page. She moved up quickly, and in 2005 she was named West Africa bureau chief. While in that role, she earned a 2006 George Polk Award for her reporting from the war-torn Darfur region of Sudan.

In 2009 she was named South Asia correspondent, and she remained based in New Delhi, India, for almost three years, before returning to Africa to head the Johannesburg bureau. "When I arrived in South Africa in 2011 as a correspondent, it was too late to meet [Nelson] Mandela," she recalled in her 2013 *Times* essay, written following the death of the South African statesman, whose antiapartheid struggles she had heard about as a child in Kenya. "But in many ways I live in the nation he made. Among my friends are many interracial couples. A black hand intertwined with a white one at the movies or at the grocery store no longer draws long, hard stares. . . . When I look at the butterscotch faces these unions produce, so much like my own, I remember just how far this nation has come."

In 2014 Polgreen was lured away from writing to accept the post of deputy international editor, soon followed by editorial director of NYT Global, charged with expanding the paper's digital presence outside the United States, especially in Spanish-speaking countries. It was while she was engaged in that gratifying pursuit that she was approached in late 2016 by the *Huffington Post*, whose founder, Arianna Huffington, was stepping down as editor-in-chief to launch a wellness startup.

Polgreen took what she called the "unmissable opportunity" to head a major digital news platform, and quickly began to make her mark—first by formalizing the colloquial name commonly used for the outlet, which under Polgreen officially changed its name from the *Huffington Post* to *HuffPost*. She also looked to broaden the site's appeal. "For me, the [2016 presidential] election was a kind of road-to-Damascus moment," Polgreen told Claire Landsbaum for *The Cut* (20 Apr. 2017). "I was happily working at the *New York Times* and on a great career trajectory there, and the day after the election a lot of us rubbed the sleep off our eyes and said, 'What are we doing here?' That's no knock on the *New York Times*, which is an extraordinary journalistic institution. But because I spent most of my childhood in Kenya and Ghana and most of my

career as a foreign correspondent, I've thought a lot about how important it is for people to have access to high-quality journalism at every level of the socio-economic ladder." *HuffPost*, she asserted, was not "a liberal or conservative organization," but was rather characterized by "a broad humanist kind of populism" with core principles in support of universal human rights. "We really want to be serving the moment we're living in," she told Landsbaum. Her mission at the online publication, she has told interviewers, is to unite people over "fundamental kitchen table interests."

In her dedication to that mission, Polgreen's path at *HuffPost* has not been trouble-free, with some critics asserting the publication still leans too far to the left and others decrying a continuing preponderance of lightweight, clickbait articles. There have been financial difficulties, as well: in early 2019, parent company Verizon laid off twenty *HuffPost* staffers, shuttering the entire opinion and health sections of the publication.

PERSONAL LIFE

Polgreen, the recipient of the 2018 Randy Shilts Award for LGBTQ Coverage, realized she was gay when she was in college. "I always knew there was something different about me, but I didn't know how to put my finger on it," she told Hicklin. "When I got to college, I met other lesbians and I was, like, Oh, this is who I am, I get it, I see it now. It was really like a light went on and suddenly this very clear thing about myself that had always been a subtext became text, and that was a remarkable thing." She had a strong role model in one of her uncles, who had been in an open, long-term gay relationship for years.

She is married to documentary photographer Candace Feit, whom she met on assignment in Africa. While stationed in socially conservative African societies, the two had to be exceptionally discreet, circumstances that Polgreen has said can be exhausting to deal with. "My last posting for the *New York Times* was in South Africa, where . . . there are huge problems around homophobia and violence, particularly against queer African women," Polgreen told Hicklin, "So it was a tremendous relief to come back to the U.S. and be safely ensconced in New York City."

SUGGESTED READING

Bhuiyan, Johana. "HuffPost Editor in Chief Lydia Polgreen Said She Wouldn't Have Chosen to Cover President Trump as Entertainment." *Vox*, 12 Feb. 2018, www.vox.com/2018/2/12/17006082/lydia-polgreen-huffington-post-code-media-2018-arianna-huffington. Accessed 8 May 2019.

Ember, Sydney. "Huffington Post Hires Senior New York Times Editor." *The New York Times*, 6 Dec. 2016, www.nytimes.com/2016/12/06/business/media/huffington-post-hires-senior-new-york-times-editor.html. Accessed 8 May 2019.

Hicklin, Aaron. "Lydia Polgreen: Meet the Queer Black Woman Changing Journalism." *Out*, 31 Mar. 2017, www.out.com/out-exclusives/2017/3/31/lydia-polgreen-meet-queer-black-woman-changing-journalism. Accessed 8 May 2019.

Landsbaum, Claire. "Lydia Polgreen Wants to Bring HuffPost Back to the People." *The Cut*, 20 Apr. 2017, www.thecut.com/2017/04/lydia-polgreen-on-the-huffington-posts-new-direction.html. Accessed 8 May 2019.

Lehman, Susan. "Lydia Polgreen on Leaving to Lead *Huffington Post*: 'Hardest Decision I've Ever Made.'" *The New York Times*, 21 Dec. 2016, www.nytimes.com/2016/12/21/insider/lydia-polgreen-on-leaving-to-lead-huffington-post-hardest-decision-ive-ever-made.html. Accessed 8 May 2019.

Polgreen, Lydia. "A Racial Acceptance That Resonates." *The New York Times*, 5 Dec. 2013, www.nytimes.com/2013/12/05/world/africa/a-racial-acceptance-that-resonates.html. Accessed 8 May 2019.

Stiny, Andy. "St. John's Grad, Globe-Trotting Journalist, to Deliver Address." *Santa Fe New Mexican*, 18 May 2018, www.santafenewmexican.com/life/features/st-john-s-grad-globe-trotting-journalist-to-deliver-address/article_57474087-dbab-5c33-8ff7-487f7b1397f8.html. Accessed 8 May 2019.

—*Mari Rich*

Dan Porter

Date of birth: June 13, 1966
Occupation: Entrepreneur

Dan Porter is a tech entrepreneur who created an app-based sports network called Overtime. The mobile app features high-school game highlights, culled from a national network of over 1,000 stringers. In early 2018, a clip of Virginia senior Mac McClung, captured by a local Overtime stringer, went viral, and was featured on ESPN's *SportsCenter*. "While there are lots of digital media companies focused on high school sports, Overtime has a different angle: It doesn't care about scores, stats and recruiting narratives," Peter Kafka explained for *Recode* (14 Feb. 2018). "It's focused instead on a couple dozen athletes it thinks have the charisma to become

internet stars." The company has enjoyed an enthusiastic response from high-profile investors, including NBA superstar Kevin Durant. Porter, the son of college professors, founded Overtime with Zack Weiner, the former founder of a sports media company called the Sports Quotient, in 2016. At the time, Porter was the head of digital operations for the talent agency William Morris Endeavor (WME). Before that, Porter oversaw the sale of a digital company called OMGPOP, along with the hit game *Draw Something*, to the mobile game developer Zynga for $200 million in 2012. Porter has worked for a number of other start-ups—including Ticketweb and Speedle—but actually began his career as a high school teacher. He joined the fledgling nonprofit Teach for America when it started in the 1990s and was later named the organization's president.

EARLY LIFE AND TEACH FOR AMERICA

Porter was born on June 13, 1966. Both of his parents were professors, and in an interview with Jeremy Shinewald and Miles Lasater for *Smart People Should Build Things: The Venture for America Podcast* (19 May 2015), Porter described his upbringing as very "academic." He attended the independent Quaker Friends Central School in Wynnewood, Pennsylvania, where he started a jazz band. He wrote music for his senior project and graduated in 1984. Porter attended Princeton University. Though he dreamed of being a rockstar, he wrote his senior thesis on the avant-garde movement in jazz and graduated with a bachelor's degree in history in 1988.

Porter told Shinewald that after graduating, he first got a job in the music industry, but quickly left. On the suggestion of a friend, he began looking for a job as a teacher after he heard about a nationwide teacher shortage. He had few qualifications. He had "never volunteered, never taught, never worked with kids," he recalled to Shinewald. Still, in August 1989 he found a job as a teacher at Clara Barton High School in the Crown Heights neighborhood of Brooklyn. He had been teaching for about ten months when he was approached about joining the staff of the Teach for America program, which was then new. A former Princeton classmate, Wendy Kopp, wrote for her senior thesis a proposal for a national teaching program, akin to the two-year Peace Corps. Kopp's goal was twofold, Jodi Wilgoren wrote for the *New York Times* (12 Nov. 2000): "To get bright young missionaries"—i.e., recent graduates of mostly Ivy League schools— "into some of the nation's neediest classrooms and to create a cadre of civic leaders conscious of the challenges of education and poverty." After graduation, Kopp oversaw the launch of the nonprofit Teach for America.

Porter was one of Teach for America's first hires in 1990. Based on his brief teaching experience, he helped design recruitment and selection criteria. He was eventually named the organization's president. Over the course of his four and a half years with Teach for America, Porter realized he was most interested in the entrepreneurial aspects of the organization, or as he put it to Shinewald, "the idea that you could come in, have a problem, sit around with a bunch of people, come up with an idea and just do it." "It took me a while to process that . . . this whole kind of idea around building something and creating something was separate from just the idea of education," he said. As a former musician, he found that entrepreneurship satisfied his creative impulses in a way that education alone did not.

EARLY BUSINESS CAREER

Porter left Teach for America in 1994, and, after five years of concurrent study, earned a master's degree in Latin American history, with a focus on nineteenth-century Mexico, from New York University (NYU) in 1995. He applied to business school and was admitted, but chose to take a job in finance, working for a chemical company, instead. As he explained to Shinewald, he was underqualified for the position and had to learn the basics of business and finance, reading a book under his desk, on the job. In 1998, he left to join TicketWeb, a San Francisco–based online ticketing company started by Porter's roommate. The company counted only three employees, but over the course of Porter's three-year tenure, he helped grow TicketWeb to over seventy employees. They sold the company to their largest competitor, Ticketmaster, in 2000. During the tail end of Porter's time at Ticketweb, he launched his own start-up called Speedle. Porter described it to Rob MacKay for the *Princeton Alumni Weekly* (4 July 2001), saying, "It's like the Billboard charts, but based on what people e-mail around to each other." His description of the site sounds, to a contemporary reader, a little bit like Twitter or Reddit, tracking trending articles and topics. Regardless, Speedle folded in 2001, due in part to a lack of investor enthusiasm after the September 11 terrorist attacks. Porter moved back to New York, and he took a job with Bertelsmann, a mass media corporation, running the company's "twelve CDs for a penny" club. In 2005, Porter got a job with Virgin USA through a recruiter. As the senior vice president of corporate development, Porter was responsible for launching new Virgin brand businesses in the United States, including Virgin Music Festivals. As time went on Porter became interested in video games, and eventually left Virgin to take a job with a gaming company.

DRAW SOMETHING AND OMGPOP

Porter took a job with a company called I'm in Like with You. The company, founded by Charles Forman, began as a dating site in 2006. "The entire company started as a joke, honestly," Forman recalled to Brian X. Chen and Jenna Wortham for the *New York Times* (25 Mar. 2012). Only when he realized that users were spending a lot of time on the site did he decide to expand it into a gaming site called OMGPOP. Porter was named chief executive of the company in December 2008. The office at OMG-POP, a tiny room with a single window shared among seven people, was very different from the luxurious corporate digs at Virgin. Porter began raising money for the company but recalls having to walk out on the street to get cell phone reception. Still, he described the atmosphere to Shinewald as "energizing." The company began designing and launching web-based games, but soon moved to Facebook and mobile. By 2012, the company had made thirty-five games but had yet to land a hit. They were projected to run out of money by summer. In early February, the company released a mobile game called *Draw Something*. A twist on the game *Pictionary*, *Draw Something* was a version of an earlier OMGPOP web-based drawing game called *Draw My Thing*. *Draw My Thing* was competitive and, like *Pictionary*, timed; users raced against the clock to guess answers. Porter led the design team to create *Draw Something*, which functions a bit differently. He got the idea for it while playing catch with his son and his son's friend in Brooklyn's Prospect Park. He challenged the boys to toss a football back and forth one hundred times without dropping it. "I had this moment where I thought, that's exactly what the game is," he told Chen and Wortham. "This game is like catch because we're working collaboratively together to try to achieve something." There are no time limits or losers in *Draw Something*; the object of the game is to keep it going.

Within weeks, *Draw Something* had been downloaded over 35 million times, and its users had generated more than 1 billion drawings. In March, Zynga, then a giant in social gaming, bought the company for $200 million. The acquisition was a huge boon for Porter—he shared the wealth by rehiring designers that the company had been forced to lay off before the deal went through—but ultimately, it was far less of a boon for Zynga. The popularity of *Draw Something* quickly waned, and Porter, who had taken a job with Zynga as vice president of general management, left in 2013.

WME AND OVERTIME

Porter left Zynga to take a job with the talent agency William Morris Endeavor (WME). The agency represents actors and writers in the entertainment business, and Porter helped build a digital content and talent pool. He also created a social media division in the company, signing YouTube stars like Germán Garmendia. Porter also continued to work building and designing apps. With some of the former OMGPOP crew, he launched Tally, a community newsfeed, in 2014, and Overtime in 2016. Porter left WME in 2016 to focus on Overtime. In February 2019, the sports network garnered over $23 million in funding—investors included Victor Oladipo of the Indiana Pacers and NBA All-Star Carmelo Anthony—to develop autonomous production capabilities. Overtime plans to expand its original programming, creating more video shows like their existing *Hype School* on Snapchat, *Kevin Durant Film School*, and *Overtime Challenge*. "You can't build a next-generation sports network off of 15-second clips," Zack Weiner, Overtime's president, told Sahil Patel for *Digiday* (21 Feb. 2019). "You can build a community and a brand, and capture proprietary content in a cheap way—which will still be a big part of the business—but we knew we had to get into longer-form content." The company opened a production office in Los Angeles to support this aim. After a partnership with Converse, Porter also expressed a desire to launch an Overtime apparel business.

PERSONAL LIFE

Since 2017, Porter has been an adjunct professor at NYU, teaching courses on entrepreneurship. He is married to filmmaker Melanie Judd. They have two sons and live in Brooklyn.

SUGGESTED READING

Chen, Brian X, and Jenna Wortham. "A Game Explodes and Changes Life Overnight at a Struggling Start-Up." *The New York Times*, 25 Mar. 2012, www.nytimes.com/2012/03/26/technology/draw-something-changes-the-game-quickly-for-omgpop.html. Accessed 5 Mar. 2019.

Kafka, Peter. "Overtime Wants to Turn High School Jocks into Social Media Stars." *Recode*, 14 Feb. 2018, www.recode.net/2018/2/14/17009016/overtime-mac-maclung-funding-dan-porter-omgpop-kevin-durant-andreessen. Accessed 4 Mar. 2019.

MacKay, Rob. "The Speedle of Light." *Princeton Alumni Weekly*, 4 July 2001, www.princeton.edu/paw/web_exclusives/more/more_25.html. Accessed 4 Mar. 2019.

Patel, Sahil. "With $23m in Fresh Funding, Overtime Wants to Move Beyond Viral Dunk Clips to Build a 'Next-Generation Sports Network.'" *Digiday*, 21 Feb. 2019, digiday.com/media/sports-media-startup-overtime/. Accessed 5 Mar. 2019.

Porter, Dan. "Interview with Dan Porter, Former Teacher and CEO of Teach of America, Creator of Draw Something, Board Member of Venture for America." Interview by Jeremy Shinewald and Miles Lasater. *Smart People Should Build Things: The Venture for America Podcast*, 19 May 2015, omny.fm/shows/smart-people-should-build-things-the-venture-for-a/b-est-of-interview-with-dan-porter-former-teacher. Accessed 2 Mar. 2019.

Wilgoren, Jodi. "Wendy Kopp, Leader of Teach for America." *The New York Times*, 12 Nov. 2000, www.nytimes.com/2000/11/12/education/wendy-kopp-leader-of-teach-for-america.html. Accessed 4 Mar. 2019.

—Molly Hagan

Ayanna Pressley

Date of birth: February 3, 1974
Occupation: Politician

In September 2018, Boston City Council member Ayanna Pressley bested Representative Michael Capuano, a ten-term incumbent, in the Democratic primary for Massachusetts's Seventh Congressional District. With no Republican challenger in the general election, Pressley officially became the first black woman elected to the US Congress from Massachusetts in November of that year.

Pressley had galvanized a group of voters hungry for change, campaigning with the slogan Change Can't Wait. Wilnelia Rivera, a political strategist who worked on Pressley's campaign, told Katharine Q. Seelye and Matt Flegenheimer for the *New York Times* (5 Sept. 2018): "Our strategy was to expand the electorate and ignite the base. We trained new activists to engage in a new form of political campaign and to reach the pool of people who don't normally vote." Pressley's team relied heavily on social media and chose not to run traditional broadcast television ads, though they ran a Spanish-language ad on Telemundo and Univision. According to John Walsh, a former chair of the state Democratic Party, a typical primary in the Seventh District would draw about 60,000 voters. In 2018, 102,000 voters showed up to the polls, with Pressley winning nearly 60,000 votes.

Pressley's historic upset was one of a multitude of progressive victories by women of color in the 2018 midterms. Others included Alexandria Ocasio-Cortez, a Latina who bested nine-term congressman Joseph Crowley, one of the party's highest-ranking members, in New York's Fourteenth District, and Rashida Tlaib, a Muslim Palestinian American who won a seat in

Michigan's Thirteenth District after the incumbent, longtime representative John Conyers Jr., resigned due to sexual harassment allegations.

Pressley, an only child raised by a single mother, made a compelling case for her particular bona fides on the campaign trail. She had worked for Senator John Kerry for over a decade and served nearly as long on Boston City Council, but it was her perseverance through poverty and trauma, she argued, that made her uniquely qualified to challenge the status quo in Washington. In a campaign ad posted to Twitter and on the trail, she stated, "It is my fundamental belief that the people closest to the pain should be closest to the power."

EARLY LIFE AND EDUCATION

Pressley was born in Chicago, Illinois, on February 3, 1974, and grew up in the city's Lincoln Park neighborhood. Her mother, Sandra, was a social worker, tenants' rights organizer, and legal secretary, and raised Pressley alone. The two shared a deep bond; Pressley later described her to Michael Levenson and Stephanie Ebbert for the *Boston Globe* (8 Sept. 2018) as "my shero and bedrock and foundation." Sandra Pressley died in 2011. Pressley's father, Martin Terrell, struggled with heroin addiction and spent Pressley's youth in and out of prison. Pressley's early years were rife with uncertainty, she recalled to Seelye and Astead W. Herndon for the *New York Times* (1 Sept. 2018). "Coming home to an eviction notice on the door. Coming home alone. I'm an only child. My mother was raising me alone. We couldn't afford child care; child care hours didn't work according to her schedule." She also endured a decade of sexual abuse as a child, though she has chosen not to elaborate further.

Although money was tight, Pressley's mother enrolled Pressley in ballet, cello, and ballroom-dancing classes. She also found a way to get Pressley a partial scholarship to the progressive Francis W. Parker School, a top-ranked private school in Chicago. Pressley has described Parker as a refuge from the trauma of other aspects of her life.

Pressley exhibited a skill for public speaking as a child, attending her grandfather's Rise and Shine Missionary Baptist Church. When she was ten years old, she volunteered on her first political campaign for Harold Washington, who became Chicago's first black mayor in 1983. In high school, Pressley was elected president of the student government. She was also a cheerleader and competed on the debate team. Outside of school, Pressley did voice-over work and modeled for Planned Parenthood ads that appeared on public buses. When she graduated from Parker in 1992, Pressley gave the commencement address and was named "most likely to be mayor of Chicago."

Photo by Franmarie Metzler via Wikimedia Commons

INTRODUCTION TO POLITICS

Pressley moved to Boston to attend Boston University. During her two years there, she was elected student president of her college and a student senator. She also began interning for US Representative Joseph P. Kennedy II. The summer of her freshman year, Pressley was raped by someone she knew. "You just never get over it. I'm not over it," she later told Bob Oakes for *Morning Edition* (31 Mar. 2011).

During Pressley's sophomore year, her mother, who was working as an executive assistant at Time Warner in New York, lost her job. Pressley dropped out of school, taking odd jobs as a receptionist, a barback, and a caterer to help support her mother. After two years of cobbling together rent money, Pressley got a job on Senator John Kerry's reelection campaign. She went on to work for Kerry for thirteen years, serving first as scheduler, then as constituent services director, and finally as political director. She left Kerry's staff in 2009 to run for Boston City Council, with a specific mission to help the city's girls and young women. In her farewell speech in 2018, she recalled the motivation behind her decision to run, as quoted by Christopher Gavin for *Boston.com* (6 Dec. 2018): "I wanted to fight for girls, not be their voice, but to lift up their voices, their stories, their struggles, and their ideas to create room and space and dignity for them at the policy table and in committee hearings."

During the campaign, her mother, Pressley recalled to Levenson and Ebbert, "was my not-so-secret weapon" with potential voters. "She used to make these little bags called 'Sandy's Candies,'" Pressley said. Pressley won the election, becoming the first black woman to serve on the council and went on to win several more terms.

"CHANGE CAN'T WAIT"

Pressley, then a five-term councilor, declared her intention to run for Congress in January 2018. The Seventh District includes most of the city of Boston and is the only congressional district in the state that counts a majority of nonwhite constituents. With her decision to mount a challenge to popular incumbent Michael Capuano, David S. Bernstein opined for *WGBH News* (31 Jan. 2018), Pressley "willfully broke the long-standing code of Massachusetts politics—the one that forbids Democrats from challenging incumbents from their own party." Primary challenges are rare in Massachusetts, a state where all elected representatives to the US Congress are Democrats. The city of Boston has a deeply entrenched political machine that has long supported political dynasties, most notably the Kennedys. (The Seven District encompasses parts of John F. Kennedy's former congressional district.) Political insiders in Boston fretted that Pressley, certain to lose, would only stand to make enemies, hurting her chances at a run for higher office in the future. But for Pressley, the bid was a calculated risk. Her father, who now lives in North Carolina, recalled how Pressley presented him with detailed research before announcing her candidacy. "Ayanna studies things before she goes into it," he told Levenson and Ebbert.

Pressley hoped to capture the fervor of the new progressive Left. She and her opponent, Capuano, had few ideological differences—both acknowledged that they would vote the same on most occasions—but Pressley cast herself as an activist fighting to establish a new order. "I'm not running to keep things as they are," Pressley told Seelye and Herndon. "I'm running to change them." A close friend put it a different way: "She didn't grow up here, she didn't have 14 cousins who ran different precincts for her, she didn't have a mom and dad who went to high school with so and so. There is a shift happening in this city . . . Ayanna is the face of that shift—generationally, racially and in terms of gender."

Capuano was endorsed by Boston mayor Marty Walsh and enjoyed the support of the city's formidable political establishment. He also received endorsements from former governor Deval Patrick and prominent Congress members John Lewis and Maxine Waters. Pressley, however, enjoyed the support of Maura Healey, the state's popular attorney general and, just before the election, received endorsements from the city's major newspapers, the *Boston Globe* and the *Boston Herald*—a rarity for a challenger. In what was widely considered a boon for Pressley, the state's two senators, Elizabeth Warren and Ed Markey, refused to endorse a candidate in the race. In September, Pressley won an impressive seventeen-point victory over Capuano and, without a Republican opponent, secured her congressional seat.

IN OFFICE

Pressley occupies the former congressional office of her idol, Shirley Chisholm, the first black member of Congress and the first black person and woman to ever seek a nomination for president by a major party. Representative Katie Hill of California originally drew the office but gave it to Pressley.

During her campaign, Pressley said in one impassioned speech, as quoted by Seelye and Herndon, "This is not just about resisting and affronting [President Donald] Trump. Because the systemic inequalities and disparities that I'm talking about existed long before that man occupied the White House." In her first year in office, Pressley cosponsored several bills seeking to address those inequities. She also spearheaded a bill that would extend postpartum Medicaid coverage to combat rising maternal mortality rates, an issue that disproportionately affects black women.

PERSONAL LIFE

Pressley met Conan Harris, then the manager of the antiviolence campaign StreetSafe Boston, in 2011. She challenged him, asking why he was not doing more to help young girls, and they later had got to know each other better when he gave her a ride home. They married in 2014. When not in Washington, DC, Pressley lives in Dorchester, Massachusetts, with Harris and her stepdaughter, Cora.

SUGGESTED READING

Bernstein, David S. "Explaining the Mystery: Why Ayanna Pressley Is Running for Congress." *WGBH News*, 31 Jan. 2018, www.wgbh.org/news/2018/01/31/explaining-mystery-why-ayanna-pressley-running-congress. Accessed 11 May 2019.

Gavin, Christopher. "Ayanna Pressley Bids City Council Farewell in Impassioned Speech." *Boston.com*, Boston Globe Media, 6 Dec. 2018, www.boston.com/news/politics/2018/12/06/ayanna-pressley-boston-city-council-farewell. Accessed 11 May 2019.

Levenson, Michael, and Stephanie Ebbert. "The Life and Rise of Ayanna Pressley." *Boston Globe*, 8 Sept. 2018, www.bostonglobe.com/metro/2018/09/08/the-life-and-rise-ayanna-pressley/pqdppGFPoZPSEwo3Ko23BJ/story.html. Accessed 11 May 2019.

Oakes, Bob. "Boston City Councilor Reveals She Was Raped at Local College." *Morning Edition*, WBUR, 31 Mar. 2011, www.wbur.

org/news/2011/03/31/ayanna-pressley.   Accessed 11 May 2019.

Seelye, Katharine Q. "Ayanna Pressley Upsets Capuano in Massachusetts House Race." *The New York Times*, 4 Sept. 2018, www.nytimes.com/2018/09/04/us/politics/ayanna-pressley-massachusetts.html. Accessed 11 May 2019.

Seelye, Katharine Q., and Astead W. Herndon. "Ayanna Pressley Seeks Her Political Moment in a Changing Boston." *The New York Times*, 1 Sept. 2018, www.nytimes.com/2018/09/01/us/politics/ayanna-pressley-massachusetts.html. Accessed 11 May 2019.

Seelye, Katharine Q., and Matt Flegenheimer. "Ayanna Pressley's Victory: A Political Earthquake That Reflects a Changed Boston." *The New York Times*, 5 Sept. 2018, www.nytimes.com/2018/09/05/us/politics/ayanna-pressley-massachusetts-elect.html. Accessed 11 May 2019.

—*Molly Hagan*

Pat Quinn

Date of birth: December 16, 1948
Occupation: Former governor of Illinois

Pat Quinn is a politician who has worked on behalf of consumers, taxpayers, and working-class citizens his entire career. He has held several elected positions, including lieutenant governor and governor of Illinois.

EARLY LIFE AND EDUCATION
Pat Quinn was born on December 16, 1948, in Chicago, Illinois, to Eileen Quinn and Patrick Joseph Quinn Sr. The oldest of three sons, he spent his first years in Chicago, and when he was two years old, the family moved to Hinsdale, a suburb west of Chicago. His mother was a secretary in Hinsdale public schools, and his father was an executive for Catholic Cemeteries of Chicago.

Quinn attended St. Isaac Jogues Elementary School in Hinsdale and Fenwick High School in Oak Park. During high school, he was the captain of the cross-country team. After graduating in 1967, he enrolled in Georgetown University Edmund A. Walsh School of Foreign Service.

After earning a bachelor's degree in international economics in 1971, Quinn became involved in several grassroots movements and petition drives. He later returned to school and earned a law degree from Chicago's Northwestern University School of Law in 1980.

In a 2010 interview with a *Chicago Tribune* reporter, Ellen Quinn relayed how her son's activism started early: as a ten-year-old, he

marshaled a group of neighborhood boys to help clean up an unkempt lot and turn it into a ballpark. Quinn credits his Catholic education and his parents for instilling in him a strong sense of patriotism and commitment to public service. He also was shaped by the civil rights movement and Vietnam War of the 1960s and 1970s.

POLITICAL CAREER
Quinn started his political career by working as a community organizer for Dan Walker's gubernatorial campaign. From 1973 to 1975, Quinn worked in Governor Walker's administration, first as a liaison to the public and later as an assistant in the Illinois Industrial Commission. During his time in law school, Quinn continued his activism by forming the Coalition for Political Honesty with the goal to combat corruption and promote ethics in government. One of his first actions with the Coalition was a successful petition drive to end the long-standing practice of Illinois legislators receiving their entire term's salary on the first day they took office. In 1976 he began a petition drive to amend the Illinois Constitution to reduce the number of legislators in the General Assembly. The question was put on the November 1980 ballot, and voters approved the amendment.

In 1982 Quinn, a Democrat, was elected Commissioner of the Cook County Board of (Property) Tax Appeals. During his four-year term, he helped rid the office of corrupt practices. In 1983 Quinn was instrumental in setting up the Citizens Utility Board, a consumer advocacy group for fair utility rates and practices.

Quinn successfully ran for Illinois State Treasurer in 1990, once again focusing on corruption and ethics by helping to pass the Illinois Whistleblower Reward and Protection Act. He also proposed an act barring state employees from demanding political contributions from businesses they inspect, which resulted in the Inspector Act being passed in 2002.

After serving one term as state treasurer, Quinn ran for secretary of state in 1994, the US Senate in 1996, and lieutenant governor in 1998. He lost each election but continued to stay active in politics. In 2001 he walked across Illinois to raise awareness for health care. The following year, he again ran for lieutenant governor with a campaign based on reform and an honest government that would work to empower citizens. In November Quinn won the election with Rod Blagojevich his running mate for governor.

As lieutenant governor, Quinn focused on health care, consumer issues, honest government, the environment, and aiding the military and their families. He implemented several new programs and spearheaded new legislation, including the Military Family Relief Act and the Let Them Rest in Peace Act, the latter of which bans protests at military funerals. He continued his fight to clean up Illinois government and politics, including attempts to reform the Illinois State Toll Highway Authority and the pay-to-play system used to grant government contractors awards.

After the Illinois House and Senate impeached Governor Blagojevich for abuse of power and corruption in 2009, Quinn was sworn in as governor. One of Quinn's first acts was to sign Executive Order 1 (2009), which established the Illinois Reform Commission to make the government more ethical and transparent. He also passed a $3-billion economic stimulus act to provide funds for capital construction and job creation.

In 2010 Quinn campaigned against Republican Bill Brady and won the governorship by a narrow margin. His achievements during this term included signing legislation approving same-sex marriage and abolishing the death penalty in Illinois. His term, however, was marred by his inability to reverse the state's growing debt and reform its public-employee pension program.

In November 2014 Quinn lost the gubernatorial campaign to Republican Bruce Rauner. In his first public appearance after losing the election, Quinn reiterated his intent to continue to advocate for citizens' and consumers' rights. He neither announced nor ruled out his intent to run for office again.

IMPACT

Quinn's career in politics corresponds to his work as a reformer and activist. He has attempted to empower citizens and taxpayers while reducing the power of the entrenched Democratic machine in Chicago and Springfield, Illinois. One of his most successful achievements as governor was abolishing the death penalty.

PERSONAL LIFE

Quinn is divorced and has two adult sons: David and Patrick IV.

SUGGESTED READING

"Ex-Gov. Pat Quinn Pushes Consumer Rights, Blasts Bruce Rauner's Budget." *Northwest Herald*, 27 Feb. 2015, www.nwherald.com/2015/02/27/ex-gov-pat-quinn-pushes-consumer-rights-blasts-bruce-rauners-budget/awdru3x/. Accessed 15 Sept. 2015.

Felsenthal, Carol. "Does Pat Quinn Have a Personal Life?" *Chicago*. Tribune Publishing, 20 Oct. 2014, www.chicagomag.com/Chicago-Magazine/Felsenthal-Files/October-2014/Pat-Quinn-Personal-Life/. Accessed 15 Sept. 2015.

Jaeger, Bethany. "Pat Quinn Sworn in as Illinois' 41st Governor." *Illinois Issues*, U of Illinois at Springfield, Jan. 2009, illinoisissuesblog.blogspot.com/2009/01/. Accessed 15 Sept. 2015.

Lester, Kerry. "Pat Quinn's Mom Shows Toughness, Love on the Campaign Trail." *Daily Herald*, 6 Nov. 2010, www.dailyherald.com/article/20101106/news/711079965/. Accessed 15 Sept. 2015.

"Pat Quinn." *Reboot Illinois*. Reboot Illinois, 2014. Web. 15 Sept. 2015.

Stepanek, Marcia. "Pat Quinn—A Man Politicians Love to Hate." *Illinois Issues*, U of Illinois at Springfield, 8 Feb. 1980, www.lib.niu.edu/1980/ii800204.html. Accessed 15 Sept. 2015.

—*Barb Lightner*

Kirthiga Reddy

Date of birth: 1971
Occupation: Business executive

Kirthiga Reddy is a venture partner for the Japanese conglomerate SoftBank. In this role, she advises the company's $100 billion Vision Fund, which invests in industries that, SoftBank believes, are poised to revolutionize technology in the decades and even centuries to come. Prior to her job at SoftBank, Reddy spent eight years at the social-networking giant Facebook. She launched Facebook's expansion into India in 2010 and was named one of *Fast Company* magazine's 100 Most Creative People in 2013. Her time at Facebook India, she told a group at *Fortune*'s Most Powerful Women International Summit in London in 2019, "was a vivid example of the power of technology to transform lives." During her tenure, Facebook's usership in India grew from 8 million to about 130 million users—even as the company ran afoul of the country's regulators. Reddy left Facebook India in 2016, though she continued to work with Facebook, out of its California headquarters, until 2018. In 2019, Reddy sought to assuage fears about the Vision Fund, and criticism that its enormous investments, doled out at a minimum of $100 million to a few start-ups, might inflate valuations and make it difficult for smaller start-ups to compete. She described the sizable investments at the *Fortune* event as "bold" and, ultimately, "long-term." She further described tech as an ecosystem, with companies working across sectors as technology advances. "The [fundraising] environment has changed," she said.

EARLY LIFE AND EDUCATION

Kirthiga Reddy was born to a middle-class family in India. Her mother received little schooling because her family deemed it unnecessary for a woman to complete high school. "Her parents said, 'You know enough math to do your laundry and grocery bills, you don't need to study further,'" Reddy recalled to Masoom Gupte for India's *Economic Times* (16 July 2015). Her father was a government worker, and because of his job, the family moved every four years. Reddy and her sister spent their formative years in big cities like Mumbai and Chennai, but also small towns like rural Dandeli, known for its wildlife preserve. Unlike her mother's family, Reddy's parents believed it was important for their daughter to receive an education. According to her LinkedIn profile, she graduated with a degree in computer science and engineering from Dr. Babasaheb Ambedkar Marathwada University, Aurangabad, in 1992. She was second in her class and won an award for all-around excellence.

After graduation, Reddy moved with her parents to Nagpur in central India. She got a job with Yashavant Kanetkar, a computer science author, whose books are foundational texts in engineering schools. Reddy worked as a software programmer and helped Kanetkar develop programming examples to illustrate important concepts in his books. Reddy enjoyed the small, start-up-like atmosphere of the company, but hoped to pursue a graduate degree. "I started studying for my GMAT then"—her graduate management admission test—"and I vividly remember my colleagues doing flashcards during breaks to help me work on my GMAT scores," she told Gunjeet Sra for *India Today* magazine (11 Nov. 2011). Reddy was accepted to Syracuse University in the United States, becoming the first person in her family to study abroad. She graduated with an MS degree in computer engineering in 1995.

EARLY CAREER

Upon her graduation, Reddy took a job with the computer hardware and software manufacturer Silicon Graphics. In 2000, she became the company's youngest director of engineering. She left Silicon Graphics to earn her MBA degree at Stanford University. She graduated in 2003 as an Arjay Miller scholar, meaning that she was in the top ten percent of her class. Reddy took a job with a company called Good Technology in Sunnyvale, California. The company was later acquired by the telecommunications company Motorola in 2008. The same year, Reddy became the director of Good India, the company's Indian division. Moving back to India was a difficult career decision, she told Sra. "Change is hard although, in hindsight, it was a great career decision and led to [a job with Facebook] that I consider a once-in-a-lifetime opportunity," she said. In 2009, she joined the software company

Phoenix Technologies, where, as a vice president and general manager, she led a team serving the United States, India, Japan, South Korea, and Taiwan.

FACEBOOK INDIA

In 2010, Reddy was tapped to run Facebook India, based out of Hyderabad. She brought with her Facebook's "flat culture," as she described it to Jeff Chu for *Fast Company* (13 May 2013). A flat organization structure means fewer boundaries between executives and staff. Reddy explained, "You're not here to do just what you're told. You're here to see gaps and to act upon them." It was a vast departure for many Indian hires who were more familiar with hierarchical and bureaucratic workplaces, but Reddy credits the approach for Facebook India's initial success. In 2010, Facebook had about 8 million Indian users, in a country of about 1.2 billion people. By the end of 2012, the site had over 71 million users. Surging usership could more directly be attributed to the company's Facebook for Every Phone initiative. In 2011, the company made a deal with various phone companies in India (and in the Philippines, Latin America, and Africa) to offer free access to Facebook on low-end phones for ninety days, even if the user did not have a data plan.

By 2014, Facebook India had over 100 million users; by 2016, the site had over 130 million users. Reddy worked with advertisers hoping to target Indian users. Facebook's founder and CEO, Mark Zuckerberg, worked with Indian politicians to bring internet access to more Indians, many of whom had never been online before. Zuckerberg framed the mission as a charitable endeavor, though he was primarily interested in drawing more users to Facebook, not the Internet at large. He called the project Internet.org. After its launch in 2015, it was rechristened Free Basics. As early critics pointed out, Free Basics allowed access to certain sites, while necessarily excluding others—a violation of net neutrality, "the principle that phone companies and internet providers should not be allowed to prioritise certain sites and services, since this could fundamentally alter the level playing field of the internet," Rahul Bhatia explained for the *Guardian* (12 May 2016). Facebook became a gatekeeper, deciding which sites Indians with the service would be allowed to see. A fierce debate about net neutrality emerged, and companies that had partnered with Facebook and Free Basics began to withdraw their participation. It is unclear how involved Reddy, the managing director of Facebook in India, was with Free Basics, but Bhatia's investigative piece for the *Guardian* suggests that the project was valuable enough to require significant personal attention from both Zuckerberg and Facebook's chief operating officer, Sheryl Sandberg.

In early 2016, the Indian government made a ruling on net neutrality that effectively made Free Basics illegal. Reddy stepped down days later. A Facebook spokesperson presented her departure as separate from the failure of Free Basics. "As she had planned for some time, Kirthiga Reddy is moving back to the U.S. to work with the teams in Headquarters," a Facebook spokesperson said as quoted by *Reuters* (12 Feb. 2016). "During her time in India, Kirthiga was not involved in our Free Basic Services efforts."

SOFTBANK VISION FUND

Reddy returned to the United States and spent the next two years working as a managing global clients partner and emerging markets lead. In 2018, she joined the Japanese conglomerate SoftBank Group Corporation. SoftBank was founded in the early 1980s as a telecommunications company. In 2018, it was a multinational conglomerate that owns and invests in companies across a spectrum of industries. In 2010, SoftBank's charismatic chairman and CEO Masayoshi Son released a 300-year-plan for the company, which has become one of the most valuable in the world; the plan culminates in the singularity, a hypothetical future point at which technology will supersede human intelligence. The philosophies illustrated in the plan fuel the company's investments in areas like artificial intelligence (AI) and the "Internet of Things" (IoT).

In 2017, SoftBank launched a $100 billion investment arm called the Vision Fund, then the largest tech fund in history. Early investments included the ride-sharing service Uber, the real estate company, WeWork, and a Beijing-based transportation company called Didi Chuxing. Reddy was hired as a venture partner for the Vision Fund in 2018. As a venture partner, she works closely with Deep Nishar, the fund's senior managing partner for the Americas, on investing in what she describes as "frontier technologies" like AI, robotics, bioengineering, and quantum computing. Such technologies "will enable the next stage of the information revolution," and address the most challenging societal and industrial problems, according to a profile of her on the *SoftBank Vision Fund* website (2019).

In 2018, Reddy and six other women executives who had earlier worked at Facebook co-founded a seed investment fund called F7. The group focuses on funding female-led ventures. Reddy also serves as chair of the Stanford Business School Management Board.

PERSONAL LIFE

Reddy and her husband, Devanand Reddy, live in the San Francisco Bay Area with their two daughters, Ashna and Ariya.

SUGGESTED READING

Bhatia, Rahul. "The Inside Story of Facebook's Biggest Setback." *The Guardian*, 12 May 2016, www.theguardian.com/technology/2016/may/12/facebook-free-basics-india-zuckerberg. Accessed 17 Sept. 2019.

Chu, Jeff. "Most Creative People 2013: 4. Kirthiga Reddy—The Global Mobile All-Star." *Fast Company*, 13 May 2013, www.fastcompany.com/3009243/4-kirthiga-reddy. Accessed 17 Sept. 2019.

"Facebook India MD Kirthiga Reddy Stepping Down." *Reuters*, 12 Feb. 2016, de.reuters.com/article/facebook-india/facebook-india-md-kirthiga-reddy-stepping-down-idUSKCN0VL2AL. Accessed 17 Sept. 2019.

Gupte, Masoom. "Kirthiga Reddy's Role Model: Her Mother." *The Economic Times*, 16 July 2015, economictimes.indiatimes.com/magazines/panache/kirthiga-reddys-role-model-her-mother/articleshow/48096349.cms. Accessed 17 Sept. 2019.

Lev-Ram, Michal. "SoftBank Partner: Fundraising 'Environment Has Changed.'" *Fortune*, 5 June 2019, fortune.com/2019/06/05/softbank-kirthiga-reddy-mpw/. Accessed 17 Sept. 2019.

Reddy, Kirthiga. "Kirthiga Reddy." *Lean In*, 2019, leanin.org/stories/kirthiga-reddy. Accessed 17 Sept. 2019.

Sra, Gunjeet. "Face to Face with Kirthiga Reddy." *India Today*, 11 Nov. 2011, www.indiatoday.in/magazine/supplement/story/20111121-kirthiga-reddy-facebook-india-education-women-leaders-749624-2011-11-11. Accessed 17 Sept. 2019.

—*Molly Hagan*

Barbara Jane Reyes

Date of birth: 1971
Occupation: Poet

Barbara Jane Reyes has used poetry as a bridge between her life in the United States and that of her extended family in the Philippines. Each collection of poems builds on the earlier one, as Reyes within them moves from autobiography to witness to muse or deity. Of her Filipina heritage and the challenge of publishing, Reyes told Emily Wilson for *California Magazine* (29 Aug. 2018), "I could complain for a very long time that there are no Filipina-authored books of poetry out in the world, or I can write like hell and be real aggressive about publishing. If there are a few of us doing that, pretty soon you have a presence."

Asked for advice she might offer young writers, Reyes told Melissa Sipin for *Tayo Literary Magazine* (22 Dec. 2013), "If the story is meant to be written, then it will be written, and it's up to you to figure out how to get to that point that you're ready to write it. For me, it meant years of practice, and going to school to continue my education as a writer, immersing myself in a structured, professional environment with writers and professors who would push my aesthetic and literary boundaries, and oftentimes push them hard."

EARLY LIFE

Born in the Philippine capital of Manila, Reyes came with her family to the area around San Francisco Bay when she was two years old and grew up there. She is one of four daughters, all of whom were expected to attend prestigious institutes of higher education. As a child, her Filipina heritage of myths and stories was important to her, as she told Sipin: "When I was very young, my mother's mother would tell me stories that really stayed with me; I mostly remember the story of the god who formed people out of mud, and baked them in a large earthen oven. . . . The undercooked ones were Caucasians, the overcooked ones Africans, and the just-right ones were us. This meant something to me, and my world view was formed around her stories." Other stories that influenced her were parables from the Bible and Aesop's fables.

Reyes's early religious experience affected her writing, as she told Craig Santos Perez for *Jacket2* (10 May 2011): "I haven't attended church in years, nor have I recently recited the rosary or a novena, but I remember the hum and buzz of the congregation, being a part of that, as in the call and response of the Litany of the Blessed Virgin. You feel like one intoning body in this shared spiritual experience, tapping into a higher power."

As an adolescent, Reyes frequented San Francisco's famed City Lights Books and read poetry. She wrote both poetry and fiction. She also observed the use of multiple languages within her extended family, whose members spoke two Filipino languages, Tagalog and Ilocano, along with English. Reyes tried to analyze which language was appropriate for various kinds of communication. She uses those languages in her writing, along with "Tagalish" or "Taglish," a blend of Tagalog and English, which was also spoken within her family. Standard American English was the language of school.

EDUCATION AND EARLY CAREER

While still at University of California Berkeley earning a bachelor's degree in ethnic studies,

Photo by Oscarb via Wikimedia Commons

Reyes helped edit the magazine *Maganda*. She also took advantage of the Kearny Street Workshop, which was founded in 1972 and is the nation's oldest Asian Pacific American multidisciplinary arts organization. Kearny Street connects new voices with established writers and artists, as well as offering exhibits, readings, and performances. The example of Jessica Hagedorn, the Filipina performance artist and writer, encouraged Reyes to get her work out of notebooks and into the world. Being asked to read a poem at Kearny Street also fired up her ambition as a poet. In 2018, she was an honoree of the APAture Focus Award; APA is an abbreviation for Asian and Pacific Americans; *APAture* is the journal Kearny Street publishes.

After completing her undergraduate degree, Reyes earned a master of fine arts degree with a concentration in poetry from San Francisco State University. Of her decision to earn an MFA, Reyes told Sipin, "I always say that one need not get an MFA to be a writer, and I truly believe this. I chose that route for myself because I needed critical and involved feedback, which I was not getting from my own community. . . . There was no challenge here, no critical eye on the work, and no language to help me better understand my process so that I could hone it, improve upon it. So in this way, the MFA was necessary for me, in order to be challenged and pushed."

The pushing was successful: her first full-length collection, *Gravities of Center*, was published in 2003. In 2007, she began teaching at Mills College in Oakland, where she is a visiting assistant professor of creative writing. She is also an adjunct professor in the Yuchengco

Philippine Studies program at the University of San Francisco, where she has taught since 2009. In 2011 she also started teaching at San Francisco State University as a lecturer in the creative writing department. Of her teaching, she told Abigail Licad for *Hyphen Magazine* (5 Nov. 2014), "As a teacher of literature, one of my major concerns is maintaining the balance between literary study, and covering social, cultural, historical matters in the works. There is a lot we learn about culture and history, from discussing genre, form, and various narrative strategies and literary techniques."

POETA EN SAN FRANCISCO AND CHAP BOOKS

Reyes's second volume of poetry, *Poeta en San Francisco*, was published in 2005. It is written in multiple languages, including Spanish and Tagalog, as well as English. Some of the sections in Tagalog, the national language of the Philippines, is written in its original script, Baybayin. In addition to these languages, Reyes incorporates street talk, propaganda, and other contemporary idiomatic language in her poems. The concerns of the poems include the history of colonialism as well as contemporary life in San Francisco.

The work is structured as a triptych, or a work with three parts, bracketed by a prologue and an epilogue. The three sections are named "orient," "dis-orient," and "re-orient." In his summary of the prologue, Danny Thanh Nguyen wrote for *Indiana Review* (Summer 2007), "Reyes is not just sorting through the bones of her native Philippines—its history of Spanish colonialism, of US occupation—she is also trying to find voices for the dead fallen in the name of globalization, those who cannot speak."

The Academy of American Poets awarded the collection the James Laughlin Award. As James Longenbach wrote for *American Poet* (Fall 2006), "If William Blake were alive and well and sitting on a eucalyptus branch in the hills above the bay, this is the poetry he would aspire to write."

In 2008, Reyes published two chapbooks of poetry, *Easter Sunday* and *Cherry*. Four years later, she published *For the City that Nearly Broke Me*, her third chapbook.

DIWATA

Diwata, published in 2010, was an outgrowth of Reyes's affinity for myths of her native land and particularly for mermaids, which have been present in many of her works. It was a finalist for the California Book Award and won the Global Filipino Literary Award for Poetry.

As Reyes told Sipin, "I started writing *Diwata*, really by revisiting the mythic women voices and personae which have always populated my work. . . . This mermaid who encounters the executed revolutionaries made her way into *Diwata*

in my 'Duyong' poems, where I've written five different mermaid personae, who speak with a certain amount of emotional maturity, distance, ambivalence that she's cultivated over her long, long life and mythical status as an observer/witness of human lives."

Reyes explained the mythic creatures in this work to Santos Perez saying, "Because I don't know the names of so many of my ancestors, because I do not know the details of their lives, I invent, I speculate, I turn to myth-making." She has also invented some of the mythic stories, combining a number of sources.

TO LOVE AS ASWANG

Reyes published *To Love as Aswang* in 2015. The work's imaginative cover art leads the reader into the text with images of both the tree of life and the Ouroboros, a serpent depicted eating its own tail, signifying a return to the beginning or the cyclical nature of life.

The poems explore the nature of the Filipina experience, particularly that of sex and shaming because of colonial and imperial forces, of both Spain and the United States. Aswang in Philippine myth is a monster; she has been linked to perceived female boundary-breaking and has served as a scapegoat. As April Joseph wrote in a review of the collection for *Tayo Literary Magazine* (7 Nov. 2016), "Reyes's work is a bridge that Aswang resides over, not merely to sing the horrors and atrocities within Pinay culture, but to invite us all to stand on the bridge together, as witness, to be touched and transformed by the fire." ("Pinay" is a colloquial term for "Filipina.")

INVOCATION TO DAUGHTERS

Reyes's fifth poetry collection, *Invocation to Daughters*, published in 2017, was a finalist for the 2018 California Book Award. It is a collection of psalms, odes, and prayers for Filipina women and girls. This liturgical context is a rich form, given that the Philippines is home to the world's third-largest Roman Catholic population. Some sections resemble biblical texts, particularly the Gospel of Saint John, the most mystical of the accounts of Christ's life, and bringing Juana de la Cruz (a feminine form of Saint Juan de la Cruz) into the text as a type of everywoman.

The daughters of the collection are understood as Pinays, grappling with patriarchy and a colonial past. Reyes wrote primarily in English with Spanish and Tagalog interspersed in the language. The first two languages are part of the experience of the conquered people, but also reflect contemporary Filipino experience. Tagalog, as Reyes told Therese Konopelski for *Letra Latinas* (28 Sept. 2018), "brings Filipino core values into the work—concerns and practices of reciprocity, collectivity, community, and collaboration, over the individual, what I like to call, 'we' culture."

Reyes also told Konopelski that part of the impetus for this collection was violence committed against two Filipina women, Mary Jane Veloso and Jennifer Laude. Veloso is the only Filipina on death row in Indonesia, sentenced for trying to smuggle heroin into the country, which she said she was duped into doing. Laude, a transgender woman, was murdered in 2014 by a United States Marine.

PERSONAL LIFE

Reyes is married to Oscar Bermeo, who was born in Ecuador and is also a poet; they live in Oakland, California. As she told Sipin, "I am married to a poet who also has a public life, and so poetic discussion happens with us in the course of our everyday, in our morning commute, at the grocery store, at the dinner table." Together the couple runs Doveglion Press, which focuses on political writing.

Reyes hikes and kayaks, finding poetry and rhythm in her striding and paddling. Although she finds poetry in her private life, she told Sipin, "I typically take my autobiographical self out of the work, because I believe it limits me; there's only so much about myself and my private life that I am willing to share with readers, with others." She is on the board of Philippine American Writers and Artists (PAWA).

SUGGESTED READING

Longenbach, James. "Opening the Eyes Wider Still." Review of *Poeta en San Francisco*, by Barbara Jane Reyes. *American Poet*, vol. 31, 2006, p. 11, www.barbarajanereyes.com/wp-content/uploads/2016/08/american-poet.pdf. Accessed 30 Nov. 2018.

Nguyen, Danny Thanh. Review of *Poeta en San Francisco*, by Barbara Jane Reyes. *Indiana Review*, vol. 29, no. 1, 2007, pp. 198–99, www.barbarajanereyes.com/wp-content/uploads/2016/08/indiana-review.pdf. Accessed 30 Nov. 2018.

Reyes, Barbara Jane. "Art Talk with Poet Barbara Jane Reyes." Interview by Rebecca Sutton. *Art Works*, National Endowment for the Arts, 23 May 2017, www.arts.gov/art-works/2017/art-talk-poet-barbara-jane-reyes. Accessed 12 Nov. 2018.

Reyes, Barbara Jane. Interview by Melissa R. Sipin. *Tayo Literary Magazine*, 22 Dec. 2013, www.tayoliterarymag.com/barbara-jane-reyes. Accessed 9 Nov. 2018.

Reyes, Barbara Jane. "Q&A: Writes Barbara Jane Reyes, 'I Am Not Your Ethnic Spectacle.'" Interview by Emily Wilson. *California Magazine*, Cal Alumni Association UC Berkeley, 29 Aug. 2018, alumni.berkeley.edu/california-magazine/just-in/2018-08-29/barbara-jane-reyes-filipino-poet. Accessed 9 Nov. 2018.

Reyes, Barbara Jane. "Talking with Barbara Jane Reyes." Interview by Craig Santos Perez. *Jacket2*, 10 May 2011, jacket2.org/commentary/talking-barbara-jane-reyes. Accessed 17 Nov. 2018.

SELECTED WORKS

Gravities of Center, 2003; *Poeta en San Francisco*, 2005; *Diwata*, 2010; *To Love as Aswang*, 2015; *Invocation to Daughters*, 2017

—*Judy Johnson*

Jessie Reyez

Date of birth: June 12, 1991
Occupation: Singer-songwriter

Jessie Reyez is a Canadian singer-songwriter of Colombian descent known for her gutting vocals and sharp, honest lyrics—including those that make up the powerful single "Body Count," which advocates for women's sexual liberation in a society she perceives as dominated by gender double standards. After capitalizing on her experience with the Toronto mentorship program the Remix Project, she released her first extended play (EP), *Kiddo*, in 2017 and has steadily gained momentum in the music industry ever since. *Kiddo* features her hit single "Figures," about a bad breakup. She turned another song on that record, "Gatekeeper," into an approximately twelve-minute, poignant short film about her experience being propositioned by an anonymous industry professional whom she later revealed as Noel "Detail" Fisher—a producer who has worked with Beyoncé and Drake—earlier in her career. The film was nominated for an MTV Video Music Award (VMA) for Video with a Message and inspired other artists, including Bebe Rexha and Tinashe, to come forward about their experiences with Fisher. Reyez released her second EP, *Being Human in Public*, in 2018.

Considered an artist to watch, some of her earliest musical inspirations came from reggae music, but her output can more easily be compared to R & B singers like Amy Winehouse and SZA. She has, in multiple interviews, such as that with Emilia Petrarca for *W* magazine (11 May 2017), described her genre-bending style as "Quentin Tarantino music," after the frenetic filmmaker. "It's violent soul music," she told Yezmin Villarreal for *Billboard* (5 Jan. 2018). "It's romantic, it's bloody, it's heaven, it's hell." Reyez, who had yet to release a full-length album as of late 2018, won Breakthrough Artist of the Year at Canada's Juno Awards that year, and she has collaborated with prominent artists like DJ Calvin Harris, Latin superstar Romeo Santos, and rapper Eminem.

Photo by FeldBum via Wikimedia Commons

EARLY LIFE

Jessica "Jessie" Reyez was born in Toronto, Canada, on June 12, 1991. The daughter of Colombian immigrants, she spent her early childhood in a multicultural enclave of the city. "When I went to school, I didn't know a lick of English, but it was okay because there were so many immigrants in the area, a lot of the kids didn't speak a lick of English either," she told Samantha Edwards for Toronto's weekly *Now* (10 Oct. 2018). "It was normal to have a wicked accent." Looking back, she has often expressed that growing up in and around a diverse city like Toronto was crucial to developing a unique, authentic musical style. Eventually, the family moved to Brampton, a city in the Greater Toronto Area. At her new, majority white school, she was often teased for the way she spoke. As an adult, she says the experience helped her develop a thicker skin.

In addition to exposing her to salsa, merengue, and cumbia, Reyez's father taught her how to play the guitar while her older brother got her listening to reggae, and she started writing poems as an adolescent. In the seventh grade, a teacher offered some pivotal encouragement regarding her writing. "She said, 'this is dope,' and went as far as to tell my parents, 'I don't know if you know, but your daughter is lit with the pen!'" Reyez recalled to Geena Kloeppel for *Spin* (26 June 2017). Still, according to Reyez, she did not write anything worthwhile until her first heartbreak as a teenager. "I needed to get that pain out," she told Kloeppel.

In high school, Reyez was mostly interested in music and dancing. Long evenings spent at hip-hop dance class caused her to suffer academically. Though she insists she was not a great singer as a teen, she auditioned for a girl group. She failed to make the cut, but manager Tyse Saffuri was intrigued enough to offer her a brief mentorship. Reyez told Kloeppel that Saffuri's advice helped push her in the right direction.

EARLY CAREER

After graduating from high school and declining to go to college, Reyez began performing songs she had written herself at Toronto clubs and on the street. At that point, however, she decided to follow her family to Miami, Florida. After eighteen years of waiting, the family's American visas had been approved. Rather than live in Toronto on her own, she decided to follow her family to the United States. She got a job as a bartender, but the city's party culture became the primary drain of her time. "People party all the time, and if you're working in the industry, you're sleeping all day and at the club all night, day after day," she told Slava Pastuk for *Noisey* (23 Oct. 2014). "I did that for a year, I completely neglected my music. The only musical thing I did was playing the guitar at the beach when everyone was coming down after a long night."

Reyez, frustrated with the slow pace of trying to get her music produced, after talking to producer Doc McKinney, decided she needed to jumpstart her career by taking matters into her own hands. She asked a friend to shoot a music video for a song that she had written while she was still living in Canada. Driven by a deep sense of urgency, she edited the video herself and posted it on her *Facebook* page. One person who saw it referred her to Toronto's Remix Project, a collaborative academy for artists from low-income backgrounds.

Reyez saw the Remix Project as an opportunity to learn and practice her craft. Once she had applied, she scrounged together enough money for a flight to Toronto to audition and gained admittance. The change proved to be just the kind of motivation she needed, and she made the most of her time there in 2014: "It took me out of the environment of clubs and brought me into a focused setting where everyone is a dreamer and ambitious and taking advantage of their opportunity," she told Pastuk. She was still a student there when she caught the attention of Chicago rapper King Louie, who had come to the academy to conduct a workshop. Having enjoyed her song "Status," he asked Reyez to collaborate with him on a song. The two jammed together; Reyez played "Status" and King Louie freestyled over her guitar. From that seed of an idea came the song "Living in the Sky," released in 2014. Chance the Rapper heard the song and posted on Twitter about it, Reyez told Karen Bliss for *Billboard* (5 Sept. 2017), "and things have just been rolling since."

KIDDO

Reyez teamed up with the Toronto-based production agency Mad Ruk Entertainment, who sent her to a writing camp in Sweden. There, she met producers Priest and the Beast and Shy Carter, who worked with her on channeling her emotions regarding a difficult breakup into her song "Figures." The song was released in 2016 and would eventually reach number fifty-eight on the Billboard Canadian Hot 100 chart. Her second single, "Shutter Island," released in early 2017, introduced listeners to the gonzo side of Reyez, who sings, "I'm crazy just like Galileo / My straight jacket's custom-made though." The song "comes out swinging," Tom Twardzik wrote for the pop culture website *PopDust* (24 Jan. 2017). "The orchestration sinks beneath heavy bass and a piercing drum machine. Reyez's voice in the verses swerves from aggressive sarcasm to light falsetto. But in the chorus, she lets loose the power behind it. The vocal dexterity she exercises is impressive and the sarcastic humor of her lyrics is perfect." When asked about the song's inspiration, Reyez responded to Kajal Patel for the music website *Pigeons & Planes* (25 Jan. 2017), "Have you heard 'Figures?' It's about the same guy . . . but I was angrier this time."

Both songs and their accompanying videos garnered attention for the newcomer and the debut EP, *Kiddo*, on which they appear, released in April 2017 to largely positive reviews. That year, she performed the aching ballad "Figures" at the Black Entertainment Television (BET) Awards to great acclaim and took the stage on NBC's *Late Night with Seth Meyers*. Meanwhile, another song off the EP, "Gatekeeper," and its accompanying short film (nominated for a Video Music Award (VMA)) attracted yet more attention, and she was featured on both the hit Calvin Harris song "Hard to Love" and Romeo Santos's song "Un Vuelo a La," included on his album *Golden*. The collaboration with Harris marked a personal milestone for Reyez, who, years before, had tried to sneak the DJ her mixtape during one of his performances. With her talent more fully recognized, including being honored with the award for Breakthrough Artist of the Year at Canada's Juno Awards, 2018 also brought further opportunities for collaboration, including cowriting Harris's massive hit with Dua Lipa, "One Kiss." Additionally, she appears on the songs "Nice Guy" and "Good Guy" on Eminem's record *Kamikaze* (2018).

BEING HUMAN IN PUBLIC

Always continuing to write her own material, Reyez released songs such as "Apple Juice" in advance of putting out her second EP, *Being Human in Public*, in October 2018. Chris DeVille, who reviewed the record for *Stereogum* (18 Oct. 2018), wrote that it contained "some of the more evocative lyrics I've encountered this year." He added, "Her voice sounds like the fiery taste in your throat after shooting whiskey. . . . She's one of those personalities too big to contain, except she seems to know exactly when to rein herself in and when to let loose." A. D. Amorosi, writing for *Variety* (19 Oct. 2018), called Reyez a "major new voice," describing the EP as "more accessible than her previous work." The record is marked by contrast, from the anguished soul ballad "Apple Juice" to the flippant hip-hop song "F—— Being Friends." Inspired by her work with Santos, she sings entirely in Spanish on the gentle acoustic track "Sola." She even offers up a feminist "rallying cry," as DeVille described it, on "Body Count." The video for that song, reminiscent of the similarly masochistic "Shutter Island," features her being burned at the stake.

The multitude of personas on the record fits Reyez's definition of "being human in public." For her, that means "being honest. Being the way you are inside your house and in the safety of privacy, but being that way outdoors too. And being OK with it. Wearing your flaws right on the surface and accepting them," she told Keryce Chelsi Henry for *Forbes* (19 Oct. 2018). "To me, being human is clearing that barrier and seeing yourself as you are." To further promote the EP, she embarked on a North American tour, which included dates in her native Canada as well as in US cities such as San Francisco and Chicago.

In interviews, Reyez has expressed that she appreciates having time to herself and has increasingly branched out into yoga and meditation. At the same time, she is extremely family oriented, inviting her parents on tour and bringing them on stage with her during the acceptance of her 2018 Juno Award.

SUGGESTED READING

DeVille, Chris. "Jessie Reyez Is Really Good and You Should Listen to Her." Review of *Being Human in Public*, by Jessie Reyez. *Stereogum*, 18 Oct. 2018, www.stereogum.com/2018411/jessie-reyez-being-human-in-public-review/franchises/the-week-in-pop. Accessed 12 Nov. 2018.

Edwards, Samantha. "A Day in the Life of Jessie Reyez, Toronto's Next Big Pop Star." *Now*, 10 Oct. 2018, nowtoronto.com/music/features/jessie-reyez-interview-cover-story. Accessed 12 Nov. 2018.

Pastuk, Slava. "Toronto's Jessie Reyez Connects with King Louie on Unlikely Terms." *Noisey*, 23 Oct. 2014, noisey.vice.com/en_us/article/65nknr/jessie-reyez-was-saved-by-the-remix-project. Accessed 12 Nov. 2018.

Reyez, Jessie. "Jessie Reyez' Realness Will Not Be Diluted." Interview by Geena Kloeppel. *Spin*, 26 June 2017, www.spin.com/featured/jessie-reyez-interview. Accessed 12 Nov. 2018.

———. "Jessie Reyez Talks Her New EP, *Being Human in Public*." Interview by Keryce Chelsi Henry. *Forbes*, 19 Oct. 2018, www.forbes.com/sites/kerycehenry/2018/10/19/jessie-reyez-talks-her-new-ep-being-human-in-public. Accessed 12 Nov. 2018.

Twardzik, Tom. "Listen to the Newest Single by Upcoming R&B Hitmaker Jessie Reyez." Review of "Shutter Island," by Jessie Reyez. *PopDust*, 24 Jan. 2017, www.popdust.com/jessie-reyez-shutter-island-2210511020.html. Accessed 12 Nov. 2018.

Villarreal, Yezmin. "2018 Preview: Jessie Reyez, the Next Queen of Outspoken R&B." *Billboard*, 5 Jan. 2018, www.billboard.com/articles/columns/pop/8092582/jessie-reyez-queen-outspoken-rb-2018-preview. Accessed 12 Nov. 2018.

—*Molly Hagan*

Matthew Rhys

Date of birth: November 8, 1974
Occupation: Actor

Some actors are breakout stars. Others hone their crafts for years in small parts on stage and screen, getting a bigger role here and there, and are ultimately rewarded with accolades for the unique perspectives they bring to the characters they portray. The latter is the case for Matthew Rhys, a Welsh actor who has been working professionally since the late 1990s but who only more recently came into his own with his vivid portrayal of a conflicted Soviet spy named Philip Jennings in FX's acclaimed period television drama *The Americans* (2013–18).

The Americans was heralded for its compelling story line, portrayal of family conflicts, and exploration of 1980s espionage. In the series, Rhys's character can no longer bear to live a double life in America. His troubled conscience brings him into conflict with his wife, Elizabeth, played by Keri Russell, who remains a true believer in the Soviet system. Rhys discussed *The Americans*' main characters in an interview with Maureen Ryan for the *New York Times* (30 May 2018), saying: "These two were plucked at an incredibly early age to do this. They were indoctrinated. It wasn't a choice that came later in life with maturity and hind- and foresight. . . . What you saw in Philip was someone emerging from that going, 'Actually, this isn't right. And it's not for me.'"

In 2018, Rhys earned an Emmy Award for his performance in the show's final season, and he had earned roles in a number of big-budget films, including *The Post* (2017) and *Mowgli: Legend of the Jungle* (2018).

EARLY LIFE AND EDUCATION

Matthew Rhys was born in Cardiff, Wales, on November 8, 1974. He has an older sister named Rachel, who became a television producer. His mother was a teacher, while his father was the headmaster of a local school. According to Rhys, his father was never very strict with his children at home. "He was good like that," Rhys said to Gerard Gilbert for the *Independent* (8 Sept. 2012). "He spent all day and every day being the disciplinarian; by the time he came home he enjoyed being more of the fun dad."

Rhys spent much of his childhood being interested in rugby and farming. In addition to participating in the biannual national performing arts festival as well as youth theater, he developed an interest in acting, in part through his friend Ioan Gruffudd, who became a leading man in the Horatio Hornblower series of television movies between 1998 and 2003 and starred in a host of television series and films. Rhys followed Gruffudd (who is a year older and attended the same primary and high school) to the Royal Academy of Dramatic Art (RADA) in London, ultimately earning the prestigious Patricia Rothermere Scholarship. "Rada was a slap in the face," he told Gilbert. "The work rate there is big. I had friends at university and they were doing six hours of lectures every week and you're doing 12 hours a day sometimes and worked Saturdays as well. It wasn't this wild, raucous drinking, having a good time I thought it might have been. But the training is phenomenal, so it's a trade-off."

Soon after graduation, Rhys appeared in the film *House of America* (1997) and the British

Photo by Icla via Wikimedia Commons

television series *Backup* (1997). Meanwhile, his performance on stage at the Royal Court Theatre alongside Paul Bettany in a production of *Stranger's House* in 1997 secured him an American agent.

ACTING ON BOTH SIDES OF THE ATLANTIC

At the suggestion of his agent, Rhys went to Los Angeles in 1998 during pilot season and quickly landed a role in Julie Taymor's *Titus* (1999), an adaptation of William Shakespeare's play *Titus Andronicus* (ca. 1594) that starred Anthony Hopkins in the lead role. "I thought, 'Oh, L.A.'s great! You just walk up and get big movies. It's brilliant.' Then I went back nine years consecutive and couldn't catch a cold," he explained to Cynthia Littleton for *Variety* (4 June 2014). Over the next several years, he found small roles in television miniseries like *Metropolis* (2000), television movies like *The Lost World* (2001), films such as *Peaches* (2000) and *Very Annie Mary* (2001), and the series finale of the long-running detective show *Columbo* (2003).

Rhys had some better success on stage in his native United Kingdom, where he won the leading role in the West End adaptation of the 1967 film *The Graduate*, in which his character is seduced by an older woman, played onstage by Kathleen Turner. While the role helped elevate his profile during the popular show's run in 2000 and further connected him with Hollywood celebrities, afterward he again found his career without another big project to take it to the next level; at the same time, he did appear in some notable roles, including in the independent film *Love and Other Disasters* (2006), with Brittany Murphy, and as poet Dylan Thomas in *The Edge of Love* (2008), costarring Keira Knightley, Sienna Miller, and Cillian Murphy.

Rhys's greatest success of the period, however, came in 2006, when he was asked to play Kevin Walker on the ensemble American network television series *Brothers & Sisters*, which ran for five seasons until 2011. The ABC show costarred Calista Flockhart, Rachel Griffiths, Sally Field, and Rob Lowe and focused on the trials and triumphs of an upper-middle-class family in California. Rhys's character was gay, but that was not meant to be his defining attribute. "The creator, Jon Robin Baitz, was very clear he didn't want campness about him," Rhys said to Gilbert. "He didn't want a coming-out story, in fact he wanted it as inconsequential as possible—the lawyer who's the brother who happens to be gay. That was the brief."

THE AMERICANS

After *Brothers & Sisters* ended in 2011, Rhys found work portraying John Jasper in a two-part television adaptation of Charles Dickens's unfinished 1870 novel *The Mystery of Edwin Drood*, which aired in January 2012. Having maintained

an affinity for the theater, he also returned to the stage that month to portray Jimmy Porter in an Off-Broadway revival of *Look Back in Anger*. Later that same year, in a remake of *The Scapegoat*, he took on the dual role of two men with the same face; the film was based on the 1957 novel by Daphne du Maurier.

Although Rhys's work up until this point in his career had been favorably received, it was not until he won the role of Philip Jennings in the acclaimed FX television series *The Americans* that he was widely recognized for his talents. He impressed series creator and executive producer Joe Weisberg in the first reading for the especially complex part, which included his failing to flinch after an especially hard slap from his eventual costar, Keri Russell. "The genius of Matthew Rhys was very obvious at the start," Weisberg told Michael Sebastian for *Esquire* (30 May 2018).

In the show, which started airing in 2013, Rhys portrayed a Soviet secret agent living in the United States during the 1980s with his wife, Elizabeth (portrayed by Russell), a fellow Soviet agent, and their two American-born children, who initially know nothing about their parents' double lives. Although the series, which begins around the time of Ronald Reagan's inauguration as president of the United States in 1981, initially had a mission-of-the-week feel, it quickly morphed in the first season into something more like a family drama, as the Jennings had to weave through their conflicting responsibilities to each other, their children, and the Soviet state. The depiction of such relationships, particularly between Philip and Elizabeth, was among the biggest draws for Rhys. "When I first read the script, I just thought, this is insane. I've never seen a relationship like this. . . . the extremity that they have to live in, then balancing that with the domestic tension. It was that multi-layered aspect of it that grabbed me. Then on top of that, you stick a spy thriller, a bit of action," he explained to Craig McLean for the *Telegraph* (31 May 2013). "It's got the lot." Early on, Philip's character becomes disenchanted with his spy work. Elizabeth, however, remains committed to the Soviet cause.

OTHER PROJECTS AND RECOGNITION

More in demand as *The Americans* continued, Rhys simultaneously earned further roles in a variety of film and television projects, including in Steven Spielberg's high-profile film *The Post* (2017), in which he played the military analyst Daniel Ellsberg. In 1971, Ellsberg released portions of a top-secret Pentagon study of the US government's actions regarding the Vietnam War. The film starred Tom Hanks as *Washington Post* editor Ben Bradlee and Meryl Streep as *Post* owner Katharine Graham.

In 2018, the same year in which *The Americans* concluded, Rhys also appeared in *Death and Nightingales*, a historical drama miniseries based on a 1992 novel by Eugene McCabe, and as John Lockwood, a colonial hunter, in *Mowgli: Legend of the Jungle*, a motion-capture film based on the stories of Rudyard Kipling and directed by Andy Serkis. His next film role will again find him acting alongside Hanks in *A Beautiful Day in the Neighborhood*, set for release in 2019, in which Hanks portrays Fred Rogers, the creator of the long-running preschool show *Mister Rogers' Neighborhood* (1968–2001).

Throughout the six-season run of *The Americans*, Rhys and Russell were widely celebrated for their performances. In the *Washington Post* (18 Sept. 2018), Sonny Bunch proclaimed, "Philip's transformation would only have been believable with the work of a first-rate actor, and Rhys delivered the goods." The show was a darling of professional critics and was nominated for numerous awards, but only began winning awards in its final season. In 2018, Rhys, who had been nominated in both 2016 and 2017, won the Emmy Award for Outstanding Lead Actor in a Drama Series, and executive producers Joel Fields and Weisberg won the Emmy for Outstanding Writing for a Drama Series. In 2019, the show earned the Golden Globe Award for Best Television Series–Drama. When asked about acting after *The Americans*, Rhys has expressed his gratitude for the series but also a desire to experience something new again: "One of the great luxuries in this business is working, but I think even better than that is if you get to do something completely different in your next job. So, if I find something as free and far from Philip Jennings as possible, then I'd be over the moon," he told Shirley Li for *Entertainment Weekly* (29 May 2018).

PERSONAL LIFE
Rhys and his former costar, Keri Russell, confirmed that they were in a romantic relationship in 2014. The couple live in New York City's Brooklyn borough, where much of the series was filmed, and have a son together, who was born in 2016. Russell also has two children from her previous marriage. Rhys has been teaching his son the Welsh language, which he speaks fluently. "How much he'll retain growing up in New York I don't know," Rhys told John Hazleton for *Screen Daily* (5 July 2018). "But he'll have a lot of trips home and he'll have a dad who will only speak to him in Welsh, so that might help."

SUGGESTED READING
Bunch, Sonny. "Matthew Rhys and *The Americans* Finally Get Their Due at the Emmys." Review of *The Americans*, created by Joe Weisberg. *The Washington Post*, 18 Sept. 2018, www.washingtonpost.com/news/act-four/wp/2018/09/18/matthew-rhys-and-the-americans-finally-get-their-due-at-the-emmys. Accessed 31 Dec. 2018.

Gilbert, Gerard. "Matthew Rhys: 'We'd Troll Off to LA and Try to Nick Jobs off the Americans.'" *Independent*, 8 Sept. 2012, www.independent.co.uk/news/people/profiles/matthew-rhys-wed-troll-off-to-la-and-try-to-nick-jobs-off-the-americans-8106987.html. Accessed 3 Jan. 2019.

Margulies, Julianna, and Matthew Rhys. "Julianna Margulies, Matthew Rhys on Divas, Theater and Unrequited Love." Interview by Cynthia Littleton. *Variety*, 4 June 2014, variety.com/2014/tv/awards/1201210794-1201210794. Accessed 3 Jan. 2019.

McLean, Craig. "Matthew Rhys Interview for *The Americans*: 'Our Scripts Go to the CIA for Approval.'" *The Telegraph*, 31 May 2013, www.telegraph.co.uk/culture/tvandradio/10078177/Matthew-Rhys-interview-for-The-Americans-Our-scripts-go-to-the-CIA-for-approval.html. Accessed 3 Jan. 2019.

Russell, Keri, and Matthew Rhys. "Keri Russell and Matthew Rhys Break Down the 'Devastating' Finale of *The Americans*." Interview by Maureen Ryan. *The New York Times*, 30 May 2018, www.nytimes.com/2018/05/30/arts/television/keri-russell-matthew-rhys-the-americans.html. Accessed 31 Dec. 2018.

Sebastian, Michael. "The Moment Everything Changed for Matthew Rhys." *Esquire*, 30 May 2018, www.esquire.com/entertainment/a20965189/matthew-rhys-the-americans-series-finale-interview. Accessed 31 Dec. 2018.

SELECTED WORKS
Titus, 1999; *Brothers & Sisters*, 2006–11; *The Edge of Love*, 2008; *The Mystery of Edwin Drood*, 2012; *The Americans*, 2013–18; *The Post*, 2017; *Death and Nightingales*, 2018

—*Christopher Mari*

Sarah Richardson

Date of birth: October 22, 1971
Occupation: Designer and television personality

Even as a child, the future Canadian television designer Sarah Richardson had developed a reputation as a formidable decorator, seamster, and chef. She distances herself from the inevitable comparisons to Martha Stewart, the older American homemaking media mogul. Richardson got her start as a set designer for decorating shows in the 1990s but went on to become one of Canada's most popular television designers. She has hosted numerous HGTV Canada home-renovation shows, including *Room Service, Sarah 101, Design Inc., Sarah's House, Sarah's Cottage, Real Potential, Sarah's Rental Cottage,* and *Sarah Off the Grid.* In 2010 she won a Gemini Award, the Canadian equivalent to the Emmy Award, for hosting *Sarah's House* with Tommy Smythe.

On her television programs, Richardson, sometimes aided by her frequent collaborator Smythe, tackles gut renovations and small, do-it-yourself (DIY) projects with enthusiasm and humor. Canadians, and her myriad international fans, have watched Richardson at work with her design firm, Sarah Richardson Design, in *Design Inc.* and followed along as she and her family built an off-the-grid dream home in rural Ontario in *Sarah Off the Grid.* For many, Richardson is a friendly and familiar face, having hosted decorating programs for the better part of two decades.

Richardson has parlayed her television success into other ventures as well. She was, for a time, a contributing design editor for *Canadian Home and Country Magazine,* and her design advice has also appeared in prominent design magazines, such as *Good Housekeeping, Country Living, House & Home, Style at Home,* and *House Beautiful,* as well as national newspapers. She went on to write two best-selling books: *Sarah Style: An Inspiring Room-by-Room Guide to Designing Your Perfect Home* (2014) and *At Home: Sarah Style* (2015), which features recipes and photographs of Richardson's own homes. She has also launched an eponymous product line that partners with major manufacturers to produce household textiles, furniture, wallpaper, and stationery.

EARLY LIFE AND EDUCATION

Sarah Richardson was born on October 22, 1971, to Douglas Richardson and Susan Cuddy. She has an older brother and two younger half-brothers. Her father taught art history at the University of Toronto and took her on tours of old English churches. Her designer mother worked for the old City of Toronto. Richardson's parents divorced when she was five; by that time, young Richardson had already taught herself to sew. She also exhibited an early flair for marketing. In fourth grade, she drew a hopscotch court down her entire street and solicited a local children's television program to interview her about it.

Richardson attended Whitney Junior Public School and Havergal College, a girl's boarding school in Toronto, where she earned the nickname Mother for her handy domestic know-how. "She was always sophisticated beyond her years," her childhood friend Andrea Lenczner recalled in an interview with Francine Kopun for the *Toronto Star* (2 Jan. 2010). "On weekends, I don't know what I was doing—stealing cigarette

Photo by Michael Stewart/Getty Images

butts and smoking them. Sarah would be making duck à l'orange." Richardson graduated in 1989.

As a visual art student at the University of Western Ontario in London, Richardson decorated fellow classmates' residences, custom-tailored party dresses, and threw dinner parties. She graduated with a bachelor's degree in 1993.

INITIAL CAREER

Through a university acquaintance, Richardson landed a job as a prop stylist for a show called *Home Style,* produced by Michael Prini. She also worked as a set decorator and production designer for the Prini-produced entertaining program *Savoir Faire.* "Working behind the scenes for intense, 16-hour days, I learned what went into a great TV show and what made people succeed—drive and limitless energy, and knowing how to work collaboratively as part of a creative community," she told Marjo Johne for the *Globe and Mail* (5 May 2008).

In 1996, as a favor to a friend, Richardson appeared as a guest on *Real Life.* Over the next several years, she founded a Toronto-based interior design firm, Sarah Richardson Design, and went on to appear on *Real Life* fifty times before crafting a proposal for her own design show, called *Room Service,* cocreated and coproduced with Prini. The first episode aired in 2000. On *Room Service,* Richardson tackled low-budget renovation projects and led viewers through DIY craft tutorials. "The early episodes were sometimes corny and laboured," Kopun wrote, but *Room Service* quickly gained a following. It aired on HGTV Canada for five seasons and eventually made its way to US airwaves too.

In 2004 Richardson launched *Design Inc.*, a reality show about her design firm that ran for four seasons and more than sixty episodes. Her team included fellow designers Tommy Smythe and Tanya Bonus, as well as stylists Natalie Hodgins, Kate Stuart, and Lindsay Mens. The show, also coproduced with Prini, captured the ups and downs of the design business, from "the sofas that don't fit" and "the fabric on backorder" to "the downpours on install days," Patrick J. Hamilton wrote for *Apartment Therapy* (8 July 2011). "Honesty and truth are really important core principles to the programming that we create," Richardson told Hamilton. "It doesn't help the design community as a whole, or even the do it yourselfer, to be made to feel that everything is just perfect in my world. Because guess what? It's *far* from it. To me it's more about how you solve those projects, how you navigate, how you conduct yourself that's more informative."

SARAH'S HOUSE AND SARAH 101
In 2007 Richardson premiered *Sarah's House*. Each season followed the renovation of an entire home. Over the course of the show's four seasons, Richardson raised the degree of difficulty—from putting in a pool and designing landscapes in season 2, to overseeing renovations on a fifty-acre farm in season 3, to building a house on an empty lot and customizing that prototypical suburban home in season 4. *Sarah's House* also introduced Smythe as a cohost. Smythe, who became a popular television star in his own right, often serves as Richardson's foil, the acerbic wit to her earnest team leader. For her work on that program, she received the 2010 Gemini Award for Best Host in a Lifestyle/Practical Information, or Performing Arts Program or Series.

In 2008, while still working on *Sarah's House*, Richardson shot *Sarah's Cottage*, in which she and her family renovate their beach cottage in Georgian Bay. The series aired beginning the following April. She later produced a similar miniseries, called *Sarah's Rental Cottage*, which aired in April 2015. The miniseries follows Richardson, her husband, Alexander "Alex" Younger, and Smythe as they renovate a 1950s island cabin near Ontario's Parry Sound. The cabin was made available to rent after the show concluded.

As they were wrapping up *Sarah's House*, Richardson and Smythe premiered *Sarah 101* in 2011. The two-season show tackles smaller projects with modest budgets—an oversized bedroom, a finished basement, for example—while touting the "building blocks," as Richardson puts it in the show's teaser, of good design. "We wanted to be able to focus on helping people realize dramatic changes in their spaces through the use of an interesting combination of materials, sources, furniture, fabrics, you name it," she told Hamilton. "In my view, there's nothing wrong with a good old-fashioned decorating project to make a huge change."

Richardson next put together a short-lived show called *Real Potential*, which debuted in September 2013. In each of its thirteen episodes, she tours potential properties with homebuyers and renovates a single room of their selected house according to a budget.

SARAH OFF THE GRID
Touted as her most ambitious project to date, Richardson set out to build an off-the-grid home in tiny Creemore, Ontario, for her family. Richardson and Younger had bought the property and been working on drawings of the house for four years before they premiered *Sarah Off the Grid* in September 2017. The show chronicles Richardson's quest to build the home—she and Younger served as general contractors—while maintaining her business and caring for her family. True to the title of the show, the finished house exists off the main power grid, supplying its own water, heat, electricity, and sewage management. Built on a hundred-acre property, the 5,000-square-foot home runs on sixty solar panels and is partially heated by wood stoves and fireplaces.

Season 2 of *Sarah Off the Grid* began airing in April 2019. Having finished her own home, Richardson set her sights on renovating a small Victorian house, also in Creemore, as a vacation rental property. Richardson was drawn to the house's bay window and how the light streamed into the kitchen and dining room. "That's what I love about old houses, that challenge of taking those pieces that are here now . . . the real success story is if you can take something old and make it amazing for new and now and next. That's the bigger accomplishment," she told Dianne Daniel for the *Toronto Sun* (22 Apr. 2019).

Also in the spring of 2019, Richardson launched a web video series called *SR Design Life* to chronicle some of her other projects and to present question-and-answer sessions. She and Younger also returned to their cottage to renovate the exterior.

PERSONAL LIFE
Richardson and Younger, the founder of Design Lab, a marketing and advertising agency, first met in primary school, when Younger was in Richardson's older brother's class. They were married in 2005 and have two daughters, Robin (b. 2006) and Fiona (b. ca. 2009). The couple are frequent collaborators, and Richardson's onscreen work has often chronicled changes in their family life, including her pregnancies and their move to Creemore.

SUGGESTED READING
Daniel, Dianne. "Sarah Off the Grid Season Two Debuts." *Toronto Sun*, 22 Apr. 2019,

torontosun.com/life/homes/sarah-off-the-grid-season-two-debuts. Accessed 17 June 2019.

Hamilton, Patrick J. "Apartment Therapy Interviews: Sarah Richardson." *Apartment Therapy*, 8 July 2011, www.apartmenttherapy.com/at-interviews-sara-richardson-150567. Accessed 17 June 2019.

Johne, Marjo. "Sarah Richardson, 36." *The Globe and Mail*, 5 May 2008, www.theglobeandmail.com/report-on-business/sarah-richardson-36/article18450218. Accessed 17 June 2019.

Kopun, Francine. "Home Truths: Design Dynamo Can't Lay Off." *Toronto Star*, 2 Jan. 2010. *Press Reader*, www.pressreader.com/canada/toronto-star/20100102/284627483559797. Accessed 17 June 2019.

Richardson, Sarah. "Sarah Richardson on Her New Book, and How She Celebrates the Holiday." Interview by Emma Reddington. *Chatelaine*, 1 Dec. 2014, www.chatelaine.com/home-decor/qa-sarah-richardson-book-holiday-season. Accessed 19 June 2019.

SELECTED WORKS

Sarah's House, 2007–11; *Sarah 101*, 2011–12; *Sarah Style: An Inspiring Room-by-Room Guide to Designing Your Perfect Home*, 2014; *At Home: Sarah Style*, 2015; *Sarah's Rental Cottage*, 2015; *Sarah Off the Grid*, 2017–

—*Molly Hagan*

Photo by Peabody Awards/Jana Lynn French via Wikimedia Commons

Krysten Ritter

Date of birth: December 16, 1981
Occupation: Actor

When Krysten Ritter first appeared on screen as star of the Netflix series *Jessica Jones*, based on the Marvel Comics character of the same name, she inhabited the role so fully that viewers could perhaps be forgiven for believing that she was born into that role and had never played anything else. Indeed, much of the media coverage of the series identified the role as Ritter's big break, a description that is fitting yet fails to tell the whole story. Initially a teen model who was first spotted at a Pennsylvania mall, Ritter transitioned into acting by her twenties and soon filled her résumé with an array of small parts and more extensive stints on series such as *Veronica Mars* and *Breaking Bad*. She costarred in several television series, including the acclaimed yet poorly scheduled *Don't Trust the B—— in Apartment 23* and appeared in a number of films. Her role in *Jessica Jones*, however, presented a compelling challenge to the actor as well as an opportunity to showcase the skills honed after nearly two decades in the entertainment industry. "Jessica Jones is such a great part, and I do serious work on it. I feel really creatively fulfilled," Ritter told Estelle Tang for *Elle* (17 Nov. 2017). "I get to do stunts and great drama and work with great scene partners and also be funny. That's a high bar."

Ritter has expressed dissatisfaction with many of the roles available to her in the wake of her rise to fame, noting that she has no interest in playing the wife of an actor her father's age. She has made it clear, however, that when opportunities do not exist, she will create them. As a musician, writer, and director, Ritter has recorded music with her band Ex Vivian, written both screenplays and the 2017 novel *Bonfire*, and directed an episode for season 3 of *Jessica Jones*. "I'm a really proactive girl," she told Tang. "I don't wait for people to tell me."

EARLY LIFE AND EDUCATION

Krysten Ritter was born on December 16, 1981, in Bloomsburg, Pennsylvania. She grew up in the town of Benton. When Ritter was twelve, her parents, Garry and Kathi, divorced. Ritter remained with her mother, and the pair moved to the small rural town of Shickshinny. In Shickshinny, the family lived on a farm, and Ritter spent a portion of her teen years raising cows and chickens. Ritter's mother later remarried and had a second daughter.

Although Ritter left rural Pennsylvania when she was in her late teens, she later noted in interviews that the culture and values she absorbed during her childhood greatly influenced her development as an adult. "I sort of still have that early-bird-gets-the-worm mentality," she told Sara Benincasa for *Bust* (Feb.–Mar. 2018). "If you don't need it, don't buy it. The clean plate club—finish everything on your plate. I grew up with humble, small-town values like that, and they do totally stick with you. I really understand the value of a dollar and the value of hard work. I have a small house. I just like to live a simple life."

As a teenager, Ritter initially considered becoming a pediatric cardiologist, inspired by the work of the doctors who helped address her sister's heart murmur. However, Ritter's career trajectory shifted dramatically when she was fifteen, when a scout for the major modeling agency Elite Model Management spotted her at a mall. After signing with Elite, Ritter spent the next years balancing her high school studies with modeling work, traveling to New York and other locations during weekends and vacations. She also spent time abroad, living and working in Italy and Japan. Ritter graduated from Northwest Area High School in 2000.

EARLY CAREER

As a teenager, Ritter enjoyed modeling work, which she described to Scott Feinberg for the *Hollywood Reporter* (5 July 2012) as "awesome." "Immediately, I felt like I fit in," she told Feinberg. "Meeting the other models, who were also kind of weird looking, and tall, and skinny, I was like, 'Wow, I feel more like myself here.'" Over the years, however, Ritter observed that models who did not attain a certain notability and book an adequate amount of work within a few seasons did not experience lasting success in the profession, which prompted her to begin to assess her options. "I just wanted to like, figure out a way to stay in New York and do something that I loved," she recalled to Feinberg.

After switching agencies, Ritter began to pursue work as an actor, initially in commercials. She booked the first commercial role for which she auditioned, earning a part in a Dr. Pepper commercial. Although she was ultimately cut out of the commercial, the successful audition boded well for Ritter's career as an actor, which continued to develop over the subsequent years. Ritter soon found early roles in both television and film, appearing in episodes of series such as *Law & Order*, *One Life to Live*, and *Whoopi*, as well as in films such as *Mona Lisa Smile* (2003). She began to obtain recurring roles in television series midway through the decade, playing a substantial role in the second season of the teen mystery drama *Veronica Mars*. She went on to appear in multiple episodes of series such as *Gilmore Girls* and *'Til Death* and costarred in the 2009 web series *Woke Up Dead*. She appeared in an episode of the teen drama *Gossip*

Girl that was intended to be a backdoor pilot for a spin-off series set in the 1980s, but the series was not picked up. Ritter remained active in film as well, playing supporting roles in comedies such as *27 Dresses* (2008) and *Confessions of a Shopaholic* (2009).

MAJOR ROLES

Ritter gained further critical attention beginning in 2009, when she appeared in the second season of the widely acclaimed drama *Breaking Bad*. The actor played Jane Margolis, a recovering heroin addict who, after beginning a relationship with major character Jesse (Aaron Paul), experiences a relapse that leads to her tragic death. Filming the character's final episode was a particularly challenging appearance for Ritter, who had to do her best to feign death while Paul's Jesse grieved. "It was emotional witnessing someone grieving for your death," she recalled to Sam Briger for *Fresh Air* (14 May 2018). "I'm a very sensitive person and Aaron Paul was really—his performance was so amazing—and he was so distraught and so devastated and crying and on my chest and trying to revive me so violently that it was intense." *Breaking Bad* was nominated for the Emmy Award for best drama series following its second season, and Ritter's performance received widespread praise.

Following *Breaking Bad*, Ritter costarred in the short-lived television series *Gravity* as well as the 2011 film *L!fe Happens*, which she also cowrote. In 2012, she began to costar in the ABC comedy series *Don't Trust the B—— in Apartment 23*, in which she played a manipulative party girl, Chloe, who habitually scams and then drives away her roommates. After new roommate June (Dreama Walker) refuses to be intimidated, however, the pair become friends and engage in a variety of hijinks. *Don't Trust the B—— in Apartment 23* received generally positive reviews and amassed a devoted fan base during its two seasons. However, the network's scheduling choices and a variety of extenuating circumstances proved detrimental to the show's overall viewership. "They didn't tell anybody we were coming back, they didn't tell anybody we moved nights, and then the election, and then there was the hurricane. It was just one thing after another," Ritter recalled to Matt Goldberg for *Collider* (11 Mar. 2014). "The odds were not in our favor. It was just a disaster. And then for some reason they aired [the episodes] out of order." *Don't Trust the B—— in Apartment 23* was ultimately canceled after two seasons.

In 2014, Ritter returned to the world of *Veronica Mars* for a sequel film set nearly a decade after the conclusion of the series. She had not expected to return to her role but quickly became reacquainted with the character of Gia, a supporting character in the television series who plays a crucial role in the film. "As soon as I read her dialogue—she's got a specific cadence and rhythm when she talks fast—she's specific. So as I read it, I was like, 'Okay, I know what to do with this,'" she told Goldberg. Although the filmmakers were unable to fund the film through traditional means, they raised funding for the film through the crowdfunding website *Kickstarter*. In addition to *Veronica Mars*, Ritter appeared in several other films in 2014, including *Big Eyes*, *Listen Up Philip*, and *Asthma*.

JESSICA JONES AND BONFIRE

Perhaps the most significant moment in Ritter's career to date came in November 2015, when the first season of the series *Jessica Jones* was made available on Netflix, a streaming-media content provider. Based in part on the Marvel Comics series *Alias*, published between 2001 and 2004, the series focuses on the title character, a young woman with superpowers who works as a private investigator while coping—poorly—with her past trauma. The series was the second series based on Marvel properties produced by Netflix, all of which, although ostensibly set in the same universe as the non-Netflix Marvel shows and Marvel Cinematic Universe, feature a darker tone and themes than their non-Netflix counterparts. After multiple auditions and screen tests, Ritter claimed the role of Jessica, a challenging character whose portrayal relies heavily on Ritter's body language and facial expressions. "I am doing the most work when I'm not saying lines," she told Briger. "It's been ingrained in me in my training. . . . If you don't have anything going on in your head you're not interesting to watch. So I would say that the bulk and the majority of my work is when I have no lines."

Following the series' debut, critics praised the show and particularly Ritter's performance, which earned her nominations for the Critics' Choice Television Award for Best Actress in a Drama Series and the Saturn Award for Best Actress on Television, both in 2016. Ritter reprised the role of Jessica Jones in *The Defenders*, a 2017 team-up series that brought together the stars of *Jessica Jones* as well as fellow Netflix Marvel shows *Daredevil*, *Luke Cage*, and *Iron Fist*. Season 2 of *Jessica Jones* premiered on Netflix in March 2018, and the following month, Netflix announced that a third season had been ordered. Ritter later revealed that she would be directing an episode of season 3 and expressed excitement about making her directorial debut.

Amid filming *Jessica Jones* and *The Defenders*, Ritter completed her debut novel, *Bonfire*. Published in 2017, the novel is a thriller about an environmental lawyer who returns to her small hometown to investigate happenings there. For Ritter, the process of publishing her first book was a "scary" one, as she told Tang, "this is something I made with my brain and my hands. . . . and now here it is—it exists." Reviews of *Bonfire* leaned positive, with many critics praising Ritter's prose and her depiction of the novel's protagonist.

PERSONAL LIFE

Ritter has commented in interviews that she has no business manager and prefers to oversee all her financial dealings herself, a somewhat unusual choice among actors. "I'm a creative person who also has a pretty good business mind, thank God," she told Benincasa. "There are people who are way more talented, but I have a business savvy and a level of obsession that allows me to find these things that I love so much and make them my job. So I never actually feel like I'm working, because I play."

In addition to acting and writing, Ritter sings and plays in her band, Ex Vivian, and is an avid knitter. She has collaborated with the website *We Are Knitters* to design a variety of knitting patterns.

Ritter has been dating musician Adam Granduciel, front man for the rock band the War on Drugs, since 2014.

SUGGESTED READING

Benincasa, Sara. "Krysten Ritter on the Emotional Toll of Playing Jessica Jones." *Bust*, Feb.–Mar. 2018, bust.com/tv/194360-krysten-ritter-jessica-jones-cover-story.html. Accessed 9 Nov. 2018.

Briger, Sam. "'I'm Just So Invested': Krysten Ritter on Becoming 'Jessica Jones.'" *Fresh Air*, NPR, 14 May 2018, www.npr.org/2018/05/14/610954817/i-m-just-so-invested-krysten-ritter-on-becoming-jessica-jones. Accessed 9 Nov. 2018.

Feinberg, Scott. "Krysten Ritter, Star of Raunchy ABC Comedy, on Playing Everyone's Favorite 'B——.'" *The Hollywood Reporter*, 5 July 2012, www.hollywoodreporter.com/race/krysten-ritter-abc-dont-trust-bicth-apt-23-345574. Accessed 9 Nov. 2018.

Ritter, Krysten. "Krysten Ritter Talks *Veronica Mars* Movie, Returning to the Character, *Don't Trust the B——*, Her Top 5 Films of 2013, and More." Interview by Matt Goldberg. *Collider*, 11 Mar. 2014, collider.com/veronica-mars-movie-krysten-ritter-interview. Accessed 9 Nov. 2018.

——. "Krysten Ritter Wants More Complicated, Imperfect, Not-Always-Pretty Characters." Interview by Estelle Tang. *Elle*, 17 Nov. 2017, www.elle.com/culture/books/a13795415/krysten-ritter-bonfire-interview. Accessed 9 Nov. 2018.

——. "Superhero and the City." Interview by Emma Brown. *Interview*, 23 Nov. 2015, www.interviewmagazine.com/culture/

krysten-ritter-jessica-jones. Accessed 9 Nov. 2018.

Stacey, Michelle. "Krysten Ritter's Life Motto: Go Hard as a Motherf-cker." *Women's Health*, 11 Oct. 2017. www.womenshealthmag.com/life/g19945076/krysten-ritter-interview. Accessed 9 Nov. 2018.

SELECTED WORKS

Veronica Mars, 2005–6; *Gilmore Girls*, 2006–7; *Woke Up Dead*, 2009; *Breaking Bad*, 2009–10; *Gravity*, 2010; *Don't Trust the B—— in Apartment 23*, 2012–13; *Veronica Mars*, 2014; *Big Eyes*, 2014; *Jessica Jones*, 2015–; *The Defenders*, 2017

—*Joy Crelin*

Johan Rockström

Date of birth: December 31, 1965
Occupation: Scientist and sustainability researcher

For Johan Rockström, solutions for addressing global climate change and related sustainability and resilience concerns go far beyond commonly recommended initiatives such as ending the use of fossil fuels. "We focus all our attention on coal, oil and natural gas, but when you look at the agenda overall, that's the easier part of the climate challenge," he told Annette Ekin for the European Commission magazine *Horizon* (22 Oct. 2018). "The much more challenging part is water, soil, biodiversity, nitrogen, phosphorus, the bio dimension of the economy and of the climate challenge." As the codirector of the Potsdam Institute for Climate Impact Research and a former head of the Stockholm Environment Institute and Stockholm Resilience Centre, Rockström looks to research and to educate the world about the intersecting systems crucial to life on earth and humankind's detrimental impact on many of those systems. As a leading environmental researcher, he has advised governments and international organizations.

Rockström is particularly known for advancing the idea that the planet has certain boundaries (among them, global temperature and ozone levels) that if crossed could trigger large-scale, irreversible, and potentially devastating environmental changes. While the challenges that concept presents are daunting, Rockström has continually asserted that human society can mitigate the existing damage and prevent further planetary boundaries from being crossed. "Technology alone will not do the job," he told Diane Toomey for the Yale School of Forestry and Environmental Studies blog, *YaleEnvironment360*

(23 Sept. 2015). "It will require behavioral change and new values. We need a mind shift. We need to reconnect our human societies with biospheres, and we need to work with nature, not against it."

EARLY LIFE AND EDUCATION

Rockström was born in 1965 in Finspång, Sweden. He spent much of his early childhood near São Paolo, Brazil, because of his father's career in asphalt manufacturing. The family later moved to Milan, Italy, when he was about nine. Rockström eventually returned to Sweden, where he attended secondary school in Karlskrona. Interested in studying agriculture after completing secondary school, he feared that his lack of experience with farm work would prove to be a disadvantage. He later took an unpaid job at a farm, helping with tasks like feeding cows.

Rockström went on to enroll in the Swedish University of Agricultural Sciences, where he earned a master's degree in 1992. He next attended the Institut National Agronomique Paris-Grignon (now part of AgroParisTech), doing a degree project in Niger and completing an advanced agronomy degree in 1993. He then moved on to Stockholm University, where he earned a licentiate of philosophy in 1995 and his doctorate in natural resources management in 1997. He returned to Niger for his doctoral work.

RESEARCH AND TEACHING CAREER

Rockström began his career in land and water management, working for the Swedish International Development Cooperation Agency in

Photo by Stefanie Loos via Wikimedia Commons

eastern and southern Africa in 1998. He served as an associate professor of integrated water resource management at the University of Zimbabwe for a time and as a senior lecturer and regional research coordinator for the UNESCO-IHE Institute for Water Education in Delft, the Netherlands from 2000 to 2004.

In 2003 Rockström's career trajectory shifted somewhat, however, when Bert Bolin, a Swedish professor and climate research leader, recruited him to become the executive director of the Stockholm Environment Institute. The institute is dedicated to researching environmental issues and making recommendations regarding Swedish environmental policy. Rockström joined the institute as executive director in 2004 and held that position until 2012.

Additionally, over the next years Rockström worked both to facilitate environmental research and to teach the next generation of researchers. In 2007 he became the founding director of the Stockholm Resilience Centre (SRC) at Stockholm University, which researches sustainability, interactions between different social and ecological systems, and humankind's role within the earth's biosphere. He also began teaching courses at Stockholm University and became a full professor of natural resource management there by mid-2012. In the fall of 2014, Rockström also held a visiting professorship at the University of Cambridge in England.

Although perhaps best known for his focus on climate change and the human impact on the biosphere, Rockström also remained active in water resilience and coauthored the preface to the 2014 book *Water Resilience for Human Prosperity*.

PLANETARY BOUNDARIES

Rockström has been most outspoken about the concept of planetary boundaries. First developed by Rockström and a multinational group of colleagues in 2009 and updated in 2015, the concept specifies that the earth's environment has nine natural boundaries that will lead to serious—even catastrophic—planetary upheaval if crossed. "These nine processes are the ones that regulate the stability of the earth system," he explained to Toomey. "Once quantified, they give us the safe operating space of the hardwired biophysical process of the earth's system. They have nothing to do with humans. It's really the biophysical boundaries." Those boundaries relate to, among other issues, climate change, ozone depletion, the loss of biodiversity, ocean acidification, and land system change (that is, land being converted from one type of environment, such as forest, into another, such as farmland).

According to Rockström and his colleagues, moving past those boundaries—and thus out of the so-called safe operating space—puts pressure on the planet's interconnected systems. That, in turn, could cause dramatic environmental changes to take place. While he noted in interviews that several boundaries had been crossed by 2015, he expressed that it was not too late to prevent humankind from exceeding the remaining boundaries and that some progress could be made in mitigating the damage done.

Rockström has publicized the concept of planetary boundaries through academic papers, speaking appearances, and books. He and Anders Wijkman cowrote *Bankrupting Nature: Denying Our Planetary Boundaries* (2012), which makes economic arguments for taking climate action. That same year Rockström published his first collaboration with established nature photographer Mattias Klum, *The Human Quest: Prospering within Planetary Boundaries*. Mixing text with photographs, *The Human Quest* presents the human impact on the natural world and suggests potential means of addressing issues such as climate change. About that project, Rockström said, "We wanted to combine the rational, science, with the emotional, photography. Our book summarizes the science, and shows the damage, but also the beauty we need to preserve," as quoted by Brian Clark Howard for *National Geographic* (18 June 2012). Rockström and Klum reunited to produce the 2015 book *Big World, Small Planet: Abundance within Planetary Boundaries*, which likewise combines photography with discussion of critical issues facing the earth and its population.

THE ANTHROPOCENE

Particularly key to Rockström's approach to environmental research, sustainability, and resilience is the argument that the earth has entered the early stages of a new era known as the Anthropocene, the successor to the Holocene period, when humankind had no effect on the earth's environment on a macro level. "From 8,000 years back all up until the mid-1950s . . . we see no evidence of humans affecting the resilience and stability of the entire earth system," he told Toomey. "Then something happens in the mid-1950s, which is clearly the exponential rise of human pressure on the planet. And then these exponential rises are multiple, from greenhouse gases all the way to loss of biodiversity, eutrophication, deforestation, land degradation, pollution of water." By the 2010s, humankind had "become a global force of change at the planetary scale, surpassing the magnitude and frequency of natural changes to the planet," he asserted to Toomey. Addressing that issue, Rockström emphasizes the importance of setting and adhering to specific, measurable goals—such as creating national budgets for elemental fertilizers and following a "carbon law" halving carbon emissions each decade—and transforming behaviors and societies.

In addition to more academic forms of outreach, Rockström supplied his expert view of the future for the 2016 documentary *Before the Flood*, produced by well-known actor Leonardo DiCaprio. He has also given several TED Talks and written opinion pieces for prominent popular publications like the *Guardian* in the United Kingdom.

ADDITIONAL LEADERSHIP ROLES

Over the course of his career, Rockström has chaired or helped lead numerous environmental organizations and programs, including the Earth League, the Education & Agriculture Together (EAT) Foundation and SRC advisory boards, and the New York Academy of Sciences. He has even advised the Swedish government, the United Nations (UN), and the World Economic Forum on issues of sustainability and climate.

Rockström has been widely recognized for his contributions to environmental science. He has received many honors, including the Royal Swedish Academy of Forestry and Agriculture's 2007 Georg and Greta Borgström Prize, *Fokus* magazine's Swede of the Year 2009 designation, the Zoological Society of London's 2015 Award for Conservation Innovation, and the 2017 Hillary Institute of International Leadership laureate. He was also made a knight of the French Legion of Honor in 2016.

In 2018 Rockström became chief scientist at Conservation International. That October he added to the duty of codirector of Germany's Potsdam Institute for Climate Impact Research alongside economics professor Ottmar Edenhofer. Rockström also joined the University of Potsdam as a professor of earth system science. Through both roles, he sought to continue his mission to protect humankind's future on earth and to combat both climate-change denial and the belief that sustainability and economic success are incompatible. "At the end of the day, you can't be 100 percent sustainable," he told Toomey. "But I think it's fair to say today that we have enough evidence that we can actually deliver sustainable economic development. We're saying that people and the planet can go hand-in-hand."

PERSONAL LIFE

Rockström met his wife, a veterinarian named Ulrika, at the Swedish University of Agricultural Sciences. They have three children. When not working internationally, Rockström lives in Rindö, an island in Sweden. In keeping with his research and public work, he and his family remain committed to sustainability in their private life: they raise livestock, grow their own vegetables, cycle, and take vacations by train or sailboat.

SUGGESTED READING

Howard, Brian Clark. "'The Human Quest' Shows How to Prosper within Planetary Boundaries." *National Geographic*, 18 June 2012, blog.nationalgeographic.org/2012/06/18/the-human-quest-shows-how-to-prosper-within-planetary-boundaries. Accessed 16 Aug. 2019.

McGrath, Matt. "Climate Change: 'Hothouse Earth' Risks Even If CO2 Emissions Slashed." *BBC News*, 6 Aug. 2018, www.bbc.co.uk/news/amp/science-environment-45084144. Accessed 16 Aug. 2019.

McPherson, Stephanie M. "Johan Rockström: Presenting a Framework for Preserving Earth's Resilience." *MIT News*, 26 Sept. 2017, news.mit.edu/2017/johan-rockstrom-framework-for-preserving-earth-resilience-0926. Accessed 16 Aug. 2019.

Monahan, Matthew. "Welcome to the Anthropocene." *Edmund Hillary Fellowship*, 6 June 2018, stories.ehf.org/johan-rockstrom-anthropocene-d825e490f1eb. Accessed 16 Aug. 2019.

Rockström, Johan. "Eliminating Coal, Oil and Natural Gas Is the Easy Part of Fighting Climate Change—Johan Rockström." Interview by Annette Ekin. *Horizon: The EU Research & Innovation Magazine*, 22 Oct. 2018, horizon-magazine.eu/article/eliminating-coal-oil-and-natural-gas-easy-part-fighting-climate-change-johan-rockstr-m.html. Accessed 16 Aug. 2019.

Siegfried, Alina. "Johan Rockström Announced as 2017 Global Hillary Laureate." *Edmund Hillary Fellowship*, 13 June 2017, stories.ehf.org/johan-rockström-announced-as-2017-global-hillary-laureate-f1117c33de84. Accessed 16 Aug. 2019.

Toomey, Diane. "One Scientist's Hopeful View on How to Repair the Planet." *YaleEnvironment360*, Yale School of Forestry and Environmental Studies, 23 Sept. 2015, e360.yale.edu/features/one_scientists_hopeful_view_on_how_to_repair_the_planet. Accessed 16 Aug. 2019.

SELECTED WORKS

Bankrupting Nature: Denying Our Planetary Boundaries, 2012 (with Anders Wijkman); *The Human Quest: Prospering within Planetary Boundaries*, 2012 (with Mattias Klum); *Big World, Small Planet: Abundance within Planetary Boundaries*, 2015 (with Mattias Klum)

—Joy Crelin

Sally Rooney

Date of birth: February 20, 1991
Occupation: Writer

Irish writer Sally Rooney has been widely described as one of the great novelists of the millennial generation for her unsparing explorations of love, isolation, and yearning, and for her sharp, unvarnished prose, which seamlessly weaves in modern modes of communication like instant messages, text messages, and emails. She earned such recognition not long after the publication of her first novel, *Conversations with Friends* (2017), a zeitgeist-defining romance about two young women who befriend an older married couple in 2010s Dublin. The novel received rapturous acclaim upon its release and a number of literary honors.

Rooney's sophomore effort, *Normal People* (2018), which chronicles the complicated friendship and romance between two Trinity College students, similarly received near universal praise. It earned a litany of awards, including the longlist for the Man Booker Prize in 2018, helping to propel Rooney to the forefront of the international literary scene. Yet despite her newfound status, the author remained unassuming and down-to-earth. As she told Ellen Barry for the *New York Times* (31 Aug. 2018), "I can't help feeling that I am not a very important person, and being treated like one gives me strange feelings."

EARLY LIFE AND EDUCATION

The middle of three children, Sally Rooney was born in 1991 in Castlebar, a small town in northwestern Ireland. Her mother, Marie Farrell, served as director of the town's community arts center, Linenhall; her father, Kieran Rooney, worked as a technician for Telecom Éireann, a telecommunications company. Rooney's parents were socialists who raised her, her younger sister, and her older brother to embrace Marxist values. They were also bibliophiles who encouraged their children to read.

Following her parents' influence, Rooney developed a Marxist vision of the world and a love of reading from a young age. However, as she told Alex Clark for the *Guardian* (25 Aug. 2018), she took to the latter pursuit in "a very flimsy way" as an adolescent, reading anything that piqued her interest. This undisciplined nature carried over to school, which Rooney did not particularly enjoy, in part due to her distrust of authority figures. Instead, she found solace surfing the Internet. As she explained to Lauren Collins for the *New Yorker* (31 Dec. 2018), "I was someone who, in a very disorganized way, was thirsty for knowledge. I liked having access to anything I wanted to know."

Photo by Richard Kendal / Barcroft Images / Barcroft Media via Getty Images

As a teenager, Rooney began channeling her multifarious interests through writing. At age fifteen she joined a creative writing group, for which she contributed biweekly stories. Though those stories were "rubbish," as Rooney put it to Clark, the experience prompted her to pursue a career in writing. After graduating from St. Joseph's Secondary School, an all-girls Catholic institution in Castlebar, she won acceptance to Trinity College, Ireland's most prestigious university, where she studied English literature.

In her early years at Trinity, Rooney had two of her poems published in the *Stinging Fly*, a Dublin literary magazine. Besides writing, she became involved in competitive debating, an academic activity that allowed her to flaunt her rhetorical skills. At twenty-two, she became the top competitive debater in Europe after winning the 2013 European University Debating Championships. She ultimately stopped debating, however, after finding it to be immoral.

RISE TO LITERARY PROMINENCE

Rooney first entered the literary scene in 2015 with the publication of her essay titled "Even If You Beat Me" in the *Dublin Review*. Chronicling her experiences as a competitive debater, the incisive essay caught the attention of Tracy Bohan, a literary agent with the Wylie Agency. Bohan eventually picked up the polished manuscript for *Conversations with Friends*, the first draft of which Rooney had written in just three months while simultaneously pursuing a master's degree in American literature at Trinity. In 2016, the manuscript was purchased by the venerable

London publishing house Faber & Faber in a seven-way auction.

Rooney originally conceived *Conversations*, about two university students who befriend a glamorous older married couple, as a short story. The story, however, grew too long, prompting her to turn it into a novel. Told from the first-person perspective of a precocious twenty-one-year-old woman named Frances, the novel follows Frances, an aspiring poet and communist, as she navigates the trials of adulthood as a student at Trinity College. Bobbi, Frances's best friend and ex-girlfriend, is a fellow Trinity student with whom she writes and recites spoken-word poetry at open-mike nights around Dublin. The two women's lives take on a new tenor after they enter the orbit of Melissa, a well-known writer and photographer, and her husband Nick, a handsome B-list actor. The foursome's relationship becomes severely strained, however, after Frances commences a secret affair with Nick.

When *Conversations with Friends* was published in 2017, Rooney was quickly hailed by critics as a significant voice of the millennial generation for her ability to authentically capture the experience of being young in the 2010s. Many reviewers made note of Rooney's deft integration of online communication (emails, texts, and instant messages) into her prose, her disarmingly detailed handling of sex and relationships, and her timely exploration of millennial social, political, and economic concerns. In a representative review for the *New Yorker* (24 July 2017), Alexandra Schwartz called the novel "a bracing study of ideas," commenting that Rooney "writes with a rare, thrilling confidence, in a lucid and exacting style uncluttered with the sort of steroidal imagery and strobe flashes of figurative language that so many dutifully literary novelists employ."

Besides garnering laudatory critical praise, *Conversations* received further attention thanks, in part, to buzz generated by everyone from acclaimed novelist Zadie Smith to actor Sarah Jessica Parker. Among other literary honors, the novel earned Rooney the 2017 *Sunday Times/Peters Fraser + Dunlop Young Writer of the Year Award*, in association with the University of Warwick, and was featured on numerous publications' lists of best books of the year, including *Vogue*, *Slate*, and *Elle*.

NORMAL PEOPLE

Rooney was named editor of the *Stinging Fly* in November 2017. Then, just a little over a year after her debut book was released, Rooney published her second novel, *Normal People* (2018), which also became an immediate and highly lauded best seller. After it was made available in the United Kingdom in 2018, it was released in the United States in early 2019.

Similar to *Conversations*, the novel began as a series of short stories, one of which, "At the Clinic," appeared in the London-based literary magazine the *White Review* in 2016. That story centers around two main characters, Marianne and Connell, whose complex romantic relationship is given more in-depth treatment in *Normal People*. A love story highlighted by class differences, the novel takes place between 2011 and 2015, tracking gifted students Marianne and Connell as they go through an on-again, off-again relationship from their time in high school in a small Irish town to their years as undergraduates at Trinity College. While Marianne is a privileged but awkward outcast, Connell is a popular and handsome jock whose mother works as a housekeeper for Marianne's family. However, their trajectories reverse once they enter college, which ultimately tests the limits of their friendship-cum-romance.

Many critics commented on the immediacy and universal appeal of the novel, which alternates between Marianne's and Connell's points of view. In a review for the *New York Times* (15 Apr. 2019), Andrew Martin assessed *Normal People* in relation to Rooney's debut, writing that her "novels have the unusual power to do what realist fiction was designed to do: bring to light how our contemporaries think and act in private (which these days mostly means off the internet), and allow us to see ourselves reflected in their predicaments." Meanwhile, writing for the *Guardian* (8 Jan. 2019), Sian Cain declared *Normal People* to be "the literary phenomenon of the year," calling it a "zeitgeist novel" that "has trapped a moment—in this case, our new sense of collective precariousness—whether individual, economic or political."

Before it was even published, *Normal People* was included on the longlist for the prestigious Man Booker Prize in July 2018. Though the novel did not make the Booker shortlist, it received a slew of other literary honors, including Waterstones Book of the Year 2018, the 2018 Costa Book Award in the novel category, and the Book of the Year at the 2019 British Book Awards. Brett Wolstencroft, a judge for the latter awards, which are commonly referred to as the "Nibbies," called *Normal People* "that rare thing, a sublime work of literary fiction that exquisitely renders a universal experience: being young, finding love, friendship and, ultimately, a sense of self," as quoted by Matthew Wilson in the *Guardian* (13 May 2019).

FURTHER WORK

Though Rooney has often been pigeonholed as a millennial writer, she has said that her sole aim has always been to speak for herself. In April 2019, she landed a fellowship at the New York Public Library's Dorothy and Lewis B. Cullman

Center for Scholars and Writers. As she explained to Clark about her writing experiences up to that point, "When I'm writing something everything falls into place. When I'm not writing, stuff keeps happening to me and there's nowhere to put it all."

Meanwhile, in 2018 the BBC had announced that it was partnering with Rooney to adapt *Normal People* for the small screen. In 2019, the streaming service Hulu placed a straight-to-series order for the adaptation.

PERSONAL LIFE

Rooney had a long-term relationship with John Prasifka, a high school math teacher whom she met during her time at Trinity College.

SUGGESTED READING

Barry, Ellen. "Greeted as the First Great Millennial Author, and Wary of the Attention." *The New York Times*, 31 Aug. 2018, www.nytimes.com/2018/08/31/world/europe/sally-rooney-ireland.html. Accessed 26 Aug. 2019.

Cain, Sian. "Normal People: How Sally Rooney's Novel Became the Literary Phenomenon of the Decade." *The Guardian*, 8 Jan. 2019, www.theguardian.com/books/2019/jan/08/normal-people-sally-rooney-novel-literary-phenomenon-of-decade. Accessed 26 Aug. 2019.

Clark, Alex. "Conversations with Sally Rooney: The 27-Year-Old Novelist Defining a Generation." *The Guardian*, 25 Aug. 2018, www.theguardian.com/books/2018/aug/25/sally-rooney-interview-normal-people-conversations-with-friends. Accessed 26 Aug. 2019.

Collins, Lauren. "Sally Rooney Gets in Your Head." *The New Yorker*, 31 Dec. 2018, www.newyorker.com/magazine/2019/01/07/sally-rooney-gets-in-your-head. Accessed 26 Aug. 2019.

Martin, Andrew. "Is Sally Rooney's New Novel as Great as Her First?" Review of *Normal People*, by Sally Rooney. *The New York Times*, 15 Apr. 2019, www.nytimes.com/2019/04/15/books/review/normal-people-sally-rooney.html. Accessed 26 Aug. 2019.

Schwartz, Alexandra. "A New Kind of Adultery Novel." Review of *Conversations with Friends*, by Sally Rooney. *The New Yorker*, 24 July 2017, www.newyorker.com/magazine/2017/07/31/a-new-kind-of-adultery-novel. Accessed 26 Aug. 2019.

Wilson, Matthew. "Sally Rooney Trumps Michelle Obama to Book of the Year Title." *The Guardian*, 13 May 2019, www.theguardian.com/books/2019/may/13/sally-rooney-trumps-michelle-obama-to-book-of-the-year-title. Accessed 26 Aug. 2019.

—*Chris Cullen*

Sahle-Work Zewde

Date of birth: February 21, 1950
Occupation: President of Ethiopia

After a long and successful career as a diplomat, Sahle-Work Zewde was appointed president of Ethiopia on October 25, 2018. Although presidential duties are largely ceremonial in that country, many political observers were quick to point out that the position carries great symbolic weight and societal importance. Her ascendance to the presidency was seen as part of an especially auspicious series of events given that Ethiopia's newly elected prime minister Abiy Ahmed, a reformist, had recently appointed a cabinet in which half the members were women, including Defense Minister Aisha Mohammed, and Muferiat Kamil, who is responsible for important police and domestic intelligence matters as leader of Ethiopia's Ministry of Peace.

On the social-media site *Twitter*, Fitsum Arega, the prime minister's chief of staff and spokesperson, wrote, "In a patriarchal society such as ours, the appointment of a female head of state not only sets the standard for the future but also normalizes women as decision-makers in public life."

Commenting on her presidency, as well as on the gender composition of the new cabinet, Sahle-Work said in an early parliamentary speech, quoted by Elias Gebreselassie for *Al Jazeera* (27 Oct. 2018), "If the current change in Ethiopia is headed equally by both men and women, it can sustain its momentum and realize a prosperous Ethiopia free of religious, ethnic and gender discrimination."

EARLY LIFE AND EDUCATION

Sahle-Work was born on February 21, 1950, in Addis Ababa, the largest city in Ethiopia. It has been the capital of the country since the late nineteenth century and is home to many institutions of higher learning, including Addis Ababa University and the National School of Music. The cosmopolitan city is also the site of numerous museums, government offices, and former imperial palaces, as well as the National Library and Archives, making it a center of Ethiopian culture.

The future president was the eldest of four girls in her family. Although girls in more rural areas often lack educational opportunities, learning was extremely important to her father, a senior officer in the imperial army, and he arranged for her to attend the Lycée Guébré-Mariam (also known as Lycée franco-éthiopien Guébré-Mariam), a highly regarded international school that enjoys support from the French government. (France and Ethiopia enjoy a strong diplomatic and economic relationship, and there

Photo by J.Marchand via Wikimedia Commons

are several French educational institutions in Ethiopia.) There she remained to complete both her primary and secondary education. She did well enough to earn a college scholarship, and at seventeen she traveled to France to attend the University of Montpellier (Université de Montpellier), where she studied natural science. According to a short biographical sketch posted on the Ethiopian Ministry of Foreign Affairs site, Sahle-Work was in France for nine years before deciding to return to her native country to become a public servant. "Service is my passion, especially serving a country and serving a cause," she later told the author of a blog post on the Ministry of Foreign Affairs site, looking back on her career. "I have been a civil servant all my life and public service has been the core of my life."

Sahle-Work began her professional career in Ethiopia as a public relations officer at the Ministry of Education, and she eventually worked her way up to become the head of her department.

DIPLOMATIC CAREER
Looking for a new challenge, Sahle-Work then joined the Ministry of Foreign Affairs, where she became an ambassador. From 1989 to 1993 she was assigned to Dakar, the capital of the African nation of Senegal, and she was subsequently made a permanent representative (head of a country's diplomatic mission to an international organization) to the Intergovernmental Authority on Development (IGAD), an eight-country trade bloc aimed at promoting food security, environmental protection, and humanitarianism. She also served from 1993 to 2002 as the ambassador

to Djibouti, a former French territory at the intersection of the Red Sea and the Gulf of Aden that was undergoing a civil war for part of that time. "When the government appointed me to Djibouti, I was very reluctant to accept it," she recalled to the *Official Blog of MFA Ethiopia*. "I thought being a woman in a Muslim country might not be conducive to getting the two countries closer." However, the foreign minister encouraged her to take the position anyway, for which, she said, she was later grateful. "Looking back, my best years in my diplomatic life were in Djibouti where I can see the impact of my work." She credits that experience with showing her the importance of mentorship, saying, "I try to do the same for others. In mission trips and delegates meetings, I take others with me and . . . allow them to experience diplomacy both by observing as well as acting. I allow them to fail and rise."

In 2002 she was assigned to France; made permanent representative to the United Nations Educational, Scientific and Cultural Organization (UNESCO), which is based in Paris; and given responsibility for diplomatic ties with Tunisia and Morocco. From 2006 to 2009, she was the permanent representative of Ethiopia to the African Union, a continent-wide group consisting of more than fifty nations; permanent representative to the United Nations Economic Commission for Africa (UNECA); and director general for African affairs in the Ministry of Foreign Affairs of Ethiopia.

In 2009 Sahle-Work began leading the newly established United Nations Integrated Peacebuilding Office in the Central African Republic (also known as Bureau Intégré de l'Organisation des Nations Unies en Centrafrique or BINU-CA), whose mission was to quell tensions in the Central African Republic, a country bordered by Chad, Sudan, and the Democratic Republic of the Congo that had been the site of periodic civil war for years.

Sahle-Work's UN career continued to rise; in early 2011 Secretary-General Ban Ki-moon appointed her as the first director-general of the UN office in Nairobi, and under her leadership, the newly created office (one of just four such headquarters in the world) gained in stature and importance. She remained in that post until 2018, when Secretary-General António Guterres, a former Portuguese prime minister who had assumed the position after Ban Ki-moon, made her his special representative to the African Union and head of the United Nations Office to the African Union (UNOAU), a position at the level of under-secretary-general.

PRESIDENCY
Sahle-Work did not hold that position long, however. In April 2018 Abiy Ahmed, a former

member of the Ethiopian National Defense Force and the United Nations Peace Keeping Force in Rwanda, became the fifteenth prime minister of Ethiopia. Chair of the ruling Ethiopian People's Revolutionary Democratic Front (EPRDF) and the Oromo Democratic Party, one of the four coalition parties that make up the EPRDF, he immediately embarked on a series of social and economic reforms. He released thousands of political prisoners, pardoned exiled dissidents, opened major industries to foreign investment, and brokered a peace agreement with neighboring Eritrea, which had long been embroiled in a territorial dispute with Ethiopia. He was also responsible for what political observers characterized as something of a "pink wave," appointing ten female ministers to his twenty-person cabinet and making Ethiopia the third country in Africa, after Rwanda and Seychelles, to achieve full gender balance in their cabinets.

After President Mulatu Teshome stepped down in October 2018, Abiy tapped Sahle-Work to replace him, and she agreed. She was unanimously approved by the Ethiopian parliament and sworn into office on October 25 for a six-year term.

Sahle-Work was listed by *Forbes* magazine as one of the 100 most powerful women in the world in 2018. In her capacity as Ethiopia's president, she has vowed to address women's rights and asserted at her swearing-in ceremony, as quoted by Gebreselassie, "I know today I have said a lot about female empowerment, but expect me to be even more vocal in the coming years about female rights and equality."

PERSONAL LIFE

Sahle-Work is married and has two sons. She is fluent in French and English in addition to Amharic, the official language of her country and the second-most commonly spoken Semitic language in the world, after Arabic.

SUGGESTED READING

Ahmed, Hadra, and Kimiko de Freytas-Tamura. "Ethiopia Appoints Its First Female President." *The New York Times*, 25 Oct. 2018, www.nytimes.com/2018/10/25/world/africa/sahlework-zewde-ethiopia-president.html. Accessed 11 Jan. 2019.
"Ethiopia Appoints Career Diplomat Sahle-Work Zewde as Africa's Only Female President." *The Telegraph*, 25 Oct. 2018, www.telegraph.co.uk/news/2018/10/25/ethiopia-appointscareer-diplomat-sahle-work-zewde-africas-female/. Accessed 11 Jan. 2019.
Ethiopian Ministry of Foreign Affairs. "Celebrating Ethiopian Women: Ambassador Sahle-Work Zewde." *MFA Blog*, 22 Mar. 2018, mfaethiopiablog.wordpress.com/2018/03/22/celebrating-ethiopian-women-ambassador-sahle-work-zewde/. Accessed 11 Jan. 2019.
Gebreselassie, Elias. "Who is Sahle-Work Zewde, Ethiopia's First Female President?" *Al Jazeera*, 27 Oct 2018, www.aljazeera.com/news/2018/10/sahle-work-zewde-ethiopia-female-president-181027134726828.html. Accessed 11 Jan. 2019.
Ruiz, Michelle. "Sahle-Work Zewde Is Ethiopia's First Woman President and Africa's Only Serving Female Head of State." *Vogue*, 25 Oct. 2018, www.vogue.com/article/sahle-work-zewde-elected-president-of-ethiopia. Accessed 11 Jan. 2019.
Shaban, Abdur Rahman Alfa. "Forbes 2018 Most Powerful Women: Ethiopia President Sole African." *Africa News*, Euro News, 7 Dec. 2018, www.africanews.com/2018/12/07/forbes-2018-most-powerful-women-ethiopia-president-sole-african/. Accessed 11 Jan. 2019.

—*Mari Rich*

Alvin Salehi

Date of birth: ca. 1990
Occupation: Technologist and policymaker

Alvand "Alvin" Salehi is a senior technology advisor in the White House Office of the Federal Chief Information Officer (CIO). Hired during the Obama administration in 2015, Salehi oversaw the release of the White House's first official federal source code policy, requiring government agencies to "release 20 percent of any new code they commission as open source software, meaning the code will be available for anyone to examine, modify, and reuse in their own projects," Klint Finley explained for *Wired* (11 Aug. 2016). It was the US government's first meaningful shift to open source code—code that is accessible to everyone—over proprietary, or closed source code—code owned and guarded as a trade secret by a private entity. Crucially, the policy also allowed for government agencies to share code with each other. Transparency and innovation are two goals of the open source policy; cost-effectiveness is another. At the tech festival SXSW in 2018, Salehi said he hoped to crack down on duplicative government software procurement. For years, tech companies have profited from the federal government with contracts that prevent individual government agencies from sharing elements of their software with one another. "The US government has been spending up to $6 billion per year on duplicative software," he said, as quoted by John Holden of the *Irish Times* (15 Mar. 2018). Salehi, with former US CIO Tony Scott, launched an open source platform called

Code.gov to facilitate this policy in November 2016. "Our goal is to make *Code.gov* the nation's primary platform for sharing and improving government software," he told Steffanie Agnew for *SXTX State* (7 Mar. 2018), a website of the Texas State University School of Journalism and Mass Communication.

Salehi, who also had short stints at the Energy and State departments, was named a research affiliate at Harvard Law School's Berkman Klein Center for Internet and Society in 2017. In 2018, he appeared on the *Forbes* list of 30 Under 30 in the law and policy category, and the Fed 100, a list of exceptional people working in federal technology compiled by the website *Federal Computer Week (FCW)*. Also that year, he was named a Millennium Fellow at the Atlantic Council, a think tank focused on international affairs.

EARLY LIFE AND EDUCATION

Salehi was born Alvand Abdolsalehi to parents Mohsen and Shahla in Orange County, California. He has a sister, Emon, and a brother, Ali. He is a first-generation Iranian American. Salehi earned his bachelor's degree in broadcast journalism and political science from the University of Southern California (USC) in 2010. During his senior year, he served as the executive producer of Annenberg TV News, the school's student-produced nightly news program. He went on to earn a master's degree in communication management from USC in 2013, and graduated from the USC Gould School of Law in 2013. He was admitted to the California Bar the same year. According to his personal *LinkedIn* page, after graduation, Salehi clerked for the late Judge Arthur Alarcon on the US Court of Appeals for the Ninth Circuit and served as general counsel for the data company Bolt Analytics.

EARLY GOVERNMENT CAREER

In 2014, Salehi joined the Department of Energy as a presidential management fellow at the Advanced Research Projects Agency–Energy (ARPA-E). ARPA-E is modeled after the Defense Advanced Research Projects Agency (DARPA) at the Pentagon, a government agency that invests in audacious new technologies for the military. In the 1960s, DARPA created an early computer network system, ARPANET, that provided the basis for the modern-day Internet. In the same vein, ARPA-E is a government agency that promotes and funds research into innovative energy technologies. In 2015, Salehi joined the State Department as a foreign affairs officer in cyber and telecommunications. In that role, he worked to expand internet access in sub-Saharan Africa.

FEDERAL SOURCE CODE POLICY

In November 2015, Salehi joined the Office of the Federal CIO as senior technology advisor under President Barack Obama. His hiring came amid a years-long effort to open communications between government agencies. In 2014, in the Second Open Government National Action Plan, the federal government made a commitment to improve access to federal source code. Two years later, in March 2016, the CIO offered a draft of what would become the federal source code policy. The nonprofit *Sunlight Foundation*, which advocates for greater transparency in the US government, supported the draft. "We believe that making more of the software built by or for the federal government open source will improve how the federal government works and save agencies money," the organization said in a public comment on the draft policy (11 Apr. 2016). It added: "Externally, some projects may have much broader societal relevance, like the NASA Nebula project that grew into OpenStack, or the Accumulo software from the NSA." This kind of cross-pollination is common elsewhere. For instance, the European Union (EU) made a point of embracing open source software for government services as early as 2003, and the US Department of Defense (DoD) released a memo regarding open source policy in 2009. Over the years, critics have argued that open source software is vulnerable to attack and unsafe. The Pentagon feels differently. As Kelsey Atherton put it for the *Verge* (14 Nov. 2017): "Open-source software is . . . more secure than closed-source software, by its very nature: the code is perpetually scrutinized by countless users across the planet, and any weaknesses are shared immediately." NASA launched an open source platform in 2012.

The official federal source code policy, released in August 2016, specifically required two things: code reuse and an open source code pilot program. The code reuse provision addressed duplicative software procurement specifically. It stipulated that code commissioned for one government agency, from 2016 onward, could be used by another. The unprecedented open source code pilot program stipulates that each government agency must make at least 20 percent of any new commissioned code available to the public as open source software. To facilitate this second stipulation, the CIO launched Code.gov in November 2016. Salehi and Scott were the platform's primary architects.

CODE.GOV AND ANET

"I've spoken with so many people over the years who have expressed a sincere interest in improving government websites," Salehi told Agnew. "And occasionally, this desire is born out of frustration—someone might log onto a government site and find that it's not functioning the way they expect it to. Ideally, with *Code.gov*, they would be able to submit a fix to that issue right then and there." *Code.gov* inventories code across federal agencies. The site began with forty-five projects available to the public. As of February 2019, there were nearly five thousand searchable projects on the site. *Code.gov* launched at an uncertain moment in US history. In May 2017, Salehi appeared at the annual O'Reilly Open Source Convention, or OSCON, in Austin, Texas, and he addressed questions about the future of *Code.gov* under the administration of President Donald Trump. "This is a completely nonpartisan issue, as it should be," he said. "Code.gov is here to stay." He suggested that the cost-saving value of the project appeals to the new president. He also described one of the projects, through the DoD, available to public on the site.

In 2015, a program called Advisor Network, or ANET, was created for the North American Treaty Organization (NATO) military and civilians in Afghanistan to log interactions and training with Afghan officials. Members of the Defense Digital Service (DDS), private sector experts hired by the DoD, first encountered the program in Kabul in 2016. (At the O'Reilly convention, Salehi admiringly described them as the "tech SWAT team of the federal government.") One DDS advisor, in an interview with Issie Lapowsky for *Wired* (27 May 2017) compared the ANET interface to "early Netscape Navigator," a web browser from the 1990s. Reports took users hours to file and download. DDS coders in Kabul and Washington, DC, worked together using GitHub, a popular open source hosting service, to build a beta version of a streamlined ANET by early 2017. It was not perfect—though it took users significantly less time to create reports—and after its completion, the DDS team released ANET as open source software. The software, Salehi argued, could prove useful to other government agencies like the State Department or the US Agency for International Development. "This is a side of open source that offers the potential of technology to help bolster the safety of Americans abroad and the ability of the software itself to help troops and their advisors fulfill their objectives," he said at O'Reilly. Inspired by *Code.gov*, the state of California launched a similar platform in late 2018 called Code California.

PERSONAL LIFE

Salehi, who lives in Alexandria, Virginia, is guarded about his personal life; when contacted for a story by the *Washington Post* in 2016, he answered questions but declined to give his age. The human-interest story told how, one afternoon in May 2016, Salehi was on his way to a meeting when he saw a man steal a woman's purse. Salehi took off in pursuit, driving the man toward the White House, where he was arrested. "It was like one of those movies that you never think will happen in real life," Salehi told Peter Hermann for the *Washington Post* (2 May 2016). "As the person begins running, everything slows down around you. You have no idea what you're supposed to do. Your instinct kicks in, and it just happens." Salehi was modest about his act of bravery. "I never thought my first involvement in a crime would be stopping a robbery near the White House," he said.

SUGGESTED READING

Agnew, Steffanie. "Preview: America's Code: Open Sourcing Government Software." *SXTX State*, 7 Mar. 2018, sxtxstate.com/2018/03/preview-americas-code-open-sourcing-government-software/. Accessed 16 Feb. 2019.

Atherton, Kelsey. "The Pentagon Is Set to Make a Big Push toward Open Source Software Next Year." *The Verge*, 14 Nov. 2017, www.theverge.com/2017/11/14/16649042/pentagon-department-of-defense-open-source-software. Accessed 16 Feb. 2019.

Finley, Klint. "Open Source Won. So, Now What?" *Wired*, 11 Aug. 2016, www.wired.com/2016/08/open-source-won-now/. Accessed 16 Feb. 2019.

Holden, John. "Irish Tech Firms Make Their Mark at the Ever-Growing SXSW Event." *The Irish Times*, 15 Mar. 2018, www.irishtimes.com/business/innovation/irish-tech-firms-make-their-mark-at-the-ever-growing-sxsw-event-1.3427007. Accessed 16 Feb. 2019.

Lapowsky, Issie. "Meet the Nerds Coding Their Way through the Afghanistan War." *Wired*, 27 May 2017, www.wired.com/2017/05/meet-nerds-coding-way-afghanistan-war/. Accessed 16 Feb. 2019.

"Sunlight's Comments on the Proposed U.S. Open Source Software Policy." *Sunlight Foundation*, 11 Apr. 2016, sunlightfoundation.com/2016/04/11/sunlights-comments-on-the-proposed-u-s-open-source-software-policy/. Accessed 19 Feb. 2019.

—*Molly Hagan*

Sarkodie

Date of birth: July 10, 1988
Occupation: Rapper

Sarkodie is one of the most popular music artists in Ghana. He raps in a Ghanaian hybrid genre called hiplife, a blend of hip-hop and highlife, another Ghanaian genre that originated in the twentieth century and draws on traditional Akan music. Hiplife was born in the 1990s, created by British-born Ghanaian artist Reggie Rockstone. When he returned to Ghana in 1994, he began rapping in his native language, Twi, a dialect of Akan. Since then, the genre has been nurtured by people like Dr. Duncan, the radio DJ who discovered Sarkodie and a host of other hiplife talents.

Sarkodie is the first truly international hiplife star. He was the first Ghanaian artist to win a BET Award for Best International Artist Africa in 2012, and he won the Best Hip-Hop Award at the MTV Africa Music Awards in 2014. He has performed around the world, and in 2015, sold out the legendary Apollo Theatre in Harlem, New York, as a headliner. Since his debut album, *Makye* (2009), Sarkodie has risen to become hiplife royalty. "When the history of these times in African music is read back to generations after us, there shall only be a few names at the top of the column for hip-hop," a reviewer for the Nigerian website *Pulse* (11 Sept. 2017) wrote. "Sarkodie will be right up there, his story inspiring, his music captivating, and his efforts for the culture trailblazing."

EARLY LIFE

Sarkodie was born Michael Kwesi Owusu Addo on July 10, 1988. The fourth of five children, he was raised by a single mother, Emma Maame Aggrey, in Tema, east of the Ghanaian capital of Accra, on the Atlantic coast. His father, a Michael Jackson fan, named him after the pop star. Sarkodie chose his stage name because two of his father's wealthy friends were named Sarkodie; he equated the name with success. Drawn early to hip-hop, he performed songs by Obrafour, then hiplife's reigning superstar, as a young student at Achimota Preparatory School before beginning to write songs of his own. Sarkodie was also heavily influenced by the rapid flow of New York rapper Busta Rhymes. Sarkodie modeled himself in Busta's image. "I always start with the rhythm like a drummer, and then I find the lyrics to fit it," he told Halifu Osumare for the book *The Hiplife in Ghana: West African Indigenization of Hip-Hop* (2012). Sarkodie graduated from Methodist Day Secondary School in Tema. Teachers remember him as an average but respectful student who always turned in assignments on time. Sarkodie went on to earn a certificate in graphic design through the Tema branch of IPMC College of Technology. He was offered a job in advertising but turned it down, breaking the news to his family: he wanted to pursue a career in music.

EARLY CAREER

Sarkodie was discovered as a teenager by radio DJ Isaac "Dr. Duncan" Williams of Dom 106.3

Photo by Owula kpakpo via Wikimedia Commons

Radio. "He was the one who believed in my talent ever since he saw me as a young guy growing up," Sarkodie told a reporter for *Ghana Web* (2 June 2008). "I wouldn't have been here today if not for Duncan." Sarkodie performed at street carnivals sponsored by Dr. Duncan, where underground rappers competed for recognition—always rapping in the local Twi language. Through those events, Sarkodie eventually earned time on Dr. Duncan's star-making radio program, *Kasahari*. Duncan, who became Sarkodie's first manager, introduced Sarkodie to local hiplife producer Edward Nana Poku Osei (known as Hammer), who had worked with Obrafour and other hiplife stars early in their careers. In 2008, Sarkodie scored a feature on the hit song "You Dey Craze" by fellow Ghanaian rapper Edem. His own first hit song was "Baby," featuring Mugeez of the group R2Bees. He recalls the first time he heard it on the radio. "I was at the barbershop, when all of a sudden I heard [it]," he told the Ghanaian music blog *Afromusion* (1 Sept. 2011). "I kept it to myself." He released his debut album, *Makye*, in 2009. One of the songs on that album, "Borga" featuring J-Town, takes aim at Ghanaians living abroad. ("Borga" is a slang term for Ghanians who return from overseas.) The lyrics emphasize Sarkodie's own allegiance to Ghana and to his hometown, Tema. He raps in Twi, but the translated lyrics say, in part: "Someone is in Canada he needs to go begging for his daily meal / A lot of these borga are not truthful you would have known life in the West is not that easy / [When] you live and work in Ghana / At the very least you have somewhere to sleep."

It was an explosive debut: in 2010, Sarkodie swept the Ghana Music Awards, taking home five awards, including Artist of the Year. In 2011, Sarkodie released lead singles from his next album, Rapperholic (2012), including the hit "U Go Kill Me," an enormously popular song that fueled the Azonto dance craze, first popularized by Ghanaian soccer player Asamoah Gyan during the 2010 World Cup tournament. Another song, "Saa Okodie No," featuring his childhood hero Obrafour, describes the passing of the torch from one hiplife legend to another. The success of Rapperholic earned Sarkodie another Ghana Music Award for Artist of the Year, and a BET Award for Best International Artist Africa.

SARKOLOGY AND MARY

Sarkodie released his third album, Sarkology, in 2014. The thirty-track album features a host of artists including Obrafour and Nigerian singer Davido. Davido appears on the album's lead single "Gunshot." Other hits include "Illuminati," and "Down on One," featuring Ghanaian-English artist Fuse ODG. Jacob Roberts-Mensah of Ghana Web (24 Jan. 2014) described the album as an extension of Sarkodie's earlier record, Rapperholic, suggesting that it "should've been called Rapperholic II," as it covers "the same topics of overcoming haters, winning a Grammy, faith and being the best MC." Still, he wrote, "Sarkodie shows that he is very aware of his prominence in (Ghana) rap and (Ghana) music history as a whole throughout the album in songs like 'Preach' and 'Y'all Already Know.'" Robert-Mensah concluded that Sarkodie "does very well on this album to further blur the lines between (Ghana) rap/hiplife and hip-hop, not necessarily being boxed in or defined by either genre." Also in 2014, Sarkodie won the Best Hip-Hop Award at the MTV Africa Music Awards and performed with American singer Miguel at the awards ceremony.

Sarkodie's fourth album, Mary, was released on his own Sarkcess Records in 2015—the same year he headlined a show at New York's legendary Apollo Theatre in Harlem. Mary is dedicated to his grandmother who died in 2012. His grandmother was a highlife fan and had encouraged Sarkodie to add more traditional instrumentation to his music. The album is an attempt to honor her request. Sarkodie's innovative use of traditional Ghanaian music, Jesse Brent wrote in his review in Afropop Worldwide (18 Sept. 2015), makes Mary "an especially important moment for Ghanaian music." The album's upbeat lead single, "Mewu," features the singer-songwriter Akwaboah. Brent praised its "terrific production." Like the rest of the album, "Mewu" was recorded with live instruments in the studio. It took Sarkodie and his team nearly two years to complete the album. Brent described the title track, which features Sarkodie singing in Twi, as the "most compelling moment" on the album, as well as the moment "in which hiplife and highlife meet most convincingly." Sarkodie takes stock of his roots in other ways. On the album's last track, "Sarkcess Story," Sarkodie recalls how far he has come from his impoverished upbringing. "Think about where I came from / No shoes, no shirts, no cars, and no income," he raps. As if to emphasize his ascension, he was invited to give a speech at Harvard University the next year called "The Art of the Hustle."

HIGHEST

Sarkodie released his next album, Highest, in 2017. That album was inspired by the birth of his daughter, Adalyn, nicknamed Titi, the previous year to his longtime girlfriend, Tracy, whom he married in 2018. "As far as Africa is concerned I really have nothing to prove and it's only right I crown my current state as the highest!" he told Jameelah Wilkerson for The Hype magazine (19 Oct. 2017). A reviewer for Pulse described the album as a "victory lap." The "music matches his ambitions," they concluded. The album opens with the UK–based Ghanaian poet, Suli Breaks, dramatically praising Sarkodie—"He is the one that wields the microphone of legend . . . the beast who wrestled with rap legacy and came out victorious"—before the beat drops and Sarkodie starts rapping. The album's lead single, "Pain Killer," features Nigerian singer Runtown. The beat of the song, Sabo Kpade wrote for Okay-Africa (9 Feb. 2017), is "recognizably Ghanaian" for its syncopated percussion and flutes. Other singles from the album include "Come to Me," featuring R & B singer Bobii Lewis. In 2018, Sarkodie released a stand-alone single called "Rush Hour." In early 2018, Sarkodie's friend and fellow musician, singer Ebony Reigns, was killed in a car accident. He recorded a song called "Wake Up Call" about road safety.

In 2013, Sarkodie launched his own fashion line called the Sark Collection; it shuttered in 2017. He has been a brand ambassador for Samsung, Tigo Telecommunications, and the dairy manufacturer Fan Milk. In 2017, Forbes Africa ranked Sarkodie ninth on its list of the "top ten most bankable artists in Africa," and in 2018, at the age of twenty-nine, he appeared on the Forbes Africa 30 Under 30 list of influential people in the creatives category.

SUGGESTED READING

"'Highest' Is Sarkodie's Entertaining Victory Lap." Pulse, 11 Sept. 2017, www.pulse.ng/entertainment/music/album-review-highest-is-sarkodies-entertaining-victory-lap/czmf5q3. Accessed 17 Mar. 2019.

Kpade, Sabo. "Sarkodie and Runtown's 'Pain Killer' Is the Best Song You'll Hear This Week."

OkayAfrica, 9 Feb. 2017, www.okayafrica. com/sarkodie-runtown-pain-killer-download/. Accessed 17 Mar. 2019.

Osumare, Halifu. *The Hiplife in Ghana: West African Indigenization of Hip-Hop.* Palgrave Macmillan, 2012.

Roberts-Mensah, Jacob. Review of *Sarkology*, by Sarkodie. *Ghana Web*, 24 Jan. 2014, www. ghanaweb.com/GhanaHomePage/entertainment/Sarkodie-s-Sarkology-An-album-review-298722. Accessed 17 Mar. 2019.

"Sarkodie Devotes His Whole Time on Rap Music." *Ghana Web*, 2 June 2008, www. ghanaweb.com/GhanaHomePage/entertainment/Sarkodie-devotes-his-whole-time-on-rap-music-193764. Accessed 15 Mar. 2019.

"Sarkodie: On Life, Music and Everything in Between." *Afromusion*, 1 Sept. 2011, afromusion.wordpress.com/2011/09/10/sarkodie-on-life-music-and-everything-in-between/. Accessed 17 Mar. 2019.

Wilkerson, Jameelah. "Five Questions with Sarkodie." *The Hype*, 19 Oct. 2017, www.thehypemagazine.com/2017/10/five-questions-with-sarkodie/. Accessed 17 Mar. 2019.

SELECTED WORKS

Rapperholic, 2012; *Sarkology*, 2014; *Mary*, 2015; *Highest*, 2017

—Molly Hagan

Riad Sattouf

Date of birth: May 5, 1978
Occupation: Cartoonist

Riad Sattouf is best known for *L'Arabe du futur*, a graphic novel series that has sold well over two million copies and been translated into more than twenty languages. *The Arab of the Future*, as the series is known in English, is a memoir of Sattouf's youth, which he spent in France, Libya, and Syria. An example of bande dessinée—a highly respected genre of French comics—*The Arab of the Future* has invited positive comparisons to other popular graphic memoirs, including Art Spiegelman's *Maus: A Survivor's Tale* (1991), about his parents' survival during the Holocaust, and Marjane Satrapi's acclaimed *Persepolis* (2000), about her flight from Iran.

"*The Arab of the Future* has become that rare thing in France's polarized intellectual climate: an object of consensual rapture, hailed as a masterpiece in the leading journals of both the left and the right," Adam Shatz wrote for the *New Yorker* (12 Oct. 2015). Sattouf told Shatz, however, that he did not intend to make a political statement or position himself as an expert on the Arab world. "If I had written a book about a village in southern Italy or Norway, would I be asked about my vision of the European world?" he wondered to Shatz. Sattouf admitted to Olivia Snaije for the *Guardian* (28 Oct. 2015), "It's inevitable that people ask me my opinion. I knew Syria in the 1980s but I can't say I know anything about Syria today. I'm no more informed about the situation in the Middle East than the average person who watches TV."

Snaije explained the universal appeal of the graphic novels, writing, "Sattouf's work is laced with astute observations of human beings. His memoirs often dwell on their failings: hypocrisy, cowardice, bullying. Yet there's humour too—mainly because his humans are so helplessly absurd." Sattouf, who was labeled an Arab while living in France and considered a foreigner when living in the Middle East, has credited his understanding of human nature to being required to straddle two very different cultures. "When you're an outsider, you observe other people more," he told Rachel Cooke for the *Guardian* (27 Mar. 2016). "I still do this. I'm a watcher. Cartoonists are by definition outsiders: they're outside literature, art, the establishment."

EARLY LIFE AND EDUCATION

Riad Sattouf was born in 1978 in Paris. In *The Arab of the Future*, he refers to his parents by the pseudonyms Clémentine and Abdel-Razak. His mother, a native of France, met his father, who hailed from a small Syrian village near Homs, while both were studying at the Sorbonne in the early 1970s. He has one younger brother. Besides employing pseudonyms, Sattouf has been hesitant to divulge certain details of his life, arguing that he may want to use them in future books, and he has been known to disseminate falsehoods to throw journalists off track.

When Sattouf was two years old, his father received an offer to teach at Oxford; but insulted that the letter from England misspelled his name, he instead accepted a post at a university in Libya. There, the family was provided with a house, but because Libyan leader Muammar al-Qaddafi had outlawed private property, they were not given a key. One day, while Sattouf was out with his parents for several hours, another family claimed occupancy; and they had to search for another abandoned house in which to live. Food was generally scarce, and they often subsisted just on bananas—all that was available in Libya's denuded marketplaces.

After Qaddafi decreed that Libya's professors must relocate to farms to work the land, Abdel-Razak, a great believer in pan-Arab unity, got a job teaching in Syria and moved the family to the village of Ter Maaleh, where he'd grown up. In Syria, Clémentine chafed against the tradition that women in the devoutly Sunni area

Photo by Selbymay via Wikimedia Commons

were treated as second-class citizens and Sattouf was tormented by his cousins, who bullied him and beat him up.

Sattouf found solace in the care packages of French comic books his grandmother sent him from Brittany, France, and he began drawing cartoons himself. He also enjoyed spending summers back in France and told Terry Gross for the National Public Radio show *Fresh Air* (9 Nov. 2015), "It was like, you know, arriving in a huge toy store. I don't know how to tell you—there was light everywhere, there was people everywhere, cars everywhere. . . . I was loving that." In 1990, Sattouf's parents separated. Clémentine and her two sons moved to Brittany. The three lived in a public housing complex, subsisting with the help of government benefits for several years before Clémentine found work as a medical secretary.

Sattouf continued to be bullied in school in France. He thus spent much of his time as a teenager in his room, reading comic books and drawing. After earning his baccalauréat, the equivalent of a high school diploma, Sattouf studied applied art for a time in Nantes, and then attended the Gobelins School of the Image, a visual arts school in Paris, where he took up animation.

CAREER AS A CARTOONIST

Sattouf earned his first contract in 1998, shortly after graduating. He quickly caught the eye of Guy Delcourt, the owner of a publishing house specializing in cartoons. In 2000, Delcourt published Sattouf's first book, *Petit Verglas*, based on a story line by Éric Corbeyran. Other volumes

in the series were published in 2001 and 2002. Sattouf won greater attention with the 2004 young-adult book whose title translates to "My Circumcision"; the three-volume coming-of-age series *Les pauvres aventures de Jérémie* (*The Poor Adventures of Jeremiah*) (2003–05); and the 2005 graphic novel *Retour au collège* (Back to school), for which he spent two weeks embedded in an elite high school in a wealthy section of Paris.

In 2004, Sattouf began contributing a weekly comic strip to the popular satirical magazine *Charlie Hebdo*. His strip, *La vie secrète des jeunes* (The secret life of youth), was based on conversations he overheard in the Métro and on the streets of Paris. In 2006, he published the first volume in the *Pascal Brutal* comic series, which takes place in an imagined future where the poor are banned from Paris, Russian society is in tatters, and the pan-Arab world has become a utopia thanks to the leadership of the cartoonist himself. Later volumes were released in 2007, 2009, and 2014.

In addition to his cartooning, Sattouf soon began working as a scriptwriter and film director. His first film, *Beaux Gosses* (released internationally as *The French Kissers*), a comedic yet sensitive portrayal of an adolescent boy trying to fit in, was released in 2009. It garnered a César Award (the French equivalent to an Oscar) for best debut film of the year. His next cinematic effort was *Jacky au royaume des filles* (*Jacky in the Kingdom of Women*), a 2014 picture that takes place in a land where women hold the power and men are forced to wear burqa-like veils.

After working at *Charlie Hebdo* for ten years, Sattouf left the magazine in 2014. The only cartoonist of Middle Eastern descent at the publication, Sattouf had typically avoided editorial meetings because of his unwillingness to participate in the raucous political debates that ensued, and he also expressed some misgivings about the editors' confrontational satirical style. After two Muslim terrorists stormed the publication's offices and killed twelve people in 2015, however, Sattouf contributed a final *La vie secrète des jeunes* strip. The comic depicted a young North African man asserting that although he cared little for the magazine, it was wrong to kill someone over a cartoon.

In 2014, Sattouf began writing the weekly strip *Les cahiers d'Esther* (Esther's Notebooks) for the French newsmagazine *L'Obs*. The comics, based on stories recounted to Sattouf by the young daughter of a friend, were later collected and republished in multiple volumes. The first volume in the series, *Les cahiers d'Esther: Histoires des mes 10 ans* (*Story of My 10 years*), was released in 2016, followed by three later volumes depicting Esther's eleventh, twelfth, and thirteenth years between 2017 and 2019. *Les cahiers d'Esther* was also adapted into a television cartoon that aired on the Canal network.

Simultaneously, Sattouf published the first graphic novel—*L'Arabe du futur: Une jeunesse au Moyen-Orient (1978–1984)*—in the reported five-volume *L'Arabe du futur* series in 2014. Sattouf had started to seriously consider writing about his early life in the Arab world in 2011. "Maybe I was a little afraid of writing about my family. But mostly, I didn't want to be considered The Arab Cartoonist. I wanted to do other things first. So I waited, and I waited," he told Cooke of why he had not written an autobiographical comic earlier. "Then, in 2011, a part of my family had to leave Homs, and I had to help them, and I had a lot of difficulties in France getting authorisation. I sat there thinking: oh, God, I want to make a comic about this. And then I realised . . . if I'm going to do that, I have to tell the whole story right from the beginning." The resulting critically acclaimed series evocatively depicts France in the blues and grays of the coast of Brittany, Libya in yellows reminiscent of desert sands, and Syria in light reds and pinks meant to mimic ferrous soil.

Volume one was awarded the Grand prix RTL de la bande dessinée, Prix BD Stas/Ville de Saint-Étienne, and Angoulême International Comics Festival Fauve d'or. The second volume in the series, *Une juenesse au Moyen-Orient (1984–1985)* was published in 2015; followed by volume three, covering 1985 to 1987, in 2016; and volume four, detailing the time between 1987 to 1992, in 2018. *L'Arabe du futur* began being translated and published in English as the *Arab of the Future: A Childhood in the Middle East* in 2015.

HONORS AND PERSONAL LIFE

In addition to his César, Sattouf's laurels include the 2003 Angoulême International Comics Festival René Goscinny Award for volume one of *Les pauvres aventures de Jérémie*; the 2007 Jacques Lob Prize for volume two of *Pascal Brutal*; the 2008 Globes de Cristal Award for *La vie secrète des jeunes*; and the 2010 Angoulême International Comics Festival Fauve d'or for volume three of *Pascal Brutal*.

PERSONAL LIFE

Sattouf and his partner, a comic-book editor, live in Paris, France. They have a son.

SUGGESTED READING

Chute, Hillary. "Comics of Violence and Nostalgia from War-Torn Syria." Review of *The Arab of the Future 3: A Childhood in the Middle East, 1985–1987*, by Riad Sattouf, *Brothers of the Gun: A Memoir of the Syrian War*, by Marwan Hisham and Molly Crabapple, and *The Unwanted: Stories of the Syrian Refugees*, by Don Brown. *The New York Times*, 12 Oct. 2018, www.nytimes.com/2018/10/12/books/review/arab-of-the-future-3-riad-sattouf.html. Accessed 28 July 2019.

Sattouf, Riad. "Riad Sattouf: Not French, Not Syrian . . . I'm a Cartoonist." Interview by Rachel Cooke. *The Guardian*, 27 Mar. 2016, www.theguardian.com/books/2016/mar/27/riad-sattouf-arab-of-the-future-interview. Accessed 28 July 2019.

Sattouf, Riad. "Riad Sattouf Interview: 'I Didn't Want to Be the Guy of Arab Origin Who Makes Comics about Arab People.'" Interview by Angelique Chrisafis. *The Guardian*, 30 Sept. 2016, www.theguardian.com/books/2016/sep/30/riad-sattouf-interview-graphic-novelist. Accessed 28 July 2019.

Sattouf, Riad. "*Arab of the Future* Chronicles the Challenges of a Cross-Cultural Childhood." Interview by Terry Gross. *Fresh Air*, National Public Radio, 9 Nov. 2015, www.npr.org/2015/11/09/455303187/arab-of-the-future-chronicles-the-challenges-of-a-cross-cultural-childhood. Accessed 28 July 2019.

Shatz, Adam. "Drawing Blood." *The New Yorker*, 12 Oct. 2015, www.newyorker.com/magazine/2015/10/19/drawing-blood. Accessed 28 July 2019.

Snaije, Olivia. "Riad Sattouf Draws on Multicultural Past for *The Arab of the Future*." *The Guardian*, 28 Oct. 2015, www.theguardian.com/books/2015/oct/28/riad-sattouf-draws-on-his-own-multicultural-past-for-the-arab-of-the-future-books. Accessed 28 July 2019.

SELECTED WORKS

Les pauvres aventures de Jérémie, 2003–05; *La vie secrète des jeunes*, 2004–15; *Retour au collège*, 2005; *Les cahiers d'Esther*, 2014– ; *L'Arabe du futur: Une juenesse au Moyen-Orient*, 2014–

—Mari Rich

Melanie Scrofano

Date of birth: December 20, 1981
Occupation: Actor

Canadian actor Melanie Scrofano reached a new level in her career in 2016 when she first appeared in the title role on *Wynonna Earp*, a science-fiction Western show on the SyFy Channel that proved to be a hit. Scrofano credited much of the show's popularity to fans' eagerness for strong female characters. She defined such a character as one who "just gets on getting on, even when it's not pretty, and even if there's some swearing and tears along the way," as she told Sage Young for *Bustle* (27 July 2018).

And she took the inspirational potential of her lead role seriously, striving to give back to supportive fans and acknowledging the impact of entertainment on viewers. "It does affect people's lives," she told Young of the show. "It either makes them laugh in really dark times, or it makes them think about people in their lives differently, or it makes them see themselves in a way they never saw themselves and it gives them strength. I think that inspires me to really work harder than I would if I didn't think it was reaching anybody."

Before her breakthrough Scrofano had amassed a steady stream of television credits in her native Canada, appearing in such shows as the CBC dramedy *Being Erica* in 2010 and the teen hit *Degrassi: The Next Generation* in 2013. She also had minor roles in several films, with the most prominent productions being the horror movie *Saw VI* (2009) and the 2014 remake of the 1987 film *RoboCop*. As she received attention for *Wynonna Earp* she continued to appear in other shows as well. These included the political drama *Designated Survivor* in 2016, the Canadian sitcom *Letterkenny* (2016–), and the crime drama *Bad Blood* beginning in 2018.

EARLY LIFE AND EDUCATION

Melanie Neige Scrofano was born and grew up in Ottawa, Ontario. Her mother was of French-Canadian descent and had a government job. Her father, of Italian descent, was an engineer. "I think being Italian-Canadian is very different than being Italian-American, which is what we usually see on TV or in the movies," she told A. R. Wilson for *TV, Eh?*, a website devoted to Canadian television (30 Oct. 2018). "There's a certain flavor to it." Scrofano picked up a love of storytelling from her father, an interest in music from her mother, who played the piano, and an affinity for cooking from her Italian grandmother.

Scrofano began modeling in Canada at the age of thirteen. Finding success, by the time she was sixteen she was often traveling between Ottawa, Toronto, and Montreal for jobs. Her agent eventually suggested that she try her hand at acting, and though she had not considered that as a career, she came to find she was better suited to it than she was to modeling. (One of her earliest roles, in fact, was playing a model.) The experience opened her eyes to the exciting, if daunting, prospects that could lie ahead. "I realized how much there was to acting," she told Liz Allemang, for *Panoram Italia* (5 Dec. 2012). "You could work on it forever and never become a real actor. There's always room for improvement. . . . In acting, the possibilities for who you portray and how you portray are limitless."

Photo by iDominick via Wikimedia Commons

EARLY ACTING CAREER

Early on in her acting career Scrofano "paid her dues" with an array of bit parts. Her first credited role came in 2002, when she appeared in season six of an MTV anthology program called *Undressed*, known for its depictions of relationships among young people. The following year she portrayed the girlfriend of a police officer in an episode of the television miniseries *Mob Stories*. In 2006 she moved to Toronto permanently to help establish a foothold in the Canadian television industry. To support herself, she spent a short time as a barista at a Starbucks coffeeshop.

As with many novice actors, Scrofano's career continued in a similarly low-profile vein for some time. She built up a portfolio of parts in such shows as *Naked Josh* (2004), *Beautiful People* (2006), *Jeff Ltd.* (2006), and *Supernatural* (2007). In addition to appearances in series, she took roles in television movies including *Anne of Green Gables: A New Beginning* (2008). In 2009 she played cult member Leslie Van Houten in the biopic *Manson*, which depicted the days leading up to the infamous 1969 Tate-La Bianca murders. That same year marked her turn as Gena in *Saw VI*, which, if not a blockbuster, was at least part of a well-known series of films and, therefore, her most notable appearance to that point. In the film, her character pretends to be pregnant in an unsuccessful effort to avoid being killed by the franchise's sadistic murderer.

Higher-profile parts followed. In 2010 Scrofano had significant roles on two Canadian television series, the mockumentary *Pure Pwnage* and the comedy *Being Erica*. from 2012 to

2014 she had a recurring role in *The Listener*, a show about a young paramedic with paranormal powers. Film appearances included the horror thriller *Nurse 3D* (2013) and the big-budget *RoboCop* (2014). In 2014 she also appeared in two similarly titled but quite different Canadian films: *Wolves*, a supernatural drama directed by David Hayter, and *We Were Wolves*, an independent film about two brothers who reconcile after the death of their father. She then had a recurring role in the series *Gangland Undercover* (2015).

WYNONNA EARP

After years of minor parts, Scrofano earned a new level of fame in 2016. That year she appeared in the title role in *Wynonna Earp*, which debuted on the cable TV channel SyFy. Based on a comic book created by Beau Smith, the show's premise is that the descendants of storied gunslinger Wyatt Earp are forced to battle demons and other supernatural beings. "It's a plot that allows viewers to enjoy a unique blend of genres, mixing elements of paranormal thriller and horror with a modern western vibe," Eric Volmers wrote for the *Calgary Herald* (31 Mar. 2016). "Our protagonist gets to blast away at demons with both Wyatt's supernaturally enhanced Peacemaker and any number of bad-ass assault rifles. She gets to ride motorcycles, chug shots of whisky and exercise that new-found prowess in hand-to-hand combat." The action takes place, for the most part, in Purgatory, a mysterious small town where Wynonna and her sister Waverly grew up and where "revenants," resurrected outlaws from Wyatt Earp's time, roam around wreaking havoc. Wyatt Earp's former sidekick, Doc Holliday (played by Tim Rozon), has also been resurrected and serves (eventually) as a love interest for Wynonna.

The show, helmed by Calgary-based director Emily Andras, proved to be quite popular and critically successful. "If a sci-fi Western is even remotely your thing, the charms of *Wynonna Earp* are impossible to resist," Jordan Crucchiola wrote for *Vulture* (10 Aug. 2018), for example. The show also invited frequent comparison to cult hits such as *Buffy the Vampire Slayer*. Like *Buffy* before it, *Wynonna Earp* earned a particularly enthusiastic fan base, self-styled as "Earpers." The fandom even gained a measure of attention in the television world for its cohesion and kindness; stories abounded of fans chipping in when a fellow member of the community faced a health emergency or natural disaster or simply needed a place to stay during a convention. Even on Twitter, known for being a hotbed of vitriol, fans remained upbeat. Passionate fans were instrumental in winning the series the 2018 E! People's Choice Award in the category of sci-fi/fantasy show—despite its absence from the initial ballot—by mounting a write-in campaign.

Scrofano readily acknowledged the importance of the fans in the show's success, and therefore her own. "We wouldn't be here without the Earpers," she told Crucchiola after three seasons had aired, but she also noted the challenges of having such an invested fanbase. "At the end of the day, we are storytellers. The thing that becomes tricky—and this is not exclusive to our show—is you have to balance what people would like to see and what is honest to the people who created it."

OTHER ROLES

While *Wynonna Earp* launched Scrofano's career to new heights, it was not her only project of 2016. She additionally appeared that year on the television series *Damien* and *Designated Survivor* in recurring roles. She also had a part in the debut season of the Canadian sitcom *Letterkenny*, playing the character Mrs. McMurray, and regularly appeared on later seasons as well after the show proved successful. Along with her starring role as Earp, these projects raised her profile, especially in Canada.

In 2018 Scrofano took on a role as a mob-wife-turned-informant in the television series *Bad Blood*. Another Canadian production, the show is a dramatization of the life of Montreal Mafia boss Vito Rizzuto, known in the news as the "Teflon Don." "Every time I came to set, I had to go to some dark places," Scrofano told Wilson of her experience of the character. "You know, she's either angry or crying or terrified. . . . You shoot those things and you get really emotional and, afterwards, the world just moves on, but you still felt all those things and you really need a hug."

PERSONAL LIFE

Scrofano and her husband, Jeff, had a son in 2013 and another in 2017. Although she has revealed little about her personal life to the media, her second pregnancy was notable for coinciding with the development of *Wynonna Earp*'s second season. Initially, Scrofano was worried about revealing her pregnancy to Andras, fearing that the showrunner would be upset or that it would prove disruptive to the shooting schedule. "I broke down in my doctor's office," Scrofano recalled to Maureen Ryan for *Variety* (7 July 2017). "I was terrified. I was scared that she would be mad, or feel like I was doing it to her somehow." Rather than being upset, however, Andras simply wrote the pregnancy into the show, and at the end of the season, Wynonna gives birth to a baby girl. Scrofano's second son was born shortly after production ended.

Scrofano continued to do many of her own stunts for the duration of the filming, noting that she did not want to let her fellow actors down or cause doubt in the industry that a pregnant woman could be a worthy costar, even in a physically demanding action role. "I was so tired all the time," she admitted to Ryan. "But the whole experience—now that I've done that, I feel like I can literally do anything."

SUGGESTED READING

Allemang, Liz. "The Many Lives of Melanie Scrofano." *Panoram Italia*, 5 Dec. 2012, www.panoramitalia.com/index.php/2012/12/05/the-many-lives-of-melanie-scrofano/. Accessed 3 Jan. 2019.

Scrofano, Melanie. "*Wynonna Earp* Star Melanie Scrofano Doesn't Want You Calling Her Show 'Cheesy.'" Interview by Jordan Crucchiola. *Vulture*, 10 Aug. 2018, www.vulture.com/2018/08/wynonna-earp-season-3-melanie-scrofano-interview.html. Accessed 3 Jan. 2019.

Scrofano, Melanie, and Emily Andras. "*Wynonna Earp* Exclusive: Showrunner Emily Andras and Star Melanie Scrofano Break Down That Big Reveal." Interview by Maureen Ryan. *Variety*, 7 July 2017, variety.com/2017/tv/features/wynonna-earp-emily-andras-melanie-scrofano-news-exclusive-1202476757/. Accessed 3 Jan. 2019.

Volmers, Eric. "Calgary-Shot Wynonna Earp Ready for Action." *Calgary Herald*, 31 Mar. 2016, calgaryherald.com/entertainment/television/calgary-shot-wynonna-earp-ready-to-action. Accessed 3 Jan. 2019.

Wilson, A. R. "Bad Blood: Melanie Scrofano on Valentina, Shooting Emotional Scenes, and Wynonna Earp." *TV, Eh?*, 30 Oct. 2018, www.tv-eh.com/2018/10/30/bad-blood-melanie-scrofano-on-valentina-shooting-emotional-scenes-and-wynonna-earp/. Accessed 3 Jan. 2019.

Young, Sage. "Why the Women of 'Wynonna Earp' Feel So Real, According to Star Melanie Scrofano." *Bustle*, 27 July 2018, www.bustle.com/p/why-the-women-of-wynonna-earp-feel-so-real-according-to-star-melanie-scrofano-9870333. Accessed 3 Jan. 2019.

Yu, Alan. "How *Wynonna Earp* Built the World's Nicest TV Fandom." *Vulture*, 23 July 2018, www.vulture.com/2018/07/wynonna-earp-fandom-earpers.html. Accessed 3 Jan. 2019.

SELECTED WORKS

Saw VI, 2009; *Pure Pwnage*, 2010; *Being Erica*, 2010; *The Listener*, 2012–14; *Gangland Undercover*, 2015; *Damien*, 2016; *Designated Survivor*, 2016; *Letterkenny*, 2016– ; *Wynonna Earp*, 2016– ; *Bad Blood*, 2018

—*Mari Rich*

Kierra Sheard

Date of birth: June 20, 1987
Occupation: Gospel singer

Kierra "Kiki" Sheard was born into a gospel dynasty. Her mother, Karen Clark Sheard, is a member of the Grammy Award–winning gospel group the Clark Sisters and a successful gospel solo artist. Her maternal grandmother, Mattie Moss Clark, was a choir director and is considered a pioneer of modern gospel music. Sheard continued her family's legacy by becoming a successful gospel singer in her own right and bringing the genre to a new generation of listeners. As Kelly Carter stated, as quoted by Patrick Cole for the *Light* (21 Jan. 2007), she "does what her mother and aunts did so famously . . . take church music and make it accessible to a mainstream ear." Her legacy notwithstanding, Sheard is an individual artist, incorporating elements of hip-hop and R & B in her music, musical elements absent from her maternal family's work. She often collaborates with her younger brother, an R & B producer. Predictably, her music sometimes runs afoul of gospel purists, but critics praise her ability to continually incorporate contemporary sounds into her music. Sheard got her start in the music business at ten, when she appeared on a song called "The Will of God" on her mother's 1997 solo debut album. Her performance won her a coveted Stellar Award. She released her own debut album, *I Owe You*, featuring the hit song "You Don't Know," at the age of sixteen in 2004. In 2010, she appeared in a film called *Preacher's Kid*. In 2013, Sheard and her famous family—her father is a well-known pastor in Detroit—appeared on a season of a reality television show called *The Sheards* on BET. By 2019, Sheard, well known for the hit song "God in Me" with gospel duo Mary Mary, had released six studio albums, founded a youth ministry, and designed a line of plus-sized clothing called Eleven60. In 2019, it was announced that Sheard would play her mother in a Clark Sisters biopic for Lifetime.

GOSPEL MUSIC ROYALTY

Kierra Sheard was born on June 20, 1987. She grew up in the Greenwich Park neighborhood of Detroit. Her grandmother, Mattie Moss Clark, was a legendary songwriter and choir director. A pioneer of modern gospel music, Clark shepherded her five daughters—Jacky Clark Chisholm, Denise Clark Bradford, Elbernita "Twinkie" Clark Terrell, Dorinda Clark Cole, and Sheard's mother, Karen Clark Sheard—to gospel fame as the Clark Sisters. The Detroit-born Clark Sisters rose to prominence in the era of Motown, and scored crossover hit songs such as "Is My Living in Vain" (1980) and the megahit

Photo by Johnny Louis/FilmMagic via Getty Images

"You Brought the Sunshine" in 1981. The Clark Sisters, who continued to perform into 2019, are considered one of the most influential acts in gospel music. Sheard's father, Bishop John Drew Sheard, is the pastor of the Greater Emmanuel Institution Church of God in Christ in Detroit. Sheard's younger brother, John Drew "J. Drew" Sheard II, is an R & B music producer. She began singing in the choir at her father's church—a place so familiar to her that she has jokingly referred to it as her second sibling—when she was just six years old. At ten, she was featured on her mother's 1997 Grammy-nominated solo debut album, *Finally Karen*, appearing on the song "The Will of God." The song (sometimes called "The Safest Place") was recorded live at the Bailey Cathedral in Detroit. Young Sheard's performance—an uncanny interpretation of the run-heavy Clark sound—was so impressive that she won a Stellar Award for Best Children's Performance for it in 1997.

I OWE YOU

Sheard continued to perform with her mother throughout her childhood. In an episode of the BET web series called #BLX, she recalled her first talent show. She had chosen to sing the hit R & B song "The Boy Is Mine," a duet featuring singers Brandy and Monica. Her mother came to a rehearsal before the show. "My mom came in, she changed my song on the spot in front of everybody, I was so embarrassed," Sheard said, as quoted by Christine Thomasos for the *Christian Post* (12 Feb. 2015). The elder Sheard informed her daughter that she would be singing the hymn "His Eye Is on the Sparrow" instead. Sheard performed the version as it was sung by

hip-hop legend Lauryn Hill in the popular 1993 film *Sister Act II*. "That changed my life because that's who I am today," Sheard said. "As a Christian singer, she told me to not be ashamed of what I do."

Thanks to her early success with "The Will of God," as well as other songs she had been featured on, record companies were vying to sign Sheard. Sheard released her debut album, *I Owe You*, in 2004. *I Owe You*—coproduced by Grammy Award–winning hip-hop producer Rodney Jerkins and Sheard's brother, among others—reached number one on the Billboard Gospel Album chart and cracked the top thirty on the Billboard R & B/Hip-Hop chart. Stan North, for the blog *Gospel Flava* (7 Sept. 2004), began his favorable review with a line that sums up Sheard's music career to date: "This isn't her grandmother's music." He went on to describe *I Owe You* as a "shimmering and auspicious debut." The Jerkins-produced "You Don't Know" from that album won a Dove Award from the Gospel Music Association (GMA) for Urban Recorded Song of the Year.

Sheard graduated from Walled Lake Central High School in 2005. She released a remix album called *Just Until . . .* the same year. That album peaked at number ten on the Billboard Top Gospel Albums chart and became a surprise hit in Japan.

GRAMMY-NOMINATED ALBUMS

Sheard's second studio album, *This Is Me*, debuted at number one on the Billboard Top Gospel Album chart in 2006. It was nominated for a Grammy Award for Best Contemporary R & B Gospel Album and won the 2007 Dove Award for Urban Album of the Year. Paul Poulton for *Cross Rhythms* (19 Oct. 2006), the British Christian media website, offered reserved praise: "Kiki continues her push towards becoming one of the main players in the gospel arena, with a good-looking set of songs." He concluded, "Possibly not quite as impactful as her stunning debut but still slickly produced R & B gospel." In 2008, Sheard released her third album, *Bold Right Life*. The album received an enthusiastic response from critics. Dave Derbyshire of *Cross Rhythms* (14 Mar. 2009) wrote that Sheard was "really finding her own sound, morphing an R & B vibe and Clark Sisters–style harmonies into worship music for a new generation who might otherwise find praise and worship . . . a bit boring." *Bold Right Life* was nominated for a Grammy Award for Best Contemporary R & B Gospel Album.

Also in 2008, Sheard sang with the gospel duo Mary Mary on the single "God in Me." The song peaked at number five on the Billboard R & B/Hip-Hop chart and at number one on the Billboard Hot Gospels Songs chart. "God in Me" remained one of Sheard's most popular songs into 2019. In 2009, Sheard released *Kiki's Mixtape*, an extended play (EP) featuring remixes and several new songs. The following year, she appeared in the musical drama *Preacher's Kid* (2010), starring LeToya Luckett-Walker, and the drama *Blessed and Cursed* (2010). In 2011, Sheard graduated from Wayne State University with a bachelor's degree in English.

FREE AND OTHER PROJECTS

Sheard's next album, *Free* (2011), was released by her family's record label Karew Records—the name is a portmanteau of Karen and Drew—which was created in 2009. "I've never wrestled in my mind so much as I have around the time of when I was writing this record," Sheard recalled, as quoted by Cole. She looked to excise bad experiences and reach out to others who might be going through hard times. "I wanted to put in my music freedom . . . from dysfunctional relationships [and] from what you may have done or gone through," Sheard explained. Continuing, she stated, "So many of us in the church, we've been taught to pacify our issues rather than deal with them . . . I just wanted to be free and really grow." In the album, a full collaboration with her brother, Sheard leaned into the R & B sounds that made "God in Me" so popular.

In 2014, Sheard released *Graceland*. The album, also produced by J. Drew, samples iconic Clark Sisters renditions such as "There Is a Balm in Gilead" and "He'll Turn Your Scars into Stars." *Graceland*'s overall sound, however, was compared to secular pop artists such as Beyoncé and Rihanna. Reviewers singled out the inspirational, hip-hop-inspired song "2nd Win" for particular praise. Both *Free* and *Graceland* peaked at number one on the Billboard Top Gospel Albums chart.

In 2013, Sheard and her family appeared on a season of a BET reality television series called *The Sheards*. In 2015, Sheard served as a celebrity judge on BET's gospel singing competition show, *Sunday's Best*. The same year, she released an eight-track EP called *LED*. In 2019, Sheard was featured on singer and producer Sir the Baptist's single "Showing Off."

PERSONAL LIFE

In 2011, Sheard was briefly engaged to Welton T. Smith IV, the pastor and founder of the New Life Family Church in Detroit. She founded a youth ministry, named after her album *Bold Right Life*, in 2009. In 2015, Sheard launched a plus-size clothing line called Eleven60, named after her mother's birth month and year. In 2019, the popular line was made available through Macy's department store.

SUGGESTED READING

Cole, Patrick, and Kelly Carter. "Gospel Singer Kierra Sheard Asserts Her Independence on a High-Energy New Album." *The Light*, Praise Indy, 21 Jan. 2007, praiseindy.com/1480492/gospel-singer-kierra-sheard-asserts-her-independence-on-a-high-energy-new-album/. Accessed 21 June 2019.

Derbyshire, Dave. Review of *Bold Right Life*, by Kierra Sheard. *Cross Rhythms*, 14 Mar. 2009, www.crossrhythms.co.uk/products/Kierra_Sheard/Bold_Right_Life/50224/. Accessed 21 June 2019.

North, Stan. Review of *I Owe You*, by Kierra Sheard. *Gospel Flava*, 7 Sept. 2004, www.gospelflava.com/reviews/kierrasheard.html. Accessed 21 June 2019.

Poulton, Paul. Review of *This Is Me*, by Kierra Sheard. *Cross Rhythms*, 19 Oct. 2006, www.crossrhythms.co.uk/products/Kierra_Kiki_Sheard/This_Is_Me/18937/. Accessed 21 June 2019.

Sheard, Kierra. "Being: Kierra Sheard." Interview by Britni Daniella. *Ebony*, 24 Mar. 2017, www.ebony.com/entertainment/being-kierra-sheard/. Accessed 21 June 2019.

Thomasos, Christine. "Kierra Sheard Reminisces about Life Changing Start in Gospel Music." *Christian Post*, 12 Feb. 2015, www.christianpost.com/news/kierra-sheard-reminisces-about-life-changing-start-in-gospel-music.html. Accessed 21 June 2019.

SELECTED WORKS

I Owe You, 2004; *This Is Me*, 2006; *Bold Right Life*, 2008; *Free*, 2011; *Graceland*, 2014

—*Molly Hagan*

Ben Simmons

Date of birth: July 20, 1996
Occupation: Basketball player

When the Philadelphia 76ers selected Ben Simmons as the first overall pick in the 2016 National Basketball Association (NBA) Draft, the moment was in many ways the culmination of years of enthusiasm and speculation that had surrounded the young athlete since his early days on the court. The son of former basketball player Dave Simmons, who played professionally in Australia, Simmons began playing the sport himself as a young child. He soon attracted significant attention for his skills playing for the Australian junior national team and then in the United States at Montverde Academy in Florida. During his single season with Louisiana State University, he further demonstrated the talents that made him one of the most talked-about prospective draft picks of 2016.

Photo by Keith Allison via Wikimedia Commons

Simmons, however, focused more on the game than on the hype surrounding him. "For me, there's only one thing you can do; play as hard as you can, and do what you need to do on the floor. And that's play your game," he said, as reported by Steve Duck for *Complex Australia* (21 Aug. 2018). Nevertheless, Simmons had significant goals in mind upon joining the 76ers, which prior to his drafting had not won a championship since 1983. "I believe we can win a ring but it comes down to everyone playing their role," he told Conor Duffy and Roscoe Whalan for *ABC* (30 Jan. 2018). "It's not easy. It takes time. It may not happen this year or next year, but we're going to get there."

EARLY LIFE AND EDUCATION
Benjamin David Simmons was born on July 20, 1996, in Fitzroy, Victoria, Australia. He was the second of two children born to Dave and Julie Simmons and grew up with four older half-siblings. Simmons's father was an American-born former professional basketball player who played for several teams in the Australian National Basketball League, including the Melbourne Tigers, over the course of more than a decade. As a child growing up in Newcastle, Australia, Simmons learned to play basketball from his father at a young age. Although he also played and enjoyed Australian rules football, he particularly excelled at basketball and soon began playing against much older children. As a teenager, he attended Box Hill Senior Secondary College near Melbourne, where he became a valuable contributor to the school's basketball team. He also played for the junior Australian national team at events

such as the 2012 FIBA U17 World Championship, where the team claimed second place.

Seeking to progress further as a basketball player, Simmons moved to the United States in 2013, transferring to Montverde Academy, a private preparatory school in Florida. Simmons eventually joined the school's varsity basketball team, where he showcased skills on the court that gained him significant attention from local fans. "It was crazy when I had little kids waiting outside the locker room as a sophomore," he told David Sygall for the *Sydney Morning Herald* (15 Aug. 2017). "Then in my senior year I used to come out of the locker room and it was packed. I couldn't leave for an hour because there were so many people just waiting." During his time at Montverde, Simmons also gained the attention of colleges hoping to recruit him, and he ultimately committed to attending Louisiana State University (LSU).

LOUISIANA STATE UNIVERSITY
After graduating from Montverde Academy in 2015, Simmons enrolled in LSU, where he joined the LSU Tigers men's basketball team. The team competed in the Southeastern Conference (SEC) of Division I of the National Collegiate Athletic Association (NCAA), the highest division of collegiate sports. Simmons was heavily touted as one of the best young players in the world and a savior for the LSU basketball program. However, he soon became unhappy with the treatment of athletes under NCAA rules, which prevented student athletes from being paid for their work while still enabling them to serve as advertisements and profit centers for the university athletics departments. He later described the business of college sports as "dirty business" in an interview with Maverick Carter for *Uninterrupted* (2017). Although Simmons had made it clear that he intended to spend only a single year at LSU, the university featured him prominently in advertising and also required him to participate in numerous media-focused activities, which he disliked.

Over the course of the 2015–16 college basketball season, Simmons lived up to the hype. He amassed impressive statistics, averaging 19.2 points, 11.8 rebounds, and 4.8 assists per game. Simmons led the SEC in total rebounds and field goals and was third in total points with 632. Yet despite his strong performance, the Tigers had a middling season, earning an SEC win-loss record of 11–7. The team tied for third in the SEC and competed in the conference tournament but ultimately lost to Texas A&M University in the semifinals. The Tigers did not compete in the 2016 NCAA Tournament.

Although Simmons had a productive season during his single year at LSU, he later suggested that he may have benefited from immediately entering the NBA Draft after high school. "I think I would have learned a lot more being around professional athletes," he told Carter during his first season as a professional player. "Looking at it now, I don't really even know what I learned, financially, or just being a person at LSU. I think I've learned a lot more . . . being a pro, than I did at LSU."

PROFESSIONAL BASKETBALL

Following his year in Louisiana, Simmons entered the 2016 NBA Draft to the wide expectation that he would be the top selection. Indeed, on June 23, 2016, the Philadelphia 76ers chose him as the first overall pick in the draft, a position that reflected not only the level of media attention that had surrounded him since high school but also the extent of the skills he demonstrated on the court. Simmons signed a rookie contract with the team in early July. He devoted that summer to preparing for his NBA career rather than joining the Australian national team at the Rio De Janeiro Olympic Games, as some observers had expected. However, he later announced his intention to rejoin the Australian team for the 2020 Olympics.

Simmons had planned to play for the 76ers during the 2016–17 season, and some fans and sports commentators were optimistic that his addition to the team would be the change needed to propel Philadelphia to new heights. Some even suggested he could make the 76ers contenders for the NBA championship, which the team had not won in several decades. Both Simmons's plans and fans' expectations changed, however, when Simmons broke a bone in his foot during the preseason training camp. The injury required him to undergo surgery and extensive rehabilitation, preventing him from playing in what would have been his rookie season.

Although the injury represented a disappointing setback for Simmons and the team, Simmons remained positive about his future. "I'm looking forward to just rehabbing every day and getting stronger," he was quoted as saying in an article posted to the *NBA*'s website (26 Oct. 2016). "I want to be the best at what I'm doing now and that's rehab. . . . I'll have my first game eventually. My time will come."

PHILADELPHIA 76ERS

Simmons finally made his NBA debut on October 18, 2017, appearing in Philadelphia's 2017–18 season opener against the Washington Wizards. Although the 76ers ultimately lost the game by five points, Simmons made a substantial contribution to the team, scoring eighteen points, ten rebounds, and five assists. He went on to put forth a dominant performance in his first ten games, becoming the first player in the NBA ever to record at least 100 rebounds, 80

assists, and 170 points that quickly to begin a season. Milestones continued to pile up as his strong play continued. In March 2018 he became just the third rookie ever to make it to 1,000 points, 500 assists, and 500 rebounds, joining NBA legends Magic Johnson and Oscar Robertson

Over the course of his rookie season, Simmons averaged 15.8 points, 8.1 rebounds, and 8.2 assists per game, earning four rookie of the month selections. He played a major role in the success of the 76ers, who rode a season-ending winning streak to a 52–30 record, good for third place in the NBA's Eastern Conference. Entering the play-offs for the first time since 2012, the 76ers beat the Miami Heat in the first round and advanced to the conference semifinals. There they lost to the Boston Celtics four games to one.

After the 2017–18 season, Simmons's strong performance was recognized when he was awarded NBA Rookie of the Year honors. He was also unanimously named to the NBA All-Rookie First Team. Although pleased with his performance, Simmons often expressed the desire for continued improvement, which he noted differentiated him from some other professional players. "Guys get [to the NBA] and they're comfortable. They're happy to be where they are, they're happy with the money they make and they're happy just to be in the league," he told Duck. "There's differences between certain guys in the league, where they're just happy to play and then there's guys who wanna get better and continue to grow and get to the next level."

Before the 2018–19 season began, many basketball commentators expected Simmons and teammate Joel Embiid to lead Philadelphia on a deep playoff run, especially following the departure of rival superstar LeBron James from the Eastern Conference. However, Simmons had a more immediate goal in mind. "I wanna be an All-Star," he told Olgun Uluc for *Fox Sports Australia* (17 Aug. 2018). "Those are the best players in the league. I think setting myself up for little goals like that along the way just keeps me motivated." While the 76ers began the season with somewhat mixed results, Simmons consistently performed well early on. In October 2018, the 76ers exercised the fourth-year option of his rookie contract, ensuring team control through the 2019–20 season.

PERSONAL LIFE

In addition to playing basketball, Simmons enjoys playing video games. Among his favorites was the NBA 2K series, for which he appeared on the cover of the Australian edition of the game NBA 2K19. A dual citizen of the United States and Australia, Simmons lived primarily in the former after entering the NBA but enjoyed returning to Australia, where many of his friends and family members remained. He noted in interviews that he especially appreciated the laid-back culture of his birthplace. "We're so down to earth and love our sports and just love having a good time," he explained to Duffy and Whalen. "I think that's one of the things that I miss."

Simmons dedicated portions of his visits to Australia to promoting the sport of basketball and attempting to develop the skills of talented young players. His efforts included children's basketball camps, during which he sought to give meaningful advice and support to the young attendees. "I have a great opportunity now to be able to give back to the kids here, and to Australian basketball," he told Oliver Kay for the *Pick and Roll* (20 Aug. 2018). "[To] just be a good role model to them, and just [be] someone they can look up to and lean on."

SUGGESTED READING

Duffy, Conor, and Roscoe Whalan. "Ben Simmons on the NBA Limelight, Coming Home to Australia, Donald Trump and Olympic Gold." *ABC*, 30 Jan. 2018, www.abc.net.au/news/2018-01-30/ben-simmons-home-and-family-keep-me-humble/9369826. Accessed 9 Nov. 2018.

Kay, Oliver. "Ben Simmons' Basketball Camp Demonstrates His Passion for Australian Hoops." *The Pick and Roll*, 20 Aug. 2018, pickandroll.com.au/ben-simmons-camp-passion-australian-hoops/. Accessed 9 Nov. 2018.

"No. 1 Pick Ben Simmons Says No Timetable for Return from Broken Foot." *NBA*, 26 Oct. 2016, www.nba.com/article/2016/10/26/philadelphia-76ers-ben-simmons-no-timetable-return. Accessed 9 Nov. 2018.

Simmons, Ben. "Kneading Dough: Ben Simmons." Interview with Maverick Carter. *Uninterrupted*, 2017, www.uninterrupted.com/watch/CiQZqsrP/kneading-dough-ben-simmons?playlist=N4M8xKh5. Accessed 9 Nov. 2018.

Simmons, Ben, and Christian Petracca. "Interview: Ben Simmons and Christian Petracca Discuss Pressure, Pre-Game Fits and 'Astroworld.'" Interview by Steve Duck. *Complex Australia*, 21 Aug. 2018, www.complex.com/sports/2018/08/ben-simmons-christian-petracca/. Accessed 9 Nov. 2018.

Sygall, David. "The Hype Around Louisiana State University Star Ben Simmons Is Warranted, but It's a Long Way to the Top If You Want to Pick and Roll." *Sydney Morning Herald*, 15 Aug. 2015, www.smh.com.au/sport/basketball/the-hype-around-louisiana-state-university-star-ben-simmons-is-warranted-but-its-a-long-way-to-the-top-if-you-want-to-pick-and-roll-20150815-gizs4d.html. Accessed 9 Nov. 2018.

Uluc, Olgun. "Ben Simmons' Goal for the 2018–19 NBA Season: I Wanna Be an All-Star." *Fox Sports Australia*, 17 Aug. 2018, www.foxsports.com.au/basketball/nba/ben-simmons-goal-for-the-201819-nba-season-i-wanna-be-an-allstar/news-story/e76fc10f4545aa0fec9a739858c94bc1?nk=369635d09ab9ee2c65d6dbd94d8072f2-1541862135. Accessed 9 Nov. 2018.

—*Joy Crelin*

Simon Sinek

Date of birth: October 9, 1973
Occupation: Leadership expert

Simon Sinek is a motivational speaker and best-selling author known for a 2009 TEDx Talk called "How Great Leaders Inspire Action." One of the TED brand's most famous lectures, it has been viewed over 42 million times. In the video, Sinek, a marketer who trained as a cultural anthropologist, shares a "discovery" that he claims profoundly changed his worldview. Using such diverse examples as Apple, a computer company, and Dr. Martin Luther King Jr., the late civil rights leader, Sinek identifies a concept he calls the golden circle. In his TEDx talk he drew three circles arranged in a bull's eye to illustrate his point. The third circle, the outer layer, represents "what." All companies, he said, know what they do. The second circle represents "how." Some companies, he said, know how they do what they do. The innermost circle represents "why." Very few companies, he said, know why they do what they do, outside of making money. Apple ("Think different") and King ("I have a dream"), Sinek argues, were successful because they could identify this elusive "why," and they used it to inspire people to buy what they were selling. "People don't buy what you do, they buy why you do it," he concluded. The talk's success set the stage for Sinek's first book, *Start with Why: How Great Leaders Inspire Everyone to Take Action*, published in 2009. Sinek is also the author of *Leaders Eat Last: Why Some Teams Pull Together and Others Don't* (2014), about good leadership and fostering cooperation; *Together Is Better: A Little Book of Inspiration* (2016), an illustrated parable about leadership; and *The Infinite Game* (2018), about building companies that last.

Sinek is also known for "Millennials in the Workplace," a 2016 viral interview with entrepreneur Tom Bilyeu for *Inside Quest* in which Sinek addressed the working lives of members of the millennial generation, which generally refers to people who were born in the 1980s or 1990s. Sinek's various opinions about millennials drew

Photo by Startwithwhy via Wikimedia Commons

enthusiastic and heated responses from the Internet. Sinek argued that members of the Millennial generation "were told that they were special all the time" and earned "participation medals for coming in last." He described a generation of people with precipitously low self-esteem, unable to comprehend a world in which they are not constantly celebrated. Later, Sinek discussed the interview with Rachel Browne for the *Sydney Morning Herald* (4 Feb. 2017). "It touched a nerve," he said. "For a lot of people who lead millennials, it gave them some insight. The overwhelming majority of millennials said: 'Thank you, we feel understood.' That was very heartening."

EARLY LIFE AND EDUCATION

Simon Sinek was born to parents Susan and Steve Sinek in Wimbledon, England, in 1973. Sinek's mother, who is of Hungarian Jewish descent, published a baking cookbook in 2013. Sinek has a sister named Sara Sinek Toborowsky, with whom he is extremely close and who serves as the co-CEO of Start with Why, Sinek's consultancy. As a young child, Sinek and his family lived all over the world, spending time in London and Johannesburg, South Africa, where his grandparents lived. Sinek's family moved to New Jersey when he was teenager. He attended Northern Valley Regional High School in Demarest and graduated in 1991. He studied cultural anthropology at Brandeis University in Waltham, Massachusetts. Sinek was particularly interested in ethnography, or the study of how people live in their environments. This line of inquiry would later inspire his views on

business culture and leadership. He graduated with a bachelor's degree in 1995. Sinek briefly attended the City University of London with the intention of becoming a lawyer, but quickly decided against pursuing that career. He took a job in marketing, with Euro RSCG (rebranded Havas Worldwide in 2012), instead. He also worked for the New York–based British advertising firm Ogilvy & Mather. Sinek launched his own advertising and marketing company, Sinek Partners, in 2002. His clients came to include General Electric and ABC Sports.

START WITH WHY

In 2005, Sinek suffered a crisis of purpose. "Superficially, life was good—but I was putting all my energy into acting happy," he told Gregory Zuckerman for *Brandeis Magazine* (Summer 2017). "I had lost my passion and was embarrassed to admit I was struggling." He added: "I knew what I did and how I did it, but not why I did it." He began asking friends and clients more "why" questions, like why do you work in a particular industry? But also, why do you get up in the morning? Asking people to explain themselves in this way, he found, seemed to inspire them. To better explain his idea to a client in Vancouver, Sinek began drawing circles on paper—the birth of the golden circle. The client was so impressed he told his CEO, who paid Sinek $5,000 for a consulting session. "I realized I can make a living helping other companies and entrepreneurs discover their own why," he told Zuckerman. In 2007 he started a consultancy, Start with Why, in New York. He began traveling as a consultant and public speaker, expounding on the golden circle.

Jennifer Walzer, the CEO of a company called Backup My Info! (acquired by j2Global/ KeepItSafe in 2014) wrote about her experience working with Sinek in an article for the *New York Times* (16 Sept. 2009). "Mr. Sinek's approach started with an internal analysis. And by internal, I mean he sat me and my team down to find out what motivated each of us," she wrote. After much discussion and thought, she discovered that she had founded her company to help people, and that most of her employees shared this motivation. "The process of figuring this out was exciting and painful and ultimately revealing," in terms of hiring staff and building her company, she wrote. The same year, 2009, Sinek gave his enormously popular TEDx Talk, and published his first book, *Start with Why: How Great Leaders Inspire Everyone to Take Action*. In addition to explaining his golden circle concept, Sinek included in the book what he calls the science of why. Citing psychiatrist and neuroscientist Peter Whybrow of the University of California, Los Angeles (UCLA), Sinek claimed that the "how" and "why" circles correspond to the limbic system of the brain, "where gut decisions come from," he explained to Zuckerman. "Our limbic brain is powerful enough to drive behavior that sometimes contradicts our rational and analytical understanding of a situation."

Zuckerman and others have duly pointed out that the human brain is more complex than this rather neat assessment of it. Zuckerman also notes that similar ideas—collectively known as limbic system theory—have been around since the 1950s. But Sinek, who offers no empirical evidence of his claims, remains unequivocal about the science of why. "The power of why is not opinion," he told Zuckerman. "It's biology." *Start with Why* became a New York Times Best Seller, inspiring, in 2017, a workbook called *Find Your Why: A Practical Guide to Discovering Purpose for You and Your Team*, which Sinek wrote with David Mead and Peter Docker.

LEADERS EAT LAST
Sinek published his second book, *Leaders Eat Last: Why Some Teams Pull Together and Others Don't*, in 2014. The title, he explained to Alec Hogg for South Africa's *Biz News* (1 Mar. 2016), "is a metaphor just like we feed our children before we feed ourselves." True leadership, he said, is "not about being in charge, it's about taking care of those in our charge." The book collects Sinek's observations working with various company teams as a consultant. Teams with leaders that fostered environments of cooperation and trust were most successful. (He uses the military, where people risk their lives for one another, as an extreme example.) Sinek writes that leaders must build a circle of safety, a multifaceted concept that has to do with building interdependence among team members. Like *Start with Why*, Sinek uses science to back up his ideas. He writes that leaders are tasked with balancing various brain chemicals. Companies that focus on results to the detriment of their employees' well-being over-prioritize the rush of so-called "selfish" chemicals, endorphins and dopamine, which Sinek says are necessary for helping individuals survive and thrive. Leaders must also learn to value oxytocin, "chemical love," and serotonin, the "leadership chemical," responsible for pride in others, both of which create social bonds, thus ensuring the long-term survival of the group. Michael Schein of *Forbes* (13 June 2018) criticized Sinek for using scientific jargon to peddle pedestrian ideas. Mocking Sinek's allusions to the limbic system and dopamine, Schien wrote: "Is all this accurate? Who cares? Sinek knows scientific lingo is one of the best ways to sell ideas . . . . Straight talk and common sense only go so far. Sometimes it pays to over-complicate your simple messages."

TOGETHER IS BETTER AND THE INFINITE GAME
In 2016, Sinek published a picture book called *Together Is Better: A Little Book of Inspiration*, illustrated by Ethan M. Aldridge. The book is a parable about leadership told through the playground adventures of three young children. It also contains inspirational quotes from thinkers and authors. Sinek worked with a company called 12.29 to design a custom scent, "the smell of optimism," based on the story, which is part of the experiential design of physical copies of the book. In 2018, Sinek published a book called *The Infinite Game*. In it, he addresses competition, urging business leaders to view their competitors as rivals, not adversaries to be beaten. In an "infinite game"—a longer view of one's business—there are no winners and losers, only those that get ahead and those that fall behind, Sinek argues. The idea goes back to Sinek's core philosophy: only those businesses that know why they exist, that have a purpose larger than the product they are selling, will last.

SUGGESTED READING
Browne, Rachel. "Millennials Are Not Lazy, Just Misunderstood: Author and Speaker Simon Sinek." *The Sydney Morning Herald*, 4 Feb. 2017, www.smh.com.au/national/nsw/millennials-are-not-lazy-just-misunderstood-author-and-speaker-simon-sinek-20170201-gu3527.html. Accessed 21 Jan. 2019.

Hogg, Alec. "SA-Raised Ted Talks Star Simon Sinek on What Makes Great Leaders—and Bad Ones." *BizNews*, 1 Mar. 2016, www.biznews.com/leadership/2016/03/01/sa-raised-ted-talks-star-simon-sinek-on-what-makes-great-leaders-and-bad-ones. Accessed 21 Jan. 2019.

Schein, Michael. "Author Simon Sinek Is Full of Hot Air (And Other Reasons You Should Follow His Lead)." *Forbes*, 13 June 2018, www.forbes.com/sites/michaelschein/2018/06/13/simon-sinek-is-full-of-fluff-and-other-reasons-you-should-follow-his-lead/. Accessed 21 Jan. 2019.

Walzer, Jennifer. "What You Need to Understand to Improve Your Hiring." *The New York Times* 16 Sept. 2009, boss.blogs.nytimes.com/2009/09/16/what-you-need-to-understand-to-improve-your-hiring/. Accessed 21 Jan. 2019.

Zuckerman, Gregory. "The Workforce Whisperer." *Brandeis Magazine*, Summer 2017, www.brandeis.edu/magazine/2017/summer/featured-stories/sinek.html. Accessed 21 Jan. 2019.

SELECTED WORKS
Start with Why, 2009; *Leaders Eat Last*, 2014; *Together Is Better*, 2016; *The Infinite Game*, 2018

—*Molly Hagan*

Josh Singer

Date of birth: 1972
Occupation: Screenwriter

One of Hollywood's top screenwriters, Josh Singer is known for crafting scripts that are based on real-life people and major historical events. An alumnus of Yale and Harvard University, Singer began his scriptwriting career in the early 2000s working on such television shows as *The West Wing* before moving on to feature films. His first feature, *The Fifth Estate*, about the rise of the whistleblower website *WikiLeaks*, was produced in 2013. Though poorly received, the cyber thriller helped pave the way for his next script, *Spotlight*, which chronicles the team of journalists who uncovered the Catholic Church child sex abuse scandal in the Boston area during the early 2000s. Universally praised by critics, the film, which was directed and cowritten by Tom McCarthy, earned Singer an Academy Award for best original screenplay.

Singer has since written acclaimed scripts for two other features: *The Post* (2017), a drama about the *Washington Post*'s publication of the Pentagon Papers, cowritten with Liz Hannah and directed by Steven Spielberg; and *First Man* (2018), a biopic about iconic astronaut Neil Armstrong directed by Damien Chazelle and adapted from James R. Hansen's same-titled 2005 biography. An insatiable researcher, Singer has strived for the utmost accuracy and authenticity in dramatizing historical figures and events. As he explained to Matt Grobar for *Deadline* (7 Jan. 2019), "We make myths. We make stories that people hold onto, and believe in, and so we have a profound responsibility in how we make those myths, especially when we're telling stories about history."

EARLY LIFE AND EDUCATION

Josh Singer was born in 1972 in Philadelphia, Pennsylvania, to Bruce and Rebecca Singer. He was raised in a Jewish household in the Philadelphia suburb of Ambler. His father, who died in 2012, was a prominent local dentist. Singer has credited both of his parents with instilling in him a hard work ethic and an indomitable will to succeed.

From an early age, Singer became captivated by the power of storytelling. Through his parents' influence, he gravitated toward books that centered around moral and ethical dilemmas, such as Madeleine L'Engle's science fantasy novel *A Wrinkle in Time* (1962). Writing and music served as major forms of expression for Singer, who penned prose sketches as a child and sang in his synagogue's choir. He became involved in the arts at Upper Dublin High School, in Fort Washington, Pennsylvania, where he wrote for

Photo by NASA/Aubrey Gemignani via Wikimedia Commons

the student newspaper, acted in musicals, and was a standout member of the school's a cappella singing group.

A talented, high-achieving student, Singer graduated as class valedictorian from Upper Dublin High in 1990, after which he attended Yale University. At Yale, he double majored in mathematics and economics and sang in the university's famed a cappella group, the Whiffenpoofs. Upon graduating magna cum laude, Singer moved to New York to work as a business analyst for the consulting firm McKinsey & Company. It was while working in that staid role that he turned again to writing as a creative outlet.

Singer's writing efforts eventually led to him working at the Children's Television Workshop (now the Sesame Workshop). He worked there for a few months before pursuing a joint graduate degree in law and business at Harvard University. While there he started writing at least two hours every day to determine if he had anything of worth to say. That experiment and a series of entertainment summer internships, including ones with Nickelodeon and the Disney Channel, helped redirect Singer's career focus. "When I was working at these places, I kept getting more interested in the script and the writing," Singer told Kate Erbland for *IndieWire* (4 Nov. 2015) "I kept wanting to get closer to actually *making* stuff, as opposed to being an executive of some sort."

TELEVISION TO FEATURE FILMS

Singer's desire to become a screenwriter prompted him to move to Los Angeles after graduating from Harvard Law School in 2001. He did so with his parents' blessing, resolving to give it three years before returning to a more stable career. As part of his plan to break into the industry, Singer first focused his attention on television, and on the advice of an insider, he wrote a spec script for his favorite show, *The West Wing*. His script, which centered on the Israeli-Palestinian conflict, eventually found its way into the hands of John Wells, an executive producer for the political drama series. Upon taking over the show from creator Aaron Sorkin in 2004, Wells hired Singer to serve as one of its staff writers on the strength of his script.

Singer worked on *The West Wing* for its final three seasons from 2004 to 2006, during which he wrote or cowrote six episodes and was promoted to executive story editor. During that time, he learned the intricacies of screenwriting from Wells and colleagues like Debora Cahn, who taught him the importance of adding not just exposition, but emotional depth to scenes. Over the next five years, Singer wrote for such television shows as *Law & Order: Special Victims Unit*, *Lie to Me*, and *Fringe*, before venturing off on his own to write features. As he put it to Steven Rea for the *Philadelphia Inquirer* (14 Jan. 2016), "I gradually became a little bored with writing other people's worlds, other people's characters."

In 2012, a spec feature Singer wrote about the American composer George Gershwin helped him land a deal to write *The Fifth Estate*, which was released in October of the following year. An exploration of twenty-first century journalism, the film chronicles the founding of the whistleblowing website *WikiLeaks* by Australian computer programmer Julian Assange. It focuses on Assange's relationship with German technology activist Daniel Domscheit-Berg, a former WikiLeaks spokesperson. Singer partly based his script on two books: Domscheit-Berg's *Inside WikiLeaks: My Time with Julian Assange at the World's Most Dangerous Website* (2011) and *WikiLeaks: Inside Julian Assange's War on Secrecy* (2011) by British journalists David Leigh and Luke Harding.

Structured as a coming-of-age story about Domscheit-Berg, *The Fifth Estate*, which was directed by Bill Condon, was panned by critics, most of whom found fault with its lack of narrative focus. Despite being distributed by Steven Spielberg's DreamWorks Pictures and boasting a dynamic lead performance by Benedict Cumberbatch as Assange, the film also performed poorly at the box office. "I thought my career was over," Singer admitted to Julia Hanna in a profile for the *Harvard Business School* website (3 Sept. 2018).

SPOTLIGHT AND THE POST

Despite its shortcomings, *The Fifth Estate* opened other career opportunities for Singer, who in late 2012 was hired by director Tom McCarthy to write the script for *Spotlight*, which tells the true story of the *Boston Globe*'s Spotlight investigative reporting team who helped uncover the Catholic priest child abuse scandal in the early 2000s. He spent part of the next two years researching and writing the complex script with McCarthy, during which he made extensive trips to Boston and conducted lengthy interviews with the journalists involved, including longtime *Globe* editor Walter "Robby" Robinson, who oversaw the Spotlight team's Pulitzer Prize–winning investigation. "Josh is one of the best reporters I've ever known," Robinson told Hanna. "Over the course of two years he dug out of us everything we knew—and then some."

Even as *Spotlight* started filming in 2014, Singer and McCarthy rewrote scenes on the set to get them right. Their painstaking work paid off, and upon being released in 2015, *Spotlight* received universal acclaim from critics. Featuring an ensemble cast headed by Michael Keaton (who portrays Robinson), Mark Ruffalo, Rachel McAdams, Liev Schrieber, and Stanley Tucci, the docudrama offers a blow-by-blow account of the Spotlight investigation, highlighting the sweeping impact of institutional blindness and the power of investigative journalism. As Singer explained to Carla Iacovetti for *Creative Screenwriting* (25 Jan. 2016), "We wanted to spark or rekindle an interest in accurate and accountable journalism. When there is this kind of accountability among good journalists working together, it has a lasting effect on the public."

Singer and McCarthy received several honors for their script, including an Academy Award, British Academy of Film and Television Arts (BAFTA) Award, and Writers Guild of America Award, all for best original screenplay. *Spotlight* received six Academy Award nominations in total, and in addition to best screenplay, it took home the coveted award for best picture. It was also a box-office success, grossing $98 million worldwide on a budget of $20 million.

Spotlight put Singer on the radar of many high-profile Hollywood directors, most notably Steven Spielberg, who hired him to do rewrite work on *The Post* (2017). Like Singer's first two features, *The Post* reflects the exciting world of journalism. Set in 1971, the film provides a thrilling, true-to-life account of the *Washington Post*'s frantic efforts to publish the Pentagon Papers, a then-classified trove of documents detailing the United States' involvement in the Vietnam War. It stars Meryl Streep as the *Post*'s trailblazing owner and publisher, Katharine Graham, and Tom Hanks as the newspaper's famed executive editor, Ben Bradlee.

The Post followed a lightning-fast, forty-five-day production schedule, during which Singer rewrote scenes daily with the film's first-time screenwriter, Liz Hannah. A celebration of First Amendment rights, the timely film was released in time for awards season in December 2017 and received mostly positive reviews. It earned six Golden Globe nominations, including one for Singer and Hannah for best screenplay, and two Oscar nominations for best picture and best actress (for Streep).

FIRST MAN AND BEYOND

Singer next wrote the screenplay for the Neil Armstrong biopic *First Man*, which is partly based on the biography of the same name by James R. Hansen. He had first started working on the script for the film in 2014, following a fruitful meeting with the young visionary director Damien Chazelle, whose breakthrough second feature, the music-themed drama *Whiplash*, was released that year. The two resolved to create a provocative portrait of Armstrong that was grounded in fact and authenticity. Consequently, in writing *First Man*, Singer not only consulted Hansen's text, but also conducted interviews with Armstrong's first wife, Janet, his two sons, Mark and Rick, and numerous former astronauts and National Aeronautics and Space Administration (NASA) personnel. Those efforts resulted in a script that shed light on aspects of Armstrong's life and character that were previously unknown to the public, such as the death of his two-year-old daughter Karen from brain cancer. "The space program has been painted in gossamer tones," Singer told Julia Hanna. "To me, Neil Armstrong's journey is more about his endurance and stoicism in the face of tremendous loss than his incredible skills and abilities."

Set against the backdrop of the 1960s space race between the United States and the Soviet Union, *First Man* focuses on the eight-year period of Armstrong's life leading up to his historic Apollo 11 manned landing on the moon on July 20, 1969. Premiering at the 2018 Venice International Film Festival, the film was met with wide critical acclaim for its deeply nuanced portrait of Armstrong (who was portrayed by Ryan Gosling) and visceral, first-person look at human spaceflight. Sadly, its release was marred by a controversy over Singer and Chazelle's decision not to depict the planting of the American flag during the film's climactic moon landing sequence. Though not a politically motivated artistic choice, the resulting controversy caused by the omission had a negative impact on the film's box-office performance, and it grossed just over $100 million worldwide on a $59 million budget.

That controversy notwithstanding, *First Man* received numerous accolades, most notably the Academy Award for best visual effects. Singer himself earned a number of honors for his script, including a BAFTA Award nomination for best adapted screenplay. In conjunction with the film's release, he published an annotated script for *First Man*, which highlighted his meticulous attention to detail and authenticity. In his *Deadline* interview with Matt Grobar, Singer said, "I'm not going to stop trying to say things with known history, and trying to learn from history, and sharing those lessons with the world."

In 2018, it was announced that Singer had penned a biopic about the legendary American composer Leonard Bernstein. Tentatively titled *Bernstein*, it will be directed by and star Bradley Cooper and produced by Steven Spielberg and Martin Scorsese.

PERSONAL LIFE

Singer has been married to the American novelist Laura Dave since 2012. They have a young son, Jacob, and divide their time between Los Angeles and New York City.

SUGGESTED READING

Hanna, Julia. "Moving Pictures." *Harvard Business School*, 3 Sept. 2018, www.alumni.hbs.edu/stories/Pages/story-bulletin.aspx?num=6746. Accessed 26 Mar. 2019.

Iacovetti, Carla. "Spotlight: The Burden of Truth." *Creative Screenwriting*, 25 Jan. 2016, creativescreenwriting.com/spotlight-the-burden-of-truth/. Accessed 26 Mar. 2019.

Singer, Josh. "'First Man' Scribe on the Value of Truth-Telling Art in Troubled Times." Interview by Matt Grobar. *Deadline*, 7 Jan. 2019, deadline.com/2019/01/first-man-josh-singer-oscars-screenwriting-interview-1202521005/. Accessed 26 Mar. 2019.

Singer, Josh. "How 'Spotlight' Screenwriter Josh Singer Recovered from 'The Fifth Estate' with Another Journalism Film." Interview by Kate Erbland. *IndieWire*, 4 Nov. 2015, www.indiewire.com/2015/11/how-spotlight-screenwriter-josh-singer-recovered-from-the-fifth-estate-with-another-journalism-film-54871/. Accessed 26 Mar. 2019.

Singer, Josh. "On Movies: Q&A with Ambler Native, 'Spotlight' Writer, Oscar Nominee Josh Singer." Interview by Steven Rea. *The Philadelphia Inquirer*, 14 Jan. 2016, www.philly.com/philly/entertainment/movies/20160117_On_Movies__Q_A__Ambler_native___Spotlight__writer__Oscar_nominee_Josh_Singer.html. Accessed 26 Mar. 2019.

Singer, Josh. "Shtumi in the Spotlight: How to Turn an Info-Heavy Story into Riveting Drama." *MovieMaker*, 17 Nov. 2015, www.moviemaker.com/archives/moviemaking/screenwriting/shtumi-in-the-spotlight/ Accessed 26 Mar. 2019.

SELECTED WORKS
The West Wing, 2004–6; *The Fifth Estate*, 2013; *Spotlight*, 2015; *The Post*, 2017; *First Man*, 2018

—*Chris Cullen*

Glenn Slater

Date of birth: 1968
Occupation: Lyricist

For a musical to work, "it needs to feel effortless," the acclaimed lyricist Glenn Slater told Melanie Votaw for the pop culture and entertainment site *Reel Life with Jane* (4 June 2016). "It needs to feel like you're hearing those characters spontaneously lifting their voices into song. Otherwise, the illusion is shattered." Over nearly three decades, Slater has done just that, writing musicals for both the stage and screen that have effortlessly enraptured audiences. He is best known for his collaborative partnership with the legendary composer Alan Menken, with whom he has written songs for Broadway productions and film and television projects. With Menken, Slater has received a number of honors, including Tony Award nominations for his work on the hit Broadway musicals *The Little Mermaid* (2008) and *Sister Act* (2011); a Grammy Award for the song "I See the Light," featured in the Disney 3-D animated film *Tangled* (2010); and an Emmy Award nomination for "A New Season," a song that was featured on ABC's 2015–16 musical comedy television series *Galavant*, which he and Menken also executive-produced.

Additionally, Slater has often collaborated with the English composer Andrew Lloyd Webber. He earned a third Tony Award nomination for providing lyrics for Webber's *School of Rock*, a musical adaptation of the eponymous 2003 Jack Black film that debuted on Broadway in 2015. Slater's latest Broadway effort with Menken, *A Bronx Tale*, a musical adaptation of Chazz Palminteri's 1989 play of the same name, premiered in 2016.

EARLY LIFE AND EDUCATION
Glenn Slater was born to a Jewish family in 1968 in Brooklyn, New York. He was raised in East Brunswick, a town in central New Jersey. Slater's parents were devoted fans of musical theater and reportedly started taking him to Broadway shows when he was a young child; the first show he ever saw was a revival of the 1959 musical *Gypsy* that starred Angela Lansbury. Broadway cast albums "were always playing at our house," Slater recalled to Guillermo Nazará in an interview for the *Primera Fila* blog (27 Aug. 2015). From a young age, he added, "my ears and

fingers became deeply attuned to 'musical theater' as a language." Slater also studied piano for a number of years.

Though he did not foster aspirations of becoming a performer, Slater developed an affinity for storytelling and songwriting. It was not until his junior year at East Brunswick High School, however, that he became involved in musical theater. At that time, Slater was playing in a rock cover band but had grown frustrated with his older bandmates' unwillingness to play songs he was writing. Those frustrations were quelled after his school's drama teacher, Elliott Taubenslag, posted a notice that asked students to submit songs for a teenage-themed musical he was putting together. Slater volunteered and was charged with setting student poems to music and with writing the lyrics to several songs.

Taubenslag's musical, *How I Survived High School*, won multiple awards at a drama competition and was soon turned into a fringe theater production with professional actors. Slater helped rework the show for a much smaller cast, and though it did not fare particularly well with critics upon opening in 1986, he has said that it had a major influence on his career. "That was literally the spark that got me on this path," he told Ilana Keller for the *Asbury Park Press* (7 Apr. 2016).

Upon graduating from East Brunswick in 1986, Slater attended Harvard University, where he concentrated in English. Throughout his time there, he continued to write songs for the theater, serving as a member of Harvard's historic Hasty Pudding Club. As a junior, he composed the music for its Prohibition-era production called *Whiskey Business*.

ROAD TO BROADWAY
Slater graduated from Harvard in 1990, after which he moved back to New York City with the intention of becoming a professional composer. He soon came to the disheartening realization that his skills were grossly inferior to those of established composers, however. "I realized, there was no way I was going to keep up with these guys," he explained to Caryn Robbins for *Broadway World* (1 June 2016), "and if I actually wanted to have a career in the theater, I needed to switch gears."

Consequently, Slater gave up composing and remade himself as a lyricist. He applied and was accepted to New York's renowned BMI Lehman Engel Musical Theatre Workshop, where he learned the intricacies behind writing and constructing theater songs and how to collaborate with composers. To earn income, Slater worked as a copywriter, and over a period of several years, he led a "double life" writing advertisements during the day and songs at night, as he told Votaw. That hard work paid off, and in 1996, he won the prestigious Kleban Prize, which is named for the late lyricist Edward Kleban and is awarded annually to the most promising librettist and lyricist in American musical theater.

With the prize money, Slater was able to quit his job as a copywriter and focus full-time on songwriting. A workshop performance of an unproduced play Slater wrote eventually brought him to the attention of the Walt Disney Company. As a tryout with the company, Slater was invited to write songs for an animated film called "Marco Polo," which was written by screenwriter Joss Whedon, who had recently contributed to the computer animation Toy Story (1995). The film, expectedly, went unproduced, but Slater's songs impressed executives enough to later put him in contact with the eight-time Academy Award–winning composer Alan Menken.

Meanwhile, in 2001, Slater wrote the lyrics for the Off-Broadway musical comedy revue Newyorkers, which received a Lucille Lortel Award nomination for outstanding musical. He also contributed additional lyrics to the song "Paris through the Window" for the Broadway production of A Class Act (2001), a musical loosely based on the life of Edward Kleban, who died of oral cancer at age forty-eight in 1987.

PARTNERSHIP WITH MENKEN

Slater's first collaboration with Menken came in 2004 on the Disney Western-themed animated film Home on the Range. Though initially intimidated by Menken, who is best known for his scores for such Disney animated films as The Little Mermaid (1989), Beauty and the Beast (1991), Aladdin (1992), and Pocahontas (1995), Slater has said that the two instantly clicked and that they understood each other's musical language right away. As he put it to Ruthie Fierberg for Playbill (21 Nov. 2016), "We come to songwriting from two directions. Alan is all intuition. It's just an instinct, whereas I'm all head."

Slater next collaborated with Menken on a Broadway musical adaptation of the latter's The Little Mermaid. In writing additional songs for the musical, which features such popular numbers as "Part of Your World" and "Under the Sea," he adhered closely to the pop-oriented style and intentions of its original lyricist, Howard Ashman. (Ashman, Menken's longtime songwriting partner, had died of AIDS in 1991.) The Little Mermaid debuted at the Lunt-Fontanne Theatre in New York in January 2008 and earned Slater his first Tony Award nomination for best original musical score (along with Menken and Ashman); it ran for 685 performances before closing in August 2009.

Following The Little Mermaid, Slater and Menken co-created a 1970s musical reimagining of the 1992 hit comedy film Sister Act. Opening at the Broadway Theatre in April 2011, the musical won Slater his second Tony nomination for best score. After running for 561 performances on Broadway, Sister Act became a successful national and international touring production.

In 2012, Slater and Menken's gospel-driven riff on another 1992 Hollywood comedy, Leap of Faith, had its Broadway premiere at New York's St. James Theatre. Despite receiving tepid reviews and being a commercial flop, the musical received a Tony Award nomination that year for best musical.

TANGLED AND LLOYD WEBBER COLLABORATIONS

Concurrently, Slater and Menken created music for both film and television. The duo wrote nineteen original songs for Disney's 3D computer-animated film Tangled, which was released in 2010 and raked in nearly $600 million worldwide. Loosely inspired by the nineteenth-century Brothers Grimm fairy tale Rapunzel, the film features the hit pop ballad "I See the Light," for which Slater and Menken received a 2011 Grammy Award for Best Song Written for Visual Media, as well as Oscar and Golden Globe nominations.

In the wake of Tangled's success, Slater and Menken teamed up with that film's screenwriter, Dan Fogelman, to create the Monty Python–inspired musical comedy series Galavant. It premiered on ABC in 2015 and aired for two seasons. A song from the series, titled "A New Season," garnered the pair an Emmy Award nomination for outstanding original music and lyrics in 2016. While working on Galavant, whose episodes featured several songs each, Slater said that he and Menken wrote songs almost every other day, a pace that stood in stark contrast to their film and theater projects, which generally have years-long gestation periods. Still, he explained to Keller, "The process of writing the actual songs is the same on the micro level. For every medium, you get a script or a story, [and] you find the moments that are the most emotionally resonant."

Slater has taken this approach while working with other collaborators, the most notable of which include the English musical theater giant Andrew Lloyd Webber, the visionary behind such landmark Broadway productions as Cats (1982) and Phantom of the Opera (1988). He wrote songs for Lloyd Webber's highly anticipated sequel to the latter musical, Love Never Dies, which opened on London's West End in 2010. Health problems and crew changes ultimately resulted in the cancellation of a planned Broadway production, though the show did go on to be staged in Toronto, Canada, and Melbourne, Australia.

Nevertheless, Slater enjoyed much more success on his next collaboration with Webber, a musical adaptation of the 2003 comedy film *School of Rock*, which starred Jack Black as a slacker-turned-substitute teacher who inspires kids through rock music. Featuring a book written by *Downton Abbey* creator Julian Fellowes, music by Lloyd Webber, and lyrics by Slater, the musical remained largely faithful to the original version. After making its Broadway debut at the Winter Garden Theatre in December 2015, it ran on Broadway for 1,309 performances before closing in January 2019. It received mostly positive reviews and earned Slater his third career Tony Award nomination for best score.

A BRONX TALE AND BEYOND

Slater's fourth Broadway collaboration with Menken, a musical adaptation of Chazz Palminteri's play *A Bronx Tale* (1989), premiered on Broadway in December 2016. The original one-man show inspired an eponymous hit 1993 coming-of-age gangster film, directed by and starring Robert De Niro. Codirected by De Niro and four-time Tony Award winner Jerry Zaks, who helmed a 2007 Broadway revival of Palminteri's one-man show, the 1960s doo wop-and-pop-infused musical was generally well received by critics and played seven hundred performances before closing in August 2018. It also launched a national tour that fall. In writing songs for *A Bronx Tale*, Slater worked closely with Palminteri and his other collaborators, which included producer Tommy Mottola, to capture the sound of the era. "My job," he explained to Alan Ash for the *OnStage Blog* (6 Mar. 2018), "was to listen to what everybody had to say, to find the common ground and to bring everyone together to find the spine of the show."

Slater and Menken also cowrote the opening number, "The Great Beyond," for Seth Rogen's raunchy, R-rated animated feature *Sausage Party* (2016). The following year saw the worldwide premiere of Slater's 1950s beatnik jazz musical *Beatsville*, with music and lyrics written by his wife, Wendy Leigh Wilf, herself a composer-lyricist and musician. Slater wrote the book for the musical, which opened at the Asolo Repertory Theatre in Sarasota, Florida, and is based on Roger Corman's 1959 cult horror film *A Bucket of Blood*.

Slater has continued to work with Menken on other projects. They cowrote two songs ("Life After Happily Ever After" and "Wind in My Hair") for Disney's made-for-television animated film *Tangled: Before Ever After* (2017), and Slater provided lyrics for music featured in the spinoff series *Tangled*, which premiered in 2017. The duo later created the track "Full-Throated Love Song," which was featured in the Will Ferrell and John C. Reilly comedy detective vehicle *Holmes & Watson* (2018). Menken praised Slater's intelligence to Fierberg and compared him to Howard Ashman "in terms of his ability to get the essence of what a musical style of songs calls for in a lyric and also twist it and apply it to the effect of a new musical."

PERSONAL LIFE

Slater and Wilf reside in New York City with their children, Benjamin and Daniel.

SUGGESTED READING

Ash, Alan. "A Chat with Glenn Slater: Giving Voice to Belmont Avenue." *OnStage Blog*, 6 Mar. 2018, www.onstageblog.com/new-blog-1/2018/3/6/glenn-slater-giving-voice-to-belmont-avenue. Accessed 30 Dec. 2018.

Fierberg, Ruthie. "What Makes Alan Menken and Glenn Slater the Head and Heart Team." *Playbill*, 21 Nov. 2016, www.playbill.com/article/what-makes-alan-menken-and-glenn-slater-the-head-and-heart-team. Accessed 30 Dec. 2018.

Keller, Ilana. "Glen Slater: The Man behind the Music." *Asbury Park Press*, 7 Apr. 2016, www.app.com/story/entertainment/theater/2016/04/07/glenn-slater-man-behind-music/82497434/. Accessed 30 Dec. 2018.

Slater, Glenn. "BWW Interview – Lyricist Glenn Slater Talks SCHOOL OF ROCK, TANGLED & Possible GALAVANT Stage Show." Interview by Caryn Robbins. *Broadway World*, 1 June 2016, www.broadwayworld.com/article/BWW-Interview-Lyricist-Glenn-Slater-Talks-SCHOOL-OF-ROCK-TANGLED-Possible-GALAVANT-Stage-Show-20160601. Accessed 30 Dec. 2018.

Slater, Glenn. "Interview: Broadway/Disney Lyricist Glenn Slater Talks 'School of Rock,' 'Galavant,' & More – Pt. 1." Interview by Melanie Votaw. *Reel Life with Jane*, 4 June 2016, www.reellifewithjane.com/2016/06/interview-lyricist-glenn-slater. Accessed 30 Dec. 2018.

SELECTED WORKS

The Little Mermaid (with Alan Menken), 2008; *Tangled* (with Menken), 2010; *Sister Act* (with Menken), 2011; *School of Rock* (with Andrew Lloyd Webber), 2015; *Galavant* (with Menken), 2015–16; *A Bronx Tale* (with Menken), 2016; *Beatsville* (with Wendy Leigh Wilf), 2017

—*Chris Cullen*

George Springer

Date of birth: September 19, 1989
Occupation: Baseball player

Outfielder George Springer proved he could excel at every level of baseball, but it was his knack for postseason heroics that made him a true star. After being called up to the Houston Astros in 2014, he helped transform one of the worst teams in Major League Baseball (MLB) to one of the best while demonstrating his ability to perform especially well under pressure. This was most evident when the Astros won the 2017 World Series against the Los Angeles Dodgers to secure the franchise's first title in its more than fifty years of existence. Over the seven-game series, Springer hit five home runs, becoming just the third player in MLB history to accomplish such a feat, and was named the World Series Most Valuable Player (MVP). However, he often downplayed his own success while emphasizing teamwork and pure effort. "I just think [the postseason is] one of those times where the lights get brighter, the stage gets a little bit bigger, and I think guys tend to concentrate more," he told Jesse Dougherty for the *Washington Post* (12 Oct. 2018). "You hone in on stuff."

A baseball player from early childhood, Springer earned attention from scouts in high school and at the University of Connecticut before being drafted by the Astros in 2011. After progressing quickly through the minor leagues, he joined an Astros team that was soon loaded with young talent. Their rise to success brought new pressure to perform, but Springer remained focused on enjoying his sport. "This is a game where the best part is looking in the stands and watching kids with their moms and dads," he told Tom Verducci for *Sports Illustrated* (3 Aug. 2017). He continued, "I believe it's my job to try to make as many people's days as positive as I can. I'm having the best time of my life, not only to have a chance to play and live out my dream, but to see kids enjoying the game."

EARLY LIFE AND EDUCATION

George Chelston Springer III was born on September 19, 1989, in New Britain, Connecticut. Springer grew up in an athletic family that was particularly devoted to baseball: his father and grandfather had both played the sport when they were younger; his sisters, Nicole and Lena, played softball; and his mother, Laura, coached softball in addition to teaching gymnastics. Springer himself displayed a talent for the sport early in life, and he spent much of his childhood practicing his baseball skills with his father. "George loved defensive drills," Springer's father told Richard Justice for *MLB.com* (28 Sept. 2017). "He loved to run. He loved to track down balls. On windy days in particular, I'd hit them at various heights, over his head, everything. His combination of energy and drive and the ability to take angles and to anticipate was extraordinary."

Growing up only about two hours' drive from Boston, Massachusetts, Springer often

Photo by Keith Allison via Wikimedia Commons

accompanied his family to Fenway Park, where they watched Red Sox games. He was also inspired by his local minor-league team, the New Britain Rock Cats, an affiliate of the Minnesota Twins. At the age of eight, Springer had a memorable encounter with Rock Cats player Torii Hunter, who would later play for several major-league teams. "He changed my life," Springer recalled to Verducci. "I got a chance to play catch at the time with what I thought was a big leaguer. I didn't know any better. He's playing on a big diamond in a stadium with lights and a big scoreboard. It made me want to play baseball even more."

As a teenager, Springer spent a year at New Britain High School, where he played baseball and earned appreciation from his coaches for his determination and humility. He later transferred to Avon Old Farms, a boys' boarding school in Avon, Connecticut. Springer spent three years there, playing both baseball and soccer. A major contributor to the school's baseball team, he was voted most outstanding player for his senior season. Springer graduated in 2008.

During high school, Springer attracted considerable attention from MLB scouts, but he committed to playing for the University of Connecticut (UConn). For that reason, many teams passed him over in the 2008 MLB Draft, though the Minnesota Twins finally selected him in the forty-eighth round. Although Springer did aspire to play baseball professionally, he decided not to sign but to pursue a college education as planned. "I wanted to go to school," he told Rhett Bollinger for *MLB.com* (30 May 2018) of his decision. "I think it was an important time in my life where I felt school was the best option for me to grow physically and mentally and to learn all aspects of the game and in life. So I went."

Springer enrolled at UConn, the institution his parents had both attended, where he majored in history. Known for its strong athletic programs, the university competes in Division I of the National Collegiate Athletic Association (NCAA), the highest-ranked level of college sports. Springer joined the UConn baseball program as a freshman and quickly proved that he would be a key team member, earning Big East Conference Rookie of the Year honors for his debut season. He remained at the school for three years, accumulating a .348 batting average, 196 runs batted in (RBIs), and 76 stolen bases along with a school-record 46 home runs and 220 runs scored. In his final season with the team, Springer was named Big East Player of the Year, among other awards and nominations. He left UConn in 2011 to focus on his professional baseball career.

MLB DRAFT AND THE MINOR LEAGUES

Springer reentered the MLB Draft in June 2011. With his improved skills and track record of college success, he drew attention from many teams and was expected to be a high selection. His years of additional training paid off when the Houston Astros chose him in the first round as the eleventh overall pick. Springer's selection made him the then highest-drafted UConn baseball player and represented a vast improvement over his previous draft position. After an extended negotiation with the Astros, Springer signed with the team on August 15 of that year for a $2.52 million bonus.

As is typical in baseball, Springer began his career in the minor leagues, working his way through various affiliate teams. In August 2011 he joined the Tri-City ValleyCats, a Class A Short Season team based in Troy, New York. Although the team was among the lowest-level teams affiliated with the Astros, Springer was prepared to give his full effort. "If I have to run into a wall, I will," he told Don Amore for the *Hartford Courant* (19 Aug. 2011). "If I have to climb a wall, so be it. I'm a guy who just goes out and plays as hard as I can and has a lot of fun."

Having joined the ValleyCats late in the 2011 season, he played in only eight games with the team prior to the short season's conclusion. The following year Springer began the season with the Class A Advanced Lancaster JetHawks before moving up to the Double A Corpus Christi Hooks. He advanced to the Triple A Oklahoma City RedHawks in June 2013. Throughout the minors, Springer hit for both power and average, showed speed in stealing bases, and played strong defense in the outfield. By 2014 he was considered one of the top prospects in baseball.

HOUSTON ASTROS

Although Springer opened the 2014 season with the RedHawks, he was soon called up to the Astros, making his major-league debut on April 16, 2014. He went on to play seventy-eight games with the Astros that season and in May was named American League (AL) Rookie of the Month. After injuring his leg, however, he spent considerable time on the disabled list and was shut down for the season. He still finished his rookie campaign with twenty home runs, though he also struck out often. He ultimately helped the team to a 70–92 record, a considerable improvement on its franchise-worst 51–111 performance in 2013.

Springer returned to the Astros at the start of the 2015 season. That year he cut down his strikeout rate, which helped raise his batting average to .276, though he missed sixty games with a fractured wrist and his power declined somewhat with sixteen home runs. Despite Springer's injury, the Astros continued their upward trajectory, finishing second in the AL West at 86–76 and earning a wild card play-off spot. The game marked the first postseason appearance of Springer's career and the first for the Astros since 2005. After defeating the New York Yankees in the AL Wild Card Game, the Astros went on to compete against the Kansas City Royals in the AL Division Series (ALDS), ultimately losing three games to two.

The 2016 season was slight step back for the Astros, as the team finished third in the AL West with an 84–78 record and did not make the postseason. For Springer, however, the season was productive, as he was healthy the whole year and succeeded as a leadoff hitter. He led the AL in both game appearances (162) and plate appearances (744), across which he hit 29 home runs and 29 doubles.

WORLD SERIES CHAMPION

The 2017 season represented a turning point for the Astros, as Springer and other young players the organization had cultivated over a lengthy rebuilding process led the team to an impressive regular-season record of 101–61, the best in the AL West and second-best in the AL overall. Springer himself set new career highs with a .283 batting average, 34 home runs, 85 RBIs, and a .522 slugging percentage. His strong play earned him his first All-Star Game spot and first Silver Slugger Award. Entering the postseason, the team beat the Red Sox three games to one in the ALDS before moving on to the AL Championship Series (ALCS), where they defeated the Yankees four games to three. With that victory the Astros secured an appearance in the World

Series, just the second in the franchise's more than fifty-year history and first since the team's switch from the National League (NL) to the AL in 2013.

The Astros' World Series trip was especially meaningful for many fans as Houston had experienced severe flooding and other damage from Hurricane Harvey a few months before. Facing the LA Dodgers—the only NL team with a superior regular-season record—the Astros played a highly competitive series that went to the full seven games. Although he had struggled at times during the play-offs, here Springer proved a difference-maker. He hit five home runs over the course of the series, becoming one of only three players ever to do so in a single World Series and the first to hit home runs in four consecutive games of the same series. He also set World Series records with eight total extra-base hits and twenty-nine total bases. The Astros ultimately beat the Dodgers four games to three to win the franchise's first World Series title. In light of his contributions to the Astro's victory, Springer was named the World Series MVP, an honor he appreciated but downplayed in favor of the team's accomplishments. "To earn this is great. It's an honor," he told Anthony Castrovince for *MLB. com* (2 Nov. 2017). "But it's not about me. It's about the team and what the team has done."

Springer had another solid year in 2018, finishing the regular season with a .265 average, 22 home runs, and 26 doubles across 140 games en route to a second All-Star Game selection. The Astros again finished first in the AL West, improving their record to 103–59. The team swept Cleveland in the ALDS but lost the ALCS to the Red Sox, who went on to beat the Dodgers in that year's World Series.

PERSONAL LIFE

Since 2014, Springer has served as a spokesperson for the Stuttering Association for the Young (SAY), an organization dedicated to the well-being of children and teens who stutter. He endured bullying as a child because of his own stutter but came to accept it as simply a part of himself.

Springer married Charlise Castro, a personal trainer and former softball player, in January 2018.

SUGGESTED READING

Amore, Dom. "Springer Takes Initial Cuts with Astros." *Hartford Courant*, 19 Aug. 2011, www.courant.com/sports/hc-xpm-2011-08-19-hc-springer-with-astros-0820-20110819-story.html. Accessed 15 Feb. 2019.

Bollinger, Rhett. "Springer Was Twins' 48th-Round Pick in 2008." *MLB. com*, 30 May 2018, www.mlb.com/news/twins-drafted-george-springer-in-2008/c-278355430. Accessed 15 Feb. 2019.

Castrovince, Anthony. "Springer Swats His Way to MVP Honors." *MLB.com*, 2 Nov. 2017, www.mlb.com/news/george-springer-named-world-series-mvp/c-260386660. Accessed 15 Feb. 2019.

Dougherty, Jesse. "George Springer and the Inexplicable Art of Thriving in October." *The Washington Post*, 12 Oct. 2018, www.washingtonpost.com/sports/2018/10/12/george-springer-inexplicable-art-thriving-october. Accessed 15 Feb. 2019.

Justice, Richard. "For Springer Family, Success Is Relative." *MLB.com*, 28 Sept. 2017, www.mlb.com/news/george-springer-puts-family-teammates-first/c-256089288. Accessed 15 Feb. 2019.

"SAY Spokesperson George Springer." *SAY*, www.say.org/say-spokesperson-george-springer. Accessed 15 Feb. 2019.

Verducci, Tom. "How the Astros' George Springer Learned to Embrace the Game—and Himself." *Sports Illustrated*, 3 Aug. 2017. www.si.com/mlb/2017/08/03/george-springer-houston-astros. Accessed 15 Feb. 2019.

—*Joy Crelin*

Ed Stafford

Date of birth: December 26, 1975
Occupation: Explorer

In 2010 Ed Stafford became the first person in recorded history to have walked the length of the Amazon River, a feat that took him two years and four months and earned him a coveted place as a Guinness World Record holder. He chronicled his journey in a book and television documentary, and his expedition brought him high praise, including from Ranulph Fiennes, the legendary British explorer and one of Stafford's idols. Of his accomplishment, Stafford noted to Max Williams for *Square Mile* (13 Feb. 2017), "I think it's quite cool that I'm the only human to ever do something, and I don't mean to sound egotistic but it is cool, isn't it? I feel like we spend our lives trying to fit in. I'm not that sort of person, I wanted to stray away from the norm and do something that everybody told me was impossible. I was determined to prove them wrong."

Stafford has parlayed that achievement into the development of television exploration and adventure series, which both consider the limits of human endurance and provide insights into such diverse issues as conservation and mental health. He also works as a motivational speaker, encouraging both adults and children to explore

Photo by Pete Mcbride/National Geographic/Getty Images

the natural world as a way to reach their full potential and cure themselves of bad habits, such as screen addiction. Additionally, he is an active ambassador for Land Rover, the Scouts, and the Youth Adventure Trust.

EARLY LIFE AND EDUCATION

Ed Stafford was born in England on December 26, 1975. Adopted as a baby by lawyers Barbara and Jeremy Stafford, he was raised in Leicestershire. (His father, who had long suffered bouts of illness and struggles with cancer, died in 1999.) He also has a sister, Janie. Spending a good deal of time outdoors from a young age, he was actively involved with the Scouts and was named Cub of the Year in 1986. Additionally, he enjoyed playing rugby as he was growing up.

Stafford has admitted in interviews that he has grappled with having been adopted. After completing his expedition to the Amazon, he sought out his birth family, not because he was unhappy with the family that had loved and raised him, but simply because he wanted to know about them. He learned his birth parents, who had given him up for adoption when they were teenagers, later married and had two sons.

After receiving his education largely at Uppingham, a boarding school, and Newcastle University, where he earned a degree in geography in 1997, Stafford joined the British Army. During his military career, he attained the rank of captain and served in Northern Ireland. Although he did acquire some valuable skills, Stafford recalled to Williams, "I didn't particularly enjoy the Army. Well, I made some good friends and had a laugh but the seriousness of being in the military

meant that I never really relaxed. I would get the shudders just looking at the barbed wire that surrounds most camps in the UK. Even though I learnt a lot, I was glad to leave once my commission was up." He retired from the army in 2002.

Instead of pursuing an office job like brokering stocks as he initially considered, Stafford started working with the expedition company Trekforce. The expeditions he led, often for younger people, typically focused on conservation projects. Meanwhile, he also worked alongside the United Nations in Afghanistan during the lead-up to the country's first presidential elections after the US–led invasion in 2001, assisting with security and logistics.

WALKING THE AMAZON

By early 2007 Stafford had developed the idea of walking the entire length of the Amazon River, a trek of more than four thousand miles, and had committed, along with fellow expedition leader Luke Collyer, to making the dream a reality. Stafford has admitted that the thrill of the challenge and the prospect of recognition were the foundation of his decision to undertake the expedition, but he also knew that it could help increase conservation awareness and raise money for select charities. In an interview with Nick Davidson for *Outside* magazine (21 Sept. 2010), Stafford explained that he got the idea after having explored Central American and Asian jungles and then doing an online search: "I'd never been to the Amazon, and I wanted to do a big expedition there. I'm not a great kayaker, so it was a bit of a no-brainer. I just thought, 'Has anybody walked it?' thinking somebody must have, but they hadn't. It ended up being a far bigger expedition than kayaking it would have been."

To put together enough money for the trip, Stafford and Collyer needed to find backers. Eventually, they secured funding and equipment from corporate sponsors and, largely with the help of an expedition website that Stafford maintained with blog updates, he received further donations throughout the journey. He and Collyer began the trek on April 2, 2008, at a source of the Amazon River on the southern coast of Peru. Collyer left after three months of hiking, and Stafford continued to work his way toward the Atlantic Ocean, eventually with the help of his guide Gadiel "Cho" Sanchez Rivera, a Peruvian forestry worker.

Throughout the remainder of the expedition, approximately two years, Stafford and Cho slogged through the rainforest over very difficult terrain and under intense physical and mental strain. In addition to periods when they ran out of food and money, their medical insurance lapsed, and their GPS broke, they faced dangers that included being held at arrowpoint by members of the Asháninkas, who believed the expeditioners to be dangerous trespassers. Ultimately, the calm explorers were let go once it was understood that they posed no threat.

RECOGNITION AND BECOMING A TELEVISION EXPLORER

On August 9, 2010, after endless, grueling days of carrying heavy rucksacks, Stafford and Cho reached the Atlantic Ocean. Not long after the success was announced, Stafford began to be showered with accolades, including officially recognition as a Guinness World Record holder. He was named among *National Geographic*'s Adventurers of the Year 2010 as well as a European Adventurer of the Year 2011 at an event in Stockholm, Sweden. He was also presented with the Mungo Park Medal by the Royal Scottish Geographical Society. Also in 2011 footage he shot along the Amazon was released as a television documentary titled *Walking the Amazon*, and his memoir about his experiences was published in the United Kingdom as *Walking the Amazon: 860 Days. The Impossible Task. The Incredible Journey.* and in the United States with the subtitle *860 Days. One Step at a Time.*

Now internationally recognized, Stafford began working with the Discovery Channel on programs about exploration and adventuring. The first of these series was *Naked and Marooned with Ed Stafford*, which was released in the United Kingdom in 2013 and as *Naked Castaway* in the United States that same year. The premise of the series was to drop Stafford onto the uninhabited island of Olorua in the Pacific Ocean, without food, water, equipment, or even clothing. After making a grass skirt, Stafford spent the next sixty days attempting to survive. His experiences there were also chronicled in his book *Naked and Marooned: One Man. One Island. One Epic Survival Story* (2014). The isolation of living alone on that tropical island gave him a new perspective on himself and even sent him into therapy afterward. Stafford noted of his experience to Williams, "Isolation is easy if you are completely honest with yourself and have nothing to hide. It's like a big mirror to yourself and there is nowhere to hide. My new self-awareness has caused many changes, all life-changing. I wouldn't change the 60-day isolation period for anything in the world—but would I want to go through that again? No thank you."

FURTHER TELEVISION PROJECTS

The first season of another series, *Marooned with Ed Stafford*, in which he was sent to a variety of isolated locations without supplies for ten-day periods, premiered in 2014 and followed along similar lines. Among the places he traveled to were Botswana, Venezuela, Borneo, Thailand, and Rwanda, as well as other parts of the world.

In his next program, *Ed Stafford: Into the Unknown* (2015), he went to remote locations in West Papua, Zambia, Brazil, Ethiopia, and Siberia to look at inexplicable markings that have shown up on satellite images and have confounded scientists. A second season of *Marooned* that aired in 2016 saw him test his limits in challenging places in such countries as Mongolia, Namibia, and Norway. Then the 2017 series *Ed Stafford: Left for Dead* followed him as he was given ten days to emerge from forests, deserts, and mountains using only his survival instincts and carrying nothing more than his own camera to film his experiences.

Ed Stafford: First Man Out, which aired in 2019, was formatted as a series of competitions between Stafford and a different survival expert each episode as the two raced to see who could come out of a difficult trek using only a limited number of supplies. Against his competitors, Stafford had to escape from isolated locations in places such as Borneo, Kazakhstan, Mongolia, and Thailand.

Meanwhile, his 2019 three-part documentary series *60 Days on the Streets*—in which he lived on the streets of London, Glasgow, and Manchester to better understand the homelessness crisis in Great Britain—was a bit of a departure for him. Speaking about his decision to undertake the experiment, he told Adrian Lobb for the *Big Issue* (14 Mar. 2019), "Like everyone, I have seen homelessness rise over the last years. And it seemed to be getting worse faster. How has the situation got to this, why are there so many people on the street? I thought it would be a huge challenge to sleep rough for 60 days to try and find out a little bit more about this world."

PERSONAL LIFE

Ed Stafford married Laura Bingham, a fellow adventurer, in 2016. The couple met shortly after she had sailed across the Atlantic Ocean in a thirty-eight-foot trimaran for almost two months. She was researching a cycling trip across South America when she emailed him to pick his brain. They spoke on the phone and later met for a drink. Within three months, they were engaged. Their son, Ran, was born in 2017, and they live in rural Leicestershire.

SUGGESTED READING
Fox-Leonard, Boudicca. "Babies in the Jungle? It's Safer Than the Car! Explorers Ed Stafford and Laura Bingham on Parenting." *The Telegraph*, 8 Nov. 2018, www.telegraph.co.uk/family/parenting/babies-jungle-safer-car-explorers-ed-stafford-laura-bingham. Accessed 7 July 2019.

Hann, Michael. "Naked, Marooned and in Therapy: Secrets of the Soul-Baring King of Survival TV." *The Guardian*, 24 Jan. 2019, www.

theguardian.com/tv-and-radio/2019/jan/24/naked-marooned-and-in-therapy-ed-stafford-soul-baring-king-of-survival-tv. Accessed 7 July 2019.

Stafford, Ed. "Best Job in the World: Ed Stafford, Explorer." Interview by Max Williams. *Square Mile*, 13 Feb. 2017, squaremile.com/features/ed-stafford-explorer-interview. Accessed 7 July 2019.

Stafford, Ed. "60 Days on the Streets: I Begged beside Big Issue Sellers. I Made More Money." Interview by Adrian Lobb. *The Big Issue*, 14 Mar. 2019, www.bigissue.com/interviews/60-days-on-the-streets-i-begged-beside-big-issue-sellers-i-made-more-money. Accessed 7 July 2019.

Stafford, Ed. "Walking the Amazon: Interview with Ed Stafford." Interview by Nick Davidson. *Outside*, 21 Sept. 2010, www.outsideonline.com/1810886/walking-amazon-interview-ed-stafford. Accessed 7 July 2019.

SELECTED WORKS

Walking the Amazon, 2011; *Naked and Marooned with Ed Stafford*, 2013; *Ed Stafford: Into the Unknown*, 2015; *Ed Stafford: Left for Dead*, 2017; *Ed Stafford: First Man Out*, 2019

—*Christopher Mari*

Fiona Staples

Date of birth: ca. 1985
Occupation: Comics artist and illustrator

Comic book artist Fiona Staples earned much attention in the industry with the series *Saga*, an original collaboration with writer Brian K. Vaughan that debuted in 2012. Although she had already begun to make a name for herself working on established DC Comics titles and a few well-received original works with various writers, *Saga* quickly made her one of the most acclaimed illustrators in comics—a field with notably few high-profile female creators. The series consistently sold well and drew critical praise; for example, in 2018 *Vulture* named Staples's art from the first page of the first issue one of North America's one hundred most influential comic pages of all time.

Staples has won numerous industry honors for her art, including multiple Eisner and Harvey awards. Yet she has remained open to continual change and stylistic shifts, always seeking improvement. "If anything, I've learned it's okay for the look of the comic to evolve over time," she told Abraham Riesman for *Vulture* (23 Oct. 2018), discussing *Saga* in particular. "It's never too late to fix stuff."

EARLY LIFE AND EDUCATION

Staples was born in Calgary, Alberta, Canada, and loved to draw from a young age. As a child she enjoyed Richard Scarry's Busytown books, and later was enchanted by fantasy works such as George MacDonald's *The Princess and the Goblin* and Brian Jacques's Redwall series. She also read comic books, particularly Archie comics, which she found accessible due to each issue's standalone story compared to the intricate, long-running plot lines of popular superhero comics. Staples' parents encouraged her interest in art, and by the time she was in high school she had decided to attend art school and attempt to somehow earn a living as an artist.

Staples attended the Alberta College of Art and Design, with a major in visual communications. She worked in a comic book store, Comic-Kazi, while in college, which gave her a window into the true variety in comic book genres, themes, and art. A class in narrative illustration that included a project in comic books helped her see how the illustrations could enhance storytelling within the genre. Indeed, Staples would later credit her college experience with helping shape her entire approach to the creative process. "They teach you how to teach yourself," she said in an interview for *GraphicNovelReporter* (2011). "How to be critical and how to look at your own work, to see where you need to improve and how to take criticism from others. The whole critiquing process is drilled into you in college. That's something that I keep going back to."

Photo by Sergei Scurfield via Wikimedia Commons

EARLY CAREER

While still in college, Staples created art for the comic series Done to Death. A vampire-focused satire, it was a collaboration with writer Andrew Foley, a fellow Canadian, who she met on a message board for creators. The first of its five issues came out as she graduated, and she and Foley promoted it at the 2006 San Diego Comic-Con. At that event she made connections that helped her find further work, initially mainly as a colorist. She worked on various projects including for Image Comics, the magazine 2000AD, and WildStorm, an imprint of major publisher DC Comics.

Early in her career, Staples drew images in pen and ink and scanned them to be colored digitally with programs such as Photoshop. Soon, however, she switched to working fully in the digital realm, which she found to be a quicker way to create. While her skill in this technique began to attract admirers, it came with the drawback of a lack of physical copies of early sketches, which are popular collector's items among comic fans. As Staples joked to George Gene Gustines for the New York Times (8 July 2015), "My art dealer is pretty much perpetually disappointed by me."

Among Staples's next projects was creating the art for writer Aaron Williams's comic North 40, which debuted in 2009. The genre-defying supernatural story received mixed reviews, but the art was widely praised. Staples also worked on the WildStorm limited series Secret History of the Authority: Hawksmoor (2008) with writer Mike Costa and the 2010 series Mystery Society with writer Steve Niles. These projects solidified her status as an up-and-coming talent in the world of comics. Staples was nominated for an Eisner Award as penciller on North 40 and for 2011 Joe Schuster Awards as an outstanding comic book artist and cover artist.

DEVELOPING SAGA

Through Niles, Staples was introduced to Brian K. Vaughan, the acclaimed writer of the comic series Y: The Last Man (2002–8) and Runaways (2003–7). Vaughan was already familiar with her work and reached out to her about doing the art for a planned series based on ideas he had been forming since childhood. She agreed, and the two developed Saga, a sprawling science fiction fantasy centered on a young family trying to escape an interplanetary war. They launched the series in 2012 as an ongoing monthly book. It was published by Image Comics, which allowed it to be fully creator-owned—Staples and Vaughan retained all rights and control over the property.

Staples drew on many sources in developing the look of Saga, extrapolating off Vaughan's basic descriptions of characters. "He'll usually give me a sentence or two, explaining what animal the creature looks like and maybe what they're wearing, and then I try to execute that in a way that fits in with our universe and what that character's role is supposed to be," she told John Martin for the Observer (12 July 2017). At the beginning of the partnership, Staples asked Vaughn if the characters needed to be white. Receiving a negative answer, she gave East Asian characteristics to the character Marko while picturing his wife Alana with dark skin. These lead characters were already humanoid aliens of different races—the former sporting horns and the latter wings—so the allusion to real-world ethnicity only underscored the social themes at play. Alana and Marko's respective planets are at war, their love is forbidden, and their daughter Hazel—another central character—is biracial.

Staples rendered Alana, Marko, and Hazel in pen-and-ink style. Her backgrounds were typically done in a more painterly style, with a debt to Japanese animation, video games, and historical architecture. Her natural artistic tendencies helped form the characteristic organic look of the Saga world: "Drawing mechanical stuff is what takes me the longest to do, and I don't really enjoy it that much," she told Douglas Wolk for Time (5 Aug. 2013). "I told Brian that, and I don't know if he planned it all along, but one of our main settings is a wooden rocket ship." Staples also created the cover art for each issue of Saga and lettered the story's narration in her own natural handwriting.

SAGA'S SUCCESS

Saga quickly drew comparisons to hugely popular franchises such as Final Fantasy and Star Wars for its narrative breadth. It also earned attention for its refusal to maintain the dominant mode of white males as the default for comic book heroes. In subtle ways, the comic addresses modern concerns such as racism and gender identity. As Staples noted to Martin, it was "clear since the beginning that we'd be confronting heavy subject matter. I trust Brian, both as an intelligent writer and a decent person, to treat emotionally-charged topics in a thoughtful way."

The series soon became a favorite of both critics and general readers, with the first collected volume reaching the New York Times Best Sellers list for graphic books in 2012. Staples's art was consistently praised: "Her designs, expressions and coloring all make 'Saga' look unlike anything else currently on the stands," wrote Adam W. Kepler for the New York Times (26 Oct. 2012). With an M rating for violence and sexual content, however, Saga did attract some controversy, eventually appearing on the

American Library Association's list of most-challenged books in 2014.

Regardless of such objections, the series was nominated for multiple Hugo Awards, the most prestigious award for science fiction. In 2017, *Saga* won four Eisner Awards, the most of any comic. Staples was honored as best penciller/inker and best cover artist along with sharing the award for best continuing series with Vaughan. However, the following year, after fifty-four issues collected into nine book-size volumes, Staples and Vaughan decided to take an extended hiatus from the project. "It took seven years to get the story to this point, and being under intense deadline pressure nearly the whole time was starting to wear me out," Staples told Christian Holub for *Entertainment Weekly* (28 Aug. 2018).

ARCHIE REBOOT
While working on *Saga*, Staples still managed to find time for other projects. In honor of the seventy-fifth anniversary of the comic book character Archie Andrews, first introduced in 1941, Staples joined veteran writer Mark Waid in a reboot of the Archie series. While the iconic red-headed high school student and his friends had appeared in many forms over the years, they had largely stuck to the same signature artistic style. Now, however, Staples was tasked with overhauling the look of the series for contemporary audiences. As she remarked to Gustines, "Mike Pell, the president of Archie, just told me to make him cute. Make Archie someone the girls would fight over."

The reset began a new numbered series, intended to draw new attention to the new look. Still, Staples suggested that her work sought to retain the essence of the venerable franchise. "We don't want to change more than necessary," she told Gustines. "We're sticking to the spirit of Archie and the design of the characters. I don't think I changed any of the major features of the characters so much as I drew them in my own style."

Staples and Waid's take on *Archie* was a success, winning critical praise and the intended media attention. The fact that Staples was a female creator working on an iconic comics industry property—one with a history of less-than-feminist portrayals of female characters—also attracted significant notice. "It's hard not to be constantly aware of your gender and your place in the industry," she said to Gustines. "But I think things are only improving for women creators. If you compare now to almost ten years ago, which is when I started, there were fewer women." Though she left the series after the first three issues, her mark was felt as the reinvigorated Archie franchise expanded into other ventures. Meanwhile, Staples remained vocal about

wanting to see even greater gender equality and diversity in the comic book world, noting that it would better reflect audiences. As she told Martin "That diversity is what's causing the market to grow."

SUGGESTED READING
Amin, Shaan. "The Sprawling, Empathetic Adventure of Saga." *The Atlantic*, 28 Mar. 2018, www.theatlantic.com/entertainment/archive/2018/03/saga-comic-series-image-issue-50/556481/. Accessed 7 Nov. 2018.

Staples, Fiona. "Artist Unmasking: Fiona Staples." *GraphicNovelReporter*, 2011, www.graphicnovelreporter.com/authors/brian-k-vaughan/news/interview-090110. Accessed 7 Nov. 2018.

———. "The Comic Book Artist Fiona Staples Gives Archie a Makeover." Interview by George Gene Gustines. *The New York Times*, 8 July 2015, www.nytimes.com/2015/07/12/arts/the-comic-book-artist-fiona-staples-gives-archie-a-makeover.html. Accessed 7 Nov. 2018.

———. "Graphic Books Best Sellers: Fiona Staples Talks About 'Saga.'" Interview by Adam W. Kepler. *The New York Times*, 26 Oct. 2012, artsbeat.blogs.nytimes.com/2012/10/26/graphic-books-best-sellers-fiona-staples-talks-about-saga/. Accessed 7 Nov. 2018.

———. "How *Saga* Comics Artist Fiona Staples Drew a Masterpiece." Interview by Abraham Riesman. *Vulture*, 23 Oct. 2018, www.vulture.com/2018/10/saga-comics-artist-fiona-staples-sketches-script.html. Accessed 7 Nov. 2018.

———. "'Saga' Artist Fiona Staples on Making Comics in a Digital Era." Interview by John Martin. *Observer*, 12 July 2017, observer.com/2017/07/saga-artist-fiona-staples-interview/. Accessed 7 Nov. 2018.

———, Fiona, and Brian K. Vaughan. "Brian K. Vaughan and Fiona Staples Explain Why Saga Is Taking a Hiatus after That Stunning Cliffhanger." Interview by Christian Holub. *Entertainment Weekly*, 28 Aug. 2018, ew.com/books/2018/08/28/brian-k-vaughan-fiona-staples-saga-hiatus/. Accessed 7 Nov. 2018.

Wolk, Douglas. "Masters of the Universe." *Time*, 5 Aug. 2013, p. 54. *TOPICsearch*, search.ebscohost.com/login.aspx?direct=true&db=tth&AN=89516881&site=eds-live. Accessed 7 Nov. 2018.

SELECTED WORKS
Mystery Society (with Steve Niles and Ashley Wood), 2010; North 40 (with Aaron Williams), 2009–10; Saga (with Brian K. Vaughan), 2012– ; Archie (with Mark Waid), 2015

—Judy Johnson

Simon Stephens

Date of birth: February 6, 1971
Occupation: Playwright

Simon Stephens is an award-winning British playwright and one of the most prolific theater writers of his generation. He has written dozens of original plays and adaptations since his debut, *Bluebird*, in 1998. Stephens told Patrick Healy for the *New York Times* (4 Oct. 2012) that he views himself as an "action designer and story designer." He painstakingly plots out his plays before writing a word of dialogue. Thanks to his prodigious outlining, he wrote his celebrated 2006 play *Motortown* in four days. Stephens's plays embody the dramaturgy he preaches: "Dramatic narrative needs present tense action," he told Kate Kellaway for the *Guardian* (29 Aug. 2009). People tend to see life as "something that happens to them," he said. A playwright must reorient this view, asking not "Why is this happening to me?" but "Why am I doing this?" he said. Among Stephens's best-known works are the plays *Punk Rock*, about a school shooting in England, and *Harper Regan*, about a woman in the throes of a midlife crisis. His 2012 adaptation of Mark Haddon's 2003 novel *The Curious Incident of the Dog in the Night-Time* won a record-breaking seven Laurence Olivier Awards. It premiered on Broadway in 2014, picking up five Tony Awards, including best new play. Stephens serves as associate playwright at the Royal Court Theatre and an artistic associate at the Lyric Hammersmith, another theater that produces new work in London.

EARLY LIFE AND EDUCATION

Stephens was born in Stockport, a suburb of Manchester in Northern England, on February 6, 1971. His father was an electronics salesman and his mother was a schoolteacher. He attended the Tithe Barn School and the all-boys Stockport School. Stephens's teenage years were anguished, unhappy ones. "As a teenager, I had immense periods of misery," Stephens recalled to Kellaway. "If it hadn't been for [the rock band] the Smiths I would have been an even more unhappy person." In addition to music, Stephens found solace in long philosophical conversations with his general studies teacher, James Sidley. "If I were to choose one teacher throughout school . . . who I would give credit to me being a writer, it would be James Sidley," Stephens wrote for the education website *Tes* (23 Feb. 2019). Sidley encouraged Stephens's writing, giving him reading lists and writing exercises. "He read my work seriously and told me when it wasn't good enough and when it was," Stephens wrote. Stephens went on to attend the University of York, where

Photo by Ben Gabbe via Getty Images

he studied history and began writing plays. After graduation, he moved to Edinburgh, Scotland, where he worked at a café and wrote after his shifts at night; he also attempted to work as a DJ, but with little success. In 1993 he joined the post-punk rock band the Country Teasers, of which he was a member for over a decade before officially quitting in 2005. However, by that time, he had already become less active in the band and earned a teaching certificate at the Institute of Education. After a year of training, he took a job as a schoolteacher at East Brook School in Dagenham, England. He left the school after a year, when he was offered a role as the resident dramatist at the Royal Court in 2000.

BLUEBIRD AND OTHER EARLY PLAYS

Stephens's first professional play, *Bluebird*, premiered at the Royal Court Theatre in 1998. The play follows a London cab driver named Jimmy over the course of a night. Jimmy interacts with his passengers, who philosophize about life and love. He is also reunited with his ex-wife, whom he has not seen since the death of their daughter several years before. *Bluebird* won praise upon its premiere. It made its American debut over a decade later, playing Off-Broadway in 2011. Though Jimmy is supposed to be played by an actor in his thirties, that production starred fifty-year-old English stage legend Simon Russell Beale.

Bluebird launched Stephens's career. The same year it premiered, 1998, he received his first play commission. His next play, *Herons*, premiered at the Royal Court in 2001. *Herons* features a cast of teens who struggle to survive in the violent streets of their East London neighborhood. It received lukewarm reviews. *Port* (2002), Stephens's next play, fared much better with critics following its premiere at Manchester's Royal Exchange Theater. Set in Stockport, the play follows the coming-of-age of a working-class girl named Rachel between 1988 and 2002. It won a Pearson Award for Best Play. Of a 2013 production, critic Susannah Clapp, writing for the *Guardian* (2 Feb. 2013), observed: "More than any modern drama I have seen, *Port* conveys a sense of personal history lived from within. . . . This is as close to biography as you will get on stage."

Stephens served as a tutor for the Royal Court's Young Writers Program between 2001 and 2005. During that time he also wrote a play called *One Minute* (2003), about the abduction of a young girl, and *Christmas*, about a night at an East London pub just before the titular holiday, which premiered at the Pavilion Theatre in Brighton in 2003. In 2004, Stephens premiered a play called *Country Music* at the Royal Court. In it, protagonist Jamie, from a rough world like the one depicted in *Herons*, goes to prison for murder. The play was written on commission. While writing it, Stephens taught a playwriting course at a prison in London. "In the play, I tried to do service to some of the wit and grace of the men I met in my workshops," Stephens later wrote for the *Guardian* (25 June 2010). "I tried to write [Jamie] Carris not as a convict but as a lover, a brother and a father; I tried to make him into a human being." Stephens premiered his play *On the Shore of the Wide World* at the Royal Exchange Theater in Manchester in 2005. (It later transferred to the National Theatre.) The play follows three generations of a Stockport family. Though critics offered weak praise, *Wide World* won the Olivier Award for best play in 2006.

HARPER REGAN AND MORE RECENT PLAYS

In 2006, Stephens's *Motortown*, about a soldier returning from the Iraq War, premiered at the Royal Court Theatre. That same year, Stephens served as the first resident dramatist at the National Theatre, where his next play, *Harper Regan*, premiered in 2008. In it, a middle-aged woman is beset by crisis. She returns to her hometown—Stockport—to reconcile with her parents and reckon with her husband's terrible secret, revealed in the play's second act. In his *New York Times* review (10 Oct. 2012) for a 2012 Off-Broadway production of the play, Ben Brantley wrote that the main character's journey home "feels almost Homeric, an odyssey that seems to embrace all the essential primal acts of life and death, of sex and violence." However, Brantley wrote, *Harper Regan* is also "specifically and resonantly topical, a portrait of a world

in which technology and the noise it generates only underscore the loneliness that pervades a crowded planet."

Stephens's play *Pornography*, written in 2005, had been commissioned by the Deutsches Schauspielhaus in Hamburg, Germany, and had been staged four times in that country by the time of its UK premiere at the Edinburgh Theatre Festival in 2008. The play was inspired by the terrorist bombings that took place in London on July 7, 2005, and explores the humanity of a suicide bomber. Stephens's thirty-minute, philosophical monologue *Sea Wall* also premiered in 2008, at the Bush Theatre. In 2019, that play ran Off-Broadway on a double bill with British playwright Nick Payne's monologue *A Life*.

Stephens premiered his next play, *Punk Rock*, at the Lyric Hammersmith in 2009. The play, set in Stockport, was inspired by the Columbine massacre, a 1999 school shooting in Colorado. Michael Billington, writing for the *Guardian* (9 Sept. 2009), praised the play, comparing it favorably to the 2006 musical adaptation of *Spring Awakening*, a classic nineteenth-century German play about the anguish of youth. Billington wrote that *Punk Rock* "confronts young people as they really are, and builds inexorably towards its tragic and violent climax."

In 2010, Stephens wrote a musical called *Marine Parade*, and premiered *A Thousand Stars Explode in the Sky*, which he wrote with dramatists David Eldridge and Robert Holman, at the Lyric Hammersmith. This was followed in 2011 by *Wastwater* and a translation of Norwegian Jon Fosse's *Eg er vinden* (*I Am the Wind*). In 2012, Stephens collaborated with German director Sebastian Nübling and Estonian designer Ene-Liis Semper to create a divisive, experimental play called *Three Kingdoms* at the Lyric. His satire *The Trial of Ubu* also premiered that year at the Hampstead Theatre.

THE CURIOUS INCIDENT OF THE DOG IN THE NIGHT-TIME

In 2012, Stephens premiered three plays: a coming-of-age play called *Morning* at the Lyric; his new translation of Henrik Ibsen's 1879 play *A Doll's House* at the Young Vic; and his adaptation of Haddon's *The Curious Incident of the Dog in the Night-Time* at the National Theatre. Stephens had met Haddon through the National Theatre in 2006. Haddon had been approached numerous times about adapting his best-selling novel into a musical, but Haddon felt the story would work much better as a play without music, and asked Stephens to write it. The book and the play follow the story of a teenager with autism who becomes obsessed with solving the murder of his neighbor's dog. Stephens won praise for his adaptation, and the canny choices he made in rendering the first-person tale in dialogue. The play transferred to the West End, and earned a record-breaking seven Olivier Awards, including best new play. The play premiered on Broadway in 2014, won five Tony Awards including best new play, before closing in 2016.

Stephens's play *Birdland*, about a successful rock star, premiered at the Royal Court in 2014. Billington, again writing for the *Guardian* (10 Apr. 2014), rated it four out of five stars and described it as "ceaselessly inventive." That same year, Stephens premiered a critically praised play, set in Stockport, called *Blindsided* at the Royal Exchange.

In 2015, Stephens wrote an adaption of Bizet's opera *Carmen* called *Carmen Disruption*. It premiered at the Almeida Theatre in London. He also wrote a new translation of Anton Chekov's *The Cherry Orchard*, wrote a monologue for the Young Vic called *Song from Far Away*, and premiered a love story called *Heisenberg* Off-Broadway at the Manhattan Theater Club in New York City, which played on Broadway in 2016. Also in 2016, Stephens wrote a new adaptation of Bertolt Brecht's musical *The Threepenny Opera* for the National Theatre. In 2017, he worked with musician Karl Hyde from the British electronic group Underworld and director Scott Graham, to create a verbatim play—meaning that the words spoken onstage are taken from interviews with real people—called *Fatherland*. The play explores the relationship between fathers and sons. That same year, Stephens wrote a new translation of Chekov's *The Seagull* for the Lyric. He also wrote a stage adaptation of Luchino Visconti's 1943 film *Obsession*, which is, in turn, based on the 1934 noir classic *The Postman Always Rings Twice*.

PERSONAL LIFE
Stephens lives in East London with his family. He is married to Polly Heath, and the couple have three children: Oscar, Stanley, and Scarlett.

SUGGESTED READING

Billington, Michael. "Birdland Review—Ceaselessly Inventive Critique of Rock Stardom." Review of *Birdland*, by Simon Stephens, directed by Carrie Cracknell. *The Guardian*, 10 Apr. 2014, www.theguardian.com/stage/2014/apr/10/birdland-rock-stardom-theatre-review-royal-court. Accessed 19 Apr. 2019.

Brantley, Ben. "Sometimes You Just Need to Get Away." Review of *Harper Regan*, by Simon Stephens, directed by Gaye Taylor Upchurch. *The New York Times*, 10 Oct. 2012, www.nytimes.com/2012/10/11/theater/reviews/mary-mccann-in-harper-regan-at-atlantic-theater-company.html. Accessed 19 Apr. 2019.

Clapp, Susannah. Review of *Port*, by Simon Stephens, directed by Marianne Elliott. *The Guardian*, 2 Feb. 2013, www.theguardian. com/stage/2013/feb/03/port-lyttelton-simon-stephens-review. Accessed 19 Apr. 2019.

Healy, Patrick. "Specializing in Secrets and Their Dear Cost." *The New York Times*, 4 Oct. 2012, www.nytimes.com/2012/10/07/theater/specializing-in-secrets-and-their-dear-cost.html. Accessed 19 Apr. 2019.

Kellaway, Kate. "How Simon Stephens's Plays Are Galvanizing the British Theatre." *The Guardian*, 29 Aug. 2009, www.theguardian.com/stage/2009/aug/30/simon-stephens-theatre-punk-rock. Accessed 19 Apr. 2019.

Stephens, Simon. "Simon Stephens: 'Mr. Sidley Was Like No Teacher I'd Never Known." *Tes*, 23 Feb. 2019, www.tes.com/news/simon-stephens-mr-sidley-was-no-teacher-id-never-known. Accessed 19 Apr. 2019.

Stephens, Simon. "Drama in the Wings: Why Theatre in Prison Matters." *The Guardian*, 25 June 2010, www.theguardian.com/stage/theatreblog/2010/jun/25/theatre-in-prisons-country-music. Accessed 19 Apr. 2019.

SELECTED WORKS
Bluebird, 1998; *Port*, 2002; *On the Shore of the Wide World*, 2005; *Harper Regan*, 2008; *Punk Rock*, 2009; *The Curious Incident of the Dog in the Night-Time*, 2012

—Molly Hagan

Beth Stevens

Date of birth: 1970
Occupation: Neurologist

Beth Stevens is a neurologist whose work revealed the role microglia cells play in the neuronal "pruning" that occurs in brain development and their potential to cause or contribute to neurodevelopmental and neurodegenerative diseases such as autism, Alzheimer's disease, schizophrenia, and Huntington's disease.

EARLY LIFE AND EDUCATION
Beth Stevens was born in Brockton, Massachusetts, in 1970. She received her bachelor's degree in 1993 from Northeastern University. Upon completing her undergraduate work, she moved to Washington, DC. She applied for a position in a lab at the National Institutes of Health (NIH) but was turned away because of her lack of research experience. She took a job as a server at a nearby Chili's restaurant and returned to the NIH, résumé in hand, each week. A few months later, she was contacted by neuroscientist R. Douglas Fields. He was willing to take her on in his lab, where he was studying the role glial cells play in insulating neurons. (Glial

cells are the non-neuronal cells in the brain, which serve largely structural and maintenance roles, in contrast to the more-famous neuron's job of transmitting thoughts and encoding memories.) Scientists had known about microglial cells for some time, but little was known about them before Stevens took an interest and built her life's work around them.

She completed her work and received a PhD from the University of Maryland, College Park, in 2003. In 2005 she moved across the country to begin postdoctoral work at Stanford University in the lab of neuroscientist Ben Barres. When Stevens joined, little was known about how the brain went about pruning excess neurons over the course of development. (The brain initially forms about twice as many neurons as it will need for optimal function, which are pruned away over the course of the first three decades of life.) Stevens and Barres focused their research on the pruning process for neurons associated with vision.

THE ROLE OF MICROGLIAL CELLS IN BRAIN DEVELOPMENT AND DISEASE

In 2007, Stevens made her first major discovery alongside Barres. She had found an unusual protein in the brain: a protein called C1q that was only known previously to serve as a "tag" to mark damaged cells, microbes, and debris in the body for destruction by the immune system. The paper they published in the journal *Cell* later that year demonstrated that, in mice at least, these protein tags were marking developing neurons for elimination; they were part of the mysterious pruning process. As further evidence of this claim, Stevens and Barres demonstrated that mice genetically engineered to not produce the tagging protein had difficulty in pruning their neurons.

In 2008, Stevens opened her own lab at Harvard University and dedicated it to answering the questions her research with Barres had raised. By 2012, Stevens had reached a second major breakthrough in her research with the discovery that microglial cells were responsible for pruning.

Microglial cells, which make up about 10 percent of the brain's total cell count, were well known at the time for serving as the brain's housekeepers. They were considered analogous to the body's macrophages, white blood cells that engulf and digest microbes and other unwanted material in the body. Stevens called microglia the "Pac-Man" cells of the brain for their behavior. Stevens had observed microglia in mouse brains in the act of engulfing and digesting otherwise healthy neurons that had been tagged for elimination.

In 2015 Stevens published further research showing mice that did not produce a particular tagging protein of the type she observed during her work at the NIH were protected from age-related cognitive decline. They did not suffer from age-related synapse loss and performed better on learning and memory tests. Without the protein to tell microglia to remove old neurons, they were left untouched even as the mice grew old.

Stevens continued to probe the disease-related implications of her research by teaming up with Harvard schizophrenia researchers Steve McCarroll and Aswin Sekar, as well as immunologist Mike Carroll. Together they identified a specific gene, named C4, involved in producing a tagging protein that affects the tagging-and-elimination process Stevens had been studying. Published in early 2016, this research generated a new theory that schizophrenia may in fact be a disease of over-pruning.

IMPACT

Stevens's work has upended the conventional understanding of microglia and the brain's pruning process, and in doing so she has opened new avenues in the research of neurodevelopmental and neurodegenerative diseases such as autism, schizophrenia, Alzheimer's, Parkinson's, or Huntington's disease.

In September 2015, Stevens was awarded one of twenty-four MacArthur Foundation "genius" grants for her groundbreaking work. Stevens works at her Stevens Lab at Harvard, as well as the F. M. Kirby Neurobiology Center at Boston Children's Hospital. In both capacities she continues to explore the relationship between glia, neurons, brain development, and disease.

PERSONAL LIFE

Stevens is married to Rob Graham. The couple has a daughter Riley.

SUGGESTED READING

Blakemore, Erin. "Ask a MacArthur Genius: How Does the Brain Remodel Itself?" *The Washington Post.* Washington Post, 12 Oct. 2015, www.washingtonpost.com/news/speaking-of-science/wp/2015/10/12/ask-a-macarthur-genius-how-does-the-brain-remodel-itself/?utm_term=.3c8f377ef01b. Accessed 29 Jan. 2019.

Fliesler, Nancy. "Beth Stevens: A Transformative Thinker in Neuroscience." *Vector.* Boston Children's Hospital, 29 Sept. 2015, vector.childrenshospital.org/2015/09/beth-stevens-a-transformative-thinker-in-neuroscience/. Accessed 29 Jan. 2019.

Giles, Matt. "Big Idea: The Brain's Best-Kept Secret." *Popular Science.* Bonnier, 22 Dec. 2015, www.popsci.com/big-idea-brains-best-kept-secret. Accessed 29 Jan. 2019.

Hughes, Virginia. "Microglia: The Constant Gardeners." *Nature*. MacMillan, 31 May 2012, www.nature.com/news/microglia-the-constant-gardeners-1.10732. Accessed 29 Jan. 2019.

Mukherjee, Siddhartha. "Runs in the Family." *The New Yorker*. Condé Nast, 28 Mar. 2016, www.newyorker.com/magazine/2016/03/28/the-genetics-of-schizophrenia. Accessed 29 Jan. 2019.

Piore, Adam. "The Rogue Immune Cells That Wreck the Brain." *MIT Technology Review*, 4 Apr. 2016, www.technologyreview.com/s/601137/the-rogue-immune-cells-that-wreck-the-brain/. Accessed 29 Jan. 2019.

Zeliadt, Nicholette. "Beth Stevens: Casting Immune Cells as Brain Sculptors." *Spectrum*. Simons Foundation, 24 Sept. 2015, www.spectrumnews.org/news/profiles/beth-stevens-casting-immune-cells-as-brain-sculptors/. Accessed 29 Jan. 2019.

—*Kenrick Vezina*

Hannah Storm

Date of birth: June 13, 1962
Occupation: Television sports journalist

Hannah Storm is one of the most recognizable faces and names in television sports broadcasting. A graduate of the University of Notre Dame, Storm launched her career in the early 1980s, a time when there were few opportunities for women in the sports broadcasting world. Encountering widespread rejection and sexism, she took a job as a disc jockey at a heavy metal radio station and gradually worked her way up the broadcasting ladder. In 1989, she became the first female sportscaster at CNN, and over the next three decades, achieved several other distinctions. During an illustrious tenure at NBC from 1992 to 2002, Storm became the first woman to solo host Major League Baseball (MLB) coverage, while also covering three Olympic Games and other major sporting events. In 2008, following a five-year stint at CBS as host of *The Early Show*, she joined ESPN, where she has established herself as one of the leading sports network's signature personalities. Among other responsibilities, she hosts weekday and Sunday morning editions of *SportsCenter*, ESPN's flagship program.

The recipient of numerous awards, Storm has also founded her own production company, authored two books, and started her own eponymous charitable foundation. In 2018 she became part of the first female announcing team to cover a National Football League (NFL) game for Amazon Prime's *Thursday Night Football* coverage. Addressing the subject of gender bias in sports journalism, she explained to Kevin Draper in an interview for the *New York Times* (26 Sept. 2018), "If you are smart, if you do your homework, if you care, and then you have decades of experience, those are the things that matter."

EARLY LIFE AND EDUCATION

Storm was born Hannah Lynn Storen on June 13, 1962, in Oak Park, Illinois, and was raised in an Irish Catholic family. She developed an early love of sports through her father, Mike Storen, who, after serving in the Marine Corps, became a top sports executive. Described by Monte Burke for *Forbes* (9 Oct. 2009) as "the Forrest Gump of American sports franchises," Mike Storen held executive roles with such professional basketball franchises as the Chicago Zephyrs, Baltimore Bullets, and Indiana Pacers, before serving as commissioner of the American Basketball Association (ABA) from 1973 to 1974. Among other innovations, he helped design that league's iconic red, blue, and white basketballs.

Due to her father's profession, Storm, along with her two brothers, had a peripatetic childhood, which she characterized as "a journey of cities, pro leagues and franchises" in a self-penned article for ESPN (18 June 2011). Attending seven schools in twelve years, she has said that the experience of constantly being the new girl in school taught her how to be outgoing. Growing up, she also learned how to be comfortable around prominent professional athletes and coaches, who were often at her family's home.

Storm spent her last two years of high school at Westminster Schools, a private school in Atlanta, Georgia, where she ran track and acted in plays. Describing herself to Burke as a "huge ham," she also served as her school's mascot. Originally wanting to be an actor, Storm eventually opted to pursue a career in television sports broadcasting by the time she graduated from Westminster. Following in the footsteps of her father, who was then serving as president of the National Basketball Association (NBA)'s Atlanta Hawks, she went to the University of Notre Dame, in South Bend, Indiana. There, she majored in political science and communications.

Storm's path to becoming a sports broadcaster began at Notre Dame. She served as a stage manager for Notre Dame football's Sunday morning replay show, which was hosted by the legendary broadcaster Harry Kalas, and anchored a sports program on the university's local radio station. Every summer during college, Storm worked unpaid internships at various television stations to gain further experience; this included doing sports reporting for a local NBC affiliate. To support herself financially, she waited tables.

Photo by Unknown via Wikimedia Commons

SUCCEEDING WITHOUT A ROAD MAP

Upon graduating from Notre Dame in 1983, Storm embarked on her sports broadcasting career. At the time, few women were going into the field, and those who tried met with much resistance. Consequently, Storm's early experiences in trying to land a job proved humbling. "It just wasn't done," she told Heather Wood Rudúlph for *Cosmopolitan* (28 Dec. 2015). "There wasn't really a road map for what I wanted to do." By her own admission, she received "hundreds" of rejections from television stations around the country; many came in demeaning fashion, as when one station director told her, "I would not hire a woman to do sports even over my dead body," she noted to Rudúlph.

Following an enlightening jogging session with her father, whom she has credited with teaching her tenacity and the importance of always maintaining a positive attitude, Storm decided to shift her focus to radio broadcasting, which offered more job opportunities. She began answering hundreds of want ads, and eventually landed a job as a late-night DJ at a heavy metal radio station in Corpus Christi, Texas. At the urging of the station's producers, she changed her last name to "Storm," which they felt sounded better on the radio. The station was situated in the middle of farm country, and Storm has fondly recalled her time there, in which she interviewed bands like Black Sabbath, Heart, and Mötley Crüe.

All the while, Storm continued applying to television jobs, in hopes of returning to sports. In 1985, she got a gig as a sportscaster for an ABC radio affiliate in Houston, Texas, after showing up in the station's lobby and presenting her résumé to the program director. Storm's tireless persistence paid off, and in 1989, following a stint covering sports for an NBC television affiliate in Charlotte, North Carolina, she was hired by CNN to serve as the then-fledgling cable network's first female sportscaster—after they made her take a quiz to prove her sports knowledge.

Storm spent three years at CNN, during which she anchored *Sports Tonight* and other primetime sports programs. She also covered baseball and hosted the Goodwill Games for CNN's sister network TNT. "I got a lot of hate mail," she admitted to Rudúlph. "There was a segment of our viewership that needed to get used to seeing a woman deliver sports."

TENURES AT NBC AND CBS

Storm's profile rose considerably once she joined NBC in 1992. She was at the national network just a short while before she achieved one of her life goals: hosting an Olympic Games telecast. After hosting the 1992 Wimbledon Championships, Storm was assigned to host late-night telecasts of that year's Summer Olympics in Barcelona, Spain. She went on to host two more Olympic Games for the network, as well as other major sporting events like the World Series.

Storm's coverage of NBA and MLB games for NBC helped her become a household name in the sports world. She spent several years serving as an NBA sideline reporter and then later became the host of the *NBA on NBC*. She also covered Women's National Basketball Association (WNBA) games, serving as that league's first play-by-play announcer during its inaugural season in 1997. Meanwhile, from 1994 to 2000, she hosted NBC's MLB coverage, becoming the first woman ever to do so in a solo capacity.

In 2002, after spending a decade at NBC, Storm realized another longtime goal—hosting a morning network show—when she moved to CBS to host *The Early Show*. She held that role for five years, during which she covered major national stories like Hurricane Katrina and the 2004 presidential election, as well as interviewing national political figures like George W. Bush, Barack Obama, and John McCain, and cultural icons like Paul McCartney, Elton John, and Justin Timberlake.

According to Storm, the live format of *The Early Show* helped make her a stronger and more flexible interviewer. As she noted to Burke, "We would go from a serious segment to something totally goofy to something about getting gravy stains out of your tablecloth." Storm's flexibility as a reporter led CBS to occasionally assign her other responsibilities like hosting episodes of the network's award-winning newsmagazine *48 Hours* and cohosting its coverage of the Macy's Thanksgiving Day Parade.

ESPN AND BEYOND

Storm made her return to sports broadcasting in 2008, after CBS opted, for financial reasons, to not renew her contract. Turning down an opportunity to remain with CBS in a different capacity, she decided to interview with ESPN for a new live morning *SportsCenter* anchor position. Despite her wealth of experience, Storm had to go through a rigorous interview process to land the job, which included auditioning and interviewing with more than half a dozen people. Nevertheless, the national cable sports network, which is in Bristol, Connecticut, hired her, and it was not long before she became one of its signature talents.

As cohost of ESPN's live, three-hour weekday edition of *SportsCenter*, Storm is responsible for writing her scripts for on-air interviews and highlights, and for delivering breaking news reports. Drawing on the hard news background she acquired on *The Early Show*, she often brings panelists onto the show to discuss issues that are relevant to the sports world, from domestic violence to racism to sexual orientation and gender identity. As she told Rudúlph, "It's directing the conversation, and advancing it in a meaningful way."

Storm's responsibilities at ESPN also include hosting an NFL Sunday morning edition of *SportsCenter*. Upon debuting in that role in 2014, she became the first woman to solo host the flagship program. In addition, Storm hosts and executive produces the network's primetime interview specials, *In Focus with Hannah Storm* and *Face to Face with Hannah Storm*. Known for her earnest but easygoing interviewing style, she has interviewed many of the world's most distinguished athletes, including LeBron James, David Beckham, Michael Phelps, Peyton Manning, and Derek Jeter.

In conjunction with her arrival at ESPN, Storm founded Brainstormin' Productions, which has produced award-winning documentary films for the network and other branded content. She made her producing debut in 2010 with *Unmatched*, a documentary made for ESPN's *30 for 30* film series that chronicles the longstanding rivalry and friendship of tennis legends Martina Navratilova and Chris Evert. She has since produced and directed short and long-form pieces about NBA Hall of Famer Shaquille O'Neal, WNBA legend Sheryl Swoopes, and the late professional golfer Payne Stewart, among others.

In 2018, Storm added to her list of firsts when she became part of the first all-woman booth to call an NFL game. Along with veteran sportscaster Andrea Kremer, she provided commentary and analysis for Amazon Prime Video's live streaming coverage of eleven *Thursday Night Football* games during that year's NFL season.

In her interview with Kevin Draper, Storm explained, "I am really excited in the big picture, at having young women, men, all sorts of people, to understand that football and sports is for everyone."

PERSONAL LIFE

Aside from her duties at ESPN and Brainstormin' Productions, Storm runs the Hannah Storm Foundation, which raises awareness and funds to treat children born with vascular birthmarks. She founded the charitable organization in part due to being born with a port-wine stain birthmark under her left eye, which she often speaks publicly about.

Storm has authored two books: *Notre Dame Inspirations: The University's Most Successful Alumni Talk about Life, Spirituality, Football and Everything Else* (2006), which features a collection of stories about thirty-two prominent Notre Dame alumni; and *Go Girl! Raising Healthy, Confident and Successful Girls through Sports* (2002; with Mark Jenkins), a guide about how parents can successfully navigate their daughters' involvement in sports. She has also written articles for such publications as *Notre Dame Magazine*, *Cosmopolitan*, and *The Hollywood Reporter*.

Storm lives in Greenwich, Connecticut, with her husband, the NBC sportscaster Dan Hicks, whom she met while the two were working at CNN. The couple have three daughters: Hannah, Ellery, and Riley. Among many other honors, Storm was named the 2018 Woman of Influence by *Multichannel News* for her work as a journalist, producer, and director.

SUGGESTED READING

"About Hannah." *Hannahstorm.com*, hannah-storm.com/#about. Accessed 22 Dec. 2018.

Barron, David. "Hannah Storm Long on Gumption." *Houston Chronicle*, 12 Sept. 2010, www.chron.com/life/article/Hannah-Storm-long-on-gumption-1718050.php. Accessed 22 Dec. 2018.

Burke, Monte. "Off the Field with Hannah Storm." *Forbes*, 9 Oct. 2009, www.forbes.com/2009/10/08/hannah-storm-sportscenter-lifestyle-sports-espn.html#3471df945baf. Accessed 22 Dec. 2018.

Storm, Hannah. "Get That Life: How I Became One of TV's First Woman Sports Broadcasters." Interview by Heather Wood Rudulph. *Cosmopolitan*, 28 Dec. 2015, www.cosmopolitan.com/career/interviews/a51015/get-that-life-hannah-storm-sportscenter-broadcaster/. Accessed 22 Dec. 2018.

Storm, Hannah. "I Sat Next to Elvis." *ESPN*, 18 June 2011, www.espn.com/espn/commentary/news/story?page=storm-110617. Accessed 22 Dec. 2018.

Storm, Hannah, and Andrea Kremer. "For Hannah Storm and Andrea Kremer, History in the Broadcast Booth." Interview by Kevin Draper. *The New York Times*, 26 Sept. 2018, www.nytimes.com/2018/09/26/sports/thursday-night-football-andrea-kremer-hannah-storm.html. Accessed 22 Dec. 2018.

—*Chris Cullen*

Trevor Story

Date of birth: November 15, 1992
Occupation: Baseball player

In May 2011, nearly thirty scouts visited Irving High School in Texas to observe a practice session held by the school's varsity baseball team. The player who drew them there was shortstop Trevor Story, a senior member of the team who had been identified as a major prospect in that year's Major League Baseball (MLB) Draft. Although the attention and expectations of those scouts might have easily thrown Story off his game, the talented young player was not so easily rattled. "I wouldn't say I'm nervous," he told Corbett Smith for *SportsDay HS* (4 May 2011) at the time. "I'm excited. We'll just have to wait and see where I end up." Where Story ended up turned out to be the Colorado Rockies, which drafted him as the forty-fifth overall pick in the 2011 MLB Draft.

After about five years in the minor leagues, playing for Rockies affiliate teams such as the Modesto Nuts and the Albuquerque Isotopes, Story joined the Rockies at the start of the 2016 season. He immediately distinguished himself by scoring two home runs in his first game, an achievement followed by Player of the Week and Rookie of the Month honors. Although Story struggled in the 2017 season, that fall brought his first postseason appearance and the Rockies' first since 2009. The Rockies' 2017 and 2018 postseason campaigns ultimately proved unsuccessful, but Story remained confident and focused. "Just sticking with the process, and I know that sounds cliché, but that really is truly what it is for me," he told Michael Spencer for *CBS Denver* (21 Aug. 2018).

EARLY LIFE AND EDUCATION

Trevor John Story was born to Ken and Teddie Story on November 15, 1992, in Irving, Texas. Story's father worked as a firefighter for the Irving Fire Department. His mother, a former banker, worked for and eventually headed the nonprofit organization Irving Cares. A fan of baseball, Story's father taught both him and his older brother, Tyler, the basics of the sport, and

Story reportedly began playing T-ball at the age of four. He progressed as an athlete over the later years, drawing inspiration both from his father and from established baseball players such as outfielder Ken Griffey Jr. and shortstop Derek Jeter. In addition to playing baseball, Story visited Colorado occasionally on ski trips and enjoyed watching the Dallas Cowboys professional football team.

Upon beginning high school, Story joined the Irving High School baseball and football teams and quickly proved his strength as an athlete. His baseball coach promoted him to the varsity team late in his first season, and Story remained with that team for the rest of his high school career, later dropping football to focus on baseball. Story's promotion not only gave him the opportunity to play alongside his brother, who was already a varsity player, but further enabled him to demonstrate his strong aptitude for the sport and showcase his skills as shortstop. A versatile athlete, he served as a pitcher when one was needed and at one point reached a speed of ninety-six miles per hour with a pitch. Story also performed well as a hitter, achieving a batting average of nearly .500 during his senior season. The teen also strove to improve his batting further by working with batting coach Brandon Sherard, with whom he would continue to work as a professional player.

Story's strong performance on the Irving High School varsity team drew the attention of major-league scouts, many of whom attended the team's games and practices to observe him and his teammates. Although pleased with his abilities as a shortstop, some scouts were unsure

Jennifer Linnea Photography

whether his batting skills, though impressive in high-school games, would measure up in the majors. Story, however, was unphased by criticism of his offensive play. "Being a shortstop, my first priority is defense," he told Andrew T. Fisher in an interview for *Purple Row* (25 Aug. 2011). "The offensive criticism honestly motivates me to prove my bat. I know I can swing it and it will show soon."

Story graduated from Irving High School in 2011. He had planned to attend Louisiana State University after high school, having been offered a scholarship, but instead entered the 2011 MLB Draft and pursued a professional career immediately.

MINOR LEAGUES

In early June 2011, the Colorado Rockies selected Story as the forty-fifth overall draft pick. For Story, that development was unexpected. "I went into the draft with low expectations, just hoping that everything would work out for the best, and it certainly did," he told Fisher. "I really had no idea of which team I would be chosen by, but it was a high honor to be selected by the Colorado Rockies." Putting aside his earlier plans to enroll in college, he signed with the team on July 9 of that year, receiving a signing bonus of $915,000. Days later, he was playing for the Casper Ghosts, then the rookie-level affiliate of the Rockies. Story played the remainder of that season with the Ghosts before moving on to the Class A Asheville Tourists for the 2012 season.

In March 2013, Story joined the Modesto Nuts, the Rockies' Class A Advanced affiliate. Although he struggled at first, his performance improved during the 2014 season, which he began in Modesto. Speaking of his strategy, he told Jen Mac Ramos for *Purple Row* (15 Oct. 2014): "It was really getting back to what I've always done as a hitter, offensively, in high school and really getting back to my roots as a hitter. Really just being more disciplined at the plate, and not swinging at bad pitches." Although he primarily played shortstop for minor-league teams such as the Nuts, as he had since high school, he also tried out the second-base and third-base positions to test his capabilities and learn new skills.

In late June 2014, Story moved to the Double-A Tulsa Drillers. He went on to play with the Salt River Rafters of the Arizona Fall League during the fall of 2014. Story then began the 2015 season with the Double-A New Britain Rock Cats and went on to complete the season with the Triple-A Albuquerque Isotopes.

COLORADO ROCKIES

Having performed well during major-league spring training in early 2016, Story was called up to Rockies at the beginning of the 2016 season. He debuted with the Rockies during the regular-season opener on April 4, 2016, against the Arizona Diamondbacks. The Rockies defeated the Diamondbacks, 10–5, and Story himself scored two home runs during the game. He went on to score at least one home run in each of his first six games, setting an MLB record. In recognition of his early achievements with the Rockies, Story was named the NL Rookie of the Month for April and National League (NL) Player of the Week twice, once in April and once in July. That season, Story played in ninety-seven games with the Rockies and achieved sixty-seven runs, twenty-seven home runs, and a batting average of .272. He also put forth a strong defensive performance as shortstop, achieving a fielding percentage of .977. Despite Story's efforts, the Rockies struggled during the season, finishing third out of five in the NL West with a record of seventy-five wins to eighty-seven losses and did not qualify for a postseason berth.

Story's second season with the Rockies was challenging from an offensive perspective and was hampered, in part, by a shoulder injury Story incurred in May 2017, which required him to be placed on the disabled list and to complete a brief rehabilitation assignment in Albuquerque before returning to the Rockies. Over 145 games with the team, Story managed only twenty-four home runs—three fewer than in his ninety-seven-game debut season—and a lower batting average of .239. However, he performed far better on defense and achieved a fielding percentage of .982, the second-highest among shortstops in the NL. "If you don't get the job done offensively, you have to get it done defensively as a shortstop. I take that very much to heart," he told Eric Goodman and Les Shapiro in an interview for their radio show, *Afternoon Drive with Goodman and Shapiro* (7 Mar. 2018). "I just love playing defense. It's fun to me." Although he told Goodman and Shapiro that he had not performed as well offensively as he had hoped, he "learned a lot about [him]self" that season and hoped that those lessons would help him in 2018.

POSTSEASON DREAMS

The Rockies once again finished the regular season in third place in the NL West. Despite that, the 2017 postseason—their first since 2009—proved an exciting opportunity for the team, which received a spot in the NL Wild Card Game. The franchise also had yet to win a World Series, and for both the team and its fans, the 2017 postseason represented a chance to begin a new chapter. Facing off against the Diamondbacks, the Rockies made a strong effort, and Story himself scored a home run. However, the Rockies ultimately fell to the Diamondbacks, 8–11, ending the team's hopes of World Series glory.

During the 2018 regular season, Story missed several games due to an elbow injury. He nevertheless played in 157 games with the Rockies, achieving eighty-eight runs, a batting average of .291, and a fielding percentage of .979. He ranked second in the league for home runs (37) and fourth for runs batted in (108), doubles (42), and strikeouts (168). Most impressively, in September 2018, Story smashed records with a 505-foot-long homer, then the longest in MLB history. In recognition of his achievements, Story was selected for the 2018 NL All-Star Game and received an NL Silver Slugger Award, given to the best offensive player in each position.

For Story and his teammates, however, the most significant goal was to return to postseason competition and progress farther than in 2017. "We want the West, no doubt," he told Kyle Newman for the *Denver Post* (29 Sept. 2018). The Rockies ended the regular season ranked second in the NL West and proceeded to the Wild Card Game, where they defeated the Chicago Cubs, 2–1. They then competed in the National League Division Series (NLDS) but ultimately lost all three games to the Milwaukee Brewers.

PERSONAL LIFE

Story married Mallie Crow in November 2018 in Grapevine, Texas. The two had begun dating in high school. The couple live near Dallas during the offseason.

SUGGESTED READING

Newman, Kyle. "Clinching a Postseason Berth Is Nice, but the Rockies Now Have Tunnel Vision on First Division Title." *Denver Post*, 29 Sept. 2018, www.denverpost.com/2018/09/29/rockies-tunnel-vision-division-title. Accessed 12 Apr. 2019.

Smith, Corbett. "Meet Irving's Trevor Story: The Shortstop Who Attracted 28 Scouts to a Practice This Season." *SportsDay HS*, Dallas Morning News, 5 May 2011, sportsday.dallasnews.com/high-school/highschoolheadlines/2011/05/04/meet-irving_s-trevor-story-the-shortstop-who-attracted-28-scouts-to-a-practice-this-season. Accessed 12 Apr. 2019.

Spencer, Michael. "Trevor Story: Confidence the Key to Rockies Success Right Now." *CBS Denver*, 21 Aug. 2018, denver.cbslocal.com/2018/08/21/trevor-story-colorado-rockies. Accessed 12 Apr. 2019.

Story, Trevor. "Afternoon Drive: Trevor Story on His Off Season and How His Teammates Help Him Grow." Interview by Eric Goodman and Les Shapiro. *Afternoon Drive with Goodman & Shapiro*, Mile High Sports, audioboom.com/posts/6712105-afternoon-drive-trevor-story-on-his-off-season-and-how-

his-teammates-help-him-grow. Accessed 12 Apr. 2019.

Story, Trevor. "Purple Row Interviews Rockies 1st Round Pick Trevor Story." Interview by Andrew T. Fisher. *Purple Row*, SB Nation, 25 Aug. 2011, www.purplerow.com/platform/amp/2011/8/25/2381977/purple-row-interviews-trevor-story-rockies. Accessed 12 Apr. 2019.

Story, Trevor. "Rockies Prospect Trevor Story Adjusting to New Positions." Interview by Jen Mac Ramos. *Purple Row*, SB Nation, 15 Oct. 2014, www.purplerow.com/2014/10/15/6982551/rockies-prospect-trevor-story-interview-position-change. Accessed 12 Apr. 2019.

Sylte, Allison. "Meet Colorado Rockies Shortstop Trevor Story." *9News.com*, KUSA-TV, 6 Apr. 2016, www.9news.com/article/sports/mlb/colorado-rockies/meet-colorado-rockies-shortstop-trevor-story/123066665. Accessed 12 Apr. 2019.

—*Joy Crelin*

Yvonne Strahovski

Date of birth: July 30, 1982
Occupation: Actor

Australian-born actor Yvonne Strahovski often describes her sudden success in Hollywood as something of a fairy tale—which is perhaps ironic given the tough personas for which she is best known. Strahovski, who got her start in Australian stage and television, first came to the attention of American audiences in 2007, just a few years out of school. In a whirlwind, she was selected as the female lead on the cult-favorite NBC series *Chuck*: CIA agent Sarah Walker, who could brutally take down an enemy with martial-arts moves while wearing four-inch stilettos. When *Chuck* ended in 2012, Strahovski jumped to the other side of the law-enforcement equation, joining the cast of the beloved, long-running series *Dexter* as Hannah McKay, the love interest of the show's serial killer protagonist—and a serial killer herself. In recent years Strahovski has garnered increased fame as Serena Joy Waterford, a reprehensible but complex villain in Hulu's dystopian drama *The Handmaid's Tale*, which is based on a novel by Margaret Atwood. "That's the fun of it I think, for an actor," Strahovski told Marika Aubrey for the arts and theater website *Aussie Theatre* (14 Sept. 2013). "You get to be so many different people in a lifetime."

Strahovski has also played on Broadway. The versatile actor has appeared on the big screen in

Photo by Dominick D via Wikimedia Commons

such films as *The Guilt Trip* (2012), *The Astronaut Wives Club* (2015), *He's Out There* (2018), and *The Predator* (2018), choosing projects from a wide variety of genres, including drama, comedy, science fiction, and horror.

EARLY YEARS
The actor was born Yvonne Jaqueline Strzechowski on July 30, 1982, in Werrington Downs, a suburb of Sydney, the capital of the Australian state of New South Wales. Some sources mistakenly list her place of birth as Maroubra, a beachside suburb not too far away; she has clarified that her parents longed to live near the ocean and eventually moved to the more-desirable Maroubra when she was about five. Her father worked as an electrical engineer and her mother was a lab technician and they immigrated to Australia from a repressive communist regime in Poland. Strahovski is their only child. Growing up in Maroubra, she relished being outdoors and could often be found camping, rock climbing, and hiking.

She was an exceptionally studious child who excelled throughout school. Because she spoke Polish at home rather than English, Strahovski walked around all day with a dictionary in her hand; each time she heard an unfamiliar word, she would look it up, write it on the back of her hand, and use it as many times as possible, in order to absorb it.

She acknowledges that she was a bit of a ham. "I remember being the lanky, goofy, acne-covered child who was always clowning around in front of a home video camera," she told Luaine Lee for the New Zealand newspaper *Stuff* (6

June 2017). "And there was just never any question in my mind that I wanted to go down this [career] path." She performed in a number of school productions.

EDUCATION AND EARLY CAREER
After graduating from Santa Sabina College, a Catholic school in Strathfield, in 2000, Strahovski entered Western Sydney University's drama program, also known as Theatre Nepean. Strahovski's parents would have preferred her to pursue medicine or law, but they supported her decision. She earned money while in school by waiting tables, a physically demanding job she has likened to going to the gym for hours on end, and also worked as an usher at a local cinema.

The hard work, she has explained, was well worth it in that it allowed her to chase her dreams of a professional acting career. "As I've gotten older, I think I've come to realize that it really is about storytelling and about reflecting life and life reflecting art," she mused to Lee. "And you always learn something from watching art of any kind. You always take something away from it because you can't help but have it reflect on you, and hold up a mirror to your own personal life."

After graduating from Theatre Nepean in 2005, Strahovski cofounded a small theater company and began booking occasional commercials. In 2004 she appeared in an episode of the action-comedy series *Double the Fist*, and the following year she won a recurring role on the short-lived Australian drama *Headland* (stylized as *headLand*), which chronicled the romantic exploits of a group of university students in New South Wales.

CHUCK
On a whim, Strahovski decided to accompany a group of friends who were traveling to the United States to audition in advance of pilot season. While there she found an American manager. She soon sent in an audition tape to the creators of *Chuck*, which centers on a young computer geek who inadvertently downloads critical government secrets into his brain. After being called in to read lines with Zachary Levi, who was playing the titular protagonist, Strahovski felt hopeful. Passing through the gates of the studio, she called her parents to tell them she might not be returning to Australia as quickly as planned.

That confidence was warranted: she was hired to play Sarah Walker, the beautiful CIA agent assigned to protect the main character, and quickly found a small shared apartment in the Hollywood Hills. Urged to adopt a stage name, Strahovski instead changed the spelling of her name to more accurately reflect its phonetic pronunciation. After the pilot was picked up by the network, she eventually found a place of her own and settled into her new life in the United States.

The series won two Emmy Awards for outstanding stunt coordination—a nod to Strahovski's physical prowess as well, as she did most of her own stunts. In 2011, in recognition of her derring-do, she was also named woman of the year at *Cosmopolitan*'s Fun Fearless Female of the Year, as well as favorite actress. While it was regularly threatened with cancellation because of lackluster ratings, *Chuck* aired until 2012 thanks to the efforts of its passionate fan base, which was small but vocal.

GOLDEN BOY AND OTHER PROJECTS

When *Chuck* ended, Strahovski returned to her stage roots briefly. She appeared in a Broadway revival of Clifford Odets's *Golden Boy* as the lead's crush, Lorna, and earned glowing reviews, such as the one notoriously discerning critic Charles Isherwood wrote for the *New York Times* (6 Dec. 2012). "The icily beautiful Ms. Strahovski, making a striking Broadway debut, brings out the velvety heart beating under Lorna's cool, hardened-steel exterior," Isherwood opined. "Slinging Lorna's tart wisecracks with the expertise of a 1930s B-movie star, she also manages to turn her borderline stereotypical character into a rounded human being."

During *Chuck*'s run, Strahovski had also appeared in the 2011 action thriller *Killer Elite*, opposite Jason Statham, Clive Owen, and Robert De Niro, and shortly after the series went off the air, she landed a part in the big-screen comedy *The Guilt Trip* (2012), starring Seth Rogen and Barbra Streisand. Her next recurring television role came during the seventh season of the hit Showtime crime series *Dexter*. The quirky show starred Michael C. Hall as a forensic investigator who moonlights as a serial killer in order to advance justice—he kills only other killers who have somehow eluded capture—and Strahovski was cast as Hannah McKay, a fellow killer with whom Dexter falls in love. Her character became a fan favorite and returned for the critically acclaimed show's eighth and final season.

Following *Dexter*'s series finale (which caused some consternation among die-hard fans of the show), Strahovski steadily worked in a variety of roles. She starred, for example, in the 2014 fantasy-horror film *I, Frankenstein*; played another CIA agent in the 2014 television miniseries *24: Live Another Day*; was part of the ensemble cast of 2015's period piece *The Astronaut Wives Club*; and had roles in the 2016 films *All I See Is You* and *Manhattan Night*.

In 2018 Strahovski appeared in two horror films, *He's Out There* and *The Predator* (a remake of *Aliens*, the iconic Ridley Scott franchise), and she also returned to her native Australia to film the psychological thriller *Angel of Mine*, slated for release in August 2019. It was, she noted, the first time she had been called upon to use an Australian accent in many years.

THE HANDMAID'S TALE

Strahovski's largest post-*Dexter* audience has come courtesy of the hit Hulu drama *The Handmaid's Tale*, which began airing in 2017. It follows the denizens of Gilead, a dystopian future America in which less privileged women known as handmaids are forced to bear children for infertile couples of higher social status. In it, she plays Serena Joy Waterford, the wife of a high-ranking official whose handmaid Offred (played by Elisabeth Moss) longs to escape Gilead and reunite with her own family.

"There's a reason people are comparing Hulu's adaptation of Margaret Atwood's dystopian novel *The Handmaid's Tale* to our current political climate," Patti Greco wrote for *Cosmopolitan* (26 Apr. 2017). "It's about a world where women's rights are stripped away in a totalitarian return to 'traditional values.' It also features protests, terrorism, and a character who's already drawn comparisons to Ivanka Trump [for their complicity]." Never having read the novel before taking that part, Strahovski was immediately fascinated by her character. "I found her quite mesmerising, because I didn't have all the answers to her," she explained to Jane Albert for *Vogue Australia* (6 July 2018). She added, "So, to me, all that loneliness, bitterness and emotional instability were the first things I noticed about this character, and I loved the complexity of her."

For her work on the show, Strahovski was nominated for Emmy and Golden Globe Awards in 2018 and 2019, respectively. At press time, the third season of *The Handmaid's Tale* was scheduled to start airing in June 2019.

PERSONAL LIFE

Strahovski announced at the 2017 Emmy Awards that she had married fellow actor Tim Loden in a quiet private ceremony. Their honeymoon consisted of a cross-country road trip with their dogs, making stops to camp, hike, and go fly-fishing. In October 2018 she gave birth to a son; she mentioned in interviews the challenges of concealing her pregnancy while shooting *Handmaid*. Strahovski and her family live in Los Angeles.

SUGGESTED READING

Albert, Jane. "Australian Actress Yvonne Strahovski Talks Motherhood and *The Handmaid's Tale*." *Vogue Australia*, 6 July 2018, www.vogue.com.au/celebrity/interviews/australian-actress-yvonne-strahovski-talks-motherhood-and-the-handmaids-tale/news-story/666eef5dabaf23e05cc5911282625cb2. Accessed 6 May 2019.

Isherwood, Charles. "The Sweet Science vs. the Stradivarius." Review of *Golden Boy*, directed by Bartlett Sher. *The New York Times*, 6 Dec. 2012, www.nytimes.com/2012/12/07/theater/reviews/golden-boy-directed-by-bartlett-sher.html. Accessed 6 May 2019.

Lee, Luaine. "How Aussie Actress Yvonne Strahovski Made It into Hollywood's Closed Society." *Stuff*, 6 June 2017, www.stuff.co.nz/entertainment/tv-radio/93334941/the-handmaids-tale-how-aussie-actress-yvonne-strahovski-made-it-into-hollywoods-closed-society. Accessed 6 May 2019.

Strahovski, Yvonne. "How We Do What We Do." Interview by Marika Aubrey. *Aussie Theatre*, 14 Sept. 2013, aussietheatre.com.au/blogs/how-we-do-what-we-do/doyvonne-strahovski-marika-aubrey. Accessed 6 May 2019.

Strahovski, Yvonne. "*The Handmaid's Tale*'s Yvonne Strahovski on Serena Joy's Role in the Rise of Gilead." Interview by Patti Greco. *Cosmopolitan*, 26 Apr. 2017, www.cosmopolitan.com/entertainment/tv/a9564607/yvonne-strahovski-serena-joy-the-handmaids-tale-interview. Accessed 6 May 2019.

Vineyard, Jennifer. "*The Handmaid's Tale*: Yvonne Strahovski on the Harrowing Finale and Serena's Murky Future." *The New York Times*, 11 July 2018, www.nytimes.com/2018/07/11/arts/television/the-handmaids-tale-yvonne-strahovski-interview-season-2-finale.html. Accessed 6 May 2019.

Wyatt, Edward. "Super Nerd Is Out to Save the World." *The New York Times*, 30 Sept. 2007, www.nytimes.com/2007/09/30/arts/television/30wyatt.html. Accessed 6 May 2019.

SELECTED WORKS

Headland, 2005; *Chuck*, 2007–12; *Killer Elite*, 2011; *The Guilt Trip*, 2012; *Dexter*, 2012–13; *The Astronaut Wives Club*, 2015; *The Handmaid's Tale*, 2017–; *The Predator*, 2018

—*Mari Rich*

Mark Stucky

Date of birth: Septmber 11, 1958
Occupation: Test pilot

Mark "Forger" Stucky has a unique job: he is the lead test pilot for SpaceShipTwo, the spacecraft that Sir Richard Branson hopes to use (in combination with its mother ship, White Knight Two) to make commercial suborbital spaceflight possible. On SpaceShipTwo, "space tourists" would be taken to the edge of space, where they would experience a few minutes of weightlessness and see the curvature of the Earth. Branson's company Virgin Galactic is one of several private space ventures—which include Elon Musk's Space X and Jeff Bezos's Blue Origin—that hope to take spaceflight out of the purview of governments and into the hands of private individuals. Yet to do that, Branson must rely on highly skilled test pilots who have had extensive training, both in the military and with the National Aeronautics Space Administration (NASA), to give his spacecraft the necessary shakedowns to prove it will be reliable time and again. He has found such a lead test pilot in Mark Stucky.

Stucky believes SpaceShipTwo is one of the most innovative crafts out there—part spacecraft, part fighter jet, part business jet—and something that will impress both future paying customers and future historians of aeronautics. In an interview with Noah Davis for *Popular Mechanics* (7 May 2015), Stucky described the key ingredients in the making of a good test pilot: "I think the main thing is the interest in learning and not just flying from point A to point B. You're trying to understand what makes an airplane fly, what makes it better, and all the theory that goes into it. It's a different kind of flying—really high-risk. I'd say there is a good percentage of pilots that would have no interest in being a test pilot because of the perceived danger."

EARLY LIFE AND EDUCATION

The son of Paul and Lidia Stucky, Mark Paul Stucky was born September 11, 1958 and grew up in Salina, Kansas. One of Mark's first memories was watching John Glenn's orbital flight on February 20, 1962—a moment that captivated both the young boy and the nation at large because it demonstrated that the United States could compete with the Soviet Union in outer space. Stucky recalled to Noah Davis in *Popular Mechanics*: "One of my earliest memories was John Glenn's flight. I was enthralled by the concept of flying in space. I knew that to do that, you had to be a test pilot. I wanted to do that from a young age, even though I never thought it would be possible."

Part of the reason why young Mark did not think he would ever become an astronaut was that his father, Paul, was a Mennonite, a Protestant Christian denomination that rejects military service. Because of his beliefs, the elder Stucky was a conscientious objector during World War II, and worked at a Civilian Public Service camp in Puerto Rico. Although Paul, as a physics instructor at a local college, had an appreciation for the space program, since American astronauts at that time came from the military, Paul saw no way that his son would ever become one.

Yet the idea of becoming a test pilot and an astronaut long lingered in Mark's mind. Although he did not bring up the subject with his father for years, he continued to read about piloting and the space program in magazines like *National Geographic*. One story in that magazine got him interested in the emerging sport of hang gliding. At thirteen, he discussed the sport with his father, who eventually agreed to split the costs of a glider. After his first flight, on May 15, 1974, near Wilson Lake, Kansas, young Mark was hooked. His love of gliding—he later switched to paragliding, which uses a glider more like a parachute, with no rigid structure—would become a lifelong passion, culminating in his coauthoring the 2006 book, *Paragliding: A Pilot's Training Manual*, with Mike Meier.

Stucky went to Kansas State University, earning a bachelor's degree in physical science in 1980. (In 1992, he would earn his MS in aviation systems at the University of Tennessee Space Institute.) As an undergraduate, he often missed classes in favor of gliding around the flint hills of the area.

PILOTING CAREER

With the dream of becoming an astronaut still in the back of his mind, Stucky joined the US Marines in 1980, over the objections of his father. In 1982, he was accepted into flight school, initially joining a training squadron flying F-4 Phantoms out of Yuma, Arizona. As a young pilot he got a reputation for being highly skilled—and having excellent eyesight—as well as a reputation for being a bit of a showoff. One such example: in 1985 he got within a few dozen feet of a Soviet bomber over the Sea of Japan and took a picture of it. During his thirteen years in the Marines, he would also fly F-18s and serve as a test pilot at Naval Air Station Point Mugu and Naval Weapons Center China Lake, both in California. During the Persian Gulf War (1990–91), he flew combat missions against Saddam Hussein's armed forces in Iraq.

Upon leaving the Marines in March 1993, Stucky joined NASA as an aerospace research pilot, during which time he applied for the astronaut corps several times, hoping that he would one day fly on a Space Shuttle mission. Yet he never made the cut. He compared attempting to become an astronaut to winning the Miss America pageant in his interview with Nicholas Schmidle for the *New Yorker* (20 Aug. 2018): "You can be one of fifty very talented and beautiful women, but you can't *plan* on winning. There's an element of luck involved."

Stucky remained at NASA until 1999, spending three years training and instructing future astronauts at the Johnson Space Center and then another three years as a research pilot at the Dryden Flight Research Center. During this period he flew, in 1997, the SR-71 Blackbird, billed as the world's fastest spy jet, and got to see the curvature of the Earth at 80,000 feet.

He also worked as a consultant, in 1998, on a manned hypersonic-research jet. As a consultant he met Burt Rutan, an engineer and designer who had founded an innovative airplane company, Scaled Composites.

But Stucky's time at Dryden soon soured him on staying with NASA. The problem stemmed from the fact that manned missions were not as popular as the new drone systems then emerging. With the writing on the wall, Stucky decided to resign. "It is disappointing to me that the world's premier flight-test organization could consider going for extended periods without any . . . piloted research projects," he wrote in his resignation letter to NASA, as quoted by Schmidle. "Dryden established its reputation by making the impossible possible but increasingly we seem content to make the possible impossible."

Upon leaving NASA he became a commercial pilot for United Airlines, where he worked as a first officer on the B-737, 757, 767 and A-319/320 aircrafts, from 1999 to 2003. Although friends said he would hate being a commercial pilot, Stucky found that he enjoyed it. One of the more upsetting things that happened to him during this period was learning that the Space Shuttle *Columbia* burned up upon reentry from a mission in February 2003. Stucky had trained three of the seven astronauts on board: Col. Rick Husband, Lt. Col. Michael Anderson, and Kalpana Chawla. It was the second shuttle mission to end with the loss of life of all its astronauts onboard; the first had been the *Challenger*, which killed all seven astronauts aboard in January 1986. Owing to the perceived dangers in the reusable launch vehicle, the Space Shuttle program ended in 2011. "When NASA first designed the shuttle, they said one would fly every two weeks and that the failure rate would be one in 100,000," Stucky said to Steve Chawkins for the *Los Angeles Times* (8 Feb. 2003). "But any thinking astronaut has to realize that there's about a 2-percent chance they won't be coming home. That's the realistic success rate right now, but it's not necessarily one that we as a nation can stomach."

During this time, Stucky was also working as a mortgage salesman for Pacific Republic Mortgage, but the idea of a deskbound life did not sit well with him. He rejoined the military in July 2003, this time with the US Air Force. In addition to serving as the director of education at the USAF Test Pilot School, he would also serve combat duty during the Iraq War and as Flight Test Squadron Commander, Deputy Operations Group Commander in the 412th Operations Group.

WORKING WITH SCALES COMPOSITES AND VIRGIN GALACTIC

In April 2009, Stucky left the Air Force to become a test pilot with Rutan's Scaled Composites. He had long been fascinated with the work Rutan was doing. Five of Rutan's planes were in the National Air and Space Museum, and his SpaceShipOne—an experimental air-launched rocket-powered aircraft—had been the first manned private spacecraft to go suborbital (briefly reaching outer space but not orbiting the Earth). The craft used a hybrid rocket motor to accomplish this feat on June 21, 2004.

As a test pilot for Scaled Composites, now owned by Northrop Grumman, Stucky was tasked with ensuring that SpaceShipTwo and its carrier plane, White Knight Two, would be ready for space tourists to use to enjoy rides to the edge of space. "Beyond his primary position as a test pilot, [Stucky] has been an instrumental and critical part of our programs, working as a design engineer, instructor pilot, project pilot, technical adviser and even a mentor to others," Kevin Mickey, the president of Scaled Composites, remarked, as quoted in a *Northrop Grumman* press release (1 Nov. 2013). "His dedication to the advancement of flight testing and the enthusiastic pursuit of discovery personify the spirit of Scaled Composites, and illustrate the vital role Scaled plays in the Northrop Grumman portfolio."

Scaled Composites' client for these vehicles was Virgin Galactic, a subsidiary of the Virgin Group, which is headed by British billionaire Richard Branson. Virgin's plan to send paying tourists into suborbital spaceflight received an enormous setback in October 2014, when pilot Michael Alsbury, a good friend of Stucky's, was killed when his test vehicle crashed in California. Shortly after Alsbury's death, Virgin asked Stucky to come aboard as lead test pilot for Virgin Galactic. At the time of his appointment, Stucky said, as quoted by *Space Daily* (27 Jan. 2015): "It is an honor for me to join the Virgin Galactic team on the home stretch of the flight test program and help turn Sir Richard's vision of the first commercial spaceline into reality. I firmly believe the success of this program will go beyond fulfilling the dreams of our astronaut customers but will lay the foundation for follow-on technologies that will benefit mankind in ways we may not yet fathom."

Although the accident was a heavy blow for Stucky, it did not prevent him from seeing the potential SpaceShipTwo had for the future of aeronautics. Stucky worked with designers and engineers to improve the spacecraft's design and performance by carrying out extensive engine and glide tests to ensure its safety and reliability. After a new design was revealed in 2016, Stucky and his copilot Dave Mackay continued to train to make sure SpaceShipTwo's return to supersonic flight would be a resounding success. In April 2018, almost four years after Alsbury's death, Stuck and Mackay completed the first powered flight of the newly redesigned ship. In the *Telegraph* (5 Apr. 2018), Sarah Knapton quoted Branson as seeing outer space as now being "tantalisingly close."

SUGGESTED READING

Chawkins, Steve. "Former NASA Test Pilot Airs Grief over Astronauts." *Los Angeles Times*, 8 Feb. 2003, articles.latimes.com/2003/feb/08/local/me-pilot8. Accessed 16 Oct. 2018.

Davis, Noah. "Tough Jobs: Experimental Aircraft Test Pilot." *Popular Mechanics*, 7 May 2015, www.popularmechanics.com/flight/a15380/tough-jobs-experimental-aircraft-test-pilot/. Accessed 17 Oct. 2018.

Gibbs, Yvonne, Editor. "Former Pilots: Mark P. Stucky." *NASA.gov*, 7 Aug. 2017, www.nasa.gov/centers/armstrong/news/Biographies/Pilots/bd-dfrc-p020.html. Accessed 17 Oct. 2018.

Knapton, Sarah. "Virgin Galactic Completes First Powered Flight since Fatal Crash in 2014." *The Telegraph*, 5 Apr. 2018, www.telegraph.co.uk/science/2018/04/05/virgin-galactic-completes-first-powered-flight-since-fatal-crash/. Accessed 17 Oct. 2018.

"Scaled Composites' Mark Stucky Earns 2013 Iven C. Kincheloe Award from the Society of Experimental Pilots." *Northrop Grumman*, 1 Nov. 2013, news.northropgrumman.com/news/releases/scaled-composites-mark-stucky-earns-2013-iven-c-kincheloe-award-from-the-society-of-experimental-pilots. Accessed 17 Oct. 2018.

Schmidle, Nicholas. "Virgin Galactic's Rocket Man." *The New Yorker*, 20 Aug. 2018, www.newyorker.com/magazine/2018/08/20/virgin-galactics-rocket-man. Accessed 17 Oct. 2018.

"Virgin Galactic Appoints Mark Stucky as Pilot." *Space Daily*, 27 Jan. 2015, www.space-daily.com/reports/Virgin_Galactic_Appoints_Mark_Stucky_as_Pilot_999.html. Accessed 16 Oct. 2018.

—*Christopher Mari*

Nicola Sturgeon

Date of birth: July 19, 1970
Occupation: First minister of Scotland

Nicola Sturgeon is the first minister of Scotland, the leader of the Scottish National Party (SNP), and a politician who has advocated for Scotland's independence since her youth.

EARLY LIFE AND EDUCATION

Nicola Sturgeon was born on July 19, 1970, in Irvine, Scotland. She grew up in Dreghorn, a small working-class village in North Ayrshire. Her father, Robin Sturgeon, was an engineer; her mother, Joan Sturgeon, was a dental nurse. Sturgeon attended Greenwood Academy in North Ayrshire.

Although neither of her parents were overly political, Sturgeon developed a strong interest in government and politics at an early age. When she was sixteen, she became a member of the pro-independence Scottish National Party and a political left-wing activist. She also worked on her first political campaign. She introduced herself to Kay Ullrich, who was running for a seat in Parliament, by knocking on her door and volunteering to help with her campaign.

Sturgeon has credited her interest in politics and her political views with her disdain for Margaret Thatcher, the prime minister of the United Kingdom during the 1980s, and everything that the Conservative Party stood for. Thatcher's policies had a deeply adverse effect on the heavily industrial area of North Ayrshire, where coal mine pits were closed as part of Thatcher's reforms and miners at some of the remaining mines walked out of work, leaving many families without income. Many large industrial employers left the area during the Thatcher years.

Sturgeon studied law at the University of Glasgow and graduated in 1992. That same year, she ran for a seat in the UK Parliament. After losing the election, she continued her political activism, giving a speech in a Glasgow square during a pro-independence rally. Although lacking the finesse of a seasoned politician, the twenty-one-year-old impressed SNP leaders with her seriousness and commitment to helping Scotland achieve independence. Following a legal traineeship in Glasgow, she worked at Drumchapel Law Centre. In 1997 Sturgeon ran for Parliament again, and once again lost.

POLITICAL CAREER

In 1998, UK Parliament passed the Scotland Act 1998, which allowed for the creation of a devolved Scottish Parliament. The newly formed parliament could govern on certain matters in Scotland separate from the UK Parliament. The first elections for Scottish Parliament were held in 1999. Sturgeon was elected as a member of the Scottish Parliament (MSP) representing Glasgow that same year. At that time, the Labour Party and the Liberal Democrat Party formed a majority coalition, and as a member of the opposition party.

In 2004, Sturgeon planned to run for leader of the SNP to replace John Swinney, who was stepping down. Then Alex Salmond, who had served as SNP leader from 1990 to 2000, announced his plan to run again for the party's top position. Sturgeon withdrew her candidacy and ran as Salmond's deputy. Salmond and Sturgeon ran on a joint ticket, with Salmon elected as SNP leader and Sturgeon as deputy leader of the SNP. As deputy leader, Sturgeon worked to increase support for the SNP and increase its membership. She also worked to gain support for independence for Scotland.

The year 2007 was a pivotal year for the SNP. The party won the highest number of seats in the Scottish Parliament for the first time since devolution. Following the election, Salmond became the first minister of Scotland and Sturgeon was appointed deputy first minister. She served as the MSP for the Glasgow Govan constituency from 2007 to 2011. Following a boundary change that expanded Govan to create the new Glasgow Southside constituency, Sturgeon was elected as the MSP for Glasgow Southside. She was the cabinet secretary for health and wellbeing from 2007 to 2012 and for infrastructure, investment, and cities from 2012 to 2014.

In November 2014 Scotland held a referendum on independence from the United Kingdom. Voters rejected independence by 55 percent to 45 percent. Following the "No" vote, Salmond resigned as party leader and as first minister. Sturgeon ran unopposed to replace him and was elected party leader. Sturgeon was sworn in on November 20, 2014, as the first female and fifth first minister of Scotland since devolution.

Shortly after becoming first minister, Sturgeon announced her goal to create a nation that was both socially democratic and socially just. Upon taking office, she assigned the cabinet, which included some promotions, reassignments, and the replacement of two incumbents. Sturgeon made it clear that she was making a stand on gender equality by assigning a cabinet that was evenly divided between male and female ministers. The new cabinet was generally accepted by the opposition parties. Among Sturgeon's plans for Scotland are raising the minimum wage, increasing spending for public services, providing greater welfare benefits, and offering free university education. She has also made a goal of the removal of the Trident program, which includes a naval base in Scotland and submarines armed with nuclear weapons that patrol waters off Scotland's coast. Sturgeon also seeks to increase Scotland's powers through more devolution and greater involvement in the United Kingdom's politics.

IMPACT

As party leader, Sturgeon has sought to increase party membership and gain support for the SNP among Scotland's voters.

PERSONAL LIFE

Sturgeon married Peter Murrell, the chief executive of the SNP, in 2010. They live in Glasgow.

SUGGESTED READING

Adam, Karla. "Why Scottish Politician Nicola Sturgeon Has Been Called 'The Most Dangerous Woman in Britain.'" *The Washington Post,* 10 June 2015, www.washingtonpost.com/news/worldviews/wp/2015/06/10/why-scottish-politician-nicola-sturgeon-has-been-called-the-most-dangerous-woman-in-britain/. Accessed 27 Sept. 2019.

Black, Andrew. "Family and friends speak about the Nicola Sturgeon they know." Nov. 19, 2014, BBC. www.bbc.com/news/uk-scotland-scotland-politics-30105263.

Black, Andrew. "Nicola Sturgeon Announces New Scottish Cabinet." *BBC,* 19 Nov. 2014, www.bbc.com/news/uk-scotland-scotland-politics-30138550. Accessed 27 Sept. 2019.

Curwen, Lesley. "Introducing . . . Nicola Sturgeon: First Lady of Scotland." *Global: The International Briefing.* Nexus Strategic Partnerships, www.global-briefing.org/2015/01/introducing-nicola-sturgeon-first-lady-of-scotland/.

Sturgeon, Nicola. Interview by Robert Siegel. "Scottish First Minister: 'Independent Scotland Would Be a Powerful Voice'." *National Public Radio,* 11 June 2015, www.npr.org/2015/06/11/413711331/scottish-first-minister-independent-scotland-would-be-a-powerful-voice. Accessed 27 Sept. 2019.

Torrance, David. "What Makes Nicola Sturgeon Tick?" *Telegraph,* 25 Apr. 2015, www.telegraph.co.uk/news/politics/nicola-sturgeon/11561233/What-makes-Nicola-Sturgeon-tick.html. Accessed 27 Sept. 2019.

—*Barb Lightner*

Charlie Sykes

Date of birth: November 11, 1954
Occupation: Political commentator

Charlie Sykes was once among the most influential conservative voices in Wisconsin. As a radio talk-show host, he cheered conservative Republicans who adhered to his brand of fiscal and personal responsibility, civility, free markets, and strict constitutionalism. He was beloved by his fans for more than twenty-three years, until Donald Trump became the Republican frontrunner and nominee for president in 2016. Sykes could not abide Trump's political positions, or, most especially, his incivility, his appeal to nativism, and his hints of racial bias. Sykes's hard line against Trump caused his listeners to turn on him. Looking back, Sykes said in an interview with Robin Young for the Boston public radio program *Here and Now* (10 Feb. 2017): "I had expected Donald Trump would not be elected, and that as a result, there would be this reckoning where we would actually have to confront what had happened to the conservative media, the irresponsible media—the sites like Infowars and Breitbart and Drudge and what Rush Limbaugh had done to conservatism—and that there would be some sort of a sorting out. Instead, as a result of the election, all of those elements have been empowered."

Sykes ended his show in December 2016 to examine his own role in helping nativist elements to take over the Republican Party, and he has sought to find ways to return conservatism to its original values. His 2017 book *How the Right Lost Its Mind* is his most thorough examination of these efforts and has met with acclaim.

EARLY LIFE AND EDUCATION

Charles J. Sykes was born in Seattle, Washington, on November 11, 1954, the only son of Jay G. and Katherine Sykes. The central figure of young Charlie's life was his father, who had been a US Army code breaker in World War II and went on to earn a law degree from the University of Washington. The elder Sykes worked at various times as a lawyer, journalist, and professor, but above all else his son described him as a contrarian. "If you put him in a room with ten people, he would find a way of disagreeing with eight of them," Sykes told Kurt Chandler

Photo by Kris Connor/Getty Images for NAMM

for *Milwaukee Magazine* (1 July 2000). "It was just his personality. He was not mean, he was just kind of playful. And he just couldn't stand pompous self-righteousness."

Politics was central to the Sykes family. Both father and son supported Senator Eugene McCarthy, a candidate in the 1968 Democratic presidential primaries, because McCarthy wanted to end the war in Vietnam. Jay Sykes was McCarthy's state campaign director in Wisconsin, and Charlie, then aged thirteen, worked as a page at the Democratic National Convention that year in Chicago. McCarthy ultimately lost the nomination to Vice President Hubert Humphrey, though Sykes told Chandler that he still regards McCarthy as "one of the noblest, most honorable men in American politics." A few years later, however, Sykes became disillusioned with the brand of liberalism he saw driving the antiwar movement. "It's one thing to think that war is immoral," he told Chandler. "It's another thing to think that America is this awful, terrible place in the world. . . . I sensed that liberalism, instead of this free spirit, was becoming this rigid and constant moral hectoring. Things started to change."

This change of heart marked the beginning of Sykes's political transformation. By the time he enrolled in college at the University of Wisconsin–Milwaukee, he was becoming more conservative. At age eighteen he converted to Roman Catholicism, after being raised without religion. As a freshman at UWM and still a Democrat—albeit one opposed to abortion—he ran for the state legislature against Republican incumbent Jim Sensenbrenner and lost badly.

JOURNALIST AND AUTHOR
Upon earning his bachelor's degree in English in 1975, Sykes began working as a journalist for the *Northeast Post*, a weekly newspaper, and then the *Milwaukee Journal*. He made a name for himself at the *Journal* working the City Hall beat, often jousting with Mayor Henry Maier. In 1982 he took a job as a staff writer at *Milwaukee Magazine*, becoming its editor in 1984.

Sykes put his stamp on the magazine, writing columns, features, and investigative journalism. He attacked Wisconsin politicians, both Republicans and Democrats, when he felt they were not living up to standards of good governance. Most notably, he tapped his father, then a professor at the University of Wisconsin–Milwaukee, to write a piece about academia. Jay Sykes finished the piece, which criticized his fellow professors for neglecting their students and engaging in inconsequential scholarship, four days before dying suddenly of a heart attack.

Jay Sykes's academia piece would help his son transition from being a journalist to an author. Based on interest from a literary agent,

Sykes decided to expand his father's article into an entire book critiquing the state of American higher education. The result, *ProfScam: Professors and the Demise of Higher Education* (1988), would be the first of many books for Sykes, and it launched him on a career in political commentary.

TALK RADIO CELEBRITY
After leaving journalism in 1988, Sykes made a brief foray into government public relations work for Dave Schulz, the Milwaukee County executive. The job was not the right fit, and he left in March 1989. He soon found his new vocation in the budding field of conservative call-in radio talk shows, an increasingly popular genre spearheaded by Rush Limbaugh. Sykes got his start occasionally filling in for local hosts Kathleen Dunn and Mark Belling. In May 1992 Belling's station, WISN, hired Sykes for his own show but did not sign him to a contract. In June 1993 he left WISN for WTMJ, where Dunn's show aired, and where Sykes would find a home for more than two decades. Of this early period, Sykes recalled to Young: "I was very excited back in the 1990s to realize that we were part of creating an alternative media. That we were moving from a period where a handful of elite media titans, sitting in perhaps Manhattan, would decide what people would see and what they would talk about. Now suddenly, you had this proliferation of different voices."

During his run, Sykes became one of the most powerful conservative voices on Wisconsin radio. His program became one of the top-rated shows in the state, in large part because of the intelligent and gleeful way Sykes demolished progressive political ideas and touted conservative policy and Wisconsin Republican politicians like Scott Walker (ultimately the state's governor) and Paul Ryan (ultimately the Speaker of the House of Representatives).

Conservative listeners ate up everything Sykes said throughout the years, until he grew vocally critical of Donald Trump, the real estate tycoon who ran for the 2016 Republican nomination for president. Sykes was uncomfortable with Trump's vicious political rhetoric, which appealed to nativism, nationalism, and populism, sometimes with bigoted overtones. At the same time, Trump appeared to be weak on traditional conservative values near to Sykes's heart, like free markets, strict constitutionalism, and, in personal conduct, civility. Although other conservative commentators began lining up behind Trump when he became the Republican nominee, Sykes, along with a handful of other conservatives such as columnists George Will and David Brooks, declared himself in the "never Trump" camp. Before long, Sykes's fans began turning on him. "Basically the music score of my last six months was 'We're not listening to you again,' 'What's up with you?' 'Betrayal,'" Sykes said to Mark Z. Barabak for the *Los Angeles Times* (30 Jan. 2017). "Some could have been trolls from Macedonia. Others were prominent Republican women from Waukesha I've known for 20 years."

THE CONTRARIAN CONSERVATIVE

After Trump won the presidency in November 2016, defeating Democrat Hillary Clinton, Sykes decided to end his radio show in December. He did so believing that he was no longer a part of what the Republican Party now represented after the election of Trump. He also believed that conservative talk shows like his had contributed to the rise of racist, sexist, and xenophobic elements that were becoming louder voices in the Republican Party. Since that time, he has been a contributor to MSNBC and NPR, among other media outlets, and has written for the *New York Times*, the *Wall Street Journal, Politico, Salon, USA Today*, the *National Review*, and the *Weekly Standard*, where he has expressed regret for his inadvertent participation in the corruption of conservatism and has discussed ways conservatives can return to their core principles.

In his 2017 book *How the Right Lost Its Mind*, Sykes provides a history of modern conservatism, diagnoses its problems, and offers a road to recovery. In a review for the *Washington Post* (4 Oct. 2017), Carlos Lozada noted, "He calls for fellow 'contrarian conservatives' to return to first principles, revitalize their policy proposals, break free from the influence of lobbyists and address the 'legitimate grievances' of Trump supporters while separating them from the authoritarian and racist elements of Trump's base."

PERSONAL LIFE

Sykes has been married three times. His first marriage, to Christine Libbey, took place in May 1975 when he was twenty years old. The couple had a daughter and divorced three years later. In 1980 he married Diane Schwerm (now Diane Sykes, a judge on the US Court of Appeals for the Seventh Circuit). This marriage produced two children and ended in divorce in 1999. His current marriage, to Janet Riordan, an opera singer, began in 2000. He also has two grandchildren. He lives in Mequon, Wisconsin.

SUGGESTED READING

Barabak, Mark Z. "How a Top Conservative Radio Host Took on Trump, Lost His Audience and Faith, but Gained a New Perspective." *Los Angeles Times*, 30 Jan. 2017, www.latimes.com/politics/la-na-pol-sykes-talk-radio-2017-story.html. Accessed 25 Jan. 2019.
Chandler, Kurt. "Charlie's Bully Pulpit." *Milwaukee Magazine*, 1 July 2000, www.milwaukeemag.com/charlies-bully-pulpit. Accessed 25 Jan. 2019.
"Charlie Sykes." *WNYC*, 2019, www.wnyc.org/people/charlie. Accessed 25 Jan. 2019.
Lozada, Charles. "It's Like 'What Happened,' but for Conservatives." Review of *How the Right Lost Its Mind*, by Charles Sykes. *The Washington Post*, 21 Nov. 2018, www.washingtonpost.com/news/book-party/wp/2017/10/04/its-like-what-happened-but-for-conservatives. Accessed 25 Jan. 2019.
Sykes, Charles. *How the Right Lost Its Mind*. St. Martin's P, 2017.
Sykes, Charles. "Radio Host Charlie Sykes Says Conservative Media Will Give Cover to Trump." Interview by Robin Young. *Here and Now*, WBUR, 13 Feb. 2017, www.wbur.org/hereandnow/2017/02/10/charlie-sykes. Accessed 25 Jan. 2019.

SELECTED WORKS

ProfScam: Professors and the Demise of Higher Education, 1988; *The Hollow Men: Politics and Corruption in Higher Education*, 1990; *A Nation of Victims: The Decay of the American Character*, 1992; *Dumbing Down Our Kids: Why American Children Feel Good about Themselves but Can't Read, Write, or Add*, 1995; *The End of Privacy: The Attack on Personal Rights at Home, at Work, On-Line, and in Court*, 1999; *50 Rules Kids Won't Learn in School: Real-World Antidotes to Feel-Good Education*, 2007; *A Nation of Moochers: America's Addiction to Getting Something for Nothing*, 2012; *Fail U.: The False Promise of Higher Education*, 2016; *How the Right Lost Its Mind*, 2017

—*Christopher Mari*

Tamim bin Hamad Al Thani

Date of birth: June 3, 1980
Occupation: Emir of Qatar

His Highness Sheik Tamim bin Hamad Al Thani became emir of Qatar on June 25, 2013, following his father's abdication. At thirty-three, he is the youngest leader of a Middle Eastern state.

EARLY LIFE AND EDUCATION

Tamim bin Hamad Al Thani was born on June 3, 1980, into the powerful Al Thani dynasty that has ruled Qatar since the mid-1800s. At the time of his birth, his grandfather, Khalifa bin Hamad Al Thani, was emir of Qatar. In 1995, his father, Hamad bin Khalifa Al Thani, overthrew Khalifa in a bloodless coup and became emir. Tamim's mother, Mozah bint Nasser Al Missned, is the second of his father's three wives.

The fourth eldest son, he has ten brothers and thirteen sisters.

Tamim grew up amid immense wealth and was educated at schools in Great Britain. He attended the elite private school Sherborne International in Dorset, achieving his A levels in 1997. He graduated from the Royal Military Academy in Sandhurst in 1998. Shortly after leaving the academy, he was commissioned as a second lieutenant in the Qatar armed forces.

POLITICAL CAREER

Sports are an important part of Qatar's culture, and hosting major sports events is an important part of its positioning in the global community. Tamim is an avid athlete and worked as a sports administrator before becoming emir. He was the president of the Al Sadd Sports Club from 1999–2000 and became the president of the Qatar Olympic Committee in the early 2000s and a member of the International Olympic Committee in 2002. He has helped Qatar land several significant sports events, including the 2006 Asian Games, the 2014 FINA Swimming World Championships, and the 2022 FIFA World Cup. He headed the unsuccessful bid for the 2020 Summer Olympics in Doha and has served on the organizing committees of several sporting events. In 2005 he founded Qatar Sport Investments and later negotiated its purchase of the Paris Saint-Germain football and handball teams.

Hamad designated Tamim the heir apparent in 2003 after his older brother, Jasim bin Hamad bin Khalifa Al Thani, renounced his claim to the throne. His father groomed Tamim for the position, and Tamim worked alongside his father in running the country. Tamim chaired the board of directors of the Qatar Investment Authority, the Supreme Council for the Environment and Natural Reserves, the Supreme Council for Information and Communication Technology (2005), and the Supreme Education Council. In 2009 he became the deputy commander in chief of Qatar's armed forces.

In June 2013 Emir Hamad bin Khalifa Al Thani announced his plan to abdicate the throne for the purpose of providing a smooth transition to the younger generation of leaders. This was a break with tradition in Gulf Arab nations, where most power transfers involuntarily or upon the death of a ruler. For two days, Qatari citizens visited the Emir Diwan, Qatar's seat of government, to pledge their allegiance to Tamim as the new emir.

On June 25, 2013, Tamim became emir of Qatar. In his inaugural speech, he expressed his intent to continue his father's foreign policies to pursue the goals of the Qatar National Vision 2030, a long-range development plan for Qatar that was developed in 2008.

The next day, Tamim named his cabinet, about half of which were new members. He appointed Abdullah bin Nasser bin Khalifa Al Thani the prime minister and interior minister, signaling a greater emphasis on domestic affairs than foreign policy and the desire to further develop Qatar's infrastructure and diversify its economy.

Upon becoming the head of state, Tamim became the commander-in-chief of the armed forces. He retained his positions as president of the board of directors of the Qatar Investment Authority and chair of the Qatar 2022 Supreme Committee (now the Supreme Committee for Delivery and Legacy) and chairs the Supreme Council for Economic Affairs and Investment and the Supreme Committee for Coordination and Follow-up.

In January 2016 Tamim reshuffled his cabinet in part to boost economic recovery in response to declining oil prices and to shed the cabinet of ministers from his father's reign. He also cut state spending and implemented austerity measures to address Qatar's first budget deficit in fifteen years.

IMPACT

Tamim bin Hamad Al Thani has sought to increase Qatar's influence in both regional and international spheres. He has met with heads of states and other political and military leaders in countries throughout the world, including Russia, Italy, France, Nigeria, Djibouti, Eritrea, Mexico, Canada, the United States, Pakistan, Bosnia and Herzegovina, and the Chechen Republic in order to strengthen bilateral relations and discuss issues of mutual concern, such as the Syrian conflict and security. He has also sought to end the aggression against the Palestinians, a major source of regional conflict, and has funded reconstruction in the Gaza Strip.

PERSONAL LIFE

Tamim has two wives and six children. He married Jawaher bint Hamad bin Suhaim Al Thani, his second cousin, in 2005 and Anoud bint Mana al-Hajra in 2009.

SUGGESTED READING

Al Harami, Jaber. "500 Days of Sheikh Tamim's Rule." *Peninsula*. Peninsula Newspaper, p. 9. 25 Dec. 2014, www.dev.thepeninsulaqatar.com/uploads/2016/08/10/pdf/ThePeninsulaDecember252014.pdf. Accessed 8 Dec. 2018.

"The Emir." *Government of Qatar*. Government of Qatar, 2016, portal.www.gov.qa/wps/portal/about-qatar/theemir. Accessed 8 Dec. 2018.

Dickinson, Elizabeth. "Focus Turns to Domestic Policy under Qatar's new Emir." *National*. Abu Dhabi Media, 14 Dec. 2013, www.

thenational.ae/world/focus-turns-to-domestic-policy-under-qatar-s-new-emir-1.287414. Accessed 8 Dec. 2018. Web.

"Inside Perspective: His Highness Sheikh Tamim Bin Hamad Al Thani, Emir, Qatar." *The Business Year, 2017.* www.thebusinessyear. com/qatar-2017/foreword-to-the-business-year-qatar-2017/foreword. Accessed 8 Dec. 2018.

"Profile: Qatar Emir, Sheikh Tamim bin Hamad Al Thani." *BBC*. BBC, 25 June 2013, www. bbc.com/news/world-middle-east-23046307. Accessed 8 Dec. 2018.

"Qatar's New Emir Sheikh Tamim Bin Hamad Al-Thani Seen Maintaining Country's Role as Power Broker." *NDTV.* NDTV Convergence Limited, 25 June 2013. Web. 5 Apr. 2016.

"Who's Who in Qatar: The People of Qatar You Should Know About." *Marhaba.* Marhaba, 10 Aug. 2014, www.marhaba.qa/whos-who-in-qatar-the-people-of-qatar-you-should-know-about/. Accessed 8 Dec. 2018.

—*Barb Lightner*

Photo by François GOGLINS via Wikimedia Commons

Dominic Thiem

Date of birth: September 3, 1993
Occupation: Tennis player

"I admire all the players who make it to the top in tennis because it's really tough," tennis player Dominic Thiem said in an interview for the *Association of Tennis Professionals (ATP) Tour* website (23 May 2015). He added, "Of course, I watch the best and try to learn something from them." As Thiem's performance on the court since the start of his professional tennis career in 2011 has demonstrated, his strategy of observing and learning from the best has been undoubtedly successful. A tennis player from the age of six, Thiem competed on the junior level as a teenager and spent several years on the lower-tier professional circuits prior to beginning regular ATP Tour play in 2014. His first ATP Tour title, won in France in 2015, was the first of many. His performance in the prestigious Grand Slam events likewise signaled that Thiem was a key player to watch. He confirmed his top-ten position in 2018 and 2019, during which he made two consecutive attempts to claim the singles title at Roland-Garros, also known as the French Open. Although he ultimately lost in the finals of both tournaments, Thiem sought to move forward rather than dwell on previous close calls. "I don't need that much time in order to reflect on everything. It's in the past. I can't change anything," he said of the Noventi Open in an interview for the *Gerry Webber World* website (13 June 2016). "I'm more focused on the future."

EARLY LIFE AND EDUCATION

Thiem was born in Wiener Neustadt, Austria, on September 3, 1993, the first of two sons born to tennis coaches Wolfgang and Karin Thiem. His father began to work for a Vienna tennis school headed by coach Günter Bresnik when Thiem was about eleven. Thiem began playing the sport at the age of six, and his younger brother, Moritz, later followed in his footsteps. In addition to tennis, Thiem enjoyed playing soccer and became an avid fan of Britain's Chelsea Football Club. Thiem later commented in interviews that had he not pursued a professional tennis career, he would have liked to have played soccer professionally.

Throughout his childhood and adolescence, Thiem honed his tennis skills in a variety of competitive environments and gained valuable experience that served him well in his later career. "Clay is my favourite surface. I grew up on it, but also I like hard courts," he told the *ATP Tour* website. "What I like more about clay is you have a little bit of Plan B. If you don't play so well, you can grind it out a little bit and that's what I like." After his father joined the staff of Bresnik's tennis school, Thiem began taking lessons with the coach. Bresnik served as Thiem's coach for much of his early career.

EARLY CAREER

As a teenager, Thiem competed extensively on the International Tennis Federation (ITF) Junior Circuit and distinguished himself in his division by winning singles titles at events such as the 2010 Yucatán World Cup and the 2011 Orange Bowl International Tennis Championship. He likewise competed in junior-level competitions at some of the prestigious tournaments known as the Grand Slam of tennis—the Australian Open, Roland-Garros, Wimbledon, and the US Open—but had limited success at those events. Despite being best known as a singles player, he also competed in doubles matches during his junior career.

The decision to go professional was somewhat daunting for Thiem, who understood that success on the junior-level circuit does not always translate into success at the senior level. "In the juniors you are kind of a star, but just because you are a good junior doesn't mean you will be a good pro," he told Greg Garber for *ESPN* (12 Mar. 2014).

Following his professional debut in 2012, Thiem competed in lower-level professional events held as part of the ITF Futures tour and the ATP Challenger Tour. Success in these tours enables players to move up in the ranks of tennis professionals and potentially to compete in the top-tier ATP Tour, also known as the ATP World Tour. Thiem won his first ITF Futures title in the Czech Republic in 2012 and several additional singles titles at Futures events in 2012 and 2013. He won his first title on the ATP Challenger Tour at the Kenitra tournament in Morocco in late 2013. In addition, Thiem qualified to compete in a couple of individual ATP Tour events.

Thiem began competing extensively on the ATP Tour in 2014. In August of that year he made it to finals at the Kitzbühel tournament in Austria, where he ultimately lost to Belgian player David Goffin. Although the loss was disappointing, Thiem found the intense level of competition at top-tier competitions highly motivating. "I must say I am excited not to be playing in the Futures and Challenger matches," he told Garber. "These big tournaments, yeah, they get you going. I like to compete and these are the best players in the game." Thiem made his first senior-level Grand Slam appearance in the 2014 Australian Open, where he progressed to the round of sixty-four before being eliminated. He went on to appear in all four Grand Slam events that year and made it to the round of sixteen in the US Open before being defeated by Czech player Tomáš Berdych. Thiem was also active in doubles play in the Grand Slam tournaments between 2014 and 2016.

ATP TOUR SUCCESS

As Thiem became acclimated to high-level professional play, he found increasing success on the ATP Tour. He managed several quarterfinal and semifinal finishes over the course of the 2015 tour season. The twenty-one-year-old won his first ATP Tour title at the Open de Nice Côte d'Azur in May of that year. "It's something really, really special," he told the *ATP Tour* website about his victory. "I think it doesn't matter which age, but I'm happy that I made it at a quite a young age. It was a perfect week for me, and I'm happy that I won the title in a really, really good final." Thiem went on to win additional titles at tournaments in Croatia and Switzerland.

In light of such successes, some tennis commentators began to describe Thiem as a member of the next generation of tennis stars, a designation of which Thiem was skeptical. "It's nice to hear," he told Ava Wallace for the *Washington Post* (31 July 2017). "But I think we still have to win a lot of matches and win a lot of titles to deserve to be called like that, to be the next big things in tennis." In addition to his overall success as a player, Thiem also received significant attention for his strong single-handed backhand, which he described to Garber as a strategy—implemented by Bresnik—that enabled him "to be more aggressive in the points."

Thiem won four ATP Tour singles titles in 2016 and finished the year with an ATP Tour ranking of eighth in the world. He continued to compete in Grand Slam events and performed especially well at Roland-Garros, where he progressed to the semifinals in both 2016 and 2017. The year 2017 also saw Thiem achieve fourth-round finishes at the Australian Open, Wimbledon, and the US Open. Thiem's strong performance in 2017, including the title at a tournament in Brazil and several other high-ranking finishes, raised his ATP singles ranking to fifth. He was also a member of the winning Team Europe at the first-ever Laver Cup.

GRAND SLAM CONTENDER

In 2018 Thiem won ATP Tour titles at events in Argentina, France, and Russia, and performed well at other competitions, including the Australian Open and the US Open. The most significant moment of the season, however, came at Roland-Garros, where Thiem successfully progressed to the final round, his first in a Grand Slam event. Although he ultimately lost to Spanish player Rafael Nadal, the competition solidified Thiem's standing as a Grand Slam contender and provided further motivation for the athlete. "I was super-motivated from that point to be able to live that moment again, to play a grand slam final and be again that close to such a big goal which I had set up from the very beginning of my career," he told Simon Cambers for the official *Roland-Garros* website (3 Dec. 2018).

In early 2019 Thiem announced he had split from longtime coach Bresnik and began training instead with coach Nicolás Massú. The 2019 ATP Tour started off strong for Thiem, who beat renowned Swiss player Roger Federer in the BNP Paribas Open in Indian Wells, California, to win his first Masters title. He then beat Russian player Daniil Medvedev in Spain's Barcelona Open in April. He was somewhat less successful in the early Grand Slams, losing in the round of sixty-four in the Australian Open. However, Thiem sought to remain focused on each individual match rather than on thoughts of winning tournaments. "If you think about the fourth round before the first one, you're probably out before the second. Of course, you look at the draw, but you quickly learn as a young player to focus on each round as it happens," he told Alex Maxifahrer for the *Red Bull* website (15 Jan. 2019). "That's the secret of the big players—they take every match, every round and every opponent 100 percent seriously." In May 2019 Thiem returned to Roland-Garros and once again reached the finals. Just as in 2018, however, he faced off against Nadal, who ultimately proved victorious. Although an early-round elimination at Wimbledon followed, Thiem's strong performance overall made him a major competitor on the ATP Tour, and he was ranked fourth among the tour's players by July 2019.

PERSONAL LIFE

Thiem has attributed his success on the tennis court not only to his skill and training but also to aspects of his personality. "I consider myself mentally strong," he explained to Cambers. "Even if I have really bad losses or shocking losses, I still come back a while after to play good tennis again."

In keeping with the Austrian policy of compulsory military service, he joined the Austrian military for four weeks in 2014, completing a reduced period of service designed to avoid conflicting with his tennis career. When not playing or training elsewhere, Thiem lives in Lichetenwörth, Austria.

SUGGESTED READING

Briggs, Simon. "Dominic Thiem Exclusive Interview: On His Love of Chelsea, Who the Best Footballer on Tour Is, and Why Equal Pay Is Imperative." *The Telegraph*, 23 Apr. 2019, www.telegraph.co.uk/tennis/2019/04/23/dominic-thiem-exclusive-interview-love-chelsea-best-footballer. Accessed 12 July 2019.

Cambers, Simon. "Heirs to the Throne, Part IV: Dominic Thiem." *Roland-Garros*, 3 Dec. 2018, www.rolandgarros.com/en-us/article/heirs-to-the-throne-part-4-dominic-thiem. Accessed 12 July 2019.

Maxifahrer, Alex. "5 Things Dominic Thiem Is Saying about His Grand Slam Goals for 2019." *Red Bull*, 15 Jan. 2019, www.redbull.com/in-en/dominic-thiem-grand-slam-goals. Accessed 12 July 2019.

Thiem, Dominic. "First-Time Winner Spotlight: Dominic Thiem." *ATP Tour*, 23 May 2015, www.atptour.com/en/news/nice-final-2015-first-time-winner-thiem. Accessed 12 July 2019.

Thiem, Dominic. "Five Questions with Dominic Thiem." Interview by Greg Garber. *ESPN*, 12 Mar. 2014, www.espn.com/tennis/story/_/id/10593953/tennis-five-questions-dominic-thiem. Accessed 12 July 2019.

Thiem, Dominic. Interview. *Gerry Webber World*, 13 June 2016, www.gerryweber-open.de/en/tournament/interviews/interview/interview-with-dominic-thiem-13-06-2016. Accessed 12 July 2019.

Wallace, Ava. "Dominic Thiem: An Heir to Tennis's Throne during an Age of Royalty." *The Washington Post*, 31 July 2017, www.washingtonpost.com/sports/tennis/dominic-thiem-an-heir-to-tenniss-throne-during-an-age-of-royalty/2017/07/31/47500888-7628-11e7-9eac-d56bd5568db8_story.html. Accessed 12 July 2019.

—*Joy Crelin*

Tessa Thompson

Date of birth: October 3, 1983
Occupation: Actor

Tessa Thompson is an actor best known for her roles in the films *For Colored Girls*, *Dear White People*, and *Creed*.

EARLY LIFE AND EDUCATION

Tessa Lynne Thompson was born on October 3, 1983, in Los Angeles, California. Her father, Marc Anthony Thompson, is a musician from Panama. She attended Santa Monica High School, where she participated in school plays, including a performance of William Shakespeare's *A Midsummer Night's Dream*, in which she played the role of Hermia.

Following high school, Thompson continued her education at Santa Monica College in Santa Monica, California. There she studied cultural anthropology and took acting classes. She did not have enough credits to graduate and elected to take a lecture course given by members of the Los Angeles Women's Shakespeare Company. The group's founder, Lisa Volpe, asked Thompson to do a reading and subsequently cast her as Ariel in their production of Shakespeare's *The Tempest*.

Through her role in *The Tempest*, Thompson was cast in a production of Shakespeare's *Romeo and Juliet* produced by the Boston Court Performing Arts Center in Pasadena, California, in 2003. This version, called *Romeo and Juliet: Antebellum New Orleans, 1836*, took the play out of Verona and set it in the French Quarter. The production was successful with critics, and Thompson received an Image Award nomination from the National Association for the Advancement of Colored People (NAACP) for her performance as Juliet.

LIFE'S WORK

Thompson starred in two succeeding shows at the Boston Court, *Summertime* (2004) and *Pera Palas* (2005), before making her transition to film and television. After two weeks of auditions in Los Angeles, she received her first television role. She guest starred on the crime drama series *Cold Case* (2005), on which she played the victim of an unsolved 1930s murder in one episode. That same year, she secured a recurring role on the comedy drama series *Veronica Mars* (2004–7). That series ran for three seasons and Thompson appeared in the second season as Jackie Cook, the daughter of a famous baseball player. While shooting *Veronica Mars*, Thompson continued to work in theater with a role in the play *Indoor/Outdoor* (2006).

Thompson also made her big screen debut in 2006, in the horror film *When a Stranger Calls* (2006). She received her first film accolade for her role in the drama *Mississippi Damned* (2009); based on the director Tina Mabry's experiences growing up in Tupelo, Mississippi, the film was praised by critics, and Thompson won the grand jury prize for best actor at the American Black Film Festival that year for her role as a struggling pianist. Following *Mississippi Damned*, Thompson appeared on several television series, including the law drama *Private Practice* in 2009, the superhero drama *Heroes* in the same year, and in a few episodes of the police drama *Detroit 1-8-7* in 2010 and 2011.

Her next major film role was in the drama *For Colored Girls* (2010). Based on the play by Ntozake Shange, the film looks at the lives of nine African American women and the challenges they face. Thompson plays Nyla Adrose, a dance student who lies to her family and friends about getting an abortion. Although the film received generally negative reviews, the cast was applauded for their performances, including Thompson, who won a Black Reel Award for best breakthrough performance. Thompson stated that the role was very special for her because she had been a fan of the original play since she was a teenager.

Thompson landed her next two recurring roles in television series in 2012 with the period drama *Copper* and *666 Park Avenue*. On the big screen, Thompson starred in the satirical comedy *Dear White People* (2014), about racial hypocrisy at a college. For her role as a biracial student, she received numerous accolades, including an Image Award nomination for outstanding actress in a motion picture and a 2014 Gotham Independent Film Award for best breakthrough actor.

After appearing in the period drama *Selma* (2014) as civil rights activist Diane Nash, Thompson costarred in the boxing drama *Creed* (2015). An installment in the popular *Rocky* series (1976–2015), *Creed* was critically acclaimed, and Thompson won an Image Award and an African American Film Critics Association Award for best supporting actress.

IMPACT

Since becoming involved in acting in the early 2000s, Thompson has worked consistently in theater, film, and television. For her critically acclaimed performances, she has won an Image Award, a Black Reel Award, and a grand jury prize at the American Black Film Festival.

PERSONAL LIFE

Thompson lives in Los Angeles and enjoys traveling solo in her spare time to India and Europe.

SUGGESTED READING

Behrens, Deborah. "Tessa Thompson Returns to Shakespeare as Rosalind." *This Stage Magazine*. LA Stage Alliance, 11 July 2012, thisstage.la/2012/07/tessa-thompson-returns-to-shakespeare-as-rosalind/. Accessed 8 Dec. 2018.

Dockterman, Eliana. "*Creed*'s Tessa Thompson on Why She's More Than Just a Cliché Movie Girlfriend." *Time*, 30 Nov. 2015, time.com/4129487/creed-tessa-thompson-cliche-movie-girlfriend/. Accessed 8 Dec. 2018.

Houston, Shannon M. "Tessa Thompson Breaks the Mold." *Paste Magazine*. Paste Media Group, 28 May 2014, www.pastemagazine.com/articles/2014/05/the-hollywood-race-tessa-thompson-and-the-myth-of.html. Accessed 8 Dec. 2018.

Lange, Maggie. "Creed Star Tessa Thompson: Hollywood's Miss Independent." *GQ*. Condé Nast, 25 Nov. 2015, www.gq.com/story/tessa-thompson-wcw. Accessed 8 Dec. 2018.

Peoples, Lindsay. "Tessa Thompson on Race, Hollywood, and Her Impending Stardom." *New York Magazine*. New York Media, 12 Feb. 2016, www.thecut.com/2016/02/meet-tessa-thompson.html. Accessed 8 Dec. 2018.

SELECTED WORKS

Veronica Mars, 2005–6; *Detroit 1-8-7*, 2010–11; *Copper*, 2012–13; *Mississippi Damned*, 2009; *For Colored Girls*, 2010; *Dear White People*, 2014; *Creed*, 2015

—*Patrick G. Cooper*

Tinashe

Date of birth: February 6, 1993
Occupation: Singer and actor

Tinashe is a multidimensional singer who has collaborated with musicians such as Britney Spears, Katy Perry, and Nicki Minaj. She has been compared to Aaliyah, Beyoncé, and Janet Jackson. "I consider myself a pop artist who makes R&B-tinged pop music," she told Michael Cragg for *Guardian* (12 June 2017). Studios and radio stations, therefore, find it difficult to place her music in a clear-cut category, such as urban or rhythm and blues. This can result in less airtime for her music, but her popularity continues to rise. Her debut album reached number seventeen on the Billboard 200 list, and in 2015, she won a YouTube Music Award. She released her second album, *Joyride*, in 2018. The same year, Tinashe appeared on the twenty-seventh season of CBS's *Dancing with the Stars*.

CHILDHOOD AND EDUCATION

Tinashe Jorgensen Kachingwe was born in Kentucky to Aimie and Michael Kachingwe. Her mother, who hails from the Midwest, teaches physical therapy at California State University, Northridge. Her father, an immigrant from Zimbabwe, teaches acting at California State Polytechnic University, Pomona. Her parents played a great deal of music in their home; Zimbabwean culture promotes vocal music. She was inspired as a child by singers like Michael Jackson, Sade, and Janet Jackson. Tinashe knew she wanted to perform from a young age, and her father initially booked her baby modeling jobs. Tinashe's parents encouraged her aspirations, moving the family first to Chicago before settling in Los Angeles in 2001. But neither parent was the stereotypical stage parent, as Tinashe told Will Lavin for *SoulCulture* (21 Nov. 2012), "I was very much the driving force in my career. . . . my parents were just really supportive of me as opposed to grooming me. I don't think they were ever pushing me or anything."

At age five she began gaining acting credits, first earning a guest voice role on an episode of the animated children's show *Franklin* in 1997, before appearing in the made-for-television film *Cora Unashamed* (2000). In the early 2000s, she appeared on *America's Most Talented Kid*, singing Alicia Keys' hit "Falling." By age eleven, she had a black belt in Tae Kwon Do. In addition, she had a modeling career and played piano and violin. She was also cast as an extra in *The Polar Express* (2004), starring Tom Hanks, and *Akeelah and the Bee* (2006). Tinashe then appeared as a recurring character in the children's series *Out of Jimmy's Head*, from 2007 to 2008, and in the comedy series *Two and a Half Men*, from 2008 to 2009.

EARLY MUSIC CAREER

Tinashe tested out of school at fifteen, and shortly after, in 2007, she joined the Stunners, a female quintet. The group appeared first on the 2007 soundtrack to the Nickelodeon show *iCarly*. In 2010, the Stunners were the opening act for twenty shows of singer Justin Bieber's first world tour. Tinashe told Lauren Nostro for *Noisey* (6 Dec. 2013), "Every time we performed the stadiums were packed, which was such an amazing experience because there are just so many people there and the energy is incredible. The whole girl group experience was a really great learning experience." The group split in 2011, with each member pursuing her own career. Tinashe, who had been the unofficial lead singer and composed some of the songs, focused on her music. She has stated that the experience she gained being in the studio and touring with the Stunners was a benefit to her career.

When Tinashe turned eighteen, around 2011, she built a studio in her home to record and mix her music. She told Cragg, "I learned how to record in big studios and how to engineer and create songs." In 2012, Tinashe created her first mixtape, *In Case We Die*, in sixteen days. That tape led to a deal with RCA/Sony. Several other mixtapes followed, including the thirteen-cut *Black Water*, which she created in a month when it became clear that her first album would not be ready in 2013.

Photo by Drew de Fawkes via Wikimedia Commons

AQUARIUS

Tinashe released her debut album, *Aquarius*—named for her astrological sign—in 2014. She worked with several other performers to produce the album, including Boi-1da, Dev Hynes, Stuart Matthewman, T-Minus, and Mike WiLL Made-It. The lead single from the album, "2 On" featuring SchoolBoy Q, reached number twenty-four on the Billboard Hot 100 chart, her only song to break the top one hundred. It then achieved platinum status. One interlude, the song "Deep in the Night," was first composed when Tinashe was six, with the help of her piano teacher to score it properly. The album gave Tinashe the opportunity to meld her major influences—alternative music, hip-hop, and rhythm and blues—into a unique blend. She recorded some of the songs in her bedroom, hoping to connect with listeners through an authenticity sometimes lacking in polished studio recordings. *Aquarius* earned Tinashe a Black Entertainment Television (BET) Award nomination for new artist in 2015.

The same year, she was asked by Janet Jackson to perform with singers Ciara and Jason Derulo during the Janet Jackson Dance Tribute at the 2015 BET Awards. She then began building a fan base while touring with Nicki Minaj and Katy Perry in 2015. While touring she was influenced by world music, which she began incorporating into her own music.

MIXTAPES

In 2015, Tinashe self-released the mixtape *Amethyst* as a thank you to her fans. Shortly after, she announced that she was working on her second album, however the project was slow moving with no set release date. On social media sites, she accused RCA of focusing more on singer Zayne Malik's debut solo album than on her project. To get her record label to move faster, she leaked her own music, including the songs "Party Favors" featuring Young Thug and "Player" featuring Chris Brown.

Because of the long delay in getting her sophomore album out, Tinashe eventually decided to pull some of the tracks intended for that work and release them as a separate mixtape. Titled *Nightride* (2016), *Rolling Stone* placed the mixtape on their Twenty Best R & B Albums of 2016 list. The mixtape varied from the type of music she had released before. As she told Raisa Bruner for *Time* (5 Apr. 2018), "I don't like being told what to do. It's easy for people to marginalize you—if they hear you do a certain type of song, they expect that from you every time. But that's so boring!"

Despite a career stall after the release of *Nightride*, Tinashe was not daunted. As she told Cragg, "Things haven't always gone according to my original plan, but that's life, and things change. However long it takes, I know I will get to my end goal. I'm never going to stop. I will make music forever." Instead, she focused on other endeavors, including endorsing products like Dr. Pepper and John Frieda's hair-care line, thus presenting her music to new audiences. She also appeared in designer Alexander Wang's Fall 2016 campaign video. In 2017, she appeared in two episodes of the drama series *Empire*.

JOYRIDE

Tinashe's sophomore album, *Joyride*, was finally released in 2018. Looking back on the time it took to produce the album, Tinashe told Dee Lockett for *Vulture* (Apr. 2018), "I made the mistake of even talking about the project too soon. When I look back on the entire journey of it, I'm very thankful for the time that it did take. It pushed me to create the version of the album that is coming out now. It was important that it ended up taking as long as it did." The album release party was held at Sony Hall, which RCA rented for the event.

Tinashe admitted that in developing the album, she created about two hundred songs and had three versions of the recording. About 20 percent of the first draft made the cut for the final album. As a self-confessed perfectionist, she found letting go of the material difficult. As she told Lockett, "When you're a super perfectionist, set unreasonably high expectations, and don't hit them, you can be hard on yourself. I'm my harshest critic because I put the most pressure on myself." Tinashe sees herself as a storyteller, even though not all the stories she puts into her music are from her own life. In addition to her own experiences, she will use and reweave stories that friends have told her or completely make up the story line.

With the album, Tinashe resisted the label's attempt to slot her into a specific genre, telling Lockett, "They were trying to make me one thing . . . when really I can be a melting pot of different things. That's what makes people human: We have different dimensions. To expect that from a music artist or the music itself is just very simple-minded."

In 2018, Tinashe appeared on *Dancing with the Stars*. She was eliminated during the fourth round after performing a three-dancer tango with Brandon Armstrong and Amy Purdy. Tinashe then joined singer and actor Vanessa Hudgens in a televised live version of the musical *Rent*, playing Mimi Marquez, for Fox Live in early 2019.

PERSONAL LIFE

Tinashe lives in Hollywood Hills in Los Angeles, where she built a home studio to record and produce her music. Tinashe, who speaks Shona, the first language of her father, has two younger brothers, Thulani and Kudzai. They sometimes accompany her when she creates music videos.

SUGGESTED READING

Bruner, Raisa. "R&B Triple Threat Tinashe Hits Her Stride on New Album *Joyride*." Review of *Joyride*, by Tinashe. *Time*, 5 Apr. 2018, time. com/5228975/tinashe-hits-her-stride-on-new-album-joyride/. Accessed 14 Dec. 2018.

Cragg, Michael. "Tinashe: 'If You're a Black Singer, You're Either Beyoncé or Rihanna.'" *The Guardian*, 12 June 2017, www.theguardian.com/music/2017/jun/12/tinashe-if-black-singer-either-beyonce-rihanna. Accessed 12 Dec. 2018.

Kachingwe, Tinashe. "Tinashe: Are You Ready?" Interview by Lauren Nostro. *Noisey*, 6 Dec. 2013, noisey.vice.com/en_us/article/6w7x46/tinashe-black-water-interview. Accessed 31 Dec. 2018.

Kachingwe, Tinashe. "Tinashe Is Not a Music Industry Prisoner." Interview by Dee Lockett. *Vulture*, Apr. 2018, www.vulture.com/2018/04/tinashe-on-releasing-joyride-setbacks-and-taking-control.html. Accessed 13 Dec. 2018.

Lavin, Will. "Bridging the Rhythmic Gap: Tinashe Talks Stage, Stunners & Reverie." *Soul Culture*, 21 Nov. 2012, soulculture.com/features/interviews/bridging-the-rhythmic-gap-tinashe-talks-stage-stunners-reverie/. Accessed 8 Jan. 2019.

Scarano, Ross. "Tinashe." *Complex*, Feb./Mar. 2016, www.complex.com/music/tinashe-interview-2016-cover-story. Accessed 8 Dec. 2018.

SELECTED WORKS

Aquarius, 2014; *Nightride*, 2016; *Joyride*, 2018

—Judy Johnson

Christina Tosi

Date of birth: November 9, 1981
Occupation: Chef and television personality

"I was never raised to take myself so seriously when baking," chef and television personality Christina Tosi told Alex Witchel for the *New York Times* (3 May 2011). "My whole approach is to look in cupboards and throw a bunch of stuff together. It can't really be bad if it's coated in chocolate and butter. Just enjoy yourself." Since 2008, Tosi has showcased that distinctive culinary point of view through her bakery Milk Bar, a popular and critically acclaimed business known for mingling sweet and savory flavors and offering unique treats that evoke the tastes and comforts of home.

Trained in the pastry arts at the French Culinary Institute, Tosi launched her culinary career in New York City's fine-dining scene but ultimately discovered that her own culinary approach was incompatible with the formal, elegant desserts she was often tasked with making. However, she soon found a home for her personal creations within the Momofuku restaurant group, providing baked goods and desserts for chef David Chang's restaurants before launching Momofuku Milk Bar—later known simply as Milk Bar—as a standalone operation. Although the business grew over the subsequent decade, a major turning point came in 2017, when a significant outside investment enabled Tosi to begin a concerted effort to expand Milk Bar's operations nationwide. While the company's sudden success and whirlwind of expansion may have proven daunting for some chefs, Tosi takes such developments as a source of inspiration. "I am at my very best when I'm in over my head," she told Maria Aspan for *Inc.* (Mar./Apr. 2018). "You reach into these depths of your mind that you would otherwise never really be forced to tap into."

EARLY LIFE AND EDUCATION

Christina Tosi was born in Ohio in 1981. Her father was an agricultural economist who worked for the US Department of Agriculture, and her mother was an accountant. Her parents divorced when she was a teenager, and her mother later remarried. She and her older sister, Angela, grew up largely in Springfield, Virginia, part of the extended Washington, DC, metropolitan area.

As a child, Tosi was a somewhat picky eater but enjoyed experimenting with food, creating unusual combinations of ingredients that would influence her later approach to designing desserts. A baker from a young age, she dreamed of one day owning a bakery, an aspiration she described to Witchel as "the other little-girl dream besides being a princess." In addition to her culinary interests, she was focused on excelling academically with the goal of attending college, in keeping with her parents' emphasis on the role of education in ensuring future success. A "no-nonsense person" as a child and teenager, as Tosi described her younger self to Mary H. K. Choi for *Eater* (5 Sept. 2017), she was dedicated to both her education and her extracurricular activities, which included cross-country.

Tosi attended Robert E. Lee High School, from which she graduated in 1999. After high school, she enrolled in the University of Virginia to study electrical engineering, as she felt drawn to mathematics and science. However, it soon became clear to Tosi, as she spent many nights staying up late baking, that her chosen area of

Photo by Christina Tosi via Wikimedia Commons

study—and indeed, college itself—was not a good fit. Following a period of study abroad in Italy, she completed her education, with a focus on math and Italian, at Virginia's James Madison University at an accelerated pace. "I realized after my first year that college was not for me, so I took as many classes as I could and graduated in three years," she told Aspan of the experience. "Then I had to ask myself, what is that one thing I could do that's going to make me excited about waking up in the morning and that I'll never get sick of?" The answer to that question, as Tosi told Aspan, was a simple one: "making cookies."

EARLY CAREER

Prior to graduating from college, Tosi had begun her career in the culinary field by taking a position at a local microbrewery, where she worked initially as a member of the front-of-house staff and later in the kitchen. After her graduation, she moved to New York City to study pastry arts at the French Culinary Institute, an institution later renamed the International Culinary Center. During that period, she supported herself by working as a host and server in various New York restaurants. She went on to secure her first pastry position at Bouley, a critically acclaimed French restaurant in New York's Tribeca neighborhood. In addition to that role, she gained additional experience through a variety of informal gigs in the food industry as well as a stint with the culinary magazine *Saveur*. Knowing that she needed to be present to get a job, she took an unpaid position at veteran chef Wylie Dufresne's noted molecular-gastronomy restaurant wd~50 before eventually becoming a paid

employee of the popular establishment. In addition to her work in the kitchen, Tosi played an essential role in helping wd~50's leadership navigate health-department bureaucracy, handling crucial paperwork to ensure the restaurant's continued operation.

For Tosi, her challenging work in fine dining was a formative aspect of her early career and a key test of her commitment to her chosen field. "I think that in a large way is where I developed grit and I got my chops," she told Sarah Polus for the *Washington Post* (10 Nov. 2018). "When you first get out of a school, I'm a big believer that you go and work in the hardest place in your profession to really gut-check whether or not you mean it, and whether or not you have what it takes." However, her time in fine dining also taught her that she did not enjoy working as a pastry chef in such environments, as she appreciated the elegant desserts being created but did not connect with them on a personal level. "I think with other chefs, the ones that are successful are the ones who speak from the truest part of who they are, and some of them are fine dining chefs," she told Polus. "That's just not who I am. I was raised by women who were like, 'Eat this cookie. Take this plate of bars to a bake sale,' and that's how my love for food grew."

MOMOFUKU

Following Tosi's successful handling of wd~50's health-department paperwork, Dufresne recommended her to chef David Chang to help with similar food-safety paperwork for his Momofuku restaurant group; she ultimately began to work for him in an administrative capacity. Her responsibilities soon expanded to include operational tasks such as managing payroll and procuring supplies for Chang's Momofuku Noodle Bar and the additional restaurants he went on to open under the Momofuku brand, including Ssäm Bar and Momofuku Ko. Unlike in some of her earlier restaurant experiences, Tosi identified with Chang's culinary point of view and dedication to creating food that was both delicious and approachable. She likewise impressed her employer with her own ability to create inventive desserts, many of which she baked at home during her free time and later brought in to work as snacks for the office. Following the opening of Ssäm Bar, Chang tasked Tosi with creating a dessert to be featured on the restaurant's menu, and she went on to create a variety of desserts and baked goods for the Momofuku restaurants.

After several years with Momofuku, Tosi had the opportunity to expand her bakery offerings further in 2008, when a retail space next to one of Chang's restaurants in New York's East Village became available. With support and seed funding from her employer, she opened the bakery

Momofuku Milk Bar. The venture was immediately successful. "I had a moment on opening morning—at like 4 or 5 a.m.—baking cookies with the three people who were crazy enough to follow me down this path," Tosi recalled to Aspan. "Then we opened the door, and there was a line around the corner, down the block. It was like a cannon ball and we were off." In addition to making a variety of items for the Momofuku restaurants, Momofuku Milk Bar began retail operations out of its new storefront and went on to expand into online sales and additional retail locations elsewhere in the city.

FIRST YEARS OF MILK BAR

Following its launch in 2008, Momofuku Milk Bar gained widespread acclaim for its unique offerings, which often featured unusual combinations of flavors and textures that appealed to a wide range of customers. Particularly successful items included a pie with a decadent, buttery filling served in a toasted oat crust; a cookie featuring sweet flavors as well as salty additions such as pretzels and potato chips, known as the Compost Cookie; and soft-serve ice cream designed to taste like the sweet milk left in a cereal bowl after the cereal has been eaten. For Tosi, such desserts were creative yet also evoked flavors with which many customers would be deeply familiar. "Even people who don't cook home-cooked meals often know what a home-cooked meal is, and those foods and flavors and ingredients are found in the aisles of the grocery store," she told Polus. "So it's kind of leveraging the flavors that are connected to your heartstrings, that you already know. And for me, it's finding a way to re-create them and rediscover them."

In light of the success of Milk Bar's cookies, cakes, and other offerings, Tosi began writing and releasing cookbooks revolving around the bakery, beginning in 2011 with *Momofuku Milk Bar*. As the store expanded throughout New York City and began to make a profit, it became increasingly popular as a business in its own right rather than through its association with the Momofuku brand. As such, Tosi and her colleagues began to remove Momofuku from the bakery's name around 2012, referring to it simply as Milk Bar. The year 2012 also saw Tosi win the prestigious James Beard Award for Rising Star Chef of the Year in honor of her work at Milk Bar, and a partnership with model Karlie Kloss resulted in the creation of the gluten-free cookie line Karlie's Kookies.

GREATER EXPANSION AND OTHER VENTURES

Tosi opened the first Milk Bar location outside of New York in 2013 with the beginning of business at a new, international store in Toronto, Canada, and a Washington, DC, store opened its doors in 2015. That same year, Tosi won the James Beard Award for Outstanding Pastry Chef; published her second cookbook, *Milk Bar Life*; and was tapped to begin serving as a judge on the popular network cooking competition shows *MasterChef* and *MasterChef Junior*. When asked about her involvement with *MasterChef*, she explained to Amy Wilkinson for *Entertainment Weekly* (20 May 2015), "Even after a long day at work in the kitchen, going home and watching these home cooks love food so much—for some reason I just always found it perfect parts thrilling and invigorating and challenging and emotional."

In 2017, Milk Bar received a large investment from the venture-capital firm RSE Ventures, which Tosi planned to use to expand the company's reach further. Having already branched out to Nevada, she went on to open Milk Bar locations in states such as California and Massachusetts, and the company amassed a total of sixteen locations by early 2019. Always exploring creative opportunities, Milk Bar collaborated with the clothing brand Madewell in 2017, and in 2018 Tosi partnered with the brand Pyrex on a collection of decorated food-storage containers. In the meantime, she had also published a third cookbook, titled *Milk Bar: All about Cake* (2018).

PERSONAL LIFE

Tosi married Will Guidara, a restaurateur and co-owner of the Make It Nice restaurant group, in 2016. They live in Manhattan. In addition to baking, Tosi enjoys growing houseplants and running.

SUGGESTED READING

Choi, Mary H. K. "Christina Tosi Has a Cookie." *Eater*, 5 Sept. 2017, www.eater.com/2017/9/5/16213430/christina-tosi-profile-milk-bar. Accessed 10 May 2019.

Leve, Ariel. "Christina Tosi: 'My Diet Was Crazy for the First 27 Years of My Life.'" *The Guardian*, 21 Apr. 2012, www.theguardian.com/lifeandstyle/2012/apr/22/christina-tosi-milk-bar-interview. Accessed 10 May 2019.

Severson, Kim. "For Christina Tosi, Building a Dessert Empire Is Not All Milk and Cookies." *The New York Times*, 12 Feb. 2019, www.nytimes.com/2019/02/12/dining/christina-tosi-milk-bar.html. Accessed 10 May 2019.

Tosi, Christina. "5 Minutes with: Milk Bar Founder Christina Tosi." Interview by Sarah Polus. *The Washington Post*, 10 Nov. 2018, www.washingtonpost.com/arts-entertainment/2018/11/10/minutes-with-milk-bar-founder-christina-tosi. Accessed 10 May 2019.

Tosi, Christina. "How Milk Bar's Christina Tosi Went from Momofuku Employee to Bakery Chain CEO." Interview by Maria Aspan.

Inc., Mar./Apr. 2018, www.inc.com/maga-zine/201804/maria-aspan/christina-tosi-milk-bar-momofuku-bakery.html. Accessed 10 May 2019.

Tosi, Christina. "MasterChef: Meet 'Scary but Friendly' New Judge Christina Tosi." Interview by Amy Wilkinson. *Entertainment Weekly*, 20 May 2015, ew.com/article/2015/05/20/masterchef-meet-scary-friendly-new-judge-christina-tosi/. Accessed 10 May 2019.

Witchel, Alex. "Christina Tosi, a Border-Crossing Pastry Chef." *The New York Times*, 3 May 2011, www.nytimes.com/2011/05/04/dining/04feed.html. Accessed 10 May 2019.

—*Joy Crelin*

Molly Tuttle

Date of birth: 1993
Occupation: Musician and singer-songwriter

Photo by cp_thornton via Flickr

Despite being in her mid-twenties when she released her first solo full-length record in 2019, Molly Tuttle displayed the talents of a virtuoso guitarist and banjo player twice her age. Hailing from a bluegrass background, Tuttle has crossed genres to impress lovers of folk and Americana music as well. The praise stems from her stellar flat-picking, clawhammer, and cross-picking styles, which have wowed listeners, as well as from her skills as a singer and songwriter of considerable depth and sensitivity. She developed her musical abilities with the help and encouragement of her father, Jack Tuttle, whose own passion for bluegrass music exposed her to the recordings of flat-picking greats like Clarence White, Doc Watson, and Tony Rice at a young age.

After collaborating with her family and other notable bluegrass musicians on recordings and in performances, Tuttle struck out on her own, producing the acclaimed recordings *Rise* (2017), her debut EP, and *When You're Ready* (2019), her first full-length album. These recordings have added to her growing fan base as well as to her list of accomplishments, which have included winning the award for Guitar Player of the Year, presented at the International Bluegrass Music Association (IBMA) Awards, in 2017 and 2018, and being named Instrumentalist of the Year at the 2018 Americana Honors & Awards.

Yet more than anything else, Tuttle hopes to use her talents and experience to inspire future musicians. "I love seeing any young person trying to play one of my songs or just learning something from me," she remarked to Rick Kreiser for the *Bakersfield Californian* (21 May 2019). "One of my goals is to inspire the next generation, especially young girls, to play guitar. I think if girls see a woman doing something, it helps them think, 'I can do that, too.'"

EARLY LIFE

Molly Tuttle was born in 1993 and raised in California's San Francisco Bay area. She has two brothers: Sullivan, who plays guitar, and Michael, who plays the mandolin. Her father, Jack Tuttle, a bluegrass musician and instructor, plays a wide variety of instruments. While he did end up playing different styles, his daughter recalled in an interview with Jon Weisberger for the *Bluegrass Situation* (13 July 2018), "What my dad always loved was bluegrass. He grew up playing bluegrass, and that's really what he studied and what he loves."

Though initially drawn to the violin and piano, Tuttle started playing guitar at around eight, developing flat-picking and clawhammer guitar styles largely under the tutelage of her father. She later learned how to play mandolin and banjo as well, beginning to perform with her father when she was just about eleven. Around that time, because she was going to bluegrass jams and was impressed with the singing she saw there, she also decided to take voice lessons from a local instructor.

In 2007 Tuttle and her father collaborated on and released the bluegrass album *The Old Apple Tree*. Jack Tuttle also put together his own family band with the young vocalist and instrumentalist AJ Lee, called the Tuttles with AJ Lee, when his children became skilled enough to perform with him. Tuttle performed with the band, particularly at festivals, in shows on the weekends, eventually maturing to the point where she could help her father with arrangements.

Beyond her father, Tuttle had a number of musical idols and a bolstering bluegrass community growing up. She recalled to Weisberger, "When I was a kid I looked up to Laurie Lewis, Kathy Kallick, Keith Little, Bill Evans, my dad— all these Bay Area people. There's a really great scene there and they were all so supportive of me." Later she would come to love such eclectic musical artists as folk rocker Bob Dylan, indie rocker Neko Case, and roots artist Gillian Welch. Because her musical tastes moved beyond bluegrass, she was later able to incorporate a wide variety of musical genres into her own work.

WORKING WITH OTHER MUSICIANS

Upon graduating from Palo Alto High School, Tuttle moved to the East Coast to study guitar performance and songwriting at Berklee College of Music in Boston, Massachusetts, in its American Roots Music Program. Of her decision to attend the prestigious institution, she told Mark Small for *Berklee Today* (Fall 2018), "Of all the music schools I looked at, Berklee seemed to offer more styles than the others and had the amazing American Roots program. It seemed to me that going there would expand the way I thought about music and open my ears to other styles." Continuing to perform while attending classes, in 2012 she competed, along with her father, in a duet contest for the radio variety show *A Prairie Home Companion* and received recognition for her musicianship, including being named Best Female Vocalist by the Northern California Bluegrass Society.

Also while at Berklee, she met the fellow students with whom she would form the band the Goodbye Girls, combining old-time music, bluegrass, and Swedish folk music. Her fellow band members included Allison de Groot on banjo, Lena Jonsson on fiddle, and Brittany Karlson on bass. In addition to touring in Jonsson's native Sweden, the Goodbye Girls recorded the EP *Going to Boston* in 2014. That same year Tuttle also recorded a five-track EP with fiddler John Mailander titled *Molly Tuttle and John Mailander*.

GOING SOLO

In 2015, about a year after graduating from Berklee, Tuttle moved to Nashville, Tennessee, the center of country and bluegrass music. Though beginning to really focus on making her dream of a solo project a reality, she performed with the Goodbye Girls and put out the full-length album *Snowy Side of the Mountain* with the band in 2016. That same year she was named the Momentum Instrumentalist of the Year from the International Bluegrass Music Association (IBMA).

Tuttle eventually recorded her first solo EP, *Rise*, which was released in 2017. To help her during the recording, she brought on board Mailander, bassist Todd Phillips, banjo player Wesley Corbett, and backing vocalists Kai Welch and Kathy Kallick, among others. Welch also supplied instrumental contributions and produced the EP. The singer-songwriter and multi-instrumentalist Darrell Scott also appeared on the recording.

Although she had powerful professional musicians supporting her, *Rise* gave Tuttle an opportunity to showcase not only her gifts as a singer and instrumentalist, but also as a songwriter. She wrote or cowrote every song on the EP, including "You Didn't Call My Name," which won Best Song of the Year at the 2018 International Folk Music Awards. Other notable songs on *Rise* include "Friend and a Friend" and the opening track "Good Enough." In a review for *Bluegrass Today* (2 Apr. 2018), Lee Zimmerman said of *Rise*, "Ultimately, despite its abbreviated seven song setlist, *Rise* accomplishes all its title suggests—that is, to provide a platform for an artist who has already ascended to certain prominence, her relative youth notwithstanding. It not only elevates her stature, but affirms her artistic inclinations as well."

The EP also garnered Tuttle significant recognition. In 2017 the IBMA Awards named her Guitar Player of the Year, making her the first woman to receive the award in that category. The following year she was again celebrated at the IBMA Awards, winning Guitar Player of the Year for a second time; Missy Raines's "Swept Away," in which Tuttle had a part, won Recorded Event of the Year. Tuttle was also nominated for Emerging Artist of the Year, Female Vocalist of the Year, Album of the Year for *Rise*, and Song of the Year for "You Didn't Call My Name." At the 2018 Americana Honors & Awards, she won Instrumentalist of the Year.

WHEN YOU'RE READY

In 2019 Tuttle emerged from the studio with her first full-length solo record, *When You're Ready*, produced by Ryan Hewitt, who had previously worked with the Lumineers and the Avett Brothers. As she had on *Rise*, Tuttle wrote all the songs, either solo or in collaboration with songwriters such as Welch, Sarah Siskind, and Maya de Vitry. Among the standout songs are "Sit Back and Watch It Roll," "Take the Journey," "Make My Mind Up," and "Sleepwalking," all of which highlight her emotive singing and her gifts as an instrumentalist.

When You're Ready received considerable praise upon its release. Jewly Hight, writing for *NPR Music* (28 Mar. 2019), declared, "Tuttle applies remarkable precision to her pursuit of clarity. That's even a central theme of her lyrics: consciously reckoning with indecision or intuition, honestly acknowledging incompatibility, cultivating intimacy based on people seeing each other for who they are."

OTHER INVOLVEMENT

In addition to her work as a recording and touring musician, Tuttle has taught beginner, advanced, and intermediate guitar classes at music camps, including Targhee Music Camp, ar the Grand Targhee Ski Resort in Alta, Wyoming. She enjoys teaching because it enables her to pass on her knowledge to a new generation.

Tuttle also supports alopecia awareness. Alopecia is an autoimmune disease that causes hair loss. Tuttle herself has had the condition since a young age. She has used her growing profile to help the public develop a better understanding and to promote self-acceptance among those like her who live with alopecia. In an interview with Hight for *NPR Music* (29 Aug. 2017), she explained, "[Alopecia] doesn't affect your health at all, but it effects how you see yourself, how others see you. I've had a feeling my whole life that this was something I could offer the alopecia community with my music, and vice-versa, kind of offer the music community awareness about people who are dealing with hair loss, and tying it in to accepting everyone for who they are."

SUGGESTED READING

Hight, Jewly. "Every Note Rings Clear on Molly Tuttle's 'When You're Ready.'" Review of *When You're Ready*, by Molly Tuttle. *NPR Music*, National Public Radio, 28 Mar. 2019, www.npr.org/2019/03/28/706971355/first-listen-molly-tuttle-when-you-re-ready. Accessed 25 July 2019.

Kreiser, Rick. "Bluegrass and Beyond: Molly Tuttle Ready to Wow at Guitar Masters Show." *The Bakersfield Californian*, 21 May 2019, www.bakersfield.com/entertainment/music/bluegrass-and-beyond-molly-tuttle-ready-to-wow-at-guitar/article_ac0e9d48-7801-11e9-ab1c-bb1137427746.html. Accessed 25 July 2019.

Tuttle, Molly. "A Desire to Inspire: A Conversation with Molly Tuttle." Interview by Jon Weisberger. *The Bluegrass Situation*, 13 July 2018, thebluegrasssituation.com/read/a-desire-to-inspire-a-conversation-with-molly-tuttle/. Accessed 24 July 2019.

Tuttle, Molly. "World Cafe Nashville: Molly Tuttle." Interview by Jewly Hight. *NPR Music*, National Public Radio, 29 Aug. 2017, www.npr.org/sections/world-cafe/2017/08/29/546730707/world-cafe-nashville-molly-tuttle. Accessed 25 July 2019.

Tuttle, Molly, and Sierra Hull. "Young Bluegrass Virtuosos." Interview by Mark Small. *Berklee Today*, Fall 2018, www.berklee.edu/berklee-today/fall-2018/young-bluegrass-virtuosos. Accessed 25 July 2019.

Zimmerman, Lee. Review of *Rise*, by Molly Tuttle. *Bluegrass Today*, 2 Apr. 2018, bluegrass-today.com/rise-molly-tuttle. Accessed 31 July 2019.

SELECTED WORKS

Going to Boston (with the Goodbye Girls), 2014; *Snowy Side of the Mountain* (with the Goodbye Girls), 2016; *Rise*, 2017; *When You're Ready*, 2019

—Christopher Mari

Karen Uhlenbeck

Date of birth: August 24, 1942
Occupation: Mathematician

Beginning a college math class might be a mundane event for many students, but for mathematician Karen Uhlenbeck, it was a career-shaping moment. "I didn't know that you could even be a mathematician when I was growing up," she recalled to Clara Moskowitz for *Scientific American* (27 Mar. 2019). "But in my freshman college calculus class, as soon as I grasped that you had certain rules and could do all sorts of interesting things within the framework of mathematics, I just fell in love with it."

Uhlenbeck's love of mathematics drove her not only to complete a doctorate in the subject and begin a lengthy career as a professor, but also to investigate a host of complex topics in the field and, in so doing, join the ranks of its most accomplished figures. In recognition of her groundbreaking work in areas such as minimal surfaces and gauge theory, she has received a host of honors, including the prestigious MacArthur Fellowship. In 2019 she became the first woman to receive the Abel Prize, among the highest honors in mathematics, from the Norwegian Academy of Science and Letters.

Although Uhlenbeck's wide-ranging body of work has won her widespread acclaim, she remains primarily attracted to the challenge of understanding new and complex ideas. "I find that I am bored with anything I understand," she wrote in a 1996 autobiographical sketch published in *Math Horizons*.

EARLY LIFE AND EDUCATION

Uhlenbeck was born Karen Keskulla on August 24, 1942, in Cleveland, Ohio. She was the first of four children born to Arnold Keskulla, an

Photo by George Bergman via Wikimedia Commons

engineer, and Carolyn Keskulla, a painter and art teacher. When Uhlenbeck was a child, the family moved to New Jersey and settled in the rural community of West Millington. Thanks both to her environment and to the influence of her parents, Uhlenbeck grew up enjoying outdoor activities such as hiking and for a time considered pursuing a career in forestry. She was also an inquisitive child and avid reader who was particularly drawn to physics and began reading books on astrophysics at the age of twelve.

As a high school student, Uhlenbeck enjoyed playing sports and also played clarinet in the school band. Her parents were both the first in their families to attend college, and they encouraged Uhlenbeck to pursue a college education as well. After graduating from high school in 1960, she enrolled in the University of Michigan, where she originally planned to study physics.

Upon taking an honors-level calculus class, however, Uhlenbeck shifted her focus to mathematics. "I still remember when I first saw the rigorous definition of a derivative, which involves taking the limit of difference quotients to give meaning to an expression that looks at first glance to be zero divided by zero," she recalled to Isaac Chotiner for the New Yorker (28 Mar. 2019). "I was so excited I turned to a friend next to me and said, 'Are you allowed to do that?'" In addition to developing a fascination with pure mathematics, Uhlenbeck was pleased that mathematics, unlike physics, was largely solitary and did not involve extensive laboratory work, which she disliked. She continued to study high-level mathematics while studying abroad in Germany during her junior year and went on to earn her bachelor's degree from the University of Michigan in 1964.

After completing her undergraduate studies, Uhlenbeck decided to pursue a graduate degree at New York University's Courant Institute of Mathematical Science. She remained there for a year before relocating to Massachusetts, as her then husband was pursuing his own graduate studies at Harvard University. Uhlenbeck herself enrolled in Brandeis University, where she continued to study mathematics while receiving funding from the National Science Foundation (NSF) Graduate Fellowship. After earning her master's degree in 1966, she went on to complete her doctorate at the same institution, completing the thesis "The Calculus of Variations and Global Analysis" under the supervision of adviser Richard Palais. Uhlenbeck earned her PhD in 1968.

TEACHING CAREER

Although as a child Uhlenbeck had resisted the idea of becoming a teacher, she was drawn into that occupation after leaving Brandeis, beginning a nearly five-decade career as a university-level educator. She struggled at times during her early career due to discriminatory hiring policies at certain colleges and universities, which were still reluctant to hire women. Nevertheless, she was able to find employment, although her options were sometimes limited. "Looking back now I realize that I was very lucky," she told Kenneth Chang for the New York Times (19 Mar. 2019). "I was in the forefront of a generation of women who actually could get real jobs in academia." Uhlenbeck began her career as an instructor at the Massachusetts Institute of Technology (MIT) in 1968 and the following year moved to California. There she spent two years as a lecturer at the University of California (UC), Berkeley.

In 1971, Uhlenbeck attained her first professorship, becoming an assistant professor at the University of Illinois at Urbana-Champaign. During her years at the university, she rose to the position of associate professor and received a fellowship from the Sloan Foundation. She moved to the University of Illinois's Chicago campus in 1977 and then to the University of Chicago in 1983 to become a full professor. In 1987 the University of Texas at Austin offered her a position as the Sid W. Richardson Foundation Regents' Chair in Mathematics. She accepted and remained in that role until her retirement in 2014, after which she was named professor emerita.

In addition to her primary academic positions, Uhlenbeck held visiting professorships and similar positions at a host of institutions throughout her career, including Northwestern University, Harvard University, the Max Planck

Institute for Mathematics in Germany, and the Mathematics Research Centre at the United Kingdom's Warwick University. She also spent several periods as a member of the Institute for Advanced Study at Princeton University and in 1997 was named a distinguished visiting professor there. Uhlenbeck remained affiliated with the institute following her retirement from the University of Texas, after which she returned to New Jersey.

MATHEMATICAL RESEARCH

Over the course of her career, Uhlenbeck's research has dealt with a variety of complex mathematical concepts that often overlap with physics. She became particularly recognized for her work on soap bubbles, which take on various shapes to surround the largest amount of space while having the least and lowest-energy amount of surface area possible. Predicting the shapes of such soap bubbles, whether real or theoretical, proved thorny for mathematicians. "You can ask a question of when you have a soap bubble in this n-dimensional space," she explained to Chang. "You don't know ahead of time what the shapes of those minimal soap bubbles are going to be." Uhlenbeck worked to develop techniques for addressing such questions, which fall within the category of optimization problems.

Uhlenbeck also devoted a portion of her career to the Yang-Mills equations, which among physicists are key to areas of study such as string theory and gauge theory. "When I started in the field, these equations were not very well-defined mathematically," she told Chotiner. "They have a large invariance, and looking at them is a little wobbly, meaning you can move the answers around a lot, and you have the same physical thing but your mathematical description of this physical thing has a lot of indeterminacy in it. And I realized that, to treat these equations as standard mathematical equations, you had to destroy this indeterminacy and make the equation more rigid." Uhlenbeck became well known for her approach to those equations as well as her investigations of integral systems and bubbling (a technique in which complex phenomena can be viewed on a larger scale and thus be better understood).

Due to the nature of the topics she explores, Uhlenbeck has collaborated both with experts in physics and with other mathematicians, despite having been long drawn to the supposed solitude of her field. "I like to work alone, and I do most of my thinking alone, but I find it absolutely necessary to have other people to talk to now. I need to see how my ideas are panning out," she told Moskowitz. "If I don't have a collaborator I often end up solving a problem and then don't publish because I lose interest." In addition to collaborating with other researchers, Uhlenbeck has

influenced numerous developments in mathematics through her groundbreaking work.

RECOGNITION

For her influential contributions to mathematics and physics, Uhlenbeck has received widespread recognition from bodies both within and outside of her chosen fields. In 1983 the John D. and Catherine T. MacArthur Foundation named her among that year's group of thinkers to receive the MacArthur Fellowship, sometimes known as the "genius grant," a five-year monetary award that enables its recipients to pursue projects of their choice in their respective fields. Uhlenbeck went on to be inducted into the American Academy of Arts and Sciences in 1985 and the National Academy of Sciences (NAS) in 1986. In 2000 she received the National Medal of Science; then in 2007 she was awarded the American Mathematical Society's Steele Prize for Seminal Contribution to Research. She also received honorary doctorates from the University of Illinois and the University of Michigan, among other institutions.

In addition to her numerous contributions to mathematics, Uhlenbeck received notice for being one of few female mathematicians working in the United States during the early part of her career. Although she noted in interviews that she avoided interacting extensively with other women during her days as a student and early career, as such interactions were somewhat discouraged, she began to establish herself as a mentor for younger female mathematicians as she reached a later point in her career. "I looked around and talked with my other women colleagues and we said, 'Where are the women coming behind us?'" she explained to Chotiner. Among other initiatives, Uhlenbeck launched a program for women in mathematics with the support of the Institute for Advanced Study.

A major milestone in Uhlenbeck's career came in March 2019, when the Norwegian Academy of Science and Letters announced that she was the recipient of that year's Abel Prize in recognition of "her pioneering achievements in geometric partial differential equations, gauge theory and integrable systems, and for the fundamental impact of her work on analysis, geometry and mathematical physics," as quoted by Chotiner. Uhlenbeck was the first woman to receive the prestigious mathematics award, which had been given since 2003. In addition to prestige, the award came with a prize of six million kroner, or more than $700,000. For Uhlenbeck, the award was welcome yet surprising. "I'm not quite sure what it means to me," she told Moskowitz. "Right now, it means I have a lot of interviews, and there are a lot of young women looking up to me. I hope I'll grow into it."

PERSONAL LIFE

Uhlenbeck met her first husband, biophysicist Olke Uhlenbeck, while they were both attending the University of Michigan. They married in 1965 and divorced by 1976. She later married Robert Williams, a fellow mathematician and professor. They live in New Jersey.

SUGGESTED READING

Al-Khalili, Jim. "A Biography of Karen Uhlenbeck." *Abel Prize*, 2019, www.abelprize.no/c73996/binfil/download.php?tid=74107. Accessed 10 May 2019.

Chang, Kenneth. "Karen Uhlenbeck Is First Woman to Win Abel Prize for Mathematics." *The New York Times*, 19 Mar. 2019, www.nytimes.com/2019/03/19/science/karen-uhlenbeck-abel-prize.html. Accessed 10 May 2019.

Roberts, Siobhan. "In Bubbles, She Sees a Mathematical Universe." *The New York Times*, 8 Apr. 2019, www.nytimes.com/2019/04/08/science/uhlenbeck-bubbles-math-physics.html. Accessed 10 May 2019.

Uhlenbeck, Karen. "Coming to Grips with Success: A Profile of Karen Uhlenbeck." *Math Horizons* vol. 3, no. 4, Apr. 1996. *Celebratio Mathematica*, celebratio.org/Uhlenbeck_K/article/515. Accessed 10 May 2019.

Uhlenbeck, Karen. "The 'Fantastic' Feeling of a Breakthrough: Q&A with Math Prize Winner Karen Uhlenbeck." Interview by Clara Moskowitz. *Scientific American*, 27 Mar. 2019, www.scientificamerican.com/article/the-fantastic-feeling-of-a-breakthrough-q-a-with-math-prize-winner-karen-uhlenbeck. Accessed 10 May 2019.

Uhlenbeck, Karen. "A Groundbreaking Mathematician on the Gender Politics of Her Field." Interview by Isaac Chotiner. *The New Yorker*, 28 Mar. 2019, www.newyorker.com/news/q-and-a/groundbreaking-mathematician-karen-uhlenbeck-on-the-politics-of-her-field/amp. Accessed 10 May 2019.

Uhlenbeck, Karen. "Karen Uhlenbeck on Being the First Woman to Receive the Abel Prize." *IAS*, 2019, www.ias.edu/ideas/karen-uhlenbeck-being-first-woman-receive-abel-prize. Accessed 10 May 2019.

—*Joy Crelin*

Lauren Underwood

Date of birth: October 4, 1986
Occupation: Politician

Lauren Underwood was one of nineteen people with a background in the sciences who ran for the House of Representatives in the midterm elections of 2018. In the wake of that election, the former nurse also, at age thirty-two, became the youngest black woman ever elected to Congress. She told Steve Inskeep for *NPR* (12 Mar. 2019), "I am black. I know I'm black. The people in the 14th [district] know I'm black, and I am a millennial, and I'm a woman. And so do I have an interesting perspective on issues that impact those demographic groups directly? Sure." Underwood was one of several black women who had become interested in running for office in the wake of movements such as Black Lives Matter and #MeToo. As Melanie Campbell, president of the National Coalition on Black Civic Participation and convener of the Black Women's Roundtable Public Policy Network, told Deborah Barfield Barry for *USA Today* (19 Mar. 2018), "Black women are recognizing more and more the power we have in our vote. It's not just electing public officials but being elected ourselves."

EARLY LIFE AND EDUCATION

Lauren Ashley Underwood was born in Mayfield Heights, Ohio, and her family moved to Naperville, Illinois, when she was three. At eight, she was diagnosed with a heart condition, supraventricular tachycardia. The care she received motivated her to go into a career in health care.

While in high school Underwood was a student member of the fair housing commission in Naperville, a prosperous Chicago suburb. She took seriously the charges citizens made against landlords who discriminated against them.

After graduating from Neuqua Valley High School in Naperville in 2004 and winning a

Photo by U.S. House of Representatives via Wikimedia Commons

scholarship, Underwood entered the nursing program at the University of Michigan in Ann Arbor. There she enrolled in a course on the politics and policy of nursing, which, as she told Jeffrey Mervis for *Science* (18 Oct. 2018), "opened up a new world for me. While my nursing school colleagues were spending summers working in an [intensive care unit], I went to Capitol Hill in 2006 and interned for Senator [Barack] Obama."

EARLY CAREER

Underwood went on to Johns Hopkins University, where she earned a joint master's degree in nursing and public health in 2009. After graduating, she became counselor for science and public health and later executive assistant to Health and Human Services Secretary Kathleen Sebelius. Her tasks then included managing the paper flow necessary to implement the Affordable Care Act.

Once the law was fully implemented, Underwood moved into the area of bio-preparedness. She worked to prevent public health emergencies, such as outbreaks of Ebola and the Zika virus, as well as working on the response to the water crisis created by lead poisoning in Flint, Michigan.

Her supervisor, Nicole Lurie, who hired her as an assistant, told Mervis, "Any task I asked Lauren to do, it didn't matter how outlandish it was, she just got it done. At times, like in Flint, we'd be working with a community that was terrified and angry. So it was important to talk to the person in the street, explain what was going on and understand their concerns. Then we could develop a strategy to meet their needs."

Through Georgetown University's online master's degree program, Underwood also taught future nurse practitioners.

DECIDING TO RUN FOR CONGRESS

In response to the presidency of Donald Trump, Underwood was part of a national move, particularly among Democrats and women, to run for Congress in 2018. Her campaign focused on three key areas: family, healthcare, and jobs. Within those arenas, she gave particular attention to the opioid crisis and the need for coverage for detox and rehab; paid family leave and equal pay; and infrastructure improvements as a means of both creating jobs and increasing the quality of life in her district. She also was clear that climate change and rollbacks on clean air and water initiatives affected public health outcomes. Capitalizing on the Fourteenth District's proximity to the Illinois Research and Development Corridor and Fermi National Accelerator Laboratory, Underwood favored increased use of clean energy.

Underwood observed the negative effect of Trump's trade war with China on the farmers in her district and made that a campaign issue. She also discussed the separation of migrant families at the US–Mexico border, which distressed many in her district. Her ideas on health care, however, were a key factor in her election. Representative Randy Hultgren, the Republican incumbent, had first pledged to vote against any legislation that would remove protections for coverage of pre-exiting conditions. Less than a month later, he reneged on that pledge, which angered Underwood and many others.

At that point, she filed the necessary paperwork to run for office. During the 2018 elections, health care was overwhelmingly cited as a concern amid attempts to destroy or weaken the Affordable Care Act. Hultgren voted with Trump's policies and priorities 96 percent of the time, a fact Underwood repeatedly highlighted during her campaign.

WINNING HER SEAT

Underwood won the primary election with 57 percent of the vote, handily beating out six other contenders to be on the ballot in November 2018. She defeated Hultgren in the general election with more than 52 percent of the vote, winning all seven counties in Illinois's Fourteenth District, which voted for Donald Trump in 2016.

Underwood is part of one of the most diverse freshman classes in congressional history, and hopes to be part of a change in Congress's effectiveness. As she told Guy Stephens for Illinois's Northern Public Radio (18 Jan. 2019), "I believe that what we seek to accomplish in the Congress should be done on a bipartisan basis. We've begun that outreach to other Republican freshmen in particular. They have a number of incoming folks that we've had a chance to get to know. And I'm excited about working with my new colleagues doing that."

She became one of 102 women in the House of Representatives in 2019, 89 of them Democrats. Underwood stayed busy during the seven weeks between the 2018 election and her inauguration on January 3, 2019. Underwood helped write a letter from freshman members of Congress, detailing their priorities and goals, hoping to have an impact on the legislative agenda. By the time Underwood and her cohort were sworn into office, the federal government was undergoing a shutdown over spending. Many of her constituents, including air traffic controllers working without pay, were affected by the shutdown.

CONFRONTING IMMIGRATION ISSUES

Between December 2018 and May 2019, five migrant children trying to enter the United States across the US–Mexico border died in Border Patrol custody. Underwood said during a congressional hearing, as quoted by Joel Rose for National Public Radio's *All Things Considered*

(22 May 2019), "At this point with five kids that have died, 5,000 separated from their families, . . . the evidence is really clear that this is intentional. It's intentional. It's a policy choice being made on purpose by this administration, and it's cruel and inhumane."

In March 2019 Underwood questioned Homeland Security Secretary Kirstjen Nielsen about the effects of the Trump administration's policy of separating children from their parents at the border. Underwood later tweeted that the children in question were "at risk for learning delays, mental health issues, and assorted illness. . . . Sec. Nielsen had few answers for me and showed herself to be uninformed on the impact of her Department's policies. That won't fly anymore."

SAVING WOMEN AND CHILDREN

One of Underwood's priorities is the health of black women. In April 2019, along with Congresswoman Alma Adams of North Carolina, Underwood launched the Black Maternal Health Caucus. The group joined with the Black Mamas Matter Alliance, which is led by women and aims to improve the health of women of color. Black women are four times as likely to die in childbirth as other groups, and their babies are twice as likely to die prematurely. As Underwood told Tanya A. Christian for *Essence* (June 2019), "The statistics around Black maternal health are more than just numbers—they are the horrifying reality for too many women and families in America."

Underwood's committee assignments include the House Committee on Education and Labor, the House Committee on Homeland Security, and the House Committee on Veteran's Affairs, as well as the House Democratic Steering and Policy Committee. As a member of the Future Forum, she joins other young Democratic members of Congress who focus on working for the next generation of Americans. She is also a member of the Congressional Black Caucus and the LGBT Equality Caucus. Underwood is a member of the Congressional Gun Violence Prevention Taskforce, with a desire to address the nation's gun violence. She cosponsored a bill making background checks for gun purchases mandatory.

Of her continued commitment to preserving insurance coverage for preexisting conditions such as her own, Underwood told Bret McCabe for *Johns Hopkins Magazine* (Spring 2019), "The work I'm embarking on is an extension of my nursing practice, an opportunity to ensure that millions and millions of Americans have high-quality health care coverage so that they can lead healthy, productive lives."

LOOKING AHEAD

On August 20, 2019, Underwood joined 125 other House Democrats who had come out in favor of impeaching President Trump. Underwood issued a statement of her position, citing the report of Special Counsel Robert Mueller, which "lays out substantial evidence that the president's campaign worked with a foreign adversary to influence an election" and that Trump has indicated he would welcome foreign influence in the 2020 election as well. She went on to state, "Let me be clear: No one wins when Congress is compelled to investigate impeachment or bring about articles of impeachment. This is a tragedy for our country."

Five Republicans who are seeking to regain her seat for their party in 2020 were swift to criticize her decision as being out of step with the wishes of her constituents. There are thirteen Democratic delegates of eighteen for Illinois; eight of those thirteen have come out in favor of an impeachment inquiry. The fact that during the 2016 election, the Illinois state board of elections was hacked by Russian interference strengthened her resolve.

In June 2019 Underwood announced she would run for a second term. She told Rick Pearson for *Chicago Tribune* (29 June 2019), "I'm ready to continue taking courageous steps in defending our community and being a partner in bringing our voices to Washington. I'm representing you, and it's the biggest honor of my life."

PERSONAL LIFE

When Congress is in session, Underwood shares an apartment with another woman new to Congress, Representative Katie Hill, from California's Twenty-Fifth District. Underwood avoids discussing policy on social media. As she told Inskeep, "I am happy to speak in paragraph statements to talk about the solutions because—guess what—problems are not always illustrated in 140 characters, and solutions are not always illustrated in 140 characters." Her sister, Lindsey Underwood, is an editor for the Smarter Living section of *New York Times*.

SUGGESTED READING

Alter, Charlotte. "How Women Candidates Changed American Politics in 2018." *Time*, 7 Nov. 2018, time.com/5446556/congress-women-pink-wave/. Accessed 5 Sept. 2019.

Alter, Charlotte. "Lauren Underwood's Unlikely Congressional Bid Is All about Health Care." *Time*, 2 Nov. 2018, time.com/5442702/lauren-underwood-health-care-illinois-14/. Accessed 5 Sept. 2019.

Berry, Deborah Barfield. "Black Women Candidates for Congress Say They're Reclaiming Their Time." *USA Today*, 15 Mar. 2018,   www.usatoday.com/story/news/

politics/2018/03/15/black-women-candi-dates-congress-say-theyre-reclaiming-their-time/426463002/. Accessed 5 Sept. 2019.

Christian, Tanya A. "10 Things We're Talk-ing About." *Essence*, vol. 50, no. 2, June 2019, pp. 51–52, www.questia.com/magazine/1P4-2242708263/10-things-we-re-talking-about.

Inskeep, Steve. "Meet Freshman Demo-cratic Rep. Lauren Underwood of Il-linois." *NPR*, 12 Mar. 2019, www.npr.org/2019/03/12/702464519/meet-freshman-democratic-rep-lauren-underwood-of-illinois. Accessed 5 Sept. 2019.

Mervis, Jeffrey. "Lauren Underwood Runs on Progressive Values in Seeking House Seat." *Science*, 18 Oct. 2018, www.sciencemag.org/news/2018/10/lauren-underwood-runs-pro-gressive-values-seeking-house-seat. Accessed 5 Sept. 2019.

Rose, Joel. "Democrats Clash with Homeland Security Secretary over Migrant Children Deaths." *NPR*, 22 May 2019, www.npr.org/2019/05/22/725845379/democrats-clash-with-homeland-security-secretary-over-migrant-children-deaths. Accessed 5 Sept. 2019.

—*Judy Johnson*

Ewine van Dishoeck

Date of birth: June 13, 1955
Occupation: Astrophysicist

Outer space is not empty space: the vast distanc-es between stars are filled with a very thin gas. The larger concentrations of this gas—interstel-lar clouds, which are the birthplaces of new stars and planets—are comprised of molecules that provide the building blocks for future solar sys-tems. To better understand these molecules is to better understand the origins of our own solar system, and ultimately perhaps the origin of life itself. Bridging the gap between the molecular and the astronomical is the field of astrochemis-try—the study of molecules in our universe and their interaction with radiation.

One of the world's leading experts in this field is Ewine van Dishoeck, "the world's most wide-ly-cited astrophysicist" according to the Uni-versity of Gothenburg-Chalmers University of Technology, which presented her with the 2014 Gothenburg Lise Meitner Award. Van Dishoeck received numerous other awards for her pioneer-ing work, including the prestigious Kavli Prize in 2018 for her contributions to astrochemistry. In her interview with Adam Hadhazy for the Ka-vli Foundation (Summer 2018), she remarked:

"The overall story told by astrochemistry is, what is our origin? Where do we come from, how were we built? How did our planet and Sun form? That ultimately leads us to try to discover the basic building blocks for the Sun, the Earth, and us. It's like Legos—we want to know what pieces were in the Lego building set for our solar system."

EARLY LIFE AND EDUCATION

Ewine Fleur van Dishoeck was born on June 13, 1955, and raised in Leiden, the Netherlands. Her father was a doctor and eventually served as a professor at Leiden University; her mother was an elementary school teacher. She went to elementary school at a Montessori institution and played the violin, enjoying a happy child-hood. Yet from an early age she was also groomed for professional success. "My parents clearly had an academic career for me in mind," she wrote in her autobiography for the Kavli Prize (2018). "My birth announcement shows a baby wear-ing a stethoscope crawling toward the university with the motto 'vires acquirit eundo' ('she will gather strength along the way'; from Virgilius' *Ae-neid*). This turned out to be a very appropriate quote. My parents got only one aspect wrong: I never had any inclination to study medicine."

Van Dishoeck's first moment of apprecia-tion for science came in 1969, when her family was temporarily living in San Diego, California. There, as a teenager in the public junior high school, her love of science blossomed under the tutelage of a teacher she found inspiring. After returning to the Netherlands, she discovered a passion for chemistry, and especially molecular chemistry, while in high school. She decided to pursue a chemistry degree at Leiden University beginning in 1973 and became interested in chemical physics and quantum chemistry before graduating cum laude with a bachelor's degree in chemistry in 1976. She earned a second bach-elor's degree, in mathematics, in 1977.

GRADUATE STUDIES AND FELLOWSHIP

Van Dishoeck continued her graduate studies at Leiden, earning a master's degree (summa cum laude) in chemistry in 1980. While working on her master's research projects, she decided she wanted to pursue quantum chemistry for her PhD, but the Leiden professor who special-ized in that field had died. To stay at Leiden, she would need to change her field of study—something she was reluctant to do. However, she learned about new research on interstellar mol-ecules, and in 1979 was introduced to Harvard University professor Alexander Dalgarno, one of the world's leading experts in the emerging field of astrochemistry.

Dalgarno immediately invited her to come to Harvard to study for several months, and he

Photo by IAU/M. Zamani via Wikimedia Commons

eventually became her PhD advisor. In her Kavli Prize autobiography, van Dishoeck called Dalgarno her "lifelong mentor," noting that "he set the tone with his phenomenal knowledge, his clarity, his love of science and constant drive for excellence and integrity, and his agility in moving easily between molecular physics and astronomy." Thanks to a grant brokered by University of Leiden professor Harm Habing, her other PhD advisor, van Dishoeck officially remained at Leiden for her doctorate, but made frequent trips to Harvard. She subsequently earned her PhD (cum laude) in 1984. Her thesis was on photodissociation (the separation of a chemical compound by the action of light) and the excitation of interstellar molecules.

After completing her doctoral work, van Dishoeck became a junior fellow at the Harvard Society of Fellows, where she worked from 1984 to 1987. At Harvard, she studied "how rapidly a molecule falls apart under UV radiation and what are the basic molecular processes by which this occurs," as she told Nick Zagorski for *PNAS* (15 Aug. 2006). In addition, she studied how certain molecules could be used to better understand the processes occurring in nebulae and other interstellar clouds. During this period, she also served as a visiting member at the Institute for Advanced Study from 1984 to 1988, and as a visiting professor at Princeton University from 1987 to 1988.

RESEARCHING MOLECULES IN SPACE
Van Dishoeck moved to California in 1988 to take up a position as an assistant professor of cosmochemistry at the California Institute of

Technology (Caltech), where she served until 1990. Here she used her skills in molecular diagnostics to better understand how planets and stars are formed. Much of her work was made possible by the development of ground-based telescopes like the James Clerk Maxwell Telescope (JCMT) and the Caltech Submillimeter Observatory (CSO), which considerably improved detecting power. "These regions in which stars and planets are being formed are basically very dusty," she explained to Zagorski, "and that means they are completely black at the optical range. It's only when you go to longer wavelengths that you start to find something."

In 1990, van Dishoeck returned to Leiden University to teach as a senior lecturer. Returning to her home country and alma mater appealed to her for a variety of reasons, but two of the great ones were that she was given grant money to start a research group and was guaranteed time to do research on the short-wavelength spectrometer (SWS) on the European Space Agency's (ESA) upcoming Infrared Space Observatory (ISO) satellite. The ISO was finally launched in 1995—the same year van Dishoeck became a full professor of molecular astrophysics at Leiden—marking the first time that scientists could obtain infrared data on space bodies outside of Earth's atmosphere. "That was important because in infrared wavelengths, you can see not just gas-phase molecules but also solid-state species," van Dishoeck told Zagorski. "That gave me an infrared complement to what I was doing at the submillimeter telescopes, which was important . . . You need both wavelengths to put the story together."

The ISO mission was an enormous success. Van Dishoeck and her team were able to learn more about the chemical makeup of the regions in which new stars are formed, and they also identified new solid-state molecules. Along the way they solidified the importance of the young field of astrochemistry.

ASTROCHEMISTRY PIONEER
Improving technology allowed van Dishoeck to continually refine and expand her groundbreaking work. Notably, she conducted further research with the ISO's successor, the Spitzer Space Telescope, which the National Aeronautics and Space Administration (NASA) launched in 2003. She and her team studied icy and dusty protoplanetary disks and discovered not only water, ammonium, and methane, but also hydrogen cyanide and acetylene gases, which form the building blocks of amino acids and nucleic acids—both key components for the development of life. "I am fortunate to be part of one of these big legacy programs in which you give a group of people . . . a large amount of observation time with the caveat that your data become public

immediately," she remarked to Zagorski about the Spitzer mission. "So it's basically a program you're carrying out for the community."

Van Dishoeck was also centrally involved with the planning and development of several next-generation instruments. These included the Herschel Space Laboratory, which was launched by the ESA in 2009 and worked until 2013. The largest infrared telescope ever built, it was able to pierce the dustiest and coldest corners of our galaxy. Van Dishoeck was the leader of a Herschel program that detected the presence of water at remote distances, including in various types of protostars.

Additionally, van Dishoeck was deeply involved with the Atacama Large Millimeter/submillimeter Array (ALMA) in Chile. Composed of sixty-six radio telescopes in the Atacama Desert, ALMA began full operations in 2013, and was capable of observing electromagnetic radiation at millimeter and submillimeter wavelengths. It is the first truly international astronomical observatory. According to her colleagues, van Dishoeck's role in overseeing the development of ALMA was critical, as she persuaded scientists from around the world to collaborate on the project. "She has a way that is very persuasive and positive," astrophysicist Reinhard Genzel said, as quoted in 2018 on the *Kavli Prize* website. "And she has been able to communicate this positivity to young people and science organisations. It is a terrific gift."

WINNING THE KAVLI PRIZE

Throughout her distinguished career, van Dishoeck received numerous awards for her pioneering work. Some of the more notable ones include the 2000 Spinoza Prize from the Netherlands Organization for Scientific Research (NWO); the 2001 Bourke Award from the Royal Society of Chemistry (RSC); the 2014 Gothenburg Lise Meitner Award; the World Cultural Council's (WCC) 2015 Albert Einstein World Award of Science, and the 2018 James Craig Watson Medal from the National Academy of Sciences (NAS). Yet perhaps her highest-profile honor was the 2018 Kavli Prize, an award that recognizes leading scientists for their contributions to their respective fields.

The Kavli Prizes, first presented in 2008 as a partnership between the Norwegian Academy of Science and Letters, the Kavli Foundation in the United States, and the Norwegian Ministry of Education and Research, each carry a stipend of $1 million—about the equivalent monetary award of a Nobel Prize. In addition to the prize money, winners receive a scroll and a gold medal, which is presented by the Norwegian monarch. According to the *Kavli* website, van Dishoeck received the award in astrophysics "for

her seminal work on revealing the chemical and physical processes in interstellar clouds, where stars and planets form. Her work has contributed to a breakthrough of astrochemistry, demonstrating how molecules form and evolve during the transformation of a cloud into stellar systems like our own." She was just the second person to win the prize individually, rather than share it with others in their field.

In addition to her awards, van Dishoeck received recognition through numerous institutional positions and professional memberships. She was notably an external scientific member of the Max Planck Institute Extraterrestrial Physics, a member of the Royal Dutch Academy of Sciences, and a member of the US National Academy of Sciences. In 2007 she became the scientific director of the Netherlands Research School for Astronomy (NOVA), and from 2007 to 2017 she was the director general of the European Southern Observatory. In 2018 she became the president of the International Astronomical Union (IAU).

PERSONAL LIFE

Van Dishoeck married Tim de Zeeuw, an astronomer, on July 26, 1984. In her spare time, she enjoys camping and hiking, cooking, reading, music, and art. She has a love of art that connects with astronomy.

SUGGESTED READING

"Ewine van Dishoeck." *The Kavli Prize*, 2018, kavliprize.org/prizes-and-laureates/laureates/ewine-van-dishoeck. Accessed 3 Dec. 2018.

"Ewine van Dishoeck: Profile." *Leiden University*, www.universiteitleiden.nl/en/staffmembers/ewine-van-dishoeck/publications#tab-2. Accessed 5 Dec. 2018.

"Homepage of Ewine F. van Dishoeck." *Leiden University*, home.strw.leidenuniv.nl/~ewine/. Accessed 3 Dec. 2018.

Van Dishoeck, Ewine. "2018 Kavli Prize in Astrophysics: A Conversation with Ewine van Dishoeck." Interview by Adam Hadhazy. *The Kavli Foundation*, Summer 2018. kavlifoundation.org/science-spotlights/2018-kavli-prize-astrophysics-conversation-ewine-van-dishoeck#.XAfqJq3MwdU. Accessed 5 Dec. 2018.

Van Dishoeck, Ewine Fleur. "Autobiography." *The Kavli Prize*, 2018, kavliprize.org/sites/default/files/Ewine%20van%20Dishoeck%20-%20autobiography.pdf. Accessed 3 Dec. 2018.

Walchover, Natalie, and Olena Shmahalo. "Ewine van Dishoeck, the Netherlander Who Traced Water's Origin." *Quanta Magazine*, 1 Nov. 2018, www.quantamagazine.org/ewine-van-dishoeck-the-netherlander-who-traced-waters-origin-20181101/. Accessed 9 Jan. 2019.

Zagorski, Nick. "Profile of Ewine F. van Dishoeck." *PNAS*, vol. 103, no. 33, 2006, pp. 12229–31, doi:10.1073/pnas.0604740103. Accessed 3 Dec. 2018.

—*Christopher Mari*

Gary Vaynerchuk

Date of birth: November 14, 1975
Occupation: Entrepreneur

Gary Vaynerchuk, popularly known as Gary Vee, is a media entrepreneur, best-selling author, and wine guru. Vaynerchuk is the cofounder of the successful marketing firm VaynerMedia. He was an early adopter of social media who now advises companies that are eager to reach consumers in more specific and targeted ways. Vaynerchuk's initial popularity came in 2006, when he launched the successful video blog *Wine Library TV*. In simply produced tasting videos, Vaynerchuk cast himself as a populist wine critic, urging consumers to buck the snobbery of the wine world and follow their palate. His carnivalesque videos made him an early internet sensation. The world of wine offered a begrudging welcome, but Vaynerchuk had his sights set on other industries. VaynerMedia, founded in 2009, developed other companies including VaynerSmart, a tech marketing firm, and Vayner-Sports, a sports agency focused on personal branding. Vaynerchuk's business success is a testament to his charismatic personality and his own personal brand. He has authored a number of best-selling books, all part-business and part-self-help guides, including *Crush It!: Why Now Is the Time to Cash In on Your Passion* (2009), *The Thank You Economy* (2011), and *#AskGary-Vee: One Entrepreneur's Take on Leadership, Social Media and Social Awareness* (2016). He is also a popular speaker. Despite his ventures into other industries, Vaynerchuk did not leave behind wine entirely. In 2018, he launched Empathy Wines, a company that allows farmers to sell wine directly to consumers at, ideally, lower cost and higher profit.

EARLY LIFE AND EDUCATION

Gary Vaynerchuk was born in Babruysk, Belarus, on November 14, 1975. He has a younger brother, A. J., who cofounded VaynerMedia with him and works as his business partner, and a younger sister named Liz. His family immigrated to Queens, New York, in 1978, before settling in Edison, New Jersey. His father, Sasha, owned a wine store called Shopper's Discount Liquors;

Photo by Vaynermedia via Wikimedia Commons

his mother, Tamara, was a homemaker. As a child in the early 1980s, Vaynerchuk became an ardent New York Jets fan; football was his entry point into American culture. "It represented so much," he told Zach Schonbrun for the *New York Times* (28 Dec. 2018). "We were starting to make it in America. That was the way I broke through. It is the American thing for me." Vaynerchuk exhibited an entrepreneurial flair from a young age. He set up a string of lemonade stands, advertising them like a franchise, with makeshift signs posted around his suburban neighborhood. As a middle school student at John Adams Middle School, he joined a baseball card club and began selling baseball cards, toys, and action figures. His interest in business, he told Chuck O'Donnell for *My Central Jersey* (20 Feb. 2018), was inspired by his family's store. "Clark, New Jersey, was where my dad's first liquor store was and where I kind of went to the store on weekends and smelled the thoughts of a family business," he recalled. "Not only can it be traced to, but it has made such a greater impact on me than I even allude to." He began working at the store when he was fourteen.

Vaynerchuk's family—and the family business—moved to Springfield when Vaynerchuk was in high school. He graduated from North Hunterdon High School in Annandale in 1994. He then attended Mount Ida College (now a part of UMASS Amherst) in Newton, Massachusetts. After graduating in 1998, he returned to Springfield to work at his father's store.

WINE LIBRARY

In 1994 Vaynerchuk, then a freshman in college, started using the Internet. He saw the web's advantages over brick-and-mortar businesses. "I was like, 'Wait a minute. We don't need 8,000 liquor stores. I can just build this,'" he recalled to Daniel Roberts for *Fortune* (8 Dec. 2014). In 1997, while still a student, he launched a website called *WineLibrary.com*, which soon became one of the first e-commerce wine businesses. His father allotted Vaynerchuk an ad budget and freedom to run the site however he wanted. He took advantage of early marketing boons, making sure that *WineLibrary.com* would appear in Google searches for "wine." The Vaynerchuks later renamed Shoppers Discount Liquors the Wine Library to match the website, which had greatly increased sales. The store had once enjoyed annual revenues of about $3 million; by 2003, the Wine Library was making over $45 million each year. In 2006, Vaynerchuk launched a video blog called *Wine Library TV*. The videos were informal with a low-production value; their real draw was Vaynerchuk. Over time, Vaynerchuk, who began the practice of over-enunciating his own name with pauses as "Vay-Ner-Chuk," began to develop a fast-talking, free-wheeling persona. He presented himself as the antidote to the perceived snobby, stodgy exclusivity of other wine critics and the wine industry at large. His spit bucket bore the logo of the New York Jets. Using contemporary parlance, *Wine Library TV* quickly went viral—though Vaynerchuk faced plenty of criticism. "Many people who I respected were disappointed when I started *Wine Library TV*," Vaynerchuk told Eric Asimov, the wine critic for the *New York Times* (8 Sept. 2009). He added, "They thought I was dumbing down wine, but I always knew I was one of the biggest producers of new wine drinkers in the world, and people are realizing it now." In 2007, Vaynerchuk solidified his mainstream appeal as a wine critic when he appeared as a guest on *Late Night with Conan O'Brien*. He sought to build the comedian's palate, making him taste grass doused in grapefruit juice, wet rocks, cherries covered in dirt and tobacco, and a stalk of asparagus wrapped in a sweaty sock.

BOOK DEAL AND VAYNERMEDIA

In 2008, Vaynerchuk published the book *Gary Vaynerchuk's 101 Wines: Guaranteed to Inspire, Delight, and Bring Thunder to Your World*. The title makes reference to the colloquial title of *Wine Library TV*: "The Thunder Show, a.k.a. the Internet's Most Passionate Wine Program." In 2009, the British wine magazine *Decanter*—a publication that embodies the elitist wine world Vaynerchuk disagreed with—ranked him number forty on its list of the fifty most influential people in wine. By then, however, Vaynerchuk

sought to apply his marketing skills to other industries. "It's about stories," he told Asimov. "If I can tell the story to America, whether it's Riesling or a boxer from Harlem, it will sell." The same year, Vaynerchuk signed a seven-figure, ten-book deal with the publisher HarperStudio. The first book from that deal was an entrepreneur's self-help guide called *Crush It!: Why Now is the Time to Cash In on Your Passion* (2009). The best-selling book launched Vaynerchuk's lucrative career as a traveling speaker.

Also in 2009, Vaynerchuk and his brother, A. J., founded the marketing firm VaynerMedia. The company focuses on social media marketing. Vaynerchuk saw himself as an underdog in the world of wine; he held a similar outlook when he entered the world of marketing. "When I first started it, everyone was like, 'Oh, Mr. A-lot-of-Twitter-followers thinks he can compete in this world,'" he told Roberts. "And we've not only competed, we will be considered a new standard." They soon began working with Fortune 500 companies like General Electric, Unilever, PepsiCo, and Hulu.

He published his second book, *The Thank You Economy*, in 2011. In it, Vaynerchuk writes about how businesses can harness social media to win customers. "It is self-evident that the world of communication has fundamentally changed and Vaynerchuk again seems to be out in front of it," Robert Rosenthal wrote in his review of the book for *HuffPost* (25 Mar. 2011). In Vaynerchuk's next book, *Jab, Jab, Jab, Right Hook: How to Tell Your Story in a Noisy Social World* (2013), Vaynerchuk expanded on this theme. He defines individual brands as a story that businesses tell consumers. "There is no sale without a story," he writes in the book. "No knockout without the setup."

VIDEO BLOGS AND VAYNER EXPANSIONS

After several years of success, Vaynerchuk officially ended *Wine Library TV* after its thousandth episode in 2011; he launched a new video blog called *#AskGaryVee* in 2014. He later collected hundreds of his answers from that show—which explores a range of topics related to branding and entrepreneurship—in his book *#AskGaryVee: One Entrepreneur's Take on Leadership, Social Media and Social Awareness* (2016). Ken Yeung wrote in a review of the book for *Venture Beat* (28 Feb. 2016), stating, "For anyone looking for a 'Getting Started' book, this publication is going to be your go-to guide." In 2015, Vaynerchuk launched *DailyVee*, an intimate video blog offering entrepreneurial wisdom and a glimpse into his everyday life.

In 2016, Vaynerchuk launched an offshoot company of VaynerMedia called VaynerSmart, focusing on tech and the Internet of Things. For instance, the company has built skills for

Amazon Alexa in relation to various brands. In 2017, under the Vayner umbrella, Vaynerchuk absorbed and rebranded a sports agency called VaynerSports. VaynerSports hopes to help athletes develop their personal brands through social media, with an eye toward post-sports life. The same year, Vaynerchuk and his brother created VaynerX, which serves as the parent company of VaynerMedia and its other associated companies. VaynerX is also the parent company of Vaynerchuk's other projects, including the Gallery Media Group, which controls his 2017 acquisition of the women's lifestyle company PureWow; Tracer, a data platform for marketing efficiency; and the Sasha Group, a consulting service for start-up business which was launched in 2018.

In 2018, Vaynerchuk published the self-help business guide *Crushing It! How Great Entrepreneurs Build Their Business and Influence—And How You Can Too*. The same year, he cofounded Empathy Wines, a winery that focuses on promoting the farmers and sells wine directly to the consumer.

PERSONAL LIFE

Vaynerchuk and his wife, Lizzie, were married in 2004. They have two children: Misha and Xander. Vaynerchuk has professed a passionate desire to own the professional football team the New York Jets, telling Schonbrun, "I'd like to buy the Jets at 68 years old and win six Super Bowls before I die."

SUGGESTED READING

Asimov, Eric. "Pop Goes the Critic." *The New York Times*, 8 Sept. 2009, www.nytimes.com/2009/09/09/dining/09pour.html. Accessed 9 Aug. 2019.

O'Donnell, Chuck. "How Gary Vaynerchuk's Childhood in Edison Helps Him Crush It in Business." *My Central Jersey*, USA Today, 20 Feb. 2018, www.mycentraljersey.com/story/news/local/people/2018/02/20/how-gary-vaynerchuks-childhood-edison-helps-him-crush-business/345216002/. Accessed 9 Aug. 2019.

Roberts, Daniel. "Is Gary Vaynerchuk for Real?" *Fortune*, 8 Dec. 2014, fortune.com/2014/12/08/is-gary-vaynerchuk-vaynermedia-for-real/. Accessed 9 Aug. 2019.

Rosenthal, Robert. "Who Is Gary Vaynerchuk and What Is the Thank You Economy?" Review of *The Thank You Economy*, by Gary Vaynerchuk. *HuffPost*, 25 Mar. 2011, www.huffpost.com/entry/who-is-gary-vaynerchuk-an_b_840179. Accessed 9 Aug. 2019.

Schonbrun, Zach. "The Self-Described Jets Owner-in-Waiting Will Tailgate for Now." *The New York Times*, 28 Dec. 2018, www.nytimes.com/2018/12/28/sports/gary-vaynerchuk-jets-owner.html. Accessed 9 Aug. 2019.

Vaynerchuk, Gary. *Jab, Jab, Jab, Right Hook: How to Tell Your Story in a Noisy Social World*. HarperCollins, 2013. *Google Books*, books.google.com/books/about/Jab_Jab_Jab_Right_Hook.html?id=JQYwAAAAQBAJ. Accessed 9 Aug. 2019.

Yeung, Ken. "Review: Gary Vaynerchuk's New Book Taught Me 369 Lessons about Business." Review of *#AskGaryVee: One Entrepreneur's Take on Leadership, Social Media and Self-Awareness*, by Gary Vaynerchuk. *Venture Beat*, 28 Feb. 2016, venturebeat.com/2016/02/28/review-gary-vaynerchuks-new-book-taught-me-369-lessons-about-business/. Accessed 9 Aug. 2019.

SELECTED WORKS

Crush It!: Why Now Is the Time to Cash In on Your Passion, 2009; *The Thank You Economy*, 2011; *#AskGaryVee: One Entrepreneur's Take on Leadership, Social Media and Social Awareness*, 2016; *Crushing It! How Great Entrepreneurs Build Their Business and Influence—And How You Can Too*, 2018

—Molly Hagan

Seema Verma

Occupation: Policy consultant and government official

On March 14, 2017, Seema Verma was sworn in as the head of the Centers for Medicare and Medicaid Services (CMS), a post in which she works under the US Secretary of Health and Human Services Alex M. Azar II, and oversees an annual budget in the vicinity of $1 trillion. CMS has charge of much more than Medicare and Medicaid, however, as Verma explained to Janelle Morrison for *Carmel Monthly* (Sept. 2017). "We also run Obamacare and implement large pieces of the Obamacare program. We are also responsible for the safety and quality of nursing health facilities and for hospitals and laboratories. We have so many different pieces that we are looking at, and so when I look back at this, I want to make sure that we have continued to ensure that Americans have access to the best healthcare system in the world."

Despite such assertions, Verma's appointment, like that of most appointees in the administration of US President Donald Trump, has been the subject of a great deal of partisan sentiment. That extends even to her time in the private sector, when she was founder and chief executive officer of SVC, a national health policy consultancy, and it is difficult to find coverage of her that does not either unquestioningly tout her actions or vilify them.

Verma is best known for her role as the architect of the Healthy Indiana Plan (HIP), a 2007 health insurance pilot program, under Indiana governors Mitch Daniels and Mike Pence. Pence went on to serve as Trump's vice president and was responsible for pushing Verma's appointment to the CMS. HIP 2.0, as the plan became known, was celebrated by conservatives for its emphasis on personal responsibility and accountability. Critics of the plan, on the other hand, pointed out that it called for even the most destitute residents of the state to pay premiums—a seemingly draconian requirement for poor families that might mean the difference between putting food on the table or obtaining health coverage. The most centrist view is that at least the plan allowed right-leaning Indiana politicians like Pence to support expanding Medicaid at a time when many other states were refusing, on principle, to accept Obamacare funds to do so.

EARLY YEARS AND EDUCATION

Verma's parents immigrated from India to the United States. She was born in Virginia, but her date of birth is not readily available. It is known that she has at least one sister, because a woman identified as such attended her CMS swearing-in ceremony.

Verma's father, Jugal Verma, has told journalists that he is a "staunch Democrat," and that Verma was raised in a Democratic family. He told Jessica Glenza, writing for the *Guardian* (4 Dec. 2016), of being amazed by his daughter's habit of giving money to a homeless man on her way to work each day. By her own account, Verma had a peripatetic upbringing. "Growing up, we lived in a lot of different places," she recalled to Morrison, including Joplin, Missouri, the outskirts of Washington, DC, and Taiwan. "Living in the greater Indianapolis area is the longest that I've lived in any one place."

In 1993 Verma earned her bachelor's degree in life sciences from the University of Maryland, College Park. She then received a master's degree in public health from Johns Hopkins University in Baltimore, Maryland, in 1996.

HEALTH CARE ADMINISTRATOR AND CONSULTANT

Verma served as the vice president of planning for the Health and Hospital Corporation of Marion County, Indiana, and as a director with the Association of State and Territorial Health Officials (ASTHO) in Washington, DC, before launching SVC in 2001. The Indianapolis-based consulting company soon counted several state governments—including Indiana, Iowa,

Kentucky, Maine, Michigan, Ohio, and Tennessee—as clients. She made it something of a specialty to help states set up and administer their Medicaid expansion programs under the Affordable Care Act, more commonly known as Obamacare since it was one of President Barack Obama's signature pieces of legislation. "It gave me the opportunity to gain a national perspective on healthcare issues that went beyond Indiana," Verma recalled to Morrison. "I think that our company did a lot of cutting-edge work, and we became the company that folks would look to when they were thinking about doing something innovative in their healthcare programs."

In Kentucky, SVC's innovations included requiring Medicaid recipients to fulfill a so-called work activity requirement, which could include unpaid community service, to be eligible to receive health insurance coverage. In Ohio, a plan designed by SVC required Medicaid recipients to be barred from public health insurance until they had paid off their premium arrears. Representative Charlie Brown, Indiana's ranking Democrat on the House's public health committee, told Glenza that SVC's recommendations were "about saving the dollars by any means possible." SVC's Medicaid expansion plan for Indiana has gotten the most attention in the press, however. As Jake Harper wrote for NPR's *Shots* (29 Nov. 2016), "Indiana's unique Medicaid expansion was designed to appeal to conservatives. HIP 2.0 asks covered people to make a small monthly payment to access health insurance. A missed payment can result in six-month lockout from insurance coverage. Those provisions aren't allowed under traditional Medicaid, but Indiana got a federal waiver to implement them."

Glenza, while admitting that HIP 2.0 expanded Medicaid to some 400,000 Indiana residents, described it as "a plan meant to mimic the commercial market, as a financial lesson for its recipients. It remains one of the most complex and punitive Medicaid expansions in the country, an outlier in a system of state-run safety nets largely free for the poor."

Although Pence awarded Verma the Sagamore of the Wabash for distinguished service to the state and/or governor, her tenure at the helm of SVC was not without political controversy. In 2014 journalists at the *Indianapolis Star* uncovered what seemed to be a clear conflict of interest: by then, SVC had been awarded more than $3.5 million in state contracts during a period when Verma was concurrently employed in a division of Hewlett-Packard (HP), one of Indiana's Medicaid vendors that had won $500 million in state contracts.

FEDERAL APPOINTMENT

Despite these issues, on November 29, 2016, acting upon Pence's recommendation,

President-elect Donald Trump nominated Verma for the position of CMS administrator. Policy analyst Joan Alker echoed the sentiments of many upon hearing the news, telling Harper, "It is a good thing that she has experience with Medicaid . . . But I think if you look at the totality of the Trump administration's picks today—Congressman [Dr. Thomas E.] Price as well as Ms. Verma—this represents potentially a very damaging and chaotic restructuring of the Medicaid program." Price, who was at that time Trump's nominee for secretary of the US Department of Health and Human Services, had already come out in favor of severely cutting Medicaid funding. (Price resigned from the cabinet position in September 2017.) Alker was also troubled that Verma, who, as director of CMS, would report to Price, would institute "cuts and more stringent requirements" that would effectively take health insurance away from current and potential Medicaid recipients.

For her part, Verma saw the new role as a natural one for her. "The president was very clear that he didn't want to just rely on the traditional D.C. folks and wanted to bring people from outside of the beltway that have more practical experience, more private-sector experience," she told Morrison. "My work in Indiana has given me a better sense of how policy is actually implemented on a day-to-day basis and how it's going to impact someone's life or how it's going to impact a medical practice or hospital. I think that experience is unique."

During Verma's hearing before the Senate Finance Committee, she made plain her belief in the adage that people should lift themselves up by their own bootstraps, saying that her presence before the committee was "a testament to the fact that the American dream is very much alive for those willing to work for it." The hearing went smoothly, and on March 14, 2017, she was sworn in, taking her oath of office on a copy of the Hindu Bhagavad Gita and becoming the second Indian American woman in the Trump administration, after Nikki Haley, Trump's first ambassador to the United Nations.

THE TRUMP ADMINISTRATION

In an interview for *Forbes* (5 Dec. 2017), Avik Roy asked Verma about her ongoing priorities. "I think decisions about healthcare should really be at the patient and doctor level," she replied. "We need to empower our patients with information. . . . We want to move across all of our programs, Medicaid, Medicare, and our exchange programs, that concept of patient empowerment. It's putting out more information for individuals and structuring the programs in a way that incentivize our beneficiaries to be active consumers of their healthcare."

Although such stated priorities strike many as relatively benign, some consequences of Verma's tenure could have severe repercussions for certain patients. In January 2018, for example, the Trump administration reversed Obama-era guidance regarding Medicaid funds, making it harder for low-income patients in certain states to get health care, including such needed basic procedures as cancer screenings and well-woman exams, at Planned Parenthood clinics—a development that negatively affects approximately 60 percent of Planned Parenthood patients who rely on Medicaid or other public programs to pay for care.

With issues of such importance on the table, a loud outcry greeted Verma's tweet of October 31, 2018, which some users of social media saw as frivolous. The tweet in question pictured a man in a T-shirt with the words "Medicare for All" printed on it. Verma had captioned the photo, "This year's scariest Halloween costume goes to . . ." and later tweeted: "Did I get your attention? Good. People are right. Medicare for All isn't a joke. It's a multi-trillion drain on the American economy that will bankrupt future generations."

Watchdog organization Citizens for Responsibility and Ethics in Washington (CREW) did not consider the matter frivolous and filed a formal complaint against Verma, alleging that she was using her official government Twitter account just days before the contentious midterm elections to suggest that the government disapproves of Medicare for all, which was included in the platform of former Democratic presidential candidate Senator Bernie Sanders. The organization contended that Verma had been in violation of the Hatch Act, which bars federal employees from using their offices, work resources, and social media accounts for political purposes.

PERSONAL LIFE

Verma is married to Sanjay Mishra, a child psychiatrist. They have a daughter, Maya, and a son, Shaan.

SUGGESTED READING

Glenza, Jessica. "Trump's Pick for Key Health Post Known for Punitive Medicaid Plan." *The Guardian*, 4 Dec. 2016, www.theguardian.com/us-news/2016/dec/04/seema-verma-trump-centers-medicare-medicaid-cms. Accessed 7 Dec. 2018.

Harper, Jake. "Trump Picks Seema Verma to Run Medicare and Medicaid." *Shots: Health News from NPR*, 29 Nov. 2016, www.npr.org/sections/health-shots/2016/11/29/503762324/trump-picks-seema-verma-to-run-medicare-and-medicaid. Accessed 7 Dec. 2018.

Morrison, Janelle. "Seema Verma: A Carmel Resident in Charge of American Healthcare." *Carmel Monthly*, Sept. 2017, carmelmonthly-magazine.com/seema-verma-carmel-resident-charge-american-healthcare. Accessed 7 Dec. 2018.

Newkirk, Vann R. "Seema Verma's Austere Vision for Medicaid." *The Atlantic*, 17 Feb. 2017, www.theatlantic.com/politics/archive/2017/02/seema-vermas-vision-for-medicaid/517077/. Accessed 7 Dec. 2018.

Ravindranath, Mohana. "Lawmakers Tee Up Telemedicine Priorities." *Politico Morning eHealth*, 16 Nov. 2018, www.politico.com/newsletters/morning-ehealth/2018/11/16/lawmakers-tee-up-telemedicine-priorities-416833. Accessed 7 Dec. 2018.

Roy, Avik. "CMS Chief Seema Verma Speaks about Her Top Health Care Policy Priorities." *Forbes*, 5 Dec. 2017, www.forbes.com/sites/theapothecary/2017/12/05/cms-chief-seema-verma-speaks-about-her-top-health-care-policy-priorities/#35d9dd8d2f4d. Accessed 7 Dec. 2018.

—*Mari Rich*

Hans Vestberg

Date of birth: 1965
Occupation: Business executive

In August 2018 Hans Vestberg became the CEO of telecom giant Verizon, and as Prashant S. Rao and Michael J. de la Merced wrote for the *New York Times* (8 June 2018), "the changing of the guard comes at a time when the wireless industry as a whole is grappling with new technologies and a wave of consolidation."

Vestberg, who added the role of chairman in March 2019, has made fifth-generation (5G) mobile communication a focus at Verizon. His appointment, Rao and de la Merced wrote, "underscores the importance Verizon places on that technology, which will greatly increase download speeds and lay the wireless foundation for self-driving cars and smart appliances." Some of the promises made about 5G may seem the stuff of science fiction—many industry insiders assert that 5G will usher in an era in which physicians use sophisticated virtual-reality gear to operate on patients from remote locations and smart cars communicate with one another to avoid accidents—but Vestberg is a true believer. "5G is way more than just a step up from current wireless technology," he told Katie Kuehner-Hebert for *Chief Executive Magazine* (15 Apr. 2019). "It's a quantum leap that will bring an era of radically new possibilities across all areas of technology."

Whatever the future holds for 5G, there is no question that Vestberg is at the vanguard of the telecommunications industry. Verizon's network assets, according to the company's website, encompass "the country's leading 4G LTE network, the largest 5G test-bed in the U.S., the nation's biggest residential fiber network, a global internet backbone and undersea cable network carrying much of the world's internet traffic, and fiber assets in 45 of the top 50 markets in the U.S."

EARLY YEARS AND EDUCATION

Hans Vestberg was born in 1965 in Hudiksvall, a small city located alongside a picturesque bay in the Swedish province of Hälsingland. Although the English-language media has not covered the details of his childhood extensively, he often speaks to reporters about his early love of sports. In an essay posted on the professional networking site LinkedIn (8 Feb. 2016), he wrote, "Since I was very young, sport has been one of my greatest passions. In my youth I played all kinds of sports, but as I grew older my favorite sport became team handball." Explaining that handball is played in more than 160 countries and that in Sweden it is one of the most popular sports after soccer, he asserted, "My formation as a leader comes very much from the roots of being part of a team."

Vestberg was not only passionate about the sport—which requires players to throw a ball into the opposing team's goal, using their hands to pass it—he was good enough to play

Photo by Pombo Photography via Wikimedia Commons

in Sweden's national league as a youth and had even hoped to turn professional.

Instead of pursuing that goal, however, he opted to attend Sweden's University of Uppsala. There, in 1991, he earned a bachelor's degree in business administration and economics.

ERICSSON

After graduating from Uppsala with high honors, Vestberg began working for Ericsson, a Swedish telecommunications company founded in the 1870s. He was assigned to work in the travel expenses department, located in his hometown of Hudiksvall, and over the next several years he steadily climbed the corporate ladder, taking on various roles in China, Brazil, Chile, and Mexico at various times. In 2007 he became Ericsson's chief financial officer (CFO), and in 2009 he was named CEO.

"What Mr. Vestberg lacks in technical skills—he's the first non-engineer to run Ericsson since it was founded 137 years ago—he makes up for in chutzpah and the belief that better communications can improve society; very Ericsson and very Swedish," Margareta Pagano wrote for the *Independent* (11 Jan. 2014). "One of his first moves on taking over was to come up with the expression the Networked Society, describing the latest technological revolution that will see us all connected to everything and everyone over the next few decades—the Internet of Things."

OPPORTUNITIES AND CHALLENGES

Under Vestberg's leadership, Ericsson, whose researchers held some 27,000 patents, began to focus less on hardware and more on software and services. "The infrastructure we provide is the same in a remote town in Africa or New York or an archipelago in Sweden: we use the same system and the chips inside the phone are the same. Even if you buy a Finnish, Korean or American phone—it will be Ericsson on the inside," he explained to Pagano. "So it's about the cost of the handset. . . . For every $10 drop in the price of a handset, there will be another 100 million or so new subscribers."

Vestberg was particularly excited about the possibilities posed by the big data generated by all those users. "Around 30 per cent of carbon emissions could be reduced by using information from mobile data more efficiently for managing traffic, water control and in many other ways," he told Pagano. "The Estonians are already reading data from mobiles to reduce car congestion, while the use of mobiles in emerging countries like Africa and India for healthcare is just at the beginning. The possibilities are endless as live surveillance connectivity sends information to companies to improve dramatically their way of working, but also for society."

Despite his enthusiasm, Vestberg found that being at the helm of a company that provided 40 percent of the world's mobile traffic, with well over 100,000 employees, meant steep challenges. Ericsson embarked on a cost-cutting program in 2014; however, that effort proved insufficient. In mid-July 2016 Ericsson, amid growing competition from companies like Huawei, announced that it would eliminate thousands of jobs and severely reduce its research and development budget to compensate for a steep drop in net profits. Industry publications pointed out that since Vestberg had been appointed CEO in 2010, the company's stock had lost almost a third of its market value. By contrast, during that same period the Stockholm Stock Exchange index had risen sharply. It did not help matters that Ericsson had been embroiled in investigations by the US Department of Justice and the US Securities and Exchange Commission (SEC) over possible violations of the Foreign Corrupt Practices Act—violations for which Vestberg, as CFO and CEO, would have had responsibility. On July 25 board members unanimously voted to oust him and installed then CFO Jan Frykhammar as interim CEO in his stead. Upon news of his departure, Ericsson stock rose 5 percent.

VERIZON

It thus came as something of a surprise to those in the telecommunications industry when Verizon announced in early 2017 that it was reorganizing into three main divisions and that Vestberg would be heading a newly formed Network and Technology team. The company released a statement, quoted by Todd Spangler in *Variety* (31 Mar. 2017) that the restructuring would provide "greater organizational agility to continue to lead the market with our wireless and fiber services, scale and expand our media and telematics businesses, and maintain the leadership in network reliability and new technology that is a Verizon trademark."

Vestberg's initial title was chief technology officer and president of Global Networks, but in August 2018 he was elevated to CEO. Then in March 2019, he was also named chairman of the company, which employs 150,000 people. When Verizon filed its 2019 Notice of Annual Meeting of Shareholders and Proxy Statement with the SEC, it was revealed that in 2018 Vestberg had been compensated some $22 million, including a base salary of $1.23 million, a bonus of $1 million, and stock awards of more than $16 million, along with generous nonequity incentives.

He has announced that moving forward, Verizon will be strongly focused on 5G mobile: the month after he assumed the chairmanship, 5G service launched in Chicago and Minneapolis, and Denver and Providence followed soon after. By the end of 2019, Verizon expects to offer its

5G Ultra Wideband network in up to thirty cities across the country.

PERSONAL LIFE

Vestberg, his spouse, and two children live in New Jersey. He has told interviewers that he attempts to turn off his mobile devices on the weekend to focus on his family. He is fluent in Swedish, English, Spanish, and Portuguese.

Vestberg was a founding member of the International Telecommunications Union (ITU) Broadband Commission for Sustainable Development, which seeks to encourage better broadband infrastructure in developing nations and underserved communities. He appears frequently at such high-profile industry events as the Mobile World Congress and the Consumer Electronics Show.

Additionally, he serves on the Leadership Council of the United Nations' Sustainable Development Solutions Network, where he helped conceive of the UN Sustainable Development Goals. He is also a board member of the World Childhood Foundation, which was launched by Queen Silvia of Sweden to fight child abuse and exploitation.

Vestberg maintains his lifelong love of sports, especially handball. He has served as head of both the Swedish Handball Federation (2007–16) and the Swedish Olympic Committee (2016–18). He has also coached a youth handball team, and in his LinkedIn essay he wrote, "I still hold out hope for handball's world domination."

SUGGESTED READING

Charlton, Alistair. "Microsoft CEO Race—Profile of Hans Vestberg." *International Business Times*, 17 Jan. 2014, www.ibtimes.co.uk/microsoft-ceo-race-profile-hans-vestberg-1432569. Accessed 9 July 2019.

Kuehner-Hebert, Katie. "For Verizon's CEO Hans Vestberg, the 5G Future Is Now." *Chief Executive Magazine*, 15 Apr. 2019, chiefexecutive.net/for-verizons-ceo-hans-vestberg-the-5g-future-is-now. Accessed 9 July 2019.

Moritz, Scott. "Verizon's New CEO Is Said to Weigh Top-Level Shakeup in 5G Push." *Bloomberg*, 9 Oct. 2018, www.bloomberg.com/news/articles/2018-10-09/verizon-s-new-ceo-is-said-to-weigh-top-level-shake-up-in-5g-push. Accessed 9 July 2019.

Pagano, Margareta. "Is Ericsson Chief Hans Vestberg the Most Connected Man in the World?" *The Independent*, 11 Jan. 2014, www.independent.co.uk/news/business/analysis-and-features/is-ericsson-chief-hans-vestberg-the-most-connected-man-in-the-world-9052875.html. Accessed 9 July 2019.

Rao, Prashant S., and Michael J. de la Merced. "At Verizon, a Changing of the Guard as It Pursues 5G." *The New York Times*, 8 June 2018, www.nytimes.com/2018/06/08/business/verizon-lowell-mcadam-hans-vestberg.html. Accessed 9 July 2019.

Spangler, Todd. "Verizon Hires Ex-Ericsson CEO Hans Vestberg, Eyes U.S. Internet Pay-TV Launch." *Variety*, 31 Mar. 2017, variety.com/2017/digital/news/verizon-ericsson-hans-vestberg-internet-pay-tv-launch-1202020130. Accessed 9 July 2019.

Vestberg, Hans. "How Coaching Teen Sports Made Me a Better Leader." *LinkedIn*, 8 Feb. 2016, www.linkedin.com/pulse/how-coaching-teen-sports-made-me-better-leader-hans-vestberg. Accessed 9 July 2019.

—*Mari Rich*

Hezekiah Walker

Date of birth: December 25, 1962
Occupation: Singer and pastor

Bishop Hezekiah Walker is a Grammy Award–winning gospel singer and senior pastor at the Love Fellowship Tabernacle in Brooklyn, New York. Nicknamed the Hip Hop Pastor, Walker has recorded with rapper P. Diddy and has boasted rappers such as Lil' Kim and Foxy Brown as his congregants. Since Walker founded the Love Fellowship Crusade Choir in 1985, the choir has recorded more than a dozen records and won two Grammy Awards.

Still, most of Walker's work is local. "I come out of the neighborhood, I come out of the culture," Walker told Dan Deluca for the Youngstown, Ohio, *Vindicator* (27 Oct. 2003). "I know what it's like when, because of your surroundings, you feel you're never going to go nowhere. You're never going to get out, because you have no positive influences. All you have is your style, your music." Walker was raised in the Fort Greene housing projects in Brooklyn but founded his ministry in nearby East New York. In 1993, the year Walker opened his Pentecostal church in a former factory on Pacific Street, East New York reached a two-decade high for the number of homicides in a single precinct; as New York newspapers ran lurid articles about the neighborhood, Walker opened his doors, offering spiritual counsel to residents struggling with extreme poverty and drug addiction. The role of the church is "not just to preach and sing," Walker told Joyce Shelby for the *New York Daily News* (28 July 2008), "but to care for the people."

Articles about Walker have pointedly noted the bishop's extraordinary wealth, though Walker

Photo by Jemal Countess/Getty Images for Family Federation for a Heavenly USA

shuns the idea that his lavish lifestyle has any bearing on his work. "The kids today watch the hip-hop culture on videos, and they see the money, the jewelry, the diamonds and the easy sex," he told Chris Hedges for the *New York Times* (21 Apr. 2001). "They want to experience that. I am here to say that there is a penalty paid when you do not obtain these things the right way."

EARLY LIFE AND EDUCATION

Hezekiah "Hez" Walker was born in Brooklyn on December 25, 1962, and grew up in the Fort Greene public housing projects. His was a deeply religious home, Hedges reported, "where dancing, drinking and watching movies were not allowed." Walker, his brothers Melvin and Richard, and sisters Viola and Velina were raised by their mother, Gladys Lee Walker, a social worker. His father died when Walker was fourteen years old.

Walker was inspired to join a choir when he was eight, after hearing the gospel song "One More Day." He teared up, he recalled to Hedges, and was overcome by "a strange feeling." Walker continued to sing in a choir and began writing gospel songs as a teenager and student at Park West High School. With a small ensemble, he traveled to sing in Japan. He went on to study sociology at Long Island University. After graduation, he worked for Xerox in Stamford, Connecticut.

When Walker was twenty-one years old, his mother collapsed en route to church and died. He was devastated. He quit his job and, for months, could barely be roused to bathe himself. Facing eviction, he prayed, he told Hedges, and

wrote a gospel song called "I'll Make It." The song would provide the fruitful seed of Walker's entire career.

LOVE FELLOWSHIP CRUSADE CHOIR

Walker founded the Love Fellowship Crusade Choir in 1985. They sang the classic hymn "Jesus Is the Light of the World," at their first rehearsal. The twelve-person choir has grown to more than one hundred members. In 1987, they released their debut LP, *I'll Make It*, featuring Walker's song, through the small, now defunct Pennsylvania label Sweet Rain. It was a surprise success, reaching the number-twelve slot on the Billboard Top Gospel Albums chart in 1988. The choir also released their second album, *Oh Lord We Praise You* (1990), through Sweet Rain, but in 1992, they signed with Benson Records. They released their third album, *Focus on Glory* (1992), the same year. That album reached number five on the Top Gospel Albums chart, and Walker and the choir began to tour.

Performing nationally and internationally, Walker told Tony Cummings for the British Christian media website *Cross Rhythms* (31 Jan. 2007), he was surprised by the hypocrisy of other gospel acts. "Gospel music was just a job for them," Walker said. "They didn't have the ministry at heart. That bothered me a lot. When I got around them, we all were anointed on stage, but after the concert was over, behind stage, it was a different thing." This disillusionment with the music industry may have pushed Walker further toward his ministry, which was, in 1993, just getting off the ground.

GRAMMY AWARDS AND CHART TOPPERS

The choir's next album, *Live in Toronto* (1993), broke the top ten, peaking at number three on the Top Gospel Albums chart. Their next two live albums, *Live in Atlanta at Morehouse College* (1994) and *Live in New York . . . By Any Means* (1995), fared equally well. *Live in Atlanta* earned the group their first Grammy Award for Best Gospel Album by a Choir or Chorus in 1994.

In 1996, Walker and his choir appeared on the soundtrack for the popular movie *The Preacher's Wife*, starring Whitney Houston. They can be heard backing Cissy Houston, a Grammy Award–winning gospel singer and Whitney's mother, on the song "The Lord Is My Shepherd."

Two albums, *Live in London at Wembley* (1997) and *Live at Love Fellowship Tabernacle* (1998), followed. Of the latter, David Faulkner praised solo performances by Walker and singer Stayze Burnett in his review for *Cross Rhythms* (1 Dec. 1998). "Lyrics largely reflect evangelical individualism and the music is mostly conservative," he wrote. "Nevertheless this [album] exudes class."

In 1999, Walker and the choir released the Grammy-nominated *Family Affair*, followed by the Grammy Award–winning *Love Is Live!* (2001), and *Family Affair II: Live at Radio City Music Hall* (2002). The choir was also nominated for the NAACP Image Award for Gospel Artist–Traditional in 2002. It appeared on R & B singer R. Kelly's two-disc album *Happy People/U Saved Me* in 2004, which stirred controversy because of its dual themes of spiritual and carnal love. The choir went on to produce the anniversary album *20/85 The Experience* (2005), and the 2008 album *Souled Out* yielded the choir's first number-one hit single, "Souled Out," in 2009.

Azusa: The Next Generation (2013) spent three weeks at number one on the Billboard Top Gospel Album chart. That album's hit single, "Every Praise," spent six nonconsecutive months at number one on the Billboard Gospel Airplay chart, a rare feat in any genre. It remains one of Walker's most enduring songs. The follow-up, *Azusa—The Next Generation 2: Better* (2016), spent three weeks at number one on the Top Gospel Album chart and yielded the number-one hit single "Better." The music video for the song features Walker singing with choirs in South Africa, Italy, France, and the United States.

LOVE FELLOWSHIP TABERNACLE

Walker recalled a harrowing but serendipitous incident to Clem Richardson for the *New York Daily News* (5 Feb. 2001). Performing with the choir at the McDonald's Gospelfest, an annual gospel festival in Newark, New Jersey, a woman slipped Walker a note. After his performance, he read it in his seat. It was a suicide note to her mother that she wanted Walker to deliver. Walker searched desperately for the woman, but when he found her, she told him that hearing the music had made her reconsider. "I realized I had something about me that could change people," he told Richardson. "I was praying for and with people. People were asking me for counseling. I woke up one day and realized I was doing the work of a minister. While I was struggling over the decision, God spoke to me and told me I could make a difference in people's lives. So I accepted the call."

Walker studied at the Hugee Theological Seminary and New York School of the Bible and was ordained as a minister in 1993. The same year, in November, Walker and his choir opened Love Fellowship Tabernacle in a former factory on Pacific Street in Brooklyn's East New York neighborhood. Walker's first parishioners were young people, many of them sex workers or struggling with addiction. Services became so popular that Walker decided to move the thousand-member church to a larger location a couple of streets away on Liberty Avenue on Easter Sunday in 1996.

Rapper Sean "P. Diddy" Combs sought Walker's counsel after the death of a close friend, rapper Biggie Smalls, who was murdered in 1997. The connection has served as a conduit between other hip-hop artists and Walker, earning him his enduring nickname. Walker sang on Diddy's unreleased gospel album, *Thank You*, and in 2000, Walker, along with Mario Winans, appeared on the Diddy song "Best Friend."

As Walker's ministry grew in popularity, he opened a new branch of Love Fellowship Tabernacle in Willingboro, New Jersey, in 1998, which moved across the river to Bensalem, Pennsylvania, in 2000. He also created the Covenant Keepers International Fellowship, which includes member churches in the Carolinas, Pennsylvania, California, Minnesota, and abroad. Walker was named a bishop of the Pentecostal church in 2008.

Walker's ministry extends beyond the walls of the church, though. He also became the co-host of a daily radio program, *Afternoon Praise* on 1190 WLIB, New York City's twenty-four-hour gospel station. In February 2017, Walker signed an $80 million deal with the city to build a new church and low-income housing on property he owns in Brooklyn.

PERSONAL LIFE

Walker and Monique Williams met as teenagers at a city pool. She joined his choir, and he later proposed in song in front of four thousand people at a gospel concert in May 1992. The couple were married on Christmas Day that same year and had a daughter named Kyasia Monet Walker in 1993. They later separated.

SUGGESTED READING

Cummings, Tony. "Hezekiah Walker: Gospel Star, Choir Leader Extraordinary and Hip Hop Pastor." *Cross Rhythms*, 31 Jan. 2007, www.crossrhythms.co.uk/articles/music/Hezekiah_Walker_Gospel_star_choir_leader_extraordinary__hiphop_Pastor/25823/p1. Accessed 12 Nov. 2018.

Deluca, Dan. "The Hip Hop Pastor." *The Vindicator*, 27 Oct. 2003, www.vindy.com/news/2003/oct/27/the-hip-hop-pastor/?print. Accessed 11 Nov. 2018.

Faulkner, David. "Pastor Hezekiah Walker Presents the LFT Church Choir." Review of *Live at Love Fellowship Tabernacle*, by LFT Church Choir. *Cross Rhythms*, 1 Dec. 1998, www.crossrhythms.co.uk/products/Pastor_Hezekiah_Walker_Presents_The_LFT_Church_Choir/Recorded_Live_At_Love_Fellowship_Tabernacle/5803. Accessed 12 Nov. 2018.

Hedges, Chris. "Gospel Message, Rap Style; To a Brooklyn Preacher, Good Works Yield a

Fortune." *The New York Times*, 21 Apr. 2001, www.nytimes.com/2001/04/21/nyregion/gospel-message-rap-style-to-a-brooklyn-preacher-good-works-yield-a-fortune.html. Accessed 10 Nov. 2018.

Richardson, Clem. "Minister Who Raised the Roof: Faith Made Rev. Walker into a Grammy Winner." *The New York Daily News*, 5 Feb. 2001, www.nydailynews.com/archives/boroughs/minister-raised-roof-faith-made-rev-walker-grammy-winner-article-1.905159. Accessed 12 Nov. 2018.

Shelby, Joyce. "Rev. Hezekiah Walker, 'Hip-Hop Pastor,' to Become Pentecostal Bishop." *The New York Daily News*, 28 July 2008, www.nydailynews.com/new-york/brooklyn/rev-hezekiah-wlaker-hip-hop-pastor-pentecostal-bishop-article-1.346808. Accessed 12 Nov. 2018.

Thomasos, Christine. "Bishop Hezekiah Walker Embarks on $80M NYC Building Project for Affordable Housing in Brooklyn." *The Christian Post*, 24 Feb. 2017, www.christianpost.com/news/bishop-hezekiah-walker-80-million-affordable-housing-brooklyn-175751. Accessed 13 Nov. 2018.

SELECTED WORKS

I'll Make It, 1987; *Live in Atlanta at Morehouse College*, 1994; *Love Is Live!*, 2001; *Azusa: The Next Generation*, 2013

—*Molly Hagan*

Daniel Wanjiru

Date of birth: May 26, 1992
Occupation: Runner

Long-distance runner Daniel Wanjiru gained notoriety in 2017, when he finished first at the prestigious London Marathon, while still relatively new to competitive marathon running. A talented athletics competitor since primary school, Wanjiru began competing in events overseen by the International Association of Athletics Federations (IAAF) in 2010 and competed in his first IAAF marathon in 2014. He won his first IAAF marathon in 2016, finishing the Amsterdam Marathon in an impressive two hours, five minutes, and twenty-one seconds. Although new to the world of high-profile marathon competitions at the time, Wanjiru did not allow doubts about his own abilities or the strengths of his fellow runners to distract him from his goals. "I will not fear anyone because they have trained just like me and we will be running on the same course," he told Elias Makori and Benard Rotich for the *Daily Nation* (22 Apr. 2017).

EARLY LIFE AND EDUCATION

Daniel Kinyua Wanjiru was born in Kenya on May 26, 1992. He grew up in Kirinyaga County in central Kenya, where he lived with his mother, Delilah Wanjiru. Wanjiru developed an interest in the sport of athletics, particularly running, as a child. He began competing in athletics events in 2004, while attending Kianjege Primary School. As his skills and experience as a runner increased, he began to dream of one day competing in and winning major running events, especially high-profile international competitions such as the London Marathon. He was particularly inspired by the success of runner David Nyaga, later known as Daham Najim Bashir, who lived and trained in Wanjiru's area of Kenya during Wanjiru's teen years.

As a teenager, Wanjiru attended Mutitu Secondary School, where he continued to compete as a runner. He completed his secondary schooling in 2008. Looking to develop his athletic abilities further and seriously pursue a career in the sport, Wanjiru moved to neighboring Embu County to train. He ultimately joined a training camp operated by runner Jason Mbote, who remained his coach throughout the subsequent years.

EARLY RUNNING CAREER

While athletics events are held under the supervision of a variety of institutions, including schools, the bulk of major national and international events in the sport—which encompasses running and a variety of other track and field events—are governed by the IAAF and its regional member federations. Wanjiru began

Photo by Katie Chan via Wikimedia Commons

competing in IAAF running events in Kenya in 2010, placing eleventh in the Nairobi Standard Chartered Half Marathon with a time of one hour, two minutes, and fifty-three seconds that year. He continued to compete in half marathons—races measuring roughly 13.1 miles (21.1 kilometers) in length—over the course of 2011 and 2012. He also made appearances in shorter races, including ten-kilometer (about 6.2 miles) events. In July 2012, Wanjiru claimed his first first-place finish in an IAAF event, winning the ten-kilometer Le Miglia di Agordo race in Italy with a time of twenty-nine minutes and fifty-three seconds. His success in that race hinted at the young runner's potential, and subsequent events further cemented his status as a strong competitor. Wanjiru competed in nine IAAF events in 2013 and took first place in two of them, the Radenci Half Marathon in Slovenia and the Karlovy Vary Half Marathon in the Czech Republic. He also finished third in a fifteen-kilometer (about 9.3 miles) event in Switzerland that year.

MARATHON DEBUT

Wanjiru made his debut appearance in an IAAF marathon in October 2014, when he traveled to Germany to compete in the Frankfurt Marathon. With a course measuring about 26.2 miles (42.2 kilometers) in length, a marathon represents a significant challenge for any runner and one of the highest levels of competition for elite athletes. Wanjiru performed well during his first IAAF marathon, finishing seventh with a time of two hours, eight minutes, and eighteen seconds. He competed in shorter races as well, winning the 2014 Krems Wachau Half Marathon in Austria in September. Wanjiru did not compete in any IAAF marathons in 2015, but did put forth impressive performances in two half marathons, placing second in the Ras Al Khaimah International Half Marathon in the United Arab Emirates in February and winning the Praha Half Marathon in the Czech Republic the following month.

In 2016, Wanjiru won the Praha Half Marathon for the second year in a row, beating his previous time by over thirty seconds. He also competed in two IAAF marathons, beginning with the Praha Marathon in May 2016. Wanjiru placed fourth in the event with a time of two hours, nine minutes, and twenty-five seconds. He went on to achieve a key milestone in October of that year, defeating numerous, more experienced runners to win the Netherlands' Amsterdam Marathon. "I'm very excited for my win. I really need one and the time was right for me since I had prepared really well," he told Charity Wanja for *Citizen Digital* (18 Oct. 2016) after the event. "The race was very challenging but I kept faith and went for

it. I did not want to think of other champions I was running against." In addition to facilitating Wanjiru's first IAAF marathon win, his time of two hours, five minutes, and twenty-one seconds represented his official personal best marathon time.

LONDON MARATHON

Having achieved an elite-level marathon time, Wanjiru qualified to compete in the 2017 Virgin Money London Marathon. Often referred to as the London Marathon, the event is widely considered one of the most prestigious marathons in the world and its winners earn sizable prizes as well as significant attention from the media and potential sponsors. To prepare for the race, Wanjiru continued to train primarily in Embu and Kirinyaga Counties, which he told Makori and Rotich were "perfect for athletics" due to their proximity to Mount Kenya and the resulting altitude. Although Wanjiru faced strong competition from his fellow runners, he remained sure of his abilities and chances in the event. "I have done enough training and I started early preparations once I was listed as one of the elites for London and I'm confident I will win the race," he told Makori and Rotich. "I just want to be on the podium as a winner."

On April 23, 2017, more than forty thousand competitors raced through the streets of London, Wanjiru among them. Finishing the race with a time of two hours, five minutes, and forty-eight seconds, Wanjiru beat Ethiopian runner Kenenisa Bekele by nine seconds to claim first place. In interviews following the marathon, he commented that he had particularly appreciated the race's many spectators, whose excitement and cheers helped propel him to victory. Although Wanjiru's success in London earned him $130,000 in prize money, as well as worldwide recognition, he expressed the desire to keep his success from changing him. "I know it will come with many challenges, but I have come from far and will remain that humble boy from Kanyekine, Kirinyaga," he told Ayumba Ayodi for the *Daily Nation* (Apr. 2017). "Distractions will always be there, but I trust in God to help me avoid bad groups and bad influence." Following the marathon, he returned to Kenya to resume training, with the goal of competing for Kenya in the IAAF World Championships in Athletics.

Following his London Marathon performance, Wanjiru was selected to compete in the marathon event at the IAAF World Championships, held in London in August 2017. "I'm very excited to be part of Team Kenya," he told Wanja for *Citizen Digital* (23 May 2017) following his selection. "It has always been my dream to represent my country. My training is tailored to win a gold medal for Kenya." Wanjiru finished eighth in the marathon at the World Championships, achieving a time of two hours, twelve minutes, and sixteen seconds. In addition to his high-profile marathons, Wanjiru competed in a variety of shorter IAAF events during 2017, placing fourth in the Heerenberg Montferland Run, a fifteen-kilometer race held in the Netherlands.

2018 MARATHONS

Although Wanjiru competed in several shorter IAAF events in 2018, he focused particularly on marathons, beginning with his attempt to defend his title in London. The return to the London Marathon represented a challenge for Wanjiru, who struggled with a knee injury throughout early 2018, including during the time he spent preparing for the marathon. Nevertheless, he sought to focus less on such challenges and more on his own performance. "I believe in my training, and I'll do my own race," he told Andy Edwards for *Race News Service* before the event, as reported by RunBlogRun (21 Apr. 2018). During the marathon, held on April 22, Wanjiru completed the race with a time of two hours, ten minutes, and thirty-five seconds and ultimately placed eighth.

By November 2018, Wanjiru had recovered from his injury and was preparing to compete in the New York City Marathon, to which he took a more cautious approach than previous marathons. "The New York course is not so friendly, so I'm not thinking much about lowering my PB," he told Gilbert Kiprotich for *Citizen Digital* (16 Oct. 2018) about his goals for the race. "Of course being my first race after shaking off injury I cannot be over ambitious, but I know I will run a good race." Held on November 4, the race was a relatively successful one for Wanjiru, who placed fifth with a time of two hours, ten minutes, and twenty-one seconds. In addition to the London and New York marathons, Wanjiru competed in half marathons in the United States and the United Kingdom, as well as a ten-kilometer race in the Netherlands in which he placed fourth.

PERSONAL LIFE

Wanjiru is married to Sarah Njeri, with whom he has two children: Shalin and Fidel-Thomas. When not competing or training elsewhere, he lives in Kirinyaga County. In addition to winning prize money from his successful races, Wanjiru has been sponsored by the athletic-wear brand Adidas.

SUGGESTED READING

Ayodi, Ayumba. "'I Met Prince William and Harry, but That Won't Get into My Head.'" *Daily Nation*, Apr. 2017, www.nation.co.ke/sports/athletics/1100-3903844-view-asAMP-msj616/index.html. Accessed 15 Mar. 2019.

Kiprotich, Gilbert. "Injury Free Wanjiru Working to Conquer New York." *Citizen Digital*, 16 Oct. 2018, citizentv.co.ke/sports/injury-free-wanjiru-working-to-conquer-new-york-215392/. Accessed 15 Mar. 2019.

Makori, Elias, and Benard Rotich. "Mark the Name Daniel Wanjiru in London Marathon." *Daily Nation*, 22 Apr. 2017, www.nation.co.ke/sports/athletics/Mark-the-name-Daniel-Wanjiru-in-London-Marathon/1100-3900028-et0far/. Accessed 15 Mar. 2019.

Parry, Richard. "Daniel Wanjiru Wins the Men's Elite Race at the London Marathon." *Evening Standard*, 23 Apr. 2017, www.standard.co.uk/sport/daniel-wanjiru-wins-the-mens-elite-race-at-the-london-marathon-a3521471.html. Accessed 15 Mar. 2019.

Wanja, Charity. "Joy and Dance as Amsterdam King Wanjiru Returns Home." *Citizen Digital*, 18 Oct. 2016, citizentv.co.ke/sports/joy-and-dance-as-amsterdam-king-wanjiru-returns-home-145733/. Accessed 15 Mar. 2019.

Wanja, Charity. "'Tailored to Win'—Wanjiru Out to Rock London Again." *Citizen Digital*, 23 May 2017, citizentv.co.ke/sports/tailored-to-win-wanjiru-out-to-rock-london-again-166599/. Accessed 15 Mar. 2019.

Wanjiru, Daniel. "2018 Virgin Money London Marathon Diary: Daniel Wanjiru Interview Pre London Marathon 2018 by Andy Edwards, Race News Service." Interview by Andy Edwards. *RunBlogRun*, 21 Apr. 2018, www.runblogrun.com/2018/04/daniel-wanjiru-interview-pre-london-marathon-2018-by-andy-edwards-race-news-service.html. Accessed 15 Mar. 2019.

—Joy Crelin

Brad Watson

Date of birth: July 24, 1955
Occupation: Author

Mississippi native Brad Watson is an award-winning novelist and short-story writer whose work has drawn comparisons to that of William Faulkner for its southern gothic elements, dark themes, and poetic prose stylings. A former aspiring actor who held odd jobs (including garbage collector) before turning to literature and becoming a longtime college professor, Watson did not publish his first book of fiction, the award-winning short-story collection *Last Days of the Dog-Men* (1996), until he reached his forties. However, he went on to earn a reputation as a "masterful novelist," as fellow author Silas House proclaimed for *Salon.com* (21 July 2016), etching his place among America's leading

Photo by Pool ANDERSEN/GAILLARDE/Gamma-Rapho via
Getty Images

contemporary writers with works that often challenge readers' expectations.

Watson's works include the widely acclaimed novels *The Heaven of Mercury* (2002) and *Miss Jane* (2016), as well as the short-story collection *Aliens in the Prime of Their Lives* (2010). Each features his trademark strange yet deeply nuanced and complex characters, traversing the full spectrum of humanity.

EARLY LIFE AND EDUCATION

The middle of three brothers, Watson was born on July 24, 1955, in Meridian, Mississippi. He grew up there in a middle-class home "where books were far from prized possessions," as Susanna Felts noted for the literary website *Chapter 16* (22 Apr. 2011). Consequently, Watson did not read much growing up, save for pulp novels. A self-described loner and daydreamer, he often passed the time as a boy by taking solitary walks into the woods near the family home. This helped him develop an early sensibility to his surrounding environs, a quality that would later mark his fiction.

Unlike his two brothers, Watson was generally well-behaved and even timid as a child, so much so that he was often teased by his siblings and peers. As a result, he resolved to become a tougher version of himself, which led to a disaffected and rebellious adolescence, one that was characterized by binge-drinking, fighting, and petty hijinks. He was even arrested after various incidents. At Meridian High School, Watson channeled his demons through sports and theater, the latter of which he had stumbled into thanks to a junior high teacher. His passion for

performing prompted him to move to Los Angeles, California, after high school to pursue a career as an actor.

Despite receiving the support of his open-minded parents, Watson's acting dreams proved to be short-lived after he failed to land on-screen work. He ended up working a series of odd jobs, including as the lone employee of a small garbage collection business. Watson eventually returned to Meridian after his older brother was killed in a car accident. He took over running a small dive bar his father had bought, but it soon went bankrupt due to his poor business practices. Though he made plans to become a carpenter, at the urging of his family he subsequently enrolled at Meridian Junior College (MJC).

It was at MJC that the foundations of Watson's literary career took shape. There, he was unexpectedly placed in an honors-level English class taught by Niles "Buck" Thomas, a respected scholar of southern literature. In Thomas's class, Watson read works by such important and influential southern writers as William Faulkner, Mark Twain, Flannery O'Connor, and Robert Penn Warren. "For the first time I read great works seriously, with attention, with excellent guidance, with enthusiasm," he explained to Sarah Anne Johnson for the *Fiction Writers Review* (20 Mar. 2018), "It was an awakening."

EARLY CAREER

Watson's "awakening" ultimately led to him becoming a writer. After graduating from MJC he attended Mississippi State University, where he studied under author Price Caldwell, known for such short stories as "Gordon at Church" and "Tarzan Meets the Department Head." Upon receiving a bachelor's degree in English in 1978, he enrolled in the master of fine arts (MFA) program at the University of Alabama (UA), in Tuscaloosa, Alabama. There, he was mentored by the award-winning and fellow Meridian-bred author Barry Hannah.

Throughout his studies, Watson immersed himself in his craft, writing "a big box-full of bad stories," as he told Johnson, that he would eventually burn. By the time he earned his MFA in writing and American literature, he had published several stories in small literary magazines. However, to earn a living, he moved to the Alabama Gulf Coast and became a reporter, even giving up fiction writing for a time due to frustration with his output. He covered local news and later served as an editor for the *Montgomery Advertiser*. As a journalist, however, he was often uncomfortable with the newsroom atmosphere because of his tendency to empathize with subjects, even those accused of crimes or otherwise involved in trouble. Watson would later attribute this to his background in creative writing, rather than journalism like his newspaper colleagues:

"Writing fiction, in terms of dealing with your characters, is all about empathy. All about figuring out this or that person's humanity, her and his human-ness," he explained to Matthew Neill Null for *Electric Literature* (12 July 2016).

In 1988, following his stint as a journalist and time working at an advertising agency, Watson returned to Tuscaloosa to become an adjunct professor of creative writing at UA. Over the next eight years he returned to writing short stories, often with dissatisfying results. In an interview for the journal *Fiction Southeast* (3 Nov. 2014), Watson noted that he acquired a folder of rejection slips "about an inch thick" compared to a file of acceptance letters "about a millimeter thin . . . I'd got to the point that I didn't think it was ever going to happen. I wasn't going to stop writing, but I was going to stop hoping for a 'publishing career.'" However, on the strength of a piece that appeared in *Story* magazine, he was contacted by W. W. Norton & Company, which published his first book, the short-story collection *Last Days of the Dog-Men*, in 1996.

Featuring eight stories populated by peculiar characters living on the margins in rural Mississippi with their beloved dogs, the collection received widespread praise. It went on to win the prestigious Sue Kaufman Award for First Fiction from the American Academy of Arts and Letters, boosting Watson to a new level of recognition.

THE HEAVEN OF MERCURY AND SECOND STORY COLLECTION

In 1997, following the success of *Last Days*, Watson was hired at Harvard University, in Cambridge, Massachusetts. He spent five years there as a Briggs-Copeland lecturer in fiction, during which he wrote his debut novel, *The Heaven of Mercury*. Published by W. W. Norton in 2002, the novel, whose title derives from Dante's *Divine Comedy* (1320), is set in the fictional town of Mercury, Mississippi, during the first quarter of the twentieth century. It centers around the would-be romance between an obituary writer, Finus Bates, and his lifelong love, the elusive Birdie Wells.

Mixing in pathos with humor, jumping back and forth in time, and focusing on themes of love, death, and racism, *Heaven of Mercury* provides a wide-ranging portrait of the human condition, with memorable secondary characters that include a necrophiliac mortician and a former slave turned medicine woman. The novel garnered universal acclaim from critics and received several literary honors, including being named a finalist for the National Book Award and winning fiction awards from the Southern Book Critics Circle and the Mississippi Institute of Arts and Letters. It also drew praise from fellow writers, including Watson's former mentor Hannah, who compared to the writing to that of the masters of Irish literature.

Heaven of Mercury helped solidify Watson's status as an important American fiction author. The recognition led to him serving as a writer-in-residence at several schools, including the University of West Florida, the University of California at Irvine, and the University of Mississippi. In 2005, Watson joined the faculty of the then-new MFA program at the University of Wyoming, in Laramie, Wyoming. He eventually became director of the university's creative writing program, teaching courses on subjects including American literature, foreign literature in translation, and the publishing business.

In 2010, Watson published his second short-story collection, *Aliens in the Prime of Their Lives*, which was named a finalist for the PEN/Faulkner Prize in Fiction, among other honors. Written in the southern gothic tradition and tackling such themes as loneliness and divorce, the collection includes stories that were previously published in the *New Yorker* and *Granta*. Two stories, "Visitation" and "Alamo Plaza," won PEN/O. Henry awards and were included in the *PEN/O. Henry Prize Stories* collections in 2010 and 2011, respectively.

MISS JANE AND BEYOND

In 2011 Watson was awarded a Guggenheim Foundation fellowship. He then set out to finish a novel he had been working on since 2002, and from 2012 to 2015 he focused exclusively on that project. The result was his second novel, *Miss Jane*, published by W. W. Norton in 2016. It is based on the life of his mysterious great-aunt, Mary Ellis "Jane" Clay, who never married and was unable to have children due to a birth defect. Watson met his great-aunt, who died in 1975, just once as a boy, but became interested in writing a novel about her after coming across an old photograph of her in a flirtatious pose. Because no member of his family knew what medical condition she had suffered from, Watson did extensive research to help identify a credible one for her fictional iteration, Jane Chisolm.

The novel follows Jane as she cautiously navigates the world around her and the people who inhabit it. That world is again the fictional town of Mercury, Mississippi, which is populated by suspecting neighbors and townsfolk who become intrigued by Jane's condition. Unlike Watson's debut novel, *Miss Jane* features a more tempered prose style and is less concerned with the subject of race, instead delving deep into the complexities of Jane's rich inner life. Like his previous works, the book was well-received by critics, many of whom especially praised the realistic, balanced portrayal of the American South.

Throughout Watson's work, the depth of the characters is another strength frequently noted by reviewers. Much of this comes from his careful yet natural writing process, as he explained to Johnson: "I work instinctively, at first, trying to find the voice, understand who the people are, what the problem is, get a sense of what it's all about and why I even ought to write about it." This attention to his craft earned the author various awards and honors, which in addition to his Guggenheim fellowship included a grant from the National Endowment for the Arts and residencies from the Lannan Foundation and the Aspen Institute.

PERSONAL LIFE

"Warm, affable, funny and blunt, Watson's personality is a mirror of his writing," Richard Farrell wrote for the online literary journal *Numéro Cinq* (Dec. 2011), despite the author's own suggestion that he was a "misanthrope." Watson was married as a teenager between his junior and senior years of high school, and the couple had a son, Jason, before divorcing. He later married Nell Hanley, a writer and horse trainer, with whom he had another son, Owen.

SUGGESTED READING

"About Brad." *Brad Watson*, 2019, wiltonbradwatson.com/about/. Accessed 4 Jan. 2019.

Watson, Brad. "Author in the Prime of His Life." Interview by Susanna Felts. *Chapter 16*, 22 Apr. 2011, chapter16.org/author-in-the-prime-of-his-life/. Accessed 4 Jan. 2019.

Watson, Brad. "Making the Little Monsters Walk: Interview with Brad Watson—Richard Farrell." Interview by Richard Farrell. *Numéro Cinq*, Dec. 2011, numerocinqmagazine.com/2011/12/16/making-the-little-monsters-walk-an-interview-with-brad-watson/. Accessed 4 Jan. 2019.

Watson, Brad. "Author Interview Series: Brad Watson." *Fiction Southeast*, 3 Nov. 2014, fictionsoutheast.com/author-interview-series-brad-watson/. Accessed 4 Jan. 2019.

Watson, Brad. "Brad Watson on Scoundrels, Medical Mysteries & Building His New Novel Out of a Family Secret." Interview by Matthew Neill Null. *Electric Literature*, 12 July 2016, electricliterature.com/brad-watson-on-scoundrels-medical-mysteries-building-his-new-novel-out-of-a-family-secret-8602f30ee885. Accessed 4 Jan. 2019.

Watson, Brad. "'Something Was Wrong with Aunt Jane': Brad Watson on the Uncommon Woman behind His New Novel, Writing Difference and the Appeal of 'Fly-Over' Country." Interview by Silas House. *Salon.com*, 21 July 2016, www.salon.com/2016/07/20/something_was_wrong_with_aunt_jane_brad_watson_on_the_uncommon_woman_behind_his_new_novel_writing_difference_and_the_appeal_of_fly_over_country/. Accessed 4 Jan. 2019.

Watson, Brad. "Interesting Problems: An Interview with Brad Watson." Interview by Sarah Anne Johnson. *Fiction Writers Review*, 20 Mar. 2018, fictionwritersreview.com/interview/interesting-problems-an-interview-with-brad-watson/. Accessed 4 Jan. 2018.

SELECTED WORKS

Last Days of the Dog-Men, 1996; *The Heaven of Mercury*, 2002; *Aliens in the Prime of Their Lives*, 2010; *Miss Jane*, 2016

—*Chris Cullen*

Jessica Watson

Date of birth: May 18, 1993
Occupation: Sailor and writer

In May 2010, Australian Jessica Watson returned home after sailing around the world in a thirty-four-foot yacht. The sixteen-year-old had completed the treacherous seven-month voyage alone. By the time she sailed into Sydney Harbor after 210 days at sea, Watson, greeted by thousands of supporters, including Australian prime minister Kevin Rudd, had become a national celebrity. Rudd spoke to the gathered crowd and described Watson as "Australia's newest hero," as quoted by Mary Papadakis for the *Herald Sun* (15 May 2010). Watson responded, "I don't consider myself a hero. I'm an ordinary girl who believed in a dream. You don't have to be someone special or anything special to achieve something amazing."

Watson went on to publish an edited collection of her popular at-sea blog posts titled *True Spirit: The Aussie Girl Who Took On the World*, in 2010. That same year, she released a documentary, *210 Days: Around the World with Jessica Watson*, created from the video diary she shot before and during her voyage and narrated by business magnate Sir Richard Branson. She was named the national Young Australian of the Year 2011 for her exceptional voyage and was awarded a medal of the Order of Australia (OAM) in 2012.

Watson later led the youngest team ever to compete in Australia's competitive Sydney-to-Hobart yacht race in 2011 and became involved with a start-up revolving around a marine community website called *Deckee* in 2015. Priding herself in setting further challenges and diversifying her career goals, she published her first novel, titled *Indigo Blue*, in 2018.

Photo by Sheba_Also via Wikimedia Commons

EARLY LIFE

Watson was born on May 18, 1993, and raised mostly in Queensland, Australia. Her father, Roger, worked as a businessman and her mother, Julie, is an occupational therapist. Brought up without a television, Watson spent a lot of time outside, and she and her family often went camping. Alongside her sisters Emily and Hannah and brother, Tom, Watson learned to sail at a sailing camp when she was in the fourth grade. Her mother reckoned that she was the least likely member of the family to continue sailing because she was so shy. In her book *True Spirit*, Watson even describes her young self as "pretty much afraid of everything." But sailing captured Watson in a way that other activities had not. Soon, she was taking part in regular classes and club racing. For around five years, she lived with her family on a cabin cruiser, called the *Home Abroad*, that they used to travel along the coast when not moored at a marina, picking up knowledge of navigation and maintenance as she helped crew the boat.

As a child, Watson struggled with severe dyslexia, but she eventually found inspiration in Jesse Martin's book *Lionheart: A Journey of the Human Spirit* (2000), which her mother read to her when she was around eleven. The book describes how, in 1999, an eighteen-year-old Martin became the youngest person to make a solo nonstop sailing voyage around the world. She was also captivated by the story of Ellen MacArthur, who completed the Vendée Globe, a solo nonstop yacht race around the world, at the age of twenty-four. "It was Jesse's book that first gave me the idea for my journey but certainly Ellen's

[2002 book *Taking On the World*] been a huge inspiration," Watson told Christopher Clarey for the *New York Times* (24 Dec. 2011). "She just fought so incredibly hard for everything that she did achieve. Like she says and like I've always believed as well, it's not about being a girl. Her record was the fastest *person* around the world. I didn't want to go for youngest girl around the world; I wanted to go for youngest person."

PREPARING FOR THE VOYAGE

Watson began preparing for her journey and working to convince her parents she was capable years before she officially announced her intention to sail single-handedly around the globe. In addition to garnering thousands of miles of coastal and ocean sailing experience, she earned qualifications in and learned skills regarding offshore safety, diesel engines, stitching sails, nutrition, radio operations, celestial navigation, and first aid. She served on the crews of various voyages and skippered a journey across the Tasman Sea. "Before I left, the longest voyage I'd been on was 14 days straight, though I had almost 10,000 miles sea time through the Tasman, Pacific, and the Southern Arctic Oceans," she told Ryan Bradley for *National Geographic* (6 Dec. 2010).

With the help of her family and sponsors she had also wooed, Watson, along with volunteers, meticulously stripped and outfitted the boat that expert sailor Don McIntyre had bought for her, named *Ella's Pink Lady*. "For me, the most important thing was preparation and the amazing team of people around me, who just wouldn't have let me leave unless I was ready," she added to Bradley. "You need an incredible amount of support to achieve something like this, and I was lucky." In an interview with Watson for *The Australian* (21 Sept. 2013), Trent Dalton wrote that before Watson left, her father knew *Ella's Pink Lady* well enough to picture the yacht's "hull screws and nuts and bolts in his sleep."

Still, after Watson announced her endeavor, lay people and expert sailors alike expressed serious concerns. Watson's parents were particularly scrutinized, accused of both, as Dalton put it, "stage-parenting" and "child neglect." While some media outlets reported that the Queensland government was threatening to stop the voyage, others included quotes from Phil Reeves, minister for child safety, clarifying that the government was not going to prevent her from achieving her dream. Nevertheless, critics described Watson's plan as reckless and Watson herself as too inexperienced to face the dangers of the open ocean alone. Despite her many supporters, among them Jesse Martin, such criticism gained steam when her boat collided with a large cargo ship on a trial run in September 2009. She had been asleep at the time of the crash, in which *Ella's Pink Lady* lost its mast.

SAILING AROUND THE WORLD

Undeterred, Watson and a newly repaired *Ella's Pink Lady* left Sydney Harbor on October 18, 2009. Julie Watson told a reporter for the *Sydney Morning Herald* (18 Oct. 2009) that Watson remained upbeat and excited for the voyage. "She said to me, 'Mum, I am going to get up tomorrow and sail around the world,'" her mother recalled.

On November 19, a little more than a month into her voyage, Watson crossed the equator. Poignantly, she spent Christmas near Point Nemo, the point in the ocean farthest away from any land and known as one of the remotest places on Earth. With the cabin decorated and wearing a festive crown, Watson recorded a short video diary entry on that day. In it, she said she planned to open the Christmas presents her family had sent with her. On January 13, 2010, she rounded Cape Horn, the southernmost tip of South America. This was a major milestone; Cape Horn is an extremely difficult passage that has claimed the lives of thousands of sailors. A few weeks later, crossing the South Atlantic, she experienced her first (and second, third, and fourth) knockdown, meaning that the mast of her boat dipped below horizontal and into the sea. She had no choice but to endure the storm, which lasted for hours, belted in below deck. Of the second knockdown, Watson later wrote in her memoir, "It would be more accurate to say that *Ella's Pink Lady* was picked up, thrown down a wave, then forced under a mountain of breaking water and violently turned upside down." After rounding South Africa's Cape of Good Hope in February, she was back in Australian waters by April. On May 15, 2010, she completed her voyage, sailing back into the harbor in Sydney just three days prior to turning seventeen.

LIFE AFTER THE VOYAGE

Watson returned to Sydney a celebrity, though there was some controversy over the classification of her achievement. After the eighteen-year-old Martin made it back from his historic voyage in 1999, the World Sailing Speed Record Council (WSSRC) abolished its "youngest" category. Watson knew she would not be in the running for an official record, but the other sailing experts further argued that she had not sailed far enough above the equator for her journey to be considered a true circumnavigation of the globe.

Proud, regardless, of having successfully navigated approximately 23,000 nautical miles and accomplished her goal to sail solo nonstop around the world, Watson was then tasked with more mundane but significant activities like finishing high school—which she accomplished in

2011—and earning her driver's license. She published her book *True Spirit* (2010) and embarked on a tour to promote it. After being named the national Young Australian of the Year early in 2011, she traveled to Laos as a youth representative for the United Nations World Food Programme (WFP). Watson was also honored with a medal of the Order of Australia in 2012 for her contributions to the world of sailing and for setting an example to other young Australians.

On December 26, 2011, Watson skippered the youngest crew to ever compete in the Sydney-to-Hobart race, one of the country's most celebrated sailing events. The race, covering 628 nautical miles, runs across the Tasman Sea from Sydney to Hobart, Tasmania. "It's a whole new skill set I've had to learn," Watson told Clarey. "You are coming from around the world, which is all about slow and steady. . . . It was about having a good general knowledge of everything and being able to keep your head in the right place for that amount of time, whereas this voyage is a sprint, and I'm part of a team." The team finished second in its division, and Watson was awarded the Jane Tate Memorial Trophy for being the first female skipper to cross the finish line.

PURSUING OTHER CHALLENGES

Watson then decided to invest further in her education, earning a bachelor's degree in media and communications from Deakin University in 2016. In 2015, the same year in which she visited Syrian refugees in Lebanon and Jordan on behalf of WFP, she began working with and serving as communications manager for a start-up called *Deckee*. "It brings together the things that I love, working with the marine industry, sailors and boaties," she told a reporter for *Sunshine Coast Daily* (14 Oct. 2015). "It hasn't really been done before and this is a great opportunity to bring the marine world together online." The website collects community reviews of marinas, products, and other services. With the launch of a mobile app in 2018, *Deckee* also acts as a navigational and forecast tool.

Watson further built on her education by earning an MBA from the Australian Institute of Management (AIM) Business School in 2017. She went on to become a consultant with Deloitte Australia's Human Capital Practice in May 2018 and continued her work as a corporate speaker.

That same year, Watson published a novel for younger readers titled *Indigo Blue*. In it, a high school girl named Alex moves in with her aunt in a tiny lakeside town in Queensland. She has trouble making friends at her new school and devotes herself to restoring an old yacht. It contains elements of folklore and magical realism. Inspired by her own early experiences reading about sailing, and hoping to inspire other young girls to sail, she started writing the novel in 2014.

PERSONAL LIFE
Though Watson has focused increasingly on other pursuits, she still makes time to sail and indulge in her passion.

SUGGESTED READING
Barbeler, David, and Jessica Marszalek. "Solo Sailor Watson Suffers Yacht 'Knockdown.'" *Brisbane Times*, 24 Jan. 2010, www.brisbanetimes.com.au/national/queensland/solo-sailor-watson-suffers-yacht-knockdown-20100124-mrzp.html. Accessed 4 Apr. 2019.

Clarey, Christopher. "Sydney to Hobart with a Teenager at the Helm." *The New York Times*, 24 Dec. 2011, www.nytimes.com/2011/12/25/sports/yacht-racing-sydney-to-hobart-without-an-adult-on-board.html. Accessed 4 Apr. 2019.

Dalton, Trent. "2010: Jessica Watson, Solo Sailor." *The Australian*, 21 Sept. 2013, www.theaustralian.com.au/life/weekend-australian-magazine/jessica-watson-solo-sailor/news-story/9c16a74dd7d6d6fc0a927d2b6ca5f077. Accessed 4 Apr. 2019.

Papadakis, Mary. "Teen Hero Sheds Tears to Be Home." *Herald Sun*, 15 May 2010, www.heraldsun.com.au/news/im-so-proud-of-my-voyage-of-a-lifetime-says-solo-sailor-jessica-watson/news-story/fef9d406d28d054e603c097a4a615296?sv=42305dca066ac1b89bef9a8c84527892&nk=d799b638d0c8ecf7352d72e258ce19a7-1555075334. Accessed 12 Apr. 2019.

Watson, Jessica. "The Circumnavigator: Jessica Watson." Interview by Ryan Bradley. *National Geographic*, 6 Dec. 2010, www.nationalgeographic.com/adventure/features/adventurers-of-the-year/2010/jessica-watson-2010. Accessed 4 Apr. 2019.

Watson, Jessica. *True Spirit: The Aussie Girl Who Took On the World*. Hachette Australia, 2010.

"Where Are They Now: Jessica Watson Embarks on New Career." *Sunshine Coast Daily*, 14 Oct. 2015, www.sunshinecoastdaily.com.au/news/jess-on-course-for-new-job/2806128. Accessed 6 Apr. 2019.

—*Molly Hagan*

Paula Mae Weekes

Date of birth: December 23, 1958
Occupation: Politician

Paula Mae Weekes became the president of the Republic of Trinidad and Tobago in 2018.

Photo by Sean Drakes/Getty Images

Though the position is largely ceremonial—the prime minister holds more power—Weekes's ascension is significant. At the time, Trinidad and Tobago was the only nation in Latin America and the Caribbean to have a woman head of state. Weekes is a former lawyer who served for many years as a judge. She developed a reputation for her eviscerating commentary, which she displayed when she was asked if there was anything that she would like people to know before she was sworn into office. Weekes told a reporter for *Trinidad and Tobago Newsday* (8 Feb. 2018): "I'm surprised that people who should know better have applied to me for favors. I would like them to desist. That will save them some embarrassment. I've never done it, and I'm not going to start now."

Weekes assumed her job at a difficult moment in her country's history. Trinidad and Tobago is a small Caribbean nation off the coast of Venezuela. A former colony (of Spain, then France, then Great Britain), Trinidad and Tobago declared independence in 1962. Low oil prices have hit the oil-rich nation hard. Crime, violence, and corruption plague the country as well. In her inaugural address, Weekes identified the feelings of hopelessness that many citizens felt. Experts, she said, "tell us that T&T is perilously close to the point of no return—crime, corruption, racism, abysmal public services and an ineffective judicial system, among other problems are so thick on the ground that all hope is lost; that we will soon be, if are not already there, a failed state, however defined." But Weekes advocated hope and action, urging citizens to work together to engender change.

EARLY LIFE AND EDUCATION

Paula Mae Weekes was born on December 23, 1958. Her mother, Phyllis Weekes, gave her the middle name Noelle, because she was born just before Christmas. Weekes's father, an insurance agent and sailor, left the family when she was very young. She and her late younger brother, Robert, were raised by their mother in Port-of-Spain, the country's capital.

As a child, Weekes attended Miss Ritchie's Private School, Tranquility Government Primary School, and Bishop Anstey High School. She devoured the Chronicles of Narnia series and continues to count herself an admirer of author C. S. Lewis; she even quoted him—"this is a good world gone wrong but it still retains the memory of what ought to have been"—in her inaugural address. (Like Weekes, Lewis was also a devout Anglican.) Unsurprisingly, Weekes showed academic promise early. "There was never any trouble with Paula in school," her mother recalled to Angela Pidduck for the *Trinidad Express* (3 Mar. 2018). "She would do her homework while waiting for me to collect her after school. I remember one of my co-workers foresaw her as some chief justice or some great person." The elder Weekes went on: "There was nothing above or beyond Paula-Mae because whatever she puts her mind to, she will do it. But she never liked the limelight."

Upon graduation, Weekes enrolled at the University of the West Indies at Cave Hill in Barbados in 1977. She chose to study law after a friend's father, a judge, lamented that none of his children were interested in the profession. Weekes seized on the inspiration. She graduated in 1980 with a Bachelor of Law degree with honors. She earned a legal education certificate from the school's Hugh Wooding Law School in 1982 and was called to the bar later that year.

LAW CAREER

Weekes began her law career in the office of the Director of Public Prosecutions (DPP), the country's criminal law department. She worked for the DPP for eleven years and went into private practice in 1993. In 1996, she was approached by Trinidad and Tobago's Supreme Court chief justice Michael de la Bastide about a change of career. She soon became a judge on the criminal division of the country's high court. During her time on the bench, she developed a formidable reputation. "No one could make you feel like a blithering idiot like Justice Weekes," one attorney recalled to *Newsday*. She became a fellow of the Commonwealth Judicial Education Institute in 2000. The same year, her brother, Robert, died of kidney failure caused by HIV. His death had an enormous effect on her. She took a more serious interest in the country's poor public health system and, to assuage her grief, began running marathons. "I've seen written after I started running that it is a metaphor for life and it really is," she told Joel Julien for the *Trinidad and Tobago Guardian* (6 Feb. 2018). "When you feel 'oh my God I can't go another step' you tell yourself, 'all right just make it to that lamppost and we will see where you go after that' and that is what it was."

Weekes was promoted to the Court of Appeals in 2005. She enjoyed being part of a panel of judges, she told a reporter for *Newsday* (7 Feb. 2018), but admitted that she and the other judges sometimes had "some very fiery conversations" about their verdicts. She retired in 2016. In 2017, she was sworn in as an appellate judge in Turks and Caicos for a three-year term. (The court sits for brief periods each year.) She also began teaching classes in criminal law, like cross-examination, at Hugh Wooding Law School.

PRESIDENT OF TRINIDAD AND TOBAGO

Keith Rowley, a geologist and veteran politician, was elected prime minister of Trinidad and Tobago in 2015. In January 2018, he nominated Weekes to replace outgoing President Anthony Carmona, whose term was set to end in March. In Trinidad and Tobago, presidential candidates are nominated by the ruling party, the People's National Movement (PNM) in this case. The opposition party (the United National Congress, at the time of Weekes's nomination) may also nominate a candidate if they so choose. The president is elected through the Electoral College, comprising all the members of the Senate and of the House of Representatives. Kamla Persad-Bissessar, opposition leader and the country's former prime minister, was pleased by Rowley's nominee. She and her party opted not to field a candidate of their own. Weekes, the only candidate in the race, was thus deemed elected without a vote several weeks later. In an early interview as president-elect, Weekes expressed a desire to address issues facing young people and crime.

Weekes was sworn in as the sixth president of Trinidad and Tobago on March 19, 2018. In her inaugural address, she defined her role as president as "humble first servant." She keeps an office in the Parliament building, but only appears there by appointment. The president has one legal adviser, though Weekes would prefer a legal department.

SHINING A SPOTLIGHT

In early 2018, Weekes conceded that, in her new position, she would have to "resist the temptation of feeling I know how a matter ought to be resolved," she told *Newsday*. Aware that the president had little independent power, she further admitted that her role is "in some respects at the end of the day . . . a glorified rubber stamp." The president, in fact, is tasked with making several important appointments, but she did recognize one other important power: her ability to speak, and offer guidance, with the authority of the office both publicly and behind closed doors. Some problems, she told *Newsday*, require "someone in a position to shine a spotlight on them who doesn't fear any backlash."

In 2018, the high court voted to decriminalize gay sex, exciting fury among anti-gay protesters. Weekes urged calm and understanding. "I think in terms of the State and the law all citizens and all persons under the protection of our jurisdiction should have equal treatment whatever their gender, whatever their sexual orientation, whatever their race we need to have absolute equality across the board," she said, as quoted by Julien. In January 2019, Weekes used her office to shine a spotlight on the country's education system. In a veiled reference to newly drafted education policy, Weekes implored parents, students, and teachers to place less stock in awards and competition and view education more holistically. In her speech, Weekes said that there were plenty of people with multiple degrees that, greedy and amoral, made for poor citizens. "From my vantage point as President of the Republic of Trinidad and Tobago, it would seem that it is time to do a complete overhaul of the education system if we are to have any chance of producing the individuals that we want and need to lead this country into the future," she said, as quoted by Rishard Khan for the *Guardian* (8 Jan. 2019).

PERSONAL LIFE

Weekes enjoys traveling, cooking, and cultivating orchids. She once attempted to climb Mount Kilimanjaro but suffered a bad bout of altitude sickness that prevented her from completing the climb. She has run four marathons. She lives with her elderly mother in Diego Martin.

A lifelong Anglican, Weekes served as chancellor of the Anglican Diocese of Trinidad and Tobago from 1997 to 2018. She also served as the superintendent of the Sunday school at her church. As a member of the church, Weekes has held workshops on restorative justice, an approach that values community rehabilitation over prison sentences.

SUGGESTED READING

"'I Want to Let the Light In.'" *Trinidad and Tobago Newsday*, 7 Feb. 2018, newsday.co.tt/2018/02/07/i-want-to-let-the-light-in. Accessed 20 Jan. 2019.

Julien, Joel. "Social Media Talk Stuns President-Elect: I'm Not a Lesbian." *Trinidad and Tobago Guardian*, 6 Feb. 2018, ftp.guardian.co.tt/news/2018-02-05/i'm-not-lesbian. Accessed 21 Jan. 2019.

Khan, Rishard. "President: Scholars Need to Help Reform T&T." *Trinidad and Tobago Guardian*, 8 Jan. 2019, www.guardian.co.tt/news/president-scholars-need-to-help-reform-tt-6.2.752339.85da70867a. Accessed 20 Jan. 2019.

"'My Life No Longer My Own.'" *Newsday*, 8 Feb. 2018, newsday.co.tt/2018/02/08/my-life-no-longer-my-own. Accessed 20 Jan. 2019.

Pidduck, Angela. "Nothing above or beyond Paula Mae." *Trinidad Express*, 3 Mar. 2018, www.trinidadexpress.com/news/local/nothing-above-or-beyond-paula-mae/article_35d28234-1fbf-11e8-9731-97049b6f160d.html. Accessed 20 Jan. 2019.

—*Molly Hagan*

Chrissie Wellington

Date of birth: February 18, 1977
Occupation: Triathlete

Chrissie Wellington is a retired professional triathlete and four-time Ironman Triathlon World Champion. She was honored as an Officer of the British Empire in 2015.

EARLY LIFE AND EDUCATION

Christine Ann Wellington was born on February 18, 1977, in Bury St. Edmunds, United Kingdom. She attended a local state school, Downham Market High School, where she was active in different sports, including gymnastics, swimming, and running. She continued her education at Birmingham University in Birmingham, United Kingdom, where she graduated with a first-class honors degree in geography.

After traveling the world for two years, Wellington pursued her master's degree at the University of Manchester in Manchester, United Kingdom. She graduated in October 2001. Around this time, she began dealing with body image issues that led her to suffer from anorexia and bulimia. With the help of her family, Wellington recovered and started working for the UK Department for Environment, Food and Rural Affairs (DEFRA). There she helped work on the country's water and sanitation policies and took part in negotiations at the United Nations' World Summit on Sustainable Development (WSSD). While working for the government, Wellington remained passionate about sports, and in 2002, she entered her first marathon and finished in three hours. She finished her first triathlon race in third place in May 2004. Later in 2004 she competed in two Olympic-distance triathlons.

She took a sabbatical from DERFA in September 2004 to work for a nongovernmental organization (NGO) in Nepal. She did some more traveling and returned to her DERFA job in May 2006. Her first major race was the 2006 amateur world triathlon championships, where she won first place in her age group. This major win inspired her to quit her job at NERFA to turn professional.

CAREER AS A PROFESSIONAL TRIATHLETE

Wellington started her career as a professional triathlete under Australia's national triathlon coach Brett Sutton. She has stated that the controversial coach (he was suspended for two years for sexual misconduct with a minor) trained her so hard she would cry some days, but that he was highly influential in her life. Sutton saw Wellington's potential and although she was a rookie who had never competed in a long-distance triathlon, he entered her in the Ironman World Championships in Kona, Hawaii, in October 2007. Wellington finished the race in first place, with the second-fastest time by a woman in the running leg. Since Wellington was only a rookie who had turned professional ten months earlier, her first place win in Ironman was considered a remarkable feat.

Following this first major victory, Wellington subsequently won first in the October 2008 and 2009 Ironman World Championships. At the Ironman European Championships in July 2008, she finished first with the second-fastest time to date by a woman. In addition to the Ironman wins, Wellington competed in other triathlons, including the 2008 Alpe d'Huez Triathlon in France, where she finished second overall. Later that year, Wellington and Sutton ended their professional relationship as coach and trainee.

Under her new coach Simon Lessing, Wellington set triathlon records at the Challenge Roth race in Germany in July 2009. After only a short time working with Lessing, Wellington decided to leave his tutelage to train by herself. She again set a course record at the Ironman World Championship in October 2009. Illness forced Wellington to drop out of the 2010 Ironman race. She called it the hardest decision of her life, but subsequent tests showed that she was suffering from strep throat, pneumonia, and West Nile virus.

After taking time to recover from her illnesses, Wellington beat her own record in the Ironman South Africa race on April 10, 2011. That July, she set a new world record for a woman at the Challenge Roth race. On September 24, 2011, just weeks before the next Ironman World Championships, Wellington crashed her bicycle while training. She suffered serious injuries, including a torn pectoral muscle that made it painful for her to swim. She competed in the race regardless of her injuries. She swam more slowly than usual and was forced to start twenty-one minutes behind the leader. During the bicycle leg of the race, she got a flat tire but did not stop. Despite these setbacks, Wellington won the race by almost three minutes. In post-race interviews Wellington stated she was in severe pain during the race.

After her win at the 2011 Ironman World Championship, Wellington took a break in 2012 to promote her acclaimed autobiography, *A Life without Limits: A World Champion's Journey* (2012). Wellington announced her retirement in February 2012. In an article posted on her blog, she explained that her passion for the sport had not diminished, but she wished to pursue new challenges and experiences, including charity work, public speaking, and policy development.

IMPACT

During her professional athletic career, Wellington was unrivaled as a female triathlete. She broke numerous records in the Ironman World Championships and various other endurance races around the world. As a symbol of strength and endurance, she became a role model for other athletes around the world. Since retiring from triathlons, she has become a patron of various charities, including Girls Education Nepal and Envision, a UK youth empowerment organization. She was honored as an Officer of the British Empire in December 2015.

PERSONAL LIFE

Wellington gave birth to a daughter in December 2015. She and her husband, Tom Lowe, live in Bristol, United Kingdom.

SUGGESTED READING

Churchill, L. "New Year Honours: Bristol's Four-Time Ironman World Champ Chrissie Wellington among Those Awarded." *Bristol Post*. Local World, 30 Dec. 2015. Accessed 2 May 2016.

Cracknell, James. "Ironman World Champion Chrissie Wellington Weighs Up Cycling for London 2012." *Telegraph*. 18 Nov. 2009, www.telegraph.co.uk/sport/olympics/triathlon/6599308/Ironman-world-champion-Chrissie-Wellington-weighs-up-cycling-for-London-2012.html. Accessed 25 Feb. 2019.

Goodchild, Sophie. "Meet Chrissie Wellington, the World's Fittest Woman." *Evening Standard*. 10 Feb. 2010, www.standard.co.uk/lifestyle/health/meet-chrissie-wellington-the-worlds-fittest-woman-6755182.html. Accessed 25 Feb. 2019.

Lobby, Mackenzie. "Chrissie Wellington Raises the Intensity." *ESPN*. 1 May 2014, www.espn.com/espnw/news-commentary/

article/10860898/espnw-chrissie-wellington-four-time-ironman-world-champion-set-tackle-three-highest-peaks-united-kingdom-4321-challenge. Accessed 25 Feb. 2019.

McRae, Donald. "Chrissie Wellington: I Have Got Nothing to Prove to Anyone Anymore." *Guardian*. 20 Feb. 2012, www.theguardian.com/sport/2012/feb/20/chrissie-wellington-ironman-triathlete. Accessed 25 Feb. 2019.

—*Patrick G. Cooper*

Photo by Keith Allison via Wikimedia Commons

Carson Wentz

Date of birth: December 30, 1992
Occupation: Football quarterback

Standing at six feet, five inches tall and weighing almost 240 pounds, boasting above-average arm strength and athleticism, and possessing a high football acumen, Carson Wentz was considered a prototype quarterback entering the National Football League (NFL). After enjoying a standout career at North Dakota State University (NDSU), Wentz was selected by the Philadelphia Eagles with the number two overall pick of the 2016 NFL Draft. Arriving in Philadelphia hailed as "the franchise's savior," as Zach Berman wrote for the *Philadelphia Inquirer* (4 Feb. 2019), he amassed a number of NFL and Eagles records as a rookie. He then effectively established himself as one of the league's best quarterbacks during his sophomore season in 2017, earning his first career Pro Bowl nod and second-team All-Pro honors. That year Wentz led the Eagles to a scorching 11–2 start and was the frontrunner for the league's Most Valuable Player (MVP) Award before suffering a season-ending knee injury.

Philadelphia went on to win Super Bowl LII without Wentz, and some analysts began questioning his future despite his early success. He returned as the Eagles' starter during the 2018 season and in eleven games posted the highest single-season completion percentage (69.6 percent) in franchise history. The Eagles went just 5–6 in those games, however, and another injury cut Wentz's season short for the second year in a row. The team again performed well without him, and rumors swirled that his intense, uncompromising personality had caused tension in the locker room. Regardless, the Eagles awarded Wentz a record-breaking contract extension in June 2019, signaling their faith in him as the team's long-term starter. As the talented quarterback explained to Berman, "I'm excited to put all this behind me, the injuries, and then do everything I can to just be healthy, stay healthy,

and get back on this driver's seat. I'm excited for where this team's heading."

EARLY LIFE

Carson James Wentz was born on December 30, 1992, in Raleigh, North Carolina, but moved with his family to North Dakota at the age of three. He was raised in the state capital of Bismarck. Wentz's father, Doug, a bank loan officer, and his mother, Cathy, who worked for the American Heart Association, divorced before he entered elementary school. Hyperactive as a child, Wentz channeled much of his energy into sports and other activities. He found a willing playmate in his older brother, Zach, with whom he shared a close bond and was extremely competitive. As Wentz recalled in a self-penned article for the *Players' Tribune* (25 Apr. 2016), "Baseball, football, checkers, number of plates consumed at a buffet—it did not matter what we were doing, everything was a competition."

Though his brother was admittedly the better athlete growing up, Wentz looked up to him as a role model and used him as a gauge for his own athletic development. Wentz was nonetheless a natural athlete himself and played competitively in six sports as a youth. It was football, however, that proved to be his favorite. "It was a faster pace, the contact, the competitiveness," Wentz told Tim McManus for *ESPN* (7 Sept. 2017). "I loved every aspect of it."

Wentz grew up rooting for the closest NFL team, the Minnesota Vikings, and idolizing the perennial Pro Bowl quarterback Brett Favre, who played for the rival Green Bay Packers. Drawn to Favre's gunslinger mentality and childlike on-field exuberance, Wentz dreamed of following in his footsteps one day. However, after joining the Bismarck youth football league in fifth grade, he started out not as a quarterback but as a running back, a position that allowed him to showcase his agility and toughness.

HIGH SCHOOL AND COLLEGE CAREER

Despite his reputation for toughness, when Wentz entered Bismarck's Century High School as a freshman, he stood just five feet, eight inches tall and weighed 125 pounds. Consequently, he initially served as a receiver, cornerback, free safety, and kick returner for Century's varsity football team. He also played on the school's baseball and basketball teams. After undergoing a nine-inch growth spurt, Wentz was moved to quarterback during his senior year, in which he led Century to the state semifinals. An academic standout as well, he graduated as the valedictorian of his class in 2011.

Despite those achievements, Wentz was lightly recruited by major Division I college football programs, with his only offer in the top-level Football Bowl Subdivision (FBS) coming from Central Michigan University. As a result, he opted to remain close to home and accepted a scholarship to attend North Dakota State University (NDSU), which competes in the Football Championship Subdivision (FCS). Wentz was given the redshirt designation as a freshman for development purposes. He then spent his next two seasons as the backup quarterback, watching as NDSU won three consecutive FCS titles.

While serving as backup, Wentz devoted himself to bulking up his lanky frame and to mastering the pro-style offense of the NDSU Bison. "He was a tall, lanky kid with a superstrong arm and speed," his teammate Zach Vraa noted to Greg Bishop for *Sports Illustrated* (27 Apr. 2016). "He picked things up faster than anybody I've ever seen." By the time he became the Bison's starting quarterback as a redshirt junior in 2014, Wentz had increased his weight to nearly 240 pounds. The added size further bolstered his game, and in his two seasons as a starter, he amassed a record of 20–3, leading the Bison to two more FCS national titles. As Wentz put it in the *Players' Tribune* article, "In high school, I learned how to lead a team for the first time. And in college, I learned how to win championships."

Despite missing eight games during his senior season due to a broken wrist, Wentz returned to play in the 2016 FCS national championship game and ultimately finished third in school history in career passing yards (5,115), touchdown passes (45), and completions (392). Meanwhile, he was twice recognized as the Academic All-American of the Year by the College Sports Information Directors of America. He graduated from NDSU with a degree in health and physical education, finishing with a perfect 4.0 grade-point average.

EAGLES' FRANCHISE QUARTERBACK

After his strong senior year, many analysts and scouts projected Wentz as a potential first round selection in the 2016 NFL Draft. His draft stock rose considerably, however, following impressive performances at several showcase events prior to the draft, namely the Senior Bowl and the NFL Scouting Combine, in which he displayed his arm strength, mobility, and intellect. This, combined with his prototypical size, immediately put him on the radar of several teams that held the top picks in the draft and were in need of an elite quarterback. Eagles general manager Howie Roseman, then the team's executive vice president of football operations, said to Austin Murphy for *Sports Illustrated* (2 May 2016), "I was struck by the presence he had, the leadership he showed in a setting with all sorts of guys from bigger schools."

The Eagles ultimately selected Wentz with the second overall pick, which made him the highest-drafted FCS quarterback in NFL history. In May 2016, he signed a four-year contract with the Eagles worth approximately $26.6 million. Wentz nonetheless entered the team's annual training camp that summer with the understanding that he would likely spend his rookie year developing behind incumbent starter Sam Bradford and backup quarterback Chase Daniel. Those plans changed, however, after the Eagles traded Bradford to the Minnesota Vikings eight days before the start of the 2016 regular season. Despite having barely played in the preseason, Wentz was designated the Eagles' starter by first-year head coach Doug Pederson.

Undaunted, Wentz began his NFL career by leading the Eagles to a 3–0 start, in which he threw for a combined 769 yards with five touchdown passes and no interceptions. Though he went through typical rookie growing pains as the season wore on, he started all sixteen games for the Eagles, who finished with a 7–9 record. He established a single-season franchise and NFL rookie record with 379 completions, and his 3,782 passing yards marked the fourth-highest total by a rookie in league history. During the season, Eagles center Jason Kelce spoke of Wentz's intangible qualities to Kevin Van Valkenburg for *ESPN* (28 Nov. 2016): "I think the best quarterbacks are always guys you naturally gravitate toward. Carson's work ethic, the confidence he shows, his competitiveness, all that leads to you wanting to fight for him that much harder."

MVP-CALIBER SEASON AND ACL INJURY

During the 2017 season Wentz not only solidified his status as the Eagles' franchise quarterback, but also made a case for being one of the NFL's best signal callers. He guided Philadelphia to a blistering 11–2 start, in which he threw for 3,296 passing yards and an NFL-best thirty-three touchdown passes, which established a franchise single-season record. Meanwhile, he threw just seven interceptions in those games. Wentz's breakthrough season came to a sudden halt, however, after he tore the anterior cruciate ligament (ACL) in his left knee in week fourteen, forcing him to undergo season-ending surgery. At the time, he was leading the NFL in a number of statistical categories for a quarterback and was considered the frontrunner for the league MVP Award.

As Wentz recovered from surgery, Eagles backup quarterback Nick Foles took his place and proceeded to author one of the most memorable fill-in jobs in NFL history. The team secured the top play-off seed in the National Football Conference (NFC) with a 13–3 record and advanced to Super Bowl LII. There, the Eagles upset the heavily favored New England Patriots to claim their first-ever Super Bowl title. While Wentz was happy to see his teammates succeed, it was also difficult for him to be stuck on the sidelines. "Obviously, it was frustrating watching," he told Berman. "Nick's a heck of a player. But at the same time, there's the real emotions that . . . I want to be out there."

Despite missing the Eagles' Super Bowl run, Wentz was named to his first Pro Bowl team and earned second-team All-Pro honors following the 2017 season. He also ranked third in MVP voting. He finished second in the NFL in touchdown passes, and his 101.9 passer rating ranked fourth in the league. Wentz was one of just four quarterbacks in NFL history to record at least thirty-three passing touchdowns and a 100-plus passer rating in their first or second season. The Eagles organization remained excited about their quarterback of the future despite his significant injury. "You just look at his whole sports life and the success he's had," coach Pederson said of Wentz to Lorenzo Reyes for *USA Today* (12 Oct. 2017) during the season. "He's the right player for the Philadelphia Eagles."

2018 SEASON RETURN AND CONTRACT EXTENSION

Entering the 2018 season, Wentz was ranked third overall in the annual NFL Top 100 Players survey—the highest-ever debut ranking on that list. Still, he was forced to miss the first two weeks of that season while continuing to recover from his ACL injury. Wentz went on to make eleven starts for the Eagles, passing for 3,074 yards, twenty-one touchdowns, and seven interceptions. He ranked third in the NFL with a franchise-best 69.9 completion percentage and finished seventh in the league with a career-high 102.2 passer rating. The Eagles, however, struggled overall, going just 5–6 in his starts.

Hampered by a nagging back injury, Wentz was shut down by the team during the last month of the season. Foles reassumed the starting role and rallied the Eagles to the postseason, though they ultimately lost in the divisional round to the New Orleans Saints. In the immediate wake of that loss, reports emerged that anonymous Eagles players and employees blamed Wentz for the team's 2018 struggles, characterizing him as selfish and egotistical. Wentz denied certain allegations, such as that he had refused to run plays designed for Foles but did admit his personality could be challenging. "I know I'm not perfect, I know I have flaws. So I'm not going to sit here and say it was inaccurate and completely made up," he told Berman. "You look at it and be like, 'Well, if someone did have this perception of me, why? What have I done wrong? What can I get better at?'"

Wentz quickly won the public support of the Eagles front office, coaches, and teammates. Then, after letting Foles leave the team in free agency, the Eagles proved their full commitment to Wentz in June 2019, when they signed him to a four-year contract extension worth $128 million. The contract included a record-setting more than $107 million in guaranteed money through the 2024 season. "The blueprint is always, 'Can you find a franchise quarterback?' Is he going to be the personality and the leader and the talent that you want?" Eagles owner Jeffrey Lurie said, as quoted by Daniel Gallen for *PennLive* (6 June 2019). "We're very, very lucky to have somebody like Carson. . . . A highly competitive, very Type-A personality, demanding, very smart, obsessed with winning and winning big, respected by everybody. Just you can't really draw it up much better."

PERSONAL LIFE

Wentz married Madison Oberg in July 2018. A devout Christian, in 2017 he founded the Audience of One (AO1) Foundation, a faith-based charitable organization serving various communities worldwide. He was also involved in the Mission of Hope program in Haiti. Wentz's favorite hobbies included hunting and fishing.

SUGGESTED READING

Berman, Zach. "Eagles Quarterback Carson Wentz Reflects on Challenging Year, Recent Criticism: 'I Know I'm Not Perfect.'" *The Philadelphia Inquirer*, 4 Feb. 2019, www.inquirer.com/eagles/carson-wentz-eagles-playoffs-mike-groh-nick-foles-acl-injury-selfish-20190204.html. Accessed 29 July 2019.

Bishop, Greg. "Inside the Low-Profile Life of Top QB Prospect Carson Wentz." *Sports Illustrated*, 27 Apr. 2016, www.si.com/nfl/2016/04/27/nfl-draft-2016-carson-wentz-north-dakota-state. Accessed 29 July 2019.

Gallen, Daniel. "Carson Wentz, Philadelphia Eagles Agree to Four-Year Contract Extension Reportedly Worth $128 Million, Including Record Guarantee." *PennLive*, 6 June 2019, www.pennlive.com/philadelphiaeagles/2019/06/carson-wentz-philadelphia-eagles-agree-to-four-year-contract-extension.html. Accessed 29 July 2019.

Murphy, Austin. "Art of the Deals: How QBs Goff, Wentz and Lynch Got Drafted." *Sports Illustrated*, 2 May 2016, www.si.com/nfl/2016/05/03/nfl-draft-jared-goff-carson-wentz-paxton-lynch-first-round. Accessed 29 July 2019.

Van Valkenburg, Kevin. "How Eagles Rookie QB Carson Wentz Won Teammates' Trust." *ESPN*, 28 Nov. 2016, www.espn.com/nfl/story/_/id/18147502/how-carson-wentz-won-philadelphia-eagles-teammates-being-less-perfect-nfl-2016. Accessed 29 July 2019.

Wentz, Carson. "How We Play Football in North Dakota." *The Players' Tribune*, 25 Apr. 2016, www.theplayerstribune.com/en-us/articles/carson-wentz-north-dakota-state-nfl-draft. Accessed 29 July 2019.

Wentz, Carson. "Q&A with Eagles Quarterback Carson Wentz." Interview by Tim McManus. *ESPN*, 7 Sept. 2017, www.espn.com/blog/nfceast/post/_/id/77700/qa-with-eagles-quarterback-carson-wentz. Accessed 29 July 2019.

—*Chris Cullen*

Zach Williams

Date of birth: March 5, 1981
Occupation: Musician

Redemption stories are among the most powerful stories human beings can experience and share with one another. That concept is very clear to Zach Williams, who spent years living a drug-addled, alcohol-fueled life as a rock musician, only to give it up in 2012 because he felt he had a calling to be closer to God. He quit his band and returned home, content to be involved with his local Baptist church, eventually serving as a campus director and worship leader. "I was running from all these things that I was trying to succeed so hard at but failed. I was trying to put the blame on everybody else, but instead it was all my fault and I just needed to own up to it and be a man about it," he said to Jeannie Law for the *Christian Post* (24 Oct. 2016).

Through his work singing at church, Williams came into contact with a producer and songwriter from Essential Music Publishing who suggested they collaborate on Christian music. His first album with Essential Records, *Chain Breaker* (2016), produced a slew of worship music chart hits and went on to become a Grammy Award–winning record in 2018. Following this success, Williams continued to hope that his music would resonate powerfully with audiences, and that his story of redemption would connect with others in need. He sought to give back through charitable works connected with his church, and in late 2018, he performed for inmates at a prison in Nashville, Tennessee. The performance was captured as the EP *Survivor: Live from Harding Prison* (2018).

EARLY LIFE AND EDUCATION

Zach Williams was raised in the area of Jonesboro, Arkansas, by devoutly Christian parents. His father, who worked in construction, led worship services; and his mother sang in their church. Throughout his childhood, he would later emphasize in interviews, he was comforted by his closeness with God. Although his dad was a musician, Williams never played an instrument himself when he was young; instead, his passion was sports.

In high school, Williams's skills on the basketball court were so keen that college scouts soon took an interest in him. However, he also began partying with classmates and experimenting with drugs and alcohol, behavior that effectively killed his chances for a Division I scholarship. Eventually he would admit that the people he chose to hang out with as a young adult proved to be detrimental to him. "For me, the crowd that I was around had a lot to do with the things that I got involved in. I kind of ran from the Lord. I felt like the Lord had a calling

Photo by John Shearer/Getty Images

on my life at an early age but it scared me," he explained to Law.

Despite missing out on his athletic scholarship, he played basketball in a men's intramural league and eventually secured a full scholarship to a junior college. Unfortunately, the partying lifestyle again got the better of him, as drugs and alcohol began to exert an even greater influence in his life. Then, before playing his first college game, he tore several ligaments in his ankle and was benched for the entire season, putting an end to his basketball dreams. His inability to play basketball prompted him to turn his attention elsewhere, and he discovered his roommate's guitar. After teaching himself to play, he realized his love for music and songwriting. In an interview with Carla Hinton for the *Oklahoman* (15 Apr. 2017), Williams recalled, "It was like the Lord had other plans. When I started playing guitar, I fell in love with music and I never really looked back at sports again."

HARD LIVING AND CHRISTIAN CONVERSION

Music and living the lifestyle of a rock star became so central to Williams's life that he dropped out of college shortly before completing a design degree. He returned home to work with his father's construction company and pursue music after work hours, playing wherever he could. He believed that no matter how hard he partied at night, as long as he got up in the morning to work with his father, he would be fine.

Around 2007, as Williams was struggling through a divorce, he helped form a rock band, Zach Williams and the Reformation. His role in the group involved playing acoustic guitar, providing lead vocals, and songwriting. The band released two albums independently, *Electric Revival* (2009) and *A Southern Offering* (2011) and began to tour widely across the southern United States and also in Europe. Williams's wild lifestyle continued unabated until 2011, when he received a warning from a doctor that he had the early stages of esophageal cancer. Though the doctor told him to change the way that he lived, it took another year before a radical change took place in his life, which came in large part through an invitation to a local church.

Williams and his second wife, Crystal, were asked to attend a local church and found they were met with much love and support. They began getting involved with the congregation as much as possible through a wide variety of events. Yet although Williams was on the road to a more positive lifestyle, he later noted that he did not fully embrace his renewed Christian identity until he was on a tour with his band and heard Big Daddy Weave's "Redeemed" playing on the radio. For Williams, who had listened to Christian music while working alongside his father, it felt as if God had been speaking directly to him. He needed to clean up his life and make a change for the better. "God just spoke to me in that moment and gave me a glimpse of what my life would be like if I turned to Him and used my music for His glory. So I called my wife from Spain, I quit my band and came home and we started going to church," he told Hinton.

AWARD-WINNING RECORDING ARTIST

When Williams quit his band in 2012 and began attending and volunteering at Central Baptist Church in Jonesboro, he initially had no intention of returning to recording or performing music, apart from the duties he took on when he was eventually invited to serve as a campus director and worship leader for the church. Then one day, while at Central Baptist's flagship church, he made an impression on someone in attendance that altered his expectations of the future. Recalling how this development occurred, he told Jim Asker for *Billboard* (12 Dec. 2017), "I was . . . just happy to sing worship on Sundays and be part of the community. One Sunday, I just happened to be at their flagship church and [songwriter and producer] Jonathan Smith happened to be in church. He asked me to have coffee with him; one thing led to another and we were writing songs together."

In 2016, Williams signed with Provident Label Group's Essential Records as a Christian solo artist. His first single, "Chain Breaker," about how Jesus had released him from his vices, held the top spot on the Billboard Christian Airplay chart for fifteen weeks. Cowritten with Smith and Mia Fieldes, the song had secured his signing. It also reached the number-one position on the Billboard Hot Christian Songs chart and went on to earn him his first Grammy Award nomination for Best Contemporary Christian Music Performance/Song. Williams released his debut full-length album in the worship music genre, also titled *Chain Breaker*, digitally later in 2016 and in physical format early the next year. The record additionally features the track "Old Church Choir," which also hit the top of the Christian charts.

In 2018, Williams was nominated in the Top Christian Artist category at the Billboard Music Awards, and "Old Church Choir" was nominated for Top Christian Song. At the 2018 Grammy Awards he won the trophy for Best Contemporary Christian Music Album for *Chain Breaker*.

CONTINUED MUSICAL INFLUENCE

Williams's third single off of *Chain Breaker*, "Fear Is a Liar," peaked at number three on the Billboard Christian Airplay chart. The song describes how fear is humanity's greatest enemy and can be used by the devil to keep people from living their lives in freedom. "For anybody who was struggling with fear or going through something, I hope this song gives them hope, to call the devil out," he explained to Markos Papadatos for *Digital Journal* (6 Apr. 2018). Another song from the album, "Survivor," similarly moved up the chart to claim the third position.

In his work with his church, Williams also became involved with ministering to prisoners. The Tennessee-based program Men of Valor asked him to come and perform live for a group of inmates, and he did so at a Nashville prison in 2018. He even recorded a live album there, the EP *Survivor: Live from Harding Prison* (2018), following in the footsteps of his musical hero Johnny Cash, who also performed for inmates and recorded albums from prisons. "You could tell every one of these guys were just grateful we were there," Williams said to Jeannie Law for the *Christian Post* (12 Oct. 2018). "They don't get stuff like this very often. We weren't going in and trying to exploit these guys or just do something to make a record. We just wanted to go in and hang out and play some music for these guys."

The live EP was later nominated for a 2019 Grammy for Best Contemporary Christian Music Album. In June 2019 "Rescue Story," the first single off of Williams's sophomore full-length album of the same name, was released. When asked about his career, he told Asker, "I'm just going to continue to work hard, keep writing and hope that anyone that hears my music or comes to a show will also see the message of Christ in me. That's all I ask for."

PERSONAL LIFE

Williams and his wife, Crystal, had two children together. The musician noted that his family contributed greatly to his success, a fact that helped keep him humble and grounded. "My wife and kids stay home, while I travel a lot. My wife holds the fort down at home. She's the rock for our family, so that I can do what I love to do," he said to Papadatos.

SUGGESTED READING

"About." *Zach Williams*, www.zachwilliams-music.com/about. Accessed 9 Sept. 2019.

Law, Jeannie. "Christian Singer Zach Williams Records New Album Live from Prison." *The Christian Post*, 12 Oct. 2018, www.christian-post.com/news/christian-singer-zach-wil-liams-records-new-album-live-from-prison.html. Accessed 9 Sept. 2019.

Williams, Zach. "Rocker-Turned-Christian Musician Zach Williams Breaks Free from Drugs and Alcohol with 'Chain Breaker'." Interview by Jeannie Law. *The Christian Post*, 24 Oct. 2016, www.christianpost.com/news/former-rocker-zach-williams-breaks-free-destructive-lifestyle-drugs-alcohol-chain-breaker-inter-view.html. Accessed 9 Sept. 2019.

Papadatos, Markos. "Zach Williams Talks Grammy Win, 'Fear Is a Liar,' Lauren Daigle." *Digital Journal*, 6 Apr. 2018, www.digitaljournal.com/entertainment/music/zach-williams-talks-grammy-win-fear-is-a-liar-lauren-daigle/article/519217. Accessed 9 Sept. 2019.

Williams, Zach. "Zach Williams Discusses Concert Tour." Interview by Carla Hinton. *The Oklahoman*, 15 Apr. 2017, oklahoman.com/article/5545544/zach-williams-discusses-con-cert-tour. Accessed 9 Sept. 2019.

Williams, Zach. "Zach Williams on His Chart-Topping 2017: 'I Am Doing What God Wants Me to Do.'" Interview by Jim Asker. *Billboard*, 12 Dec. 2017, www.billboard.com/articles/columns/chart-beat/8070257/zach-williams-interview-chart-topping-2017. Accessed 9 Sept. 2019.

SELECTED WORKS

Electric Revival (with Zach Williams and the Reformation), 2009; *A Southern Offering* (with Zach Williams and the Reformation), 2011; *Chain Breaker*, 2016; *Survivor: Live from Harding Prison*, 2018

—*Christopher Mari*

Whitney Wolfe Herd

Date of birth: Jul7 1, 1989
Occupation: Entrepreneur

Whitney Wolfe Herd, a tech entrepreneur, has made a name for herself as one of the richest self-made women in the United States. "Some users of [her app] Bumble . . . are lucky enough to swipe right and find love, a new friend or a job opportunity," Madeline Berg wrote for *Forbes* (11 July 2018). "Wolfe Herd, though, may be the luckiest of all: The app, which *Forbes* values at $1 billion, has brought its 29-year-old founder a $230 million fortune."

That mention of "swiping right" refers to the mechanism by which users of Bumble browse the matchmaking app on their mobile devices: swiping left when a profile is of no interest to them and right when they glimpse a possible match. The now-ubiquitous method was popularized a few years earlier at Tinder, another dating app that Wolfe Herd helped launch. Despite Tinder's massive success, she parted ways with the company in 2014, because of insurmountable tensions with its male cofounders, and she later filed a sexual-harassment lawsuit that netted her $1 million when it settled.

The bitter experience, during which Wolfe Herd was subjected to vicious online trolling and anonymous vitriol, deeply influenced Bumble,

Photo by Patrick T. Fallon/Bloomberg via Getty Images

whose advertising features such catchphrases as "Be the CEO your parents always wanted you to marry" and "We're not playing the field, we're leveling it." Wolfe Herd recalled crying for months and told Kimya Kavehkar for *Paper Magazine* (7 Mar. 2016) of her realization: "You know what? I'm okay, I'm healthy, I have a support system. There's definitely a 13-year-old out there who has zero support system, and they're reading [sexist] stuff like this about themselves. How does that make them feel? So if I am in this position to change that, it's pretty much my duty to do so."

Bumble's mission and ethos are strongly rooted in female empowerment: with Bumble, if both a man and woman swipe right on each other, indicating mutual interest, the woman must make contact or the match cannot proceed. "If you look at where we are in the current heteronormative rules surrounding dating, the unwritten rule puts the woman a peg under the man—the man feels the pressure to go first in a conversation, and the woman feels pressure to sit on her hands," Wolfe Herd explained to Leora Yashari for *Vanity Fair* (7 Aug. 2015). "If we can take some of the pressure off the man and put some of that encouragement in the woman's lap, I think we are taking a step in the right direction, especially in terms of really being true to feminism. I think we are the first feminist, or first attempt at a feminist dating app."

EARLY YEARS AND EDUCATION
Whitney Wolfe Herd was born in 1989 in Salt Lake City, Utah, to property developer Michael Wolfe and homemaker Kelly Wolfe. She has one younger sister, Danielle. When the future entrepreneur was in elementary school, her family took an extended sabbatical in Paris, France, where she learned to speak French.

Back in Utah, she attended Judge Memorial Catholic High School, and after graduating in 2007, she entered Southern Methodist University (SMU) in Dallas, Texas. There she hoped to study marketing, but ironically, she was not admitted to the school's Temerlin Advertising Institute for Education and Research and was forced instead to go with her second choice: international studies at SMU's Dedman College of Humanities and Sciences.

She launched her first entrepreneurial venture at age nineteen, while still in college. In the aftermath of the catastrophic BP *Deepwater Horizon* oil spill in the Gulf of Mexico, she began crafting bamboo tote bags and sending the money from their sale to the nonprofit Oceans Future Project; when celebrities like Nicole Richie and Kate Bosworth began sporting the accessory, the enterprise took off.

The Kappa Kappa Gamma sorority sister studied abroad during her junior year, attending the Sorbonne, in Paris. She graduated in 2011 and traveled to Southeast Asia to volunteer in orphanages.

EARLY TECH CAREER
After returning from Asia, Wolfe Herd settled in Los Angeles and took a job at a start-up incubator called Hatch Labs, which was run by digital-media business IAC, the owners of the online-dating behemoth Match.com. She was attracted to the tech field, she has told interviewers, because of its potential to make a positive impact on society. While working at Hatch, she met Sean Rad, a driven entrepreneur working on an app for retail loyalty cards called Cardify. In 2012, after Cardify had failed to take off as hoped, Rad invited Wolfe to collaborate with him on a new venture.

Joined by a small team of computer coders and designers, they came up with the idea for a dating app that would allow users to swipe through the Facebook profiles of local singles. Wolfe Herd's contributions included the name of the app, Tinder, which she reportedly thought of while reminiscing about the fireplace at her family's vacation cabin. Named the vice president of marketing, she also had the idea of marketing the new app on college campuses—a major contributor to its early success.

HARASSMENT
During those heady early days, Wolfe Herd briefly dated her direct supervisor, Justin Mateen. When the relationship ended, Mateen became verbally abusive, threatened retaliation if she became involved with anyone else, and stripped

her of her cofounder title; instead of disciplining him, Rad, the CEO, blamed Wolfe Herd and terminated her. Although she tried to resolve the matter on her own, in 2014, unable to bear the tension and animosity, Wolfe Herd filed a lawsuit for sexual harassment. It was settled for an estimated $1 million, but in the interim, she received a steady stream of online abuse and bullying from anonymous trolls. "I was being told the ugliest things by complete strangers, and they were having full debates about me," she recalled to Clare O'Connor for *Forbes* (12 Dec. 2017). "I wasn't running for office. I wasn't trying to be on a reality show. I was just a girl who left somewhere."

Of her decision to file the suit, Wolfe Herd told Alyson Shontell for *Business Insider* (27 Jan. 2015), "It wasn't about the money. It was about my hard work. I had been erased from the company's history. . . . I'm not here to take credit fully for Tinder. It's about the team, and I think I played a really important role in the team. I was there from inception of this app that's now known by the world."

BUMBLE

Once that ugly period was behind her, Wolfe Herd moved back to Texas and began thinking of her next step, hoping to do something to address online bullying. She envisioned launching a women-only social network called Merci, which would focus on positivity and empowerment. One day, however, she received an email from Russian entrepreneur Andrey Andreev, the founder of the massive global dating site Badoo, whom she had met years before. He proposed that she join Badoo now that she was free of Tinder. Not wanting to sign on as anyone's employee, she pitched Merci to him instead. Andreev was receptive to the idea of a women-centric brand but believed that the two should stick with what they both knew best: dating sites. Luckily for Wolfe Herd, the Tinder settlement had not included a non-compete clause, and together the pair launched a new site, Bumble, with Andreev as majority owner and Wolfe Herd as founder, CEO, and minority owner.

The app went live in December 2014 and attracted 100,000 downloads in its first month alone. Within twelve months, it had racked up more than 15 million unique conversations and 80 million matches. By the end of 2017, Bumble boasted 22 million registered users, and by early 2019, that number had rocketed to 47 million.

Much of that success has been attributed to the innovations Wolfe Herd had insisted on: a female user was required to initiate any one-on-one contact with a male user (the rule did not hold for same-gender matches); initial contact had to occur within twenty-four hours of the swiped match, to encourage women to be proactive and confident; and men could not use the shirtless mirror selfies so popular on Tinder. "For the first time in the tech space, the woman has been encouraged to be on an even playing field," she told Yashari. She added, "On Bumble, by having the lady make the first move, [the man] doesn't feel rejection or aggression—he feels flattered. That one little shift . . . guides the conversation in a very different way, and that sets the tone for that conversation, that relationship, that friendship, whatever that is, to be a confident one."

ATTRACTING NOTICE

In addition to the dating function, Bumble added BFF, a service that focuses on platonic female friendships, in 2016, and Bizz, a business networking service for young women, in 2017. Also in 2016 Wolfe Herd and Andreev invested heavily in Chappy, a dating app for the gay community that asks users to rank potential suitors on a scale that includes such categories as "Mr. Right," "Mr. Right Now," and "Mr. Who Knows."

In 2018 Wolfe Herd made news headlines when she adopted a ban on images of weaponry within the Bumble app, with the notable exception of armed, uniformed members of military and law enforcement. She made the decision in the wake of the Parkland, Florida, school shooting and felt that such images were not conducive to the safe, kind environment she had striven to build.

That same year Bumble was sued by Tinder's parent company, Match, which accused it of having too similar a business model and alleging patent and trademark violations. Berg posited in her *Forbes* article that the lawsuit was a reaction to Wolfe Herd's refusal of the Match Group's $450 million buyout offer in 2017. Bumble countersued for damages, alleging buyout talks were used to steal Bumble's trade secrets. As of late 2018, the two companies were still involved in complex litigation proceedings.

Bumble purchased airtime during the 2019 Super Bowl to air a commercial starring legendary tennis player Serena Williams. Notable for being directed by a woman, the spot extols the company's mission of helping women "make the first move—in life, in love, in business."

Wolfe Herd has been included on numerous lists of the most important women in tech by such outlets as *Forbes, Time, Elle, Business Insider*, and *TechCrunch*.

PERSONAL LIFE

In December 2013 the entrepreneur was on a ski vacation in Aspen, Colorado, when a friend introduced her to Michael Herd, a restaurateur and energy businessman. The pair were engaged in June 2015 and married Positano, Italy, in

October 2017. The couple live in Austin, Texas, where Bumble is headquartered.

SUGGESTED READING

Berg, Madeline. "Bumble's Whitney Wolfe Herd Swiped Right to a $230 Million Fortune." *Forbes*, 11 July 2018, www.forbes.com/sites/maddieberg/2018/07/11/whitney-wolfe-heard-bumble-net-worth/. Accessed 18 Jan. 2019.

Kavehkar, Kimya. "Whitney Wolfe: The Matchmaker." *Paper Magazine*, 7 Mar. 2016, www.papermag.com/whitney-wolfe-bumble-it-girls-1647547057.html. Accessed 18 Jan. 2019.

Macon, Alexandra. "Bumble Founder Whitney Wolfe's Whirlwind Wedding Was a True Celebration of Southern Italy." *Vogue*, 5 Oct. 2017, www.vogue.com/article/bumble-founder-whitney-wolfe-michael-herd-positano-wedding. Accessed 18 Jan. 2019.

O'Connor, Clare. "Billion-Dollar Bumble: How Whitney Wolfe Herd Built America's Fastest-Growing Dating App." *Forbes*, 12 Dec. 2017, www.forbes.com/sites/clareoconnor/2017/11/14/billion-dollar-bumble-how-whitney-wolfe-herd-built-americas-fastest-growing-dating-app/. Accessed 18 Jan. 2019.

Shontell, Alyson. "What It's Like to Found a $750 Million Startup, Go through a Sexual-Harassment Lawsuit, and Start All Over by Age 25." *Business Insider*, 27 Jan. 2015, www.businessinsider.com/tinder-co-founder-whitney-wolfe-and-bumble-2015-1. Accessed 18 Jan. 2019.

Thurmond, Sarah. "Queen Bee." *Austin Monthly*, Aug. 2015, www.austinmonthly.com/AM/August-2015/Queen-Bee. Accessed 18 Jan. 2019.

Yashari, Leora. "Meet the Tinder Co-Founder Trying to Change Online Dating Forever." *Vanity Fair*, 7 Aug. 2015, www.vanityfair.com/culture/2015/08/bumble-app-whitney-wolfe. Accessed 18 Jan. 2019.

—*Mari Rich*

Letitia Wright

Date of birth: October 31, 1993
Occupation: Actor

In 2018 actor Letitia Wright enjoyed a remarkable breakout year, most noted for her fan-favorite turn in the critically acclaimed box-office smash *Black Panther* as the irreverent, charming tech genius Shuri, the younger sister of the titular superhero. Just months later she reprised the role in the ensemble blockbuster *Avengers:*

Photo by Gage Skidmore via Wikimedia Commons

Infinity War, establishing her as part of the next generation of stars in the hugely popular Marvel Cinematic Universe. Wright also appeared in director Steven Spielberg's *Ready Player One* and the Liam Neeson–led action film *The Commuter* in 2018, making her the year's top actor in terms of domestic box-office earnings.

Yet while her rise to success was rapid, Wright insisted that her devotion to her art would remain. "I pride myself on keeping it the same as when I came into acting, to not just change the lane and take everything, just because it may have a big name or a big budget," she told Alex Ritman for the *Hollywood Reporter* (7 Nov. 2018). "Am I right for this part? Is this what I should be playing? If something feels off in my spirit, I know that's God's way of saying, 'You shouldn't do that.'"

EARLY LIFE

Letitia Wright was born in Georgetown, Guyana, on October 31, 1993. Her mother was a teacher and an accountant; her father did agricultural and security work. When not in school, her time was spent surrounded by her extended family, which included cousins, aunts, grandmothers, and a great-grandmother. Work, in her family's mindset, consisted of doing practical things, not anything remotely artistic. "Art, music, acting, there is not an industry there," Wright said in an interview with Jenny Comita for *W Magazine* (23 July 2018). But she felt an early calling for something more in her life, though acting specifically was not at the forefront of her mind. It was her family's decision to move to the United Kingdom that supplied opportunities for other pursuits. "I was only 8 years old, but I felt like, This is my chance!" she told Comita.

Wright's family settled in Tottenham, a working-class part of London, where she strove to replicate her classmates' accents. "I would practice at home, to feel more accepted," she told Comita. "That's probably where the acting started." When she was twelve, Wright's instinctive acting nature came into its own when she was asked to play pioneering African American civil rights icon Rosa Parks in her school's Black History Month play. She so impressed everyone with her perfect Alabama accent that the show was later restaged at a nearby community theater. Emboldened, she continued to act.

As a teenager, Wright was inspired to take her acting seriously after seeing *Akeelah and Bee* (2006), an independent film about an African American girl skilled at spelling. She found that she could relate to the movie's protagonist in a way she had never done before. She then began trying to score a talent agent by distributing her credentials—including a head shot she took in the bathroom mirror—door-to-door across London. After that proved fruitless, she began emailing casting directors in earnest. None replied, and her parents were skeptical of the whole endeavor, but she persisted. "I kept nagging one in particular until the receptionist got sick of me and was finally like, 'Okay, just come in.'" Wright recalled to Comita. "I did the reading and got signed on the spot. My mom was like, 'Wow, this really is a thing!'"

EARLY ACTING CAREER

At age sixteen, Wright enrolled at the London Identity School of Acting. The school had been established in 2003 by actor-agent Femi Oguns to supply more diverse talent to the British film industry. After seeing Wright perform in classes, Oguns immediately signed her to his in-house talent agency and began promoting her. Her first role came on the longtime BBC hospital program *Holby City* in 2011. Further appearances on British television soon followed, most notably on the acclaimed series *Top Boy* in 2011. That year she also made her film debut, in the low-budget crime movie *Victim*.

Wright continued to rack up credits and experience. Among her roles were a small part in the 2012 film *My Brother the Devil* and appearances on the series *Coming Up* (2013), *Chasing Shadows* (2014), *Banana* (2015), and *Cucumber* (2015). She also earned praise for her performance in an episode of the cult favorite *Doctor Who* in 2015.

Wright's first starring role came in 2015, when she appeared in the coming-of-age drama *Urban Hymn* by acclaimed director Michael Caton-Jones. In the film Wright portrays a troubled teenager with a sensational singing voice who must choose between the people who have brought her down and the care worker who inspires her to a better life. Set against the backdrop of the 2011 England riots, which were a response to the Great Recession and high unemployment, the film provided Wright with an opportunity to create an inspirational character. Caton-Jones had high praise for the actor, comparing her talent to that of Leonardo DiCaprio, whom the director had worked with in one of his breakthrough roles. "She was just fascinating from the beginning, loose and fluid," Caton-Jones told Dalya Alberge for the *Guardian* (4 Apr. 2015). "My instinct is she can be as big as she wants. Letitia is just gobsmackingly brilliant. The camera loves her. She has an emotional honesty." Critics agreed, as Wright's performance earned her a nomination as most promising newcomer at the 2016 British Independent Film Awards.

DEPRESSION AND CONVERSION

Urban Hymn brought Wright to the attention of Hollywood, and she appeared poised to immediately take the next step toward stardom. However, by 2015 she was struggling with deep depression that consumed her private life. She could function while on set or working, but whenever she was alone, she found herself filled with anxiety. "When I wasn't acting I was full of fear and doubt, trying to fill this void inside of me any way I could: drinking, smoking," she told Comita. "It was bad."

Although Wright initially kept her struggles to herself, she later opened up to interviewers about the experience in the hope of inspiring others who might be going through similar challenges. Looking back, she felt that much of the problem came from a desire for acceptance from others as a person and as an artist. This damaged her sense of self-worth; cruel comments on social media could be devastating. For Wright, the answer was faith, which she discovered after joining some actor friends at a Bible study. "I needed to take a break from acting," Wright recalled in an interview on British television, as quoted in *Relevant* magazine (21 Feb. 2018). "I went on a journey to discover my relationship with God, and I became a Christian. It really just gave me so much love and light within myself. I felt secure, like I didn't need validation from anyone else, or getting a part. My happiness wasn't dependent on that, it was dependent on my relationship with God."

The experience proved to be revelatory, so much so that Wright seriously considered giving up acting to pursue her newly found Christian faith with as much vigor as she could muster. Notably, she turned down the chance to appear in a film starring Nicole Kidman, among many other offers. However, she ultimately felt that acting was indeed her calling and returned to work reinvigorated. Yet she now had the confidence to take on only projects she truly felt were right for her. "Anything I attach myself to needs to have a purpose," she told Comita. "If it feels like a red light in any way, I don't do it."

Wright continued to find success after her brief break from acting. In 2016 she appeared in the second season of the sci-fi series *Humans* as Renie, a girl pretending to be a robot. The next year she was featured in an episode of the acclaimed anthology series *Black Mirror*. That performance earned her a Primetime Emmy Award nomination for outstanding supporting actress.

MARVEL CINEMATIC UNIVERSE

While the television projects Wright took on helped get her back into acting, the film roles she agreed to following her spiritual awakening led to her true breakout in 2018. She appeared in four feature films released that year, all of which went on to box-office success. Her parts in *The Commuter*, a thriller starring Liam Neeson, and in famed director Stephen Spielberg's adaptation of the hit sci-fi novel *Ready Player One* were small but helped raise her profile in Hollywood. However, it was her role as Shuri in the groundbreaking *Black Panther* that rocketed Wright to fame as an up-and-coming star.

In both Marvel's comics and films, Shuri is the younger sister of T'Challa, the superhero Black Panther. A princess of the ultra-technologically advanced African country of Wakanda, she is also one of the world's smartest scientists. In the *Black Panther* film, critics and fans alike considered Wright's Shuri a scene-stealer as she creates all sorts of impressive gadgets, including upgrades to her brother's battle suit. Wright won much praise for her playful, enthusiastic portrayal of the tech genius as an easygoing teenager ever ready to tease her big brother and also capable of fighting her own fights. According to Joanna Robinson for *Vanity Fair* (7 Feb. 2018), *Black Panther* director Ryan Coogler described Shuri as "the love and the light" of the film.

Later in 2018 Wright reprised the role of Shuri with a brief but important appearance in *Avengers: Infinity War*, which set numerous box-office records and became one of the highest-grossing movies of all time. She was also contracted to continue in the Marvel Cinematic Universe with *Avengers: Endgame* (2019) and an eventual *Black Panther* sequel. Wright embraced the enthusiastic response to Shuri wholeheartedly, noting especially the role's potential to inspire young people. She also stated her commitment to furthering diversity in the film industry however possible. "Let's venture out and do projects with people of different ethnicities," she told Robinson. "Just an equality across the board."

In recognition of her rapid ascent to the spotlight, Wright received the EE Rising Star Award from the British Academy of Film and Television Arts (BAFTA) in 2019. That year she also appeared in the Amazon Studios film *Guava Island*, starring Donald Glover and Rihanna.

SUGGESTED READING

Alberge, Dalya. "Letitia Wright, Britain's Newest Rising Screen Star, Says Black Actors Need More Positive Roles." *The Guardian*, 4 Apr. 2015, www.theguardian.com/film/2015/apr/05/letitia-wright-britains-rising-screen-star-michael-caton-jones-leonardo-dicaprio. Accessed 11 Apr. 2019.

"'Black Panther' Breakout Star Letitia Wright Shares How Christianity Changed Her Life." *Relevant*, 21 Feb. 2018, relevantmagazine.com/culture/black-panther-breakout-star-letitia-wright-shares-testimony-british-talk-show. Accessed 11 Apr. 2019.

Comita, Jenny. "How Letitia Wright Finally Took Control of Her Career by Saying 'No.'" *W*, 23 July 2018, www.wmagazine.com/story/letitia-wright-black-panther-w-magazine-cover. Accessed 11 Apr. 2019.

Ritman, Alex. "'Black Panther' Breakout Letitia Wright on How Faith Rescued Her from a 'Very Dark Place.'" *The Hollywood Reporter*, 7 Nov. 2018, www.hollywoodreporter.com/features/black-panther-star-letitia-wright-how-faith-saved-her-1158459. Accessed 11 Apr. 2019.

Robinson, Joanna. "Black Panther Breakout Letitia Wright Smashes Disney Princess Expectations." *Vanity Fair*, 7 Feb. 2018, www.vanityfair.com/hollywood/2018/02/black-panther-who-plays-shuri-letitia-wright-profile. Accessed 11 Apr. 2019.

SELECTED WORKS

Urban Hymn, 2015; *Humans*, 2016; *Black Mirror*, 2017; *The Commuter*, 2018; *Black Panther*, 2018; *Ready Player One*, 2018; *Avengers: Infinity War*, 2018; *Guava Island*, 2019; *Avengers: Endgame*, 2019

—Christopher Mari

Tom Wright

Date of birth: September 8, 1957
Occupation: Architect

With its iconic sail-shaped design, the Burj Al Arab (Tower of the Arabs) hotel in Dubai, in the United Arab Emirates (UAE), has wowed observers as a marvel of modern architecture and opulence since its unveiling in 1999. Often

Photo by Frogmoretom via Wikimedia Commons

billed as the world's only seven-star hotel, it has become a lasting symbol for the city of Dubai, which has undergone unprecedented growth and development since the early 1990s. Had it not been for the creative genius of British architect Tom Wright, however, the hotel, which forms the centerpiece of the Jumeirah Beach Resort, might have never emerged as the iconic structure it is today. Wright served as the hotel's design director while working for global engineering giant Atkins and, in the years since, has built a strong international reputation for his forward-thinking yet practical designs, which often take on nautical themes.

After launching his architecture career in the early 1980s, Wright joined Atkins in 1991 and remained with the company for more than two decades, during which he helped to significantly grow its architecture division. Since 2013 he has run and operated his own high-end architectural practice, WKK, with two former Atkins design directors. The firm, which is based in the United Kingdom, has designed and built a wide array of stunning development projects, from office towers to mixed-use spaces, in locations all over the world, and has also lent its vision to cruise ships.

EARLY LIFE AND EDUCATION

Tom Wright was born on September 8, 1957, in Croydon, a neighborhood in South London, England. His parents were schoolteachers. At an early age, Wright, who was naturally creative and artistic, became drawn to architecture, which is "one of the most enduring forms of art," as he wrote in a self-penned article for the *Atkins* website (10 Dec. 2007). "Once a building is built,

people have to live in it, work in it, play in it," he added. "You affect their mood and life in a big way."

When Wright was eighteen years old, his father took him sailing for the first time, igniting a lifelong passion for the sport and for the sea that would have a major influence on his architectural designs. After graduating from the prestigious Royal Russell School, located in the Addington area of Croydon, he attended Kingston Polytechnic in southwest London, where he studied architecture. In 1983 he qualified as an architect and became a member of the Royal Institute of British Architects, a global professional organization.

CREATING A GLOBAL ICON

Shortly after qualifying, Wright joined Marshall, Haines and Barrow, a small architectural firm in London. He quickly earned a series of promotions, rising from associate to senior associate in a matter of years. During that time, the firm won a number of design competitions. In 1986, when the firm merged with Lister Drew Associates, a larger outfit based in West London, to form Lister Drew Haines Barrow, Wright helped establish an office for the practice in Central London. Over the next five years, he oversaw the practice's design projects, becoming a director and helping it grow into one of the largest architectural practices in the United Kingdom.

When Lister Drew Haines Barrow was acquired by the engineering consultancy giant Atkins in 1991, Wright was assigned to head the company's newly created architecture arm. He had only been with Atkins for eighteen months when the company was approached by the government of Dubai to supply design ideas for a new project that would replace the 615-room Chicago Beach Hotel, which had opened as the city's first resort residence in 1977. Named design director on the project, Wright was given two weeks to devise a structure that would come to serve as an icon for Dubai as it remodeled itself as an ultramodern and sophisticated international tourist destination. As he put it to Hannah Baldock for *Building* magazine (27 Jan. 2000), "We had to design a building that would become a symbol not of Dubai's past but of its future."

The result was the Burj Al Arab, which Wright designed to look like a traditional Arabian dhow sail setting out to sea. His initial sketches for the hotel were immediately accepted, and in 1994 he moved his family to Dubai to oversee the design and construction of the Jumeirah Beach Resort Development. One of Wright's first decisions included building the hotel on an artificial island nearly 300 meters offshore, which would prevent it from casting a shadow over its sister properties on the Jumeirah settlement. Complex engineering feats were nonetheless required to create the hotel's low-lying foundation on the island.

Taking five years to complete with a team of over 250 designers, the fifty-six-story, 202-room Burj Al Arab officially opened in December 1999, to coincide with the new millennium. At 1,053 feet, it was then the tallest hotel in the world; it has since been surpassed by four other hotels, three of which are in Dubai. The hotel, which is made of steel, glass, and concrete, also quickly earned the distinction of being the most luxurious, thanks to twenty-four-carat gold leaf and marble interiors and amenities such as reception desks and private butlers on every floor.

FORWARD-THINKING VISION
Wright's innovative designs for the Burj Al Arab made the hotel look unique; he wanted it to become an iconic image for the city of Dubai, "like the Opera House in Sydney [Australia] or the Eiffel Tower in Paris," he told Baldock. The hotel has since become one of the most photographed buildings in the world. Among other things, it features the world's tallest atrium at 590 feet—formed by its massive V-shaped mast design—and a nearly 700-feet-high helipad, which has been used for various sporting events, including a tennis match between Roger Federer and Andre Agassi in 2005.

Often marketed as the only seven-star hotel in the world, the Burj Al Arab, which is situated across from the award-winning, wave-shaped Jumeirah Beach Hotel, has been often criticized for its shameless opulence. The five-star-rated property nonetheless transformed Atkins into a major global architecture player, as the company soon won commissions for other resort developments in the Middle East and Asia. Upon returning to the United Kingdom, Wright was charged with running the design teams for those commissions, as well as further building Atkins's international architecture business. "Design should be uplifting, within its context, for the people interacting with it," he explained in his article for the *Atkins* website. "It doesn't have to be massively different, but the end result has to have a sense of harmony and balance that is enjoyable."

Over the next decade Wright coordinated projects for Atkins in places all over the world, helping the company build a reputation for practical, out-of-the-box designs. This included the Regatta Apartments in Jakarta, Indonesia, a mixed-development complex of eleven skyscrapers that Atkins began construction in 2009. Overlooking the Java Sea, the skyscrapers resemble elegant yachts and are each named after major port cities of the world. In 2010 another project led by Wright, a four-tower luxury residential complex called the Millennium Residence, opened in Bangkok, Thailand.

Wright played an instrumental role in establishing Atkins's world-class design team, which by 2013 had 650 architects operating in 150 countries. This growth paved the way for him to venture out on his own, and in September of that year he left Atkins with two longtime colleagues, design directors Hakim Khennouchi and Geku Kuruvilla, to form a new global company called WKK, also based in the United Kingdom.

WORK WITH WKK
WKK became committed to focusing on efficient and innovative high-end projects that had a strong sense of context. As he did with the Burj Al Arab, Wright always factors in a project's cultural and historical surroundings when coming up with his initial designs. While still at Atkins, he explained to Carlos Silva for the *Slovenia Times* (7 May 2010), "What we [the design team] are looking for is a place which is seeking an identity, something to be known and recognised for—a town which wants to be put on the map."

Carrying on their mission at Atkins, Wright and his partners have designed and created developments all over the world that redefine the landscapes they are situated in. Among them include the South Quarter in Jakarta, a mixed-use sustainable development complex that features office buildings, retail spaces, and apartments. The high-end, earth-toned complex features understated architectural elements that pay homage to Indonesia's natural environment. Construction on phase 1 of the complex, which received several architectural awards, was completed in October 2015.

In November 2015 construction was completed on another WKK concept, the Capital Fort in Sofia, Bulgaria. The mixed-use development consists of a twenty-eight-floor aerodynamic office tower and an L-shaped low-rise building that houses retail and conference facilities. The tower overlooks Vitosha Mountain and stands 413 feet high, making it the tallest building in Bulgaria. It has since come to be regarded as one of Sofia's most recognizable landmarks.

Meanwhile, Wright and his partners have conceptualized several development projects for Limassol, Cyprus, helping to make the scenic coastal city an up-and-coming tourist destination. Among these is a high-rise commercial office building called the Oval, which opened in Limassol's business district in April 2017. Featuring an egg-shaped design inspired by round pebbles on the city's shoreline, the sixteen-story, 216-feet-high structure is the highest office building in Cyprus. By the time the Oval opened, construction had already begun on another WKK project in Limassol called One, a mixed-use tower featuring luxury apartments and retail units.

With WKK, Wright has continued to take inspiration from ships, for such projects as the Hanging Gardens building in Bahrain, which draws on the dhow ships on which the Burj Al Arab is also based as well as on its legendary namesake, and the mixed-use Centaurus development in Islamabad, Pakistan, which includes a hotel shaped like a menacing sail.

CRUISE SHIPS OF THE FUTURE

Wright's architectural endeavors have also extended to ship design. While at Atkins, he helped design Royal Caribbean International's *Oasis of the Seas*, a nearly 1,200-feet-long cruise liner that can carry 5,400 passengers at full occupancy. Upon its launch in 2009, the ship, which is highlighted by an open-air urban park, became the largest cruise ship in the world. Wright later teamed up with Royal Caribbean again with WKK, designing the exterior of their cruise ship *Quantum of the Seas*. For that ship, he conceptualized a multifunction entertainment facility called the Seaplex, which became the largest active indoor space at sea, and the Northstar viewing pod, in which passengers can soar over the ocean.

Wright, however, saved his most revolutionary designs for Celebrity Cruises' *Edge*, a 2,918-passenger ship that made its maiden voyage in December 2018. The ship, which cost $1 billion to make, features a number of industry firsts, most notably a tennis court–sized cantilevered passenger platform called the Magic Carpet, which serves a variety of functions as it moves up and down the ship, from an embarkation station at its lowest position to a specialty restaurant at its highest. Wright devised the one-of-a-kind innovation, along with others, such as a pair of two-story martini glass–shaped hot tubs and a rooftop garden, to reinforce the ship's larger concept of having a greater connection with the ocean. "We've got store rooms of brilliant ideas," he told Teresa Machan, who reviewed the ship for the *Telegraph* (1 Dec. 2018). "It's just a case of marrying the right ideas with the right ship."

Under Wright's direction, WKK has enjoyed profits every year since its inception. The company has since grown to a team of twenty architects and designers.

PERSONAL LIFE

Wright lives with his family in West Sussex, a county in southern England. An avid seafarer, he spends much of his spare time sailing on his yacht. He has said that he dreams of taking ten years off to sail around the world.

SUGGESTED READING

Baldock, Hannah. "The Wow Factor." *Building*, 27 Jan. 2000, www.building.co.uk/focus/the-wow-factor/2666.article. Accessed 30 Nov. 2018.

Hurst, Will. "Burj Al Arab Architect Leaves Atkins to Set Up Rival Practice." *Building*, 20 Sept. 2013, www.building.co.uk/news/burj-al-arab-architect-leaves-atkins-to-set-up-rival-practice/5060871.article. Accessed 3 Dec. 2018.

Machan, Teresa. "'The Rule Book Has Been Ripped Up'—A First Look at the $1 Billion Cruise Ship." *The Telegraph*, 1 Dec. 2018, www.telegraph.co.uk/travel/cruises/articles/all-aboard-the--1-billion-dollar-ship. Accessed 3 Dec. 2018.

"Projects." *WKK*, WKK Architects, 2018, wkkarchitects.com. Accessed 4 Dec. 2018.

"Tom Wright." *Celebrity Edge Fact Sheets*, www.celebritycruisespresscenter.com/pdf/core_press_materials_edge/EDGE-FactsSheet.pdf. Accessed 30 Nov. 2018.

Wright, Tom. "Fighting Gravity." *Atkins*, 10 Dec. 2007, www.atkinsglobal.com/en-gb/angles/all-angles/fighting-gravity. Accessed 30 Nov. 2018.

Wright, Tom. "The Wright Approach to Architecture." Interview by Carlos Silva. *The Slovenia Times*, 7 May 2010, www.sloveniatimes.com/the-wright-approach-to-architecture. Accessed 30 Nov. 2018.

—*Chris Cullen*

Jean Wyllys

Date of birth: March 10, 1974
Occupation: Politician

"Having gone from poverty to parliament via *Big Brother* and Brazil's first gay-rights election platform, Jean Wyllys must rank among the most postmodern of politicians," Jonathan Watts wrote for the *Guardian* (26 Jan. 2014). After emerging as the victor on the hit television competition, Wyllys, as Watts explained, "triumphed in a more traditional popularity contest five years later."

That year, 2010, Wyllys was elected to the National Congress of Brazil, thus becoming the first openly gay elected official in a country where systemic homophobia remains the norm. "It is a difficult battle to fight. Sometimes I feel like Don Quixote, you know?" Wyllys—often compared to the San Francisco politician and gay rights activist Harvey Milk, who was assassinated in the late 1970s—told Tom Phillips for the *Guardian* (27 Jan. 2012). "But this is my vocation. My calling. I feel that I need to be here."

Wyllys's gay rights activism had long angered Brazil's conservative political establishment, and he had been employing bodyguards for years, but that comparison to Milk began to seem chillingly prescient in 2018, when he became the subject of a targeted social media campaign that painted him as a deviant and pedophile. He began receiving credible death threats, and after a close friend, Rio de Janeiro city councillor and human rights activist Marielle Franco, was fatally shot in March of that year after delivering a speech, Wyllys became increasingly concerned for his own safety. At his request, he was provided with a bulletproof car and official police escort for official events, but his uneasiness mounted.

In January 2019, just as he was scheduled to be sworn in for a third term in office, he released a note from an undisclosed overseas location, informing the public that he had left Brazil because of the threats and would not be returning. "For the future of this cause, I need to be alive. I do not want to be a martyr," he said, as quoted by Francesca Paris for *NPR* (25 Jan. 2019). "I'm very proud of what [I've accomplished]. . . . But I'm human and I reached my limit."

EARLY LIFE AND EDUCATION

Jean Wyllys de Matos Santos was born on March 10, 1974, in Alagoinhas, a small town in the northeastern Brazilian state of Bahia. It was a region of extreme poverty, and his home, like most others in his neighborhood, lacked electricity and running water. It was not unusual for Wyllys and his six siblings to go to bed hungry. One sister died of typhoid at a young age. His mother, who worked washing clothes at the nearby Pojuca River, and his father, an alcoholic automotive worker, were both illiterate. Wyllys tried as best he could to help the family make ends meet, selling popcorn and sweets on the street as a child.

Despite those dire circumstances, Wyllys intuitively understood the value of education, and he worked hard to gain admission to a Catholic boarding school, where the left-leaning priests lent him books and spoke to him about social justice. He told Phillips that the priests urged him to read "everything, from the Bible to Mario Vargas Llosa" and asserted, "What my parents couldn't give me the church did."

Wyllys attended the Federal University of Bahia, a large public university in Salvador, tuition-free, and there he earned a degree in journalism. Some sources state that he also earned a master's degree in literature, with a specialization in Bahian culture.

Wyllys later embarked on a career in journalism and academia, teaching communications at the Federal University of the State of Rio de

Photo by Ministério da Cultura via Wikimedia Commons

Janeiro; in 2001 he published a book of *cronicas* ("chronicles" or "columns") titled *Aflitos* (generally translated as "the afflicted"), which won Brazil's Prêmio Copene de Cultura e Arte.

In 2005, he auditioned for the Brazilian version of the televised reality show *Big Brother*, claiming to be motivated by intellectual curiosity about the show's social dynamics. *Big Brother* had been created in the Netherlands in 1999 and was later syndicated internationally in more than fifty countries. As in other countries, the Brazilian version, which debuted in 2002, places a group of young contestants together in a specially constructed house, where they are filmed twenty-four hours a day. Over the course of the competition, as personal dramas and conflicts develop, contestants are voted out each week by their housemates (as well as by audience members who call in their votes), until only one remains to win the cash prize.

Much to the surprise of many, when the seventy-nine-day competition was over, Wyllys, the first openly gay contestant in the history of the show, had won, thanks to his popularity with the viewing audience, who were charmed by his wit and outsized personality. He had received 50 million call-in votes and was widely credited with starting a national discussion on gay rights and homophobia. "It [was] a surprise that homophobia became the theme of the most popular TV show of the country," Wyllys told Kevin Truong for *NBC News* (24 Oct. 2017), explaining that week after week his housemates felt free to make fun of his manner of speaking and to openly air their prejudices. "When I was there what happened [to me] was the same [thing] that happens every day with [LGBTQ people] in Brazil," he asserted, referring to the lesbian, gay, bisexual, transgender, and queer community. Wyllys later wrote a memoir, *Ainda Lembro* (I still remember).

POLITICAL CAREER

"Those expecting Wyllys to disappear after his 15 minutes of fame were mistaken," Phillips wrote of Wyllys's subsequent entry into the political sphere. Wyllys—who served for a time as a reporter for the news program *Mais Você*; a commentator on the radio show *Amigas Invisíveis*; and a columnist for *G Magazine*, a Brazilian publication aimed at gay men—entered the political arena in 2010, vying for a seat in his country's bicameral Congresso Nacional (National Congress). A member of the Socialism and Liberty party, he quickly became known for his focus on LGBTQ rights. "I've been insisting the LGBTQ movement should have a positive agenda. I mean not only defending matters against violence, which, yes, is always present in the LGBTQ community, but also mainly [working for an] extension of rights," Wyllys told Truong. He explained that LGBTQ people were facing multipronged attacks from religious fundamentalists, conservative members of the military, and congressional officials from rural areas—all of whom had banded together to turn back the clock on even the meager advances that had been made in recent years. For example, a federal judge ruled in 2017 that homosexuality could be considered a disease, thereby reversing a 1999 decision put forth by Brazil's Federal Council of Psychology prohibiting that diagnosis; that same year, a gay-focused art show had been shut down after pressure from conservative groups. "My fear is that Brazil will become a theocratic republic," Wyllys told Watts. "I'm worried they could restrict liberties for ethnic, religious and sexual minorities."

Wyllys was putting himself, according to Phillips, "on the frontline of an increasingly venomous feud with a legion of outspoken and unashamedly radical evangelical preachers." Not unlike the United States, Phillips explained, the country had made moves toward tolerance and legal equality for LGBTQ individuals, but these had drawn the ire of "firebrand pastors who conduct exorcisms of lesbians and gay men and pronounce that African-Brazilian religions are the work of 'Satanás.'"

"Jean Wyllys de Matos Santos does not pick the easy battles, nor does he pick the vote-winning ones," Donna Bowater and Priscilla Moraes wrote for the *Independent* (6 Apr. 2015). Among the varied pieces of legislation Wyllys introduced in Congress were the government regulation of prostitution, the lifting of restrictions on abortion, and the government funding of sex reassignment surgeries and hormonal treatment for transgender people. Such actions made him a target of popular televangelists such as Silas Malafaia, and he also made a particular enemy of fellow representative Jair Bolsonaro, who became president of Brazil in 2018 and who never forgot that during one contentious 2016 debate, Wyllys had imprudently spit on him in anger.

Once Bolsonaro ascended to the presidency, many of Wyllys's worst fears seemed to be confirmed. Although same-sex unions had been legally recognized in Brazil since 2004, and same-sex marriages legal since 2013, during the first day of his administration, the new president removed the LGBTQ community from the list of groups covered by the country's human rights ministry, and many feared that their hard-earned rights would be placed in jeopardy. Bolsonaro's new human rights minister, Damares Alves, who had declared that diversity was a threat to family values, said upon taking office, "Girls will be princesses and boys will be princes. There will be no more ideological indoctrination of children and teenagers in Brazil."

Soon, thanks at least in some part to Bolsonaro's heated rhetoric, physical attacks on the LGBTQ community increased significantly, with more than seventy assaults taking place in just one ten-day span after the election. Wyllys, long a target of accusations that he was perverted or sacrilegious, found the slanderous charges against him escalating further, with pedophilia among the most egregious allegations. "I saw my reputation destroyed by lies, and I, powerless, unable to do anything," he said, as quoted by Paris. "People have no idea what it's like to be the target."

Following the assassination of Marielle Franco, who had been happily engaged to her partner, Monica Benicio, at the time of her death, matters came to a head for Wyllys, who considers the legalization of same-sex marriage in Brazil as one of his proudest accomplishments. Although he had been elected to a third term in the 2018 elections, he could not envision living for four more years under such conditions.

He sent his letter of resignation from an undisclosed location, announcing his intention to spend time writing and working on a doctoral degree. On his *Twitter* account, he asserted: "We did a lot for the common good. And we will do much more when the new time comes, it doesn't matter if we do it by different means!"

Bolsonaro and his son tweeted in the wake of the resignation, with the older man posting a "thumbs-up" emoji and the younger writing, "Go with God and be happy." (They claim, however, that those tweets were not a direct response to Wyllys's news.)

Wyllys's seat will be taken by David Miranda, an openly gay councilman from Rio de Janeiro who is married to the American journalist Glenn Greenwald. Soon after that news broke, Miranda's Twitter account featured a message aimed squarely at Bolsonaro: "Check your emotions. One LGBT is leaving, but another is entering. See you in Brasília."

PERSONAL LIFE

In 2015, Wyllys was featured on *CEO World Magazine*'s list of top fifty global personalities with an outstanding commitment to diversity. The following year, an independent Brazilian filmmaker released the documentary *Entre os homens de bem* (*The Stranger in the House*), about Wyllys's life and career.

Wyllys is said to be fond of Saint George, known for slaying dragons, and Phillips reported him displaying a large painting of the Catholic saint in his former apartment in Rio de Janeiro.

SUGGESTED READING

Biller, David. "Gay Brazilian Congressman Resigns, Citing Death Threats." *Bloomberg News*, 24 Jan. 2019, www.bloomberg.com/news/articles/2019-01-24/gay-brazilian-congressman-resigns-his-seat-citing-death-threats. Accessed 4 Mar. 2019.

Bowater, Donna, and Priscilla Moraes. "Brazil's Only Openly Gay MP Jean Wyllys de Matos Santos Leads the Fight to Legalise Abortion." *Independent*, 6 Apr. 2015, www.independent.co.uk/news/world/americas/brazils-only-openly-gay-mp-jean-wyllys-de-matos-santos-leads-the-fight-to-legalise-abortion-10158565.html. Accessed 4 Mar. 2019.

Garcia, Michelle. "Brazil's Only Gay Congressman Flees Country Fearing Violence." *Out Magazine*, 25 Jan. 2019, www.out.com/news-opinion/2019/1/25/jean-wyllys-brazil-gay-congressman-violence. Accessed 4 Mar. 2019.

Paris, Francesca. "I Do Not Want to Be a Martyr." *NPR*, 25 Jan. 2019, www.npr.org/2019/01/25/688647722/i-do-not-want-to-be-a-martyr-openly-gay-lawmaker-leaves-brazil. Accessed 4 Mar. 2019.

Phillips, Tom. "Jean Wyllys, Brazil's First Openly Gay MP, Takes Fight to the Religious Right." *The Guardian*, 27 Jan. 2012, www.theguardian.com/world/2012/jan/27/brazil-openly-gay-mp-jean-wyllys. Accessed 4 Mar. 2019.

Truong, Kevin. "Reality TV Star-Turned-Politician Fights 'Moral Terror' of Brazil's Far Right." *NBC News*, 24 Oct. 2017, www.nbcnews.com/feature/nbc-out/reality-tv-star-turned-politician-fights-moral-terror-brazil-s-n813686. Accessed 4 Mar. 2019.

Watts, Jonathan. "Voices of Brazil: The Politician Who Won *Big Brother*." *The Guardian*, 26 Jan. 2014, www.theguardian.com/world/2014/jan/26/voices-of-brazil-the-politician-jean-wyllys-big-brother. Accessed 4 Mar. 2019.

—*Mari Rich*

Andrew Yang

Date of birth: January 13, 1975
Occupation: Entrepreneur

Andrew Yang, the founder of a nonprofit training program for entrepreneurs called Venture for America, is a dark-horse candidate for the Democratic nomination for president in 2020. Yang's campaign centers on one bold policy proposal: universal basic income (UBI). His version of UBI could more accurately be described as a guaranteed minimum income—giving people enough money so that, theoretically, each American could live above the poverty line. Yang proposes sending a thousand dollars each month, amounting to a twelve-thousand-dollar stipend each year, to each American over the age of eighteen. Unlike existing welfare programs—food stamps, for example—the money could be spent however the receiver sees fit. But it would be misleading to describe UBI as a welfare program. Every person, regardless of income, would receive it. Yang has termed his proposal a Freedom Dividend, or informally, a "tech check."

Yang argues that automation and artificial intelligence will soon lead to mass unemployment, citing Amazon as responsible for the closure of shopping malls and the loss of a host of retail jobs, for example. He maintains that tech-related job loss will only continue and expand. "It's not immigrants causing these problems," Yang told Lizette Chapman and Ryan Teague Beckwith for *Bloomberg* (12 Sept. 2019), dismissing a prevailing argument of the Republican Party. "It's technology."

Amid a crowded field of Democratic contenders, Yang's campaign has drawn fervent supporters, particularly in Silicon Valley and among tech workers around the country. Elon Musk, the founder of SpaceX and Tesla, is a fan, but so are ordinary people concerned that government is undereducated about and woefully ill-equipped to address radical, emerging changes in technology.

EARLY LIFE AND EDUCATION

Andrew Yang was born in Schenectady, New York, on January 13, 1975, to immigrants who had come from Taiwan in the 1960s and met as graduate students at the University of California, Berkeley. They married in 1971. His father, Kei-Hsiung Yang, was a researcher at IBM and generated nearly seventy patents during

Photo by Gage Skidmore via Wikimedia Commons

his career. His mother, Nancy Yang, worked as a systems administrator for the State University of New York (SUNY); she later became a well-known pastel artist. Yang's brother is named Lawrence, after Berkeley's Lawrence Hall of Science.

Yang grew up in upstate New York. He attended the elite preparatory school Phillips Exeter Academy in Exeter, New Hampshire, for two years and graduated in 1992. He then went on to study economics and political science at Brown University and, after graduating in 1996, attended Columbia Law School. Yang earned his juris doctorate in 1999 and spent "five unhappy months," as he recalled in a CNN op-ed (30 July 2019), as a corporate attorney for Davis Polk and Wardwell.

Yang quit and founded Stargiving, a tech start-up that aimed to raise funds for charity. After it failed, he took jobs in the mobile software and health-care software industries. In 2006 he became the CEO of Manhattan GMAT, a test-preparation company that was eventually sold to Kaplan, an education corporation, in 2009. Yang received a payout of several million dollars from the deal.

VENTURE FOR AMERICA

In 2011, Yang founded the nonprofit Venture for America. Like the nonprofit organization Teach for America, which matches recent college graduates with struggling schools, Venture for America matches recent college graduates with tech start-ups in more than a dozen economically insecure cities, such as Detroit, Michigan; Cleveland, Ohio; and St. Louis, Missouri. Yang

hoped to lure students away from Wall Street and other corporate jobs. "I wanted to create a path for smart young people to go out and build things, not toil away on corporate mergers that just shifted money from one millionaire's account to another," he wrote for CNN.

Venture for America is basically a training program for entrepreneurs. Fellows spend two years with a start-up, earning a modest salary. Yang's vision for Venture for America was two-pronged: train young entrepreneurs and create jobs. In 2014, he published a book touting his enthusiasm for projects like Venture for America, titled *Smart People Should Build Things: How to Restore Our Culture of Achievement, Build a Path for Entrepreneurs, and Create New Jobs in America*.

Venture for America's mission won praise early. Before a single fellow had been selected, President Barack Obama honored Yang as a 2011 White House Champion of Change. But Venture for America failed to create the kind of aggressive change Yang sought. He set an ambitious goal of creating one hundred thousand jobs, but in eight years, Venture for America, by its own account, created fewer than four thousand jobs.

Yang left his position as CEO and board member in the summer of 2017. He had become disillusioned with its purpose even as he was lauded as a visionary. He came to realize that start-ups alone were not equipped to address the seismic changes roiling American life. In an interview with Russell Brandom for the *Verge* (17 Apr. 2019), Yang put it this way: "Imagine being this celebrated entrepreneur, and then feeling like your work is like a wall of sand in front of a tidal wave. And people keep asking, 'How did you build the wall of sand?'"

THE WAR ON NORMAL PEOPLE

In 2018, Yang published a second book refuting his earlier ideas, titled *The War on Normal People: The Truth about America's Disappearing Jobs and Why Universal Basic Income Is Our Future*. The book provides an argument for the animating purpose of Yang's presidential campaign, a universal basic income. Yang's predictions in the absence of UBI are grim. He paints economic decline in purely human terms, translating economic instability to a rise in events like "deaths of despair," including suicide and overdose deaths, which are already alarmingly on the rise. "Normal people" like those working manufacturing and retail jobs will suffer and grow increasingly isolated from more prosperous workers in places like Silicon Valley, where the average starting salary was nearing $200,000 by 2018. A reviewer for *Kirkus Reviews* described *The War on Normal People* as a "provocative work of social criticism."

This outlook fueled Yang's presidential ambition. "People think [Republican president] Donald Trump is a problem. No, Donald Trump is a symptom of this ongoing transformation," Yang told Brandom. Of that transformation, he added, "That is literally what drove me to run for president. I thought to myself, realistically, my choices are to watch the society come apart or try and galvanize energy around meaningful solutions."

YANG 2020

Yang launched his bid for president in November 2017. He frequently explains his motivation for running with statements such as "We are undergoing the greatest economic transformation in our history, and we are dealing with it by pretending nothing is happening," as he put in for CNN. He makes for an unorthodox candidate, one who is more comfortable speaking like a self-deprecating software engineer than a politician. Emily Witt observed for the *New Yorker* (18 July 2019) that his stump speech sounds more like a TED Talk. Witt noted that his favorite campaign trail wisecrack is "the opposite of Donald Trump is an Asian man who likes math." (Indeed, Yang is one of only a handful of Asian Americans ever to have sought a major-party nomination for president and actively campaigns on his heritage.) Yang's one-liner met with mixed reactions from Asian Americans and others, with some criticizing it for perpetuating the model-minority stereotype, and others accepting it as self-deprecating, in-group humor.

Journalists and pundits were baffled initially by Yang's decision to run. Kevin Roose, a reporter and columnist who covers technology at the *New York Times*, met Yang when he was the head of Venture for America. In 2017, Yang had called Roose and told him that he planned to run for president. "And at first, I was very confused—I was like, president of the food co-op? The homeowners association? What could you possibly mean by running for president?" Roose recalled to Michael Barbaro for the *New York Times'* podcast *The Daily* (12 Sept. 2019).

In Brandom's estimation, Yang reached a "tipping point" in February 2019, when he appeared on an episode of the popular *Joe Rogan Experience* podcast, hosted by comedian Joe Rogan. Rogan's followers, many of them interested in tech and futurism, helped catapult Yang to internet fame. Memes featuring the candidate multiplied, and he began to accrue a serious following of progressives, libertarians, and former supporters of both President Trump and Senator Bernie Sanders. Adherents call themselves the Yang Gang and wear hats with the acronym MATH ("Make America Think Harder") printed on them. At the same time Yang's campaign has struggled to distance itself from trolls and meme creators who latched onto some of Yang's economic ideas but exhibit racist and anti-Semitic agendas.

POLICY

Most coverage of Yang's campaign has focused on his Freedom Dividend proposal, to be paid for by a value-added tax on consumption in an effort to redistribute wealth from corporate tech giants and other beneficiaries of automation. He was the first US presidential candidate to center a campaign on UBI, though the concept had been around for decades and a handful of countries around the world—and the state of Alaska through its petroleum fund—have tested it with some success.

Yang has touted a host of other policy proposals, including legalized marijuana, a dual-key fail-safe for nuclear launch decisions, Puerto Rico statehood, electronic campaigning and voting, and a new postal banking system. Among other solutions to technological shifts, Yang wants to establish a government agency that will educate officials on issues like artificial intelligence and data privacy that they are charged with addressing through laws and regulations. But he seemed content to be seen primarily as a one-issue candidate, if only because UBI encapsulates a worldview that Yang called "human-centered capitalism," in which work and well-being are measured in human terms, such as satisfaction and health, rather than purely economic terms like gross domestic product (GDP). His focus on UBI has also been a key factor to the longevity of his candidacy. "Candidates who advertise about a specific issue have an easier time targeting the people that are likely to give to them," Connor Farrell, a progressive fund-raising consultant, told Chapman and Beckwith. "You'll make more money spending less money."

Yang won enough support to make the significantly winnowed third Democratic debate in September 2019, the first to feature the ten most popular Democratic nominees for president on one stage. At that debate, Yang announced that his campaign would run its own small-scale UBI test, giving ten American families one thousand dollars each month for a year. Within the week, nearly a half million Americans entered the raffle to participate. Questioned immediately about its legality, experts deemed the unusual action a permissible campaign advertising strategy. The unconventional move underscored his unconventional candidacy.

PERSONAL LIFE

Yang met his wife, Evelyn (Lu) Yang, at Columbia. The couple married in early 2011. Evelyn, a marketing manager at the cosmetics company L'Oréal, became a stay-at-home parent to their two sons, one of whom has autism; Yang has argued that, with his proposed Freedom Dividend, labor like hers would be recognized.

SUGGESTED READING

Brandom, Russell. "Andrew Yang Is the Candidate for the End of the World." *The Verge*, 17 Apr. 2019, www.theverge.com/2019/4/17/18408685/andrew-yang-2020-president-democrat-candidate-policies-universal-basic-income-reddit-twitter. Accessed 13 Sept. 2019.

Chapman, Lizette, and Ryan Teague Beckwith. "Andrew Yang Brings Silicon Valley's Upstart Spirit to 2020 Bid." *Bloomberg*, 12 Sept. 2019, www.bloomberg.com/news/articles/2019-09-12/can-andrew-yang-win-in-2020-inside-his-unorthodox-campaign. Accessed 12 Sept. 2019.

Roose, Kevin. "His 2020 Campaign Message: The Robots Are Coming." *The New York Times*, 10 Feb. 2018, www.nytimes.com/2018/02/10/technology/his-2020-campaign-message-the-robots-are-coming.html. Accessed 17 Sept. 2019.

Roose, Kevin. "An Interview with Andrew Yang, an Outsider at Tonight's Democratic Debate." Interview by Michael Barbaro. *The Daily*, The New York Times, 12 Sept. 2019, www.nytimes.com/2019/09/12/podcasts/the-daily/andrew-yang-democratic-debate.html. Accessed 14 Sept. 2019.

Yang, Andrew. "Andrew Yang: What I Learned from Five Unhappy Months as a Corporate Lawyer." *CNN*, 30 July 2019, www.cnn.com/2019/07/26/opinions/andrew-yang-2020-economic-vision-lift-americans/index.html. Accessed 12 Sept. 2019.

Witt, Emily. "How Andrew Yang's Robot Apocalypse Can Heal a Divided Nation." *The New Yorker*, 18 July 2019, www.newyorker.com/news/news-desk/how-andrew-yangs-robot-apocalypse-can-heal-a-divided-nation. Accessed 17 Sept. 2019.

—*Molly Hagan*

Kevin Young

Date of birth: November 8, 1970
Occupation: Poet

Kevin Young is one of America's most acclaimed, versatile, and prolific poets. He is the recipient of a Guggenheim Foundation Fellowship and a MacDowell Colony Fellowship and was inducted into the American Academy of Arts and Sciences in 2016. Described by Dwight Garner for the *New York Times* (16 Apr. 2018) as "a maximalist, a putter-inner, an evoker of roiling appetites,"

Young is known for crafting allusive but accessible poems that investigate race and culture on both a personal and collective level. Over the past three decades, he has produced eleven books of poetry, two of which, *Jelly Roll: A Blues* (2003) and *Blue Laws: Selected & Uncollected Poems 1995–2015* (2016), were longlisted for the National Book Award; his 2018 poetry collection, *Brown*, was a New York Times Notable Book. An equally esteemed scholar, he has also authored two award-winning works of nonfiction, *The Grey Album: On the Blackness of Blackness* (2012) and *Bunk: The Rise of Hoaxes, Humbug, Plagiarists, Phonies, Post-Facts, and Fake News* (2017), and has edited eight anthologies.

In 2017, Young became the first African American to be named poetry editor of the *New Yorker*, a prestigious post he continues to hold. He also serves as the director of the Harlem-based Schomburg Center for Research in Black Culture, which is part of the New York Public Library system. In both positions, Young has resolved to highlight an all-encompassing range of voices, selecting work that reflects the true breadth of poetry. In an article for *Time* (7 Mar. 2019), he explained, "To me, poetry has long been alive. It's continuing to live and it's also thriving right now. I'm interested in capturing that aliveness."

EARLY LIFE AND EDUCATION

An only child, Kevin Lowell Young was born on November 8, 1970, in Lincoln, Nebraska. His parents both hailed from rural, Jim Crow Louisiana and were the first in their respective families to attend college. His father, the late Paul E.

Photo by Larry D. Moore via Wikimedia Commons

Young, was an ophthalmologist. His mother, Dr. Azzie Young, is an accomplished chemist with a doctorate from the University of Nebraska and a master's degree from Harvard's Kennedy School of Government, who later worked as the director of the Mattapan Community Health Center in Boston, Massachusetts. Because of his parents' academic and professional obligations, Young had a peripatetic upbringing, moving six times before the age of ten. His family eventually settled in Topeka, Kansas, where he spent the bulk of his adolescence.

In Topeka, Young and his family attended the same church that was formerly pastored by the Reverend Oliver Brown, an iconic civil rights activist who famously launched a lawsuit—*Brown v. Board of Education of Topeka*—that helped lead to the desegregation of public schools in the United States. Though Reverend Brown died in 1961, Young has recalled feeling his presence whenever he entered the church. Fascinated by history and the past, he developed an early fondness for books and the written word. He gravitated toward poetry, and at age thirteen, discovered a gift for writing verse after a teacher championed his work during a summer writing workshop at Topeka's Washburn University.

Young wrote poetry throughout his time at Topeka West High School, and after graduating from there in 1988, he attended Harvard University in Cambridge, Massachusetts. He became a major fixture on the university's lively literary scene, helping to revive an obscure black journal called *Diaspora* and joining the Dark Room Collective, a legendary black poets' group. "He always knew what he wanted to do," his friend and fellow Collective member, the Pulitzer Prize–winning novelist Colson Whitehead, recalled to Matthew Schneier for the *New York Times* (7 Nov. 2017). "When most people were dabbling, he was working. He was well on his way when most of us were listening to Nirvana and wearing dirty clothes."

A pupil of the late renowned poets Seamus Heaney and Lucie Brock-Broido, Young graduated from Harvard with a degree in English and American literature in 1992. He then landed a highly coveted Wallace Stegner Fellowship in Poetry from Stanford University, in California, where, as per program requirements, he studied creative writing for two years. He transferred to the writing program at Brown University, in Providence, Rhode Island, and graduated with his MFA in 1996.

EARLY CAREER

Young started publishing individual works of poetry as an undergraduate at Harvard. Winning an award from the American Academy of Poets as a freshman, he became known as the university's "Young Black Poet," a moniker he resented.

Through the influence of the Dark Room Collective, however, he dedicated himself to an aesthetic that represented life in all its forms. It was during this time that Young came to the realization that "poetry was not this thing in the atmosphere," as he told Robert P. Baird for *Esquire* (6 Nov. 2017). "You have to look in your backyard. That's the stuff to write about."

Young kept this artistic aim in mind while writing his first book of poetry, *Most Way Home*, which was published by William Morrow in 1995. Drawing on the oral storytelling tradition of the American South, the book traverses the variegated landscape of the African American experience, featuring a collection of poems that revolve around the concept of home. It was selected for the National Poetry Series by the award-winning poet Lucille Clifton and won the Zacharis First Book Award from the American literary journal *Ploughshares*.

Over the next decade, Young established a reputation as one of his generation's leading poets. He published "Langston Hughes," his first poem in the *New Yorker*, in 1999, and two years later, released his second collection of poetry, *To Repel Ghosts* (2001). The latter, inspired by the paintings and lifestyle of artist Jean-Michel Basquiat, marked the first installment of an American trilogy called *Devil's Music*. The second installment of that trilogy, *Jelly Roll* (2003), an inventive, blues-based collection of love poems, won the Paterson Poetry Prize, and was a finalist for the National Book Award and the Los Angeles Times Book Prize. It was followed by *Black Maria* (2005), a collection of verse that riffs on the language and themes of film noir.

While writing and publishing his own poetry, Young edited anthologies such as *Giant Steps: The New Generation of African American Writers* (2000), a collection of various literary works by black authors born after 1960, and *John Berryman: Selected Poems* (2004), which highlights the achievements of the Pulitzer Prize–winning poet's early work. Young also entered the realm of academia, teaching at the University of Georgia and Indiana University before being named the Atticus Heygood Professor of Creative Writing and English at Emory University in 2005. Emory later recognized him with a Charles Howard Candler Professorship. He additionally became the curator of Emory's Raymond Danowski Poetry Library, which houses a collection of 75,0000 volumes of rare and modern poetry.

AWARD-WINNING POET AND SCHOLAR

Young held his distinguished professorship and curatorial position at Emory for eleven years, during which he continued to produce a prolific output of work that reflected his broad range of interests. His fifth collection of poetry, *For the Confederate Dead* (2007), is an energetic jazz-and-blues-influenced exploration of African American culture and the legacy of the Civil War, featuring poems inspired by famous personages as well as personal relationships, it received the Quill Award in Poetry in 2007 and the Paterson Award for Sustained Literary Achievement in 2008. Young's sixth collection, *Dear Darkness* (2008), is largely an autobiographical meditation on food, family, and memory, offering a heartfelt ode to Louisiana's culture and traditions.

In 2011, Young released *Ardency: A Chronicle of the Amistad Rebels*, about Mende abductees from Sierra Leone who seized control of their captors' slave ship, *La Amistad*. Written over the course of twenty years and featuring poems characterized by syntactical shifts, puns, repetition, and vernacular utterances, the collection showcases Young's unique style and won an American Book Award from the Before Columbus Foundation in 2012.

That same year Young published his first book of nonfiction, *The Grey Album: On the Blackness of Blackness*, whose title refers to musician Danger Mouse's eponymous 2004 mashup album of the Beatles' *The White Album* and rapper Jay-Z's *The Black Album*. A mélange of literary and cultural criticism, the book highlights the birth of the traditional African American trickster figure and assesses black art's larger contribution to American culture. Helping to establish Young as a major critic, it received a number of honors, including the Graywolf Nonfiction Prize and the PEN Open Book Award. In a review for the *New York Times* (15 Mar. 2012), Dwight Garner described *The Grey Album* as "equal parts blues shout, church sermon, interpretive dance, TED talk, lit-crit manifesto and mixtape," calling it "an ambitious blast of fact and feeling, a nervy piece of performance art."

Young's eighth collection of poetry, *Book of Hours*, was released in 2014 to wide acclaim. Inspired by his father's death and his son's birth, the book explores the dichotomy between grief and joy. Among other honors, it won the 2015 Lenore Marshall Prize for Poetry, which the American Academy of Poets awards each year to the most outstanding book of poetry published in the United States during the previous year. In his award citation, A. Van Jordan wrote, as quoted on Young's official website, that *Book of Hours* "exemplifies what poetry can do in the world when language works at its full power," containing poems that "hold emotion taut on each line while allowing for the nimbleness of language to drape over them, bringing tension between the heart and the mind, as Young consistently surprises us with profound elegance."

Young followed *Book of Hours* with *Blue Laws: Selected and Uncollected Poems 1995–2015* (2016), which gathers standout works from the first two decades of the poet's career,

along with self-described "B sides" and "bonus tracks." *Blue Laws* was recognized by numerous publications as one of the best poetry collections of 2016 and was longlisted for the prestigious National Book Award.

SECURING TWO LEADING POSTS

In 2016, Young moved from Atlanta to New York to become director of the New York Public Library's Schomburg Center for Research in Black Culture. The research institution was founded in 1926 by Arturo Schomburg, a black historian from Puerto Rico. In his role as director, Young manages a vast collection of books, manuscripts, photographs, films, and print ephemera that showcase the legacies of known and unknown black artists. "I'm not an archivist by training," he explained in the *Time* article. "But by temperament, I love thinking about history and how it talks to now."

It was Young's work as an archivist and anthologist that led David Remnick to name him the successor to Paul Muldoon as poetry editor of the *New Yorker* in 2017. In that plum role, which disqualifies him from publishing his own poems in the prestigious magazine, Young sifts through hundreds of submissions from contemporary poets every week. According to Remnick, the magazine's editor-in-chief, "Kevin has made it his business to represent from all over the range of human voices," as he told Karen Grigsby Bates for *NPR's Morning Edition* program (25 Apr. 2018). "And week after week, even though I've followed these things for years, I'm being introduced to poets and names I hadn't met before." Also in 2017, Young published his second nonfiction book, *Bunk: The Rise of Hoaxes, Humbug, Plagiarists, Phonies, Post-Facts, and Fake News*, which provides a cultural history of hoaxes in America. Tracing a legacy of lies and deception over several centuries, from the Shakespeare forgers in the eighteenth century to the chicanery of circus impresario P. T. Barnum in the nineteenth century, and culminating with the polarizing presidency of Donald J. Trump, *Bunk* confronts the idea of truth in an uncertain social and political climate marked by a proliferation of "fake news." The book was showered with critical praise and received a number of literary honors, including winning the Anisfield-Wolf Book Award in Nonfiction and being longlisted for the National Book Award.

Young's 2018 collection of poetry, *Brown*, honors the history and impact of black culture and centers around the notion of "Brownness," with references to important figures like musician James Brown, abolitionist John Brown, and the Reverend Oliver Brown. It includes poems that focus on Young's childhood in Kansas and on other influential American cultural icons. In a review for *Commonweal* (2 Dec. 2018), Anthony

Domestico wrote that *Brown* "displays [Young's] versatility at every turn," calling it "deeply personal and expansively political, the best of his distinguished career."

PERSONAL LIFE

Young is known to be an inveterate collector of rare books and other ephemera. According to friends, he has "a taste for the finer things" and is "a reveler in the sensual pleasures of art, food, clothing," as noted by Schneier.

Young married Kate Tuttle, a book critic and editor, in 2005. They reside in New York with their two children.

SUGGESTED READING

Abrams, et al. "12 Leaders Who Are Shaping the Next Generation of Artists." *Time*, 7 Feb. 2019, time.com/longform/art-leaders-next-generation/. Accessed 23 June 2019.

Baird, Robert P. "Can Kevin Young Make Poetry Matter Again?" *Esquire*, 6 Nov. 2017, www.esquire.com/entertainment/a13135556/kevin-young-poetry/. Accessed 23 June 2019.

Domestico, Anthony. "A Literary Omnivore's Dream." *Commonweal*, 22 Dec. 2018, www.commonwealmagazine.org/literary-omnivores-dilemma. Accessed 23 June 2019.

Garner, Dwight. "Scorching, Sophisticated New Work from Two of America's Leading Poets." *New York Times*, 16 Apr. 2018, www.nytimes.com/2018/04/16/books/review-wade-in-water-tracy-k-smith-brown-kevin-young.html. Accessed 23 June 2019.

Schneier, Matthew. "In an Age of Fake News, a Historian of the Hoax." *The New York Times*, 7 Nov. 2017, www.nytimes.com/2017/11/07/books/kevin-young-new-yorker-bunk.html. Accessed 23 June 2019.

Smith, Talmon Joseph. "Kevin Young Has Had Just about Enough of This Bullsh——." *The Village Voice*, 22 Apr. 2018, www.villagevoice.com/2018/04/22/kevin-young-has-had-just-about-enough-of-this-bullshit/. Accessed 23 June 2019.

Young, Kevin. "Kevin Young Examines All Things 'Brown.'" Interview by Karen Grigsby Bates. *NPR*, 25 Apr. 2018, www.npr.org/2018/04/25/605597014/kevin-young-examines-all-things-brown. Accessed 23 June 2019.

SELECTED WORKS

Most Way Home, 1995; *Jelly Roll*, 2003; *The Grey Album*, 2012; *Book of Hours*, 2014; *Blue Laws*, 2016; *Bunk*, 2017; *Brown*, 2018

—Chris Cullen

Zedd

Date of birth: September 2, 1989
Occupation: Musician

In 2011 Anton "Zedd" Zaslavski sent a Myspace message that would dramatically alter the course of his life and career. An aspiring electronic musician, he contacted deejay-producer Skrillex and sent the more established artist a sample of his work, which Skrillex enjoyed. Over the next several years, Zedd went from an opening act for Skrillex to a prominent artist in his own right, releasing a variety of extended-play (EP) recordings and official remixes prior to the release of his debut album, *Clarity*, in 2012. The title single from that album went on to win the Grammy Award for Best Dance Recording, a shocking milestone for Zedd. "When I got a nomination for a Grammy, I was like, 'Wait, these people actually know my music?'" he recalled to Chris Martins for *Billboard* (10 Aug. 2017). He followed *Clarity* with the 2015 album *True Colors*, the Top Dance/Electronic Album at the 2016 Billboard Music Awards.

While Zedd continued to experience significant success with his subsequent works, which included critically acclaimed singles such as "Stay" (2017) and "The Middle" (2018), he remained committed to evolving as an artist and opposed to constraints like musical genres. "It's boring to stay the same," he explained to David Drake for *Rolling Stone* (1 June 2015). "It's important for me that my fans known I'm Zedd the musician, not Zedd the EDM DJ. And if I decide

Photo by Mingle Media TV via Wikimedia Commons

to make an acoustic album . . . that's still me. My heart is in there."

EARLY LIFE AND MUSICAL EDUCATION

Zedd was born Anton Zaslavski in the Soviet Union (now Russia) on September 2, 1989. At the age of three, he moved to Dansenberg, Germany, with his family, and they later settled in the city of Kaiserslautern. Music featured prominently in Zedd's childhood: his father, Igor, was a teacher who also played guitar, and his mother, Marina, played and taught piano. Zedd began playing piano himself at the age of four and began writing his own songs as a child. Although he initially focused on classical music, his interests later shifted to genres of rock such as metal, and he began playing drums as a preteen. During his teen years, Zedd played in the metal band Dioramic alongside his older brother, Arkadi, and had his first experiences of touring and playing music in front of live audiences.

While in his teens, Zedd began to develop an interest in electronic music and was particularly inspired by Justice, an electronic duo made up of French musicians Gaspard Augé and Xavier de Rosnay. "I just thought [their music] was really great-sounding, from a sound design aspect," he explained to Zack O'Malley Greenburg for *Forbes* (14 Aug. 2013). "And musically, it was just really interesting, and I had no clue how to do that." He drew inspiration from electronic artists such as Daft Punk and Skrillex as well as from older rock groups such as the Beatles and Queen. As he delved into making electronic music of his own, beginning around 2009, he began to use the name Zedd, a nickname he had been given in school taken from the first letter of his last name.

EARLY CAREER

Zedd quickly gained attention for his work after sending remixes he had made to a variety of contests. A key moment in his career came in 2011, when he sent a song he had been working on to the American electronic artist and record producer Skrillex through the social-networking site Myspace. Skrillex was impressed by Zedd's work and helped the young artist obtain representation, and the two went on to tour together. Although touring with Skrillex was a significant milestone for Zedd, he later commented on how different the experience was from headlining his own tours several years later. "My production, as an opening act, was just a folding table," he recalled to Greenburg for *Forbes* (14 Nov. 2017). "And between me and the next DJ, who was Porter Robinson, I looped the song, and he came on stage, and while the song was looping, we switched tables into his laptop, and then I was like, 'Thanks, guys!' And I'd walk off the stage and he'd start."

In addition to touring, Zedd remained active as a remix artist and began to release official remixes for artists such as Lady Gaga, who later hired him to produce tracks for her 2013 album *ARTPOP*. He released an EP record, *Autonomy*, in 2011 and followed that record with various other EPs and singles as well as remixes of his own tracks and songs by other artists.

In 2012 Zedd released his first full-length album, *Clarity*. The album received attention thanks to the title track, which featured vocals by the British singer Foxes that Zedd later revealed had been a late addition to the song. "I was actually really close [to] not even putting ["Clarity"] on the album because I was not happy with the way the vocals sounded," he told the official website of the *Grammy Awards* (2 Dec. 2014). "A few days before deadline my manager [brought] me Foxes' [music] and . . . I was like, 'That's exactly the kind of voice I want for 'Clarity.'" The song went on to win the Grammy Award for Best Dance Recording, further establishing Zedd as an electronic artist to watch.

MAJOR ARTIST

Over the years following the release of *Clarity*, Zedd continued to experience commercial and critical success and to make music with a variety of collaborators. In 2014 he collaborated with pop singer Ariana Grande on the single "Break Free," which went triple platinum in the United States. The following year saw the release of Zedd's second album, *True Colors*, which included popular singles such as "I Want You to Know," featuring singer Selena Gomez. "I got really lucky that every collaborator really trusted my vision, even if it was outside of their comfort zone," he told Drake about his many musical collaborations. "Every single person I worked with trusted my vision, and at the point where we recorded vocals, the songs weren't always done. Sometimes they were really raw. It was like, just trust me. I'm not gonna do anything that's not great." A concept album in which each song stood for a different color, *True Colors* won Top Dance/Electronic Album at the Billboard Music Awards. A documentary on the making of *True Colors* premiered at the Los Angeles Film Festival in 2016.

As Zedd's popularity among fans of electronic and pop music grew, his concerts became increasingly elaborate events that he likened in interviews to film or theater performances due to their strong visual components. During 2017 he was involved in a number of high-profile concerts, including various performances as part of a residency at Las Vegas's OMNIA Nightclub. The residency continued throughout 2017, and in early 2018, the Hakkasan Group, which operates several Las Vegas venues including

OMNIA, announced that Zedd was extending his residency with performances through 2020.

The artist also engaged in political activism during that year, working with the American Civil Liberties Union (ACLU) to organize a concert protesting US president Donald Trump's ban on travelers from a group of Muslim-majority countries. When speaking about the concert, Zedd explained that while he was not affected personally by the ban, the issue felt "personal" to him due to his own immigrant background, as he told *CNN* (11 Mar. 2017). "It just sparked something in me and I decided to start speaking up," he explained. "Although I'm a musician, I'm also a human being and I have my own opinion. I feel like I have a right to express my thoughts." In addition to Zedd himself, the concert, known as Welcome!, featured performances by Skrillex, Halsey, and Imagine Dragons.

HIT SINGLES

Although Zedd had experienced substantial success with his earlier strategies for releasing albums and singles, in 2017 he began to experiment with releasing new tracks shortly after they were completed rather than waiting to include them on an album. He launched that strategy in February of that year with the release of the song "Stay," featuring singer Alessia Cara. "That was the first time I finished a song essentially, and put it out right away," Zedd told Greenburg for *Forbes* (14 Nov. 2017). "It sounded fresh. I don't know how fresh 'Stay' would have sounded if I released it two years from now, when the rest of my album is done. I want to try that for a little while." The song went on to be nominated for the Grammy Award for Best Pop Duo/Group Performance. Zedd revisited that release strategy in 2018 for his song "The Middle," featuring Maren Morris and Grey, which went on to be nominated for the Grammy Awards for Best Pop Duo/Group Performance, Song of the Year, and Record of the Year. In May 2019 Zedd announced plans for a new tour, Orbit, and sparked rumors that the artist would release a third album. The Orbit tour was set to begin in September of that year.

Despite making a name for himself as an electronic artist during the first decade of his career, Zedd often stated in interviews that he did not necessarily envision himself remaining in that genre forever. "I personally see myself as a musician in the first place," he told Greenburg in 2013. "You know, I don't want to say I will be a producer and DJ for the rest of my life. I can totally see myself being in another band in five years, if that's what my heart and soul wants to do, if that's what will make me happy I'm totally happy to just not DJ anymore." He reiterated that point when speaking to Greenburg in 2017, expressing a desire to begin performing with live instrumentation at some point in the future.

PERSONAL LIFE

Zedd moved to the United States while working on the Lady Gaga album *ARTPOP*. He owns a house in the Hollywood Hills, where he maintains a home studio, and also has a home in Kaiserslautern. In keeping with both his career and his musical upbringing, he continues to play instruments such as piano, a fact that sometimes surprises collaborators who are unaware of his background. "[A recording artist] was singing and I turned around and started improvising," Zedd recalled to Martins. "He's like, 'I didn't know you could play piano.' I was like, 'How am I going to make music if I don't know how to play music?'" In addition to his musical pursuits, Zedd enjoys playing poker and board games.

SUGGESTED READING

Greenburg, Zack O'Malley. "Zedd Ahead: Meet the Next Big Star of Electronic Music." *Forbes*, 14 Aug. 2013, www.forbes.com/sites/zackomalleygreenburg/2013/08/14/zedd-ahead-meet-the-next-big-star-of-electronic-music. Accessed 14 June 2019.

Martins, Chris. "Zedd, Dance Music's Anti-Bro, on Making Hits for Selena, Kesha and Liam and Why DJs Should 'Speak Up' on Trump." *Billboard*, 10 Aug. 2017, www.billboard.com/articles/news/cover-story/7896990/zedd-interview-billboard-cover-story-2017. Accessed 14 June 2019.

Zaru, Deena. "Zedd Organizes Concert to Speak Out against Trump's Travel Ban." *CNN*, 11 Mar. 2017, www.cnn.com/2017/03/11/politics/zedd-donald-trump-travel-ban-aclu-concert/index.html. Accessed 14 June 2019.

Zedd. "From A to Zedd: The 30 Under 30 Cover Interview." Interview by Zack O'Malley Greenburg. *Forbes*, 14 Nov. 2017, www.forbes.com/sites/zackomalleygreenburg/2017/11/14/from-a-to-zedd-the-30-under-30-cover-interview. Accessed 14 June 2019.

"Zedd." *TheDJList*, thedjlist.com/djs/zedd/info. Accessed 14 June 2019.

Zedd. "Zedd on What He's Learned from Skrillex, Lady Gaga and the Beatles." Interview by David Drake. *Rolling Stone*, 1 June 2015, www.rollingstone.com/music/music-news/zedd-on-what-hes-learned-from-skrillex-lady-gaga-and-the-beatles-42445. Accessed 14 June 2019.

"Zedd Reveals How 'Clarity' Crystallized." *Grammy Awards*, 2 Dec. 2014, www.grammy.com/grammys/news/zedd-reveals-how-clarity-crystallized. Accessed 14 June 2019.

—*Joy Crelin*

Volodymyr Zelensky

Date of birth: January 25, 1978
Occupation: Politician

In April 2019, Ukrainian comedian Volodymyr Zelensky (also known as Vladimir Zelenskiy) was elected president of Ukraine in a landslide victory. Zelensky, who hails from the country's industrial southeast, rose to fame in the late 1990s and early 2000s with Kvartal 95 (Quarter 95), a comedy troupe that grew into a production company. He became one of Ukraine's most popular celebrities, and in 2015, began starring in a television show called *Servant of the People* (*Sluga naroda*) as Vasyl Holoborodko, a schoolteacher who is elected president after his rousing YouTube rant about government corruption goes viral. Zelensky's political rise is a profound example of life imitating art. As a political candidate, he ran largely on the popularity of his television character, with a new political party—the Servant of the People Party—named after his show. Eschewing in-depth interviews and, until the day before the run-off election, debates, his unorthodox campaign was almost entirely digital. He won voters through comedic performances and short online videos. Despite misgivings about his qualifications, he successfully ousted the deeply unpopular incumbent President Petro Poroshenko. Zelensky is Ukraine's first Jewish president, a remarkable sign of the times given the country's anti-Semitic past—including pogroms in the nineteenth and twentieth centuries and the murder of an estimated 1.5 million Ukrainian Jews during the Holocaust—and thriving contemporary far-right groups.

EARLY LIFE AND EDUCATION

Volodymyr Zelensky was born in Kryvyi Rih, a predominantly Russian-speaking industrial city in southeastern Ukraine, on January 25, 1978. At the time, Ukraine was a part of the Soviet Union. Zelensky grew up in the town's central district, Kvartal 95. His father, Oleksandr Zelensky, a Doctor of Economics, was head of the computer science department at the local branch of Kyiv National Economic University (KNEU). His mother, Rimma Zelenska, worked as an engineer.

During his childhood, Zelensky's family lived briefly in Erdenet, Mongolia. They returned to Kryvyi Rih after four years. Zelensky attended School Number 95, and later, studied law at KNEU's Kryvyi Rih Economic Institute with the ambition of becoming a diplomat.

Zelensky, who began performing comedy in college, launched his performing career on a popular competitive Russian television improv-quiz show called *KVN* (*Klub veselikh i nanodchivikh*, Club of the funny and inventive

people), while he was still a student. In 1997, he won a campus-wide mock presidential election as a member of the fictitious, anticorruption Clean Ukraine party. That same year he and his comedy team won an international comedy competition in Moscow. The victory made him a local celebrity. In an interview with Anthony Kao for *Cinema Escapist* (22 Aug. 2017), Zelensky described his evolution from law student to comedian as a happy accident. "Sometimes you think you totally control the situation, but in reality it's like you're guided in some way, as if destiny is building your career in a way that you didn't intend."

KVARTAL 95

Zelensky cofounded the *KVN* comedy team Kvartal 95, named after the district where he grew up. From 1999 to 2003, the team dominated *KVN* competitions. In 2003, Zelensky and his team launched Kvartal 95 as an independent production company and teamed up with a television channel called 1+1, owned by Ukrainian oligarch Ihor Kolomoisky. Throughout the 2000s and 2010s, 1+1 produced a number of Kvartal 95 shows.

Zelensky was soon ubiquitous in Ukrainian media, becoming one of the country's most popular celebrities. In 2006, he won a Ukrainian version of the reality television program *Dancing with the Stars*. He was involved in a number of television shows as a writer, producer, and/or actor, including *Svaty* (Matchmakers, 2008–). He also starred in films such as *Lubov v bolshom gorode* (*No Love in the City*, 2009), a romantic comedy about three Russian expats living in

Photo by The Presidential Office of Ukraine via Wikimedia Commons

New York City who are cursed with impotence until they find true love. In 2012, Zelensky starred in a comedy called *Rževski protiv Napoleona*, (Rževski versus Napoleon), in which he plays the titular French emperor. Zelensky codirected, cowrote, and starred in Kvartal 95's 2018 comedy feature *Ya, Ty, Vin, Vona*.

SERVANT OF THE PEOPLE

Zelensky and Kvartal 95 first came up with the idea for *Servant of the People* in the early 2000s. They initially envisioned it as a reality show, in which ordinary people would sell themselves as political candidates and viewers would vote for them. "Back then, the political situation in Ukraine wasn't so challenging," Zelensky told Kao. "Despite the fact that people weren't very interested in politics at the time, we still somehow fantasized about and came up with the idea of a commoner becoming the head of state." The scripted show premiered in 2015.

On the show, Zelensky plays a schoolteacher named Vasyl Holoborodko who rants to his class about corruption in politics—a rousing call to decency that resonated for many of the show's Ukrainian viewers. Holoborodko's speech is recorded by a student and posted on the Internet where it goes viral. Once elected to the presidency—with over 60 percent of the popular vote—Holoborodko, known as the "People's President," and his crew of everymen humorously try to outwit villains and do well by their countrymen. In 2016, at least a year before there was any suggestion that Zelensky might run for office himself, Katherine Jacobsen of *Foreign Policy* magazine (13 Dec. 2016) wrote that *Servant of the People* offered a tantalizing vision of real democracy in Ukraine. She noted the show's pointed lampooning of government officials, and quoted Zelensky as saying, "The best way to make sure Ukrainians don't come to accept the current state of affairs as normal is to put these [political] absurdities in a new format." The show became so popular that Fox Studios purchased adaptation rights; Netflix made the show internationally available starting in 2017. A film called *Servant of the People* 2 was released in 2016. Notably, Zelensky spent much of his campaign filming the show's third season, which was released just before the election.

FROM COMEDIAN TO CANDIDATE

To understand Zelensky's election—or even why *Servant of the People* so deeply captured the Ukrainian imagination—one must first understand the history of Ukraine during the late twentieth and early twenty-first centuries. After the Soviet Union's collapse in 1991, a historical divide reemerged. For centuries, Ukraine has sought to reconcile tensions between its Ukrainian-speaking, pro-European western region, and its Russian-speaking, pro-Russian eastern region and Crimea. In 2004, Ukrainians took to the streets after Viktor Yanukovych, a pro-Russian presidential candidate, won an election through massive voter fraud. The unrest sparked the Orange Revolution, and the pro-European candidate, Viktor Yushchenko, eventually took office. Yanukovych was lawfully elected president in 2010, but in November 2013, Ukrainians took to the streets again, in what became known as the Maidan Revolution. The Maidan Revolution saw the ouster of Yanukovych, but in retaliation, Russia illegally annexed Crimea, a pro-Russian autonomous region within Ukraine, in March 2014. At the same time, Russia began funding separatist groups in eastern Ukraine, sparking the ongoing Donbas War a month later. By 2019, the conflict had cost more than 13,000 lives and displaced more than 2 million people. In addition to Ukraine's geopolitical woes, the country is ruled by a corrupt oligarchy.

The exploits of politicians and oligarchs had provided rich fodder for Zelensky and his comedy troupe since their inception, but around the time of the Maidan Revolution and the events that followed, the elite's tolerance for satire began to wane. Zelensky's wife, comedy writer and Kvartal 95 member Olena Zelenska, recalled 2014 as the year she and her husband began to think seriously about participating in politics, not merely satirizing them. "Most politicians took our humor with dignity, the way it should be, like in the United States where you can call the president anything," she said in an interview with Anna Nemtsova for the *Daily Beast* (30 Apr. 2019). "But in the last five years authorities indicated 'the game is over'. . . . That's when we decided to do something, to save our democracy. When TV channels one by one fell under the leadership's control, we realized if we didn't act, we'd end up in the same situation as Russia."

Zelensky announced his candidacy for president at the stroke of midnight on New Year's Day 2019 on the 1+1 holiday broadcast. He was among a staggering thirty-nine candidates running against incumbent president Petro Poroshenko. The first round of the election took place on March 31, 2019. Zelensky led the pack with 30 percent of the vote—Poroshenko came in second with less than 16 percent of the vote. The results forced a run-off election. On the eve of voting, Zelensky agreed to debate Poroshenko at the Olimpiyskiy Stadium in Kiev. Of his own unexpected popularity, Zelensky told Poroshenko, as quoted by Joshua Yaffa for the *New Yorker* (22 Apr. 2019), "I am the result of your mistakes."

On April 22, 2019, Zelensky won the presidency with 73 percent of the vote. He was sworn into office on May 20, 2019. In his inauguration speech, he dissolved the parliament, which was dominated by members of Poroshenko's party, and called for new elections to be held in July 2019 instead of October. He also called on members of the public to apply to join the Servant of the People party as parliamentary candidates. Zelensky's party appeared to win a parliamentary majority in the July election.

Despite his pledge to end corruption, Zelensky's continuing relationship with Kolomoisky, the owner of 1+1, has raised concerns. Although Kvartal 95 continues to sell content to 1+1, Zelensky denies that he has any further business connections with Kolomoisky. The oligarch went into self-imposed exile after he was accused of defrauding Ukraine's largest bank of over $5 billion in 2016. His financial and legal resources, including his personal lawyer, were integral to Zelensky's campaign, and though Zelensky has repeatedly denied that Kolomoisky has any influence over him, the billionaire's return to Ukraine, just days before Zelensky's inauguration, has complicated that view.

PERSONAL LIFE

Zelensky met his wife, Olena (Kiyashko) Zelenska, in high school in Kryvyi Rih. Zalenska is a scriptwriter and longtime member of Kvartal 95. The couple were married in 2003 and have two children, Oleksandra and Kyrylo.

SUGGESTED READING

Jacobsen, Katherine. "How a Fictional President Is Helping Ukrainians Rethink Their Absurd Politics." *Foreign Policy*, 13 Dec. 2016, foreignpolicy.com/2016/12/13/how-a-fictional-president-is-helping-ukrainians-rethink-their-absurd-politics/. Accessed 22 July 2019.

Nemtsova, Anna. "Ukraine's Funny New First Lady Is Dead Serious, Just Like Her Husband." *Daily Beast*, 30 Apr. 2019, www.thedailybeast.com/ukraines-funny-new-first-lady-olena-zelenska-is-dead-seriousjust-like-her-husband. Accessed 22 July 2019.

Yaffa, Joshua. "Can the Actor Who Ruled Ukraine on TV Do It in Real Life?" *The New Yorker*, 22 Apr. 2019, www.newyorker.com/news/news-desk/can-the-actor-who-ruled-ukraine-on-tv-do-it-in-real-life. Accessed 22 July 2019.

Zelensky, Vladimir. "Interview: Vladimir Zelenskiy on Playing Ukraine's President in 'Servant of the People.'" By Anthony Kao. *Cinema Escapist*, 22 Aug. 2017, www.cinemaescapist.com/2017/08/interview-vladimir-zelenskiy-playing-ukraines-president-servant-people/. Accessed 22 July 2019.

—Molly Hagan

Jane Zhang

Date of birth: October 11, 1984
Occupation: Singer-songwriter

Pop singer Jane Zhang skyrocketed to fame in the early 2000s as a contestant on China's hit singing competition show *Super Girl*. She earned the nickname "Dolphin Princess" for her ability to hit dizzying high notes, including the so-called "whistle note," like her idol, American pop star Mariah Carey. In 2009, Zhang appeared on *The Oprah Winfrey Show*. By then, she was a superstar in China. She had been named China's best female artist three years running—by 2019, she had won the award eight times—and had garnered fifteen number one hit singles. In 2016, Zhang released her first English-language single aimed at an American audience. Produced by legendary American producer Timbaland, "Dust My Shoulders Off" became the first single by a Chinese artist to break the top five on the iTunes download chart. Zhang released her first English-language album, *Past Progressive*, in 2019.

Zhang is one of a slew of Chinese artists looking for crossover success in the US music market. Unlike popular Korean acts such as the boy band BTS or some of the Latin American music stars who have found success in the United States, Zhang chose to make her debut in English rather than her first language, Mandarin. Although some artists, such as Robyn, a pop artist originally from Sweden, have found success singing in English, this approach makes it harder to distinguish crossover artists from their US counterparts. Zhang, who introduced herself to a US audience with an elaborate and playful music video, hopes to distinguish herself in other ways.

EARLY LIFE AND EDUCATION

Jane Zhang was born Zhang Liangying in Chengdu, in China's Sichuan province, on October 11, 1984. Her father was a truck driver. Her mother, Zhang Guiying, worked as an office assistant. Zhang had always dreamed of becoming a singer. She was inspired by Mariah Carey, an American pop singer known for her extraordinary vocal range. "Her voice makes me think about how to sing the songs well, how to release your emotions to everyone," Zhang recalled to Mesfin Fekadu for the Associated Press (31 Jan. 2017). "The first time I heard her music I didn't learn English yet so I didn't understand the lyrics . . . I just feel that her voice is amazing, and I can really feel the things she told." Later, after Zhang had graduated with a degree in English from Sichuan University, she checked Carey's lyrics again. "It just [meant] the same thing I felt," she said. "So I totally think her voice, her songs crossed the culture." Zhang's parents divorced when she was thirteen, and when she was fifteen, her father died, leaving her and her mother in financial straits. To help earn money, Zhang began singing in local bars after school.

SUPER GIRL

The Chinese reality television program *Super Girl* became a pop-culture phenomenon when it premiered in 2004. Its official title, including the name of the show's sponsor, translated to *Mongolian Cow Sour Yogurt Super Girl Contest*. Based on popular programs such as Britain's *Pop Idol* and the United States' *American Idol*, *Super Girl* featured female singers from different regions of China. There had been similar talent programs broadcast locally in China, but *Super Girl* was the first nationally televised show of its kind. In a country where state-owned television stations often broadcast military officials singing patriotic songs, David J. Lynch wrote for *China Daily* (26 May 2005), the flashy, participatory *Super Girl* was an immediate hit. The show capitalized on China's growing prosperity and a desire for individual expression. "If such a program happened five or 10 years ago, I don't think it would have been so influential," one contestant from 2004 told Lynch. "I don't think the ordinary people would have opened themselves up to participate."

Zhang was one of the 120,000 hopefuls—ranging in age from four to eighty-nine—to audition for the show in 2005. She steadily rose through the competition, the rules of which are more complex than those of its American and British counterparts. She often sang English-language songs such as Christina Aguilera's "Reflection," Carey's "Hero," and "Don't Cry for Me Argentina," from the musical *Evita*, and eventually landed on the show's finale. Over 400 million viewers tuned in to watch the show. Zhang came in third place; Li Yuchun, who garnered a staggering 3.5 million votes, was named the winner. In 2007, the Chinese government banned text voting on the show; after a three-year suspension, it banned the show altogether in 2011. Officially, regulators considered the show, which often ran for more than three hours, too long, though many suspected that the government was threatened by the show's large viewership, financial success, and democratic structure.

SUPERSTARDOM IN CHINA

Zhang may have not won *Super Girl*, but her appearance on the show won her a recording contract. "It began with a dream, a dream that exists inside all of us. I participated in the show because of my pure passion for singing," she recalled to Chen Nan for *China Daily* (15 May 2015). "But after that, it became a whole different thing." Zhang released her first album, *The*

Photo by Sherriff via Wikimedia Commons

One, in 2006. It was followed by *Update* in 2007 and *Believe in Jane* in 2010. Discussing the latter album, Zhang told Han Bingbin and Qin Zhongwei for *China Daily* (22 Aug. 2010) that she struggled to reconcile her fans' desire for plaintive love songs with the music she really wanted to make. "Hopefully, I can contribute more of my own thoughts to the making of future albums," she said. Promoting *Believe in Jane*, Zhang embarked on an ambitious world tour called "I Believe." In 2011, she released an album called *Reform*; it was more energetic and upbeat than her earlier offerings, and Zhang expressed some concern about how her fans would react. "Sure, I'm worried, but I don't want to be worried," she told Han and Qin for *China Daily* (7 June 2011). "I don't want to shoulder too many public expectations. I have my own expectations, too, and I will be the kind of singer I want to be." Still, the album divided fans. In 2013, Zhang took time off to reflect, to paraphrase her interview with Chen, on what kind of singer she wanted to be. In 2014, she returned to the spotlight, releasing an album called *The Seventh Sense*. It was met with lukewarm reviews. In 2015, Zhang appeared on a popular reality television show for professional singers called *I Am A Singer*.

"DUST MY SHOULDERS OFF" AND AMERICA DEBUT

In 2016, Zhang teamed up with American music producer Timbaland on a song called "Dust My Shoulders Off." It was not Zhang's first English-language song, but it marked her first serious bid to enter the American market. The song broke the top five on the iTunes download chart, and its beguiling video garnered millions of views. The "Dust My Shoulders Off" video is a kaleidoscope of art and pop culture references. It features Zhang in a series of famous paintings including Vincent van Gogh's *Self-Portrait*, Johannes Vermeer's *Girl with a Pearl Earring*, Andrew Wyeth's *Christina's World*, and Edvard Munch's *The Scream*. (It also features references to boxer Mike Tyson and the film *Men in Black*.) The impressive video was hard-earned for Zhang and her staff, who spent forty-eight continuous hours shooting it. "I was painted over and over again throughout the production. It was painful to remove the makeup. My face was swollen after we finished the shooting for the second painting," Zhang recalled to the *BBC* (21 Dec. 2016). The elaborate video served as a strategic introduction to Zhang's work. "Stars have to be beautiful or sexy in Chinese-language music videos, or the stars' dance moves have to be shown clearly," the video's director, Liao Jen Shuai, told the *BBC*. "I told her that I have to let the audience remember your cool and fun personality. I have to let them know you are a brave singer who loves challenges. To break into the US market, this is the thing that matters."

Zhang released her second English single, "Work for It," in 2017. She performed alongside British pop star Harry Styles and American R & B singer Miguel at the Victoria's Secret Fashion Show in Shanghai the same year. Zhang released her debut English-language album, *Past Progressive*, in 2019. It was a long time in the making. In a 2017 interview, Zhang said that she had been working on it for the previous two or three years at that point. The album includes the song "Fighting Shadows," featuring rapper Big Sean, from the film *Terminator Genisys* (2015), and "Body First," the album's third single. In many ways, *Past Progressive*—the title is a term for an English verb tense that refers to something that was happening in the past continuously or over time, e.g., "I was running errands all day yesterday"—is the musically diverse album Zhang has been looking to make her entire career. "Compared to repeating the same work, the process of making this album makes every day more fulfilling, giving myself more enthusiasm, motivation and goals for music," Zhang said, as quoted by *Billboard* (10 May 2019). "The 16 songs you hear are about my work and life. It was my biography of music, and is Past Progressive."

PERSONAL LIFE

Zhang married longtime boyfriend Feng Ke, the CEO of her management company, in 2016. The union angered Zhang's mother, who accused Feng of lying to Zhang—the couple first began dating when Zhang was nineteen; he was still married—and exploiting her finances. The couple divorced in 2018.

SUGGESTED READING

Chen Nan. "'Dolphin Princess' Finds Her Voice 10 Years On." *China Daily*, 15 May 2015, www.chinadaily.com.cn/life/2015-05/15/content_20722364.htm. Accessed 20 June 2019.
"Could Jane Zhang Become China's First Global Pop Star?" *BBC*, 21 Dec. 2016, www.bbc.com/news/world-asia-china-38179767. Accessed 20 June 2019.
"C-Pop Superstar Jane Zhang Releases English Debut Album, 'Past Progressive.'" *Billboard*, 10 May 2019, www.billboard.com/articles/news/international/8510967/china-jane-zhang-english-debut-album-past-progressive. Accessed 20 June 2019.
Fekadu, Mesfin. "Chinese Singer Jane Zhang Gets the Timbaland Touch." *Associated Press*, 31 Jan. 2017, apnews.com/7a6b443f9fc047cf8d4f7044488ea7d4. Accessed 20 June 2019.
Han, Bingbin, and Qin Zhongwei. "Jane Zhang Liangying's No Plain Jane." *China Daily*, 22 Aug. 2010, www.chinadaily.com.cn/life/2010-08/22/content_11185343.htm. Accessed 20 June 2019.
Lynch, David J. "China Under Spell of Mighty 'Super Girl.'" *China Daily*, 26 May 2005, www.chinadaily.com.cn/english/doc/2005-05/27/content_446335.htm. Accessed 20 June 2019.

SELECTED WORKS

The One, 2006; *Update*, 2007; *Believe in Jane*, 2010; *Past Progressive*, 2019

—*Molly Hagan*

Karen Zoid

Date of birth: August 10, 1978
Occupation: Singer-songwriter

Karen Zoid is one of South Africa's most influential rock musicians. With an impressive oeuvre of award-winning albums, recorded in both English and Afrikaans, Zoid has been dubbed South Africa's "Queen of Rock." In the early 2000s, her songs served as the soundtrack to the lives of so many young South African fans that cultural observers often refer to it as the "Zoid Generation."

Alluding to the 1994 dismantling of the repressive and racist apartheid system in South African, Zoid tried explaining the carefree appeal of rock music such as hers to Simon Robinson for *Time* (11 Apr. 2004). "People across the globe are trying to be individuals rather than part of a group," Zoid said. "The new generation is living free. We have a democracy now. We don't care about politics."

Zoid does not, however, want to be pigeon-holed into appealing only to a particular generation of music lover. "When I was sixteen I discovered Pink Floyd, which is so after the fact," she recalled to Therese Owen for *IOL* (16 Feb. 2011). "I hope that one day a sixteen-year-old will discover my music in their parents' music collection and it will mean something to them."

In addition to her recording career, Zoid has become a television celebrity in her home country, presiding over multiple seasons of the talk show *Republiek van Zoid Afrika*. On the show, she interviews notable figures and performs with her musical guests. She also served for a time as a judge on the South African version of the televised talent competition *The Voice*.

Zoid maintains an active social media presence and owes much of her current success to such global online platforms as *iTunes*. She told Herman Eloff for the South African news outlet *Channel 24* (19 Sept. 2017) that we are currently "living in a time when anyone can put anything on the internet." She asserted, "To stand out among the masses you need to put your heart and soul into it. You have to put your very best out there and then people will take notice."

EARLY LIFE AND EDUCATION
Zoid was born Karen Louise Greeff on August 10, 1978, in Brussels, Belgium, where her father, a career diplomat, was then posted. Her early years were split between Belgium and Johannesburg, South Africa. The Johannesburg township of Soweto was home to activists Nelson Mandela and Desmond Tutu, and the area was a hub of the ultimately successful anti-apartheid movement.

When Zoid was just nine years old, her mother died of cancer. Unable to fully cope, she descended into drug addiction during her teens and became estranged from her father. Discussing her past, Zoid released an open letter, posted on *Facebook*, on July 13, 2016. Headed "An open letter to someone who needs hope," Zoid wrote: "By the time I was twenty I had overdosed four times, and lost too many friends to death by overdose or suicide. I have been free from drugs for almost seventeen years now. It just doesn't even feel like the person I am writing about is actually me anymore." She concluded, "Whatever your vice is, whatever your pain is, there is always a way out. Don't give up—ever."

Zoid's addiction affected both her personal relationships and her education. As a teenager, she ran away to Cape Town, a city on South Africa's southwest coast, but she later reconciled with her father. She attended the National Arts School in Johannesburg but dropped out before graduating. In 1996, she studied drama at The School for the Creative Economy (AFDA), before earning her matric certificate—the South

African equivalent of a general education diploma (GED)—by taking correspondence courses.

Throughout most of her early life, Zoid had played in bands and busked on the street to earn money. Although she was most often part of punk or metal groups, she cites gentler singer/songwriters like Joni Mitchell, whom she listened to as a child, as major influences, because they wrote about the travails and joys of ordinary, everyday life. In the late 1990s, Zoid shifted her attention to focus on music as a career.

BECOMING THE QUEEN OF ROCK
In 2001, Zoid was signed to major label EMI on the strength of her experience with local punk and metal bands. In June of that year, her debut album, *Poles Apart*, was released to near universal acclaim. *Poles Apart*, "arrived just as a new wave of South African rock acts were starting to make their presence felt, particularly Afrikaans bands," Stephen Segerman wrote in a review included on *South African Rock Encyclopedia* (Dec. 2001). "The movement needed a figurehead, and in a year in which the ladies led the pop-rock procession from the front, it got just that. Up stepped this smart, confident, vulnerable, funny, sneering, sweet, blonde rocker, with a sack of great songs, and an enthusiasm and belief in her and our music that should be bottled." *Poles Apart*, which included the infectious anthem "Afrikaners Is Plesierig," garnered numerous laurels, including two Geraas Music Awards, in the categories of best newcomer and best rock album, and was nominated for the South African Music Association (SAMA) Award for Rock Album of the Year.

Her sophomore effort, *Chasing the Sun* (2003), fared similarly well, earning Zoid three of the five Geraas Music Awards for which she was nominated: best songwriter, best album, and best rock album. That year she was named one of the top-six rising stars of South Africa by the South Africa *Sunday Times* newspaper and landed on multiple other lists of top public figures.

In 2005, Zoid released of her third well-received album, *Media*, and earned gold status for her earlier releases. The same year, she received an invitation to play at a charity concert organized by Mandela, who had served as South Africa's president between 1994 and 1999. The concert included performances by South African legend Johnny Clegg and the internationally famous band Queen. In 2008, the same year she was awarded the SAMA Award for Best Female Artist, she played at a celebration of Mandela's ninetieth birthday.

After the releases of her next three albums, *Postmodern World* (2007), *Ultimate Zoid* (2009), and *Terms & Conditions* (2010), Zoid was so firmly established in the South African music scene that she was often described as something of a *grande dame*. Zoid, Owen asserted, "created a unique space for herself. Before her there was no Afrikaans female singer who played rock 'n' roll guitar like a boy. There was no Afrikaans female artist who was that aggressive on stage . . . . She earned respect among men because she knows music and how to deliver it well."

ACTING AND HOSTING

In 2010, Zoid's popularity led to a starring role in the film *Susanna van Biljon*, playing a woman from a small South African town who longs to have a professional singing career. She then released the album *Zoid Afrika* (2012). In 2014, Zoid began hosting a talk show called *Die Republiek van Zoid Afrika* on the South African television network KykNet. The first episode was broadcast on July 10 of that year and quickly became a hit. Among its most popular features was the concluding segment, in which Zoid performs a duet with the musical guest of the day, including such notables as Kurt Darren and Zolani Mahola. Beginning in the second season, Zoid recorded the numbers and released them on *iTunes*: they regularly appeared on the local *iTunes* chart and, between 2015 and 2016, she released four volumes of collected songs from the show.

Die Republiek van Zoid Afrika was not without controversy, however, despite audiences' fondness for both Zoid and the show's format. She raised the ire of many observers, for example, when she had as her guest singer Steve Hofmeyr, who had made seemingly pro-apartheid statements. "The idea of my TV show is to have conversations with people that have made a mark in South Africa. Steve certainly fits the profile," Zoid explained to Rudi Massyn for *Empire Road Interviews* (16 Sept. 2015). "I think it is important that we stay in conversation with people from different religious, sexual and political orientation than ourselves in this country. How will we grow or understand love if we boycott each other?"

ENGLISH AND AFRIKAANS ALBUMS

Zoid returned to music in 2015, with the release of *Drown Out the Noise*, her first English-language work in several years. "It was time for an English album again. I've been working on a lot of Afrikaans projects lately, which I absolutely love, but I needed to do something for a wider audience this time," she explained to Herman Eloff for *Channel 24* (30 Apr. 2015). "I wanted to go big." She followed *Drown out the Noise* with 2017's *Op Die Oomblik (Deel Een)*, an extended play (EP) of Afrikaans tunes that was officially released on the South African holiday of Spring Day. The lead single from the album, "Vir Jou," landed immediately atop the South African music charts. From 2016 to 2017, Zoid also served

as one of the judges on the South African version of the juggernaut talent competition *The Voice*, a franchise that has proven popular in some sixty countries. Over the course of her career, almost thirty of Zoid's tunes have appeared at number one.

PERSONAL LIFE

In 2004, Zoid married fellow guitarist Don Reinecke, with whom she had long collaborated musically. They had a son together in early 2007, before divorcing in 2010.

SUGGESTED READING

Eloff, Herman. "Karen Zoid: I Only Know Now Who I Really Am." *Channel 24*, 19 Sept. 2017, www.channel24.co.za/Music/News/karen-zoid-i-only-know-now-who-i-really-am-20170919. Accessed 6 Jan. 2019.

Eloff, Herman. "25 Minutes with Karen Zoid and a Whole String of Social Media Notifications on My Phone." *Channel 24*, 30 Apr. 2015, www.channel24.co.za/Music/News/25-minutes-with-Karen-Zoid-and-a-whole-string-of-social-media-notifications-on-my-phone-20150430. Accessed 6 Jan. 2019.

Jordaan, Dirk. "A New Voice for SA Rock." *Channel 24*, 1 Mar. 2002, www.news24.com/xArchive/Archive/A-new-voice-for-SA-rock-20010731. Accessed 6 Jan. 2019.

Owen, Therese. "A New Life on Her Terms." *IOL*, 16 Feb. 2011, www.iol.co.za/entertainment/music/a-new-life-on-her-terms-1027049. Accessed 6 Jan. 2019.

Robinson, Simon. "That's Kwaito Style." *Time*, 11 Apr. 2004, content.time.com/time/magazine/article/0,9171,610043,00.html. Accessed 6 Jan. 2019.

Segerman, Stephan. Review of *Poles Apart*, by Karen Zoid. *South African Rock Encyclopedia*, Dec. 2001, www.rock.co.za/legends/2000plus/karen_zoid_poles_apart.html. Accessed 4 Feb. 2019.

Zoid, Karen. "My Interview with Karen Zoid." Interview by Rudi Massyn. *Empire Road Interviews*, 16 Sept. 2015, empireroadinterviews.wordpress.com/2015/09/16/my-interview-with-karen-zoid/. Accessed 6 Jan. 2019.

SELECTED WORKS

Poles Apart, 2001; *Chasing the Sun*, 2003; *Media*, 2005; *Post Modern World*, 2007; *Ultimate Zoid*, 2009; *Terms & Conditions*, 2010; *ZOID AFRIKA*, 2012; *Drown out the Noise*, 2015; *Op Die Oomblik (Deel Een)*, 2017

—*Mari Rich*

OBITUARIES

Paul Allen

Born: Seattle, Washington; January 21, 1953
Died: Seattle, Washington; October 15, 2018
Occupation: Computer software executive, investor

Paul Allen was the co-creator of the renowned computer software company, Microsoft. Along with his childhood friend, Bill Gates, Allen worked throughout his twenties to create a software program that is still largely used today.

Paul Allen was born in 1953 to Kenneth and Faye Allen, who were both librarians at the University of Washington. Allen, and his childhood friend, Bill Gates, attended Lakeside School. In 1971, Allen attended the University of Washington, and that same year, he and Gates started a company, Traf-O-Data. Allen dropped out of college in 1973 and followed Gates to Cambridge, Massachusetts. There, Allen recognized a need for software in the 1975 Altair 8800. He and Gates wrote a version of the computer language BASIC for Altair personal microcomputers. After Gates dropped out of Harvard in 1975 the two friends moved to Albuquerque, New Mexico, to begin work on "Micro-soft." Four years later Allen and Gates decided to move their business to Seattle, Washington. In 1980, the company, IBM, contacted Microsoft to create an operating system for its new computer. Allen and Gates modified an operating system called D-QOS, calling it Microsoft Disk Operating System (MS-DOS), which soon became the preferred operating system for computers. When Allen was diagnosed with Hodgkin's Disease in 1982, treatment limited his involvement with the running of Microsoft. Though he left Microsoft in the capacity he once held, Allen did return in 1990 to serve on the Board of Directors for ten years. In 1985, Allen set up a software company called Asymetrix, and then in 1986 set up an investment research firm, Vulcan Ventures. In 1988, Allen bought the NBA franchise, the Portland Trail Blazers and eventually the Seattle Seahawks, too. In 1992, he and David Liddle, consulting professor of Computer Science at Stanford University co-founded Interval Research, a research think tank, which closed its doors in 2000. Allen also founded Starwave in 1993, which was later purchased by Disney in 1998. Among his investments were Telescan, Metricom, Lone Wolf, Harbinger-EDI Services, Cardinal Technologies, and Virtual Vision. Allen also bought 80 percent of the company, Ticketmaster. In 1994 he formed the Paul Allen Group to keep track of his technology and information investments. Allen also set up several philanthropic foundations, including the Paul G. Allen Family Foundation and the Allen Spinal Cord Atlas.

Paul Allen died of non-Hodgkin's lymphoma at the age of 65. He is survived by his sister, Jody Patton, and her family.

See *Current Biography* 1998

Thomas J.J. Altizer

Born: Cambridge, Massachusetts; September 28, 1927
Died: Stroudsburg, Pennsylvania; November 28, 2018
Occupation: Theologian

Thomas JJ Altizer was a main proponent of the 1960s theological movement "God is Dead." Altizer and his colleagues published several works of their theories on religion, and the rise of the Evangelical right is often attributed to the attention put on Altizer's Christian-atheist beliefs and teachings.

Thomas Jonathan Jackson Altizer was born in 1927 to Jackson and Frances Altizer. Altizer graduated from Stonewall Jackson High School in 1944 and then attended the College of the University of Chicago in 1947, after serving in the army during WWII. He obtained a BA in 1948, an MA in theology in 1952, and a PhD in the history of religions in 1955 from the Divinity School of the University of Chicago. In 1954, Altizer became an assistant professor of religion at Wabash College, where he began examining and expanding the prominent Nietzsche theory, "God is Dead." He moved to Emory University in 1956 as an assistant professor in Bible and religion. Once at Emory, Altizer began to publish articles and books on his religious beliefs, being, the traditional Christian image of God as a transcendent creator is obsolete; that organized Christianity has obscured the true spirit of faith by its ecclesiastical forms; and that although God came to Earth in the person of Christ, God died on the cross with Christ. Moving on from such negatives, however, Altizer argues that God entered the world as Christ and that ever since then God has become more immanent in the universe. In 1965, many of Altizer's publications on the theory of "God is Dead," began attracting media attention. Due to his notoriety in the religious community, he was blocked from being a priest but served as a minister at an Episcopal mission in the south of Chicago. In 1968, Altizer moved to the State University of New York at Stony Brook to teach English and in 1996 moved to the Poconos, PA.

Thomas Altizer was married and divorced three times and is survived by his daughter, Katharine, his son, John, and two grandchildren.

See *Current Biography 1967*

Bibi Andersson

Born: Stockholm, Sweden; November 11, 1935
Died: Stockholm, Sweden; April 14, 2019
Occupation: Swedish Actress

Berit Elisabet Andersson, known professionally as Bibi Andersson, was a protégée among the exclusive collective of actors working with Swedish filmmaker Ingmar Bergman. Her start in television soap advertisements at age fifteen with Bergman quickly progressed to a career in Swedish and American stage and film beginning in 1956 and continuing through 2010. She achieved international fame and received awards from multiple countries.

She was born Berit Elisabet Andersson to Stockholm businessman, Josef Andersson and social worker mother, Karin Mansson. Andersson had an older sister Gerd, who became a successful ballerina with the Swedish Royal Opera. Their parents divorced when the girls were young, and Karin remained supportive of their dancing and acting ambitions. At fourteen Andersson worked as a movie extra, and at fifteen she debuted in Ingmar Bergman's Bris soap advertisement. She studied at Terserus Drama School and the Royal Dramatic Theatre School (1954–1956).

While Bergman remained influential in her success, Andersson also worked in American and international productions with other directors: Vilgot Sjöman in *The Mistress* (1962) and *My Sister, My Love* (1966); Ralph Nelson in *Duel at Diablo* (1966); Leonardo Bercovici in *Story of a Woman* (1969); John Huston in *The Kremlin Letter* (1970); and Robert Altman in *The Quintet* (1979). Andersson was admired for her innocence, subtlety, sensitivity, naturalness, free-spiritedness, depth, and complexity. Her roles ranged from devoted wife in *The Seventh Seal* (1956), dual role of boyhood sweetheart/hitchhiker in *Wild Strawberries* (1957), pregnant teen in *Brink of Life* (1957), lesbian in *The Night of the Tribades* (1977), to psychiatrist in *I Never Promised You a Rose Garden* (1977). Among her later productions were: *Poor Butterfly* (1986), *The Lost Prince* (2003), *The Frost* (2009).

Andersson won many Best Actress awards for her performances: (1951) Swedish television prize for *Miss Julie*; (1958) Cannes Film Festival for *Brink of Life*; (1963) Swedish Silver Bear for *The Mistress*; (1966) National Society of Film Critics for *Persona*; (1966) French Film Academy for *My Sister, My Love*; (1971) British Film Academy for *The Touch*; and (1975) National Society of Film Critics for *Scenes from a Marriage*.

Bibi Andersson is survived by her third husband Gabriel Mora Baeza, daughter Jenny Matilde Grede (from her first marriage), sister Gerd Andersson, and nephew Lars Bethke.

See *Current Biography 1978*

Moshe Arens

Born: Kaunas, Lithuania; December 27, 1925
Died: Savyon, Israel; January 7, 2019
Occupation: Israeli aeronautical engineer, researcher, diplomat, and politician

A renowned aeronautical engineer, politician, and early mentor of Benjamin Netanyahu, Moshe Arens was a leading Israeli statesman who served as defense minister, minister without portfolio, and ambassador.

Moshe Arens was born in Lithuania and moved to New York City in 1939 following the Nazi occupation of Poland. Arens graduated from George Washington High School before serving two years in the Engineers Corps where he was discharged with the rank of Sergeant First Class. After the war, he recommenced his studies at the Massachusetts Institute of Technology (MIT), earning a Bachelor of Science in Mechanical Engineering degree. After three years in the newly established State of Israel, Arens returned to America to study for a . Master of Science degree in Aeronautical Engineering from the California Institute of Technology (Caltech). Pursuing his aeronautical passion, Arens spent the next 15 years working on jet engine development and served as the Deputy Direct General at Israel Aircraft Industries from 1962 to 1971. An active participant in Herut Party politics since its formation in 1948, Arens was elected to the Knesset in 1974, before becoming chairman of the Knesset Foreign Affairs and Defense Committee in 1977. Arens served in various government positions, from Minister without Portfolio to Minister of Foreign Affairs and Minister of Defense. In 1992, Arens quit politics after Likud's defeat at the ballot box, although he returned in 1999 when Benjamin Netanyahu appointed him Minister of Defense. When Likud, however, lost the elections in 2003, Arens lost his seat for the final time. Upon retiring from his political work, Arens dedicated his time to researching and writing about the Jewish Military Union (ŻZW) who fought alongside the Jewish Combat Organisation (ŻOB) in the Warsaw Ghetto uprising. Arens wrote many articles on the revolt, as well as the book, *Flags Over the Warsaw Ghetto*.

Moshe Arens is survived by his wife Muriel, his sons, Yigal and Raanan, and daughters, Aliza and Rut.

See *Current Biography 1989*

Dominick Argento

Born: York, Pennsylvania; October 27, 1927
Died: Minneapolis, Minnesota; February 20, 2019
Occupation: Composer

Dominick Argento was a composer known primarily for his lyric opera works. He was commissioned by many major performing groups and orchestras across the United States and created new work well into his eighties. His awards include a Pulitzer Prize for music, and a Grammy.

Dominick Argento was born on October 27, 1927, to a family of Sicilian immigrants in York, Pennsylvania. He hated music classes in elementary school but learned to play piano, nonetheless. Shortly after graduating high school, Argento was drafted into the army where he worked as a cryptographer. After the war, and thanks to funding from the GI Bill, he attended the Peabody Conservatory in Baltimore to pursue piano performance but quickly switched to composition. He eventually graduated with both a bachelor's degree and master's degree. He also studied for a year in Florence, Italy, thanks to a scholarship from the US–Italy Fulbright Commission. He earned a PhD from the Eastman School of Music, Rochester, New York, before returning to Florence, Italy, for a year on a Guggenheim Fellowship. Upon his return, he taught at the Eastman School and became director of Hilltop Opera in Baltimore, MD. In 1958, Argento began teaching at the University of Minnesota, where he was commissioned by various performing groups from around the United States. He remained until 1997, holding the rank of Professor Emeritus in later years. Although he was well known for his instrumental works, most of his music was written for voices. He was a pioneer of lyric opera in the United States, emphasizing the power of the human voice in operatic, choral, and solo contexts. Some of his most famed works include the surrealist opera *Postcard from Morocco* (1971), *Casanova's Homecoming* (1984), and *The Dream of Valentino* (1993). He holds many awards and accolades—in 1975, Argento received the Pulitzer Prize for music for his song cycle *From the Diary of Virginia Woolf*. In 1979, he was elected to the American Academy of Arts and Letters, and in 1997 he was named Composer Laureate to the Minnesota

Orchestra. In 2004, he won a Grammy Award for best contemporary classical composition for *Casa Guidi*.

Dominick Argento is not survived by any immediate family.

See *Current Biography 1977*

Paddy Ashdown

Born: New Delhi, India; February 27, 1941
Died: Norton-sub-Hamdon, England; December 22, 2018
Occupation: Politician, diplomat

Paddy Ashdown was the first party leader of the Liberal Democrats, a UK political party that rose in popularity during the late 1980s and throughout the 1990s. Ashdown was known for bridging the political differences between the two additional leading parties, the Labours and the Conservatives.

Jeremy John Durham Ashdown was born in 1941 to John and Lois Ashdown. As a member of Great Britain's Indian Army, Ashdown and his family lived in India until his father retired and moved them to Northern Ireland. He attended Bedford School outside of London and in 1959 enrolled in the Royal Marines, where he served for twelve years. Ashdown then served for five years as the first secretary for the British Mission for the United Nations (UN). He then moved to England to pursue a career in business and quickly became involved in local politics in Yeovil, England, joining the Liberal Party. In 1983, Ashdown was elected as a Liberal to Parliament and in 1988 was elected leader of the Social and Liberal Democratic (SLD) party. As party leader, Ashdown pledged to incorporate both liberal and conservative philosophies and during the early 1990s raised the party in popularity, following PM John Major's takeover succeeding Margaret Thatcher. Then, in 1992, Ashdown publicly admitted to an affair with his secretary; however, the admission did not hinder his performance in the election polls. In 1997, the Labours won the majority, though the Liberal Democrats remained a third party in UK politics. Ashdown retired from politics in 2002 and was appointed as High Representative for Bosnia-Herzegovina. He was appointed President of UNICEF UK in 2009; and in 2015, Ashdown chaired the Liberal Democrats election campaign and extensively campaigned against Brexit. He published his memoirs, entitled *A Fortunate Life*, in 2009.

Paddy Ashdown is survived by his wife, Jane, their daughter, Kate, and their son, Simon.

See *Current Biography 1992*

Max Azria

Born: Sfax, Tunisia; January 1, 1949
Died: Houston, Texas; May 6, 2019
Occupation: Fashion designer

Max Azria was the world-famous fashion designer, who created the women's clothing brand BCBGMAXAZRIA. He was also the chairman and CEO of BCBG Max Azria Group, which ran over 20 brands.

Max Azria, born on January 1, 1949, in Sfax Tunisia. He was the youngest of six children, raised in southeastern France, until his family moved to Paris in 1963. In Paris, Azria began working for a women's apparel line as a designer. After eleven years with the company, Azria moved to Los Angeles and launched "Jess" retail women's apparel boutiques. In 1989, Azria launched BCBG Max Azria, named "Bon Chic, Bon Genre." In 1996, BCBG Max Azria runway collection was first shown at New York Fashion Week. In 1998, Azria was inducted into the Council of Fashion Designers of America. Azria launched a line of couture gowns in 2004, called "Max Azria Atelier," and in 2006, Azria released a ready-to-wear collection, "Max Azria." In 1998, Azria acquired Hervé Léger fashion house, and in 2007, he relaunched Herve Leger with his own designs. At the 2008 New York Fashion Week, Azria presented three of his collections, making him the first American designer to produce three shows during a single fashion week. In 2009, along with his daughter, Joyce, Azria created BCBGeneration. Azria left BCBG in 2016, and the company filed for bankruptcy in 2017. That same year, Azria joined ZappLight, an LED light bulb and bug zapper company, as CEO and partner. As of 2006, there were over 550 BCBG Max Azria boutiques worldwide. His designs were worn by many celebrities, including Sharon Stone, Alicia Keys, Halle Berry, and Fergie. He collaborated with Miley Cyrus in 2009 for his BCBGeneration collection.

Max Azria is survived by his second wife, Lubov, and his six children, Michael, Joyce, Marine, Chloe, Anais, and Agnes.

See *Current Biography 2000*

Leonard L. Bailey

Born: Takoma Park, Maryland; August 28, 1942
Died: Redlands, California; May 12, 2019
Occupation: Surgeon

Leonard Bailey was an American surgeon who specialized in heart transplantation. During his career, he performed more than 200 transplants on young mammals for the sake of his research, hoping to engage with the problem of congenital heart defects in infants. Apart from contributing to this burgeoning body of research, he built a center for children's cardiac surgery at Loma Linda University in Southern California.

Leonard Lee Bailey was born on August 28, 1942, to chef Nelson Bailey and nurse Catherine (Long) Bailey. After graduating from Columbia Union College in 1964, he received his PhD from Loma Linda University, School of Medicine in 1969. In the 1970s, he completed a residency at the Hospital for Sick Children in Toronto, Canada. When this sparked his interest in congenital heart diseases, he became an assistant professor at Loma Linda University's School of Medicine in 1976, focusing on heart transplantation in young mammals. In 1984, Bailey attracted global attention when he transplanted the heart of a baboon into an ailing young girl, Stephanie Fae Beauclair—named Baby Fae by the media. The child, born with half a heart, died twenty-one days after the surgery. However, the controversial case remains in the public eye, infamous for the ethical and moral challenges it presented to the medical world and beyond. Bailey remained focused on pediatric heart surgery for the rest of his career, performing many more infant heart transplants. Indeed, the year after Baby Fae's surgery, he completed the first successful transplant in an infant using the heart of a human donor. He ceased performing operations in 2017.

Leonard Bailey is survived by his two sons Brooks and Connor, and two granddaughters.

See *Current Biography 1999*

Russell Baker

Born: Loudoun County, Virginia; August 14, 1925
Died: Leesburg, Virginia; January 21, 2019
Occupation: Columnist and author

Russell Baker was a two-time Pulitzer prize-winning writer, a columnist for the *New York Times*, and a respected author. His satirical style and sharp political insight were a staple of the American political and literary scene for over six decades.

Russell Wayne Baker was born and raised in Loudoun County, Virginia. He received a scholarship to Johns Hopkins University in 1942, although his studies were interrupted by a stint in the U.S. Navy, before graduating in 1947 with a bachelor's degree. Baker's journalistic career began at *The Baltimore Sun*, where he worked his way up from a night police reporter to White

House Correspondent. Drawn by his droll and witty reporting, he moved to the *New York Times*, where he spent eight years covering politics before receiving his own column. From 1962 to 1998, Baker was the writer of "The Observer", a column that focused on politics and the experience of ordinary American life. His prose was distinctive thanks to his spare use of language, and although he often covered politics with an amused detachment, he was passionate about covering poverty as faced by everyday Americans. Branching out into television, Baker became the host of *Masterpiece Theatre*. Over his extensive literary career, Baker wrote or edited seventeen books, and was elected as Fellow of the American Academy of Arts and Sciences in 1993. To date, he is one of only six people to win a Pulitzer Prize for both Journalism, which he won in 1979 for his "Observer" column, and Arts & Letters, which he won in 1982 for his autobiography, *Growing Up*.

Russell Baker was married to Miriam Nash, who died in 2015. Baker is survived by his four children, Allen, Kasia, Michael, and Phyllis.

See *Current Biography 1980*

Kaye Ballard

Born: Cleveland, Ohio; November 20, 1925
Died: Rancho Mirage, California; January 21, 2019
Occupation: Comedian, singer, television and Broadway actress

Kaye Ballard had a long career as an American actress, singer, comedian, and nightclub performer. She performed on Broadway, as well as starring in the NBC sitcom *The Mothers-in-Law*. Her catchphrase in sketches and on television was "Good luck with your MOUTH!"

Catherine Gloria Balotta was one of four first-generation Italian American children, born to immigrant parents from Calabria, southern Italy. By the 1940s, Ballard had joined the Spike Jones touring revue and started to develop the physical comedy and stand-up routines that would make her name famous. In 1946, Ballard was offered a place in a Broadway revue of *Three to Make Ready* as it was about to go on tour, which she took and appeared across the country. Her theater success continued in 1954 when she won the part of Helen of Troy in a John Latouche and Jerome Moross musical called *The Golden Apple*. The role saw her originating the song ""Lazy Afternoon" that later went on to be recorded by other artists, including Barbra Streisand. When Ballard first released the song, she included on the flip side the first known

recording of the Peggy Lee and Frank Sinatra standard "Fly Me to the Moon." At the pinnacle of her career, Ballard played an ugly stepsister in the CBS television special of Rodgers and Hammerstein's *Cinderella*, alongside Julie Andrews. Ballard's next role in 1961 was for the musical *Carnival!*, where she enjoyed a two-year Broadway run. Ballard then pursued opportunities in television, including a recurring role on *The Doris Day Show*, and as Kaye Buell in NBC's *The Mothers-In-Law*. In 1995, Ballard was recognized by the Palm Springs Walk of Stars with a Golden Palm Star, and in 2006 published her autobiography, *How I Lost 10 Pounds in 53 Years*.

Kaye Ballard never married and left no immediate survivors.

See *Current Biography 1969*

Elizabeth Barrett-Connor

Born: Evanston, Illinois; April 8, 1935
Died: La Jolla, California; June 10, 2019
Occupation: Doctor, researcher, and professor

Elizabeth Barrett-Connor was an epidemiologist and professor who specialized in women's health and aging. She completed studies on conditions like cardiovascular disease and osteoporosis and led the Diabetes Prevention Program Outcomes Study. One of her methods was eventually appropriated by the European Prospective Investigation into Cancer and Nutrition and the UK Biobank study. She received many awards for her work.

Elizabeth Louise Barrett-Connor was born on April 8, 1935, the only child of Florence Hershey and chemical engineer William Barrett. She studied zoology at Mount Holyoke College, graduating in 1956. After earning her medical degree at Cornell University in 1960, she completed her medical residency at the University of Texas Southwestern Medical Center. She then carried out postdoctoral research at the London School of Hygiene & Tropical Medicine, earning a diploma in Clinical Medicine of the Tropics in 1965. Subsequently, she worked in epidemiology at the University of Miami, and then in the faculty of the Department of Family Medicine and Public Health at the University of California San Diego School of Medicine. In 1972, she started the Rancho Bernardo Heart and Chronic Disease Study, recruiting around 70% of Rancho Bernardo's population and collecting data for over four decades. Over the course of her career, Barrett-Connor served as president of the American Public Health Association, the American Epidemiological Society, the American Heart Association Epidemiology Council, and the Society for Epidemiologic Research. In 2018, she was given the Endocrine Society's Fred Conrad Koch Lifetime Achievement Laureate Award for her work on endocrine physiology and hormones in relation to cardiovascular disease, diabetes, osteoporosis, and breast cancer.

Elizabeth Barrett-Connor is survived by her husband James Connor, her three children Caroline, Jonathan, and Steven, and her two step-children Susan and James-Davis.

See *Current Biography 1999*

Birch Bayh

Born: Terre Haute, Indiana; January 22, 1928
Died: Easton, Maryland; March 14, 2019
Occupation: Senator

Birch Bayh was the liberal Senator from Indiana, who campaigned for gender equality and was the driving force behind Title IX.

Birch Evans Bayh Jr. was born on January 22, 1928, in Terre Haute, Indiana, where he attended New Goshen High School. From 1946 to 1948, he served as Military Police with the U. S. Army in occupied Germany, before returning to study at the Purdue University School of Agriculture in 1951. Bayh's foray into politics started when he was elected to the Indiana House of Representatives in 1954 where, at the age of 26, he was the youngest Speaker to date. A farmer and a lawyer, he was Democratic Floor Leader in 1962 when he was elected to the Senate. As a freshman senator, Bayh was made the chairman of the Senate Judiciary's subcommittee on constitutional amendments and remained in that role for two decades. Bayh spearheaded two constitutional amendments: The 25th amendment dealt with the transition of power in the case of presidential death, disability, or resignation, while the 26th amendment sought to reduce the voting age to 18 years old, instead of the previous 21. Bayh was the only non-Founding Father to have ever authored two constitutional amendments in U. S. history. Bayh co-authored and introduced Title IX of the higher Education Act of 1965, which states that no student should be discriminated on the basis of sex from programs or activities receiving federal funding. Bayh drafted the language that barred sex discrimination at schools and colleges and expanded sports programs to women. He additionally authored the Juvenile Justice and Delinquency Prevention Act and co-authored the Bayh–Dole Act. Bayh almost ran for president in both 1972 and 1976 but had to drop out for familial obligations. Bayh held his seat in the Senate for three terms, until he lost in 1980.

Birch Bayh is survived by his second wife, Katherine Bayh, and his sons, Birch Evans Bayh III and Christopher.

See *Current Biography 1965*

Wendy Beckett

Born: Johannesburg, South Africa; February 25, 1930
Died: Quidenham, Norfolk, United Kingdom; December 26, 2018
Occupation: Nun, art critic

Wendy Beckett devoted her life to the Catholic church as a nun. However, in the 1990s, Beckett became known for her knowledge and critique of art. She was commissioned by the BBC to create several documentary series, where she became known for her large owl-like glasses and distinctive lisp.

Wendy Beckett was born in Johannesburg, South Africa, to Aubrey and Dorothy Beckett and at the age of two moved with her family to Edinburgh, Scotland. She attended Catholic boarding school; and at the age of 16, Beckett joined the Sisters of Notre Dame de Namur. In 1950, the order sent her to Oxford University, where Beckett lived for four years and studied literature. She then attended teacher's school in Liverpool and moved to South Africa in 1954 to teach. She taught for fifteen years until the Vatican granted Beckett permission to pursue a life of solitude and contemplation. At this time, she moved to the Carmelite Monastery in Norfolk, where she remained in solitude throughout the 1970s. In 1980, Beckett was given permission by the order to study art. She began to learn about art history; and in the late 1980s, Beckett decided to use her knowledge to earn money for the order. Her first book, *Women Contemporary Artists*, was published in 1988, followed by several pieces for newspapers and magazines. In 1991, Beckett was asked to do a filmed documentary on the British National Gallery. The documentary was very successful, and Beckett was asked to film a six-part series, *Sister Wendy's Odyssey*. Her second series, *Sister Wendy's Grand Tour*, was released in 1994, and her third, *Sister Wendy's Story of Painting*, was released in 1997. Beckett continued to critique art after her show ended and remained devout and often silent.

Wendy Beckett is survived by her brother.

See *Current Biography 1998*

Robert (Bob) Bergland

Born: Roseau, Minnesota; July 22, 1928
Died: Roseau, Minnesota; December 9, 2018
Occupation: Congressman, Secretary of Agriculture

Robert (Bob) Bergland was a liberal Democrat who served as a congressman under President Jimmy Carter. He spent most of his life advocating for America's farmers and consumers, though his advocacy and support was not always welcomed.

Robert Selmer Bergland was born to Selmer and Mabel, one of four siblings. After graduating from Roseau High School, Bergland attended the University of Minnesota School of Agriculture and in 1948 joined the National Farmers Union (NFU) as a field representative. In 1961, Bergland was named chairman of the Minnesota Agricultural Stabilization and Conservation Service and was then promoted to Midwest regional director. Bergland was elected to the House of Representatives in 1970 and was reelected three times. He was named to the Cabinet during his last term. Under President Carter, Bergland was appointed agriculture secretary. While in Congress, he served on the Agriculture Committee and guided policies relating to price supports for farmers and federal food-stamp programs. From 1981–1982 he served as president of Farmland-Eaton World Trade and then became executive vice president and general manager of the National Rural Electric Cooperative Association (NRECA). Bergland retired in 1994.

Bob Bergland is survived by his wife, Helen; five children: Franklyn, Allan, Bill, Dianne, and Linda; eighteen grandchildren; and sixteen great-grandchildren. He was predeceased by his two sons, Jon and Stevan.

See *Current Biography 1977*

Robert L. Bernstein

Born: New York, New York; January 5, 1923
Died: Manhattan, New York; May 27, 2019
Occupation: Publisher, human rights activist

Robert L. Bernstein was a publisher and human rights activist who worked as the President and CEO of Random House for 25 years. He also founded the famous NGO Human Rights Watch.

Robert L. Bernstein was born to a Jewish family in New York on January 5, 1923. He graduated from Harvard University with a BSc in 1944, before starting his career in publishing as an office boy for Simon & Schuster in 1946. In 1956, he moved to Random House, where he succeeded Bennett Cerf as CEO ten years later. He served as the president of Random House for 25 years. He soon became interested in writers whose work could not be published because of restrictions in their own countries and ensured that famed dissidents such as Andrei Sakharov, Yelena Bonner, Václav Havel, Jacobo Timerman, Xu Wenli, and Wei Jingsheng were able to be published around the world. He established the Fund for Free Expression, which was to be the parent organization of Helsinki Watch, an NGO established to monitor the former Soviet Union's compliance with the Helsinki Accords. Numerous "Watch Committees" then followed and in 1988 merged to become Human Rights Watch. Bernstein won numerous awards and accolades for his work in Human rights, including the Human Rights Award from the Lawyers Committee for Human Rights and the Florina Lasker Award from the New York Civil Liberties Union. In 1988, Yale Law School honored him by creating the Robert L. Bernstein Fellowships in International Human Rights at Yale Law School. He was later also honored by the NYU School of Law that established the Robert L. Bernstein Fellowship in International Human Rights in 2006 and the Robert L. Bernstein Institute for Human Rights in 2015. He received honorary doctorates from numerous universities including Swarthmore College, The New School, Bard College, Bates College, and Yale University.

Robert L. Bernstein is survived by his wife of 69 years, Helen, along with three sons, a sister, ten grandchildren and four great-grandchildren.

See *Current Biography 1987*

Bernardo Bertolucci

Born: Parma, Italy; March 16, 1941
Died: Rome, Italy; November 26, 2018
Occupation: Film director

Bernardo Bertolucci was film director and screenplay writer notorious for such films as *Last Tango in Paris* (1972), which caused controversy for its explicit sex scenes, and *The Last Emperor* (1987), which received nine Oscar awards, including Best Director and Best Adapted Screenplay.

Bernardo Bertolucci was born to Attilio and Ninetta Bertolucci. His father was a well-known poet and his mother was a schoolteacher, so Bertolucci began writing at a very young age. By the age of fifteen he received several literary awards for his first book and at sixteen years old began making 16 mm films. In 1961, Bertolucci was hired as a production assistant by Pier Paolo Pasolini, for the filming of *Accattone [Vagabond]*. At this time Bertolucci also attended the University of Rome but did not complete his degree. One year later, at the age of twenty-two, he directed his first film, *The Grim Reaper*. He then directed, *Before the Revolution*, in 1964. During the 1970s, Bertolucci collaborated extensively with cinematographer Vittorio Storaro and other international filmmakers, which elevated his reputation in the film industry. Some of the films that lead to this prominence in the industry included *The Spider's Stratagem* (1970) and *The Conformist* (1970). During this same time, in 1972, Bertolucci directed *Last Tango in Paris*, a controversial film due to its explicit sex scenes, including scenes of rape. Criminal charges were filed against Bertolucci, who served four months in prison and lost his civil rights for five years. This controversy even further propelled Bertolucci's notoriety, and he was extremely successful in directing *1900* (1977), *Luna* (1979), and *The Tragedy of a Ridiculous Man* (1981). In 1987, Bertolucci directed the Oscar-winning film, *The Last Emperor*, which received a total of nine Oscars. Later films include: *The Sheltering Sky* (1990), *Little Buddha* (1993), *Stealing Beauty* (1996), *Besieged* (1998), *The Triumph of Love* (2001), *The Dreamers* (2003), and *Me and You* (2012). Besides several Oscar awards, Bertolucci also received a Golden Lion and an honorary Palme d'Or.

Bernardo Bertolucci is survived by his second wife, Clare Peploe.

See *Current Biography 1974*

Belisario Betancur

Born: Amagá, Colombia; February 4, 1923
Died: Bogotá, Colombia; December 7, 2018
Occupation: President of Colombia

Belisario Betancur served as the 26th President of Colombia. During his term in office, Betancur attempted to forge peace with guerilla rebels in the country but was unsuccessful following an attack on the Colombian Palace of Justice.

Belisario Betancur Cuartas was born on February 4, 1923, to Rosendo Betancur and Ana Otilia Cuartas. His mother gave birth to twenty-two children, but only five survived. He attended the Universidad Pontificia Bolivariana (UPB) and in 1955 graduated with a degree in law and economics. While obtaining his degree, Betancur worked as a deputy in the Antioquia Departmental Assembly and as a representative to the National Chamber. In 1963, he served as Minister of Labor and from 1975 to 1977 was

the Ambassador to Spain. Betancur ran twice for presidency before winning the election in 1982. During his presidency, Betancur negotiated extensively with rebel groups active in the country, in a bid to bring an end to the armed attacks plaguing the country. His government managed to secure an amnesty, which saw 1500 fighters freed from prison. However, the ceasefires he negotiated with leading armed groups were short-lived. Betancur was sitting in office during the guerilla attacks on the Palace of Justice in 1985, during which over 100 people were killed. Betancur was prohibited from running for a second term, as he was suspected of being involved with the imprisonment and killing of several guerillas following the Palace attacks. The country's most fatal natural disaster, a volcano eruption in which over 25,000 people died, also occurred during Betancur's presidency. Following his presidency, Betancur became a senior officer in the Club of Rome and served as president of the Pan American Health Organization (PAHO). He also worked as a journalist and writer, and published numerous books on politics, economics, sociology, and education.

Belisario Betancur is survived by his son Diego, his daughters Maria Clara and Beatriz, and his second wife, Dalia Rafaela Navarro Palmar.

See *Current Biography 1985*

James H. Billington

Born: Bryn Mawr, Pennsylvania; June 1, 1929
Died: Washington, DC; November 20, 2018
Occupation: Historian, Librarian of Congress

James H. Billington spent three decades leading the Library of Congress from 1987 to 2015. He was responsible for the Library's massive digitization as the world entered the digital age and oversaw the transition of library materials into the digital form.

James Hadley Billington was born in Pennsylvania to Nelson and Jane Billington. Billington's father never went to college but was an avid reader, and he transmitted this scholarship to his son at an early age. Billington graduated as valedictorian of his class at Princeton University. He then completed his doctorate at Oxford University and later entered the army in 1953 at the end of the Korean War. Billington joined the history faculty at Harvard in 1957. In 1958, he published his most notable work, titled *Mikhailovsky and Russian Populism*, about influential Russian journalist Nikolai Mikhailovsky. He was commended for focusing on more moderate political advocates and for breaking the tendency to focus solely on Russian extremism. In 1962, Billington moved to Princeton University and spent over a decade teaching history as an associate professor. In 1966, Billington published *The Icon and the Axe: An Interpretive History of Russian Culture*, which summarized over 1,000 years of Russian history through an exploration of organized religion in Russia's development. Billington's scholarship earned him the position of Director of the Woodrow Wilson International Center for Scholars. President Ronald Reagan submitted Billington's nomination; and in September of 1987, Billington was sworn in as the thirteenth Librarian of Congress. During his time as director, he established the Library of Congress's National Digital Library Program that digitized many of the library's resources and made them available online. He also formed the World Digital Library in partnership with the United Nations Educational, Scientific and Cultural Organization (UNESCO) to make materials from libraries around the world available online. He has also controversially acquired Twitter's digital archive of tweets, arguing that it will be important for future historians to understand life in the early twentieth century.

Billington is survived by his wife, Marjorie Anne Brennan, and their four children, Susan, Anne, James Jr., and Thomas.

See *Current Biography 1989*

Kathleen Blanco

Born: New Iberia, Louisiana; December 15, 1942
Died: Lafayette, Louisiana; August 18, 2019
Occupation: Governor

In November 2003 Kathleen Blanco, who broke new ground for women in her more than 20 years of public service in Louisiana, became the first woman elected governor of the state. Her leadership was sorely tested in 2005 by Hurricane Katrina, which ravaged the state and flooded most of New Orleans when the levees failed.

Of Cajun heritage, Kathleen Babineaux Blanco was born and raised in the heart of Cajun country. Her father, Louis, owned a carpeting business, and her mother, Lucille stayed home to raise the couple's eight children.

In 1960 Blanco enrolled at the University of Louisiana at Lafayette, where she earned a BS degree in business education. (She met her husband, a football coach, there.) She then began teaching business classes at Breaux Bridge High School but was forced to resign when she began showing signs of being pregnant with her first child.

For a time, Blanco ran her own polling and marketing research firm, worked as a bookkeeper, and, from 1979 to 1980, served as a district manager for the state Census Office. In 1983 she ran successfully for the office of state representative of District 45, becoming the first woman elected to represent the people of Lafayette County in the state legislature. She served in that capacity from 1984 to 1989, during which time she was a member of the state legislature's house education committee and transportation, highways, and public-works committee. In 1989 Blanco became the first woman elected to the Louisiana Public Service Commission (PSC), which she then chaired from 1993 to 1994. She was elected lieutenant governor, the state's second-highest office, in 1995, working under Republican governor Mike Foster.

Though many polls taken in the days before the 2003 gubernatorial election had her trailing, Blanco, a conservative democrat, defeated her Republican opponent, Bobby Jindal, with 52 percent of the vote, and took her oath of office in both English and Cajun French. The early months of her tenure were largely uneventful, but that changed with Katrina. Although she tried to get New Orleans residents to evacuate, she was overwhelmed by the chaos and devastation ripping through her state; and when the storm was over, she shared much of the blame for how badly rescue and recovery operations had been mismanaged.

Blanco announced in 2017 that she had incurable cancer, first discovered in her eye, some of that censure turned to public sympathy.

Kathleen Blanco died while in hospice care and is survived by her husband, Raymond; her mother; five children (Raymond Jr., Karmen Blanco-Hartfield, Monique Boulet, Nicole Blanco, and Pilar Blanco Eble); and 13 grandchildren.

See *Current Biography 2004*

William Blum

Born: New York, New York; March 6, 1933
Died: Arlington, Virginia; December 9, 2018
Occupation: Journalist

William Blum is most known for his book *Rogue State: A Guide to the World's Only Superpower*, famously mentioned by former leader of Al-Qaeda, Osama Bin-Laden. Blum's commitment to ending hostile American foreign policy had skyrocketed him to fame, and his books have since been translated into a dozen languages.

William Blum was born in the Brooklyn borough of New York City to Jewish immigrants from Poland, Isadore Blum and Ruth Katz, on March 6, 1933. He enrolled in City College and graduated with a degree in accounting, spending the first few years after college moving between programming and accounting jobs at multiple companies. Blum took a job as an employee of the State Department with the hopes of becoming a Foreign Service officer. However, US involvement in the Vietnam War led him to quit, and he organized and participated in demonstrations against the war during this time. In 1967, Blum founded the DC–based *Washington Free Press* in an effort to fight "intellectualism." During the 1970s, Blum traveled throughout the United States, South America, and Europe to cover US involvement in its overhaul of the democratically elected Socialist president of Chile, Salvador Allende. This alerted Blum to how powerful the Central Intelligence Agency (CIA) had become in pushing American political agendas internationally, and he later wrote and published numerous novels on the subject, including *The CIA: A Forgotten History* and *Killing Hope*. In 1998, Blum published an essay about how the United States had given Iraq chemical and biological warfare capabilities in the 1980s, becoming one of the ten most censored stories of 1998. It also earned him an "Excellence in Journalism" Award from Project Censored.

William Blum is survived by his wife, Adelheid Zöfel and his son Alexander Blum.

See *Current Biography 2007*

Jim Bouton

Born: Newark, New Jersey; March 8, 1939
Died: Great Barrington, Massachusetts; July 10, 2019
Occupation: Baseball player, sportscaster, and author

Jim Bouton was a top-ranking major-league baseball pitcher until his arm gave out in 1965. He continued to play for five more years as a journeyman relief hurler, using an ingenious, elusive knuckleball to compensate for his loss of brute speed and then embarked on a successful career as a sportscaster.

James Alan Bouton was born to George H. Bouton, a businessman, and Trudy (Vischer) Bouton, who raised their family in New Jersey, and, later, Illinois. Physically a late starter, he was short for his age in childhood and did not immediately display a superiority in athletics, but by dint of effort he eventually developed prowess as a baseball player.

In 1957 Bouton entered Western Michigan University, where he vacillated between business and liberal arts before finally settling on a business finance major. On the basis of his pitching for the university's freshman baseball team he was granted a scholarship at the beginning of his sophomore year, but a proffered contract with the American League's New York Yankees was more attractive, and he signed with the team on Thanksgiving Day in 1958.

In 1962 Bouton moved up to the mother club in New York as a relief pitcher, and he became a starter with the Yankees the following year. In the 1964 World Series he won two games for the Yankees, but in 1965, when his arm gave out, his stats worsened considerably. Early in the 1967 season, when his record was 1–0, the Yankees shipped him back to the minors in Syracuse, and the following year he was sold to the Seattle Angels.

In 1970 Bouton published the best-selling book *Ball Four; My Life and Hard Times Throwing the Knuckleball in the Big Leagues*, a candid, iconoclastic diary of the 1969 season that delighted the reading public but greatly angered his fellow baseball insiders. In September of that year he joined the staff of WABC-TV in New York City as sports correspondent, gaining fame for his irrepressible comic sense and enthusiasm.

Among other activities, Bouton served as a delegate at the 1972 Democratic National Convention, tried his hand at acting (playing a killer in the 1973 film *The Long Goodbye* and appearing in a short-lived television series based on *Ball Four* in 1976), and wrote a handful of other books. He even returned to the field briefly, eight years into his retirement, starting five games for the Atlanta Braves at the age of 39.

Jim Bouton is survived by his wife, Paula Kurman; two sons, Michael and David (the latter was adopted from Korea as a child); two stepchildren, Lee and Hollis Kurman; six grandchildren; and a brother, Robert. (He was predeceased by his daughter, Laurie, who was killed in a car crash in 1997, and another brother, Peter, who died just a few months before him.)

See *Current Biography 1971*

Sydney Brenner

Born: Germiston, South Africa; January 13, 1927
Died: Singapore; April 5, 2019
Occupation: South African Molecular Biologist, Nobel laureate

Sydney Brenner received over twenty-two prestigious awards from many countries during his extensive career, including a 2002 Nobel Prize with John Sulston and H. Robert Horvitz in Physiology or Medicine. His nine-year Worm Project studies on *Caenorhabditis elegans*, a tiny soil-dwelling nematode, led to breakthroughs in cell death in diseases such as AIDS, stroke, myocardial infarction, Alzheimer's, and cancer.

Brenner was born in Germiston, South Africa, to Morris Brenner, a cobbler, and Lena Blacher, illiterate immigrants from Lithuania and Russia. Brenner attended kindergarten for free at the request of the teacher, a customer of his father. He taught himself to read, then finished three years of school requirements in one year entering fourth grade at the age of six. Brenner found the public library to be "a source of knowledge and the means to acquire it by reading" and developed an interest in science, especially biology. By fourteen he received a scholarship and was studying physics, chemistry, botany, and zoology at the University of Witwatersrand in Johannesburg from which he received a Master of Science in 1947. Failing and having to repeat Medicine and Surgery, he received his Bachelor of Medicine in 1951. In 1952 he received a scholarship to the University of Oxford in England where he became fascinated by genetic mutations, molecular biology, and the work of Drs. Crick and Watson on the double-helix structure of DNA. After he earned his doctoral degree in chemistry in 1954, Brenner visited and conducted research at the California Institute of Technology (Caltech) and the Virus Laboratory at the University of California, Berkeley and made friends with biologists of the "Phage School" in the United States. With Crick's assistance he was offered a position at the British Medical Research Council's (MRC) Cambridge laboratory, the foremost center in DNA research. Brenner's team identified mRNA, a new type of RNA, a discovery that earned him numerous honors and is considered one of his greatest achievements. In 1982, Brenner helped found the Institute of Molecular and Cell Biology in Singapore and in 1986 became director of the MRC's Molecular Genetics Unit while working part of the year at Scripps Research Institute in California and at the University of Cambridge School of Clinical Medicine until 1996. In 1996, he founded The Molecular Sciences Institute in Berkeley retiring in 2001.

Sydney Brenner is survived by one stepson, Jonathan, from his over fifty-year marriage to May Balkind and their three children: Stefan, Belinda, and Carla.

See *Current Biography 2007*

Harold Brown

Born: New York City, New York; September 19, 1927
Died: Rancho Santa Fe, California; January 4, 2019
Occupation: Nuclear physicist and U. S. Secretary of Defense

Harold Brown was a nuclear physicist and U. S. Secretary of Defense under President Jimmy Carter from 1977 to 1981. During his career, Brown made significant contributions towards the development of plutonium, the Polaris missile, and nuclear warheads.

Born in Brooklyn, New York, Harold Brown was a child prodigy who was fascinated by mathematics and physics. He graduated from the Bronx High School of Science at the age of 15, with a grade average of 99.5. Aged 17, he graduated summa cum laude from Columbia University with a Bachelor of Science and the Green Memorial Prize for the best academic record. He remained at Columbia where he was awarded a PhD in physics at the age of 21. After a brief stint of teaching and engaging in postdoctoral research, Brown joined the Radiation Laboratory at the University of California, Berkeley, (UC-Berkeley) where he contributed to the construction of the Polaris missile and the development of plutonium. His scientific career continued at UC where he became the director of the UC Radiation Laboratory at Livermore in 1960 and led the team responsible for developing nuclear warheads. Brown served as a consultant to several federal agencies and was the senior science advisor at the 1958 Conference on the Discontinuance of Nuclear Tests. Under his leadership as the President of the California Institute of Technology (Caltech), from 1969 to 1977, Brown was instrumental in admitting the first female undergraduates. Brown was the first natural scientist to become Secretary of Defense, where he sought to review the defense organization and bring efficient change to the agency. Upon leaving the Pentagon, he moved to teach at the Paul H Nitze School of Advanced International Studies at Johns Hopkins University. Brown was a partner at the investment firm Warburg Pincus, as well as serving on the boards of many companies including CBS, IBM, and Mattel.

Harold Brown was married to Colene D. McDowell, who died in 2018. Brown is survived by his daughters Deborah and Ellen, sister Leila Brennet, and two grandchildren.

See *Current Biography 1977*

Mario Buatta

Born: New York, New York; October 20, 1935
Died: New York, New York; October 15, 2018
Occupation: Interior designer

Mario Buatta added a unique touch to every room he designed. At the height of his fame, Buatta was responsible for the interior decoration of the homes of numerous esteemed celebrities and social elites such as Barbara Walters, Malcolm Forbes, and Henry Ford II.

Mario Buatta was born on Staten Island in 1935 to Olive and Felix Buatta and was the grandchild of Italian immigrants. His father was a bandleader and former performer. From a young age, Buatta showed a strong interest in drawing and was originally encouraged to pursue architecture by his grandfather. However, by his teen years he had developed a strong interest in collecting antique furniture after tagging along with his aunt to antique shows and purchased his first piece of antique furniture at the age of twelve: a Sheraton writing desk. He disliked the white walls and white furniture of his own home and often marveled at the antique furniture that filled his aunt's home. Upon his first trip to England, Buatta fell in love with classic English country style homes and continued to make repeated trips back to England yearly to draw further inspiration. In 1964, Buatta met his future mentor John Fowler, who has been credited with the original modern English country home style. Buatta spent many years learning from Fowler and developing his own personal style, and by the 1970s Buatta had begun to stir the Interior Design world. Notably, he decorated a sitting room for the Kips Bay Decorator Show House with large amounts of lacquer, glazed walls, and ribbons and bows strung throughout the room. At the time, Buatta's decoration was divisive but instantly drew attention, and by the 1980s he had become one of the most sought-after decorators in the United States. Buatta always emphasized that his work was merely a recommendation—the client always had the final decision in their space. Buatta, aptly named "Prince of Chintz" for his near-constant use of chintz, a cotton printed fabric with a glazed finish, is remembered for his clashing yet harmonious color use and purposefully mismatched fabrics and designs that "Buatta"-fied every room he designed.

Mario Buatta was never married. He is survived by his brother, Joseph.

See *Current Biography 1991*

George H. W. Bush

Born: Milton, Massachusetts; June 12, 1924
Died: Houston, Texas; November 30, 2018
Occupation: Former President of the United States and businessman

George Bush served as the 41st president of the United States from 1989 to 1993 and the 43rd vice president from 1981 to 1989. Prior to these positions, he was a member of the United States House of Representatives, the U.S. ambassador to the United Nations, and Director of Central Intelligence. The Republican politician was the longest-lived president in American history before being surpassed by Jimmy Carter in March 2019.

George Herbert Walker Bush was born on June 12, 1924, to Prescott Sheldon Bush and Dorothy (Walker) Bush. Graduating from Phillips Academy, he enlisted in the U.S. Navy during the aftermath of the Pearl Harbor attack and became one of the youngest aviators at just 18 years old. He then studied economics at Yale University, graduating in 1948. In the early 1960s, Bush became an agent of the U.S. Central Intelligence Agency. In 1963, he began his political career, becoming chairman of the Harris County, Texas Republican Party. From this, he advanced to the U.S. House of Representatives in 1966, to chairman of the Republican National Committee in 1973, and to Chief of the U.S. Liaison Office in the People's Republic of China the year after. Finishing his stint as Director of Central Intelligence in 1977, he became chairman of the Executive Committee of the First International Bank in Houston, part-time professor of Administrative Science at Rice University's Jones School of Business, and director of the Council on Foreign Relations. After an unsuccessful run for president, he became vice president to Ronald Reagan for two consecutive terms. He ran for president once again in the 1988 campaign, defeating Democrat Michael Dukakis. During his time as president, he dealt with issues such as theunification of Germany, the 1991 collapse of the Soviet Union, and the Gulf War of 1990. His administration was partially responsible for negotiating the North American Free Trade Agreement (NAFTA). He also used the position to highlight the importance of voluntary service, creating the Points of Light Foundation in 1990. In the 1992 presidential race, Bush was defeated by Democrat Bill Clinton. He remained active in the political arena for the rest of his life, witnessing his son George W. Bush serve as the 43rd president of the United States from 2001 to 2008.

George H. W. Bush is survived by his sons, George, Jeb, Neil, and Marvin, and his daughter Dorothy.

See *Current Biography 1999*

Valery Fyodorovich Bykovsky

Born: Pavlovsky Posad, Russia; August 2, 1934
Died: Moscow, Russia; March 27, 2019
Occupation: Soviet Cosmonaut

Valery Bykovsky was the 11th person to enter space and held the unbroken record for the longest solo spaceflight to date.

Valery Fyodorovich Bykovsky was born on August 2, 1934, in Pavlovsky Posad, a town around 40 miles east of Moscow. As a young man, he traveled often thanks to his father's role in the Ministry of Railways, including seven years of his youth that was spent in Iran. Originally drawn to be a sailor, a talk at school piqued his interest in flying, and he joined the Moscow City Aviation Club. In 1955, Bykovsky graduated from the Kachinsk Military Aviation Academy with full marks in flying and combat training and began his career as the chief pilot in the 23rd Interceptor Flight Regiment of the 17th Air Division in the Soviet Air Force. He was promoted to senior lieutenant military pilot, 3rd Class, by the time he tested to become a cosmonaut in 1959. Bykovsky was selected for the first cohort of Soviet space cosmonaut trainees in March 1960. He flew three times to space, logging a total of 20 days, 17 hours, and 47 minutes in Earth's orbit. First, Bykovsky was the pilot of Vostok 5, the former Soviet Union's fifth spaceflight and the 11th worldwide; then in 1976, Bykovsky was the commander of Soyuz 22; finally in 1978, Bykovsky took part in the Interkosmos mission with Sigmund Jähn, Germany's first citizen in space, to deliver supplies to the Salyut 6 space station. Bykovsky then worked as a cosmonaut trainer, and in 1988 left the space program to serve as the House of Soviet Sciences and Culture in Berlin. In 1990, Bykovsky retired from public life, aged 56. He had been named a Hero of the Soviet Union and was awarded the Order of Lenin and the Order of the Red Star.

Valery Fyodorovich Bykovsky is survived by his wife, Valentina, and son, Sergei.

See *Current Biography 1965*

Patrick Caddell

Born: Rock Hill, South Carolina; May 19, 1950
Died: Charleston, South Carolina; February 16, 2019
Occupation: Pollster, Political firm consultant

Patrick Caddell was a pollster and political consultant to major politicians including presidential candidates Jimmy Carter and Joe Biden.

Patrick Caddell was born on May 19, 1950, in the small town of Rock Hill, South Carolina, the son of a Coast Guard officer, Newton Pascal Caddell and mother, Janie (Burns) Caddell. He attended Harvard University and was still an undergraduate senior when he was employed by George McGovern to work as a pollster for his 1972 presidential campaign. He then gained notoriety as an advisor for Jimmy Carter's successful campaign in 1976. He returned to work with Carter in 1980 and worked for Gary Hart in 1984, Joe Biden in 1988, and Jerry Brown in 1992. Known by many as "The oracle of American Politics," Caddell gained renown for his insight into public opinion, focusing especially on voter unrest and alienation. He also returned to South Carolina as a guest lecturer at the College of Charleston. Caddell grew discontented with the Democratic Party leadership, leaving the Democratic Party in 1988, and relocated to Los Angeles, where he began to work as a writer and producer on *The West Wing*, as well as consulting on various films, including *Running Mates, Air Force One, Outbreak,* and *In the Line of Fire.* He also worked as a consultant for the marketing campaign of Francis Ford Coppola's 1979 film *Apocalypse Now.* He continued to conduct research on voter unrest and dissatisfaction for his company, *Caddell Associates.* He also consulted and wrote for various news outlets and online publications. Using his theory of voter alienation, Caddell largely predicted the success of Donald Trump. He became a regular contributor to *Fox News,* and during that time he also formed a close relationship with Breitbart leader Steve Bannon, leading to him working as an informal advisor on Donald Trump's 2016 campaign. He also worked in an official capacity as an advisor to Republican Robert Mercer, who was a major fundraiser for Donald Trump's candidacy.

Patrick Caddell is survived by his daughter, Heidi, and his three grandchildren. He is also survived by a brother, Daniel, and a sister, Patricia.

See *Current Biography 1979*

Mortimer Maxwell Caplin

Born: New York, New York; July 11, 1916
Died: Chevy Chase, Maryland; July 15, 2019
Occupation: Lawyer and educator

Mortimer Caplin served as the commissioner of the Internal Revenue Service (IRS) under John F. Kennedy and Lyndon B. Johnson.

Mortimer Maxwell Caplin's mother was the former Lillian Epstein. His father, Daniel, was an assistant director of health education in the New York City school system. Caplin, who had one sister, Jeanne, attended John Adams High, where he captained the swimming team, acted in plays, and joined the honor society. He graduated in 1933.

Enrolling at the University of Virginia, Caplin majored in economics and political science. He was elected to the Phi Beta Kappa Society and was a member of the Virginia Players drama group and the university boxing team. Although he fought for half his senior year with a broken bone in one hand, he won the National Collegiate Athletic Association (NCAA) middleweight title. He received his BS degree in 1937 and then entered the University of Virginia Law School. In 1940 he graduated first in his class with an LLB degree. (New York University Law School awarded him a JSD degree in 1953.)

Caplin began his legal career as a law clerk to US Circuit Judge Armistead Dobie; and in 1941 he joined the law firm of Paul, Weiss, Rifkind, Wharton & Garrison. He served in World War II with the U. S. Navy; and in 1950 he returned to the University of Virginia to become a professor at the Law School, specializing in tax and corporate law. (Among his students were Edward and Robert Kennedy.) In 1958 and 1959 he testified before the House Ways and Means Committee on the general revision of the Internal Revenue Code, and he also was a member of President John F. Kennedy's task force on taxation.

Acknowledged as one of the country's leading tax experts, he often cited Will Rogers's adage that "the income tax has made more liars out of the American people than golf has."

In 1961 Kennedy appointed Caplin as Commissioner of Internal Revenue. In that capacity he aggressively pursued tax cheats, persuaded Congress to require that expenses of more than $25 be itemized if they were claimed as deductions, introduced a centralized computer system to audit returns efficiently, and developed a strong reputation for being fair-minded and reasonable.

He stepped down from the post in mid-1964, returning to the University of Virginia as a visiting professor for the next two decades. In later years he was fond of telling people that he owed his professional success to the advice of his college boxing coach, who told him: "Punch hard, punch first and keep on punching."

Mortimer Caplin was predeceased in 2014 by his wife, the former Ruth Sacks, a painter, designer, and arts advocate whom he had married in 1942. One of his daughters, Mary Ellen, died in 1977. He is survived by his sons, Lee, Michael, and Jeremy; a daughter, Cate; eight grandchildren; and three great-grandchildren.

See *Current Biography 1961*

Carol Channing

Born: Seattle, Washington; January 31, 1921
Died: Rancho Mirage, California; January 15, 2019
Occupation: Actress and performer

Carol Channing was a celebrated Broadway actress, most famously known for her repeated role as Dolly in *Hello Dolly!*

Born Carol Elaine Channing in Seattle, Washington, Channing grew up in San Francisco, California. An only child, she discovered performance arts early. She went to study drama and dance at Bennington College in Vermont and worked in small roles and understudy parts until her big break in 1949. Channing originated the role of flapper Lorelei Lee in the musical *Gentlemen Prefer Blondes*. The show ran for two years, and Channing then played Lorelei on tour for another year afterward. This led to her being featured on the covers for both *Time* and *Life* magazines. Over the next decade, she appeared on Broadway in numerous musicals, from *Wonderful Town* to *Show Girl*, while also creating her own nightclub act. In 1964, her next career-defining role was Dolly in *Hello, Dolly!* at the St. James Theatre. The show went on to win 10 Tony Awards, including one for Channing. While she dabbled in movies, her only real success was in *Thoroughly Modern Millie* in 1967, for which she received an Academy Award nomination and a Golden Globe. Returning time and again to the role of Dolly, Channing claimed to have performed the role over 5000 times, touring 30 cities, and visiting Britain, Australia, Japan, and China. Upon news of her death, the lights of Broadway were dimmed in Channing's honor, while a crowd congregated outside the St. James Theatre for the anniversary of the opening of the original production of *Hello, Dolly!*

Carol Channing is survived by her only son, Channing.

See *Current Biography 1964*

Roy Clark

Born: Meherrin, Virginia; April 15, 1933
Died: Tulsa, Oklahoma; November 15, 2018
Occupation: Country singer

Roy Clark was well known for his appearance as host of the long-running television variety show, *Hee Haw*, which ran for almost thirty years. Clark released many country songs throughout his life, many of which hit top music charts, including "The Tips of My Fingers."

Roy Clark was born to Hester and Lillian Clark, the oldest of five children. His mother was a pianist and his father occasionally played the guitar, fiddle, or banjo with local bands. Clark would accompany his father at square dances and by the age of 14 had won two national banjo competitions. At the age of 17, Clark performed on television for the Grand Ole Opry and then spent eighteen months touring the country playing backup guitar for several country musicians. At this time, Clark also obtained his airplane pilot license, a hobby he continued throughout his life. In 1954, Clark was asked to join Jimmy Dean's band as lead guitarist and performed with the band on several television programs. In 1960, Clark moved to Las Vegas to be lead guitarist for Hank Penny and also worked extensively with Wanda Jackson. It was at this time Clark first appeared on *The Tonight Show.* In the mid-1960s he was asked to host a weekday country variety show, *Swingin' Country.* In 1964, Clark released his first hit, "The Tips of My Fingers," and after his variety show ended, began hosting a sketch comedy program, *Hee Haw,* which aired from 1969 until 1997. That same year, Clark also released a cover of "Yesterday When I Was Young," which reached many top music charts. Clark won a Grammy Award in 1983 and became a member of the Grand Ole Opry in 1987. He then published his autobiography, *My Life—In Spite of Myself,* in 1994. In 2009, Clark was inducted into the Country Music Hall of Fame.

Roy Clark is survived by his wife of 62 years, Barbara, their five children, Roy, Michael, Terry, Susan, and Diane, and four grandchildren.

See *Current Biography 1978*

Johnny Clegg

Born: Bacup (Lancashire), England; June 7, 1953
Died: Johannesburg, South Africa; July 16, 2019
Occupation: Musician

Long before Paul Simon, Peter Gabriel, and other rock musicians attempted to merge the rhythms of African music with Western styles, Johnny Clegg was doing so; perhaps even more notable is that he was composing and performing his music in a South Africa divided by the government-sanctioned system of racial segregation known as apartheid.

Although Johnny Clegg was born in a former mill town in northwest England, his early years were peripatetic: His biological father, Dennis Clegg, and his mother, Muriel, a jazz singer of Lithuanian-Jewish descent who had been born in what was then Rhodesia, divorced soon after his birth. In 1954 he and his mother moved to Israel with his maternal grandfather. The family returned to Rhodesia in 1955, and Clegg was raised on a farm in Gwelo (now Gweru) until he was six. In 1960 Muriel married Dan Pienaar, a South African journalist whose love of native African music and passionate anti-apartheid views greatly influenced Clegg. The family moved to South Africa, and Clegg sometimes accompanied his new stepfather on journalistic visits to the country's all-black townships.

Clegg attended the all-white Athlone Boys' High School, where he learned to play the guitar and immersed himself in native African music—an activity then strictly forbidden to whites under South African law. In 1968 he ran away from home and for about a month lived among the Zulus in an otherwise all-black township. The police ultimately returned him home; but undeterred, he continued to visit the hostels where migrant Zulu miners lived and played their music. He was arrested by the police several times for fraternizing with blacks.

Clegg studied anthropology at the University of Witwatersrand; and after earning his degree, he stayed on as a lecturer. At night, he secretly performed at private venues with black musician Sipho Mchunu. They called their duo Juluka (the Zulu word for "sweat") and released several popular albums, despite a government ban on playing music that mixed English and Zulu lyrics.

In 1985 Clegg formed a new band, Savuka (a Zulu term translated as "we have risen"). Their first album, *Third World Child* (1987), was a critical success and sold more than two million copies internationally, and several other award-winning albums followed. Savuka toured the globe, and Clegg's performance of high-kicking Zulu dances became a beloved feature of his concerts for his fans. The early 1990s, one of the periods of Clegg's greatest renown, coincided with the gradual dismantling of government-sanctioned segregation in South Africa; and on May 10, 1994, Clegg played at the inauguration of South Africa's first black president, the revered anti-apartheid activist Nelson Mandela. (Among his most popular songs has long been "Asimbonanga," a tribute to Mandela.)

Johnny Clegg, who was diagnosed with pancreatic cancer in 2015, is survived by his second wife, Jenny (nee Bartlett), whom he married in 1989, and their two sons, Jesse and Jaron.

See *Current Biography 2005*

Geraldyn "Jerrie" M. Cobb

Born: Norman, Oklahoma; March 5, 1931
Died: Florida March 18, 2019
Occupation: American aviator and astronaut candidate

Geraldyn "Jerrie" Cobb began flying at twelve, earned a pilot and commercial license by eighteen, flew an AT-6 to Peru at twenty-one, and was well along her career path. The first woman to pass astronaut testing, she was unable to achieve space flight when the training program closed. Cobb was inducted into the National Aviation Hall of Fame in 2012.

Geraldyn "Jerrie" Cobb was born on March 5, 1931, to U. S. Air Force Lieutenant Colonel William Harvey Cobb and Helena Butler Stone. At twelve Cobb's father taught her to fly his Waco biplane. Horse ranching and plane waxing provided flying money. After a year at Oklahoma College for Women, Cobb left to become a commercial and flight instructor at eighteen and began teaching veterans flying, navigation, and meteorology at an aviation school. She flew charters, dusted crops, and did pipeline patrol.

In 1952, Cobb became the only female ferry pilot in the United States flying commercial and military planes, including B-17's, T-6G's, and C-46's to foreign countries. Cobb established two weight-class world records and an altitude record with Aero Commanders followed by a 1957 long-distance, nonstop record flying from Guatemala City to Oklahoma City. In 1959, she established a world speed record of 226.148 miles per hour and in 1960 broke her altitude record by flying to 37,010 feet. Cobb's accomplishments led to an invitation from the National Aeronautics and Space Administration (NASA) for astronaut training at the Lovelace's Woman in Space Program in Albuquerque, New Mexico, in 1960. Even though Cobb's performance was rated "extraordinary" and she proved that women were just as, or more capable in some ways than men for space travel, the Lovelace program shut down; and she did not become the first women in space. A Soviet Union woman went to space in 1963, and American Sally Ride flew the Space Shuttle Challenger on June 18, 1983. Cobb turned to solo missionary flights of supplies and medications to indigenous tribes in the Amazon Rainforest and surveying new routes across the rainforest and Andes Mountains.

Cobb achieved Woman of the Year in Aviation and Pilot of the Year in 1959, received the Amelia Earhart Gold Medal of Achievement, the Harmon International Trophy in 1973, Nobel Peace Prize nomination in 1981 and held Fédération Aéronautique Internationale Gold Wings (Paris, France). Her life inspired a 2005 book by Margaret A. Weitekamp, *Right Stuff, Wrong Sex: America's First Women in Space Program (Gender Relations in the American Experience)* and *Mercury 13*, a 2018 Netflix documentary.

See *Current Biography 1961*

Thad Cochran

Born: Pontotoc, Mississippi; December 7, 1937
Died: Oxford, Mississippi; May 30, 2019
Occupation: Politician and attorney

William Thad Cochran was a Republican politician who served in the House of Representatives for six years before becoming a Senator for Mississippi.

William Thad Cochran was born on December 7, 1937, to Emma Grace and William Holmes Cochran in Pontotoc, Mississippi. He graduated valedictorian from Byram High School before pursuing a BA at the University of Mississippi, majoring in Psychology and minoring in Political Science. He graduated in 1959, and quickly joined the US Navy where he was an ensign until 1961. In 1965, he received a Juris Doctor from the University of Mississippi School of Law, and went on to practice law for seven years. In 1968, Cochran, then a Democrat, was selected by Lamar Alexander to serve as chairman of the Citizens for Nixon-Agnew in Mississippi. In 1972, he was recruited by lawyer Mike Allred and oilman Billy Mounger to run for Congress as a Republican. He went on to become Representative for the 4th District, with Charles Evers, an independent, splitting the Democratic vote. He was reelected for two further consecutive terms, in 1974 and 1976. In 1978, he became State Senator and was the first republican to win a statewide election in Mississippi for over a century. For decades, he faced no serious challengers, and even ran unopposed in several elections. In total, he served for seven terms in the Senate, retiring in April 2018. Though he did not gain widespread media coverage, Cochran was known to be a highly influential politician, especially behind the scenes, where he put his decades of experience to work through private deals and meetings, outside of the public eye. In 2006, *Time* magazine named him one of "America's 10 Best Senators," calling him "The Quiet Persuader." He had an A+ rating from the National Rifle Association (NRA) due to his support for pro-gun legislation. In 2017, he was one of 22 senators to sign a letter urging President Donald Trump to withdraw the United States from the Paris Agreement.

William Thad Cochran is survived by his wife, Kay, his brother, Nielsen, two children, Thaddeus and Katherine, and three grandchildren.

See *Current Biography 2002*

Rafael Hernández Colón

Born: Ponce, Puerto Rico, United States; October 24, 1936
Died: San Juan, Puerto Rico, United States; May 2, 2019
Occupation: Governor, Puerto Rico

Rafael Hernández Colón, a Popular Democratic Party member, served fourth and sixth terms as governor of Puerto Rico from 1973 to 1977 and 1985 to 1993. He promoted maintaining commonwealth status while many pushed for full statehood or complete independence. Many thought of him as a Hispanic version of John F. Kennedy.

Rafael Hernández Colón was born in Ponce, Puerto Rico, to Rafael Hernández Matos and Dora Colón Clavell. His father was a distinguished attorney from 1926 to 1957 and remained an associate justice on the Supreme Court into the 1960s. Colón had a comfortable life without financial worries or exposure to poverty or slums. He pursued his curiosity of bureaucracy and power politics and interest in law and government at Johns Hopkins University in Baltimore, Maryland, graduating in 1956. His thesis at Hopkins, which he continued during law school, examined the political ties between Puerto Rico and the United States. Colón sent his thesis to Governor Luis Muñoz Marín who had it distributed throughout U. S. libraries. Colón graduated first in his class with an LLB in 1959 from the University of Puerto Rico.

Colón practiced law in Ponce, Puerto Rico, joined the Popular Democratic Party run by Marín since its inception in the mid-1930s, and was appointed by Marín to the Public Service Commission in 1960 serving until 1962. In 1965 he became attorney general for two years after which he opened a law firm before entering and winning a Senate seat in 1968. Democrats controlled the Senate but lost the House of Representatives during the term of Luis Ferré, a pro-statehood millionaire industrialist of the New Progressive Party with ties to mainland Republicans. Colón became president of the Senate in 1969 and gubernatorial pick for 1972. In 1973, he was the youngest governor to be elected. He advocated for commonwealth status, more autonomy, better control of shipping rates, granting of radio frequencies, and island-mainland airline route planning. Colón won, and Popular Democrats controlled the legislature.

Colón faced trouble with tourism, sugar industries, bailouts, manufacturing closings, unequal wealth distribution and a 1973–1974 oil crisis. Losing in 1977, Colón returned to win in 1984 serving until 1993, when he stepped down from the Democratic Party.

He married his first wife, Lila Mayoral Wirshing in 1959. After her death in 2003 he married Nelsa López.

Colón is survived by his wife Nelsa López and his children, Juan Eugenio, JoséAlfredo, Rafael, and Dora.

See *Current Biography 1973*

Tim Conway

Born: Willoughby, Ohio; December 15, 1933
Died: Los Angeles, California; May 14, 2019
Occupation: Actor, comedian, writer, director

Tim Conway was an actor and comedian who rose to fame on the Carol Burnett Show in the 1970s. Throughout his career he earned six Emmys and a Golden Globe for his writing and performances.

Tim Conway was born Thomas Daniel Conway on December 15, 1933, to Sophia Murgoi and Daniel Conway in Willoughby, Ohio. His father was an Irish immigrant, and his mother was Romanian. He attended Bowling Green State University and majored in television and radio, before enlisting in the army from 1956 to 1958. After his discharge, he returned to Cleveland where he worked in television with Ernie Anderson, appearing on the morning film show *Ernie's Place* and writing comedic skits. He then moved to New York and gained a spot on ABC's *The Steve Allen Show.* Conway later rose to national fame thanks to his role in the 1960's sitcom *McHale's Navy,* for which he earned an Emmy and a Laurel Award. He became most well known for his appearances on *The Carol Burnett Show* from 1975 to 1978. His work on the show earned him a Golden Globe Award and four Emmy Awards—three for performance and one for writing. He was known for creating interesting characters, many of which reappeared on film and television. He also did voice work for numerous shows and films, including *SpongeBob SquarePants, The Simpsons, Scooby-Doo* and *The Wild Thornberrys.* His work with Disney earned him a Disney Legend award in 2004, and included starring roles in films from the 1970s such as *The World's Greatest Athlete* and *The Apple Dumpling Gang,* and lending his voice to films such as *Hercules.* He earned yet another Emmy in 2008 for his work as a guest actor on *30 Rock.* In 2013, his memoir *'What's So*

Funny? My Hilarious Life' reached *The New York Times* Best Seller list as soon as it was published.

Tim Conway is survived by his wife of 35 years, Charlene, his stepdaughter, his six children, and two granddaughters.

See *Current Biography 1980*

Douglas M. Costle

Born: Long Beach, California; July 27, 1939
Died: McLean, Virginia; January 13, 2019
Occupation: Politician

Douglas M. Costle was a politician who designed the United States Environmental Protection Agency (EPA) before serving as the EPA Administrator.

Born in Long Beach, California on July 27, 1939, Douglas Michael Costle grew up in the Pacific Northwest. He spent much of his youth outdoors, and this shaped his passion for environmental protection. He studied for a bachelor's degree at Harvard University and graduated in 1961, before receiving a juris doctor degree (JD) from the University of Chicago Law School in 1964. He joined the bar in Washington DC and in California, as well as serving in the United States Army Reserve, where he specialized in military intelligence. From 1964 to 1965, Costle was a trial attorney for the Civil Rights Division of the Justice Department, before becoming an attorney for the Economic Development Administration. In 1967, he moved to San Francisco and became an associate attorney for Kelso, Cotton, Seligman, and Ray. He went on to become the senior associate at the San Francisco urban planning firm Marshall, Kaplan, Gans, and Kahn. In 1970, Costle headed the study by the President's Advisory Council on Executive Organizations as the Senior Staff Associate for Environmental and Natural Resources. Costle became a Fellow of the Woodrow Wilson International Center for Scholars in 1971, before becoming the Deputy Commissioner of the Connecticut Department of Environmental Protection. He went on to become the Commissioner. In 1975, he became a consultant to the EPA on land-use policies. Also in 1975, he worked at the Congressional Budget Office as the Assistant Director for Natural Resources and Commerce. From 1977 until 1981, Costle served as the Administrator of the EPA under President Jimmy Carter. In 1987, Costle served as the dean of the Vermont Law School and co-founded the Institute for Sustainable Communities with Vermont Governor Madeleine Kunin in 1991.

Douglas M. Costle is survived by his wife, Elizabeth, his daughter Caroline, and his son, Douglas Jr.

See *Current Biography 1980*

John C. Culver

Born: Rochester, Minnesota; August 8, 1932
Died: Washington, DC; December 27, 2018
Occupation: Politician

John Chester Culver was a U.S. Congressman who represented Iowa in the House of Representatives from 1965 to 1975 and in the Senate from 1975 to 1981. Culver, a Democrat, was known for his liberal views and voting record.

John Chester Culver was born on August 8, 1932, to Mary and William Culver and raised in Cedar Rapids, Iowa. He attended Harvard University, where he played on the football team alongside future Senator Edward Kennedy. He studied for a year as the Lionel de Jersey Harvard Scholar at Emmanuel College, Cambridge University before serving in the U.S. Marine Corps from 1955 to 1958. After graduating from Harvard Law School, Culver worked as a legislative assistant for Senator Kennedy. In 1964, he was elected to the House of Representatives, ousting the Republican incumbent, James Bromwell. He was openly critical of the Vietnam War and of the methods used by the House Un-American Activities Committee, on which he served. In addition, he was one of the few House members to vote against the 1967 bill that would have made it a federal crime to burn the American flag because he believed the act fell under the Constitutional protection of free speech. He served five terms in the House before being elected to the Senate in 1974, winning the race for the seat vacated by the retirement of his fellow Democrat Harold Hughes. During his single term in the Senate, Culver established the Culver Commission, which helped modernize the Senate's procedures. Culver proudly maintained a liberal voting record despite the conservative movement that elected Ronald Reagan as president and led to Culver losing his seat in the Senate to Republican Chuck Grassley. After leaving office, Culver practiced law in Washington and had retired from the firm of Arent Fox shortly before his death. He served as interim director for the Institute of Politics at Harvard University in 2010 and afterwards remained a member of its advisory committee.

John C. Culver is survived by his wife, Mary Jane Cheechi; three daughters, Catherine, Rebecca, and Christina; two sons, John and Chet; his sister, Katherine; and eight grandchildren.

See *Current Biography 1979*

Dick Dale

Born: Boston, Massachusetts; May 4, 1937
Died: Loma Linda, California; March 16, 2019
Occupation: Guitarist

Dick Dale was an influential guitarist, known for fathering the Surf Guitar music wave. Though he rose in popularity during the early 1960s, he drew attention in the 1990s for his song "Misirlou" in the hit film, *Pulp Fiction*.

Richard Anthony Monsour (nickname Dick Dale) was born on May 4, 1937, to James and Sophia, who lived outside Boston, Massachusetts. As a young child, he learned to play the piano, trumpet, ukulele, and eventually guitar. His uncle taught Dale to play the tarabaki (a traditional Greek drum), and he soon learned to play the guitar using different rhythm styles and alternative picking to replace drumming. Dale graduated from Washington Senior High School in El Segundo, California in 1955. After graduating, he began playing at local country western rockabilly bars and was given the nickname Dick Dale. Because of his loud amplifiers and heavy gauge strings, Dale became known as the "Father of Heavy Metal." Dale and Leo Fender made a custom Fender amp, called the "Single Showman Amp." During the early 1960s, Dale played at the Rendezvous Ballroom in Balboa, California, where he is known to have created the surf music phenomenon. Dale released his first album, *Surfers' Choice* in 1962, after which he was asked to perform on *The Ed Sullivan Show*. In the 1970s, Dale developed colorectal cancer and stop performing for several years. Then in 1979 he had a leg amputated due to an infected swimming injury. In 1986, Dale released a new album, for which he was nominated for a Grammy. In 1994, with the use of his song "Misirlou" in the film *Pulp Fiction*, a new wave of fans found Dale. He was inducted into the Musicians Hall of Fame and Museum in 2009 and in 2011 was inducted into the Surfing Walk of Fame. During his career, Dale recorded over 20 albums.

Dick Dale is survived by his wife, Lana, and his son, James.

See *Current Biography 2001*

Evelyn Y. Davis

Born: Amsterdam, the Netherlands; August 16, 1929
Died: Washington, DC; November 4, 2018
Occupation: Activist, Financial Journalist, and Philanthropist

Evelyn Y. Davis was an activist who was known for her work advocating for shareholder rights and stricter corporate governance. She was editor and publisher of the investor newsletter "Highlights and Lowlights" and president of the Evelyn Y. Davis Foundation.

Evelyn Yvonne was born on August 16, 1929, to Herman DeJong, a neurologist, and Marianne Witteboon DeJong, a psychologist, in Amsterdam, the Netherlands. During World War II, the Nazis arrested the DeJongs, who had Jewish roots, while Herman DeJong was in the United States on business. They were imprisoned in concentration camps in the Netherlands and Czechoslovakia. After their release, Davis and her brother, Rudolph, joined their father in Baltimore, Maryland, in 1942. Her parents divorced after the war. In 1947, she graduated high school in Catonsville, Maryland, and then studied business administration at Western Maryland College and George Washington University but did not complete her degree. Her father's death in 1956 left her with a sizeable inheritance that she began investing in companies and public bonds. She became a shareholder activist and well-known corporate gadfly, attending shareholder meetings and raising questions on issues such as chief executives' salaries, the overseas political affiliations of companies, and board election protocols. Davis often wore costumes to help make her points and draw attention to her advocacy, which is credited with helping advance stricter rules for corporate governance. From 1965 until 2011, Davis published her annual newsletter, "Highlights and Lowlights" and sold it for $600 a copy. She owned shares in over 80 companies and used her investment returns and earnings from her newsletter to fund her charitable foundation, the Evelyn Y. Davis Foundation, which donated millions of dollars to universities, hospitals, journalism foundations, and art centers.

Evelyn Y. Davis was divorced four times but kept the last name of her first husband, William Henry Davis, and had no children.

See *Current Biography 2007*

Doris Day

Born: Cincinnati, Ohio; April 3, 1922
Died: Carmel Valley Village, California; May 13, 2019
Occupation: Actor, singer, activist

Doris Day was an actor and singer who rose to fame in the 1950s. She is considered to be one of the most successful female actors of the twentieth century, after ranking number one at the box office four times and receiving seven consecutive Laurel Awards as the top female box-office star.

Doris Day was born Doris Mary Kappelhoff on April 3, 1922, in Cincinnati, Ohio, to Alma Sophia and William Joseph Kappelhoff. She was interested in dance from an early age, performing locally throughout her childhood and adolescence but was injured in a car accident in 1937, which ruled out a career as a dancer. She discovered a passion for singing while recovering from her accident, which her mother encouraged by insisting she take singing lessons. Day began to find work as a vocalist on the local radio and in restaurants. She soon started to work along major bandleaders and recorded her first hit, *"Sentimental Journey"* while working with the Les Brown band in 1945. Over the next year, Day had six other top ten hits. In 1948, she was cast for a role in the musical film *Romance on the High Seas,* which marked the beginning of her career as a movie star. Day gradually took on more dramatic roles, and her first dramatic role as singer Ruth Etting in *Love Me or Leave Me* was a critical success. By the 1960s, Day was an actor first and foremost, and a singer second, performing in a wave of successful romantic comedies, alongside thrillers and dramas. Throughout her film career, Day received nine Laurel Award nominations for best female performance, counting four wins, and six Golden Globe nominations. Day's third husband Martin Melcher died in 1968, and it was revealed that he and lawyer Jerome Rosenthal had left Day deeply in debt and committed her to a television show and numerous TV specials without her consent. She took on the work, hosting *The Doris Day Show,* but largely retired from acting after the end of its five-year run. In 1978, she founded a charity, the Doris Day Animal Foundation, which continues to be active today.

Doris Day is survived by her only grandchild, Ryan Melcher.

See *Current Biography 1954*

Fernando de la Rúa

Born: Córdoba, Argentina; September 15, 1937
Died: Loma Verde, Argentina; July 9, 2019
Occupation: Politician

Fernando de la Rúa was a politician who held the office of President of Argentina from 1999 to 2001.

Fernando de la Rúa was born on September 15, 1937, to Antonio de la Rúa Catani and Eleonora Felisa Bruno. He attended a military boarding school before studying law at Córdoba National University and graduated with a law degree from Buenos Aires University at the age of 21. De la Rúa began his political career as a member of the centrist Unión Cívica Radical party, serving as a legal adviser to the interior ministry under President Arturo Illia. In March 1973, he was elected senator. In September 1973, de la Rúa ran as the vice-presidential candidate on Ricardo Balbín's ticket in the presidential election, but Balbín lost to Juan Perón in a landslide. De la Rúa served three terms as senator and one term as a lawmaker in Argentina's lower house of Congress. Following the 1994 amendment of the Constitution of Argentina, Buenos Aires ran its inaugural mayoral election, and de la Rúa became the first elected mayor of the city in 1996. On October 24, 1999, de la Rúa won the presidential race as part of the Alianza, a center-left coalition between the UCR and Frepaso parties. De la Rúa inherited a national deficit and soon found himself dealing with both a corruption scandal that led to the resignation of his vice president, Carlos Álvarez, and an economic crisis. A banking panic in November 2001 led the de la Rúa administration to impose a limit on bank withdrawals, igniting mass protests that escalated to riots and looting and resulted in the deaths of over 20 people. Amidst these riots, de la Rúa's Economy Minister Domingo Cavallo resigned, along with the rest of the cabinet. On the evening of December 20, 2001, de la Rúa presented his formal resignation and took off from the presidential palace in a helicopter, a dramatic exit that became infamous as a symbol of his failed presidency. In the years following de la Rúa's resignation, Argentina experienced further economic and political crisis, further cementing his legacy.

Fernando de la Rúa is survived by his wife, Inés Pertiné; their three children, Agustina, Antonio, and Fernando; and 11 grandchildren.

See *Current Biography 2001*

Yogesh Chander Deveshwar

Born: Lahore, India; February 4, 1947
Died: Gurugram, India; May 11, 2019
Occupation: Businessman

Yogesh Chander Deveshwar was an Indian businessman who chaired one of India's largest and most successful companies, ITC Limited, for over 15 years.

Yogesh Chander Deveshwar was born on February 4, 1947, in Lahore, then British India. He studied mechanical engineering at the Indian Institute of Technology (IIT) in Delhi, graduating in 1968. He also studied management for six weeks at Harvard University, and took a course at Cornell University on managing hotels. After graduating, Deveshwar joined ITC Limited, then a tobacco company, as a management trainee. In 1974, he took over as the factory manager in ITC's Packaging and Printing Plant in Chennai. In 1984, he was appointed as a main board director before becoming CEO in 1996. He gained control of the company during an uncertain time and is largely credited for ITC's successful diversification. Under his control, ITC went from being largely a cigarette manufacturer to becoming a diversified conglomerate spanning IT, hotels, food, agricultural products, paper, consumer products, and more. He also drove the company to become more sustainable—in 2004, ITC became the first Indian organisation to submit a sustainability report as per the guidelines of the Global Reporting Initiative. Under his leadership, ITC received the World Business Award given by the United Nations Development Program, the International Chamber of Commerce, and the International Business Leader's Forum. Deveshwar was the longest-serving CEO of an Indian company. He also served as the President of the Confederation of Indian Industry and was a member of the Board of Governers in the Indian School of Business and the Indian Institute of Management. In 2011, Deveshwar was awarded the Padma Bhushan, India's third-highest civilian award; and in 2013 he was listed as the best performing CEO in India by the Harvard Business Review, as well as 7th in the World.

Yogesh Chander Deveshwar is survived by his wife, Bharti, and his children, Gaurav and Garima, and many grandchildren.

See *Current Biography 2005*

John D. Dingell

Born: Colorado Springs, Colorado; July 8, 1926
Died: Dearborn, Michigan; February 7, 2019
Occupation: Politician

John D. Dingell was a democratic representative for Michigan. He is the longest serving member of the United States Congress, having served nearly 60 years in the House of Representatives.

John D. Dingell was born to Grace and John Dingell Sr. in Colorado Springs, Colorado, on July 8, 1926, as the Dingells were in Colorado during this time seeking a cure for John Dingell Sr's tuberculosis. As soon as they were able, the family returned to Michigan, where Democratic candidate John Sr. was elected representative of the Michigan's 15th District in 1932. Dingell first attended Georgetown Preparatory School, and then the House Page School, serving as a page for the US House of Representatives from 1938 to 1943. In 1944, Dingell joined the Army, where he was ordered to serve in the planned US invasion of Japan. However, due to President Truman's use of the atomic bomb, Dingell was never required to travel to Japan. He left the Army to attend Georgetown University and graduated with a BSc in chemistry in 1949, before pursuing a Juris Doctor, graduating in 1952. He worked in a variety of fields between 1952 and 1955—first as a lawyer in private practice, then as a research assistant to US District Court judge Theodore Levin, as a Congressional employee, a forest ranger, and finally as assistant prosecuting attorney for Wayne County. In 1955, Dingell's father died and Dingell won a special election to succeed him as representative of Michigan's 15th district. He won a full term in 1956 and proceeded to be reelected 29 times, receiving over 60% of the vote in all but two elections. In 1995, he became the Dean of the United States House of Representatives and is one of only four people to serve in the House for 50 years. In 2013, Dingell became the longest serving member of Congress, and upon retiring in 2015, he had served 21,571 days in the House of Representatives.

John D. Dingell is survived by his wife, Rep. Debbie Dingell, and his three children, John, Christopher, and Jennifer.

See *Current Biography 1983*

Albert J. Dunlap

Born: Hoboken, New Jersey; July 26, 1937
Died: Ocala, Florida; January 25, 2019
Occupation: Executive

Albert J. Dunlap was an American corporate executive, first known for his aggressive leadership style, who later became famous for his elaborate scams. He was known on Wall Street as "Chainsaw Al" and has been named "World's worst CEO" by many influential outlets.

Albert John Dunlap was born on July 26, 1937, in Hoboken, New Jersey. After graduating from West Point with a BSc in Engineering, he served in the U.S. Army for three years. His first position in business was at Kimberly-Clark, which he joined in 1963 before moving to Sterling Pulp & Paper and quickly becoming CEO. In 1974, he moved to Nitec, a paper-mill company based in Niagara Falls, NY, but was fired after two years. In 1976, the company faced an audit by Arthur Young, which revealed fraud indicating that Nitec's $5 million profit for the year was actually a $5.5 million loss. Although Nitec tried to sue Dunlap for fraud, the company was forced out of business, and Dunlap continued with his career regardless. In 1983, he was hired as the president and CEO of Lily Tulip Cup, whose stock rose 900% under his leadership. In 1994, he was headhunted by Scott Paper, which he took on and sold two years later for more than double the valuation he inherited. He took away over $100million from the deal. In 1996, Dunlap, by now known as one of corporate America's top turnaround artists, became the chairman and CEO of Sunbeam, and the company's shares went up 52%, as a result. However, it quickly became clear that Dunlap was achieving his successes through fraudulent means. A few years after taking over Sunbeam, the company went bankrupt, and Dunlap was forced to contend with charges of fraud brought forward by the U.S. Securities Exchange Commission (SEC). Dunlap paid a $500,000 civil penalty and in 2002, was barred from ever running a public company again.

Albert John Dunlap is survived by his wife Judy Dunlap, and son Troy.

See Current Biography 1998

Okwui Enwezor

Born: Calabar, Nigeria; October 23, 1963
Died: Munich, Germany; March 15, 2019
Occupation: Curator

Okwui Enwezor was a renowned art curator and the only person to curate both the Venice Biennale and Documenta. During his career, Enwezor curated numerous shows, wrote six books, and taught at universities worldwide on art history.

Okwui Enwezor was born on October 23, 1963, into an influential family in Nigeria. He attended the University of Nigeria before moving to New York to study political science at the New Jersey City University. After graduating in 1987, Enwezor began to study poetry, conceptual art, and art criticism. In 1993, Enwezor created the *Nka Journal of Contemporary African Art*. Then, in 1996, he gained notoriety for curating "In/Sight" at the Guggenheim, which was the first show to depict African art surrounding colonial withdrawal and African independence. Enwezor then became the artistic director of the second Johannesburg Biennale from 1996 to 1997 and became an adjunct curator at the Art Institute of Chicago in 1998. In 1998, he became the artistic director of Documenta 11 in Germany until 2002, where he was the first non-European to hold the position. From 2005 to 2009, Enwezor was the Dean of Academic Affairs and Senior Vice President for the San Francisco Art Institute and served as a visiting professor at many global universities. In 2012, he organized "The Rise and Fall of Apartheid" at the International Center for Photography in New York. The next year, Enwezor became the curator for the Venice biennale 2015. During his career, Enwezor authored and co-authored six books and wrote as a critic and editor for numerous journals. In 2006, he won the Frank Jewett Mather Award for art criticism and was ranked 42 in *ArtReview*'s list of the 100 most powerful figures in contemporary art. Enwezor was the director of the Haus der Kunst in Munich, Germany, before stepping down for health reasons in 2018.

Information regarding Okwui Enwezor's survivors is unavailable.

See Current Biography 2002

Hussain Muhammad Ershad

Born: Dinhata, West Bengal, India; February 1, 1930
Died: Dhaka, Bangladesh; July 14, 2019
Occupation: Former President of Bangladesh

The People's Republic of Bangladesh gained its independence from Pakistan in 1971, and for much of its time as an independent nation it has been plagued with grinding poverty and other problems. Lieutenant General Ershad, who attained power in a bloodless coup in March 1982 and ruled throughout that decade, had a decidedly mixed record but did succeed in making some strides, most notably, strengthening relations with the United States and initiating ambitious infrastructure projects.

The son of Muhammad Maqbul Hussain and his wife, Begum Majida Khatun, Hussain Muhammad Ershad was born in what was then a part of British India. His father was one of the principal lawyers of the Rangpur District Bar Association. Ershad attended Carmichael College in Rangpur and then entered the University of Dhaka, graduating with a BA degree in 1950.

After completing his studies at the officers' training school at Kohut, West Pakistan, Ershad was commissioned in September 1952 as an infantry officer in the Pakistani army and later held military posts of increasing rank. He saw combat duty in the 1965 India-Pakistan war as a company commander, and while Bangladesh, in alliance with India, was waging its struggle for independence from Pakistan in 1971, Ershad was in command of an infantry battalion in the province of Sind. After the establishment of the newly independent People's Republic of Bangladesh, Ershad chose repatriation. Promoted to colonel, he was appointed in December 1973 as the first Adjutant General of the new Bangladesh Army.

In December 1978 Ziaur Rahman—who had assumed the national presidency in April of the previous year and was leading the country back to civilian rule—appointed Ershad as chief of staff of the army and soon after that as lieutenant general.

There was strong opposition to President Zia, as he was known, within his own army; and on May 30, 1981 he was assassinated by mutinous officers. Although officially the military remained neutral in the campaign for the new presidential election scheduled for November 1981, and Ershad denied that he had political ambitions, a few months after Abdus Sattar triumphed at the polls, Ershad and other top military officers assumed virtual control of the presidential palace. On March 24, 1982, Ershad officially ousted Sattar, imposed martial law, suspended the constitution, dissolved Parliament, imposed a dusk-to-dawn curfew, and placed troops in control of all key points. The following year he proclaimed himself president and held that post until 1990, when he was ousted in an uprising.

After his ouster, he was arrested on more than two dozen charges. Although he was acquitted of many, he was convicted of corruption and imprisoned for six years. Despite that checkered history, he was elected to Parliament in 2008, 2014, and 2018; and at the time of his death, he was the opposition leader.

Hussain Muhammad Ershad was twice divorced, he is survived by three sons and a daughter.

See *Current Biography 1984*

Neil Estern

Born: New York, New York; April 18, 1926
Died: Sharon, Connecticut; July 11, 2019
Occupation: Sculptor

Neil Estern fashioned statues and busts of such towering figures in American history as President Franklin Delano Roosevelt and President John F. Kennedy. During an early stint as a toy designer, he created another American icon: a 35-inch doll named Patti Playpal, which was introduced in 1959 and became an enduring success for its manufacturer.

An only child, Neil Estern was raised in Brooklyn by his parents, Molly and Marc, a negotiator for a toy-industry trade group. Starting early in life, he enjoyed making things out of clay, and at age 12, he began taking classes in drawing and painting at the Pratt Institute. Estern attended the School of Industrial Arts (later renamed the High School of Art and Design), in Manhattan, where at that time each student took four art classes daily.

Having decided that he was far more interested in fine art than commercial art, like many of his classmates, Estern enrolled at the Tyler School of Fine Arts, a division of Temple University, in Philadelphia. He also took classes at the Barnes Foundation, in nearby Merion. In 1947 Estern earned both a BFA degree and a BS degree in education from the Tyler School—the latter for practical reasons, in case he was unable to support himself as an artist.

Estern soon discovered that he had little chance of earning a living as a fine artist, not least because his specialty—realist, or classical, art—was no longer in vogue among the buyers and sellers of art; rather, the demand was for abstract, or nonrepresentational, work. With the help of his father, he got a job as a wax modeler with the Ideal Toy Co., molding heads, limbs, and torsos for dolls. In the late 1950s he created Patti Playpal, examples of which sell to collectors for hundreds of dollars today.

In the early 1960s he got a big break when he was commissioned to sculpt a marble bust of the recently assassinated John F. Kennedy for display at Brooklyn's Grand Army Plaza. Other high-profile assignments steadily followed, including likenesses of New York City mayor Fiorello H. La Guardia, displayed on a pedestal in Greenwich Village; Eleanor Roosevelt, at the National Cathedral in Washington; Irving Berlin, at the Music Box Theater in Manhattan; and Senator Claude Pepper, at the Pepper Museum in Tallahassee. Among his most famed pieces is a massive sculpture of Franklin Roosevelt seated in a wheelchair, on display at Washington's West Potomac Park. (A separate sculpture of his beloved terrier, Fala, sits at his feet.) He was a two-time president of the National Society of Sculptors.

Neil Estern is survived by his wife, Anne Graham; a daughter, Victoria; two sons, Peter and Evan; and three grandchildren.

See *Current Biography 2008*

Martin S. Feldstein

Born: New York, New York; November 25, 1939
Died: Boston, Massachusetts; June 11, 2019
Occupation: Economist

Martin S. Feldstein was a conservative economist who served as president of the National Bureau of Economic Research (NBER) for over 30 years. He also published widely about economic policy and worked as an advisor for numerous U. S. Presidents.

Martin Stuart Feldstein was born on November 25, 1939, in New York City to a Jewish family. He studied at Harvard University before attending Nuffield College, Oxford, and obtaining a DPhil (same as PhD) in Economics. He stayed on as an Oxford Fellow until 1967, when he joined the Harvard faculty. He became a tenured professor of economics in 1969 and was appointed George F. Baker Professor of Economics in 1984. Over his academic career, he published numerous influential papers and was a graduate teacher and advisor to many successful politicians, economists, and academics. In 1977, Feldstein was awarded the John Bates Clark Medal of the American Economic Association (AEA), a prize given to an economist under the age of 40 regarded to have made the greatest contribution to economic science. He wrote widely on issues relating to economic policy and

frequently contributed to the *Wall Street Journal*. He was also the recipient of several honorary degrees. Outside of academia, Feldstein played an active role within the area of public policy, chairing the board of economic advisors for President Reagan, and acting as an advisor for President Bush and President Obama. Later in his career, he served as a consultant to the U. S. Department of Defense (DoD), and on the board of directors of the Council on Foreign Relations (CFR), the Trilateral Commission, The Group of 30, and the National Committee on United States–China Relations. He also served as president of the National Bureau of Economic Research from 1978 to 2008.

Martin Feldstein is survived by his wife, Kathleen, two daughters, and four grandchildren.

See *Current Biography 1983*

Albert Finney

Born: Salford, England; May 9, 1936
Died: London, England; February 7, 2019
Occupation: Actor

Albert Finney was a leading British actor known for his work in film, television, and theatre. He won multiple awards throughout his career, including two BAFTAs (British Academy of Film and Television Arts), an Emmy, and three Golden Globes.

Albert Finney was born on May 9, 1936, to Alice and Albert Finney in Salford. He attended the Royal Academy of Dramatic Art (RADA) and graduated in 1956. Upon graduating from RADA, he joined the Royal Shakespeare Company. He began to perform in shows filmed for the BBC, and in 1960, he made his first film appearance in *The Entertainer*. His breakthrough came later that year with his role in *Saturday Night and Sunday Morning*, which was the third most popular film in Britain that year. In 1963, he starred in the Academy-award winning film *Tom Jones* and was voted ninth most popular box office star of the year. He continued to split his time between stage and film, taking on a season of plays at the National Theatre, before co-starring with Audrey Hepburn in *Two For the Road* (1967). In 1974, Finney found himself once again in the box office spotlight, starring as Hercule Poirot in *Murder on the Orient Express*. He continued to act in film, television, and stage roles from the 1970s to the 2000s, with a standout role in *Erin Brockovich* (2000). In 2002, his portrayal of Winston Churchill in *The Gathering Storm* won him a BAFTA, an Emmy, and a Golden Globe Award. Throughout his film and television career, Finney received numerous awards and accolades. He was nominated for five Academy Awards; thirteen BAFTAs, two of which he won; nine Golden Globes, three of which he won; and one winning Emmy. For his stage acting work, Finney was nominated for two Tony Awards, and won one Laurence Olivier Award, and three Evening Standard Theatre Awards. He declined the offer of a CBE in 1980, and also refused a knighthood in 2000.

Albert Finney is survived by his son, Simon, and his third wife Pene Delmage.

See *Current Biography 1963*

Keith Flint

Born: London, England; September 17, 1969
Died: Essex, England; March 4, 2019
Occupation: Singer, dancer

Keith Flint was a singer, dancer, and avid motorcycle racer best known for being the front man of alternative electronic band The Prodigy, performing on two UK number one singles, 'Firestarter' and 'Breathe.'

Keith Flint was born on September 17, 1969, to Clive and Yvonne Flint in London, though his family soon moved to suburban Essex. He was expelled from the Boswell School in Chelmsford at the age of 15 for being disruptive. He soon took on work as a roofer. He began attending raves and met DJ Liam Howlett at local club *The Barn*. He encouraged Howlett to play his own music and offered to perform alongside him as a dancer with friend Leeroy Thornhill. The three were soon joined by MC Maxim Reality and together formed a successful electronic dance act The Prodigy. In 1996, Flint became the band's official front man, performing vocals on the hit single 'Firestarter', and swiftly after, on 'Breathe.' He continued to perform and record lead vocals for many of The Prodigy's tracks including 'Baby's Got a Temper' (2002) and 'Omen' (2009), which peaked at Number 5 and Number 4 on the UK Charts, respectively. Flint became known for his unpolished, punk-inspired style and energetic performances. In 2012, he recorded the single 'War' with dubstep artist Caspa. He further experimented with solo projects, including punk band Flint. However, none were as successful or as long-lived as The Prodigy, whose seven studio albums all debuted at Number 1 on the UK Albums Chart. Flint was a keen motorcyclist and raced in numerous competitions. He also owned a motorcycle team, Team Traction Control. He continued to tour with The Prodigy until the month before his death in 2019. Soon after his death, it was revealed that his death was a suicide. In a campaign to raise awareness about

male suicide and to pay tribute to Flint, fans returned the single 'Firestarter' to the charts, where it reached Number 57 in the UK Weekly Charts, and Number 13 in the Billboard Charts for Dance/Electronic Digital Songs Sales.

See *Current Biography 2009*

Peter Fonda

Born: New York, New York; February 23, 1940
Died: Los Angeles, California; August 16, 2019
Occupation: Actor

For generations, the name "Fonda" has been an emblem of Hollywood. Henry Fonda was one of the best-loved film actors of all time. Jane Fonda is a two-time Oscar winner. Bridget Fonda is a star in her own right. Yet for Peter Fonda—son of Henry, younger brother of Jane, and father of Bridget—being the child of a Hollywood legend was sometimes problematic, especially as he and Henry were often at odds.

Peter Fonda was born to Henry and socialite Frances Ford Seymour (Brokaw) Fonda, who committed suicide in 1950, when he was 10. Less than a year later, he shot himself in the stomach, claiming it was an accident.

Fonda attended Omaha University; and in 1960, he starred in *The Golden Fleece* at the Omaha Community Playhouse. He followed that regional role less than a year later with his Broadway debut, in *Blood, Sweat and Stanley Poole*, for which he won a New York Drama Critics' Circle Award. He made his television debut in a 1962 episode of the police drama *Naked City*, and his big-screen debut as Dr. Mark Cheswick in the 1963 feature *Tammy and the Doctor*.

Fonda starred as a leather-clad biker named Heavenly Blues in the Roger Corman film *The Wild Angels* (1966); and the picture's tremendous popularity, along with Fonda's much-publicized trial for possession of marijuana, suddenly made him a symbol of the 1960s counterculture. He next appeared in another Corman picture, *The Trip* (1967), which had a screenplay by Jack Nicholson and an appearance by Dennis Hopper. Afterwards, Fonda proposed to Hopper that they make their own film. With the writer Terry Southern, they came up with a script about two stoners who score big with a cocaine deal and then set off on their Harley-Davidson choppers on a pilgrimage to New Orleans. Fonda, as producer, raised $350,000 to make the film, which Hopper directed, and they co-starred as Wyatt (nicknamed Captain America) and Billy, respectively. Jack Nicholson played George Hanson, an alcoholic lawyer.

For nearly three decades, the film, *Easy Rider* (1969), was seen as the defining moment of Fonda's screen career. It is also seen by many as the film of the late 1960s, much the way that the Woodstock music festival is seen as the concert of that era.

Easy Rider kept Fonda in starring roles for more than a decade; and although that era represented the peak of his career, he remained busy over the next half-century, appearing in such films as *Futureworld* (1976), *The Passion of Ayn Rand* (1999), *Back When We Were Grown-Ups* (2004), and the 2007 remake of *3:10 to Yuma*.

Peter Fonda died of lung cancer and is survived by his third wife, Margaret; his sister, Jane; daughter, Bridget; son, Justin; two stepsons, Thomas McGuane and Wills DeVogelaere; a stepdaughter, Lexi DeVogelaere; a half-sister, Amy Fonda Fishman; and one grandson.

See *Current Biography 1998*

Albert Frère

Born: Fontaine-l'Évêque, Belgium; February 4, 1926
Died: Gerpinnes, Belgium; December 3, 2018
Occupation: Businessman

Albert Frère was a Belgian businessman who used successful investments to create a media, utilities, and oil empire and amassed billions of dollars in wealth, making him the richest man in Belgium.

Albert Frère was born on February 4, 1926, to Oscar and Madeleine Frère in Belgium's coal and steel region. His father, a nail and chain merchant, died when he was 17, and Frère left school early to help run the family business. The nail company became profitable in the post-World War II reconstruction period, and Frère's shrewd investment in steel factories led to him controlling virtually the entire steel industry in the Belgian region of Charleroi by the 1970s. In 1979, when the Belgian government nationalized the industry, Frère sold his enterprises to the state and used the windfall to expand into finance, establishing the Swiss holding company Pargesa with Paul Desmarais, a Canadian entrepreneur. Frère and Desmarais took over Groupe Bruxelles Lambert in 1982 to manage their investments. Frère bought and sold significant stakes in blue-chip conglomerates and engineered multinational mergers and acquisitions. His active promotion of international consolidation, including the merger he engineered in 2007 between waste and water company Suez SA, a CNP subsidiary, and French utility Gaz de France (GDF), helped advance the economic integration of Europe. He became the richest man in Belgium and among the richest in Europe, with a net worth estimated by Forbes at close to $6 billion. King Albert II of Belgium gave Frère the title of baron in 1994. Frère was married twice, first to Nelly Poplimont and then to Christine Henning, and had three children. A son from his second marriage, Charles-Albert, died in a car accident in 1999. Frère jointly owned Château Cheval Blanc vineyard in Saint-Émilion, France, with Bernard Arnault, the chairman of French luxury-goods firm LVMH. He retired as chief executive of Groupe Bruxelles Lambert in 2015.

Albert Frère is survived by his son, Gérald, and his daughter, Ségolène.

See *Current Biography 2002*

Bruno Ganz

Born: Zürich, Switzerland, March 22, 1941
Died: Zürich, Switzerland; February 16, 2019
Occupation: Actor

Bruno Ganz was a well-known stage and film actor who worked in both German and English. He was widely regarded as one of the most prominent and highly skilled German-language actors, and his career spanned over fifty years.

Bruno Ganz was born on March 22, 1941, in Zürich to a Swiss factory worker father and a northern Italian mother. He was always interested in acting, and by the time he reached university, decided to devote himself to it as a career. In 1960, Ganz made his screen debut in *Der Herr mit der schwarzen Melone* (The gentleman with the black melon), but did not gain cinematic fame until many years later. His theatrical debut in 1961 was more successful, and Ganz dedicated himself almost entirely to the stage until the late 1970s. In 1970, he co-founded the theatre company "Schaubühne" in Berlin, with Peter Stein. In 1973, he was named Actor of the Year by German theatre magazine *Theater heute*. He finally made his film breakthrough in the 1976 film *Sommergäste* (Summer Guests), and quickly became well-known in Germany and abroad. He worked with famous directors such as Warner Herzog, Wim Wenders, Ridley Scott, and Francis Ford Coppola. In 1996, he became the fifth actor in more than a century to receive the Iffland-Ring, an award given to the "most significant and most worthy actor of German-speaking theatre." Outside of Germany, he is perhaps best known for starring as Adolf Hitler in the Academy Award nominated *Der Untergang* (Downfall), a historical war drama about the end of Hitler's life, which appeared in 2004. He is also known for his starring roles in *Unknown* (2011), *The Counselor* (2013), and *The Party* (2017).

Bruno Ganz is survived by his long-time partner, Ruth Walz, and a son, Daniel, from his marriage to Sabine, from whom he was separated but not divorced.

See *Current Biography 2006*

Alan García Pérez

Born: Lima, Peru; May 23, 1949
Died: Lima, Peru; April 17, 2019
Occupation: Former President of Peru

Alan Gabriel Ludwig García Pérez, a thirty-six-year-old lawyer regarded as hope for democracy's survival, was elected president of crisis-ridden Peru on July 28, 1985. García was elected to the Constituent Assembly in 1978, served in the National Congress starting in 1980, and became General Secretary of Alianza Popular Revolucionaria Americana (APRA) in 1982.

APRA was founded in 1924 as a militant leftist movement changing to a moderate social democratic movement influential in Peruvian politics. Both of García's parents—Carlos García Ronceros, an accountant, and Nytha Pérez Rojas, a teacher—belonged to APRA, and García became active in the youth organization at eleven. He graduated with a law degree from Universidad Nacional Mayor de San Marcos in 1973 and continued studies in Spain and France, acquiring a doctor of law from Universidad Complutense de Madrid before returning to Lima in 1977. García, a top APRA candidate, won a 1980 to 1985 seat on the National Congress and in 1982 was elected Secretary General of the party assuring him presidential candidacy. In 1985 Peru suffered from increasing inflation, high unemployment, excessive foreign debt, flood damage, and violent military campaigns. García campaigned against the International Monetary Fund (IMF) and foreign investors. He favored restricting foreign-debt payments, greater national self-sufficiency, agricultural growth, selective tariff increases, anti-narcotics campaigns, and consideration of historical and racial issues for peacefully dealing with guerrilla organizations. García's election was initially promising. Anti-narcotics campaigns were launched with United States and Columbia's help, cocaine-processing laboratories were raided, officials were dismissed for illegal drug involvement and civilian deaths during guerrilla raids, inflation slowed, cost of living rose, fighter plane orders were canceled, and official's salaries were frozen. García's debt plan was criticized by U. S. and Cuban officials, and conditions in the country continued to decline as did his popularity. After his term, accusations of embezzling and kickbacks resulted in a nine-year exile to Paris. He returned to Peru to join the presidential race of 2001, which he lost. García won the 2006 elections, but his second term was as unsuccessful as his first. He was eliminated in the first round of his 2016 run. García shot himself as police officers attempted to arrest him during a corruption and bribery investigation.

García is survived by his second wife, Maria del Pilar Nores Bodereau and their four children, a daughter from his first marriage to Carla Buscaglia, and a son from an affair with Roxanne Cheesman.

See *Current Biography 1985*

Jack Gargan

Born: Philadelphia, Pennsylvania; October 20, 1930
Died: Bangkok, Thailand; November 4, 2018
Occupation: Politician

Jack Gargan was a financial consultant and politician who served as chairman of the Reform Party and was best known for his support of third-party candidates and his campaigns to set term limits for all members of U.S. Congress.

John J. "Jack" Gargan was born on October 20, 1930, to John and Frances Gargan, along with one brother, James. His father died in 1932. Gargan graduated from Prospect Park High School in 1948 and went on to serve in both the US Navy and the US Army. Following his military service, he graduated from Birmingham-Southern College with a degree in business administration and moved to Florida, where he attended Stetson University College of Law. In 1984, Gargan founded the International Association of Registered Financial Consultants (IARFC) and served as the association's president and CEO. In 1990, he created the Throw the Rascals Out (THOR) group and led a two-year campaign, running advertisements in major newsletters across the United States that denounced Congress for voting to increase legislative salaries and advocated overthrowing every congressional incumbent and setting term limits. He led the campaign to draft Ross Perot into the 1992 presidential race and served as the second chairman of the Reform Party started by Perot until he was voted out in 2000. Gargan ran for Governor of Florida in 1994 and ran on the Reform Party ticket for a seat in the House of Representatives in 1998 and 2002. He garnered a significant number of votes as a third-party candidate but did not win any of these elections.

He retired as a financial consultant; and in 2005, he moved to Thailand, where he married his second wife, Paniwan, thirty-three years his junior.

Jack Gargan is survived by his four children, his grandchildren, and his great-grandchildren.

See *Current Biography 2001*

Leslie H. Gelb

Born: New Rochelle, New York; March 4, 1937
Died: New York, New York; August 31, 2019
Occupation: Journalist and government official

Leslie Gelb has been called "a unique star in American foreign policy" and "a patriot in its noblest definition." He had a distinguished career as both a federal government official and a journalist and is perhaps best known for compiling the Pentagon Papers, the landmark study that revealed many previously hidden aspects of the United States' involvement in the Vietnam War, while working for the U.S. Department of Defense in 1967.

Leslie Gelb's parents, Max and Dorothy, were Jewish immigrants from Hungary who toiled 14 hours a day running a small corner store. Gelb inherited that work ethic, taking on jobs as a dishwasher and parking valet to pay his way through Tufts University, where he studied government and philosophy and in 1959 earned a bachelor's degree, with honors. He next enrolled at Harvard, where he received a master's degree in 1961 and doctorate in 1964, both in government.

After graduating, Gelb became an assistant professor in government at Wesleyan University, and in 1967 he joined the U.S. Department of Defense as the deputy director of the policy-planning staff; a year later he was promoted to director. In 1968 and 1969, he served as the acting deputy assistant secretary of defense for policy planning and arms control.

Earlier, in June 1967, the U.S. secretary of defense, Robert S. McNamara, had assigned Gelb to establish a task force to answer 100 questions for a classified study on the Vietnam War. The study, which later became known as the Pentagon Papers, examined the United States' activities in Southeast Asia, specifically in regard to the events that began with the French control of what was then Indochina and expanded into a full-scale war that involved hundreds of thousands of American troops.

After Richard Nixon took office, Gelb left the Defense Department to become a senior fellow at the Brookings Institution. Four years later the *New York Times* hired him as a correspondent; there, from 1973 to 1977, he wrote more than 300 articles. He alternated between government service and journalism for the remainder of his career, serving in the Jimmy Carter administration, for example, and being named a *New York Times* national security correspondent.

Leslie Gelb died of renal failure. He is survived by his wife, Judith; their children, Adam, Caroline and Alison; and five grandsons.

See *Current Biography 2003*

Murray Gell-Mann

Born: Manhattan, New York; September 15, 1929
Died: Santa Fe, New Mexico; May 24, 2019
Occupation: Physicist

Murray Gell-Mann was a physicist well known for his research into quarks, quantum physics, and nuclear physics. In 1969, he was awarded the Nobel Prize for Physics.

Murray Gell-Mann was born on September 15, 1929, in Manhattan, New York, to Pauline and Arthur Isidore Gell-Mann, who were both Jewish immigrants from the Austro-Hungarian Empire, present day Ukraine. Gell-Mann was always fascinated by nature and mathematics and graduated valedictorian from his high school before going to study physics at Yale University. After his graduation in 1948, he pursued a PhD in physics at the Massachusetts Institute of Technology (MIT) under Victor Weisskopf, graduating in 1951. He then worked briefly as a visiting professor at the University of Illinois (1952–1953), and as a visiting associate professor at Columbia University and an associate professor for a year at the University of Chicago (1954–1955). He then moved to the California Institute of Technology (Caltech), where he worked as a professor from 1955 to 1993, collaborating with Richard Feynman and Richard Earl Block, among others, on diverse groundbreaking research projects. He specialised in nuclear physics, and made numerous discoveries, developing models and classificatory schemes that have proven important to further research in nuclear and quantum physics. He is particularly well known for coining the term 'quark' and contributing to their discovery. In 1969, Gell-Mann was awarded the Nobel Prize in Physics for his work discovering and classifying elementary particles and their interactions. He also researched String Theory extensively throughout the 1970s and 1980s, contributing greatly to its popularity among american researchers. In 1994, he published a successful popular science book *The Quark and the Jaguar: Adventures in the Simple and the Complex*. Over his career, Gell-Mann won numerous award and accolades, including the American Academy of Achievement's Golden Plate Award, the Ernest Orlando Lawrence Award, and the Albert Einstein Medal. He was also awarded honorary doctorates from universities including Cambridge, Columbia, Oxford, and Yale.

Murray Gell-Mann is survived by his children, Nicholas and Elizabeth, and his stepson.

See *Current Biography 1998*

Georgie Anne Geyer

Born: Chicago, Illinois; April 2, 1935
Died: Washington, DC; May 15, 2019
Occupation: Journalist

Georgie Anne Geyer was a foreign correspondent famous for interviewing some of the world's most notorious leaders, including Saddam Hussein and Fidel Castro.

Georgie Anne Geyer was born on April 2, 1935, in Chicago's working-class Far South Side, where her father ran a dairy business. She attended Northwestern University, graduating from the Medill School of Journalism in 1956. She also spent a year at the University of Vienna on a Fulbright Scholarship. Geyer was fluent in Spanish, Portuguese, German, and Russian. After graduating, she worked briefly for the *Southtown Economist* in Chicago, before pursuing a career as a reporter with the *Chicago Daily News* from 1959 to 1974. Although she started as a reporter for the news desk, she quickly became an important foreign correspondent. After leaving the newspaper, she started writing as a syndicated columnist, her work appearing in over 100 newspapers across the United States, including the *Times*. In 1973, she became the first Western reporter to interview Saddam Hussein. Other notable interviewees include Yasser Arafat, Anwar Sadat, King Hussein of Jordan, Muammar al-Gaddafi, the Ayatollah Khomeini, Juan and Eva Perón, and Fidel Castro, whom she wrote a book about. Geyer travelled extensively, being particularly drawn to the Middle East, Africa, and Latin America, where she brought attention to the conflicts between dictators and guerrilla fighters. She also provided extensive coverage of the Angolan Civil War. During her career, she published five books, wrote countless articles, and appeared regularly on news talk shows. Geyer was diagnosed with tongue cancer in 2007, and was no longer able to participate in speaking engagements or interview people. Still, she continued to write a column until late in life. Geyer held twenty-one honorary degrees from a range of universities and colleges, as well as numerous journalism awards and prizes.

Georgie Anne Geyer never married and had no immediate survivors.

See *Current Biography 1986*

Kenneth A. Gibson

Born: Enterprise, Alabama; May 15, 1932
Died: West Orange, New Jersey; March 29, 2019
Occupation: Politician

Kenneth A. Gibson, an independent Democrat, holds the distinction of being the first elected African American mayor of a major city, Newark, New Jersey. He faced high incidences of crime, drug use, unemployment, welfare, slum housing, high taxes, infant mortality, volatile racial clashes, and a city verging on bankruptcy.

Kenneth A. Gibson was the oldest son born to Willie Gibson, a butcher, and Daisy, a seamstress and later nursing home aide. After Willie built his family a home with an indoor toilet, his salary was cut; and they could no longer stay in Enterprise, Alabama, so they moved to Newark. Gibson played saxophone and worked as a porter while maintaining honors in high school. After two years of factory work, Gibson joined the 65th Engineer Battalion of the U. S. Army in Hawaii and continued his engineering studies. In 1963, his civil engineering degree led to a position with the Newark Housing Authority. His younger brother, Harold, became a Newark policeman. Gibson was active in civil rights, the Urban League, the National Association for the Advancement of Colored People (NAACP), the Congress of Racial Equality (CORE), the Young Men's Christian Association (YMCA), Young Women's Christian Association (YWCA), and Newark's Business and Industry Coordinating Council. He was named Man of the Year by the Newark Junior Chamber of Commerce in 1964. Gibson lost the 1966 mayoral election but won in 1970. Three other black men were elected to the city council in Newark at a time when blacks comprised 62 percent and Spanish-speaking 10 percent of the population of 400,000. Gibson focused on keeping major corporations in Newark. City finances, tax packages, and the predominately black Board of Education and predominately white Teachers Union strike, were all settled with compromises. During his sixteen years he improved health services and rehabilitated or had new housing units built; but the unemployment rate increased, and a third of high school students did not graduate. In 1976 he was the first African American president of the U.S. Conference of Mayors; in 1979 he received the U.S. Senator John Heinz Award; and in 1986, after 16 years of being the longest-serving mayor in Newark, he lost the mayoral election. Gibson opened an engineering consulting company in 1998 and was indicted for bribery and misappropriation of funds in 2001, but the jury failed to reach an agreement that lead to a mistrial.

Gibson is survived by two daughters, Cheryl and Joanne, a stepdaughter, Joyce Byron and Kennon Hunter from his second marriage to Muriel Cook, and his third wife Camille whom he married in 2004.

See *Current Biography 1971*

Nathan Glazer

Born: New York, New York; February 25, 1923
Died: Cambridge, Massachusetts; January 19, 2019
Occupation: Sociologist, intellectual, and author

Nathan Glazer was an urban sociologist and seen as a defining member of the neoconservative circle of academics.

Nathan Glazer, born on February 25, 1923, in New York, was a first-generation Jewish Polish American who grew up in East Harlem. He attended the City College of New York, which throughout the 1940s, was seen as a radical institution. It was here that Glazer learned and celebrated Marxism and was hostile to Soviet-Communism. During the outbreak of World War II, Glazer would become increasingly convinced that communism was a greater threat to the United States than capitalism. He graduated in 1944, and his first job was at the *Contemporary Jewish Record*, which became known as the *Commentary*. He published his first book, *The Lonely Crowd*, with David Riesman and Reuel Denney in 1950, which is perceived as a seminal work on American society. In 1960, Glazer briefly edited *The Committee of Correspondence Newsletter* at Harvard University, but soon dropped this project and began writing articles about ethnic groups in New York City. These would eventually be collected and published in 1963 as the book *Beyond the Melting Pot: The Negroes, Puerto Ricans, Jews, Italians and Irish of New York City.* In 1962–1963, Glazer worked at the Kennedy administration's Housing and Home Finance Agency before accepting a teaching position at Berkeley in 1963. In 1965, Glazer was one of the first contributors to *The Public Interest* magazine, which would go on to be a staple of neoconservative publications. He edited the magazine from 1973 to 2005. Glazer was an advocate of preserving buildings, and under Lyndon Johnson's presidency, he was a consultant with the Model Cities Program. In 1969, Glazer started teaching at Harvard University, in a position created to focus on the problems of cities. Throughout the 1980s and 1990s, he continued to publish books and papers on race and ethnicity, including his

book, *We Are All Multiculturalists Now* in 1997. Glazer sat on the committee for the National Academy of Sciences (NAS).

Nathan Glazer is survived by his second wife, Sulochana, and his children, Glazer Khedouri, Elizabeth Glazer and Sophie Glazer.

See *Current Biography 1970*

William Goldman

Born: Highland Park, Illinois; August 12, 1931
Died: New York, New York; November 16, 2018
Occupation: Novelist, screenwriter, playwright

William Goldman was a writer best known for his Academy Award–winning screenplays for *Butch Cassidy and the Sundance Kid* and *All the President's Men* and for the screen adaptations of his novels *The Princess Bride* and *Marathon Man*.

William Goldman was born to Maurice and Marion Goldman. Goldman attended Oberlin College, where he first developed an interest in creative writing. He graduated from Oberlin with a BA in 1952. He was then drafted into the military and discharged in 1954. He later attended Columbia University and obtained his Master's degree in 1956. His first novel, *The Temple of Gold* was published in 1957.Collaborating with his older brother, playwright James Goldman, and their friend, composer John Kander, Goldman wrote three plays that all opened on Broadway but had short, unsuccessful runs. It was the success of his screenplay for the film *Harper* (1966), starring Paul Newman, that launched his career as a screenwriter. While teaching creative writing at Princeton University, Goldman wrote his first original screenplay, *Butch Cassidy and the Sundance Kid* (1969), which became the highest-grossing film of 1969 and won four Academy Awards, including best original screenplay. Goldman published his two most famous novels, *The Princess Bride* in 1973 and *Marathon Man* in 1974. He wrote the script for *All the President's Men* (1976), for which he received an Academy Award for best adapted screenplay. For most of the 1980s, Goldman focused on publishing novels and a memoir, *Adventures in the Screen Trade*, before returning to Hollywood by adapting two of his novels into films: *Heat* (1986), directed by Michael Mann, and the well-beloved *The Princess Bride* (1987), directed by Rob Reiner. Goldman also wrote the screenplay adaptation of Stephen King's novel *Misery* into the 1990 film of the same name. In his later career, Goldman was highly sought after as a script doctor, doing uncredited work on films such as *A Few Good Men* (1992), *Indecent Proposal* (1993), and *Dolores Claiborne* (1995).

In total, Goldman wrote more than 20 novels and more than 20 screenplays.

William Goldman is survived by his partner, Susan Burden, his daughter, Jenny Goldman, and a grandson. His other daughter, Susanna Goldman, died in 2015.

See *Current Biography 1995*

Paul Gregory

Born: Waukee, Iowa; August 27, 1920
Died: Desert Hot Springs, California; December 25, 2015
Occupation: Producer

Paul Gregory was a 1950s film, television, and theater producer. His most noted work included his 1955 television adaptation of *The Night of the Hunter*.

James Burton Lenhart (later changed to Paul Gregory) was born on August 27, 1920, outside of Des Moines, Iowa, to James and Esther. When Gregory was a teenager, his father abandoned his family, and his mother was forced to send Gregory to live with relatives in London, as she could not afford to support five children during the Great Depression. Once he returned from London, Gregory got a job reading the newspaper for the local radio. After graduating from Lincoln High School in 1939, Gregory moved to Hollywood in an effort to become famous. He landed a few small roles with MGM movies, while also managing a drugstore. He then joined an agent company, MCA, where Gregory began working with Charles Laughton. He left MCA in 1950 and joined Laughton in producing a reading tour. During the 1950s and 1960s, Gregory produced seventeen Broadway plays and in 1955, along with Laughton, produced the film adaptation of *The Night of the Hunter*. In 1958, Gregory produced *The Naked and the Dead*, his last film. He won an Emmy Award for his 1955 television adaptation of *The Caine Mutiny Court-Martial*.

Paul Gregory does not have any immediate survivors.

See *Current Biography 1956*

B. J. Habibie

Born: Parepare, South Sulawesi, Indonesia; June 25, 1936
Died: Jakarta, Indonesia; September 11, 2019
Occupation: President of Indonesia

Bacharuddin Jusuf Habibie—better known simply by the initials B.J.—was the third president of Indonesia; appointed to the role in 1998, he served just a 512-day tenure as the country's leader.

Habibie was born June 25, 1936, on one of the largest of the more than 3,000 islands that make up Indonesia. He was the fourth of the eight children of Alwi Abdul Jalil Habibie and R. A. Tuti Marini Puspowardojo.

In 1948, when Habibie's father was appointed head of the Department of Agriculture of the State of East Indonesia, the family moved to Ujung Pandang, then known as Macassar. Across the street from where the Habibies lived was billeted a young military commander who had distinguished himself in battles against Dutch forces in the war for Indonesia's independence: Suharto. The Habibies became friends with Suharto, and when Habibie's father died, Suharto and the 13-year-old boy developed a virtual father-son relationship.

Habibie went to high school in Bandung, Java, and graduated in 1954. In the mid-1960s, he earned a doctorate in aeronautical engineering from the Technischen Hochschule. He then worked at the German aircraft company Messerschmitt-Böolkow-Blohm (MBB) and became vice president and director for technology application, as well as the head of the Advanced Technology and Aeronautics Division.

In 1974, Suharto requested that he return to Indonesia to serve as an adviser on the development of high-technology industries like aircraft construction, shipbuilding, and other defense-related industries. Four years later, he was appointed minister of state for research and technology; and for the next 20 years, he oversaw the government's various state-owned high-tech industries, including Industri Pesawat Terbang Nusantara (Nusantara Aircraft Industry (IPTN)), which spent $2 billion in developing Indonesian passenger airplanes and jets.

Habibie became one of Suharto's longest-serving cabinet members, and his loyalty was rewarded in 1998, when Suharto chose him as his vice-presidential running mate. That year Suharto, who exerted tyrannical control over the electoral process, easily won election to a seventh term. He was forced to step down on May 21, however, in the midst of a worsening economic crisis, a steady succession of student protests, and riots to protest a steep increase in the price of gas.

Suharto turned power over to Habibie, who promised to address longstanding issues of corruption, nepotism, and human-rights abuses. Many observers predicted he'd last fewer than 100 days in office, given his seeming inability to mitigate the economic crisis, he had inherited and his failure to clamp down on corruption. He quickly lost any semblance of public and parliamentary support, and in the run-up to the 1999 presidential elections, he was voted down by his party and did not appear on the ballot.

Bacharuddin Jusuf Habibie was predeceased in 2010 by his wife, Hasri Ainun (née Besari), and his memoir of their decades together, *Habibie and Ainun*, was turned into a film in 2012. He is survived by their sons, Ilham Akbar and Tareq Kamal.

See *Current Biography 1998*

Roy Hargrove

Born: Waco, Texas; October 16, 1969
Died: New York, New York; November 2, 2018
Occupation: Jazz trumpet player

Roy Hargrove was a prominent neo-traditionalist jazz musician during the 1980s and 1990s. His improvisational skills created a new era in the jazz genre.

Roy Anthony Hargrove was born on October 16, 1969, in Waco, Texas. From a young age, Hargrove was very interested in music, and first learned the cornet at the age of nine. He played with local bands in Dallas throughout middle and high school and was discovered by famous trumpeter Wynton Marsalis. He subsequently began performing with big-name musicians as a teenager, and by 17, Hargrove had toured Europe and Japan. In 1989, at the age of 20, Hargrove decided to form his own quintet. Many believed him to be too young, but by the release of his first album in 1993, *With the Tenors of Our Time*, he had become acknowledged as one of the main forces in the modern jazz scene. His up-and-coming reputation led to a scholarship at Berklee College of Music in Boston, MA, where Hargrove developed a competitive edge. Over the next few years, he performed with numerous established artists such as Frank Morgan, James Williams, and Larry Willis. Although he recorded numerous albums during this time, including *Public Eye* (1990), *Tokyo Sessions* (1991), and *Beauty and the Beast* (1992), his big break in 1992 was when he played with saxophonist Sonny Rollins in Carnegie Hall. He gained respect for his jazz solos amongst critics and became

a more established name in the jazz genre. In 1995, Hargrove founded Roy Hargrove's Big Band, which focused on a more traditional jazz sound to the likes of Duke Ellington and Count Basie. That same year, he beat out Wynton Marsalis as trumpeter of the year in the Down Beat Readers Poll. He continued his musical career in New York, where he settled in lower Manhattan and continued to release music for the rest of his life.

Roy Hargrove is survived by his mother; his wife, Aida; his daughter, Kamala; and his brother, Brian.

See *Current Biography 2000*

Valerie K. Harper

Born: Suffern, New York; August 22, 1939
Died: Los Angeles, California; August 30, 2019
Occupation: American actress

Valerie Kathryn Harper made her television debut in 1970 mesmerizing viewers as the brash, but loveable, Rhoda Morgenstern on *The Mary Tyler Moore Show* for which she won three Emmys. Harper's career started with dancing and improvisation with Second City and *Story Theatre* on Broadway in 1970–1971. Harper earned a Tony Award nomination for her role in the 2010 Broadway play *Looped*.

Valerie Harper was born in Suffern, New York, to a sales executive father, Howard Harper, and a nurse mother, Iva McConnell. Harper's older sister, Leanne, became a folk singer and younger brother, Merrill (who later was known as Don), went into logging. Howard's lighting fixture sales position kept the family moving from the likes of Oregon, Massachusetts, New Jersey, Michigan, and California before the family finally settled in Jersey City, New Jersey, in 1951. Her parent's divorced in 1956. Harper began dancing lessons at six aspiring to become a ballerina. At sixteen she danced behind the Rockettes at Radio City Music Hall followed by the chorus line in *Li'L Abner* in Las Vegas and Paramount film in 1959. Harper began drama lessons while taking New York chorus positions in *Take Me Along* (1959), *Wildcat* (1960), and *Subways Are for Sleeping* (1961). Harper studied improvisation with Paul Sills and Viola Spolin when she joined the comedy troupe Second City in the 1960s, and early in 1970s she was picked to perform in *Story Theatre*. While in Los Angeles for *Story Theatre*, Harper auditioned for the role of Rhoda Morgenstern for *The Mary Tyler Moore Show* and was hired immediately. During 1970–1971 Harper alternated between *The Mary Tyler Moore Show*, *Story Theatre*, and another play with Second City, *Metamorphoses*. She was awarded an Emmy for Outstanding Performance by an Actress in a Supporting Role in Comedy in 1971, 1972, and 1973. In 1974, she had her own spin-off series, *Rhoda*, and received first place in the Nielsen ratings. In 1975, Harper received Emmy and Golden Globe awards for Outstanding Lead Actress in a Comedy Series. *Rhoda* ran until 1977. Harper had numerous appearances in television, films, comedy series, stage, dance competitions, and did character voices on *The Simpsons* until 2018. Harper was also an active Democrat involved in causes, picketing in labor disputes, anti-war demonstrations, working on prison reform, and in the Poor People's March on Washington.

Harper is survived by her husband Tony Cacciotti whom she married in 1987 and their adopted daughter, Cristina Harper.

See *Current Biography 1975*

Judith Rich Harris

Born: Brooklyn, New York; February 10, 1938
Died: Middletown, New Jersey; December 29, 2018
Occupation: Psychology researcher

Judith Rich Harris was a child development psychologist, well known for her published work *The Nurture Assumption: Why Children Turn Out the Way They Do*, which suggested adult's personalities were influenced more by genetics and childhood social groups than by parent's rearing.

Judith Rich Harris was born to Sam and Frances Rich in Brooklyn, New York, before moving to Tucson, Arizona, for her father's health. Harris attended Tucson High School and then Arizona State University, before transferring to Brandeis University, where she graduated magna cum laude in 1959. Harris then received a master's degree in psychology from Harvard University in 1961, and she and her husband moved to New Jersey to work for Bell Labs. There, Harris developed a mathematical model for visual information processing and co-authored two textbooks on developmental psychology. In 1994, Harris published her theory of child development, which focused on children being more influenced by genes and peers than by parents. Her theory received the American Psychological Association's George A. Miller Award for Outstanding Recent Article in General Psychology. Harris published a book on this same theory in 1998, called *The Nurture Assumption: Why Children Turn Out the Way They Do*. Then in 2006, Harris published another book, *No Two Alike: Human*

Nature and Human Individuality, theorizing why identical twins raised in the same household have different personalities. Much of her work ran contrary to popular psychologist theory and created debate around its validity.

Judith Rich Harris is survived by her husband, Charles, her two daughters, Nomi and Elaine, and four grandchildren.

See *Current Biography 1999*

Robert J. L. Hawke

Born: Bordertown, Australia; December 9, 1929
Died: Northbridge, Australia; May 16, 2019
Occupation: Politician

Robert J. L. Hawke was an Australian Labor Party politician best known for serving as the 23rd Prime Minister of Australia for over eight years.

Robert James Lee Hawke was born on December 9, 1929, in Bordertown, South Australia, the second child ofClem, a Congregationalist minister, and Edith, a schoolteacher. His uncle Albert was the Labor Premier of Western Australia between 1953 and 1959. Hawke joined the Labor party at the age of 18. He graduated in 1952 from the University of Western Australia with a BA and Bachelor of Laws. He then won a Rhodes Scholarship to attend the University of Oxford, where he studied Philosophy, Politics, and Economics (PPE) before undertaking an undergraduate thesis, graduating with a Bachelor of Letters in 1956. That same year he accepted a scholarship to undertake doctoral studies in arbitration law at the Australian National University. He soon left to become a research officer at the Australian Council of Trade Unions (ACTU) and was elected ACTU President in 1969. In 1972, he was elected as Federal President of the Labor Party. Serving as President to both organisations placed significant strain on Hawke, who suffered a physical collapse in 1979. This led him to publicly announce his alcoholism in a television interview and begin rehabilitation. This policy of honesty ultimately worked in his favour, as he became an increasingly popular public figure throughout this time. He was appointed to the Shadow Cabinet that same year, as Shadow minister for Industrial Relations. He became a new favorite for Leader of the Labor Party and led them to a landslide victory in a snap election in 1983. He became the 23rd Prime Minister of Australia on March 11, 1983. His government became known for financial reform, social reform, a successful public health campaign regarding HIV/ Aids, and several important environmental decisions. Ultimately, Hawke was at the helm of the country until he resigned in 1991. After leaving Parliament, he entered the business world, taking on numerous directorships and consultancy positions. He remained aligned with the Labor party and supported them on numerous occasions throughout his later life.

Robert J. L. Hawke is survived by his wife Blanche, and three children from his first marriage, Susan, Stephen, and Rosslyn.

See *Current Biography 1983*

Ágnes Heller

Born: Budapest, Hungary; May 12, 1929
Died: Lake Balaton, Hungary; July 19, 2019
Occupation: Philosopher, writer, educator, and social activist

Virtually unknown by the general public, Ágnes Heller was a giant among her peers in academia for her explorations of Marxism, ethics, and modernity. A teen during World War II, she was deeply influenced by the horrors of the war, and in particular the murder by Nazis of Heller's father and millions of other civilians. (Heller and her mother evaded capture by the Nazis during the war and remained in Budapest after it ended.) "I was always interested in the question: How could this possibly happen? How can I understand this?" she once told an interviewer. "How could this happen? How could people do things like this? So, I had to find out what morality is all about, what is the nature of good and evil, what can I do about crime, what can I figure out about the sources of morality and evil? That was the first inquiry. The other inquiry was a social question: What kind of world can produce this? What kind of world allows such things to happen? What is modernity all about? Can we expect redemption?"

As an undergraduate at Eötvös Loránd University (formerly, and still often called, the University of Budapest), she briefly considered studying physics and chemistry but ultimately turned to philosophy and social theory. She embraced the tenets of Marxism, but she later recognized the enormous disparity between Marx's ideas about just societies and the nature of the societies set up in his name. In 1952 Heller completed her undergraduate work and entered a PhD program at the Hungarian Academy of Sciences, writing her thesis on the nineteenth-century Russian socialist and philosopher Nikolay Gavrilovich Chernyshevsky. She completed it in 1955 and joined the faculty of the University of Budapest as an assistant professor of philosophy.

As part of a circle of like-minded political theorists known collectively as the Budapest school of socialist philosophy, she was subjected to persecution by government agents. In the late 1970s, under governmental pressure, she and her family immigrated to Australia, where she taught at La Trobe University, in a Melbourne suburb, for nearly a decade. In 1986 she and her family moved to New York City, where she joined the faculty of the New School. (She retired from her post there in 2009 and spent her last years living in Budapest and lecturing around the world.)

A prolific author, she wrote or co-wrote dozens of books throughout her career, including *The Theory of Need in Marx* (1976); *A Theory of History* (1982), *Everyday Life* (1984), *A Theory of Modernity* (1999), *The Concept of the Beautiful* (1999), and *The Immortal Comedy: The Comic Phenomenon in Art, Literature, and Life* (2005).

Ágnes Heller was vacationing at the summer resort of the Hungarian Academy of Sciences when her lifeless body was found floating in a lake. She is survived by a son, György Fehér, and a daughter, Zsuzsanna Hermann.

See *Current Biography 2008*

Stephen Hillenburg

Born: Fort Sill, Oklahoma; August 21, 1961
Died: San Marino, California; November 26, 2018
Occupation: Marine biologist, animator, voice actor

Stephen McDannell Hillenburg is most famously known for being the creator of the highly popular children's animated series *SpongeBob SquarePants*. In addition to animation and voice acting for the series, Hillenburg was a passionate marine biologist and educator.

Stephen McDannell Hillenburg was born on August 21, 1961, to his father, Kelly, and mother, Nancy, at a U. S. Army fort in Oklahoma. From a young age, Hillenburg developed a passion for the ocean, particularly fueled by his interest in oceanographer, Jacques Cousteau. It was also at this time Hillenburg developed his love for illustration, often combining these two passions by illustrating ocean scenes. He attended Savanna High School in California and then, in 1984, graduated from Humboldt State University with a degree in natural-resource planning and interpretation. After graduating, Hillenburg got a job at the Orange County Marine Institute educating the public about marine science and maritime history. At the institute he became a marine biology teacher. During this time, Hillenburg became interested in comic book illustrations and created a comic book called *Intertidal Zone*, which became the inspiration for the animated television series *SpongeBob SquarePants*. In 1989, after enrolling in the California Institute of the Arts, he created his first animated short films, *The Green Beret* and *Wormholes*. In 1993, Hillenburg became director of the Nickelodeon series *Rocko's Modern Life*. Then, in 1997, he proposed *SpongeBob SquarePants* to Nickelodeon, and it became the network's first original Saturday-morning animated series. It first aired in 1999 and by 2001 was the highest rated children's series on television. In 2004, Hillenburg created a film companion to the series, *The SpongeBob SquarePants Movie*. The series is scheduled to end in 2019, with a third movie to air in 2020. Hillenburg and his wife, Karen set up the United Plankton Charitable Trust in 2005, and it endows numerous organizations, totaling over 500,000 dollars annually. *SpongeBob SquarePants* has been nominated for 17 Emmy Awards.

Stephen Hillenburg is survived by his wife, Karen, and their son, Clay.

See *Current Biography 2003*

Tony Hoagland

Born: Fort Bragg, North Carolina; November 19, 1953
Died: Santa Fe, New Mexico; October 23, 2018
Occupation: Poet

Anthony "Tony" Dey Hoagland was an award-winning poet, known for his dry sense of humor and his use of everyday items in his writing.

Tony Hoagland, along with his twin brother, were born on November 19, 1953, in Fort Bragg, North Carolina, to Peter and Patricia, but moved several times throughout the country during his youth because his father was in the military. Hoagland received his bachelor's degree from the University of Iowa and his master's from the University of Arizona. After graduating, Hoagland taught creative writing at the University of Houston. In 1992, Hoagland published his first collection of poetry, "Sweet Ruin." Over his career, Hoagland published seven collections of poems, with his last being "Priest Turned Therapist Treats Fear of God." Hoagland was known for his use of juxtaposition and his incorporation of everyday items into his writing. During his career in writing Hoagland won many literary awards, including the Academy Award in Literature from the American Academy of Arts and Letters and the Mark Twain Award from the Poetry Foundation. In 2003, his collection, "What

Narcissism Means to Me," was a finalist for the National Book Critics Circle Award.

Tony Hoagland is survived by his wife, Katherine Lee.

See *Current Biography 2011*

Fritz Hollings

Born: Charleston, South Carolina; January 1, 1922
Died: Isle of Palms, South Carolina; April 6, 2019
Occupation: American Senator

"Fritz" Hollings, a conservative Democrat known for his controversial stands, was Governor of South Carolina from 1959 to 1963 and United States Senator from 1966 to 2005. During his nearly four decades in public service he oversaw desegregation in South Carolina in 1960, endorsed John F. Kennedy for president, admitted that hunger was a problem in his region, voted against the 1991 war in Iraq and was later against the 2003 invasion, and supported worldwide ocean and marine mammal protections.

Ernest "Fritz" Hollings was born on January 1, 1922, to a family of wealthy paper mill owners that went bankrupt during the Great Depression. Hollings borrowed money from an uncle in order to attend The Citadel receiving a BA in 1942. As an army officer he won seven campaign stars before being discharged with the rank of captain. He obtained an LLB degree from the University of South Carolina School of Law in 1947. In 1948, he began a career as a member of the South Carolina House of Representatives and served as speaker pro tempore from 1951 to 1954. Hollings became Governor in 1958. After the civil rights demonstrations he criticized President Eisenhower and declared protestors would not be tolerated, he protested examination of voting records in a county where none of the black residents were registered, and he also integrated public schools, raised teachers' salaries, fought for import restrictions to protect the textile industry, and pushed for educational innovation and reform. In 1963 when his term as governor ended, he returned to practicing law. In 1970 his book, *The Case against Hunger: A Demand for a National Policy* was published. Hollings won a seat as senator in 1966 with a number of accomplishments before retiring in 2004. He offered low-income taxpayers a tax relief program, supported federal funding for day care, supported the banning of unregulated dumping into ocean and coastal waters, promoted the Marine Mammals Protection Act, and helped to establish the National Oceanic and Atmospheric Administration (NOAA), proposed amendments to the Deepwater Port bill that would bar ownership of ports by oil companies, and supported increased defense spending.

Ernest Hollings is survived by his sons Michael Milhous Hollings and Ernest Frederick "Fritzie" Hollings III, daughter Helen Hayne Reardon and several grandchildren.

See *Current Biography 1982*

Lee A. Iacocca

Born: Allentown, Pennsylvania; October 15, 1924
Died: Bel Air, Los Angeles, California; July 2, 2019
Occupation: Automobile Executive

Lee A. Iacocca, a top Ford Executive that held numerous high-ranking corporate positions, was known for his marketing prowess and was recognized for developing numerous Ford cars including the Mustang, the Mark III, the Maverick, and the Econoline Truck.

Lido Anthony "Lee" Iacocca was born on October 15, 1924, to Italian immigrants Nicola and Antoinette Iacocca. His father, Nicola, built a real estate empire and became a millionaire after the Depression financially ruined him. Iacocca enrolled in Lehigh University after graduating high school in 1942. He maintained excellent grades and graduated with a degree in Industrial Engineering in 1945. He received his master's degree in Mechanical Engineering from Princeton and went to Dearborn for an executive trainee program for the Ford Company. Iacocca worked in engineering and sales with Ford and received recognition in 1956 after the launch of his '56 for 56' campaign, centered around buying a new Ford for only $56 a month. It was so successful in the Philadelphia area that it was launched nationwide and resulted in the sale of 72,000 additional cars. Iacocca was soon promoted to truck marketing manager of the Ford division, and he moved back to Dearborn to take the role. By 1960, he oversaw both car and truck marketing, and by the age of thirty-six he was named vice-president and general manager of the Ford division. His vision for speed resulted in the creation of the Mustang, which went on to become one of the most successful cars in Detroit history, selling 417,800 in the first year and continuing Iacocca's upwards trajectory and success in the Ford company. In 1970, Iacocca was named president of the Ford Company, and brought the Maverick (1969) and Pinto (1970) to market as President, both successful models that emphasized affordability. Iacocca was hired in 1978 as President of Chrysler Corporation. Iacocca subsequently served on the board of multiple companies and established the Iacocca Family Foundation in 1984 for diabetes research.

Lee A. Iacocca is survived by two children, Kathryn and Lia, and eight grandchildren.

See *Current Biography 1988*

Ricky Jay

Born: Brooklyn, New York; June 26, 1946
Died: Los Angeles, California; November 24, 2018
Occupation: Magician, actor, and writer

Ricky Jay was a Guinness World Record holding magician, actor, consultant, and writer who largely influenced the world of magic in the twentieth century. Throughout his career, Jay appeared in many television series, films, and wrote eleven books.

Richard Jay Potash was born on June 26, 1946, to Shirley and Samuel and raised in Elizabeth, New Jersey. Jay was first introduced to magic as child, by his grandfather, Max Katz. Jay performed his first public magic show on the television show, *Time for Pets*, at the age of seven. As a teenager, Jay played shows throughout Manhattan, until he moved to Ithaca, New York, to pursue his education. Though he attended five different schools, Jay never graduated with a formal degree. During the 1970s, Jay returned to New York and performed magic as an opening act for performers like Ike and Tina Turner and EmmyLou Harris. In 1970, Jay appeared for the first time on *The Tonight Show*. In the late 1970s, Jay moved to Los Angeles, where he was able to perform on more television series, including *American Masters* (1996), *The X-Files* (2000), *Deadwood*(2004), *Get On* (2014), and *Sneaky Pete* (2019). Jay also appeared in numerous films, including *House of Games* (1987), *Ricky Jay and His 52 Assistants* (1996), *The Spanish Prisoner* (1997), and *State and Main* (2000). He was additionally a magic consultant for films such as *The Escape Artist* (1987), *The Prestige* (2006), and *Ocean's Thirteen* (2007). Throughout his career, Jay authored eleven books, many of which were influential magic books, including *Cards as Weapons* (1977), *Learned Pigs and Fireproof Women* (1986), and *Jay's Journal of Anomalies* (2001). He held a Guinness world record for throwing a playing card 190 feet at 90 miles per hour, a trick which he regularly incorporated in his magic shows.

Ricky Jay is survived by his wife, Chrisann Verges.

See *Current Biography 1994*

Daniel Johnston

Born: Sacramento, California; January 22, 1961
Died: Waller, Texas; September 11, 2019
Occupation: Singer, songwriter, artist

Little known among the general public, Daniel Johnston nonetheless had many high-profile fans among his musical peers, including David Bowie, Tom Waits, and Kurt Cobain, who often wore a Johnston T-shirt in public.

Daniel Johnston was the youngest of five children in a Christian fundamentalist family. His father, Bill, was an engineer, and his mother, Mabel, was a homemaker. During Johnston's childhood he was subject to frequent bursts of hyperactivity; when calmer, he mostly read comic books and drew his own.

Johnston attended Abilene Christian University for a year, then transferred to a branch of Kent State University, where he studied art and met an undergraduate named Laurie, for whom he wrote hundreds of songs of unrequited love. Johnston recorded some on cassettes, with hand-drawn cartoons on their covers. He gave most of the tapes to passersby. Meanwhile, his grades plummeted, and he quit college. In 1983, he moved into his brother's home in Texas and got a job at AstroWorld, a theme park. In his free time, he continued to write songs, often accompanying himself on his nephew's toy chord organ.

After a string of other moves and odd jobs, he settled in Austin, where he passed around his homemade tapes on the streets; one impressed the local band Glass Eye, whose members invited Johnston to open for them in 1985. The audience's response was enthusiastic. Later that year an MTV crew came to Austin to film the city's music scene, and the documentary included footage of Johnston introducing himself and waving around a copy of his tape *Hi, How Are You.*

Thanks to that film and his growing reputation in Austin, Johnston acquired a manager, and in 1986 *Hi, How Are You* and another album, *Yip/Jump Music*, were released on a small label. Around that time Johnston's behavior became increasingly erratic. After hitting his manager in the head with a lead pipe and being found screaming while standing in a creek, he was admitted to a psychiatric facility.

Released into his parents' care, he continued to record, and his subsequent albums included *Songs of Pain* and *More Songs of Pain*, released in 1988 and remastered in 2003; and *Artistic Vice* (1991), *Fun* (1994), *Rejected Unknown* (2001), *Fear Yourself* (2003), *The Late Great Daniel Johnston: Discovered Covered* (2004), and the greatest-hits compilation *Welcome to My World* (2006).

Despite his artistic output, Johnston continued to exhibit disturbing behaviors on a regular basis, getting arrested for defacing the Statue of Liberty, for example, and wresting control of his father's small aircraft and crash-landing it. In later years, he withdrew from performing and earned income by selling his drawings and cartoons.

Daniel Johnston died at the age of 58, shortly after being treated for kidney problems. He is survived by his siblings.

See *Current Biography 2010*

Donald Keene

Born: New York, New York; June 18, 1922
Died: Tokyo, Japan; February 24, 2019
Occupation: Scholar, historian, writer, and translator

Donald Lawrence Keene was an eminent specialist in Japanese Culture and Literature. He translated many major works and contributed to the widespread popularization of Japanese Literature in the Anglophone world.

Donald Lawrence Keene was born on June 18, 1922, in Brooklyn, New York, the son of a trading merchant. He enrolled at Columbia University in 1938 after skipping two grades. In 1940, he bought a copy of Arthur Waley's translation of *The Tale of Genji* for 49 cents in a Times Square bookstore. He was so enthralled by the book that it prompted him to pursue a life of studying Japanese literature. In 1942, he entered the U.S. Navy Japanese Language School to learn Japanese and served as an interpreter in battle zones during WW2. At the end of the war he travelled to Tokyo and Nikkô before returning to Columbia to earn his MA. He travelled extensively as a young academic, pursuing graduate studies at Harvard University and Cambridge University, then earning a doctorate from Columbia in 1949. He then began graduate studies at Kyoto University. In 1960, he took a professorship at Columbia, where he remained for five decades. During his time as a postgraduate student and professor, Keene published many papers on Japanese literature. He also worked on numerous translations, including major classical works by writers such as Matsuo Bashô, Yoshida Kenkô and Chikamatsu Monzaemon, and twentieth century novels by writers such as Abe Kôbô, Mishima Yukio, and Dazai Osamu. His four-volume history of Japanese literature has become the standard work in Japanese studies. Keene was the recipient of many awards and accolades as well as honorary doctorates from over 10 universities worldwide. He also received the Japanese Order of the Rising Sun Award in 1975 and 1993, and the Order of Culture in 2008. In 2012, after the 2011 Tōhoku earthquake and tsunami, Keene retired from Columbia and acquired Japanese citizenship.

Donald Lawrence Keene is survived by his adopted son, Seiki, a samisen player.

See *Current Biography 1988*

Herbert Kelleher

Born: Camden, New Jersey; March 12, 1931
Died: Dallas, Texas; January 3, 2019
Occupation: Founder of Southwest Airlines

Herbert Kelleher was an American billionaire, airline executive, and lawyer. He was a co-founder and CEO, as well as chairman emeritus of Southwest Airlines.

Herbert David Kelleher was born on March 12, 1931, in Camden, New Jersey, and raised in Audubon, New Jersey. He graduated from Haddon Heights High School before earning a bachelor's degree from Wesleyan University. While studying at Wesleyan, Kelleher was named the Olin Scholar from New York University (NYU), where he had been a Root-Tilden Scholar and had a place on the *New York University Law Review*. Kelleher received his law degree (LL.B.) in 1956 cum laude, before he was admitted to the New Jersey State Bar. For two years he clerked for a New Jersey Supreme Court Justice, before joining the Newark law firm of Lum, Biunno and Tompkins. He relocated to San Antonio, Texas, in 1961, where he became a partner in the law firm of Matthews, Nowlin, Macfarlane & Barrett. During this time, Kelleher met Texas businessman Rollin King and banker John Parker, and together they conceived of the airline that became Southwest Airlines. The first flight took off in 1971. Kelleher acted as the legal counsel and operational advisor before becoming general counsel. Lamar Muse served as CEO of Southwest Airlines until 1978, and Kelleher was installed as Chairman of the Board the same year. In 1981, Kelleher was appointed the full-time CEO and President of Southwest Airlines, and he served in that position until March 2001, when he stepped down as CEO and president. In 2008, Kelleher stepped down as Chairman of the Board. Upon his retirement, Kelleher was given the title of Chairman Emeritus and had an office at the Southwest Airlines headquarters until his death. From 2010 to 2013, Kelleher became the chair of the Federal Reserve Bank of Dallas board of directors.

Herbert David Kelleher is survived by his wife, Joan; his daughters, Julie and Ruth; and his sons, Michael and David.

See *Current Biography 2001*

Wim Kok

Born: Bergambacht, Netherlands; September 29, 1938
Died: Amsterdam, Netherlands; October 20, 2018
Occupation: Prime Minister of the Netherlands

Wim Kok served as the Prime Minister of the Netherlands from 1994 until 2002. During his time in office, Kok worked to reduce taxation, create employment, legalize same-sex marriage, and euthanasia.

Willem (Wim) Kok was born on September 29, 1938, to Willem Kok and Neeltje de Jager in South Holland. Kok attended Nyenrode Business University and in 1961 began his career at the Netherlands Association of Trade Unions. There he served as chairman from 1973 until 1982. With the forming of Federatie Nederlandse Vakbeweging (FNV), Kok served as chair until 1986. At this time, Kok was elected to the House of Representatives and was shortly after elected as Parliamentary Leader of the Labour Party, that same year. In 1989, Kok became both Deputy Prime Minister of the Netherlands and Minister of Finance, at which he served until his election as Prime Minister in 1994. He was then reelected in 1998, holding his premiership until 2002. During his time as Prime Minister, Kok focused on tax reduction and creating employment. He was also responsible for the legalization of same-sex marriage and euthanasia in the Netherlands. During his time in office, Kok also led the first Purple Coalition of social democrats and liberals. In 2002, Kok announced an early resignation, tied to allegations in a government-commissioned report by the NIOD Institute for War, Holocaust, and Genocide Studies and the 1995 fall of Srebrenica. At this time, Kok also stepped down as Labour Party Leader and retired from active politics. In 2002, Kok became a lobbyist for the European Union (EU). In 2003, Kok was given the Honorary title of Minister of State. In 2004, he headed a review of the Lisbon Strategy, and in 2007 he headed the Amato Group, that worked to rewrite the Treaty of Lisbon.

Wim Kok is survived by his wife, Rita, and their children, Carla, Marcel, and Andre.

See *Current Biography 2003*

Christopher C. Kraft, Jr.

Born: Phoebus, Virginia; February 28, 1924
Died: Houston, Texas; July 22, 2019
Occupation: Aerospace engineer

During the course of his long career, Christopher C. Kraft, Jr., directed America's first piloted orbital flights, oversaw the Apollo 11 lunar landing, and led the Johnson Space Center in Houston, among other pioneering accomplishments.

As a young man, Kraft was known for his baseball prowess; for a time, he considered a career as a pro ball player, but in high school he discovered an affinity for mathematics and began to consider engineering instead. In 1941 he entered Virginia Polytechnical Institute at Blacksburg. He first studied mechanical engineering but later switched to the new department of aeronautical engineering, earning a BS degree in that field in 1944. Rejected for World War II military service because of a childhood injury, Kraft joined the staff of the Langley Research Laboratory of the National Advisory Committee for Aeronautics in 1945. From the beginning Kraft was involved in projects that paved the way for the space program, including developing ground control techniques for the X-1 experimental rocket plane and other aircraft.

With the development of the U. S. space program, spurred by the launch of the first space satellite, Sputnik I, by the Soviet Union in 1957, Kraft became one of the original members of the American space team. As flight director of Project Mercury, Kraft directed each of the six one-man Mercury flights from behind the scenes, beginning with the first suborbital flight of Alan B. Shepard in May 1961, as well as the unmanned test launches that preceded them. After the successful conclusion of the Mercury program, Kraft took leadership roles in Project Gemini, which involved two-man flights of longer duration that proved a spacecraft could stay in orbit long enough to reach the moon, and in the Apollo manned lunar exploration project.

Journalists sometimes say that Kraft literally "wrote the book" for the National Aeronautics and Space Administration (NASA), referring to a series of notebooks he compiled and continually revised throughout the early years of the space program. He is credited with devising protocols for use beyond the Earth's atmosphere and for originating the idea of a "mission control" that places authority in a ground-based flight director rather than leaving it in the hands of a possibly less-than-calm astronaut soaring through space.

In 1972 Kraft was made director of the manned spacecraft center (renamed the Johnson Space Center the following year), and he held that post until his retirement in 1982. Besides overseeing the remaining Apollo missions, in that capacity he oversaw projects involving Skylab, the first crewed space station, and the first space shuttle flights.

Upon his death, NASA released a statement that read: "America has truly lost a national treasure today. . . . We stand on his shoulders as we reach deeper into the solar system, and he will always be with us on those journeys."

Christopher C. Kraft, Jr. is survived by his wife, Betty Anne, and their children, Kristi-Anne and Gordon.

See *Current Biography 1966*

Judith Krantz

Born: New York, New York; January 9, 1928
Died: Los Angeles, California; June 22, 2019
Occupation: American Romance Novelist

Judith Krantz is known for once being the world's highest paid commercial novelist, writing numerous romance bestsellers centered mainly around the working rich and their relationships with one another.

Judith Krantz was born on January 9, 1928, as the second of three children to Jack and Mary Tarcher. From a young age, Krantz was very interested in reading and attended the exclusive Birch Wathen School in New York City. Krantz attended Wellesley College, earning a degree in English, and then moved to France for a year, where she became fluent in French and worked in the fashion industry. She returned to New York and began working for *Good Housekeeping*, where she became the magazine's fashion accessories editor. In 1956, Krantz left *Good Housekeeping* and began work as a freelance nonfiction writer for many large magazines including *Cosmopolitan*, *McCall's*, and *Ladies Home Journal*. After relocating to Los Angeles in 1971, Krantz became West Coast contributing editor of *Cosmopolitan*. Her first novel, *Scruples*, was picked up by her future agent Morton Janklow. The book was published in March 1978 and reached the number one position on the *New York Times* Bestseller List four months later, remaining on the *Times* list for a year and selling over 220,000 copies. It was praised for its departure from typical romance novels and blatant sexuality, characterizing wealth in a way that had never been done before. The paperback rights of Krantz's second novel, *Princess Daisy*, was sold to Bantam Books for over $3 million dollars and remains the highest price ever paid for reprint rights of a fiction novel. Prior to *Princess Daisy's* release in 1980, it was already number one on the *New York Times* Bestseller list and later became the number one fiction paperback of 1981. Krantz's third novel, *Mistral's Daughter*, also met commercial success after its release in 1982. Krantz continued to release novels until 1998, releasing ten books over two decades and selling over 85 million copies in 50 languages.

Judith Krantz is survived by her two sons, Tony and Nicholas, and two grandchildren.

See *Current Biography 1982*

Karl Lagerfeld

Born: Hamburg, Germany; September 10, 1933
Died: Neuilly-sur-Seine, France; February 19, 2019
Occupation: Fashion designer, creative director, artist, photographer, and caricaturist

Karl Lagerfeld was, above all, a fashion designer known as a driving force behind iconic fashion houses Fendi and Chanel. Alongside design, he pursued diverse creative interests including illustration and photography.

Karl Otto Lagerfeld was born on September 10, 1933, in Hamburg, Germany, to Elisabeth and businessman Otto Lagerfeld. He was always interested in the arts, considering French artists to be his main inspiration. He attended the Lycée Montaigne in Paris where he continued to study drawing. In 1955, Lagerfeld won a coat design competition sponsored by the International Wool Secretariat and befriended Yves Saint Laurent, who won the dress category. He was soon hired by Pierre Balmain, working as his assistant and apprentice until 1958, when he became the artistic director for Jean Patou. In 1964, he moved to Rome to study art history and worked for a number of brands including Tiziano, Chloé, and Valentino. In 1967, he was hired by Fendi and stayed loyal to the fashion house for the rest of his life. Lagerfeld was hired as chief designer by Coco Chanel in the 1980s and became known for the modern revival of the brand. In 1984, he began his own brand, *Karl Lagerfeld,* though he was most well known as the creative force behind Chanel's new look. Throughout his career in fashion, he collaborated with many big names in the industry. In 2010, he was presented with an award created for him by the Couture Council at the Fashion Institute of Technology, The Couture Council Fashion Visionary Award. Later in life, Lagerfeld also worked as a caricaturist, publishing political cartoons in the German newspaper *Frankfurter Allgemeine Zeitung* (FAZ) from 2013. He also worked throughout his career as a costume designer, illustrator, and fashion photographer. In 2015,

Lagerfeld won the British Fashion Award for Outstanding Achievement.

Karl Lagerfeld is survived by his iconic Birman cat, Choupette.

See *Current Biography 1982*

Niki Lauda

Born: Vienna, Austria; February 22, 1949
Died: Zürich, Switzerland; May 20, 2019
Occupation: Racing driver

Niki Lauda, two-time Grand Prix Champion, was one of the top motor racers in the world. He was known for his perfectionism, determination, and fearlessness while racing.

Niki Lauda was born on February 22, 1949, in Vienna, Austria, as one of two sons to a wealthy papermill owner. He loved cars from an early age and by fourteen he was disassembling Volkswagens. Lauda dropped out of school at eighteen to enter mountain-racing. In the 1969 racing season, Lauda won eight events and placed second in six. Team manager Kurt Bergmann noticed that Lauda improved with increasing horsepower; and in 1970, Lauda convinced an Austrian bank to sponsor $20,000 for him to compete in a Formula II racing event. By the end of 1971, Lauda managed to borrow $90,000 for a Formula I event in 1972. That year he gained no points in Grand Prix racing but won the British Formula II championship. As the debts caught up, Lauda spent most of 1973 racing lucrative touring-car races, winning upwards of $10,000 dollars on top of his starting money. Lauda's skill was noticed by Enzo Ferrari, founder of the Ferrari motor racing team, and he was invited to join the Ferrari team in late 1973. Racing for Ferrari, Lauda won the Grand Prix in Spain and the Netherlands and placed second in Belgium and France. In 1975, Lauda gave Ferrari its first victory in twenty years at the Monaco Grand Prix and won a number of other Grand Prix races in the same season. Lauda won the Grand Prix again the following year. In August of 1976, Lauda got into a severe crash in Nürburgring, West Germany, that left him with second and third degree burns to his face and hands, a concussion, a broken collar bone, and numerous other fractures. Lauda managed to recover and return to racing only 42 days after the accident, finishing fourth at the Italian Grand Prix. His accident left him with severe disfigurement, but many who knew him noted that it never shrouded Lauda's vibrant personality.

Niki Lauda is survived by his wife, Birgit, and his five children.

See *Current Biography 1980*

Stan Lee

Born: New York, New York; December 28, 1922
Died: Los Angeles, California; November 12, 2018
Occupation: Comic book writer, editor, publisher

Stan Lee is the creator of the Avengers superhero comics and the writer and publisher of Marvel Comics' most popular superheroes, including Spider-Man and the Fantastic Four.

Stanley Martin Lieber was born on December 28, 1922, to his Jewish-Romanian immigrant parents, Celia and Jack. He attended DeWitt Clinton High School and developed an interest in writing from a young age. In high school, Lee had a part-time job writing obituaries for a news service, until he graduated high school early in 1939 and joined the WPA Federal Theater Project. This same year, Lee became an assistant at Timely Comics division of *Pulp Magazine*. It was there Lee wrote his first comic book as text filler, *Captain America Foils the Traitor's Revenge*, under the pseudonym, Stan Lee. His first actual comic (non-filler) was "The Destroyer" in *Mystic Comics #6*, in 1941. By the end of 1941, Lee, who was only 19 years old, became interim editor of the Comics division, a position he held until 1972. In 1942, Lee joined the United States Army to serve in WWII, during which time he continued to write comics for the *Timely Comics*, weekly. After the war, Lee returned to the magazine, but in the late 1950s, Lee was asked by Marvel Comics to create a superhero team in response to the success of the DC Comic team, "Justice League of America." The first superheroes Lee created were The Fantastic Four, to be followed by the Hulk, Iron Man, X-Men, and most successful, Spider-Man. Lee also made a team, comprised of several of his characters, called The Avengers. By 1966, *The Amazing Spider-Man* became Marvel Comics' top-selling comic, and throughout the 1960s addressed many real-world social issues. In 1967, one of the first African American characters in comics was introduced, the Black Panther. Though Lee stopped writing monthly comic books in 1972, he continued as the face of Marvel Comics. In 1981, Lee moved to Los Angeles to help spearhead the Marvel TV and film adaptations (often appearing in cameo roles) of his comics. Lee continued to write for Marvel, and in the 2000s also wrote for DC Comics. Over his career, Lee won several awards for his comics and their associate television and film adaptations. In 2001, Lee started POW! Entertainment.

Stan Lee is predeceased by his wife, Joan Boocock, and is survived by their daughter, Joan Cecilia.

See *Current Biography 1993*

Andrea Levy

Born: London, England; March 7, 1956
Died: London, England; February 14, 2019
Occupation: Author

Andrea Levy was an author whose stories chronicled the Windrush generation. Her work focused heavily on migration and on the experiences of being black, British, and a woman.

Andrea Levy was born on March 7, 1956, in London, England, to Jamaican parents . Her father had immigrated to the United Kingdom on the HMT *Empire Windrush* in 1948, and her mother had joined him in 1949 on a banana boat. She grew up on a council estate, attending Highbury Hill Grammar School before leaving to study textile design and weaving at Middlesex Polytechnic. Levy claimed to have read her first book at the age of 23, and began to read widely. She quickly became dissatisfied with the lack of black British voices in literature. For Levy, writing was primarily a way to understand where she came from. She studied in Alison Fell's Creative Writing Class at City Lit in 1989 for seven years, struggling to get her work published. In 1994, her first novel, *Every Light in the House Burnin'* was published to favorable reviews. Her second novel, *Never Far from Nowhere* (1996) was longlisted for the Orange Prize. It was with her fourth novel, *Small Island* (2004) that Levy reached widespread recognition. The novel, which focused on the Windrush generation, highlighting the interwoven history of Britain and Jamaica, won the Whitbread Book of the Year Award, the Orange Prize, and the Commonwealth Writers' Prize. It was also adapted for stage (2019) and BBC television (2009). In 2005, Levy was elected a fellow of the Royal Society of Literature. Her fifth and final novel, *The Long Song* (2010) won the Walter Scott Prize and was shortlisted for the Man Booker prize. It was adapted for BBC television in 2018. Her works provided a nuanced portrayal of Caribbean immigrants and their children in Britain, and it has been met with widespread acclaim the world over.

Andrea Levy is survived by her husband, Bill, and two stepdaughters.

See *Current Biography 2010*

Li Peng

Born: Shanghai, China; October 20, 1928
Died: Beijing, China; July 22, 2019
Occupation: Prime Minister of the People's Republic of China

The appointment of Li Peng as prime minister in November 1987, made him the head of 46 million members of the Chinese Communist party, and he became internationally known early in his tenure as the "butcher of Beijing," for his role in the bloody 1989 suppression of the Tiananmen Square democracy movement.

Li is the son of the writer Li Shuoxun, who became one of the Communist Party's earliest martyrs when he was executed by members of Chiang Kai-shek's Nationalist party in 1930. At the age of three, Li was adopted by his father's close friend, Zhou Enlai, and his wife, Deng Yingchao, who sent him to live in what were then the Communist guerrilla headquarters in Shensi Province and Chongqing to be educated. He completed his engineering studies at the Yan'an Institute of Natural Sciences and became a member of the Communist party in 1945.

In 1948 Li went to Moscow to obtain further training in electrical engineering at the Moscow Power Institute, and he remained in the Soviet Union for seven years. Upon his return to China, by then a Communist republic under the leadership of Mao Zedong and Li's foster father, Zhou Enlai, he spent the next several years overseeing hydroelectric plants; he escaped the persecution suffered by Soviet-trained Chinese during that period of tumult, terrorism, and purges, only because of Zhou's influence.

Li enjoyed a rapid rise in the party after Mao's death in 1976, becoming national minister of power industries in 1981, Central Committee member in 1982, and Politburo member in 1985. In 1987 he was appointed acting prime minister and named to the five-man standing committee of the Politburo.

He never ascended, however, to general secretary, the top post in the Party, and most observers cite his role in encouraging the army's disastrous assault on unarmed students and workers in Tiananmen Square in mid-1989, which left hundreds of the pro-democracy protesters dead. He strenuously defended himself, blaming the elderly behind-the-scenes leader Deng Xiaoping for the decision to send in troops, and he was given a second term as prime minister in 1993. He retired in 2002.

Li's death was announced by the state-run news agency.

Li Peng is survived by his wife, Zhu Lin, and his children: Li Xiaolin, Li Xiaopeng, Li Xiaoyong. In addition to the events in Tiananmen Square, immortalized in an iconic photo of a lone protester bravely facing down a tank, he is most remembered for his promotion of the Three Gorges Dam on the Yangtze River, the construction of which displaced more than a million people.

See *Current Biography 1988*

Gene Littler

Born: San Diego, California; July 21, 1930
Died: San Diego, California; February 15, 2019
Occupation: Golfer

Gene Littler was a professional American golfer, nicknamed "Gene the Machine." Renowned for having a solid temperament and reliable game, he was an inductee to the World Golf Hall of Fame in 1990.

Gene Alec Littler was born on July 21, 1930, in San Diego, California, and developed his love of golf from playing on area courses in his youth. Littler graduated from San Diego State University in 1951 before enrolling and serving in the US Navy. Aged just twenty-three, he won the California State Amateur and the US Amateur, as well as playing in the 1953 US Walker Cup Team. In 1954, he managed the unlikely feat of winning the San Diego Open as an amateur and quickly turned pro afterward. Littler was narrowly beaten in the US Open of 1954, losing by one stroke to Ed Furgol. In 1955, he won four tournaments, including the Tournament of Champions in Las Vegas—his first of three consecutive victories. Only once, from 1954 to 1979, did Littler place out of the top 60 of the PGA Tour Money List and that was in 1972 due to being sidelined by surgery after the discovery of a cancerous lymph node. Littler quickly recovered from that to win three tournaments, including the St. Louis Children's Hospital Classic in July 1973. He also won the Ben Hogan Award as the comeback player of the year, as well as the Bob Jones Award from distinguished sportsmanship. Littler's victory at the 1975 Bing Crosby National Pro-Am competition marked the first, and to date only, time a player has won the event as both an amateur and a professional. Between 1961 and 1975, Littler was a member of the US Ryder Cup Teams seven times, and in 1961 he won his only major championship, the US Open. Throughout the 1980s and 1990s, Littler participated in the Senior PGA Tour and won eight times before being inducted to the World Golf Hall of Fame in 1990.

Gene Littler is survived by his wife, Shirley; his daughter, Suzanne; and his son, Curt.

See *Current Biography 1956*

Richard G. Lugar

Born: Indianapolis, Indiana; April 4, 1932
Died: Annandale, Virginia; April 28, 2019
Occupation: Politician

Richard G. Lugar had two notable terms as Mayor of Indianapolis prior to serving as Senator from Indiana and as chairman on the Senate Foreign Relations Committee. He was a moderate Republican open to working with Democrats to accomplish goals.

Marvin and Bertha (Green) Lugar were prominent leaders in their Indianapolis, Indiana, community when fourth-generation Richard was born. Lugar's accomplishments started early with Eagle Scout recognition, graduating first in his class at Shortridge High School, co-president of the student body, and graduating top of his class at Denison University in Ohio. He served as president of the American Students Association while receiving two advanced degrees as a Rhodes Scholar at Pembroke College, Oxford. He attended the U. S. Navy's Officer Candidate School (OCS) and had a position as an intelligence briefer to the chief of naval operations. Returning home, Lugar spent seven years reviving the family livestock and grain operations and food production equipment plant. He served as vice-president on the Indianapolis School Board (1964–1966) and in 1967 became the first Republican Mayor of Indianapolis in twenty years. Lugar's Unigov bill proposing consolidation of Indianapolis with Marion County passed and went into effect in 1970. The city increased from 82 to 388 square miles, the population went from 520,000 to over 750,000; and overnight, Indianapolis became the eleventh largest city in the nation and received several Federal Block grants, the first for $1,300,000. Lugar, a long-time supporter of President Nixon, earned the title of "Nixon's favorite mayor," which opened doors to his 1971 position of president of the National League of Cities, involvement in national politics, and running for senate. Elected in 1977 he retained his seat until 2013. During this time Lugar's focus was foreign affairs. He was chairman of the Foreign Relations Committee from 1985 to 1987 and 2003–2007. Nixon sent Lugar to the Philippines where he was instrumental in Corazon Aquino's presidential win over Ferdinand Marcos's fraudulent election. Georgia Democratic Senator Sam Nunn and Lugar created the Nunn-Lugar Cooperative Threat Reduction Program in 1991, devoting billions of dollars to working with the Soviet Union to decommission and deactivate nuclear weapons. After a loss in 2013, he opened the Lugar Center dedicated to research for global problems, and educating the public, policymakers, and future leaders.

Richard Lugar is survived by his wife Charlene Smeltzer of sixty-three years, four sons, Mark, Robert, John, and David, thirteen grandchildren, and seventeen great-grandchildren.

See *Current Biography 1977*

Manuel Lujan, Jr.

Born: San Ildefonso, Pueblo, New Mexico: May 12, 1928
Died: Albuquerque, New Mexico: April 25, 2019
Occupation: American congressman and Secretary of the Interior

Manuel Lujan Jr. was the only Hispanic Republican when he served in the House of Representatives from 1969 to 1989. He was nominated Secretary of the Interior in 1988 by President-elect George W. Bush, a position that had the role of balancing environmental protection and development of natural resources since the 1964 Wilderness Act. Lujan believed we could achieve both goals.

Manual Lujan Jr. was born on May 12, 1928, to Manuel Sr., owner of Manuel Lujan Insurance Agency and three term Republican mayor of Santa Fe, and Lorenzita (Romero) Lujan. He was the eighth of eleven children. Lujan received a BA from the College of Santa Fe in 1950. He worked for his father from 1948 to 1968, expanded the business in 1964, and maintained part ownership throughout his congressional terms. During the 1968 election, Lujan campaigned by appealing to the ethnic pride of the customarily Democratic Hispanic's and for balancing the federal budget. Lujan served on the House Interior and Insular Affairs Committee from 1969 to 1989. He was a ranking Republican during Reagan's first term; but also supported initiatives of Democratic chairmen Morris Udall. Although he introduced legislation to delay an opening of 700 acres in the El Capitan Wilderness area of New Mexico to gas and oil exploration, he cosponsored similar explorations to move forward in the Arctic National Wildlife Refuge, supported nuclear power and development over endangered species. In 1985, after Reagan rejected Lujan for secretary of the interior, he became the ranking Republican on the Science, Space, and Technology Committee, where he had been a member since 1977 and served until 1989. Lujan served on the National Commission on Space panel and after watching the tragic *Challenger* space shuttle explosion, he criticized the National Aeronautics and Space Administration (NASA) and pushed for better management while supporting establishing bases on the moon and Mars. Often Lujan angered environmentalists by his favoring of development and industry. He supported timber harvesting over the disruption of Spotted Owl habitat and renewed a forty-year water contract to guarantee water to the Orange Cove Irrigation District prior to an impact study requested by the Environmental Protection Agency (EPA). Lujan held his position as Secretary of the Interior until his retirement at the end of Bush's presidency in 1993.

Manuel Lujan Jr. is survived by his wife, Jean Kay Couchman, and four children, Terra Kay Everett, Barbara Frae, Robert Jeffrey, and Noah Lujan.

See *Current Biography 1989*

Galt MacDermot

Born: Montreal, Quebec, Canada; December 18, 1928
Died: Staten Island, New York; December 17, 2018
Occupation: Canadian American Pianist and composer

Galt MacDermot is known for composing over thirteen musicals heavily influenced by African rhythms and numerous instrumental compositions outside of the stage with his group New Pulse Jazz Band.

Arthur Terence Galt MacDermot was born on December 18, 1928, to Terence and Elizabeth MacDermot. His father, an educator and diplomat, was high commissioner and ambassador to multiple countries from 1950 to 1961, representing Canada to South Africa, Greece, Israel, and Australia. MacDermot was exposed to music at a young age; his father would regularly play piano, and his mother was a dancer. While MacDermot learned how to play the violin and piano from a young age, he did not become interested in music until high school when he discovered the music of Pete Johnson and Duke Ellington. After his family moved to South Africa for his father's work, MacDermot enrolled in the University of Cape Town (UCT) and graduated with a degree in music composition and the organ. He was heavily influenced by the music he heard in the black African neighborhoods, namely "quaylas," a South African version of rock and roll. With this influence, he began to compose his own music. MacDermot returned to Montreal in 1954 and began working for the Westmount Baptist Church as an organist and choirmaster. He spent weekends playing piano in a jazz trio. In 1961, he moved his family to England and released his best-selling hit "African Waltz," later moving back to New York City where he supported himself and his family

solely on making demo records for publishers. In 1967, MacDermot began writing music for a book that would later become the soundtrack to the internationally known musical *Hair*. By 1969, *Hair* had grossed millions of dollars and was being performed internationally. His later work included *Two Gentlemen of Verona*, which later won a Tony Award.

Galt MacDermot is survived by his wife Marlene, his sister Anne, five children; Vincent, Molly, Yolanda, Sarah, and Elizabeth; seven grandchildren; and two great-grandchildren.

See *Current Biography 1984*

Warren MacKenzie

Born: Kansas City, Missouri; February 16, 1924
Died: Stillwater, Minnesota; December 31, 2018
Occupation: American Potter

Warren MacKenzie is known for creating tens of thousands of functional pottery pieces included serving bowls, baking dishes, mugs, jars, and teapots. He was recognized for gaining recognition of contemporary ceramics as a form of craft and expression.

Warren MacKenzie was born on February 16, 1924, to Fred and Adelaide MacKenzie in Kansas City, Missouri. MacKenzie was drafted into the US Army two years after entering the School of the Art Institute, and he became a silk-screen technician, where he designed and made training charts. After the end of World War II, he was transferred to Japan where he worked in a Japanese-run printing plant. He made many acquaintances with Japanese artists, who helped him later display an exhibition of abstract geometric paintings in Japan. MacKenzie returned to Chicago, but due to all of the painting classes being full, he was forced to register for a ceramics class, initially hating it, but soon fell in love with pottery-making after reading *A Potter's Book* at the recommendation of another student. After graduating in 1947 and marrying Alixandra Kolesky, MacKenzie moved to St. Paul, Minnesota, to establish a crafts program with his wife at the St. Paul Gallery and School of Art. In 1948, he gained an apprenticeship from Bernard Leach and spent a year learning from him and later developed a close personal relationship that would last until Leach's death in 1979. He and his wife made thousands of pieces under Leach and developed their skills to the point where they were able to divest creatively into other styles of pottery. After returning to the United States from England in 1952, MacKenzie spent many years teaching at numerous studios and universities before he and his wife established

Stillwater studio, focused on producing pots for everyday use. MacKenzie had dozens of exhibitions, lectures, workshops, and demonstrations in the United States and internationally, becoming one of the most well-known potters in the world. MacKenzie was named an honorary fellow of the American Craft Council in 1981 and of the National Council of Education in the Ceramic Arts in 1982, later nominated by ceramics Monthly to be one of the world's twelve best potters.

Warren MacKenzie is survived by his daughters, Tamsyn, Shawn, Erica, and Mark.

See *Current Biography 1994*

Penny Marshall

Born: New York, New York; October 15, 1943
Died: Los Angeles, California; December 17, 2018
Occupation: Actress and director

Penny Marshall is known for her role as Laverne De Fazio on *Laverne and Shirley*, later becoming one of the only female film directors in Hollywood in the 1990s.

Penny Marshall was born on October 15, 1943, as the third child to Tony and Marjorie Marshall. Marshall was exposed to the arts from a young age, dancing in her mother's tap-dancing school from the age of three and performing with the dance troupe the Marshallettes that her mother organized and coached. She enrolled at the University of New Mexico, briefly studying psychology before she dropped out to marry football player Michael Henry. Shortly after divorcing Henry, Marshall supported herself by working as a secretary and dance teacher. In 1967, Marshall moved to Los Angeles and made her first television appearance on an episode *The Danny Thomas Hour* in 1968. She married actor and director Rob Reiner in 1971, continuing to work numerous small roles in television shows such as *The Odd Couple*, *The Bob Newhart Show*, *The Super*, and *Paul Sand in Friends and Lovers*. Marshall was later cast in *Laverne and Shirley*, a show centered around two witty young women who share a basement apartment. Though successful, the show ended in 1983 after contract disputes and slipping ratings. She was invited by Academy Award-winning director James L. Brooks to direct *Big*, which received overwhelmingly positive reviews, and its star Tom Hanks received an Academy Award nomination for his portrayal. Following *Big*'s success, Marshall later directed *Awakenings* (1990), *A League of Their Own* (1992), *Riding in Cars* (2001), and *Bewitched* (2005). In the mid-2000s, Marshall guest-starred on many television shows

including *Entourage* (2006), *Portlandia* (2012), and *The Odd Couple* (2016).

Penny Marshall is survived by her sister, Ronny; her daughter, Tracy Reiner; and three grandchildren.

See *Current Biography 1992*

Willie McCovey

Born: Mobile, Alabama; January 10, 1938
Died: Palo Alto, California; October 31, 2018
Occupation: Baseball Player

Willie McCovey is known as the leading power hitter of the San Francisco Giants from 1967 to 1980.

Willie Lee McCovey was born on January 10, 1938, to Frank and Ester McCovey. His father was a railroad laborer, and McCovey was the seventh of ten children. McCovey played many sports while growing up, including baseball, football, softball, and basketball. He pursued sports in high school, playing end on his football team and quarterback of a team in the men's league. One of McCovey's playground directors alerted Alex Pompez, a scout for the Giants, about McCovey's athletic prowess. McCovey dropped out and went to Los Angeles to look for full-time work. Shortly after his arrival, the Giants reached out and asked McCovey to come to their tryout camp in Melbourne, Florida. McCovey was signed to the Giants farm team in Sandersville, Georgia, for $175 a month. He jumped around to different teams, playing with Dallas and Phoenix over the next few years in the Pacific Coast League. In 1959, the Giants called McCovey to San Francisco for his major league debut against Philadelphia on July 30, 1959, where he won National League Rookie of the Year Award. In the 1962 World Series, McCovey hit a game-winning home run against the New York Yankees. This led manager Alvin Dark to start him nearly every game, boosting McCovey's morale and leading to stronger performance in both his hitting and outfield positions. Following the death of his father and multiple foot and ankle injuries, McCovey's averages dropped. After Herman Franks replaced Dark in 1965 and settled McCovey permanently at first base, McCovey regained his strength as a player and became one of the highest-averaging players in the league in hits and runs. In 1969, McCovey achieved his best performance to date, standing fourth in the National League for home runs and runs batted in (RBIs). McCovey retired in 1980, finishing his career as a six-time All-Star with a .270 batting average, 521 home runs, and 1,555 RBIs. He was later inducted in the National Baseball Hall of Fame in 1986.

Willie Lee McCovey is survived by his wife, Estela, his daughter, Allison, and three grandchildren.

See *Current Biography 1970*

Zhores Aleksandrovich Medvedev

Born: Tbilisi, Georgia, USSR; November 14, 1925
Died: London, England; November 15, 2018
Occupation: Biologist, writer

Zhores Medvedev was a Soviet biologist, writer, and dissident who criticised Lysenkoism and Stalinist repression. He was declared insane, confined to a mental institution, and stripped of his citizenship because of his defiance.

Zhores Aleksandrovich Medvedev and his twin brother, Roy, were born on November 14, 1925 to Yulia, a cellist, and Alexander Medvedev, a Marxist philosopher. Their father was arrested in the 1930s and died in Siberia. This eventually prompted Roy to study history. Zhores, on the other hand, studied natural sciences at the Timiryazev Agricultural Academy, where he gained a PhD. At the time, Soviet agricultural science was dominated by Lysenkoism, a pseudoscience that promised rapid advancements in farming. Zhores wrote over 100 scientific papers on biology but also became a prolific contributor to underground literature protesting Soviet policies. Notably, he wrote a book exposing Lysenko as a fraud. While Lysenko was, indeed, discredited, the Soviet government did not appreciate Medvedev's defiance, and he was dismissed of his post as head of the department of molecular biology at the Institute of Medical Radiology in Obninsk. In May 1970 he was arrested and confined to a mental institution. Several famed writers and scientists protested his detention, and after 19 days he was released. Alongside his brother, he published a book about his ordeal, in which he wrote that over 250 Soviet citizens were being held in mental asylums for political reasons. He published many more books abroad critiquing Soviet policies. He moved to London in 1973 to take a one-year job at the National Institute for Medical Research, accompanied by his son Dimitri, and wife Rita, a fellow scientist. Upon arrival, he was told that his Soviet citizenship had been revoked. He continued to work as a scientist and writer and remained an expatriate until his death in 2018, despite Gorbachev having reinstated his citizenship in 1990.

Zhores Medvedev is survived by his wife Rita, their son, Dimitri, four grandchildren and three great-grandchildren. Another son, Sasha, predeceased him.

See *Current Biography 1973*

W.S. Merwin

Born: New York, New York; September 30, 1927
Died: Haiku, Hawaii; March 15, 2019
Occupation: Poet

W.S. Merwin was a Pulitzer-prize winning poet who became the seventeenth United States Poet Laureate. During his career, Merwin published over twenty-five volumes of poems and translated eighteen others.

William Stanley Merwin was born on September 30, 1927, and raised in New Jersey, until the age of nine, when his family moved to Scranton, Pennsylvania. As a child, Merwin would write hymns for his father, who was a Presbyterian minister. Merwin attended Princeton University and then in 1952, moved to Spain with his wife, Dorothy Jeanne Ferry. In Spain, Merwin tutored poet, Robert Grave's son. He also collaborated with Dido Milroy to write a play. After his divorce from Ferry, he eventually married Milroy and they moved to London. In 1956, Merwin took a fellowship at the Poet's Theater in Boston, where he became the playwright-in-residence. In 1960, Merwin released a volume of poetry, *The Drunk in the Furnace*. And in 1962, he became poetry editor for *The National*. During this time, Merwin also translated numerous works of Spanish, French, Latin, and Italian. In the late 1970s, Merwin moved to Hawaii, where he lived for the rest of his life. His 2005 volume, *Migration: New and Selected Poems*, won the National Book Award for poetry, and *The Shadow of Sirius*, won the 2009 Pulitzer Prize for poetry. The Library of Congress named Merwin the seventeenth United States Poet Laureate in 2010. That same year, Merwin and his third wife, Paula Dunaway, founded The Merwin Conservancy, which became one of the world's largest collections of rare palm trees. Merwin published his last book in 2016, titled *Garden Times*. Throughout his career, Merwin won numerous awards, and in 2006, a street near is childhood home was named WS Merwin Way.

W.S. Merwin was predeceased by his wife, Paula, who died in 2017.

See *Current Biography 1999*

Edmund Morris

Born: Nairobi, Kenya; May 27, 1940
Died: Danbury, Connecticut; May 24, 2019
Occupation: Biographer

Edmund Morris was a Pulitzer Prize-winning biographer of Theodore Roosevelt and Ronald W. Reagan's authorized biographies.

Arthur Edmund Morris was born on May 27, 1940, in Nairobi, Kenya, to Eric and May Morris. His parents were British, and his father was an airline pilot. Morris attended the Prince of Wales School in Nairobi. Morris went on to study music and history at Rhodes University in Grahamstown, South Africa, for one year before relocating to London to work advertising copy jobs and finally immigrating to the United States to explore writing further. Morris joined the *New York Times* staff as a contributing editor for a year and in 1971, Morris worked on a biographical study of Josef Lhévinne, a Russian pianist for WNCN radio. After writing a screenplay based on Theodore Roosevelt's life, Morris was solicited to write a short biography. *The Rise of Theodore Roosevelt* published in 1979 and later won a Pulitzer Prize and American Book Award. In October 1985, Morris agreed to write the biography of Ronald Reagan and was soon given access to the presidential papers, high-level aides, and presidential retreats under the condition that he would not write the book until the end of the presidency in 1989, and would not release it until 1991. His high level of access as well as his known literary prowess made the Reagan biography highly anticipated and led to Random House making the highest advance for a novel to date for over $3 million dollars. The highly anticipated biography, titled *Dutch: A Memoir of Ronald Reagan*, was released in 1999. Morris continued to write, releasing *Theodore Rex* in 2002 and a third sequel in 2010 titled *Colonel Roosevelt*.

Edmund Morris is survived by his wife Sylvia.

See *Current Biography 1989*

Robert Morris

Born: Kansas City, Missouri; February 9, 1931
Died: Kingston, New York; November 28, 2018
Occupation: Sculptor

Robert Morris was a renowned sculptor, credited as one of the major proponents of Minimalism in American Art. Over the course of his career, he also made contributions to land art, performance, painting and conceptual art.

Robert Eugene Morris was born on February 9, 1931, in Kansas City, Missouri, to Lora Pearl Morris and Robert Obed Morris. He studied art at the Kansas City Art Institute, then at the California School of Fine Arts in the early 1950s. He also served in Korea and Japan with the Army Corps of Engineers, before attending Reed College in Oregon from 1953 to 1955.

He lived in San Francisco, and focused on Abstract Expressionist paintings, which he showed in his first two solo exhibitions, as well as dance, performance, and film. He then moved to New York City in 1959 with his first wife, Simone Forti. There, he began creating sculptures influenced by Dadaism, which led to his first New York solo show at the Green Gallery in 1963. He studied for a master's degree in art history at Hunter College in Manhattan and soon began teaching there, which he continued to do into his later years. He pioneered a minimalist sculptural style and was represented by the Leo Castelli and Sonnabend Galleries in New York. In 1966 he began to publish a series of essays, called "Notes on Sculpture," in *Artforum* magazine, which further cemented his importance in the Art World. He became an important figure at the forefront of Abstraction and Minimalism in American Sculpture and is well known for his massive multipart sculptures of the 1980s, comprised of a wide variety of materials, including casts of body parts and skeletons. However, his work was not constrained to one particular style. Alongside sculpture, he created land art, conceptual art, performance, film, and dance. His myriad contributions to Modern Art were documented in a retrospective exhibition at the Guggenheim Museum in 1994, attesting to the variety and depth of his work. A collection of his essays, titled "Continuous Project Altered Daily" was also published in 1993.

He is survived by a daughter, Laura Morris; a sister, Donna Caudle, and his third wife, Lucile Michels Morris, whom he married in 1984.

See *Current Biography 1971*

Toni Morrison

Born: Lorain, Ohio; February 18, 1931
Died: Bronx, New York; August 5, 2019
Occupation: Novelist

With the critical and popular success of her 1977 novel, *Song of Solomon*, Toni Morrison's place in contemporary American literature was assured, and that status was further cemented when she garnered a 1988 Pulitzer Prize for her masterwork *Beloved* (1987), which follows the travails of Sethe, an escaped slave who has become one of the most indelible protagonists in fiction. In 1993 Morrison reached the pinnacle of her profession, winning a Nobel Prize in Literature for "novels characterized by visionary force and poetic import," and "giving life to an essential aspect of American reality," in the words of the Swedish Academy. (She was the first black woman ever to gain that laurel.)

The author was born Chloe Ardelia Wofford in a working-class community not far from Cleveland. During the Depression her father, George, toiled as a car washer, welder in a local steel mill, and road construction worker, and he later found steady work as a shipyard welder. Her mother, the former Ramah Willis, was a strong-willed woman who never hesitated to speak up when she saw an injustice.

Morrison graduated from high school in 1949, and four years later she earned a bachelor's degree from Howard University, an all-black school in Washington, DC. Somewhat aimless, she then earned a master's degree in English at Cornell and embarked on a teaching career. In 1964 she took a job as a textbook editor for a subsidiary of Random House, the publishing conglomerate. There, she developed a short story she had written at Howard into a novel, *The Bluest Eye*, which was published in 1969. *The Bluest Eye* is the story of two young sisters living in a tiny, provincial black community in Ohio in 1941 and their friendship with Pecola Breedlove, a homely, outcast little girl so mercilessly victimized by her parents and narrow-minded neighbors that she eventually retreats into insanity.

That debut novel established Morrison as an astute observer of contemporary black America, and she was often asked to write social commentary for mass market publications. Concurrently, she remained a senior editor at Random House's New York headquarters and became a staunch advocate for other black writers. Her own writing career took another step forward in late 1973 with the publication of *Sula*, an examination of an intense, 40-year friendship between two women.

In addition to *Beloved*, Morrison's later novels, which also met near-universal acclaim, included *Tar Baby* (1981), *Jazz* (1992), *Paradise* (1998), *Love* (2003), *A Mercy* (2008), and *Home* (2012).

The Toni Morrison Society, which continues to celebrate her life and work, was founded in 1993. In 2012 Barack Obama, who often cited her as a favorite author, awarded her the Presidential Medal of Freedom.

Toni Morrison died from complications of pneumonia and is survived by her son, Harold, and three grandchildren. She was predeceased in 2010 by her other son, Slade, with whom she collaborated on multiple children's books.

See *Current Biography 1979*

Robert Gabriel Mugabe

Born: Kutama, Mashonaland, Zimbabwe; February 21, 1924
Died: Singapore; September 6, 2019
Occupation: Former Zimbabwean president

During the 1960s and 1970s, when the African nation of Zimbabwe was in a state of turmoil, Robert Mugabe, the head of the Zimbabwe African National Union (ZANU), was the most militant of the black nationalist leaders seeking to overthrow the white-minority government and establish majority rule. "Genuine independence," he declared, "can only come out the barrel of a gun." The first prime minister and later president of the country once it had gained independence, he ultimately became known as a strongman and tyrant.

The son of a village carpenter, Robert Gabriel Mugabe was born in what was then the British colony of Southern Rhodesia. Educated in Roman Catholic mission schools, he began his career as a teacher while still a teen. In 1950, he entered the University of Fort Hare, in South Africa, qualifying for a degree in a year.

Returning to Southern Rhodesia, he immersed himself in the nationalist struggle against the white-minority government; and in 1960, he joined the newly formed National Democratic Party (NDP). After the NDP was banned by the colonial government in late 1961, Mugabe joined with Joshua Nkomo's nationalist group, Zimbabwe African People's Union (ZAPU). Racial unrest led to a ban on ZAPU as well, and after being arrested several times for political agitation, Mugabe fled to Tanzania.

In mid-1963, Mugabe helped form a more radical organization, the Zimbabwe African National Union (ZANU). The following year he was arrested and spent a decade in detention. Although ZANU and ZAPU merged into the Patriotic Front (PF) and waged fierce guerilla warfare, the white government maintained its rule without much difficulty.

In 1980, the Rhodesian government accepted mediation from Britain and the United States, helping establish majority rule and free elections. Mugabe was considered a revolutionary hero and elected to head the first government of the new country, re-named Zimbabwe, as prime minister on March 4 of that year. His party became known as the Zimbabwe African National Union-Patriotic Front (ZANU-PF).

During the first two years of Mugabe's rule, Zimbabwe prospered, but soon the country entered a period of growing unrest, due to a large-scale drought, rising unemployment, rampant corruption, the slow progress of land reform, and multiple disputed elections.

Despite that, Mugabe remained in power through 2017, when his own party placed him under house arrest and forced him to step down. He was the world's oldest head of state—and the only leader Zimbabweans had known since gaining independence 37 years before. International observers noted that he had presided over the decline of one of the most prosperous nations in Africa.

Robert Mugabe died at Gleneagles Hospital, in Singapore, where he was being treated for an undisclosed illness. He is survived by his second wife, Grace (an unpopular figure who had been his secretary and mistress during his first marriage); daughter, Bona; two sons, Robert Jr. and Bellarmine Chatunga; and a stepson, Russell Goreraza. His son, Michael, predeceased him in 1996.

See *Current Biography 2013*

Kary B. Mullis

Born: Lenoir, North Carolina; December 28, 1944
Died: Newport Beach, California; August 7, 2019
Occupation: Biochemist

Kary B. Mullis invented a simple but powerful technique for rapidly synthesizing billions of copies of any given fragment of Deoxyribonucleic acid (DNA), the molecule that contains the genetic code. The polymerase chain reaction, or PCR, as the technique is called, has since revolutionized medicine, forensics, biotechnology, paleontology, comparative biology, and the many other fields. It also won Mullis the Nobel Prize for Chemistry in 1993.

The future biochemist was the second of four sons born to Cecil, a salesman, and Bernice, a real-estate broker. His interest in science can be traced to his youth; he has recounted, for example, that at 17 he learned to make rocket fuel out of potassium nitrate and sugar.

While attending the Georgia Institute of Technology on a National Merit Scholarship, Mullis founded his own chemical-manufacturing company and also reportedly developed a device that used brain waves (which he generated by having his subjects look at pictures of scantily clad women) to turn lights on. After earning his BS degree in chemistry in 1966, he entered the University of California at Berkeley (UC-Berkeley), where, besides studying biochemistry, he immersed himself in the then-flourishing counterculture and earned a reputation as a free spirit.

After he obtained his PhD in 1972, he settled in Kansas City and temporarily abandoned his scientific career to try writing fiction. When he

realized that his literary gifts were limited, he accepted a series of postdoctoral fellowships, and in about 1979, he accepted a job as a biochemist at the Cetus Corporation, in California. Mullis was hired to synthesize oligonucleotide probes, or short stretches of single-stranded DNA, which other Cetus scientists could then use to isolate target genes or nucleotide sequences from a sample of DNA. In early 1983, thanks to improvements in the procedure for synthesizing oligonucleotides, Mullis found himself with free time, which he filled with a project of his own design: figuring out how to determine the identity of a nucleotide at a specific point in a given stretch of DNA.

It was at Cetus that Mullis made his Nobel-worthy discovery, publishing a description of his technique in a 1985 issue of *Science*, and in 1986 he described it in a paper published in the *Cold Spring Harbor Symposia on Quantitative Biology*. The patent for the process was granted in 1987, and soon after that Cetus announced the invention of the Thermal Cycler, a relatively inexpensive and automatic system for using the PCR. Although some colleagues predicted that because of his personal eccentricities he would never be recognized with a Nobel, in 1993 they were proven wrong.

Mullis, who had an acknowledged history of using alcohol and illicit drugs, had quit Cetus in 1986 and busied himself primarily on the lecture circuit thereafter.

Kary B. Mullis died of heart and respiratory failure brought on by pneumonia. Thrice divorced, he is survived by his fourth wife, Nancy; a daughter; two sons, Christopher and Jeremy; two of his three brothers; and two grandchildren.

See *Current Biography 1996*

Art Neville

Born: New Orleans, Louisiana; December 17, 1937
Died: New Orleans, Louisiana; July 22, 2019
Occupation: Singer and keyboardist

Art, Charles, Aaron, and Cyril Neville performed for decades together as the Neville Brothers, a musical act that embodied the sound of New Orleans with their rich gumbo of rock, soul, jazz, funk, doo-wop, reggae, country, and gospel.

Art Neville was the oldest of the sons born to Arthur (a day laborer) and Amelia (a homemaker) Neville. (The family also included two sisters.) When he was about three years old, he accompanied his grandmother to a church she had been hired to clean and saw an organ for the first time. Intrigued, he learned to play early on, and as a teenager he joined the local group the Hawketts, singing lead on their big hit "Mardi Gras Mambo."

After spending several years in the U.S. Navy in the 1950s, Neville began working with producer Allen Toussaint and—along with his brothers in various configurations—formed a series of groups, including the Neville Sounds and the Meters. The Meters, now widely celebrated for popularizing New Orleans funk and influencing generations of hip-hop artists, began to gain some national attention in the mid-1970s, when they opened for the Rolling Stones. The brothers also worked as solo artists, and Art Neville gained a reputation as a solid studio musician, playing backup on recordings by such popular artists as Little Richard and Lee Dorsey.

In 1976, calling themselves the Wild Tchoupitoulas, the brothers released an eponymous album of Mardi Gras music; and the following year, they released the simply titled *The Neville Brothers*. Recording under that new name, they later released *Fiyou on the Bayou* (1981), *Nevillization* (1984), *Treacherous* (1986), *Uptown* (1987), *Yellow Moon* (1989), *Brother's Keeper* (1990), *Treacherous Too* (1991), *Family Groove* (1992), *Live on Planet Earth* (1994), and *The Very Best of the Neville Brothers* (1997). Although the albums rarely topped charts, the brothers gained a particularly strong reputation for their rollicking live performances.

Suffering from a variety of health problems, Neville retired in 2018. Upon his death, Louisiana governor John Bel Edwards paid tribute to him, saying that he "took the unique sound of New Orleans and played it for the world to enjoy."

Art Neville is survived by his wife, Lorraine; a sister, Athelgra; a son, Ian; and two daughters, Arthel and Amelia Neville, as well as by brothers Aaron and Cyril. (Charles had died in 2018.)

See *Current Biography* 1998

Don Newcombe

Born: Madison, New Jersey; June 14, 1926
Died: Los Angeles, California; February 19, 2019
Occupation: Professional baseball pitcher

Don Newcombe was an American professional baseball pitcher who played in both the Negro league and Major League Baseball teams, for the Newark Eagles, Brooklyn and Los Angeles Dodgers, Cincinnati Reds, and the Cleveland Indians.

Donald Newcombe, known by fans as "Newk," was born on June 14, 1926, in Madison, New Jersey. He attended Jefferson High School and was a baseball fan from a young age. As the school did not have its own baseball team, Newcombe started to play semi-professional baseball while still in high school. From 1944 to 1945, Newcombe played for the Negro National League team the Newark Eagles, before being signed by the Dodgers. A pioneer alongside catcher, Roy Campanella, Newcombe was one of the first players in the first racially integrated baseball team, the Nashua Dodgers of the New England League. Newcombe was promoted to the Montreal Royals of the AAA International League in 1948, before making his debut for the Brooklyn Dodgers in 1949. He was only the third-ever African American pitcher in major league baseball (MLB) and helped the team celebrate 17 victories. Along with his teammates Jackie Robinson, Roy Campanella, and Larry Doby of the Cleveland Indians, Newcombe was one of the first black players to be named to an All-Star Team, as well as being named Rookie of the Year. From 1950 to 1952, Newcombe was a staple of MLB, helping the Dodgers take 39 wins, before having to enroll in military service during the Korean War. His record was 149–90 with an ERA of 3.6, and throughout the decade of his professional career, Newcombe completed 136 games. He was awarded the first ever Cy Young Award for the best pitcher in the combined major leagues and was named the National League's Most Valuable Player (MVP). In the late 1970s, Newcombe returned to the Dodger organization to serve as the Director of Community Affairs; and in 2009, he was named the Special Adviser to the Chairman. In 2016, Newcombe was inducted into the Baseball Reliquary's Shrine of the Eternals.

Don Newcombe is survived by his wife, Karen; his sons Brett and Don Jr.; his stepson, Chris Peterson, and his daughter, Kellye Roxanne.

See *Current Biography* 1957

Jessye Norman

Born: Augusta, Georgia; September 15, 1945
Died: New York, New York; September 30, 2019
Occupation: Opera singer

Jessye Norman rose from a childhood in the segregated American South to fame as one of the most recognizable divas in the world. The singer "didn't achieve world-class status by being subtle," a reviewer once wrote for the *Washington Post* (12 May 1993). "It was her glorious voice and magnificent stage presence that made her one of the most sought-after Wagnerian sopranos singing today."

Norman was born on September 15, 1945, in Augusta, Georgia, to Silas, an insurance broker, and Janie (King), a secretary. Both parents were music lovers, and as a child, she often heard her father sing in Augusta's Mount Calvary Baptist Church. Her mother was an avid amateur pianist, and Norman and her four siblings all took piano lessons from an early age.

While scrubbing the kitchen each weekend—her regular assigned task—Norman discovered Metropolitan Opera radio broadcasts and immediately became enamored by singers like Leontyne Price and Maria Callas; she soon began adding arias to her own vocal repertoire.

At 16 Norman entered the annual Marian Anderson Foundation scholarship auditions held in Philadelphia. Her trip was financed by small contributions from her classmates. Although she did not win, during the trip she met a voice teacher from Howard University who recommended that she be awarded a full scholarship to the school.

In 1967, Norman earned her Bachelor of Music degree cum laude from Howard and began studying at the University of Michigan. The next few years found her embarking on a State Department-sponsored arts tour of South America and winning the International Music Competition in Munich. As a result of that victory, she was offered a three-year contract with the Deutsche Oper Berlin, and more opportunities later arose in Milan, London, and other world capitals.

In 1973 she made her New York debut at Lincoln Center, and a decade later she finally made her long-awaited debut with the Metropolitan Opera, performing in Berlioz's *Les Troyens* (The Trojans) and singing the roles of both Cassandra and Dido in some performances.

Over the course of her career, Norman became celebrated for her commanding presence, and among her signature roles was that of the title character in Richard Strauss's *Ariadne auf Naxos*. Critics found her robust voice to be particularly suited to Wagner and Strauss as well. (A prolific recording artist, she was especially acclaimed for her version of Strauss's *Four Last Songs*.)

Invited to perform the French national anthem in Paris on the 200th anniversary of Bastille Day, Norman also sang at the inaugurations of Ronald Reagan and Bill Clinton. Among her laurels were five Grammy Awards (four for her recordings and one for lifetime achievement), the prestigious Kennedy Center Honor, and the National Medal of Arts.

Jessye Norman died of septic shock and multiple organ failure related to a spinal cord injury she suffered in 2015; she is survived by a brother, James, and a sister, Elaine.

See *Current Biography 1976*

Sono Osato

Born: Omaha, Nebraska; August 29, 1919
Died: Manhattan, New York; December 26, 2018
Occupation: Ballet dancer, actress

Sono Osato was a Japanese American ballet dancer, broadway performer, and actress who rose to fame in the 1930s dancing with the Ballets Russes de Monte Carlo.

Sono Osato was born in Omaha, Nebraska, on the August 29, 1919, to a Japanese father, Shoji Osato, and an Irish-French Canadian mother, Frances Fitzpatrick. In 1925, they moved to Chicago. Then, when she was eight years old, Osato's mother took her to Europe for two years. While in Monte Carlo they attended a performance of Cléopâtre by the famous Ballets Russes company, which prompted Osato to start ballet classes when she returned home in late 1929. She began her dance career at the age of fourteen with the Ballets Russes de Monte Carlo, as their youngest member, first American dancer, and first member of Japanese descent. In 1941 she joined the American Ballet Theatre and enjoyed success in New York. Following the Japanese attack on Pearl Harbor, Osato's father was arrested and detained under the U. S. Japanese American Internment policy. Osato struggled to keep working as a ballerina, as she was unable to tour with her troupe due to travel restrictions imposed on Japanese Americans. She retired from the American Ballet Theatre to focus on her family with husband, real estate developer Victor Elmaleh. However, she continued to perform on Broadway, receiving a Donaldson Award in 1943 for her role as principal dancer in *A Touch of Venus* choreographed by Agnes de Mille. In 1944 she originated the role of all-American girl, Ivy Smith in *On the Town* choreographed by Jerome Robbins. In the late 1940s and early 1950s, she pursued a brief career as an actress, appearing with Frank Sinatra in the film *The Kissing Bandit*. In 1980, she published an autobiography detailing her life and groundbreaking career, *Distant Dances*. In 2006, she founded the Sono Osato Scholarship in Graduate Studies at Career Transition for Dancers, an organization that helps dancers retire from performance into diverse and varied professions.

She is survived by her sons, Niko and Antonio Elmaleh, and three grandchildren.

See *Current Biography 1945*

Amos Oz

Born: Jerusalem, Israel; May 4, 1939
Died: Tel-Aviv-Yafo, Israel; December 28, 2018
Occupation: Writer

Amos Oz was an Israeli writer and political commentator who was known worldwide for his poignant portrayal of Israeli family life, as well as his scrutiny of Israeli politics.

Amos Klausner was born on May 4, 1939, in Jerusalem to Fania and Yehuda Arieh Klausner, two Eastern European immigrants. His mother suffered from depression and committed suicide when Amos was twelve. Two years later, Oz became a Labor Zionist and left home to join Kibbutz Hulda. There, he was adopted by the Huldai family and changed his surname to "Oz," the Hebrew word for "strength." He began to write during his free time, focussing on political and personal Jewish trauma. After finishing his three years of mandatory regular army service, he was sent by his kibbutz to study philosophy and Hebrew literature at the Hebrew University of Jerusalem. He graduated in 1963 and started teaching in the kibbutz high school, while continuing to write. In 1960, Oz married Nily Zuckerman, and they had three children. He published his first book, *Where the Jackals Howl*, a collection of short stories, in 1965. His first novel, *Another Place*, appeared in 1966. Oz soon became a leading figure of the Israeli literary "New Wave" movement. He published 40 books—14 of them novels, and nearly 500 articles and essays. Notable works included bestseller *My Michael* (1968), *The Hill of Evil Counsel* (1976), *A Perfect Peace* (1982), *Black Box* (1988), *To Know a Woman* (1989), *Don't Call It Night* (1995) and *The Same Sea* (1999). He became known for casting an unflinching eye on Israeli politics, famously advocating for a two-state solution to the Palestinian conflict. His novels revolved around Israeli family life, with realism at the forefront of his writing. He won many prizes and awards, including the Bialik prize in 1986, the French Legion of Honour in 1997, the Israel prize for literature in 1998, and an Honorary degree from the University of Milan in 2015.

He is survived by his wife Nily Zuckerman, his son Daniel, and two daughters, Fania and Gallia.

See *Current Biography 1983*

Ieoh Ming (I. M.) Pei

Born: Guangzhou, China; April 26, 1917
Died: Manhattan, New York; May 16, 2019
Occupation: Architect

Ieoh Ming (I. M.) Pei was a world-famous architect, most known for his design of the glass pyramid entrance to the Louvre Museum in Paris and the Chinese American East Building addition to the National Gallery of Art in Washington DC.

Ieoh Ming Pei was born on April 26, 1917, to Tsuyee Pei and Lien Kwun Chwong. Pei's mother passed away while Pei was still young, and his family eventually relocated to Shanghai where he attended the prestigious St. John's Middle School. Pei moved to the United States to study and graduated from the Massachusetts Institute of Technology (MIT) with a degree in architecture in 1940. Pei became a US citizen in 1954 and obtained his master's degree in architecture from Harvard University. He was hired by the real estate firm Webb & Knapp as the director of the architectural division, and soon went on to establish his own firm: I. M. Pei and Partners. Pei's firm had many famous early projects, included the Mile High Center in Denver (1955), the Place Ville-Marie in Montreal (1961), and the Kips Bay Plaza in Manhattan (1962). The Everson Museum of Art in Syracuse, New York, was Pei's first breakthrough project, in which four galleries were connected by bridges, and brought Pei wider recognition for his work. He followed with the design of the JFK Airport Domestic Terminal in 1970 and the John Hancock Building in Boston three years later. In 1979, Pei designed a library at Harvard University that would hold John F. Kennedy's books, which resulted in him winning the Gold Medal from the American Institute of Architects (AIA). In 1983, Pei was chosen by French president François Mitterrand to design a series of extensions for the Louvre. Perhaps Pei's most notable work, is the designed 70-foot glass pyramid that functions as the entrance to the museum and is now one of the Louvre's most defining architectural features. In 1983, Pei was honored as the fifth recipient of the International Pritzker Award, and in 1989 he was chosen as a recipient of the Praemium Imperiale from the Japan Art Association, considered to be an equivalent of a Nobel Prize for achievement in the arts.

Ieoh Ming (I. M.) Pei is survived by three children; Chien, Li, and Liane; and several grandchildren and great-grandchildren. He was predeceased by his son, T'ing.

See *Current Biography 1990*

César Pelli

Born: San Miguel de Tucumán, Tucumán, Argentina; October 12, 1926
Died: New Haven, Connecticut; July 19, 2019
Occupation: Architect

Through the skillful use of modern technology and industrialized materials, César Pelli was able to resolve with uncommon success the age-old conflict between art and the pragmatic demands of financial restraint and client specifications. His refined style stamped such iconic buildings as the United States Embassy in Tokyo and the Pacific Design Center in Los Angeles.

César Pelli was born to Victor V. Pelli, a civil servant, and Teresa S. (Suppa) Pelli, an educator. His grandfather had immigrated to Argentina from Italy in the nineteenth century. After five years of study at the University of Tucumán, Pelli received a diploma in architecture cum laude in 1949, choosing the field because it combined history and art, which he loved. During the following two years he worked as director of design at OFEMPE, a government organization, in Tucumán. In 1952 he went to the United States to continue his education at the University of Illinois. Although his intention had been to spend nine months abroad, he remained there for two years to earn his MSc degree in architecture and immediately afterward became an associate architect in the firm of Eero Saarinen & Associates. Saarinen died in 1961, but Pelli remained with the firm to complete various projects until 1964. (Among his best-known projects of this period were the TWA Flight Center at Kennedy Airport in New York and two new residential colleges at Yale that, while modernist, evoked the university's historic masonry buildings.) He next moved to the West Coast, and there he experimented with innovative glass facades, designing several buildings covered in "skins" that offered eye-catching reflections of the sky.

Pelli didn't open his own eponymous firm until 1977, when he was selected to design a renovation and expansion of the New York City's Museum of Modern Art (MoMA), which was completed in 1984. The company became especially renowned for its skyscrapers: the Petronas Twin Towers in Malaysia that Pelli designed had the distinction of being the tallest buildings in the world for several years, and other projects helped define the skylines of their cities, including the Salesforce Tower, now the tallest building in San Francisco; the International Finance Centre in Hong Kong; the Wells Fargo tower in Minneapolis; and the Goldman Sachs tower in Jersey City, among others.

A one-time dean of Yale's School of Architecture, Pelli won hundreds of awards over the course of his career, including the 1995 gold medal of the American Institute of Architects (AIA).

César Pelli was 92 when he died: he is survived by his sons—Rafael, an architect, and Denis, a professor of psychology and neural science—as well as by two grandchildren. He was predeceased in 2016 by his ex-wife, Diana Balmori, a landscape architect with whom he frequently collaborated, even after their 2001 divorce.

See *Current Biography 1983*

Ross Perot

Born: Texarkana, Texas; June 27, 1930
Died: Dallas, Texas; July 9, 2019
Occupation: Businessman and politician

Ross Perot, a brash billionaire who amassed his fortune in the early computer services industry, has been called one of the most unlikely candidates ever to run for president.

Henry Ray Perot was the second son of Gabriel Elias Perot, a cotton broker, and his wife, Lulu May, a former secretary-turned-homemaker. At the age of 12, he legally changed his name to Henry Ross Perot. The family's first-born son had died at the age of three, but Perot had one older sister, Bette.

Perot worked from the age of seven, breaking horses for a dollar each (and suffering numerous injuries in the process) and selling garden seeds and Christmas cards door-to-door. At the age of 13, he achieved the rank of Eagle Scout, only 16 months after joining the Boy Scouts– a feat that takes most boys at least three years.

Following his graduation from Texarkana High School in 1947, Perot enrolled at Texarkana Junior College. In 1949, thanks to his fervent petitioning, he was admitted to the U.S. Naval Academy, in Annapolis. He was sworn in as a midshipman at age 19, served on aircraft carriers during the Korean War, and remained in the navy until 1957.

Perot later joined I.B.M. in Dallas as a computer salesman and once fulfilled his annual quota in just three weeks. When his supervisors spurned his suggestions to deal in software and technical support, he quit; and in 1962, he founded the computer services firm Electronic Data Systems. The company went public in 1968, and Perot became one of the richest men in the nation.

Perot captured the imagination of the public with his swashbuckling form of activism: In 1969, he chartered two planes, loaded them with 30 tons of supplies, and flew to Southeast

Asia in an attempt to free American POWs. In 1979, in the midst of an Islamic revolution in Iran, he mounted a commando raid on a prison to free two employees being held for ransom.

In 1984, Perot sold Electronic Data Systems to General Motors for $2.5 billion in cash and stock; but four years later he founded another company, Perot Systems, which he sold to Dell for almost $4 billion in 2009. Consistently generous, he gave millions to schools, hospitals, and other institutions throughout his life. He was best known, however, for his badly failed presidential candidacies, in 1992 and 1996, when he ran on a populist platform of restoring a homespun, Norman Rockwell-inspired vision of America.

Ross Perot died of leukemia at the age of 89. He is survived by his wife, Margo; his sister, Bette; his five children, Ross Jr., Nancy, Suzanne, Carolyn, and Katherine; 16 grandchildren; and three step-grandchildren.

See *Current Biography 1996*

Luke Perry

Born: Mansfield, Ohio; October 11, 1966
Died: Burbank, California; March 4, 2019
Occupation: Actor

Luke Perry was an American actor who became famous for his starring role in the television series *Beverly Hills, 90210*.

Coy Luther "Luke" Perry III was born on October 11, 1966, in Mansfield, Ohio, and raised in Fredericktown, Ohio. He attended Fredericktown High School, where he played the role of Freddie Bird, the school mascot. Perry moved to Los Angeles after graduating to pursue acting, and supported himself working odd jobs, including at a doorknob factory and at an asphalt paving company. Work was slow for Perry, until he appeared in a music video in 1985, and by 1988 he had auditioned over 250 times before receiving his first acceptance. Perry's name was made in 1989, when he starred as Dylan McKay on Fox's teen drama, *Beverly Hills, 90210*. He kept this role from 1989–1995, and then from 1998–2000. Perry appeared on Broadway in 2001 in a *Rocky Horror Picture Show* Revival, and in 2004 appeared in a London West End production of *When Harry Met Sally*. While only enjoying minor success in movies, he appeared in *Buffy the Vampire Slayer*, *8 Seconds*, *The Fifth Element*, and *Once Upon a Time in Hollywood*. Perry also contributed voice-over work for numerous animated series, often playing the part of himself. His final television role was as Frederick "Fred" Andrews in the CW series *Riverdale*.

Luke Perry is survived by his fiancée, Wendy Madison Bauer, and his children, Jack and Sophie.

See *Current Biography 1998*

Ferdinand Piëch

Born: Vienna, Austria; April 17, 1937
Died: Rosenheim, Bavaria; August 25, 2019
Occupation: German automobile executive

Ferdinand Piëch may not be a widely recognized name but evidence of his achievements is visible on the streets and raceways in the popular names of Porsche, Audi, and Volkswagen. Born into an auto dynasty as grandson to Ferdinand Porsche, designer of Adolph Hitler's Volkswagen, the "people's car," and developer and founder of the Porsche sports-car company, at a young age Piëch aspired to and succeeded in becoming an automotive businessman and engineering legend.

Ferdinand Karl Piëch was born on April 17, 1937. His father, Anton, a lawyer, developed a VW beetle prototype in 1938 and during WWII became CEO of Volkswagen, directing manufacturing of automobiles, aircraft engines, and tank parts. Louise Porsche, Piëch's mother, and her brother Ferry co-owned Porsche's headquarters in Stuttgart, Germany. Piëch focused on automotive studies and toying with the engine in his Porsche while studying at the Swiss Technical University in Zurich. He started work in 1968 as engine tester at Porsche's headquarters in Stuttgart and became head of research and development that same year. Investing millions of dollars into race car development paid off in a 240-mile-per-hour Porsche 917 winning the 1970 Le Mans competition in France. Family squabbles prompted his mother and uncle to bar family members from holding management posts compelling Piëch to become director of special projects in research and development at Volkswagen's Audi division. He developed the five-cylinder gas engine and four-wheel drive system before becoming head of Audi in 1988. In 1993, Piëch took over as Volkswagen's chief executive officer, taking the company from minus $1.1 billion to earnings of over $1.2 billion by 1998. He reduced board members, managers, employee hours, and pay, streamlined manufacturing, and hired López de Arriortúa and seven of his colleagues from General Motors in 1993. The following years saw controversy, criminal investigations, and accusations of stolen confidential documents and designs. Legal battles involving López, GM, and Volkswagen followed causing López to resign in 1994. In

1997, Piëch introduced the Passat and in 1998 the inexpensive Lupo minicar. In July 1998, all charges against López were dropped, and two months later Piëch introduced the new Volkswagen Beetle. Gambling on the growth of ultra-luxury cars, Volkswagen purchased Lamborghini and Bugatti.

Ferdinand Piëch is survived by thirteen children, three from his second marriage to Ursula (nee Plasser), five from a first marriage to Corina von Planta, two from a relationship with Marlene Porsche, and at least three from other relationships.

See *Current Biography 1999*

followed by *The Green Dark* in 1988 and *The Bird Catcher* in 1998. Her poetry echoed themes of motherhood, divorce, love, and marriage. *The Bird Catcher* gained widespread attention, and as a result, she was awarded the National Book Critics Circle Award. Ponsot continued writing, releasing the poetry collection *Easy* in 2009 at the age of 88. Her final collection, titled *Collected Poems*, was published in 2016.

Marie Ponsot is survived by seven children; Monique, Denis, Antoine, William, Christopher, Matthew, and Gregory, sixteen grandchildren, and nine great-grandchildren.

See *Current Biography 1999*

Marie Ponsot

Born: New York; New York; April 6, 1921
Died: New York, New York; July 5, 2019
Occupation: Poet and Literary Critic

Marie Ponsot was a famed poet known for writing about love, divorce, and family.

Marie Ponsot was born Marie Birmingham on April 6, 1921, in Brooklyn, New York, to William and Marie Candee Birmingham. She attended Richmond Hill High School in Queens and later went to obtain her bachelor's degree from St. Joseph's College for Women before earning her master's in seventeenth-century literature from Columbia University. During World War II, she worked at a bookstore. After a car accident that fractured her femur, she moved with a friend to Paris, where she worked as an archivist for the United Nations Educational, Scientific and Cultural Organization (UNESCO) and studied at the Sorbonne. She met classmate Lawrence Ferlinghetti, who would later publish her work, and her husband, French painter Claude Ponsot. In 1950, after the birth of their first child and pregnant with a second, Ponsot and her husband moved back to the United States where Ponsot supported herself and her husband through freelance translating and writing. Ponsot continued writing poetry independently, publishing work through magazines. Ferlinghetti had since established a bookstore in San Francisco and accepted Ponsot's *True Minds* as the fifth in a poetry series he was publishing, following the release of Ginsberg's groundbreaking *Howl and Other Poems True Minds* was the only book that Ponsot released for nearly 25 years. By 1961, still living in New York, Ponsot had begun teaching at Queens College while raising seven children. Her marriage ended in divorce in 1970, and Ponsot relocated to Jamaica Hills in Queens to focus on her writing. In 1981, Ponsot resumed publishing her work with the release of *Admit Impediment*,

Hal Prince

Born: New York, New York; January 30, 1928
Died: Reykjavik, Iceland; July 31, 2019
Occupation: Theatrical producer and director

A young Harold "Hal" Prince was dubbed the "Boy Wonder" of Broadway when he co-produced *The Pajama Game* in 1954. He followed that smash musical with a string of iconic hits—including *West Side Story*, *A Funny Thing Happened on the Way to the Forum*, and *Fiddler on the Roof*—that defined theater-going for a generation and established his reputation as a talented figure who could address themes of underlying seriousness that were simultaneously entertaining and intellectually stimulating.

Prince was born Harold Smith Jr.; his parents, Harold Sr. and Blanche divorced when he was a child, and his mother soon remarried, to Milton Prince, a well-to-do stockbroker. Aspiring to be a playwright, thanks in some part to the influence of Blanche, an ardent theatergoer, Prince attended the University of Pennsylvania, and upon graduating in 1948 he returned to his native New York and found work doing odd jobs for director George Abbott. His career trajectory was interrupted by a brief stint in the military, but when his tour of duty ended, he resumed work as an assistant stage manager for Abbott's musical *Wonderful Town*, which premiered in 1953.

While *Wonderful Town* was running, Prince and Robert E. Griffith, who had worked together stage-managing Abbott's shows, decided to produce a musical themselves. The result was *The Pajama Game*, a lighthearted take on labor troubles in a pajama factory, which opened in 1954 to enthusiastic reviews and earned Prince a Tony as producer of the year's best musical. It was the first of a record-breaking 21 he would win over the course of his career. (The 21st Tony was a lifetime achievement award, garnered in 2006.)

Critics often cite *Cabaret*, which opened in 1966 with Prince both producing and directing, as a pivotal point in both his career and musical theater. Although Broadway was thought to be losing relevance in an age of rock-n-roll and political discontent, the show, with its dark themes and acknowledgment of the tawdrier aspects of life, sparked a resurgence of interest in younger patrons.

Prince, who frequently collaborated with the celebrated lyricist Stephen Sondheim, sometimes set records only to break them himself. *Fiddler on the Roof*, for example, opened on September 22, 1964, and had a record-setting total of 3,242 performances, making it the longest-running show in Broadway history at the time; that number pales, however, in comparison to the current record-holder, Prince's *Phantom of the Opera*, which in 2012 became the first Broadway production ever to mount 10,000 performances and that remains the longest-running show in Broadway history by a wide margin.

Hal Prince died after a brief illness at the age of 91. He is survived by his wife of more than five decades, Judy Chaplin; his son, Charles, an orchestra conductor; his daughter, Daisy, a theater director; and three grandchildren.

See *Current Biography 1971*

Lee Radziwill

Born: New York, New York; March 3, 1933
Died: New York, New York; February 15, 2019
Occupation: Socialite and Princess

Caroline Lee Radziwill (usually known as Princess Lee Radziwill) was a renowned American socialite and the younger sister of First Lady Jacqueline Bouvier Kennedy. She also had a career as a public relations executive and as an interior designer.

Caroline Lee Bouvier was born on March 3, 1933, in New York City, New York to Janet Lee and John Bouvier III, and attended Potomac School in Washington, DC before attending Miss Porter's School in Farmington, Connecticut. Radziwill enrolled to study at Sarah Lawrence College, but left after a year to study art in Italy. In 1959, she married Prince Stanisław Albrecht "Stash" Radziwiłł, a London real-estate investor and socialite. Together they had two children but divorced in 1974. After the death of her brother-in-law, John F. Kennedy, Radziwill's relationship with her sister, Jacqueline Kennedy, was the subject of much gossip and analysis by the press. It was claimed that Radziwill was responsible for introducing her sister to her future husband, Aristotle Onassis. In 1972, Radziwill

hired a documentary filmmaker to work on a film about her extended family, particularly, the Beales, or as they were known "Big Eddie" and "Little Eddie," who were a mother and daughter who lived in isolation in a deteriorating house in Long Island, New York. The documentary, "Grey Gardens" was wildly successful and adapted into a television movie in 2009. Radziwill was famous for being a prominent socialite, frequenting the company of artists and celebrities such as The Rolling Stones and Truman Capote, Rudolf Nureyev, and Margot Fonteyn. Radziwill worked briefly as an actress, before founding an interior design firm in 1976. She went on to serve as a public relations executive for Giorgio Armani from 1986 to 1994.

Lee Radziwill is survived by her daughter, Anna Christina, daughter-in-law Carole Radziwill, and her half-brother, Jamie Auchincloss.

See *Current Biography 1977*

Charles A. Reich

Born: New York, New York; May 20, 1928
Died: San Francisco, California; June 15, 2019
Occupation: Writer, professor, and lawyer

Charles Reich was a Yale Law School Professor and writer whose 1970 book *The Greening of America* became a *New York Times* bestseller. A manifesto on the counterculture of the 1960s, *The Greening of America* made Reich a celebrity and became a canonical text of the time.

Charles Alan Reich was born on May 20, 1928, to Dr. Carl and Eleanor Reich, who later divorced, and his brother Peter. He attended City and Country School in Greenwich Village and the Lincoln School of Teachers College. Reich earned a bachelor's degree in history from Oberlin College in 1949. Reich went on to Yale Law School, during which time he clerked for Justice Hugo L. Black of the United States Supreme Court and worked at two law firms, Cravath, Swaine & Moore LLP in New York and Arnold, Fortas & Porter in Washington DC. Reich taught at Yale Law School from 1960 until 1974, where his students included Bill Clinton and Hillary Rodham. His 1964 article, "The New Property", defended the individual's right to privacy and freedom against government privilege. In 1970, the article was cited in a landmark administrative law case, *Goldberg v Kelly*, in which the Supreme Court ruled to broaden its conceptualization of property to include licenses, contracts, and welfare benefits. The same year, Reich's most famous work, *The Greening of America*, first appeared as a 39,000-word extract in *The New Yorker*, with the book going on to become a bestseller despite a mixed reaction from critics. Reich later said that the book effectively "did me in as far as academe was concerned." He moved to San Francisco in 1974 and taught at the University of California, Santa Barbara, and the University of San Francisco School of Law. He published an autobiography, *The Sorcerer of Bolinas Reef* in 1976, in which he revealed that he was gay, although he stated that he was never defined by his sexuality. Reich was active in LGBT rights activism during the 1970s. He returned to Yale Law School from 1991 to 1995 as a visiting professor.

Charles Reich is survived by his nephew, Daniel Reich, and his niece, Alice Reich.

See *Current Biography 1972*

Ogden R. Reid

Born: New York, New York; June 24, 1925
Died: Waccabuc, New York; March 2, 2019
Occupation: Editor and Congressman

Ogden R. Reid was an American politician and diplomat who was the U.S. Ambassador to Israel, as well as serving as a six-term United States Representative from Westchester County as both a Republican and a Democrat.

Ogden Rogers Reid, known to his friends as "Brownie," was born on June 24, 1925, in New York City to the publishing family of Helen Rogers Reid and Ogden Mills Reid. He graduated from Deerfield Academy in 1943 and enlisted as a private in the U. S. Army. He was discharged as a First Lieutenant in 1946 and later served as a Captain in the Army Reserves. He graduated from Yale University in 1949 and served as publisher, president, and editor of the family-owned newspaper, the *New York Herald Tribune* from 1955 until 1958. During this time, he was also the director of the Panama Canal Company, before becoming the U. S. Ambassador to Israel in 1959. Reid first ran for Congress in 1962 and was elected to the eighty-eighth Congress, serving for ten years as a Republican. In 1972, Reid switched parties to join the Democratic Party, as he felt he could not support Richard Nixon as President. At the end of his term in 1974, Reid declined re-election. While he served in Congress, Reid sponsored 85 pieces of legislation and co-sponsored a further 99. Reid later served in the administration of Governor Hugh Carey, as Commissioner of Environmental Conservation.

Ogden R. Reid is survived by his wife, Mary Louise Reid, and their six children, David, Stewart, Michael, William, Ogden, and Elisabeth Taylor.

See *Current Biography 1956*

Meshulam Riklis

Born: Istanbul, Turkey; December 2, 1923
Died: Tel Aviv, Israel; January 25, 2019
Occupation: Financier and businessman

Meshulam Riklis was a Turkish-born Israeli businessman and financier. Riklis is credited with being one of the first businessmen to acquire companies using solely credit, earning him the designations of "takeover artist" and "corporate raider."

Meshulam Riklis was born on December 2, 1923, in Istanbul, Turkey, to Jewish parents who were emigrating from Russia to Israel. He grew up in Tel Aviv. He served with the British Army in Europe during World War II and soon moved to the United States in 1947 with his first wife and daughter. There, he taught Hebrew as a part time job while studying mathematics at Ohio State University. He graduated in 1950, before becoming a junior stock analyst for Piper Jaffray. Riklis created the Rapid-American Corporation in 1966. Upon establishing his financial empire, Riklis returned to Ohio State to complete a master degree in finance, during which time he wrote his thesis "Expansion through Financial Management" that discussed the techniques he used to take over failing businesses. He insisted that if he had sufficient cash, he could buy almost any business on credit alone. Pioneering this technique of using borrowed cash to fund corporate takeovers, Riklis became a controversial business tycoon. At the pinnacle of his financial success, Riklis claimed to have had a net worth of around a billion dollars. However, his tactics nearly cost him his livelihood on multiple occasions, as indeed, making long-term investments with equally long-term debt was always a game of financial risk. As famous for his love life as his entrepreneurship, Riklis was married three times—first to his childhood sweetheart, then to the infamous actress Pia Zadora. A close friend of Ariel Sharon, Riklis was a fervent supporter of Israel. Over his life, he donated around $190 million to Israeli charities and pro-Israel causes.

Meshulam Riklis is survived by his wife, Tali, his sons Ira and Kristofer, and daughters, Marcia and Kady.

See *Current Biography 1971*

Alice M. Rivlin

Born: Philadelphia, Pennsylvania; March 4, 1931
Died: Washington, DC; May 14, 2019
Occupation: American economist

Alice M Rivlin, was an American economist and served as Vice Chair of the Federal Reserve, Director of the White House Office of Management and Budget, and was the founding Director of the Congressional Budget Office.

Alice Mitchell Rivlin, born Georgianna Alice Mitchell, on March 4, 1931, to father, Allan C.G. Mitchell, and mother Georgianna Peck (Fales) Mitchell. Rivlin spent her early years in Bloomington, Indiana, where her father was the head of physics at Indiana University; he also contributed to the development of the atomic bomb as part of the Manhattan Project. Rivlin graduated from Bryn Mawr College in 1952. After a short break in Europe working on the Marshall Plan, Rivlin earned her PhD in economics from Harvard University in 1958. During her career, Rivlin interspersed government positions with stints at the Brookings Institution, a Washington think tank, from 1957 to 1966, 1969 to 1975, 1983 to 1993, and 1999 to her death. From 1968 to 1969 Rivlin served as Assistant Secretary for Planning and Evaluation, United States Department of Health, Education, and Welfare (HEW). When the Congressional Budget Office (CBO) was founded in 1975, Rivlin was appointed the first director. In this role she shaped the CBO into a trusted authority charged with providing Congress with nonpartisan, reliable data on the fiscal consequences of proposed legislation. Rivlin, a Democrat, was vocal in her criticism of Reaganomics during her tenure at the CBO. Despite largely being praised for their impartiality, Rivlin and her team were not without critics, including the Reagan and Clinton administrations. She later went on to serve as deputy director of the Office of Management and Budget (OMB), from 1993 to 1994, and then director of the OMB, from 1994 to 1996, selected by President Bill Clinton. Rivlin was the vice chair of the Federal Reserve from 1996 to 1997. In 1983, she won a MacArthur Foundation Genius award. In 2012, she received a Foremother Award from the National Research Center for Women & Families. She authored three books, a column in *The Los Angeles Times*, as well as many articles for Brookings.

Alice M. Rivlin is survived by her husband, Sidney, her children, Catherine, Allan, and Douglas, and four grandchildren.

See *Current Biography 1982*

Cokie Roberts

Born: New Orleans, Louisiana; December 27, 1943
Died: Washington, DC; September 17, 2019
Occupation: Broadcast journalist

Beloved and trusted by millions of fans of National Public Radio (NPR) and ABC News, Cokie Roberts explained the world of Washington politics from an insider's perspective, while blazing a trail for other female journalists.

Covering the operations of Congress came naturally to Roberts, who grew up in a prominent political family. She was born Mary Martha Corinne Morrison Claiborne Boggs, on December 27, 1943, the daughter of (Thomas) Hale Boggs, a Democratic congressman, and Corinne Morrison (Claiborne) Boggs, who was elected to her husband's seat in the U.S. House of Representatives after the airplane on which he was a passenger disappeared in Alaska in 1972. Between them, the couple represented Louisiana in Congress for almost 50 years. The youngest of three children, Roberts was given the nickname "Cokie" by her brother, Thomas, who had difficulty pronouncing the word "Corinne."

Roberts attended Wellesley College, earning a BA in political science in 1964 and embarked on a career reporting and producing for various news outlets in Washington, New York, and Los Angeles. In 1974, she moved to Greece, where she began working as a stringer for CBS News radio. Upon returning to the United States in 1977, she was recruited by NPR to cover Congress, joining Linda Wertheimer and Nina Totenberg to form a formidable trio of talented female journalists at the station.

In 1981, Roberts and Wertheimer became correspondents for the weekly PBS television show *The Lawmakers*; and as the regular congressional correspondent on the prestigious *MacNeil/Lehrer NewsHour* on which she appeared from 1984 to 1987, Roberts attracted even greater national attention. At about the same time, Roberts also began appearing frequently on the Sunday-morning ABC television program *This Week with David Brinkley*, alongside the regular panelists Sam Donaldson and George Will.

In 1988, ABC made the unprecedented step of offering Roberts a contract that allowed her to be the network's Washington correspondent for ABC News and a regular panelist on the Brinkley show as well as a senior political analyst three days a week for NPR. Among her most popular posts were co-anchoring the Sunday morning political affairs program *This Week*, alongside Sam Donaldson, from 1996 to 2002, and fielding questions from NPR listeners on the long-running segment *Ask Cokie*.

The author of such books as *Ladies of Liberty: The Women Who Shaped Our Nation* (2008) and *Capital Dames: The Civil War and the Women of Washington, 1848–1868* (2015), she once told an interviewer, "As close up and as personally as I saw [the American political system] and saw all of the flaws, I [also] understood all of the glories of it."

The winner of an Edward R. Murrow Award for outstanding contribution to public radio, Roberts died of breast cancer.

Cokie Roberts is survived by her husband, Steven, a journalist; her two children, Lee and Rebecca; and six grandchildren.

See *Current Biography 1994*

Kevin Roche

Born: Dublin, Ireland; June 14, 1922
Died: Guildford, Connecticut; March 1, 2019
Occupation: Architect

Irish American architect, Kevin Roche, was responsible for the design and master planning for over 200 buildings, both in the United States and abroad, including the Metropolitan Museum of Art ("The Met") and the Ford Foundation building in New York City.

Eamonn Kevin Roche was born on June 14, 1922, in Dublin and raised in Cork, Ireland. He graduated from the University College Dublin (UCD) in 1945 and immediately went to work with Irish architect, Michael Scott. In 1946, he moved to London to work with Maxwell Fry, before applying to graduate programs at Harvard, Yale, and the Illinois Institute of Technology. Accepted at all three schools, Roche elected to go to Illinois to study under Ludwig Mies van der Rohe. By 1950, he had worked at the planning office for the UN Headquarters building in New York and had joined the firm of Eero Saarinen and Associates. There, he met his future partner, John Dinkeloo. In 1954, he became the Principal Design Associate to Saarinen and assisted on every one of his projects until Saarinen's death in 1961. In 1966, Roche and Dinkeloo formed Kevin Roche John Dinkeloo and Associates LLC and went on to complete 12 of the major unfinished Saarinen projects, including the TWA Flight Center at JFK Airport, the CBS Headquarters in New York, and the John Deere Headquarters in Moline, Illinois. Kevin Roche John Dinkeloo and Associates became masters of corporate headquarters, constructing office buildings, banks, art centers and museums, and part of the Bronx Zoo. In 1982, Roche

was one of the first recipients of the Pritzker Prize and used the $100,000 prize money to endow the Eero Saarinen Chair of Architecture at Yale in memory of Eero Saarinen. Alongside his architectural business, Roche was a trustee of the American Academy in Rome, the American Academy of Arts and Letters, a member of the U. S. Commission of Fine Arts, and a member of the National Academy of Design.

Kevin Roche is survived by his wife, Jane, and children, Eamon, Paud, Denis, Anne, and Alice.

See *Current Biography 1970*

Nicolas Roeg

Born: London, England; August 15, 1928
Died: London, England; November 23, 2018
Occupation: Director, cinematographer

Nicolas Roeg was a British director and cinematographer whose work was characterised by a dizzying narrative style and experimental imagery. At the height of his career, in the 1970s, he was seen by many to be one of the leading British directors of his time.

Nicolas Roeg was born on August 15 1928, in London, to Jack Roeg and Mabel Gertrude. In 1947, after completing National Service, Roeg began working as an apprentice at Marylebone Studios. In fact, Roeg claimed that he only entered the film industry due to the studio being across the road from his home. There, he made tea and worked as a clapper-boy before moving up the ranks to the role of camera operator on several major films including *Tarzan's Greatest Adventure* (1959) and *The Trials of Oscar Wilde* (1960). He then graduated to work as a cinematographer on films such as David Lean's *Lawrence of Arabia* (1962) and François Truffaut's *Fahrenheit 451* (1966). In the late 1960s, Roeg moved into directing with *Performance*, which he co-directed with Donald Cammell. Roeg's solo directorial debut, *Walkabout* (1971), filmed in Australia, was also his last film as cinematographer. Over the ten years that followed, Roeg directed numerous films, such as *Don't Look Now* (1973), *The Man Who Fell to Earth* (1976), starring David Bowie, *and Bad Timing* (1980), starring Theresa Russell, who he married in 1982, and directed again in several films. His visionary style, characterised by fragmented, disjointed, and sometimes disturbing images, has been met with widespread critical acclaim. Many of his later works, however, had minimal release or went straight to television or video. In 1999, the British Film Institute named his films *Don't Look Now* and *Performance* the eighth and forty-eighth greatest British films of all time, respectively.

Roeg is survived by his third wife, actor Harriet Harper; by four sons from his first marriage, Luc, Waldo, Sholto, and Nico; and by two sons of his second marriage, Max and Statten.

See *Current Biography 1996*

Nancy Grace Roman

Born: Nashville, Tennessee; May 16, 1925
Died: Germantown, Maryland; December 25, 2018
Occupation: Astronomer

Nancy Grace Roman was an American astronomer credited with the early development of the Hubble Space Telescope.

Nancy Grace Roman was born on May 16, 1925, in Nashville, Tennessee, to music teacher Georgia Smith Roman, and geophysicist Irwin Roman, both of whom she considered to be a major influence in her interest in science. From an early age she was fascinated by space, even going on to organize an astronomy club while in fifth grade. In 1946 she earned a bachelor's degree in astronomy from Swarthmore College, Pennsylvania. She received her doctorate from the University of Chicago in 1949, in the same field. Upon graduation, she continued at the University of Chicago first as a postdoctoral student, then as instructor, and was ultimately appointed assistant professor becoming the first woman on the faculty in the department of Astronomy and Astrophysics. She also worked at the Yerkes Observatory. However, it soon became clear that as a woman, she would struggle to gain tenure at the university so she left to find work elsewhere. Later, she was hired to work in radio astronomy at the Naval Research Laboratory. Roman then joined the National Aeronautics and Space Administration (NASA) in 1959, six months after the agency was opened. She became their chief of astronomy, and their first-ever female executive. Roman promoted space-based astronomy and, most notably, had direct oversight into the early development of what became the Hubble Space telescope, leading many to call her "The Mother of Hubble." In 1979, Dr. Roman retired from NASA but not before earning the Women in Aerospace Lifetime Achievement Award and the Exceptional Scientific Achievement Award. After leaving NASA, she continued to work with contractors supporting the Goddard Space Flight Center in Maryland. She promoted professional opportunities for women scientists through the American Association of University Women, speaking frequently in schools and universities.

Roman leaves no immediate survivors.

See *Current Biography 1960*

Theodore Isaac Rubin

Born: Brooklyn, New York; April 11, 1923
Died: New York, New York; February 16, 2019
Occupation: Psychiatrist and author

Theodore Rubin was a psychiatrist and author whose novel *Lisa and David* was turned into an Academy Award-nominated movie. Rubin became the face of psychotherapy for post-war American culture.

Theodore Isaac Rubin, known as Ted, was born on April 11, 1923, and raised in Brooklyn, New York. He attended Far Rockaway High School in Queens before attending Brooklyn College. After a stint in the U.S. Navy, Rubin received his medical degree from the University of Lausanne in Switzerland. He then moved to Los Angeles where he was a resident at the Los Angeles VA Hospital, before returning to Brooklyn's Downstate Medical School to specialize in psychiatry. Rubin trained in German American as an analyst at the Karen Horney's American Institute for Psychoanalysis, where he eventually joined the faculty in 1960 and served for many years as the institute's president. Alongside his work at the Institute, Rubin kept a private practice in Manhattan, as well as writing extensively. The release of *David and Lisa*, a movie based on his novel, propelled Rubin into the spotlight. A for-television remake was produced in 1998 by Oprah Winfrey. Rubin wrote extensively across genres, from fiction to nonfiction and self-help. He also contributed a column to *Ladies' Home Journal* and appeared on television to talk about therapy, mental health, and daily emotional struggles.

Theodore Rubin's wife, Eleanor, passed away in 2017, and he is survived by his sons Jeffrey and Eugene, and his daughter, Trudy.

See *Current Biography 1980*

Francisco Mauro Salzano

Born: Cachoeira do Sul, Brazil; July 27, 1928
Died: Porto Alegre, Brazil; September 28, 2018
Occupation: Geneticist

Francisco Mauro Salzano was a Brazilian geneticist of international acclaim best known for his work researching indigenous populations in South America.

Francisco Mauro Salzano was born to Francisco and Onelia Salzano on July 27, 1928 in Cachoeira do Sul, a town in Southern Brazil. His father, who was a doctor and on the board of directors for the Secretary of Health, wanted him to become a doctor, but Salzano didn't pass the entrance exam. Instead, he studied Natural History at the Federal University of Rio Grande do Sul in Porto Alegre. There, he also studied biology and zoology before moving into genetics, a field that was still in its inception at the time. He gained his doctorate in Biology at the University of São Paolo in 1955, and soon received a fellowship from the Rockefeller Foundation for postdoctoral training in human genetics at the University of Michigan. In 1960 he returned to the Federal University of Rio Grande do Sul as an assistant professor of genetics. He became head of the university's genetics department in 1981. During his Career, Salzano published over a thousand academic articles. He became known as a pioneer in the field of genetics and conducted extensive genetic research on Brazil's indigenous population, focusing especially on the Chavante people of Central Brazil. With his research, he hoped to answer questions relating to the migration and population of the Americas, as well as provide insights into the relationship between disease and deoxyribonucleic acid(DNA). He received various prizes for his work, including the Admiral Álavaro Alberto Award in 1994, courtesy of the Brazilian National Council for Scientific and Technological Development. In 2010, he was awarded an honorary doctorate from the Paul Sabatier University in Toulouse, France. During his time as a professor, Salzano mentored 46 PhD and 48 MSc students, leaving a lasting mark on the field of genetics within Brazil and worldwide.

Francisco Mauro Salzano is survived by his sons Felipe and Renato, and five grandchildren.

See *Current Biography 2006*

Edward P. G. Seaga

Born: Boston, Massachusetts; May 28, 1930
Died: Miami, Florida; May 28, 2019
Occupation: Politician

Edward Seaga was a Jamaican politician and the fifth Prime Minister of Jamaica from 1980–1989.

Edward Philip George Seaga was born on May 28, 1930, in Boston, Massachusetts, to Philip George Seaga and Erna (Maxwell) Seaga. His parents were both originally from Jamaica and returned there when Seaga was three. Seaga returned to the United States to earn a bachelor of arts degree in social sciences from Harvard University in 1952. Prior to becoming a politician, he set up his own record label, West Indies Recording Limited, in 1959. He sold the company when he was elected as a Member of Parliament for the Jamaica Labor Party (JLP) in 1962. Seaga held this seat for 43 years, the longest serving MP in Jamaican history. He served as minister of welfare and development and as minister of finance before becoming leader of the JLP in 1974, a position he held for thirty years. During his term as Prime Minister, Seaga severed Jamaica's ties with Cuba and solidified ties with the United States, securing financial aid from the Reagan administration and David Rockefeller, which helped to rebuild the country's economy following independence. Seaga supported Reagan's much-criticized invasion of the island nation of Grenada in 1983. He is credited with building Jamaica's financial infrastructure and developing its cultural heritage during his time as Prime Minister but was criticized for a lack of progress in tackling poverty and unemployment. He was defeated in the 1989 election by Michael Manley. Seaga continued as Leader of the Opposition until his retirement from politics in 2005. He was appointed as a member of the Privy Council by Queen Elizabeth II in 1981 and was awarded the Order of the Nation by the Jamaican Government in 2002.

Edward Seaga is survived by his wife Carla and their daughter, and his three children from his first marriage.

See *Current Biography 1981*

Shehu Shagari

Born: Shagari village, Nigeria; February 25, 1925
Died: Abuja, Nigeria; December 28, 2018
Occupation: Politician

Shehu Shagari was the first democratically elected President of Nigeria, and also served seven times in ministerial or cabinet posts throughout his political career.

Shehu Usman Aliyu Shagari was born to Aliyu and Mariamu Shagari on February 25, 1925, in Shagari village, Nigeria, where his father was village head. In fact, it was Shehu Shagari's great-grandfather, Ahmadu Rufa'i, who initially founded the village and took the name Shagari as his family name. Shehu Shagari, raised as a Sunni muslim, started his education in a Quranic school and eventually attended Kaduna College, known for its elite and famous alumni. Shagari then trained and worked as a teacher, before entering politics in 1951, when he became the secretary of the Northern People's Congress in Sokoto. In 1954 he was elected into public office for the first time, as a member for the federal House of Representatives for Sokoto west. He served as a minister in a number of cabinet positions over the next several years, as well as holding various commissioner positions. Notably, during his time as commissioner of finance for Nigeria, he also served as a governor for the World Bank and was a member of the International Monetary Fund (IMF) Committee. In 1978, Shagari was a founding member of the National Party of Nigeria. He was chosen by his party as the presidential candidate for Nigeria's first general election the next year and won. In 1981, he navigated a massive fall in oil prices marking the end of the oil boom in Nigeria. Amid economic decline and allegations of corruption, his presidency lost credibility and popularity. He was re-elected in 1983, but after a few months in office he was overthrown by General Muhammadu Buhari in a military coup that ushered in a long period of military rule.

Shehu Shagari is survived by two of his three wives, as well as many children and grandchildren.

See *Current Biography* 1980

Ntozake Shange

Born: Trenton, New Jersey; October 18, 1948
Died: Bowie, Maryland; October 27, 2018
Occupation: Playwright, poet, author

Ntozake Shange was a playwright and poet whose work aimed to capture and popularize the lived experiences of women of color.

Ntozake Shange was born Paulette Linda Williams on October 18, 1948, to Paul and Eloise Williams, in Trenton, New Jersey. Shange was interested in poetry from an early age, and her parents fostered her artistic education, encouraging her to write and attend readings. When she was eight, her family moved to St. Louis, Missouri. There, Shange attended a non-segregated school, where she faced racist attacks and bullying. Shange returned to New Jersey in her teenage years and went on to attend Columbia University, graduating cum laude with a degree in American Studies before pursuing a master's degree in the same field at the University of Southern California. In her first year at college, Shange got married. However, the relationship was short-lived. This contributed to her depression; and in 1971, Shange attempted suicide. Her later recovery led her to change her name to Ntozake Shange, Xhosa for "she who carries her own things" and "she who walks like a lion." In 1975, after completing her master's, Shange returned to New York City, where she quickly became a well-recognized poet and playwright. Her first, and most famous play, *For Colored Girls*

Who Have Considered Suicide / When the Rainbow Is Enuf, was produced, ending up on Broadway. It won her several prizes, including the Obie award, the Outer Critics Circle award, and the AUDELCO award. Shange coined the term "choreopoem" to describe the ground-breaking dramatic form she created with the piece, which told the stories of women of color across the United States. Shange wrote many other plays, including *Spell No. 7*, and an adaptation of Bertolt Brecht's *Mother Courage and Her Children*, which won her another Obie award. She was also a renowned poet, having published 19 collections of poetry throughout her life, alongside six novels, five children's books, and three essay collections.

Ntozake Shange is survived by her two sisters, Ifa Bayeza and Bisa Williams, her brother, Paul T Williams Jr, her daughter Savannah Shange, and granddaughter Harriet Shange Watkins.

See *Current Biography* 1978

Anne Rivers Siddons

Born: Fairburn, Georgia; January 9, 1936
Died: Charleston, South Carolina; September 11, 2019
Occupation: Novelist; former journalist

Anne Rivers Siddons is the author of *Heartbreak Hotel*, *Peachtree Road*, *Colony*, *Downtown*, *Low Country*, and several other novels whose heroines, like her, are natives of the United States South. Although her "commitment" to the South is "absolute," in her words, she always tried to escape the mindset associated with the stereotypical southern belle and with the romanticized notions about the South that have long manifested themselves in popular culture.

The only child of Marvin Rivers, a prosperous lawyer, and the former Katherine Kitchens, a high-school secretary, the writer was born Sybil Anne Rivers on January 9, 1936. Like six generations of her ancestors, she was raised in the South Carolina town of Fairburn. After her high-school graduation, in 1954, Siddons enrolled at Auburn University, in Alabama. She studied architecture before changing her major to illustration. As an undergraduate she joined a sorority and "did the things I thought I should," as she once told an interviewer, referring to societal expectations that she would focus on marriage and family rather than career. She was far from totally compliant, however, and one year she was barred from editing the school paper because she had written an op-ed in support of integration.

Siddons earned a bachelor of applied arts degree in 1958 and embarked on a career in advertising illustration. She soon discovered a talent for writing copy as well; and in 1963, she joined the staff of *Atlanta* magazine. In the early 1970s, she received a letter from Larry Ashmead, an editor at Doubleday, who had admired some of her *Atlanta* articles and wondered whether she might be interested in writing a book. She agreed, and the result was a collection of essays, *John Chancellor Makes Me Cry* (1975), and a semiautobiographical novel, *Heartbreak Hotel* (1976). Although both were well received, her real breakthrough success came in 1988 with *Peachtree Road*, a saga about Atlanta in the decades following World War II, as told through the eyes of two cousins.

Siddons enjoyed steady and sustained popularity throughout the rest of her career, often appearing on bestseller lists. Her final novel, *The Girls of August*, was published in 2014 and told the story of a group of longtime friends who gather annually for a beach vacation.

"The South is hard on women, partly because of the emphasis on looks and charm," she once explained to an interviewer, "No matter what I did, I always ended up with this hollow feeling. It finally hit me. That's why I wrote: I am writing about the journey we take to find out what lives in that hole."

Anne Rivers Siddons died at the age of 83 from lung cancer. She is survived by her stepchildren (David, Kem, Rick, and Lee) and three step-grandchildren. Her husband, Heyward Siddons, predeceased her in 2014.

See *Current Biography 2005*

John Singleton

Born: Los Angeles, California; January 6, 1968
Died: Los Angeles, California; April 28, 2019
Occupation: American film director and screenwriter

At the age of twenty-three, John Singleton was the youngest filmmaker and first African American to be nominated for an Academy Award for Best Director of his semiautobiographical 1991 film *Boyz N the Hood*. The films that followed from 1993 to 2005, although often commended for their social vision, did not receive the same acclaim.

John Daniel Singleton was born to teenage parents who never married. After putting themselves through college, Danny Singleton worked as a mortgage broker and Sheila Ward worked as a pharmaceutical sales executive. John spent his first eleven years with his mother after which he moved in with his father. At the age of nine, Singleton saw films as his career and began writing screenplays in his teens. He enrolled in the University of Southern California's Filmic Writing Program winning the school's Jack Nicholson Writing Award for Best Feature-length Screenplay in his junior and senior years. Internships introduced him to influential people, and his writing ability opened doors to securing an agent at Creative Artists Agency while he was in college. Singleton wrote *Boyz N the Hood* during college and agreed to sell the script to Columbia Pictures in 1990 as long as he had the role of director. *Boyz N the Hood*, a film based on Singleton's life experiences, dealt with three friends struggling with life in the ghetto, race, relationships, and violence but with anti-gang and antiviolence messages. While violence, riots, thirty injuries and one death caused by rival gangs accompanied twenty of the July theater openings, the film went on without further issues to gross around $100 million. The next two films, *Poetic Justice* (1993) and *Higher Learning* (1995) received both criticisms and praise but not the popularity of his first production. Singleton stated that his first three films were "coming-of-age, coming-of-consciousness;" and he went on to filming "his first adult movie" *Rosewood* (1996), a historical drama and someone else's script based on the 1923 Florida Rosewood massacre in a black logging town. *Baby Boy* (2001) was another coming-of-age film. His other works were varied from private-eye hero in *Shaft* (2000), street racing in *2 Fast 2 Furious* (2003), crime thriller in *Four Brothers* (2005), thriller in *Abduction* (2011), and included the series *Billions* and *Empire* (2010s) and *Snowfall* (2017).

John Singleton is survived by his daughters Hadar and Cleopatra.

See *Current Biography 1997*

Phil Solomon

Born: New York, New York; January 3, 1954
Died: Boulder, Colorado; April 20, 2019
Occupation: American experimental filmmaker

Phil Solomon's experimental films were exhibited across the United States and Europe, he won numerous awards for his videos, films, and teaching, received a variety of grants, and yet is not widely known. Solomon combined chemicals, old films made by others, his films, and an optical printer to manipulate each frame to create new work. A process he described as "artistic introversion" made with a "secret magic machine" to make art that emphasized poetic form, visual rhymes, and metaphor that somehow emulated his life experiences.

Phil Stewart Solomon was born on January 3, 1954, to parents, Samuel David Solomon and Ruth Ann Rosencrantz, co-owners of a rental car company. Hoping their son would be a physician, they bought him chemistry sets and a microscope for encouragement. His father enjoyed taking 8 mm family films and showing them was a family treat. Solomon grew up hooked on television, and by age 14, was making his own 8 mm films. He admired the works of poets like Emily Dickinson, landscape painters like Frederick Church, composers like Charles Ives, directors like Ingmar Bergman, and filmmakers like Orson Wells. Solomon's intentions were veterinary school when he enrolled at State University of New York (SUNY), but he switched to film to pursue poetic and artistic filmmaking after taking cinema courses by noted experimental "art" filmmakers. While at SUNY Solomon produced *Night Light* (1975), a well-received senior thesis project, containing scenes of clouds, children playing with flashlights, lightning storms, and nighttime bombing scenes. In 1978, Solomon entered a graduate program at Massachusetts College of Art in Boston, began teaching filmmaking, cinema aesthetics and analysis, and made his film, *Passage of the Bride* (1978). The film won first prize in the 1979 New England Student Film Festival and was nominated for an Academy Award as best student film of the year in experimental works. After earning an MFA he became a teaching assistant at Harvard University winning a Distinction in Teaching Award (1981). His film *The Secret Garden* (1988) combined footage of water with scenes from *Wizard of Oz* to emulate Adam and Eve leaving the Garden of Eden. He won an honorable mention at Black Maria Film and Video Festival where he also won first place for six other films during his career. *Remains to Be Seen* and *Exquisite Hour* (both 1989) were about the death of his parents and both received recognition and won awards. Solomon started teaching at the University of Colorado, Boulder, where he became good friends and collaborator with Stan Brakhage, whose work he was strongly influenced by. *Innocence and Despair* (2002), described by Solomon as "an underwater lullaby for my hometown in another time, an engulfed cathedral of innocence and loss," became one of 30 works for Underground Zero, a collaborative project on the 9/11 terrorist attacks. *Film Comment* magazine in a 2010 poll tied Solomon and Brakhage for fifth place out of fifty avant-garde filmmakers for the prior decade.

Phil Solomon is survived by his sister Shelly Solomon Klein, niece Jamie Baressi, and nephew Matthew Klein.

See *Current Biography 2007*

Bart Starr

Born: Montgomery, Alabama; January 9, 1934
Died: Birmingham, Alabama; May 26, 2019
Occupation: Professional football player and coach

Bart Starr was a professional football player for the Green Bay Packers and was the only quarterback in National Football League (NFL) history to lead a team to three consecutive league championships.

Bart Starr was born on January 9, 1934, in Montgomery Alabama, to Benjamin Bryan and Lula Starr. He had a younger brother, Hilton E. Starr, who died in 1946 from tetanus. Starr attended Sidney Lanier High School in Montgomery and led their football team to an undefeated season in his junior year. He received a scholarship to play football at the University of Alabama, where he became the starting quarterback, safety, and punter during his sophomore year. Starr eloped with Cherry Morton in 1954; they kept their marriage a secret at the time, as married athletes were liable to have their scholarships revoked in the 1950s. Starr sustained a serious back injury during a hazing initiation in college, which later disqualified him from military service and disrupted his playing during university. Starr was selected by the Green Bay Packers in the 17th round of the 1956 NFL Draft, with the 200th overall pick. During his 16 seasons with the Packers, Starr won five NFL championships, including wins in three consecutive years, the only quarterback in NFL history to do so. He was named the NFL's most valuable (MVP) player in 1966. He led the Packers to win the first two Super Bowls in 1967 and 1968 and was named MVP in both games. He was inducted into the Pro Football Hall of Fame in 1977. Starr had surgeries on his throwing arm in 1971 and retired from football. He served as the Packers' quarterback coach in 1972, before a brief stint as a broadcaster for CBS. He rejoined the Packers as head coach in 1974, a role he held until 1983. In his later life, Starr and his wife supported many charitable organizations, including founding their own charity supporting young people in Wisconsin.

Bart Starr is survived by his wife, Cherry, his son Bart Starr, Jr., three grandchildren and three great-grandchildren.

See *Current Biography 1968*

John Paul Stevens

Born: Chicago, Illinois; April 20, 1920
Died: Fort Lauderdale, Florida; July 16, 2019
Occupation: Supreme Court justice

John Paul Stevens, a moderate conservative, was the 101st justice to serve on the Supreme Court of the United States. Over the course of his decades-long tenure, he gained a reputation as fair and open-minded, willing to question his own beliefs and assumption, and to carefully consider the opinions of his fellow jurists.

John Paul Stevens was the youngest of four sons born to Ernest James and Elizabeth (Street) Stevens. His father operated the Stevens and LaSalle hotels, among other enterprises.

Stevens was a bright child—able to beat adults at the complex game of bridge—and later, at the University of Chicago, where he earned a BA in 1941, he was a member of Phi Beta Kappa. Soon after the United States entered World War II, he joined the Navy, and from 1942 to 1945 he was stationed in Washington, DC, as an intelligence officer. When he returned to Chicago at the end of the war, he enrolled in Northwestern University School of Law, and in 1947 graduated first in his class. Before joining a series of prestigious law firms, he clerked for a year for Supreme Court Justice Wiley Rutledge.

An expert in antitrust law, Stevens served in the early 1950s as associate counsel of the House Judiciary Committee's subcommittee on the study of monopoly power and as a member of the Attorney General's National Committee to Study Antitrust Laws.

Stevens later came to the attention of President Richard Nixon, who on October 14, 1970 appointed him a judge of the Seventh Circuit Court of Appeals. He spent five years on the federal bench in Chicago, where he came to be rated as one of the twelve leading appeals court judges in the country. In 1975, when it appeared that Associate Justice William O. Douglas might have to step down after 36 years on the Supreme Court, President Gerald Ford acted on the advice of the American Bar Association (ABA) screening committee and nominated Stevens to replace him.

Stevens was confirmed unanimously and sworn in on December 19, 1975. Over the course of his almost 35 years on the bench, he wrote major opinions on the death penalty, the role of government agencies in making regulations, and the limits of presidential power. With the Supreme Court moving to the right thanks to new appointments, by the time he stepped down, he was considered one of the body's more liberal justices—one known for sparring with the ultra-conservative Justice Antonin Scalia.

Following his retirement, Stevens never hesitated to make his opinions known, writing numerous essays, op-eds, and books for a lay readership. (He shocked many in the legal community when he took the unusual step of speaking out openly against the confirmation of Trump Supreme Court pick Brett Kavanaugh.)

John Paul Stevens died at the age of 99 after suffering a stroke and is survived by his two daughters.

See *Current Biography 1976*

Ellen O. Tauscher

Born: Newark, New Jersey; November 15, 1951
Died: Palo Alto, California; April 29, 2019
Occupation: American politician and diplomat

Ellen O. Tauscher was a centrist Democrat serving as Representative of the East Bay suburbs of San Francisco and Oakland, California, from 1997 to 2009 when she left to serve as a diplomat under President Barack Obama. In 2009, she was confirmed as Under Secretary of State for Arms Control and International Security Affairs. Tauscher was one of the first women and the youngest at age twenty-five to earn a seat on the New York Stock Exchange (NYSE).

Ellen O. Tauscher was born in East Newark, New Jersey, as Ellen O'Kane to a father who managed a grocery store and a mother who worked as a secretary. She was the first in her family to attend college. She honored her parents' commitment to her education by earning a BS in special education from Seton Hall University in New Jersey, in 1974. Tauscher spent 14 years on Wall Street employed at Bache Securities and Drexel Burnham Lambert where she worked to improve the American Stock Exchange (AMEX) [now known as NYSE American, and more recently as NYSE MKT].

After her marriage to William Tauscher in 1989 the couple moved to the San Francisco area where she both started her business, Child-Care Registry Inc., and co-wrote *The ChildCare Sourcebook* with Kathleen Candy.

Tauscher worked with Dianne Feinstein on two Senate campaigns (1992 and 1994) before running for and winning a seat in California's 10th District in 1996. Her commitments were to fiscal responsibility, a balanced budget and deficit reduction; abortion rights; environmental safety; and a ban on assault-style weapons. In Washington DC she found support in the Blue Dog Democrats and later the moderate-to-conservative New Democrat Coalition (NDC), which she joined. Tauscher was assigned to the Armed Services Committee, where she tackled nuclear security issues, and the Transportation and Infrastructure Committee, where she endeavored to improve highway and public transportation in her district. She also addressed affordable childcare, funding for aging schools and libraries, and teacher training. During her terms (1996–2009) Tauscher supported background checks and waiting periods for gun purchases, funding for women's health initiatives, equal pay, and abortion rights. After her 2009 House resignation she was confirmed as Under Secretary of State for Arms Control and International Security Affairs, serving as diplomat in the Obama administration until 2012. She successfully negotiated the New Strategic Arms Reduction Treaty of 2010 that resulted in the lowest nuclear arsenals levels of the United States and Russia since the 1950s.

Ellen O. Tauscher is survived by her daughter Katherine from her first marriage to William Tauscher, which ended in divorce.

See *Current Biography 2001*

Stanley Tigerman

Born: Chicago, Illinois; September 20, 1930
Died: Chicago, Illinois; June 3, 2019
Occupation: Architect and designer

Stanley Tigerman was an accomplished American architect and designer who worked on around 390 projects and was responsible for over 175 built structures. He designed exhibition installations for various museums, both national and international, published several books, and created products for the Swid Powell Company.

Stanley Tigerman was born on September 20, 1930, in Chicago, Illinois, to typist Emma Stern and engineer Samuel Tigerman. He was interested in music from a young age, learning piano and eventually studying jazz in high school. Tigerman briefly attended the Massachusetts Institute of Technology (MIT). He then spent four years in the U. S. Navy, participating in the Korean War. A prior apprenticeship with architect George Fred Keck sparked his interest in architecture, and after his military service he worked for A. J. Del Bianco, Milton Schwartz, and Skidmore Owings & Merrill on various architectural projects. Despite his lack of an undergraduate degree, he interviewed with the Yale School of Architecture in 1958 and was later admitted to a graduate program. During this period, he worked for school chairman, Paul Rudolph's architecture business. He graduated in 1961. From 1964 to 2017, Tigerman ran his own practice, Stanley Tigerman and Associates Ltd., which was later called Tigerman McCurry

Architects. He worked at the University of Illinois at Chicago's School of Architecture, also co-founding Archeworks, a nonprofit organization in Chicago dedicated to assisting students interested in urban planning. During his lengthy career, he played a large role in the architectural group the Chicago Seven. He is best known for several designs: the Illinois Holocaust Museum and Education Center, the Illinois Regional Library for the Blind and Physically Handicapped, and the former Powerhouse Energy Museum in Illinois. He additionally worked on projects in Portugal, Germany, Japan, and Bangladesh. His practice created luxury homes, but also designed structures like the Pacific Garden Mission, a homeless shelter, and an animal shelter. He retired in 2017.

Stanley Tigerman married three times and had two children. He is survived by his wife Margaret McCurry, his son Judson Tigerman, and his daughter Tracy Leigh Hodges.

See *Current Biography 2001*

Rip Torn

Born: Temple, Texas; February 6, 1931
Died: Lakeville, Salisbury, Connecticut; July 9, 2019
Occupation: Actor

Rip Torn was a versatile performer who tackled roles on both stage and screen, including a scene-stealing stint on *The Larry Sanders Show*, one of the most popular and provocative sitcoms of the 1990s.

The actor was born Elmore Rual Torn Jr. and took the nickname Rip from his father, who worked as an economist. He studied drama at the University of Texas and served as a military policeman for two years during the Korean War. After leaving the army, he moved to New York to study at the Actors Studio. In 1956 he won a small, uncredited part in the Southern gothic film *Baby Doll*, directed by Elia Kazan and written by Tennessee Williams; and over the next few years he became a fixture on the television anthology series that were then popular, like *Kraft Theatre*, *Playhouse 90*, and the *Hallmark Hall of Fame*.

His first Broadway appearances were in Williams's plays directed by Kazan. In 1956 he portrayed Brick in *Cat on a Hot Tin Roof*; and three years later he was in the original cast of *Sweet Bird of Youth*, earning a Tony nomination for his performance of Tom Finley, a supporting character. Later, he took on the lead role of drifter Chance Wayne, replacing Paul Newman. (When *Sweet Bird of Youth* was adapted for television in

1989, an older Torn played Tom's vengeful father; similarly, in a 1984 adaptation of *Cat on a Hot Tin Roof*, he played the patriarch.)

Torn worked steadily throughout the years, appearing on and off Broadway and making such disparate films as the biblical potboiler *King of Kings* (1961), in which he played Judas; the David Bowie film *The Man Who Fell to Earth* (1976); the comedic sci-fi hit *Men in Black* (1997); and the action flick *RoboCop 3* (1993).

From 1992 to 1998 he played Artie, a curmudgeonly but loyal producer, on *The Larry Sanders Show*, which starred comedian Larry Shandling. He garnered six Emmy Award nominations for outstanding supporting actor in a comedy series, winning the award in 1996. Other laurels were harder to come by: he was nominated only once for a Tony, for his performance in *Sweet Bird of Youth*, and only once for an Academy Award, for his portrayal of a backwoodsman in *Cross Creek* (1983).

Some observers thought Torn might have had a more illustrious career if not for his personal antics; in 1968, while filming with the equally volatile Norman Mailer, the two got into a serious physical altercation, and he once pulled a knife on fellow actor Dennis Hopper. In later years he was arrested on drunken-driving charges several times, and he was once caught breaking into a bank at night armed with a loaded gun.

Torn was married twice—the first time to actress Ann Wedgeworth, whom he divorced, and then to actress Geraldine Page, who predeceased him in 1987.

Rip Torn is survived by his longtime partner, Amy Wright; four daughters; two sons; and four grandchildren.

See *Current Biography 1977*

Gloria Vanderbilt

Born: New York City, New York; February 20, 1924
Died: New York City, New York; June 17, 2019
Occupation: Fashion designer, artist, actress, author, heiress and socialite

Gloria Laura Vanderbilt was an American heiress and socialite who went on to become a fashion designer, artist, actress, and author. In her youth, she was embroiled in a highly publicized child custody battle between her mother and her paternal aunt, each seeking control of the funds she was to inherit after the death of her father. Later in her life, she was well known for starting a line of designer jeans.

Gloria Laura Vanderbilt was born on February 20,1924, in New York the only child of Reginald Claypoole Vanderbilt and Gloria Morgan.

As a teenager, she became a fashion model featured in *Harper's Bazaar*. She attended the Art Students League of New York, licensing some of her artwork to Hallmark Cards and Bloomcraft. She then became devoted to acting, joining a Broadway show and appearing in multiple television programmes, such as *The Love Boat* and *The Oprah Winfrey Show*. In the 1970s and 1980s Vanderbilt flourished in her career as a fashion designer, creating lines of scarves, jeans, dresses, blouses, and other apparel. She later focused once again on visual art, opening a successful exhibition called "Dream Boxes" in 2001 and returning in 2007 for another exhibition at the Southern Vermont Arts Center. She wrote two books, four memoirs, and three novels, also writing for *The New York Times*, *Elle*, and *Vanity Fair*. In 2016, she wrote an additional book with her son, CNN anchor Anderson Cooper, entitled *The Rainbow Comes and Goes: A Mother and Son on Life, Love, and Loss*. That same year, a documentary called *Nothing Left Unsaid: Gloria Vanderbilt & Anderson Cooper*, was released, focusing on Vanderbilt's history.

Gloria Vanderbilt was married four times and had four children. She is survived by three sons.

See *Current Biography 1972*

Sander Vanocur

Born: Cleveland, Ohio; January 8, 1928
Died: Santa Barbara, California; September 16, 2019
Occupation: News commentator

In an era when presidential debates are routinely televised, it's easy to forget what a landmark it was considered when John F. Kennedy and Richard M. Nixon faced off on September 26, 1960—the first time in U.S. history that major party presidential candidates had debated on national television. Sander Vanocur played a significant role in that event, as one of the journalists questioning the pair.

Sander "Sandy" Vanocur (born Alexander Vinocur) is the son of Louis and Rose Vinocur, who divorced when the newsman and his sister, Roberta, were young. (He and his father, a lawyer, spelled their surnames differently.) Vanocur graduated from Western Military Academy in 1946 and Northwestern University in 1950. He later studied at the London School of Economics, and in 1952, he entered the U.S. Army, serving two years in Austria and Germany.

Returning to England after his discharge, Vanocur joined the staff of the Manchester *Guardian* as a reporter. Not too long afterwards he began his career as a news broadcaster when, as a sideline to his job with the *Guardian*, he did a weekly analysis for the North American Service of the BBC. He also wrote for the London *Observer* and for a short time served as a "stringer" for the Columbia Broadcasting System (CBS). As a reporter in England he covered a wide variety of assignments, including the retirement of Winston Churchill and the romance of Princess Margaret and Group Captain Peter Townsend.

In 1955, Vanocur joined the city staff of the *New York Times*, and two years later he became a correspondent for NBC News. In 1960, Vanocur was assigned to cover John F. Kennedy's bid for the Democratic Presidential nomination, and he followed the campaign trail for months, through the primary elections, the Democratic National Convention in Los Angeles, and the election. When Kennedy was instated in the White House in January 1961, Vanocur took on the White House beat, and he became particularly noted for his rapport with the sometimes reticent First Lady, Jacqueline Kennedy. While at NBC he conducted what would turn out to be one of the last interviews with Senator Robert F. Kennedy before his 1968 assassination.

Later in his career, Vanocur worked at such outlets as the Public Broadcasting Corporation, the *Washington Post*, and ABC. He also worked on a freelance basis, and in that capacity, in 1992, he helped moderate a lively debate between George H.W. Bush, Bill Clinton, and Texas business tycoon and longshot candidate Ross Perot.

In addition to his work as a correspondent, Vanocur taught at Duke University, consulted at the Center for the Study of Democratic Institutions, and hosted shows on the *History Channel*.

Sander Vanocur died of the complications of dementia and is survived by his second wife, Virginia; his son Christopher; a stepdaughter, Daphne; and two grandchildren. His first wife, Edith, predeceased him in 1975; his other son, Nicholas, predeceased him in 2015.

See Current Biography 1963

Agnes Varda

Born: Ixelles, Brussels, Belgium; May 30, 1928
Died: Paris, France; March 29, 2019
Occupation: French filmmaker

Agnes Varda was a woman in a field dominated by men. A professional photographer, director, and writer; she would come to be known as "mother of French New Wave." Her first film, *La Pointe Courte* (1954), was not as highly acclaimed as many of her works that followed, such as *Cleo de cinq a sept [Cleo, from 5 to 7]*

(1962), *Le Bonheur [Happiness]* (1965), and *Les Creatures* (1966), and *Lions Love* (1969).

She was born Arlette Varda on May 30, 1928, only daughter of five children of Greek engineer, Eugene Jean Varda, and French mother, Christiane (Pasquet) Varda. Varda spent her youth in the city of Sete near the filming location of *La Pointe Courte[The Short Point]*. She began her studies at College de Sete before studying literature and psychology at Sorbonne in Paris, painting and sculpture at École du Louvre, and photography at Vaugirard School of Photography. Varda worked as the official photographer for Theatre National Populaire and also as reporter and photographer for magazines from 1951 until 1961. Varda produced two short publicity travelogues followed by a documentary of a pregnant women's view of life in the slums, *Opera mouffe* (1958) which won a prize at the Brussels Experimental Film Festival. With the backing of businessman, Georges de Beauregard, Varda produced her feature-length film released as *Cleo de cinq a sept* (1962) in England and *Cleo from 5 to 7* in the United States. Critics considered the film brilliant, and it was awarded the Prix Méliès. The story follows an egotistical pop singer's two hours waiting for a cancer diagnosis that transforms her to a person able to give and receive affection. Her next film, *Salut les Cubains* (1963), was successful in France and Cuba and won the Bronze Lion award at the Venice Film Festival in 1964. The non-political documentary set to Cuban dance rhythms about Fidel Castro's revolution was a combination of 1,500 still photographs from a trip to Cuba. Varda made numerous films right up to a couple of years before her death. Her first digital film, *Gleaners* (2001) won a European Film Award and *Faces Places* (2017) won an Oscar for documentary. Varda herself was given an L'Œil d'or at the Cannes International Film Festival in 2015, an honorary Palme d'Or in 2016, and honorary Academy Award for her contributions to cinema in 2017.

Agnes Varda is survived by her son Mathieu with husband Jacques Demy, and daughter Rosalie from an earlier relationship with Antoine Bourseiller.

See Current Biography 1970

Binyavanga Wainaina

Born: Nakuru, Kenya; January 18, 1971
Died: Nairobi, Kenya; May 21, 2019
Occupation: Author

Binyavanga Wainaina was a memoirist who in 2014 revealed he was gay. The timing was significant—and brave. In many African countries, gay men were being rounded up and beaten by mobs, and laws were enacted that banned same-sex relationships. Although he was widely censured on his native continent, Wainaina was named one of *Time* magazine's 100 most influential people that year.

Kenneth Binyavanga Wainaina was born on January 18, 1971, the son of a hairdresser and a business executive. In his 2014 essay, he writes of sensing he was gay from the age of five. While he had trouble conforming to the strictures of school life, he found solace in imported cultural icons like the Bee Gees and Michael Jackson, and he read voraciously.

In 1991, he left Kenya to study commerce at the University of Transkei in South Africa. Wainaina did not take well to his studies; he stopped attending class and moved into an outbuilding with only a mattress and some books. In 1996 he moved to Cape Town, where he wrote food and travel articles and worked as a professional cook. He returned to Kenya in 2001, renting a room in a hostel on the periphery of a Nairobi slum. Later, he earned his master's degree in creative writing from the University of East Anglia.

In 2002 Wainaina's autobiographical novella, *Discovering Home*, won the prestigious Caine Prize for African Writing. Buoyed by his success, Wainaina and a group of artists, writers, and intellectuals in Nairobi used the prize money to found a literary journal called *Kwani?* in 2003. In the mid-2000s, while living in London, he wrote a scathing e-mail to the editor of the literary magazine *Granta*, criticizing the naïveté of an old issue that centered on the African continent. Later, he tweaked the missive, and the magazine published it under the headline "How to Write about Africa." "In your text, "treat Africa as if it were one country," he wrote sarcastically. "Never have a picture of a well-adjusted African on the cover of your book, or in it, unless that African has won the Nobel Prize."

Wainaina published a memoir called *One Day I Will Write about This Place* in 2011; it was well received by critics and was given a boost with U.S. readers when Oprah Winfrey's magazine included it on its summer reading list. It was, however, missing a very important part of Wainaina's identity. He rectified that omission when he published what he called a "Lost Chapter" in January 2014. In the piece, Wainaina imagines telling his mother, on her deathbed, that he is gay, thus announcing it to the reading public.

Wainaina suffered a stroke in 2015 and revealed that he was HIV-positive the following year. While he planned to wed his boyfriend in 2019, he died before the ceremony could take place.

Binyavanga Wainaina is survived by his partner, and his three siblings.

See *Current Biography 2015*

Patricia M. Wald

Born: Torrington, Connecticut; September 16, 1928
Died: Washington, DC; January 12, 2019
Occupation: Judge, Attorney

Patricia Ann McGowan Ward was a judge and attorney best known for her work as assistant attorney general under Jimmy Carter.

Patricia Ann McGowan Wald was born an only child to Joseph McGowan and Margaret O'Keefe in Torrington, Connecticut, on September 16, 1928. Her father left when she was two years old, and Wald was raised by her mother and extended family. Most of her relatives were factory workers, and after joining them during the summers, Wald decided to devote herself to protecting labour rights and working people. She received a private scholarship and was able to attend Connecticut College for Women, studying government. She was then awarded a Pepsi-Cola fellowship enabling her to attend Yale Law School, one of only 12 women in a class of 200. She pursued jobs as a legal clerk and worked in private practice for a small time before leaving to raise her five children. She returned to work six years later, taking on part-time roles in consulting and research. Wald joined the United States Department of Justice in 1967 as an attorney, which marked the beginning of a wide-ranging career as an attorney working to improve the United States' legal system, focusing mainly on Health and Social policy. In 1979, she was nominated by President Jimmy Carter to the District of Columbia Circuit, where she served as Chief Judge from 1986 to 1991. After retiring from federal service, Wald became the United States representative to the International Criminal Tribunal for the Former Yugoslavia, where she oversaw many trials of high-ranking officers accused of genocide. Throughout her career, Ward received widespread recognition for her contributions to the legal system and to human rights causes. She was awarded over twenty honorary degrees and received numerous accolades, such as the American Lawyer Hall of Fame Lifetime Achievement Award in 2004, and in 2013, the Presidential Medal of Freedom.

Patricia Wald is survived by her three daughters, and two sons.

See *Current Biography 2000*

Immanuel Maurice Wallerstein

Born: New York, New York; September 28, 1930
Died: Branford, Connecticut; August 31, 2019
Occupation: Sociologist

Immanuel Maurice Wallerstein is best known for his groundbreaking and hugely influential "world-systems" analysis of the global capitalist system, its origins, its evolution, and what he saw as its inherent inequalities.

Immanuel Maurice Wallerstein's parents, Menachem Lazar (a rabbi-turned-physician) and Sara Günsberg (an artist), often discussed world affairs around the dinner table. As a teenager he became interested in India's struggle for independence from Great Britain, which it won officially in 1947, the year he enrolled at Columbia University. There, as a result of political debates and his participation in an international youth congress, he switched his focus to Africa; during those years he studied colonialism on that continent at the École des Hautes Études en Sciences Sociales (EHESS), in Paris. At the time Paris was a breeding ground for radical intellectual and political thought: the city, and the time he spent there, were formative for Wallerstein.

Wallerstein earned his BA in 1951. He then served two years in the U.S. Army before returning to Columbia to earn his MA (1954) and PhD (1959). Having received a Ford Foundation African Fellowship, he conducted research for his doctoral thesis on the colonial systems and independence movements in Ghana and the Ivory Coast; at the time he was one of the only social scientists in his area of expertise to do his fieldwork in Africa. His study of colonialism and independence in Africa is seen by many as a precursor to his world-systems analysis of the global economy as well as his subsequent critique of globalization and U.S. hegemony.

The 1968 student revolt at Columbia was a crucial turning point in Wallerstein's career, as his sympathy for the progressively minded students cost him standing among his colleagues; and in 1971 he moved to McGill University, in Montreal, to teach sociology. Five years later he moved to the State University of New York (SUNY) at Binghamton, becoming a distinguished professor and remaining there until 1999. In 2000 he became a senior researcher at Yale University.

In 1974, Wallerstein published the first volume of *The Modern World-System*, creating an instant sensation. The book focused on transformations in early modern Europe, which, he argued, had led to the birth of the capitalist system. The concept was groundbreaking because it saw not the nation-state but the global capitalist economy as the basic unit of analysis for modern social change. He followed that in 1980 with Volume II of *The Modern World-System*, and nine years later Volume III was released.

After the publication of that third volume, Wallerstein—also the author of dozens of other influential articles and books—spent much of his time attempting to revolutionize the social sciences, largely through his positions as president of the International Sociological Association (ISA).

Immanuel Maurice Wallerstein died of an infection and is survived by his wife, Beatrice; daughter, Katharine; stepchildren, Susan and Robert; and five grandchildren.

See *Current Biography 2009*

Mary Warnock

Born: Winchester, England; April 14, 1924
Died: Savernake Forest, England; March 20, 2019
Occupation: Philosopher and writer

Helen Mary Warnock was a renowned philosopher, known for her inquiry into human fertilization, embryo research, and surrogacy.

Helen Mary Warnock, born Helen Mary Wilson, on April 14, 1924, was the youngest of seven children born to Ethel and Archibald Wilson, though her father died before her birth. In 1942, she studied classics at Lady Margaret Hall, Oxford, and though her studies were interrupted by WWII, she eventually graduated in 1948. She married Geoffrey Warnock, philosopher and vice-chancellor at Oxford in 1949. She became a fellow of philosophy at St Hugh's College, Oxford from 1949 until 1966. During this time, she wrote extensively about contemporary ethics, Sartre and existentialism, and published three books on the subjects between 1963 and 1970. From 1972 until 1976, Warnock was a Talbot Research Fellow at Lady Margaret Hall, during which time she published *Imagination*, and then became a senior research fellow at St Hugh's College from 1976 until 1984. In 1985, Warnock was made an honorary fellow at St Hugh's and then went on to become mistress of Girton College, Cambridge, until 1991. After retiring, Warnock served on public committees and helped publish *The Uses of Philosophy* (1992), *Imagination and Time* (1994) and *An Intelligent Person's Guide to Ethics* (1998). During her time teaching, Warnock created a report in 1978, which highlighted the need for "Statementing" children with learning disabilities in mainstream schools, to provide them with special educational support. From 1979 to 1984, Warnock sat on a Royal Commission on Environmental Pollution, and from 1982 to 1984, she chaired a committee of Inquiry into Human Fertilization and Embryology, which eventually advised the Human Fertilization and Embryology Act of 1990. Warnock was also an advocate for euthanasia. During her career, Warnock earned several honorary degrees and was given the title Baroness Warnock in 1985 and sat in the House of Lords as a cross-bencher until 2015.

Mary Warnock is survived by her children, Felix, James, Boz, and Kitty. She was predeceased by her daughter, Fanny.

See *Current Biography 2005*

Pernell Whitaker

Born: Norfolk, Virginia; January 2, 1964
Died: Virginia Beach, Virginia; July 14, 2019
Occupation: Boxer

Pernell "Sweet Pea" Whitaker, who won a gold medal at the 1984 Summer Olympics and became a champion in four different weight classes, was especially lauded in the boxing world for the deft way he avoided his opponent's punches, bobbing around the ring in a masterfully elusive manner.

Whitaker learned to box as a child at a recreation center near the housing project where his parents, Raymond and Novella, were raising him and his six siblings. By the time he was 13, he was fighting sailors who came to the center from a nearby naval base.

While an amateur in the lightweight division, Whitaker took home a silver medal from the 1982 World Boxing Championships (WBC) and won gold at the 1983 Pan-American Games and the 1984 Summer Olympics in Los Angeles. Ultimately, he compiled an impressive amateur record of 201 wins and just 14 losses, with 91 of the wins by knockout.

Whitaker made his professional debut as a lightweight in 1984, beating his opponent by technical knockout in just two rounds. After a 10-bout string of victories, he defeated Roger Mayweather, the North American Boxing Federation (NABF) lightweight champion, in March 1987, and captured the first of his numerous professional titles.

Lacking a true rival in the lightweight division (135–139 pounds), he moved up in weight class in 1993 and fought James "Buddy" McGirt for the WBC welterweight title. Whitaker won, and thus became only the fourth boxer in history to win titles in both the lightweight and welterweight divisions. Later that year he faced the Mexican legend Julio César Chávez, and in an exceedingly controversial and unpopular ruling, the match ended in a draw. Although Whitaker retained his welterweight title, the result haunted him for years.

In 1995, Whitaker, who also held the World Boxing Association (WBA) super welterweight title for a time, moved up another weight class and fought the former world junior middleweight champion, Julio César Vásquez, for the WBA junior middleweight crown. He won a unanimous decision, joining an elite corps of boxers who had gained titles in at least three different weight classes, and that year, *Ring* magazine named him the world's best fighter, pound for pound.

In 1997, after having successfully defended his World Boxing Council (WBC) welterweight title 13 times, Whitaker faced the undefeated Oscar De La Hoya for the welterweight belt. In what was widely seen as the most humiliating result since his fight with Chávez, the judges ruled against him in a unanimous (but still controversial) decision. Although he continued to fight, his performances were lackluster, and he was disqualified multiple matches after testing positive for cocaine. In his later years, he trained younger boxers and sold autographs to support himself.

Pernell Whitaker was killed by a car when crossing the street. He is survived by his sons, Devon, Dominique, and Dantavious, and his daughter, Tiara. His son Pernell Jr. died in 2015.

See *Current Biography 1998*

Michael H. Wilson

Born: Toronto, Ontario, Canada; November 4, 1937
Died: Toronto, Ontario, Canada; February 10, 2019
Occupation: Politician and Statesman

Michael Holcombe Wilson was a Canadian politician who served as Canada's Ambassador to the United States.

Michael Holcombe Wilson was born on November 4, 1937, in Toronto, Ontario, Canada. He attended Upper Canada College before enrolling in Trinity College at the University of Toronto. Wilson entered politics by running for president in 1983, although he dropped out of the race before the elections and backed the winning candidate, President Brian Mulroney. As part of Mulroney's government after the 1984 Canadian elections, Wilson was appointed to be Minister of Finance. In this role, he reformed the previous tax system to lower rates and remove many special provisions; he was also instrumental in the negotiations for the Canada-United States Free Trade Agreement. Although unpopular with consumers, Wilson was also responsible for the Goods and Services Tax that has been in place since 1990. After seven years in Finance, Wilson became the Minister of International Trade, as well as the Minister for Industry, Science, and Technology. In this role, he participated in negotiating the North American Free Trade Agreement (NAFTA). Wilson served in several high-profile university positions in Canada, as the Chancellor of Trinity College from 2003 to 2007, and the Chancellor of the University of Toronto from 2012–2018. Upon the loss of his son to suicide, Wilson became a prominent mental health advocate, establishing the Cameron Parker Holcombe Wilson Chair in Depression Studies at the University of Toronto, as well as sitting on the board, and eventually becoming the board chair, for the Mental Health Commission of Canada. Wilson was appointed as an Officer of the Order of Canada in 2003 and promoted to Companion of the Order of Canada in 2010. In 2006, Wilson was appointed as Canadian Ambassador to the United States but stepped down in 2008.

Michael H. Wilson is survived by his wife, Margie, son Geoff, and daughter Lara.

See *Current Biography 1990*

Nancy Wilson

Born: Chillicothe, Ohio; February 20, 1937
Died: Pioneertown, California; December 13, 2018
Occupation: Singer and actress

Nancy Wilson was a well-known jazz and rhythm and blues singer who rose to fame in the 1960s with the chart-topping hits *Tell Me the Truth* and *How Glad I Am*.

Nancy Sue Wilson was born to Olden Wilson and Lillian Ryan in Chillicothe, Ohio, on February 20, 1937. She grew up loving music, and her parents supported her by buying records and encouraging her to sing in church choirs and perform for her family. Wilson sang in clubs throughout her teenage years before going to college to study teaching. However, she dropped out after one year to pursue her dream of becoming a singer and joined a big band. In 1959, she relocated to New York City, and quickly became a regular at the Blue Morocco Club, in the Bronx. Capitol Records signed her in 1960 and went on to release five Nancy Wilson albums over the next two years, following the success of her debut single, 'Guess Who I Saw Today.' She collaborated and worked on over 50 further albums and singles, many of which hit the charts. Wilson won her first Grammy for the album *How Glad I Am* in 1964. Wilson also appeared on a number of television shows and films, even hosting her own Emmy award-winning series on NBC between 1967 and 1968. In 1990, she received a star on the Hollywood Boulevard Walk of Fame. Further awards and accolades include the National Endowment of the Arts (NEA) Jazz Masters Fellowship in 2004, the National Association for the Advancement of Colored People (NAACP) Image Award for Best Recording Jazz Artist in 2005, and Oprah Winfrey's Legends Award. In 2005, Wilson was also honored for her activism, receiving a plaque at the International Civil Rights Walk of Fame, located at the Martin Luther King Jr. National Historic Site. Throughout her career, she won 3 Grammy awards and was nominated seven times.

Nancy Wilson is survived by her son Kacy, from her first marriage, her daughters Samantha and Sheryl, from her second marriage, her two sisters, and five grandchildren.

See *Current Biography 1997*

Harris Wofford

Born: Manhattan, New York; April 9, 1926
Died: Washington, DC; January 21, 2019
Occupation: Attorney, Politician

Harris Wofford was an attorney and US Senator known for his support of progressive legislation and civil rights. He served as an advisor to John F. Kennedy and also held Pennsylvania's Senate seat for three years.

Harris Llewellyn Wofford Jr. was born in Manhattan, New York, to Estelle Allison and Harris Llewellyn Wofford on April 9, 1926. When he was 11, he toured the world for six months with his widowed grandmother. Notably, they visited India where Wofford learned about Mahatma Gandhi, and spent time in Rome, where they witnessed a fascist parade just after Italy withdrew from the League of Nations. These experiences sparked a lifelong interest in civil and human rights causes. He received his law degree from Yale Law School in 1954, then quickly began a career of public service as a legal assistant with the United States Commission on Civil Rights. He was a proud supporter of the Civil Rights Movement in the South in the 1950s, and became an advisor to Martin Luther King Jr. His political career truly began when he joined John F. Kennedy's presidential campaign in 1960. In 1961, Kennedy named him Special Assistant to the President for Civil Rights. Wofford also helped found the Peace Corps, serving as its assistant director between 1964 and 1966. Between 1966 and 1985, he stepped back from politics to serve as the head of State University of New York (SUNY), then Bryn Mawr College, before deciding to pursue private law practice. He returned to politics in 1986, serving first as the Chairman of the Pennsylvania Democratic Party, then as the state's Secretary of Labor and Industry, before being elected to represent Pennsylvania in the Senate from 1991 to 1994. Later, Wofford served on the boards of several charities and organisations and continued to do so until the end of his career.

Harris Wofford is survived by his husband, Matthew Charlton, and three children, Susanne, Daniel, and David, and six grandchildren.

See *Current Biography 1992*

Herman Wouk

Born: New York, New York; May 27, 1915
Died: Palm Springs, California; May 17, 2019
Occupation: Author

"Setting aside the years at war, I have had no other aim or occupation than that of writing," Herman Wouk once wrote. "In the good hours when words are flowing well it seems there is hardly a pleasanter way to spend one's time on earth." Thus Wouk, author of *The Caine Mutiny* (1951), *Marjorie Morningstar* (1955), and *The Winds of War* (1971), among other novels, summed up a long literary career.

Herman Wouk, born on May 27, 1915, was the son of Russian-Jewish immigrants, Abraham Isaac and Esther (Levine) Wouk. His father began work in this country as a laundry laborer at $3 a week and eventually became a well-known industrialist. Wouk spent his early years in the Bronx; and after graduating from Townsend Harris Hall High School, he entered Columbia University, majoring in comparative literature and philosophy.

By 1934, Wouk had managed to acquire not only a bachelor's degree but the invaluable experience of editing the college humor magazine and writing two varsity shows. This extracurricular activity led to his being hired after graduation to work as a "gagman" grinding out material for radio comedians.

With the outbreak of World War II in Europe, Wouk went to work for the United States Treasury, writing and producing radio shows to promote the sale of bonds. Soon after Pearl Harbor, he enlisted in the U. S. Navy; and in 1943 he enlivened the tedium of sea duty by writing a novel, *Aurora Dawn*, which earned him a publishing contract. He followed that with a semi-autobiographical novel, *The City Boy* (1948); and while neither garnered much attention, his next effort, *The Caine Mutiny*, proved to be a blockbuster. A drama set on the high seas, the book (whose protagonist, Philip F. Queeg, was played by Humphrey Bogart in the 1954 Hollywood adaptation) sold more than three million copies in the United States alone and won the Pulitzer Prize.

He enjoyed equal critical success with two other war novels: *The Winds of War* (1971), which took place in the period between 1939 to the attack on Pearl Harbor, and *War and Remembrance* (1978), which concluded with the dropping of the atom bomb. The books later formed the basis for popular television miniseries that starred Robert Mitchum and aired in 1983 and 1988, respectively.

Aside from those occasional critical successes, Wouk was often pilloried by critics, who charged him with overwrought plotting and clumsy dialogue. The public, however, did not share those sentiments, and Wouk's books regularly landed on bestseller lists. His last, a memoir, *Sailor and Fiddler: Reflections of a 100-Year-old Author*, was published in 2016.

Herman Wouk died just ten days before his 104th birthday. He was said to be working on a new book at the time. He was predeceased by his wife, Betty, in 2011. A son, Abraham, died in a childhood accident. He is survived by two children, Iolanthe and Joseph; three grandchildren; and two great-grandchildren.

See *Current Biography 1952*

Franco Zeffirelli

Born: Florence, Italy; February 12, 1923
Died: Rome, Italy; June 15, 2019
Occupation: Theatrical and operatic director

Franco Zeffirelli was renowned for his extravagant opera productions and popular big-screen adaptations of the classics.

Born on February 12, 1923, Gian Franco Corsi Zeffirelli, was the son of businessman Ottorini Corsi and the former Adelaide Garosi, a fashion designer, who were not married to each other at the time of his birth. (The Corsi family originated in Vinci, near Florence, and has connections with the family of Leonardo da Vinci.) Zeffirelli, as he preferred to be called, attended the Accademia di Belle Arti in Florence, graduating in 1941 and going on, at his father's behest, to study architecture at the University of Florence. There he became director of the university's theater company and helmed several local productions.

In 1943, when he was 20, Zeffirelli was swept up in the war. Italy was then under German occupation, and he fought against the Nazis for a year as a partisan. He then worked as an interpreter attached to the Scots Guards. During this period he met a number of British theater people then serving with the armed forces in Italy and found his imagination fired. The war ended in 1945 and Zeffirelli, against parental wishes, abandoned his architectural studies and went to Rome. He began his theatrical career in 1945 as a radio actor; and in 1946 he joined Luchino Visconti's Morelli-Stoppa Company, as an actor and stage manager.

Two small roles were enough to convince Zeffirelli that his future did not lie in acting, and thereafter he occupied himself staging a wide variety of operas at such iconic venues as La Scala and the Royal Opera House in Covent Garden. American audiences were introduced to him in 1962, when his acclaimed Old Vic production of *Romeo and Juliet* went on tour.

Zeffirelli made his debut at the Metropolitan Opera House on March 6, 1964, handling direction, sets, and costumes in a triumphant production of Verdi's *Falstaff*. For the next four decades, his work at the Met drew large, appreciative audiences. He was best-known in America, however, for the 1968 film version of *Romeo and Juliet*, which grossed more than $50 million and introduced Shakespeare to countless young viewers who might never have read the play. He enjoyed other success with film adaptations of Shakespeare's *The Taming of the Shrew* (1967), starring Elizabeth Taylor and Richard Burton, and *Hamlet* (1990), starring Mel Gibson, as well as with film versions of such operas as *La Traviata* (1982) and *Otello* (1986), the latter starring Plácido Domingo.

Zeffirelli, who had a long affair with acclaimed director Luchino Visconti, always described himself as homosexual, rather than gay—a term he found inelegant. In addition to his artistic career, he was twice elected to the Italian Parliament, as an ultraconservative.

Franco Zeffirelli died at the age of 96 and is survived by two sons, Giuseppe and Luciano, whom he adopted as adults.

See *Current Biography 1964*

CLASSIFICATION BY PROFESSION

ACTIVISM
Natalie Diaz
Amanda Nguyen
Suzan Shown Harjo

ARCHITECTURE
Alejandro Aravena
Tom Wright

ART
Cecily Brown
Njideka Akunyili Crosby
Maurizio Cattelan
Pierre Charpin
Peter Doig
Tommy Hollenstein
Jarrett J. Krosoczka
Simone Leigh
Yuyi Morales
Katie Paterson
Fiona Staples

BUSINESS
Chris Anderson
Mary Callahan Erdoes
Stacey Cunningham
Morgan DeBaun
Laura Deming
Anne Fulenwider
Andrew Haldane
Belinda Johnson
Marie Kondo
Kai-Fu Lee
Jessica Lessin
Lori Lightfoot
Yusaku Maezawa
Rose Marcario
Sundar Pichai
Dan Porter
Kirthiga Reddy
Simon Sinek
Gary Vaynerchuk
Hans Vestberg
Whitney Wolfe Herd
Andrew Yang

COMEDY
Tiffany Haddish

DANCE
Rennie Harris

EDUCATION
Fadlo R. Khuri

ENTERTAINMENT
Germán Garmendia

FICTION
Fredrik Backman
Esi Edugyan
Álvaro Enrigue
Sunetra Gupta
Joe Hill
Joel Thomas Hynes
James Kaplan
Karl Ove Knausgaard
Jarrett J. Krosoczka
Evangeline Lilly
Meg Medina
Yuyi Morales
Ryan North
Sally Rooney
Riad Sattouf
Brad Watson

FILM
Zaradasht Ahmed
Kris Aquino
Nicole Beharie
Alia Bhatt
Shane Carruth
Olivia Colman
Ana de Armas
Kevin Feige
Henry Golding
James Gunn
Tiffany Haddish
Remy Hii
Joel Thomas Hynes
Brie Larson
Evangeline Lilly
Ma Dong-seok
Hasan Minhaj
Jason Momoa
Ryan Murphy
Matthew Rhys
Krysten Ritter
Melanie Scrofano
Josh Singer
Yvonne Strahovski
Tessa Thompson
Letitia Wright

FOOD
Cristeta Comerford
Nina Compton
Duff Goldman
Rachel Khoo
Christina Tosi

GOVERNMENT
Scott Gottlieb
Donald Hopkins
Robert Lighthizer
Jelena McWilliams
Alvin Salehi

HISTORY
Rutger Bregman
Claudia Goldin
Yuval Noah Harari

JOURNALISM
Iona Craig
Eliza Griswold
Jessica Lessin
Rachel Nichols
Lydia Polgreen
Hannah Storm

MODELING
Jourdan Dunn

MUSIC
Lauren Alaina
Jason Aldean
Isabel Bayrakdarian
Alia Bhatt
Cardi B
Brandi Carlile
Jekalyn Carr
Eric Church
Luis Fonsi
Destra Garcia
Ludwig Göransson
Matt Haimovitz
Barbara Hannigan
Niall Horan
Joel Thomas Hynes
Jason Isbell
Hayley Kiyoko
Paul MacAlindin
Post Malone
Maluma
Cassper Nyovest
Jessie Reyez
Sarkodie
Kierra Sheard
Glenn Slater
Tinashe
Molly Tuttle
Hezekiah Walker
Zach Williams
Zedd
Jane Zhang
Karen Zoid

NONFICTION
Rutger Bregman
Claudia Goldin
Ross Edgley

Yuval Noah Harari
James Kaplan
Karl Ove Knausgaard
Marie Kondo
Jarrett J. Krosoczka
James Martin
Meghan McCain
Simon Sinek
Gary Vaynerchuk
Jessica Watson

ONLINE PERSONALITY
Tyler "Ninja" Blevins

POETRY
Natalie Diaz
Eliza Griswold
Ben Lerner
Ada Limón
Barbara Jane Reyes
Kevin Young

POLITICS, FOREIGN
Diane Abbott
John Bercow
Kolinda Grabar-Kitarović
Rami Hamdallah
Queen Mathilde of Belgium
Viktor Orbán
Otto Pérez Molina
Sahle-Work Zewde
Nicola Sturgeon
Tamim bin Hamad Al Thani
Volodymyr Zelensky

POLITICS, U.S.
Dan Crenshaw
Ro Khanna
Lori Lightfoot
Meghan McCain
Debbie Mucarsel-Powell
Rachel Notley
Alexandria Ocasio-Cortez
Maité Oronoz Rodríguez
Ayanna Pressley
Pat Quinn
Charlie Sykes
Lauren Underwood
Seema Verma
Paula Mae Weekes
Jean Wyllys

RADIO
Dave Fennoy

RELIGION
James Martin

SCIENCE
James P. Allison
Lucinda Backwell

Regina Barzilay
Daniel J. Bernstein
Joy Buolamwini
Laura Deming
Alan Duffy
Paul Falkowski
Kuki Gallmann
Claudia Goldin
Gita Gopinath
Scott Gottlieb
Sunetra Gupta
Jonathan Haidt
Mona Hanna-Attisha
Lisa Harvey-Smith
Jedidah Isler
Paul L. Modrich
Natalie Panek
Johan Rockström
Ed Stafford
Beth Stevens
Mark Stucky
Karen Uhlenbeck
Ewine Fleur van Dishoeck

SPORTS
Canelo Álvarez
Nolan Arenado
Mike Babcock
Beauden Barrett
Cody Bellinger
Janene Carleton
Fabiano Caruana
Bryson DeChambeau
Michelle Dorrance
Kyle Dubas
Ross Edgley
John John Florence
Chris Froome
Maya Gabeira
Johnny Gaudreau
Lydia Hall
Jayna Hefford
Gerlinde Kaltenbrunner
Isabelle Kelly
Sam Kerr
Virat Kohli
KuroKy (Kuro Takhasomi)
Jocelyne Lamoureux-Davidson
Becky Lynch
Pippa Mann
J. D. Martinez

Bo Levi Mitchell
Saina Nehwal
Katie Nolan
Katelyn Ohashi
Shohei Ohtani
Naomi Osaka
Ben Simmons
George Springer
Trevor Story
Dominic Thiem
Daniel Wanjiru
Jessica Watson
Chrissie Wellington
Carson Wentz

TECHNOLOGY
Regina Barzilay

TELEVISION
Kris Aquino
Nicole Beharie
Nicole Byer
Cardi B
Olivia Colman
Nina Compton
Ana de Armas
Dave Fennoy
Duff Goldman
Tiffany Haddish
Remy Hii
Abby Huntsman
Joel Thomas Hynes
Rachel Khoo
January LaVoy
Evangeline Lilly
Hasan Minhaj
Jason Momoa
Ryan Murphy
Katie Nolan
Matthew Rhys
Sarah Richardson
Krysten Ritter
Melanie Scrofano
Yvonne Strahovski
Christina Tosi
Letitia Wright

THEATER
Nicole Beharie
Christian Borle
Simon Stephens

LIST OF PROFILES